International Financial Management

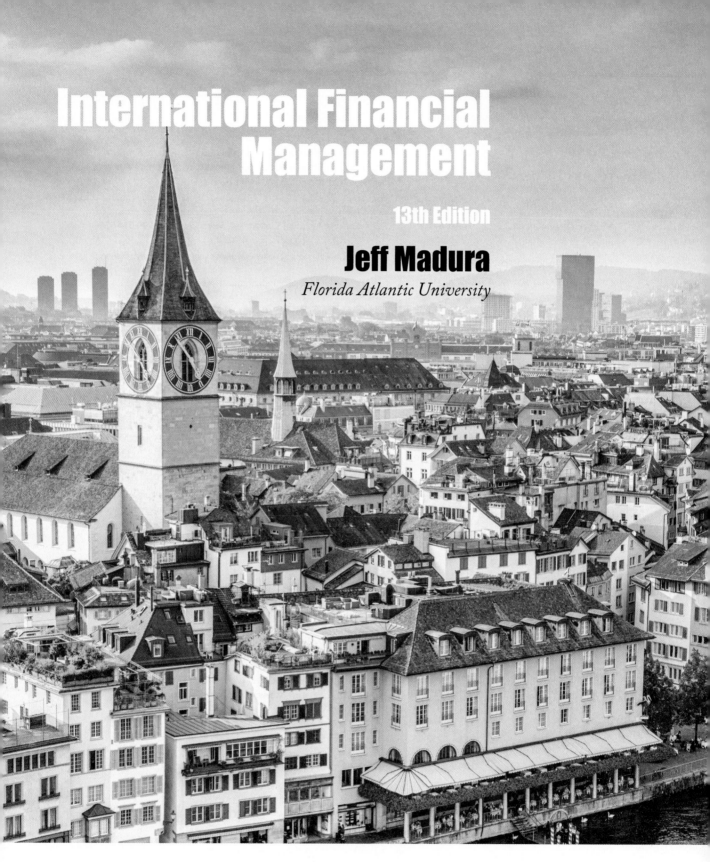

International Financial Management

13th Edition

Jeff Madura
Florida Atlantic University

CENGAGE
Learning®

Australia • Brazil • Mexico • Singapore • United Kingdom • United States

International Financial Management, 13th Edition
Jeff Madura

SVP, General Manager for Social Sciences, Humanities & Business: Erin Joyner

Executive Product Director: Mike Schenk

Sr. Product Team Manager: Joe Sabatino

Project Manager: Julie Dierig

Content Developer: Stacey Lotkoski, MPS

Product Assistant: Denisse A Zavala-Rosales

Marketing Manager: Nathan Anderson

Content Project Manager: Nadia Saloom

Media Developer: Mark Hopkinson

Manufacturing Planner: Kevin Kluck

Marketing Communications Manager: Sarah Greber

Marketing Coordinator: Hillary Johns

Production Service: Lumina Datamatics, Inc.

Sr. Art Director: Michele Kunkler

Internal and Cover Designer: Tippy McIntosh

Cover Image: AleksandarGeorgiev/ E+/Getty Images

Intellectual Property Analyst: Brittani Morgan

Project Manager: Nick Barrows

Library of Congress Control Number: 1234567890

Student Edition ISBN: 978-1-337-09973-8

Loose Leaf Edition ISBN: 978-1-337-26996-4

Cengage Learning
20 Channel Center Street
Boston, MA 02210
USA

Cengage Learning is a leading provider of customized learning solutions with employees residing in nearly 40 different countries and sales in more than 125 countries around the world. Find your local representative at **www.cengage.com.**

Cengage Learning products are represented in Canada by Nelson Education, Ltd.

To learn more about Cengage Learning Solutions, visit **www.cengage.com.**

Purchase any of our products at your local college store or at our preferred online store **www.cengagebrain.com.**

Printed in Canada
Print Number: 01   Print Year: 2016

Dedicated to my mother Irene

Brief Contents

PART 1: The International Financial Environment   1
1 Multinational Financial Management: An Overview   3
2 International Flow of Funds   33
3 International Financial Markets   63
4 Exchange Rate Determination   103
5 Currency Derivatives   131

PART 2: Exchange Rate Behavior   185
6 Government Influence on Exchange Rates   187
7 International Arbitrage and Interest Rate Parity   227
8 Relationships among Inflation, Interest Rates, and Exchange Rates   257

PART 3: Exchange Rate Risk Management   295
9 Forecasting Exchange Rates   297
10 Measuring Exposure to Exchange Rate Fluctuations   325
11 Managing Transaction Exposure   355
12 Managing Economic Exposure and Translation Exposure   393

PART 4: Long-Term Asset and Liability Management   415
13 Direct Foreign Investment   417
14 Multinational Capital Budgeting   437
15 International Corporate Governance and Control   477
16 Country Risk Analysis   503
17 Multinational Capital Structure and Cost of Capital   527
18 Long-Term Debt Financing   551

PART 5: Short-Term Asset and Liability Management   575
19 Financing International Trade   577
20 Short-Term Financing   595
21 International Cash Management   611

Appendix A: Answers to Self-Test Questions   643
Appendix B: Supplemental Cases   656
Appendix C: Using Excel to Conduct Analysis   676
Appendix D: International Investing Project   684
Appendix E: Discussion in the Boardroom   687
Appendix F: Use of Bitcoin to Conduct International Transactions   695
Glossary   697
Index   705

Contents

Preface, xix

About the Author, xxvi

PART 1: The International Financial Environment   1

1: MULTINATIONAL FINANCIAL MANAGEMENT: AN OVERVIEW   3

1-1 Managing the MNC, 4

    1-1a How Business Disciplines Are Used to Manage the MNC, 4

    1-1b Agency Problems, 4

    1-1c Management Structure of an MNC, 6

1-2 Why MNCs Pursue International Business, 8

    1-2a Theory of Comparative Advantage, 8

    1-2b Imperfect Markets Theory, 8

    1-2c Product Cycle Theory, 9

1-3 Methods to Conduct International Business, 10

    1-3a International Trade, 10

    1-3b Licensing, 10

    1-3c Franchising, 11

    1-3d Joint Ventures, 11

    1-3e Acquisitions of Existing Operations, 11

    1-3f Establishment of New Foreign Subsidiaries, 12

    1-3g Summary of Methods, 12

1-4 Valuation Model for an MNC, 13

    1-4a Domestic Model, 14

    1-4b Multinational Model, 14

    1-4c Uncertainty Surrounding an MNC's Cash Flows, 17

    1-4d Summary of International Effects, 20

    1-4e How Uncertainty Affects the MNC's Cost of Capital, 21

1-5 Organization of the Text, 21

2: INTERNATIONAL FLOW OF FUNDS   33

2-1 Balance of Payments, 33

    2-1a Current Account, 33

    2-1b Financial Account, 35

    2-1c Capital Account, 36

    2-1d Relationship between the Accounts, 37

2-2 Growth in International Trade, 37

    2-2a Events That Increased Trade Volume, 37

    2-2b Impact of Outsourcing on Trade, 39

    2-2c Trade Volume among Countries, 40

    2-2d Trend in U.S. Balance of Trade, 42

2-3 Factors Affecting International Trade Flows, 43

    2-3a Cost of Labor, 43

2-3b Inflation, 44

2-3c National Income, 44

2-3d Credit Conditions, 44

2-3e Government Policies, 44

2-3f Exchange Rates, 48

2-4 International Capital Flows, 52

2-4a Factors Affecting Direct Foreign Investment, 52

2-4b Factors Affecting International Portfolio Investment, 53

2-4c Impact of International Capital Flows, 53

2-5 Agencies That Facilitate International Flows, 55

2-5a International Monetary Fund, 55

2-5b World Bank, 56

2-5c World Trade Organization, 57

2-5d International Finance Corporation, 57

2-5e International Development Association, 57

2-5f Bank for International Settlements, 57

2-5g OECD, 58

2-5h Regional Development Agencies, 58

3: INTERNATIONAL FINANCIAL MARKETS   63

3-1 Foreign Exchange Market, 63

3-1a History of Foreign Exchange, 63

3-1b Foreign Exchange Transactions, 64

3-1c Foreign Exchange Quotations, 70

3-1d Derivative Contracts in the Foreign Exchange Market, 74

3-2 International Money Market, 75

3-2a European and Asian Money Markets, 76

3-2b Money Market Interest Rates among Currencies, 76

3-2c Risk of International Money Market Securities, 77

3-3 International Credit Market, 78

3-3a Syndicated Loans in the Credit Market, 78

3-3b Bank Regulations in the Credit Market, 79

3-3c Impact of the Credit Crisis, 79

3-4 International Bond Market, 80

3-4a Eurobond Market, 80

3-4b Development of Other Bond Markets, 81

3-4c Risk of International Bonds, 81

3-4d Impact of the Greece Crisis, 82

3-5 International Stock Markets, 83

3-5a Issuance of Stock in Foreign Markets, 83

3-5b Issuance of Foreign Stock in the United States, 84

3-5c Comparing the Size among Stock Markets, 85

3-5d How Governance Varies among Stock Markets, 86

3-5e Integration of International Stock Markets and Credit Markets, 87

3-6 How Financial Markets Serve MNCs, 88

Appendix 3: Investing in International Financial Markets, 95

4: EXCHANGE RATE DETERMINATION   103

4-1 Measuring Exchange Rate Movements, 103

4-2 Exchange Rate Equilibrium, 104

4-2a Demand for a Currency, 105

4-2b Supply of a Currency for Sale, 106

4-2c Equilibrium Exchange Rate, 106

4-2d Change in the Equilibrium Exchange Rate, 107

4-3 Factors That Influence Exchange Rates, 108

4-3a Relative Inflation Rates, 109

4-3b Relative Interest Rates, 110

4-3c Relative Income Levels, 111

4-3d Government Controls, 112

4-3e Expectations, 112

4-3f Interaction of Factors, 114

4-3g Influence of Factors across Multiple Currency Markets, 115

4-3h Impact of Liquidity on Exchange Rate Adjustments, 116

4-4 Movements in Cross Exchange Rates, 116

4-5 Capitalizing on Expected Exchange Rate Movements, 117

4-5a Institutional Speculation Based on Expected Appreciation, 118

4-5b Institutional Speculation Based on Expected Depreciation, 119

4-5c Speculation by Individuals, 120

4-5d The "Carry Trade", 120

5: CURRENCY DERIVATIVES   131

5-1 Forward Market, 131

5-1a How MNCs Use Forward Contracts, 131

5-1b Bank Quotations on Forward Rates, 132

5-1c Premium or Discount on the Forward Rate, 133

5-1d Movements in the Forward Rate over Time, 134

5-1e Offsetting a Forward Contract, 134

5-1f Using Forward Contracts for Swap Transactions, 135

5-1g Non-Deliverable Forward Contracts, 135

5-2 Currency Futures Market, 136

5-2a Contract Specifications, 136

5-2b Trading Currency Futures, 137

5-2c Credit Risk of Currency Futures Contracts, 138

5-2d Comparing Currency Futures and Forward Contracts, 138

5-2e How MNCs Use Currency Futures, 139

5-2f Speculation with Currency Futures, 141

5-3 Currency Options Market, 142

5-3a Currency Options Exchanges, 142

5-3b Over-the-Counter Currency Options Market, 142

5-4 Currency Call Options, 142

5-4a Factors Affecting Currency Call Option Premiums, 143

5-4b How MNCs Use Currency Call Options, 144

5-4c Speculating with Currency Call Options, 145

5-5 Currency Put Options, 148

5-5a Factors Affecting Currency Put Option Premiums, 149

5-5b How MNCs Use Currency Put Options, 149

5-5c Speculating with Currency Put Options, 150

5-6 Other Forms of Currency Options, 152

5-6a Conditional Currency Options, 152

5-6b European Currency Options, 154

Appendix 5A: Currency Option Pricing, 165

Appendix 5B: Currency Option Combinations, 169

Part 1 Integrative Problem: The International Financial Environment, 183

PART 2: Exchange Rate Behavior   185

6: GOVERNMENT INFLUENCE ON EXCHANGE RATES   187
6-1 Exchange Rate Systems, 187
> *6-1a Fixed Exchange Rate System, 187*
> *6-1b Freely Floating Exchange Rate System, 189*
> *6-1c Managed Float Exchange Rate System, 190*
> *6-1d Pegged Exchange Rate System, 191*
> *6-1e Dollarization, 197*
> *6-1f Black Markets for Currencies, 197*

6-2 A Single European Currency, 198
> *6-2a Monetary Policy in the Eurozone, 198*
> *6-2b Impact on Firms in the Eurozone, 199*
> *6-2c Impact on Financial Flows in the Eurozone, 199*
> *6-2d Impact of Eurozone Country Crisis on Other Eurozone Countries, 199*
> *6-2e Impact of a Country Abandoning the Euro, 202*

6-3 Direct Intervention, 203
> *6-3a Reasons for Direct Intervention, 203*
> *6-3b The Direct Intervention Process, 204*
> *6-3c Direct Intervention as a Policy Tool, 207*
> *6-3d Speculating on Direct Intervention, 208*

6-4 Indirect Intervention, 209
> *6-4a Government Control of Interest Rates, 209*
> *6-4b Government Use of Foreign Exchange Controls, 210*

Appendix 6: Government Intervention during the Asian Crisis, 218

7: INTERNATIONAL ARBITRAGE AND INTEREST RATE PARITY   227
7-1 Locational Arbitrage, 227
> *7-1a Gains from Locational Arbitrage, 228*
> *7-1b Realignment due to Locational Arbitrage, 228*

7-2 Triangular Arbitrage, 229
> *7-2a Gains from Triangular Arbitrage, 230*
> *7-2b Realignment due to Triangular Arbitrage, 232*

7-3 Covered Interest Arbitrage, 232
> *7-3a Covered Interest Arbitrage Process, 232*
> *7-3b Realignment due to Covered Interest Arbitrage, 234*
> *7-3c Arbitrage Example When Accounting for Spreads, 235*
> *7-3d Covered Interest Arbitrage by Non-U.S. Investors, 236*
> *7-3e Comparing Different Types of Arbitrage, 236*

7-4 Interest Rate Parity (IRP), 236
> *7-4a Derivation of Interest Rate Parity, 237*
> *7-4b Determining the Forward Premium, 238*
> *7-4c Graphic Analysis of Interest Rate Parity, 240*
> *7-4d How to Test Whether Interest Rate Parity Holds, 242*
> *7-4e Does Interest Rate Parity Hold?, 242*
> *7-4f Considerations When Assessing Interest Rate Parity, 243*

7-5 Variation in Forward Premiums, 244
> *7-5a Forward Premiums across Maturities, 244*
> *7-5b Changes in Forward Premiums over Time, 245*

8: RELATIONSHIPS AMONG INFLATION, INTEREST RATES, AND EXCHANGE RATES   257

8-1 Purchasing Power Parity (PPP), 257

   8-1a Interpretations of Purchasing Power Parity, 257

   8-1b Rationale behind Relative PPP Theory, 258

   8-1c Derivation of Purchasing Power Parity, 258

   8-1d Using PPP to Estimate Exchange Rate Effects, 259

   8-1e Graphic Analysis of Purchasing Power Parity, 260

   8-1f Testing the Purchasing Power Parity Theory, 263

   8-1g Does Purchasing Power Parity Exist?, 265

8-2 International Fisher Effect (IFE), 266

   8-2a Deriving a Country's Expected Inflation Rate, 266

   8-2b Estimating the Expected Exchange Rate Movement, 267

   8-2c Implications of the International Fisher Effect, 267

   8-2d Derivation of the International Fisher Effect, 270

   8-2e Graphic Analysis of the International Fisher Effect, 272

   8-2f Testing the International Fisher Effect, 273

   8-2g Limitations of the IFE Theory, 274

   8-2h IFE Theory versus Reality, 275

   8-2i Comparison of IRP, PPP, and IFE Theories, 275

Part 2 Integrative Problem: Exchange Rate Behavior, 286

Midterm Self-Exam, 287

PART 3: Exchange Rate Risk Management   295

9: FORECASTING EXCHANGE RATES   297

9-1 Why Firms Forecast Exchange Rates, 297

9-2 Forecasting Techniques, 299

   9-2a Technical Forecasting, 299

   9-2b Fundamental Forecasting, 299

   9-2c Market-Based Forecasting, 303

   9-2d Mixed Forecasting, 306

9-3 Assessment of Forecast Performance, 307

   9-3a Measurement of Forecast Error, 307

   9-3b Forecast Errors among Time Horizons, 308

   9-3c Forecast Errors over Time Periods, 308

   9-3d Forecast Errors among Currencies, 308

   9-3e Comparing Forecast Errors among Forecast Techniques, 309

   9-3f Graphic Evaluation of Forecast Bias, 309

   9-3g Statistical Test of Forecast Bias, 311

   9-3h Shifts in Forecast Bias over Time, 312

9-4 Accounting for Uncertainty Surrounding Forecasts, 312

   9-4a Sensitivity Analysis Applied to Fundamental Forecasting, 313

   9-4b Interval Forecasts, 313

10: MEASURING EXPOSURE TO EXCHANGE RATE FLUCTUATIONS   325

10-1 Relevance of Exchange Rate Risk, 325

10-2 Transaction Exposure, 326

   10-2a Estimating "Net" Cash Flows in Each Currency, 328

   10-2b Transaction Exposure of an MNC's Portfolio, 329

10-2c Transaction Exposure Based on Value at Risk, 332

10-3 Economic Exposure, 335

10-3a Exposure to Foreign Currency Depreciation, 336

10-3b Exposure to Foreign Currency Appreciation, 337

10-3c Measuring Economic Exposure, 337

10-4 Translation Exposure, 340

10-4a Determinants of Translation Exposure, 340

10-4b Exposure of an MNC's Stock Price to Translation Effects, 342

11: MANAGING TRANSACTION EXPOSURE   **355**

11-1 Policies for Hedging Transaction Exposure, 355

11-1a Hedging Most of the Exposure, 355

11-1b Selective Hedging, 355

11-2 Hedging Exposure to Payables, 356

11-2a Forward or Futures Hedge on Payables, 356

11-2b Money Market Hedge on Payables, 357

11-2c Call Option Hedge on Payables, 357

11-2d Comparison of Techniques for Hedging Payables, 360

11-2e Evaluating Past Decisions on Hedging Payables, 363

11-3 Hedging Exposure to Receivables, 363

11-3a Forward or Futures Hedge on Receivables, 363

11-3b Money Market Hedge on Receivables, 364

11-3c Put Option Hedge on Receivables, 364

11-3d Comparison of Techniques for Hedging Receivables, 367

11-3e Evaluating Past Decisions on Hedging Receivables, 370

11-3f Summary of Hedging Techniques, 370

11-4 Limitations of Hedging, 371

11-4a Limitation of Hedging an Uncertain Payment, 371

11-4b Limitation of Repeated Short-Term Hedging, 371

11-5 Alternative Methods to Reduce Exchange Rate Risk, 373

11-5a Leading and Lagging, 374

11-5b Cross-Hedging, 374

11-5c Currency Diversification, 374

Appendix 11: Nontraditional Hedging Techniques, 388

12: MANAGING ECONOMIC EXPOSURE AND TRANSLATION EXPOSURE   **393**

12-1 Managing Economic Exposure, 393

12-1a Assessing Economic Exposure, 394

12-1b Restructuring to Reduce Economic Exposure, 395

12-1c Limitations of Restructuring Intended to Reduce Economic Exposure, 398

12-2 A Case Study on Hedging Economic Exposure, 398

12-2a Savor Co.'s Assessment of Economic Exposure, 398

12-2b Possible Strategies for Hedging Economic Exposure, 400

12-3 Managing Exposure to Fixed Assets, 401

12-4 Managing Translation Exposure, 402

12-4a Hedging Translation Exposure with Forward Contracts, 403

12-4b Limitations of Hedging Translation Exposure, 403

Part 3 Integrative Problem: Exchange Risk Management, 412

PART 4: Long-Term Asset and Liability Management   415

13: DIRECT FOREIGN INVESTMENT   417

13-1 Motives for Direct Foreign Investment, 417
  13-1a Revenue-Related Motives, 417
  13-1b Cost-Related Motives, 418
  13-1c Comparing Benefits of DFI among Countries, 420
13-2 Benefits of International Diversification, 421
  13-2a Diversification Analysis of International Projects, 422
  13-2b Diversification among Countries, 424
13-3 Host Government Impact on DFI, 424
  13-3a Incentives to Encourage DFI, 425
  13-3b Barriers to DFI, 425
13-4 Assessing Potential DFI, 427
  13-4a A Case Study of Assessing Potential DFI, 427
  13-4b Evaluating DFI Opportunities That Pass the First Screen, 429

14: MULTINATIONAL CAPITAL BUDGETING   437

14-1 Subsidiary versus Parent Perspective, 437
  14-1a Tax Differentials, 437
  14-1b Restrictions on Remitted Earnings, 438
  14-1c Exchange Rate Movements, 438
  14-1d Summary of Factors That Distinguish the Parent Perspective, 438
14-2 Input for Multinational Capital Budgeting, 439
14-3 Multinational Capital Budgeting Example, 441
  14-3a Background, 441
  14-3b Analysis, 442
14-4 Other Factors to Consider, 443
  14-4a Exchange Rate Fluctuations, 444
  14-4b Inflation, 447
  14-4c Financing Arrangement, 447
  14-4d Blocked Funds, 450
  14-4e Uncertain Salvage Value, 451
  14-4f Impact of Project on Prevailing Cash Flows, 452
  14-4g Host Government Incentives, 453
  14-4h Real Options, 453
14-5 Adjusting Project Assessment for Risk, 454
  14-5a Risk-Adjusted Discount Rate, 454
  14-5b Sensitivity Analysis, 454
  14-5c Simulation, 457

Appendix 14: Incorporating International Tax Law in Multinational Capital Budgeting, 469

15: INTERNATIONAL CORPORATE GOVERNANCE AND CONTROL   477

15-1 International Corporate Governance, 477
  15-1a Governance by Board Members, 477
  15-1b Governance by Institutional Investors, 478
  15-1c Governance by Shareholder Activists, 478
15-2 International Corporate Control, 479
  15-2a Motives for International Acquisitions, 479
  15-2b Trends in International Acquisitions, 479

15-2c Barriers to International Corporate Control, 480

15-2d Model for Valuing a Foreign Target, 481

15-3 Factors Affecting Target Valuation, 482

15-3a Target-Specific Factors, 482

15-3b Country-Specific Factors, 483

15-4 A Case Study of Valuing a Foreign Target, 484

15-4a International Screening Process, 484

15-4b Estimating the Target's Value, 485

15-4c Uncertainty Surrounding the Target's Valuation, 487

15-4d Changes in Market Valuation of Target over Time, 487

15-5 Disparity in Foreign Target Valuations, 488

15-5a Expected Cash Flows of the Foreign Target, 488

15-5b Exchange Rate Effects on Remitted Earnings, 489

15-5c Required Return of Acquirer, 489

15-6 Other Corporate Control Decisions, 490

15-6a International Partial Acquisitions, 490

15-6b International Acquisitions of Privatized Businesses, 490

15-6c International Divestitures, 491

15-7 Corporate Control Decisions as Real Options, 492

15-7a Call Option on Real Assets, 492

15-7b Put Option on Real Assets, 493

16: COUNTRY RISK ANALYSIS   503

16-1 Country Risk Characteristics, 503

16-1a Political Risk Characteristics, 503

16-1b Financial Risk Characteristics, 506

16-2 Measuring Country Risk, 507

16-2a Techniques for Assessing Country Risk, 508

16-2b Deriving a Country Risk Rating, 509

16-2c Comparing Risk Ratings among Countries, 511

16-3 Incorporating Risk in Capital Budgeting, 512

16-3a Adjustment of the Discount Rate, 512

16-3b Adjustment of the Estimated Cash Flows, 512

16-3c Analysis of Existing Projects, 515

16-4 Preventing Host Government Takeovers, 516

16-4a Use a Short-Term Horizon, 516

16-4b Rely on Unique Supplies or Technology, 516

16-4c Hire Local Labor, 516

16-4d Borrow Local Funds, 516

16-4e Purchase Insurance, 517

16-4f Use Project Finance, 517

17: MULTINATIONAL CAPITAL STRUCTURE AND COST OF CAPITAL   527

17-1 Components of Capital, 527

17-1a Retained Earnings, 527

17-1b Sources of Debt, 528

17-1c External Sources of Equity, 529

17-2 The MNC's Capital Structure Decision, 530

17-2a Influence of Corporate Characteristics, 531

17-2b Influence of Host Country Characteristics, 531

17-2c Response to Changing Country Characteristics, 532

17-3 Subsidiary versus Parent Capital Structure Decisions, 533
17-3a Impact of Increased Subsidiary Debt Financing, 533
17-3b Impact of Reduced Subsidiary Debt Financing, 533
17-3c Limitations in Offsetting a Subsidiary's Leverage, 534
17-4 Multinational Cost of Capital, 534
17-4a MNC's Cost of Debt, 534
17-4b MNC's Cost of Equity, 534
17-4c Estimating an MNC's Cost of Capital, 535
17-4d Comparing Costs of Debt and Equity, 535
17-4e Cost of Capital for MNCs versus Domestic Firms, 536
17-4f Cost-of-Equity Comparison Using the CAPM, 537
17-5 Cost of Capital across Countries, 539
17-5a Country Differences in the Cost of Debt, 540
17-5b Country Differences in the Cost of Equity, 541

18: LONG-TERM DEBT FINANCING   **551**
18-1 Debt Denomination Decision of Foreign Subsidiaries, 551
18-1a Foreign Subsidiary Borrows Its Local Currency, 551
18-1b Foreign Subsidiary Borrows Dollars, 553
18-2 Debt Denomination Analysis: A Case Study, 553
18-2a Identifying Debt Denomination Alternatives, 553
18-2b Analyzing Debt Denomination Alternatives, 554
18-3 Loans Facilitate Financing, 555
18-3a Using Currency Swaps, 555
18-3b Using Parallel Loans, 556
18-4 Debt Maturity Decision, 559
18-4a Assessment of the Yield Curve, 559
18-4b Financing Costs of Loans with Different Maturities, 559
18-5 Fixed versus Floating Rate Debt Decision, 560
18-5a Financing Costs of Fixed versus Floating Rate Loans, 560
18-5b Hedging Interest Payments with Interest Rate Swaps, 561
Part 4 Integrative Problem: Long-Term Asset and Liability Management, 572

PART 5: Short-Term Asset and Liability Management   **575**

19: FINANCING INTERNATIONAL TRADE   **577**
19-1 Payment Methods for International Trade, 577
19-1a Prepayment, 577
19-1b Letters of Credit, 578
19-1c Drafts, 580
19-1d Consignment, 581
19-1e Open Account, 581
19-1f Impact of the Credit Crisis on Payment Methods, 581
19-2 Trade Finance Methods, 581
19-2a Accounts Receivable Financing, 582
19-2b Factoring, 582
19-2c Letters of Credit (L/Cs), 583
19-2d Banker's Acceptances, 583
19-2e Medium-Term Capital Goods Financing (Forfaiting), 586
19-2f Countertrade, 586

19-3 Agencies That Facilitate International Trade, 587

    19-3a Export-Import Bank of the United States, 587

    19-3b Private Export Funding Corporation, 589

    19-3c Overseas Private Investment Corporation, 589

20: SHORT-TERM FINANCING   595

20-1 Sources of Foreign Financing, 595

    20-1a Internal Short-Term Financing, 595

    20-1b External Short-Term Financing, 596

    20-1c Access to Funding during a Credit Crisis, 596

20-2 Financing with a Foreign Currency, 596

    20-2a Motive for Financing with a Foreign Currency, 597

    20-2b Potential Cost Savings from Financing with a Foreign Currency, 597

    20-2c Risk of Financing with a Foreign Currency, 598

    20-2d Hedging the Foreign Currency Borrowed, 599

    20-2e Reliance on the Forward Rate for Forecasting, 600

    20-2f Use of Probability Distributions to Enhance the Financing Decision, 601

20-3 Financing with a Portfolio of Currencies, 602

21: INTERNATIONAL CASH MANAGEMENT   611

21-1 Multinational Working Capital Management, 611

    21-1a Subsidiary Expenses, 611

    21-1b Subsidiary Revenue, 612

    21-1c Subsidiary Dividend Payments, 612

    21-1d Subsidiary Liquidity Management, 612

21-2 Centralized Cash Management, 613

    21-2a Accommodating Cash Shortages, 614

21-3 Optimizing Cash Flows, 614

    21-3a Accelerating Cash Inflows, 614

    21-3b Minimizing Currency Conversion Costs, 615

    21-3c Managing Blocked Funds, 617

    21-3d Managing Intersubsidiary Cash Transfers, 617

    21-3e Complications in Optimizing Cash Flow, 617

21-4 Investing Excess Cash, 618

    21-4a Benefits of Investing in a Foreign Currency, 618

    21-4b Risk of Investing in a Foreign Currency, 619

    21-4c Hedging the Investment in a Foreign Currency, 620

    21-4d Break-Even Point from Investing in a Foreign Currency, 621

    21-4e Using a Probability Distribution to Enhance the Investment Decision, 622

    21-4f Investing in a Portfolio of Currencies, 623

    21-4g Dynamic Hedging, 625

    Part 5 Integrative Problem: Short-Term Asset and Liability Management, 631

    Final Self-Exam, 633

Appendix A: Answers to Self-Test Questions, 643

Appendix B: Supplemental Cases, 656

Appendix C: Using Excel to Conduct Analysis, 676

Appendix D: International Investing Project, 684

Appendix E: Discussion in the Boardroom, 687

Appendix F: Use of Bitcoin to Conduct International Transactions, 695

Glossary, 697

Index, 705

Businesses evolve into multinational corporations (MNCs) so that they can capitalize on international opportunities. Their financial managers must be able to assess the international environment, recognize opportunities, implement strategies, assess exposure to risk, and manage that risk. The MNCs most capable of responding to changes in the international financial environment will be rewarded. The same can be said for the students today who may become the future managers of MNCs.

Intended Market

International Financial Management, 13th Edition, presumes an understanding of basic corporate finance. It is suitable for both undergraduate and master's level courses in international financial management. For master's courses, the more challenging questions, problems, and cases in each chapter are recommended, along with special projects.

Organization of the Text

International Financial Management, 13th Edition, is organized to provide a background on the international environment and then to focus on the managerial aspects from a corporate perspective. Managers of MNCs will need to understand the environment before they can manage within it.

The first two parts of the text establish the necessary macroeconomic framework. Part 1 (Chapters 1 through 5) introduces the major markets that facilitate international business. Part 2 (Chapters 6 through 8) describes relationships between exchange rates and economic variables and explains the forces that influence these relationships.

The rest of the text develops a microeconomic framework with a focus on the managerial aspects of international financial management. Part 3 (Chapters 9 through 12) explains the measurement and management of exchange rate risk. Part 4 (Chapters 13 through 18) describes the management of long-term assets and liabilities, including motives for direct foreign investment, multinational capital budgeting, country risk analysis, and capital structure decisions. Part 5 (Chapters 19 through 21) concentrates on the MNC's management of short-term assets and liabilities, including trade financing, other short-term financing, and international cash management.

Each chapter is self-contained so that professors can use classroom time to focus on the more comprehensive topics while relying on the text to cover other concepts. The management of long-term assets (Chapters 13 through 16 on direct foreign investment, multinational capital budgeting, multinational restructuring, and country risk analysis) is covered before the management of long-term liabilities (Chapters 17 and 18 on capital structure and debt financing) because the financing decisions depend on the investment decisions. Nevertheless, these concepts are explained with an emphasis on how the management of long-term assets and long-term liabilities is integrated. For example, multinational capital budgeting analysis demonstrates how the feasibility of a foreign project may depend on the financing mix. Some professors may prefer to teach the chapters on managing long-term liabilities prior to teaching the chapters on managing long-term assets.

The strategic aspects, such as motives for direct foreign investment, are covered before the operational aspects, such as short-term financing or investment. For professors who prefer to cover the MNC's management of short-term assets and liabilities before the management of long-term assets and liabilities, the parts can be rearranged because they are self-contained.

Professors may limit their coverage of chapters in some sections where they believe the text concepts are covered by other courses or do not need additional attention beyond what is in the text. For example, they may give less attention to the chapters in Part 2 (Chapters 6 through 8) if their students take a course in international economics. If professors focus on the main principles, they may limit their coverage of Chapters 5, 15, 16, and 18. In addition, they may give less attention to Chapters 19 through 21 if they believe that the text description does not require elaboration.

Approach of the Text

International Financial Management, 13th Edition, focuses on financial management decisions that maximize the value of multinational corporations. The text offers a variety of methods to reinforce key concepts so that instructors can select the methods and features that best fit their teaching styles.

- *Part-Opening Diagram.* A diagram is provided at the beginning of each part to illustrate how the key concepts covered in that part are related.
- *Objectives.* A bulleted list at the beginning of each chapter identifies the key concepts in that chapter.
- *Examples.* The key concepts are thoroughly described in the chapter and supported by examples.
- *Web Links.* Websites that offer useful related information regarding key concepts are provided in each chapter.
- *Summary.* A bulleted list at the end of each chapter summarizes the key concepts. This list corresponds to the list of objectives at the beginning of the chapter.
- *Point/Counter-Point.* A controversial issue is introduced, along with opposing arguments, and students are asked to determine which argument is correct and to explain why.
- *Self-Test Questions.* A "Self-Test" at the end of each chapter challenges students on the key concepts. The answers to these questions are provided in Appendix A.
- *Questions and Applications.* A substantial set of questions and other applications at the end of each chapter test the student's knowledge of the key concepts in the chapter.
- *Critical Thinking Question.* At the end of each chapter, a critical thinking question challenges the students to use their skills to write a short essay on a specific topic that was given attention in the chapter.
- *Continuing Case.* At the end of each chapter, the continuing case allows students to use the key concepts to solve problems experienced by a firm called Blades, Inc. (a producer of roller blades). By working on cases related to the same MNC over a school term, students recognize how an MNC's decisions are integrated.
- *Small Business Dilemma.* The Small Business Dilemma at the end of each chapter places students in a position where they must use concepts introduced in the chapter to make decisions about a small MNC called Sports Exports Company.
- *Internet/Excel Exercises.* At the end of each chapter are exercises that expose the students to applicable information available at various websites, enable the application of Excel to related topics, or provide a combination of these. *Integrative*

Problem. An integrative problem at the end of each part integrates the key concepts of chapters within that part.

■ *Midterm and Final Examinations.* A midterm self-exam is provided at the end of Chapter 8, which focuses on international macro and market conditions (Chapters 1 through 8). A final self-exam is provided at the end of Chapter 21, which focuses on the managerial chapters (Chapters 9 through 21). Students can compare their answers to those in the answer key provided.

■ *Supplemental Cases.* Supplemental cases allow students to apply chapter concepts to a specific situation of an MNC. All supplemental cases are located in Appendix B.

■ *Running Your Own MNC.* This project allows each student to create a small international business and apply key concepts from each chapter to run the business throughout the school term. The project is available in the textbook companion site (see the "Online Resources" section).

■ *International Investing Project.* This project (located in Appendix D) allows students to simulate investing in stocks of MNCs and foreign companies and requires them to assess how the values of these stocks change during the school term in response to international economic conditions. The project is also available on the textbook companion site (see the "Online Resources" section).

■ *Discussion in the Boardroom.* Located in Appendix E, this project allows students to play the role of managers or board members of a small MNC that they created and to make decisions about that firm. This project is also available on the textbook companion site (see the "Online Resources" section).

■ The variety of end-of-chapter and end-of-part exercises and cases offer many opportunities for students to engage in teamwork, decision making, and communication.

Changes to this Edition

All chapters in the 13th edition have been updated to include recent developments in international financial markets, and in the tools used to manage a multinational corporation. In particular, the following chapters were revised substantially:

■ Chapter 2 has been revised to reflect the balance-of-payments format that is consistent with the recent format used by the U.S. government for reporting the specific accounts.

■ Chapter 3 has been revised to improve flow between sections, and to update the manipulation of exchange rates in the foreign exchange market.

■ Chapter 6 now includes a section on black markets for currencies, and a section on the recent challenges of the European Central Bank (ECB) to stabilize financial conditions in the eurozone.

■ Chapter 8 has been revised substantially to synthesize the relationships between the Fisher effect, purchasing power parity (PPP), and the international Fisher effect (IFE).

■ Chapter 9 has been reorganized to improve the flow.

■ Chapter 10 has been revised to improve flow between sections, and to direct attention to the value at risk method for assessing exchange rate exposure.

■ Chapter 13 now includes a new case study example.

■ Chapter 14 now includes more detailed information about how managers (and students) can use spreadsheets to facilitate the international capital budgeting process and apply sensitivity analysis.

■ Chapter 18 has been revised to improve the flow between sections.

Online Resources

The textbook companion site provides resources for both students and instructors.

Students: Access the following resources by going to **www.cengagebrain.com** and searching **ISBN 9781337099738**: Running Your Own MNC, International Investing Project, Discussion in the Boardroom, Key Terms Flashcards, and chapter Web links.

Instructors: Access textbook resources by going to **www.cengage.com**, logging in with your faculty account username and password, and using **ISBN 9781337099738** to search for instructor resources or to add instructor resources to your account.

Instructor Supplements

The following supplements are available to instructors.

- *Instructor's Manual.* Revised by the author, the Instructor's Manual contains the chapter theme, topics to stimulate class discussion, and answers to end-of-chapter Questions, Case Problems, Continuing Cases (Blades, Inc.), Small Business Dilemmas, Integrative Problems, and Supplemental Cases.
- *Test Bank.* The expanded test bank, which has also been revised by the author, contains a large set of questions in multiple choice or true/false format, including content questions as well as problems.
- *Cognero™ Test Bank.* Cengage Learning Testing Powered by Cognero™ is a flexible online system that allows you to: author, edit, and manage test bank content from multiple Cengage Learning solutions; create multiple test versions in an instant; deliver tests from your LMS, your classroom, or wherever you want. The Cognero™ Test Bank contains the same questions that are in the Microsoft® Word Test Bank. All question content is now tagged according to Tier I (Business Program Interdisciplinary Learning Outcomes) and Tier II (Finance-specific) standards topic, Bloom's Taxonomy, and difficulty level.
- *PowerPoint Slides.* The PowerPoint Slides provide a solid guide for organizing lectures. In addition to the regular notes slides, a separate set of exhibit-only PPTs are also available.

Additional Course Tools

Cengage Learning Custom Solutions

Whether you need print, digital, or hybrid course materials, Cengage Learning Custom Solutions can help you create your perfect learning solution. Draw from Cengage Learning's extensive library of texts and collections, add your own original work, and/or create customized media and technology to match your learning and course objectives. Our editorial team will work with you through each step, allowing you to concentrate on the most important thing—your students. Learn more about all our services at **www.cengage.com/custom**.

MindTap

Feel confident as you use the most engaging digital content available to transform today's students into critical thinkers. Personalize your course to match the way you teach and your students learn. Improve outcomes with real-time insight into student progress, and save time. All while your students engage with your course content, enjoy the flexibility of studying anytime and anywhere, stay connected with the MindTap Mobile app, and earn better grades.

MindTap Instant Access Code ISBN: 9781337270021.

Acknowledgments

Several professors reviewed previous versions of this text and influenced its content and organization. They are acknowledged below in alphabetical order.

Tom Adamson, Midland University

Raj Aggarwal, University of Akron

Richard Ajayi, University of Central Florida

Alan Alford, Northeastern University

Yasser Alhenawi, University of Evansville

H. David Arnold, Auburn University

Robert Aubey, University of Wisconsin

Bruce D. Bagamery, Central Washington University

James C. Baker, Kent State University

Gurudutt Baliga, University of Delaware

Laurence J. Belcher, Stetson University

Richard Benedetto, Merrimack College

Bharat B. Bhalla, Fairfield University

Rahul Bishnoi, Hofstra University

P. R. Chandy, University of North Texas

Prakash L. Dheeriya, California State University – Dominguez Hills

Benjamin Dow, Southeast Missouri State University

Margaret M. Forster, University of Notre Dame

Lorraine Gilbertson, Webster University

Charmaine Glegg, East Carolina University

Anthony Yanxiang Gu, SUNY – Geneseo

Anthony F. Herbst, Suffolk University

Chris Hughen, University of Denver

Abu Jalal, Suffolk University

Steve A. Johnson, University of Texas – El Paso

Manuel L. Jose, University of Akron

Dr. Joan C. Junkus, DePaul University

Rauv Kalra, Morehead State University

Ho-Sang Kang, University of Texas – Dallas

Mohamamd A. Karim, University of Texas – El Paso

Frederick J. Kelly, Seton Hall University

Robert Kemp, University of Virginia

Coleman S. Kendall, University of Illinois – Chicago

Dara Khambata, American University

Chong-Uk Kim, Sonoma State University

Doseong Kim, University of Akron

Elinda F. Kiss, University of Maryland

Thomas J. Kopp, Siena College

Suresh Krishnan, Pennsylvania State University

Merouane Lakehal-Ayat, St. John Fisher College

Duong Le, University of Arkansas – Little Rock

Boyden E. Lee, New Mexico State University

Jeong W. Lee, University of North Dakota

Michael Justin Lee, University of Maryland

Sukhun Lee, Loyola University Chicago

Richard Lindgren, Graceland University

Charmen Loh, Rider University

Carl Luft, DePaul University

Ed Luzine, Union Graduate College

K. Christopher Ma, KCM Investment Co.

Davinder K. Malhotra, Philadelphia University

Richard D. Marcus, University of Wisconsin – Milwaukee

Anna D. Martin, St. Johns University

Leslie Mathis, University of Memphis

Ike Mathur, Southern Illinois University

Wendell McCulloch Jr., California State University – Long Beach

Carl McGowan, University of Michigan – Flint

Fraser McHaffie, Marietta College

Edward T. Merkel, Troy University

Stuart Michelson, Stetson University

Scott Miller, Pepperdine University

Jose Francisco Moreno, University of the Incarnate Word

Penelope E. Nall, Gardner-Webb University

Duc Anh Ngo, University of Texas – El Paso

Srinivas Nippani, Texas A&M University

Andy Noll, St. Catherine University

Vivian Okere, Providence College

Edward Omberg, San Diego State University

Prasad Padmanabhan, San Diego State University

Ali M. Parhizgari, Florida International University

Anne Perry, American University

Rose M. Prasad, Central Michigan University

Larry Prather, East Tennessee State University

Abe Qastin, Lakeland College

Frances A. Quinn, Merrimack College

Mitchell Ratner, Rider University

David Rayome, Northern Michigan University

S. Ghon Rhee, University of Rhode Island

William J. Rieber, Butler University

Mohammad Robbani, Alabama A&M University

Ashok Robin, Rochester Institute of Technology

Alicia Rodriguez de Rubio, University of the Incarnate Word

Tom Rosengarth, Westminster College

Atul K. Saxena, Georgia Gwinnett College

Kevin Scanlon, University of Notre Dame

Michael Scarlatos, CUNY – Brooklyn College

Jeff Schultz, Christian Brothers University

Jacobus T. Severiens, Kent State University

Vivek Sharma, University of Michigan – Dearborn

Peter Sharp, California State University – Sacramento

Dilip K. Shome, Virginia Tech University

Joseph Singer, University of Missouri – Kansas City

Naim Sipra, University of Colorado – Denver

Jacky So, Southern Illinois University – Edwardsville

Luc Soenen, California Polytechnic State University – San Luis Obispo

Ahmad Sohrabian, California State Polytechnic University – Pomona

Carolyn Spencer, Dowling College

Angelo Tarallo, Ramapo College

Amir Tavakkol, Kansas State University

G. Rodney Thompson, Virginia Tech

Stephen G. Timme, Georgia State University

Daniel L. Tompkins, Niagara University

Niranjan Tripathy, University of North Texas

Eric Tsai, Temple University

Joe Chieh-chung Ueng, University of St. Thomas

Mo Vaziri, California State University

Mahmoud S. Wahab, University of Hartford

Ralph C. Walter III, Northeastern Illinois University

Hong Wan, SUNY – Oswego

Elizabeth Webbink, Rutgers University

Ann Marie Whyte, University of Central Florida

Marilyn Wiley, University of North Texas

Rohan Williamson, Georgetown University

Larry Wolken, Texas A&M University

Glenda Wong, De Paul University

Shengxiong Wu, Indiana University – South

J. Jimmy Yang, Oregon State University

Bend Mike Yarmuth, Sullivan University

Yeomin Yoon, Seton Hall University

David Zalewski, Providence College

Emilio Zarruk, Florida Atlantic University

Stephen Zera, California State University – San Marcos

In addition, many friends and colleagues offered useful suggestions that influenced the content and organization of this edition, including Kevin Brady (Florida Atlantic University), Kien Cao (Foreign Trade University), Inga Chira (California State University, Northridge), Jeff Coy (Penn State – Erie), Sean Davis (University of North Florida), Luis Garcia-Feijoo (Florida Atlantic University), Dan Hartnett, Victor Kalafa, Sukhun Lee (Loyola University Chicago), Pat Lewis,Marek Marciniak (West Chester University), Thanh Ngo (East Carolina University), Arjan Premti (University of Wisconsin – Whitewater), Nivine Richie (University of North Carolina – Wilmington), Garrett Smith (University of Wisconsin – Whitewater), Jurica Susnjara (Kean University), Alex Tang (Morgan State University), and Nik Volkov (Mercer University).

I also benefited from the input of many business owners and managers I have met outside the United States who have been willing to share their insight about international financial management.

I appreciate the help and support from the people at Cengage Learning, including Joe Sabatino (Sr. Team Product Manager), Mike Reynolds (Retired), Nate Anderson (Marketing Manager), Brad Sullender and Stacey Lutkoski (Content Developers) and Denisse A Zavala-Rosales (Product Assistant). Special thanks are due to Nadia Saloom (Content Project Manager) and Nancy Ahr (Copyeditor) for their efforts to ensure a quality final product.

Jeff Madura
Florida Atlantic University

About the Author

Dr. Jeff Madura is presently Emeritus Professor of Finance at Florida Atlantic University. He has written several successful finance texts, including *Financial Markets and Institutions* (in its 12th edition). His research on international finance has been published in numerous journals, including *Journal of Financial and Quantitative Analysis*; *Journal of Banking and Finance*; *Journal of Money, Credit and Banking*; *Journal of International Money and Finance*; *Financial Management*; *Journal of Financial Research*; *Financial Review*; *Journal of International Financial Markets, Institutions, and Money*; *Global Finance Journal*; *International Review of Financial Analysis*; and *Journal of Multinational Financial Management*. Dr. Madura has received multiple awards for excellence in teaching and research, and he has served as a consultant for international banks, securities firms, and other multinational corporations. He served as a director for the Southern Finance Association and the Eastern Finance Association, and he is also former president of the Southern Finance Association.

The International Financial Environment

Part 1 (Chapters 1 through 5) provides an overview of the multinational corporation (MNC) and the environment in which it operates. Chapter 1 explains the goals of the MNC, along with the motives and risks of international business. Chapter 2 describes the international flow of funds between countries. Chapter 3 describes the international financial markets and how these markets facilitate ongoing operations. Chapter 4 explains how exchange rates are determined, and Chapter 5 provides background on the currency futures and options markets. Managers of MNCs must understand the international environment described in these chapters in order to make proper decisions.

1
Multinational Financial Management: An Overview

CHAPTER OBJECTIVES

The specific objectives of this chapter are to:

■ identify the management goal and organizational structure of the MNC,

■ describe the key theories about why MNCs engage in international business,

■ explain the common methods used to conduct international business, and

■ provide a model for valuing the MNC.

Multinational corporations (MNCs) are defined as firms that engage in some form of international business. Their managers conduct international financial management, which involves international investing and financing decisions that are intended to maximize the value of the MNC. The goal of these managers is to maximize their firm's value, which is the same goal pursued by managers employed by strictly domestic companies.

Initially, firms may merely attempt to export products to a certain country or import supplies from a foreign manufacturer. Over time, however, many of these firms recognize additional foreign opportunities and eventually establish subsidiaries in foreign countries. Dow Chemical, IBM, Nike, and many other firms have more than half of their assets in foreign countries. Some businesses, such as ExxonMobil, Fortune Brands, and Colgate-Palmolive, commonly generate more than half of their sales in foreign countries. It is typical also for smaller U.S. firms to generate more than 20 percent of their sales in foreign markets; examples include Ferro (Ohio) and Medtronic (Minnesota). Many technology firms, such as Apple, Facebook, and Twitter, expand overseas in order to capitalize on their technology advantages. Many smaller private U.S. firms such as Republic of Tea (California) and Magic Seasoning Blends (Louisiana) generate a substantial percentage of their sales in foreign markets. Seventy-five percent of U.S. firms that export have fewer than 100 employees.

International financial management is important even to companies that have no international business. The reason is that these companies must recognize how their foreign competitors will be influenced by movements in exchange rates, foreign interest rates, labor costs, and inflation. Such economic characteristics can affect the foreign competitors' costs of production and pricing policies.

This chapter provides background on the goals, motives, and valuation of a multinational corporation.

1-1 Managing the MNC

The commonly accepted goal of an MNC is to maximize shareholder wealth. Managers employed by the MNC are expected to make decisions that will maximize the stock price and thereby serve the shareholders' interests. Some publicly traded MNCs based outside the United States may have additional goals, such as satisfying their respective governments, creditors, or employees. However, these MNCs now place greater emphasis on satisfying shareholders; that way, the firm can more easily obtain funds from them to support its operations. Even in developing countries (e.g., Bulgaria and Vietnam) that have just recently encouraged the development of business enterprise, managers of firms must serve shareholder interests in order to secure their funding. There would be little demand for the stock of a firm that announced the proceeds would be used to overpay managers or invest in unprofitable projects.

The focus of this text is on MNCs whose parents wholly own any foreign subsidiaries, which means that the U.S. parent is the sole owner of the subsidiaries. This is the most common form of ownership of U.S.-based MNCs, and it gives financial managers throughout the firm the single goal of maximizing the entire MNC's value (rather than the value of any particular subsidiary). The concepts in this text apply generally also to MNCs based in countries other than the United States.

1-1a How Business Disciplines Are Used to Manage the MNC

Various business disciplines are integrated to manage the MNC in a manner that maximizes shareholder wealth. Management is used to develop strategies that will motivate and guide employees who work in an MNC and to organize resources so that they can efficiently produce products or services. Marketing is used to increase consumer awareness about the products and to monitor changes in consumer preferences. Accounting and information systems are used to record financial information about revenue and expenses of the MNC, which can be used to report financial information to investors and to evaluate the outcomes of various strategies implemented by the MNC. Finance is used to make investment and financing decisions for the MNC. Common finance decisions include:

- whether to discontinue operations in a particular country,
- whether to pursue new business in a particular country,
- whether to expand business in a particular country, and
- how to finance expansion in a particular country.

These finance decisions for each MNC are partially influenced by the other business discipline functions. The decision to pursue new business in a particular country is based on comparing the costs and potential benefits of expansion. The potential benefits of such new business depend on expected consumer interest in the products to be sold (marketing function) and expected cost of the resources needed to pursue the new business (management function). Financial managers rely on financial data provided by the accounting and information systems functions.

1-1b Agency Problems

Managers of an MNC may make decisions that conflict with the firm's goal of maximizing shareholder wealth. For example, a decision to establish a subsidiary in one location versus another may be based on the location's appeal to a particular manager rather than on its potential benefits to shareholders. A decision to expand a subsidiary may be motivated by a manager's desire to receive more compensation rather than to enhance the value of the MNC. This conflict of goals between a firm's managers and shareholders is often referred to as the **agency problem**.

The costs of ensuring that managers maximize shareholder wealth (referred to as *agency costs*) are normally larger for MNCs than for purely domestic firms for several reasons. First, MNCs with subsidiaries scattered around the world may experience larger agency problems because monitoring the managers of distant subsidiaries in foreign countries is more difficult. Second, foreign subsidiary managers who are raised in different cultures may not follow uniform goals. Some of them may believe that the first priority should be to serve their respective employees. Third, the sheer size of the larger MNCs can also create significant agency problems, because it complicates the monitoring of managers.

EXAMPLE   Two years ago, Seattle Co. (based in the United States) established a subsidiary in Singapore so that it could expand its business there. It hired a manager in Singapore to manage the subsidiary. During the last two years, sales generated by the subsidiary have not grown. Even so, the manager hired several employees to do the work that he was assigned to do. The managers of the parent company in the United States have not closely monitored the subsidiary because it is so far away and because they trusted the manager there. Now they realize that there is an agency problem. The subsidiary is experiencing losses every quarter, so its management must be more closely monitored. ●

Lack of monitoring can lead to substantial losses for MNCs. The large New York–based bank JPMorgan Chase & Co. lost at least $6.2 billion and had to pay more than $1 billion in fines and penalties after a trader in its office in London, England, made extremely risky trades. The subsequent investigation revealed that the bank had maintained poor internal control and failed to provide proper oversight of its employees.

Parent Control of Agency Problems   The parent corporation of an MNC may be able to prevent most agency problems with proper governance. The parent should clearly communicate the goals for each subsidiary to ensure that all of them focus on maximizing the value of the MNC and not of their respective subsidiaries. The parent can oversee subsidiary decisions to check whether each subsidiary's managers are satisfying the MNC's goals. The parent also can implement compensation plans that reward those managers who satisfy the MNC's goals. A common incentive is to provide managers with the MNC's stock (or options to buy that stock at a fixed price) as part of their compensation; thus the subsidiary managers benefit directly from a higher stock price when they make decisions that enhance the MNC's value.

EXAMPLE   When Seattle Co. (from the previous example) recognized the agency problems with its Singapore subsidiary, it created incentives for the manager of the subsidiary that aligned with the parent's goal of maximizing shareholder wealth. Specifically, it set up a compensation system whereby the manager's annual bonus is based on the subsidiary's earnings. ●

Corporate Control of Agency Problems   In some cases, agency problems can occur because the goals of the entire management of the MNC are not focused on maximizing shareholder wealth. Various forms of corporate control can help prevent these agency problems and thus induce managers to make decisions that satisfy the MNC's shareholders. If these managers make poor decisions that reduce the MNC's value, then another firm might acquire it at the lower price and hence would probably remove the weak managers. Moreover, institutional investors (e.g., mutual and pension funds) with large holdings of an MNC's stock have some influence over management because they will complain to the board of directors if managers are making poor decisions.

Institutional investors may seek to enact changes, including removal of high-level managers or even board members, in a poorly performing MNC. Such investors may also band together to demand changes in an MNC, as they know that the firm would not want to lose all of its major shareholders.

How SOX Improved Corporate Governance of MNCs   One limitation of the corporate control process is that investors rely on reports by the firm's own managers for information. If managers are serving themselves rather than the investors, they may exaggerate their performance. There are many well-known examples (such as Enron and WorldCom) in which large MNCs were able to alter their financial reporting and hide problems from investors.

Enacted in 2002, the Sarbanes-Oxley Act (SOX) ensures a more transparent process for managers to report on the productivity and financial condition of their firm. It requires firms to implement an internal reporting process that can be easily monitored by executives and the board of directors. Some of the common methods used by MNCs to improve their internal control process are:

■   establishing a centralized database of information,
■   ensuring that all data are reported consistently among subsidiaries,
■   implementing a system that automatically checks data for unusual discrepancies relative to norms,
■   speeding the process by which all departments and subsidiaries access needed data, and
■   making executives more accountable for financial statements by personally verifying their accuracy.

These systems make it easier for a firm's board members to monitor the financial reporting process. In this way, SOX reduced the likelihood that managers of a firm can manipulate the reporting process and therefore improved the accuracy of financial information for existing and prospective investors.

1-1c Management Structure of an MNC

The magnitude of agency costs can vary with the MNC's management style. A centralized management style, as illustrated in the top section of Exhibit 1.1, can reduce agency costs because it allows managers of the parent to control foreign subsidiaries and thus reduces the power of subsidiary managers. However, the parent's managers may make poor decisions for the subsidiary if they are less informed than the subsidiary's managers about its setting and financial characteristics.

Alternatively, an MNC can use a decentralized management style, as illustrated in the bottom section of Exhibit 1.1. This style is more likely to result in higher agency costs because subsidiary managers may make decisions that fail to maximize the value of the entire MNC. Yet this management style gives more control to those managers who are closer to the subsidiary's operations and environment. To the extent that subsidiary managers recognize the goal of maximizing the value of the overall MNC and are compensated in accordance with that goal, the decentralized management style may be more effective.

Given the clear trade-offs between centralized and decentralized management styles, some MNCs attempt to achieve the advantages of both. That is, they allow subsidiary managers to make the key decisions about their respective operations while the parent's management monitors those decisions to ensure they are in the MNC's best interests.

Exhibit 1.1 Management Styles of MNCs

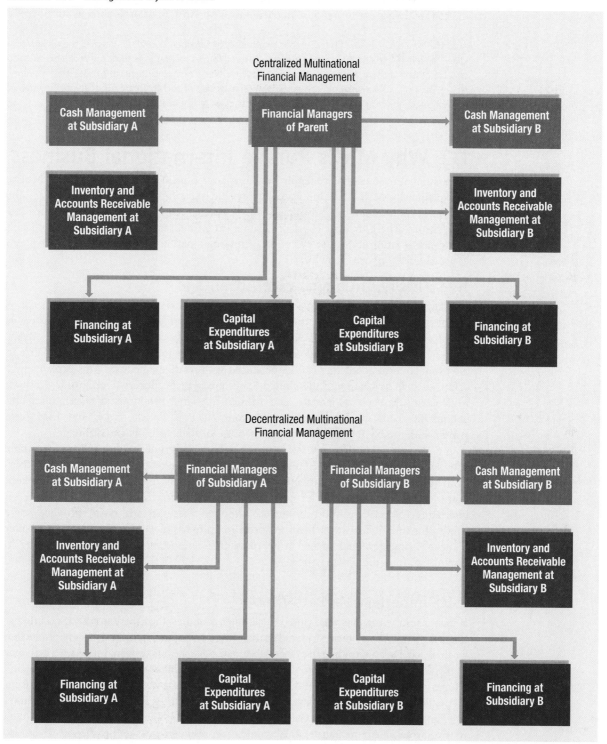

How the Internet Facilitates Management Control   The Internet simplifies the process for the parent to monitor the actions and performance of its foreign subsidiaries.

EXAMPLE   Recall the example of Seattle Co., which has a subsidiary in Singapore. Using the Internet, the foreign subsidiary can e-mail updated information in a standardized format that reduces language problems and also send images of financial reports and product designs. The parent can then easily track the inventory, sales, expenses, and earnings of each subsidiary on a weekly or monthly basis. Thus using the Internet can reduce agency costs due to international aspects of an MNC's business. ●

1-2 Why MNCs Pursue International Business

Multinational business has generally increased over time. Three commonly held theories to explain why MNCs are motivated to expand their business internationally are the (1) theory of comparative advantage, (2) imperfect markets theory, and (3) product cycle theory. These theories overlap to some extent and can complement each other in developing a rationale for the evolution of international business.

1-2a Theory of Comparative Advantage

Specialization by countries can increase production efficiency. Some countries, such as Japan and the United States, have a technology advantage, whereas others, such as China and Malaysia, have an advantage in the cost of basic labor. Because these advantages cannot easily be transported, countries tend to use their advantages to specialize in the production of goods that can be produced with relative efficiency. This explains why countries such as Japan and the United States are large producers of electronic products while countries such as Jamaica and Mexico are large producers of agricultural and handmade goods. Multinational corporations such as Oracle, Intel, and IBM have grown substantially in foreign countries because of their technology advantage.

A country that specializes in some products may not produce other products, so trade between countries is essential. This is the argument made by the classical theory of comparative advantage. **Comparative advantages** allow firms to penetrate foreign markets. Many of the Virgin Islands, for example, specialize in tourism and rely completely on international trade for most products. Although these islands could produce some goods, it is more efficient for them to specialize in tourism. That is, the islands are better off using some revenues earned from tourism to import products than attempting to produce all the products they need.

1-2b Imperfect Markets Theory

If each country's markets were closed to all other countries, then there would be no international business. At the other extreme, if markets were perfect and thus the factors of production (such as labor) easily transferable, then labor and other resources would flow wherever they were in demand. Such unrestricted mobility of factors would create equality in both costs and returns and thus would remove the comparative cost advantage, which is the rationale for international trade and investment. However, the real world suffers from **imperfect market** conditions where factors of production are somewhat immobile. There are costs and often restrictions related to the transfer of labor and other resources used for production. There also may be restrictions on transferring funds and other resources among countries. Because markets for the various resources used in production are "imperfect," MNCs such as the Gap and Nike often capitalize on a foreign country's particular resources. Imperfect markets provide an incentive for firms to seek out foreign opportunities.

1-2c Product Cycle Theory

One of the more popular explanations as to why firms evolve into MNCs is the **product cycle theory**. According to this theory, firms become established in the home market as a result of some perceived advantage over existing competitors, such as a need by the market for at least one more supplier of the product. Because information about markets and competition is more readily available at home, a firm is likely to establish itself first in its home country. Foreign demand for the firm's product will initially be accommodated by exporting. As time passes, the firm may feel the only way to retain its advantage over competition in foreign countries is to produce the product in foreign markets, thereby reducing its transportation costs. The competition in those foreign markets may increase as other producers become more familiar with the firm's product. The firm may develop strategies to prolong the foreign demand for its product. One frequently used approach is to differentiate the product so that competitors cannot duplicate it exactly. These phases of the product cycle are illustrated in Exhibit 1.2. For instance, 3M Co. uses one new product to enter a foreign market, after which it expands the product line there.

There is, of course, more to the product cycle theory than summarized here. This discussion merely suggests that, as a firm matures, it may recognize additional opportunities outside its home country. Whether the firm's foreign business diminishes or expands over time will depend on how successful it is at maintaining some advantage over its competition. That advantage could be an edge in its production or financing approach that reduces costs or an edge in its marketing approach that generates and maintains a strong demand for its product.

Exhibit 1.2 International Product Life Cycle

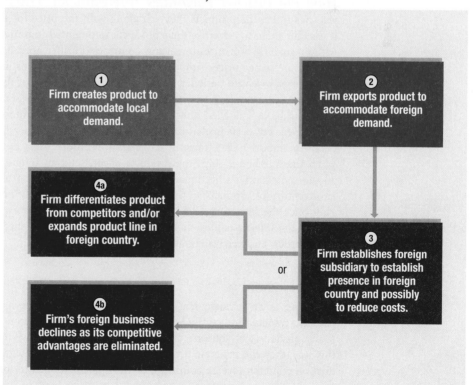

1-3 Methods to Conduct International Business

Firms use several methods to conduct international business. The most common methods are:

■   international trade,
■   licensing,
■   franchising,
■   joint ventures,
■   acquisitions of existing operations, and
■   establishment of new foreign subsidiaries.

Each method will be discussed in turn, with particular attention paid to the respective risk and return characteristics.

1-3a International Trade

WEB

www.trade.gov/mas/ian
Outlook of international
trade conditions for each
of several industries.

International trade is a relatively conservative approach that can be used by firms to penetrate markets (by exporting) or to obtain supplies at a low cost (by importing). This approach entails minimal risk because the firm does not place any of its capital at risk. If the firm experiences a decline in its exporting or importing, it can normally reduce or discontinue that part of its business at a low cost.

Many large U.S.-based MNCs, including Boeing, DuPont, General Electric, and IBM, generate more than $4 billion in annual sales from exporting. Nonetheless, small businesses account for more than 20 percent of the value of all U.S. exports.

How the Internet Facilitates International Trade   Many firms use their websites to list the products they sell along with the price for each product. This makes it easy for them to advertise their products to potential importers anywhere in the world without mailing brochures to various countries. Furthermore, a firm can add to its product line or change prices simply by revising its website. Thus importers need only check an exporter's website periodically in order to keep abreast of its product information.

Firms also can use their websites to accept orders online. Some products, such as software, can be downloaded directly by the importer via the Internet. Other products must be shipped, but even in that case the Internet makes it easier to track the shipping process. An importer can transmit its order for products via e-mail to the exporter, and when the warehouse ships the products it can send an e-mail message to the importer and to the exporter's headquarters. The warehouse may also use technology to monitor its inventory of products so that suppliers are automatically notified to send more supplies once the inventory falls below a specified level. If the exporter has multiple warehouses, the Internet allows them to operate as a network; hence if one warehouse cannot fill an order, another warehouse will.

1-3b Licensing

Licensing is an arrangement whereby one firm provides its technology (copyrights, patents, trademarks, or trade names) in exchange for fees or other considerations. Many producers of software allow foreign companies to use their software for a fee. In this way, they can generate revenue from foreign countries without establishing any production plants in foreign countries, or transporting goods to foreign countries.

1-3c Franchising

Under a **franchising** arrangement, one firm provides a specialized sales or service strategy, support assistance, and possibly an initial investment in the franchise in exchange for periodic fees, allowing local residents to own and manage the units. For example, McDonald's, Pizza Hut, Subway, and Dairy Queen have franchises that are owned and managed by local residents in many foreign countries. As an example, McDonald's typically purchases the land and establishes the building. It then leases the building to a franchisee and allows the franchisee to operate the business in the building for a specified number of years (such as 20 years), but the franchisee must follow standards set by McDonald's when operating the business. Because franchising by an MNC often requires a direct investment in foreign operations, this is referred to as a **direct foreign investment (DFI)**.

1-3d Joint Ventures

A **joint venture** is a venture that is jointly owned and operated by two or more firms. Many firms enter foreign markets by engaging in a joint venture with firms that already reside in those markets. Most joint ventures allow two firms to apply their respective comparative advantages in a given project. Joint ventures often require some degree of DFI, while the other parties involved in the joint ventures also participate in the investment.

For instance, General Mills, Inc., joined in a venture with Nestlé SA so that the cereals produced by General Mills could be sold through the overseas sales distribution network established by Nestlé. Xerox Corp. and Fuji Co. (of Japan) engaged in a joint venture that allowed Xerox to penetrate the Japanese market while allowing Fuji to enter the photocopying business. Kellogg Co. and Wilmar International Ltd. have established a joint venture to manufacture and distribute cereals and snack products in China. Wilmar already has a wholly owned subsidiary in China, and it is participating in the venture. Joint ventures between automobile manufacturers are numerous because each manufacturer can offer its own technological advantages. General Motors has ongoing joint ventures with automobile manufacturers in several different countries, including the former Soviet states.

1-3e Acquisitions of Existing Operations

Firms frequently acquire other firms in foreign countries as a means of penetrating foreign markets. Such acquisitions give firms full control over their foreign businesses and enable the MNC to quickly obtain a large portion of foreign market share. Acquisitions represent direct foreign investment because MNCs directly invest in a foreign country by purchasing the operations of target companies.

EXAMPLE   Google, Inc., has made major international acquisitions to expand its business and improve its technology. It has acquired businesses in Australia (search engines), Brazil (search engines), Canada (mobile browser), China (search engines), Finland (micro-blogging), Germany (mobile software), Russia (online advertising), South Korea (weblog software), Spain (photo sharing), and Sweden (videoconferencing). ●

However, the acquisition of an existing corporation could lead to large losses because of the large investment required. In addition, if the foreign operations perform poorly then it may be difficult to sell the operations at a reasonable price.

Some firms engage in partial international acquisitions in order to obtain a toehold or stake in foreign operations. This approach requires a smaller investment than that of a full international acquisition and so exposes the firm to less risk. On the other hand, the firm will not have complete control over foreign operations that are only partially acquired.

1-3f Establishment of New Foreign Subsidiaries

Firms can also penetrate foreign markets by establishing new operations in foreign countries to produce and sell their products. Like a foreign acquisition, this method requires a large direct foreign investment. Establishing new subsidiaries may be preferred to foreign acquisitions because the operations can be tailored exactly to the firm's needs. In addition, a smaller investment may be required than would be needed to purchase existing operations. However, the firm will not reap any rewards from the investment until the subsidiary is built and a customer base established.

1-3g Summary of Methods

The methods of increasing international business extend from the relatively simple approach of international trade to the more complex approach of acquiring foreign firms or establishing new subsidiaries. International trade and licensing are usually not viewed as examples of DFI because they do not involve direct investment in foreign operations. Franchising and joint ventures tend to require some investment in foreign operations but only to a limited degree. Foreign acquisitions and the establishment of new foreign subsidiaries require substantial investment in foreign operations and account for the largest portion of DFI.

Many MNCs use a combination of methods to increase international business. For example, IBM and PepsiCo engage in substantial direct foreign investment yet also derive some of their foreign revenue from various licensing agreements, which require less DFI to generate revenue.

EXAMPLE The evolution of Nike began in 1962 when Phil Knight, a student at Stanford's business school, wrote a paper on how a U.S. firm could use Japanese technology to break the German dominance of the athletic shoe industry in the United States. After graduation, Knight visited the Unitsuka Tiger shoe company in Japan. He made a licensing agreement with that company to produce a shoe that he sold in the United States under the name Blue Ribbon Sports (BRS). In 1972, Knight exported his shoes to Canada. In 1974, he expanded his operations into Australia. In 1977, the firm licensed factories in Taiwan and Korea to produce athletic shoes and then sold the shoes in Asian countries. In 1978, BRS became Nike, Inc., and began to export shoes to Europe and South America. As a result of its exporting and its direct foreign investment, Nike's international sales reached $1 billion by 1992 and now exceed $8 billion per year. ●

The effects of international business on an MNC's cash flows are illustrated in Exhibit 1.3. In general, the cash outflows associated with international business by the U.S. parent are used to pay for imports, to comply with its international arrangements, and/or to support the creation or expansion of foreign subsidiaries. At the same time, an MNC receives cash flows in the form of payment for its exports, fees for the services it provides within international arrangements, and remitted funds from the foreign subsidiaries. The first diagram in this exhibit illustrates the case of an MNC that engages in international trade; its international cash flows therefore result either from paying for imported supplies or from receiving payment in exchange for products that it exports.

The second diagram illustrates an MNC that engages in some international arrangements (which could include international licensing, franchising, or joint ventures). Any such arrangement may require cash outflows of the MNC in foreign countries to cover, for example, the expenses associated with transferring technology or funding partial

Exhibit 1.3 Cash Flow Diagrams for MNCs

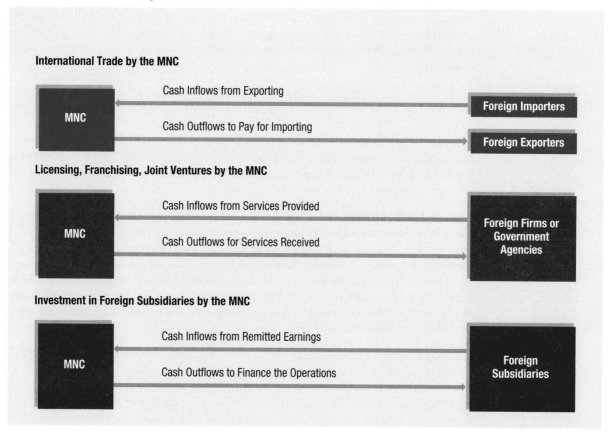

investment in a franchise or joint venture. These arrangements generate cash flows for the MNC in the form of fees for services (e.g., technology, support assistance) that it provides.

The third diagram in Exhibit 1.3 illustrates the case of an MNC that engages in direct foreign investment. This type of MNC has one or more foreign subsidiaries. There can be cash outflows from the U.S. parent to its foreign subsidiaries in the form of invested funds to help finance the operations of the foreign subsidiaries. There are also cash flows from the foreign subsidiaries to the U.S. parent in the form of remitted earnings and fees for services provided by the parent; all of these flows can be classified as remitted funds from the foreign subsidiaries.

1-4 Valuation Model for an MNC

The value of an MNC is relevant to its shareholders and its debt holders. When managers make decisions that maximize the firm's value, they also maximize shareholder wealth (assuming that the decisions are not intended to maximize the wealth of debt holders at the expense of shareholders). Given that international financial management should be conducted with the goal of increasing the MNC's value, it is useful to review some basics of valuation. There are numerous methods of valuing an MNC, some of which lead to the same valuation. The method described in this section reflects the key factors affecting an MNC's value in a general sense.

1-4a Domestic Model

Before modeling an MNC's value, consider the valuation of a purely domestic firm in the United States that does not engage in any foreign transactions. The value (V) of the purely domestic firm is commonly specified as the present value of its expected dollar cash flows:

$$V = \sum_{t=1}^{n} \left\{ \frac{E(CF_{\$,t})}{(1+k)^t} \right\}$$

Here $E(CF_{\$,t})$ denotes expected cash flows to be received at the end of period t; n is the number of future periods in which cash flows are received; and k represents not only the weighted average cost of capital but also the required rate of return by investors and creditors who provide funds to the MNC.

Dollar Cash Flows The dollar cash flows in period t represent funds received by the firm minus funds needed to pay expenses or taxes or to reinvest in the firm (such as an investment to replace old computers or machinery). The expected cash flows are estimated from knowledge about various existing projects as well as other projects that will be implemented in the future. A firm's decisions about how it should invest funds to expand its business can affect its expected future cash flows and therefore can affect the firm's value. Holding other factors constant, an increase in expected cash flows over time should increase the value of a firm.

Cost of Capital The required rate of return (k) in the denominator of the valuation equation represents the cost of capital (including both the cost of debt and the cost of equity) to the firm and is, in essence, a weighted average of the cost of capital based on all of the firm's projects. In making decisions that affect its cost of debt or equity for one or more projects, the firm also affects the weighted average of its cost of capital and thus the required rate of return. If the firm's credit rating is suddenly lowered, for example, then its cost of capital will probably increase and so will its required rate of return. Holding other factors constant, an increase in the firm's required rate of return will reduce the value of the firm because expected cash flows must be discounted at a higher interest rate. Conversely, a decrease in the firm's required rate of return will increase the value of the firm because expected cash flows are discounted at a lower required rate of return.

1-4b Multinational Model

An MNC's value can be specified in the same manner as a purely domestic firm's value. However, consider that the expected cash flows generated by a U.S.-based MNC's parent in period t may be coming from various countries and may be denominated in different foreign currencies.

The foreign currency cash flows will be converted into dollars. Thus the expected dollar cash flows to be received at the end of period t are equal to the sum of the products of cash flows denominated in each currency j multiplied by the expected exchange rate at which currency j could be converted into dollar cash flows by the MNC at the end of period t:

$$E(CF_{\$,t}) = \sum_{j=1}^{m} [E(CF_{j,t}) \times E(S_{j,t})]$$

Here $CF_{j,t}$ represents the amount of cash flow denominated in a particular foreign currency j at the end of period t, and $S_{j,t}$ denotes the exchange rate at which the foreign currency (measured in dollars per unit of the foreign currency) can be converted to dollars at the end of period t.

Valuation of an MNC That Uses Two Currencies

An MNC that does business in two currencies could measure its expected dollar cash flows in any period by multiplying the expected cash flow in each currency by the expected exchange rate at which that currency could be converted to dollars and then summing those two products.

It may help to think of an MNC as a portfolio of currency cash flows, one for each currency in which it conducts business. The expected dollar cash flows derived from each of those currencies can be combined to determine the total expected dollar cash flows in the given period. It is easier to derive an expected dollar cash flow value for each currency before combining the cash flows among currencies within a given period, because each currency's cash flow amount must be converted to a common unit (the dollar) before combining the amounts.

EXAMPLE

Carolina Co. has expected cash flows of $100,000 from local business and 1 million Mexican pesos from business in Mexico at the end of period t. Assuming that the peso's value is expected to be $.09 when converted into dollars, the expected dollar cash flows are:

$$
\begin{aligned}
E(CF_{\$,t}) &= \sum_{j=1}^{m} [E(CF_{j,t}) \times E(S_{j,t})] \\
&= \text{\$ CF from U.S. operations } + \text{ \$ CF from operations in Mexico} \\
&= \$\,100{,}000 + [1{,}000{,}000 \text{ pesos } \times (\$.09)] \\
&= \$\,100{,}000 + \$\,90{,}000 \\
&= \$190{,}000.
\end{aligned}
$$

The cash flows of $100,000 from U.S. business were already denominated in U.S. dollars and therefore did not have to be converted. ●

Valuation of an MNC That Uses Multiple Currencies

The same process as just described can be employed to value an MNC that uses many foreign currencies. The general formula for estimating the dollar cash flows to be received by an MNC from multiple currencies in one period can be written as follows:

$$
E(CF_{\$,t}) = \sum_{j=1}^{m} [E(CF_{j,t}) \times E(S_{j,t})]
$$

EXAMPLE

Assume that Yale Co. will receive cash in 15 different countries at the end of the next period. To estimate the value of Yale Co., the first step is to estimate the amount of cash flows that it will receive at the end of the period in each currency (such as 2 million euros, 8 million Mexican pesos, etc.). Second, obtain a forecast of the currency's exchange rate for cash flows that will arrive at the end of the period for each of the 15 currencies (such as euro forecast = $1.40, peso forecast = $.12, etc.). The existing exchange rate can be used as a forecast for the future exchange rate, but there are many alternative methods (as explained in Chapter 9). Third, multiply the amount of each foreign currency to be received by the forecasted exchange rate of that currency in order to estimate the dollar cash flows to be received due to each currency. Fourth, add the estimated dollar cash flows for all 15 currencies in order to determine the total expected dollar cash flows in the period. The previous equation captures the four steps just described. When applying that equation to this example, $m = 15$ because there are 15 different currencies. ●

Valuation of an MNC's Cash Flows over Multiple Periods

The entire process described in the example for a single period is not adequate for valuation because most MNCs have multiperiod cash flows. However, the process can be easily adapted to estimate the total dollar cash flows for all future periods. First, apply the same process described for a single period to all future periods in which the MNC will receive cash flows; this will generate an estimate of total dollar cash flows to be received in every period in the future. Second, discount the estimated total dollar cash flow for each period at the weighted cost of capital (k) and then sum these discounted cash flows to estimate the value of this MNC.

The process for valuing an MNC receiving multiple currencies over multiple periods can be expressed formally as:

$$V = \sum_{t=1}^{n} \left\{ \frac{\sum_{j=1}^{m}[E(CF_{j,t}) \times E(S_{j,t})]}{(1+k)^t} \right\}$$

Here $CF_{j,t}$ is the cash flow denominated in a particular currency (which may be dollars) and $S_{j,t}$ denotes represents the exchange rate at which the MNC can convert the foreign to the domestic currency at the end of period t. Whereas the previous equation is applied to single-period cash flows, this equation considers cash flows over multiple periods and then discounts those flows to obtain a present value.

Because the management of an MNC should be focused on maximizing its value, the equation for valuing an MNC is extremely important. According to this equation, the value (V) will increase in response to managerial decisions that increase the amount of its cash flows in a particular currency (CF_j) or to conditions that increase the exchange rate at which that currency is converted into dollars (S_j).

To avoid double counting, cash flows of the MNC's subsidiaries are considered in the valuation model only when they reflect transactions with the U.S. parent. Therefore, any expected cash flows received by foreign subsidiaries should not be counted in the valuation equation unless they are expected to be remitted to the parent.

The denominator of the valuation model for the MNC remains unchanged from the original valuation model for the purely domestic firm. However, note that the weighted average cost of capital for the MNC is based on funding some projects involving business in different countries. Hence any decision by the MNC's parent that affects the cost of its capital supporting projects in a specific country will also affect its weighted average cost of capital (and required rate of return) and thereby its value.

EXAMPLE

Austin Co. is a U.S.-based MNC that sells video games to U.S. consumers; it also has European subsidiaries that produce and sell the games in Europe. The firm's European earnings are denominated in euros (the currency of most European countries), and these earnings are typically remitted to the U.S. parent. Last year, Austin received $40 million in cash flows from its U.S. operations and 20 million euros from its European operations. The euro was valued at $1.30 when remitted to the U.S parent, so Austin's cash flows last year are calculated as follows:

Austin's total
$ cash flows last year = $ cash flows from U.S. operations + $ cash flows from foreign operations
= $ cash flows from U.S. operations + [(euro cash flows) × (euro exchange rate)]
= $40,000,000 + [(20,000,000 euros) × ($1.30)]
= $40,000,000 + $26,000,000
= $66,000,000

Assume that Austin Co. plans to continue its business in the United States and Europe for the next three years. As a basic valuation model, the firm could use last year's cash flows to estimate each future year's cash flows; then its expected cash flows would be $66 million for each of the next three years. Its valuation could be estimated by discounting these cash flows at its cost of capital. ●

1-4c Uncertainty Surrounding an MNC's Cash Flows

The MNC's future cash flows (and therefore its valuation) are subject to uncertainty because of its exposure not only to domestic economic conditions but also to international economic conditions, political conditions, and exchange rate risk. These factors are explained next, and Exhibit 1.4 complements the discussion.

Exposure to International Economic Conditions   To the extent that a foreign country's economic conditions affect an MNC's cash flows, they affect the MNC's valuation. The cash inflows that an MNC receives from sales in a foreign country during a given period depends on the demand by that country's consumers for the MNC's products, which in turn is affected by that country's national income in that period. If economic conditions improve in that country, consumers there may enjoy an increase in their income and the employment rate may rise. In that case, those consumers will have more money to spend and their demand for the MNC's products will increase. This illustrates how the MNC's cash flows increasing because of its exposure to international economic conditions.

However, an MNC can also be adversely affected by its exposure to international economic conditions. If conditions weaken in the foreign country where the MNC does business, that country's consumers suffer a decrease in their income and the employment rate may decline. Then those consumers have less money to spend, and their demand for the MNC's products will decrease. In this case, the MNC's cash flows are reduced because of its exposure to international economic conditions.

When Facebook went public in 2012, the registration statement acknowledged its exposure to international economic conditions: "We plan to continue expanding our operations abroad where we have limited operating experience and may be subject to increasing business and economic risks that could affect our financial results."

Exhibit 1.4   How an MNC's Valuation Is Exposed to Uncertainty (Risk)

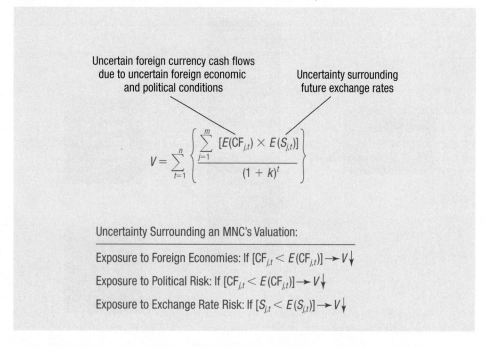

Uncertain foreign currency cash flows due to uncertain foreign economic and political conditions

Uncertainty surrounding future exchange rates

$$V = \sum_{t=1}^{n} \left\{ \frac{\sum_{j=1}^{m} [E(CF_{j,t}) \times E(S_{j,t})]}{(1+k)^t} \right\}$$

Uncertainty Surrounding an MNC's Valuation:

Exposure to Foreign Economies: If $[CF_{j,t} < E(CF_{j,t})] \rightarrow V\downarrow$

Exposure to Political Risk: If $[CF_{j,t} < E(CF_{j,t})] \rightarrow V\downarrow$

Exposure to Exchange Rate Risk: If $[S_{j,t} < E(S_{j,t})] \rightarrow V\downarrow$

International economic conditions can also affect the MNC's cash flows indirectly by affecting the MNC's home economy. Consider that when a country's economy strengthens and hence its consumers buy more products from firms in other countries, the firms in those other countries experience stronger sales and cash flows. Therefore, the owners and employees of these firms have more income. When they spend a portion of that higher income locally, they stimulate their local economy.

Conversely, if the foreign country's economy weakens and hence its consumers buy fewer products from firms in other countries, then the firms in those countries experience weaker sales and cash flows. The owners and employees of these firms therefore have less income, and if they reduce spending locally their local economy weakens.

There is much international trade between the United States and Europe. European countries under weak economic conditions tend to reduce their demand for U.S.-made products. The result may be weaker economic conditions in the United States, which may lead to lower national income and higher unemployment there. Then U.S. consumers would have less money to spend and so would reduce their demand for the products offered by U.S.-based MNCs. In recent years, the financial press has featured extensive coverage on how bad economic conditions in European countries adversely affect the U.S economy. Similarly, research has documented that U.S. stock market performance is highly sensitive to economic conditions in Europe.

The effects on international economic conditions are illustrated in Exhibit 1.5, which shows how weak European conditions can affect the valuations of U.S.-based MNCs. The top string of effects (from left to right) in this exhibit indicate how weak European economic conditions cause a decline in the demand for the products made by U.S. firms. The result is weaker cash flows of the U.S.-based MNCs that sell products either as exports or through their European subsidiaries to European customers. However, there

Exhibit 1.5 Potential Effects of International Economic Conditions

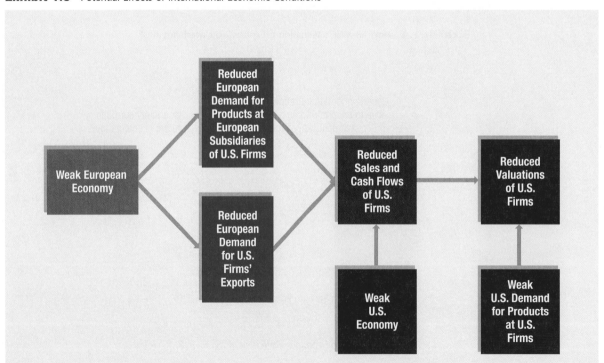

is an additional adverse effect of the weak European economy on U.S.-based MNCs and even on domestic U.S. firms. As the U.S.-based MNCs experience weaker cash flows, they may reduce their workforce or the number of hours that employees work. Furthermore, the profits earned by their owners are reduced. Thus not only the employees but also the owners of U.S.-based MNCs have less money to spend, so all U.S. firms will likewise experience reduced sales and cash flows. This means that a weak European economy, in addition to reducing European demand for the products of U.S.-based MNCs, also weakens the U.S. economy and thus reduces U.S. demand for those products.

EXAMPLE

Recall from the original example for Austin Co. that it has expected annual cash flows of $40 million from its U.S. operations. If Europe experiences a recession, however, then Austin expects reduced European demand for many U.S. products, and this will adversely affect the U.S. economy. Under these conditions, the U.S. demand for Austin's computer games would decline, reducing its expected annual cash flows due to U.S. operations from $40 million to $38 million. A European recession would naturally result in reduced European demand for Austin's video games, so the company reduces its expected euro cash flows due to European operations from 20 million euros to 16 million euros. ●

Exposure to International Political Risk   Political risk in any country can affect the level of an MNC's sales. A foreign government may increase taxes or impose barriers on the MNC's subsidiary. Alternatively, consumers in a foreign country may boycott the MNC if there is friction between the government of their country and the MNC's home country. Political actions like these can reduce the cash flows of an MNC. The term "country risk" is commonly used to reflect an MNC's exposure to a variety of country conditions, including political actions such as friction within the government, government policies (such as tax rules), and financial conditions within that country.

EXAMPLE

In 2015, Russia banned many different food items that were imported from the United States. This action was in retaliation for some U.S. sanctions imposed on Russia. The ban by Russia reduces the sales and cash flows of some U.S.-based MNCs that previously exported to Russia. Those MNCs have nothing to do with the sanctions imposed on Russia, yet they are adversely affected by the political relations between the United States and Russia. ●

Exposure to Exchange Rate Risk   If the foreign currencies to be received by a U.S.-based MNC suddenly weaken against the dollar, then the MNC will receive a lower amount of dollar cash flows than expected. Therefore, the MNC's cash flows will be reduced.

EXAMPLE

Recall from the previous example that Austin Co. now anticipates a European recession and so has revised its expected annual cash flows to be 16 million euros from its European operations. The dollar cash flows that Austin will receive from these euro cash flows depend on the exchange rate at the time those euros are converted to dollars. If the exchange rate is expected to be $1.30, then Austin's cash flows are predicted as follows.

$$\begin{aligned}\text{Austin's \$ cash flows resulting}\\ \text{from European operations} &= \text{Austin's cash flows in euros} \times \text{euro exchange rate}\\ &= 16{,}000{,}000 \text{ euros} \times \$1.30\\ &= \$20{,}800{,}000\end{aligned}$$

However, if Austin believes that the anticipated European recession will cause the euro's value to weaken and be worth only $1.20 when the euros are converted into dollars, then its estimate of the dollar cash flows from European operations would be revised as follows.

$$\begin{aligned} \text{Austin's \$ cash flows resulting} \\ \text{from European operations} &= \text{Austin's cash flows in euros} \times \text{euro exchange rate} \\ &= 16{,}000{,}000 \text{ euros} \times \$1.20 \\ &= \$19{,}200{,}000 \end{aligned}$$

Thus Austin's expected dollar cash flows are reduced as a result of reducing the expected value of the euro at the time of conversion into dollars.

This conceptual framework can be used to understand how MNCs such as Facebook and Google are affected by exchange rate movements. Google now receives more than half of its total revenue from outside the United States as it provides advertising for non-U.S. companies targeted at non-U.S. users. Consequently, Google's dollar cash flows are favorably affected when the currencies it receives appreciate against the dollar over time.

As Facebook attracts more users in Europe, it will attract more demand for advertising by European firms and therefore will receive more cash flows in euros. As it sells more ads to firms in other countries, it will receive more cash flows in their respective currencies. Its international revenue as a percentage of total revenue has consistently increased over the last five years and is now approaching 50 percent. As Facebook's international business continues to grow, its estimated dollar cash flows in any period will necessarily become more sensitive to the exchange rates of these currencies relative to the dollar. If the revenue it receives is denominated in currencies that appreciate against the dollar over time, then its dollar cash flows and valuation will increase. Conversely, if the revenue it receives is denominated in currencies that depreciate against the dollar over time, its dollar cash flows and valuation will decrease. ●

Many MNCs have cash outflows in one or more foreign currencies because they import supplies or materials from companies in other countries. When an MNC anticipates future cash outflows in foreign currencies, it is exposed to exchange rate movements but in the opposite direction. If those foreign currencies strengthen, then the MNC will require more dollars to obtain the foreign currencies needed to make its payments. This dynamic reduces the MNC's dollar cash flows (on a net basis) overall and so diminishes its value.

1-4d Summary of International Effects

Exhibit 1.4 summarized how an MNC's expected cash flows and valuation are subject to uncertainty through exposure to international conditions. Up to this point, the possible impact of each international condition on an MNC's cash flows has been treated in isolation. In reality, however, an MNC must consider the impact of all international conditions so that it can determine the resulting effect on its cash flows.

EXAMPLE

Recall the original example of Austin Co., a U.S.-based MNC that expects to generate $40 million annually in cash flows from its operations in the United States and 20 million euros annually in cash flows from its operations in Europe over the next three years. Assume that Austin anticipates a possible European recession during this period and therefore revises its expectations as follows to reflect that possibility.

1. The company expects that a European recession will adversely affect the U.S. economy and result in reduced U.S. demand for its video games; it therefore reduces its estimated dollar cash flows from U.S. operations to $38 million annually over the next three years.

2. Austin expects that a European recession will result in a reduced European demand for its video games, so it lowers its estimated euro cash flows from European operations to 16 million euros annually over the next three years.

3. The firm expects that a European recession will weaken the euro and hence lowers its estimate of the euro's value to $1.20 over the next three years. Altogether, then, Austin's expected annual cash flows for each of the next three years are now calculated as follows:

Austin's total expected $ cash
flows each year = $ cash flows from U.S. operations + $ cash flows from foreign operations
                = $ cash flows from U.S. operations + [(euro cash flows) × (euro exchange rate)]
                = $38,000,000 + [(16,000,000 euros) × ($1.20)]
                = $38,000,000 + $19,200,000
                = $57,200,000

Comparing these estimates to those in the original example reveals how each of the three revisions in expectations affects expected cash flows. The expected dollar cash flows from U.S. operations are reduced. The expected euro cash flows are reduced and the expected exchange rate is lower; both of these factors reduce the estimate of dollar cash flows from foreign operations. The expected annual dollar cash flows for Austin in the original example were $66 million, whereas the revised expectation is only $57.2 million. This example clearly illustrates just how adversely an MNC's cash flows can be affected by exposure to international conditions. ●

1-4e How Uncertainty Affects the MNC's Cost of Capital

If there is suddenly more uncertainty about an MNC's future cash flows, then investors will expect to receive a higher rate of return. Thus more uncertainty increases the return on investment required by investors (and thus the MNC's cost of obtaining capital), which lowers the firm's valuation.

EXAMPLE   Because Austin Co. does substantial business in Europe, its value is strongly influenced by how much revenue it expects to earn from that business. As a result of some events that occurred in Europe today, economic conditions in Europe are subject to considerable uncertainty. Although Austin does not change its
forecasts of expected cash flows, it is concerned that the actual flows could deviate substantially from
those forecasts. The increased uncertainty surrounding these cash flows has increased the firm's cost of capital, because its investors now require a higher rate of return. In other words, the numerator (estimated cash
flows) of the valuation equation has not changed but the denominator has increased owing to the
increased uncertainty surrounding the cash flows. Thus the valuation of Austin Co. has decreased. ●

If the uncertainty surrounding conditions that influence cash flows declines, the uncertainty surrounding cash flows of MNCs also declines and results in a lower required rate of return and cost of capital for MNCs. Consequently, the valuations of MNCs increase.

1-5 Organization of the Text

The chapters in this textbook are organized as shown in Exhibit 1.6. Chapters 2 through 8 discuss international markets and conditions from a macroeconomic perspective, focusing on external forces that can affect the value of an MNC. Although financial managers cannot control such forces, they can control the extent of their firm's exposure to them. These chapters focus on macroeconomic concepts that serve as a foundation for international financial management.

Chapters 9 through 21 take a microeconomic perspective and focus on how the financial management of an MNC can affect its value. Financial decisions by MNCs are commonly classified as either investing decisions or financing decisions. In general, investing decisions by an MNC tend to affect the numerator of the valuation model because such decisions affect expected cash flows. In addition, investing decisions by the MNC that alter the firm's weighted average cost of capital may also affect the denominator of the valuation model. Long-term financing decisions by an MNC tend to affect the denominator of the valuation model because they affect its cost of capital.

Exhibit 1.6   Organization of Chapters

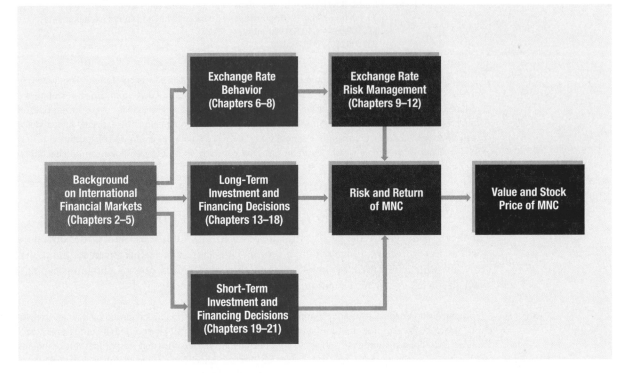

SUMMARY

- The main goal of an MNC is to maximize shareholder wealth. When managers are tempted to serve their own interests instead of those of shareholders, an agency problem exists. Multinational corporations tend to experience greater agency problems than do domestic firms because managers of foreign subsidiaries might be tempted to make decisions that serve their subsidiaries instead of the overall MNC. Proper incentives and communication from the parent may help to ensure that subsidiary managers focus on serving the overall MNC.

- International business is encouraged by three key theories. The theory of comparative advantage suggests that each country should use its comparative advantage to specialize in its production and rely on other countries to meet other needs. The imperfect markets theory suggests that imperfect markets render the factors of production immobile, which encourages countries to specialize based on the resources they have. The product cycle theory suggests that, after firms are established in their home countries, they commonly expand their product specialization in foreign countries.

- The most common methods by which firms conduct international business are international trade, licensing, franchising, joint ventures, acquisitions of foreign firms, and formation of foreign subsidiaries. Methods such as licensing and franchising involve little capital investment but distribute some of the profits to other parties. The acquisition of foreign firms or formation of foreign subsidiaries requires substantial capital investments but offers the potential for large returns.

- The valuation model of an MNC shows that the MNC's value is favorably affected when its expected foreign cash inflows increase, the currencies denominating those cash inflows increase, or the MNC's required rate of return decreases.

Conversely, the MNC's value is adversely affected when its expected foreign cash inflows decrease, the values of currencies denominating those cash flows decrease (assuming that they have net cash inflows in foreign currencies), or the MNC's required rate of return increases.

POINT COUNTER-POINT

Should an MNC Reduce Its Ethical Standards to Compete Internationally?

Point Yes. When a U.S.-based MNC competes in some countries, it may encounter some business norms there that are not allowed in the United States. For example, when competing for a government contract, firms might provide payoffs to the government officials who will make the decision. Yet in the United States, a firm will sometimes take a client on an expensive golf outing or provide skybox tickets to events. This is no different than a payoff. If the payoffs are bigger in some foreign countries, the MNC can compete only by matching the payoffs provided by its competitors.

Counter-Point No. A U.S.-based MNC should maintain a standard code of ethics that applies to any country, even if it is at a disadvantage in a foreign country that allows activities that might be viewed as unethical. In this way, the MNC establishes more credibility worldwide.

Who Is Correct? Use the Internet to learn more about this issue. Which argument do you support? Offer your own opinion on this issue.

SELF-TEST

Answers are provided in Appendix A at the back of the text.

1. What are typical reasons why MNCs expand internationally?

2. Explain why unfavorable economic or political conditions affect the MNC's cash flows, required rate of return, and valuation.

3. Identify the more obvious risks faced by MNCs that expand internationally.

QUESTIONS AND APPLICATIONS

1. Agency Problems of MNCs
a. Explain the agency problem of MNCs.
b. Why might agency costs be larger for an MNC than for a purely domestic firm?

2. Comparative Advantage
a. Explain how the theory of comparative advantage relates to the need for international business.
b. Explain how the product cycle theory relates to the growth of an MNC.

3. Imperfect Markets
a. Explain how the existence of imperfect markets has led to the establishment of subsidiaries in foreign markets.
b. If perfect markets existed, would wages, prices, and interest rates among countries be more similar or less similar than under conditions of imperfect markets? Why?

4. International Opportunities
a. Do you think the acquisition of a foreign firm or licensing will result in greater growth for an MNC? Which alternative is likely to have more risk?
b. Describe a scenario in which the size of a corporation is not affected by access to international opportunities.
c. Explain why MNCs such as Coca-Cola and PepsiCo, Inc., still have numerous opportunities for international expansion.

5. International Opportunities Due to the Internet
a. What factors cause some firms to become more internationalized than others?
b. Offer your opinion on why the Internet may result in more international business.

6. Impact of Exchange Rate Movements Plak Co. of Chicago has several European subsidiaries that remit earnings to it each year. Explain how appreciation of the euro (the currency used in many European countries) would affect Plak's valuation.

7. Benefits and Risks of International Business As an overall review of this chapter, identify possible reasons for growth in international business. Then list the various disadvantages that may discourage international business.

8. Valuation of an MNC Hudson Co., a U.S. firm, has a subsidiary in Mexico, where political risk has recently increased. Hudson's best guess of its future peso cash flows to be received has not changed. However, its valuation has declined as a result of the increase in political risk. Explain.

9. Centralization and Agency Costs Would the agency problem be more pronounced for Berkely Corp., whose parent company makes most major decisions for its foreign subsidiaries, or Oakland Corp., which uses a decentralized approach?

10. Global Competition Explain why more standardized product specifications across countries can increase global competition.

11. Exposure to Exchange Rates McCanna Corp., a U.S. firm, has a French subsidiary that produces wine and exports to various European countries. All of the countries where it sells its wine use the euro as their currency, which is the same currency used in France. Is McCanna Corp. exposed to exchange rate risk?

12. Macro versus Micro Topics Review the Table of Contents and indicate whether each of the chapters from Chapter 2 through Chapter 21 has a macro or micro perspective.

13. Methods Used to Conduct International Business Duve, Inc., desires to penetrate a foreign market with either a licensing agreement with a foreign firm or by acquiring a foreign firm. Explain the differences in potential risk and return between a licensing agreement with a foreign firm and the acquisition of a foreign firm.

14. International Business Methods Snyder Golf Co., a U.S. firm that sells high-quality golf clubs in the United States, wants to expand internationally by selling the same golf clubs in Brazil.

a. Describe the trade-offs that are involved for each method (such as exporting, direct foreign investment, etc.) that Snyder could use to achieve its goal.

b. Which method would you recommend for this firm? Justify your recommendation.

15. Impact of Political Risk Explain why political risk may discourage international business.

16. Impact of 9/11 Following the terrorist attack on the United States on September 11, 2001, the valuations of many MNCs declined by more than 10 percent. Explain why the expected cash flows of MNCs were reduced, even if they were not directly hit by the terrorist attacks.

Advanced Questions

17. International Joint Venture Anheuser-Busch (which is now part of AB InBev due to a merger), the producer of Budweiser and other beers, has engaged in a joint venture with Kirin Brewery, the largest brewery in Japan. The joint venture enabled Anheuser-Busch to have its beer distributed through Kirin's distribution channels in Japan. In addition, it could utilize Kirin's facilities to produce beer that would be sold locally. In return, Anheuser-Busch provided information about the American beer market to Kirin.

a. Explain how the joint venture enabled Anheuser-Busch to achieve its objective of maximizing shareholder wealth.
b. Explain how the joint venture limited the risk of the international business.
c. Many international joint ventures are intended to circumvent barriers that normally prevent foreign competition. What barrier in Japan did Anheuser-Busch circumvent as a result of the joint venture? What barrier in the United States did Kirin circumvent as a result of the joint venture?
d. Explain how Anheuser-Busch could have lost some of its market share in countries outside Japan as a result of this particular joint venture.

18. Impact of Eastern European Growth The managers of Loyola Corp. recently had a meeting to discuss new opportunities in Europe as a result of the recent integration among Eastern European countries. They decided not to penetrate new markets because of their present focus on expanding market share in the United States. Loyola's financial managers have developed forecasts for earnings based on the 12 percent market share (defined here as its percentage of total European sales) that Loyola currently has in Eastern Europe. Is 12 percent an appropriate estimate for next year's Eastern European market share? If not, does it likely overestimate or underestimate the actual Eastern European market share next year?

19. Valuation of an MNC Birm Co., based in Alabama, is considering several international opportunities in Europe that could affect the value of its firm. The valuation of its firm is dependent on four factors: (1) expected cash flows in dollars, (2) expected cash flows in euros that are ultimately converted into dollars, (3) the rate at which it can convert euros to dollars, and (4) Birm's weighted average cost of capital. For each opportunity, identify the factors that would be affected.

a. Birm plans a licensing deal in which it will sell technology to a firm in Germany for $3 million; the payment is invoiced in dollars, and this project has the same risk level as its existing businesses.
b. Birm plans to acquire a large firm in Portugal that is riskier than its existing businesses.
c. Birm plans to discontinue its relationship with a U.S. supplier so that it can import a small amount of supplies (denominated in euros) at a lower cost from a Belgian supplier.
d. Birm plans to export a small amount of materials to Ireland that are denominated in euros.

20. Assessing Motives for International Business Fort Worth, Inc., specializes in manufacturing some basic parts for sports utility vehicles (SUVs) that are produced and sold in the United States. Its main advantage in the United States is that its production is efficient and less costly than that of some other unionized manufacturers. It has a substantial market share in the United States. Its manufacturing process is labor intensive. It pays relatively low wages compared to U.S. competitors, but has guaranteed the local workers that their positions will not be eliminated for the next 30 years. It hired a consultant to determine whether it should set up a subsidiary in Mexico, where the parts would be produced. The consultant suggested that Fort Worth should expand for the following reasons. Offer your opinion on whether the consultant's reasons are logical.

a. Theory of Competitive Advantage: There are not many SUVs sold in Mexico, so Fort Worth, Inc., would not have to face much competition there.
b. Imperfect Markets Theory: Fort Worth cannot easily transfer workers to Mexico, but it can establish a subsidiary there in order to penetrate a new market.
c. Product Cycle Theory: Fort Worth has been successful in the United States. It has limited growth opportunities because it already controls much of the U.S. market for the parts it produces. Thus the natural

next step is to conduct the same business in a foreign country.
d. Exchange Rate Risk: The exchange rate of the peso has weakened recently, so this would allow Fort Worth to build a plant at a very low cost (by exchanging dollars for the cheap pesos to build the plant).
e. Political Risk: The political conditions in Mexico have stabilized in the last few months, so Fort Worth should attempt to penetrate the Mexican market now.

21. Valuation of Walmart's International Business In addition to its stores in the United States, Walmart Stores, Inc., has 107 retail units in Argentina, 359 in Brazil, 395 in Canada, 412 in China, 2,296 in Mexico, and 604 in the United Kingdom. Overall, it has 6,100 retail units in foreign countries. Consider that the value of Walmart is composed of two parts, a U.S. part (due to business in the United States) and a non-U.S. part (due to business in other countries). Explain how to determine the present value (in dollars) of the non-U.S. part assuming that you had access to all the details of Walmart businesses outside the United States.

22. Impact of International Business on Cash Flows and Risk Nantucket Travel Agency specializes in tours for American tourists. Until recently, all of its business was in the United States. It just established a subsidiary in Athens, Greece, which provides tour services in the Greek islands for American tourists. It rented a shop near the port of Athens. It also hired residents of Athens who could speak English and provide tours of the Greek islands. The subsidiary's main costs are rent and salaries for its employees and the lease of a few large boats in Athens that it uses for tours. American tourists pay for the entire tour in dollars at Nantucket's main U.S. office before they depart for Greece.

a. Explain why Nantucket may be able to effectively capitalize on international opportunities such as the Greek island tours.
b. Nantucket is privately owned by owners who reside in the United States and work in the main office. Explain possible agency problems associated with the creation of a subsidiary in Athens, Greece. How can Nantucket attempt to reduce these agency costs?
c. Greece's cost of labor and rent are relatively low. Explain why this information is relevant to Nantucket's decision to establish a tour business in Greece.

d. Explain how the cash flow situation of the Greek tour business exposes Nantucket to exchange rate risk. Is Nantucket favorably or unfavorably affected when the euro (Greece's currency) appreciates against the dollar?
Explain.

e. Nantucket plans to finance its Greek tour business. Its subsidiary could obtain loans in euros from a bank in Greece to cover its rent, and its main office could pay off the loans over time. Alternatively, its main office could borrow dollars and would periodically convert dollars to euros to pay the expenses in Greece. Does either type of loan reduce the exposure of Nantucket to exchange rate risk? Explain.

f. Explain how the Greek island tour business could expose Nantucket to political country risk.

23. Valuation of an MNC Yahoo! has expanded its business by establishing portals in numerous countries, including Argentina, Australia, China, Germany, Ireland, Japan, and the United Kingdom. It has cash outflows associated with the creation and administration of each portal. It also generates cash inflows from selling advertising space on its website. Each portal results in cash flows in a different currency. Thus the valuation of Yahoo! is based on its expected future net cash flows in Argentine pesos after converting them into U.S. dollars, its expected net cash flows in Australian dollars after converting them into U.S. dollars, and so on. Explain how and why the valuation of Yahoo! would change if most investors suddenly expected that the dollar would weaken against most currencies over time.

24. Uncertainty Surrounding an MNC's Valuation Carlisle Co. is a U.S. firm that is about to purchase a large company in Switzerland at a purchase price of $20 million. This company produces furniture and sells it locally (in Switzerland), and is expected to earn large profits every year. The company will become a subsidiary of Carlisle and will periodically remit its excess cash flows due to its profits to Carlisle Co. Assume that Carlisle Co. has no other international business. Carlisle has $10 million that it will use to pay for part of the Swiss company and will finance the rest of its purchase with borrowed dollars. Carlisle Co. can obtain supplies from either a U.S. supplier or a Swiss supplier (in which case the payment would be made in Swiss francs). Both suppliers are very reputable and there would be no exposure to country risk when using either supplier. Is the valuation of the total cash flows of Carlisle Co. more uncertain if it

obtains its supplies from a U.S. firm or a Swiss firm? Explain briefly.

25. Impact of Exchange Rates on MNC Value Olmsted Co. has small computer chips assembled in Poland and transports the final assembled products to the parent, where they are sold by the parent in the United States. The assembled products are invoiced in dollars. Olmsted Co. uses Polish currency (the zloty) to produce these chips and assemble them in Poland. The Polish subsidiary pays the employees in the local currency (zloty), and Olmsted Co. finances its subsidiary operations with loans from a Polish bank (in zloty). The parent of Olmsted will send sufficient monthly payments (in dollars) to the subsidiary in order to repay the loan and other expenses incurred by the subsidiary. If the Polish zloty depreciates against the dollar over time, will that have a favorable, unfavorable, or neutral effect on the value of Olmsted Co.? Briefly explain.

26. Impact of Uncertainty on MNC Value Minneapolis Co. is a major exporter of products to Canada. Today, an event occurred that has increased the uncertainty surrounding the Canadian dollar's future value over the long term. Explain how this event can affect the valuation of Minneapolis Co.

27. Exposure of MNCs to Exchange Rate Movements Arlington Co. expects to receive 10 million euros in each of the next 10 years. It will need to obtain 2 million Mexican pesos in each of the next 10 years. The euro exchange rate is presently valued at $1.38 and is expected to depreciate by 2 percent each year over time. The peso is valued at $.13 and is expected to depreciate by 2 percent each year over time. Review the valuation equation for an MNC. Do you think that the exchange rate movements will have a favorable or unfavorable effect on the MNC?

28. Impact of a Recession on an MNC's Value If a U.S. recession occurred without any change in interest rates, identify the part of the MNC valuation equation that would most likely be affected.

29. Exposure of MNCs to Exchange Rate Movements Because of the low labor costs in Thailand, Melnick Co. (based in the United States) recently established a major research and development subsidiary there that it owns. The subsidiary was created to improve new products that the parent of Melnick can sell in the United States (denominated in dollars) to U.S. customers. The subsidiary pays its local employees in baht (the Thai currency). The subsidiary has a small amount of sales denominated in baht, but its expenses are much larger than its revenue. It has just obtained a large loan denominated in baht that will be used to expand its subsidiary. The business that the parent of Melnick Co. conducts in the United States is not exposed to exchange rate risk. If the Thai baht weakens over the next three years, will the value of Melnick Co. be favorably affected, unfavorably affected, or not affected? Briefly explain.

30. Shareholder Rights of Investors in MNCs
MNCs tend to expand more when they can more easily access funds by issuing stock. In some countries, shareholder rights are very limited, and the MNCs have limited ability to raise funds by issuing stock. Explain why access to funding is more severe for MNCs based in countries where shareholder rights are limited.

31. MNC Cash Flows and Exchange Rate Risk
Tuscaloosa Co. is a U.S. firm that assembles phones in Argentina and transports the final assembled products to the parent, where they are sold by the parent in the United States. The assembled products are invoiced in dollars. The Argentine subsidiary obtains some material from China, and the Chinese exporter is willing to accept Argentine pesos as payment for these materials that it exports. The Argentine subsidiary pays its employees in the local currency (pesos), and finances its operations with loans from an Argentine bank (in pesos). Tuscaloosa Co. has no other international business. If the Argentine peso depreciates against the dollar over time, will that have a favorable, unfavorable, or neutral effect on Tuscaloosa Co.? Briefly explain.

32. MNC Cash Flows and Exchange Rate Risk
Asheville Co. has a subsidiary in Mexico that develops software for its parent. It rents a large facility in Mexico and hires many people in Mexico to work in the facility. Asheville Co. has no other international business. All operations are presently funded by Asheville's parent. All the software is sold to U.S. firms by Asheville's parent and invoiced in U.S. dollars.

a. If the Mexican peso appreciates against the dollar, does this have a favorable effect, unfavorable effect, or no effect on Asheville's value?

b. Asheville Co. plans to borrow funds to support its expansion in the United States. The Mexican interest rates are presently lower than U.S. interest rates, so Asheville obtains a loan denominated in Mexican pesos in order to support its expansion in the United States.

Will the borrowing of pesos increase, decrease, or have no effect on its exposure to exchange rate risk? Briefly explain.

33. Estimating an MNC's Cash Flows Biloxi Co. is a U.S. firm that has a subsidiary in China. The subsidiary reinvests half of its net cash flows into operations and remits half to the parent. Biloxi Co. has expected cash flows from domestic business equal to $10,000,000 and the Chinese subsidiary is expected to generate 100 million Chinese yuan at the end of the year. The expected value of yuan at the end of the year is $.13. What are the expected dollar cash flows of the parent of Biloxi Co. in one year?

34. Uncertainty Surrounding an MNC's Cash Flows
a. Assume that Bangor Co. (a U.S. firm) knows that it will have cash inflows of $900,000 from domestic operations, cash inflows of 200,000 Swiss francs due to exports to Swiss operations, and cash outflows of 500,000 Swiss francs at the end of the year. While the future value of the Swiss franc is uncertain because it fluctuates, your best guess is that the Swiss franc's value will be $1.10 at the end this year. What are the expected dollar cash flows of Bangor Co?

b. Assume that Concord Co. (a U.S. firm) is in the same industry as Bangor Co. There is no political risk that could have any impact on the cash flows of either firm. Concord Co. knows that it will have cash inflows of $900,000 from domestic operations, cash inflows of 700,000 Swiss francs due to exports to Swiss operations, and cash outflows of 800,000 Swiss francs at the end of the year. Is the valuation of the total cash flows of Concord Co. more uncertain or less uncertain than the total cash flows of Bangor Co.? Explain briefly.

35. Valuation of an MNC Odessa Co., Midland Co., and Roswell Co. are U.S. firms in the same industry and have the same valuation as of yesterday, based on the present value of future cash flows of each company. Odessa Co. obtains a large amount of its supplies invoiced in euros from European countries, and all of its sales are invoiced in dollars. Midland has a large subsidiary in Europe that does all of its business in euros and remits profits to the U.S. parent every year. Roswell Co. has no international business. Assume that as of this morning an event occurred that you believe will cause a substantial depreciation of the euro against the dollar over time. Assume that this event will not change the business operations of the firms mentioned in this question. Which firm will have the highest valuation based on your expectations? Briefly explain.

36. Impact of Uncertainty on an MNC's Valuation Assume that Alpine Co. is a U.S. firm that has direct foreign investment in Brazil as a result establishing a subsidiary there. Political conditions have changed in Brazil, but the best guess by investors of the future cash flows per year for Alpine Co. has not changed. Yet there is more uncertainty surrounding the best guess of Alpine's cash flows. In other words, the distribution of possible outcomes above and below the best guess has expanded. Would the change in uncertainty cause the prevailing value of Alpine Co. to increase, decrease, or remain unchanged? Briefly explain.

37. Exposure of MNC Cash Flows
a. Rochester Co. is a U.S. firm that has a language institute in France. This institute attracts Americans who want to learn the French language. Rochester Co. charges tuition to the American students in dollars. It expects that its dollar revenue from charging tuition will be stable over each of the next several years. Its total expenses for this project are as follows: It rents a facility in Paris, and makes a large rent payment each month in euros. It also hires several French citizens as full-time instructors, and pays their salary in euros. It expects that its expenses denominated in euros will be stable over each of the next several years. If the euro appreciates against the dollar over time, should this have a favorable effect, unfavorable effect, or no effect on the value of Rochester Co.? Briefly explain.
b. Rochester considers a new project in which it would also attract people from Spain, and the institute in France would teach them the French language. It would charge them tuition in euros. The expenses for this project would be about the same as the expenses of the project described above for the American students. Assume that euros to be generated by this project would be stable over the next several years. Assume that this project is about the same size as the project for American students. For either project, the expected annual revenue is just slightly larger than the expected annual expenses. Is the valuation of net cash flows subject to a higher degree of exchange rate risk for this project or for the project for American students? Briefly explain.

Critical Thinking

Impact of International Environment of MNC Cash Flows Conduct an online search to review a recent annual report of the operations of any publicly traded U.S.-based MNC. Write a brief essay in which you describe how the MNC's cash flows are exposed to the international environment. Is the MNC you selected most exposed to a particular currency? If so, how would depreciation of that currency against the dollar affect the value of the MNC? Is the MNC exposed to economic conditions in a particular foreign country? If so, describe how a change in the conditions of that country could adversely affect the MNC's cash flows.

Discussion in the Boardroom

This exercise can be found in Appendix E at the back of this textbook.

Running Your Own MNC

This exercise can be found on the *International Financial Management* text companion website. Go to www.cengagebrain.com (students) or www.cengage.com/login (instructors) and search using **ISBN 9781133947837**.

BLADES, INC. CASE

Decision to Expand Internationally

Blades, Inc., is a U.S.-based company that has been incorporated in the United States for three years. Blades is a relatively small company, with total assets of only $200 million. The company produces a single type of product, roller blades. Due to the booming roller blade market in the United States at the time of the company's establishment, Blades has been quite successful. For example, in its first year of operation, it reported a net income of $3.5 million. Recently, however, the demand for Blades' "Speedos," the company's primary product in the United States, has been slowly tapering off, and Blades has not been performing well. Last year, it reported a return on assets of only 7 percent. In response to the company's annual report for its most recent year of operations, Blades' shareholders have been pressuring the company to improve its performance; its stock price has fallen from a high of $20 per share three years ago to $12 last year. Blades produces high-quality roller blades and employs a unique production process, but the prices it charges are among the top 5 percent in the industry.

In light of these circumstances, Ben Holt, the company's chief financial officer (CFO), is contemplating his alternatives for Blades' future. There are no other cost-cutting measures that Blades can implement in the United States without affecting the quality of its product. Also, production of alternative products would require major modifications to the existing plant setup. Furthermore, and because of these limitations, expansion within the United States at this time seems pointless.

Holt is considering the following: If Blades cannot penetrate the U.S. market further or reduce costs here, why not import some parts from overseas and/or expand the company's sales to foreign countries? Similar strategies have proved successful for numerous companies that expanded into Asia in recent years to increase their profit margins. The CFO's initial focus is on Thailand. Thailand has recently experienced weak economic conditions, and Blades could purchase components there at a low cost. Holt is aware that many of Blades' competitors have begun importing production components from Thailand.

Not only would Blades be able to reduce costs by importing rubber and/or plastic from Thailand due to the low costs of these inputs, but it might also be able to augment weak U.S. sales by exporting to Thailand, an economy still in its infancy and just beginning to appreciate leisure products such as roller blades. Although several of Blades' competitors import components from Thailand, few are exporting to the country. Long-term decisions would also eventually have to be made; perhaps Blades, Inc., could establish a subsidiary in Thailand and gradually shift its focus away from the United States if its U.S. sales do not rebound. Establishing a subsidiary in Thailand would also make sense for Blades due to its superior production process. Holt is reasonably sure that Thai firms could not duplicate the high-quality production process employed by Blades. Furthermore, if the company's initial approach of exporting works well, establishing a subsidiary in Thailand would preserve Blades' sales before Thai competitors are able to penetrate the Thai market.

As a financial analyst for Blades, Inc., you are assigned to analyze international opportunities and risk resulting from international business. Your initial assessment should focus on the barriers and opportunities that international trade may offer. Holt has never been involved in international business in any form and is unfamiliar with any constraints that may inhibit his plan to export to and import from a foreign country. Holt has presented you with a list of initial questions you should answer.

1. What are the advantages Blades could gain from importing from and/ or exporting to a foreign country such as Thailand?

2. What are some of the disadvantages Blades could face as a result of foreign trade in the short run? In the long run?

3. Which theories of international business described in this chapter apply to Blades, Inc., in the short run? In the long run?

4. What long-range plans other than establishment of a subsidiary in Thailand are an option for Blades and may be more suitable for the company?

Small Business Dilemma

Developing a Multinational Sporting Goods Corporation

In every chapter of this text, some of the key concepts are illustrated with an application to a small sporting goods firm that conducts international business. These "Small Business Dilemma" features allow students to recognize the dilemmas and possible decisions that firms (such as this sporting goods firm) may face in a global environment. For this chapter, the application is on the development of the sporting goods firm that would conduct international business.

Last month, Jim Logan completed his undergraduate degree in finance and decided to pursue his dream of managing his own sporting goods business. Logan had worked in a sporting goods shop while going to college, and he had noticed that many customers wanted to purchase a low-priced football. However, the sporting goods store where he worked, like many others, sold only top-of-the-line footballs. From his experience, Logan was aware that top-of-the-line footballs had a high markup and that a low-cost football could possibly penetrate the U.S. market. He also knew how to produce footballs. His goal was to create a firm that would produce low-priced footballs and sell them on a wholesale basis to various sporting goods stores in the United States. Unfortunately, many sporting goods stores began to sell low-priced footballs just before Logan was about to start his business. The firm that began to produce the low-cost footballs already provided many other products to sporting goods stores in the United States and therefore had already established a business relationship with these stores. Logan did not believe that he could compete with this firm in the U.S. market.

Rather than pursue a different business, Logan decided to implement his idea on a global basis. Although football (as it is played in the United States) has not been a traditional sport in foreign countries, it has become more popular in some foreign countries in recent years. Furthermore, the expansion of cable networks in foreign countries would allow for much more exposure to U.S. football games in those countries in the future. To the extent that this would increase the popularity of football (U.S. style) as a hobby in the foreign countries, it would result in a demand for footballs in foreign countries. Logan asked many of his foreign friends from college days if they recalled seeing footballs sold in their home countries. Most of them said they rarely noticed footballs being sold in sporting goods stores but that they expected the demand for footballs to increase in their home countries. Consequently, Logan decided to start a business of producing low-priced footballs and exporting them to sporting goods distributors in foreign countries. Those distributors would then sell the footballs at the retail level.

Logan planned to expand his product line over time once he identified other sports products that he might sell to foreign sporting goods stores. He decided to call his business "Sports Exports Company." To avoid any rent and labor expenses, Logan planned to produce the footballs in his garage and to perform the work himself. Thus his main business expenses were the cost of the materials used to produce footballs and expenses associated with finding distributors in foreign countries who would attempt to sell the footballs to sporting goods stores.

1. Is Sports Exports Company a multinational corporation?

2. Why are the agency costs lower for Sports Exports Company than for most MNCs?

3. Does Sports Exports Company have any comparative advantage over potential competitors in foreign countries that could produce and sell footballs there?

4. How would Jim Logan decide which foreign markets he would attempt to enter? Should he initially focus on one or many foreign markets?

5. The Sports Exports Company has no immediate plans to conduct direct foreign investment. However, it might consider other less costly methods of establishing its business in foreign markets. What methods might the Sports Exports Company use to increase its presence in foreign markets by working with one or more foreign companies?

Internet/Excel Exercises

The website address of the Bureau of Economic Analysis is www.bea.gov.

1. Use this website to assess recent trends in direct foreign investment (DFI) abroad by U.S. firms. Compare the DFI in the United Kingdom with the DFI in France. Offer a possible reason for the large difference.

2. Based on the recent trends in DFI, are U.S.-based MNCs pursuing opportunities in Asia? In Eastern Europe? In Latin America?

Online Articles with Real-World Examples

Find a recent article online that describes an actual international finance application or a real-world example about a specific MNC's actions that reinforces one or more of the concepts covered in this chapter.

If your class has an online component, your professor may ask you to post your summary there and provide the web link of the article so that other students can access it. If your class is live, your professor may ask you to summarize your application in class. Your professor may assign specific students to complete this assignment for this chapter or may allow any students to do the assignment on a volunteer basis.

For recent online articles and real-world examples applied to this chapter, consider using the following search terms (and include the current year as a search term to ensure that the online articles are recent).

1. company AND repatriated foreign earnings
2. Inc. AND repatriated foreign earnings
3. company AND currency effects
4. Inc. AND currency effects
5. company AND country risk
6. Inc. AND country risk
7. direct foreign investment
8. joint venture AND international
9. licensing AND international
10. multinational corporation AND risk

2
International Flow of Funds

CHAPTER OBJECTIVES

The specific objectives of this chapter are to:

- explain the key components of the balance of payments,

- explain the growth in international trade activity over time,

- explain how international trade flows are influenced by economic and other factors,

- explain how international capital flows are influenced by country characteristics, and

- introduce the agencies that facilitate the international flow of funds.

Many MNCs are heavily engaged in international business, such as exporting, importing, or direct foreign investment (DFI) in foreign countries. The transactions arising from international business cause money flows from one country to another. The balance of payments is a measure of international money flows and is discussed in this chapter.

Financial managers of MNCs monitor the balance of payments so that they can determine how the flow of international transactions is changing over time. The balance of payments can indicate the volume of transactions between specific countries and may even signal potential shifts in specific exchange rates. Thus it can have a major influence on the long-term planning and management by MNCs.

2-1 Balance of Payments

The **balance of payments** is a summary of transactions between domestic and foreign residents for a specific country over a specified period of time. It represents an accounting of a country's international transactions for a period, usually a quarter or a year. It accounts for transactions by businesses, individuals, and the government.

A balance-of-payments statement is composed of the current account, the capital account, and the financial account.

2-1a Current Account

The **current account** measures the flow of funds between one country and all other countries due to purchases of goods and services or to income generated by assets. The main components of the current account are payments between two countries for (1) merchandise (goods) and services, (2) primary income, and (3) secondary income.

Payments for Goods and Services   Merchandise exports and imports represent tangible products, such as smartphones and clothing, that are transported between countries. Service exports and imports represent tourism and other services (such as legal, insurance, and consulting services) provided for customers based in other countries. Service exports by the United States result in an inflow of funds to the United States, while service imports by the United States result in an outflow of funds.

The difference between total exports and imports is referred to as the **balance of trade**. A deficit in the U.S. balance of trade means that the value of merchandise and services exported by the United States is less than the value of merchandise and services that it imports. Before 1993, the balance of trade was based solely on merchandise exports and imports. In 1993, it was redefined to also include service exports and imports.

Primary Income Payments   A second component of the current account is **primary income** (also sometimes referred to as **factor income** in the past), which is mostly composed of income earned by MNCs on their DFI (investment in fixed assets in foreign countries that can be used to conduct business operations), and also income earned by investors on portfolio investment (investments in foreign securities). Thus, primary income received by the United States reflects an inflow of funds into the United States. Primary income paid by the United States to foreign companies or investors reflects an outflow of funds from the United States. Net primary income represents the difference between the primary income receipts and the primary income payments.

Secondary Income   The third main component of the current account is **secondary income** (also sometimes referred to as **transfer payments**), which represents aid, grants, and gifts from one country to another. Net secondary income represents the difference between the secondary income receipts and the secondary income payments.

Examples of Payment Entries   Exhibit 2.1 shows several examples of transactions that would be reflected in the current account. Every transaction generating a U.S. cash inflow (exports and income receipts by the United States) represents a credit to the current account, and every transaction generating a U.S. cash outflow (imports and income payments from the United States) represents a debit to the current account. Therefore, a large current account deficit indicates that the United States is sending more cash abroad to buy goods and services or to pay income than it is receiving for its sales of goods and services.

Actual Current Account Balance   The components of a country's current account balance can be evaluated to recognize how its flow of funds with other countries is influenced by international trade and income payments. To illustrate, the U.S. current account balance in the year 2014 is summarized in Exhibit 2.2, segmented by the components described above. Components that result in cash inflows to the United States are denoted by a plus sign, while components that result in cash outflows from the United States have a minus sign.

Notice from Exhibit 2.2 that the U.S. receipts (cash inflows) due to exports of merchandise were valued at $1,635 billion (see line 1) and U.S. payments (cash outflows) for imports of merchandise were valued at $2,372 billion (see line 2). Thus the net receipts (cash inflows minus cash outflows) due to merchandise were −$737 billion (computed as $1,635 billion − $2,372 billion in line 3). The U.S. receipts due to service exports were $710 billion (see line 4), while U.S. outflow payments due to service imports were $478 billion (see line 5), resulting in net receipts due to services of $232 billion (computed as $710 billion − $478 billion in line 6). Thus the value of U.S. service exports exceeded the value of U.S. service imports, but the value of U.S. merchandise exports was much smaller than the value of U.S. merchandise imports. Consequently, the United States had a negative balance of trade in 2014.

Exhibit 2.2 also shows that primary income received (cash inflows) by the United States was $819 billion (see line 7), while primary income payments made (cash outflows) by the United States were $601 billion (see line 8). Secondary income received by the United States was $125 billion (see line 10), while secondary income payments sent by the United States were $249 billion (see line 11). Overall, the U.S. current account balance (line 13) was −$411 billion in 2014. The main reason for the large

Exhibit 2.1 Examples of Current Account Transaction

INTERNATIONAL *TRADE* TRANSACTION	U.S. CASH FLOW POSITION	ENTRY ON U.S. BALANCE-OF-PAYMENTS ACCOUNT
J.C. Penney purchases clothing produced in Indonesia that it will sell in its U.S. retail stores.	U.S. cash outflow	Debit
Individuals in the United States purchase leather goods over the Internet from a firm based in Italy.	U.S. cash outflow	Debit
The Mexican government pays a U.S. consulting firm for consulting services provided by the firm.	U.S. cash inflow	Credit
Home Depot headquarters in the United States purchases lumber from Canada that it uses in assembling kitchen cabinets.	U.S. cash outflow	Debit
A university bookstore in Ireland purchases textbooks produced by a U.S. publishing company.	U.S. cash inflow	Credit
INTERNATIONAL PRIMARY *INCOME* TRANSACTION	**U.S. CASH FLOW POSITION**	**ENTRY ON U.S. BALANCE-OF-PAYMENTS ACCOUNT**
A U.S. investor receives a dividend payment from a French firm in which she purchased stock.	U.S. cash inflow	Credit
The U.S. Treasury sends an interest payment to a German insurance company that purchased U.S. Treasury bonds one year ago.	U.S. cash outflow	Debit
A Mexican company that borrowed dollars from a bank based in the United States sends an interest payment to that bank.	U.S. cash inflow	Credit
INTERNATIONAL SECONDARY *INCOME* TRANSACTION	**U.S. CASH FLOW POSITION**	**ENTRY ON U.S. BALANCE-OF-PAYMENTS ACCOUNT**
The United States provides aid to Costa Rica in response to a flood in Costa Rica.	U.S. cash outflow	Debit
Switzerland provides a grant to U.S. scientists to work on cancer research.	U.S. cash inflow	Credit

deficit was that the value of U.S. merchandise imports (cash outflows) was so much larger than the value of merchandise exports (cash inflows).

2-1b Financial Account

The **financial account** measures the flow of funds between countries that are due to (1) direct foreign investment, (2) portfolio investment, and (3) other capital investment.

Direct Foreign Investment The financial account keeps track of a country's payments for new DFI over a given period (such as a specific quarter or year). Payments representing DFI in the United States (such as the acquisition of a U.S. firm by a non-U.S. firm) are recorded as a positive number in the U.S. financial account, because funds are flowing into the United States. Conversely, payments representing a U.S.-based MNC's DFI in another country are recorded as a negative number because funds are being sent from the United States to another country. Examples of DFI by the United States include an MNC's payments to complete its acquisition of a foreign company, to construct a new manufacturing plant in a foreign country, or to expand an existing plant in a foreign country.

Portfolio Investment The financial account also keeps track of a country's payments for new portfolio investment (investment in financial assets such as stocks or bonds) over a given period (such as a specific quarter or year). Thus a purchase of Heineken International (Netherlands) stock by a U.S. investor is classified as portfolio investment because it

Exhibit 2.2   Summary of Current Account in the Year 2014 (billions of $)

	COMPONENT OF CURRENT ACCOUNT	VALUE IN BILLIONS OF DOLLARS FOR 2014
(1)	U.S. receipts for merchandise exports	+$1,635
(2)	U.S. payments for merchandise imports	−$2,372
(3) = (1)−(2)	U.S. net receipts for merchandise	−$737
(4)	U.S. receipts for service exports	+$710
(5)	U.S. payments for service imports	−$478
(6) = (4)−(5)	U.S. net service receipts	+$232
(7)	U.S. receipts due to primary income	+$819
(8)	U.S. payments of primary income	−$601
(9) = (7)−(8)	U.S. net primary income receipts	+$218
(10)	U.S. receipts due to secondary income	+$125
(11)	U.S. payments of secondary income	−$249
(12) = (10)−(11)	U.S. net secondary income receipts	−$124
(13) = (3) + (6) + (9) + (12)	U.S. current account balance	−$411

Source: Survey of Current Business, 2015.

represents a purchase of foreign financial assets without changing control of the company. This transaction is recorded as a negative number for the U.S. financial account (a debit), as it reflects a payment from the United States to another country. If a U.S. firm purchased all of Heineken's stock in an acquisition, this transaction would result in a transfer of control and therefore would be classified as DFI instead of portfolio investment.

Other Capital Investment   A third component of the financial account consists of other capital investment, which represents transactions involving short-term financial assets (such as money market securities) between countries. In general, DFI measures the expansion of firms' foreign operations, whereas portfolio investment and other capital investment measure the net flow of funds due to financial asset transactions between individual or institutional investors.

2-1c Capital Account

The **capital account** measures the flow of funds between one country and all other countries due to financial assets transferred across country borders by people who move to a different country, or due to sales of patents and trademarks. The sale of patent rights by a U.S. firm to a Canadian firm is recorded as a positive amount (a credit) to the U.S. capital account because funds are being received by the United States as a result of the transaction. Conversely, a U.S. firm's purchase of patent rights from a Canadian firm is recorded as a negative amount (a debit) to the U.S. capital account because funds are being sent from the United States to another country.

In general, the financial account items represent very large cash flows between countries, whereas the capital account items are relatively minor (in terms of dollar amounts) when compared with the financial account items. Thus the financial account is given much more attention than the capital account when attempting to understand how a country's investment behavior has affected its flow of funds with other countries during a particular period.

2-1d Relationship between the Accounts

If a country has a negative current account balance, then it should have a positive financial and capital account balance (and vice versa). This implies that if it sends more money out of the country than it receives from other countries due to international trade and income payments, it receives more money from other countries than it spends on foreign investments.

For example, if a country's DFI in other countries exceeds the amount of DFI by other countries into that country, this will result in a negative number (debit) for that country's financial account, because more funds are leaving that country than are coming into it. However, DFI in other countries generates primary income receipts for the country engaging in the investment. Therefore, the higher level of DFI by that country will cause it to receive more primary income from other countries, which results in a positive number (credit) for its current account balance because more primary income is coming into that country than is leaving it.

WEB

www.bea.gov
Update of the current
account balance and
international trade
balance.

Errors and Omissions and Reserves   The balance-of-payments account also includes a category of errors and omissions, because measurement errors commonly occur when attempting to measure the value of funds transferred between two countries.

2-2 Growth in International Trade

The United States has benefited from international trade. First, such trade has created some U.S. jobs, especially in industries where domestic firms have a technology advantage. International trade has caused a shift of production to countries that can produce products more efficiently. In addition, it ensures more competition among the firms that produce products, which forces the firms to keep their prices low. Hence U.S. consumers have more product choices, and at lower prices, as a result of international trade.

WEB

www.census.gov/foreign
-trade/index.html
This provides several
links to additional details
about the U.S. balance
of trade.

2-2a Events That Increased Trade Volume

International trade has increased substantially over time, which has strongly affected multinational corporations. First, it has enabled some MNCs to obtain materials at lower prices. Second, it has allowed many MNCs to increase their sales and expand their operations.

The development of international trade is the result of numerous efforts by governments to remove cross-border restrictions. Some of the more important historical events that increased trade activity are discussed next.

Fall of the Berlin Wall   In 1989, the Berlin Wall separating East Germany from West Germany was torn down. This symbolic event led to improved relations between Eastern and Western Europe and also encouraged free enterprise in all Eastern European countries and the privatization of businesses that were owned by the government. Finally, the Berlin Wall's removal led to major reductions in trade barriers in Eastern Europe. Many MNCs began to export products there, and others capitalized on the cheap labor costs by importing supplies from that region.

Single European Act   In the late 1980s, industrialized countries in Europe agreed to make regulations more uniform and to remove many taxes on goods traded among themselves. This agreement, which was formalized by the Single European Act of 1987, was followed by a series of negotiations among the countries to achieve uniform policies by 1992. The act allows firms in a given European country greater access to supplies from firms in other European countries.

Many firms, including European subsidiaries of U.S.-based MNCs, have capitalized on this agreement by attempting to penetrate markets in border countries. By producing more of the same product and distributing it across European countries, firms are better able to achieve economies of scale. Best Foods (now part of Unilever) was one of many MNCs that increased efficiency by streamlining manufacturing operations in response to reduced trade barriers.

NAFTA   As a result of the North American Free Trade Agreement (NAFTA) of 1993, trade barriers between the United States and Mexico were eliminated. Some U.S. firms attempted to capitalize on this by exporting goods that had previously been restricted by barriers to Mexico. Other firms established subsidiaries in Mexico to produce their goods at a lower cost than was possible in the United States before selling them in the United States. The removal of trade barriers essentially allowed U.S. firms to penetrate product and labor markets that were previously inaccessible.

The removal of trade barriers between the United States and Mexico allows Mexican firms to export some products to the United States that were previously restricted. Thus U.S. firms that produce these goods are now subject to competition from Mexican exporters. Given the low cost of labor in Mexico, some U.S. firms have lost some of their market share. These effects are most pronounced in labor-intensive industries, such as clothing.

WEB

europa.eu/about-eu
/basic-information
/money/euro/index_en
.htm
Information about the
euro.

GATT   Within a month of the NAFTA accord, the momentum for free trade continued with a General Agreement on Tariffs and Trade (GATT) accord. This particular agreement was the conclusion of the so-called Uruguay round of trade negotiations that had begun seven years earlier. It called for the reduction or elimination of trade restrictions on specified imported goods over a 10-year period across 117 countries. This accord has generated more international business for firms that had been unable to penetrate foreign markets because of trade restrictions.

The European Union   The European Union (EU) consists of 28 European countries that subscribe to the free movement of products, services, and capital among the member countries. The EU's philosophy promotes strong competition among MNCs, because it allows MNCs in any EU country to export to the other EU countries without restrictions. Prior to 2004, EU membership consisted of only Western European countries (Austria, Belgium, Denmark, Finland, France, Germany, Greece, Iceland, Italy, Luxembourg, the Netherlands, Portugal, Spain, Sweden, and the United Kingdom). In 2004, the EU expanded into Eastern Europe by adding Cyprus, the Czech Republic, Estonia, Hungary, Latvia, Lithuania, Malta, Poland, Slovakia, and Slovenia. These countries were followed by Bulgaria and Romania in 2007 and Croatia in 2013. Because wages in the Eastern European member countries are substantially lower than in Western European countries, many MNCs have established manufacturing plants there to produce goods for export to Western Europe. Today, the EU countries in aggregate have a total population of more than 500 million people, and account for about one-fourth of the world's gross domestic product (GDP).

While the EU has been successful at achieving general agreement on the free movement of products, services, and capital among EU countries, it has been less successful at guiding a standard immigration policy. Those EU countries that are more open to immigration have argued that the immigrants should be dispersed evenly (in proportion to population) across the EU countries. However, other EU countries have serious concerns about immigration. Consequently, many countries within the EU are presently implementing immigration policies that serve their own interests.

If EU country governments are forced to abide by a standard rigid immigration policy that differs substantially from their own philosophy, they might consider leaving the EU. In June 2016, the United Kingdom's voters voted to exit the EU. The complete exit of the United Kingdom from the EU may take at least two years. The potential impact of this historic event on the United Kingdom and Europe in general is subject to much disagreement. Some analysts suggest that the United Kingdom will suffer a major recession, while other analysts suggest that it will be more efficient without involvement in the EU bureaucracy, and that other countries in the EU might also consider exiting.

The exit of a country from the EU could have major implications for its own citizens and companies. In particular, the country's exporting firms could be subject to trade restrictions imposed by other EU countries. Furthermore, the country might impose its own trade restrictions on any imports arriving from other EU countries. Thus, just as the reduction in trade restrictions allowed for growth in international trade, the imposition of new trade restrictions might reduce international trade for a country. Yet, all companies within the country are not affected in the same manner by new trade restrictions. While exporting firms based in that country are adversely affected if new restrictions are imposed by other countries on its exports, domestic firms that focus on serving the local market and face much competition from foreign exporters are favorably affected if new restrictions are imposed on products imported by the country.

Inception of the Euro   In 2002, 11 countries that were members of the EU adopted the euro as a new currency in place of their local currency. Over time, 8 additional EU countries also adopted the euro. To qualify for participation in the so-called eurozone (the geographic area containing countries that have adopted the euro), a country must be a member of the EU, and its government must meet specified fiscal responsibility limitations on its budget deficit and total debt. Some EU countries (such as the United Kingdom) have decided not to participate in the euro. Nineteen of the 28 EU members participate in the eurozone; some other members may adopt the euro once their governments satisfy the fiscal responsibility guidelines.

When MNCs in the eurozone engage in transactions with each other, they do not need to convert one currency to another. Thus they avoid exposure to exchange rate risk on these transactions, which encourages MNCs to pursue trade within the eurozone. International trade between countries in the eurozone has increased following their adoption of the euro. All of the countries that have adopted the euro as their local currency are subject to the same monetary policy, which is explained in detail in Chapter 6.

Other Trade Agreements   In June 2003, the United States and Chile signed a free trade agreement to remove tariffs (government-imposed taxes) on products traded between the two countries. In 2006, the Central American Trade Agreement (CAFTA) was implemented; this pact allowed for lower tariffs and regulations on trade between the United States, the Dominican Republic, and four Central American countries. The United States has also established trade agreements with many other countries, including Singapore (2004), Morocco (2006), Oman (2009), Peru (2009), Jordan (2010), Bahrain (2010), and South Korea (2012). During the 2008–2011period, when the global economy was weak, momentum for trade agreements subsided as some governments became more concerned about protecting their own country's companies and local jobs. In 2016, the United States signed the Trans-Pacific Partnership, an agreement among 12 nations on the Pacific Rim including Australia, Canada, Japan, Mexico, New Zealand, and Singapore.

2-2b Impact of Outsourcing on Trade

The term **outsourcing** refers to the process of subcontracting to a third party. In the context of multinational financial management, outsourcing consists of subcontracting to a third party in another country to provide supplies or services that were previously produced internally. Under this definition, outsourcing increases international trade activity because it means that MNCs now purchase products or services from another country. For example, technical support for computer systems used in the United States is commonly outsourced to India or other countries.

Outsourcing allows MNCs to conduct operations at a lower cost. The reason is that the expenses incurred from paying a third party are less than those incurred if the MNC itself produces the product or service. Many MNCs argue that they cannot compete globally without outsourcing some of their production or services. Outsourcing by MNCs has created many jobs in countries where wages are low. However, outsourcing by U.S.-based MNCs is sometimes criticized because it may reduce jobs in the United States. These MNCs might counter that, if they had not outsourced, they would have shut down some labor-intensive operations because labor expenses are too high in the United States to compete on a global basis.

There are many opinions about outsourcing but no simple solutions. Often people have opinions about outsourcing that are inconsistent with their own behavior.

EXAMPLE

As a U.S. citizen, Rick says he is embarrassed by U.S. firms that outsource their labor services to other countries as a means of increasing their value because this practice eliminates jobs in the United States. Rick is president of Atlantic Co. and says the company will never outsource its services. Atlantic Co. imports most of its materials from a foreign company. It also owns a factory in Mexico, and the materials produced there are exported to the United States.

Rick recognizes that outsourcing may replace jobs in the United States, but he does not realize that importing materials or operating a factory in Mexico may also replace U.S. jobs. When questioned about his use of foreign labor markets for materials and production, he explains that the high manufacturing wages in the United States force him to rely on lower-cost labor in foreign countries. However, the same argument could be used by other U.S. firms that outsource services.

Rick owns a Toyota, a Samsung smartphone and tablet, and Adidas clothing. He argues that these non-U.S. products are a better value for the money than their U.S. counterparts. His friend Nicole suggests that Rick's consumption choices are inconsistent with his "create U.S. jobs" philosophy. She explains that she only purchases U.S. products. She owns a Ford automobile (produced in Mexico), an Apple iPad and iPhone (produced in China), and Nike clothing (produced in Indonesia). ●

Managerial Decisions about Outsourcing Managers of a U.S.-based MNC may argue that they produce their products in the United States to create jobs for U.S. workers. However, when the same products can be easily duplicated in foreign markets for one-fifth of the cost, shareholders may pressure the managers to establish a foreign subsidiary or to engage in outsourcing. Shareholders could argue that the managers are failing to maximize the MNC's value as a result of their commitment to creating U.S. jobs. The MNC's board of directors, which governs all major managerial decisions, could pressure the managers to move some of the production outside the United States. The board should consider the potential savings that could occur from this strategy, but it must also consider the possible adverse effects due to bad publicity or to bad morale among its remaining U.S. workers. If production cost could be substantially reduced outside the United States without a loss in quality, then a possible compromise is to restrict foreign production to accommodating any growth in the firm's business. That way, the outsourcing strategy would not adversely affect the employees already involved in production.

2-2c Trade Volume among Countries

Some countries rely more heavily on international trade than do others. The annual international trade volume of the United States is typically between 10 and 20 percent of its annual GDP. Based on this ratio, the United States is less reliant on trade than many other developed countries. Canada, France, Germany, and other European countries rely more heavily on trade than does the United States. For instance, Canada's volume of exports and imports per year is valued at more than 50 percent of its annual GDP. The annual international trade volume of European countries is typically between 30 and 40 percent of their respective GDPs. The annual trade volume of Japan is typically between 10 and 20 percent of its GDP, much as in the United States.

WEB

http://trade.gov
The international trade conditions outlook for each of several industries.

Trade Volume between the United States and Other Countries The dollar value of U.S. exports to various countries during 2015 is shown in Exhibit 2.3, where amounts are rounded to the nearest billion. For example, exports to Canada were valued at $251 billion.

Exhibit 2.3 Distribution of U.S. Exports by Country (2015, billions of $)

Source: U.S. Census Bureau, 2016.

The proportion of total U.S. exports to various countries is shown in the upper portion of Exhibit 2.4. About 19 percent of all U.S. exports are to Canada and 16 percent are to Mexico.

The proportion of total U.S. imports from various countries is shown in the lower part of Exhibit 2.4. Canada, China, Mexico, and Japan are the key exporters to the United States; together, they account for more than half of the value of all U.S. imports.

2-2d Trend in U.S. Balance of Trade

Any country's balance of trade can change substantially over time. Shortly after World War II, the United States experienced a large balance-of-trade surplus because Europe relied on U.S. exports as it was rebuilt. During the last decade, the United States has experienced large balance-of-trade deficits, due to strong U.S. demand for imported

Exhibit 2.4 Distribution of U.S. Exports and Imports by Country (2015).

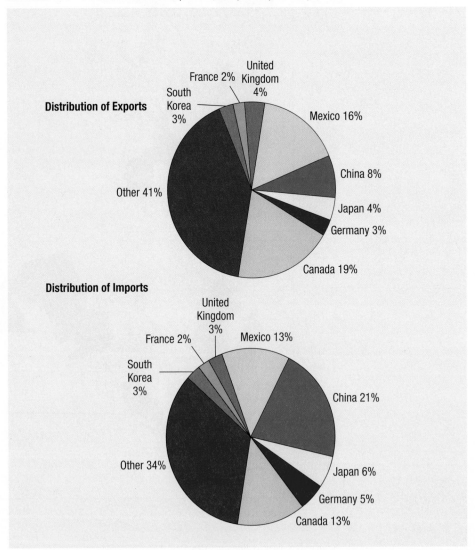

Source: *U.S. Census Bureau, 2016.*

Exhibit 2.5   U.S. Balance of Trade over Time (Quarterly)

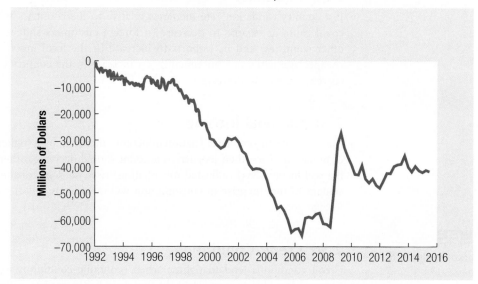

Source: U.S. Dept. of Commerce, Bureau of Economic Analysis, Census Bureau, Federal Reserve.

products that are produced at a lower cost than similar products can be produced in the United States.

The quarterly trend in the U.S. balance of trade is shown in Exhibit 2.5. Much of the U.S. trade deficit is due to a trade imbalance with just two countries: China and Japan. In recent years, the U.S. annual balance-of-trade deficit with China has exceeded $300 billion.

2-3 Factors Affecting International Trade Flows

Because international trade can significantly affect a country's economy, it is important to identify and monitor the factors that influence it. The most influential factors are:

- cost of labor,
- inflation,
- national income,
- credit conditions,
- government policies, and
- exchange rates.

WEB

http://research
.stlouisfed.org/fred2
Information about
international trade,
international
transactions, and the
balance of trade.

2-3a Cost of Labor

The cost of labor varies substantially among countries. Many of China's workers earn wages of less than $300 per month, so it is not surprising that China's firms commonly make products that require manual labor—at a much lower cost than most countries in Europe and North America. Within Europe, wages of Eastern European countries tend to be much lower than wages of Western European countries. Firms in countries where labor costs are low typically have an advantage when competing globally, especially in labor-intensive industries.

2-3b Inflation

If a country's inflation rate increases relative to the countries with which it trades, this could cause its exports to decrease (if foreign customers shift to cheaper alternatives in other countries) and its imports to increase (if the local individuals and firms shift to cheaper alternatives). Consequently, an increase in the country's inflation may cause its current account to decrease.

2-3c National Income

If a country's income level (national income) increases by a higher percentage than those of other countries, then its current account should decrease, other things being equal. As the real income level (adjusted for inflation) rises, so does consumption of goods. A percentage of that increase in consumption will most likely reflect an increased demand for foreign goods.

WEB

http://export.gov
/logistics/
Information about tariffs
on imported products.
Click on any country
listed, and then click on
Trade Regulations.
Review the import
controls set by that
country's government.

2-3d Credit Conditions

Credit conditions tend to tighten when economic conditions weaken because corporations are less able to repay debt. In that case, banks are less willing to provide financing to MNCs, which can reduce corporate spending and further weaken the economy. As MNCs reduce their spending, they also reduce their demand for imported supplies. The result is a decline in international trade flows.

An unfavorable credit environment also may reduce international trade by making it difficult for some MNCs to obtain the funds needed for purchasing imports. Many MNCs that purchase imports rely on letters of credit, which are issued by commercial banks on behalf of the importers and consist of a promise to make payment upon delivery of the imports. If banks fear that an MNC will be unable to repay its debt because of weak economic conditions then they might refuse to provide credit, and such an MNC will be unable to purchase imports without that credit.

2-3e Government Policies

Theories about the advantages of free trade are commonly given much attention in classrooms, but these theories are less popular when the country's unemployment rate increases in response to a large balance-of-trade deficit. A job created in one country may be lost in another, which causes countries to battle for a greater share of the world's exports.

Government policies can have a major influence on which firms within an industry attain the most market share worldwide. These policies affect the legislating country's unemployment level, income level, and economic growth. Each country's government wants to increase its exports because more exports lead to more production and income, and may also create jobs. Moreover, a country's government generally prefers that its citizens and firms purchase products and services locally (rather import them) because doing so creates local jobs.

An easy way to start an argument among students (or professors) is to ask what they think their country's international trade policy should be. People whose job prospects are significantly influenced by international trade tend to have strong opinions on this subject.

Governments of countries with a weak economy tend to become more creative and aggressive with policies that are intended to boost their exports or reduce imports. There are several types of policies often used to improve the balance of trade and thereby to create jobs within a country.

WEB

www.commerce.gov
General information
about import restrictions
and other trade-related
information.

Restrictions on Imports
Some governments prevent or discourage imports from other countries by imposing trade restrictions. Of these, the most commonly used are tariffs and quotas. When a country's government imposes a tax on imported goods (known as a **tariff**), the tax is commonly passed on from the importer to the consumer. Consequently, consumers pay more to purchase foreign goods. Many governments impose tariffs on imported cars as a means of encouraging the exporter to establish local subsidiaries that will manufacture the cars (and create local jobs). Tariffs imposed by the U.S. government are, on average, lower than those imposed by other governments. Even so, some U.S. industries are more highly protected by tariffs than are others. American apparel products and farm products have historically received more protection against foreign competition through high tariffs on related imports.

In addition to tariffs, a government can reduce its country's imports by enforcing a **quota**, or a maximum limit that can be imported. Quotas have frequently been applied to a variety of goods imported by the United States and other countries. In fact, weakening economic conditions in 2008–2012 led many countries to implement barriers intended to protect some of their industries.

Subsidies for Exporters
A government may offer subsidies to its domestic firms so that they can produce products at a lower cost than their global competitors. The demand for exports produced by those firms is higher as a result of these subsidies.

EXAMPLE   Many firms in China receive free loans or free land from the government. Thus they incur a lower cost of operations and can therefore price their products lower. Lower prices, in turn, enable these subsidized firms to capture a larger share of the global market. ●

Firms in some countries receive subsidies from the government provided that the manufactured products are then exported. The exporting of products that were produced with the help of government subsidies is commonly referred to as **dumping**. These firms may be able to sell their products at a lower price than any of their competitors in other countries. Some subsidies are more obvious than others, and it could be argued that every government provides subsidies in some form.

Restrictions on Piracy
Government restrictions on piracy vary among countries. A government can affect international trade flows by its *lack* of restrictions on piracy. A government that does not act to minimize piracy may indirectly reduce imports and may even discourage MNCs from exporting to that market.

EXAMPLE   In China, piracy is very common. Individuals (called pirates) manufacture video games and DVDs that look almost exactly like the original product produced in the United States and other countries. They then sell the games and DVDs on the street at a price that is lower than the price of the original product; in fact, they even sell the games and DVDs to retail stores. In addition, websites offer downloadable movies and games that have been pirated. Consequently, local consumers obtain copies of imports rather than actual imports. According to the U.S. film industry, as many as 90 percent of the movies (which are the intellectual property of U.S. firms) sold as DVDs or downloaded in China may be pirated. It has been estimated that U.S. producers of video, music, and software lose billions of dollars in sales each year to piracy in China. The Chinese government periodically promises to crack down, but piracy remains prevalent there. ●

As a result of piracy, China's demand for imports is lower. Piracy is one reason why the United States has a large balance-of-trade deficit with China. However, this deficit would still be large even if piracy were eliminated.

Environmental Restrictions
When a government imposes environmental restrictions, local firms experience higher costs of production. Those costs could put local firms

at a disadvantage compared with firms (in other countries) that are not subject to the same restrictions. Some governments have considered loosening or entirely eliminating environmental restrictions as a means to ensure that local firms can compete globally. Of course, such a policy will be in clear conflict with the objectives of that country's environmental groups. A person's opinion about the appropriate policy is often based in large part on whether local jobs or a clean environment is considered to be the most important criterion.

Labor Laws   Labor laws vary among countries, which might allow for pronounced differences in the labor expenses incurred by firms among countries. Some countries have more restrictive laws that protect the rights of workers. In addition, some countries have more restrictive child labor laws. Firms based in countries with more restrictive laws will incur higher expenses for labor, other factors being equal. For this reason, their firms may be at a disadvantage when competing against firms based in other countries.

Business Laws   Some countries have more restrictive laws on bribery than others. Firms based in these countries may not be able to compete globally in some situations, such as when government officials of an agency soliciting specific services from MNCs expect to receive bribes from the MNCs attempting to secure that business.

Tax Breaks   The government in some countries may allow tax breaks to firms that operate in specific industries. Although it need not be a subsidy, this practice is still a form of government financial support that could benefit firms that export products. For example, U.S.-based MNCs can benefit from tax breaks when investing in research and development and also when investing in equipment and machinery.

Country Trade Requirements   A government may require that MNCs complete various forms or obtain licenses before they can export products to its country. Such requirements often result in delays simply because the government is inefficient in validating the forms or licenses. The process might even be *purposely* inefficient in order to discourage exporters and thereby, indirectly, protect jobs within a country.

Bureaucracy (whether international or not) is a strong trade barrier. Furthermore, it is difficult to prove that a country's government is purposely trying to prevent trade and is therefore in violation of free trade agreements. Even with the available advances in technology (such as the possibility of online forms), many governments still respond slowly to requests by other country's exporters to export products to their country. Given that some governments are slow, it is also possible that other governments are purposely slow as a form of retaliation that could hinder trade and so protect local jobs. Bureaucratic delays discourage some MNCs from pursuing business in other countries.

Government Ownership or Subsidies   Some governments maintain ownership in firms that are major exporters. The Chinese government has granted billions of dollars of subsidies over the years to its auto manufacturers and auto parts suppliers. The U.S. government bailed out General Motors in 2009 by investing billions of dollars to purchase a large amount of its stock.

Country Security Laws   Some U.S. politicians have argued that international trade and foreign ownership should be restricted when U.S. security is threatened. Despite the general support for this opinion, there is disagreement regarding which specific U.S. business and transactions deserve protection from foreign competition. Consider, for example, the following questions.

1. Should the United States purchase military planes only from a U.S. producer even when Brazil could produce the same planes for half the price? The trade-off is a larger budget deficit against increased security. Is the United States truly safer with planes produced in the United States? Are technology secrets safer when production occurs in the United States by a domestic firm?

2. If military planes are manufactured only by a U.S. firm, should there be any restrictions on foreign ownership of that firm? Note that foreign investors own a portion of most large publicly traded companies in the United States.

3. Should foreign ownership restrictions be imposed on investors based in some countries but not on those based in other countries, or should owners based in *any* foreign country be banned from business transactions that might threaten U.S. security? Is the threat that the producing firm's owners could sell technology secrets to enemies? Is a firm with only U.S. owners immune to that threat? If some foreign owners are acceptable, then which countries are considered to be acceptable?

4. What products should be viewed as a threat to U.S. security? Suppose, for instance, that military planes are produced by strictly U.S. firms; what about all the components that are used in the planes' production? Some of the components used in U.S. military plane production are produced in China and imported by the plane manufacturers.

To appreciate the extent of disagreement on such issues, try to obtain a consensus answer on any of these questions from your fellow students. If students without hidden agendas cannot agree on an answer, imagine the level of disagreement among owners or employees of U.S. and foreign firms that have much to gain (or lose) from whatever international trade and investment policy is implemented. It is difficult to distinguish between a trade or investment restriction that enhances national security versus one that unfairly protects a U.S. firm from foreign competition. This same dilemma is faced not only by the United States, of course, but also by most other countries.

Policies to Punish Country Governments   International trade policy issues have become even more contentious over time. Although some people advocate free trade without restrictions, many other people want their government to impose new trade restrictions that would punish other country governments that do not enforce environmental laws or child labor laws, or that commit human rights violations. Every international trade convention now attracts a large number of protesters, all of whom have their own agendas.

The managers of each MNC cannot be responsible for resolving these international trade policy conflicts. However, they should at least recognize how a particular international trade policy affects their competitive position in the industry and how policy changes could affect their future position.

Summary of Government Policies   Every government implements some policies that may give its local firms an advantage in the battle for global market share, so the playing field is probably not level across all countries. However, no formula can ensure a completely fair contest for market share. Most governments are pressured by their constituents to implement trade restrictions that create local jobs and give their local firms an exporting advantage. However, a country's imposition of new trade restrictions will often trigger retaliation.

EXAMPLE   Assume that a large number of agriculture firms in the United States have lost business recently because local consumers have begun buying vegetables imported from the country of Vegambia at much lower prices. Having laid off many employees as a result, these firms decide to lobby their political representatives. The agriculture firms argue that:

- vegetables from Vegambia are unfairly priced because Vegambia's government gives tax breaks to the firms that grow the vegetables,
- there is speculation that the vegetables imported from Vegambia have caused illness among some consumers, and
- Vegambia allows its children to work at an earlier age than the age allowed in the United States.

In response to this lobbying, the U.S. government decides to impose restrictions on imports. Vegambia's vegetable exports to the United States consequently decline, and its unemployment rate rises. Vegambia's government decides that it can correct its unemployment rate by improving its balance-of-trade deficit. Some of its firms specialize in manufacturing toys, but sales have been weak recently because many local citizens purchase toys imported from the United States. The government of Vegambia determines that:

- the U.S. toy manufacturers have an unfair advantage because they pay low taxes (as a proportion of their income) to the U.S. government,
- the toys produced in the United States present a health risk to local children because reportedly a few children have hurt themselves while playing with these toys, and
- the U.S. government has failed to intervene in some foreign countries to prevent the production of illegal drugs that flow into Vegambia, so Vegambia should reduce U.S. imports as a form of protest.

Therefore, the government of Vegambia prohibits the importing of toys from the United States. ●

One conclusion from the preceding example is that any government can find an argument for restricting imports if it wants to increase domestic employment. Some arguments might be justified; others, less so. Naturally, countries that are adversely affected by a trade policy may retaliate in order to offset any adverse effects on employment. This means that the plan to create jobs by restricting imports may not be successful. But even when the overall employment situation for both countries is unchanged due to offsetting effects of trade policies, employment within particular industries may be changed. In this example, the agriculture firms benefit from the U.S. government policy at the expense of the toy manufacturers.

An easy way to start an argument among students (or professors) is to ask what they think the proper government policies should be in order to ensure that MNCs of all countries have an equal chance to compete globally. Given the disagreement on this topic among citizens of the same country, consider how difficult it is to achieve agreement among countries.

2-3f Exchange Rates

Each country's currency is valued in terms of other currencies through the use of exchange rates. Currencies can then be exchanged to facilitate international transactions. The values of most currencies fluctuate over time because of market and government forces (as discussed in detail in Chapter 4). If a country's currency begins to rise in value against other currencies then its current account balance should decrease, other things being equal. As the currency strengthens, goods exported by that country will become more expensive to the importing countries and thus the demand for such goods will decrease.

EXAMPLE   Accel Co. produces a standard tennis racket in the Netherlands and sells it online to consumers in the United States. This racket competes with a tennis racket produced by Malibu Co. in the United States, which is of similar quality and is priced at about $140. Accel has set the price of its tennis racket at 100 euros. Assuming that the euro's exchange rate (during the sales month in question) was $1.60, then the price of Accel's racket to U.S. consumers is $160 (i.e., 100 euros × $1.60 per euro). Because U.S. consumers could buy a Malibu racket for only $140, Accel only sold about 1,000 rackets to U.S. consumers in that month.

Since then, however, the euro's value has weakened; this month, the euro's exchange rate is only $1.20. U.S. consumers can now purchase the Accel tennis racket for $120 (100 euros × $1.20 per euro), which is less than that charged for the U.S. Malibu racket. In this month, Accel sold 5,000 rackets. The U.S. demand for this tennis racket is price-elastic (sensitive to price changes) because there are substitute products available: the increase in demand for Accel rackets led to reduced demand for tennis rackets produced by Malibu Co. ●

The two exchange rates used in the preceding example are very real. The euro was valued at about $1.60 in July 2009 and at about $1.20 (a reduction of 25 percent) in June 2010, just 11 months later. By April 2011 the euro had reached a high of $1.48, which amounted to a 23 percent increase over 9 months. But then, in July 2012, the euro reached a low of $1.24; this represented a 16 percent decrease over a period of 15 months.

This example illustrates, first of all, how much the price of a product can change in a short time in response to movements in the exchange rate. Second, it illustrates how the demand for an exported product can shift as a result of a change in the exchange rate. Third, the example shows how the demand for products of *competitors* to an exported product can change as a function of the exchange rate.

This example considered only a single product. The economic effects are much greater when one considers how the U.S. demand for *all* products imported from euro-zone countries could change in response to such a large change in the euro's value. The following example helps explain the exchange rate's effect on U.S. exports.

EXAMPLE   Malibu Co. produces tennis rackets in the United States and sells some of them to European countries. Its standard racket is priced at $140, and it competes with the Accel racket in both the U.S. and the euro-zone market. When the euro was valued at $1.60, eurozone consumers paid about 87 euros for Malibu's racket (computed as $140/$1.60 = 87.50 euros). Because this price to eurozone consumers was lower than the Accel racket price of 100 euros per racket, Malibu sold 7,000 rackets in the eurozone at that time.

When the euro's value fell to $1.20, however, eurozone consumers had to pay about 117 euros for Malibu's standard tennis racket (i.e., $140/$1.20), which is more than the 100 euros for an Accel racket. Hence Malibu sold only 2,000 rackets to eurozone consumers in this month. As those consumers reduced their demand for Malibu rackets, they increased their demand for tennis rackets produced by Accel. ●

This example was based on only one product; the cumulative effect of all exports would again be much greater. In general, the examples here suggest that, when currencies are strong against the U.S. dollar (i.e., when the dollar is weak), U.S. exports should be relatively high and U.S. imports should be relatively low. Conversely, when currencies are weak against the U.S. dollar (i.e., when the dollar is strong), U.S. exports should be relatively low and U.S. imports should be relatively high, which would enlarge the U.S. balance-of-trade deficit.

How Exchange Rates May Correct a Balance-of-Trade Deficit   A floating exchange rate could correct any international trade imbalance between two countries in the following way. A balance-of-trade deficit suggests that the country is spending more funds on foreign products than it is receiving from exports to foreign countries. This exchange of its currency (to buy foreign goods) in greater volume than the foreign demand for its currency could place downward pressure on the value of that currency. Once the country's home currency's value declines in response to these forces, the result should be more foreign demand for its products.

Why Exchange Rates May Not Correct a Balance-of-Trade Deficit A floating exchange rate will not correct any international trade imbalances when there are other forces that offset the effects of international trade flows on the exchange rate.

EXAMPLE

Because the United States normally experiences a large balance-of-trade deficit, international trade flows should place downward pressure on the dollar's value. Yet in many periods there are more financial flows into the United States (e.g., to purchase securities) than there are financial outflows. These forces offset the downward pressure on the dollar's value caused by the trade imbalance. If the value of the dollar does not weaken in such circumstances, a floating exchange rate will not correct the U.S. balance-of-trade deficit. ●

Limitations of a Weak–Home Currency Solution Even if a country's home currency weakens, there are several reasons why its balance-of-trade deficit will not necessarily be corrected. First, when a country's currency weakens, its prices become more attractive to foreign customers; hence many foreign companies lower their prices to remain competitive. Second, a country's currency need not weaken against all currencies at the same time. Therefore, a country that has a balance-of-trade deficit with many countries is unlikely to reduce all deficits simultaneously.

EXAMPLE

Despite weakening against European currencies, the dollar might strengthen against Asian currencies. Under such conditions, U.S. consumers may reduce their demand for products in European countries but increase their demand for products in Asian countries. Hence the U.S. balance-of-trade deficit with European countries may decline but the U.S. balance-of-trade deficit with Asian countries may increase. Changes of this nature would not eliminate the overall U.S. balance-of-trade deficit. ●

A third reason why a weak currency will not always improve a country's balance of trade is that many international trade transactions are prearranged and cannot be immediately adjusted. Thus exporters and importers are committed to following through on the international transactions that they agreed to complete. The lag time between weakness in the dollar and increased non-U.S. demand for U.S. products has been estimated to be 18 months or even longer. The U.S. balance-of-trade deficit could deteriorate even further in the short run when the dollar is weak because U.S. importers then need more dollars to pay for the imports they have contracted to purchase. This pattern is referred to as the **J-curve effect** and is illustrated in Exhibit 2.6. The trade balance's further decline before a reversal is a trend whose plot resembles the letter J.

Finally, a weak currency is less likely to improve the country's balance of trade to the extent that its international trade involves importers and exporters under the same ownership. Many firms purchase products that are produced by their subsidiaries in what is known as **intracompany trade**. This type of trade amounts to more than 50 percent of all international trade. Such trading will normally continue even if the importer's currency weakens.

Exchange Rates and International Friction For the many reasons just cited, a weaker home currency is seldom the best way to reduce a balance-of-trade deficit. Even so, it is not unusual for government officials to recommend this approach as a possible solution. However, all country governments cannot simultaneously weaken their home currencies. For any pair of countries, the actions by one government to weaken its currency causes the other country's currency to strengthen. As consumers in the country with the stronger currency are enticed by the new exchange rate to purchase more imports, more jobs may be created in the country with the weak currency and jobs may be eliminated in the country with the strong currency. These outcomes can lead to friction between countries.

Exhibit 2.6 J-Curve Effect

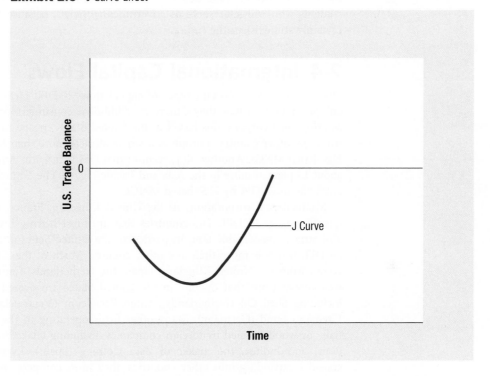

At any given moment, a group of exporters may claim that it is being mistreated and lobby its government to weaken the local currency, thus rendering its exports less expensive for foreign purchasers. When the euro is strong against the dollar, some European exporters claim that they are disadvantaged because their euro-denominated products are priced high for U.S. consumers (who must convert dollars into euros). When the euro is weak against the dollar, some U.S. exporters claim that they are disadvantaged because their dollar-denominated products are priced high for European consumers (who must convert euros into dollars). ●

It is frequently claimed by U.S. exporters and government officials that the Chinese government maintains the value of the yuan at an artificially low level against the dollar. They argue that the Chinese government should revalue the yuan upward in order to correct the large U.S. balance-of-trade deficit with China. This issue received much attention during the 2008–2012 period, when the U.S. economy was extremely weak and government officials were searching for ways to stimulate it. Some believe that if the Chinese yuan is revalued upward then U.S. exports would increase and U.S. imports would decrease. Consequently, more U.S. jobs could be created.

However, there are counterarguments that should be considered. China's government might respond that the trade imbalance is highly influenced by the difference in the cost of labor between countries and that adjusting the exchange rate could not offset such a large labor cost difference between countries. Furthermore, even if China's government revalued the yuan upward in order to make its products much more expensive for U.S. importers, would that increase demand for U.S. products? Or would it simply replace U.S. purchases from China with purchases from other countries (e.g., Malaysia, Mexico, Vietnam) where wage rates are very low? If U.S. consumers shifted their purchases to alternative low-wage countries, will U.S. government officials then argue that those countries should revalue *their* currencies so as to reduce the U.S. balance-of-trade deficit? These questions are left to be answered by today's students who will later serve as government officials, because the dispute will almost certainly still exist in the future.

2-4 International Capital Flows

One of the most important types of capital flows is DFI. Firms commonly attempt to engage in DFI so that they can reach additional consumers or utilize low-cost labor. Multinational corporations based in the United States engage in DFI more than MNCs from any other country. Europe as a whole attracts more than 50 percent of all DFI by U.S.-based MNCs. Another 30 percent of that DFI is in Latin America and Canada, with about 15 percent more in the Asia and Pacific region. The United Kingdom and Canada enjoy the most DFI by U.S.-based MNCs.

Multinational corporations in the United Kingdom, France, and Germany also frequently engage in DFI. The countries that are most heavily involved in pursuing DFI also attract considerable DFI. In particular, the United States attracts about one-sixth of all DFI, which is more than any other country. Much of the DFI in the United States comes from the United Kingdom, Japan, the Netherlands, Canada, and France. Many well-known firms that operate in the United States are owned by foreign companies, including Shell Oil (Netherlands), Citgo Petroleum (Venezuela), Canon (Japan), and Fireman's Fund (Germany). Many other firms operating in the United States are partially or wholly owned by foreign companies, including GlaxoSmithKline (United Kingdom) and Inditex, the maker of Zara clothing (Spain). Even as U.S.-based MNCs consider expanding into other countries, they must compete with foreign firms in the United States.

2-4a Factors Affecting Direct Foreign Investment

WEB

reason.org/news/show
/annual-privatization
-report-2015
Information about
privatizations around
the world together
with commentaries and
related publications.

Capital flows resulting from DFI change whenever conditions in a country change the desire of firms to conduct business operations there. Some of the more common factors that could affect a country's appeal for DFI are identified here.

Changes in Restrictions   Many countries lowered their restrictions on DFI during the 1990s, which resulted in more DFI in those countries. Many U.S.-based MNCs (including Bausch & Lomb, Colgate-Palmolive, and General Electric) have penetrated less developed countries such as Argentina, Chile, China, Hungary, India, and Mexico. New opportunities in these countries have arisen since government barriers were removed.

Privatization   Several national governments have recently engaged in privatization, which is the selling of some of their operations to corporations and other investors. Privatization is popular in Brazil and Mexico, in Eastern European countries such as Poland and Hungary, and in some Caribbean territories such as the Virgin Islands. It allows for greater international business because foreign firms can acquire operations sold by national governments.

Privatization was used in Chile to prevent a small group of investors from controlling all the shares of stock, and in France to prevent a more nationalized economy. In the United Kingdom, privatization was promoted as a way of spreading stock ownership across investors, which allowed more people to have a direct stake in the success of British industry.

The primary reason that the market value of a firm may increase in response to privatization is the anticipated improvement in managerial efficiency. Managers in a privately owned firm can focus on the goal of maximizing shareholder wealth; in contrast, a state-owned business must consider the economic and social ramifications of any decision. Also, managers of a privately owned enterprise are more motivated to ensure profitability because their careers may depend on it. For these reasons, privatized firms will search for local and global opportunities that could enhance their value. The trend toward privatization will undoubtedly create a more competitive global marketplace.

Potential Economic Growth   Countries that have greater potential for economic growth are more likely to attract DFI because firms recognize the possibility of capitalizing on that growth by establishing more business there.

Tax Rates   Countries that impose relatively low tax rates on corporate earnings are more likely to attract DFI. When assessing the feasibility of DFI, firms estimate the after-tax cash flows that they expect to earn.

Exchange Rates   Firms typically prefer to pursue DFI in countries where the local currency is expected to strengthen against their own. Under these conditions, they can invest funds to establish their operations in a country at a time when that country's currency is relatively cheap (weak). Thereafter, earnings from the new operations will have to be converted into the firm's currency at a less favorable exchange rate.

2-4b Factors Affecting International Portfolio Investment

The amount of funds invested by individual or institutional investors in a specific country is influenced by the following factors.

Tax Rates on Interest or Dividends   Investors normally prefer to invest in a country where the taxes on interest or dividend income from investments are relatively low. Investors assess their potential after-tax earnings from investments in foreign securities.

Interest Rates   Portfolio investment can also be affected by interest rates. Money tends to flow to countries with high interest rates as long as the local currencies are not expected to weaken.

WEB

www.worldbank.org
Information on capital
flows and international
transactions.

Exchange Rates   When investors invest in a security in a foreign country, their return is affected by (1) the change in the value of the security and (2) the change in the value of the currency in which the security is denominated. If a country's home currency is expected to strengthen, then foreign investors may be willing to invest in that country's securities in order to benefit from the currency movement. Conversely, if a country's home currency is expected to weaken then foreign investors may well prefer to purchase securities in other countries.

2-4c Impact of International Capital Flows

The United States relies heavily on foreign capital in many ways. First, there is foreign investment in the United States to build manufacturing plants, offices, and other buildings. Second, foreign investors purchase U.S. debt securities issued by U.S. firms and thereby serve as creditors to these firms. Third, foreign investors purchase Treasury debt securities and thus serve as creditors to the U.S. government.

Foreign investors are especially attracted to U.S. financial markets when the interest rate in their home country is lower than that in the United States. For example, investors

Exhibit 2.7 Impact of the International Flow of Funds on U.S. Interest Rates and Business Investment

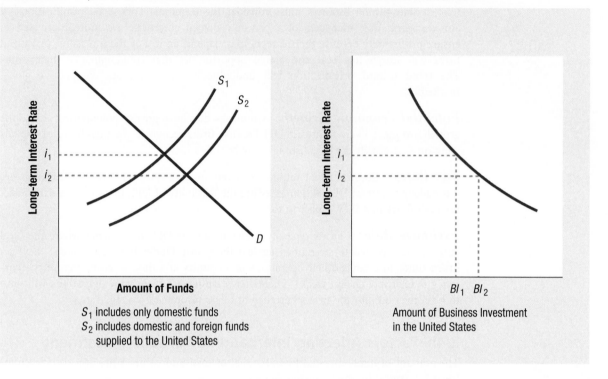

S_1 includes only domestic funds
S_2 includes domestic and foreign funds
supplied to the United States

Amount of Business Investment
in the United States

based in Japan and Europe commonly invest in U.S. debt securities when their annual interest rates are lower than the U.S. interest rates.

The impact of international capital flows on the U.S. economy is shown in Exhibit 2.7. At any time, the long-term interest rate in the United States is determined by the interaction between the supply of funds available in U.S. credit markets and the amount of funds demanded there. The supply curve S_1 in the left graph reflects the supply of funds from domestic sources. If the United States relied solely on domestic sources for its supply, then its equilibrium interest rate would be i_1 and the level of U.S. business investment (shown in the right graph) would be BI_1. But because the supply curve also includes the supply of funds from foreign sources (as shown in S_2), the equilibrium interest rate is i_2. Because of the large international capital flows to the U.S. credit markets, interest rates in the United States are lower than they would be otherwise. This allows for a lower cost of borrowing and thus a lower cost of using capital in the United States. As a result, the equilibrium level of business investment is BI_2. Because of the lower interest rate, there are more business opportunities in the United States that deserve to be funded.

Consider the long-term rate shown in the exhibit as the cost of borrowing for the most creditworthy firms; other firms would pay a premium above that rate. Without international capital flows, there would be less funding available in the United States across all risk levels and the cost of funding would be higher regardless of a firm's risk level. This would reduce the amount of feasible business opportunities in the United States.

U.S. Reliance on Foreign Funds

If Japan and China stopped investing in U.S. debt securities then U.S. interest rates would probably rise, in which case investors from other countries would be attracted to the relatively high U.S. interest rate. Thus the United States would still be able to obtain funding for its debt, but its interest rates (cost of borrowing) would rise.

In general, access to international funding has allowed more growth in the U.S. economy over time but also has made the United States more reliant on foreign investors for funding. Such reliance remains possible provided the U.S. government and U.S. firms are perceived to be creditworthy. If that trust were ever weakened, then U.S. entities would be able to obtain foreign funding only by paying a higher interest rate to compensate for the increased risk (i.e., a risk premium).

In recent years, the Federal Reserve (the U.S. central bank) has maintained the country's long-term interest rates at a very low level; this policy is intended to encourage more borrowing and stimulate the economy. Yet the low rates could also lead foreign investors to seek alternative investments offering a higher return. In that case, if the Fed wants low interest rates then it may need to supply more of the funding itself to replace those funds withdrawn by foreign investors.

WEB

www.imf.org
The latest international economic news, data, and surveys.

2-5 Agencies That Facilitate International Flows

A variety of agencies have been established to facilitate international trade and financial transactions. These agencies often represent a group of nations. A description of each of the more important agencies follows.

2-5a International Monetary Fund

The United Nations Monetary and Financial Conference held in Bretton Woods, New Hampshire, in July 1944 was called to develop a structured international monetary system. As a result of this conference, the **International Monetary Fund (IMF)** was formed. The major objectives of the IMF, as set by its charter, are to (1) promote cooperation among countries on international monetary issues, (2) promote stability in exchange rates, (3) provide temporary funds to member countries attempting to correct imbalances of international payments, (4) promote free mobility of capital funds across countries, and (5) promote free trade. It is clear from these objectives that the IMF's goals encourage the increased internationalization of business.

The IMF has played a major role in resolving international financial crises, including the Asian crisis in the late 1990s, the U.S. financial crisis of 2008–2010, and the European financial crisis of 2011–2012. In recent years it has provided considerable funding to countries such as Greece and Portugal, which have experienced large government deficits, because they are unable to obtain low-cost funding from other sources. In providing funds to these countries the IMF seeks to stabilize their economies so that their respective governments can ultimately repay the loans received from banks (and other creditors) based in various countries. In this way, the IMF aims to prevent the financial problems in these countries from spreading to other countries. The IMF is overseen by a board of governors that is composed of finance officers (such as the head of the central bank) from each of the 188 member countries; it also has an executive board consisting of 24 executive directors. This executive board is based in Washington, DC, and meets at least three times a week to discuss ongoing issues.

The IMF uses a surveillance system that closely monitors national, regional, and global financial conditions. It attempts to anticipate financial problems in member countries and offers advice to these countries on how they can reduce their exposure to potential crises. The IMF also provides technical assistance to countries in order to help them implement effective tax policies, exchange rate policies, banking systems, and legal systems.

Each member country of the IMF is assigned a quota that is based on a variety of factors reflecting its economic status. Members are required to pay this assigned quota. The amount of funds that each member can borrow from the IMF depends on its particular quota.

The financing by the IMF is measured in **special drawing rights (SDRs)**, which are a unit of account allocated to member countries to supplement currency reserves. The SDRs' value fluctuates in accordance with the value of major currencies.

One of the key duties of the IMF is its **compensatory financing facility (CFF)**, which aims to reduce the impact of export instability on the economies of member countries. Although this facility is available to all IMF members, it is used mainly by developing countries. A country experiencing financial problems resulting from reduced export earnings must demonstrate that the reduction is temporary and beyond its control. In addition, it must be willing to work with the IMF in resolving the problem.

Funding Dilemma of the IMF   The IMF typically specifies economic reforms that a country must satisfy in order to receive IMF funding, which is meant to ensure that the country uses the funds properly. However, some countries want funding without adhering to the economic reforms required by the IMF. For example, the IMF may require that a government reduce its budget deficit as a condition for receiving funding. Some governments have failed to implement these required reforms. For example, Greece received substantial funding from the IMF and was expected to reduce its massive government spending in order to reduce its budget deficit. But its government continued its spending and its large budget deficit, and in July 2015, it stopped making interest payments on the funds borrowed from the IMF.

2-5b World Bank

The **International Bank for Reconstruction and Development (IBRD)**, also referred to as the **World Bank**, was established in 1944. Its primary objective is to make loans to countries in order to reduce poverty and enhance economic development. The World Bank has been successful at reducing extreme poverty levels, increasing education, preventing the spread of deadly diseases, and improving environmental conditions.

Its main source of funds is the sale of bonds and other debt instruments to private investors and governments. The World Bank has a profit-oriented philosophy. Therefore, its loans are not subsidized but instead are extended at market rates to governments (and their agencies) that are deemed likely to repay them.

A key aspect of the World Bank's mission is the **Structural Adjustment Loan (SAL)**, established in 1980. SALs are intended to enhance a country's long-term economic growth.

Because the World Bank provides only a small portion of the financing needed by developing countries, it attempts to spread its funds by entering into **cofinancing agreements**. Cofinancing is performed in the following ways.

- *Official aid agencies.* Development agencies may join the World Bank in financing development projects in low-income countries.
- *Export credit agencies.* The World Bank cofinances some capital-intensive projects that are also financed through export credit agencies.
- *Commercial banks.* The World Bank has joined with commercial banks to provide financing for private-sector development.

WEB

www.worldbank.org
Website of the World
Bank Group.

The World Bank recently established the **Multilateral Investment Guarantee Agency (MIGA)**, which offers various forms of political risk insurance. This is an additional means (along with its SALs) by which the World Bank can encourage the development of international trade and investment.

The World Bank is one of the largest borrowers in the world. Its loans are well diversified among numerous currencies and countries, and it has received the highest credit rating (AAA) possible.

2-5c World Trade Organization

The **World Trade Organization (WTO)** was created as a result of the Uruguay round of trade negotiations that led to the GATT accord in 1993. This organization was established to provide a forum for multilateral trade negotiations and to settle trade disputes related to the GATT. The WTO began operations in 1995 with 81 member countries, and more countries have joined since then. Member countries are given voting rights that are used to render verdicts on trade disputes and other issues. World trade agreements have been signed among countries, and these agreements provide the legal foundation for facilitating international trade. Such agreements articulate how international trade must be executed so as not to violate specific social and environmental standards. Although the agreements thus contain rules, they help to promote international trade because the rules are communicated to exporters and importers alike. In other words, MNCs are more willing to pursue international trade when the rules are more transparent.

2-5d International Finance Corporation

In 1956 the **International Finance Corporation (IFC)** was established to promote private enterprise within countries. Composed of a number of member nations, the IFC works to promote economic development through the private rather than the government sector. It not only provides loans to corporations but also purchases stock, thereby becoming part owner in some cases in addition to a creditor. The IFC typically provides 10 to 15 percent of the necessary funds to the private enterprise projects in which it invests, and the rest of the project must be financed through other sources. Thus the IFC serves as a catalyst, rather than a primary supporter, for private-enterprise development projects. It traditionally has obtained financing from the World Bank but can also borrow in the international financial markets.

2-5e International Development Association

The **International Development Association (IDA)** was created in 1960 with country development objectives similar to those of the World Bank. However, its loan policy is more appropriate for less prosperous nations. The IDA extends loans at low interest rates to poor nations that cannot qualify for loans from the World Bank.

2-5f Bank for International Settlements

The **Bank for International Settlements (BIS)** attempts to facilitate cooperation among countries with regard to international transactions. It serves central banks of countries in their pursuit of financial stability. The BIS is sometimes referred to as the "central banks' central bank" or the "lender of last resort." It played an important role in supporting some of the less developed countries during international debt crises. It commonly provides financing for central banks in Latin American and Eastern European countries.

2-5g OECD

The Organisation for Economic Co-operation and Development (OECD) facilitates governance in governments and corporations of countries with market economics. It has 34 member countries as well as relationships with numerous other countries. The OECD promotes international country relationships that lead to globalization.

2-5h Regional Development Agencies

There are several other agencies whose objectives relating to economic development are more regional than global. These include, for example, the Inter-American Development Bank (focusing on the needs of Latin America), the Asian Development Bank (established to enhance social and economic development in Asia), and the African Development Bank (focusing on development in African countries). In 1990, the European Bank for Reconstruction and Development was created to help Eastern European countries adjust from communism to capitalism.

SUMMARY

- The key components of the balance of payments are the current account, the capital account, and the financial account. The current account is a broad measure of the country's international trade balance. The capital account measures the value of financial and nonfinancial assets transferred across country borders. The financial account consists mainly of payments for direct foreign investment and investment in securities (portfolio investment).

- International trade activity has grown over time in response to several government agreements to remove cross-border restrictions. In addition, MNCs have commonly used outsourcing in recent years, subcontracting with a third party in a foreign country for supplies or services they previously produced themselves. Thus outsourcing is another reason for the increase in international trade activity.

- A country's international trade flows are affected by inflation, national income, government restrictions, and exchange rates. High labor costs, high inflation, a high national income, low or no restrictions on imports, and a strong local currency tend to result in a strong demand for imports and a current account deficit. Although some countries attempt to correct current account deficits by reducing the value of their currencies, this strategy is not always successful.

- A country's international capital flows are affected by factors that influence direct foreign investment or portfolio investment. DFI tends to occur in those countries that have no restrictions and much potential for economic growth. Portfolio investment tends to occur in those countries where taxes are not excessive, where interest rates are high, and where the local currencies are not expected to weaken.

- Several agencies facilitate the international flow of funds by promoting international trade and finance, providing loans to enhance global economic development, settling trade disputes between countries, and promoting global business relationships between countries.

POINT COUNTER-POINT

Should Trade Restrictions Be Used to Influence Human Rights Issues?

Point   Yes. Some countries do not protect human rights in the same manner as the United States. At times, the United States should threaten to restrict U.S. imports from or investment in a particular country if it does not correct human rights violations. The United States should use its large international trade and investment as leverage to ensure that human rights violations do not occur. Other countries with a history of human rights violations are more likely to honor human rights if their economic conditions are threatened.

Counter-Point   No. International trade and human rights are two separate issues. International trade should not be used as the weapon to enforce human rights. Firms engaged in international trade should not be penalized by the human rights violations of a government. If the United States imposes trade restrictions to enforce human rights, the country will retaliate. Thus the U.S. firms that export to that foreign country will be adversely affected. By imposing trade sanctions, the U.S. government is indirectly penalizing the MNCs that are attempting to conduct business in specific foreign countries. Trade sanctions cannot solve every difference in beliefs or morals between the more developed countries and the developing countries. By restricting trade, the United States will slow down the economic progress of developing countries.

Who Is Correct?   Use the Internet to learn more about this issue. Which argument do you support? Offer your own opinion on this issue.

SELF-TEST

Answers are provided in Appendix A at the back of the text.

1. Briefly explain how changes in various economic factors affect the U.S. current account balance.

2. Explain why U.S. tariffs will not necessarily reduce a U.S. balance-of-trade deficit.

3. Explain why a global recession like that in 2008–2009 might encourage some governments to impose more trade restrictions.

QUESTIONS AND APPLICATIONS

1. Balance of Payments
a. What are the main components of the current account?
b. What are the main components of the capital account?

2. Inflation Effect on Trade
a. How would a relatively high home inflation rate affect the home country's current account, other things being equal?
b. Is a negative current account harmful to a country? Discuss.

3. Government Restrictions How can government restrictions affect international payments among countries?

4. IMF
a. What are some of the major objectives of the IMF?
b. How is the IMF involved in international trade?

5. Exchange Rate Effect on Trade Balance Would the U.S. balance-of-trade deficit be larger or smaller if the dollar depreciates against all currencies, versus depreciating against some currencies but appreciating against others? Explain.

6. Demand for Exports A relatively small U.S. balance-of-trade deficit is commonly attributed to a strong demand for U.S. exports. What do you think is the underlying reason for the strong demand for U.S. exports?

7. Change in International Trade Volume Why do you think international trade volume has increased over time? In general, how are inefficient firms affected by the reduction in trade restrictions among countries and the continuous increase in international trade?

8. Effects of the Euro Explain how the existence of the euro may affect U.S. international trade.

9. Currency Effects When South Korea's export growth stalled, some South Korean firms suggested that South Korea's primary export problem was the weakness in the Japanese yen. How would you interpret this statement?

10. Effects of Tariffs Assume a simple world in which the United States exports soft drinks and beer to France and imports wine from France. If the United States imposes large tariffs on the French wine, explain the likely impact on the values of the U.S. beverage firms, the U.S. wine producers, the French beverage firms, and the French wine producers.

Advanced Questions

11. Free Trade There has been considerable momentum to reduce or remove trade barriers in an effort to achieve "free trade." Yet one disgruntled executive of an exporting firm stated, "Free trade is not conceivable; we are always at the mercy of the exchange rate. Any country can use this mechanism to impose trade barriers." What does this statement mean?

12.   International Investments U.S.-based MNCs commonly invest in foreign securities.

a. Assume that the dollar is presently weak and is expected to strengthen over time. How will these expectations affect the tendency of U.S. investors to invest in foreign securities?

b. Explain how low U.S. interest rates can affect the tendency of U.S.-based MNCs to invest abroad.

c. In general terms, what is the attraction of foreign investments to U.S. investors?

13.   Exchange Rate Effects on Trade
a. Explain why a stronger dollar could enlarge the U.S. balance-of-trade deficit. Explain why a weaker dollar could affect the U.S. balance-of-trade deficit.

b. It is sometimes suggested that a floating exchange rate will adjust to reduce or eliminate any current account deficit. Explain why this adjustment would occur.

c. Why does the exchange rate not always adjust to a current account deficit?

14.   Impact of Government Policies on Trade Governments of many countries enact policies that can have a major impact on international trade flows.

a. Explain how governments might give their local firms a competitive advantage in the international trade arena.

b. Why might different tax laws on corporate income across countries allow firms from some countries to have a competitive advantage in the international trade arena?

c. If a country imposes lower corporate income tax rates, does that provide an unfair advantage?

15.   China-U.S. Balance of Trade There is an ongoing debate between the United States and China

regarding whether the Chinese yuan's value should be revalued upward. The cost of labor in China is substantially lower than that in the United States.

a. Would the U.S. balance-of-trade deficit in China be eliminated if the yuan was revalued upward by 20 percent? Or by 40 percent? Or by 80 percent?

b. If the yuan was revalued to the extent that it substantially reduced the U.S. demand for Chinese products, would this shift the U.S. demand toward the United States or toward other countries where wage rates are relatively low? In other words, would the correction of the U.S. balance-of-trade deficit have a major impact on U.S. productivity and jobs?

Critical Thinking

Cause and Effects of International Trade Conflict   Conduct an online search of the terms "international trade conflict" and also insert the prevailing month and year. You will likely see that an international trade conflict exists at the time that you conduct your search. Review the online articles on a recent conflict. Write a short essay to summarize the source of the conflict, and whether the one country's trade barriers represents retaliation due to actions by the other country. Describe the types of MNCs that are most likely to suffer from the trade conflict.

Discussion in the Boardroom

This exercise can be found in Appendix E at the back of this textbook.

Running Your Own MNC

This exercise can be found on the *International Financial Management* text companion website. Go to www.cengagebrain.com (students) or www.cengage.com/login (instructors) and search using **ISBN 9781133947837.**

BLADES, INC. CASE

Exposure to International Flow of Funds

Ben Holt, chief financial officer (CFO) of Blades, Inc., has decided to counteract the decreasing demand for Speedos roller blades by exporting this product to Thailand. Furthermore, due to the low cost of rubber and plastic in Southeast Asia, Holt has decided to import some of the components needed to

manufacture Speedos from Thailand. Holt feels that importing rubber and plastic components from Thailand will provide Blades with a cost advantage (the components imported from Thailand are about 20 percent cheaper than similar components in the United States). Currently, approximately $20 million, or

10 percent, of Blades' sales are contributed by its sales in Thailand. Only about 4 percent of Blades' cost of goods sold is attributable to rubber and plastic imported from Thailand.

Blades faces little competition in Thailand from other U.S. roller blades manufacturers. Those competitors that export roller blades to Thailand invoice their exports in U.S. dollars. Currently, Blades follows a policy of invoicing in Thai baht (Thailand's currency). Holt felt that this strategy would give Blades a competitive advantage because Thai importers can plan more easily when they do not have to worry about paying differing amounts due to currency fluctuations. Furthermore, Blades' primary customer in Thailand (a retail store) has committed itself to purchasing a certain amount of Speedos annually if Blades will invoice in baht for a period of 3 years. Blades' purchases of components from Thai exporters are currently invoiced in Thai baht.

Holt is rather content with current arrangements and believes the lack of competitors in Thailand, the quality of Blades' products, and its approach to pricing will ensure Blades' position in the Thai roller blade market in the future. Holt also feels that Thai importers will prefer Blades over its competitors because Blades invoices in Thai baht.

You, Blades' financial analyst, have doubts as to Blades' "guaranteed" future success. Although you believe Blades' strategy for its Thai sales and imports is sound, you are concerned about current expectations for the Thai economy. Current forecasts indicate a high level of anticipated inflation, a decreasing level of national income, and a continued depreciation of the Thai baht. In your opinion, all of these future developments could affect Blades financially given the company's current arrangements with its suppliers and with the Thai importers. Both Thai consumers and firms might adjust their spending habits should certain developments occur.

In the past, you have had difficulty convincing Holt that problems could arise in Thailand. Consequently, you have developed a list of questions for yourself, which you plan to present to the company's CFO after you have answered them. Your questions are listed here:

1. How could a higher level of inflation in Thailand affect Blades (assume U.S. inflation remains constant)?

2. How could competition from firms in Thailand and from U.S. firms conducting business in Thailand affect Blades?

3. How could a decreasing level of national income in Thailand affect Blades?

4. How could a continued depreciation of the Thai baht affect Blades? How would it affect Blades relative to U.S. exporters invoicing their roller blades in U.S. dollars?

5. If Blades increases its business in Thailand and experiences serious financial problems, are there any international agencies that the company could approach for loans or other financial assistance?

SMALL BUSINESS DILEMMA

Identifying Factors That Will Affect the Foreign Demand at the Sports Exports Company

Recall from Chapter 1 that Jim Logan planned to pursue his dream of establishing his own business (called the Sports Exports Company) of exporting footballs to one or more foreign markets. He has decided to initially pursue the market in the United Kingdom because British citizens appear to have some interest in football as a possible hobby, and no other firm has capitalized on this idea in the United Kingdom. (The sporting goods shops in the United Kingdom do not sell footballs but might be willing to sell them.) Logan has contacted one sporting goods distributor that has agreed to purchase footballs on a monthly basis and distribute (sell) them to sporting goods stores throughout the United Kingdom. The distributor's demand for footballs is ultimately influenced by the demand for footballs by British citizens who shop in British sporting goods stores. The Sports Exports Company will receive British pounds when it sells the footballs to the distributor and will then convert the pounds into dollars. Logan recognizes that products (such as the footballs his firm will produce) exported from U.S. firms to foreign countries can be affected by various factors.

Identify the factors that affect the current account balance between the United States and the United Kingdom. Explain how each factor may possibly affect the British demand for the footballs that are produced by the Sports Exports Company.

INTERNET/EXCEL EXERCISES

The website address of the Bureau of Economic Analysis is www.bea.gov.

1. Use this website to assess recent trends in exporting and importing by U.S. firms. How has the balance of trade changed over the last 12 months?

2. Offer possible reasons for this change in the balance of trade.

3. Go to www.census.gov/foreign-trade/balance, and obtain monthly balance-of-trade data for the last 24 months between the United States and the United Kingdom or a country specified by your professor. Create an electronic spreadsheet in which the first column is the month of concern, and the second column is the trade balance. (See Appendix C for help with conducting analyses with Excel.) Use a compute statement to derive the percentage change in the trade balance in the third column. Then go to www.oanda .com/currency/historical-rates/. Obtain the direct exchange rate (dollars per currency unit) of the British pound (or the local currency of the foreign country you

select). Obtain the direct exchange rate of the currency at the beginning of each month and insert the data in column.

4. Use a compute statement to derive the percentage change in the currency value from one month to the next in column.

5. Then apply regression analysis in which the percentage change in the trade balance is the dependent variable and the percentage change in the exchange rate is the independent variable. Is there a significant relationship between the two variables? Is the direction of the relationship as expected? If you think that the exchange rate movements affect the trade balance with a lag (because the transactions of importers and exporters may be booked a few months in advance), you can reconfigure your data to assess that relationship (match each monthly percentage change in the balance of trade with the exchange rate movement that occurred a few months earlier).

ONLINE ARTICLES WITH REAL-WORLD EXAMPLES

Find a recent article online that describes an actual international finance application or a real world example about a specific MNC's actions that reinforces one or more concepts covered in this chapter.

If your class has an online component, your professor may ask you to post your summary there and provide the web link of the article so that other students can access it. If your class is live, your professor may ask you to summarize your application in class. Your professor may assign specific students to complete this assignment for this chapter, or may allow any students to do the assignment on a volunteer basis.

For recent online articles and real world examples applied to this chapter, consider using the following search terms and include the prevailing year as a

search term to ensure that the online articles are recent:

1. U.S. AND balance of trade

2. U.S. AND international trade

3. U.S. AND outsourcing

4. U.S. AND trade friction

5. international trade AND currency effects

6. international capital flows AND currency effects

7. direct foreign investment AND currency effects

8. international trade AND inflation

9. U.S. exports AND currency effects

10. U.S. imports AND currency effects

3

International Financial Markets

CHAPTER OBJECTIVES

The specific objectives of this chapter are to describe the background and corporate use of the following international financial markets:

- foreign exchange market,

- international money market,

- international credit market,

- international bond market, and

- international stock markets.

The growth in international business over the last 30 years has led to the development of various international financial markets. Financial managers of MNCs must understand the available international financial markets so they can be used to facilitate the firm's international business transactions.

3-1 Foreign Exchange Market

Each country in the world has its own currency. An important exception is the eurozone, which consists of 19 European countries that adopted the euro as their currency. When MNCs and individuals engage in international transactions, they commonly need to exchange their local currency for a foreign currency, or exchange a foreign currency for their local currency. The **foreign exchange market** allows for the exchange of one currency for another. Large commercial banks serve this market by holding inventories of each currency so that they can accommodate requests by individuals or MNCs for currency for various transactions. Individuals rely on the foreign exchange market when they travel to foreign countries. People from the United States exchange dollars for Mexican pesos when they visit Mexico, euros when they visit Italy, or Japanese yen when they visit Japan. Some MNCs based in the United States exchange dollars for Mexican pesos when they purchase supplies in Mexico that are denominated in pesos, or exchange them for euros when they purchase supplies from Italy that are denominated in euros. Other MNCs based in the United States receive Japanese yen when selling products to Japan and may wish to convert those yen to dollars. In addition, some individuals and financial institutions speculate in the foreign exchange market by exchanging their local currency for a foreign currency that they believe will increase in value over time.

At any point in time, there is an *exchange rate* between any two currencies that specifies the rate at which one currency can be exchanged for another. In essence, the exchange rate represents the price at which one currency can be purchased with another currency. If the exchange rate of the Mexican peso is $.10, the cost of your spring break hotel in Mexico that charges 700 pesos per night would be $700 \times \$.10 = \$70$. If the exchange rate was higher (such as one peso = $.11), your cost in dollars would be higher. The exchange rate of the Mexican peso will also determine how many dollars an MNC will need to purchase supplies that are invoiced at 1 million pesos.

3-1a History of Foreign Exchange

The system for establishing exchange rates has changed over time. It has evolved from the gold standard to an agreement on fixed exchange rates to a floating rate system.

Gold Standard   From 1876 to 1913, exchange rates were dictated by the gold standard. Each currency was convertible into gold at a specified rate. Thus the exchange rate between two currencies was determined by their relative convertibility rates per ounce of gold. Each country used gold to back its currency.

When World War I began in 1914, the gold standard was suspended. Some countries reverted to the gold standard in the 1920s but abandoned it as a result of the U.S. and European banking panic during the Great Depression. In the 1930s, some countries attempted to peg their currency to the dollar or the British pound, but there were frequent revisions. As a result of instability in the foreign exchange market and the severe restrictions on international transactions during this period, the volume of international trade declined.

Agreements on Fixed Exchange Rates   In 1944, an international agreement among many countries (known as the **Bretton Woods Agreement**) called for fixed exchange rates between currencies. An exchange rate was set for each pair of currencies, and each country's central bank was required to maintain its respective local currency's value within 1 percent of the agreed-upon exchange rates. For example, when the U.S. demand for a specific foreign currency was much stronger than the supply of that currency for sale, the commercial banks that served the foreign exchange market would experience a shortage of the foreign currency, and the exchange rate would start to move outside the boundaries. Under these conditions, the Federal Reserve (the central bank of the United States) was required to intervene to balance the exchange between the two currencies (the intervention process is explained in Chapter 6) so that the exchange rate would remain stable. The system established by the Bretton Woods Agreement lasted until 1971.

By 1971 the U.S. dollar had apparently become overvalued, as the U.S. demand for some foreign currencies was substantially more than the supply of those currencies offered in exchange for dollars. Intervention by central banks could not effectively offset the large imbalance between demand and supply. Representatives from the major nations met to discuss this dilemma. This conference resulted in the **Smithsonian Agreement**, whereby the U.S. dollar's value was devalued (reset downward) relative to the other major currencies. The degree to which the dollar was devalued varied with each foreign currency. Not only was the dollar's value reset, but exchange rates were also allowed to fluctuate by 2.25 percent in either direction from the newly set rates. These boundaries of 2.25 percent were wider than the previous boundaries (of 1 percent) and thus enabled exchange rates to move within a wider range.

Floating Exchange Rate System   Even with the wider bands allowed by the Smithsonian Agreement, governments still had difficulty maintaining exchange rates within the stated boundaries. By March 1973, the official boundaries imposed by the Smithsonian Agreement were eliminated, thereby allowing exchange rates to move more freely. Since that time, the currencies of most countries have been allowed to fluctuate in accordance with market forces; however, some countries' central banks still periodically intervene in the foreign exchange market to influence the market-determined exchange rate or reduce the volatility in their respective currency's exchange rate movements.

3-1b Foreign Exchange Transactions

The foreign exchange market should not be thought of as a specific building or location where traders exchange currencies. Companies normally exchange one currency for another through a commercial bank over a telecommunications network; this is an over-the-counter market through which many transactions occur. The largest foreign exchange trading centers are in London, New York, and Tokyo, but foreign exchange transactions occur on a daily basis in cities around the world. London accounts for about 33 percent of the trading volume and New York City for about 20 percent. Thus these two markets control more than half the currency trading in the world.

Foreign Exchange Dealers serve as intermediaries in the foreign exchange market by exchanging currencies desired by MNCs or individuals. Foreign exchange dealers include large commercial banks such as Citigroup, JPMorgan Chase & Co., Barclays (United Kingdom), UBS (Switzerland), and Deutsche Bank (Germany). Dealers such as these have branches in most major cities and also facilitate foreign exchange transactions with an online trading service. Dealers that rely exclusively on online trading to facilitate such transactions include FX Connect (a subsidiary of State Street Corporation), OANDA (Canada), and XE.com (Canada). Customers establish an online account and can interact with the foreign exchange dealer's website to transmit their foreign exchange order.

In recent years, new trading platforms have been established that allow some MNCs to engage in foreign exchange transactions directly with other MNCs, thereby eliminating the need for a foreign exchange dealer. An MNC that subscribes to such a platform can indicate to the platform's other users whether it wants to buy or sell a particular currency as well as the volume desired. Some MNCs continue to use a foreign exchange dealer, often because they prefer personal attention or require more customized transactions than can be handled via trading platforms.

The average daily trading volume in the foreign exchange market now exceeds $5 trillion. The U.S. dollar is involved in about 40 percent of those transactions, and currencies from emerging countries are involved in about 20 percent of them. Most currency transactions between two non-U.S. countries do not involve the U.S. dollar. For example, a Canadian MNC that purchases supplies from a Mexican MNC exchanges its Canadian dollars for Mexican pesos; likewise, a Japanese MNC that invests funds in a British bank exchanges its Japanese yen for British pounds.

Spot Market The most common type of foreign exchange transaction is for immediate exchange. The market where these transactions occur is known as the **spot market**. The exchange rate at which one currency is traded for another in the spot market is known as the **spot rate**.

Spot Market Structure Commercial transactions in the spot market are often completed electronically with banks or other financial institutions serving as intermediaries. The exchange rate at the time determines the amount of funds necessary for the transaction.

WEB

www.oanda.com
Historical exchange rate movements. Data are available on a daily basis for most currencies.

EXAMPLE

Indiana Co. purchases supplies priced at 100,000 euros (€) from Belgo, a Belgian supplier, on the first day of every month. Indiana instructs its bank to transfer funds from its account to Belgo's account on the first day of each month. It only has dollars in its account, whereas Belgo's account balance is denominated in euros. When payment was made last month, the euro was worth $1.08; hence Indiana Co. needed $108,000 to pay for the supplies (€100,000 × $1.08 = $108,000). The bank reduced Indiana's account balance by $108,000, which was exchanged at the bank for €100,000. The bank then sent the €100,000 electronically to Belgo by increasing Belgo's account balance by €100,000. Today, a new payment needs to be made. The euro is currently valued at $1.12, so the bank will reduce Indiana's account balance by $112,000 (€100,000 × $1.12 = $112,000) and exchange it for €100,000, which will be sent electronically to Belgo.

In this way, the bank not only executes the transactions but also serves as the foreign exchange dealer. Each month the bank receives dollars from Indiana Co. in exchange for the euros it provides. In addition, the bank facilitates other transactions for MNCs in which it receives euros in exchange for dollars. The bank maintains an inventory of euros, dollars, and other currencies to facilitate these foreign exchange transactions. If the transactions cause it to buy as many euros as it sells to MNCs, then its inventory of euros will not change. However, if the bank sells more euros than it buys, then its inventory of euros will be reduced. ●

If a bank begins to experience a shortage of a particular foreign currency, it can purchase that currency from other banks. This trading between banks occurs in what is often referred to as the **interbank market**.

Some other financial institutions, such as securities firms, can provide the same services described in the previous example. Most major airports around the world also have foreign exchange centers where individuals can exchange currencies. Many cities also have retail foreign exchange offices where tourists and other individuals can exchange their currency.

Use of the Dollar in Spot Markets
The U.S. dollar is accepted as a medium of exchange by merchants in many countries; this is especially true in countries (such as Bolivia, Indonesia, Russia, Vietnam) where the home currency is weak or subject to foreign exchange restrictions. Many merchants accept U.S. dollars because they can easily use them to purchase goods from other countries.

Spot Market Time Zones
Although foreign exchange trading is conducted only during normal business hours at a given location, such hours vary among locations because of different time zones. Thus, at any given weekday time, a bank located somewhere in the world is open and ready to accommodate foreign exchange requests by MNCs.

When the foreign exchange market opens in the United States each morning, the opening exchange rate quotations are based on the prevailing rates quoted by banks in London (and other locations), where the markets have opened earlier. Suppose the quoted spot rate of the British pound was $1.80 at the previous close of the U.S. foreign exchange market but, by the time the U.S. market opens the following day, the spot rate is $1.76. Events occurring before the U.S. market opened could have changed the supply and demand conditions for British pounds in the London foreign exchange market, reducing the quoted price for the pound.

Several U.S. banks have established so-called night trading desks. The largest banks initiated night trading to capitalize on overnight foreign exchange movements and to accommodate corporate requests for currency trades. Even some medium-sized banks now offer night trading as a way of accommodating their corporate clients.

Spot Market Liquidity
The spot market for each currency is characterized by its liquidity, which reflects the level of trading activity. The more buyers and sellers there are for a currency, the more liquid the market for that currency is. The spot markets for heavily traded currencies such as the euro, the pound, and the yen are extremely liquid. In contrast, the spot markets for currencies of less developed countries are much less liquid. A currency's liquidity affects the ease with which it can be bought or sold by an MNC. If a currency is illiquid, then the number of willing buyers and sellers is limited and so an MNC may be unable to purchase or sell that currency in a timely fashion and at a reasonable exchange rate.

EXAMPLE   Bennett Co. sold computer software to a firm in Peru and received payment of 10 million units of the nuevo sol (Peru's currency). Bennett Co. wanted to convert these units into dollars. The prevailing exchange rate of the nuevo sol at the time was $.36. However, the company's bank did not want to receive such a large amount of nuevo sol because it did not expect any of its customers to need that currency. The bank was therefore willing to exchange dollars for the nuevo sol only at the lower exchange rate of $.35. ●

Attributes of Banks That Provide Foreign Exchange   The following characteristics of banks are important to customers (such as MNCs) in need of foreign exchange.

1. *Competitiveness of quote.* A savings of $.01 per unit on an order of 1 million units of currency is worth $10,000.
2. *Special relationship with the bank.* The bank may offer cash management services or be willing to make a special effort to obtain hard-to-find foreign currencies for the corporation.
3. *Speed of execution.* Banks may vary in the efficiency with which they handle an order. A corporation needing the currency will prefer a bank that conducts the transaction promptly and also handles any paperwork properly.
4. *Advice about current market conditions.* Some banks may provide assessments of foreign economies and relevant activities in the international financial environment that relate to corporate customers.
5. *Forecasting advice.* Some banks may provide forecasts of the future state of foreign economies and the future value of exchange rates.

The preceding list suggests that a corporation in need of a foreign currency should not automatically choose the bank that sells that currency at the lowest price. Most MNCs that frequently need foreign currencies develop a close relationship with at least one major bank in case they need various foreign exchange services from a bank.

Bid/Ask Spread of Banks   Commercial banks charge fees for conducting foreign exchange transactions; thus they buy a currency from customers at a slightly lower price than the price at which they sell it. This means that a bank's **bid price** (buy quote) for a foreign currency will always be less than its **ask price** (sell quote). The difference between the bid and ask prices is known as the **bid/ask spread**, which is meant to cover the costs associated with fulfilling requests to exchange currencies. A larger bid/ask spread generates more revenue for commercial banks, but represents a higher cost to individuals or MNCs that engage in foreign exchange transactions. The bid/ask spread is normally expressed as a percentage of the ask quote.

EXAMPLE   To understand how a bid/ask spread could affect you, assume you have $1,000 and plan to travel from the United States to the United Kingdom. Assume further that the bank's bid rate for the British pound is $1.52 and its ask rate is $1.60. Before leaving on your trip, you go to this bank to exchange dollars for pounds. Your $1,000 will be converted to 625 pounds (£), as follows:

$$\frac{\text{Amount of U.S dollars to be converted}}{\text{Price charged by bank per pound}} = \frac{\$1,000}{\$1.60} = £625$$

Now suppose that an emergency prevents you from taking the trip and so you now want to convert the £625 back into U.S. dollars. If the exchange rate has not changed, then you will receive only

$$£625 \times (\text{Bank's bid rate of \$1.52 per pound}) = \$950$$

Because of the bid/ask spread, you have $50 (5 percent) less than when you started. Of course, the dollar amount of your loss would be greater if you had originally converted more than $1,000 into pounds. ●

Comparison of Bid/Ask Spread among Currencies   The difference between a bid quote and an ask quote will look much smaller for currencies of lesser value. This

WEB

www.everbank.com

Individuals can open an FDIC-insured CD account in a foreign currency.

WEB

www.xe.com/fx

Allows individuals to buy and sell currencies.

differential can be standardized by measuring the spread as a percentage of the currency's spot rate.

EXAMPLE

Charlotte Bank quotes a bid price for yen (¥) of $.0070 and an ask price of $.0074; therefore, the nominal bid/ask spread in this case is $.0074 − $.0070, or just four-hundredths of a penny. Yet in percentage terms the bid/ask spread is actually slightly higher for the yen in this example than for the pound in the previous example. To prove this, consider a traveler who sells $1,000 for yen at the bank's ask price of $.0074. The traveler receives about ¥135,135 (computed as $1,000/$.0074). Suppose the traveler cancels the trip and immediately converts the yen back to dollars; then, assuming no changes in the bid/ask quotations, the bank will buy these yen back at the bank's bid price of $.007 for a total of about $946 (i.e., ¥135,135 × $.007), which is $54 (or 5.4 percent) less than what the traveler started with. This spread exceeds that of the British pound (5 percent in the previous example). ●

The bid/ask spread in percentage terms is typically computed as follows:

$$\text{Bid/ask spread} = \frac{\text{Ask rate} - \text{Bid rate}}{\text{Ask rate}}$$

This formula is used to compute the bid/ask spreads in Exhibit 3.1 for both the British pound and the Japanese yen.

Notice that these numbers coincide with those derived earlier. Such spreads are common for *retail* transactions (i.e., those serving consumers). For the larger *wholesale* transactions between banks or involving large corporations, the spread will be much smaller. The bid/ask spread for retail transactions is usually in the range of 3 to 7 percent; for wholesale transactions requested by MNCs, the spread is between .01 and .03 percent. The spread is normally larger for illiquid currencies that are less frequently traded. The bid/ask spread as defined here represents the discount in the bid rate as a percentage of the ask rate. An alternative bid/ask spread uses the bid rate (instead of the ask rate) as the denominator and thus measures the percentage markup of the ask rate above the bid rate. The spread is slightly higher when using this formula because the bid rate used in the denominator is always less than the ask rate.

In the following discussion, and in examples throughout much of the text, the bid/ask spread will be ignored. That is, only one price will be shown for a given currency so that you can concentrate on understanding other relevant concepts. These examples depart slightly from reality because the bid and ask prices are, in a sense, assumed to be equal. Although in reality the ask price will always exceed the bid price by a small amount, the implications of the examples presented here should hold nonetheless (i.e., even without accounting for the bid/ask spreads). On those occasions when the bid/ask spread contributes significantly to the concept under discussion, that spread will be accounted for.

To conserve space, some quotations show the entire bid price followed by a slash and then only the last two or three digits of the ask price.

Exhibit 3.1   Computation of the Bid/Ask Spread

CURRENCY	BID RATE	ASK RATE	ASK RATE – BID RATE / ASK RATE	=	BID/ASK PERCENTAGE SPREAD
British pound	$1.52	$1.60	$\frac{\$1.60 - \$1.52}{\$1.60}$	=	.05 *or* 5%
Japanese yen	$0.0070	$0.0074	$\frac{\$.0074 - \$.007}{\$.0074}$	=	.054 *or* 5.4%

EXAMPLE

Assume that a commercial bank's prevailing quote for wholesale transactions involving the euro is $1.0876/78. This means that the commercial bank is willing to pay $1.0876 per euro; alternatively, it is willing to sell euros for $1.0878. The bid/ask spread in this example is therefore

$$\text{Bid/ask spread} = (\$1.0878 - \$1.0876)/\$1.0878$$
$$= \text{about } .000184 \text{ or } .0184\%$$

●

Factors That Affect the Spread   The spread on currency quotations is influenced by the following factors:

Spread $= f($**Order costs, Inventory costs, Competition, Volume, Currency risk**$)$
           $+$ $+$ $-$ $-$ $+$

■ *Order costs.* Order costs are the costs of processing orders; these costs include clearing costs and the costs of recording transactions.

■ *Inventory costs.* Inventory costs are the costs of maintaining an inventory of a particular currency. Holding an inventory involves an opportunity cost because the funds could have been used for some other purpose. If interest rates are relatively high, then the opportunity cost of holding an inventory should be relatively high. The higher the inventory costs, the larger the spread that will be established to cover these costs.

■ *Competition.* The more intense the competition, the smaller the spread quoted by intermediaries. Competition is more intense for the more widely traded currencies because there is more business in those currencies. The establishment of trading platforms that allow MNCs to trade directly with each other is a form of competition against foreign exchange dealers, and it has forced dealers to reduce their spread in order to remain competitive.

■ *Volume.* Currencies that are more liquid are less likely to experience a sudden change in price. Currencies that have a large trading volume are more liquid because there are numerous buyers and sellers at any given time. This means that the market has enough depth that a few large transactions are unlikely to cause the currency's price to change abruptly.

■ *Currency risk.* Some currencies exhibit more volatility than others because of economic or political conditions that cause the demand for and supply of the currency to change abruptly. For example, currencies in countries that have frequent political crises are subject to sudden price movements. Intermediaries that are willing to buy or sell these currencies could incur large losses due to such changes in their value.

EXAMPLE

There are a limited number of banks or other financial institutions that serve as foreign exchange dealers for Russian rubles. The exchange volume of dollars for rubles is limited, which implies an illiquid market. Hence some dealers may not be able to accommodate requests of large exchange transactions for rubles, and the ruble's market value could change abruptly in response to some larger transactions. The ruble's value has been volatile in recent years, which means that dealers with an inventory of them meant to serve foreign exchange transactions are exposed to the possibility of a sharp depreciation in that currency. Given these conditions, dealers are likely to quote a relatively large bid/ask spread for the Russian ruble. ●

Like the prices of securities in many financial markets, foreign exchange prices can be subject to manipulation. In particular, a few financial institutions that serve as the main intermediaries for large foreign exchange transactions might engage in collusion by agreeing to set wider bid/ask spreads than would normally be possible if they set their quotes competitively.

In the United States, agencies such as the Justice Department, the Federal Bureau of Investigation, and the Federal Reserve attempt to ensure orderly and fair pricing in the foreign exchange market. The oversight of exchange rate pricing is challenging, however, because it can be difficult to prove that financial institutions have conspired to widen spreads.

3-1c Foreign Exchange Quotations

Exchange rate quotations for widely traded currencies, and even for many currencies that are not widely traded, are readily available on the Internet. They can be found at financial websites, at the websites of newspapers such as the *Wall Street Journal*, at the websites of foreign exchange dealers, and even by simply typing "euro-dollar exchange rate" or whatever exchange rate is wanted into a web browser. The rates are frequently updated as the exchange rates change throughout the day.

At any moment in time, the exchange rate between two currencies should be similar across the various banks that provide foreign exchange services. If there is a large discrepancy, then customers (or other banks) could profit from purchasing a large amount of the currency from the low-quoting bank and immediately selling it to the high-quoting bank. These actions would cause the low-quoting bank to quickly experience a shortage of that currency, while the high-quoting bank would quickly experience an excessive amount of that currency because it was willing to pay too much for the currency. As a result, the banks would rapidly adjust their exchange rate quotations, eliminating any discrepancy between the quotations.

Direct versus Indirect Quotations at One Point in Time
The quotations of exchange rates for currencies normally reflect the ask prices for large transactions. Quotations that report the value of a foreign currency in dollars (number of dollars per unit of other currency) are referred to as **direct quotations**, whereas quotations that report the number of units of a foreign currency per dollar are known as **indirect quotations**.. If you type, "euro-dollar exchange rate" into your web browser, the result will be 1 euro $= x$ dollars, which is a direct quotation; if you search for "dollar-euro exchange rate," the result will be 1 dollar $= x$ euros, which is an indirect quotation. Websites that provide exchange rates allow you to readily switch between direct and indirect quotations. An indirect quotation is the reciprocal (inverse) of the corresponding direct quotation.

EXAMPLE

The spot rate of the euro is quoted at $1.25. This is a direct quotation because it represents the value of the foreign currency in dollars. The indirect quotation of the euro is the reciprocal of the direct quotation:

$$(\text{Indirect quotation}) = 1/(\text{Direct quotation})$$
$$= 1/\$1.25$$
$$= .80, \text{ which means .80 euros} = \$1$$

If you initially received the indirect quotation, then you can take its inverse to obtain the direct quote. The indirect quotation for the euro is $.80, so the direct quotation is

$$(\text{Indirect quotation}) = 1/\text{Indirect quotation}$$
$$= 1/.80$$
$$= \$1.25$$

●

Direct versus Indirect Exchange Rates over Time
Exhibit 3.2 compares the direct and indirect exchange rates at two different times. Columns 2 and 3 provide quotes at the beginning of a particular period, while columns 4 and 5 provide quotes at the end of the period. For each currency, the indirect quotes at the beginning and end of

Exhibit 3.2 Direct and Indirect Exchange Rate Quotations

(1) CURRENCY	(2) DIRECT QUOTATION (dollars per unit) AT START OF PERIOD	(3) INDIRECT QUOTATION (units per dollar) AT START OF PERIOD	(4) DIRECT QUOTATION AT END OF PERIOD	(5) INDIRECT QUOTATION AT END OF PERIOD
Canadian dollar	$.66	1.51	$.70	1.43
Euro	$1.031	.97	$1.064	.94
Japanese yen	$.009	111.11	$.0097	103.09
Mexican peso	$.12	8.33	$.11	9.09
Swiss franc	$.62	1.61	$.67	1.49
U.K. pound	$1.50	.67	$1.60	.62

the period (columns 3 and 5) are the reciprocals of their respective direct quotes at the beginning and end of the period (columns 2 and 4).

Exhibit 3.2 demonstrates that, for any currency at any time, the indirect exchange rate is the inverse of the direct exchange rate. Exhibit 3.2 also shows the relationship, for each currency, between movements in the direct exchange rate and movements in the indirect exchange rate.

EXAMPLE

According to Exhibit 3.2, the Canadian dollar's direct quotation rose from $.66 to $.70 during the period. This change reflects an appreciation of the Canadian dollar: this currency increased in value over the period. Note that the Canadian dollar's indirect quotation decreased from 1.51 to 1.43 over the same time period; therefore, fewer Canadian dollars are needed to obtain a U.S. dollar at the end than at the start of the period. This change in the indirect quotation also confirms that the Canadian dollar's value has strengthened.

Note also that the Mexican peso's direct quotation changed from $.12 to $.11 during the period, reflecting a depreciation of the peso. The indirect quotation increased over the period, which means that more pesos are needed to obtain a U.S. dollar at the end than at the start of the period. This change also confirms that the peso has depreciated during this period. ●

From the relationship just described between the direct and indirect exchange rates, it follows that, if a currency's direct exchange rate is rising over time, then its indirect exchange rate must be declining over time (and vice versa).

The trend for the euro's exchange rate is shown in Exhibit 3.3. Two graphs are shown to compare movements in the direct exchange rate and indirect exchange rate of the currency. The direct exchange rate of the euro is displayed in the top graph, while the indirect exchange rate of the euro is displayed in the lower graph. In some periods (such as from June 2010 to June 2011, the direct exchange rate of the euro increased to reflect the euro's appreciation against the dollar. In such periods the indirect exchange rate of the euro declines, which represents a decrease over time in the amount of euros that equal $1. As the euro's spot rate rises, fewer euros are needed to purchase a dollar.

In other periods, such as from April 2014 to November 2015, the direct exchange rate of the euro decreased to reflect depreciation of the euro against the dollar. In such periods the indirect exchange rate of the euro increases, which represents an increase over time in the amount of euros that equal $1. As the value of the euro weakens, more euros are needed to purchase a dollar.

It is important to recognize the difference between direct and indirect exchange rates over time because both types are used in the presentations by different analysts and firms. When a discussion about depreciation of a currency is illustrated with a rising trend for that currency, the trend must be based on an indirect exchange rate.

Exhibit 3.3 Relationship over Time between the Euro's Direct and Indirect Exchange Rates

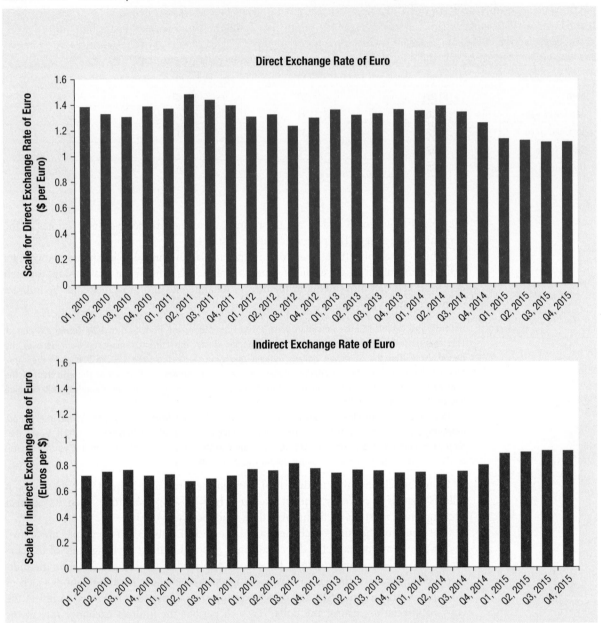

If you are conducting an extensive analysis of exchange rates, convert all exchange rates into direct quotations. In this way, you can more easily compare currencies and are less likely to make a mistake in determining whether a currency is appreciating or depreciating over a particular period.

Discussions of exchange rate movements can be confusing if some comments refer to direct quotations while others refer to indirect quotations. For consistency, the examples in this text use direct quotations unless an example can be clarified by the use of indirect quotations.

Source of Exchange Rate Quotations Updated currency quotations are provided for several major currencies on Yahoo!'s website (**finance.yahoo.com/currency-converter**).

You can select any currency for which you want an exchange rate quotation, and you can view a trend of the historical exchange rate movements for any currency. Trends are available for various periods, including 1 day, 5 days, 1 month, 3 months, 6 months, 1 year, and 5 years. As you review a trend of exchange rates, note carefully whether the exchange rate quotation is direct (value in dollars) or indirect (number of foreign currency units per dollar) so that you can properly interpret the trend. The trend indicates not only the exchange rate's direction but also the extent to which the currency has changed over time. The trend also indicates the range of exchange rates observed within a particular period. When a currency's exchange rate is extremely sensitive to economic conditions, its movements mark out a wider range.

Exchange rate quotations are also provided by many other online sources, including **www.oanda.com**. Most sources provide both direct and indirect exchange rate quotations, so be sure to check which type of quotation is being provided.

WEB

www.bloomberg.com
Cross exchange rates for
several currencies.

Cross Exchange Rates
Most tables of exchange rate quotations express currencies relative to the U.S. dollar, but in some instances, a firm will be concerned about the exchange rate between two non-dollar currencies. For example, suppose that a U.S. firm that trades with both Canada and Mexico has a large supply of Canadian dollars, but now it needs Mexican pesos to buy Mexican goods. The firm wants to use its Canadian dollars to obtain the pesos, so it needs to know the Mexican peso value relative to the Canadian dollar. The type of rate desired here is known as a **cross exchange rate** because it reflects the amount of one foreign currency per unit of another foreign currency. Cross exchange rates can be easily determined with the use of foreign exchange quotations. The relative value of any two non-dollar currencies is equal to the dollar value of one currency divided by the dollar value of the other.

EXAMPLE Recall from Exhibit 3.2 that at the start of the period, the peso was worth $.12 and the Canadian dollar was worth $.66. Under those conditions, the value of the peso in Canadian dollars (C$) is calculated as follows:

$$\text{Value of peso in C\$} = \frac{\text{Value of peso in \$}}{\text{Value of in \$}} = \frac{\$.12}{\$.66} = \text{about C\$.182}$$

Thus a Mexican peso is worth about C$.182. The cross exchange rate can also be expressed as the number of pesos that equal a single Canadian dollar. This figure can be computed by taking the reciprocal: .66/.12 = 5.5, which means that at these exchange rates a Canadian dollar is worth 5.5 pesos. ●

Cross Exchange Rates over Time
As the exchange rates of two currencies change against the U.S. dollar over time, the cross exchange rate of these currencies can change as well.

EXAMPLE Recall from Exhibit 3.2 that at the end of the period, the Mexican peso was worth $.11, while the Canadian dollar was worth $.70. Under those conditions, the value of the peso in Canadian dollars (C$) is calculated as follows:

$$\text{Value of peso in C\$} = \frac{\text{Value of peso is \$}}{\text{Value of CS in \$}} = \frac{\$.11}{\$.70} = \text{about C\$.157}$$

Because the value of the Mexican peso is lower against the Canadian dollar at the end of the period, this implies that the Mexican peso has weakened (depreciated) against the Canadian dollar over the period. The weakening of the peso against the Canadian dollar is attributed to two forces that occurred over the period: (1) the Mexican peso depreciated against the U.S. dollar, while (2) the Canadian dollar appreciated against the U.S. dollar. ●

Source of Cross Exchange Rate Quotations
Some cross exchange rates are provided online at most websites that provide exchange rate quotations including

Yahoo!'s website (**finance.yahoo.com/currency-converter**), where you can also view the recent trend of a particular cross exchange rate for periods such as 1 day, 5 days, 1 month, 3 months, or 1 year. The trend indicates the volatility of a cross exchange rate over a particular period. Two non-dollar currencies may exhibit high volatility against the U.S. dollar, but if their movements are strongly correlated, then their cross exchange rate should be relatively stable over time. For example, the values of the euro and the British pound typically move in the same direction against the dollar and, over time, also to a similar extent. For this reason, the cross exchange rate between the euro and British pound has been fairly stable.

3-1d Derivative Contracts in the Foreign Exchange Market

A currency derivative is a contract with a price that is partially derived from the value of the underlying currency that it represents. Three types of currency derivatives that are often used by MNCs are forward contracts, currency futures contracts, and currency options contracts. Each of these currency derivatives will be explained in turn.

Forward Contracts In some cases, an MNC may prefer to lock in an exchange rate at which it can obtain a currency in the future. A **forward contract** is an agreement between an MNC and a foreign exchange dealer that specifies the currencies to be exchanged, the exchange rate, and the date at which the transaction will occur. The **forward rate** is the exchange rate, specified in the forward contract, at which the currencies will be exchanged. Multinational corporations commonly request forward contracts to hedge future payments that they expect to make or receive in a foreign currency. In this way, they do not have to worry about fluctuations in the spot rate until the time of their future payments.

EXAMPLE   Today, Memphis Co. has ordered from European countries some supplies whose prices are denominated in euros. It will receive the supplies in 90 days and will need to make payment at that time. It expects the euro to increase in value over the next 90 days and therefore desires to hedge its payables in euros. Memphis buys a 90-day forward contract on euros to lock in the price that it will pay for euros at a future time.

Meanwhile, Memphis will receive Mexican pesos in 180 days because of an order it received from a Mexican company today. It expects that the peso will decrease in value over this period and wants to hedge these receivables. Memphis sells a forward contract on pesos to lock in the dollars that it will receive when it exchanges the pesos at a specified time in the future. ●

The **forward market** is the market in which forward contracts are traded. It is an over-the-counter market, and its main participants are the foreign exchange dealers and the MNCs that wish to obtain a forward contract. Many MNCs use the forward market to hedge their payables and receivables. For example, Google, Inc., normally has forward contracts in place that are valued at more than $1 billion.

Many of the large dealers that serve as intermediaries in the spot market also serve the forward market. That is, they accommodate MNCs that want to purchase euros 90 days forward with dollars. At the same time, they accommodate MNCs that want to sell euros forward in exchange for dollars.

The liquidity of the forward market varies among currencies. The forward market for euros is very liquid because many MNCs take forward positions to hedge their future payments in euros. In contrast, the forward markets for Latin American and Eastern European currencies are less liquid because there is less international trade with those countries and so MNCs take fewer forward positions. There are even some currencies for which there is no forward market.

Some quotations of exchange rates include forward rates for the most widely traded currencies. Other forward rates are not quoted on financial websites but are quoted by the banks that offer forward contracts in various currencies.

Currency Futures Contracts Futures contracts are similar to forward contracts but are sold on an exchange instead of over the counter. A **currency futures contract** specifies a standard volume of a particular currency to be exchanged on a specific settlement date. Some MNCs involved in international trade use the currency futures markets to hedge their positions. The **futures rate** is the exchange rate at which one can purchase or sell a specified currency on the settlement date in accordance with the futures contract. Thus the futures rate's role in a futures contract is similar to the forward rate's role in a forward contract.

It is important to distinguish between the *futures rate* and the *future spot rate*. The future spot rate is the spot rate that will exist at some future time and so, today, that rate is uncertain. If a U.S. firm needs Japanese yen in 90 days and if it expects the spot rate 90 days from now to exceed the current 90-day futures rate (from a futures contract) or 90-day forward rate (from a forward contract), then the firm should seriously consider hedging with a futures or forward contract.

Additional details on futures contracts, including other differences from forward contracts, are explained in Chapter 5.

Currency Options Contracts Currency options contracts can be classified as calls or puts. A **currency call option** provides the right to buy a specific currency at a specific price (called the **strike price** or **exercise price**) within a specific period of time. It is used to hedge future payables. A **currency put option** provides the right to sell a specific currency at a specific price within a specific period of time. It is used to hedge future receivables.

Currency call and put options can be purchased on an exchange. They offer more flexibility than forward or futures contracts because they are not obligations. That is, the firm can elect not to exercise the option.

Currency options have become a popular means of hedging. The Coca-Cola Co. has replaced 30 to 40 percent of its forward contracting with currency options. Although most MNCs use forward contracts, many also use currency options. Additional details about currency options, including other differences from futures and forward contracts, are provided in Chapter 5.

3-2 International Money Market

Each country has a money market whereby surplus units (individuals or institutions with available short-term funds) can transfer funds to deficit units (institutions or individuals in need of funds). Financial institutions such as commercial banks accept short-term deposits from surplus units and redirect the funds toward deficit units.

The international money market developed to accommodate the needs of MNCs. First, many MNCs borrow short-term funds in different currencies to pay for imports denominated in those currencies. Second, MNCs that need funds to support local operations may consider borrowing in a nonlocal currency that exhibits lower interest rates. This strategy is especially appropriate for firms expecting future receivables denominated in that currency. Third, MNCs may consider borrowing in a currency that they anticipate will depreciate against their home currency, as this would enable them to repay the short-term loan at a more favorable exchange rate. In this case, the actual cost of borrowing would be less than the interest rate quoted for that currency.

At the same time, some MNCs and institutional investors have incentives to invest short-term funds in a foreign currency. First, the interest rate on a short-term investment denominated in a foreign currency might exceed the interest rate on a short-term investment denominated in their home currency. Second, they may consider investing in a currency that they expect will appreciate against their home currency so that the return on their investment would be greater than the interest rate quoted for the foreign investment.

Financial institutions such as commercial banks serve this market by accepting deposits and providing loans in various currencies. These intermediaries typically also serve as dealers in the foreign exchange market.

3-2a European and Asian Money Markets

As MNCs expanded their operations in the 1970s, Europe and Asia emerged as major centers of international financial intermediation to accommodate their needs. Because the U.S. dollar was widely used even by foreign countries as a medium for international trade, there was a consistent demand for dollars in Europe and elsewhere. To conduct international trade with European countries, corporations in the United States deposited U.S. dollars in European banks. The banks accepted the deposits because they could then lend the dollars to corporate customers based in Europe. These dollar deposits in banks in Europe (and on other continents) are known as **Eurodollars** (not to be confused with the *euro*, which is the currency of many European countries today).

The growing importance of the Organization of the Petroleum Exporting Countries (OPEC) also contributed to the growth in Eurodollar deposits. Because OPEC generally requires payment for oil in dollars, the OPEC countries began to deposit a portion of their oil revenues in European banks. These dollar-denominated deposits are sometimes referred to as **petrodollars**.

Like the European money market, the **Asian money market** originated as a market involving mostly dollar-denominated deposits. This market emerged to accommodate the needs of businesses that were using the U.S. dollar (and some other foreign currencies) as a medium of exchange for international trade. These businesses could not rely on banks in Europe because of the distance and different time zones. Today, the Asian money market is centered in Hong Kong and Singapore, where large banks accept short-term deposits and make loans in various foreign currencies.

Banks within the Asian money market usually lend to each other when some banks have excess funds and other banks need more funds. The Asian money market is integrated with the European money market in that banks in Asia lend to and borrow from banks in Europe.

3-2b Money Market Interest Rates among Currencies

The money market interest rate on short-term deposits or short-term loans in a particular currency in international money markets is dependent on the supply of short-term funds provided by surplus units and the demand for short-term funds by deficit units in that currency. In general, a country that experiences both a high demand for and a small supply of short-term funds will have relatively high money market interest rates. Conversely, a country with both a low demand and a large supply of short-term funds will have relatively low money market interest rates. Money market rates tend to be higher in developing countries because they experience higher rates of inflation and faster growth, so more funds are needed (relative to the available supply) to finance that growth. The money market interest rate for a particular currency changes over time in response to changes in the supply and demand for short-term funds for that currency.

Exhibit 3.4   Comparison of 2016 International Money Market Interest Rates

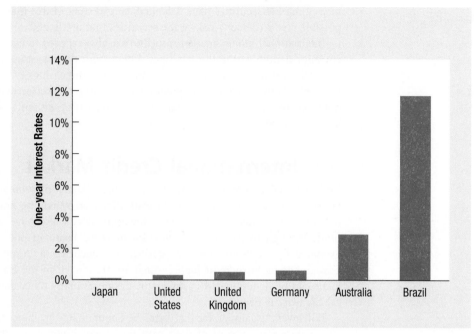

Quoted money market interest rates for various currencies are displayed in Exhibit 3.4. Notice how the money market rates vary substantially among some currencies. MNCs based in countries whose local currencies exhibit low interest rates tend to have lower financing costs.

A currency's money market is highly influenced by its respective **London Interbank Offer Rate (LIBOR)**, which is the interest rate most often charged for short-term loans between banks in international money markets. The term LIBOR is commonly used even though many international interbank transactions do not pass through London. When a currency's LIBOR rises, money market rates denominated in that currency tend to rise as well, just as U.S. money market rates tend to move with the federal funds rate (the interest rate charged on loans between U.S. banks).

The LIBOR was historically measured as the average of the rates reported by banks at a particular time. In 2012, country governments detected that some banks were falsely reporting the interest rate they offered in the interbank market in order to manipulate LIBOR and thereby boost the values of their investments that were tied to LIBOR. This scandal prompted financial markets to devise ways of determining the market interest rate in a manner that does not rely on the rates reported by participating banks.

3-2c Risk of International Money Market Securities

When MNCs and government agencies issue debt securities with a short-term maturity (one year or less) in the international money market, these instruments are referred to as **international money market securities**. MNCs typically pay a slightly higher rate than their local government when borrowing in international money markets because of a small risk premium to reflect credit (default) risk. Normally, international money market securities are perceived to be very safe, especially when they are rated high by rating agencies. And because the typical maturity of these securities is one year or less, investors are less concerned about the issuer's financial condition deteriorating by the time of maturity than if the securities had a longer-term maturity. However, some international money market securities have defaulted, so investors in this market need to consider the possible credit (default) risk of the securities that are issued.

International money market securities are also exposed to exchange rate risk when the currency denominating the securities differs from the investor's home currency. Specifically, the return on investment in the international money market security will be reduced when currency denominating the money market security weakens against the home currency. This means that, even for securities without credit risk, investors can lose money because of exchange rate risk.

3-3 International Credit Market

Multinational corporations and domestic firms sometimes obtain medium-term funds via term loans from local financial institutions or by issuing notes (medium-term debt obligations) in their local markets. However, MNCs also have access to medium-term funds through banks located in foreign markets. Loans of one year or longer that are extended by banks to MNCs or government agencies in Europe are commonly called Eurocredits or **Eurocredit loans**, which are transacted in the **Eurocredit market**. These loans can be denominated in dollars or in one of many other currencies, and their typical maturity is five years.

Borrowers usually prefer that loans be denominated in the currency of the country in which they receive most of their cash flows, which eliminates the borrower's exchange rate risk. However, the loan's interest rate depends on the currency in which the loan is denominated. Because banks in money markets accept short-term deposits and sometimes provide longer-term loans, their asset and liability maturities do not match. This misalignment can adversely affect a bank's performance during periods of rising interest rates, as the bank may have locked in a rate on its longer-term loans while the rate it pays on short-term deposits continues to rise. In order to avoid this risk, banks commonly use floating rate loans. The loan rate floats in accordance with the movement of a market interest rate, such as LIBOR. For example, a loan that is denominated in a particular currency and is provided by a bank to an MNC might be structured with an interest rate that resets every six months to the prevailing LIBOR for that currency plus 3 percent.

International credit market activity has increased over time, yet the growth is mostly concentrated in regions where economic conditions are relatively strong. Those regions tend to have more funds deposited by MNCs as well as a strong demand for loans by MNCs that are expanding their business. Conversely, lending tends to decline in regions where economic conditions are weak because MNCs are less willing to expand and thus do not borrow additional funds. Banks then are also less willing to grant loans because credit risk is higher in regions where economic conditions are weak.

3-3a Syndicated Loans in the Credit Market

Sometimes a single bank is unwilling or unable to lend the amount needed by a particular corporation or government agency. In this case, a **syndicate** of banks may be organized. Each bank within the syndicate participates in the lending. A lead bank is responsible for negotiating terms with the borrower, after which this bank organizes a group of banks to underwrite the loans. For each bank involved, syndicated loans reduce the exposure to default risk to the extent of that individual bank's participation.

Borrowers that receive a syndicated loan incur various fees besides the interest on the loan. Front-end management fees are paid to cover the costs of organizing the syndicate and underwriting the loan. In addition, a commitment fee of about .25 or .50 percent is charged annually on the unused portion of the available credit extended by the syndicate.

Syndicated loans can be denominated in a variety of currencies. The interest rate depends on the currency denominating the loan, the loan's maturity, and the creditworthiness of the borrower. Interest rates on syndicated loans are usually adjusted to reflect movements in market interest rates (such as an interbank lending rate), and the adjustment may occur every six months or every year.

3-3b Bank Regulations in the Credit Market

International banking regulations have become more standardized over time, a development that has enabled more competitive global banking. Both the Single European Act and the Basel Accord have contributed to this trend.

Single European Act   One of the most significant events affecting international banking was the **Single European Act**, which was phased in by 1992 throughout the European Union (EU) countries. Some provisions of the Single European Act of relevance to the banking industry are as follows:

■ Capital can flow freely throughout Europe.
■ Banks can offer a wide variety of lending, leasing, and securities activities in the EU.
■ Regulations regarding competition, mergers, and taxes are similar throughout the EU.
■ A bank established in any one of the EU countries has the right to expand into any or all of the other EU countries.

As a result of this act, banks have expanded across European countries. Efficiency in the European banking markets has increased because banks can more easily cross countries without concern for the country-specific regulations that prevailed in the past.

Another key provision of the act is that banks entering Europe receive the same banking powers as other banks there. Similar provisions apply to non-U.S. banks that enter the United States.

Basel Accord   In 1988, the central banks of 12 developed countries established the **Basel Accord**. Under this agreement, their respective commercial banks were required to maintain a higher level of capital (common stock and retained earnings) if they held riskier assets. A second accord (called Basel II) subjected banks to more stringent guidelines on the collateral backing their loans. In addition, in an effort to reduce failures in the banking system, this accord encouraged banks to improve their techniques for controlling operational risk.

The financial crisis of 2008–2009 revealed that banks were still highly exposed to risk, as many banks might have failed without government funding. A global committee of bank supervisors developed guidelines (informally referred to as "Basel III") aimed at enhancing the safety of the global banking system. This accord called for estimating banks' risk-weighted assets with new methods that would more properly detect the assets' level of risk and require many banks to maintain higher levels of capital. As a result of the stricter regulations, banks have maintained higher standards when extending loans to MNCs in the international credit market.

3-3c Impact of the Credit Crisis

In 2008, the United States experienced a credit crisis that affected the international credit market. The credit crisis was triggered by the substantial defaults on subprime (lower-quality) mortgages. Financial institutions in other countries, such as the United Kingdom, had also offered subprime mortgage loans and experienced high default rates. Because of the global integration of financial markets, the problems in the U.S. and U.K. financial markets spread to other markets. Some financial institutions based in Asia and Europe were common purchasers of subprime mortgages that were originated in the United States and United Kingdom. Furthermore, the resulting weakness of the U.S. and European economies reduced their demand for imports from other countries. Thus the U.S. credit crisis blossomed into an international credit crisis and increased concerns about credit risk in international markets. Creditors reduced the amount of credit that they were willing to provide, and some MNCs and government agencies were then no longer able to obtain funds in the international credit market.

3-4 International Bond Market

The international bond market facilitates the flow of funds between borrowers who need long-term funds and investors who are willing to supply long-term funds. Major investors in the international bond market include institutional investors such as commercial banks, mutual funds, insurance companies, and pension funds from many countries. Institutional investors may prefer to invest in international bond markets, rather than in their respective local markets, when they can earn a higher return on bonds denominated in foreign currencies. Borrowers in the international bond market include both national governments and MNCs.

Multinational corporations can obtain long-term debt by issuing bonds in their local markets, and they can also access long-term funds in foreign markets. They may choose to issue bonds in the international bond markets for three reasons. First, MNCs may be able to attract a stronger demand by issuing their bonds in a particular foreign country rather than in their home country. Some countries have a limited investor base, so MNCs in those countries naturally seek financing elsewhere.

Second, MNCs may prefer to finance a specific foreign project in a particular currency and thus may seek funds where that currency is widely used. Third, an MNC might attempt to finance projects in a foreign currency with a lower interest rate in order to reduce its cost of financing, although doing so would increase its exposure to exchange rate risk.

An international bond issued by a borrower foreign to the country where the bond is placed is known as a **foreign bond**. For example, a U.S. corporation may issue a bond denominated in Japanese yen that is sold to investors in Japan. In some cases, a firm may issue a variety of bonds in various countries. The currency denominating each type of bond is determined by the country where it is sold. The foreign bonds in these cases are sometimes referred to as **parallel bonds**.

3-4a Eurobond Market

Eurobonds are bonds that are sold in countries other than the country whose currency is used to denominate the bonds. They have become popular as a means of attracting funds because they circumvent registration requirements and avoid some disclosure requirements. Thus these bonds can be issued quickly and at a low cost. Eurobonds are underwritten by a multinational syndicate of investment banks and are simultaneously placed in many countries, providing a wide spectrum of fund sources to tap. U.S.-based MNCs such as McDonald's and Walt Disney commonly issue Eurobonds, and non-U.S. firms (e.g., Guinness, Nestlé, Volkswagen) also use the Eurobond market as a source of funds. Those MNCs without a strong credit record may have difficulty obtaining funds in the

Eurobond market because the limited disclosure requirements may discourage investors from trusting unknown issuers.

In recent years, governments and corporations from emerging markets such as Croatia, Hungary, Romania, and Ukraine have frequently utilized the Eurobond market. New corporations that have been established in emerging markets rely on this market to finance their growth. However, they typically pay a risk premium of at least 3 percentage points annually above the U.S. Treasury bond rate on dollar-denominated Eurobonds.

Features of Eurobonds   Eurobonds have several distinctive features. They are usually issued in bearer form, which means that no records are kept regarding ownership. Coupon payments are made yearly. Some Eurobonds carry a convertibility clause that allows for them to be converted into a specified number of shares of common stock. An advantage to the issuer is that Eurobonds typically have few, if any, protective covenants. Furthermore, even short-maturity Eurobonds include call provisions. Some Eurobonds, called **floating rate notes (FRNs)**, have a variable rate provision that adjusts the coupon rate over time according to prevailing market rates.

Denominations   Eurobonds are denominated in a number of currencies. The U.S. dollar is used most often, accounting for 70 to 75 percent of Eurobonds., However, in 2015, some U.S.-based MNCs including Coca-Cola, BlackRock, AT&T, and Kinder Morgan, issued Eurobonds denominated in euros to take advantage of the low interest rates in the eurozone. Similarly, some firms have issued debt denominated in Japanese yen in order to take advantage of Japan's extremely low interest rates. Because credit conditions and the interest rates for each currency change constantly, the popularity of particular currencies in the Eurobond market changes over time.

Secondary Market   Eurobonds have a secondary market. The market makers are in many cases the same underwriters who sell the primary issues. Euroclear, a Belgium-based financial services company, operates a settlement system that helps to inform all traders about outstanding issues for sale, thus allowing a more active secondary market.

3-4b Development of Other Bond Markets

Bond markets have developed in Asia and South America. Government agencies and MNCs in these regions use international bond markets to issue bonds when they believe they can reduce their financing costs. Investors in some countries use international bond markets because they expect their local currency to weaken in the future and prefer to invest in bonds denominated in a strong foreign currency. The South American bond market has experienced limited growth because the interest rates in some countries there are usually high. MNCs and government agencies in those countries are unwilling to issue bonds when interest rates are so high, so they rely heavily on short-term financing.

3-4c Risk of International Bonds

From the perspective of investors, international bonds are subject to four forms of risk: interest rate risk, exchange rate risk, liquidity risk, and credit (default) risk.

Interest Rate Risk   The interest rate risk of international bonds is the potential for their value to decline in response to rising long-term interest rates. When long-term interest rates rise, the required rate of return by investors rises. Therefore, the valuations of bonds decline. Interest rate risk is more pronounced for fixed rate than for floating rate bonds because the coupon rate remains fixed on fixed-rate bonds even when interest rates rise.

Exchange Rate Risk   Exchange rate risk is the potential for a bond's value to decline (from the investor's perspective) because the currency denominating the bond depreciates against the investor's home currency. As a result, the future expected coupon or principal payments to be received from the bond may convert to a smaller amount of the investor's home currency.

Liquidity Risk   Liquidity risk of bonds represents the potential for their prices to be lower at the time they are sold by investors because no consistently active market exists for them. Thus investors who wish to sell the bonds may have to lower their price in order to attract potential buyers.

Credit Risk   The credit risk of international bonds is the potential for default: interest and/or principal payments to investors to be suspended either temporarily or permanently. This risk is especially relevant in countries where creditor rights are limited, because creditors may be unable to require that debtor firms take the actions necessary to enable debt repayment.

As the credit risk of the issuing firm increases, the risk premium required by investors also increases. Any investors who want to sell their holdings of the bonds under these conditions must sell the bonds for a lower price to compensate potential buyers for the credit risk.

3-4d Impact of the Greece Crisis

In spring of 2010, Greece experienced weak economic conditions and a large increase in the government budget deficit. Investors were concerned that the government of Greece would not be able to repay its debt. Furthermore, investors learned that the government's reported budget deficits in the previous eight years were understated. A debt crisis erupted in Greece, as its government was desperate for new financing. As of March 2010, bonds issued by the government of Greece offered a 6.5 percent yield, which reflected a 4 percent annualized premium above bonds issued by other European governments (such as Germany) that also used the euro as their currency. This implies that the borrowing of the equivalent of $10 billion dollars from a bond offering would require that Greece pay an additional $400 million in interest payments every year because of its higher degree of default risk. These high interest payments caused even more concern that Greece would not be able to repay its debt.

In 2010, governments and banks in the other eurozone countries provided Greece with a bailout loan of 110 billion euros and required that Greece meet so-called austerity conditions (such as reducing its public-sector salaries and pensions) that could reduce the future budget deficit. However, Greece's budget deficit increased, and it needed another bailout of about 130 billion euros from several European governments in 2012.

Over the next few years, Greece's budget deficit continued to grow and by 2015, the government had debt of more than 300 billion euros. It needed another bailout, its third in five years. In July 2015, several European governments agreed to provide a third bailout loan of about 85 billion euros to Greece.

Contagion Effects   Because European governments served as major creditors for Greece, they were subject to credit contagion. A default by Greece on its debt could have had devastating financial effects on the European governments that provided loans, which could have prevented some of them from repaying their own debt.

The contagion concerns created by the Greece debt crisis also affected MNCs. If Greece defaulted on its debt, its government might be unable to pay some MNCs that sell products or services to Greece. In addition, the austerity measures that were imposed on Greece were intended to result in lower government pension payments to retirees, which could result in a lower demand for products or services provided by some MNCs to retirees.

The Greece crisis also forced creditors to recognize that government debt is not always risk free. Hence creditors began to assess more carefully the credit risk of other countries that had large budget deficits, such as Portugal, Spain, and Italy. Such concerns about risk reduced the access by governments of these other European countries to the debt market, as some financial institutions were no longer willing to loan them funds. In addition, those governments had to pay a higher risk premium to compensate for their credit risk, which increased their cost of borrowing funds.

WEB

www.stockmarkets.com
Information about stock markets around the world.

3-5 International Stock Markets

Just as some MNCs issue stock outside their home country, many investors purchase stocks outside their home country. There are several reasons for such a strategy. First, these investors may expect favorable economic conditions in a particular country and therefore invest in stocks of the firms in that country. Second, investors may wish to acquire stocks denominated in currencies that they expect to strengthen over time, because that would enhance the return on their investment. Third, some investors invest in stocks of other countries as a means of diversifying their portfolio. Thus their investment is less sensitive to possible adverse stock market conditions in their home country. More details about investing in international stock markets are provided in the appendix to this chapter.

3-5a Issuance of Stock in Foreign Markets

MNCs may issue stock in foreign markets for various reasons. MNCs may more readily attract funds from foreign investors by issuing stock in international markets. They have their stock listed on an exchange in any country where they issue shares, because investors in a foreign country are only willing to purchase stock if they can later easily sell their holdings locally in the secondary market. The stock is denominated in the currency of the country where it is placed.

An MNC's stock offering may be more easily digested when it is issued in several markets. The stocks of some U.S.-based MNCs are widely traded on numerous stock exchanges around the world, which gives non-U.S. investors easy access to those stocks and also gives the MNCs global name recognition. Many MNCs issue stock in a country where they will generate enough future cash flows to cover dividend payments.

EXAMPLE   Dow Chemical Co., a large U.S.-based MNC, does much business in Japan. It has supported its operations in Japan by issuing stock to investors there, which is denominated in Japanese yen. Thus Dow can use the yen proceeds to finance its expansion in Japan, and does not need to convert dollars to yen. In order to ensure that Japanese investors can easily sell the stock that they purchase, Dow Chemical Co. lists its stock on the Tokyo exchange. Because the stock listed on the Tokyo exchange is denominated in Japanese yen, Japanese investors who are buying or selling this stock need not convert to or from dollars. If Dow plans to expand its business in Japan, it may consider a secondary offering of stock in Japan. Because its stock is already listed there, it may be easy for Dow to place additional shares in that market and thereby raise equity funding for its expansion. ●

3-5b Issuance of Foreign Stock in the United States

Non-U.S. corporations that need large amounts of funds sometimes issue stock in the United States (these are called **Yankee stock offerings**) because the U.S. new-issues market is so liquid. Because many financial institutions in the United States purchase non-U.S. stocks as investments, non-U.S. firms may be able to place an entire stock offering in the United States. By issuing stock in the United States, non-U.S. firms may diversify their shareholder base; this can lessen the share price volatility induced by large investors selling shares. Investment banks and other financial institutions in the United States often serve as underwriters of stock targeted for the U.S. market, and they receive underwriting fees of about 7 percent of the issued stock's value.

Many of the recent stock offerings in the United States by non-U.S. firms have resulted from privatization programs in Latin America and Europe. That is, businesses that were previously government owned are being sold to U.S. shareholders. Given the large size of some of these businesses, their local stock markets are not large enough to digest the stock offerings. Consequently, U.S. investors are financing many privatized businesses based in foreign countries.

Non-U.S. firms that issue stock in the United States have their shares listed on a U.S. stock exchange, so that the shares placed in the United States can be easily traded in the secondary market. Firms that issue stock in the United States are normally required to satisfy stringent disclosure rules regarding their financial condition. However, they are exempt from some of these rules when they qualify for a Securities and Exchange Commission guideline (called Rule 144a) through a direct placement of stock to institutional investors.

Effect of the Sarbanes-Oxley Act on Foreign Stock Listings In 2002 the U.S. Congress passed the Sarbanes-Oxley Act, which required firms whose stock is listed on U.S. stock exchanges to provide more complete financial disclosure. However, the high cost of compliance caused many non-U.S. firms to place new issues of their stock in the United Kingdom, rather than the United States. Furthermore, some non-U.S. firms listed on U.S. stock exchanges before the Sarbanes-Oxley Act de-registered after its passage; such withdrawals may be attributed to the high cost of compliance.

American Depository Receipts Non-U.S. firms also obtain equity financing by issuing **American depository receipts (ADRs)**, which are certificates representing bundles of the firm's stock. The use of ADRs circumvents some disclosure requirements imposed on stock offerings in the United States while enabling non-U.S. firms to tap the U.S. market for funds. Examples include Cemex (ticker symbol CX, based in Mexico), China Telecom Corp. (CHA, China), Nokia (NOK, Finland), Heineken (HINKF, Netherlands), Alibaba (BABA, China), and Credit Suisse Group (CS, Switzerland).

Because ADR shares can be traded just like shares of a stock, the price of an ADR changes each day in response to demand and supply conditions. Over time, however, the value of an ADR should move in tandem with the value of the corresponding stock that is listed on the foreign stock exchange (after exchange rate effects are taken into account). The formula for calculating the price of an ADR is

$$P_{ADR} = P_{FS} \times S$$

Here P_{ADR} denotes the price of the ADR, P_{FS} is the price of the foreign stock measured in foreign currency, and S is the spot rate of the foreign currency. Holding the price of the foreign stock constant, the ADR price should move proportionately (against the dollar) with movement in the currency denominating the foreign stock. American depository receipts are especially attractive to U.S. investors who anticipate that the foreign stock will perform well and that the currency in which it is denominated will appreciate against the dollar.

EXAMPLE

WEB

www.wall-street.com
Provides links to many stock markets.

A share of the ADR of the French firm Pari represents one share of this firm's stock that is traded on a French stock exchange. The share price of Pari was 20 euros when the French market closed. As the U.S. stock market opens, the euro is worth $1.05, so the ADR price can be calculated as

$$P_{ADR} = P_{FS} \times S$$
$$= 20 \times \$1.05$$
$$= \$21 \qquad \bullet$$

If there is a difference between the ADR price and the price of the foreign stock (after adjusting for the exchange rate), then investors can use arbitrage to capitalize on this discrepancy. Over time, arbitrage will realign the prices.

EXAMPLE

WEB

finance.yahoo.com
Access to various domestic and international financial markets and financial market news; also gives links to national financial news servers.

Continuing with the previous example, assume that there are no transaction costs. If $P_{ADR} < (P_{FS} \times S)$, then ADR shares will flow back to France; they will be converted to shares of the French stock and then traded in the French market. Investors can engage in arbitrage by buying the ADR shares in the United States, converting them to shares of the French stock, and then selling those shares on the French stock exchange where the stock is listed.

The arbitrage will (1) reduce the supply of ADRs traded in the U.S. market, putting upward pressure on the ADR price, and (2) increase the supply of the French shares traded in the French market, putting downward pressure on the stock price in France. The arbitrage will continue until the discrepancy in prices disappears. ●

In reality, there are some transaction costs associated with converting ADRs to foreign shares. This means that arbitrage will occur only if the potential arbitrage profit exceeds the transaction costs. ADR price quotations are provided by various websites, such as www.adr.com.

3-5c Comparing the Size among Stock Markets

Exhibit 3.5 provides a summary of the major stock markets, although there are numerous other exchanges. Some foreign stock markets are much smaller than the U.S. markets because their firms have traditionally relied more on debt financing than on equity financing. However, recent trends indicate that firms outside the United States now issue stock more frequently, which has led to the growth of non-U.S. stock markets. The percentage of individual versus institutional ownership of shares varies across stock markets. Outside the United States, financial institutions (and other firms) own a large proportion of the shares, whereas individual investors own a relatively small proportion.

In 2000, the stock exchanges of Amsterdam, Brussels, and Paris merged to create the Euronext market; since then, the Lisbon stock exchange has also joined. In 2007, the NYSE joined Euronext to create NYSE Euronext, which represented a major step toward creating a global stock exchange. In 2012, Intercontinental Exchange (ICE) acquired NYSE Euronext. Both the NYSE and Euronext now operate as divisions of ICE. Most of the largest firms based in Europe have listed their stock on the Euronext market.

WEB

www.world-exchanges
.org
Information about the market capitalization, stock trading volume, and turnover in each stock market.

In recent years, many new stock markets have been developed. Such *emerging markets* allow foreign firms to raise large amounts of capital by issuing stock. These markets should enable U.S. firms doing business in developing countries to raise funds by issuing stock there and listing their stock on the local stock exchanges.

Exhibit 3.5 Comparison of Stock Exchanges (2015)

COUNTRY	MARKET CAPITALIZATION (billions of dollars)	NUMBER OF LISTED COMPANIES
Argentina	60	101
Australia	1,622	2,071
Brazil	823	308
Chile	225	308
China	6,270	2,635
Greece	22	244
Hong Kong	3,324	1,763
Hungary	13	48
Japan	4,485	3,470
Mexico	460	147
Norway	219	220
Slovenia	6	77
Spain	942	3,460
Switzerland	1,515	275
Taiwan	860	882
United Kingdom	6,187	2,938
United States	19,222	5,250

Source: World Federation of Exchanges.

3-5d How Governance Varies among Stock Markets

In general, stock market participation and trading activity are higher in countries where there is strong governance. Exhibit 3.6 identifies some factors that enable stronger governance and thus may increase the trading activity in a stock market. These factors are discussed next.

Rights Shareholders in some countries have more rights than those in other countries. For example, shareholders have more voting power in some countries than others, and they can have influence on a wider variety of management issues in some countries.

Legal Protection Shareholders in some countries may have more power to sue publicly traded firms if their executives or directors commit financial fraud. In general, common-law countries such as Canada, the United Kingdom, and the United States allow for more legal protection than civil-law countries such as France and Italy. Managers are more likely to serve shareholder interests when shareholders have more legal protection.

Government Enforcement A country might have laws to protect shareholders yet not adequately enforce those laws, which means that shareholders are not protected. Some countries tend to have less corporate corruption than others. In these countries, shareholders are less susceptible to major losses due to agency problems whereby managers use shareholder money for their own benefit.

Accounting Laws Beginning in 2001, the International Accounting Standards Board issued accounting rules for public companies. Many countries now require public

Exhibit 3.6 Impact of Governance on Stock Market Participation and Trading Activity

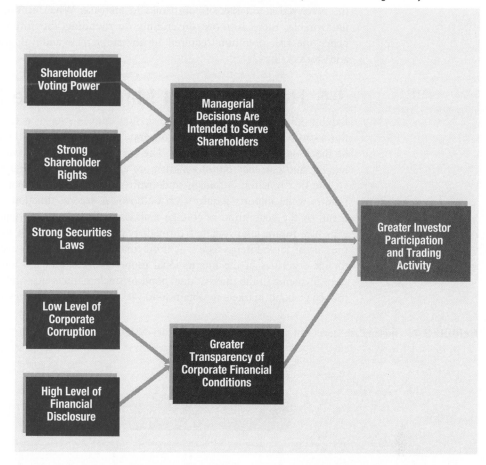

companies to use these rules in preparing their financial statements. As a result, there is more uniformity in accounting rules across countries, but there are still some differences that might make it difficult to directly compare financial statements of MNCs across countries. Shareholders are less susceptible to losses stemming from insufficient information when more transparency is required of public companies in their financial reporting.

Impact of Governance Characteristics In general, stock markets that allow more voting rights for shareholders, more legal protection, more enforcement of the laws, and more stringent accounting requirements attract more investors who are willing to invest in stocks. This allows for more confidence in the stock market and greater pricing efficiency, because there is a large set of investors who monitor each firm. A stock market that does not attract investors will not attract companies in search of funds; in this case, companies must rely either on stock markets in other countries or on credit markets (bonds and bank loans).

3-5e Integration of International Stock Markets and Credit Markets

Because the economies of countries are integrated and because stock market prices reflect the host country's prevailing and anticipated economic conditions, stock market prices are integrated across countries. Furthermore, international credit and stock markets are integrated because they are both adversely affected when conditions cause the perceived credit risk of companies to increase. When economic conditions become unfavorable, there is more uncertainty surrounding the future cash flows of firms; hence the risk premium required by investors rises and valuations of debt securities and stocks fall.

3-6 How Financial Markets Serve MNCs

Exhibit 3.7 illustrates the foreign cash flow movements of a typical MNC. These cash flows can be classified into four corporate functions, all of which generally require use of the foreign exchange markets. The spot market, forward market, currency futures market, and currency options market are all classified as foreign exchange markets.

The first function is foreign trade with business clients. Exports generate foreign cash inflows while imports require cash outflows. A second function is direct foreign investment, or the acquisition of foreign real assets. This function requires cash outflows but generates future inflows either through remitted earnings back to the MNC or through the sale of these foreign assets. A third function is short-term investment or financing in foreign securities in the international money market, and the fourth function is longer-term financing in the international bond or stock markets. An MNC may use international money or bond markets to obtain funds at a lower cost than they can be obtained locally.

Exhibit 3.7   Foreign Cash Flow Chart of a Multinational Corporation (MNC)

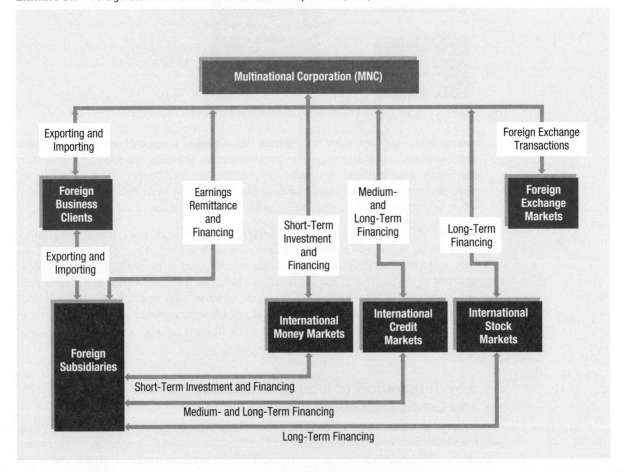

SUMMARY

- The foreign exchange market allows currencies to be exchanged in order to facilitate international trade or financial transactions. Commercial banks serve as financial intermediaries in this market. They stand ready to exchange currencies for immediate delivery in the spot market. In addition, they are also willing to negotiate forward contracts with MNCs that wish to buy and/or sell currencies in the future.

- The international money markets are composed of several large banks that accept deposits and provide short-term loans in various currencies. This market is used primarily by governments and large corporations.

- The international credit markets are composed of the same commercial banks that serve the international money market. These banks convert some of the deposits received into loans (for medium-term periods) to governments and large corporations.

- The international bond markets facilitate international transfers of long-term credit, thereby enabling governments and large corporations to borrow funds from various countries. The international bond market transactions are facilitated by multinational syndicates of investment banks that help to place the bonds.

- International stock markets enable firms to obtain equity financing in foreign countries. Thus these markets help MNCs finance their international expansion.

POINT COUNTER-POINT

Should Firms That Go Public Engage in International Offerings?

Point Yes. When a U.S. firm issues stock to the public for the first time in an initial public offering (IPO), it is naturally concerned about whether it can place all of its shares at a reasonable price. It will be able to issue its stock at a higher price by attracting more investors. It will increase its demand by spreading the stock across countries. The higher the price at which it can issue stock, the lower its cost of using equity capital. It can also establish a global name by spreading stock across countries.

Counter-Point No. If a U.S. firm spreads its stock across different countries at the time of the IPO, there will be less publicly traded stock in the United States. Thus it will not have as much liquidity in the secondary market. Investors desire stocks that they can easily sell in the secondary market, which means that they require that the stocks have liquidity. To the extent that a firm reduces its liquidity in the United States by spreading its stock across countries, it may not attract sufficient U.S. demand for the stock. Thus its efforts to create global name recognition may reduce its name recognition in the United States.

Who Is Correct? Use the Internet to learn more about this issue. Which argument do you support? Offer your own opinion on this issue.

SELF-TEST

Answers are provided in Appendix A at the back of the text.

1. Stetson Bank quotes a bid rate of $.784 for the Australian dollar and an ask rate of $.80. What is the bid/ask percentage spread?

2. Fullerton Bank quotes an ask rate of $.190 for the Peruvian currency (nuevo sol) and a bid rate of $.188. Determine the bid/ask percentage spread.

3. Briefly explain how MNCs can make use of each international financial market described in this chapter.

QUESTIONS AND APPLICATIONS

1. Motives for Investing in Foreign Money Markets Explain why an MNC may invest funds in a financial market outside its own country.

2. Motives for Providing Credit in Foreign Markets Explain why some financial institutions prefer to provide credit in financial markets outside their own country.

3. Exchange Rate Effects on Investing Explain how the appreciation of the Australian dollar against the U.S. dollar would affect the return to a U.S. firm that invested in an Australian money market security.

4. Exchange Rate Effects on Borrowing Explain how the appreciation of the Japanese yen against the U.S. dollar would affect the return to a U.S. firm that borrowed Japanese yen and used the proceeds for a U.S. project.

5. Bank Services List some of the important characteristics of bank foreign exchange services that MNCs should consider.

6. Bid/Ask Spread Utah Bank's bid price for Canadian dollars is $.7938 and its ask price is $.8100. What is the bid/ask percentage spread?

7. Bid/Ask Spread Compute the bid/ask percentage spread for Mexican peso retail transactions in which the ask rate is $.11 and the bid rate is $.10.

8. Forward Contract The Wolfpack Corp. is a U.S. exporter that invoices its exports to the United Kingdom in British pounds. If it expects that the pound will appreciate against the dollar in the future, should it hedge its exports with a forward contract? Explain.

9. Euro Explain the foreign exchange situation for countries that use the euro when they engage in international trade among themselves.

10. Indirect Exchange Rate If the direct exchange rate of the euro is $1.25, what is the euro's indirect exchange rate? That is, what is the value of a dollar in euros?

11. Cross Exchange Rate Assume Poland's currency (the zloty) is worth $.17 and the Japanese yen is worth $.008. What is the cross rate of the zloty with respect to yen? That is, how many yen equal a zloty?

12. Syndicated Loans Explain how syndicated loans are used in international markets.

13. Loan Rates Explain the process used by banks in the Eurocredit market to determine the rate to charge on loans.

14. International Markets What is the function of the international money markets? Briefly describe the reasons for the development and growth of the European money market. Explain how the international money, credit, and bond markets differ from one another.

15. Evolution of Floating Rates Briefly describe the historical developments that led to floating exchange rates as of 1973.

16. Greece Credit Crisis Explain why the Greece credit crisis can cause contagion effects throughout Europe.

17. Eurocredit Loans

a. With regard to Eurocredit loans, who are the borrowers?

b. Why would a bank desire to participate in syndicated Eurocredit loans?

c. What is LIBOR, and how is it used in the Eurocredit market?

18. Foreign Exchange You just came back from Canada, where the Canadian dollar was worth $.70. You still have C$200 from your trip and could exchange them for dollars at the airport, but the airport foreign exchange desk will only buy them for $.60. Next week, you will be going to Mexico and will need pesos. The airport foreign exchange desk will sell you pesos for $.10 per peso. You met a tourist at the airport who is from Mexico and is on his way to Canada. He is willing to buy your C$200 for 1,300 pesos. Should you accept the offer or cash the Canadian dollars in at the airport? Explain.

19. Foreign Stock Markets Explain why firms may issue stock in foreign markets. Why might U.S. firms issue more stock in Europe since the conversion to the euro in 1999?

20. Financing with Stock Chapman Co. is a privately owned MNC in the United States that plans to engage in an initial public offering (IPO) of stock so that it can finance its international expansion. At the present time, world stock market conditions are very weak but are expected to improve. The U.S. market tends to be weak in periods when the other stock markets around the world are weak. A financial manager of Chapman Co. recommends that it wait until the world stock markets recover before it issues stock.

Another manager believes that Chapman Co. could issue its stock now even if the price would be low, because its stock price should rise later once world stock markets recover. Who is correct? Explain.

Advanced Questions

21. Effects of 9/11 Why do you think the terrorist attack on the United States on September 11, 2001, was expected to cause a decline in U.S. interest rates? Given the expectations for a decline in U.S. interest rates and stock prices, how were capital flows between the United States and other countries likely affected?

22. International Financial Markets Walmart has established two retail outlets in the city of Shanzen, China, which has a population of 3.7 million. These outlets are massive and contain imports in addition to products purchased locally. As Walmart generates earnings beyond what it needs in Shanzen, it may remit those earnings back to the United States. Walmart is likely to build additional outlets in Shanzen or in other Chinese cities in the future.

a. Explain how the Walmart outlets in China would use the spot market in foreign exchange.

b. Explain how Walmart might use the international money markets when it is establishing other Walmart stores in Asia.

c. Explain how Walmart could use the international bond market to finance the establishment of new outlets in foreign markets.

23. Interest Rates Why do interest rates vary among countries? Why are interest rates normally similar for those European countries that use the euro as their currency? Offer a reason why the government interest rate of one country could be slightly higher than the government interest rate of another country, even though the euro is the currency used in both countries.

24. Interpreting Exchange Rate Quotations Today you notice the following exchange rate quotations: (a) $1 = 3.00 Argentine pesos and (b) 1 Argentine peso = .50 Canadian dollars. You need to purchase 100,000 Canadian dollars with U.S. dollars. How many U.S. dollars will you need for your purchase?

25. Pricing ADRs Today, the stock price of Genevo Co. (based in Switzerland) is priced at SF80 per share. The spot rate of the Swiss franc (SF) is $.70. During the next year, you expect that the stock price of Genevo

Co. will decline by 3 percent. You also expect that the Swiss franc will depreciate against the U.S. dollar by 8 percent during the next year. You own American depository receipts (ADRs) that represent Genevo stock. Each share that you own represents one share of the stock traded on the Swiss stock exchange. What is the estimated value of the ADR per share in 1 year?

26. Explaining Variation in Bid/Ask Spreads Go to the currency converter at finance.yahoo.com /currency-converter and determine the bid/ask spread for the euro. Then determine the bid/ask spread for a currency in a less developed country. What do you think is the main reason for the difference in the bid/ ask spreads between these two currencies?

27. Direct versus Indirect Exchange Rates Assume that during this semester, the euro appreciated against the dollar. Did the direct exchange rate of the euro increase or decrease? Did the indirect exchange rate of the euro increase or decrease?

28. Transparency and Stock Trading Activity Explain the relationship between transparency of firms and investor participation (or trading activity) in stock markets. Based on this relationship, how can governments of countries increase the amount of trading activity (and therefore liquidity)of their stock markets?

29. How Governance Affects Stock Market Liquidity Identify some of the key factors that can allow for stronger governance and therefore increase participation and trading activity in a stock market.

30. International Impact of the Credit Crisis Explain how the international integration of financial markets caused the credit crisis to spread across many countries.

31. Issuing Stock in Foreign Markets Bloomington Co. is a large U.S.-based MNC with large subsidiaries in Germany. It has issued stock in Germany in order to establish its business. It could have issued stock in the United States and then used the proceeds in order to support the growth in Europe. What is a possible advantage of issuing the stock in Germany to finance German operations? Also, why might the German investors prefer to purchase the stock that was issued in Germany rather than purchase the stock of Bloomington on a U.S. stock exchange?

32. Interest Rates among Countries As of today, the interest rates in Countries X, Y, and Z, are similar. In the next month, Country X is expected to have a weak economy, while Countries Y and Z are expected to experience a 6 percent increase in economic growth. However, conditions this month will also cause an increase in default risk of borrowers in Country Z in the next month because of political concerns, while the default risk of Countries X and Y remains unchanged. During the next month, which country should have the highest interest rate? Which country should have the lowest interest rate?

33. Greece Bailout Negotiations In July 2015, Greece was negotiating to obtain its third bailout from several European governments over a five-year period. Greece argued that austerity measures should not be imposed. Offer some reasoning for this argument. The European governments insisted on very strict austerity measures as a condition for providing loans. Offer some reasoning for the very strict austerity measures.

Critical Thinking

Impact of Shareholder Rights and Accounting Laws   Select a country outside the United States and conduct an online search to learn about the country's shareholder rights or accounting laws. Write a short essay in which you briefly describe the shareholder rights or accounting laws of that country. Would you consider investing in stocks of firms in that country based on your review of this country? Do you believe that the shareholder rights and accounting laws have encouraged the development of the stock market in this country? Explain.

Discussion in the Boardroom

This exercise can be found in Appendix E at the back of this textbook.

Running Your Own MNC

This exercise can be found on the *International Financial Management* text companion website. Go to www.cengagebrain.com (students) or www.cengage.com/login (instructors) and search using **ISBN 9781133947837**.

BLADES, INC. CASE

Decisions to Use International Financial Markets

As a financial analyst for Blades, Inc., you are reasonably satisfied with Blades' current setup of exporting "Speedos" (roller blades) to Thailand. Due to the unique arrangement with Blades' primary customer in Thailand, forecasting the revenue to be generated there is a relatively easy task. Specifically, your customer has agreed to purchase 180,000 pairs of Speedos annually, for a period of 3 years, at a price of THB4,594 (THB = Thai baht) per pair. The current direct quotation of the dollar-baht exchange rate is $.024.

The cost of goods sold incurred in Thailand (due to imports of the rubber and plastic components from Thailand) runs at approximately THB2,871 per pair of Speedos, but Blades currently only imports materials sufficient to manufacture about 72,000 pairs of Speedos. Blades' primary reasons for using a Thai supplier are the high quality of the components and the low cost, which has been facilitated by a continuing depreciation of the Thai baht against the U.S. dollar. If the dollar cost of buying components becomes more expensive in Thailand than in the United States, Blades is contemplating providing its U.S. supplier with the additional business.

Your plan is quite simple; Blades is currently using its Thai-denominated revenues to cover the cost of goods sold incurred there. During the last year, excess revenue was converted to U.S. dollars at the prevailing exchange rate. Although your cost of goods sold is not fixed contractually as the Thai revenues are, you expect them to remain relatively constant in the near future. Consequently, the baht-denominated cash inflows are fairly predictable each year because the Thai customer has committed to the purchase of 180,000 pairs of Speedos at a fixed price. The excess dollar revenue resulting from the conversion of baht is used either to support the U.S. production of Speedos if needed or to invest in the United States. Specifically, the revenues are used to cover cost of goods sold in the U.S. manufacturing plant, located in Omaha, Nebraska.

Ben Holt, Blades' CFO, notices that Thailand's interest rates are approximately 15 percent (versus 8 percent in the United States). You interpret the high interest rates in Thailand as an indication of the uncertainty resulting from Thailand's unstable economy. Holt asks you to assess the feasibility of investing Blades' excess funds from Thailand operations in Thailand at an interest rate of 15 percent. After you express your opposition to his plan, Holt asks you to detail the reasons in a detailed report.

1. One point of concern for you is that there is a trade-off between the higher interest rates in Thailand and the delayed conversion of baht into dollars. Explain what this means.

2. If the net baht received from the Thailand operation are invested in Thailand, how will U.S. operations be affected? (Assume that Blades is currently paying 10 percent on dollars borrowed and needs more financing for its firm.)

3. Construct a spreadsheet to compare the cash flows resulting from two plans. Under the first plan, net baht-denominated cash flows (received today) will be invested in Thailand at 15 percent for a 1-year period, after which the baht will be converted to dollars. The expected spot rate for the baht in 1 year is about $.022 (Ben Holt's plan). Under the second plan, net baht-denominated cash flows are converted to dollars immediately and invested in the United States for 1 year at 8 percent. For this question, assume that all baht-denominated cash flows are due today. Does Holt's plan seem superior in terms of dollar cash flows available after 1 year? Compare the choice of investing the funds versus using the funds to provide needed financing to the firm.

SMALL BUSINESS DILEMMA

Use of the Foreign Exchange Markets by the Sports Exports Company

Each month, the Sports Exports Company (a U.S. firm) receives an order for footballs from a British sporting goods distributor. The monthly payment for the footballs is denominated in British pounds, as requested by the British distributor. Jim Logan, owner of the Sports Exports Company, must convert the pounds received into dollars.

1. Explain how the Sports Exports Company could utilize the spot market to facilitate the exchange of currencies. Be specific.

2. Explain how the Sports Exports Company is exposed to exchange rate risk and how it could use the forward market to hedge this risk.

INTERNET/EXCEL EXERCISES

The Yahoo! website provides quotations of various exchange rates and stock market indexes. Its website address is www.yahoo.com.

1. Go to the Yahoo! site for exchange rate data (finance.yahoo.com/currency-converter).

a. What is the prevailing direct exchange rate of the Japanese yen?

b. What is the prevailing direct exchange rate of the euro?

c. Based on your answers to questions a and b, show how to determine the number of yen per euro.

d. One euro is equal to how many yen according to the table in Yahoo!?

e. Based on your answer to question d, show how to determine how many euros are equal to one Japanese yen.

f. Click on the euro in the first column in order to generate a historical trend of the direct exchange rate of the euro. Click on 5y to review the euro's exchange rate over the last 5 years. Briefly explain this trend (whether it is mostly upward or downward), and the point(s)at which there was an abrupt shift in the opposite direction.

g. Click on the euro in the column heading in order to generate a historical trend of the indirect exchange rate of the euro. Click on 5y to review the euro's exchange rate over the last 5 years. Briefly explain this trend, and the point(s) at which there was an abrupt shift in the opposite direction. How does this trend of the indirect exchange rate compare to the trend of the direct exchange rate?

h. Based on the historical trend of the direct exchange rate of the euro, what is the approximate percentage change in the euro over the last full year?

i. Just above the foreign exchange table in Yahoo!, there is a currency converter. Use this table to convert euros into Canadian dollars. A historical trend is provided. Explain whether the euro generally appreciated or depreciated against the Canadian dollar over this period.

j. Notice from the currency converter that bid and ask exchange rates are provided. What is the percentage bid/ask spread based on the information?

2. Go to the section on currencies within the website. First, identify the direct exchange rates of foreign currencies from the U.S. perspective. Then, identify the indirect exchange rates. What is the direct exchange rate of the euro? What is the indirect exchange rate of the euro? What is the relationship between the direct and indirect exchange rates of the euro?

3. Use the Yahoo! website to determine the cross exchange rate between the Japanese yen and the Australian dollar. That is, determine how many yen must be converted to an Australian dollar for Japanese importers that purchase Australian products today. How many Australian dollars are equal to a Japanese yen? What is the relationship between the exchange rate measured as number of yen per Australian dollar and the exchange rate measured as number of Australian dollars per yen?

ONLINE ARTICLES WITH REAL-WORLD EXAMPLES

Find a recent article online that describes an actual international finance application or a real world example about a specific MNC's actions that reinforces one or more concepts covered in this chapter.

If your class has an online component, your professor may ask you to post your summary there and provide the web link of the article so that other students can access it. If your class is live, your professor may ask you to summarize your application in class. Your professor may assign specific students to complete this assignment for this chapter, or may allow any students to do the assignment on a volunteer basis.

For recent online articles and real world examples applied to this chapter, consider using the following search terms and include the prevailing year as a search term to ensure that the online articles are recent:

1. foreign exchange market
2. foreign exchange quotations
3. company AND forward contracts
4. Inc. AND forward contracts
5. international money market
6. loan AND international syndicate
7. international capital market
8. banks AND Basel capital requirements
9. international stock listings
10. American depository receipts

Investing in International Financial Markets

WEB

money.cnn.com
Current national and international market data and analyses.

WEB

www.sec.gov/investor /pubs/ininvest.htm
Information from the Securities and Exchange Commission about international investing.

The trading of financial assets (such as stocks or bonds) by investors in international financial markets has a major impact on MNCs. First, this type of trading can influence the level of interest rates in a specific country (and therefore the cost of debt to an MNC) because it affects the amount of funds available there. Second, it can affect the price of an MNC's stock (and therefore the cost of equity to an MNC) because it influences the demand for the MNC's stock. Third, it enables MNCs to sell securities in foreign markets. So even though international investing in financial assets is not the most crucial activity of MNCs, international investing by individual and institutional investors can indirectly affect the actions and performance of an MNC. Consequently, an understanding of the motives and methods of international investing is necessary to anticipate how the international flow of funds may change in the future and how that change may affect MNCs.

Background on International Stock Exchanges

The international trading of stocks has grown over time but has been limited by three barriers: transaction costs, information costs, and exchange rate risk. But in recent years these barriers have been reduced, as explained here.

Reduction in Transaction Costs

Most countries tend to have their own stock exchanges, where the stocks of local publicly held companies are traded. Recently, however, exchanges have been consolidated within countries; this consolidation has increased efficiency and reduced transaction costs. Some European stock exchanges now have extensive cross-listings so that investors in a given European country can easily purchase stocks of companies based in other European countries.

Trades are normally conducted by electronic communications networks (ECNs), which match buyers and sellers of stocks. These networks do not have a visible trading floor; the trades are executed by a computer network. With an ECN, investors can place orders on their own computers that are then executed by the trader's computer system with the investor receiving confirmation via the Internet. Thus computers are involved in all stages of the trading process, from placement of the order to confirmation that the transaction has been executed. When there are many more buy orders than sell orders for a given stock, the computer is unable to accommodate all orders. Some buyers will then increase the price they are willing to pay for the stock. As a result, the price adjusts in response to the demand (buy orders) for the stock and the supply (sell orders) of the stock for sale recorded by the computer system. Similar dynamics would be evident on the trading floor as on the computer, but the computerized system follows documented criteria when prioritizing the execution of orders. In contrast, traders on the floor can execute some trades in ways that favor themselves at the expense of investors.

Impact of Alliances Several stock exchanges have created international alliances with the stock exchanges of other countries, thereby enabling firms to more easily cross-list their shares among various stock markets. This gives investors easier and cheaper access to foreign stocks. The alliances also allow greater integration between markets. At some point in the future, there may be one global stock market in which any stock of any country can be easily purchased or sold by investors around the world. A single global stock market would allow U.S. investors to easily purchase any stock, regardless of where the corporation is based or the currency in which the stock is denominated. The international alliances are a first step toward a single global stock market. The costs of international stock transactions have already been substantially reduced as a result of some of these alliances.

Reduction in Information Costs

The Internet provides investors with access to extensive information about foreign stocks, enabling them to make more informed decisions without having to purchase information about these stocks. Consequently, investors should be more comfortable assessing foreign stocks. Although differences in accounting rules still limit the degree to which financial data about foreign companies can be accurately interpreted or compared to data about firms in other countries, there is some momentum toward making accounting standards uniform across some countries.

Exchange Rate Risk

When investing in a foreign stock that is denominated in a foreign currency, investors are subject to the possibility that the currency denominating the stock may depreciate over time against the investor's currency. The potential for currency depreciation to induce a major decline in the stock's value is greater in emerging markets, such as Indonesia and Russia, where the local currency's value can change by 10 percent or more on a single day.

Measuring the Impact of Exchange Rates The return to a U.S. investor from investing in a foreign stock is a function of the stock's own return R, which includes the dividend, and the percentage change in the exchange rate e; thus:

$$R_\$ = (1 + R)(1 + e) - 1$$

EXAMPLE A year ago, Rob Grady invested in the stock of Vopka, a Russian company. Over the last year, the stock increased in value by 35 percent. Over this same period, however, the Russian ruble's value declined by 30 percent. Rob sold the Vopka stock today. His return is:

$$R_\$ = (1 + R)(1 + e) - 1$$
$$= (1 + .35)[1 + (-.30)] - 1$$
$$= -0.55 \text{ or } -5.5\%$$

Even though the return on this stock was more pronounced than the exchange rate movement, Rob lost money on his investment. The reason is that the exchange rate movement of −30 percent wiped out not only 30 percent of his initial investment but also 30 percent of the stock's return. ●

As the preceding example illustrates, investors should consider the potential influence of exchange rate movements on foreign stocks before investing in them. Foreign investments are especially risky in developing countries, where exchange rates tend to be volatile.

Reducing the Exchange Rate Risk of Foreign Stocks   One method of reducing exchange rate risk is to take short positions in the foreign currencies denominating the foreign stocks. For example, a U.S. investor holding Mexican stocks who expects the stocks to be worth 10 million Mexican pesos one year from now could sell forward contracts (or futures contracts) representing 10 million pesos. The stocks could be liquidated at that time, and the pesos could be exchanged for dollars at a locked-in price.

Although hedging the exchange rate risk of an international stock portfolio can be effective, it has three limitations. First, the number of foreign currency units to be converted to dollars at the end of the investment horizon is unknown. If the units received from liquidating the foreign stocks are more (less) than the amount hedged, then the investor has a net long (short) position in that foreign currency and the return will be unfavorably affected by its depreciation (appreciation). Yet even though the hedge is therefore imperfect, investors can usually hedge most of their exchange rate risk.

A second limitation of hedging exchange rate risk is that the investors may decide to retain the foreign stocks beyond the initially planned investment horizon. Of course, they can create another forward contract after the initial forward contract is completed. If they ever decide to liquidate the foreign stocks prior to the forward delivery date, the hedge will be less effective. They could use the proceeds to invest in foreign money market securities denominated in that foreign currency in order to postpone conversion to dollars until the forward delivery date. However, this prevents them from using the funds for other opportunities until that delivery date.

A third limitation of hedging is that forward rates for less widely traded currencies may not exist or may exhibit a large discount.

International Stock Diversification

A substantial amount of research has demonstrated that investors in stocks can benefit by diversifying internationally. The stocks of most firms are strongly influenced by the countries where those firms reside (although some firms are more vulnerable than others to economic conditions).

Because stock markets partially reflect the current and/or forecasted state of their respective countries' economies, they do not move in tandem. Thus the value of particular stocks that are listed in the various markets are not expected to be highly correlated. This contrasts with a purely domestic portfolio, in which most stocks often move in the same direction and by similar magnitudes.

The risk of a stock portfolio can be measured by its volatility. Investors prefer a less volatile stock portfolio because its future returns are less subject to uncertainty. The volatility of a single stock is commonly measured by its standard deviation of returns over a recent period, and the same holds for the volatility of a stock portfolio. The standard deviation of a stock portfolio is determined by the standard deviation of returns for each individual stock along with the correlations of returns between each pair of stocks in the portfolio. Thus for a two-stock portfolio:

$$\sigma_p = \sqrt{w_x^2 \sigma_x^2 + w_y^2 \sigma_y^2 + 2 w_x w_y \sigma_w \sigma_y (\text{CORR}_{xy})}$$

Here w_X is the proportion of funds invested in stock X, w_Y is the proportion of funds invested in stock Y, σ_X is the standard deviation of returns for stock X, σ_Y is the standard deviation of returns for stock Y, and CORR_{XY} is the correlation coefficient of returns between stock X and stock Y. From this equation, it should be clear that the standard deviation of returns (and therefore the risk) of a stock portfolio is positively related to the standard deviation of the individual stocks included within the portfolio and is also positively related to the correlations between individual stock returns.

Much research has documented that stock returns are driven by their country market conditions. Therefore, individual stocks within a given country tend to be highly correlated. If country economies are segmented then their stock market returns should not be highly correlated, so the individual stocks of one country are not highly correlated with individual stocks of other countries. Thus investors should be able to reduce the risk of their stock portfolio by investing in stocks among different countries.

Limitations of International Diversification   In general, correlations between stock indexes have been higher in recent years than they were several years ago. The general increase in correlations among stock market returns may have implications for MNCs that attempt to diversify internationally. To the extent that stock prices in each market reflect anticipated earnings, the increased correlations may suggest that more highly correlated anticipated earnings are expected among countries. Thus the potential risk-reduction benefits to an MNC that diversifies its business may be limited.

One reason for the increased correlations among stock market returns is increased integration of business between countries. Increased integration results in more inter-country flow of trade and capital, which increases the influence of each country on other countries. In particular, many European countries have become more integrated as regulations have been standardized throughout Europe to facilitate trade between countries. In addition, the adoption of the euro has removed exchange rate risk due to trade between participating countries.

Valuation of Foreign Stocks

When investors consider investing in foreign stocks, they need methods for valuing those stocks.

Dividend Discount Model

One valuation possibility is to use the dividend discount model with an adjustment to accommodate expected exchange rate movements. Foreign stocks pay dividends in the currency in which they are denominated. Thus the cash flow per period to U.S. investors is the dividend (denominated in the foreign currency) multiplied by the value of that foreign currency in dollars. The dividend normally can be forecast with more accuracy than the value of the foreign currency. Because of exchange rate uncertainty, the value of the foreign stock from a U.S. investor's perspective is subject to much uncertainty.

Price/Earnings Method

An alternative method of valuing foreign stocks is to apply price/earnings ratios. The expected earnings per share of the foreign firm are multiplied by the appropriate price/

earnings ratio (based on the firm's risk and industry) to determine the appropriate price of the firm's stock. Although this method is easy to use, it is subject to some limitations when applied to valuing foreign stocks. The price/earnings ratio for a given industry may change continuously in some foreign markets, especially when the industry consists of only a few firms. It is therefore difficult to determine what price/earnings ratio should be applied to a specific foreign firm. In addition, the price/earnings ratio for any particular industry may need to be adjusted for the firm's country, because reported earnings can be influenced by the firm's accounting guidelines and tax laws. Furthermore, even if U.S. investors are comfortable with their estimate of the proper price/earnings ratio, the value derived by this method is denominated in the foreign currency (because the estimated earnings are denominated in that currency). Therefore, U.S. investors would still need to consider exchange rate effects. Even if the stock is undervalued in the foreign country, it may not generate a reasonable return for U.S. investors if the foreign currency depreciates against the dollar.

Other Methods

Some investors adapt these methods when selecting foreign stocks. For example, they may first assess the macroeconomic conditions of all countries to screen out those that are expected to experience poor conditions in the future. Then they use other methods, such as the dividend discount model or the price/earnings approach, to value specific firms within the countries that are appealing.

Why Stock Valuations Differ among Countries

A stock that seems undervalued to investors in one country may seem overvalued to investors in another country. Some of the more common reasons why perceptions of a stock's valuation may vary among investors in different countries are discussed next.

Required Rate of Return   Some investors attempt to value a stock according to the present value of the future cash flows that it will generate. The dividend discount model is one of many models that employ this approach. The required rate of return that is used to discount the cash flows can vary substantially among countries, but it is always based on the prevailing risk-free interest rate available to investors plus a risk premium. For investors in the United States, the risk-free rate is typically less than 10 percent. Therefore, U.S. investors would in some cases apply a 12–15 percent required rate of return. In contrast, investors in an emerging country that has a high risk-free rate would be unwilling to accept such a low return. If they can earn a high return by investing in a risk-free asset, they would require a still higher return to invest in risky assets such as stocks.

Exchange Rate Risk   The exposure of investors to exchange rate risk from investing in foreign stocks depends on their home country. Investors in the United States who invest in a Brazilian stock are highly exposed to exchange rate risk because the Brazilian currency (the real) has depreciated substantially against the dollar over time. However, Brazilian investors are less exposed to exchange rate risk when investing in U.S. stocks because the U.S. dollar is unlikely to depreciate significantly against the Brazilian real. In fact, Brazilian investors normally benefit from investing in U.S. stocks owing to the dollar's appreciation against the real. Indeed, that appreciation is often necessary to generate an adequate return for Brazilian investors, given their high required return when investing in foreign stocks.

Taxes   The tax effects of dividends and capital gains also vary among countries. The lower a country's tax rates, the higher the share of pretax cash flows received that the investor can retain. Other things being equal, investors based in low-tax countries should value stocks higher.

The valuation of stocks by investors within a given country changes in response to changes in tax laws. Before 2003, dividend income received by U.S. investors was taxed at ordinary income tax rates, which could be nearly 40 percent for some taxpayers. This explains why many U.S. investors placed higher valuations on foreign stocks that paid low or no dividends (especially investors who were not reliant on the stocks for periodic income). The maximum tax on long-term capital gains during this period was 20 percent, a rate that increased the attractiveness of foreign stocks that paid no dividends but had the potential to generate large capital gains. In 2003, however, the maximum tax rate on both dividends and long-term capital gains was set at 15 percent. Thereafter, U.S. investors became more willing to consider foreign stocks that paid high dividends. In recent years, the maximum tax rate on dividends and capital gains has increased for high-income taxpayers, although that income is still taxed at a lower rate than ordinary income.

Methods Used to Invest Internationally

For investors attempting international stock diversification, five common approaches are available:

- direct purchases of foreign stocks,
- investment in MNC stocks,
- American depository receipts (ADRs),
- exchange-traded funds (ETFs), and
- international mutual funds (IMFs).

Each approach is discussed in turn.

Direct Purchases of Foreign Stocks

Foreign stocks can be purchased on foreign stock exchanges. Such purchases require the services of brokerage firms that can execute the trades desired by investors at the foreign stock exchange of concern. However, this approach is inefficient because of market imperfections such as insufficient information, transaction costs, and tax differentials among countries.

An alternative method of investing directly in foreign stocks is to purchase stocks of foreign companies that are sold on the local stock exchange. In the United States, for example, Royal Dutch Shell (of the Netherlands), Sony (of Japan), and many other foreign stocks are sold on U.S. stock exchanges. Because the number of foreign stocks listed on any local stock exchange is typically quite limited, this method by itself may not be adequate to achieve the full benefits of international diversification.

Brokerage firms have expanded the list of non-U.S. stocks that are available to U.S. investors. For example, Fidelity now executes stock transactions in many different countries for its U.S. investors. The transaction cost of investing directly in foreign stocks is higher than that of purchasing stocks on U.S. stock exchanges. One reason for the higher cost is that the foreign shares purchased by U.S. investors typically remain in the foreign country, and there is a cost of storing the stocks and processing records of ownership. Some brokerage firms have substantially reduced their fees for international stock transactions recently; however, they may require a larger minimum transaction value (such as $5,000) to execute the transaction. The fees may even vary among foreign stocks at a given brokerage firm. For example, the fees charged by E*Trade for executing foreign stock transactions vary with the home country of the stock.

Investment in MNC Stocks

The operations of an MNC are a form of international diversification. Like an investor with a well-managed stock portfolio, an MNC can reduce risk (variability in net cash flows) by diversifying sales not only among industries but also among countries. In this sense, the MNC as a single firm can achieve stability similar to that of an internationally diversified stock portfolio.

If MNC stocks behave like an international stock portfolio, then they should be sensitive to the stock markets of the various countries in which they operate. Yet some studies have found MNCs based in a particular country are typically affected only by their respective local stock markets and not by other stock market movements. This finding suggests that the diversification benefits from investing in an MNC are limited.

American Depository Receipts

WEB

www.adr.com
Performance of ADRs.

Another approach to investing internationally is to purchase American depository receipts (ADRs), which are certificates representing ownership of foreign stocks. More than 1,000 ADRs are available in the United States, and most are traded on the over-the-counter (OTC) stock market. An investment in ADRs may be an adequate substitute for direct investment in foreign stocks.

Exchange-Traded Funds

WEB

finance.yahoo.com/etf
Performance of ETFs.

Although investors have closely monitored international stock indexes for years, they were typically unable to invest directly in these indexes. The index was simply a measure of performance for a set of stocks but was not traded. Exchange-traded funds (ETFs) are indexes that reflect composites of stocks for particular countries; they were created so that investors could invest directly in a stock index representing any one of several countries. Some of the more popular ETFs include SPDRs (pronounced "spiders") and iShares (originally called world equity benchmark shares or WEBS).

International Mutual Funds

One last approach to consider is purchasing shares of **international mutual funds (IMFs)**, which are portfolios of stocks from various countries. Several investment firms, such as Fidelity and Vanguard, have constructed IMFs for their customers. Like domestic mutual funds, IMFs are popular because of (1) the low minimum investment necessary to participate in the funds, (2) the presumed expertise of the portfolio managers, and (3) the high degree of diversification achieved by the portfolios' inclusion of several stocks. Many investors believe an IMF can better reduce risk than a purely domestic mutual fund because the IMF includes foreign securities. An IMF represents a prepackaged portfolio, so investors who use it do not need to construct their own portfolios. Even for those who normally prefer to construct their own portfolios, the existence of numerous IMFs on the market today allows investors to select the one that most closely resembles the type of portfolio that they would construct. In addition, some investors are more comfortable when a professional manager is in charge of the international portfolio.

4

Exchange Rate Determination

CHAPTER OBJECTIVES

The specific objectives of this chapter are to:

■ explain how exchange rate movements are measured,

■ explain how the equilibrium exchange rate is determined,

■ examine factors that affect the equilibrium exchange rate,

■ explain the movements in cross exchange rates, and

■ explain how financial institutions attempt to capitalize on anticipated exchange rate movements.

WEB

www.xe.com
Real-time exchange rate quotations.

Financial managers of MNCs that conduct international business must continuously monitor exchange rates because their cash flows are highly dependent on them. They need to understand what factors influence exchange rates so that they can anticipate how exchange rates may change in response to specific conditions. This chapter provides a foundation for understanding how exchange rates are determined.

4-1 Measuring Exchange Rate Movements

Exchange rate movements affect an MNC's value because they can affect the amount of cash inflows received from exporting products or services or from a subsidiary and the amount of cash outflows needed to pay for imports of products or services. An exchange rate measures the value of one currency in units of another currency. As economic conditions change, exchange rates can change substantially. A decline in a currency's value is known as **depreciation**. When the British pound depreciates against the U.S. dollar, this means that the U.S. dollar is strengthening relative to the pound. An increase in currency value is known as **appreciation**.

When a foreign currency's spot rate at two different times are compared, the spot rate at the more recent date is denoted S and the spot rate at the earlier date is denoted as S_{t-1}. The percentage change in the value of the foreign currency over a specified period is then computed as follows:

$$\text{Percent } \Delta \text{ in foreign currency value} = \frac{S - S_{t-1}}{S_{t-1}}$$

A positive percentage change indicates that the foreign currency has appreciated over the period, and a negative percentage change indicates that it has depreciated over the period.

On some days, most foreign currencies appreciate against the dollar (although by different degrees); on other days, most currencies depreciate against the dollar (though again by different degrees). There are also days when some currencies appreciate while others depreciate against the dollar; the financial media describe this scenario by stating that "the dollar was *mixed* in trading."

EXAMPLE

Exchange rates for the Canadian dollar and the euro are shown in the second and fourth columns of Exhibit 4.1 for the months from January 1 to July 1. First, observe that the direction of the movement may persist for consecutive months in some cases but in other cases may not persist at all. The magnitude

Exhibit 4.1   How Exchange Rate Movements and Volatility Are Measured

	VALUE OF CANADIAN DOLLAR (C$)	MONTHLY % CHANGE IN C$	VALUE OF EURO	MONTHLY % CHANGE IN EURO
Jan. 1	$0.70	—	$1.18	—
Feb. 1	$0.71	+1.43%	$1.16	−1.69%
March 1	$0.70	−0.99%	$1.15	−0.86%
April 1	$0.70	−0.85%	$1.12	−2.61%
May 1	$0.69	−0.72%	$1.11	−0.89%
June 1	$0.70	+0.43%	$1.14	+2.70%
July 1	$0.69	−1.29%	$1.17	+2.63%
Standard deviation of monthly changes		1.04%		2.31%

WEB

www.bis.org/statistics
/eer/index.htm
Information on how each
currency's value has
changed against a broad
index of currencies.

of the movement tends to vary every month, although the range of percentage movements over these months is a reasonable indicator of the range of percentage movements in future months. A comparison of the movements in these two currencies suggests that they move independently of each other.

The movements in the euro are typically larger (regardless of direction) than movements in the Canadian dollar. This means that, from a U.S. perspective, the euro is a more volatile currency. The standard deviation of the exchange rate movements for each currency (shown at the bottom of the table) confirms this point. The standard deviation should be applied to percentage movements (not to the actual exchange rate values) when comparing volatility among currencies. From the U.S. perspective, some currencies (such as the Australian dollar, Brazilian real, Mexican peso, New Zealand dollar) tend to exhibit higher volatility than does the euro. Financial managers of MNCs closely monitor the volatility of any currencies to which they are exposed, because a more volatile currency has more potential to deviate far from what is expected and could have a major impact on their cash flows. ●

Foreign exchange rate movements tend to be larger for longer time horizons. Thus, if *yearly* exchange rate data were assessed the movements would be more volatile for each currency than what is shown here, but the euro's movements would still be more volatile than the Canadian dollar's movements. If *daily* exchange rate movements were assessed the movements would be less volatile for each currency than shown here, but the euro's movements would still be more volatile than the Canadian dollar's movements. A review of daily exchange rate movements is important to an MNC that will need to obtain a foreign currency in a few days and wants to assess the possible degree of movement over that period. A review of annual exchange movements would be more appropriate for an MNC that conducts foreign trade every year and wants to assess the possible degree of movements on a yearly basis. Many MNCs review exchange rates based on both short- and long-term horizons because they expect to engage in international transactions in both the near and distant future.

WEB

www.federalreserve.gov
Current and historic
exchange rates.

4-2 Exchange Rate Equilibrium

Although it is easy to measure the percentage change in a currency's value, it is more difficult to explain why the value changed or to forecast how it may change in the future. To achieve either of these objectives, the concept of an **equilibrium exchange rate** must be understood in addition to the factors that affect this rate.

Before considering why an exchange rate changes, recall that an exchange rate (at a given time) represents the *price* of a currency, or the rate at which one currency can be exchanged for another. The exchange rate always involves two currencies, but the focus in this text is on the U.S. perspective. So unless specified otherwise, the "exchange rate" of any currency is the rate at which it can be exchanged for U.S. dollars.

Like any other product sold in markets, the price of a currency is determined by the demand for that currency relative to its supply. Thus, for each possible price of a British pound, there is a corresponding demand for pounds and a corresponding supply of pounds for sale (to be exchanged for dollars). At any given moment, a currency should exhibit the price at which the demand for that currency is equal to supply; this is the equilibrium exchange rate. Of course, conditions can change over time. These changes induce adjustments in the supply of or demand for any currency of interest, which in turn creates movement in the currency's price. A thorough discussion of this topic follows.

4-2a Demand for a Currency

The British pound is used here to explain exchange rate equilibrium. The United Kingdom has not adopted the euro as its currency and continues to use the pound. The U.S. demand for British pounds results partly from international trade, as U.S. firms obtain British pounds to purchase British products. In addition, there is U.S. demand for pounds due to international capital flows, as U.S. firms and investors obtain pounds to invest in British securities. Exhibit 4.2 shows a hypothetical number of pounds that would be demanded under several different values of the exchange rate. At any point in time, there is only one exchange rate; the exhibit shows how many pounds would be demanded at various exchange rates for a given time. This *demand schedule* is downward sloping because corporations and individuals in the United States would purchase more British goods when the pound is worth less (because it takes fewer dollars to obtain the desired amount of pounds). Conversely, if the pound's exchange rate is high then corporations and individuals in the United States are less willing to purchase British goods (because the products or securities could be acquired at a lower price in the United States or other countries).

Exhibit 4.2 Demand Schedule for British Pounds

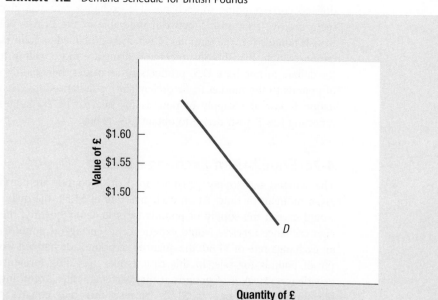

Exhibit 4.3   Supply Schedule of British Pounds for Sale

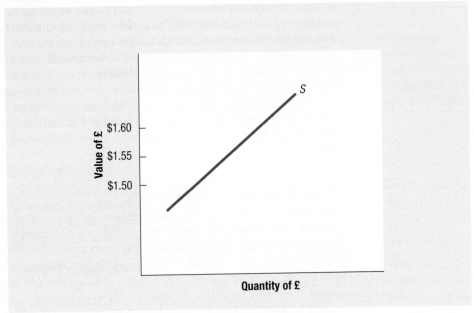

4-2b Supply of a Currency for Sale

Having considered the U.S. demand for pounds, the next step is to consider the British demand for U.S. dollars. This can be viewed as a British *supply of pounds for sale*, because pounds are supplied in the foreign exchange market in exchange for U.S. dollars.

A supply schedule of pounds for sale in the foreign exchange market can be developed in a manner similar to the demand schedule for pounds. Exhibit 4.3 shows the quantity of pounds for sale (supplied to the foreign exchange market in exchange for dollars) corresponding to each possible exchange rate at a given time. One can clearly see a positive relationship between the value of the British pound and the quantity of British pounds for sale (supplied), which is explained as follows. When the pound's valuation is high, British consumers and firms are more willing to exchange their pounds for dollars to purchase U.S. products or securities; hence they supply a greater number of pounds to the market to be exchanged for dollars. Conversely, when the pound's valuation is low, the supply of pounds for sale (to be exchanged for dollars) is smaller, reflecting less British desire to obtain U.S. goods.

4-2c Equilibrium Exchange Rate

The demand and supply schedules for British pounds are combined in Exhibit 4.4 for a given moment in time. At an exchange rate of $1.50, the quantity of pounds demanded would exceed the supply of pounds for sale. Consequently, the banks that provide foreign exchange services would experience a *shortage* of pounds at that exchange rate. At an exchange rate of $1.60, the quantity of pounds demanded would be less than the supply of pounds for sale; in this case, banks providing foreign exchange services would experience a *surplus* of pounds at that exchange rate. According to Exhibit 4.4, the equilibrium exchange rate is $1.55 because this rate equates the quantity of pounds demanded with the supply of pounds for sale.

Exhibit 4.4 Equilibrium Exchange Rate Determination

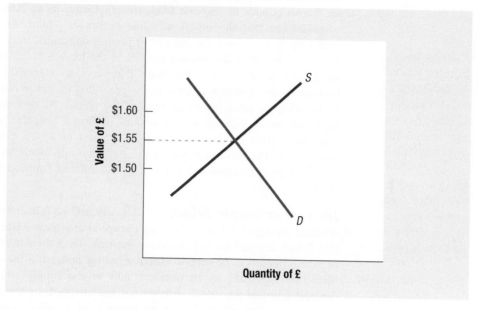

4-2d Change in the Equilibrium Exchange Rate

Changes in the demand and supply schedules of a currency force a change in the equilibrium exchange rate in the foreign exchange market. Before considering the factors that could cause changes in the demand and supply schedules of a currency, it is important to understand the logic of how such changes affect the equilibrium exchange rate. There are four possible changes in market conditions that can affect this rate, and each condition is explained with an application to the British pound. The exchange rate varies because banks that serve as intermediaries in the foreign exchange market adjust the price at which they are willing to buy or sell a particular currency in the face of a sudden shortage or excess of that currency. When reading the descriptions that follow, assume that a single bank accommodates all customers seeking to buy British pounds (to exchange dollars for pounds) as well as all who are looking to sell them (to exchange pounds for dollars). This assumption makes it easier to understand why the exchange rate adjusts to shifts in the demand or supply schedules for a particular currency. Note that the bid/ask spread quoted by banks is not needed to explain this connection.

Increase in Demand Schedule   The U.S. demand for British pounds can change at any time. Assume that the demand for British pounds in the foreign exchange market increases (depicted graphically as an outward shift in the demand schedule) but that the supply schedule of British pounds for sale has not changed. Then the amount of pounds demanded in the foreign exchange market will be more than the amount for sale in the foreign exchange market at the prevailing price (exchange rate), resulting in a shortage of British pounds. The banks that serve as intermediaries in the foreign exchange market will not have enough British pounds to accommodate demand for pounds at the prevailing exchange rate. These banks will respond by raising the price (exchange rate) of the pound. As they raise the exchange rate, there will be a decline in the amount of British pounds demanded in the foreign exchange market as well as an increase in the amount of British pounds supplied (sold) in the foreign exchange market. The banks will increase the exchange rate to the level at which the amount of British pounds demanded is equal to the amount of British pounds supplied in the foreign exchange market.

Decrease in Demand Schedule   Now suppose that conditions cause the demand for British pounds to decrease (depicted graphically as an inward shift in the demand schedule) but that the supply schedule of British pounds for sale has not changed. Under these conditions, the amount of pounds demanded in the foreign exchange market will be less than the amount for sale in the foreign exchange market at the prevailing price (exchange rate). The banks that serve as intermediaries in this market will have an excess of British pounds at the prevailing exchange rate, and they will respond by lowering the price (exchange rate) of the pound. As they reduce the exchange rate, there will be an increase in the amount of British pounds demanded in the foreign exchange market and a decrease in the amount of British pounds supplied (sold) in that market. The banks will reduce the exchange rate to the level at which the amount of British pounds demanded is equal to the amount supplied in the foreign exchange market.

Increase in Supply Schedule   The demand of British firms, consumers, or government agencies for U.S. dollars can change at any time. Assume that conditions cause that British demand for U.S. dollars to increase. Then there is an increase in the amount of British pounds to be supplied (exchanged for dollars) in the foreign exchange market (depicted graphically as an outward shift in the supply schedule) even though the demand schedule for British pounds has not changed. In this case, the amount of the currency supplied in the foreign exchange market will exceed the amount of British pounds demanded in that market at the prevailing price (exchange rate), resulting in a surplus of British pounds. The banks that serve as intermediaries in the foreign exchange market will respond by reducing the price of the pound. As they reduce the exchange rate, there will be an increase in the amount of British pounds demanded in the foreign exchange market. The banks will reduce the exchange rate to the level at which the amount of British pounds demanded is equal to the amount of British pounds supplied (sold) in the foreign exchange market.

Decrease in Supply Schedule   Now assume that conditions cause British firms, consumers, and government agencies to need fewer U.S. dollars. Hence there is a decrease in the supply of British pounds to be exchanged for dollars in the foreign exchange market (depicted graphically as an inward shift in the supply schedule), although the demand schedule for British pounds has not changed. In this case, the amount of pounds supplied will be less than the amount demanded in the foreign exchange market at the prevailing price (exchange rate), resulting in a shortage of British pounds. Banks that serve as intermediaries in the foreign exchange market will respond by increasing the price (exchange rate) of the pound. As they increase the exchange rate, there will be a reduction in the amount of British pounds demanded and an increase in the amount of British pounds supplied. The banks will increase the exchange rate to the level at which the amount of British pounds demanded is equal to the amount of British pounds supplied (sold) in the foreign exchange market.

4-3 Factors That Influence Exchange Rates

The factors that cause currency supply and demand schedules to change are discussed next by relating each factor's influence to the demand and supply schedules graphed in Exhibit 4.4. The following equation summarizes the factors that can influence a currency's spot rate:

$$e = f(\Delta INF, \Delta INT, \Delta INC, \Delta GC, \Delta EXP)$$

where

e = percentage change in the spot rate

ΔINF = change in the differential between U.S. inflation and the foreign country's inflation

ΔINT = change in the differential between the U.S. interest rate and the foreign country's interest rate

ΔINC = change in the differential between the U.S. income level and the foreign country's income level

ΔGC = change in government controls

ΔEXP = change in expectations of future exchange rates

WEB

www.bloomberg.com
Latest information from financial markets around the world.

4-3a Relative Inflation Rates

Changes in relative inflation rates can affect international trade activity, which influences the demand for and supply of currencies and therefore affects exchange rates.

EXAMPLE

Consider how the demand and supply schedules displayed in Exhibit 4.4 would be affected if U.S. inflation suddenly increased substantially while British inflation remained the same. (Assume that both British and U.S. firms sell goods that can serve as substitutes for each other.) The sudden jump in U.S. inflation should cause some U.S. consumers to buy more British products instead of U.S. products. At any given exchange rate, there would be an increase in the U.S. demand for British goods, which represents an increase in the U.S. demand for British pounds in Exhibit 4.5.

In addition, the jump in U.S. inflation should reduce the British desire for U.S. goods and thereby reduce the supply of pounds for sale at any given exchange rate. These market reactions are illustrated in Exhibit 4.5. At the previous equilibrium exchange rate of $1.55, there will now be a shortage of pounds in the foreign exchange market. The increased U.S. demand for pounds and the reduced supply of pounds for sale together place upward pressure on the value of the pound. According to Exhibit 4.5, the new equilibrium value is $1.57. If British inflation increased (rather than U.S. inflation), the opposite dynamic would prevail. ●

Exhibit 4.5 Impact of Rising U.S. Inflation on Equilibrium Value of the British Pound

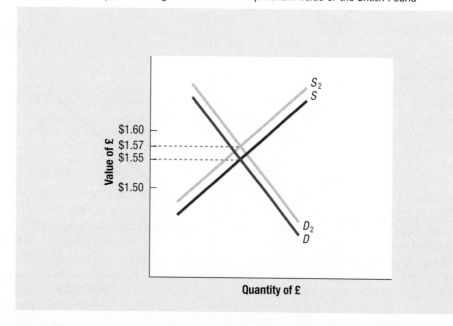

EXAMPLE

Assume there is a sudden and substantial increase in British inflation while U.S. inflation remains low. (1) How is the demand schedule for pounds affected? (2) How is the supply schedule of pounds for sale affected? (3) Will the new equilibrium value of the pound increase, decrease, or remain unchanged? Given the described circumstances, the answers are as follows: (1) The demand schedule for pounds should shift inward. (2) The supply schedule of pounds for sale should shift outward. (3) The new equilibrium value of the pound will decrease. Of course, the actual amount by which the pound's value will decrease depends on the magnitude of the shifts. Not enough information is given here to determine their exact magnitude. ●

In reality, the actual demand and supply schedules, and therefore the true equilibrium exchange rate, will reflect several factors simultaneously. The purpose of the preceding example is to demonstrate how the change in a single factor (higher inflation) can affect an exchange rate. Each factor can be assessed in isolation to determine its effect on exchange rates while holding all other factors constant. Then, all factors can be tied together to fully explain exchange rate movements.

4-3b Relative Interest Rates

Changes in relative interest rates affect investment in foreign securities, which influences the demand for and supply of currencies and thus affects the equilibrium exchange rate.

EXAMPLE

Assume that U.S. and British interest rates are initially equal but then U.S. interest rates rise while British rates remain constant. U.S. investors will likely reduce their demand for pounds, because U.S. rates are now more attractive than British rates.

Because U.S. rates now look more attractive to British investors with excess cash, the supply of pounds for sale by British investors should increase as they establish more bank deposits in the United States. In response to this inward shift in the demand for pounds and outward shift in the supply of pounds for sale, the equilibrium exchange rate should decrease. These movements are represented graphically in Exhibit 4.6. If U.S. interest rates decreased relative to British interest rates, then the opposite shifts would be expected. ●

Exhibit 4.6 Impact of Rising U.S. Interest Rates on Equilibrium Value of the British Pound

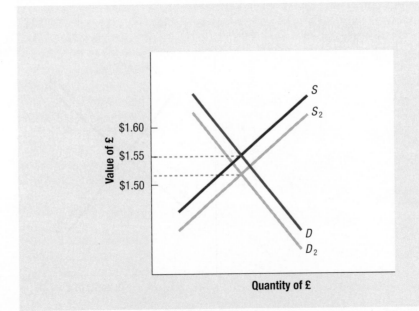

To ensure that you understand these effects, predict the shifts in both the supply and demand curves for British pounds as well as the likely impact of these shifts on the pound's value under the following scenario.

EXAMPLE

Assume that U.S. and British interest rates are initially equal but then British interest rates rise while U.S. rates remain constant. British interest rates may become more attractive to U.S. investors with excess cash, which would cause the demand for British pounds to increase. At the same time, U.S. interest rates should look less attractive to British investors, so the British supply of pounds for sale would decrease. Given this outward shift in the demand for pounds and inward shift in the supply of pounds for sale, the pound's equilibrium exchange rate should increase. ●

WEB

http://research.stlouisfed
.org/fred2
Numerous economic and
financial time series,
including balance-
of-payment statistics and
interest rates.

Many investors recognize that higher interest rates in a country could attract more funds and cause an increase in demand for the local currency. Yet they may have a better chance of benefitting from the possible appreciation if they invest in that currency before the interest rate has risen. Of course, the downside of this strategy is that the interest rate might not rise in the manner that they expect. In essence, their speculation on exchange rates also requires speculation on interest rates.

Real Interest Rates   Although a relatively high interest rate may attract foreign inflows (to invest in securities offering high yields), that high rate may reflect expectations of relatively high inflation. Because high inflation can place downward pressure on the local currency, some foreign investors may be discouraged from investing in securities denominated in that currency. In such cases it is useful to consider the **real interest rate**, which adjusts the nominal interest rate for inflation:

$$\textbf{Real interest rate} = \textbf{Nominal interest rate} - \textbf{Inflation rate}$$

This relationship is sometimes called the Fisher effect. It is explained in more detail in Chapter 8.

The real interest rate is appropriate for international comparisons of exchange rate movements because it incorporates both the nominal interest rate and inflation, each of which influences exchange rates. Other things held constant, a high U.S. real rate of interest (relative to other countries) tends to boost the dollar's value.

4-3c Relative Income Levels

A third factor affecting exchange rates is relative income levels. Because income can affect the amount of imports demanded, it can also affect exchange rates.

EXAMPLE

Assume that the U.S. income level rises substantially while the British income level remains unchanged. Consider the impact of this scenario on (1) the demand schedule for pounds, (2) the supply schedule of pounds for sale, and (3) the equilibrium exchange rate. First, the demand schedule for pounds will shift outward, reflecting the increase in U.S. income and attendant increased demand for British goods. Second, the supply schedule of pounds for sale is not expected to change. Hence the equilibrium exchange rate of the pound should rise, as shown in Exhibit 4.7. ●

This example presumes that other factors (including interest rates) are held constant. In reality, of course, other factors do not remain constant. An increasing U.S. income level likely reflects favorable economic conditions. Under such conditions, some British firms would probably increase their investment in U.S. operations, exchanging more British pounds for dollars so that they could expand their U.S. operations. In addition, British investors may well increase their investment in U.S. stocks in order to capitalize on the country's economic growth, a tendency that is also reflected in the increased sale (exchange) of pounds for U.S. dollars in the foreign exchange market. Thus the supply schedule of British pounds could increase (shift outward), which might more than offset

Exhibit 4.7 Impact of Rising U.S. Income Levels on Equilibrium Value of the British Pound

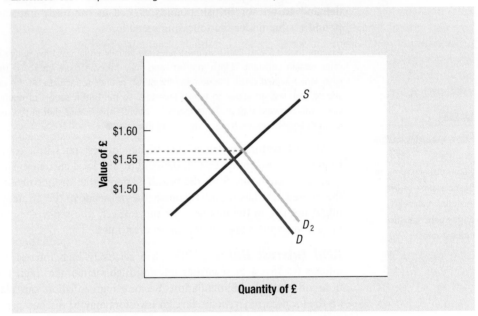

any impact on the demand schedule for pounds. Furthermore, an increase in U.S. income levels (and in U.S. economic growth) could also have an indirect effect on the pound's exchange rate by influencing interest rates. Under conditions of economic growth, the business demand for loans tends to increase and thus cause a rise in interest rates. Higher interest rates in the United States could attract more U.K.-based investors; this is another reason why the supply schedule of British pounds may increase enough to offset any effect of increased U.S. income levels on the demand schedule. The interaction of various factors that can affect exchange rates will be discussed in more detail once the other factors that could influence a currency's demand or supply schedule are identified.

4-3d **Government Controls**

A fourth factor affecting exchange rates is government controls. The governments of foreign countries can influence the equilibrium exchange rate in the following ways: (1) imposing foreign exchange barriers; (2) imposing foreign trade barriers; (3) intervening (buying and selling currencies) in the foreign exchange markets; and (4) affecting macro variables such as inflation, interest rates, and income levels. Chapter 6 covers these activities in detail.

EXAMPLE   Recall the example in which U.S. interest rates rose relative to British interest rates. The expected reaction was an increase in the British supply of pounds for sale to obtain more U.S. dollars (in order to capitalize on high U.S. money market yields). However, if the British government placed a heavy tax on interest income earned from foreign investments, such taxation would likely discourage the exchange of pounds for dollars. ●

4-3e **Expectations**

A fifth factor affecting exchange rates is market expectations of future exchange rates. Like other financial markets, foreign exchange markets react to any news that may have a future effect. News of a potential surge in U.S. inflation may cause currency traders to sell dollars because they anticipate a future decline in the dollar's value. This response places immediate downward pressure on the dollar.

Impact of Favorable Expectations

Many institutional investors (such as commercial banks and insurance companies) take currency positions based on anticipated interest rate movements in various countries.

EXAMPLE Investors may temporarily invest funds in Canada if they expect Canadian interest rates to increase, because this may cause further capital flows into Canada, which could place upward pressure on the Canadian dollar's value. By investing in securities denominated in Canadian dollars based on expectations, investors can fully benefit from the rise in the Canadian dollar's value because they will have purchased Canadian dollars before the change occurred. Although these investors face the obvious risk that their expectations may be wrong, the point is that expectations can influence exchange rates because they commonly motivate institutional investors to take foreign currency positions. ●

Impact of Unfavorable Expectations

Just as speculators can place upward pressure on a currency's value when they expect it to appreciate, they can place downward pressure on a currency when they expect it to depreciate.

WEB

www.ny.frb.org
Links to information on economic conditions that affect foreign exchange rates and potential speculation in the foreign exchange market.

EXAMPLE During the 2010–2015 period, Greece experienced a major debt crisis because of concerns that it could not repay its existing debt. Some institutional investors expected that the Greece crisis might spread throughout the eurozone, which could cause a flow of funds out of the eurozone. There were also concerns that Greece would abandon the euro as its currency, which caused additional concerns to investors who had investments in euro-denominated securities. Consequently, many institutional investors liquidated their investments in the eurozone, exchanging their euros for other currencies in the foreign exchange market. Investors who owned euro-denominated securities attempted to liquidate their positions before the euro's value declined. These conditions played a large part in the euro's substantial depreciation during this period. ●

Impact of a Currency Crisis

Sometimes a currency depreciates to such an extent that a currency crisis ensues. Many emerging markets have experienced a currency crisis. Some emerging markets seem to have a currency crisis every few years. Recent examples of countries experiencing a currency crisis include Argentina, India, and Turkey in February 2014. Although the specific conditions of each currency crisis vary among countries, an important factor in most crises is substantial uncertainty about the country's future economic or political conditions.

When a country experiences political problems, its appeal to foreign and local investors disappears. Foreign investors liquidate their investments and move their money out of the country. Local investors may follow the lead of the foreign investors by liquidating their investments and selling their local currency in exchange for the currencies of other countries so that they can move their money to a safer (more politically stable) environment.

Any concerns about a potential crisis can trigger money movements out of the country before the crisis fully develops. Yet such actions can themselves cause a major imbalance in the foreign exchange market and a significant decline in the local currency's value. That is, expectations of a crisis trigger actions that can make the crisis worse. The country's government might even attempt to impose foreign exchange restrictions in order to stabilize the currency situation, but this may create still more panic as local investors rush to move their money out of the country before restrictions are imposed.

Furthermore, some foreign exchange speculators may purposely try to capitalize on a currency crisis by borrowing the local currency that is expected to weaken and

Exhibit 4.8 Summary of How Factors Affect Exchange Rates

Trade-Related Factors

Inflation Differential
Income Differential
Government Trade Restrictions

→ U.S. Demand for Foreign Goods / Foreign Demand for U.S. Goods

→ U.S. Demand for the Foreign Currency / Supply of the Foreign Currency for Sale

→ Exchange Rate between the Foreign Currency and the Dollar

Financial Factors

Interest Rate Differential
Capital Flow Restrictions
Exchange Rate Expectations

→ U.S. Demand for Foreign Securities / Foreign Demand for U.S. Securities

→ U.S. Demand for the Foreign Currency / Supply of the Foreign Currency for Sale

exchanging it for other currencies in the foreign exchange market. Once the currency crisis occurs and the local currency's value declines substantially, they buy back that currency at a much lower price and repay their loan. Such speculation can add to the downward pressure on the currency's value.

4-3f Interaction of Factors

Transactions within foreign exchange markets facilitate either trade or financial flows. Trade-related foreign exchange transactions are generally less responsive to news. In contrast, financial flow transactions are extremely responsive to news because decisions to hold securities denominated in a particular currency often depend on anticipated changes in currency values. Sometimes trade-related factors and financial factors interact and simultaneously affect exchange rate movements.

Exhibit 4.8 separates payment flows between countries into trade-related and finance-related flows; it also summarizes the factors that affect these flows. Over a particular period, some factors may place upward pressure on the value of a foreign currency while other factors place downward pressure on that value.

The sensitivity of an exchange rate to these factors depends on the volume of international transactions between the two countries. If the two countries engage in a large volume of international trade but a small volume of international capital flows, then the relative inflation rates will likely be more influential. If the two countries engage in a large volume of capital flows, however, then interest rate fluctuations may be more influential.

EXAMPLE   Assume that Morgan Co., a U.S.-based MNC, frequently purchases supplies from Mexico and Japan and therefore desires to forecast the direction of the Mexican peso and the Japanese yen. Morgan's financial analysts have developed the following one-year projections for economic conditions.

FACTOR	UNITED STATES	MEXICO	JAPAN
Change in interest rates	−1%	−2%	−4%
Change in inflation	+2%	−3%	−6%

Assume that the United States and Mexico conduct a large volume of international trade but engage in minimal capital flow transactions. Also assume that the United States and Japan conduct very little international trade but frequently engage in capital flow transactions. The peso should be influenced most by trade-related factors because of Mexico's assumed heavy trade with the United States. The expected inflationary changes should place upward pressure on the value of the peso. Interest rates are expected to have little direct impact on the peso because of the assumed infrequent capital flow transactions between the United States and Mexico.

The Japanese yen should be most influenced by interest rates because of Japan's assumed heavy capital flow transactions with the United States. The expected interest rate changes should place downward pressure on the yen. The inflationary changes are expected to have little direct impact on the yen because of the assumed infrequent trade between the two countries. ●

Capital flows have become larger over time. A significant portion of capital flows are due to large institutional investors that commonly make large investments in securities denominated in specific currencies that may last only a day or two. The size of the capital flows can easily overwhelm trade flows. For this reason, the relationship between the factors (such as inflation and income) that affect trade and exchange rates is sometimes weaker than expected.

An understanding of exchange rate equilibrium does not guarantee accurate forecasts of future exchange rates, because that will depend in part on how the factors that affect exchange rates change in the future. Even if analysts fully realize how factors influence exchange rates, they may still be unable to predict how those factors will change.

4-3g Influence of Factors across Multiple Currency Markets

Each exchange rate has its own market, meaning its own demand and supply conditions. The value of the British pound in dollars is influenced by the U.S. demand for pounds and the amount of pounds supplied to the market (by British consumers and firms) in exchange for dollars. The value of the Swiss franc in dollars is influenced by the U.S. demand for francs and the amount of francs supplied to the market (by Swiss consumers and firms) in exchange for dollars.

In some periods, most currencies move in the same direction against the dollar. This is typically because of a particular underlying factor in the United States that has a similar impact on the demand and supply conditions across all currencies in that period.

EXAMPLE

Assume that interest rates are unusually low in the United States in a particular period, which causes U.S. firms and individual investors with excess short-term cash to invest their cash in various foreign currencies where interest rates are higher. This results in an increased U.S. demand for British pounds, Swiss francs, and euros as well as other currencies for countries in which the interest rate is relatively high (compared to the United States) and economic conditions are generally stable. Hence there is upward pressure on each of these currencies against the dollar.

Now assume that, in the following period, U.S. interest rates rise above the interest rates of European countries. This could cause the opposite flow of funds, as investors from European countries invest in dollars in order to capitalize on the higher U.S. interest rates. Consequently, there is an increased supply of British pounds, Swiss francs, and euros for sale by European investors in exchange for dollars. The excess supply of these currencies in the foreign exchange market places downward pressure on their values against the dollar. ●

It is not unusual for these European currencies to move in the same direction against the dollar because their economic conditions tend to change over time in a related manner. However, it is possible for one of the countries to experience different economic conditions in a particular period, which may cause its currency's movement against the dollar to deviate from the movements of other European currencies.

EXAMPLE | Continuing with the previous example, assume that U.S. interest rates remain relatively high compared to the European countries but that the Swiss government suddenly imposes a special tax on interest earned by Swiss firms and consumers from investments in foreign countries. Such a tax will reduce Swiss investment in the United States (and so reduce the supply of Swiss francs to be exchanged for dollars), which may stabilize the Swiss franc's value. Meanwhile, investors in other parts of Europe continue to exchange their euros for dollars to capitalize on high U.S. interest rates, which causes the euro to depreciate against the dollar. ●

4-3h Impact of Liquidity on Exchange Rate Adjustments

For all currencies, the equilibrium exchange rate is reached through transactions in the foreign exchange market; however, the adjustment process is more volatile for some currencies than others. The liquidity of a currency affects the exchange rate's sensitivity to specific transactions. If the currency's spot market is liquid, then its exchange rate will not be highly sensitive to a single large purchase or sale, so the change in the equilibrium exchange rate will be relatively small. With many willing buyers and sellers of the currency, transactions can be easily accommodated. In contrast, if a currency's spot market is illiquid, then its exchange rate may be highly sensitive to a single large purchase or sale transaction. In this case there are not enough buyers or sellers to accommodate a large transaction, which means that the price of the currency must change in order to rebalance its supply and demand. Illiquid currencies, such as those in emerging markets, tend to exhibit more volatile exchange rate movements because the equilibrium prices of their currencies adjust to even minor changes in supply and demand conditions.

EXAMPLE | The market for the Russian currency (the ruble) is not very active, which means that the volume of rubles purchased or sold in the foreign exchange market is small. Therefore, news that encourages speculators to take positions by purchasing rubles can create a major imbalance between the U.S. demand for rubles and the supply of rubles to be exchanged for dollars. So when U.S. speculators rush to invest in Russia, the result may be an abrupt increase in the ruble's value. Conversely, the ruble may decline abruptly when U.S. speculators attempt to withdraw their investments and exchange rubles back for dollars. ●

4-4 Movements in Cross Exchange Rates

Although much of this textbook focuses on movements in currency values against the dollar (reflecting a U.S. perspective), many international transactions involve the exchange of one non-dollar currency for another non-dollar currency, which is sometimes referred to as a cross exchange from a U.S. perspective.

There are distinct international trade and financial flows between every pair of countries. These flows dictate the unique supply and demand conditions for these two countries' currencies, conditions that affect movements in the equilibrium exchange rate between them. Thus a change in the equilibrium cross exchange rate between these two currencies is due to the same types of forces identified earlier in the chapter that affect the demand and supply conditions between the two currencies, as illustrated next.

Assume that the interest rates in Switzerland and the United Kingdom have been similar but that today the Swiss interest rates increased while British interest rates remain unchanged. If British investors wish to capitalize on the high Swiss interest rates, the result will be an increase in the British demand for Swiss francs. Assuming that the supply of Swiss francs to be exchanged for pounds is unchanged, the increased British demand for Swiss francs should cause the value of the Swiss franc to appreciate against the British pound. ●

The movement in a cross exchange rate over a particular period can be measured as its percentage change in that period, just as demonstrated previously for any currency's movement against the dollar. You can measure the percentage change in a cross exchange rate over some time period even when you lack cross exchange rate quotations; as shown here:

One year ago, you observed that the British pound was valued at $1.54 while the Swiss franc (SF) was valued at $.78. Today, the pound is valued at $1.60 and the Swiss franc is worth $.80. This information allows you to determine how the British pound changed against the Swiss franc over the last year:

$$\text{Cross rate of British pound one year ago} = 1.482/.78 = 1.9[\pounds 1 = SF1.9]$$
$$\text{Cross rate of British pound today} = 1.50/.75 = 2.0[\pounds 1 = SF2.0]$$
$$\text{Percentage change in cross rate of British pound} = (2.0 - 1.9)/1.9 = .05263.$$

Thus the British pound depreciated against the Swiss franc by about 5.26 percent over the last year. ●

The cross exchange rate changes when either currency's value changes against the dollar. These relationships are illustrated in Exhibit 4.9. The upper graph shows movements of the British pound value against the dollar and the Swiss franc value against the dollar; the lower graph shows the cross exchange rate (pound value against the Swiss franc). Notice the following relationships:

■ If the British pound and Swiss franc move by the same percentage against the dollar, then there is no change in the cross exchange rate. (Review the movements from year 1 to year 2 in Exhibit 4.9.)
■ If the British pound appreciates against the dollar by a greater percentage than the Swiss franc appreciates against the dollar, then the British pound appreciates against the Swiss franc. (Review the movements from year 2 to year 3 in Exhibit 4.9.)
■ If the British pound appreciates against the dollar by a smaller percentage than the Swiss franc appreciates against the dollar, then the British pound depreciates against the Swiss franc. (Review the movements from year 3 to year 4 in Exhibit 4.9.)
■ If the British pound depreciates against the dollar and the Swiss franc appreciates against the dollar, then the British pound depreciates against the Swiss franc. (Review the movements from year 4 to year 5 in Exhibit 4.9.)

4-5 Capitalizing on Expected Exchange Rate Movements

If spot exchange rates are priced properly, this implies that the foreign exchange market is *efficient*, and speculators will be unable to profit from expectations about exchange rate movements. However, if spot exchange rates are not priced properly, this implies that the foreign exchange market is not *efficient*, and there is potential for speculators to capitalize on the mispricing.

Some large financial institutions attempt to anticipate how the equilibrium exchange rate will change in the near future based on conditions identified in this chapter. These institutions may then take a position in that currency in order to benefit from their expectations.

Exhibit 4.9   Example of How Forces Affect the Cross Exchange Rate

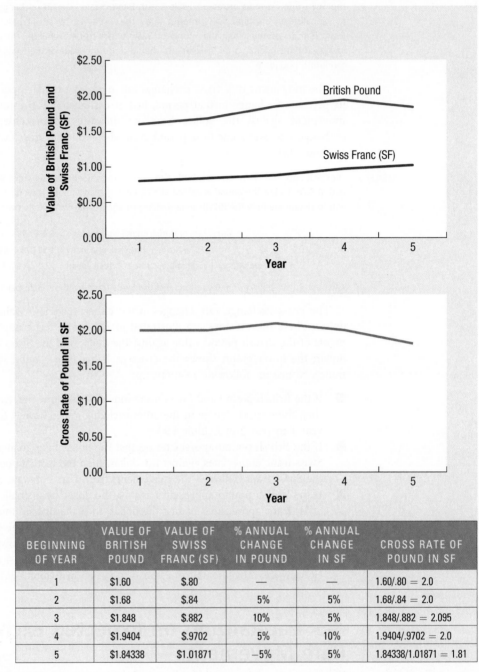

BEGINNING OF YEAR	VALUE OF BRITISH POUND	VALUE OF SWISS FRANC (SF)	% ANNUAL CHANGE IN POUND	% ANNUAL CHANGE IN SF	CROSS RATE OF POUND IN SF
1	$1.60	$.80	—	—	1.60/.80 = 2.0
2	$1.68	$.84	5%	5%	1.68/.84 = 2.0
3	$1.848	$.882	10%	5%	1.848/.882 = 2.095
4	$1.9404	$.9702	5%	10%	1.9404/.9702 = 2.0
5	$1.84338	$1.01871	−5%	5%	1.84338/1.01871 = 1.81

4-5a Institutional Speculation Based on Expected Appreciation

When financial institutions believe that a particular currency is presently valued lower than it should be in the foreign exchange market, they may consider investing in that currency now before it appreciates. They would hope to liquidate their investment in that currency after it appreciates and thus benefit from selling it for a higher price than they paid.

■ Chicago Co. expects the exchange rate of the New Zealand dollar (NZ$) to appreciate from its present level of $.50 to $.52 in 30 days.

■ Chicago Co. is able to borrow $20 million on a short-term basis from other banks.

■ Present short-term interest rates (annualized) in the interbank market are as given in the table.

CURRENCY	LENDING RATE	BORROWING RATE
U.S. dollars	6.72%	7.20%
New Zealand dollars (NZ$)	6.48%	6.96%

Given this information, Chicago Co. could proceed as follows.

1. Borrow $20 million.
2. Convert the $20 million to NZ$40 million (computed as $20,000,000/$.50).
3. Invest the New Zealand dollars at 6.48 percent annualized, which represents a .54 percent return over the 30-day period [computed as 6.48% × (30/360)]. After 30 days, Chicago Co. will receive NZ$40,216,000 [computed as NZ$40,000,000 × (1 + .0054)].
4. Use the proceeds from the New Zealand dollar investment (on day 30) to repay the U.S. dollars borrowed. The annual interest on the U.S. dollars borrowed is 7.2 percent, or .6 percent over the 30-day period [computed as 7.2% × (30/360)]. The total U.S. dollar amount necessary to repay the U.S. dollar loan is therefore $20,120,000 [computed as $20,000,000 × (1 + .006)].

If the exchange rate on day 30 is $.52 per New Zealand dollar, as anticipated, then the number of New Zealand dollars necessary to repay the U.S. dollar loan is NZ$38,692,308 (computed as $20,120,000/$.52 per New Zealand dollar).

Given that Chicago Co. accumulated NZ$40,216,000 from lending New Zealand dollars, it would earn a speculative profit of NZ$1,523,692, which is equivalent to $792,320 (given a spot rate of $.52 per New Zealand dollar on day 30). The firm could earn this speculative profit without using any funds from deposit accounts because the funds would be borrowed through the interbank market. ●

Keep in mind that the computations in the example measure the expected profits from the speculative strategy. There is a risk that the actual outcome will be less favorable if the currency appreciates to a smaller degree (and much less favorable if it depreciates).

4-5b Institutional Speculation Based on Expected Depreciation

If financial institutions believe that a particular currency is presently valued higher than it should be in the foreign exchange market, they may borrow funds in that currency now and convert it to their local currency now—that is, before the target currency's value declines to its "proper" level. The plan would be to repay the loan in that currency after it depreciates, so that the institutions could buy that currency for a lower price than the one at which it was initially converted to their own currency.

Assume that Carbondale Co. expects an exchange rate of $.48 for the New Zealand dollar on day 30. It can borrow New Zealand dollars, convert them to U.S. dollars, and lend the U.S. dollars out. On day 30, it will close out these positions. Using the rates quoted in the previous example and assuming that the firm can borrow NZ$40 million, Carbondale takes the following steps.

1. Borrow NZ$40 million.
2. Convert the NZ$40 million to $20 million (computed as NZ$40,000,000 × $.50).
3. Lend the U.S. dollars at 6.72 percent, which represents a .56 percent return over the 30-day period. After 30 days, it will receive $20,112,000 [computed as $20,000,000 × (1 + .0056)].
4. Use the proceeds of the U.S. dollar loan repayment (on day 30) to repay the New Zealand dollars borrowed. The annual interest on the New Zealand dollars borrowed is 6.96 percent, or .58 percent

over the 30-day period [computed as 6.96% × (30/360)]. The total New Zealand dollar amount necessary to repay the loan is therefore NZ$40,232,000 [computed as NZ$40,000,000 × (1 + .0058)].

If the exchange rate on day 30 is $.48 per New Zealand dollar, as anticipated, then the number of U.S. dollars necessary to repay the NZ$ loan is $19,311,360 (computed as NZ$40,232,000 × $.48 per New Zealand dollar). Given that Carbondale accumulated $20,112,000 from its U.S. dollar loan, it would earn a speculative profit of $800,640 without using any of its own money (computed as $20,112,000 − $19,311,360). ●

WEB

www.forex.com

Individuals can open a foreign exchange trading account with a small amount of money.

Most money center banks continue to take some speculative positions in foreign currencies. In fact, some banks' currency trading profits have exceeded $100 million per quarter.

The potential returns from foreign currency speculation are high for financial institutions that have large borrowing capacity. Yet because foreign exchange rates are volatile, a poor forecast could result in a large loss. Some MNCs have suffered losses of more than $1 billion due to speculation in the foreign exchange market.

WEB

www.fxcm.com

Facilitates the trading of foreign currencies.

4-5c Speculation by Individuals

There is speculation in foreign currencies even by individuals whose careers have nothing to do with foreign exchange markets. Individuals can take positions in the currency futures market or options market, as detailed in Chapter 5. Alternatively, they can set up an account at a foreign exchange trading website (such as **fxcm.com**) with a small initial amount, after which they can move their money into one or more foreign currencies. Individuals can also establish a *margin account* on some websites; in this way, they can take positions in foreign currency while financing a portion of their investment with borrowed funds.

Some speculators in the foreign exchange market have been allowed to maintain a cash amount of only 5 percent of their investment, while borrowing the remainder. This substantially magnifies the return that the speculators can earn on their speculative position. However, it also substantially magnifies their risk. When speculators borrow this amount of money, a currency's movement on a single day could wipe out their entire cash position.

Many of the websites have a demonstration (demo) that allows prospective speculators to simulate the process of speculating in the foreign exchange market. Thus speculators can determine how much they would have earned or lost by pretending to take a position with an assumed investment and borrowed funds.

Individual speculators quickly realize that the foreign exchange market remains active even after financial markets in their own country close. This means that the value of a currency can change substantially overnight while local financial markets are closed or support only limited trading. Individuals are naturally attracted by the potential for large gains, but just as with other forms of gambling, there is the risk of losing the entire investment. In that case, they would still be liable for any debt created from borrowing money to support the speculative position.

4-5d The "Carry Trade"

One of the most common strategies used by institutional and individual investors to speculate in the foreign exchange market is the *carry trade*, whereby investors attempt to capitalize on the difference in interest rates between two countries. Specifically, the strategy involves borrowing a currency with a low interest rate and investing the funds in a currency with a high interest rate. The investor may execute a carry trade for only a day or for several months. The term "carry trade" is derived from the phrase "cost of carry," which in financial markets represents the cost of holding (or carrying) a position in some asset.

Institutional and individual investors engage in carry trades, and there are brokers who facilitate both the borrowing of one currency (assuming the investor posts adequate collateral) and the investing in a different currency. There are numerous websites established by brokers that facilitate this process.

Before taking any speculative position in a foreign currency, carry traders must consider the prevailing interest rates at which they can invest or borrow in addition to their expectations about the movement of exchange rates.

EXAMPLE Hampton Investment Co. is a U.S. firm that executes a carry trade in which it borrows euros (where interest rates are presently low) and invests in British pounds (where interest rates are presently high). Hampton uses $100,000 of its own funds and borrows an additional 600,000 euros. It will pay .5 percent on its euros borrowed for the next month and will earn 1.0 percent on funds invested in British pounds. Assume that the euro's spot rate is $1.20 and that the British pound's spot rate is $1.80 (so the pound is worth 1.5 euros at this time). Hampton uses today's spot rate as its best guess of the spot rate one month from now. Hampton's expected profits from its carry trade can be derived as follows.

At Beginning of Investment Period

1. Hampton invests $100,000 of its own funds into British pounds:

   $100,000/$1.80 per pound = 55,555 pounds

2. Hampton borrows 600,000 euros and converts them into British pounds:

   600,000 euros/1.5 euros per pound = 400,000 pounds

3. Hampton's total investment in pounds:

   55,555 pounds + 400,000 pounds = 455,555 pounds

At End of Investment Period

4. Hampton receives:

   455,555 × 1.01 = 460,110 pounds

5. Hampton repays loan in euros:

   600,000 euros × 1.005 = 603,000 euros

6. Amount of pounds Hampton needs to repay loan in euros:

   603,000 euros/1.5 euros per pound = 402,000 pounds

7. Amount of pounds Hampton has after repaying loan:

   460,110 pounds − 402,000 pounds = 58,110 pounds

8. Hampton converts pounds held into U.S. dollars:

   58,110 pounds × $1.80 per pound = $104,598

9. Hampton's profit:

   $104,598 − $100,000 = $4,598

The profit of $4,598 to Hampton as a percentage of its own funds used in this carry trade strategy over a one-month period is therefore $4,598/$100,000 = 4.598%. ●

Notice the large return to Hampton over a single month, even though the interest rate on its investment is only .5 percent above its borrowing rate. Such a high return on its investment over a one-month period is possible when Hampton borrows a large portion of the funds used for its investment. This illustrates the power of financial leverage.

At the end of the month, Hampton may roll over (repeat) its position for the next month. Alternatively, it could decide to execute a new carry trade transaction in which it borrows a different currency and invests in still another currency.

Impact of Appreciation in the Investment Currency   If the British pound had appreciated against both the euro and the dollar during the month, Hampton's profits would be even higher for two reasons. First, if the pound appreciated against the euro, then each British pound at the end of the month would have converted into more euros and so Hampton would have needed fewer British pounds to repay the funds borrowed in euros. Second, if the pound also appreciated against the dollar then the remaining British pounds held (after repaying the loan) would have converted into more dollars. Thus the choice of the currencies to borrow and purchase is influenced not only by prevailing interest rates but also by expected exchange rate movements. Investors prefer to borrow a currency with a low interest rate that they expect will weaken and to invest in a currency with a high interest rate that they expect will strengthen.

When many investors executing carry trades share the same expectations about a particular currency, they execute similar types of transactions and their trading volume can have a major influence on exchange rate movements over a short period. Over time, as many carry traders borrow one currency and convert it into another, there is downward pressure on the currency being converted (sold), and upward pressure on the currency being purchased. This type of pressure on the exchange rate may enhance investor profits.

Risk of the Carry Trade

The risk of the carry trade is that exchange rates may move opposite to what the investors expected, which would cause a loss. Just as financial leverage can magnify gains from a carry trade, it can also magnify losses from a carry trade when the currency that was borrowed appreciates against the investment currency. This dynamic is illustrated in the following example.

EXAMPLE   Assume the same conditions as in the previous example but with one adjustment. Namely, suppose the euro appreciated by 3 percent over the month against both the pound and the dollar; this means that, at the end of the investment period, the euro is worth $1.236 and a pound is worth 1.456 euros. Under these conditions, Hampton's profit from its carry trade is measured below. The changes from the previous example are highlighted below.

At Beginning of Investment Period

1. Hampton invests $100,000 of its own funds into British pounds:
   100,000/$1.80 per pound = 55,555 pounds
2. Hampton borrows 600,000 euros and converts them into British pounds:
   600,000 euros/1.5 euros per pound = 400,000 pounds
3. Hampton's total investment in pounds:
   55,555 pounds + 400,000 pounds = 455,555 pounds

At End of Investment Period

4. Hampton receives:
   455,555 × 1.01 = 460,110 pounds
5. Hampton repays loan in euros:
   600,000 euros × 1.005 = 603,000 euros
6. Amount of pounds Hampton needs to repay loan in euros:
   603,000 euros/1.456 euros per pound = 414,148 pounds
7. Amount of pounds Hampton has after repaying loan:
   460,110 pounds − 414,148 pounds = 45,962 pounds
8. Hampton converts pounds held into U.S. dollars:
   45,962 pounds × $1.80 per pound = $82,731
9. Hampton's profit:
   $82,731 − $100,000 = −$17,268

In this case, Hampton experiences a loss that amounts to nearly 17 percent of its original $100,000 investment. ●

Hampton's loss is due to the euro's appreciation against the pound, which increased the number of pounds that Hampton needed to repay the euro loan. Consequently, Hampton had fewer pounds to convert into dollars at the end of the month. Because of its high financial leverage (its high level of borrowed funds relative to its total investment), Hampton's losses are magnified.

In periods when changing conditions impel carry traders to question their trade positions, many such traders will attempt to *unwind* (reverse) their positions. This activity can have a major impact on the exchange rate.

EXAMPLE Over the last several months, many carry traders have borrowed euros and purchased British pounds. Today, governments in the eurozone announced a new policy that will likely attract much more investment to the eurozone, which in turn will cause the euro's value to appreciate. Because the euro's appreciation against the pound will adversely affect carry trade positions, many traders decide to unwind their positions. They liquidate their investments in British pounds, selling pounds in exchange for euros in the foreign exchange market so that they can repay their loans in euros now (before the euro appreciates even more). Because many carry traders are simultaneously executing the same types of transactions, there is additional downward pressure on the British pound's value relative to the euro. This can result in major losses to carry traders because it means they will need more British pounds to obtain enough euros to repay their loans. ●

SUMMARY

■ Exchange rate movements are commonly measured by the percentage change in their values over a specified period, such as a month or a year. Multinational corporations closely monitor exchange rate movements over the period in which they have cash flows denominated in the foreign currencies of concern.

■ The equilibrium exchange rate between two currencies at any time is based on the demand and supply conditions. Changes in the demand for a currency or in the supply of a currency for sale will affect the equilibrium exchange rate.

■ The key economic factors that can influence exchange rate movements through their effects on demand and supply conditions are relative inflation rates, interest rates, income levels, and government controls. When these factors lead to a change in international trade or financial flows, they affect the demand for a currency or the supply of currency for sale and thus the equilibrium exchange rate. If a foreign country experiences an increase in interest rates (relative to U.S. interest rates), then the inflow of U.S. funds to purchase its securities should increase (U.S. demand for its currency increases),

the outflow of its funds to purchase U.S. securities should decrease (supply of its currency to be exchanged for U.S. dollars decreases), and there should be upward pressure on its currency's equilibrium value. All relevant factors must be considered simultaneously when attempting to predict the most likely movement in a currency's value.

■ There are distinct international trade and financial flows between every pair of countries. These flows dictate the unique supply and demand conditions for the currencies of the two countries, which affect the equilibrium cross exchange rate between their currencies. Movement in the exchange rate between two non-dollar currencies can be inferred from the movement of each currency against the dollar.

■ Financial institutions may attempt to profit from their expectation that a currency will appreciate by investing in securities denominated in that currency. They might also attempt to profit from their expectation that a currency will depreciate by borrowing that currency, exchanging it for their home currency, and paying off the loan once the borrowed currency has depreciated.

POINT COUNTER-POINT

How Can Persistently Weak Currencies Be Stabilized?

Point The currencies of some Latin American countries depreciate against the U.S. dollar on a consistent basis. The governments of these countries need to attract more capital flows by raising interest rates and making their currencies more attractive. They also need to insure bank deposits so that foreign investors who invest in large bank deposits do not need to worry about default risk. In addition, they could impose capital restrictions on local investors to prevent capital outflows.

Counter-Point Some Latin American countries have had high inflation, which encourages local firms and consumers to purchase products from the United

States instead. Thus these countries could relieve the downward pressure on their local currencies by reducing inflation. To reduce inflation, a country may have to reduce economic growth temporarily. These countries should not raise their interest rates in order to attract foreign investment because they will still not attract funds if investors fear that there will be large capital outflows upon the first threat of continued depreciation.

Who Is Correct? Use the Internet to learn more about this issue. Which argument do you support? Offer your own opinion on this issue.

SELF-TEST

Answers are provided in Appendix A at the back of the text.

1. Briefly describe how various economic factors can affect the equilibrium exchange rate of the Japanese yen's value with respect to that of the dollar.

2. A recent shift in the interest rate differential between the United States and Country A had a large effect on the value of Currency A. However, the same shift in the interest rate differential between the United

States and Country B had no effect on the value of Currency B. Explain why the effects may vary.

3. Smart Banking Corp. can borrow $5 million at 6 percent annualized. It can use the proceeds to invest in Canadian dollars at 9 percent annualized over a 6-day period. The Canadian dollar is worth $.95 and is expected to be worth $.94 in 6 days. Based on this information, should Smart Banking Corp. borrow U.S. dollars and invest in Canadian dollars? What would be the gain or loss in U.S. dollars?

QUESTIONS AND APPLICATIONS

1. Percentage Depreciation Assume the spot rate of the British pound is $1.73. The expected spot rate 1 year from now is assumed to be $1.66. What percentage depreciation does this reflect?

2. Inflation Effects on Exchange Rates Assume that the U.S. inflation rate becomes high relative to Canadian inflation. Other things being equal, how should this affect the (a) U.S. demand for Canadian dollars, (b) supply of Canadian dollars for sale, and (c) equilibrium value of the Canadian dollar?

3. Interest Rate Effects on Exchange Rates Assume U.S. interest rates fall relative to British interest rates. Other things being equal, how should this affect the (a) U.S. demand for British pounds,

(b) supply of pounds for sale, and (c) equilibrium value of the pound?

4. Income Effects on Exchange Rates Assume that the U.S. income level rises at a much higher rate than does the Canadian income level. Other things being equal, how should this affect the (a) U.S. demand for Canadian dollars, (b) supply of Canadian dollars for sale, and (c) equilibrium value of the Canadian dollar?

5. Trade Restriction Effects on Exchange Rates Assume that the Japanese government relaxes its controls on imports by Japanese companies. Other things being equal, how should this affect the (a) U.S. demand for Japanese yen, (b) supply of yen for sale, and (c) equilibrium value of the yen?

6. Effects of Real Interest Rates What is the expected relationship between the relative real interest rates of two countries and the exchange rate of their currencies?

7. Speculative Effects on Exchange Rates Explain why a public forecast by a respected economist about future interest rates could affect the value of the dollar today. Why do some forecasts by well-respected economists have no impact on today's value of the dollar?

8. Factors Affecting Exchange Rates What factors affect the future movements in the value of the euro against the dollar?

9. Interaction of Exchange Rates Assume that there are substantial capital flows among Canada, the United States, and Japan. If interest rates in Canada decline to a level below the U.S. interest rate, and inflationary expectations remain unchanged, how could this affect the value of the Canadian dollar against the U.S. dollar? How might this decline in Canada's interest rates possibly affect the value of the Canadian dollar against the Japanese yen?

10. Trade Deficit Effects on Exchange Rates Every month, the U.S. trade deficit figures are announced. Foreign exchange traders often react to this announcement and even attempt to forecast the figures before they are announced.

a. Why do you think the trade deficit announcement sometimes has such an impact on foreign exchange trading?

b. In some periods, foreign exchange traders do not respond to a trade deficit announcement, even when the announced deficit is very large. Offer an explanation for such a lack of response.

11. Comovements of Exchange Rates Explain why the value of the British pound against the dollar will not always move in tandem with the value of the euro against the dollar.

12. Factors Affecting Exchange Rates In some periods, Brazil's inflation rate was very high. Explain why this places pressure on the Brazilian currency.

13. National Income Effects Analysts commonly attribute the appreciation of a currency to expectations that economic conditions will strengthen. Yet, this chapter suggests that when other factors are held constant, increased national income could increase imports and cause the local currency to weaken. In reality, other factors are not constant. What other factor is likely to be

affected by increased economic growth and could place upward pressure on the value of the local currency?

14. Factors Affecting Exchange Rates If Asian countries experience a decline in economic growth (and experience a decline in inflation and interest rates as a result), how will their currency values (relative to the U.S. dollar) be affected?

15. Impact of Crises Why do you think most crises in countries cause the local currency to weaken abruptly? Is it because of trade or capital flows?

16. Economic Impact on Capital Flows How do you think the weaker U.S. economic conditions could affect capital flows? If capital flows are affected, how would this influence the value of the dollar (holding other factors constant)?

Advanced Questions

17. Measuring Effects on Exchange Rates Tarheel Co. plans to determine how changes in U.S. and Mexican real interest rates will affect the value of the U.S. dollar. (See Appendix C for the basics of regression analysis.)

a. Describe a regression model that could be used to achieve this purpose. Also explain the expected sign of the regression coefficient.

b. If Tarheel Co. thinks that the existence of a quota in particular historical periods may have affected exchange rates, how might this be accounted for in the regression model?

18. Factors Affecting Exchange Rates Mexico tends to have much higher inflation than the United States and also much higher interest rates than the United States. Inflation and interest rates are much more volatile in Mexico than in industrialized countries. The value of the Mexican peso is typically more volatile than the currencies of industrialized countries from a U.S. perspective; it has typically depreciated from one year to the next, but the degree of depreciation has varied substantially. The bid/ask spread tends to be wider for the peso than for currencies of industrialized countries.

a. Identify the most obvious economic reason for the persistent depreciation of the peso.

b. High interest rates are commonly expected to strengthen a country's currency because they can encourage foreign investment in securities in that country, which results in the exchange of other currencies for that currency. Yet, the peso's value has declined against the dollar over most years even though Mexican interest rates are typically much higher than U.S. interest rates. Thus it appears that the high Mexican interest rates do not attract substantial U.S. investment in Mexico's securities. Why do you think U.S. investors do not try to capitalize on the high interest rates in Mexico?

c. Why do you think the bid/ask spread is higher for pesos than for currencies of industrialized countries? How does this affect a U.S. firm that does substantial business in Mexico?

19. Aggregate Effects on Exchange Rates

Assume that the United States invests heavily in government and corporate securities of Country K. In addition, residents of Country K invest heavily in the United States. Approximately $10 billion worth of investment transactions occur between these two countries each year. The total dollar value of trade transactions per year is about $8 million. This information is expected to also hold in the future.

Because your firm exports goods to Country K, your job as international cash manager requires you to forecast the value of Country K's currency (the "krank") with respect to the dollar. Explain how each of the following conditions will affect the value of the krank, holding other things equal. Then, aggregate all of these impacts to develop an overall forecast of the krank's movement against the dollar.

a. U.S. inflation has suddenly increased substantially, while Country K's inflation remains low.

b. U.S. interest rates have increased substantially, while Country K's interest rates remain low. Investors of both countries are attracted to high interest rates.

c. The U.S. income level increased substantially, while Country K's income level has remained unchanged.

d. The United States is expected to impose a small tariff on goods imported from Country K.

e. Combine all expected impacts to develop an overall forecast.

20. Speculation

Blue Demon Bank expects that the Mexican peso will depreciate against the dollar from its spot rate of $.15 to $.14 in 10 days. The following interbank lending and borrowing rates exist:

CURRENCY	LENDING RATE	BORROWING RATE
U.S. dollar	8.0%	8.3%
Mexican peso	8.5%	8.7%

Assume that Blue Demon Bank has a borrowing capacity of either $10 million or 70 million pesos in the interbank market, depending on which currency it wants to borrow.

a. How could Blue Demon Bank attempt to capitalize on its expectations without using deposited funds? Estimate the profits that could be generated from this strategy.

b. Assume all the preceding information with this exception: Blue Demon Bank expects the peso to appreciate from its present spot rate of $.15 to $.17 in 30 days. How could it attempt to capitalize on its expectations without using deposited funds? Estimate the profits that could be generated from this strategy.

21. Speculation

Diamond Bank expects that the Singapore dollar will depreciate against the U.S. dollar from its spot rate of $.43 to $.42 in 60 days. The following interbank lending and borrowing rates exist:

CURRENCY	LENDING RATE	BORROWING RATE
U.S. dollar	7.0%	7.2%
Singapore dollar	22.0%	24.0%

Diamond Bank considers borrowing 10 million Singapore dollars in the interbank market and investing the funds in U.S. dollars for 60 days. Estimate the profits (or losses) that could be earned from this strategy. Should Diamond Bank pursue this strategy?

22. Relative Importance of Factors Affecting Exchange Rate Risk

Assume that the level of capital flows between the United States and the country of Krendo is negligible (close to zero) and will continue to be negligible. There is a substantial amount of trade between the United States and the country of Krendo and no capital flows. How will high inflation and high interest rates affect the value of the kren (Krendo's currency)? Explain.

23. Assessing the Euro's Potential Movements

You reside in the United States and are planning to make a one-year investment in Germany during the next year. Because the investment is denominated in euros, you want to forecast how the euro's value may change against the dollar over the one-year period. You expect that Germany will experience an inflation rate of 1 percent during the next year, while all other European countries will experience an inflation rate of 8 percent over the next year. You expect that the United

States will experience an annual inflation rate of 2 percent during the next year. You believe that the primary factor that affects any exchange rate is the inflation rate. Based on the information provided in this question, will the euro appreciate, depreciate, or stay at about the same level against the dollar over the next year? Explain.

24. Weighing Factors That Affect Exchange Rates Assume that the level of capital flows between the United States and the country of Zeus is negligible (close to zero) and will continue to be negligible. There is a substantial amount of trade between the United States and the country of Zeus. The main import by the United States is basic clothing purchased by U.S. retail stores from Zeus, while the main import by Zeus is special computer chips that are only made in the United States and are needed by many manufacturers in Zeus. Suddenly, the U.S. government decides to impose a 20 percent tax on the clothing imports. The Zeus government immediately retaliates by imposing a 20 percent tax on the computer chip imports. Second, the Zeus government immediately imposes a 60 percent tax on any interest income that would be earned by Zeus investors if they buy U.S. securities. Third, the Zeus central bank raises its local interest rates so that they are now higher than interest rates in the United States. Do you think the currency of Zeus (called the zee) will appreciate or depreciate against the dollar as a result of all the government actions described above? Explain.

25. How Factors Affect Exchange Rates The country of Luta has large capital flows with the United States. It has no trade with the United States and will not have trade with the United States in the future. Its interest rate is 6 percent, the same as the U.S. interest rate. Its rate of inflation is 5 percent, the same as the U.S. inflation rate. You expect that the inflation rate in Luta will rise to 8 percent this coming year, while the U.S. inflation rate will remain at 5 percent. You expect that Luta's interest rate will rise to 9 percent during the next year. You expect that the U.S. interest rate will remain at 6 percent this year. Do you think Luta's currency will appreciate, depreciate, or remain unchanged against the dollar? Briefly explain.

26. Speculation on Expected Exchange Rates Kurnick Co. expects that the pound will depreciate from $1.70 to $1.68 in one year. It has no money to invest, but it could borrow money to invest. A bank allows it to borrow either 1 million dollars or 1 million pounds for one year. It can borrow dollars at 6 percent or British pounds at 5 percent for one year. It can invest in a risk-free dollar deposit at 5 percent for one year or a risk-free British deposit at 4 percent for one year. Determine the expected profit or loss (in dollars) if Kurnick Co. pursues a strategy to capitalize on the expected depreciation of the pound.

27. Assessing Volatility of Exchange Rate Movements Assume you want to determine whether the monthly movements in the Polish zloty against the dollar are more volatile than monthly movements in some other currencies against the dollar. The zloty was valued at $.4602 on May 1, $.4709 on June 1, $.4888 on July 1, $.4406 on August 1, and $.4260 on September 1. Using Excel or another electronic spreadsheet, compute the standard deviation (a measure of volatility) of the zloty's monthly exchange rate movements. Show your spreadsheet.

28. Impact of Economy on Exchange Rates Assume that inflation is zero in the United States and in Europe and will remain at zero. U.S. interest rates are presently the same as in Europe. Assume that the economic growth for the United States is presently similar to Europe. Assume that international capital flows are much larger than international trade flows. Today, there is news that clearly signals economic conditions in Europe will be weakening in the future, while economic conditions in the United States will remain the same. Explain why and how (which direction) the euro's value would change today based on this information.

29. Movements in Cross Exchange Rates Last year a dollar was equal to 7 Swedish kronor, and a Polish zloty was equal to $.40. Today, the dollar is equal to 8 Swedish kronor, and a Polish zloty is equal to $.44. By what percentage did the cross exchange rate of the Polish zloty in Swedish kronor (i.e., the number of kronor that can be purchased with one zloty) change over the last year?

30. Measuring Exchange Rate Volatility Here are exchange rates for the Japanese yen and British pound at the beginning of each of the last five years. Your firm wants to determine which currency is more volatile as it assesses its exposure to exchange rate risk. Estimate the volatility of each currency's movements.

BEGINNING OF YEAR	YEN	POUND
1	0.008	1.47
2	0.011	1.46
3	0.008	1.51
4	0.01	1.54
5	0.012	1.52

31. Impact of Economy on Exchange Rate The country of Quinland has large capital flows with the United States. It has no trade with the United States and will not have trade with the United States in the future. Its interest rate is 6 percent, the same as the U.S. interest rate. You expect that the inflation rate in Quinland will be 1 percent this coming year, while the U.S. inflation rate will be 9 percent. You expect that Quinland's interest rate will be 2 percent during the next year, while the U.S. interest rate will rise to 10 percent during the next year. Quinland's currency adjusts in response to market forces. Will Quinland's currency appreciate, depreciate, or remain unchanged against the dollar?

32. Impact of Economy on Exchange Rate The country of Zars has large capital flows with the United States. It has no trade with the United States and will not have trade with the United States in the future. Its interest rate is 6 percent, the same as the U.S. interest rate. Its rate of inflation is 5 percent, the same as the U.S. inflation rate. You expect that the inflation rate in Zars will rise to 8 percent this coming year, while the U.S. inflation rate will remain at 5 percent. You expect that Zars's interest rate will rise to 9 percent during the next year. You expect that the U.S. interest rate will remain at 6 percent this year. Zars's currency adjusts in response to market forces and is not subject to direct central bank intervention. Will Zars's currency appreciate, depreciate, or remain unchanged against the dollar?

33. Impact of Economy on Exchange Rates The country of Vezot has massive capital flows with the United States because it has no restrictions on the movement of investment funds into or out of the country. Vezot's inflation rate just increased substantially, while the U.S. inflation rate remains unchanged. Vezot's interest rate just increased substantially, while the U.S. interest rate remains unchanged. Vezot's income level recently increased substantially, which will increase consumption of products within its country.

The U.S. income level remains unchanged. There is negligible international trade between Vezot and the United States. Vezot can easily obtain all of its imported products from border countries instead of the United States. Starting today, the United States has imposed very large taxes on U.S. importers that import products from Vezot. Vezot does not impose restrictions on imports from the United States. Vezot's currency is freely floating. Based on the information above, do you think Vezot's currency will appreciate, depreciate, or remain unchanged against the dollar? Briefly explain.

34. Foreign Exchange Transactions Assume the country of Neeland has stable and predictable international trade flows with the United States. Neeland is periodically in the news because its government might have problems repaying its debt owed to local banks. The value of its currency (the "nee") commonly declines on one day, but then jumps back up a few days later. There is much day-to-day volatility in the value of the nee. Briefly explain what types of transactions are likely causing the shifts in demand for the nee and supply of nee for sale in the foreign exchange market.

35. Weighing the Influence of Factors on Exchange Rates The New Zealand dollar's spot rate was equal to $.60 last month. New Zealand conducts much international trade with the United States but the financial (investment) transactions between the two countries are negligible. Assume the following conditions have occurred in the last year. First, interest rates increased in New Zealand but decreased in the United States. Second, inflation increased in New Zealand but decreased in the United States. Third, the New Zealand central bank intervened in the foreign exchange market by exchanging a very small amount of U.S. dollars to purchase a very small amount of New Zealand dollars. How should the New Zealand dollar change over the year based on the information provided here?

Critical Thinking

Solving a Currency Crisis   Review a recent currency crisis in a foreign country in the last year or so, using an online search term such as "currency crisis." Summarize the details of the currency crisis, and write a short essay to offer your opinion on whether the country should have attempted to impose a fixed exchange rate system for its currency to prevent the currency crisis.

Discussion in the Boardroom

This exercise can be found in Appendix E at the back of this textbook.

Running Your Own MNC

This exercise can be found on the *International Financial Management* text companion website. Go to

www.cengagebrain.com (students) or www.cengage .com/login (instructors) and search using **ISBN 9781133947837**.

BLADES, INC. CASE

Assessment of Future Exchange Rate Movements

As the chief financial officer of Blades, Inc., Ben Holt is pleased that his current system of exporting "Speedos" to Thailand seems to be working well. Blades' primary customer in Thailand, a retailer called Entertainment Products, has committed itself to purchasing a fixed number of Speedos annually for the next three years at a fixed price denominated in baht, Thailand's currency. Furthermore, Blades is using a Thai supplier for some of the components needed to manufacture Speedos. Nevertheless, Holt is concerned about recent developments in Asia. Foreign investors from various countries had invested heavily in Thailand to take advantage of the high interest rates there. As a result of the weak economy in Thailand, however, many foreign investors have lost confidence in Thailand and have withdrawn their funds.

Holt has two major concerns regarding these developments. First, he is wondering how these changes in Thailand's economy could affect the value of the Thai baht and, consequently, Blades. More specifically, he is wondering whether the effects on the Thai baht may affect Blades even though its primary Thai customer is committed to Blades over the next three years.

Second, Holt believes that Blades may be able to speculate on the anticipated movement of the baht, but he is uncertain about the procedure needed to accomplish this. To facilitate Holt's understanding of exchange rate speculation, he has asked you, Blades' financial analyst, to provide him with detailed illustrations of two scenarios. In the first, the baht would move from a current level of $.022 to $.020 within the next 30 days. Under the second scenario, the baht would move from its current level to $.025 within the next 30 days.

Based on Holt's needs, he has provided you with the following list of questions to be answered:

1. How are percentage changes in a currency's value measured? Illustrate your answer numerically by assuming a change in the Thai baht's value from a value of $.022 to $.026.

2. What are the basic factors that determine the value of a currency? In equilibrium, what is the relationship between these factors?

3. How might the relatively high levels of inflation and interest rates in Thailand affect the baht's value?. (Assume a constant level of U.S. inflation and interest rates.)

4. How do you think the loss of confidence in the Thai baht, evidenced by the withdrawal of funds from Thailand, will affect the baht's value? Would Blades be affected by the change in value, given the primary Thai customer's commitment?

5. Assume that Thailand's central bank wishes to prevent a withdrawal of funds from its country in order to prevent further changes in the currency's value. How could it accomplish this objective using interest rates?

6. Construct a spreadsheet illustrating the steps Blades' treasurer would need to follow in order to speculate on expected movements in the baht's value over the next 30 days. Also show the speculative profit (in dollars) resulting from each scenario. Use both of Holt's examples to illustrate possible speculation. Assume that Blades can borrow either $10 million or the baht equivalent of this amount. Furthermore, assume that the following short-term interest rates (annualized) are available to Blades:

CURRENCY	LENDING RATE	BORROWING RATE
Dollars	8.10%	8.20%
Thai baht	14.80%	15.40%

SMALL BUSINESS DILEMMA

Assessment by the Sports Exports Company of Factors That Affect the British Pound's Value

Because the Sports Exports Company (a U.S. firm) receives payments in British pounds every month and converts those pounds into dollars, it needs to closely monitor the value of the British pound in the future. Jim Logan, owner of the Sports Exports Company, expects that inflation will rise substantially in the United Kingdom, while inflation in the United States will remain low. He also expects that the interest rates in both countries will rise by about the same amount.

1. Given Jim's expectations, forecast whether the pound will appreciate or depreciate against the dollar over time.

2. Given Jim's expectations, will the Sports Exports Company be favorably or unfavorably affected by the future changes in the value of the pound?

INTERNET/EXCEL EXERCISES

The website of the Federal Reserve Board of Governors (www.federalreserve.gov) contains economic data, including exchange rate trends of various currencies.

1. Determine how exchange rates of various currencies have changed in recent months. Note that most of these currencies (except the British pound) may be quoted in units per dollar. In general, have most currencies strengthened or weakened against the dollar over the last three months? Offer one or more reasons to explain the recent general movements in currency values against the dollar.

2. Does it appear that the Asian currencies move in the same direction relative to the dollar? Does it appear that the Latin American currencies move in the same direction against the dollar? Explain.

3. Go to www.oanda.com/currency/historical-rates/. Obtain the direct exchange rate (C$ per currency unit) of the Canadian dollar for the beginning of each of the last 12 months. Insert this information in a column on an electronic spreadsheet. (See Appendix C for help on conducting analyses with Excel.) Repeat the process to obtain the direct exchange rate of the euro. Compute the percentage change in the value of the Canadian dollar and the euro each month. Determine the standard deviation of the movements (percentage changes) in the Canadian dollar and in the euro. Compare the standard deviation of the euro's movements to the standard deviation of the Canadian dollar's movements. Which currency is more volatile?

ONLINE ARTICLES WITH REAL-WORLD EXAMPLES

Find a recent article online that describes an actual international finance application or a real-world example about a specific MNC's actions that reinforces one or more concepts covered in this chapter.

If your class has an online component, your professor may ask you to post your summary there and provide the web link of the article so that other students can access it. If your class is live, your professor may ask you to summarize your application in class. Your professor may assign specific students to complete this assignment for this chapter, or may allow any students to do the assignment on a volunteer basis.

For recent online articles and real-world examples applied to this chapter, consider using the following search terms and include the prevailing year as a search term to ensure that the online articles are recent:

1. foreign exchange market
2. change in exchange rate
3. currency speculation
4. impact of inflation on exchange rates
5. impact of interest rates on exchange rates
6. exchange rate equilibrium
7. change in cross exchange rates
8. bank speculation in currencies
9. currency speculation by individuals
10. liquidity of foreign exchange market
11. exchange rate movement

5

Currency Derivatives

CHAPTER OBJECTIVES

The specific objectives of this chapter are to describe the characteristics and use of:

■ forward contracts,

■ currency futures contracts,

■ currency call options contracts, and

■ currency put option contracts.

A currency derivative is a contract whose price is partially derived from the value of the underlying currency that it represents. Some individuals and financial firms take positions in currency derivatives to speculate on future exchange rate movements. Multinational corporations (MNCs) often take positions in currency derivatives to hedge their exposure to exchange rate risk. Their managers must understand how these derivatives can be used to achieve corporate goals.

5-1 Forward Market

The forward market facilitates the trading of forward contracts on currencies. A **forward contract** is an agreement between a corporation and a financial institution (such as a commercial bank) to exchange a specified amount of a currency at a specified exchange rate (called the **forward rate**) on a specified date in the future. When MNCs anticipate a future need for or the future receipt of some foreign currency, they can set up forward contracts to lock in the rate at which they can purchase or sell that currency. Nearly all large MNCs use forward contracts to some extent. Some MNCs have forward contracts outstanding worth more than $100 million to hedge various positions.

Because forward contracts accommodate large corporations, the forward transaction will often be valued at $1 million or more. Forward contracts normally are not used by consumers or small firms. In cases where a bank does not know a corporation well (or does not fully trust it), the bank may request that the corporation make an initial deposit as assurance that it intends to fulfill its obligation. Such a deposit is called a compensating balance and typically does not pay interest.

The most common forward contracts are for 30, 60, 90, 180, and 360 days, although other periods are available. Yet forward contracts can be customized to the specific needs of the MNC. If an MNC wants a forward contract that allows it to exchange dollars for 1.2 million euros in 53 days, a financial institution will accommodate such a request. The forward rate of a given currency will usually vary with the length (number of days) of the forward period.

5-1a How MNCs Use Forward Contracts

MNCs use forward contracts to hedge their imports. They can lock in the rate at which they obtain a currency needed to purchase those imports.

EXAMPLE

Turz, Inc., is an MNC based in Chicago that will need 1 million Singapore dollars in 90 days to purchase Singapore imports. It can buy this currency for immediate delivery at the spot rate of $.50 per Singapore dollar (S\$). At this spot rate, the firm would need \$500,000 (calculated as S\$1,000,000 × \$.50 per Singapore dollar). However, it does not now have the funds to exchange for Singapore dollars. It could wait 90 days and then exchange U.S. dollars for Singapore dollars at the spot rate existing at that time, but Turz does not know what that rate will be. If the rate rises to \$.60 in those 90 days, then Turz will need \$600,000 (i.e., S\$1,000,000 × \$.60 per Singapore dollar), or an additional outlay of \$100,000 due solely to the Singapore dollar's appreciation.

To avoid exposure to such exchange rate risk, Turz can lock in the rate it will pay for Singapore dollars 90 days from now without having to exchange U.S. dollars for Singapore dollars immediately. Specifically, Turz can negotiate a forward contract with a bank to purchase S\$1,000,000 90 days forward. ●

The ability of a forward contract to lock in an exchange rate can create an opportunity cost in some cases.

EXAMPLE

Assume that in the previous example Turz negotiated a 90-day forward rate of \$.50 to purchase S\$1,000,000. If the spot rate in 90 days is \$.47, then Turz will have paid \$.03 per unit or \$30,000 (1,000,000 units × \$.03) more for the Singapore dollars than if it did not have a forward contract. ●

Corporations also use the forward market to lock in the rate at which they can sell foreign currencies. This strategy is used to hedge against the possibility of those currencies depreciating over time.

EXAMPLE

Scanlon, Inc., which is based in Virginia, exports products to a French firm and will receive payment of €400,000 in four months. It can lock in the amount of dollars to be received from this transaction by selling euros forward. That is, Scanlon can negotiate a forward contract with a bank to sell the €400,000 for U.S. dollars at a specified forward rate today. Assume the prevailing four-month forward rate on euros is \$1.10. In four months, Scanlon will exchange its €400,000 for \$440,000 (calculated as €400,000 × \$1.10 = \$440,000). ●

5-1b Bank Quotations on Forward Rates

Just as many large banks serve as intermediaries for spot transactions in the foreign exchange market, they also serve as intermediaries for forward transactions. They accommodate orders by MNCs to purchase a specific amount of a currency at a future time and at a specified (forward) exchange rate. They also accommodate orders by MNCs to sell a specific amount of currency at a future time and at a specified (forward) exchange rate.

Bid/Ask Spread Like spot rates, forward rates have a bid/ask spread. For example, a bank may set up a contract with one firm agreeing to sell the firm Singapore dollars 90 days from now at \$.510 per Singapore dollar; this is the ask rate. At the same time, the firm may agree to purchase (bid) Singapore dollars 90 days from now from some other firm at \$.505 per Singapore dollar.

The spread can be measured on a percentage basis, as it was for spot rates in Chapter 3. In the previous paragraph, the bid/ask spread is Bid/ask spread of 90-day forward rate of

Bid ask spread of 90-day forward rate of Singapore dollar
$$= (\$.510 - \$.505)/\$.510 = .98\%$$

The spread for a particular currency tends to be wider for forward contracts that have an obligation further into the future. For example, the bid/ask spread on a one-year forward rate is normally higher than on a 90-day contract, and a three-year forward contract will usually have a higher spread than a one-year forward contract. The market for shorter-term forward contracts tends to be more liquid, which means that banks can more easily create offsetting positions for a given forward contract. For instance, a bank that accommodates a 90-day forward purchase request on Singapore dollars may be able to offset that by accommodating some other MNC's request to sell the same number of Singapore dollars for U.S. dollars in 90 days. By satisfying these two separate requests, the bank's exposure is offset. However, if the bank accommodates a five-year forward purchase request on Singapore dollars, it may be less capable of finding an MNC that wants to sell the same amount of Singapore dollars five years forward. Hence the bank may quote a higher bid/ask spread for a five-year than for a one-year forward contract, as the five-year contract leaves the bank more exposed to the risk of appreciation in the Singapore dollar.

The spread between the bid and ask prices is wider for forward rates of currencies of developing countries, such as Chile, Mexico, South Korea, Taiwan, and Thailand. Because these markets have relatively few orders for forward contracts, banks are less able to match up willing buyers and sellers. The resulting lack of liquidity causes banks to widen the bid/ask spread when quoting forward contracts. The contracts in these countries are generally available only for short-term horizons.

5-1c Premium or Discount on the Forward Rate

The difference between the forward rate (F) and the spot rate (S) at any given time is measured by the premium:

$$F = S(1 + p)$$

Here p denotes the forward premium, or the percentage by which the forward rate exceeds the spot rate.

EXAMPLE   If the euro's spot rate is $1.40 and if its one-year forward rate has a forward premium of 2 percent, then the one-year forward rate is calculated as follows:

$$F = S(1 + p)$$
$$= \$1.40(1 + .02)$$
$$= \$1.428$$

Given quotations for the spot rate and the forward rate at any point in time, the premium can be determined by rearranging the previous equation:

$$F = S(1 + p)$$
$$F/S = 1 + p$$
$$(F/S) - 1 = p$$ ●

EXAMPLE   If the euro's one-year forward rate is quoted at $1.428 and the euro's spot rate is quoted at $1.40, then the euro's forward premium is

$$(F/S) - 1 = p$$
$$(\$1.428/\$1.40) - 1 = p$$
$$1.02 - 1 = .02 \text{ or 2 percent}$$ ●

When the forward rate is less than the prevailing spot rate, the forward premium is negative and the forward rate exhibits a discount.

EXAMPLE   If the euro's one-year forward rate is quoted at $1.35 and the euro's spot rate is quoted at $1.40, then the euro's forward premium is:

$$(F/S) - 1 = p$$
$$(\$1.35/\$1.40) - 1 = p$$
$$.9643 - 1 = -.0357 \text{ or } -3.57 \text{ percent}$$

Because p is negative, the forward rate contains a discount. ●

EXAMPLE   Assume that the forward exchange rates of the British pound for various maturities are as shown in the second column of Exhibit 5.1. These forward rates can be used to compute the forward discount on an annualized basis, as shown in the exhibit. ●

Exhibit 5.1 Computation of Forward Rate Premiums or Discounts

TYPE OF EXCHANGE RATE FOR £	VALUE	MATURITY	FORWARD RATE PREMIUM OR DISCOUNT FOR £
Spot rate	$1.681		
30-day forward rate	$1.680	30 days	$\dfrac{\$1.680 - \$1.686}{\$1.681} \times \dfrac{360}{30} = -.71\%$
90-day forward rate	$1.677	90 days	$\dfrac{\$1.677 - \$1.681}{\$1.681} \times \dfrac{360}{90} = -.95\%$
180-day forward rate	$1.672	180 days	$\dfrac{\$1.672 - \$1.681}{\$1.681} \times \dfrac{360}{180} = -1.07\%$

In some situations, a firm may prefer to assess the premium or discount on an unannualized basis. In this case, the value would not incorporate the formula's fraction that represents the number of periods per year.

Pricing   Forward rates typically differ from the spot rate for any given currency because of the differential in interest rates between the foreign country and the United States. If a currency's spot and forward rates were the same and if the foreign currency's interest rate was higher than the U.S. rate, then U.S. speculators could achieve a higher return on the foreign savings deposit than a U.S. savings deposit by following these steps: (1) purchase the foreign currency at the spot rate, (2) invest the funds at the attractive foreign interest rate, and (3) simultaneously sell forward contracts in that foreign currency for a future date when the savings deposit matures. These actions would place upward pressure on the spot rate of the foreign currency and downward pressure on the forward rate, causing the forward rate to fall below the spot rate (exhibit a discount). When the interest rate advantage of the foreign currency is more pronounced, the forward rate of the foreign currency will be more pronounced. This relationship is discussed in more detail in Chapter 7.

5-1d Movements in the Forward Rate over Time

If the forward rate's premium were constant, then over time the forward rate would move in tandem with movements in the corresponding spot rate. For instance, if the spot rate of the euro increased by 4 percent from a month ago until today, then the forward rate would also have to increase by 4 percent over the same period in order to maintain the same premium. In reality, the forward premium is affected by the interest rate differential between the two countries (as explained in Chapter 7) and can change over time. Most of the movement in a currency's forward rate is due to movements in that currency's spot rate.

5-1e Offsetting a Forward Contract

In some cases, an MNC may desire to offset a forward contract that it previously created.

EXAMPLE   On March 10, Green Bay, Inc., hired a Canadian construction company to expand its office and agreed to pay C$200,000 for the work on September 10. It negotiated a six-month forward contract to obtain C$200,000 at $.70 per unit, which would be used to pay the Canadian firm in six months. On April 10, the construction company informed Green Bay that it would not be able to perform the work as promised. Therefore, Green Bay offset its existing contract by negotiating a forward contract to sell C$200,000 for the date of September 10. However, the spot rate of the Canadian dollar had decreased over the last month, and the prevailing forward contract price for September 10 is $.66. Green Bay now has a forward contract to sell C$200,000 on September 10, which offsets the other contract it has to buy C$200,000 on September 10. The forward rate was $.04 per unit less on its sale than on its purchase, resulting in a cost of $8,000 (C$200,000 × $.04). ●

If Green Bay, Inc., negotiates the forward sale with the same bank with which it negotiated the forward purchase, then it may be able to request that its initial forward contract simply be offset. The bank will charge a fee for this service, which will reflect the difference between the forward rate at the time of the forward purchase and the forward rate at the time of the offset. Thus the MNC cannot ignore its original obligation; rather, it must pay a fee to offset that obligation.

5-1f Using Forward Contracts for Swap Transactions

A swap transaction involves a spot transaction along with a corresponding forward contract that will ultimately reverse the spot transaction. Many forward contracts are negotiated for this purpose.

EXAMPLE

Soho, Inc., needs to invest 1 million Chilean pesos in its Chilean subsidiary for the production of additional products. It wants the subsidiary to repay the pesos in one year. Soho wants to lock in the rate at which the pesos can be converted back into dollars in one year, and it uses a one-year forward contract for this purpose. Soho contacts its bank and requests the following swap transaction.

1. *Today.* The bank should withdraw dollars from Soho's U.S. account, convert the dollars to 1 million pesos in the spot market, and transmit the pesos to the subsidiary's account.
2. *In one year.* The bank should withdraw 1 million pesos from the subsidiary's account, convert them to dollars at today's forward rate, and transmit them to Soho's U.S. account.

These transactions do not expose Soho to exchange rate movements because it has locked in the rate at which the pesos will be converted back to dollars. However, if the one-year forward rate exhibits a discount, then Soho will receive fewer dollars later than it invested in the subsidiary today. Even so, the firm may still be willing to engage in the swap transaction so that it can be certain about how many dollars it will receive in one year. ●

5-1g Non-Deliverable Forward Contracts

A **non-deliverable forward contract** (NDF) is often used for currencies in emerging markets. Like a regular forward contract, an NDF is an agreement regarding a position in a specified amount of a specified currency, a specified exchange rate, and a specified future settlement date. However, an NDF does not result in an actual exchange of the currencies at the future date; that is, there is no delivery. Instead, one party to the agreement makes a payment to the other party based on the exchange rate at the future date.

EXAMPLE

Jackson, Inc., an MNC based in Wyoming, determines as of April 1 that it will need 100 million Chilean pesos to purchase supplies on July 1. It can negotiate an NDF with a local bank as follows. The NDF will specify the currency (Chilean peso); the settlement date (90 days from now); and a *reference rate*, which identifies the type of exchange rate that will be marked to market at the settlement. Specifically, the NDF will contain the following information.

- Buy 100 million Chilean pesos.
- Settlement date: July 1.
- Reference index: Chilean peso's closing exchange rate (in dollars) quoted by Chile's central bank in 90 days.

Assume that the Chilean peso (which is the reference index) is currently valued at $.0020, so the dollar amount of the position is $200,000 at the time of the agreement. At the time of the settlement date (July 1), the value of the reference index is determined, and then a payment is made from one party to another in settlement. For example, if the peso value increases to $.0023 by July 1, the value of the position specified in the NDF will be $230,000 ($.0023 × 100 million pesos). Because the value of Jackson's NDF position is $30,000 higher than when the agreement was created, Jackson will receive a payment of $30,000 from the bank.

Recall that Jackson needs 100 million pesos to buy imports. Because the peso's spot rate rose from April 1 to July 1, the company will need to pay $30,000 more for the imports than if it had paid for them on April 1. At the same time, however, Jackson will have received a payment of $30,000 due to its NDF. Thus the NDF hedged the exchange rate risk.

Suppose that, instead of rising, the Chilean peso had depreciated to $.0018. Then Jackson's position in its NDF would have been valued at $180,000 (100 million pesos × $.0018) at the settlement date, which is $20,000 less than the value when the agreement was created. In this case, Jackson would have owed the bank $20,000 at that time. Yet the decline in the spot rate of the peso means that Jackson would also pay $20,000 less for the imports than if it had paid for them on April 1. Thus an offsetting effect occurs in this example as well. ●

WEB

www.futuresmag.com
Various aspects of derivatives trading such as new products, strategies, and market analyses.

WEB

www.cmegroup.com
Time series on financial futures and option prices. The site also enables one to generate charts of historical prices.

The preceding examples demonstrate that, even though an NDF does not involve delivery, it can effectively hedge the future foreign currency payments anticipated by an MNC.

Because an NDF can specify that payments between the two parties be in dollars or some other available currency, firms can also use NDFs to hedge existing positions of foreign currencies that are not convertible. Consider an MNC that expects to receive payment in a foreign currency that cannot be converted into dollars. The MNC may use this currency to make purchases in the local country, but it may nonetheless desire to hedge against a decline in the value of that currency over the period before it receives payment. Hence the MNC takes a sell position in an NDF and uses the closing exchange rate of that currency (as of the settlement date) as the reference index. If the currency depreciates against the dollar over time, then the firm will receive the difference between the dollar value of the position when the NDF contract was created and the dollar value of the position as of the settlement date. It will therefore receive a payment in dollars from the NDF to offset any depreciation in the currency over the period of concern.

5-2 Currency Futures Market

Currency futures contracts are contracts specifying a standard volume of a particular currency to be exchanged on a specific settlement date. Thus currency futures contracts are similar to forward contracts in terms of their obligation, but they differ from forward contracts in how they are traded. These contracts are frequently used by MNCs to hedge their foreign currency positions. In addition, they are traded by speculators who hope to capitalize on their expectations of exchange rate movements. A buyer of a currency futures contract locks in the exchange rate to be paid for a foreign currency at a future time. Alternatively, a seller of a currency futures contract locks in the exchange rate at which a foreign currency can be exchanged for the home currency. In the United States, currency futures contracts are purchased to lock in the amount of dollars needed to obtain a specified amount of a particular foreign currency; they are sold to lock in the amount of dollars to be received from selling a specified amount of a particular foreign currency.

5-2a Contract Specifications

Most currency futures are traded on the Chicago Mercantile Exchange (CME), which is part of CME Group. Currency futures are available for 20 currencies at the CME. Each contract specifies a standardized number of units, as shown in Exhibit 5.2. Standardized contracts allow for more frequent trading per contract and hence for greater liquidity. For some currencies, the CME offers "E-mini" futures contracts, which specify half the number of units of a typical standardized contract. The CME also offers futures contracts on cross exchange rates (between two non-dollar currencies).

Exhibit 5.2   Currency Futures Contracts Traded on the Chicago Mercantile Exchange

CURRENCY	UNITS PER CONTRACT
Australian dollar	100,000
Brazilian real	100,000
British pound	62,500
Canadian dollar	100,000
Chinese yuan	1,000,000
Czech koruna	4,000,000
Euro	125,000
Hungarian forint	30,000,000
Indian rupee	5,000,000
Israeli shekel	1,000,000
Japanese yen	12,500,000
Korean won	125,000,000
Mexican peso	500,000
New Zealand dollar	100,000
Norwegian krone	2,000,000
Polish zloty	500,000
Russian ruble	2,500,000
South African rand	500,000
Swedish krona	2,000,000
Swiss franc	125,000

The typical currency futures contract is based on a currency value in terms of U.S. dollars. However, futures contracts are also available on some cross rates, such as the exchange rate between the Australian dollar and the Canadian dollar. Thus speculators who expect that the Australian dollar will move substantially against the Canadian dollar can take a futures position to capitalize on their expectations. In addition, Australian firms that have exposure in Canadian dollars or Canadian firms that have exposure in Australian dollars may use this type of futures contract to hedge their exposure. See www.cmegroup.com for more information about futures on cross exchange rates.

Currency futures contracts usually specify the third Wednesday in March, June, September, or December as the settlement date. There is also an over-the-counter currency futures market, where financial intermediaries facilitate the trading of currency futures contracts with specific settlement dates.

5-2b Trading Currency Futures

Firms or individuals can execute orders for currency futures contracts by calling brokerage firms that serve as intermediaries. The order to buy or sell a currency futures contract for a specific currency and a specific settlement date is communicated to the brokerage firm, which in turn communicates the order to the CME.

For example, some U.S. firms purchase futures contracts on Mexican pesos with a December settlement date in order to hedge their future payables. At the same time, other U.S. firms sell futures contracts on Mexican pesos with a December settlement date in order to hedge their future receivables.

Futures contract orders submitted to the CME are executed electronically by Globex, a computerized platform that matches buy and sell orders for each standardized contract.

Globex operates more than 23 hours of each weekday (it is closed from 4:15 p.m. to 5:00 p.m.).

EXAMPLE Assume that, as of February 10, a futures contract on 62,500 British pounds with a March settlement date is priced at $1.50 per pound. The buyer of this currency futures contract will receive £62,500 on the March settlement date and will pay $93,750 for the pounds (computed as £62,500 × $1.50 per pound plus a commission paid to the broker). The seller of this contract is obligated to sell £62,500 at a price of $1.50 per pound and therefore will receive $93,750 on the settlement date, minus the commission that it owes the broker. ●

Trading Platforms for Currency Futures There are electronic trading platforms that facilitate the trading of currency futures. These platforms serve as a broker because they execute the trades desired. The platform typically sets quotes for currency futures based on an ask price at which one can buy a specified currency for a specified settlement date and a bid price at which one can sell a specified currency. Users of the platforms incur a fee in the form of a difference between the bid and ask prices.

5-2c Credit Risk of Currency Futures Contracts

Each currency futures contract represents an agreement between a client and the exchange clearinghouse, even though the exchange has not taken a position. To illustrate, assume you call a broker to request the purchase of a British pound futures contract with a March settlement date. Meanwhile, another person unrelated to you calls a broker to request the sale of a similar futures contract. Neither party needs to worry about the credit risk of the counterparty. The exchange clearinghouse assumes the risk, and assures that you will receive whatever is owed to you as a result of your currency futures position.

To minimize its risk in such a guarantee, the CME imposes margin requirements to cover fluctuations in the value of a contract. In other words, participants must make a deposit with their respective brokerage firms when taking a position. The initial margin requirement is typically between $1,000 and $2,000 per currency futures contract. When the value of the futures contract declines over time, however, the buyer may be asked to maintain an additional margin called the "maintenance margin."

5-2d Comparing Currency Futures and Forward Contracts

Currency futures contracts are similar to forward contracts in that they allow a customer to lock in the exchange rate at which a specific currency is purchased or sold for a specific date in the future. Nevertheless, there are some differences between these contract types, which are summarized in Exhibit 5.3. Currency futures contracts are sold on an exchange through a computerized trading platform, whereas each forward contract is negotiated between a firm and a commercial bank over a telecommunications network. Because currency futures contracts are standardized, they are not as easily tailored to the firm's particular needs.

Corporations that have established relationships with large banks tend to use forward contracts rather than futures contracts because forward contracts are tailored to the precise amount of currency to be purchased (or sold) and the preferred forward date. In contrast, small firms and individuals who do not have established relationships with large banks (or who prefer to trade in smaller amounts) tend to use currency futures contracts. Margin requirements are not always required for forward contracts because of the more personal nature of the agreement. The bank knows the MNC it is dealing with and may trust it to fulfill its obligation.

Exhibit 5.3 Comparison of the Forward and Futures Markets

	FORWARD	FUTURES
Size of contract	Tailored to individual needs.	Standardized.
Delivery date	Tailored to individual needs.	Standardized.
Participants	Banks, brokers, and multinational companies. Public speculation not encouraged.	Banks, brokers, and multinational companies. Qualified public speculation encouraged.
Security deposit	None as such, but compensating bank balances or lines of credit required.	Small security deposit required.
Clearing operation	Handling contingent on individual banks and brokers. No separate clearinghouse function.	Handled by exchange clearinghouse. Daily settlements to the market price.
Marketplace	Telecommunications network.	Globex computerized trading platform with worldwide communications.
Regulation	Self-regulating.	Commodity Futures Trading Commission; National Futures Association.
Liquidation	Most settled by actual delivery; some by offset, but at a cost.	Most by offset; very few by delivery.
Transaction costs	Set by the spread between bank's buy and sell prices.	Negotiated brokerage fees.

Source: Chicago Mercantile Exchange.

Pricing Currency Futures The price of currency futures is normally similar to the forward rate for a given currency and settlement date. This relationship is enforced by the potential activity that would occur if there were significant discrepancies.

EXAMPLE Assume that the currency futures price on the British pound is $1.50 and that forward contracts for a similar period are available for $1.48. Firms may attempt to purchase forward contracts and simultaneously sell currency futures contracts. If they can exactly match the settlement dates of the two contracts, they can generate guaranteed profits of $.02 per unit. These actions will place downward pressure on the currency futures price. The futures contract and forward contracts of a given currency and settlement date should have the same price, or else guaranteed profits are possible (assuming no transaction costs). ●

5-2e How MNCs Use Currency Futures

MNCs that have open positions in foreign currencies can consider purchasing or selling futures contracts to offset their positions.

Purchasing Futures to Hedge Payables The purchase of futures contracts locks in the price at which a firm can purchase a currency.

EXAMPLE Rochester Co. orders Canadian goods and upon delivery will need to send C$500,000 to the Canadian exporter. So Rochester purchases Canadian dollar futures contracts today, thereby locking in the price to be paid for Canadian dollars at a future settlement date. By holding futures contracts, Rochester does not have to worry about changes in the spot rate of the Canadian dollar over time. ●

Selling Futures to Hedge Receivables The sale of futures contracts locks in the price at which a firm can sell a currency.

EXAMPLE Karla Co. sells futures contracts when its exports are paid for in a currency that it will not need (Karla accepts a foreign currency at the importer's request). By selling a futures contract, Karla Co. locks in the price at which it will be able to sell this currency on the settlement date. This action is especially appropriate if Karla expects the foreign currency to depreciate against its home currency. ●

The use of futures contracts to cover, or hedge, a firm's currency positions is described more thoroughly in Chapter 11.

Closing Out a Futures Position   If a firm that buys a currency futures contract decides before the settlement date that it no longer wants to maintain its position, it can close out the position by selling an identical futures contract. The gain or loss to the firm from its previous futures position will depend on the price of purchasing futures versus selling futures.

The price of a futures contract changes over time in accordance with movements in the spot rate and also with changing expectations about what the spot rate's value will be on the settlement date. If the spot rate of a currency increases substantially over a one-month period, then the futures price is likely to increase by about the same amount; in this case, the purchase and subsequent sale of a futures contract would be profitable. Conversely, a substantial decline in the spot rate should lead to a decline in the currency futures price, which means that the purchase and subsequent sale of a futures contract would result in a loss. Although purchasers of such a futures contract could decide not to close out their position under these conditions, the losses from that position could increase over time.

EXAMPLE   On January 10, Tacoma Co. anticipates that it will need Australian dollars (A$) in March when it orders supplies from an Australian supplier. Tacoma therefore purchases a futures contract specifying A$100,000 and a March settlement date (which is March 19 for this contract). On January 10, the futures contract is priced at $.53 per A$. On February 15, Tacoma realizes that it will not need to order supplies because it has reduced its production levels. Therefore, it has no need for A$ in March. It sells a futures contract on A$ with the March settlement date to offset the contract it purchased in January. At this time, the futures contract is priced at $.50 per A$. On March 19 (the settlement date), Tacoma has offsetting positions in futures contracts. However, the price when the futures contract was purchased was higher than the price when an identical contract was sold, so Tacoma incurs a loss from these positions. Tacoma's transactions are summarized in Exhibit 5.4. Move from left to right along the time line to review the transactions. The example does not incorporate margin requirements. ●

Sellers of futures contracts can close out their positions by purchasing currency futures contracts with similar settlement dates. Most currency futures contracts are closed out before the settlement date.

Exhibit 5.4   Closing Out a Futures Contract

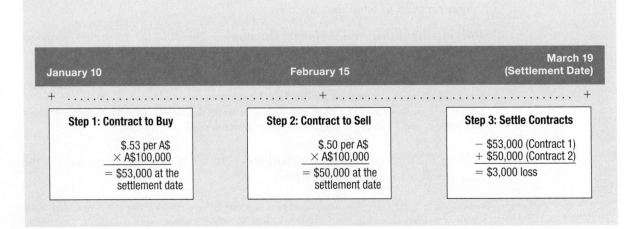

5-2f Speculation with Currency Futures

Currency futures contracts are sometimes purchased by speculators who are simply attempting to capitalize on their expectation of a currency's future movement.

Suppose that speculators expect the British pound to appreciate in the future. They can purchase a futures contract that will lock in the price at which they buy pounds at a specified settlement date. On that date, the speculators can purchase their pounds at the rate specified by the futures contract and then sell these pounds at the spot rate. If the spot rate has appreciated by this time in accordance with their expectations, then this strategy will be profitable.

Currency futures are also sold by speculators who expect that the spot rate of a currency will be less than the rate at which they would be obligated to sell it.

EXAMPLE

Suppose that, as of April 4, a futures contract specifying 500,000 Mexican pesos and a June settlement date is priced at $.09. On April 4, speculators who expect the peso to decline sell futures contracts on pesos. Assume that, on June 17 (the settlement date), the spot rate of the peso is $.08. The transactions are shown in Exhibit 5.5 (once again, the margin deposited by the speculators is not considered). The gain on the futures position is $5,000, which represents the difference between the amount received ($45,000) when selling the pesos in accordance with the futures contract versus the amount paid ($40,000) for those pesos in the spot market. ●

Of course, expectations are often incorrect. It is because of different expectations that, at any point in time, there will be some speculators wanting to purchase futures contracts and other speculators wanting to sell those same contracts.

Efficiency of the Currency Futures Market If the currency futures market is efficient, then at any time the futures price for a currency should reflect all available information. That is, the price should represent an unbiased estimate of the currency's spot exchange rate on the settlement date. For this reason, the continual use of a particular strategy to take positions in currency futures contracts should not lead to abnormal profits. Some positions will likely result in gains while others will result in losses, and the gains and losses should roughly offset over time. Research has found that in some years the futures price has been consistently higher than the corresponding spot exchange rate at the settlement date, whereas in other years the futures price has been consistently lower. This suggests that the currency futures market may be inefficient. Because these unexpected patterns are seldom observable until after they occur, it is may be difficult to consistently generate abnormal profits from speculating in currency futures.

Exhibit 5.5 Source of Gains from Selling Currency Futures

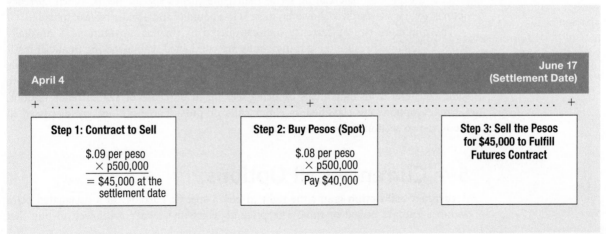

5-3 Currency Options Market

Currency options provide the right to purchase or sell currencies at specified prices up to a specified expiration date. They are available for many currencies, including the Australian dollar, British pound, Brazilian real, Canadian dollar, euro, Japanese yen, Mexican peso, New Zealand dollar, Russian ruble, South African rand, and Swiss franc.

5-3a Currency Options Exchanges

In late 1982, exchanges in Amsterdam, Montreal, and Philadelphia were the first to allow trading in standardized foreign currency options. Since that time, options have been offered on the Chicago Mercantile Exchange (CME) and the Chicago Board of Trade (CBOT). Currency options are traded through the Globex system at the CME. Thus currency options are traded virtually around the clock.

In July 2007, the CME and CBOT merged to form CME Group, which serves international markets for derivative products. The CME and CBOT trading floors were consolidated into a single trading floor at the CBOT. In addition, products of the CME and CBOT were consolidated on a single electronic platform, which reduced operating and maintenance expenses. Furthermore, the CME Group established a plan of continual innovation of new derivative products in the international marketplace that would be executed by the CME Group's single electronic platform.

The options exchanges in the United States are regulated by several agencies including the Securities and Exchange Commission and the Commodity Futures Trading Commission. Options can be purchased or sold through brokers for a commission. The commission per transaction is commonly $30 to $60 for a single currency option, but it can be much lower per contract when the transaction involves multiple contracts. Brokers require that a margin be maintained during the life of the contract. The margin is increased for clients whose option positions have deteriorated. This protects against possible losses if the clients do not fulfill their obligations.

5-3b Over-the-Counter Currency Options Market

In addition to the exchanges where currency options are available, there is an over-the-counter market where currency options are offered by commercial banks and brokerage firms. Unlike the currency options traded on an exchange, the over-the-counter market offers currency options that are tailored to the specific needs of the firm. Because these options are not standardized, all the terms must be specified in the contracts. The number of units, desired strike price, and expiration date can be set to match the client's specific needs. When currency options are not standardized, however, there is less liquidity and a wider bid/ask spread.

The minimum size of currency options offered by financial institutions is normally about $5 million. Because these transactions are conducted with a specific financial institution rather than an exchange, there are no credit guarantees. Thus the agreement made is only as safe as the parties involved. For this reason, financial institutions may require some collateral from individuals or firms seeking to purchase or sell currency options. Currency options are classified as either **calls** or **puts**. These options are discussed in the next two section sections, respectively.

5-4 Currency Call Options

A **currency call option** grants the right to buy a specific currency at a designated price within a specific period of time. The price at which the owner is allowed to buy that currency is known as the **exercise price** or **strike price**, and there are monthly expiration dates for each option.

Call options are desirable when one wishes to lock in a maximum price to be paid for a currency in the future. If the spot rate of the currency rises above the strike price, owners of call options can "exercise" their options by purchasing the currency at the strike price, which will be cheaper than the prevailing spot rate. This strategy is similar to that used by purchasers of futures contracts, but the futures contract entails an obligation whereas the currency option does not. That is, the owner can choose to let the option expire on the expiration date without ever exercising it. Owners of expired call options will have lost the premium they initially paid, but that is the most they can lose.

The buyer of a currency call option pays a *premium*, which reflects the price in order to own the option. The seller of a currency call option receives the premium paid by the buyer. In return, the seller is obligated to accommodate the buyer in accordance with the rights of the currency call option.

Currency options quotations are available at financial websites, the website of the CME Group, and the websites of major brokers. Although currency options typically expire near the middle of the specified month, some of them expire at the end of the month and are designated as EOM. Some options are listed as "European style," which means that they can be exercised only upon expiration.

A currency call option is said to be *in the money* when the present exchange rate exceeds the strike price, *at the money* when the present exchange rate equals the strike price, and *out of the money* when the present exchange rate is less than the strike price. For a given currency and expiration date, an in-the-money call option will require a higher premium than options that are at the money or out of the money.

5-4a Factors Affecting Currency Call Option Premiums

The premium on a call option represents the cost of having the right to buy the underlying currency at a specified price. For MNCs that use currency call options to hedge, the premium reflects a cost of insurance or protection.

The call option premium (denoted C) is primarily influenced by three factors:

$$C = f(\underset{+}{S - X}, \underset{+}{T}, \underset{+}{\sigma})$$

Here $S - X$ is the difference between the spot exchange rate (S) and the strike or exercise price (X), T denotes the time to maturity, and σ (sigma) captures the currency's volatility as measured by the standard deviation of its movements. The relationships between the call option premium and these factors can be summarized as follows.

- *Spot Price Relative to Strike Price.* The higher the spot rate relative to the strike price, the higher the option price will be. The increase is due to the greater probability of your buying the currency at a substantially lower price than at what you can sell it. This relationship can be verified by comparing the premiums of options for a specified currency and expiration date that have different strike prices.
- *Length of Time before the Expiration Date.* It is typically assumed that the spot rate is more likely to rise high above the strike price if it has a longer period of time to do so. A settlement date in June allows two additional months beyond April for the spot rate to move above the strike price, which explains why June option prices exceed April option prices for a specific strike price. This relationship can be verified by comparing premiums of options for a specified currency and strike price that have different expiration dates.

■ *Volatility of the Currency.* The greater the variability in the currency's price, the greater the likelihood of the spot rate rising above the strike price. This is why less volatile currencies have lower call option prices. For example, the Canadian dollar is more stable than most other currencies; if all other factors are similar, then Canadian call options should be less expensive than call options on other foreign currencies.

A currency's volatility can itself vary over time, which can affect the premiums paid on the options for that currency. When the credit crisis intensified in the fall of 2008, speculators were quickly moving their money into and out of various currencies. These actions led to increased volatility in the foreign exchange markets and also caused concerns about future volatility. As a result, option premiums increased.

5-4b How MNCs Use Currency Call Options

MNCs with open positions in foreign currencies can sometimes use currency call options to cover these positions.

Using Call Options to Hedge Payables   MNCs can purchase call options on a currency to hedge future payables.

EXAMPLE

When Pike Co. of Seattle orders Australian goods, it makes a payment in Australian dollars to the Australian exporter upon delivery. An Australian dollar call option locks in a maximum rate at which Pike can exchange dollars for Australian dollars. This exchange of currencies at the specified strike price on the call option contract can be executed at any time before the expiration date. In essence, the call option contract specifies the maximum price that Pike must pay to obtain these Australian imports. If the Australian dollar's value remains below the strike price, then Pike can purchase Australian dollars at the prevailing spot rate to pay for its imports and simply let the call option expire. ●

Options may be more appropriate than futures or forward contracts in some situations. Intel Corp. uses options to hedge its order backlog in semiconductors. If an order is canceled, then Intel has the flexibility to let the option contract expire. With a forward contract, the company would be obligated to fulfill its obligation even though the order was canceled.

Using Call Options to Hedge Project Bidding   When a U.S.-based MNC bids on foreign projects, it may purchase call options to lock in the dollar cost of the potential expenses.

EXAMPLE

Kelly Co. is an MNC based in Fort Lauderdale that has bid on a project sponsored by the Canadian government. If the bid is accepted, then Kelly will need approximately C$500,000 to purchase Canadian materials and services, but it will not know whether the bid is accepted until three months from now. In this situation, Kelly will want to purchase call options with a three-month expiration date; 10 call option contracts will cover the entire amount of potential exposure. If the bid is accepted, Kelly can use the options to purchase the Canadian dollars needed. If the Canadian dollar has depreciated over the three-month period, Kelly will likely let the options expire.

Assume that the exercise price on Canadian dollars is $.70 and that the call option premium is $.02 per unit. Kelly will pay $1,000 per option (as there are 50,000 units per Canadian dollar option), or $10,000 for the 10 option contracts. With the options, the maximum amount necessary to purchase the C$500,000 is $350,000 (computed as $.70 per Canadian dollar × C$500,000). Fewer U.S. dollars would be needed if the Canadian dollar's spot rate were below the exercise price at the time the Canadian dollars were purchased.

Even if Kelly's bid is rejected, it will exercise the currency call option (selling the C$ in the spot market) if the Canadian dollar's spot rate exceeds the exercise price before the option expires. Any gain from this exercising may partially or even fully offset the premium paid for the options. ●

Using Call Options to Hedge Target Bidding   Firms can also use call options to hedge a possible acquisition.

EXAMPLE

Morrison Co. is attempting to acquire a French firm and has submitted its bid in euros. Morrison has purchased call options on the euro because it will need euros to purchase the French company's stock. The call options hedge the U.S. firm against possible appreciation of the euro by the time the acquisition occurs. If the acquisition does not occur and the spot rate of the euro remains below the strike price, then Morrison Co. will let the call options expire. If the acquisition does not occur and the spot rate of the euro exceeds the strike price, then Morrison Co. can either exercise the options (and sell the euros in the spot market) or sell the call options it is holding. Either of these actions may offset part or all of the premium paid for the options. ●

5-4c Speculating with Currency Call Options

Because this text focuses on multinational financial management, the corporate use of currency options is more important than the speculative use. The use of options for hedging is discussed in detail in Chapter 11. Speculative trading is discussed here in order to provide more of a background on the currency options market.

Individuals may speculate in the currency options market based on their expectation of the future movements in a particular currency. Speculators who expect that a foreign currency will appreciate can purchase call options on that currency. If the spot rate of that currency does appreciate, then these speculators can exercise their options by purchasing that currency at the strike price and then selling it at the prevailing spot rate.

Just as with currency futures, for every buyer of a currency call option there must be a seller. A seller (sometimes called a **writer**) of a call option is obligated to sell a specified currency at a specified price (the strike price) up to a specified expiration date. Speculators may want to sell their call options on a currency they expect to depreciate in the future. The only way a currency call option will be exercised is if the spot rate is higher than the strike price. Thus the seller of a currency call option receives the premium when the option is purchased and can keep the entire amount if the option is not exercised. When it appears that an option will be exercised, there will still be sellers of options. However, such options will sell for high premiums due to the high risk that the option will be exercised at some point.

The net profit to a speculator from trading call options on a currency is based on a comparison of the selling price of the currency versus the exercise price paid for the currency and the premium paid for the call option.

EXAMPLE

Jim is a speculator who buys a British pound call option with a strike price of $1.40 and a December settlement date. The current spot price as of that date is about $1.39. Jim pays a premium of $.012 per unit for the call option. Assume there are no brokerage fees. Just before the expiration date, the spot rate of the British pound reaches $1.41. At this time, Jim exercises the call option and then immediately sells the pounds (to a bank) at the spot rate. In order to determine Jim's profit or loss, first compute his revenues from selling the currency. Then, from this amount subtract not only the purchase price of pounds when exercising the option but also the purchase price of the option. The computations are summarized in the following table; assume that one option contract specifies 31,250 units.

	PER UNIT	PER CONTRACT
Selling price of £	$1.41	$44,063 ($1.41 × 31,250 units)
− Purchase price of £	−1.40	−43,750 ($1.40 × 31,250 units)
− Premium paid for option	−.012	−375 ($.012 × 31,250 units)
= Net profit	−$.002	−$62 (−$.002 × 31,250 units)

Suppose that Linda was the seller of the call option purchased by Jim. Suppose also that Linda would purchase British pounds only if the option is exercised, at which time she must provide the pounds at the exercise price of $1.40. Using the information in this example, Linda's net profit from selling the call option is derived as follows.

	PER UNIT	PER CONTRACT
Selling price of £	$1.40	$43,750 ($1.40 × 31,250 units)
− Purchase price of £	−1.41	−44,063 ($1.41 × 31,250 units)
+ Premium received	+.012	+375 ($.012 × 31,250 units)
= Net profit	$.002	$62 ($.002 × 31,250 units)

As a second example, assume the following information.

- Call option premium on Canadian dollars (C$) = $.01 per unit.
- Strike price = $.70.
- One Canadian dollar option contract represents C$50,000.

A speculator who had purchased this call option decided to exercise the option shortly before the expiration date, when the spot rate reached $.74. The speculator then immediately sold the Canadian dollars in the spot market. Given this information, the net profit to the speculator is calculated as follows.

	PER UNIT	PER CONTRACT
Selling price of C$	$.74	$37,000 ($.74 × 50,000 units)
− Purchase price of C$	−.70	−35,000 ($.70 × 50,000 units)
− Premium paid for option	−.01	−500 ($.01 × 50,000 units)
= Net profit	$.03	$1,500 ($.03 × 50,000 units)

However, if the seller of the call option did not obtain Canadian dollars until the option was about to be exercised, the net profit to the seller of this call option was

	PER UNIT	PER CONTRACT
Selling price of C$	$.70	$35,000 ($.70 × 50,000 units)
− Purchase price of C$	−.74	−37,000 ($.74 × 50,000 units)
+ Premium received	+.01	+500 ($.01 × 50,000 units)
= Net profit	−$.03	−$1,500 (−$.03 × 50,000 units)

When brokerage fees are ignored, the currency call purchaser's gain will be the seller's loss. The currency call purchaser's expenses represent the seller's revenues, and the purchaser's revenues represent the seller's expenses. Yet because it is possible for purchasers and sellers of options to close out their positions, the relationship described here will not hold unless both parties establish and close out their positions at the same time.

An owner of a currency option may simply sell the option to someone else (before the expiration date) rather than exercising it. The owner could still earn a profit because the option premium changes over time to reflect the probability that the option will be exercised and the potential profit from exercising it.

Break-Even Point from Speculation The purchaser of a call option will break even if the revenue from selling the currency equals the payments made for the currency (at the strike price) plus the option premium. In other words, regardless of how many units a contract is for, a purchaser will break even if the spot rate at which the currency is sold is equal to the strike price plus the option premium.

EXAMPLE

Based on the information in the previous example, the strike price is $.70 and the option premium is $.01. Thus for the purchaser to break even, the spot rate at the time the call is exercised must be $.71 (i.e., $.70 + $.01). Of course, speculators will not purchase a call option if they think the spot rate will not surpass the break-even point before the option's expiration date. Nevertheless, calculating the break-even point is a useful exercise for any speculator deciding whether or not to purchase a particular currency call option. ●

Contingency Graph for Speculators Buying a Call Option   A **contingency graph** for the buyer of a call option compares the price paid for that option to the payoffs received under various exchange rate scenarios.

EXAMPLE

A British pound call option is available with a strike price of $1.50 and a call premium of $.02. A speculator plans to exercise the option on the expiration date (if appropriate at that time) and then immediately sell the pounds received in the spot market. Under these conditions, a contingency graph can be created to measure the profit or loss per unit (see the upper diagram in Exhibit 5.6). Observe that if the future spot rate is $1.50 or less then the net gain per unit is −$.02 (ignoring transaction costs). This represents the loss of the premium per unit paid for the option, because the option would not be exercised. At a future spot rate of $1.51, the speculator would earn $.01 per unit by exercising the option; considering the $.02 premium paid, however, the net gain would be −$.01.

At a future spot rate of $1.52, the speculator would earn $.02 per unit by exercising the option, which would offset the $.02 premium per unit. This is the break-even point. At any rate above this point, the gain from exercising the option would more than offset the premium, resulting in a positive net gain. The maximum loss to the speculator in this example is the premium paid for the option. ●

Contingency Graph for Speculators Selling a Call Option   A contingency graph for the seller of a call option compares the premium received from selling that option to the payoffs made to the option's buyer under various exchange rate scenarios.

EXAMPLE

The lower diagram in Exhibit 5.6 plots the contingency graph for a speculator who sold the call option described in the previous example; it assumes that this seller would purchase the pounds in the spot market just as the option was exercised (ignoring transaction costs). At future spot rates of less than $1.50, the net gain to the seller would be the premium of $.02 per unit (because the option would not have been exercised). If the future spot rate is $1.51, then the seller would lose $.01 per unit on the option transaction (paying $1.51 for pounds in the spot market and selling pounds for $1.50 to fulfill the exercise request). Yet this loss would be more than offset by the premium of $.02 per unit received, resulting in a net gain of $.01 per unit.

The break-even price is therefore $1.52, and the net gain to the seller of a call option becomes negative at all higher future spot rates. Notice that the contingency graphs for the buyer and seller of this call option are mirror images of one another. ●

Speculation by MNCs   Some financial institutions may have a division that uses currency options (and other currency derivatives) to speculate on future exchange rate movements. However, most MNCs use currency derivatives for hedging and not for speculation. MNCs should use shareholder and creditor funds to pursue their goal of being market leader in some product or service; it would be irresponsible if the firm instead used those funds to speculate in currency derivatives. An MNC's board of directors attempts to ensure that the MNC's operations are consistent with its goals.

Exhibit 5.6 Contingency Graphs for Currency Call Options

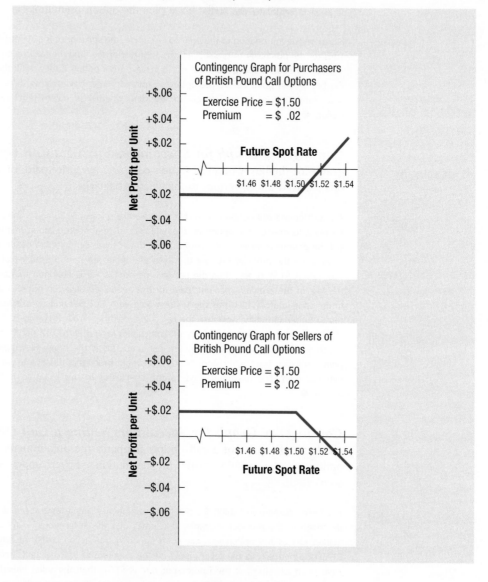

5-5 Currency Put Options

The owner of a **currency put option** has the right to sell a currency at a specified price (the strike price) within a specified period of time. As with currency call options, the owner of a put option is not obligated to exercise the option. Therefore, the maximum potential loss to the owner of the put option is the price (or premium) paid for the option contract.

The premium of a currency put option reflects the price of the option. The seller of a currency put option receives the premium paid by the buyer (owner). In return, the seller is obligated to accommodate the buyer in accordance with the rights of the currency put option.

A currency put option is said to be *in the money* when the present exchange rate is less than the strike price, *at the money* when the present exchange rate equals the strike price, and *out of the money* when the present exchange rate exceeds the strike price. For a given currency and expiration date, an in-the-money put option will require a higher premium than options that are at the money or out of the money.

5-5a Factors Affecting Currency Put Option Premiums

The put option premium (denoted *P*) is primarily influenced by three factors, as the following equation shows:

$$P = f(\underset{+}{S - X}, \underset{+}{T}, \underset{+}{\sigma})$$

As before, $S - X$ is the difference between the spot exchange rate and the strike or exercise price, T is time to maturity, and σ is the standard deviation of movements in the currency. The relationships between the put option premium and these factors, which also influence call option premiums as described previously, are summarized next.

First, the spot rate of a currency relative to the strike price is important. The lower the spot rate relative to the strike price, the more valuable the put option will be because there is a greater probability that the option will be exercised. Recall that just the opposite relationship held for call options. A second factor influencing the put option premium is the length of time until the expiration date. As with currency call options, the longer the time to expiration, the greater the put option premium will be. A longer period is associated with a greater likelihood that the currency will move into a range where it will be feasible to exercise the option. These relationships can be verified by assessing the quotations of put option premiums for a specified currency. A third factor that influences the put option premium is the currency's volatility. As with currency call options, greater variability increases the put option's premium, again reflecting a higher probability that the option may be exercised.

5-5b How MNCs Use Currency Put Options

MNCs with open positions in foreign currencies can sometimes use currency put options to cover these positions.

EXAMPLE   Assume Duluth Co. has exported products to Canada and invoiced the products in Canadian dollars (at the request of the Canadian importers). Duluth is concerned that the Canadian dollars it receives will depreciate over time. To insulate itself against such depreciation, Duluth purchases Canadian dollar put options that entitle the company to sell Canadian dollars at the specified strike price. In essence, Duluth locks in the minimum rate at which it can exchange Canadian dollars for U.S. dollars over a specified period of time. If the Canadian dollar appreciates over this period, then Duluth can let the put options expire and simply sell the Canadian dollars it receives at the prevailing spot rate. ●

At any time, some put options are deep out of the money; this means that the prevailing exchange rate is high above the exercise price. These options are cheaper (have a lower premium) because their low price makes it unlikely they will be exercised. Analogously, the exercise price of other put options is currently far above the prevailing exchange rate and so they are much more likely to be exercised; hence these options are more expensive.

EXAMPLE   Cisco Systems faces a trade-off when using put options to hedge the remittance of earnings from Europe to the United States. It can create a hedge that is cheap, but then the options can be exercised only if the currency's spot rate declines substantially. Alternatively, Cisco can create a hedge that can be exercised at a more favorable exchange rate, but then the options' premium will be higher. If Cisco's goal in using put options is simply to prevent a major loss if the currency weakens substantially, then it may prefer the inexpensive put option (low exercise price, low premium). However, if its goal is to ensure that the currency can be exchanged at a more favorable exchange rate, then Cisco should use a more expensive put option (high exercise price, high premium). By selecting currency options with an exercise price and premium that fits their objectives, Cisco and other MNCs can increase their value. ●

5-5c Speculating with Currency Put Options

Individuals may speculate with currency put options based on their expectations of the future movements in a particular currency. For example, speculators who expect that the British pound will depreciate can purchase British pound put options, which will entitle them to sell British pounds at a specified strike price. If the pound's spot rate depreciates as expected, then speculators can purchase pounds at the spot rate and exercise their put options by selling these pounds at the strike price.

Speculators can also attempt to profit from selling currency put options. The seller of such options is obligated to purchase the specified currency at the strike price from the owner who exercises the put option. Speculators who believe the currency will appreciate (or at least will not depreciate) may sell a currency put option. If the currency appreciates over the entire period, the option will not be exercised. This is an ideal situation for put option sellers because they keep the premiums received when the options were sold yet bear no cost.

The net profit to a speculator from trading put options on a currency is based on a comparison of the exercise price at which the currency can be sold versus the purchase price of the currency and the premium paid for the put option.

EXAMPLE

A put option contract on British pounds specifies the following information.

- ■ Put option premium on British pound (£) = $.04 per unit.
- ■ Strike price = $1.40.
- ■ One option contract represents £31,250.

A speculator who had purchased this put option decided to exercise the option shortly before the expiration date, when the spot rate of the pound was $1.30. The speculator purchased the pounds in the spot market at that time. Given this information, the net profit to the purchaser of the put option is calculated as follows.

	PER UNIT	PER CONTRACT
Selling price of £	$1.40	$43,750 ($1.40 × 31,250 units)
− Purchase price of £	−1.30	−40,625 ($1.30 × 31,250 units)
− Premium paid for option	− .04	−1,250 ($.04 × 31,250 units)
= Net profit	$.06	$1,875 ($.06 × 31,250 units)

Assuming that the seller of the put option sold the pounds received immediately after the option was exercised, the net profit to the seller of the put option is as follows.

	PER UNIT	PER CONTRACT
Selling price of £	$1.30	$40,625 ($1.30 × 31,250 units)
− Purchase price of £	−1.40	−43,750 ($1.40 × 31,250 units)
+ Premium received	+.04	+1,250 ($.04 × 31,250 units)
= Net profit	− $.06	−$1,875 (−$.06 × 31,250 units)

●

The seller of the put options could simply refrain from selling the pounds (after being forced to buy them at $1.40 per pound) until the spot rate of the pound rises. However, there is no guarantee that the pound will reverse its direction and begin to appreciate.

Unless the pounds are sold immediately, the seller's net loss would be still greater if the pound's spot rate continued to fall.

Whatever an owner of a put option gains, the seller loses (and vice versa). This relationship would hold in the absence of brokerage costs and if the buyer and seller of options entered and closed their positions at the same time. Of course, there are brokerage fees for currency options; these fees are similar in magnitude to those for currency futures contracts.

Contingency Graph for the Buyer of a Put Option   A contingency graph for the buyer of a put option compares the premium paid for that to the payoffs received under various exchange rate scenarios.

EXAMPLE   The upper diagram in Exhibit 5.7 shows the net gains to a buyer of a British pound put option with an exercise price of $1.50 and a premium of $.03 per unit. If the future spot rate is above $1.50 then the

Exhibit 5.7   Contingency Graphs for Currency Put Options

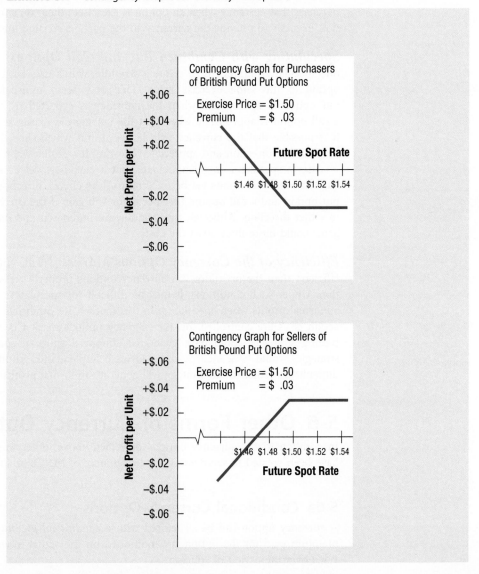

option will not be exercised. At a future spot rate of $1.48, the put option will be exercised. In that case, however, the premium of $.03 per unit entails a net loss of $.01 per unit. The break-even point in this example is $1.47, as this is the future spot rate that will generate $.03 per unit from exercising the option to offset the $.03 premium. At any future spot rates lower than $1.47, the buyer of the put option will earn a positive net gain. ●

Contingency Graph for the Seller of a Put Option

A contingency graph for the seller of a put option compares the premium received from selling that option to the payoffs made to the option's buyer under various exchange rate scenarios. The graph is shown as the lower graph in Exhibit 5.7 and is the mirror image of the contingency graph for the buyer of a put option.

For various reasons, an option buyer's net gain will not always represent an option seller's net loss. The buyer may be using call options to hedge a foreign currency rather than to speculate. In that case, the buyer does not evaluate the options position taken by measuring a net gain or loss; the option is used simply for protection. In addition, sellers of call options on a currency in which they currently maintain a position will not need to purchase that currency when an option is exercised; they can simply liquidate their position in order to provide the currency to the party exercising the option.

Speculating with Combined Put and Call Options

For volatile currencies, one speculative strategy is to create a **straddle**, which uses both a put option and a call option at the same exercise price. This may seem unusual, given that owning a put option is appropriate when the currency is expected to depreciate while owning a call option is appropriate when that the currency is expected to appreciate. However, it is possible that the currency will depreciate (at which time the put is exercised) and then reverse direction and appreciate (allowing for profits when exercising the call).

Also, a speculator might anticipate that a currency will be substantially affected by current economic events yet be uncertain of the effect's direction. By purchasing both a put option and a call option, the speculator will gain if the currency moves substantially in either direction. Although two options are purchased and only one is exercised, the gains could more than offset the costs.

Efficiency of the Currency Options Market

If the currency options market is efficient, then the premiums on currency options properly reflect all available information. Under such conditions, it may be difficult for speculators to consistently generate abnormal profits when speculating in this market. Research has found that, when transaction costs are controlled for, the currency options market is efficient. Although some trading strategies could have generated abnormal gains in specific periods, the same strategies would have incurred large losses if implemented in other periods. It is always difficult to predict which strategy will generate abnormal profits in future periods.

5-6 Other Forms of Currency Options

In addition to the currency options described above, other forms of currency options have been created to serve particular preferences of MNCs or speculators.

5-6a Conditional Currency Options

A currency option can be structured with a *conditional premium*. This means that the premium paid for the option is conditioned on the actual movement in the currency's value over the period of concern.

EXAMPLE

Jensen Co., a U.S.-based MNC, needs to sell British pounds that it will receive in 60 days. It can negotiate a traditional currency put option on pounds in which the exercise price is $1.70 and the premium is $.02 per unit.

Alternatively, Jensen can negotiate a conditional currency option with a commercial bank; this option has an exercise price of $1.70 and a *trigger* (price) of $1.74. If the pound's value falls below the exercise price by the expiration date, then Jensen will exercise the option and thereby receive $1.70 per pound; furthermore, it will not have to pay a premium for the option.

If the pound's value is between the exercise price ($1.70) and the trigger ($1.74), then the option will not be exercised and Jensen will not have to pay a premium. If the pound's value exceeds the $1.74 trigger, then Jensen must pay a premium of $.04 per unit. Note that this premium may be higher than the premium that would have been paid for a basic put option. Jensen may not mind this outcome, however, because it will receive a high dollar amount from converting its pound receivables in the spot market.

Jensen must determine whether the possible advantage of the conditional option (avoiding the payment of a premium under some conditions) outweighs the possible disadvantage (paying a higher premium than would be needed for a traditional put option on British pounds). The potential advantage and disadvantage are both illustrated in Exhibit 5.8. At exchange rates less than or equal to the trigger price ($1.74), the conditional option results in a larger payment to Jensen by the amount of the premium that would have been paid for the basic option. At exchange rates greater than the trigger price, the conditional option results in a lower payment to Jensen because its premium of $.04 exceeds the premium of $.02 per unit paid on a basic option. ●

The choice of a basic versus a conditional option depends on expectations about the currency's exchange rate over the period of concern. In the previous example, if Jensen is confident that the pound's value will not exceed $1.74 then it should prefer the conditional currency option.

Exhibit 5.8 Comparison of Conditional and Basic Currency Options

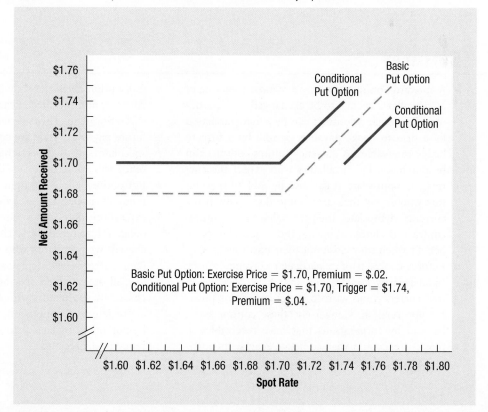

Conditional currency options are also available for U.S. firms that need to purchase a foreign currency in the near future.

EXAMPLE   A conditional call option on pounds may specify an exercise price of $1.70 and a trigger of $1.67. If the pound's value remains above the trigger of the call option, then no premium will be due for the call option. However, if the pound's value falls below the trigger, then a large premium (such as $.04 per unit) will be charged. Some conditional options require a premium if the trigger is reached at any time before the expiration date; others require a premium only if the exchange rate exceeds the trigger on the actual expiration date. ●

Firms also use various combinations of currency options. For example, a firm may purchase a currency call option to hedge payables and finance the purchase of the call option by selling a put option on the same currency.

5-6b European Currency Options

The discussion of currency options up to this point has dealt solely with so-called American-style options. European-style currency options are also available for speculating and hedging in the foreign exchange market. These are similar to American-style options except that they must be exercised on the expiration date if they are to be exercised at all. Hence such options offer less flexibility, although that is not relevant in some situations. For example, MNCs that purchase options to hedge future foreign currency cash flows will probably have no desire to exercise their options before the expiration date. If European-style options are available for the same expiration date as American-style options and can be purchased for a slightly lower premium, then some MNCs may prefer them for hedging.

SUMMARY

- A forward contract specifies a standard volume of a particular currency to be exchanged on a particular date. Such a contract can be either purchased by a firm to hedge payables or sold by a firm to hedge receivables. A currency futures contract can be purchased by speculators who expect the currency to appreciate; it can also be sold by speculators who expect that currency to depreciate. If the currency depreciates then the value of the futures contract declines, allowing those speculators to benefit when they close out their positions.

- Futures contracts on a particular currency can be purchased by corporations that have payables in that currency and wish to hedge against its possible appreciation. Conversely, these contracts can be sold by corporations that have receivables in that currency and wish to hedge against its possible depreciation.

- Call option allow the right to purchase a specified currency at a specified exchange rate by a specified expiration date. They are used by MNCs to hedge future payables. They are commonly purchased by speculators who expect that the underlying currency will appreciate.

- Put options allow the right to sell a specified currency at a specified exchange rate by a specified expiration date. They are used by MNCs to hedge future receivables. They are commonly purchased by speculators who expect that the underlying currency will depreciate.

  Call options on a specific currency can be purchased by speculators who expect that currency to appreciate. Put options on a specific currency can be purchased by speculators who expect that currency to depreciate.

POINT COUNTER-POINT

Should Speculators Use Currency Futures or Options?

Point   Speculators should use currency futures because they can avoid a substantial premium. To the extent that they are willing to speculate, they must have confidence in their expectations. If they have sufficient confidence in their expectations, they should bet on their expectations without having to pay a large premium to cover themselves if they are wrong. If they do not have confidence in their expectations, they should not speculate at all.

Counter-Point   Speculators should use currency options to fit the degree of their confidence. For example, if they are very confident that a currency will appreciate substantially, but want to limit their investment, they can buy deep out-of-the-money options.

These options have a high exercise price but a low premium and therefore require a small investment. Alternatively, they can buy options that have a lower exercise price (higher premium), which will likely generate a greater return if the currency appreciates. Speculation involves risk. Speculators must recognize that their expectations may be wrong. While options require a premium, the premium is worthwhile to limit the potential downside risk. Options enable speculators to select the degree of downside risk that they are willing to tolerate.

Who Is Correct?   Use the Internet to learn more about this issue. Which argument do you support? Offer your own opinion on this issue.

SELF-TEST

Answers are provided in Appendix A at the back of the text.

1. A call option on Canadian dollars with a strike price of $.60 is purchased by a speculator for a premium of $.06 per unit. Assume there are 50,000 units in this option contract. If the Canadian dollar's spot rate is $.65 at the time the option is exercised, what is the net profit per unit and for one contract to the speculator? What would the spot rate need to be at the time the option is exercised for the speculator to break even? What is the net profit per unit to the seller of this option?

2. A put option on Australian dollars with a strike price of $.80 is purchased by a speculator for a premium of $.02. If the Australian dollar's spot rate is $.74 on the expiration date, should the speculator exercise the option on this date or let the option expire? What is the net profit per unit to the speculator? What is the net profit per unit to the seller of this put option?

3. Longer-term currency options are becoming more popular for hedging exchange rate risk. Why do you think some firms decide to hedge by using other techniques instead of purchasing long-term currency options?

4. The spot rate of the New Zealand dollar is $.70. A call option on New Zealand dollars with a one-year expiration date has an exercise price of $.71 and a premium of $.02. A put option on New Zealand dollars at the money with a one-year expiration date has a premium of $.03. You expect that the New Zealand dollar's spot rate will rise over time and will be $.75 in one year.

a. Today, Jarrod purchased call options on New Zealand dollars with a one-year expiration date. Estimate the profit or loss per unit for Jarrod at the end of one year. [Assume that the options would be exercised on the expiration date or not at all.]

b. Today, Laurie sold put options on New Zealand dollars at the money with a one-year expiration date. Estimate the profit or loss per unit for Laurie at the end of one year. [Assume that the options would be exercised on the expiration date or not at all.]

5. You often take speculative positions in options on euros. One month ago, the spot rate of the euro was $1.49, and the one-month forward rate was $1.50. At that time, you sold call options on euros at the money. The premium on that option was $.02. Today is when the option will be exercised if it is feasible to do so.

a. Determine your profit or loss per unit on your option position if the spot rate of the euro is $1.55 today.

b. Repeat question a, but assume that the spot rate of the euro today is $1.48.

QUESTIONS AND APPLICATIONS

1. Forward versus Futures Contracts Compare and contrast forward and futures contracts.

2. Using Currency Futures
a. How can currency futures be used by corporations?
b. How can currency futures be used by speculators?

3. Currency Options Differentiate between a currency call option and a currency put option.

4. Forward Premium Compute the forward discount or premium for the Mexican peso whose 90-day forward rate is $.102 and spot rate is $.10. State whether your answer is a discount or premium.

5. Effects of a Forward Contract How can a forward contract backfire?

6. Hedging with Currency Options When would a U.S. firm consider purchasing a call option on euros for hedging? When would a U.S. firm consider purchasing a put option on euros for hedging?

7. Speculating with Currency Options When should a speculator purchase a call option on Australian dollars? When should a speculator purchase a put option on Australian dollars?

8. Currency Call Option Premiums List the factors that affect currency call option premiums and briefly explain the relationship that exists for each. Do you think an at-the-money call option in euros has a higher or lower premium than an at-the-money call option in Mexican pesos (assuming the expiration date and the total dollar value represented by each option are the same for both options)?

9. Currency Put Option Premiums List the factors that affect currency put option premiums and briefly explain the relationship that exists for each.

10. Speculating with Currency Call Options Randy Rudecki purchased a call option on British pounds for $.02 per unit. The strike price was $1.45, and the spot rate at the time the option was exercised was $1.46. Assume there are 31,250 units in a British pound option. What was Randy's net profit on this option?

11. Speculating with Currency Put Options Alice Duever purchased a put option on British pounds for $.04 per unit. The strike price was $1.80, and the spot rate at the time the pound option was exercised was $1.59. Assume there are 31,250 units in a British pound option. What was Alice's net profit on the option?

12. Selling Currency Call Options Mike Suerth sold a call option on Canadian dollars for $.01 per unit. The strike price was $.76, and the spot rate at the time the option was exercised was $.82. Assume Mike did not obtain Canadian dollars until the option was exercised. Also assume that there are 50,000 units in a Canadian dollar option. What was Mike's net profit on the call option?

13. Selling Currency Put Options Brian Tull sold a put option on Canadian dollars for $.03 per unit. The strike price was $.75, and the spot rate at the time the option was exercised was $.72. Assume Brian immediately sold off the Canadian dollars received when the option was exercised. Also assume that there are 50,000 units in a Canadian dollar option. What was Brian's net profit on the put option?

14. Forward versus Currency Option Contracts What are the advantages and disadvantages to a U.S. corporation that uses currency options on euros rather than a forward contract on euros to hedge its exposure in euros? Explain why an MNC may use forward contracts to hedge committed transactions and use currency options to hedge contracts that are anticipated but not committed. Why might forward contracts be advantageous for committed transactions, and currency options be advantageous for anticipated transactions?

15. Speculating with Currency Futures Assume that the euro's spot rate has moved in cycles over time. How might you try to use futures contracts on euros to capitalize on this tendency? How could you determine whether such a strategy would have been profitable in previous periods?

16. Hedging with Currency Derivatives Assume that the transactions listed in the first column of the table below are anticipated by U.S. firms that have no other foreign transactions. Place an "X" in the table wherever you see possible ways to hedge each of the transactions.

	FORWARD CONTRACT		FUTURES CONTRACT		OPTIONS CONTRACT	
	FORWARD PURCHASE	FORWARD SALE	BUY FUTURES	SELL FUTURES	PURCHASE A CALL	PURCHASE A PUT
a. Georgetown Co. plans to purchase Japanese goods denominated in yen.						
b. Harvard, Inc., will sell goods to Japan, denominated in yen.						
c. Yale Corp. has a subsidiary in Australia that will be remitting funds to the U.S. parent.						
d. Brown, Inc., needs to pay off existing loans that are denominated in Canadian dollars.						
e. Princeton Co. may purchase a company in Japan in the near future (but the deal may not go through).						

17. Price Movements of Currency Futures

Assume that on November 1, the spot rate of the British pound was $1.58 and the price on a December futures contract was $1.59. Assume that the pound depreciated during November so that by November 30 it was worth $1.51.

a. What do you think happened to the futures price over the month of November? Why?

b. If you had known that this would occur, would you have purchased or sold a December futures contract in pounds on November 1? Explain.

18. Speculating with Currency Futures

Assume that a March futures contract on Mexican pesos was available in January for $.09 per unit. Also assume that forward contracts were available for the same settlement date at a price of $.092 per peso. How could speculators capitalize on this situation, assuming zero transaction costs? How would such speculative activity affect the difference between the forward contract price and the futures price?

19. Speculating with Currency Call Options

LSU Corp. purchased Canadian dollar call options for **speculative** purposes. If these options are exercised, LSU will immediately sell the Canadian dollars in the spot market. Each option was purchased for a premium of $.03 per unit, with an exercise price of $.75. LSU plans to wait until the expiration date before deciding whether to exercise the options. Of course, LSU will exercise the options at that time only if it is feasible to do so. In the following table, fill in the net profit (or loss) per unit to LSU Corp. based on the listed possible spot rates of the Canadian dollar on the expiration date.

POSSIBLE SPOT RATE OF CANADIAN DOLLAR ON EXPIRATION DATE	NET PROFIT (LOSS) PER UNIT TO LSU CORP.
$.76	
.78	
.80	
.82	
.85	
.87	

20. Speculating with Currency Put Options

Auburn Co. has purchased Canadian dollar put options for speculative purposes. Each option was purchased for a premium of $.02 per unit, with an exercise price of $.86 per unit. Auburn Co. will purchase the Canadian dollars just before it exercises the options (if it is feasible to exercise the options). It plans to wait until the expiration date before deciding whether to exercise the options. In the following table, fill in the net profit (or loss) per unit to Auburn Co. based on the listed possible spot rates of the Canadian dollar on the expiration date.

POSSIBLE SPOT RATE OF CANADIAN DOLLAR ON EXPIRATION DATE	NET PROFIT (LOSS) PER UNIT TO AUBURN CO.
$.76	
.79	
.84	
.87	
.89	
.91	

21. Speculating with Currency Call Options

Bama Corp. has sold British pound call options for speculative purposes. The option premium was $.06 per unit, and the exercise price was $1.58. Bama will purchase the pounds on the day the options are exercised (if the options are exercised) in order to fulfill its obligation. In the following table, fill in the net profit (or loss) to Bama Corp. if the listed spot rate exists at the time the purchaser of the call options considers exercising them.

POSSIBLE SPOT RATE AT THE TIME PURCHASER OF CALL OPTIONS CONSIDERS EXERCISING THEM	NET PROFIT (LOSS) PER UNIT TO BAMA CORP.
$1.53	
1.55	
1.57	
1.60	
1.62	
1.64	
1.68	

22. Speculating with Currency Put Options

Bulldog, Inc., has sold Australian dollar put options at a premium of $.01 per unit, and an exercise price of $.76 per unit. It has forecasted the Australian dollar's lowest level over the period of concern as shown in the following table. Determine the net profit (or loss) per unit to Bulldog, Inc., if each level occurs and the put options are exercised at that time.

NET PROFIT (LOSS) TO BULLDOG, INC. IF VALUE OCCURS	
$.72	
.73	
.74	
.75	
.76	

23. Hedging with Currency Derivatives

A U.S. professional football team plans to play an exhibition game in the United Kingdom next year. Assume that all expenses will be paid by the British government, and that the team will receive a check for 1 million pounds. The team anticipates that the pound will depreciate substantially by the scheduled date of the game. In addition, the National Football League must approve the deal, and approval (or disapproval) will not occur for three months. How can the team hedge its position? What is there to lose by waiting three months to see if the exhibition game is approved before hedging?

Advanced Questions

24. Risk of Currency Futures

Currency futures markets are commonly used as a means of capitalizing on shifts in currency values, because the value of a futures contract tends to move in line with the change in the corresponding currency value. Recently, many currencies appreciated against the dollar. Most speculators anticipated that these currencies would continue to strengthen and took large buy positions in currency futures. However, the Fed intervened in the foreign exchange market by immediately selling foreign currencies in exchange for dollars, causing an abrupt decline in the values of foreign currencies (as the dollar strengthened). Participants that had purchased currency futures contracts incurred large losses. One prominent trader responded to the effects of the Fed's intervention by immediately selling 300 futures contracts on British pounds (with a value of about $30 million). Such actions caused even more panic in the futures market.

a. Explain why the central bank's intervention caused such panic among currency futures traders with buy positions.

b. Explain why the prominent trader's willingness to sell 300 pound futures contracts at the going market rate aroused such concern. What might this action signal to other traders?

c. Explain why speculators with short (sell) positions could benefit as a result of the central bank's intervention.

d. Some traders with buy positions may have responded immediately to the central bank's intervention by selling futures contracts. Why would some speculators with buy positions leave their positions unchanged or even increase their positions by purchasing more futures contracts in response to the central bank's intervention?

25. Estimating Profits from Currency Futures and Options One year ago, you sold a put option on 100,000 euros with an expiration date of one year. You received a premium on the put option of $.04 per unit. The exercise price was $1.22. Assume that one year ago, the spot rate of the euro was $1.20, the one-year forward rate exhibited a discount of 2 percent, and the one-year futures price was the same as the one-year forward rate. From one year ago to today, the euro depreciated against the dollar by 4 percent. Today the put option will be exercised (if it is feasible for the buyer to do so).

a. Determine the total dollar amount of your profit or loss from your position in the put option.

b. Now assume that instead of taking a position in the put option one year ago, you sold a futures contract on 100,000 euros with a settlement date of one year. Determine the total dollar amount of your profit or loss.

26. Impact of Information on Currency Futures and Options Prices Myrtle Beach Co. purchases imports that have a price of 400,000 Singapore dollars, and it has to pay for the imports in 90 days. It can purchase a 90-day forward contract on Singapore dollars at $.50 or purchase a call option contract on Singapore dollars with an exercise price of $.50. This morning, the spot rate of the Singapore dollar was $.50. At noon, the central bank of Singapore raised interest rates, while there was no change in interest rates in the United States. These actions immediately increased the degree of uncertainty surrounding the future value of the Singapore dollar over the next three months. The Singapore dollar's spot rate remained at $.50 throughout the day.

a. Myrtle Beach Co. is convinced that the Singapore dollar will definitely appreciate substantially over the next 90 days. Would a call option hedge or forward hedge be more appropriate given its opinion?

b. Assume that Myrtle Beach Co. uses a currency options contract to hedge rather than a forward contract. If Myrtle Beach Co. purchased a currency call option contract at the money on Singapore dollars this afternoon, would its total U.S. dollar cash outflows be more than, less than, or the same as the total U.S. dollar cash outflows if it had purchased a currency call option contract at the money this morning? Explain.

27. Currency Straddles Reska, Inc., has constructed a long euro straddle. A call option on euros with an exercise price of $1.10 has a premium of $.025 per unit. A euro put option has a premium of $.017 per unit. Some possible euro values at option expiration are shown in the following table. (See Appendix B in this chapter.)

	VALUE OF EURO AT OPTION EXPIRATION			
	$.90	$1.05	$1.50	$2.00
Call				
Put				
Net				

a. Complete the worksheet and determine the net profit per unit to Reska, Inc., for each possible future spot rate.

b. Determine the break-even point(s) of the long straddle. What are the break-even points of a short straddle using these options?

28. Currency Straddles Refer to the previous question, but assume that the call and put option premiums are $.02 per unit and $.015 per unit, respectively. (See Appendix B in this chapter.)

a. Construct a contingency graph for a long euro straddle.

b. Construct a contingency graph for a short euro straddle.

29. Currency Option Contingency Graphs (See Appendix B in this chapter.) The current spot rate of the Singapore dollar (S$) is $.50. The following option information is available:

■ Call option premium on Singapore dollar (S$) = $.015.
■ Put option premium on Singapore dollar (S$) = $.009.
■ Call and put option strike price = $.55.
■ One option contract represents S$70,000.

Construct a contingency graph for a short straddle using these options.

30. Speculating with Currency Straddles Maggie Hawthorne is a currency speculator. She has noticed that recently the euro has appreciated substantially against the U.S. dollar. The current exchange rate of the euro is $1.15. After reading a variety of articles on the subject, she believes that the euro will continue to fluctuate substantially in the months to come. Although most forecasters believe that the euro will depreciate against the dollar in the near future, Maggie thinks that there is also a good possibility of further appreciation. Currently, a call option on euros is available with an exercise price of $1.17 and a premium of $.04. A euro put option with an exercise price of $1.17 and a premium of $.03 is also available. (See Appendix B in this chapter.)

a. Describe how Maggie could use straddles to speculate on the euro's value.

b. At option expiration, the value of the euro is $1.30. What is Maggie's total profit or loss from a long straddle position?

c. What is Maggie's total profit or loss from a long straddle position if the value of the euro is $1.05 at option expiration?

d. What is Maggie's total profit or loss from a long straddle position if the value of the euro at option expiration is still $1.15?

e. Given your answers to the questions above, when is it advantageous for a speculator to engage in a long straddle? When is it advantageous to engage in a short straddle?

31. Currency Strangles (See Appendix B in this chapter.) Assume the following options are currently available for British pounds (£):

- Call option premium on British pounds = $.04 per unit.
- Put option premium on British pounds = $.03 per unit.
- Call option strike price = $1.56.
- Put option strike price = $1.53.
- One option contract represents £31,250.

a. Construct a worksheet for a long strangle using these options.

b. Determine the break-even point(s) for a strangle.

c. If the spot price of the pound at option expiration is $1.55, what is the total profit or loss to the strangle buyer?

d. If the spot price of the pound at option expiration is $1.50, what is the total profit or loss to the strangle writer?

32. Currency Strangles Refer to the previous question, but assume that the call and put option premiums are $.035 per unit and $.025 per unit, respectively. (See Appendix B in this chapter.)

a. Construct a contingency graph for a long pound strangle.

b. Construct a contingency graph for a short pound strangle.

33. Currency Strangles The following information is currently available for Canadian dollar (C$) options (see Appendix B in this chapter):

- Put option exercise price = $.75.
- Put option premium = $.014 per unit.
- Call option exercise price = $.76.
- Call option premium = $.01 per unit.
- One option contract represents C$50,000.

a. What is the maximum possible gain the purchaser of a strangle can achieve using these options?

b. What is the maximum possible loss the writer of a strangle can incur?

c. Locate the break-even point(s) of the strangle.

34. Currency Strangles For the following options available on Australian dollars (A$), construct a worksheet and contingency graph for a long strangle. Locate the break-even points for this strangle. (See Appendix B in this chapter.)

- Put option strike price = $.67
- Call option strike price = $.65.
- Put option premium = $.01 per unit.
- Call option premium = $.02 per unit.

35. Speculating with Currency Options Barry Egan is a currency speculator. Barry believes that the Japanese yen will fluctuate widely against the U.S. dollar in the coming month. Currently, one-month call options on Japanese yen (¥) are available with a strike price of $.0085 and a premium of $.0007 per unit. One-month put options on Japanese yen are available with a strike price of $.0084 and a premium of $.0005 per unit. One option contract on Japanese yen contains ¥6.25 million. (See Appendix B in this chapter.)

a. Describe how Barry Egan could utilize these options to speculate on the movement of the Japanese yen.

b. Assume Barry decides to construct a long strangle in yen. What are the break-even points of this strangle?

c. What is Barry's total profit or loss if the value of the yen in one month is $.0070?

d. What is Barry's total profit or loss if the value of the yen in one month is $.0090?

36. Currency Bull Spreads and Bear Spreads A call option on British pounds (£) exists with a strike price of $1.56 and a premium of $.08 per unit. Another call option on British pounds has a strike price of $1.59 and a premium of $.06 per unit. (See Appendix B in this chapter.)

Complete the worksheet for a bull spread below.

	VALUE OF BRITISH POUND AT OPTION EXPIRATION			
	$1.50	$1.56	$1.59	$1.65
Call @ $1.56				
Call @ $1.59				
Net				

a. What is the break-even point for this bull spread?
b. What is the maximum profit of this bull spread? What is the maximum loss?
c. If the British pound spot rate is $1.58 at option expiration, what is the total profit or loss for the bull spread?
d. If the British pound spot rate is $1.55 at option expiration, what is the total profit or loss for a bear spread?

37. Bull Spreads and Bear Spreads Two British pound (£) put options are available with exercise prices of $1.60 and $1.62. The premiums associated with these options are $.03 and $.04 per unit, respectively. (See Appendix B in this chapter.)

a. Describe how a bull spread can be constructed using these put options. What is the difference between using put options versus call options to construct a bull spread?
b. Complete the following worksheet.

	VALUE OF BRITISH POUND AT OPTION EXPIRATION			
	$1.55	$1.60	$1.62	$1.67
Put @ $1.60				
Put @ $1.62				
Net				

c. At option expiration, the spot rate of the pound is $1.60. What is the bull spreader's total gain or loss?
d. At option expiration, the spot rate of the pound is $1.58. What is the bear spreader's total gain or loss?

38. Profits from Using Currency Options and Futures On July 2, the two-month futures rate of the Mexican peso contained a 2 percent discount (unannualized). There was a call option on pesos with an exercise price that was equal to the spot rate. There was also a put option on pesos with an exercise price equal to the spot rate. The premium on each of these options was 3 percent of the spot rate at that time. On September 2, the option

expired. Go to www.oanda.com (or any website that has foreign exchange rate quotations) and determine the direct quote of the Mexican peso. You exercised the option on this date if it was feasible to do so.

a. What was your net profit per unit if you had purchased the call option?
b. What was your net profit per unit if you had purchased the put option?
c. What was your net profit per unit if you had purchased a futures contract on July 2 that had a settlement date of September 2?
d. What was your net profit per unit if you sold a futures contract on July 2 that had a settlement date of September 2?

39. Uncertainty and Option Premiums This morning, a Canadian dollar call option contract has a $.71 strike price, a premium of $.02, and expiration date of one month from now. This afternoon, news about international economic conditions increased the level of uncertainty surrounding the Canadian dollar. However, the spot rate of the Canadian dollar was still $.71. Would the premium of the call option contract be higher than, lower than, or equal to $.02 this afternoon? Explain.

40. Uncertainty and Option Premiums At 10:30 a.m., the media reported news that the Mexican government's political problems were reduced, which reduced the expected volatility of the Mexican peso against the dollar over the next month. The spot rate of the Mexican peso was $.13 as of 10 a.m. and remained at that level all morning. At 10 a.m., Hilton Head Co. purchased a call option at the money on 1 million Mexican pesos with an expiration date one month from now. At 11:00 a.m., Rhode Island Co. purchased a call option at the money on 1 million pesos with a December expiration date one month from now. Did Hilton Head Co. pay more, less, or the same as Rhode Island Co. for the options? Briefly explain.

41. Speculating with Currency Futures Assume that one year ago, the spot rate of the British pound was $1.70. One year ago, the one-year futures contract of the British pound exhibited a discount of 6 percent. At that time, you sold futures contracts on pounds, representing a total of £1,000,000. From one year ago to today, the pound's value depreciated against the dollar by 4 percent. Determine the total dollar amount of your profit or loss from your futures contract.

42. Speculating with Currency Options The spot rate of the New Zealand dollar is $.77. A call option on New Zealand dollars with a one-year expiration date has an exercise price of $.78 and a premium of $.04.

A put option on New Zealand dollars at the money with a one-year expiration date has a premium of $.03. You expect that the New Zealand dollar's spot rate will decline over time and will be $.71 in one year.

a. Today, Dawn purchased call options on New Zealand dollars with a one-year expiration date. Estimate the profit or loss per unit at the end of one year. [Assume that the options would be exercised on the expiration date or not at all.]

b. Today, Mark sold put options on New Zealand dollars at the money with a one-year expiration date. Estimate the profit or loss per unit for Mark at the end of one year. [Assume that the options would be exercised on the expiration date or not at all.]

43. Impact of Expected Volatility on Currency Option Premiums Assume that Australia's central bank announced plans to stabilize the Australian dollar (A$) in the foreign exchange markets. In response to this announcement, the expected volatility of the A$ declined immediately. However, the spot rate of the A$ remained at $.89 on this day, and was not affected by the announcement. The one-year forward rate of the A$ remained at $.89 on this day and was not affected by the announcement. Do you think the premium charged on a one-year A$ currency option increased, decreased, or remained the same on this day in response to the announcement? Briefly explain.

Critical Thinking

Pricing of Currency Options Review the logic regarding how currency options are priced. Consider a speculator who plans to purchase currency options for the option at the money on whatever currency has the lowest premium. He also plans to sell currency options for the option at the money on whatever currency has the highest premium. Another speculator uses a strategy of purchasing call options on Australian dollars at the money whenever the premium is relatively low (compared to the historical premiums that existed for this type of option). She also sells call options at the money on Australian dollars at the money. Write a short essay describing your opinion about the likely success of these strategies.

Discussion in the Boardroom

This exercise can be found in Appendix E at the back of this textbook.

Running Your Own MNC

This exercise can be found on the *International Financial Management* text companion website. Go to www.cengagebrain.com (students) or www.cengage.com/login (instructors) and search using **ISBN 9781133947837.**

BLADES, INC. CASE

Use of Currency Derivative Instruments

Blades, Inc., needs to order supplies two months ahead of the delivery date. It is considering an order from a Japanese supplier that requires a payment of 12.5 million yen payable as of the delivery date. Blades has two choices:

■ Purchase two call options contracts (because each option contract represents 6,250,000 yen).
■ Purchase one futures contract (which represents 12.5 million yen).

The futures price on yen has historically exhibited a slight discount from the existing spot rate. However, the firm would like to use currency options to hedge payables in Japanese yen for transactions two months in advance. Blades would prefer hedging its yen payable position because it is uncomfortable leaving the position open given the historical volatility of the yen. Nevertheless, the firm would be willing to remain unhedged if the yen becomes more stable someday.

Ben Holt, Blades' chief financial officer (CFO), prefers the flexibility that options offer over forward contracts or futures contracts because he can let the options expire if the yen depreciates. He would like to use an exercise price that is about 5 percent above the existing spot rate to ensure that Blades will have to pay no more than 5 percent above the existing spot rate for a transaction two months beyond its order date, as long as the option premium is no more than 1.6 percent of the price it would have to pay per unit when exercising the option.

In general, options on the yen have required a premium of about 1.5 percent of the total transaction amount that would be paid if the option is exercised. For example, recently the yen spot rate was $.0072, and the firm purchased a call option with an exercise price of $.00756, which is 5 percent above the existing spot rate. The premium for this option was $.0001134, which is 1.5 percent of the price to be paid per yen if the option is exercised.

A recent event caused more uncertainty about the yen's future value, although it did not affect the spot rate or the forward or futures rate of the yen. Specifically, the yen's spot rate was still $.0072, but the option premium for a call option with an exercise price of $.00756 was now $.0001512.

An alternative call option is available with an expiration date of two months from now; it has a premium of $.0001134 (which is the size of the premium that would have existed for the option desired before the event), but it is for a call option with an exercise price of $.00792.

The table below summarizes the option and futures information available to Blades:

	BEFORE EVENT	AFTER EVENT	
Spot rate	$.0072	$.0072	$.0072
Option Information			
Exercise price ($)		$.00756	$.00792
Exercise price (% above spot)		5%	10%
Option premium per yen ($)		$.0001512	$.0001134
Option premium (% of exercise price)		2.0%	1.5%
Total premium ($)		$1,890.00	$1,417.50
Amount paid for yen if option is exercised (not including premium)		$94,500	$99,000
Futures Contract Information			
Futures price		$.006912	

As an analyst for Blades, you have been asked to offer insight on how to hedge. Use a spreadsheet to support your analysis of questions 4 and 6.

1. If Blades uses call options to hedge its yen payables, should it use the call option with the exercise price of $.00756 or the call option with the exercise price of $.00792? Describe the trade-off.

2. Should Blades allow its yen position to be unhedged? Describe the trade-off.

3. Assume there are speculators who attempt to capitalize on their expectation of the yen's movement over the two months between the order and delivery dates by either buying or selling yen futures now and buying or selling yen at the future spot rate. Given this information, what is the expectation on the order date of the yen spot rate by the delivery date? (Your answer should consist of one number.)

4. Assume that the firm shares the market consensus of the future yen spot rate. Given this expectation and given that the firm makes a decision (i.e., option, futures contract, remain unhedged) purely on a cost basis, what would be its optimal choice?

5. Will the choice you made as to the optimal hedging strategy in question 4 definitely turn out to be the lowest-cost alternative in terms of actual costs incurred? Why or why not?

6. Now assume that you have determined that the historical standard deviation of the yen is about $.0005. Based on your assessment, you believe it is highly unlikely that the future spot rate will be more than two standard deviations above the expected spot rate by the delivery date. Also assume that the futures price remains at its current level of $.006912. Based on this expectation of the future spot rate, what is the optimal hedge for the firm?

SMALL BUSINESS DILEMMA

Use of Currency Futures and Options by the Sports Exports Company

The Sports Exports Company receives British pounds each month as payment for the footballs that it exports. It anticipates that the pound will depreciate over time against the U.S. dollar.

1. How can the Sports Exports Company use currency futures contracts to hedge against exchange rate risk? Are there any limitations of using currency futures contracts that would prevent the Sports Exports

Company from locking in a specific exchange rate at which it can sell all the pounds it expects to receive in each of the upcoming months?

2. How can the Sports Exports Company use currency options to hedge against exchange rate risk?

3. Are there any limitations of using currency options contracts that would prevent the Sports Exports Company from locking in a specific exchange rate at which it can sell all the pounds it expects to receive in each of the upcoming months?

4. Jim Logan, owner of the Sports Exports Company, is concerned that the pound may depreciate substantially over the next month, but he also believes that the pound could appreciate substantially if specific situations occur. Should Logan use currency futures or currency options to hedge the exchange rate risk? Is there any disadvantage of selecting this method for hedging?

INTERNET/EXCEL EXERCISES

The website of the Chicago Mercantile Exchange (www.cmegroup.com) provides information about currency futures and options.

1. Use this website to review the prevailing prices of currency futures contracts. Do today's futures prices (for contracts with the closest settlement date) generally reflect an increase or decrease from the day before? Is there any news today that might explain the change in the futures prices?

2. Does it appear that futures prices among currencies (for the closest settlement date) are changing in the same direction? Explain.

3. If you purchase a British pound futures contract with the closest settlement date, what is the futures price? Given that a contract is based on £62,500, what is the dollar amount you will need at the settlement date to fulfill the contract?

4. Go to www.nasdaqtrader.com and under "Trading Products," click on FX Options. Obtain the money currency option quotations for the Canadian dollar (the symbol is XCD) and the euro (symbol is XEU) for a similar expiration date. Which currency option has a larger premium? Explain your results.

ONLINE ARTICLES WITH REAL-WORLD EXAMPLES

Find a recent article online that describes an actual international finance application or a real-world example about a specific MNC's actions that reinforces one or more concepts covered in this chapter.

If your class has an online component, your professor may ask you to post your summary there and provide the web link of the article so that other students can access it. If your class is live, your professor may ask you to summarize your application in class. Your professor may assign specific students to complete this assignment for this chapter, or may allow any students to do the assignment on a volunteer basis.

For recent online articles and real-world examples applied to this chapter, consider using the following search terms and include the prevailing year as a search term to ensure that the online articles are recent:

1. company AND forward contract
2. Inc. AND forward contract
3. company AND currency futures
4. Inc. AND currency futures
5. company AND currency options
6. Inc. AND currency options
7. forward market
8. currency futures market
9. currency options market
10. currency derivatives

APPENDIX 5A

Currency Option Pricing

The premiums paid for currency options depend on various factors that must be monitored when anticipating future movements in currency option premiums. Because participants in the currency options market typically take positions based on their expectations of how the premiums will change over time, they can benefit from understanding how options are priced.

Boundary Conditions

The first step in pricing currency options is to recognize boundary conditions that force the option premium to be within lower and upper bounds.

Lower Bounds

The call option premium (C) has a lower bound of at least zero or the spread between the underlying spot exchange rate (S) and the exercise price (X), whichever is greater, as follows:

$$C = \textbf{MAX}(0, S - X)$$

This floor is enforced by arbitrage restrictions. For example, assume that the premium on a British pound call option is $.01, while the spot rate of the pound is $1.62 and the exercise price is $1.60. In this example, the spread ($S - X$) exceeds the call premium, which would allow for arbitrage. One could purchase the call option for $.01 per unit, immediately exercise the option at $1.60 per pound, and then sell the pounds in the spot market for $1.62 per unit. This would generate an immediate profit of $.01 per unit. Arbitrage would continue until the market forces realigned the spread ($S - X$) to be less than or equal to the call premium.

The put option premium (P) has a lower bound of zero or the spread between the exercise price (X) and the underlying spot exchange rate (S), whichever is greater, as follows:

$$P = \textbf{MAX}(0, S - X)$$

This floor is also enforced by arbitrage restrictions. For example, assume that the premium on a British pound put option is $.02, while the spot rate of the pound is $1.60 and the exercise price is $1.63. One could purchase the pound put option for $.02 per unit, purchase pounds in the spot market at $1.60, and immediately exercise the option by selling the pounds at $1.63 per unit. This would generate an immediate profit of $.01 per unit. Arbitrage would continue until the market forces realigned the spread $(X - S)$ to be less than or equal to the put premium.

Upper Bounds

The upper bound for a call option premium is equal to the spot exchange rate (S):

$$C = S$$

If the call option premium ever exceeds the spot exchange rate, one could engage in arbitrage by selling call options for a higher price per unit than the cost of purchasing the underlying currency. Even if those call options are exercised, one could provide the currency that was purchased earlier (the call option was covered). The arbitrage profit in this example is the difference between the amount received when selling the premium and the cost of purchasing the currency in the spot market. Arbitrage would occur until the call option's premium was less than or equal to the spot rate.

The upper bound for a put option is equal to the option's exercise price (X):

$$P = X$$

If the put option premium ever exceeds the exercise price, one could engage in arbitrage by selling put options. Even if the put options are exercised, the proceeds received from selling the put options exceed the price paid (which is the exercise price) at the time of exercise.

Given these boundaries that are enforced by arbitrage, option premiums lie within these boundaries.

WEB

www.ozforex.com.au
/forex-tools/tools/
fx-options-calculator
Estimates the price of
currency options based
on input provided.

Application of Pricing Models

Although boundary conditions can be used to determine the possible range for a currency option's premium, they do not precisely indicate the appropriate premium for the option. However, pricing models have been developed to price currency options. Based on information about an option (such as the exercise price and time to maturity) and about the currency (such as its spot rate, standard deviation, and interest rate), pricing models can derive the premium on a currency option. The currency option pricing model of Biger and Hull[1] is as follows:

$$C = e^{-r^*T}S \cdot N(d_1) - e^{-rT}X \cdot N(d_1 - \sigma\sqrt{T})$$

where

$$d_1 = \{\ln(S/X) + [r - r^* + (\sigma^2/2)]T\}/\sigma\sqrt{T}$$

$C =$ price of the currency call option

$S =$ underlying spot exchange rate

$X =$ exercise price

$r =$ U.S. riskless rate of interest

$r^* =$ foreign riskless rate of interest

$\sigma =$ instantaneous standard deviation of the return on a holding of foreign currency

$T =$ option's time to maturity expressed as a fraction of a year

$N(\cdot) =$ standard normal cumulative distribution function

---

[1]Nahum Biger and John Hull, "The Valuation of Currency Options," *Financial Management* (Spring 1983): 24–28.

This equation is based on the stock option pricing model (OPM) when allowing for continuous dividends. Because the interest gained on holding a foreign security (r^*) is equivalent to a continuously paid dividend on a stock share, this version of the OPM holds completely. The key transformation in adapting the stock OPM to value currency options is the substitution of exchange rates for stock prices. Thus the percentage change of exchange rates is assumed to follow a diffusion process with constant mean and variance.

Bodurtha and Courtadon[2] have tested the predictive ability of the currency option pricing model. They computed pricing errors from the model using 3,326 call options. The model's average percentage pricing error for call options was –6.90 percent, which is smaller than the corresponding error reported for the dividend-adjusted Black-Scholes stock OPM. Hence, the currency option pricing model has been more accurate than the counterpart stock OPM.

The model developed by Biger and Hull is sometimes referred to as the European model because it does not account for early exercise. European currency options do not allow for early exercise (before the expiration date), whereas American currency options do allow for early exercise. The extra flexibility of American currency options may justify a higher premium on American currency options than on European currency options with similar characteristics. However, there is not a closed-form model for pricing American currency options. Although various techniques are used to price American currency options, the European model is commonly applied to price American currency options because it can be just as accurate.

Bodurtha and Courtadon found that the application of an American currency options pricing model does not improve predictive accuracy. Their average percentage pricing error was −7.07 percent for all sample call options when using the American model.

Given all other parameters, the currency option pricing model can be used to impute the standard deviation σ. This implied parameter represents the option's market assessment of currency volatility over the life of the option.

Pricing Currency Put Options According to Put-Call Parity

Given the premium of a European call option (called C), the premium for a European put option (called P) on the same currency and same exercise price (X) can be derived from put-call parity, as follows:

$$P = C + Xe^{-rt} - Se^{-r^*}T$$

where

$$r = \text{U.S riskless rate of interest}$$
$$r^* = \text{foreign riskless rate of interest}$$
$$T = \text{option's time to maturity expressed as a fraction of the year}$$

If the actual put option premium is less than what is suggested by the put-call parity equation above, arbitrage can be conducted. Specifically, one could (1) buy the put option, (2) sell the call option, and (3) buy the underlying currency. The purchases are financed with the proceeds from selling the call option and from borrowing at the rate r. Meanwhile, the foreign currency that was purchased can be deposited to earn the foreign rate r^*. Regardless of the scenario for the path of the currency's exchange rate movement over the life of the option, the arbitrage will result in a profit. First, if the

[2]James Bodurtha and Georges Courtadon, "Tests of an American Option Pricing Model on the Foreign Currency Options Market," *Journal of Financial and Quantitative Analysis* (June 1987): 153–168.

exchange rate is equal to the exercise price such that each option expires worthless, the foreign currency can be converted in the spot market to dollars, and this amount will exceed the amount required to repay the loan. Second, if the foreign currency appreciates and therefore exceeds the exercise price, there will be a loss from the call option being exercised.

Although the put option will expire, the foreign currency will be converted in the spot market to dollars, and this amount will exceed the amount required to repay the loan and the amount of the loss on the call option. Third, if the foreign currency depreciates and therefore is below the exercise price, the amount received from exercising the put option plus the amount received from converting the foreign currency to dollars will exceed the amount required to repay the loan. Because the arbitrage generates a profit under any exchange rate scenario, it will force an adjustment in the option premiums so that put-call parity is no longer violated.

If the actual put option premium is more than what is suggested by put-call parity, arbitrage would again be possible. The arbitrage strategy would be the reverse of that used when the actual put option premium was less than what is suggested by put-call parity (as just described). The arbitrage would force an adjustment in option premiums so that put-call parity is no longer violated. The arbitrage that can be applied when there is a violation of put-call parity on American currency options differs slightly from the arbitrage applicable to European currency options. Nevertheless, the concept still holds that the premium of a currency put option can be determined according to the premium of a call option on the same currency and the same exercise price.

Currency Option Combinations

In addition to the basic call and put options just discussed, a variety of currency option combinations are available to the currency speculator and hedger. A **currency option combination** uses simultaneous call and put option positions to construct a unique position to suit the hedger's or speculator's needs. A currency option combination may include both long and short positions and will itself be either long or short. Typically, a currency option combination will result in a unique contingency graph.

Currency option combinations can be used both to hedge cash inflows and outflows denominated in a foreign currency and to speculate on the future movement of a foreign currency. More specifically, both MNCs and individual speculators can construct a currency option combination to accommodate expectations of either appreciating or depreciating foreign currencies.

In this appendix, two of the most popular currency option combinations are discussed. These are **straddles** and **strangles**. For each of these combinations, the following topics will be discussed:

- The composition of the combination
- The worksheet and contingency graph for the long combination
- The worksheet and contingency graph for the short combination
- Uses of the combination to speculate on the movement of a foreign currency

The two main types of currency option combinations are discussed next.

Currency Straddles

Long Currency Straddle

To construct a long straddle in a foreign currency, an MNC or individual would buy (take a long position in) both a call option and a put option for that currency; the call and the put option have the same expiration date and striking price.

When constructing a long straddle, the buyer purchases both the right to buy the foreign currency and the right to sell the foreign currency. Because the call option will become profitable if the foreign currency appreciates, and the put option will become profitable if the foreign currency depreciates, a long straddle becomes profitable when the foreign currency *either* appreciates or depreciates. Obviously, this is a huge advantage for the individual or entity that constructs a long straddle, as it appears that it would benefit from the position as long as the foreign currency exchange rate does not remain constant. The disadvantage of a long straddle position is that it is expensive to construct, because it involves the purchase of two separate options, each of which requires payment of the option premium. Therefore, a long straddle becomes profitable only if the foreign currency appreciates or depreciates substantially.

Long Currency Straddle Worksheet   To determine the profit or loss associated with a long straddle (or any combination), it is easiest to first construct a profit or loss worksheet for several possible currency values at option expiration. The worksheet can be set up to show each individual option position and the net position. The worksheet will also help in constructing a contingency graph for the combination.

EXAMPLE

Put and call options are available for euros (€) with the following information:

- Call option premium on euro = $.03 per unit.
- Put option premium on euro = $.02 per unit.
- Strike price = $1.05.
- One option contract represents €62,500.

To construct a long straddle, the buyer would purchase both a euro call and a euro put option, paying $.03 + $.02 = $.05 per unit. If the value of the euro at option expiration is above the strike price of $1.05, the call option is in the money, but the put option is out of the money. Conversely, if the value of the euro at option expiration is below $1.05, the put option is in the money, but the call option is out of the money.

A possible worksheet for the long straddle that illustrates the profitability of the individual components is shown below.

	VALUE OF EURO AT OPTION EXPIRATION					
	$.95	$1.00	$1.05	$1.10	$1.15	$1.20
Own a call	−$.03	−$.03	−$.03	+$.02	+$.07	+$.12
Own a put	+$.08	+$.03	−$.02	−$.02	−$.02	−$.02
Net	+$.05	$.00	−$.05	$.00	+$.05	+$.10

Long Currency Straddle Contingency Graph

A contingency graph for the long currency straddle is shown in Exhibit 5B.1. This graph includes more extreme possible outcomes than are shown in the table. Either the call or put option on the foreign currency will be in the money at option expiration as long as the foreign currency value at option expiration differs from the strike price.

There are two break-even points for a long straddle position—one below the strike price and one above the strike price. The lower break-even point is equal to the strike price less both premiums; the higher break-even point is equal to the strike price plus both premiums. Thus, for the above example, the two break-even points are located at $1.00 = $1.05 − $.05 and at $1.10 = $1.05 + $.05.

The maximum loss for the long straddle in the example occurs at a euro value at option expiration equal to the strike price, when both options are at the money. At that point, the straddle buyer would lose both option premiums. The maximum loss for the straddle buyer is thus equal to $.05 = $.03 + $.02.

Exhibit 5B.1   Contingency Graph for a Long Currency Straddle

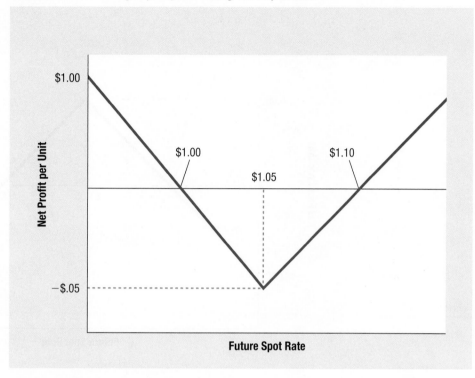

Short Currency Straddle

Constructing a short straddle in a foreign currency involves selling (taking a short position in) both a call option and a put option for that currency. As in a long straddle, the call and put option have the same expiration date and strike price.

The advantage of a short straddle is that it provides the option writer with income from two separate options. The disadvantage is the possibility of substantial losses if the underlying currency moves substantially away from the strike price.

Short Currency Straddle Worksheet and Contingency Graph

A short straddle results in a worksheet and a contingency graph that are exactly opposite to those of a long straddle.

EXAMPLE

Assuming the same information as in the previous example, a short straddle would involve writing both a call option on euros and a put option on euros. A possible worksheet for the resulting short straddle is shown below.

	VALUE OF EURO AT OPTION EXPIRATION					
	$.95	$1.00	$1.05	$1.10	$1.15	$1.20
Sell a call	+$.03	+$.03	+$.03	−$.02	−$.07	−$.12
Sell a put	−$.08	−$.03	+$.02	+$.02	+$.02	+$.02
Net	−$.05	$.00	+$.05	$.00	−$.05	−$.10

The worksheet also illustrates that there are two break-even points for a short straddle position—one below the strike price and one above the strike price. The lower break-even point is equal to the strike

Exhibit 5B.2   Contingency Graph for a Long Currency Straddle

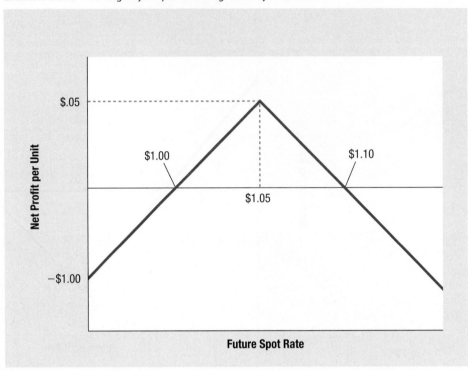

price less both premiums; the higher break-even point is equal to the strike price plus both premiums. Thus the two break-even points are located at $1.00 = $1.05 − $.05 and at $1.10 = $1.05 + $.05. This is the same relationship as for the long straddle position.

The maximum gain occurs at a euro value at option expiration equal to the strike price of $1.05 and is equal to the sum of the two option premiums ($.03 + $.02 = $.05).

The resulting contingency graph is shown in Exhibit 5B.2. ●

Speculating with Currency Straddles

Individuals can speculate using currency straddles based on their expectations of the future movement in a particular foreign currency. For example, speculators who expect that the British pound will appreciate or depreciate substantially can buy a straddle. If the pound appreciates substantially, the speculator will let the put option expire and exercise the call option. If the pound depreciates substantially, the speculator will let the call option expire and exercise the put option.

Speculators may also profit from short straddles. The writer of a short straddle believes that the value of the underlying currency will remain close to the exercise price until option expiration. If the value of the underlying currency is equal to the strike price at option expiration, the straddle writer would collect premiums from both options. However, this is a rather risky position; if the currency appreciates or depreciates substantially, the straddle writer will lose money. If the currency appreciates substantially, the straddle writer will have to sell the currency for the strike price, as the call option will be exercised. If the currency depreciates substantially, the straddle writer has to buy the currency for the strike price, as the put option will be exercised.

EXAMPLE   Call and put option contracts on British pounds (£) are available with the following information:

- Call option premium on British pounds = $.035.
- Put option premium on British pounds = $.025.
- Strike price = $1.50.
- One option contract represents £31,250.

At expiration, the spot rate of the pound is $1.40. A speculator who had bought a straddle will therefore exercise the put option but let the call option expire. Therefore, the speculator will buy pounds at the prevailing spot rate and sell them for the exercise price. Given this information, the net profit to the straddle buyer is calculated as follows:

	PER UNIT	PER CONTRACT
Selling price of £	+$1.50	$46,875 ($1.50 × 31,250 units)
− Purchase price of £	−1.40	−43,750 ($1.40 × 31,250 units)
− Premium paid for call option	−.035	−1,093.75 ($.035 × 31,250 units)
− Premium paid for put option	−.025	− 81.25 ($.025 × 31,250 units)
= Net profit	$.04	$1,250 ($.04 × 31,250 units)

The straddle writer will have to purchase pounds for the exercise price. Assuming the speculator immediately sells the acquired pounds at the prevailing spot rate, the net profit to the straddle writer will be:

	PER UNIT	PER CONTRACT
Selling price of £	+$1.40	$43,750 ($1.40 × 31,250 units)
− Purchase price of £	−1.50	−46,875 ($1.50 × 31,250 units)
+ Premium received for call option	+.035	1,093.75 ($.035 × 31,250 units)
+ Premium received for put option	+.025	781.25 ($.025 × 31,250 units)
= Net profit	−$.04	−$1,250 ($.04 × 31,250 units)

As with an individual short put position, the seller of the straddle could simply refrain from selling the pounds (after being forced to buy them at the exercise price of $1.50) until the spot rate of the pound rises. However, there is no guarantee that the pound will appreciate in the near future. ●

Note from the above example and discussion that the straddle writer gains what the straddle buyer loses, and vice versa. Consequently, the straddle writer's gain or loss is the straddle buyer's loss or gain. Thus the same relationship that applies to individual call and put options also applies to option combinations.

Currency Strangles

Currency strangles are very similar to currency straddles, with one important difference: The call and put options of the underlying foreign currency have different exercise prices. Nevertheless, the underlying security and the expiration date for the call and put options are identical.

Long Currency Strangle

Because the call and put options used in a strangle can have different exercise prices, a long strangle can be constructed in a variety of ways. For example, a strangle could be constructed in which the call option has a higher exercise price than the put option and vice versa. The most common type of strangle, and the focus of this section, is a strangle that involves buying a put option with a lower strike price than the call option that is purchased. To construct a long strangle in a foreign currency, an MNC or individual would thus take a long position in a call option and a long position in a put option for that currency. The call option has the higher exercise price.

An advantage of a long strangle relative to a comparable long straddle is that it is cheaper to construct. From previous sections, recall that there is an inverse relationship between the spot price of the currency relative to the strike price and the call option premium: the lower the spot price relative to the strike price, the lower the option premium will be. Therefore, if a long strangle involves purchasing a call option with a relatively high exercise price, it should be cheaper to construct than a comparable straddle, everything else being equal.

The disadvantage of a strangle relative to a straddle is that the underlying currency has to fluctuate more prior to expiration. As with a long straddle, the reason for constructing a long strangle is the expectation of a substantial currency fluctuation in either direction prior to the expiration date. However, because the two options involved in a strangle have different exercise prices, the underlying currency has to fluctuate to a larger extent before the strangle is in the money at future spot prices.

Long Currency Strangle Worksheet   The worksheet for a long currency strangle is similar to the worksheet for a long currency straddle, as the following example shows.

Put and call options are available for euros (€) with the following information:

- Call option premium on euro = $.025 per unit.
- Put option premium on euro = $.02 per unit.
- Call option strike price = $1.15.
- Put option strike price = $1.05.
- One option contract represents €62,500.

Note that this example is almost identical to the earlier straddle example, except that the call option has a higher exercise price than the put option and the call option premium is slightly lower.

A possible worksheet for the long strangle is shown here:

	VALUE OF EURO AT OPTION EXPIRATION					
	$.95	$1.00	$1.05	$1.10	$1.15	$1.20
Own a call	−$.025	−$.025	−$.025	−$.025	−$.025	+$.025
Own a put	+$.08	+$.03	−$.02	−$.02	−$.02	−$.02
Net	+$.055	+$.005	−$.045	−$.045	−$.045	+$.005

Long Currency Strangle Contingency Graph   Exhibit 5B.3 shows a contingency graph for the long currency strangle. Again, the graph includes more extreme values than are shown in the worksheet. The call option will be in the money when the foreign currency value is higher than its strike price at option expiration, and the put option will be in the money when the foreign currency value is below the put option strike price at option expiration. Thus the long call position is in the money at euro values above the $1.15 call option exercise price at option expiration. Conversely, the put option is in the money at euro values below the put option exercise price of $1.05.

The two break-even points for a long strangle position are located below the put option premium and above the call option premium. The lower break-even point is

Exhibit 5B.3   Contingency Graph for a Long Currency Strangle

equal to the put option strike price less both premiums ($1.005 = $1.05 − $.045); the higher break-even point is equal to the call option strike price plus both premiums ($1.195 = $1.15 + $.045).

The maximum loss for a long strangle occurs at euro values at option expiration between the two strike prices. At any future spot price between the two exercise prices, the straddle buyer would lose both option premiums (−$.045 = −$.025 − $.02).

The contingency graph for the long strangle illustrates that the euro must fluctuate more widely than with a straddle before the position becomes profitable. However, the maximum loss is only $.045 per unit, whereas it was $.05 per unit for the long straddle.

Short Currency Strangle

Analogous to a short currency straddle, a short strangle involves taking a short position in both a call option and a put option for that currency. As with a short straddle, the call and put options have the same expiration date. However, the call option has the higher exercise price in a short strangle.

Relative to a short straddle, the disadvantage of a short strangle is that it provides less income, as the call option premium will be lower, everything else being equal. However, the advantage of a short strangle relative to a short straddle is that the underlying currency has to fluctuate more before the strangle writer is in danger of losing money.

Short Currency Strangle Worksheet and Contingency Graph

The euro example is next used to show that the worksheet and contingency graph for the short strangle are exactly opposite to those of a long strangle.

EXAMPLE   Continuing with the information in the preceding example, a short strangle can be constructed by writing a call option on euros and a put option on euros. The resulting worksheet is shown below:

	VALUE OF EURO AT OPTION EXPIRATION					
	$.95	$1.00	$1.05	$1.10	$1.15	$1.20
Sell a call	+$.025	+$.025	+$.025	+$.025	+$.025	−$.025
Sell a put	−$.08	−$.03	+$.02	+$.02	+$.02	+$.02
Net	−$.055	−$.005	+$.045	+$.045	+$.045	−$.005

The table shows that there are two break-even points for the short strangle. The lower break-even point is equal to the put option strike price less both premiums; the higher break-even point is equal to the call option strike price plus both premiums. The two break-even points are thus located at $1.005 = $1.05 − $.045 and at $1.195 = $1.15 + $.045. These break-even points are identical to the break-even points for the long strangle position.

The maximum gain for a short strangle ($.045 = $.025 + $.02) occurs at a value of the euro at option expiration between the two exercise prices.

The short strangle contingency graph is shown in Exhibit 5B.4. ●

As with straddles, individuals can speculate using currency strangles based on their expectations of the future movement in a particular foreign currency. For instance, speculators who expect that the Swiss franc will appreciate or depreciate substantially can construct a long strangle. Speculators can benefit from short strangles if the future spot price of the underlying currency is between the two exercise prices.

Compared to a straddle, the speculator who buys a strangle believes that the underlying currency will fluctuate even more widely prior to expiration. In return, the speculator pays less to construct the long strangle. A speculator who writes a strangle will receive both option premiums as long as the future spot price is between the two exercise prices. Compared to a straddle, the total amount received from writing the two options is less. However, the range of future spot prices between which no option is exercised is much wider for a short strangle.

Exhibit 5B.4 Contingency Graph for a Long Currency Strangle

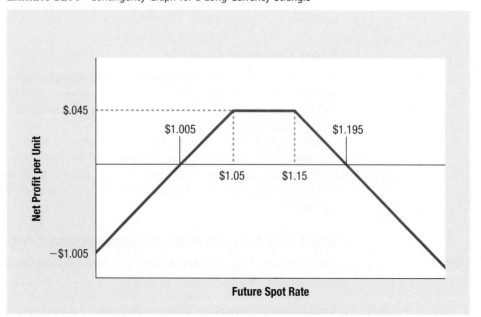

EXAMPLE Call and put option contracts on British pounds (£) are available with the following information:

- Call option premium on British pounds = $.030.
- Put option premium on British pounds = $.025.
- Call option strike price = $1.60.
- Put option strike price = $1.50.
- One option contract represents £31,250.

The spot rate of the pound on the expiration date is $1.52. With a long strangle, the speculator will let both options expire, because both the call and the put option are out of the money. Consequently, the strangle buyer will lose both option premiums:

	PER UNIT	PER CONTRACT
− Premium paid for call option	−$.030	−781.25 ($.025 × 31,250 units)
− Premium paid for put option	−.025	−$937.50 ($.030 × 31,250 units)
= Net profit	−$.055	−$1,718.75 (−$.055 × 31,250 units)

The straddle writer will receive the premiums from both the call and the put option, as neither option will be exercised by its owner:

	PER UNIT	PER CONTRACT
+ Premium received for call option	+$.030	$937.50 ($.030 × 31,250 units)
+ Premium received for put option	+.025	+781.25 ($.025 × 31,250 units)
= Net profit	$.055	$1,718.75 ($.055 × 31,250 units)

As with individual call or put positions and with a straddle, the strangle writer's gain or loss is the strangle buyer's loss or gain. ●

Currency Spreads

A variety of currency spreads exist that can be used by both MNCs and individuals to hedge cash inflows or outflows or to profit from an anticipated movement in a foreign currency. This section covers two of the most popular types of spreads: bull spreads and bear spreads. Bull spreads are profitable when a foreign currency appreciates, whereas bear spreads are profitable when a foreign currency depreciates.

Currency Bull Spreads with Call Options

A currency bull spread is constructed by buying a call option for a particular underlying currency and simultaneously writing a call option for the same currency with a higher exercise price. A bull spread can also be constructed using currency put options, as will be discussed shortly.

With a bull spread, the spreader believes that the underlying currency will appreciate modestly, but not substantially.

EXAMPLE Assume two call options on Australian dollars (A$) are currently available. The first option has a strike price of $.64 and a premium of $.019. The second option has a strike price of $.65 and a premium of $.015. The bull spreader buys the $.64 option and sells the $.65 option. An option contract on Australian dollars consists of 50,000 units.

Consider the following scenarios:

1. The Australian dollar appreciates to $.645, a spot price between the two exercise prices. The bull spreader will exercise the option he bought. Assuming the bull spreader immediately sells the Australian

dollars for the $.645 spot rate after purchasing them for the $.64 exercise price, he will gain the difference. The bull spreader will also collect the premium on the second option he wrote, but that option will not be exercised by the (unknown) buyer:

	PER UNIT	PER CONTRACT
Selling price of A$	+$.645	$32,250 ($.645 × 50,000 units)
− Purchase price of A$	−.64	−32,000 ($.64 × 50,000 units)
− Premium paid for call option	−.019	−950 ($.019 × 50,000 units)
+ Premium received for call option	+.015	+750 ($.015 × 50,000 units)
= Net profit	$.001	$50 ($.001 × 50,000 units)

Under this scenario, note that the bull spreader would have incurred a net loss of $.645 − $.64 − $.019 = −$.014/A$ if he had purchased only the first option. By writing the second call option, the spreader increased his net profit by $.015/A$.

2. The Australian dollar appreciates to $.70, a value above the higher exercise price. Under this scenario, the bull spreader will exercise the option he purchased, but the option he wrote will also be exercised by the (unknown) buyer. Assuming the bull spreader immediately sells the Australian dollars purchased with the first option and buys the Australian dollars he has to sell to the second option buyer for the spot rate, he will incur the following cash flows:

	PER UNIT	PER CONTRACT
Selling price of A$	+$.70	$35,000 ($.70 × 50,000 units)
Purchase price of A$	−.64	−32,000 ($.64 × 50,000 units)
− Premium paid for call option	−.019	−950 ($.019 × 50,000 units)
+ Selling price of A$	+.65	+32,500 ($.65 × 50,000 units)
− Purchase price of A$	−.70	−35,000 ($.70 × 50,000 units)
+ Premium received for call option	+.015	+750 ($.015 × 50,000 units)
= Net profit	$.006	$300 ($.006 × 50,000 units)

The important point to understand here is that the net profit to the bull spreader will remain $.006/A$ no matter how much more the Australian dollar appreciates. This is because the bull spreader will always sell the Australian dollars he purchased with the first option for the spot price and purchase the Australian dollars needed to meet his obligation for the second option. The two effects always cancel out, so the bull spreader will net the difference in the two strike prices less the difference in the two premiums ($.65 − $.64 − $.019 + $.015 = $.006). Therefore, the net profit to the bull spreader will be $.006 per unit at any future spot price above $.65.

Equally important to understand is the trade-off involved in constructing a bull spread. The bull spreader in effect forgoes the benefit from a large currency appreciation by collecting the premium from writing a currency option with a higher exercise price and ensuring a constant profit at future spot prices above the higher exercise price; if he had not written the second option with the higher exercise price, he would have benefited substantially under this scenario, netting $.70 − $.64 − $.019 = $.041/A$ as a result of exercising the call option with the $.64 strike price. This is the reason the bull spreader expects that the underlying currency will appreciate modestly so that he gains from the option he buys and collects the premium from the option he sells without incurring any opportunity costs.

3. The Australian dollar depreciates to $.62, a value below the lower exercise price. If the future spot price is below the lower exercise price, neither call option will be exercised, as they are both out of the money. Consequently, the net profit to the bull spreader is the difference between the two option premiums:

	PER UNIT	PER CONTRACT
− Premium paid for call option	−$.019	−$950 ($.019 × 50,000 units)
+ Premium received for call option	+.015	+750 ($.015 × 50,000 units)
= Net profit	−$.004	−$200 ($.004 × 50,000 units)

Similar to the scenario where the Australian dollar appreciates modestly between the two exercise prices, the bull spreader's loss in this case is reduced by the premium received from writing the call option with the higher exercise price. ●

Currency Bull Spread Worksheet and Contingency Graph For the Australian dollar example above, a worksheet and contingency graph can be constructed. One possible worksheet is as follows:

	VALUE OF AUSTRALIAN DOLLAR AT OPTION EXPIRATION				
	$.60	$.64	$.645	$.65	$.70
Buy a call	−$.019	−$.019	−$.014	−$.009	+$.041
Sell a call	+$.015	+$.015	+$.015	+$.015	−$.035
Net	−$.004	−$.004	+$.001	+$.006	+$.006

Exhibit 5B.5 shows the corresponding contingency graph.

Exhibit 5B.5 Contingency Graph for a Currency Bull Spread

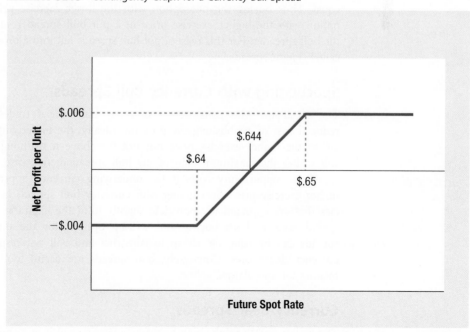

The worksheet and contingency graph show that the maximum loss for the bull spreader is limited to the difference between the two option premiums of $-\$.004 = -\$.019 + \$.015$. This maximum loss occurs at future spot prices equal to the lower strike price or below.

Also note that for a bull spread the gain is limited to the difference between the strike prices less the difference in the option premiums and is equal to $\$.006 = \$.65 - \$.64 - \$.004$. This maximum gain occurs at future spot prices equal to the higher exercise price or above.

The break-even point for the bull spread is located at the lower exercise price plus the difference in the two option premiums and is equal to $\$.644 = \$.64 + \$.004$.

Currency Bull Spreads with Put Options

As mentioned previously, currency bull spreads can be constructed just as easily with put options as with call options. To construct a put bull spread, the spreader would again buy a put option with a lower exercise price and write a put option with a higher exercise price. The basic arithmetic involved in constructing a put bull spread is thus essentially the same as for a call bull spread, with one important difference, as discussed next.

Recall that there is a positive relationship between the level of the existing spot price relative to the strike price and the call option premium. Consequently, the option with the higher exercise price that is written in a call bull spread will have the lower option premium, everything else being equal. Thus buying the call option with the lower exercise price and writing the call option with the higher exercise price involves a cash outflow for the bull spreader. For this reason, call bull spreads fall into a broader category of spreads called "debt spreads."

Also recall that the lower the spot rate relative to the strike price, the higher the put option premium will be. Consequently, the option with the higher strike price that is written in a put bull spread will have the higher option premium, everything else being equal. Thus buying the put option with the lower exercise price and writing the put option with the higher exercise price in a put bull spread results in a cash inflow for the bull spreader. For this reason, put bull spreads fall into a broader category of spreads called "credit spreads."

Speculating with Currency Bull Spreads

The speculator who constructs a currency bull spread trades profit potential for a reduced cost of establishing the position. Ideally, the underlying currency will appreciate to the higher exercise price but not far above it. Although the speculator would still realize the maximum gain of the bull spread in this case, he or she would incur significant opportunity costs if the underlying currency appreciates much above the higher exercise price. Speculating with currency bull spreads is appropriate for currencies that are expected to appreciate slightly until the expiration date. Because the bull spread involves both buying and writing options for the underlying currency, bull spreads can be relatively cheap to construct and will not result in large losses if the currency depreciates. Conversely, bull spreads are useful tools to generate additional income for speculators.

Currency Bear Spreads

The easiest way to think about a currency bear spread is as a short bull spread. That is, a currency bear spread involves taking exactly the opposite positions involved in a bull spread. The bear spreader writes a call option for a particular underlying currency and simultaneously buys a call option for the same currency with a higher exercise price. Consequently, the bear spreader anticipates a modest depreciation in the foreign currency.

Currency Bear Spread Worksheet and Contingency Graph

For the Australian dollar example above, the bear spreader writes the $.64 option and buys the $.65 option. A worksheet and contingency graph can be constructed. One possible worksheet is shown below.

	VALUE OF AUSTRALIAN DOLLAR AT OPTION EXPIRATION				
	$.60	$.64	$.645	$.65	$.70
Sell a call	+$.019	+$.019	+$.014	+$.009	−$.041
Buy a call	−$.015	−$.015	−$.015	−$.015	+$.035
Net	+$.004	+$.004	−$.001	−$.006	−$.006

The corresponding contingency graph is shown in Exhibit 5B.6.

Notice that the worksheet and contingency graph for the bear spread are the mirror image of the worksheet and contingency graph for the bull spread. Consequently, the maximum gain for the bear spreader is limited to the difference between the two exercise prices of $.004 = $.019 − $.015, and the maximum loss for a bear spread (− $.006 = −$.65 + $.64 + $.004) occurs when the Australian dollar's value is equal to or above the exercise price at option expiration.

Also, the break-even point is located at the lower exercise price plus the difference in the two option premiums and is equal to $.644 = $.64 + $.004, which is the same break-even point as for the bull spread.

Exhibit 5B.6   Contingency Graph for a Currency Bear Spread

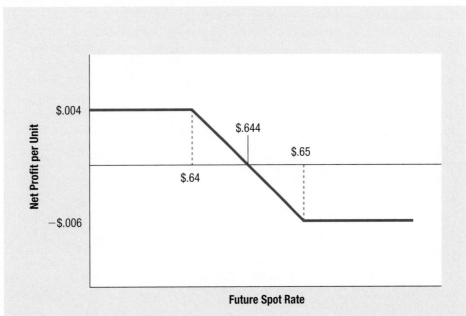

It is evident from the above illustration that the bear spreader hopes for a currency depreciation. An alternative way to profit from a depreciation would be to buy a put option for the currency. A bear spread, however, is typically cheaper to construct, as it involves buying one call option and writing another call option. The disadvantage of the bear spread compared to a long put position is that opportunity costs can be significant if the currency depreciates dramatically. Consequently, the bear spreader hopes for a modest currency depreciation.

The International Financial Environment

Mesa Co. specializes in the production of small fancy picture frames, which are exported from the United States to the United Kingdom. Mesa invoices the exports in pounds and converts the pounds to dollars when they are received. The British demand for these frames is positively related to economic conditions in the United Kingdom. Assume that British inflation and interest rates are similar to the rates in the United States. Mesa believes that the U.S. balance-of-trade deficit from trade between the United States and the United Kingdom will adjust to changing prices between the two countries, while capital flows will adjust to interest rate differentials. Mesa believes that the value of the pound is very sensitive to changing international capital flows and is moderately sensitive to changing international trade flows. Mesa is considering the following information:

- The U.K. inflation rate is expected to decline, while the U.S. inflation rate is expected to rise.
- British interest rates are expected to decline, while U.S. interest rates are expected to increase.

Questions

1. Explain how the international trade flows should initially adjust in response to the changes in inflation (holding exchange rates constant). Explain how the international capital flows should adjust in response to the changes in interest rates (holding exchange rates constant).
2. Using the information provided, will Mesa expect the pound to appreciate or depreciate in the future? Explain.
3. Mesa believes international capital flows shift in response to changing interest rate differentials. Is there any reason why the changing interest rate differentials in this example will not necessarily cause international capital flows to change significantly? Explain.
4. Based on your answer to question 2, how would Mesa's cash flows be affected by the expected exchange rate movements? Explain.
5. Based on your answer to question 4, should Mesa consider hedging its exchange rate risk? If so, explain how it could hedge using forward contracts, futures contracts, and currency options.

Exchange Rate Behavior

Part 2 (consisting of Chapters 6 through 8) focuses on critical relationships pertaining to exchange rates. Chapter 6 explains how governments can influence exchange rate movements and how such movements can affect economic conditions. Chapter 7 explores the relationships among foreign currencies. It also explains how the forward exchange rate is influenced by the difference between the interest rates of any two countries. Chapter 8 discusses prominent theories regarding the impact of inflation on exchange rates and the impact of interest rate movements on exchange rates.

6

Government Influence on Exchange Rates

CHAPTER OBJECTIVES

The specific objectives of this chapter are to:

■ describe the exchange rate systems used by various governments,

■ describe the development and implications of a single European currency,

■ explain how governments can use direct intervention to influence exchange rates, and

■ explain how governments can use indirect intervention to influence exchange rates.

As explained in Chapter 4, government policies affect exchange rates. Some government policies are specifically intended to affect exchange rates, whereas other policies are intended to affect economic conditions but indirectly influence exchange rates. Because the performance of an MNC is affected by exchange rates, financial managers need to understand how the government influences exchange rates.

6-1 Exchange Rate Systems

Exchange rate systems can be classified in terms of the extent to which the exchange rates are government controlled. Exchange rate systems normally fall into one of the following categories, each of which will be discussed in turn:

■ fixed,
■ freely floating,
■ managed float, or
■ pegged.

6-1a Fixed Exchange Rate System

In a **fixed exchange rate system**, exchange rates are either held constant or allowed to fluctuate only within very narrow boundaries. A fixed exchange rate system requires central bank intervention in order to maintain a currency's value within narrow boundaries. In general, the central bank must offset any imbalance between demand and supply conditions for its currency in order to prevent its value from changing. The specific details of how central banks intervene are discussed later in this chapter. In some situations, a central bank may reset a fixed exchange rate. That is, it will **devalue** or reduce the value of its currency against other currencies. A central bank's actions to devalue a currency in a fixed exchange rate system are referred to as **devaluation**, whereas the term *depreciation* refers to the decrease in a currency's value that is allowed to fluctuate in response to market conditions. Thus the term *depreciation* is more commonly used when describing the decrease in values of currencies that are not subject to a fixed exchange rate system.

In a fixed exchange rate system, a central bank may also **revalue** (increase the value of) its currency against other currencies. **Revaluation** refers to an upward adjustment of the exchange rate by the central bank, whereas the term *appreciation* refers to the increase in a currency's value that is allowed to fluctuate in response to market conditions. Like depreciation, appreciation is more commonly used when discussing currencies that are not subject to a fixed exchange rate system.

Bretton Woods Agreement, 1944–1971 From 1944 to 1971, most exchange rates were fixed according to a system planned at the Bretton Woods conference (held in Bretton Woods, New Hampshire, in 1944) by representatives from various countries. Because this arrangement, known as the **Bretton Woods Agreement**, lasted from 1944 to 1971, that period is sometimes referred to as the Bretton Woods era. Each currency was valued in terms of gold; for example, the U.S. dollar was valued as 1/35 ounce of gold. Because all currencies were valued in terms of gold, their values with respect to each other were fixed. Governments intervened in the foreign exchange markets to ensure that exchange rates drifted no more than 1 percent above or below the initially set rates.

Smithsonian Agreement, 1971–1973 During the Bretton Woods era, the United States often experienced balance-of-trade deficits. These deficits indicated that the dollar may have been overvalued, because the use of dollars for foreign purchases exceeded the demand by foreign countries for dollar-denominated goods. By 1971, it appeared that some currency values would need to be adjusted in order to restore a more balanced flow of payments between countries. In December 1971, a conference of representatives from various countries concluded with the **Smithsonian Agreement**, which called for a devaluation of the U.S. dollar by about 8 percent against other currencies. In addition, boundaries for the currency values were expanded to within 2.25 percent above or below the rates initially set by the agreement. Nevertheless, the imbalances in international payments continued and, as of February 1973, the dollar was again devalued. By March 1973, most governments of the major countries were no longer attempting to maintain their home currency values within the boundaries established by the Smithsonian Agreement.

Advantages of Fixed Exchange Rates A fixed exchange rate would be beneficial to a country for several reasons. First, exporters and importers could engage in international trade without concern about exchange rate movements of the currency to which their local currency is linked. Any firms that accept the foreign currency as payment would be insulated from the risk that the currency could depreciate over time. In addition, any firms that need to obtain that foreign currency in the future would be insulated from the risk of the currency appreciating over time. A second benefit is that firms could engage in direct foreign investment, without concern about exchange rate movements of that currency. They would be able to convert their foreign currency earnings into their home currency without concern that the foreign currency denominating their earnings might weaken over time. Thus the management of an MNC would be much easier.

Third, investors would be able to invest funds in foreign countries without concern that the foreign currency denominating their investments might weaken over time. Funds are needed in any country to support economic growth. Countries that attract a large amount of capital flows normally have lower interest rates, which can stimulate their economies.

Disadvantages of Fixed Exchange Rates One disadvantage of a fixed exchange rate system is that there is still a risk of the government altering its currency's value. Although an MNC is not exposed to continual movements in an exchange rate, there is always the possibility that its home country's central bank will devalue or revalue its own currency. Some central banks might need to constantly intervene in order to maintain their currency's value, which could cause concerns that they do not have the resources or ability to consistently stabilize the currency's value.

A second disadvantage is that if exchange rates are fixed and expected to remain fixed, institutional investors would invest funds in whatever country had the highest interest rate. Consequently, governments of countries with low interest rates would need to impose capital flow restrictions to prevent all local funds from flowing to countries with high interest rates.

A third disadvantage is that a fixed exchange rate system may render each country (and its MNCs) more vulnerable to economic conditions in other countries.

EXAMPLE   Assume that there are only two countries in the world: the United States and the United Kingdom. Also assume a fixed exchange rate system and that these two countries trade frequently with each other. If the United States experiences a much higher inflation rate than the United Kingdom, then U.S. consumers should buy more goods from the United Kingdom and U.K. consumers should reduce their imports of U.S. goods (because of the high U.S. prices). This reaction would reduce U.S. production and increase U.S. unemployment; it could also cause higher inflation in the United Kingdom due to the excessive demand for British goods relative to the supply of British goods produced. In this way, high U.S. inflation could cause high inflation in the United Kingdom. In the mid- and late 1960s, the United States experienced relatively high inflation and was accused of "exporting" that inflation to some European countries.

A high U.S. unemployment rate will reduce U.S. income and lead to a decline in U.S. purchases of U.K. goods. Hence productivity in the United Kingdom may decrease and unemployment may rise there. In this scenario, the United States has "exported" unemployment to the United Kingdom. ●

6-1b Freely Floating Exchange Rate System

In a **freely floating exchange rate system**, exchange rate values are determined by market forces without intervention by governments. This system is the opposite extreme of the fixed exchange rate system. Whereas a fixed exchange rate system allows only limited exchange rate movements, a freely floating exchange rate system allows for complete flexibility. A freely floating exchange rate adjusts on a continual basis in response to the demand and supply conditions for that currency.

Advantages of a Freely Floating System   One advantage of a freely floating exchange rate system is that a country is more insulated from the inflation of other countries.

EXAMPLE   Continue with the previous example in which there are only two countries, but now assume a freely floating exchange rate system, without any intervention by governments. If the United States experiences a high rate of inflation, then the resulting increased U.S. demand for U.K. goods will place upward pressure on the value of the British pound. As a second consequence of the high U.S. inflation, the reduced U.K. demand for U.S. goods will result in a reduced supply of British pounds for sale (exchanged for dollars), which will also place upward pressure on the pound's value. The pound will appreciate in response to these market forces (recall that appreciation is not allowed under the fixed rate system). This appreciation will make U.K. goods more expensive for U.S. consumers, even though U.K. producers have not raised their prices. The higher prices will simply be due to the pound's appreciation; that is, a greater number of U.S. dollars are now required to buy the same number of pounds.

In the United Kingdom, the actual price of the goods (as measured in British pounds) may be unchanged. Even though U.S. prices have increased, U.K. consumers will continue to purchase U.S. goods because they can exchange their pounds for more U.S. dollars (because of the British pound's appreciation against the U.S. dollar). ●

Another advantage of freely floating exchange rates is that a country is more insulated from unemployment problems in other countries.

EXAMPLE   Under a freely floating rate system, the decline in U.S. purchases of U.K. goods will lead to reduced U.S. demand for British pounds. Such a demand shift could cause the pound to depreciate against the dollar (under the fixed rate system, the pound would not be allowed to depreciate). This depreciation will make British goods cheaper for U.S. consumers than before, offsetting the reduced demand for these goods that may follow a reduction in U.S. income. As was true with inflation, a sudden change in unemployment will have less effect on a foreign country under a floating rate system than under a fixed rate system. ●

These examples illustrate that, in a freely floating exchange rate system, the problems experienced in one country will not necessarily be contagious. Exchange rate adjustments serve as a form of protection against "exporting" economic problems to other countries.

An additional advantage of a freely floating exchange rate system is that each government is free to implement policies irrespective of their effect on the exchange rate.

Disadvantages of a Freely Floating Exchange Rate System   In the previous example, the United Kingdom is somewhat insulated from the problems experienced in the United States because of the freely floating exchange rate system. Although an advantage for the protected country (here, the United Kingdom), this insulation can be a disadvantage for the country that initially experienced the economic problems.

EXAMPLE   If the United States experiences high inflation, then the dollar may weaken, thereby insulating the United Kingdom from the inflation (as discussed previously). From the U.S. perspective, however, a weaker U.S. dollar causes import prices to be higher. This may increase the price of U.S. materials and supplies, which in turn would increase U.S. prices of finished goods. In addition, higher foreign prices (from the U.S. perspective) can force U.S. consumers to purchase domestic products. As U.S. producers recognize that their foreign competition has been reduced by the weak dollar, they can more easily raise their prices without losing customers to foreign competition. ●

In a similar manner, a freely floating exchange rate system can adversely affect a country that has high unemployment.

EXAMPLE   If the U.S. unemployment rate is rising, then U.S. demand for imports will decrease, putting upward pressure on the dollar's value. A stronger dollar will then cause U.S. consumers to purchase foreign rather than U.S. products because the foreign products can be purchased cheaply. However, that reaction can be detrimental to the United States during periods of high unemployment. ●

As these examples illustrate, a country's economic problems can sometimes be compounded by freely floating exchange rates. Under such a system, MNCs will need to devote substantial resources to measuring and managing exposure to exchange rate fluctuations.

6-1c Managed Float Exchange Rate System

A **managed float** exchange rate system allows its currency's value to float on a daily basis, but the government can periodically intervene to achieve specific objectives. A central bank may intervene in order to maintain the currency's value within specific boundaries (that are not necessarily disclosed to the public) or as an attempt to influence local economic conditions. The managed float system differs from the freely floating exchange rate system (as defined earlier) in that governments can and sometimes do intervene to prevent their currencies from moving too far in a certain direction, or to achieve other economic conditions. The various forms of intervention used by governments to manage exchange rate movements are discussed later in this chapter.

The central banks of various countries (including Brazil, China, Denmark, Russia, and South Korea) have, at times, imposed boundaries that restrict the movement of their currency to within so-called bands. However, it is not unusual for these boundaries to be changed or removed entirely if central banks are unable to maintain their currency's value within the bands.

Countries with Floating Exchange Rates   Most large developed countries (such as the United States, the United Kingdom, Australia, and Japan) allow their currencies to float, although they may be periodically managed by their respective central banks. Exhibit 6.1 lists some countries that allow their currencies to float. Although the governments of all of these countries may periodically intervene, the degree of

Exhibit 6.1   Countries with Floating Exchange Rates (Although Government Intervention May Periodically Occur)

COUNTRY	CURRENCY	COUNTRY	CURRENCY
Afghanistan	new afghani	Mexico	peso
Argentina	peso	Norway	bone
Australia	dollar	Paraguay	guarani
Bolivia	boliviano	Peru	new sol
Brazil	real	Poland	zloty
Canada	dollar	Romania	leu
Chile	peso	Russia	ruble
Denmark	krone	Singapore	dollar
Euro participants	euro	South Africa	rand
Hungary	forint	South Korea	won
India	rupee	Sweden	krona
Indonesia	rupiah	Switzerland	franc
Israel	new shekel	Taiwan	new dollar
Jamaica	dollar	Thailand	baht
Japan	yen	United Kingdom	pound

intervention and frequency of intervention varies substantially among countries. The United States and Canada rarely intervene directly in the foreign exchange market. However, they may still implement some government policies that might be intended to have a particular impact on the value of their currency.

Criticisms of the Managed Float System   Critics argue that the managed float system allows a government to manipulate exchange rates in order to benefit its own country at the expense of others. A government may attempt to weaken its currency to stimulate a stagnant economy. The increased aggregate demand for products that results from such a policy may cause a decreased aggregate demand for products in other countries, because the weakened currency attracts foreign demand. This is a valid criticism but could apply as well to the fixed exchange rate system, where governments have the power to devalue their currencies.

6-1d Pegged Exchange Rate System

Some countries use a **pegged exchange rate** in which their home currency's value is pegged to one foreign currency or to an index of currencies. Although the home currency's value is fixed in terms of the foreign currency to which it is pegged, it moves in line with that currency against other currencies.

A government may peg its currency's value to that of a stable currency, such as the dollar, because doing so stabilizes the value of its own currency. First, this forces the pegged currency's exchange rate with the dollar to be fixed. Second, that currency will move against non-dollar currencies to the same extent as the dollar does. Because the dollar is more stable than most currencies, it will make the pegged currency more stable than most currencies. Governments might implement a pegged exchange rate when its currency is very volatile due to uncertain economic or political conditions.

Limitations of a Pegged Exchange Rate   Although countries with a pegged exchange rate may attract foreign investment because the exchange rate is expected to remain stable, weak economic or political conditions can cause firms and investors to question whether the peg will hold. A country that suffers a sudden recession may experience capital outflows as some firms and investors withdraw funds because they believe other countries offer better investment opportunities. These transactions result in an exchange of the local currency for dollars and other currencies, which puts downward pressure on the local currency's value. The central bank would need to offset this pressure by intervening in the foreign exchange market (as explained shortly), but it might not be able to maintain the peg. If the peg is broken and if the exchange rate is dictated by market forces, then the local currency's value could immediately decline substantially.

If foreign investors fear that a peg may be broken, they will quickly sell their investments in that country and convert the proceeds into their home currency. These transactions place more downward pressure on the local currency of that country. Even its own residents may consider selling their local investments and converting their funds into dollars (or some other currency) if they fear that the peg may be broken. They can exchange their currency for dollars to invest in the United States before the peg breaks, and they can leave that investment there until after the peg breaks and their local currency's value is reduced. Then these residents can sell their U.S. investments and convert the dollar proceeds into their home currency at a more favorable exchange rate. Their initial actions of converting their home currency into dollars also put downward pressure on that local currency.

For the reasons just explained, it is difficult for a country to maintain a pegged exchange rate while experiencing major political or economic problems. Even though a country whose pegged exchange rate is stable can attract foreign investment, investors will move funds to another country if they are concerned that the peg will break. Thus a pegged exchange rate system could ultimately create more instability in a country's economy. Examples of pegged exchange rate systems are given next.

WEB

http://europa.eu
Access to information about the European Union and on all related political and economic issues.

Europe's Snake Arrangement, 1972–1979   Several European countries established a pegged exchange rate arrangement in April 1972. Their goal was to maintain their currencies within established limits of each other. This arrangement became known as the **snake**. The snake was difficult to maintain, however, and market pressure caused some currencies to move outside their established limits. Consequently, some members withdrew from the snake arrangement, and some currencies were realigned.

European Monetary System (EMS), 1979–1992   In response to continued problems with the snake arrangement, the European Monetary System (EMS) was pushed into operation in March 1979. Under the EMS, exchange rates of member countries were held together within specified limits and were also tied to the European Currency Unit (ECU), a weighted average of exchange rates of the member countries. Each weight was determined by a member's relative gross national product and activity in intra-European trade. The currencies of most of these member countries were allowed to fluctuate by no more than 2.25 percent (6 percent for some currencies) from the initially established values.

The method of linking European currency values with the ECU was known as the **exchange rate mechanism** (ERM). The participating governments intervened in the foreign exchange markets to maintain the exchange rates within boundaries established by the ERM.

The European Monetary System forced participating countries to have comparable interest rates, because the currencies were not allowed to deviate much against each other and money would flow to the European country with the highest interest rate. In 1992, the German government increased its interest rates to prevent excessive spending and inflation. Other European governments were more concerned about stimulating their economies to lower their high unemployment levels, so they wanted to reduce interest rates. Yet these governments could not achieve their individual goals for a stronger economy as long as their interest rates were so strongly affected by German interest rates. As a result, some countries suspended their participation in the EMS. The governments of European countries realized that a pegged system could work only if it were set permanently. This realization provided momentum for the single European currency (the euro), which was introduced in 1999 and is discussed later in this chapter.

Mexico's Pegged System, 1994

In 1994, Mexico's central bank used a special pegged exchange rate system that linked the peso to the U.S. dollar but allowed it to fluctuate against the dollar within a band. The Mexican central bank enforced the peso's value through frequent intervention. Mexico experienced a large balance-of-trade deficit in 1994, which may have reflected an overvalued peso that encouraged Mexican firms and consumers to buy an excessive amount of imports.

Many speculators based in Mexico recognized that the peso was being maintained at an artificially high level, and they speculated on its potential decline by investing their funds in the United States. They planned to liquidate their U.S. investments if and when the peso's value weakened so that they could convert the dollars from those investments into pesos at a favorable exchange rate.

By December 1994, there was substantial downward pressure on the peso. On December 20, 1994, Mexico's central bank devalued the peso by about 13 percent. Mexico's stock prices plummeted as many foreign investors sold their shares and withdrew their funds from Mexico in anticipation of further devaluation of the peso. On December 22, the central bank allowed the peso to float freely, and it declined by another 15 percent. This was the beginning of what became known as the Mexican peso crisis. In an attempt to discourage foreign investors from withdrawing their investments in Mexico's debt securities, the central bank increased interest rates. However, the higher rates increased the cost of borrowing for Mexican firms and consumers, thereby slowing economic growth.

Mexico's financial problems caused investors to lose confidence in their peso-denominated securities, so they liquidated those positions and transferred the funds to other countries. These actions put additional downward pressure on the peso.

In the four months after December 20, 1994, the value of the peso declined by more than 50 percent against the dollar. The Mexican crisis might not have occurred if the peso had been allowed to float throughout 1994, because in that case the peso could have gravitated toward its natural level. The crisis illustrates that central bank intervention may not be able to overcome market forces, which serves as an argument for letting a currency float freely.

Asian Pegged Exchange Rates in the Late 1990s

During the late 1990s, many Asian countries such as Indonesia, Malaysia, and Thailand had their currencies pegged to the dollar. When their economies were strong, the pegged exchange rates were viewed favorably because they reduced concerns by large U.S. institutional investors that invested funds in Asia. Consequently, some Asian countries were able to rely heavily on international investment to support their growth. U.S. institutional investors invested in the equity of Asian corporations and purchased debt securities issued by Asian corporations and governments.

When the Asian economies showed signs of weakening, the institutional investors began to withdraw their funds, which resulted in a large increase in the supply of Asian currencies sold in exchange for dollars in the foreign exchange market. At the prevailing pegged exchange rate for each currency, the supply of the currency to be exchanged for dollars was greater than the U.S. demand for the currency. To maintain the pegged exchange rates, some Asian countries raised interest rates in an attempt to attract more capital flows from U.S. investors, which could increase the U.S. demand for funds.

However, higher interest rates increased the cost of debt for the corporations that borrowed locally in those Asian countries, which discouraged corporate expansion and further weakened their economies. Furthermore, this strategy was not successful in attracting more funds from the United States because U.S. investors feared that the peg would break. Therefore, the central banks of these countries could not offset the large sales of Asian currencies in exchange for dollars, and the pegged exchange rates could not be sustained. The values of many Asian currencies declined by 20 percent or more in 1998.

Because of the sharp decline in Asian currency values, some Asian governments that had financed a portion of their deficits with debt denominated in dollars needed more of their currency to pay off their debt, which caused additional problems. These conditions led to the so-called Asian crisis, which ultimately resulted in massive government bailouts by the International Monetary Fund (IMF) and some other developed countries. China was adversely affected to a smaller degree than other countries. Because it did not rely as heavily on foreign investment to support its internal growth, it did not experience an abrupt withdrawal of funds as other Asian countries experienced. More details about the Asian crisis are presented in the appendix to this chapter.

China's Pegged Exchange Rate, 1996–2005
From 1996 until 2005, China's yuan was pegged to be worth about $.12 (8.28 yuan per U.S. dollar). During this period, the yuan's value would change daily against non-dollar currencies to the same extent that the dollar did. Because of the peg, the yuan's value remained at that level even as the United States experienced a trade deficit with China of more than $100 billion annually. Politicians in the United States argued that the yuan was being held at an artificially low level by the Chinese government.

Since 2005, China has allowed the yuan to fluctuate, but it maintains the movements within boundaries. China's central bank sets the yuan exchange rate each morning (referred to as "the fix), but then allows the exchange rate to change by 2 percent during the day in response to market transactions involving purchases or sales of the yuan. One of the factors that the Chinese central bank considers when setting the exchange rate each morning is the closing exchange rate on the previous day. In this way, the central bank considers how market conditions influence the value of the yuan.

Because of the boundaries imposed by China's central bank, the yuan is much more stable against the dollar than most other currencies. However, many governments believe that the central bank of China purposely maintains a low value for the yuan, which ensures a strong foreign demand for China's exports. They argue that the yuan would be valued much higher if it was allowed to move in accordance with market forces, which would make China's exported products more expensive and reduce the balance-of-trade deficits that many countries have with China.

Venezuela's Pegged Exchange Rate
The government of Venezuela has historically pegged its currency (the bolivar) to the dollar, although there have been periodic devaluations. In January 2010, the government created a system in which it set the official rate of the bolivar so that local firms could purchase essential imports such as medicine and specific health products that are not available locally. Venezuela also set a less favorable pegged exchange rate for local firms that wish to exchange bolivars for dollars in order to purchase nonessential imports. However, some local firms are still willing to

exchange bolivars into dollars even at the less favorable exchange rate because high inflation causes some nonessential products produced locally in Venezuela to be more expensive than imported products.

Venezuela's exchange rates described above are pegged to the U.S. dollar, but the pegged rates have been periodically revised to devalue the bolivar against the dollar and other currencies. Because a devalued bolivar makes foreign products more expensive for consumers in Venezuela, it should increase the consumption of locally produced products and discourage imports of foreign products. Furthermore, the extreme reduction in the bolivar's value should make Venezuela's products cheaper for foreign firms and thus increase foreign demand for Venezuela's products. In this way, devaluation can improve Venezuela's economy and reduce its unemployment. Furthermore, because the Venezuelan government is a major exporter of oil and because those exports are denominated in dollars, the oil revenue converts into a larger amount of bolivars for Venezuela's government as a result of the devaluation. One disadvantage of the devaluation is that it allows some firms in Venezuela to increase their local prices without much concern about losing customers to foreign firms. Consequently, inflation in Venezuela has increased substantially in recent years, which reduces the purchasing power of the local residents.

Currency Boards Used to Peg Currency Values

A **currency board** is a system for pegging the value of the local currency to some other specified currency. The board must maintain currency reserves for all the currency that it has printed. This large amount of reserves may increase the ability of a country's central bank to maintain its pegged currency.

EXAMPLE

Hong Kong has tied the value of its currency, the Hong Kong dollar, to the U.S. dollar (HK$7.80 = $1.00) since 1983. Every Hong Kong dollar in circulation is backed by a U.S. dollar in reserve. Economic conditions periodically cause an imbalance in the U.S. demand for Hong Kong dollars and the supply of Hong Kong dollars for sale in the foreign exchange market. Under these conditions, the Hong Kong central bank must intervene by making transactions in the foreign exchange market that offset this imbalance. Because the central bank has successfully maintained the fixed exchange rate between the Hong Kong dollar and U.S. dollar, firms in both countries are more willing to do business with each other and are relatively unconcerned about exchange rate risk. ●

A currency board is effective only if investors believe that it will last. If investors expect that market forces will prevent a government from maintaining the local currency's exchange rate, then they will attempt to move their funds to countries in which the local currency is expected to be stronger. By withdrawing their funds from a country and converting the funds into a different currency, foreign investors put downward pressure on the local currency's exchange rate. If the supply of the currency for sale continues to exceed demand, the government will be forced to devalue its currency.

EXAMPLE

In 1991, Argentina established a currency board that pegged the Argentine peso to the U.S. dollar. In 2002, Argentina was suffering from major economic problems, and its government was unable to repay its debt. Foreign investors and local investors began to transfer their funds to other countries because they feared that their investments would earn poor returns. These actions required the exchange of pesos into other currencies, such as the dollar, and caused an excessive supply of pesos for sale in the foreign exchange market. The government could not maintain the exchange rate of 1 peso = 1 dollar because the supply of pesos for sale exceeded the demand at that exchange rate. In March 2002, the government devalued the peso to 1 peso = $.71 (1.4 pesos per dollar). Even at this new exchange rate, the supply of pesos for sale exceeded the demand, so the Argentine government decided to let the peso's value float in response to market conditions rather than set the peso's value. ●

A currency board that is expected to remain in place for a long period may reduce fears that the local currency will weaken, thereby encouraging investors to maintain their investments within the country. However, a currency board is effective only if the government can convince investors that the exchange rate will be maintained.

Interest Rates of Pegged Currencies A country that uses a currency board does not have complete control over its local interest rates because its rates must be aligned with the interest rates of the currency to which it is tied.

Recall that the Hong Kong dollar is pegged to the U.S. dollar. If Hong Kong lowers its interest rates to stimulate its economy, then its interest rates will be lower than U.S. interest rates. Investors based in Hong Kong would thus be enticed to exchange Hong Kong dollars for U.S. dollars and invest in the United States, where interest rates are higher. Because the Hong Kong dollar is tied to the U.S. dollar, the investors could exchange the proceeds of their investment back into Hong Kong dollars at the end of the investment period without concern about exchange rate risk (because the exchange rate is fixed).

If the United States raises its interest rates, Hong Kong would be forced to raise its own interest rates (on securities with similar risk as those in the United States). Otherwise, investors in Hong Kong could invest their money in the United States and earn a higher rate. ●

Even though a country may not have control over its interest rate when it establishes a currency board, its interest rate may be more stable than if it did not have a currency board. A country's interest rate will move in tandem with the interest rate of the currency to which its own currency is tied. The interest rate may include a risk premium reflecting either default risk or the risk that the currency board will be discontinued.

Exchange Rate Risk of a Pegged Currency A currency that is pegged to another currency cannot be pegged against all other currencies. If a currency is pegged to the dollar, then it will move in tandem with the dollar against all other currencies.

When the Argentine peso was pegged to the dollar (during the period 1991–2002), the dollar often strengthened against the Brazilian real and some other currencies in South America; therefore, the Argentine peso also strengthened against those currencies. Yet many exporting firms in Argentina were adversely affected by the strong Argentine peso because it made their products too expensive for importers. Because Argentina's currency board has been eliminated, the Argentine peso is no longer forced to move in tandem with the dollar against other currencies. ●

Classification of Pegged Exchange Rates Exhibit 6.2 gives examples of countries that have pegged their currency to the currency of another country. Most of these currencies are pegged to the U.S. dollar or to the euro.

Exhibit 6.2 Countries with Pegged Exchange Rates and the Currencies to Which They Are Pegged

COUNTRY	NAME OF LOCAL CURRENCY	PEGGED TO
Bahamas	dollar	U.S. dollar
Barbados	dollar	U.S. dollar
Bermuda	dollar	U.S. dollar
Brunei	dollar	Singapore dollar
Bulgaria	lev	Euro
Denmark	krone	Euro
Hong Kong	dollar	U.S. dollar
Saudi Arabia	riyal	U.S. dollar
United Arab Emirates	dirham	U.S. dollar
Venezuela	bolivar	U.S. dollar

6-1e Dollarization

Dollarization is the replacement of a foreign currency with U.S. dollars. This process is a step beyond a currency board because it forces the local currency to be replaced by the U.S. dollar. Although dollarization and a currency board both attempt to peg the local currency's value, the currency board does not replace the local currency with dollars. The decision to use U.S. dollars as the local currency cannot be easily reversed because in that case the country no longer has a local currency.

EXAMPLE

From 1990 to 2000, Ecuador's currency (the sucre) depreciated by about 97 percent against the U.S. dollar. The weakness of the currency caused unstable trade conditions, high inflation, and volatile interest rates. In an effort to stabilize trade and economic conditions, Ecuador replaced the sucre with the U.S. dollar as its currency in 2000. By November of that year, inflation had declined and economic growth had increased. Thus it appeared that dollarization had favorable effects. ●

6-1f Black Markets for Currencies

When a government sets a fixed exchange rate and imposes restrictions on residents that require them to exchange currency at that official rate, it may trigger the creation of a "black market" for foreign exchange. The term *black market* refers to an underground (illegal) network that circumvents the legal (formal) network in the economy. In some countries, the black market may be tolerated by the government to a degree, even though the market's activities may be purposely intended to circumvent the government's formal rules. A black market for foreign exchange enables residents to engage in foreign exchange transactions that may not be officially approved by the government.

In Venezuela, a black market allows residents to convert bolivars into dollars. For example, some residents may want dollars so that they can purchase nonmedical products from the United States because they are much cheaper than locally produced products. The government discourages residents from buying nonessential foreign products, so residents turn to the black market to obtain dollars for that purpose. Even though the black market exchange rate of the bolivar is lower than the official government exchange rate, residents are willing to exchange their bolivars for dollars on the black market because the U.S. prices of the products they want are sufficiently cheaper than the prices of Venezuelan goods.

For a black market to function, it needs not only residents who want to convert their local currency but also residents who can accommodate the desired currency transactions. For example, in Venezuela, the black market functions because some residents who have received dollars due to exporting or other transactions are willing to exchange them with residents who want dollars. Some residents who have dollars may participate in the black market because they can receive more bolivars per dollar in that market than if they exchanged the dollars for bolivars at the government's official exchange rate. Although the black market exchange rate is not favorable for the residents selling the local currency (such as bolivars), it is very favorable for the residents who have the currency (such as dollars) that other residents are desperately attempting to buy.

A black market for foreign exchange becomes especially active when local residents fear an impending currency crisis, because it may enable residents to move some of their money out of the country (and convert it into a different currency) before their local currency is weakened further by local political or economic conditions. Even if the black market exchange rate is not as favorable as the government rate for those trying to sell their local currency, many residents may still be willing to accept the black market exchange rate because they fear that their local currency's value will weaken over time. Such fears can cause a massive sell-off of the local currency in exchange for dollars or some other currency and can make a currency crisis even worse.

Some critics might argue that the government would be better off if it did not impose foreign exchange restrictions on the local residents, so there would be no need for a black market. However, the local government that is experiencing adverse political or economic conditions might be concerned that if it does not impose restrictions on currency transactions, its local residents will legally move most of their money out of the country.

6-2 A Single European Currency

In 1992, the Maastricht Treaty called for the establishment of a single European currency. In January 1999, the euro replaced the national currencies of 11 European countries (with official implementation for all transactions in 2002). Since then, eight more countries have converted their home currency to the euro. The countries that now use the euro as their home currency are Austria, Belgium, Cyprus, Estonia, Finland, France, Germany, Greece, Ireland, Italy, Latvia, Lithuania, Luxembourg, Malta, the Netherlands, Portugal, Slovakia, Slovenia, and Spain. The countries that participate in the euro make up a region that is referred to as the *eurozone*. These participating countries together produce more than 20 percent of the world's gross domestic product, which is more than that of the United States.

Denmark, Norway, Sweden, Switzerland, and the United Kingdom continue to use their own home currency. Some EU members from Eastern Europe (such as Bulgaria, Croatia, Czech Republic, Hungary, Poland, Romania) that have joined the European Union are eligible to participate in the euro if they meet specific economic goals, including a maximum limit on their budget deficit.

Some Eastern European countries (such as Latvia and Lithuania) initially pegged their currency's value to the euro before they officially adopted the euro as their local currency. This allowed them to assess how their economy was affected as their currency's value moved in tandem with the euro against other currencies. Once they adopted the euro as their currency, it would be more difficult for them to reverse that decision.

6-2a Monetary Policy in the Eurozone

The adoption of the euro subjects all participating countries to the same monetary policy. The **European Central Bank** (**ECB**) is based in Frankfurt and is responsible for setting monetary policy for all participating European countries. Its objective is to control inflation in the participating countries and to stabilize (within reasonable boundaries) the value of the euro with respect to other major currencies. Thus the ECB's monetary goals of price stability and currency stability are similar to those of central banks in many other countries around the world, with the difference that these goals concern a group of countries rather than a single country. It could be argued that a set of countries with the same currency and monetary policy will achieve greater economic stability than if each of these countries had its own currency and monetary policy.

However, a single European monetary policy prevents any individual European country from solving its local economic problems with its own unique policy. A particular *monetary* policy used in the eurozone during a particular period may enhance conditions in some eurozone countries while adversely affecting conditions in other eurozone countries. For example, a eurozone policy intended to reduce interest rates and stimulate economic growth might be beneficial to a eurozone country with a weak economy but could cause higher inflation in a eurozone country that already has a strong economy and is near full employment.

6-2b Impact on Firms in the Eurozone

As a result of a single currency in the eurozone, prices of products are now more comparable among European countries. Thus firms can more easily determine where they can purchase products at the lowest cost. In addition, firms can engage in international trade within the eurozone without incurring foreign exchange transactions costs because they use the same currency. The use of a single currency also encourages more long-term international trade arrangements between firms within the eurozone because they no longer have to worry about exposure to future exchange rate movements.

Firms in the eurozone may face more competition because their prices can be measured against the prices of all other firms in the same industry throughout the participating eurozone countries, not just within their own country. In addition, their performance (as measured by revenue or earnings) can be compared more easily to others because they now use the same currency.

6-2c Impact on Financial Flows in the Eurozone

A single European currency forces the risk-free interest rate offered on government securities to be similar across the participating European countries. Any discrepancy in risk-free rates would encourage investors within these countries to invest in the country with the highest rate, which would quickly realign the risk-free interest rates among them. However, the quoted interest rate may still vary between two government securities with the same maturity if they exhibit different levels of credit risk.

Investors who reside in the eurozone can now invest in euro-denominated bonds issued by governments and corporations in these countries without concern about exchange rate risk. The yields offered on bonds issued within the eurozone need not be similar, even though they are now denominated in the same currency, because the credit risk may still be higher for some issuers.

Stock prices are now more comparable among the European countries within the eurozone because they are denominated in the same currency. Investors in the participating European countries are now able to invest in stocks in these countries without concern about exchange rate risk. Thus there is more cross-border investing than there was in the past.

6-2d Impact of Eurozone Country Crisis on Other Eurozone Countries

Countries in the eurozone not only are subject to the same monetary policy, but are encouraged to do more business with each other because they all use the euro as their local currency (are not exposed to exchange rate risk). Therefore, favorable conditions in some eurozone countries will be transmitted to the other eurozone countries. However, the same rationale suggests that unfavorable conditions in some eurozone countries could likewise be transmitted to other eurozone countries. Furthermore, the eurozone arrangement might commit the government of each eurozone country (legally or politically) to bail out any other eurozone country that experiences an economic crisis. Although this arrangement may be beneficial for the eurozone countries in need of a bailout, it can be costly to the eurozone countries that finance the bailout.

EXAMPLE   Greece is one of the European countries that qualified to participate in the eurozone upon the inception of the euro as a currency in 2002. In 2010, it experienced weak economic conditions. Furthermore, the existing government at that time acknowledged that Greece's annual budget deficits in the last eight years had been substantially understated by previous government regimes. Consequently, the government was less able to obtain new loans from creditors. Its debt rating was lowered substantially by rating agencies, and at one point it was paying about 11 percent interest on its debt (versus 4 percent for governments of other eurozone countries). Its large budget deficits were partially due to very generous public-sector salaries and pensions that caused large government cash outflows and an ineffective tax system that limited the level of government cash inflows.

In response to Greece's debt crisis, governments and banks in the other eurozone countries provided a bailout loan of 110 billion euros in 2010; to obtain the loan, Greece agreed to meet so-called austerity conditions such as reducing its public-sector salaries and pensions and increasing its tax revenues. Even after receiving the loan, however, Greece's government continued to spend much more money than it generated from taxes, and in 2012, it needed another bailout. Governments and other creditors in the eurozone provided new loans of about 130 billion euros and again required that Greece satisfy specific austerity measures in order to correct its excessive spending.

Although the loans from several eurozone countries to Greece were intended to stabilize Greece's economy, they also increased the exposure of all these countries to the Greek debt crisis. If Greece's government defaulted on debt owed to governments or large banks in the eurozone, then those governments or banks that provided large loans could experience their own debt crisis. A debt crisis is closely related to a banking crisis, because the performance of banks is dependent on borrowers repaying the loans provided by banks. Many banks in the eurozone were struggling financially not only because of Greece's debt crisis but also because of massive losses due to loan defaults in the housing sector. This led to a eurozone debt crisis (also called a eurozone banking crisis).

By 2015, Greece's total public debt had grown to about 320 billion euros, and most of the loans came from governments and banks in the eurozone. Based on the estimated total value of loans provided to Greece, the countries most exposed to Greece's debt crisis were Germany (57 billion euros), France (43 billion euros), and Italy (38 billion euros). However, when considering the loans provided in proportion to the country's annual economic output, Malta, Slovenia, and Spain were the most highly exposed countries.

In July 2015, the government of Greece stated that it was unable to meet the existing loan repayment schedule, and requested additional loans amounting to about 53 billion euros from the governments of the other eurozone countries. These governments were already heavily exposed to the Greece crisis, because of the previous loans they had provided to Greece that might not be repaid. The governments recognized that Greece might be able to resolve the crisis only if it was given more loans. In addition, they recognized that the only way that they might ever recover the funds that they had previously loaned to Greece was by extending additional loans to Greece.

Yet these governments may have been concerned that Greece would not properly use the new funds to resolve its debt crisis, because Greece had failed to meet all of the austerity measures that were imposed when loans were provided in the past. Thus some governments in the eurozone may have viewed the provision of new loans to Greece as throwing good money (new loans) after bad money (previous loans that were not repaid). So while many of the governments might be in favor of Greece receiving more loans, they may have preferred not to provide the new loans themselves. Some governments in the eurozone might argue that they had already provided much funding to Greece in the past, while others might suggest that they could not afford to extend additional loans. The citizens of every eurozone country could argue that their government and local banks should give first priority to resolving financial problems within that country rather than resolving problems outside that country. ●

WEB

www.bis.org/cbanks.htm
Links to the websites of central banks around the world; some of these sites are in English.

Impact of Banking Crises within the Eurozone   During the Greece debt crisis, Portugal and Spain also experienced banking crises (primarily due to massive loan losses), while Italy and Ireland received much attention concerning their exposure to potential crises. Although each country's banking crisis is unique, some general conceptual lessons can be drawn from the eurozone debt crisis.

First, the banking industry in the eurozone is integrated because many of the banks rely on each other for funding. Consequently, the financial problems of one bank can easily spread to affect other banks in the eurozone.

Second, banks in the eurozone frequently engage in a syndicated loan, in which several banks participate in a large loan to a government agency or MNC. This causes many banks across the eurozone to be exposed whenever borrowers are unable to make timely loan repayments. Thus if any eurozone country experiences weak economic conditions that reduce the ability of its companies to repay loans, then banks throughout the eurozone may be affected.

Third, given these potential contagion effects, news about adverse conditions in any single eurozone country can trigger concerns that the problems will spread to other member countries. These concerns tend to increase the risk of securities that are traded in the eurozone. In response, institutional investors around the world may well discontinue their investments (purchases of stocks, bonds, and other securities) in the eurozone if they anticipate that one European country's problems might spread throughout the eurozone. The result is a decline in prices of securities in the eurozone, which reinforces the fear within financial markets.

Fourth, eurozone country governments do not have their own monetary policy and so must rely on fiscal policy (e.g., spending more and lowering taxes) when they experience serious financial problems. Although this type of fiscal policy can stimulate a country's economy in the short run, it results in a larger government budget deficit and could lead to concerns that the government will be unable to repay its debt in the future. In this event, the large financial institutions that normally serve as creditors to the governments of eurozone countries may no longer be willing to provide credit.

Fifth, eurozone governments rely heavily on banks within the eurozone for credit, issuing bonds that are purchased by the banks. Because banks are major creditors to their government, their performance is highly dependent on whether that government repays its debt owed to bank creditors.

ECB Role in Resolving Crises   Although the European Central Bank's role was originally conceived to be setting monetary policy, in recent years the bank's role has expanded to include providing credit for eurozone countries that are experiencing a financial crisis. However, the ECB faces a dilemma when providing credit. When providing credit to any country whose national budget deficit is excessive, the bank may signal that countries can obtain favorable credit terms irrespective of their budgets. For this reason, when providing credit to a country, the ECB imposes restrictions intended to help resolve the country's budget deficit problems over time. In particular, before lending any funds the ECB may require the receiving government to correct its budget deficit by implementing austerity measures such as higher tax rates and reduced government spending.

When the ECB can provide credit based on austerity conditions that are agreeable to the borrowing country, it may reduce the fear of a government default on existing loans and increase the likelihood that the government will resolve its economic problems. The ECB's action also reduces the uncertainty surrounding the eurozone and thus encourages institutional investors around the world to invest in that region. However, the austerity conditions could further damage the country's economy: less spending by the government normally weakens an economy, and raising taxes reduces disposable income. A government's unwillingness to accept the ECB's austerity conditions raises concerns that the government will default on all of its existing loans, which would induce contagion effects throughout the eurozone. There may also be concerns that the government will exit the eurozone and possibly lead other countries to exit as well. Consequently, financial market participants may anticipate more uncertainty in the eurozone and avoid euro-denominated investments.

Because of the trade-off faced by the ECB, any decision will likely lead to criticism. Some critics argue that the ECB should not impose austerity conditions so that countries experiencing financial problems can receive not only loans but also the proper stimulus they need. Other critics argue that the ECB's role should be limited to monetary policy and that the bank should not be providing credit. Most central banks face similar trade-offs, but the differences are more pronounced in the eurozone because it contains so many countries and their economic situations vary. Therefore, a particular policy decision may help some countries in the eurozone at the expense of others.

6-2e Impact of a Country Abandoning the Euro

If a country's government faces a crisis and is unable to obtain sufficient funding in the eurozone, it might seek to abandon the euro as its home currency. The subject of a country possibly abandoning the euro has been discussed most often with reference to Greece, because of Greece's inability to repay loans during the 2010–2015 period. However, it is possible that other eurozone countries could experience a crisis that might cause them to consider the potential impact of abandoning the euro.

A eurozone country that is experiencing trade deficit problems or weak economic conditions does not have direct control of its currency's value, as there are many other countries that participate in the euro. If the country had its own currency, then it might be able to set its exchange rate low enough that its currency (and hence its exports) become inexpensive to potential importers, which would help stimulate the economy. However, a weak home currency is not a perfect cure because it can cause higher inflation (as explained later in the chapter). In addition, if the country planned to repay its debt and if the debt was denominated in a different currency, repayment of debt with a weak currency would be more expensive.

A eurozone country that abandons the euro would no longer be subject to the prevailing monetary policy implemented by the ECB. The country's central bank could implement its own monetary policy in order to influence its local interest rate. However, a country that abandons the euro would likely be experiencing a crisis, and the typical risk-free market interest rate in such a country would likely be very high because investors tend to move their money out of countries where crises occur. Furthermore, the credit risk premium would also be high for borrowers because of the high probability that they would default on their debt. In addition to these economic implications, a country that abandoned the euro would also face political implications. If the country defaulted on its debt, it may be unable to access financing from any eurozone countries in the future.

Impact of Abandoning the Euro on Eurozone Conditions   A country's abandonment of the euro could lead to concerns that other countries might also abandon the euro. If MNCs and large institutional investors outside the eurozone feared that many countries would eventually abandon the euro, they may not be willing to invest any more funds in the eurozone due to fears of a possible collapse of the euro. Moreover, they may be concerned that existing investments in the eurozone may perform poorly when the proceeds are converted into their home currency. This concern might encourage investors to sell their assets in the eurozone now, before the euro weakens. Even local investors might sell their assets in the eurozone now and move their money into safer currencies. Thus a fear of future declines in the value of euro-denominated assets could cause the euro to weaken now.

In general, countries can more easily attract foreign investment from MNCs and large institutional investors when their local currency is expected to be stable. When the euro was created, the large number of participants in the eurozone reduced concerns about currency instability and attracted more foreign investment in eurozone countries than if each had its own local currency. Yet, because there has been a substantial amount of foreign investment in the eurozone, any concerns about the euro can now cause a much greater flow of funds out of Europe in the event that MNCs and institutional investors decide to withdraw their investments.

Furthermore, the sale of assets in the eurozone could lead to their value being reduced (apart from the currency effect). The fear that such conditions could ensue might even lead MNCs and large institutional investors *based in the eurozone* to sell their holdings of euro-based assets and move their money to a country whose currency is expected to be more stable. Such actions would place downward pressure on the value of these assets in the eurozone.

However, some critics contend that the mere threat to abandon the euro creates more problems for the eurozone than would any actual abandonment. Countries that want additional credit under favorable terms might use the threat of abandonment to obtain more funding.

6-3 Direct Intervention

A country's central bank conducts monetary policy (controls growth of the money supply) in order to maintain economic growth and low inflation. It may also intervene in the foreign exchange markets to control its currency's value. The Federal Reserve (the Fed) is the central bank of the United States, and it can attempt to control the value of the U.S. dollar with respect to other currencies. The Bank of Japan is the central bank of Japan, and it can attempt to control the value of the Japanese currency (the yen) with respect to other currencies. Because the European Central Bank (ECB) is the central bank for all countries in the eurozone, it can attempt to control the value of the euro with respect to other currencies.

6-3a Reasons for Direct Intervention

The degree to which the home currency is controlled, or "managed," varies among central banks. At one extreme, if a country had fixed exchange rates, the central bank would intervene frequently to ensure that the supply and demand conditions for its currency would maintain its fixed exchange rate. Most countries allow their currency to fluctuate, but their central banks may commonly intervene to manage exchange rates for three reasons:

- to smooth exchange rate movements,
- to establish implicit exchange rate boundaries, and
- to respond to temporary disturbances.

Smoothing Exchange Rate Movements   If a central bank is concerned that its economy will be affected by abrupt movements in the home currency's value, then it may attempt to smooth (stabilize) those currency movements over time. These actions may render business cycles less volatile. Smoothing currency movements may also reduce fears in the financial markets as well as speculative activity that could cause a major decline in a currency's value. So, in reducing exchange rate uncertainty, the central bank hopes to encourage international trade.

Establishing Implicit Exchange Rate Boundaries   Some central banks attempt to maintain their home currency rates within some unofficial, or implicit, boundaries. Analysts are often quoted as forecasting that a currency will not fall below (or rise above) some benchmark value because the central bank would intervene to prevent that from occurring. In fact, the Federal Reserve periodically intervenes to reverse the U.S. dollar's upward or downward momentum.

Responding to Temporary Disturbances   In some cases, a central bank may intervene to insulate a currency's value from a temporary disturbance. Note that the stated objective of the Fed's intervention policy is to counter disorderly market conditions.

EXAMPLE   News that oil prices might rise could cause expectations of a future decline in the value of the Japanese yen because Japan exchanges yen for U.S. dollars when it purchases oil from oil-exporting countries. Foreign exchange market speculators may exchange yen for dollars in anticipation of this decline. Central banks may therefore intervene to offset the immediate downward pressure on the yen caused by such market transactions. ●

Several studies have found that government intervention does not have a permanent effect on exchange rate movements. To the contrary, in many cases the intervention is overwhelmed by market forces. However, during a period when a country experiences much economic or political instability, currency movements might be even more volatile without direct intervention.

6-3b The Direct Intervention Process

A country's central bank can use direct intervention by engaging in foreign exchange transactions that affect the demand or supply market conditions for its currency. While the Fed does not intervene often, it can intervene directly by exchanging dollars that it holds as reserves in exchange for one or more foreign currencies in the foreign exchange market. For example, if it wanted to boost the value of the British pound against the dollar, it could contact financial institutions that serve as intermediaries for foreign exchange and exchange its U.S. dollars for British pounds. It could execute several small transactions representing the equivalent of about $10 million each, or could execute one large order with a single financial institution.

The effects of direct intervention on the value of the British pound are illustrated in Exhibit 6.3. The Fed's transactions represent an increased demand for British pounds in the foreign exchange market, which is shown as an outward shift in the demand for pounds in the left graph. Notice from the left graph that the shift in demand results in a higher equilibrium value of the British pound.

The Fed also maintains reserves in some other currencies. The transactions above caused it to exchange U.S. dollars for British pounds, so it would have some reserves in pounds. If the Fed wanted to weaken the pound's value against the dollar (or to strengthen the dollar), it could exchange some of its British pounds for U.S. dollars in the foreign exchange market. These transactions represent an increase in the supply of pounds for sale in the foreign exchange market, which is shown as an inward shift in the supply for pounds in the right graph of Exhibit 6.3. Notice from the right graph that the shift in demand results in a higher equilibrium value of the British pound.

Reliance on Reserves   Central banks of other countries commonly hold reserves in U.S. dollars that they can use in their direct intervention process if they want to strengthen their currency's value by exchanging dollars for their currency in the foreign exchange market. They also hold reserves in their own currency that they can exchange for dollars or another currency in case they want to weaken their currency's value in the foreign exchange market.

The potential effectiveness of a central bank's direct intervention is influenced by the amount of reserves it can use. For example, the central bank of China has a substantial

Exhibit 6.3   Effects of Direct Central Bank Intervention in the Foreign Exchange Market

amount of reserves that it can use to intervene in the foreign exchange market. Thus it can more effectively use direct intervention than many other Asian countries. If the central bank has a low level of reserves, it may not be able to exert much pressure on the currency's value; in that case, market forces would likely overwhelm its actions.

In the first six months of 2012, the Indian rupee declined against the dollar by about 20 percent. The Reserve Bank of India (the central bank of India) responded during this period by exchanging billions of dollars in exchange for rupees. However, the central bank's efforts were ineffective because market forces overwhelmed the direct intervention. The central bank of India holds a much smaller amount of reserves than China's central bank, and investors with funds invested in India seemed to anticipate that the direct intervention would not prevent the rupee from depreciating. Hence they liquidated their investments and fled the currency by exchanging rupees for dollars, which more than offset the actions of the Reserve Bank of India.

Frequency of Intervention   As foreign exchange activity has grown, central bank intervention has become less effective. The volume of foreign exchange transactions on a single day now exceeds the combined values of reserves at all central banks. Consequently, the number of direct interventions has declined. In 1989, for example, the Fed intervened on 97 different days. Since then, the Fed has not intervened on more than 20 days in any year.

Coordinated Intervention   Direct intervention is more likely to be effective when it is coordinated by several central banks. For example, if central banks agree that the euro's market value in dollars is too high, then they can engage in coordinated intervention in which they all use euros from their reserves to purchase dollars in the foreign exchange market. However, coordinated intervention requires the central banks to agree that a particular currency's value needs to be adjusted. Suppose a few central banks thought the euro's value was too high but that the ECB did not agree; in that case, the central banks would have to work out their differences before considering direct intervention in the foreign exchange market.

Nonsterilized versus Sterilized Intervention

When the Fed intervenes in the foreign exchange market without adjusting for the change in the money supply, it is engaging in a **nonsterilized intervention**. For example, if the Fed exchanges dollars for foreign currencies in the foreign exchange markets in an attempt to strengthen foreign currencies (weaken the dollar), the dollar money supply increases.

In a **sterilized intervention**, the Fed intervenes in the foreign exchange market and simultaneously engages in offsetting transactions in the Treasury securities markets. As a result, the dollar money supply is unchanged.

EXAMPLE   If the Fed desires to strengthen foreign currencies (weaken the dollar) without affecting the dollar money supply, then it (1) exchanges dollars for foreign currencies and (2) sells some of its holdings of Treasury securities for dollars. The net effect is an increase in investors' holdings of Treasury securities and a decrease in bank foreign currency balances. ●

The difference between nonsterilized and sterilized intervention is illustrated in Exhibit 6.4. In the upper portion of the exhibit, the Federal Reserve attempts to strengthen the Canadian dollar; in the lower portion, the Federal Reserve attempts to weaken the Canadian dollar. For each scenario, the diagram on the left shows the nonsterilized intervention and the diagram on the right shows a sterilized intervention

Exhibit 6.4 Forms of Central Bank Intervention in the Foreign Exchange Market

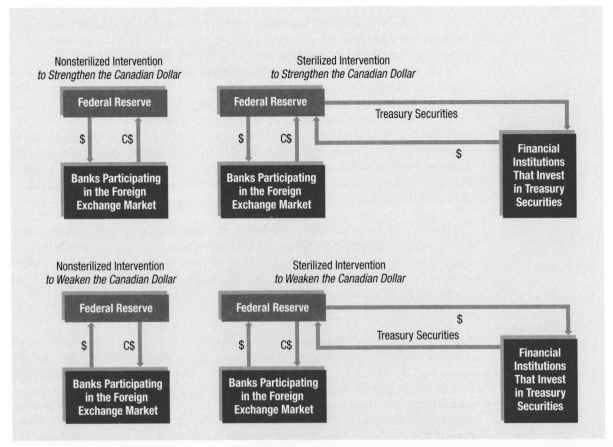

involving an exchange of Treasury securities for U.S. dollars that offsets the U.S. dollar flows resulting from the exchange of currencies. Thus the sterilized intervention achieves the same exchange of currencies in the foreign exchange market as the nonsterilized intervention, but it involves an additional transaction to prevent adjustments in the U.S. dollar money supply.

6-3c Direct Intervention as a Policy Tool

Central banks attempt to weaken their currency under some conditions and strengthen it under others. In essence, the exchange rate becomes a tool, like tax laws and the money supply, that the government can use to achieve its desired economic objectives.

Influence of a Weak Home Currency   Central banks implement direct intervention to weaken their home currency to stimulate foreign demand for products. A weak dollar, for example, can substantially boost U.S. exports and U.S. jobs; in addition, it may also reduce U.S. imports. The top part of Exhibit 6.5 shows how the Federal Reserve can use direct intervention to affect the value of the dollar in order to stimulate the U.S. economy.

Although a weak currency can reduce unemployment at home, it can lead to higher inflation. A weak dollar makes U.S. imports more expensive, thereby creating a competitive advantage for U.S. firms that sell their products in the United States. Some U.S. firms may increase their prices when the competition from foreign firms is reduced, which results in higher U.S. inflation.

Influence of a Strong Home Currency   Central banks may also implement direct intervention to strengthen their home currency, which can reduce the country's inflation. A strong home currency increases the purchasing power of local consumers and corporations that buy goods from other countries. This situation intensifies foreign

Exhibit 6.5 How Central Bank Intervention Can Stimulate the U.S. Economy

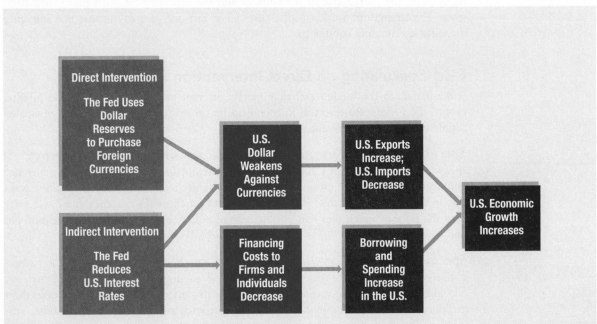

Exhibit 6.6 How Central Bank Intervention Can Reduce Inflation

competition and forces domestic producers to refrain from increasing prices. Therefore, the country's overall inflation rate should be lower if its currency is stronger, other things being equal. The top part of Exhibit 6.6 shows how the Federal Reserve can use direct intervention to affect the dollar's value and thus reduce U.S. inflation.

Although a strong currency may cure high inflation, it may also increase home unemployment because foreign products become less expensive. A currency's ideal value depends on the perspective of the country and the officials who must make such decisions. The strength or weakness of a currency is just one of many factors that influence a country's economic conditions.

6-3d Speculating on Direct Intervention

Some traders in the foreign exchange market attempt to determine when (and to what extent) the Federal Reserve will intervene so that they can capitalize on the anticipated results of the intervention effort.

Speculating on Intervention Intended to Strengthen a Currency If speculators anticipate that a central bank will attempt to strengthen a specific currency and also believe that the intervention will have its desired effects, they may take a position in that currency. In this way, they are able to purchase the currency at a lower price than the price at which they can sell the currency after the central bank intervention has had its effect.

Speculating on Intervention Intended to Weaken a Currency Alternatively, if they anticipate that a central bank will attempt to weaken a specific currency and also believe that the intervention will have its desired effects, they may take short positions in that currency by borrowing that currency and exchanging it for other currencies. Then they can reverse their transaction after the intervention has occurred. The obvious risk to these speculative strategies is that their expectations about a central bank intervening or the effects of the direct intervention may be wrong.

Central Bank Efforts to Disguise Its Strategy   The Fed normally attempts to intervene without being noticed. However, dealers at the major banks that trade with the Fed often transmit the information to other market participants. Also, when the Fed deals directly with numerous commercial banks, markets are well aware that the Fed is intervening. To hide its strategy, the Fed may pretend to be interested in selling dollars when it is actually buying dollars, or vice versa. It calls commercial banks and obtains both bid and ask quotes on currencies; that way, the banks will not know whether the Fed is considering purchases or sales of these currencies.

6-4 Indirect Intervention

The Fed can also affect the dollar's value indirectly by influencing the factors that determine it. Recall that the change in a currency's spot rate is influenced by the following factors:

$$e = f(\Delta INF, \Delta INT, \Delta INC, \Delta GC, \Delta EXP)$$

where

$e =$ **percentage change in the spot rate**

$\Delta INF =$ **change in the difference between U.S. inflation and the foreign country's inflation**

$\Delta INT =$ **change in the difference between the U.S. interest rate and the foreign country's interest rate**

$\Delta INC =$ **change in the difference between the U.S. income level and the foreign country's income level**

$\Delta GC =$ **change in government controls**

$\Delta EXP =$ **change in expectations of future exchange rates**

WEB

www.bloomberg.com
Latest information from financial markets around the world.

The central bank can influence all of these variables, which in turn can affect the exchange rate. Because these variables will probably have a more lasting impact on a spot rate than would direct intervention, a central bank may prefer to intervene indirectly by influencing these variables. Although the central bank can affect all of the variables, it is likely to focus on interest rates or government controls when using indirect intervention.

6-4a Government Control of Interest Rates

When central banks of countries increase or reduce interest rates, this may have an indirect effect on the values of their currencies.

EXAMPLE   When the Federal Reserve reduces U.S. interest rates, U.S. investors may transfer funds to other countries to capitalize on higher interest rates. This action reflects an increase in demand for other currencies and places upward pressure on these currencies against the dollar.

Conversely, if the Fed raises U.S. interest rates, foreign investors may transfer funds to the United States to capitalize on higher U.S. interest rates (especially if expected inflation in the United States is relatively low). This action reflects an increase in the supply of foreign currencies to be exchanged for dollars in the foreign exchange market, and it places downward pressure on those currencies against the dollar. ●

If the country experiences a currency crisis its central bank may raise interest rates in order to prevent a major flow of funds out of the country.

EXAMPLE Russia attracts a large amount of foreign funds from investors who want to capitalize on Russia's growth. However, when the Russian economy weakens, foreign investors flood the foreign exchange market with Russian rubles for other currencies so that they can transfer their money to other countries. The Russian central bank may raise interest rates so that foreign investors would earn a higher yield on securities if they left their funds in Russia. However, if investors still anticipate a major withdrawal of funds from the country, they will rush to sell their rubles before the value of its currency falls. These actions by investors cause the ruble's value to decline substantially. ●

The preceding example reflects the situation of countries that experienced a currency crisis in the past, including many Southeast Asian countries and many countries in Latin America. Some developing countries such as Argentina and Russia have experienced multiple currency crises. In 2014, the value of Russia's ruble declined by more than 50 percent against some currencies due to economic and political problems. The Russian central bank's direct intervention of buying rubles in the foreign exchange market with its reserves of other currencies was ineffective.

The Russian central bank also attempted indirect intervention by raising interest rates substantially to encourage local investors to invest in Russian money market securities. However, many investors moved their money into other more stable currencies, which perpetuated the decline in the ruble.

A central bank's indirect intervention commonly fails to prevent withdrawals of funds during a crisis and also increases the financing costs of the country's firms. This can reduce the amount of corporate borrowing and spending in a country, which may cause the economy to weaken further. In many cases, a currency crisis may not be avoided unless the underlying problem (such as political instability) is resolved, but a central bank is normally not the cause of political problems and it may have very little control over them.

6-4b Government Use of Foreign Exchange Controls

Some governments attempt to use foreign exchange controls (such as restrictions on the exchange of the currency) as a form of indirect intervention to maintain the exchange rate of their currency. China has historically used foreign exchange restrictions to control the yuan's exchange rate, but has partially removed these restrictions in recent years.

Intervention Warnings A central bank may announce that it is strongly considering intervention. Such announcements may be intended to warn speculators who are taking positions in a currency that benefit from appreciation in its value. An intervention warning could discourage additional speculation and might even encourage some speculators to unwind (liquidate) their existing positions in the currency. In this case there would be a large supply of that currency for sale in the foreign exchange market, which would tend to reduce its value. Thus the central bank might more effectively achieve its goal (to reduce the local currency's value) with an intervention warning than with actual intervention.

SUMMARY

- Exchange rate systems can be classified as fixed rate, freely floating, managed float, or pegged. In a fixed exchange rate system, exchange rates are either held constant or allowed to fluctuate only within very narrow boundaries. In a freely floating exchange rate system, exchange rate values are determined by market forces without intervention. In a managed float system, exchange rates are not restricted by boundaries but are subject to government intervention. In a pegged exchange rate system, a currency's value is pegged to a foreign currency (or unit of account) and moves in line with that currency (or unit) against other currencies.

■ Numerous European countries use the euro as their home currency. The single currency allows international trade among firms in the eurozone without foreign exchange expenses and without concerns about future exchange rate movements. However, countries that participate in the euro do not have complete control of their monetary policy because a single policy is applied to all countries in the eurozone. In addition, being part of the eurozone may render some countries more susceptible to a crisis occurring in some other eurozone country.

■ Governments can use direct intervention by purchasing or selling currencies in the foreign exchange market, thereby altering demand and supply conditions and hence the currencies' equilibrium values. When a government purchases a currency in the foreign exchange market, it puts upward pressure on that currency's equilibrium value. When a government sells a currency in the foreign exchange market, it puts downward pressure on the currency's equilibrium value.

■ Governments can use indirect intervention by influencing the economic factors that affect equilibrium exchange rates. A common form of indirect intervention is to increase interest rates in order to attract more international capital flows, which may cause the local currency to appreciate. However, indirect intervention is not always effective.

POINT COUNTER-POINT

Should China Be Forced to Alter the Value of Its Currency?

Point U.S. politicians frequently suggest that China needs to increase the value of the Chinese yuan against the U.S. dollar, even though China has allowed the yuan to float (within boundaries). The U.S. politicians claim that the yuan is the cause of the large U.S. trade deficit with China. This issue is periodically raised not only with currencies tied to the dollar but also with currencies that have a floating rate. Some critics argue that the exchange rate can be used as a form of trade protectionism. That is, a country can discourage or prevent imports and encourage exports by keeping the value of its currency artificially low.

Counter-Point China might counter that its large balance-of-trade surplus with the United States has been due to the difference in prices between the two countries and that it should not be blamed for the high

U.S. prices. It might argue that the U.S. trade deficit can be partially attributed to the very high prices in the United States, which are necessary to cover the excessive compensation for executives and other employees at U.S. firms. The high prices in the United States encourage firms and consumers to purchase goods from China. Even if China's yuan is revalued upward, this does not necessarily mean that U.S. firms and consumers will purchase U.S. products. They may shift their purchases from China to Indonesia or other low-wage countries rather than buy more U.S. products. Thus the underlying dilemma is not China but any country that has lower costs of production than the United States.

Who Is Correct? Use the Internet to learn more about this issue. Which argument do you support? Offer your own opinion on this issue.

SELF-TEST

Answers are provided in Appendix A at the back of the text.

1. Explain why it would be virtually impossible to set an exchange rate between the Japanese yen and the U.S. dollar and to maintain a fixed exchange rate.

2. Assume the Federal Reserve believes that the dollar should be weakened against the Mexican peso.

Explain how the Fed could use direct and indirect intervention to weaken the dollar's value with respect to the peso. Assume that future inflation in the United States is expected to be low, regardless of the Fed's actions.

3. Briefly explain why the Federal Reserve may attempt to weaken the dollar.

4. Assume the country of Sluban ties its currency (the slu) to the dollar and the exchange rate will remain fixed. Sluban has frequent trade with countries in the eurozone and the United States. All traded products can easily be produced by all the countries, and the demand for these products in any country is very sensitive to the price because consumers can shift to wherever the products are relatively cheap. Assume that the euro depreciates substantially against the dollar during the next year.

a. What is the likely effect (if any) of the euro's exchange rate movement on the volume of Sluban's exports to the eurozone? Explain.

b. What is the likely effect (if any) of the euro's exchange rate movement on the volume of Sluban's exports to the United States? Explain.

QUESTIONS AND APPLICATIONS

1. Exchange Rate Systems Compare and contrast the fixed, freely floating, and managed float exchange rate systems. What are some advantages and disadvantages of a freely floating exchange rate system versus a fixed exchange rate system?

2. Intervention with Euros Assume that Belgium, one of the European countries that uses the euro as its currency, would prefer that its currency depreciate against the U.S. dollar. Can it apply central bank intervention to achieve this objective? Explain.

3. Direct Intervention How can a central bank use direct intervention to change the value of a currency? Explain why a central bank may desire to smooth exchange rate movements of its currency.

4. Indirect Intervention How can a central bank use indirect intervention to change the value of a currency?

5. Intervention Effects Assume there is concern that the United States may experience a recession. How should the Federal Reserve influence the dollar to prevent a recession? How might U.S. exporters react to this policy (favorably or unfavorably)? What about U.S. importing firms?

6. Currency Effects on Economy What is the impact of a weak home currency on the home economy, other things being equal? What is the impact of a strong home currency on the home economy, other things being equal?

7. Feedback Effects Explain the potential feedback effects of a currency's changing value on inflation.

8. Indirect Intervention Why would the Fed's indirect intervention have a stronger impact on some currencies than others? Why would a central bank's indirect intervention have a stronger impact than its direct intervention?

9. Effects on Currencies Tied to the Dollar The Hong Kong dollar's value is tied to the U.S. dollar. Explain how the following trade patterns would be affected by the appreciation of the Japanese yen against the dollar: (a) Hong Kong exports to Japan and (b) Hong Kong exports to the United States.

10. Intervention Effects on Bond Prices U.S. bond prices are normally inversely related to U.S. inflation. If the Fed planned to use intervention to weaken the dollar, how might bond prices be affected?

11. Direct Intervention in Europe If most countries in Europe experience a recession, how might the European Central Bank use direct intervention to stimulate economic growth?

12. Sterilized Intervention Explain the difference between sterilized and nonsterilized intervention.

13. Effects of Indirect Intervention Suppose that the government of Chile reduces one of its key interest rates. The values of several other Latin American currencies are expected to change substantially against the Chilean peso in response to the news.

a. Explain why other Latin American currencies could be affected by a cut in Chile's interest rates.

b. How would the central banks of other Latin American countries be likely to adjust their interest rates? How would the currencies of these countries respond to the central bank intervention?

c. How would a U.S. firm that exports products to Latin American countries be affected by the central bank intervention? (Assume the exports are denominated in the corresponding Latin American currency for each country.)

14. Freely Floating Exchange Rates Should the governments of Asian countries allow their currencies to float freely? What would be the advantages of letting their currencies float freely? What would be the disadvantages?

15. Indirect Intervention During the Asian crisis (see Appendix 6 at the end of this chapter), some Asian central banks raised their interest rates to prevent their currencies from weakening. Yet the currencies weakened anyway. Offer your opinion as to why the central banks' efforts at indirect intervention did not work.

Advanced Questions

16. Monitoring the Fed's Interventions Why do foreign market participants monitor the Fed's direct intervention efforts? How does the Fed attempt to hide its intervention actions? The media frequently report that "the dollar's value strengthened against many currencies in response to the Federal Reserve's plan to increase interest rates." Explain why the dollar's value may change even before the Federal Reserve affects interest rates.

17. Effects of September 11 Within a few days after the September 11, 2001, terrorist attack on the United States, the Federal Reserve reduced short-term interest rates to stimulate the U.S. economy. How might this action have affected the foreign flow of funds into the United States and affected the value of the dollar? How could such an effect on the dollar have increased the probability that the U.S. economy would strengthen?

18. Intervention Effects on Corporate Performance Assume you have a subsidiary in Australia. The subsidiary sells mobile homes to local consumers in Australia, who buy the homes using mostly borrowed funds from local banks. Your subsidiary purchases all of its materials from Hong Kong. The Hong Kong dollar is tied to the U.S. dollar. Your subsidiary borrowed funds from the U.S. parent, and must pay the parent $100,000 in interest each month. Australia has just raised its interest rate in order to boost the value of its currency (Australian dollar, A$). The Australian dollar appreciates against the U.S. dollar as a result. Explain whether these actions would increase, reduce, or have no effect on:

a. The volume of your subsidiary's sales in Australia (measured in A$).

b. The cost to your subsidiary of purchasing materials (measured in A$).

c. The cost to your subsidiary of making the interest payments to the U.S. parent (measured in A$). Briefly explain each answer.

19. Pegged Currencies Why do you think a country suddenly decides to peg its currency to the dollar or some other currency? When a currency is unable to maintain the peg, what do you think are the typical forces that break the peg?

20. Impact of Intervention on Currency Option Premiums Assume that the central bank of the country Zakow periodically intervenes in the foreign exchange market to prevent large upward or downward fluctuations in its currency (the zak) against the U.S. dollar. Today, the central bank announced that it would no longer intervene in the foreign exchange market. The spot rate of the zak against the dollar was not affected by this news. Will the news affect the premium on currency call options that are traded on the zak? Will the news affect the premium on currency put options that are traded on the zak? Explain.

21. Impact of Information on Currency Option Premiums As of 10:00 a. m., the premium on a specific one-year call option on British pounds is $.04. Assume that the Bank of England had not been intervening in the foreign exchange markets in the last several months. However, it announces at 10:01 a.m. that it will begin to frequently intervene in the foreign exchange market in order to reduce fluctuations in the pound's value against the U.S. dollar over the next year, but it will not attempt to push the pound's value higher or lower than what is dictated by market forces. Also, the Bank of England has no plans to affect economic conditions with this intervention. Most participants who trade currency options did not anticipate this announcement. When they heard the announcement, they expected that the intervention would be successful in achieving its goal. Will this announcement cause the premium on the one-year call option on British pounds to increase, decrease, or be unaffected? Explain.

22. Speculating Based on Intervention Assume that you expect that the European Central Bank (ECB) plans to engage in central bank intervention in which it plans to use euros to purchase a substantial amount of U.S. dollars in the foreign exchange market over the next month. Assume that this direct intervention is expected to be successful at influencing the exchange rate.

a. Would you purchase or sell call options on euros today?

b. Would you purchase or sell futures on euros today?

23. Pegged Currency and International Trade Assume the Hong Kong dollar (HK$) value is tied to the U.S. dollar and will remain tied to the U.S. dollar. Last month, a HK\$ = 0.25 Singapore dollars. Today, a HK\$ = 0.30 Singapore dollars. Assume that there is much trade in the computer industry among Singapore, Hong Kong, and the United States and that all products are viewed as substitutes for each other and are of about the same quality. Assume that the firms invoice their products in their local currency and do not change their prices.

a. Will the computer exports from the United States to Hong Kong increase, decrease, or remain the same? Briefly explain.

b. Will the computer exports from Singapore to the United States increase, decrease, or remain the same? Briefly explain.

24. Implications of a Revised Peg The country of Zapakar has much international trade with the United States and other countries as it has no significant barriers on trade or capital flows. Many firms in Zapakar export common products (denominated in zaps) that serve as substitutes for products produced in the United States and many other countries. Zapakar's currency (called the zap) has been pegged at 8 zaps = \$1 for the last several years. Yesterday, the government of Zapakar reset the zap's currency value so that it is now pegged at 7 zaps = \$1.

a. How should this adjustment in the pegged rate against the dollar affect the volume of exports by Zapakar firms to the United States?

b. Will this adjustment in the pegged rate against the dollar affect the volume of exports by Zapakar firms to non-U.S. countries? If so, explain.

c. Assume that the Federal Reserve significantly raises U.S. interest rates today. Do you think Zapakar's interest rate would increase, decrease, or remain the same?

25. Pegged Currency and International Trade Assume that Canada decides to peg its currency (the Canadian dollar) to the U.S. dollar and that the exchange rate will remain fixed. Assume that Canada commonly obtains its imports from the United States and Mexico. The United States commonly obtains its imports from Canada and Mexico. Mexico commonly obtains its imports from the United States and Canada. The traded products are always invoiced in the exporting country's currency. Assume that the Mexican peso appreciates substantially against the U.S. dollar during the next year.

a. What is the likely effect (if any) of the peso's exchange rate movement on the volume of Canada's exports to Mexico? Explain.

b. What is the likely effect (if any) of the peso's exchange rate movement on the volume of Canada's exports to the United States? Explain.

26. Impact of Devaluation The inflation rate in Yinland was 14 percent last year. The government of Yinland just devalued its currency (the yin) by 40 percent against the dollar. Even though it produces products similar to those of the United States, it has much trade with the United States and very little trade with other countries. It presently has trade restrictions imposed on all non-U.S. countries. Will the devaluation of the yin increase or reduce inflation in Yinland? Briefly explain.

27. Intervention and Pegged Exchange Rates Interest rate parity exists and will continue to exist. The one-year interest rate in the United States and in the eurozone is 6 percent and will continue to be 6 percent. Assume that the country of Denmark's currency (called the krone) is currently pegged to the euro and will remain pegged to the euro in the future. Assume that you expect that the European central bank (ECB) to engage in central bank intervention in which it plans to use euros to purchase a substantial amount of U.S. dollars in the foreign exchange market over the next month. Assume that this direct intervention is expected to be successful at influencing the exchange rate.

a. Will the spot rate of the krone against the dollar increase, decrease, or remain the same as a result of central bank intervention?

b. Will the forward rate of the euro against the dollar increase, decrease, or remain the same as a result of central bank intervention?

c. Would the ECB's intervention be intended to reduce unemployment or reduce inflation in the eurozone?

d. If the ECB decided to use indirect intervention instead of direct intervention to achieve its objective of influencing the exchange rate, would it increase or reduce the interest rate in the eurozone?

e. Based on your answer to part (d), will Denmark's interest rate increase, decrease, or remain the same as a result of the ECB's indirect intervention?

28. Pegged Exchange Rates The United States, Argentina, and Canada commonly engage in international trade with each other. All the products traded can easily be produced in all three countries. The traded products are always invoiced in the exporting country's currency. Assume that Argentina decides to peg its currency (called the peso) to the U.S. dollar and the exchange rate will remain fixed. Assume that the Canadian dollar appreciates substantially against the U.S. dollar during the next year.

a. What is the likely effect (if any) of the Canadian dollar's exchange rate movement over the year on the volume of Argentina's exports to Canada? Briefly explain.

b. What is the likely effect (if any) of the Canadian dollar's exchange rate movement on the volume of Argentina's exports to the United States? Briefly explain.

29. Central Bank Control Over Its Currency's Value Assume that France wants to change the prevailing spot rate of its currency (euro) in order to improve its economy, while Switzerland wants to change the prevailing value of its currency (Swiss franc) in order to improve its economy. Which of these two countries is more likely to have more control over its currency? Briefly explain.

30. Coordinated Central Bank Intervention Assume that the United States has a weak economy and that the Fed wants to correct this problem by adjusting the value of the dollar. The Fed is not worried about inflation. Assume that the eurozone has a somewhat similar economic situation as the United States and the European Central Bank (ECB) wants to correct this problem by adjusting the value of the euro. The ECB is not worried about inflation. Do you think the European Central Bank and the Fed should engage in coordinated intervention in order to achieve their objectives? Briefly explain.

31. Effects of Central Bank Intervention

a. Assume that the Federal Reserve engages in intervention by exchanging a very large amount of Canadian dollars for U.S. dollars in the foreign exchange market. Should this increase, reduce, or have no effect on Canadian inflation? Briefly explain.

b. Ignore the actions of the Federal Reserve in the question above and assume that the Canadian central bank raises its interest rates. Should this increase, reduce, or have no effect on Canadian inflation? Briefly explain.

c. The Hong Kong dollar is tied to the U.S. dollar and will continue to be tied to the dollar. Given your answer in part (a), how will the intervention by the Federal Reserve affect the cross exchange rate between the Canadian dollar and the Hong Kong dollar?

32. Role of the ECB

a. Explain the dilemma that the European Central Bank (ECB) faces as it attempts to help countries with large budget deficits.

b. Describe the types of conditions that the ECB required when providing credit to countries that needed to resolve their budget deficit problems.

c. Why might these conditions have a temporary adverse effect on countries that receive credit from the ECB?

33. Impact of Abandoning the Euro

a. Explain why one country abandoning the euro could reduce the value of the euro, even if that country accounts for a very small proportion of the total production among all eurozone participants.

b. Explain why one country abandoning the euro could affect the value of the assets in the eurozone, even if that country accounts for a very small proportion of the total production among all eurozone participants.

Critical Thinking

Cause and Effects of a Currency Crisis Select a currency in a country that has experienced a crisis in the last year using an online search term such as "currency crisis." Write a short essay to describe the underlying reasons for the currency crisis. Explain how the weakness of the currency has affected economic conditions in that country. Does it appear that the currency's weakness caused the crisis in the country, or did an economic crisis in the country cause a weak currency? Did the country's central bank use direct intervention in an attempt to resolve the crisis? If so, was it successful?

Discussion in the Boardroom

This exercise can be found in Appendix E at the back of this textbook.

Running Your Own MNC

This exercise can be found on the *International Financial Management* text companion website. Go to www.cengagebrain.com (students) or www.cengage.com/login (instructors) and search using **ISBN 9781133947837**.

BLADES, INC. CASE

Assessment of Government Influence on Exchange Rates

Recall that Blades, the U.S. manufacturer of roller blades, generates most of its revenue and incurs most of its expenses in the United States. However, the company has recently begun exporting roller blades to Thailand. The company has an agreement with Entertainment Products, Inc., a Thai importer, for a three-year period. According to the terms of the agreement, Entertainment Products will purchase 180,000 pairs of "Speedos," Blades' primary product, annually at a fixed price of 4,594 Thai baht per pair. Due to quality and cost considerations, Blades is also importing certain rubber and plastic components from a Thai exporter. The cost of these components is approximately 2,871 Thai baht per pair of Speedos. No contractual agreement exists between Blades, Inc., and the Thai exporter. Consequently, the cost of the rubber and plastic components imported from Thailand is subject not only to exchange rate considerations but to economic conditions (such as inflation) in Thailand as well.

Shortly after Blades began exporting to and importing from Thailand, Asia experienced weak economic conditions. Consequently, foreign investors in Thailand feared the baht's potential weakness and withdrew their investments, resulting in an excess supply of Thai baht for sale. Because of the resulting downward pressure on the baht's value, the Thai government attempted to stabilize the baht's exchange rate. To maintain the baht's value, the Thai government intervened in the foreign exchange market. Specifically, it swapped its baht reserves for dollar reserves at other central banks and then used its dollar reserves to purchase the baht in the foreign exchange market. However, this agreement required Thailand to reverse this transaction by exchanging dollars for baht at a future date. Unfortunately, the Thai government's intervention was unsuccessful, as it was overwhelmed by market forces. Consequently, the Thai government ceased its intervention efforts, and the value of the Thai baht declined substantially against the dollar over a three-month period.

When the Thai government stopped intervening in the foreign exchange market, Ben Holt, Blades' CFO, was concerned that the value of the Thai baht would continue to decline indefinitely. Because Blades generates net inflow in Thai baht, this would seriously affect the company's profit margin. Furthermore, one of the reasons Blades had expanded into Thailand was to appease the company's shareholders. At last year's annual shareholder meeting, they had demanded that senior management take action to improve the firm's low profit margins. Expanding into Thailand had been Holt's suggestion, and he is now afraid that his career might be at stake. For these reasons, Holt feels that the Asian crisis and its impact on Blades demand his serious attention. One of the factors Holt thinks he should consider is the issue of government intervention and how it could affect Blades in particular. Specifically, he wonders whether the decision to enter into a fixed agreement with Entertainment Products was a good idea under the circumstances. Another issue is how the future completion of the swap agreement initiated by the Thai government will affect Blades. To address these issues and to gain a little more understanding of the process of government intervention, Holt has prepared the following list of questions for you, Blades' financial analyst, as he knows that you understand international financial management.

1. Did the intervention effort by the Thai government constitute direct or indirect intervention? Explain.

2. Did the intervention by the Thai government constitute sterilized or nonsterilized intervention? What is the difference between the types of intervention? Which type do you think would be more effective in increasing the value of the baht? Why? (Hint: Think about the effect of nonsterilized intervention on U.S. interest rates.)

3. If the Thai baht is virtually fixed with respect to the dollar, how could this affect U.S. levels of inflation? Do you think these effects on the U.S. economy will be more pronounced for companies such as Blades that operate under trade arrangements involving commitments or for firms that do not? How are companies such as Blades affected by a fixed exchange rate?

4. What are some of the potential disadvantages for Thai levels of inflation associated with the floating exchange rate system that is now used in Thailand? Do you think Blades contributes to these disadvantages to a great extent? How are companies such as Blades affected by a freely floating exchange rate?

5. What do you think will happen to the Thai baht's value when the swap arrangement is completed? How will this affect Blades?

SMALL BUSINESS DILEMMA

Assessment of Central Bank Intervention by the Sports Exports Company

Jim Logan, owner of the Sports Exports Company, is concerned about the value of the British pound over time because his firm receives pounds as payment for footballs exported to the United Kingdom. He recently read that the Bank of England (the central bank of the United Kingdom) is likely to intervene directly in the foreign exchange market by flooding the market with British pounds.

1. Forecast whether the British pound will weaken or strengthen based on the information provided.

2. How would the performance of the Sports Exports Company be affected by the Bank of England's policy of flooding the foreign exchange market with British pounds (assuming that it does not hedge its exchange rate risk)?

INTERNET/EXCEL EXERCISES

The website for Japan's central bank, the Bank of Japan, provides information about its mission and its policy actions. Its address is www.boj.or.jp/en.

1. Use this website to review the outline of the Bank of Japan's objectives. Summarize the mission of the Bank of Japan. How does this mission relate to intervening in the foreign exchange market?

2. Review the minutes of recent meetings by Bank of Japan officials. Summarize at least one recent meeting that was associated with possible or actual intervention to affect the yen's value.

3. Why might the foreign exchange intervention strategies of the Bank of Japan be relevant to the U.S. government and to U.S.-based MNCs?

ONLINE ARTICLES WITH REAL-WORLD EXAMPLES

Find a recent article online that describes an actual international finance application or a real world example about a specific MNC's actions that reinforces one or more concepts covered in this chapter.

If your class has an online component, your professor may ask you to post your summary there and provide the web link of the article so that other students can access it. If your class is live, your professor may ask you to summarize your application in class. Your professor may assign specific students to complete this assignment for this chapter, or may allow any students to do the assignment on a volunteer basis.

For recent online articles and real world examples applied to this chapter, consider using the following search terms and include the current year as a search term to ensure that the online articles are recent:

1. pegged exchange rate

2. Bank of China control of yuan

3. Federal Reserve intervention

4. European Central Bank intervention

5. central bank intervention

6. impact of the dollar

7. impact of the euro

8. central bank AND currency volatility

9. central bank AND weaken currency

10. central bank AND strengthen currency

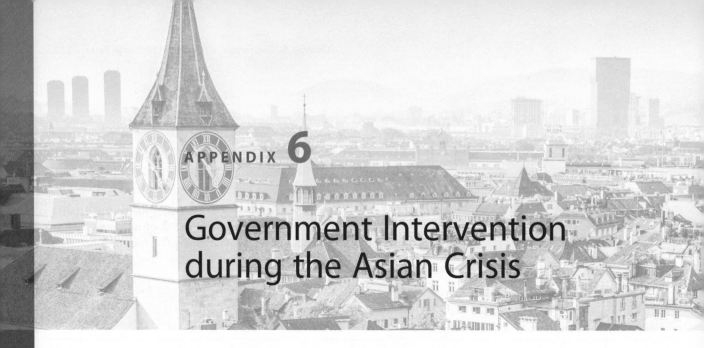

Government Intervention during the Asian Crisis

From 1990 to 1997, Asian countries achieved higher economic growth than any others. They were viewed as models for advances in technology and economic improvement. In the summer and fall of 1997, however, they experienced financial problems that led to what is known as the "Asian crisis" and resulted in the bailouts of several countries by the International Monetary Fund.

Much of the crisis is attributed to the substantial depreciation of Asian currencies, which caused severe financial problems for firms and governments throughout Asia and also in other regions. This crisis demonstrated how exchange rate movements could affect country conditions and thus affect the firms that operate in those countries.

The specific objectives of this appendix are to describe the conditions in the foreign exchange market that contributed to the Asian crisis, explain how governments intervened in an attempt to control their exchange rates, and describe the consequences of those intervention efforts. The Asian crisis offers useful lessons to governments about controlling their currency's value.

Crisis in Thailand

Until July 1997, Thailand was one of the world's fastest-growing economies. Its high level of spending and low level of saving put upward pressure on prices of real estate and products and also on the local interest rate. Normally, countries with high inflation tend to have weak currencies due to the force of purchasing power parity. Prior to July 1997, however, Thailand's currency was linked to the U.S. dollar. Thailand was an attractive site for foreign investors, who could earn a high interest rate on invested funds while being protected (until the crisis) from a large depreciation in the baht.

Bank Lending Situation

A country normally desires a large inflow of funds, which can help support its growth. In Thailand's case, however, the inflow of funds provided Thai banks with more funds than they could use for making loans. Consequently, in attempting to use all the funds, the banks made a large number of extremely risky loans. Commercial developers borrowed heavily without having to prove that the expansion was feasible. Lenders offered to lend large sums of money based solely on a developer's previous success. These loans made sense only if the economy continued its high growth, but such levels of development could not last forever.

Flow-of-Funds Situation

Apart from the bank lending situation just described, the large inflow of funds increased Thailand's susceptibility to a massive *outflow* of funds if foreign investors ever lost confidence in the Thai economy. Given the large amount of risky loans and the potential for large outflows, Thailand was sometimes described as a "house of cards" waiting to collapse.

Although the large inflow of funds put downward pressure on interest rates, the supply was offset by a strong demand for funds as developers and corporations sought to capitalize on the growth economy by expanding. Thailand's government was also borrowing heavily to improve the country's infrastructure. The sheer volume of borrowing was enough to increase interest rates, which made the debt expensive to borrowers.

Export Competition

During the first half of 1997, the U.S. dollar strengthened against the Japanese yen and European currencies, which reduced the prices of Japanese and European imports. Although the dollar was linked to the baht over this period, Thailand's products were more expensive than those of other exporters to the United States.

Pressure on the Thai Baht

The baht experienced downward pressure in July 1997 as some foreign investors recognized its potential weakness. The baht's value relative to the dollar was depressed by the large sale of baht in exchange for dollars. On July 2, 1997, the baht was detached from the dollar, after which Thailand's central bank attempted to maintain the currency's value by intervention. Specifically, it swapped its baht reserves for dollar reserves at other central banks and then used its dollar reserves to purchase the baht in the foreign exchange market (this swap agreement required Thailand to reverse this exchange by exchanging dollars for baht at a future date). The intervention was intended to offset the sales of baht by foreign investors in the foreign exchange market, but market forces overwhelmed the intervention efforts. As the supply of baht to be exchanged for dollars exceeded the U.S. demand for baht in the foreign exchange market, the government eventually had to surrender its effort to defend the baht's value. In July 1997, the value of the baht plummeted. Over a five-week period, it declined by more than 20 percent against the dollar.

Damage to Thailand

Thailand's central bank used more than $20 billion to purchase baht in the foreign exchange market as part of its direct intervention efforts. Then, because of the currency's steep decline, Thailand needed still more baht to be exchanged for the dollars required to repay the other central banks.

Thailand's banks estimated the amount of their defaulted loans at over $30 billion. Meanwhile, some corporations in Thailand had borrowed funds in other currencies (including the dollar) because the interest rates in Thailand were relatively high. This strategy backfired because the baht's weakening forced these corporations to exchange larger amounts of baht for the currencies needed to pay off the loans. Hence the corporations incurred a much higher effective financing rate (which explains the need to account for exchange rate effects when determining a loan's true cost) than if they had borrowed funds locally in Thailand. This higher borrowing cost was an additional strain on these corporations.

Rescue Package for Thailand

On August 5, 1997, the IMF and several countries agreed to provide Thailand with a $16 billion rescue package; Japan and the IMF provided $4 billion each. At the time, this was the second-largest bailout plan ever put together for a single country (Mexico had received a $50 billion bailout in 1994). In return for this monetary support, Thailand agreed to reduce its budget deficit, prevent inflation from rising above 9 percent, raise its value-added tax from 7 to 10 percent, and clean up its local banks' financial statements, which had many undisclosed bad loans.

The rescue package took time to finalize because Thailand's government was unwilling to shut down all the banks experiencing financial problems that stemmed from their overly generous lending policies. Many critics have questioned the rescue package's efficacy, as some of the funding was misallocated because of corruption in Thailand.

Spread of the Crisis throughout Southeast Asia

The crisis in Thailand was contagious to other countries in Southeast Asia. The Southeast Asian economies are fairly integrated because of the trade between countries. The crisis was expected to weaken Thailand's economy, which would reduce its demand for imports from the other countries of Southeast Asia. As the demand for those countries' products declined, so would their national income and their demand for products from other Southeast Asian countries. In this way, the effects of the crisis could spread across the region. Like Thailand, the other Southeast Asian countries had experienced high growth in recent years, leading to overly optimistic assessments of future economic conditions and thus to excessive loans being extended for projects that had a high risk of default.

These countries were also similar to Thailand in that they had relatively high interest rates and their governments tended to stabilize their currencies. As a result, these other Southeast Asian countries had attracted a large amount of foreign investment as well. Thailand's crisis made foreign investors realize that a similar crisis could befall the region's other countries. Consequently, they began to withdraw funds from these countries.

Effects on Other Asian Currencies

In July and August of 1997, the values of the Malaysian ringgit, Singapore dollar, Philippine peso, Taiwan dollar, and Indonesian rupiah declined. The Philippine peso was devalued in July. Malaysia initially attempted to maintain the ringgit's value within a narrow band, but in the end it surrendered and let the ringgit float to a level determined by market forces.

In August 1997, Bank Indonesia (the central bank) used more than $500 million in direct intervention to purchase rupiah in the foreign exchange market in an attempt to boost that currency's value. By mid-August, however, it gave up this effort and let the rupiah float to its natural level, a decision that may have been influenced by the failure of Thailand's costly efforts to maintain the baht. The market forces were simply too strong to be offset by direct intervention. On October 30, 1997, a rescue package for Indonesia was announced, but the IMF and Indonesia's government did not agree on the $43 billion package's terms until the spring of 1998. One of the main points of contention was that President Suharto wanted to peg the rupiah's exchange rate; the IMF believed that Bank Indonesia would not be able to maintain the rupiah's exchange rate at a fixed level and so the currency would come under renewed speculative attack.

Investors and firms had no confidence that the fundamental factors causing weakness in these currencies were being corrected. Therefore, the flow of funds out of the Asian countries continued. This outflow led to even more sales of Asian currencies in exchange for other currencies, which put additional downward pressure on the values of the Asian currencies.

Impact of the Asian Crisis on Hong Kong

On October 23, 1997, prices in the Hong Kong stock market declined by 10.2 percent on average; considering the three trading days before that, the cumulative four-day effect was a decline of 23.3 percent. This decline was primarily attributed to speculation that Hong Kong's currency might be devalued and that Hong Kong could experience financial problems similar to those evident in Southeast Asian countries. That Hong Kong companies could lose nearly a quarter of their market value in less than a week demonstrated the perceived exposure of Hong Kong to the crisis.

During this period, Hong Kong maintained its pegged exchange rate system (with the Hong Kong dollar tied to the U.S. dollar). However, it had to increase interest rates in order to discourage investors from transferring their funds out of the country.

Impact of the Asian Crisis on Russia

The Asian crisis caused investors to reconsider other countries where similar effects might occur. In particular, they focused on Russia. As investors lost confidence in the Russian currency (the ruble), they began to transfer funds out of Russia. In response to the downward pressure that this outflow of funds placed on the ruble, the central bank of Russia engaged in direct intervention by using dollars to purchase rubles in the foreign exchange market. It also used indirect intervention by raising interest rates to make Russia more attractive to investors, thereby discouraging additional outflows.

In July 1998, the IMF (with some help from Japan and the World Bank) organized a loan package worth $22.6 billion for Russia. The package required that Russia boost its tax revenues, reduce its budget deficit, and create a more capitalist environment for its businesses.

During August 1998, Russia's central bank intervened frequently to prevent substantial declines in the ruble. On August 26, however, it gave up its fight to defend the ruble's value, and market forces caused the ruble to decline by more than 50 percent against most currencies on that day. This led to fears of a new crisis and on the next day, "Bloody Thursday," paranoia swept stock markets around the world. Some stock markets (including the U.S. stock market) experienced declines of more than 4 percent.

Impact of the Asian Crisis on South Korea

By November 1997, seven of South Korea's conglomerates (called *chaebols)* had collapsed, and the banks that financed the operations of the chaebols were stuck with the equivalent of $52 billion in bad debt. Like banks in the Southeast Asian countries, South Korea's banks had been too willing to provide loans to corporations (especially the chaebols) without conducting a thorough credit analysis. In November, South Korea's currency (the won) declined substantially; the central bank tried using its reserves in an unsuccessful attempt to prevent a free fall in the won.

On December 3, 1997, the IMF agreed to a $55 billion rescue package for South Korea. The World Bank and the Asian Development Bank joined with the IMF to provide a standby credit line of $35 billion. In exchange for this funding, South Korea agreed to reduce its economic growth and to restrict the excessive borrowing of its conglomerates.

This restriction resulted in some bankruptcies and unemployment, because the banks could now provide loans to conglomerates only if the funding was economically justified.

Impact of the Asian Crisis on Japan

Japan was affected by the Asian crisis not only because it exports products to the affected countries but also because many of its corporations have subsidiaries located there, which means that the business performance of Japanese firms is affected by foreign economic conditions. Japan had also been experiencing its own problems. Its financial industry had been struggling, primarily because of defaulted loans. In April 1998, the Bank of Japan used more than $20 billion to purchase yen in the foreign exchange market. This effort to boost the yen's value was unsuccessful. Prime Minister Hashimoto resigned in July 1998, causing more uncertainty about the outlook for Japan.

Impact of the Asian Crisis on China

Because China had grown less rapidly than the Southeast Asian countries, it suffered few adverse economic effects from the Asian crisis. The Chinese government also had more influence on its economic conditions: it owned most of the real estate and controlled most of the banks that provided credit to support growth. As a result, China saw few bankruptcies resulting from the Asian crisis in China. China's government was also able to maintain the value of the yuan against the dollar, which limited speculative flows of funds out of China. Although interest rates increased during the crisis, they remained relatively low; hence Chinese firms could obtain funding at a reasonable cost and could continue to meet their interest payments.

Impact of the Asian Crisis on Latin American Countries

The Asian crisis also affected Latin American countries. Chile, Mexico, and Venezuela were all adversely affected because they export products to Asia, and the weakened Asian economies resulted in a lower demand for Latin American exports. In addition, the Latin American countries lost some business to other countries that switched to Asian products because the Asian currencies depreciated substantially, which made their products cheaper than those of Latin America.

These adverse effects on Latin American countries put pressure on Latin American currency values, as there was concern that speculative outflows of funds would weaken these currencies in the same way that Asian currencies had weakened. In particular, there was pressure on Brazil's currency (the real) in late October 1997.

The central bank of Brazil used about $7 billion of reserves in a direct intervention to buy the real in the foreign exchange market and protect the real from depreciation. It also used indirect intervention by raising short-term interest rates in Brazil. However, this intervention reduced economic growth because it increased the cost of borrowing for households, corporations, and government agencies in Brazil.

Impact of the Asian Crisis on Europe

Like firms in Latin America, some firms in Europe experienced a reduced demand for their exports to Asia during the crisis. In addition, they lost some exporting business to Asian exporters as a result of the weakened Asian currencies that reduced Asian prices from an importer's perspective. European banks were especially affected by the Asian crisis because they had provided large loans to numerous Asian firms that defaulted.

Impact of the Asian Crisis on the United States

The effects of the Asian crisis were felt even in the United States. Stock values of U.S. firms, such as 3M Co., Motorola, Hewlett-Packard, and Nike, that conducted much business in Asia declined. Many U.S. engineering and construction firms were adversely affected as Asian countries reduced their plans to improve infrastructure. Stock values of U.S. exporters to those countries fell because of the decline in spending by consumers and corporations in Asian countries and also because of the weakened Asian currencies, which made U.S. products more expensive. Some large U.S. commercial banks experienced significant stock price declines because of their exposure (primarily loans and bond holdings) to Asian countries.

Lessons about Exchange Rates and Intervention

The Asian crisis demonstrated the degree to which currencies could depreciate in response to a lack of confidence by investors and firms in a central bank's ability to stabilize its local currency. If investors and firms had believed the central banks could prevent the free fall in currency values, then they would not have transferred their funds to other countries and Southeast Asian currency values would not have experienced such downward pressure.

Exhibit 6A.1 shows how the exchange rates of some Asian currencies changed against the U.S. dollar during one year of the crisis (from June 1997 to June 1998). The currencies of Indonesia, Malaysia, South Korea, and Thailand all declined substantially.

The Asian crisis also demonstrated how interest rates could be affected by flows of funds out of countries. Exhibit 6A.2 illustrates how interest rates changed from June 1997 (just before the crisis) to June 1998 for various Asian countries. The increase in interest rates can be attributed to the indirect interventions (intended to prevent the

Exhibit 6A.1   How Exchange Rates Changed during the Asian Crisis (June 1997–June 1998)

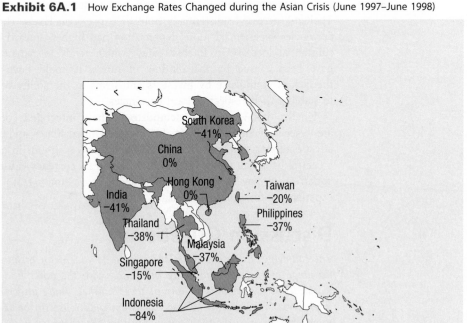

Exhibit 6A.2 How Interest Rates Changed during the Asian Crisis (Number before slash represents annualized interest rate as of June 1997; number after slash represents annualized interest rate as of June 1998)

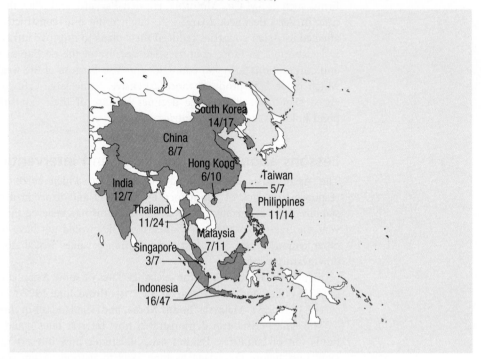

local currencies from depreciating further) or to the massive outflows of funds or to both of these conditions. In particular, the interest rates of Indonesia, Malaysia, and Thailand increased substantially from their pre-crisis levels. Those countries whose local currencies experienced more depreciation had higher upward adjustments. Because the substantial increase in interest rates (which tends to reduce economic growth) may have been caused by the outflow of funds, it could have resulted indirectly from the lack of confidence by investors and firms in the ability of the Asian central banks to stabilize their respective local currencies.

Finally, the Asian crisis demonstrated how integrated country economies actually are—especially during a crisis. Just as the United States and European economies can affect emerging markets, they are susceptible to conditions in emerging markets. Even if a central bank can withstand the pressure on its currency caused by conditions in other countries, it may not be able to insulate its economy from other countries that are experiencing financial problems.

Discussion Questions

The following discussion questions related to the Asian crisis illustrate how the foreign exchange market conditions are integrated with the other financial markets around the world. Thus participants in any of these markets must understand the dynamics of the foreign exchange market. These discussion questions can be used in several ways. They may serve as an assignment on a day that the professor is unable to attend class. They are especially useful for group exercises. The class could be segmented into small groups; each group is asked to assess all of the issues and determine a solution. Each group should have a spokesperson. For each issue, one of the groups will be randomly selected and asked to present its solution, and then other students not in that group may suggest alternative answers if they feel that the answer can be improved. Some of the issues have no perfect solution, which allows for different points of view to be presented by students.

1. Was the depreciation of the Asian currencies during the Asian crisis due to trade flows or capital flows? Why do you think the degree of movement over a short period may depend on whether the reason is trade flows or capital flows?

2. Why do you think the Indonesian rupiah was more exposed to an abrupt decline in value than the Japanese yen during the Asian crisis (even if their economies experienced the same degree of weakness)?

3. During the Asian crisis, direct intervention did not prevent depreciation of currencies. Offer your explanation for why the interventions did not work.

4. During the Asian crisis, some local firms in Asia borrowed U.S. dollars rather than local currency to support local operations. Why would they borrow dollars when they really needed their local currency to support operations? Why did this strategy backfire?

5. The Asian crisis showed that a currency crisis could affect interest rates. Why did the crisis put upward pressure on interest rates in Asian countries? Why did it put downward pressure on U.S. interest rates?

6. It is commonly argued that high interest rates reflect high expected inflation and can signal future weakness in a currency. Based on this theory, how would expectations of Asian exchange rates change after interest rates in Asia increased? Why? Is the underlying reason logical?

7. During the Asian crisis, why did the discount of the forward rate of Asian currencies change? Do you think it increased or decreased? Why?

8. During the Hong Kong crisis, the Hong Kong stock market declined substantially over a four-day period due to concerns in the foreign exchange market. Why would stock prices decline due to concerns in the foreign exchange market? Why would some countries be more susceptible to this type of situation than others?

9. On August 26, 1998, the day that Russia decided to let the ruble float freely, the ruble declined by about 50 percent. On the following day, called "Bloody Thursday," stock markets around the world (including the United States) declined by more than 4 percent. Why do you think the decline in the ruble had such a global impact on stock prices? Was the markets' reaction rational? Would the effect have been different if the ruble's plunge had occurred in an earlier time period, such as four years earlier? Why?

10. Normally, a weak local currency is expected to stimulate the local economy. Yet it appeared that the weak currencies of Asia adversely affected their economies. Why do you think the weakening of the currencies did not initially improve their economies during the Asian crisis?

11. During the Asian crisis, Hong Kong and China successfully intervened (by raising their interest rates) to protect their local currencies from depreciating. Nevertheless, these countries were also adversely affected by the Asian crisis. Why do you think the actions to protect the values of their currencies affected these countries' economies? Why do you think the weakness of other Asian currencies against the dollar and the stability of the Chinese and Hong Kong currencies against the dollar adversely affected their economies?

12. Why do you think the values of bonds issued by Asian governments declined during the Asian crisis? Why do you think the values of Latin American bonds declined in response to the Asian crisis?

13. Why do you think the depreciation of the Asian currencies adversely affected U.S. firms? (There are at least three reasons, each related to a different type of exposure of some U.S. firms to exchange rate risk.)

14. During the Asian crisis, the currencies of many Asian countries declined even though their governments attempted to intervene with direct intervention or by raising interest rates. Given that the abrupt depreciation of the currencies was attributed to an abrupt outflow of funds in the financial markets, what alternative Asian government action might have been more successful in preventing a substantial decline in the currencies' values? Are there any possible adverse effects of your proposed solution?

7

International Arbitrage and Interest Rate Parity

CHAPTER OBJECTIVES

The specific objectives of this chapter are to:

■ explain the conditions that will result in locational arbitrage and the realignments that will follow,

■ explain the conditions that will result in triangular arbitrage and the realignments that will follow,

■ explain the conditions that will result in covered interest arbitrage and the realignments that will follow,

■ explain the concept of interest rate parity, and

■ explain the variation in forward rate premiums across maturities and over time.

If discrepancies occur in the foreign exchange market, with quoted prices of currencies varying from what their market prices should be, then certain market forces will realign the rates. This realignment occurs as a result of **arbitrage**, which can be loosely defined as capitalizing on a discrepancy in quoted prices by making a riskless profit. In many cases, the strategy involves no risk and does not require that funds be tied up.

The type of arbitrage discussed in this chapter is applied to foreign exchange and international money markets and takes three common forms:

■ locational arbitrage,
■ triangular arbitrage, and
■ covered interest arbitrage

Each form will be discussed in turn.

7-1 Locational Arbitrage

Commercial banks providing foreign exchange services normally quote about the same rates on currencies, so shopping around may not lead to a more favorable rate. If the demand and supply conditions for a particular currency vary among banks then a given currency may be priced at different rates, in which case market forces will lead to realignment.

When quoted exchange rates vary among locations, participants in the foreign exchange market can capitalize on the discrepancy. Specifically, they can use **locational arbitrage**, which is the process of buying a currency at a location where it is priced cheap and then immediately selling it at some other location where it is priced higher.

EXAMPLE Akron Bank and Zyn Bank serve the foreign exchange market by buying and selling currencies. Assume that each bank is willing to buy a currency for exactly the same rate at which it is willing to sell that currency (there is no bid/ask spread). Assume the exchange rate quoted at Akron Bank for a British pound is $1.60 while the exchange rate quoted at Zyn Bank is $1.61. You could conduct locational arbitrage by purchasing pounds at Akron Bank for $1.60 per pound and then selling them at Zyn Bank for $1.61 per pound. If there is no bid/ask spread and if there are no other costs of conducting this arbitrage strategy, then your gain would be $.01 per pound. The gain is risk free in that you knew, when you purchased the pounds, how much you could sell them for. Also, you did not have to tie your funds up for any length of time. ●

Exhibit 7.1 Currency Quotes for Locational Arbitrage Example

	AKRON BANK			ZYN BANK	
	BID	ASK		BID	ASK
British pound	$1.60	$1.61	British pound	$1.61	$1.62

Locational arbitrage is normally conducted by banks or other foreign exchange dealers whose computers can continuously monitor the quotes provided by other banks. If other banks observed a discrepancy between the prices quoted by Akron Bank and Zyn Bank, then these other banks would quickly engage in locational arbitrage to earn an immediate risk-free profit.

In reality, banks have a bid/ask spread on currencies, which is their way of generating a profit from providing foreign exchange services. The following example accounts for that spread.

EXAMPLE In Exhibit 7.1, the information given previously on British pounds at both banks is revised to include a bid/ask spread. Based on these quotes, you can no longer profit from locational arbitrage. If you buy pounds at $1.61 (Akron Bank's ask price) and then sell them at $1.61 (Zyn Bank's bid price), you just break even. As this example demonstrates, locational arbitrage will not always be possible. To achieve profits from this strategy, the bid price of one bank must be higher than the ask price of another bank. ●

7-1a Gains from Locational Arbitrage

Your gain from locational arbitrage is based on two factors: the amount of money that you use to capitalize on the exchange rate discrepancy and the size of that discrepancy.

EXAMPLE The quotations for the New Zealand dollar (NZ$) at two banks are shown in Exhibit 7.2. You can obtain New Zealand dollars from North Bank at the ask price of $.640 and then sell them to South Bank at the bid price of $.645. This is considered to be one *round-trip* transaction in locational arbitrage. If you start with $10,000 and conduct one round-trip transaction, how many U.S. dollars will you end up with? The $10,000 is initially exchanged for NZ$15,625 ($10,000/$.640 per New Zealand dollar) at North Bank. Then the NZ$15,625 are sold for $.645 each to yield a total of $10,078. Thus your gain from locational arbitrage is $78. ●

Your gain may appear to be small relative to your investment of $10,000. However, consider that you did not have to tie up any of your funds. Your round-trip transaction could take place over a telecommunications network within a matter of seconds. Also, if you could use a larger sum of money for the transaction then your gains would be larger. Finally, you could continue to repeat this round-trip transaction until North Bank's ask price is no longer less than South Bank's bid price.

This example is not intended to suggest that you can finance your education with part-time locational arbitrage. As mentioned before, all foreign exchange dealers compare quotes from banks on computer terminals, which immediately signal any opportunity to employ locational arbitrage.

7-1b Realignment due to Locational Arbitrage

Quoted prices will react to the locational arbitrage strategy used by you and other foreign exchange market participants.

EXAMPLE In the previous example, the high demand for New Zealand dollars at North Bank (resulting from arbitrage activity) will cause a shortage of New Zealand dollars there. As a result of this shortage, North Bank will raise its ask price for New Zealand dollars. The excess supply of New Zealand dollars at South Bank

Exhibit 7.2 Locational Arbitrage

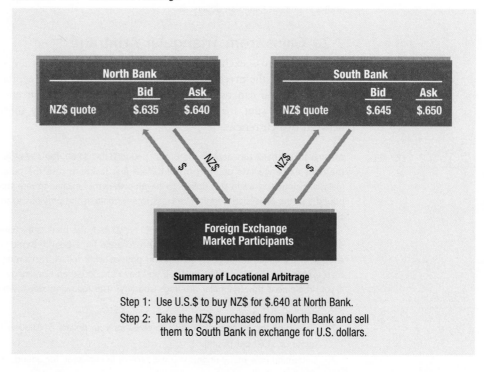

Summary of Locational Arbitrage

Step 1: Use U.S.$ to buy NZ$ for $.640 at North Bank.

Step 2: Take the NZ$ purchased from North Bank and sell
them to South Bank in exchange for U.S. dollars.

(resulting from sales of New Zealand dollars to South Bank in exchange for U.S. dollars) will force South Bank to lower its bid price. As the currency prices are adjusted, gains from locational arbitrage will be reduced. Once the ask price of North Bank is not any lower than the bid price of South Bank, locational arbitrage will no longer occur. Prices may adjust in a matter of seconds or minutes from the time when locational arbitrage occurs.

The concept of locational arbitrage is relevant because it explains why exchange rate quotations among banks at different locations will seldom differ by a significant amount. This generalization applies not only to banks on the same street or within the same city but to banks across the world. Technology allows all banks to be electronically and continuously connected to foreign exchange quotations. As a result, banks can ensure that their quotes are in line with those of other banks. They can also detect any discrepancies among quotations in real time and capitalize on those discrepancies. Thus technology enables more consistent prices among banks and reduces the likelihood of significant discrepancies in foreign exchange quotations among locations. ●

WEB

finance.yahoo.com
/currency-converter
Currency converter for
over 100 currencies with
frequent daily foreign
exchange rate updates.

7-2 Triangular Arbitrage

Cross exchange rates express the relation between two currencies that each differ from one's base currency. In the United States, the term *cross exchange rate* refers to the relationship between two non-dollar currencies.

EXAMPLE

If the British pound (£) is worth $1.60 and if the Canadian dollar (C$) is worth $.80, then the value of the British pound with respect to the Canadian dollar is calculated as follows:

$$\text{Value of £ in units of C\$} = \$1.60/\$.80 = 2.0$$

The value of the Canadian dollar in units of pounds can also be determined from the cross exchange rate formula:

$$\text{Value of C\$ in units of £} = \$.80/\$1.60 = .50$$

Note that the value of a Canadian dollar in units of pounds is simply the reciprocal of the value of a pound in units of Canadian dollars. ●

7-2a Gains from Triangular Arbitrage

If a quoted cross exchange rate differs from the appropriate cross exchange rate (as determined by the preceding formula), you can attempt to capitalize on the discrepancy. Specifically, you can use **triangular arbitrage** in which currency transactions are conducted in the spot market to capitalize on a discrepancy in the cross exchange rate between two currencies.

EXAMPLE

Assume that a bank has quoted the British pound (£) at $1.60, the Malaysian ringgit (MYR) at $.20, and the cross exchange rate at £1 = MYR8.1. Your first task is to use the pound value in U.S. dollars and Malaysian ringgit value in U.S. dollars to develop the cross exchange rate that should exist between the pound and the Malaysian ringgit. The cross rate formula in the previous example reveals that the pound should be worth MYR8.0.

When quoting a cross exchange rate of £1 = MYR8.1, the bank is exchanging too many ringgit for a pound and is asking for too many ringgit in exchange for a pound. Based on this information, you can engage in triangular arbitrage by purchasing pounds with dollars, converting the pounds to ringgit, and then exchanging the ringgit for dollars. If you have $10,000, then how many dollars will you end up with if you implement this triangular arbitrage strategy? The following steps, which are illustrated in Exhibit 7.3, will help you answer this question.

1. Determine the number of pounds received for your dollars: $10,000 = £6,250, based on the bank's quote of $1.60 per pound.
2. Determine how many ringgit you will receive in exchange for pounds: £6,250 = MYR50,625, based on the bank's quote of 8.1 ringgit per pound.
3. Determine how many U.S. dollars you will receive in exchange for the ringgit: MYR50,625 = $10,125 based on the bank's quote of $.20 per ringgit (5 ringgit to the dollar). The triangular arbitrage strategy generates $10,125, which is $125 more than you started with. ●

Exhibit 7.3 Example of Triangular Arbitrage

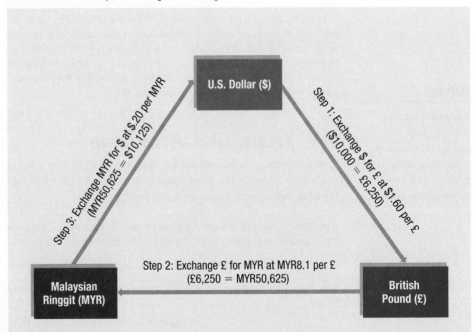

Exhibit 7.4   Currency Quotes for Triangular Arbitrage Example with Transaction Costs

	QUOTED BID PRICE	QUOTED ASK PRICE
Value of a British pound in U.S. dollars	$1.60	$1.61
Value of a Malaysian ringgit (MYR) in U.S. dollars	$.200	$.201
Value of a British pound in Malaysian ringgit (MYR)	MYR8.10	MYR8.20

Like locational arbitrage, triangular arbitrage does not tie up funds. Also, the strategy is risk free because there is no uncertainty about the prices at which you will buy and sell the currencies.

Accounting for the Bid/Ask Spread   The previous example is simplified in that it does not account for transaction costs. In reality, there is a bid and ask quote for each currency, which means that the arbitrageur incurs transaction costs that can reduce or even eliminate the gains from triangular arbitrage. The following example illustrates how bid and ask prices can affect arbitrage profits.

EXAMPLE

Using the quotations in Exhibit 7.4, you can determine whether triangular arbitrage is possible by starting with some fictitious amount (say, $10,000) of U.S. dollars and estimating the number of dollars you would generate by implementing the strategy. Exhibit 7.4 differs from the previous example only in that bid/ask spreads are now considered.

Recall that the previous triangular arbitrage strategy involved exchanging dollars for pounds, pounds for ringgit, and then ringgit for dollars. Apply this strategy to the bid and ask quotations in Exhibit 7.4. The steps are summarized in Exhibit 7.5.

Step 1. Your initial $10,000 will be converted into approximately £6,211 (based on the bank's ask price of $1.61 per pound).

Exhibit 7.5   Example of Triangular Arbitrage Accounting for Bid/Ask Spreads

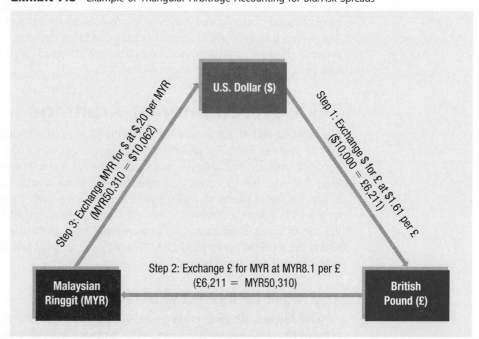

Exhibit 7.6   Impact of Triangular Arbitrage

ACTIVITY	IMPACT
1. Participants use dollars to purchase pounds.	Bank increases its ask price of pounds with respect to the dollar.
2. Participants use pounds to purchase Malaysian ringgit.	Bank reduces its bid price of the British pound with respect to the ringgit; that is, it reduces the number of ringgit to be exchanged per pound received.
3. Participants use Malaysian ringgit to purchase U.S. dollars.	Bank reduces its bid price of ringgit with respect to the dollar.

Step 2. Then the £6,211 are converted into MYR50,310 (based on the bank's bid price of MYR8.1 per pound, £6,211 × 8.1 = MYR50,310).

Step 3. The MYR50,310 are converted to $10,062 (based on the bank's bid price of $.200).

The profit is $10,062 − $10,000 = $62. The profit is lower here than in the previous example because bid and ask quotations are used. If the bid/ask spread were slightly larger in this example, then triangular arbitrage would not have been profitable. ●

7-2b Realignment due to Triangular Arbitrage

The realignment that results from triangular arbitrage activity is summarized in the second column of Exhibit 7.6. The realignment will probably occur quickly to prevent continued benefits from triangular arbitrage. The discrepancies assumed here would seldom occur at a single bank; it is much more likely that triangular arbitrage would require three transactions at three separate banks.

If any two of these three exchange rates are known, then the exchange rate of the third pair can be determined. Whenever the actual cross exchange rate differs from the appropriate cross exchange rate, the exchange rates of the currencies are not in equilibrium. Triangular arbitrage would force the exchange rates back into equilibrium.

Like locational arbitrage, triangular arbitrage is a strategy that few of us can ever exploit because the computer technology available to foreign exchange dealers can almost instantaneously detect misalignments in cross exchange rates. The point of this discussion is that triangular arbitrage will ensure that cross exchange rates are usually aligned correctly. If cross exchange rates are not properly aligned, then triangular arbitrage will take place until the rates are aligned correctly.

7-3 Covered Interest Arbitrage

The forward rate of a currency for a specified future date is determined by the interaction of demand for the contract (forward purchases) versus the supply (forward sales). Forward rates are available for many currencies at financial websites. Financial institutions that offer foreign exchange services set the forward rates, but these rates are driven by market forces (demand and supply conditions). In some cases, the forward rate may be priced at a level that allows investors to engage in a type of arbitrage that affects the volume of forward purchases or forward sales of a particular currency, and therefore affects the equilibrium forward rate. This arbitrage process and its effects on the equilibrium forward rate are described next.

7-3a Covered Interest Arbitrage Process

Covered interest arbitrage is the process of capitalizing on the difference in interest rates between two countries while covering your exchange rate risk with a forward contract. The term *covered interest arbitrage* is composed of two parts: "interest arbitrage" refers to the process of capitalizing on the difference between interest rates between two countries; "covered" refers to hedging your position against exchange rate risk.

EXAMPLE

You desire to capitalize on relatively high rates of interest in the United Kingdom and have funds available for 90 days. The interest rate is certain; only the future exchange rate at which you will exchange pounds back to U.S. dollars is uncertain. You can use a forward sale of pounds to guarantee the rate at which you can exchange pounds for dollars at some future time.

Assume the following information.

- You have $800,000 to invest.
- The current spot rate of the pound is $1.60.
- The 90-day forward rate of the pound is $1.60.
- The 90-day interest rate in the United States is 2 percent.
- The 90-day interest rate in the United Kingdom is 4 percent.

Based on this information, you should proceed as follows:

1. On day 1, convert the $800,000 to £500,000 and deposit the £500,000 in a British bank.
2. On day 1, sell £520,000 90 days forward. By the time the deposit matures, you will have £520,000 (including interest).
3. In 90 days when the deposit matures, you can fulfill your forward contract obligation by converting your £520,000 into $832,000 (based on the forward contract rate of $1.60 per pound).

The steps involved in covered interest arbitrage are illustrated in Exhibit 7.7. In this example, the strategy results in a 4 percent return over the three-month period, which is 2 percent above the return on a U.S. deposit. In addition, the return on this strategy is known on day 1, as you know when you make the deposit exactly how many dollars you will get back from your 90-day investment. ●

Exhibit 7.7   Example of Covered Interest Arbitrage

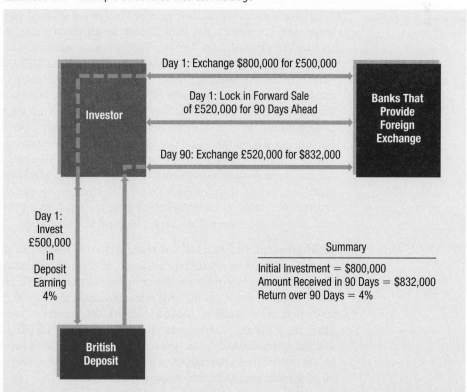

Recall that locational and triangular arbitrage do not tie up funds; thus any profits are achieved instantaneously. In the case of covered interest arbitrage, however, the funds are tied up for a period of time (90 days in our example). This strategy would not be advantageous if it earned 2 percent or less, as you could earn 2 percent on a domestic deposit. The term *arbitrage* here suggests that you can guarantee a return on your funds that exceeds the returns you could achieve domestically.

Covered interest arbitrage is sometimes interpreted to mean that the funds to be invested are borrowed locally (investors do not use their own funds). However, whether investors borrow funds locally or use their own funds, covered interest arbitrage should have a similar impact on the forward rate.

7-3b Realignment due to Covered Interest Arbitrage

As with the other forms of arbitrage, market forces resulting from covered interest arbitrage will eventually lead to market realignment. As many investors capitalize on covered interest arbitrage by executing step 2 in the example (selling British pounds forward), there is downward pressure on the 90-day forward rate. Once the forward rate has a discount from the spot rate that is about equal to the interest rate advantage, covered interest arbitrage will no longer be feasible. Because the interest rate advantage of the British interest rate over the U.S. interest rate is 2 percent in this example, the arbitrage will no longer be feasible once the forward rate of the pound exhibits a discount of about 2 percent. At that point, the U.S. investors would sell their pounds for 2 percent less than they paid for the pounds, which offsets the extra 2 percent interest rate advantage on a British investment.

Timing of Realignment   The realignment of the forward rate might not be completed until several investors execute covered interest arbitrage. The realignment does not erase the gains to those U.S. investors who initially engaged in covered interest arbitrage. Recall that they locked in their gain by obtaining a forward contract on the day that they made their investment. But their actions to sell pounds forward placed downward pressure on the forward rate. Perhaps their actions initially would have caused a small discount in the forward rate, such as 1 percent. Under these conditions, U.S. investors would still benefit from covered interest arbitrage, but not to the same degree, because the 1 percent discount partially offsets the 2 percent interest rate advantage. Although the benefits are not as great as they were initially, covered interest arbitrage should continue until the forward rate exhibits a discount of about 2 percent to offset the 2 percent interest rate advantage. Even though complete realignment may require several covered interest arbitrage transactions by different investors, this can occur within a few seconds because some institutional investors have computer platforms that will automatically place large orders if they detect that the forward rate is priced improperly. These large orders will quickly cause an adjustment in the equilibrium forward rate such that covered interest arbitrage will no longer be feasible.

Realignment Is Focused on the Forward Rate   In the previous example, only the forward rate was affected by the forces of covered interest arbitrage. It is possible that the spot rate could experience upward pressure due to the increased demand (caused by step 1 in the example). If the spot rate appreciates, then the forward rate would not have to decline by as much in order to achieve the 2 percent forward discount that would offset the 2 percent interest rate differential. Yet because the forward market is less liquid, the forward rate is more sensitive to shifts in demand (or supply) conditions caused by covered interest arbitrage; therefore the forward rate is likely to experience most if not all of the adjustment needed to achieve realignment.

EXAMPLE

Assume that, as a result of covered interest arbitrage, the 90-day forward rate of the pound declined to $1.5692 (which reflects a discount of about 2 percent from the pound's spot rate of $1.60). Consider the results from using $800,000 (as in the previous example) to engage in covered interest arbitrage after the forward rate has adjusted.

1. Convert $800,000 to pounds:

$$\$800,000/\$1.60 \ = \ \pounds500,00$$

2. Calculate accumulated pounds over 90 days at 4 percent:

$$\pounds500,000 \ \times \ 1.04 \ = \ \pounds520,000$$

3. Reconvert pounds to dollars (at the forward rate of $1.5692) after 90 days:.

$$\pounds520,000 \ \times \ \$1.5692 \ = \ \$815,984$$

4. Determine the yield earned from covered interest arbitrage:

$$(\$815,984 \ - \ \$800,000)/\$800,000 \ = \ .02, \text{ or } 2\%$$

As this example shows, the forward rate has declined to a level (by about 2 percent) that offsets the 2 percent interest rate advantage, such that future attempts to engage in covered interest arbitrage are no longer feasible. Now the return from covered interest arbitrage is no better than what U.S. investors can earn domestically. ●

7-3c Arbitrage Example When Accounting for Spreads

The following example illustrates the effects of the spread between the bid and ask quotes and of the spread between deposit and loan rates.

EXAMPLE

Suppose you are given the following exchange rates and one-year interest rates.

	BID QUOTE	ASK QUOTE
Euro spot	$1.12	$1.13
Euro one-year forward	$1.12	$1.13
	DEPOSIT RATE	LOAN RATE
Interest rate on dollars	6.0%	9.0%
Interest rate on euros	6.5%	9.5%

You have $100,000 to invest for one year. Would you benefit from engaging in covered interest arbitrage?

Observe that the quotes of the euro spot and forward rates are exactly the same whereas the deposit rate on euros is .5 percent higher than the deposit rate on dollars. It may therefore seem that covered interest arbitrage is feasible. However, U.S. investors would be subjected to the ask quote when buying euros (€) in the spot market versus the bid quote when selling those euros via a one-year forward contract.

1. Convert $100,000 to euros (ask quote):

$$\$100,000/\$1.13 \ = \ \pounds88,496$$

2. Calculate accumulated euros over one year at 6.5 percent:

$$\pounds88,496 \ \times \ 1.065 \ = \ \pounds94,248$$

3. Sell euros for dollars at the forward rate (bid quote):

$$\pounds94,248 \ \times \ \$1.12 \ = \ \$105,558$$

4. Determine the yield earned from covered interest arbitrage:

$$(\$105,558 \ - \ \$100,000)/\$100,000 \ = \ 05558, \text{ or } 5.558\%$$

The yield is less than if you had invested the funds in the United States. Thus covered interest arbitrage is not feasible. ●

7-3d Covered Interest Arbitrage by Non-U.S. Investors

In the examples so far, covered interest arbitrage was conducted as if the United States were the home country for investors. The examples could easily be adapted to make any country the home country for investors.

EXAMPLE

Assume that the one-year U.S. interest rate is 5 percent while the one-year Japanese interest rate is 4 percent. Suppose the spot rate of the Japanese yen is $.01 and that the one-year forward rate of the yen is $.01. Investors based in Japan could benefit from covered interest arbitrage by converting Japanese yen to dollars at the prevailing spot rate, investing the dollars at 5 percent, and simultaneously selling dollars (buying yen) forward. Because they are buying and selling dollars at the same price, they would earn 5 percent on this strategy, which is better than they could earn from investing in Japan.

As Japanese investors engage in covered interest arbitrage, the high Japanese demand to buy yen forward will place upward pressure on the one-year forward rate of the yen. Once the one-year forward rate of the Japanese yen exhibits a premium of about 1 percent, new attempts to pursue covered interest arbitrage would not be feasible for Japanese investors because the 1 percent premium paid to buy yen forward would offset the 1 percent interest rate advantage in the United States. ●

The concept of covered interest arbitrage applies to any two countries for which there is a spot rate and a forward rate between their currencies as well as risk-free interest rates quoted for both currencies. If investors from Japan wanted to pursue covered interest arbitrage over a 90-day period in France, they would convert Japanese yen to euros in the spot market, invest in a 90-day risk-free security in France, and simultaneously lock in the sale of euros (in exchange for Japanese yen) 90 days forward with a 90-day forward contract.

7-3e Comparing Different Types of Arbitrage

Exhibit 7.8 compares the three types of arbitrage. The threat of locational arbitrage ensures that quoted exchange rates are similar across banks at different locations; the threat of triangular arbitrage ensures that cross exchange rates are properly set; and the threat of covered interest arbitrage ensures that forward exchange rates are properly set. Any discrepancy will trigger arbitrage, which should eliminate the discrepancy. Thus arbitrage tends to ensure a more orderly foreign exchange market.

How Arbitrage Reduces Transaction Costs Many MNCs engage in transactions amounting to more than $100 million per year. Because the foreign exchange market is over the counter, there is no single consistently transparent set of exchange quotations. Hence managers of an MNC could incur large transaction costs if they consistently paid too much for the currencies they needed. However, the arbitrage process limits the degree of difference in quotations among currencies. Locational arbitrage limits the differences in a spot exchange rate quotation across locations, while covered interest arbitrage ensures that the forward rate is properly priced. Thus an MNC's managers should be able to avoid excessive transaction costs.

7-4 Interest Rate Parity (IRP)

When market forces cause interest rates and exchange rates to adjust such that covered interest arbitrage is no longer feasible, the result is an equilibrium state known as **interest rate parity (IRP)**. In equilibrium, the forward rate differs from the spot rate by a sufficient amount to offset the interest rate differential between two currencies. In the previous example, the U.S. investor receives a higher interest rate from the foreign investment; yet there is an offsetting effect because the investor must pay more per unit

Exhibit 7.8 Comparing Arbitrage Strategies

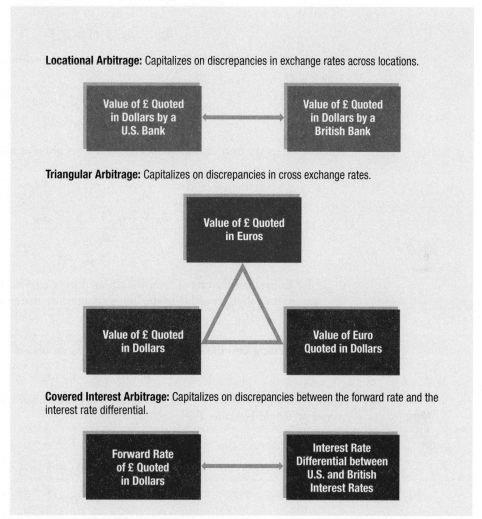

of foreign currency (at the spot rate) than is received per unit when the currency is sold forward (at the forward rate). Recall that when the forward rate is less than the spot rate, this implies that the forward rate exhibits a discount.

7-4a Derivation of Interest Rate Parity

The relationship between a forward premium (or discount) of a foreign currency and the interest rates representing these currencies according to IRP can be determined as follows. Consider a U.S. investor who attempts covered interest arbitrage. The investor's return from using this strategy can be calculated from the following information:

- the amount of the home currency (U.S. dollars, in our example) that is initially invested (A_h),
- the spot rate (S) in dollars when the foreign currency is purchased,
- the interest rate on the foreign deposit (i_f), and
- the forward rate (F) in dollars at which the foreign currency will be converted back to U.S. dollars.

With this strategy, the amount of home currency received at the end of the deposit period is

$$A_n = (A_h/S)(1 + i_f)F$$

Because F is simply S multiplied by 1 plus the forward premium p, we can rewrite this equation as

$$A_n = (A_h/S)(1 + i_f)[S(1 + p)]$$
$$= A_f(1 + i_f)(1 + p)$$

The rate of return from this investment (called R) is given as follows:

$$R = \frac{A_n - A_h}{A_h}$$
$$= \frac{[A_h(1 + i_f)(1 + p)] - A_h}{A_h}$$
$$= (1 + i_f)(1 + p) - 1$$

If IRP exists, then the rate of return R achieved from covered interest arbitrage should be equal to the rate i_h available in the home country; we therefore set

$$R = i_h$$

Now substituting into the original expression for R, we obtain

$$(1 + i_f)(1 + p) - 1 = i_h$$

After rearranging terms, we can determine what the forward premium of the foreign currency should be under IRP:

$$(1 + i_f)(1 + p) - 1 = i_h$$
$$(1 + i_f)(1 + p) = 1 + i_h$$
$$1 + p = \frac{1 + i_h}{1 + i_f}$$
$$p = \frac{1 + i_h}{1 + i_f} - 1$$

Thus, given the two interest rates of concern, the forward rate under conditions of IRP can be derived. If the actual forward rate is different from this derived forward rate, then there may be potential for covered interest arbitrage.

7-4b Determining the Forward Premium

Using the information just presented, the forward premium (or discount) can be measured based on the interest rate difference under conditions of IRP.

EXAMPLE   Assume that the Mexican peso exhibits a six-month interest rate of 6 percent and that the U.S. dollar exhibits a six-month interest rate of 5 percent. From a U.S. investor's perspective, the U.S. dollar is the home currency. According to IRP, the forward rate premium of the peso with respect to the U.S. dollar should be

$$p = \frac{1 + .05}{1 + .06} - 1$$
$$= -.0094, \text{ or } -.94\% \text{ (not annualized)}$$

Thus the six-month forward contract on the peso should exhibit a discount of about .94 percent. This means that U.S. investors would receive .94 percent less when selling pesos six months from now (based on a forward sale) than the price they pay for pesos today at the spot rate. Such a discount would offset the peso's interest rate advantage. If the peso's spot rate is $.10, then a forward discount of .94 percent results in the following calculation of the six-month forward rate:

$$
\begin{aligned}
F &= S(1 + p) \\
&= \$.10(1 - .0094) \\
&= \$.09906
\end{aligned}
$$

●

Effect of the Interest Rate Differential   The relationship predicted by IRP between the forward premium (or discount) and the interest rate differential can be approximated by the following simplified form:

$$
P = \frac{F - S}{S} \approx i_h - i_j
$$

where

p = **forward premium (or discount)**

F = **forward rate in dollars**

S = **spot rate in dollars**

i_h = **home interest rate**

i_f = **foreign interest rate**

This approximate form provides a reasonable estimate when the interest rate differential is small. Note that the variables in this equation are not annualized. In our previous example, the U.S. (home) interest rate is less than the foreign interest rate, so the forward rate contains a discount (the forward rate is less than the spot rate). The larger the degree by which the foreign interest rate exceeds the home interest rate, the larger will be the forward discount of the foreign currency specified by the IRP formula.

If the foreign interest rate is less than the home interest rate, then IRP suggests that the forward rate should exhibit a premium.

Implications   If the forward premium is equal to the interest rate differential as just described, then covered interest arbitrage will not be feasible.

EXAMPLE

Use the information on the spot rate, the six-month forward rate of the peso, and Mexico's interest rate from the preceding example to determine a U.S. investor's return from using covered interest arbitrage. Assume the investor begins with $1,000,000 to invest.

Step 1. On the first day, the U.S. investor converts $1,000,000 into Mexican pesos (MXP) at $.10 per peso:

$1,000,000/$.10 per peso = MXP10,000,000

Step 2. On the first day, this investor also sells pesos six months forward. The number of pesos to be sold forward is the anticipated accumulation of pesos over the six-month period, which is estimated as

MXP10,000,000 × (1 + .06) = MXP10,600,000

Step 3. After six months, the U.S. investor withdraws the initial deposit of pesos along with the accumulated interest, amounting to a total of 10,600,000 pesos. The investor converts the pesos into dollars in accordance with the forward contract agreed upon six months earlier. The forward rate was $.09906, so the number of U.S. dollars received from the conversion is

MXP10,600,000 × ($.09906 per peso) = $1,050,036

In this case, the investor's covered interest arbitrage achieves a return of about 5 percent. Rounding the forward discount to .94 percent causes the slight deviation from the 5 percent return. Thus using covered interest arbitrage under these circumstances generates a return that is about what the investor would receive by investing the funds domestically. This result confirms that covered interest arbitrage is not worthwhile if IRP holds. ●

Interest rate parity does not imply that investors from different countries will earn the same returns. Rather, parity reflects a comparison between foreign versus domestic investment in risk-free interest-bearing securities by a particular investor. If IRP holds, investors cannot use covered interest arbitrage to earn higher returns on a foreign investment than they could earn on a domestic investment.

WEB

www.bloomberg.com
Latest information from
financial markets around
the world.

7-4c Graphic Analysis of Interest Rate Parity

A graph can be used to compare the interest rate differential with the forward premium (or discount). The diagonal line in Exhibit 7.9 plots all points that satisfy interest rate parity.

Points Representing a Discount   For all situations in which the foreign interest rate is *higher* than the home interest rate, the forward rate should exhibit a discount approximately equal to that difference. When the foreign interest rate (i_f) exceeds the home interest rate (i_h) by 1 percent ($i_h - i_f = -1\%$), the forward rate should exhibit a discount of 1 percent. This is represented by point A on the graph. If the foreign interest rate exceeds the home rate by 2 percent then the forward rate should exhibit a discount of 2 percent (as represented by point B), and so forth.

Points Representing a Premium   For all situations in which the foreign interest rate is *lower* than the home interest rate, the forward rate should exhibit a premium approximately equal to that difference. For example, when the home interest rate exceeds

Exhibit 7.9   Illustration of Interest Rate Parity

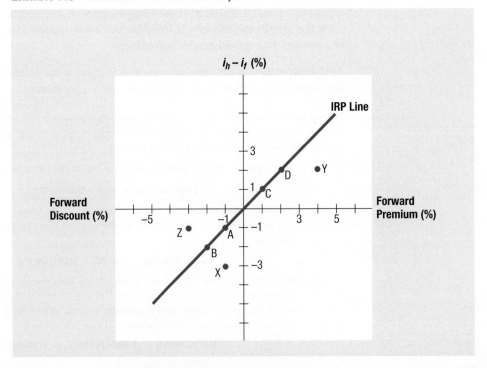

the foreign rate by 1 percent ($i_h - i_f = -1\%$), the forward premium should be 1 percent; this is represented by point C in Exhibit 7.9. If the home interest rate exceeds the foreign rate by 2 percent ($i_h - i_f = 2\%$) then the forward premium should be 2 percent, as represented by point D, and so forth.

Exhibit 7.9 can be used whether or not you annualize the rates as long as you are consistent. That is, if you annualize the interest rates to determine the interest rate differential, then you should also annualize the forward premium or discount.

Points Representing IRP

Any points lying on the diagonal line that intersects the graph's origin represent IRP. For this reason, that diagonal line is referred to as the **interest rate parity (IRP) line**. Covered interest arbitrage is not possible under conditions represented by points along the IRP line.

At any time, an individual or corporation can examine any currency to compare its forward rate premium (or discounts) to the interest rate differential with the United States. From a U.S. perspective, interest rates in Japan are usually lower than the home interest rate. Consequently, the forward rate of the Japanese yen usually exhibits a premium and may be represented by points such as C or D (or even by points above D) along the diagonal line in Exhibit 7.9. Conversely, the United Kingdom often has higher interest rates than the United States, so the pound's forward rate often exhibits a discount, which could be represented by point A or B on the graph.

A currency represented by point B has an interest rate that is 2 percent above the prevailing home interest rate. If the home country is the United States, then this means that investors who live in the foreign country and invest their funds in local risk-free securities earn 2 percent more than investors in the United States who invest in risk-free U.S. securities. Under IRP, a U.S. investor who attempted covered interest arbitrage (by investing in that foreign currency with the higher interest rate) would fail to earn any more than could be earned in the United States because the forward rate of that currency would exhibit a 2 percent discount.

A currency represented by point D has an interest rate that is 2 percent below the prevailing interest rate. If the home country is the United States, then investors who live in the foreign country and invest their funds in local risk-free securities earn 2 percent less than U.S. investors who invest in risk-free U.S. securities. Under IRP, even if those foreign investors attempt to use covered interest arbitrage by investing in the United States, they will still earn only what they could in the United States; the reason is that they would have to pay a forward premium of 2 percent when exchanging dollars for their home currency.

Points Below the IRP Line

Suppose a three-month deposit denominated in a foreign currency offers an annualized interest rate of 10 percent versus an annualized interest rate of 7 percent in the home country; this scenario is represented on the graph by $i_h - i_f = -3\%$. Assume that the foreign currency exhibits an annualized forward discount of 1 percent. The combined interest rate differential and forward discount information can be represented by point X on the Exhibit 7.9 graph. Because point X is not on the IRP line, we should expect that covered interest arbitrage will be beneficial for some investors. The investor attains an additional 3 percentage points for the foreign deposit, and this advantage is only partially offset by the 1 percent forward discount.

Now suppose that the annualized interest rate for the foreign currency is 5 percent versus 7 percent in the home country; this differential is expressed on the graph as $i_h - i_f = 2\%$. Assume, however, that the forward premium of the foreign currency is 4 percent (point Y in the graph). The high forward premium more than compensates for what the investor loses on the lower interest rate from the foreign investment.

If the current interest rate and forward rate situation is represented by point X or Y, then home country investors can engage in covered interest arbitrage. By investing in a foreign currency, they will earn a higher return (after considering the foreign interest rate and forward premium or discount) than the home interest rate. This type of activity will place upward pressure on the spot rate of the foreign currency, as well as downward pressure on the forward rate of the foreign currency, until covered interest arbitrage is no longer feasible.

Points Above the IRP Line   Now shift to the left side of the IRP line and take point Z, for example. This point represents a foreign interest rate that exceeds the home interest rate by 1 percent while the forward rate exhibits a 3 percent discount. This point, like all points to the left of the IRP line, signifies that U.S. investors would receive a lower return on a foreign than a domestic investment. The lower return normally occurs either because (1) the advantage of the foreign interest rate relative to the U.S. interest rate is more than offset by the forward rate discount (reflected by point Z), or (2) the extent by which the home interest rate exceeds the foreign rate more than offsets the forward rate premium.

For points such as these, covered interest arbitrage is feasible from the perspective of foreign investors. Consider British investors in the United Kingdom, whose interest rate is 1 percent higher than the U.S. interest rate and whose currency's forward rate (with respect to the dollar) contains a 3 percent discount (as represented by point Z). British investors will sell their foreign currency in exchange for dollars, invest in dollar-denominated securities, and engage in a forward contract to purchase pounds forward. Though they earn 1 percent less on the U.S. investment, they are able to purchase their home currency forward for 3 percent less than what they initially sold it forward in the spot market. This type of activity will place downward pressure on the spot rate of the pound, and upward pressure on the pound's forward rate, until covered interest arbitrage is no longer feasible.

7-4d How to Test Whether Interest Rate Parity Holds

An investor or firm can plot all realistic points for various currencies on a graph such as that in Exhibit 7.9 to determine whether gains from covered interest arbitrage can be achieved. The location of the points provides an indication of whether covered interest arbitrage is worthwhile. For points to the right of the IRP line, investors in the home country should consider using covered interest arbitrage, because a return higher than the home interest rate (i_h) is achievable. Of course, as investors and firms take advantage of such opportunities, the point will tend to move toward the IRP line. Covered interest arbitrage should continue until interest rate parity holds.

7-4e Does Interest Rate Parity Hold?

In order to determine conclusively whether or not interest rate parity holds, compare the forward rate (or discount) with interest rate quotations occurring at the same time. If the forward rate and interest rate quotations are not simultaneous, then results could be somewhat distorted. However, limitations in access to data make it difficult to obtain quotations that reflect the same moment of time.

Numerous academic studies have examined IRP empirically in several periods. The actual relationship between the forward rate premium and interest rate differentials generally supports IRP. Although deviations from interest rate parity do occur, they are usually too slight to make covered interest arbitrage worthwhile, as we now discuss in more detail.

7-4f Considerations When Assessing Interest Rate Parity

Even if IRP did not exist, covered interest arbitrage may still not be worthwhile after accounting for characteristics of foreign investments such as transaction costs, political risk, and differential tax laws.

Transaction Costs If an investor accounts for transaction costs, the point that indicates the actual interest rate differential and forward rate premium must then be farther from the IRP line to make covered interest arbitrage worthwhile. Exhibit 7.10 identifies the areas with potential for covered interest arbitrage *after* accounting for transaction costs: the dark shaded band surrounding the 45-degree IRP line. For points off the IRP line but still within this band, covered interest arbitrage is not worthwhile (because the excess return is offset by costs). For points to the right of (or below) the band, investors residing in the home country could gain through covered interest arbitrage; tor points to the left of (or above) the band, foreign investors could gain through such arbitrage.

Political Risk Even if covered interest arbitrage appears feasible after accounting for transaction costs, investing funds overseas is subject to political risk. Although the forward contract locks in the rate at which the foreign funds should be reconverted, there is no guarantee that the foreign government will allow the funds to be reconverted. A crisis in the foreign country could cause its government to restrict any exchange of the local currency for other currencies. In this case, the investor would be unable to use these funds until the foreign government eliminated the restriction.

Investors may also perceive a slight default risk on foreign investments, such as foreign Treasury bills, because they cannot be certain that the foreign government will

Exhibit 7.10 Potential for Covered Interest Arbitrage When Considering Transaction Costs

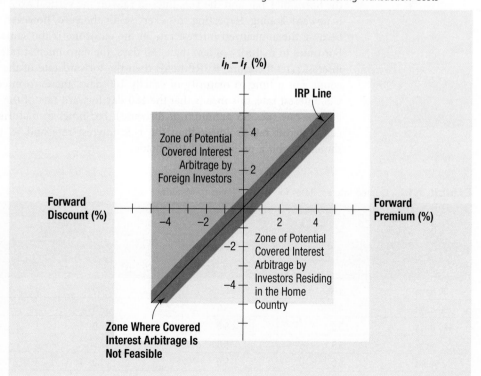

guarantee full repayment of interest and principal upon default. So because of concern that the foreign Treasury bills may default, these investors may accept a lower interest rate on their domestic Treasury bills rather than engage in covered interest arbitrage in an effort to obtain a slightly higher expected return.

Differential Tax Laws Because tax laws vary among countries, investors and firms that set up deposits in other countries must be aware of the prevailing tax laws. It may be that covered interest arbitrage is feasible in terms of before-tax but not after-tax returns. This scenario may arise when tax rates in the investor's country differ from those in the country of investment.

7-5 Variation in Forward Premiums

At any time, the forward premium varies among maturities for any particular currency. In addition, the forward premium of a particular currency with a particular maturity date also varies over time. These points are explained next.

7-5a Forward Premiums across Maturities

The *yield curve* describes the relationship, for a given moment in time, between the annualized yield of risk-free debt and the time to maturity. The yield curve for the United States normally has an upward slope, which means that the annualized interest rate is higher for longer terms to maturity. The yield curve for every country has its own unique shape. Consequently, the annualized interest rate differential between two countries will vary among debt maturities, as will the annualized forward premiums.

To illustrate these points, Exhibit 7.11 shows today's quoted interest rates for various times to maturity. If you plot a yield curve based on this data, with time to maturity on the horizontal axis and the U.S. interest rate on the vertical axis, then the U.S. yield curve is upward sloping. Repeating this exercise for the euro, however, yields a flat yield curve because the annualized interest rate in the eurozone is the same regardless of maturity. For times to maturity of less than 180 days, the euro interest rate is higher than the U.S. interest rate; therefore, if IRP holds then the forward rate of the euro will exhibit a discount. For a time to maturity of exactly 180 days, the euro interest rate is equal to the U.S. interest rate; this means that the 180-day forward rate of the euro should be equal to its spot rate (i.e., no premium or discount). For times to maturity beyond 180 days, the euro interest rate is lower than the U.S. interest rate and so the euro's forward rate should exhibit a premium (if IRP holds).

Exhibit 7.11 Quoted Interest Rates for Various Times to Maturity

TIME TO MATURITY	U.S. INTEREST (ANNUALIZED) QUOTED TODAY	EURO INTEREST (ANNUALIZED) QUOTED TODAY	INTEREST RATE DIFFERENTIAL (ANNUALIZED) BASED ON TODAY'S QUOTES	APPROXIMATE FORWARD RATE PREMIUM (ANNUALIZED) OF EURO AS OF TODAY IF IRP HOLDS
30 days	4.0%	5.0%	−1.0%	−1.0%
90 days	4.5	5.0	−.5	−.5
180 days	5.0	5.0	.0	.0
1 year	5.5	5.0	+.5	+.5
2 years	6.0	5.0	+1.0	+1.0

Now consider the implications for U.S. firms that hedge future euro payments. A firm hedging euro outflows for a date that is less than 180 days from now will lock in a euro forward rate below the existing spot rate; conversely, a firm hedging euro outflows for a date that is beyond 180 days from now will lock in a euro forward rate above the existing spot rate. Thus the amount of dollars needed by an MNC to hedge a future payment in euros will vary with the maturity date of the forward contract.

7-5b Changes in Forward Premiums over Time

Exhibit 7.12 illustrates the relationship between interest rate differentials and the forward premium over time when interest rate parity holds. Under IRP, the forward premium

Exhibit 7.12   Relationship over Time between the Interest Rate Differential and the Forward Premium

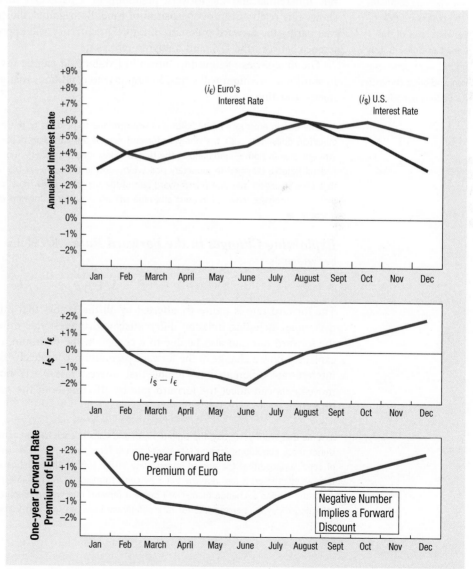

must adjust to existing interest rate conditions. In January, the U.S. interest rate is 2 percent above the euro interest rate, so the euro's forward premium must be 2 percent. By February, the U.S. and euro interest rates are the same, so the forward rate must be equal to the spot rate (and thus have no premium or discount). In March, the U.S. interest rate is 1 percent below the euro interest rate, so the euro must have a forward discount of 1 percent.

Exhibit 7.12 shows that the forward rate of the euro exhibits a premium whenever the U.S. interest rate is higher than the euro interest rate and also that the size of the premium is about equal to the size of the interest rate differential. Likewise, the forward rate of the euro exhibits a discount whenever the U.S. interest rate is lower than the euro interest rate, and the size of the premium is about equal to the size of the interest rate differential.

The middle and lower graphs of Exhibit 7.12 are related to the points plotted in Exhibit 7.9 to form the IRP line. Exhibit 7.9 shows the relationship between the interest rate differential and the forward premium for a particular time, whereas Exhibit 7.12 shows this relationship over a period of time. Both graphs illustrate that, under interest rate parity, the forward premium of a foreign currency will approximately equal the difference between the U.S. and foreign interest rate.

The time-series relationship shown in Exhibit 7.12 can be used to determine how the forward rate premium will adjust in response to conditions that affect interest rate movements over time.

WEB

www.fxstreet.com/rates
-charts/forward-rates/
Forward rates of the
Canadian dollar, British
pound, euro, Japanese
yen, and other currencies
for various periods.

EXAMPLE   Assume that interest rate parity holds and will continue to hold. As of this morning, the spot rate of the Canadian dollar was $.80, the one-year forward rate of the Canadian dollar was $.80, and the one-year interest rates in both Canada and in the United States were 5 percent. Suppose that, at noon today, the Federal Reserve engaged in monetary policy by reducing the one-year U.S. interest rate to 4 percent. In that case, under IRP the one-year forward rate of the Canadian dollar must change to reflect a 1 percent discount; otherwise, covered interest arbitrage will occur until the forward rate does exhibit a 1 percent discount. ●

Explaining Changes in the Forward Rate   Recall that the forward rate (F) can be written as

$$F = S(1 + p)$$

The forward rate is indirectly affected by all the factors that influence the spot rate (S) over time, including inflation differentials and interest rate differentials. The change in the forward rate can also be due to a change in the premium, and the previous section explained how a change in the forward premium is completely dictated by changes in the interest rate differential (assuming that interest rate parity holds). Thus interest rate movements can affect the forward rate by affecting both the spot rate and the forward premium.

EXAMPLE   Assume that, as of yesterday, the United States and Canada each had an annual interest rate of 5 percent. Under these conditions, interest rate parity should force the Canadian dollar to have a forward premium of zero. Suppose that the annual interest rate in the United States increased to 6 percent today while the Canadian interest rate remained at 5 percent. To maintain interest rate parity, commercial banks that serve the foreign exchange market will quote a forward rate with a premium of about 1 percent today, reflecting today's 1 percent interest rate differential between U.S. and Canadian interest rates. Thus the forward rate will be 1 percent above today's spot rate. As long as the interest rate differential remains at 1 percent, any future movement in the spot rate will result in a similar movement in the forward rate to retain that 1 percent forward premium. ●

SUMMARY

■ Locational arbitrage may occur if foreign exchange quotations differ among banks. The act of locational arbitrage should force the foreign exchange quotations of banks to become realigned, after which locational arbitrage will no longer be possible.

■ Triangular arbitrage is related to cross exchange rates. A cross exchange rate between two currencies is determined by the values of these two currencies with respect to a third currency. If the actual cross exchange rate of these two currencies differs from the rate that should exist, triangular arbitrage is possible. The act of triangular arbitrage should force cross exchange rates to become realigned, at which time triangular arbitrage will no longer be possible.

■ Covered interest arbitrage is based on the relationship between the forward rate premium and the interest rate differential. The size of the premium or discount exhibited by the forward rate of a currency should be about the same as the differential between the interest rates of the two countries of concern. In general terms, the forward rate of the foreign currency will contain a discount if its interest rate is higher than the U.S. interest rate.

■ If the forward premium deviates substantially from the interest rate differential, then covered interest arbitrage is possible. In this type of arbitrage, a short-term investment in some foreign currency is covered by a forward sale of that foreign currency in the future. In this manner, the investor is not exposed to fluctuation in the foreign currency's value.

■ According to the theory of interest rate parity (IRP), the size of the forward premium (or discount) should be equal to the interest rate differential between the two countries of concern. If IRP holds then covered interest arbitrage is not feasible, because any interest rate advantage in the foreign country will be offset by the discount on the forward rate. Thus covered interest arbitrage would not generate higher returns than would be generated by a domestic investment.

■ Because the forward premium of a currency (from a U.S. perspective) is influenced both by the interest rate of that currency and by the U.S. interest rate, and because those interest rates change over time, it follows that the forward premium changes over time. Thus a forward premium that is large and positive in one period, when the interest rate of that currency is relatively low, could become negative (reflecting a discount) if its interest rate rises above the U.S. level.

POINT COUNTER-POINT

Does Arbitrage Destabilize Foreign Exchange Markets?

Point Yes. Large financial institutions have the technology to recognize when one participant in the foreign exchange market is trying to sell a currency for a higher price than another participant. They also recognize when the forward rate does not properly reflect the interest rate differential. They use arbitrage to capitalize on these situations, which results in large foreign exchange transactions. In some cases, their arbitrage involves taking large positions in a currency and then reversing their positions a few minutes later. This jumping in and out of currencies can cause abrupt price adjustments of currencies and may create more volatility in the foreign exchange market. Regulations should be created that would force financial institutions to maintain their currency positions for at least one month. This would result in a more stable foreign exchange market.

Counter-Point No. When financial institutions engage in arbitrage, they create pressure on the price of a currency that will remove any pricing discrepancy. If arbitrage did not occur, pricing discrepancies would become more pronounced. Consequently, firms and individuals who use the foreign exchange market would have to spend more time searching for the best exchange rate when trading a currency. The market would become fragmented, and prices could differ substantially among banks in a region, or among regions. If the discrepancies became large enough, firms and individuals might even attempt to conduct arbitrage themselves. The arbitrage conducted by banks allows for a more integrated foreign exchange market, which ensures that foreign exchange prices quoted by any institution are in line with the market.

Who Is Correct?   Use the Internet to learn more about this issue. Which argument do you support? Offer your own opinion on this issue.

SELF-TEST

Answers are provided in Appendix A at the back of the text.

1. Assume that the following spot exchange rates exist today:

£1 = $1.50
C$ = $.75
£1 = C$2

Assume no transaction costs. Based on these exchange rates, can triangular arbitrage be used to earn a profit? Explain.

2. Assume the following information

Spot rate of £ = $1.60
180-day forward rate of £ = $1.56
180-day British interest rate = 4%
180-day US interest rate = 3%

Based on this information, is covered interest arbitrage by U.S. investors feasible (assuming that U.S. investors use their own funds)? Explain.

3. Using the information in the previous question, does interest rate parity exist? Explain.

4. Explain in general terms how various forms of arbitrage can remove any discrepancies in the pricing of currencies.

5. Assume that the British pound's one-year forward rate exhibits a discount. Assume that interest rate parity continually exists. Explain how the discount on the British pound's one-year forward discount would change if British one-year interest rates rose by 3 percentage points while U.S. one-year interest rates rose by 2 percentage points.

QUESTIONS AND APPLICATIONS

1. Locational Arbitrage Explain the concept of locational arbitrage and the scenario necessary for it to be plausible.

2. Locational Arbitrage Assume the following information:

	BEAL BANK	YARDLEY BANK
Bid price of New Zealand dollar	$.401	$.398
Ask price of New Zealand dollar	$.404	$.400

Given this information, is locational arbitrage possible? If so, explain the steps involved in locational arbitrage, and compute the profit from this arbitrage if you had $1 million to use. What market forces would occur to eliminate any further possibilities of locational arbitrage?

3. Triangular Arbitrage Explain the concept of triangular arbitrage and the scenario necessary for it to be plausible.

4. Triangular Arbitrage Assume the following information:

	QUOTED PRICE
Value of Canadian dollar in U.S. dollars	$.90
Value of New Zealand dollar in U.S. dollars	$.30
Value of Canadian dollar in New Zealand dollars	NZ$3.02

Given this information, is triangular arbitrage possible? If so, explain the steps that would reflect triangular arbitrage, and compute the profit from this strategy if you had $1 million to use. What market forces would occur to eliminate any further possibilities of triangular arbitrage?

5. Covered Interest Arbitrage Explain the concept of covered interest arbitrage and the scenario necessary for it to be plausible.

6. Covered Interest Arbitrage Assume the following information:

Spot rate of Canadian dollar	$.80
90-day forward rate of Canadian dollar	$.79
90-day Canadian interest rate	4%
90-day U.S. interest rate	2.5%

Given this information, what would be the yield (percentage return) to a U.S. investor who used covered interest arbitrage? (Assume the investor invests $1 million.) What market forces would occur to eliminate any further possibilities of covered interest arbitrage?

7. Covered Interest Arbitrage Assume the following information:

Spot rate of Mexican peso	$.100
180-day forward rate of Mexican peso	$.098
180-day Mexican interest rate	6%
180-day U.S. interest rate	5%

Given this information, is covered interest arbitrage worthwhile for Mexican investors who have pesos to invest? Explain your answer.

8. Effects of September 11 The terrorist attack on the United States on September 11, 2001, caused expectations of a weaker U.S. economy. Explain how such expectations could have affected U.S. interest rates and therefore have affected the forward rate premium (or discount) on various foreign currencies.

9. Interest Rate Parity Explain the concept of interest rate parity. Provide the rationale for its possible existence.

10. Inflation Effects on the Forward Rate Why do you think currencies of countries with high inflation rates tend to have forward discounts?

11. Covered Interest Arbitrage in Both Directions Assume that the existing U.S. one-year interest rate is 10 percent and the Canadian one-year interest rate is 11 percent. Also assume that interest rate parity exists. Should the forward rate of the Canadian dollar exhibit a discount or a premium? If U.S. investors attempt covered interest arbitrage, what will be their return? If Canadian investors attempt covered interest arbitrage, what will be their return?

12. Interest Rate Parity Why would U.S. investors consider covered interest arbitrage in France when the interest rate on euros in France is lower than the U.S. interest rate?

13. Interest Rate Parity Consider investors who invest in either U.S. or British one-year Treasury bills. Assume zero transaction costs and no taxes.

a. If interest rate parity exists, then the return for U.S. investors who use covered interest arbitrage will be the same as the return for U.S. investors who invest in U.S. Treasury bills. Is this statement true or false? If false, correct the statement.

b. If interest rate parity exists, then the return for British investors who use covered interest arbitrage will be the same as the return for British investors who invest in British Treasury bills. Is this statement true or false? If false, correct the statement.

14. Changes in Forward Premiums Assume that the Japanese yen's forward rate currently exhibits a premium of 6 percent and that interest rate parity exists. If U.S. interest rates decrease, how must this premium change to maintain interest rate parity? Why might we expect the premium to change?

15. Changes in Forward Premiums Assume that the forward rate premium of the euro was higher last month than it is today. What does this imply about interest rate differentials between the United States and Europe today compared to those last month?

16. Interest Rate Parity If the relationship that is specified by interest rate parity does not exist at any period but does exist on average, then covered interest arbitrage should not be considered by U.S. firms. Do you agree or disagree with this statement? Explain.

17. Covered Interest Arbitrage in Both Directions The one-year interest rate in New Zealand is 6 percent. The one-year U.S. interest rate is 10 percent. The spot rate of the New Zealand dollar (NZ$) is $.50. The forward rate of the New Zealand dollar is $.54. Is covered interest arbitrage feasible for U.S. investors? Is it feasible for New Zealand investors? In each case, explain why covered interest arbitrage is or is not feasible.

18. Limitations of Covered Interest Arbitrage Assume that the one-year U.S. interest rate is 11 percent, while the one-year interest rate in Malaysia is 40 percent. Assume that a U.S. bank is willing to purchase the currency of that country from you one year from now at a discount of 13 percent. Would covered interest arbitrage be worth considering? Is there any reason why you should not attempt covered interest arbitrage in this situation? (Ignore tax effects.)

19. Covered Interest Arbitrage in Both Directions Assume that the annual U.S. interest rate is currently 8 percent and Germany's annual interest rate is currently 9 percent. The euro's one1-year forward rate currently exhibits a discount of 2 percent.

a. Does interest rate parity exist?
b. Can a U.S. firm benefit from investing funds in Germany using covered interest arbitrage?
c. Can a German subsidiary of a U.S. firm benefit by investing funds in the United States through covered interest arbitrage?

20. Covered Interest Arbitrage The South African rand has a one-year forward premium of 2 percent. One-year interest rates in the United States are 3 percentage points higher than in South Africa. Based on this information, is covered interest arbitrage possible for a U.S. investor if interest rate parity holds?

21. Deriving the Forward Rate Assume that annual interest rates in the United States are 4 percent, while interest rates in France are 6 percent.

a. According to IRP, what should the forward rate premium or discount of the euro be?
b. If the euro's spot rate is $1.10, what should the one-year forward rate of the euro be?

22. Covered Interest Arbitrage in Both Directions The following information is available:

- You have $500,000 to invest.
- The current spot rate of the Moroccan dirham is $.110.
- The 60-day forward rate of the Moroccan dirham is $.108.
- The 60-day interest rate in the United States is 1 percent.
- The 60-day interest rate in Morocco is 2 percent.

a. What is the yield to a U.S. investor who conducts covered interest arbitrage? Did covered interest arbitrage work for the investor in this case?
b. Would covered interest arbitrage be possible for a Moroccan investor in this case?

Advanced Questions

23. Economic Effects on the Forward Rate Assume that Mexico's economy has expanded significantly, causing a high demand for loanable funds there by local firms. How might these conditions affect the forward discount of the Mexican peso?

24. Differences among Forward Rates Assume that the 30-day forward premium of the euro is 1 percent, while the 90-day forward premium of the euro is 2 percent. Explain the likely interest rate conditions that would cause these premiums. Does this ensure that covered interest arbitrage is worthwhile?

25. Testing Interest Rate Parity Describe a method for testing whether interest rate parity exists. Why are transaction costs, currency restrictions, and differential tax laws important when evaluating whether covered interest arbitrage can be beneficial?

26. Interest Rate Parity Implications for Russia If the U.S. interest rate is close to zero, while the interest rate of Russia is very high, what would interest rate parity suggest about the forward rate of the Russian ruble? Explain.

27. Interpreting Changes in the Forward Premium Assume that interest rate parity holds. At the beginning of the month, the spot rate of the Canadian dollar is $.70, while the one-year forward rate is $.68. Assume that U.S. interest rates increase steadily over the month. At the end of the month, the one-year forward rate is higher than it was at the beginning of the month. Yet the one-year forward discount is larger (the one-year premium is more negative) at the end of the month than it was at the beginning of the month. Explain how the relationship between the U.S. interest rate and the Canadian interest rate changed from the beginning of the month until the end of the month.

28. Interpreting a Large Forward Discount The interest rate in Indonesia is commonly higher than the interest rate in the United States, which reflects a high expected rate of inflation there. Why should Nike consider hedging its future remittances from Indonesia to the U.S. parent even when the forward discount on the currency (rupiah) is so large?

29. Change in the Forward Premium At the end of this month, you (owner of a U.S. firm) are meeting with a Japanese firm to which you will try to sell supplies. If you receive an order from that firm, you will obtain a forward contract to hedge the future receivables in yen. As of this morning, the forward rate of the yen and spot rate are the same. You believe that interest rate parity holds.

This afternoon, news occurs that makes you believe that the U.S. interest rates will increase substantially by the end of this month, and that the Japanese interest rate will not change. However, your expectations of the spot rate of the Japanese yen are not affected at all in the future. How will your expected dollar amount of receivables from the Japanese transaction be affected (if at all) by the news that occurred this afternoon? Explain.

30. Testing IRP The one-year interest rate in Singapore is 11 percent. The one-year interest rate in the United States is 6 percent. The spot rate of the Singapore dollar (S$) is $.50 and the forward rate of the S$ is $.46. Assume zero transaction costs.

a. Does interest rate parity exist?
b. Can a U.S. firm benefit from investing funds in Singapore using covered interest arbitrage?

31. Implications of IRP Assume that interest rate parity exists. You expect that the one-year nominal interest rate in the United States is 7 percent, while the one-year nominal interest rate in Australia is 11 percent. The spot rate of the Australian dollar is $.60. You will need 10 million Australian dollars in one year. Today, you purchase a one-year forward contract in Australian dollars. How many U.S. dollars will you need in one year to fulfill your forward contract?

32. Triangular Arbitrage You go to a bank and are given these quotes:

You can buy a euro for 14 pesos.
The bank will pay you 13 pesos for a euro.
You can buy a U.S. dollar for .9 euros.
The bank will pay you .8 euros for a U.S. dollar.
You can buy a U.S. dollar for 10 pesos.
The bank will pay you 9 pesos for a U.S. dollar.

You have $1,000. Can you use triangular arbitrage to generate a profit? If so, explain the order of the transactions that you would execute and the profit that you would earn. If you cannot earn a profit from triangular arbitrage, explain why.

33. Triangular Arbitrage You are given these quotes by the bank:

You can sell Canadian dollars (C$) to the bank for $.70
You can buy Canadian dollars from the bank for $.73.
The bank is willing to buy dollars for .9 euros per dollar.
The bank is willing to sell dollars for .94 euros per dollar.
The bank is willing to buy Canadian dollars for .64 euros per C$.
The bank is willing to sell Canadian dollars for .68 euros per C$.

You have $100,000. Estimate your profit or loss if you would attempt triangular arbitrage by converting your dollars to euros, and then convert euros to Canadian dollars and then convert Canadian dollars to U.S. dollars.

34. Movement in Cross Exchange Rates Assume that cross exchange rates are always proper, such that triangular arbitrage is not feasible. While at the Miami airport today, you notice that a U.S. dollar can be exchanged for 125 Japanese yen or 4 Argentine pesos at the foreign exchange booth. Last year, the Japanese yen was valued at $.01, and the Argentine peso was valued at $.30. Based on this information, the Argentine peso has changed by what percent against the Japanese yen over the last year?

35. Impact of Arbitrage on the Forward Rate Assume that the annual U.S. interest rate is currently 6 percent and Germany's annual interest rate is currently 8 percent. The spot rate of the euro is $1.10 and the one-year forward rate of the euro is $1.10. Assume that as covered interest arbitrage occurs, the interest rates are not affected, and the spot rate is not affected. Explain how the one-year forward rate of the euro will change in order to restore interest rate parity, and why it will change. Your explanation should specify which type of investor (German or U.S.) would be engaging in covered interest arbitrage, whether they are buying or selling euros forward, and how that affects the forward rate of the euro.

36. IRP and Changes in the Forward Rate Assume that interest rate parity exists. As of this morning, the one-month interest rate in Canada was lower than the one-month interest rate in the United States. Assume that as a result of the Fed's monetary policy this afternoon, the one-month interest rate in the United States declined this afternoon, but was still higher than the Canadian one-month interest rate. The one-month interest rate in Canada remained unchanged. Based on the information, the forward rate of the Canadian dollar exhibited a ___ [discount or premium] this morning that ___ [increased or decreased] this afternoon. Explain.

37. Deriving the Forward Rate Premium Assume that the spot rate of the Brazilian real is $.30 today. Assume that interest rate parity exists. Obtain the interest rate data you need from Bloomberg.com to derive the one-year forward rate premium (or discount), and then determine the one-year forward rate of the Brazilian real.

38. Change in the Forward Premium over Time Assume that interest rate parity exists and will continue to exist. As of today, the one-year interest rate of Singapore is 4 percent versus 7 percent in the United States. The Singapore central bank is expected to decrease interest rates in the future so that as of December 1, you expect that the one-year interest rate in Singapore will be 2 percent. The U.S. interest rate is not expected to change over time. Based on the information, explain how the forward premium (or discount) is expected to change by December 1.

39. Forward Rates for Different Time Horizons
Assume that interest rate parity (IRP) exists, along with the following information:

Spot rate of British pound = $1.80
6-month forward rate of pound = $1.82
12-month forward rate of pound = $1.78

a. Is the annualized 6-month U.S. risk-free interest rate above, below, or equal to the British risk-free interest rate?
b. Is the 12-month U.S. risk-free interest rate above, below, or equal to the British risk-free interest rate?

40. Interpreting Forward Rate Information
Assume that interest rate parity exists. The 6-month forward rate of the Swiss franc has a premium while the 12-month forward rate of the Swiss franc has a discount. What does this tell you about the relative level of Swiss interest rates versus U.S. interest rates?

41. IRP and Speculation in Currency Futures
Assume that interest rate parity exists. The spot rate of the Argentine peso is $.40. The one-year interest rate in the United States is 7 percent versus 12 percent in Argentina. Assume the futures price is equal to the forward rate. An investor purchased futures contracts on Argentine pesos, representing a total of 1,000,000 pesos. Determine the total dollar amount of profit or loss from this futures contract based on the expectation that the Argentine peso will be worth $.42 in one year.

42. Profit from Covered Interest Arbitrage
Today, the one-year U.S. interest rate is 4 percent, while the one-year interest rate in Argentina is 17 percent. The spot rate of the Argentine peso (AP) is $.44. The one-year forward rate of the AP exhibits a 14 percent discount. Determine the yield (percentage return on investment) to an investor from Argentina who engages in covered interest arbitrage.

43. Assessing Whether IRP Exists
Assume zero transaction costs. As of now, the Japanese one-year interest rate is 3 percent, and the U.S. one-year interest rate is 9 percent. The spot rate of the Japanese yen is $.0090 and the one-year forward rate of the Japanese yen is $.0097.

a. Determine whether interest rate parity exists, or whether the quoted forward rate is too high or too low.
b. Based on the information provided in (a), is covered interest arbitrage feasible for U.S. investors, for Japanese investors, for both types of investors, or for neither type of investor?

44. Change in Forward Rate due to Arbitrage
Earlier this morning, the annual U.S. interest rate was 6 percent and Mexico's annual interest rate was 8 percent. The spot rate of the Mexican peso was $.16. The one-year forward rate of the peso was $.15. Assume that as covered interest arbitrage occurred this morning, the interest rates were not affected, and the spot rate was not affected, but the forward rate was affected, and consequently interest rate parity now exists. Explain which type of investor (Mexican or U.S.) engaged in covered interest arbitrage, whether they were buying or selling pesos forward, and how that affected the forward rate of the peso.

45. IRP Relationship
Assume that interest rate parity (IRP) exists, along with the following information:

Spot rate of Swiss franc = $.80
6-month forward rate of Swiss franc = $.78
12-month forward rate of Swiss franc = $.81

Assume that the annualized U.S. interest rate is 7 percent for a 6-month maturity and a 12-month maturity. Do you think the Swiss interest rate for a 6-month maturity is greater than, equal to, or less than the U.S. interest rate for a 6-month maturity? Explain.

46. Impact of Arbitrage on the Forward Rate
Assume that the annual U.S. interest rate is currently 8 percent and Japan's annual interest rate is currently 7 percent. The spot rate of the Japanese yen is $.01. The one-year forward rate of the Japanese yen is $.01. Assume that as covered interest arbitrage occurs the interest rates are not affected and the spot rate is not affected. Explain how the one-year forward rate of the yen will change in order to restore interest rate parity, and why it will change. [Your explanation should specify which type of investor (Japanese or U.S.) would be engaging in covered interest arbitrage and whether these investors are buying or selling yen forward, and how that affects the forward rate of the yen.]

47. Profit from Triangular Arbitrage
The bank is willing to buy dollars for .9 euros per dollar. It is willing to sell dollars for .91 euros per dollar.

You can sell Australian dollars (A$) to the bank for $.72.

You can buy Australian dollars from the bank for $.74.

The bank is willing to buy Australian dollars (A$) for .68 euros per A$.

The bank is willing to sell Australian dollars (A$) for .70 euros per A$.

You have $100,000. Estimate your profit or loss if you were to attempt triangular arbitrage by converting your dollars to Australian dollars, then converting Australian dollars to euros, and then converting euros to U.S. dollars.

48. Profit from Triangular Arbitrage Alabama Bank is willing to buy or sell British pounds for $1.98. The bank is willing to buy or sell Mexican pesos at an exchange rate of 10 pesos per dollar. The bank is willing to purchase British pounds at an exchange rate of 1 peso =.05 British pounds. Show how you can make a profit from triangular arbitrage and what your profit would be if you had $100,000.

49. Cross Rate and Forward Rate Biscayne Co. will be receiving Mexican pesos today and will need to convert them into Australian dollars. Today, a U.S. dollar can be exchanged for 10 Mexican pesos. An Australian dollar is worth one-half of a U.S. dollar.

a. What is the spot rate of a Mexican peso in Australian dollars?

b. Assume that interest rate parity exists and that the annual risk-free interest rate in the United States, Australia, and Mexico is 7 percent. What is the one-year forward rate of a Mexican peso in Australian dollars?

50. Changes in the Forward Rate Assume that interest rate parity exists and will continue to exist. As of this morning, the one-month interest rate in the United States was higher than the one-month interest rate in the eurozone. Assume that as a result of the European Central Bank's monetary policy this afternoon, the one-month interest rate of the euro increased and is now higher than the U.S. one-month interest rate. The one-month interest rate in the United States remained unchanged.

a. Based on the information, do you think the one-month forward rate of the euro exhibited a discount or premium this morning?

b. How did the forward premium change this afternoon?

51. Forces of Triangular Arbitrage You obtain the following quotes from different banks. One bank is willing to buy or sell Japanese yen at an exchange rate of 110 yen per dollar. A second bank is willing to buy

or sell the Argentine peso at an exchange rate of $.37 per peso. A third bank is willing to exchange Japanese yen at an exchange rate of 1 Argentine peso = 40 yen.

a. Show how you can make a profit from triangular arbitrage and what your profit would be if you had $1,000,000.

b. As investors engage in triangular arbitrage, explain the effect on each of the exchange rates until triangular arbitrage would no longer be possible.

52. Return due to Covered Interest Arbitrage Interest rate parity exists between the United States and Poland (its currency is the zloty). The one-year risk-free CD (deposit) rate in the United States is 7 percent. The one-year risk-free CD rate in Poland is 5 percent and denominated in zloty. Assume that there is zero probability of any financial or political problem such as a bank default or government restrictions on bank deposits or currencies in either country. Myron is from Poland and plans to invest in the United States. What is Myron's return if he invests in the United States and covers the risk of his investment with a forward contract?

53. Forces of Covered Interest Arbitrage As of now, the nominal interest rate is 6 percent in the United States and 6 percent in Australia. The spot rate of the Australian dollar is $.58, while the one-year forward rate of the Australian dollar exhibits a discount of 2 percent. Assume that as covered interest arbitrage occurred this morning, the interest rates were not affected, the spot rate of the Australian dollar was not affected, but the forward rate of the Australian dollar was affected. Consequently interest rate parity now exists. Explain the forces that caused the forward rate of the Australian dollar to change by completing this sentence: The ___ [Australian or U.S.?] investors could benefit from engaging in covered interest arbitrage; their arbitrage would involve ___ [buying or selling?] Australian dollars forward, which would cause the forward rate of the Australian dollar to ___ [increase or decrease?].

54. Change in Forward Premium over Time Assume that the one-year interest rate in the United Kingdom is 9 percent, while the one-year interest in the United States is 4 percent. The spot rate of the pound is $1.50. Assume that interest rate parity exists. The quoted one-year interest in the United Kingdom is expected to rise consistently over the next month. Meanwhile, the quoted one-year interest rate in the United States is expected to decline consistently over the next month. Assume that the spot rate does not change over the month. Based on this information, how will the quoted one-year forward rate change over the next month?

55. Forward Rate Premiums among Maturities
Today, the annualized interest rate in the United States is 4 percent for any debt maturity. The annualized interest rate in Australia is 4 percent for debt maturities of three months or less, 5 percent for debt maturities between three months and six months, and 6 percent for debt maturities more than six months. Assume that interest rate parity exists. Does the forward rate quoted today for the Australian dollar exhibit a premium or a discount, or does your answer vary with specific conditions? Briefly explain.

56. Explaining Movements in Forward Premiums
Assume that interest rate parity holds and will continue to hold in the future. At the beginning of the month, the spot rate of the British pound is $1.60, while the one-year forward rate is $1.50. Assume that U.S. annual interest rate remains steady over the month. At the end of the month, the one-year forward rate of the British pound exhibits a discount of 1 percent. Explain how the British annual interest rate changed over the month, and whether it is higher, lower, or equal to the U.S. rate at the end of the month.

57. Forces of Covered Interest Arbitrage
Assume that the one-year interest rate in Canada is 4 percent. The one-year U.S. interest rate is 8 percent. The spot rate of the Canadian dollar (C$) is $.94. The forward rate of the Canadian dollar is $.98.

a. Is covered interest arbitrage feasible for U.S. investors? Show the results if a U.S. firm engages in covered interest arbitrage to support your answer.
b. Assume that the spot rate and interest rates remain unchanged as coverage interest arbitrage is attempted by U.S. investors. Do you think the forward rate of the Canadian dollar will be affected? If so, state whether it will increase or decrease, and explain why.

Critical Thinking

IRP Implications Since the International Credit Crisis From 2008 (when the international credit crisis occurred) through 2014, the U.S. government maintained interest rates at extremely low levels. Assume that interest rate parity existed over that time period. Write a short essay on what the U.S. interest rate conditions imply about the forward rate of the Australian dollar over this period.

Discussion in the Boardroom

This exercise can be found in Appendix E at the back of this textbook.

Running Your Own MNC

This exercise can be found on *the International Financial Management* text companion website. Go to www.cengagebrain.com (students) or www.cengage.com/login (instructors) and search using **ISBN 9781133947837**.

BLADES, INC. CASE

Assessment of Potential Arbitrage Opportunities

Recall that Blades, a U.S. manufacturer of roller blades, has chosen Thailand as its primary export target for Speedos, Blades' primary product. Moreover, Blades' primary customer in Thailand, Entertainment Products, has committed itself to purchase 180,000 Speedos annually for the next three years at a fixed price denominated in baht, Thailand's currency. Because of quality and cost considerations, Blades also imports some of the rubber and plastic components needed to manufacture Speedos from Thailand.

Lately, Thailand has experienced weak economic growth and political uncertainty. As investors lost confidence in the Thai baht as a result of the political uncertainty, they withdrew their funds from the country. This resulted in an excess supply of baht for sale over the demand for baht in the foreign exchange

market, which put downward pressure on the baht's value. As foreign investors continued to withdraw their funds from Thailand, the baht's value continued to deteriorate. Because Blades has net cash flows in baht resulting from its exports to Thailand, a deterioration in the baht's value will affect the company negatively.

Ben Holt, Blades' CFO, would like to ensure that the spot and forward rates Blades' bank has quoted are reasonable. If the exchange rate quotes are reasonable, then arbitrage will not be possible. If the quotations are not appropriate, however, arbitrage may be possible. Under these conditions, Holt would like Blades to use some form of arbitrage to take advantage of possible mispricing in the foreign exchange market. Although Blades is not an arbitrageur, Holt believes that arbitrage opportunities could offset the negative impact resulting from the baht's depreciation, which would otherwise seriously affect Blades' profit margins.

Holt has identified three arbitrage opportunities as profitable and would like to know which one of them is the most profitable. Thus he has asked you, Blades' financial analyst, to prepare an analysis of the arbitrage opportunities he has identified. This would allow Holt to assess the profitability of arbitrage opportunities very quickly.

1. The first arbitrage opportunity relates to locational arbitrage. Holt has obtained spot rate quotations from two banks in Thailand: Minzu Bank and Sobat Bank, both located in Bangkok. The bid and ask prices of Thai baht for each bank are displayed in the table below.

	MINZU BANK	SOBAT BANK
Bid	$.0224	$.0228
Ask	$.0227	$.0229

Determine whether the foreign exchange quotations are appropriate. If they are not appropriate, determine the profit you could generate by withdrawing $100,000 from Blades' checking account and engaging in arbitrage before the rates are adjusted.

2. Besides the bid and ask quotes for the Thai baht provided in the previous question, Minzu Bank has provided the following quotations for the U.S. dollar and the Japanese yen:

	QUOTED BID PRICE	QUOTED ASK PRICE
Value of a Japanese yen in U.S. dollars	$.0085	$.0086
Value of a Thai baht in Japanese yen	¥2.69	¥2.70

Determine whether the cross exchange rate between the Thai baht and Japanese yen is appropriate. If it is not appropriate, determine the profit you could generate for Blades by withdrawing $100,000 from Blades' checking account and engaging in triangular arbitrage before the rates are adjusted.

3. Ben Holt has obtained several forward contract quotations for the Thai baht to determine whether covered interest arbitrage may be possible. He was quoted a forward rate of $.0225 per Thai baht for a 90-day forward contract. The current spot rate is $.0227. Ninety-day interest rates available to Blades in the United States are 2 percent, while 90-day interest rates in Thailand are 3.75 percent (these rates are not annualized). Holt is aware that covered interest arbitrage, unlike locational and triangular arbitrage, requires an investment of funds. Thus he would like to be able to estimate the dollar profit resulting from arbitrage over and above the dollar amount available on a 90-day U.S. deposit. Determine whether the forward rate is priced appropriately. If it is not priced appropriately, determine the profit you could generate for Blades by withdrawing $100,000 from Blades' checking account and engaging in covered interest arbitrage. Measure the profit as the excess amount above what you could generate by investing in the U.S. money market.

4. Why are arbitrage opportunities likely to disappear soon after they have been discovered? To illustrate your answer, assume that covered interest arbitrage involving the immediate purchase and forward sale of baht is possible. Discuss how the baht's spot and forward rates would adjust until covered interest arbitrage is no longer possible. What is the resulting equilibrium state called?

SMALL BUSINESS DILEMMA

Assessment of Prevailing Spot and Forward Rates by the Sports Exports Company

As the Sports Exports Company exports footballs to the United Kingdom, it receives British pounds. The check (denominated in pounds) for last month's exports just arrived. Jim Logan (owner of the Sports Exports Company) normally deposits the check with his local bank and requests that the bank convert the check to dollars at the prevailing spot rate (assuming that he did not use a forward contract to hedge this payment). Logan's local bank provides foreign exchange services for many of its business customers who need to buy or sell widely traded currencies. Today, however, Logan decided to check the quotations of the spot rate at other banks before converting the payment into dollars.

1. Do you think Logan will be able to find a bank that provides him with a more favorable spot rate than his local bank? Explain.

2. Do you think that Logan's bank is likely to provide more reasonable quotations for the spot rate of the British pound if it is the only bank in town that provides foreign exchange services? Explain.

3. Logan is considering using a forward contract to hedge the anticipated receivables in pounds next month. His local bank quoted him a spot rate of $1.65 and a one-month forward rate of $1.6435. Before he decides to sell pounds one month forward, he wants to be sure that the forward rate is reasonable, given the prevailing spot rate. A one-month Treasury security in the United States currently offers a yield (not annualized) of 1 percent, while a one-month Treasury security in the United Kingdom offers a yield of 1.4 percent. Do you believe that the one-month forward rate is reasonable given the spot rate of $1.65?

INTERNET/EXCEL EXERCISE

The Bloomberg website provides quotations in foreign exchange markets. Its address is www.bloomberg.com.

Use this web page to determine the cross exchange rate between the Canadian dollar and the Japanese yen.

Notice that the value of the pound (in dollars) and the value of the yen (in dollars) are also disclosed. Based on these values, is the cross rate between the Canadian dollar and the yen what you expected it to be? Explain.

ONLINE ARTICLES WITH REAL-WORLD EXAMPLES

Find a recent article online that describes an actual international finance application or a real-world example about a specific MNC's actions that reinforces one or more concepts covered in this chapter.

If your class has an online component, your professor may ask you to post your summary there and provide the web link of the article so that other students can access it. If your class is live, your professor may ask you to summarize your application in class. Your professor may assign specific students to complete this assignment for this chapter, or may allow any students to do the assignment on a volunteer basis.

For recent online articles and real-world examples applied to this chapter, consider using the following search terms and include the current year as a search term to ensure that the online articles are recent:

1. foreign exchange AND arbitrage
2. foreign exchange AND bid/ask spread
3. covered interest arbitrage
4. currency arbitrage
5. interest rate parity
6. forward contract AND arbitrage
7. market imperfections AND interest rate parity
8. transaction costs AND interest rate parity
9. forward contract AND interest rate parity
10. forward premium AND transaction costs

8

Relationships among Inflation, Interest Rates, and Exchange Rates

CHAPTER OBJECTIVES

The specific objectives of this chapter are to:

■ explain the purchasing power parity (PPP) theory and its implications for exchange rate changes, and

■ explain the international Fisher effect (IFE) theory and its implications for exchange rate changes.

Inflation rates and interest rates can have a significant impact on exchange rates (as explained in Chapter 4) and therefore can influence the value of MNCs. Financial managers of MNCs must understand how inflation and interest rates can affect exchange rates so that they can anticipate how their MNCs may be affected.

8-1 Purchasing Power Parity (PPP)

In Chapter 4, the expected impact of relative inflation rates on exchange rates was discussed. Recall from this discussion that when a country's inflation rate rises, the demand for its currency declines as its exports decline (because of their higher prices). In addition, consumers and firms in that country tend to increase their importing. Both of these forces place downward pressure on the high-inflation country's currency. Inflation rates often vary among countries, causing international trade patterns and exchange rates to adjust accordingly. One of the most popular and controversial theories in international finance is the **purchasing power parity (PPP) theory**, which attempts to quantify the relationship between inflation and the exchange rate. This theory supports the notion developed in Chapter 4 about how relatively high inflation places downward pressure on a currency's value, but PPP is more specific about the degree by which a currency will weaken in response to high inflation.

8-1a Interpretations of Purchasing Power Parity

There are two popular forms of PPP theory, each with its own implications.

Absolute Form of PPP   The **absolute form of PPP** is based on the idea that, in the absence of international barriers, consumers will shift their demand to wherever prices are lowest. The implication is that prices of the same basket of products in two different countries should be equal when measured in a common currency. If there is a discrepancy in the prices as measured by such a common currency, then demand should shift so that these prices converge.

EXAMPLE   If the same basket of products is produced by the United States and the United Kingdom and if the price in the United Kingdom is lower when measured in a common currency, then the demand for that basket should increase in the United Kingdom and decline in the United States. Both forces would eventually cause the prices of the baskets to match when measured in a common currency. ●

The existence of transportation costs, tariffs, and quotas renders the absolute form of PPP unrealistic. If transportation costs were high in the preceding example, then demand for the baskets of products might not shift as suggested. In that case, the discrepancy in prices would continue.

Relative Form of PPP   The **relative form of PPP** accounts for such market imperfections as transportation costs, tariffs, and quotas. This version acknowledges that these imperfections make it unlikely for prices of the same basket of products in different countries to be the same when measured in a common currency. However, this form of PPP suggests that the *rate of change* in the prices of those baskets should be comparable when measured in a common currency (assuming that transportation costs and trade barriers are unchanged).

EXAMPLE

Assume that the United States and the United Kingdom trade extensively with each other and initially have zero inflation. Now suppose that the United States experiences a 9 percent inflation rate while the United Kingdom experiences a 5 percent inflation rate. Under these conditions, PPP theory suggests that the British pound should appreciate by approximately 4 percent (the difference between their inflation rates). Given British inflation of 5 percent and the pound's appreciation of 4 percent, U.S. consumers will have to pay about 9 percent more for British products than they paid in the initial equilibrium state. That value is equal to the 9 percent increase in prices of U.S. products due to U.S. inflation. The exchange rate should adjust to offset the differential in the two countries' inflation rates, in which case the prices of products in the two countries should appear similar to consumers. ●

8-1b Rationale behind Relative PPP Theory

The relative PPP theory is based on the notion that exchange rate adjustment is necessary for the relative purchasing power to be the same whether buying products locally or from another country. If that purchasing power is not equal, then consumers will shift purchases to wherever products are cheaper until purchasing power equalizes.

EXAMPLE

Reconsider the previous example but now suppose that the pound appreciated by only 1 percent in response to the inflation differential. In this case, the increased price of British products to U.S. consumers will be approximately 6 percent (5 percent inflation and 1 percent appreciation in the British pound), which is less than the 9 percent increase in the price of U.S. products to U.S. consumers. We should therefore expect U.S. consumers to continue shifting their consumption to British products. Purchasing power parity suggests that this increased U.S. consumption of British products by U.S. consumers would persist until the pound appreciated by about 4 percent. Thus, from the U.S. consumer's viewpoint, any level of appreciation lower than this would result in lower British prices than U.S. prices.

From the British consumer's viewpoint, the price of U.S. products would have initially increased by 4 percent more than British products. Thus British consumers would continue to reduce their imports from the United States until the pound appreciated enough to make U.S. products no more expensive than British products. The net effect of the pound appreciating by 4 percent is that the prices of U.S. products would increase by approximately 5 percent to British consumers (9 percent inflation minus the 4 percent savings to British consumers due to the pound's 4 percent appreciation). ●

8-1c Derivation of Purchasing Power Parity

Assume that the price indexes of the home country (h) and a foreign country (f) are equal. Now assume that, over time, the home country experiences an inflation rate of I_h while the foreign country experiences an inflation rate of I_f. Because of this inflation, the price index of products in the consumer's home country (P_h) becomes

$$P_h(1 + I_h)$$

The price index of the foreign country (P_f) will also change in response to inflation in that country:

$$P_f(1 + I_f)$$

If $I_h > I_f$ and if the exchange rate between the two countries' currencies does not change, then the consumer's purchasing power is greater for foreign than for home products. In this case, PPP does not hold. If $I_h < I_f$ and again the exchange rate remains unchanged, then the consumer's purchasing power is greater for home than for foreign products. So in this case, too, PPP does not hold.

The PPP theory suggests that the exchange rate will not remain constant but will adjust to maintain the parity in purchasing power. If inflation occurs and the exchange rate of the foreign currency changes, then the foreign price index from the home consumer's perspective becomes

$$P_f(1 + I_f)(1 + e_f)$$

where e_f represents the percentage change in the value of the foreign currency. According to PPP theory, the percentage change in the foreign currency (e_f) should be such that parity is maintained between the new price indexes of the two countries. We can solve for e_f under conditions of PPP by setting the formula for the new price index of the foreign country equal to the formula for the new price index of the home country:

$$P_f(1 + I_f)(1 + e_f) = P_h(1 + I_h)$$

Solving for e_f then yields

$$1 + e_f = \frac{P_h(1 + I_h)}{P_f(1 + I_f)}$$

$$e_f = \frac{P_h(1 + I_h)}{P_f(1 + I_f)} - 1$$

Because P_h is equal to P_f (because price indexes were assumed to be equal in both countries), the two terms cancel, which leaves

$$e_f = \frac{1 + I_h}{1 + I_f} - 1$$

This equality expresses the relationship (according to PPP) between relative inflation rates and the exchange rate. Observe that if $I_h > I_f$, then e_f should be positive, which implies that the foreign currency will appreciate when the home country's inflation exceeds the foreign country's inflation. Conversely, if $I_h < I_f$, then e_f should be negative; this implies that the foreign currency will depreciate when the foreign country's inflation exceeds the home country's inflation.

8-1d Using PPP to Estimate Exchange Rate Effects

The relative form of PPP can be used to estimate how an exchange rate will change in response to different inflation rates in two countries.

EXAMPLE   Assume that the exchange rate is initially in equilibrium. Then the home currency experiences a 5 percent inflation rate while the foreign country experiences a 3 percent inflation rate. According to PPP, the foreign currency will adjust as follows:

$$e_f = \frac{1 + I_h}{1 + I_f} - 1$$
$$= \frac{1 + .05}{1 + .03} - 1$$
$$= .0194, \text{ or } 1.94\%$$

According to this example, the foreign currency should appreciate by 1.94 percent in response to the higher inflation of the home country relative to the foreign country. If that exchange rate change does occur, then the price index of the foreign country will be as high as the index in the home country from the perspective of home country consumers. The lower relative inflation in the foreign country causes appreciation of its currency (according to PPP), which pushes the foreign price index upward from the perspective of home country consumers. When considering the exchange rate effect, price indexes of both countries rise by 5 percent from the home country perspective. Thus consumers' purchasing power is the same for foreign products and home products.

EXAMPLE

This example examines the case where foreign inflation exceeds home inflation. Suppose that the exchange rate is initially in equilibrium but then the home country experiences a 4 percent inflation rate while the foreign country experiences a 7 percent inflation rate. According to PPP, the foreign currency will adjust as follows:

$$e_f = \frac{1 + I_h}{1 + I_f} - 1$$
$$= \frac{1 + .04}{1 + .07} - 1$$
$$= -.028, \text{ or } -2.8\%$$

According to this example, the foreign currency should depreciate by 2.8 percent in response to the foreign country's higher inflation relative to that of the home country. The higher relative inflation in the foreign country causes depreciation of its currency (according to PPP) and pushes the foreign price index downward from the perspective of home country consumers. When considering the exchange rate impact, prices of both countries rise by 4 percent. Thus PPP still holds in view of the adjustment in the exchange rate. ●

The theory of purchasing power parity is summarized in Exhibit 8.1. Notice that international trade is the mechanism by which the inflation differential is theorized to affect the exchange rate. This means that PPP is more applicable when the two countries of concern engage in extensive international trade with each other. If there is not much trade between the countries, then the inflation differential will have little effect on that trade and so the exchange rate should not be expected to change.

Using a Simplified PPP Relationship   A simplified but less precise relationship based on PPP is

$$e_f \approx I_h - I_f$$

That is, the percentage change in the exchange rate should be approximately equal to the difference in inflation rates between the two countries. This simplified formula is appropriate only when the inflation differential is small or when the value of I_f is close to zero.

8-1e Graphic Analysis of Purchasing Power Parity

Using PPP theory, we should be able to assess the possible impact of inflation on exchange rates. Exhibit 8.2 is a graphic representation of PPP theory. The points on the graph indicate that, if there is an inflation differential of X percent between the home and the foreign country, then the foreign currency should adjust by X percent in response to that inflation differential.

PPP Line   The diagonal line connecting all these points together is known as the **purchasing power parity (PPP) line**. Point A in Exhibit 8.2 represents our earlier example in which the U.S. (considered the home country) and British inflation rates were assumed to be 9 and 5 percent (respectively), so that $I_h - I_f = 4\%$. Recall that these conditions led

Exhibit 8.1   Summary of Purchasing Power Parity

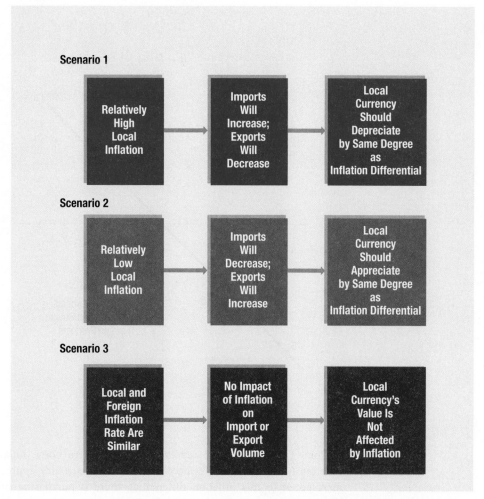

to the anticipated appreciation in the British pound of 4 percent, as illustrated by point A. Point B reflects the scenario in which the U.K. inflation rate exceeds the U.S. inflation rate by 5 percent, so that $I_h - I_f = -5\%$. This leads the British pound to depreciate by 5 percent (point B). If the exchange rate does in fact respond to inflation differentials, as PPP theory suggests, then the actual points should lie on or close to the PPP line.

PPP Line   The diagonal line connecting all these points together is known as the **purchasing power parity (PPP) line**. Point A in Exhibit 8.2 represents our earlier example in which the U.S. (considered the home country) and British inflation rates were assumed to be 9 and 5 percent (respectively), so that $I_h - I_f = 4\%$. Recall that these conditions led to the anticipated appreciation in the British pound of 4 percent, as illustrated by point A. Point B reflects the scenario in which the U.K. inflation rate exceeds the U.S. inflation rate by 5 percent, so that $I_h - I_f = -5\%$. This leads the British pound to depreciate by 5 percent (point B). If the exchange rate does in fact respond to inflation differentials, as PPP theory suggests, then the actual points should lie on or close to the PPP line.

Purchasing Power Disparity   Any points that are *off* of the PPP line represent purchasing power disparity. If the exchange rate does not move as PPP theory suggests, then there is a disparity in the purchasing power of consumers in those two countries.

Exhibit 8.2 Illustration of Purchasing Power Parity and Disparity

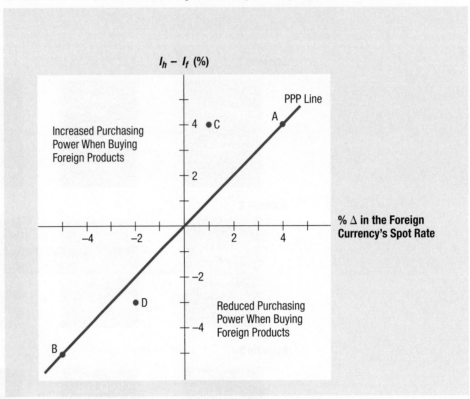

Point C in Exhibit 8.2 represents a case where home inflation I_h exceeds foreign inflation I_f by 4 percent. Yet because the foreign currency appreciated by only 1 percent in response to this inflation differential, there is purchasing power disparity. That is, home country consumers' purchasing power for foreign products has increased relative to their purchasing power for the home country's products. The PPP theory suggests that such a disparity in purchasing power should exist only in the short run. Over time, as the home country consumers take advantage of the disparity by purchasing more foreign products, upward pressure on the foreign currency's value will cause point C to move toward the PPP line. All points to the left of (or above) the PPP line represent more favorable purchasing power for foreign products than for home products.

Point D in Exhibit 8.2 represents a case where home inflation is 3 percent below foreign inflation but the foreign currency has depreciated by only 2 percent. Once again, there is purchasing power disparity: now the currency's purchasing power for foreign products has decreased relative to its purchasing power for the home country's products. The PPP theory suggests that the foreign currency in this example should have depreciated by 3 percent in order to fully offset the 3 percent inflation differential. Because the foreign currency did not weaken to this extent, home country consumers may cease to purchase foreign products. Such behavior would cause the foreign currency to weaken to the extent anticipated by PPP theory, so point D would move toward the PPP line. All points to the right of (or below) the PPP line represent greater purchasing power for home country products than for foreign products.

8-1f Testing the Purchasing Power Parity Theory

The PPP theory provides an explanation of how relative inflation rates between two countries can influence an exchange rate, and it also provides information that can be used to forecast exchange rates.

Simple Test of PPP A simple test of PPP theory is to choose two countries (such as the United States and a foreign country) and compare the differential in their inflation rates to the percentage change in the foreign currency's value during several time periods. Using a graph similar to Exhibit 8.2, we could plot each point representing the inflation differential and exchange rate percentage change for each specific time period and then determine whether these points closely resemble the PPP line as drawn in Exhibit 8.2. If the points deviate significantly from the PPP line, then the percentage change in the foreign currency is not being affected by the inflation differential in the manner that PPP theory suggests.

This simple test of PPP is applied to four different currencies from a U.S. perspective in Exhibit 8.3 (each graph represents a particular currency). The annual difference in inflation between the United States and each foreign country is represented on the vertical axis, while the annual percentage change in the exchange rate of each foreign currency (relative to the U.S. dollar) is represented on the horizontal axis. Each point on a graph represents one year during the period 1982–2014.

Although each graph shows different results, some general comments apply to all four of them. The percentage changes in exchange rates are typically much more pronounced than the inflation differentials. The annual inflation differential between the United States and the country represented in each of the four graphs is typically small, but the annual percentage change in each currency's exchange rate against the dollar is sometimes large. Thus exchange rates commonly change to a greater extent than PPP theory would predict. Similar results would occur for most currencies of developed countries. In some years, the currency actually appreciated when its inflation was higher than U.S. inflation. Overall, the results in Exhibit 8.3 indicate that the actual relationship between inflation differentials and exchange rate movements is not consistent with PPP theory.

Statistical Test of PPP A simplified statistical test of PPP can be developed by applying regression analysis to historical exchange rates and inflation differentials (see Appendix C for more information on regression analysis). To illustrate, let's focus on one particular exchange rate. The quarterly percentage changes in the foreign currency value (e_f) can be regressed against the inflation differential that existed at the beginning of each quarter as follows:

$$e_f = a_0 + a_1 \left(\frac{1 + I_{U.S.}}{1 + I_f} - 1 \right) + \mu$$

Here a_0 is a constant, a_1 is the slope coefficient, and μ is an error term. Regression analysis would be applied to quarterly data to determine the regression coefficients. The hypothesized values of a_0 and a_1 are 0 and 1, respectively. These coefficients imply that, on average, for a given inflation differential there is an equal (offsetting) percentage change in the exchange rate. The appropriate t-test for each regression coefficient requires a comparison to the hypothesized value and division by the standard error (s.e.) of the coefficient as follows:

Test for $a_0 = 0$:   **Test for $a_1 = 1$:**

$$t = \frac{a_0 - 0}{s.e. of\ a_0} \qquad t = \frac{a_1 - 1}{s.e. of\ a_1}$$

Exhibit 8.3 Comparison of Annual Inflation Differentials and Exchange Rate Movements for Four Major Countries

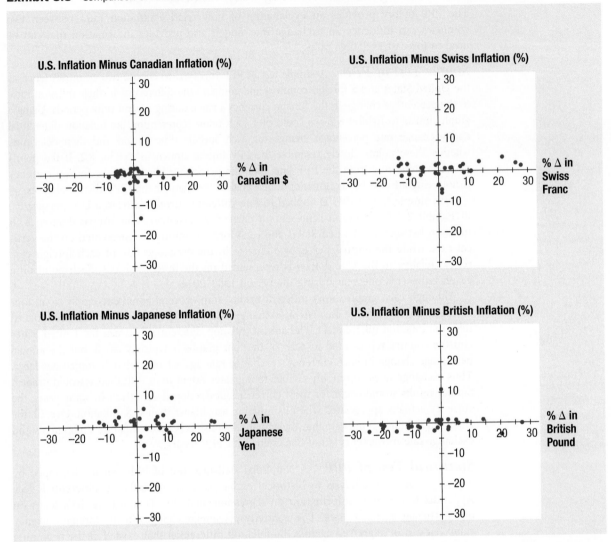

The next step is using the *t*-table to find the critical *t*-value. If either *t*-test finds that the coefficients differ significantly from what is expected, then the relationship between the inflation differential and the exchange rate is other than as stated by PPP theory. However, there is controversy over the appropriate lag time (between the inflation differential and the exchange rate) to use when making these calculations.

Results of Statistical Tests of PPP Numerous studies have been conducted to statistically test whether PPP holds. Although much research has documented how high inflation can weaken a currency's value, evidence has also been found of significant deviations from PPP. These deviations are less pronounced when longer time periods are considered, but they remain nonetheless. As a result, relying on PPP to derive a forecast of the exchange rate is subject to significant error, even for long-term forecasts.

Limitation of PPP Tests   A limitation in testing PPP theory is that the results will vary with the base period used. The base period chosen should reflect an equilibrium position because subsequent periods are evaluated in comparison with it. If the foreign currency was relatively weak for reasons other than high inflation during the base period, then most subsequent periods might erroneously show higher appreciation of that currency than predicted by PPP.

8-1g Does Purchasing Power Parity Exist?

Purchasing power parity does not normally exist because of confounding effects and because there are no substitutes for some traded products. These reasons are explained next.

Confounding Effects   The PPP theory presumes that exchange rate movements are driven completely by the inflation differential between two countries. Recall from Chapter 4, however, that a currency's spot rate is affected by several factors:

$$e_f = f(\Delta INF, \Delta INT, \Delta INC, \Delta GC, \Delta EXP)$$

where

$$e_f = \textbf{percentage change in the spot rate}$$
$$\Delta INF = \textbf{change in the differential between U.S. inflation and the foreign country's inflation}$$
$$\Delta INT = \textbf{change in the differential between the U.S. interest rate and the foreign country's interest rate}$$
$$\Delta INC = \textbf{change in the differential between the U.S. income level and the foreign country's income level}$$
$$\Delta GC = \textbf{change in government controls}$$
$$\Delta EXP = \textbf{change in expectations of future exchange rates}$$

Because exchange rate movements are not driven solely by ΔINF, the relationship between the inflation differential and exchange rate movement cannot be as simple as the PPP theory suggests.

EXAMPLE   Assume that Switzerland's inflation rate is 3 percent above the U.S. inflation rate. From this information, PPP theory would suggest that the Swiss franc should depreciate by about 3 percent against the U.S. dollar. Yet if the government of Switzerland imposes trade barriers against some U.S. exports, Switzerland's consumers and firms will not be able to adjust their spending in reaction to the inflation differential. Therefore, the exchange rate will not adjust as suggested by purchasing power parity. ●

No Substitutes for Traded Products   The idea behind PPP theory is that, as soon as prices become relatively higher in one country, consumers in the other country will stop buying imported products and instead purchase domestic products that serve as substitutes. This shift, in turn, affects the exchange rate. However, if substitute products are not available domestically, then consumers will probably continue to buy imported products.

EXAMPLE   Assume that many U.S. consumers commonly buy Swiss jewelry because they believe that the quality of the jewelry produced in Switzerland is higher than that of jewelry produced in the United States. Also assume that jewelry is the main product imported from Switzerland. If Switzerland's inflation is 3 percent higher than the U.S. inflation rate (as in the previous example), PPP suggests that U.S. consumers will shift their jewelry consumption from Switzerland (where their relative purchasing power is reduced) to the

United States (where their relative purchasing power is now stronger). Yet if the U.S. consumers think the quality of Swiss jewelry is higher, they may not view U.S. jewelry as a reasonable substitute for Swiss jewelry; thus they may continue to purchase the Swiss jewelry even though their purchasing power for Swiss jewelry is reduced. Therefore, the demand and supply conditions for the Swiss franc might not change in the manner suggested by PPP. ●

8-2 International Fisher Effect (IFE)

According to PPP, exchange rates respond to the difference in actual inflation rates of countries over the same period. But, because the actual inflation rates are not known until the period is over, they cannot be used to anticipate how exchange rates might change. Another theory, known as the **international Fisher effect (IFE) theory**, offers a specific relationship between the differential in nominal interest rates of two countries and the exchange rate movement. It suggests (1) how each country's nominal interest rate can be used to derive its expected inflation rates, and (2) how the difference in inflation rates between two countries signals an expected change in the exchange rate. These two parts are described in turn and lead to a conclusion for investors in low-interest countries who attempt to capitalize on higher interest rates in other countries.

8-2a Deriving a Country's Expected Inflation Rate

In the 1930s, the economist Irving Fisher developed a theory (now referred to as the Fisher effect) that defines the relationship between the nominal (quoted) interest rate and the expected inflation rate. The foundation of the Fisher effect is that potential savers in a country should require that their return from a local savings deposit exceed the expected rate of inflation in that country. The logic is that the savers would only be willing to save money if their savings grow at a faster rate than the prices of the products that they may buy in the future. The nominal interest rate that is offered on savings deposits represents the return to local savers, and therefore that rate should exceed the expected inflation rate in order to attract savings. This implies that the real (inflation-adjusted) interest rate should be positive:

Real interest rate = (Nominal interest rate − Expected inflation rate) > 0

By rearranging terms, the nominal interest rate can be derived as follows:

Nominal interest rate = Real interest rate + Expected inflation rate

If the real interest rate required by savers was, say, 2 percent, and if savers expected inflation to be 1 percent, then financial institutions would need to offer a nominal interest rate of 3 percent to entice potential savers to invest in deposits:

$$\textbf{Nominal interest rate} = \textbf{Real interest rate} + \textbf{Expected inflation rate}$$
$$= \textbf{2\% + 1\%}$$
$$= \textbf{3\%}$$

Assuming the real interest rate is constant over time, then any change in expected inflation over time would lead to a change in the nominal interest rate that financial institutions would have to offer on savings deposits to attract savers. For example, if expected inflation changed from 1 percent to 3 percent, financial institutions would have to offer a nominal interest rate of:

$$\text{Nominal interest rate} = \text{Real interest rate} + \text{Expected inflation rate}$$
$$= 2\% + 3\%$$
$$= 5\%$$

We cannot directly observe the expected inflation rate that a country's citizens antici-pate, because that would require obtaining the opinions of all the citizens. However, we can rearrange the terms above to derive a country's expected inflation rate:

$$\text{Expected inflation rate} = \text{Nominal interest rate} - \text{Real interest rate}$$

Thus the differential in expected inflation between countries A and B is:

$$\text{Expected inflation differential} = E(\text{INF}_A) - E(\text{INF}_B)$$
$$= (i_A - \text{Real}_A) - (i_B - \text{Real}_B)$$

Assuming that the real rate of interest required is the same for savers in all countries, $\text{Real}_A = \text{Real}_B$, the expected inflation differential can be reduced to:

$$\text{Expected inflation differential} = i_A - i_B$$

This formula is very powerful because it suggests that if the real interest rate required by savers is similar across countries, then the difference between expected inflation rates of two countries can be derived simply from the difference between their respective nominal interest rates.

EXAMPLE   Assume that the real rate of interest is 2 percent in both Canada and the United States, and assume that the nominal one-year interest rate is 13 percent in Canada versus 8 percent in the United States. Accord-ing to the Fisher effect, the expected one-year inflation rate in Canada is 13% − 2% = 11%; for the United States, it is 8% − 2% = 6%. Therefore, the difference in expected inflation over the next year between the two countries is 11% − 6% = 5%, which is equal to the difference in their nominal one-year interest rates (13% − 8% = 5%). ●

8-2b Estimating the Expected Exchange Rate Movement

Once the expected inflation rates of two countries have been derived from the nominal interest rates (based on the Fisher effect) as just described, the PPP theory can be applied to estimate how the expected inflation rate differential will affect exchange rates.

EXAMPLE   Recall from the preceding example that Canada has an expected inflation rate of 11 percent over the next year versus 6 percent in the United States. Because the expected inflation is 5 percent higher in Canada, PPP suggests that the Canadian dollar should depreciate against the U.S. dollar by about 5 percent over the next year. If the Canadian dollar depreciates by 5 percent over the next year, U.S. savers who attempted to benefit from the higher Canadian interest rate would receive 5 percent less when convert-ing Canadian dollars back to U.S. dollars than what they originally paid to obtain Canadian dollars. This would offset the 5 percent interest rate advantage that they received from investing in Canadian savings deposits instead of U.S. savings deposits. Thus their expected return from the Canadian deposits would be 8 percent, similar to the return that they could earn from a one-year savings deposit in the United States. Consequently, U.S. savers would not benefit from investing in Canadian savings deposits. ●

8-2c Implications of the International Fisher Effect

If the IFE holds, countries with high interest rates should exhibit high expected inflation (as explained by the Fisher effect), so that the currencies of these countries with relatively high expected inflation will depreciate (based on adapting the PPP theory). The level of expected depreciation is equal to the differential in nominal interest rates, which suggests that the expected depreciation should offset the advantage from investing in savings deposits in the high-interest-rate country. This implies that when U.S. nominal interest rates are relatively low, U.S. investors and MNCs would not benefit from investing in interest-bearing deposits in countries with higher interest rates.

Implications of the IFE for Foreign Investors   The implications are similar if foreign investors in countries with relatively low nominal interest rates attempt to capitalize on relatively high U.S. interest rates.

EXAMPLE   Suppose the nominal one-year interest rate is 8 percent in the United States and 5 percent in Japan, and suppose the real rate of interest is 2 percent in each country. According to the Fisher effect, the U.S. inflation rate over the next year is expected to be 6 percent (nominal interest rate of 8 percent minus real interest rate of 2 percent) while the inflation rate in Japan over the next year is expected to be 3 percent (nominal interest rate of 5 percent minus real interest rate of 2 percent). Therefore, the difference in expected inflation (U.S. expected inflation minus Japanese expected inflation) is 3 percent. Notice, once again, that the difference in expected inflation between the two countries over the next year is equal to the difference in their nominal one-year interest rates.

Applying PPP theory to the expected inflation rates of the two countries, the Japanese yen is expected to appreciate against the dollar by the expected inflation differential of 3 percent. If the Japanese yen appreciates by 3 percent over the next year, Japanese savers who attempted to benefit from the relatively high U.S. interest rate would receive 3 percent less when converting U.S. dollars back to Japanese yen at the end of the year than what they originally paid to obtain U.S. dollars. This offsets the 3 percent interest rate advantage that they would receive from investing in U.S. savings deposits instead of Japanese savings deposits. Thus their expected return from the U.S. savings deposits is 5 percent, which is similar to the return that they could earn from a one-year savings deposit in Japan. Consequently, Japanese. savers would not benefit from investing in the U.S. savings deposits. ●

Implications of the IFE for Two Non-U.S. Currencies   The international Fisher effect also applies to exchange rates involving the currencies of any two non-U.S. countries whose exchange rate systems allow exchange rates to float.

EXAMPLE   Continue with the assumption that the nominal one-year interest rate is 13 percent in Canada and 5 percent in Japan, and suppose that the real interest rate is 2 percent for savers in each country. The difference in expected inflation between Canada and Japan is 8 percent, which, applying PPP theory, should cause the Canadian dollar to depreciate by about 8 percent against the yen. Therefore, even though Japanese savers would earn an additional 8 percent interest on a Canadian savings deposit, they would receive 8 percent less when converting the Canadian dollars back to Japanese yen at the end of the year than what they originally paid for the Canadian dollars. This offsets the 8 percent interest rate advantage that they would receive from investing in Canadian savings deposits instead of Japanese savings deposits. Thus their expected return from the Canadian savings deposit is 5 percent, which is similar to the return that they could earn from a one-year savings deposit in Japan. Consequently, Japanese savers would not benefit from investing in the Canadian savings deposits. ●

Implications from Using Alternative Assumed Real Interest Rate   In the example above, the real interest rate was assumed to be 2 percent for both countries. If the real interest rate was instead assumed to be 1 percent for both countries, the difference in the two countries' expected inflation rates would still be the same, and so the conclusions in the example would also still be the same. As long as the real interest rates are assumed to be the same for the two countries that are being assessed, the difference in expected inflation rates can be derived simply from the difference in nominal interest rates between the two countries, and the conclusions would still be the same.

Implications if the Offsetting Effect Is Not Perfect   The exchange rate will not always respond to the difference in country inflation rates exactly as suggested by the IFE in every period. Thus the exchange rate's movement might not fully offset the interest rate advantage in some periods, allowing investors based in countries with low interest rates to benefit from investing in the high-interest-rate country. In other periods, the exchange rate movement might more than offset the interest rate advantage, thereby causing investors based in low-interest-rate countries to be worse off from investing in the high-interest-rate country. But the IFE theory would suggest that over several periods, the exchange rate effect should fully offset the interest rate advantage on average. Thus savers based in low-interest-rate countries will not earn higher returns on average from periodically investing in high-interest-rate countries than what they can earn domestically.

Exhibit 8.4 summarizes how the IFE theory applies to the three examples described above. Notice that the interest rate differential (second column) is equal to the expected inflation rate differential (third column) between two countries, which is equal to the degree by which the currency in the relatively high interest rate country should depreciate (fourth column). That is, a relatively high interest rate reflects a relatively high expected inflation rate, which should cause depreciation of the currency in the high-interest-rate country. This exhibit illustrates how, according to the IFE, the exchange rate movement (fourth column) is expected to offset the interest rate advantage (second

Exhibit 8.4   Summary of Application of the International Fisher Effect to Three Different Investment Scenarios

INITIAL INFORMATION ASSUMED IN THE EXAMPLES		
COUNTRY	PREVAILING NOMINAL ONE-YEAR INTEREST RATE	REAL INTEREST RATE REQUIRED BY SAVERS
Canada	13%	2%
United States	8%	2%
Japan	5%	2%

APPLICATION OF THE INTERNATIONAL FISHER EFFECT (IFE)					
SCENARIO	NOMINAL INTEREST RATE DIFFERENTIAL OF FOREIGN SAVINGS DEPOSIT VERSUS HOME DEPOSIT	EXPECTED INFLATION DIFFERENTIAL BETWEEN FOREIGN COUNTRY AND HOME COUNTRY (BASED ON FISHER EFFECT)	EXPECTED EXCHANGE RATE MOVEMENT DERIVED FROM APPLYING PPP TO EXPECTED INFLATION DIFFERENTIAL	EXPECTED RETURN ON FOREIGN SAVINGS DEPOSIT	RETURN TO SAVER WHO INVESTS IN HOME SAVINGS DEPOSIT
U.S. investor invests in Canadian bank deposit	13% − 8% = 5%	11% − 6% = 5%	−5%	13% − 5% = 8%	8%
Japanese investor invests in U.S. savings deposit	8% − 5% = 3%	6% − 3% = 3%	−3%	8% − 3% = 5%	5%
Japanese investor invests in Canadian savings deposit	13% − 5% = 8%	11% − 3% = 8%	−8%	13% − 8% = 5%	5%

WEB

www.newyorkfed.org
Exchange rate and
interest rate data for
various countries.

column), such that the expected return to investors from investing in the foreign savings deposit (fifth column) is no better than the return they could have earned domestically (sixth column).

8-2d Derivation of the International Fisher Effect

According to the IFE, the precise relationship between the nominal interest rate differential of two countries and the expected exchange rate change can be derived as follows. Note that the actual return to investors who invest in money market securities (such as short-term bank deposits) in their home country is simply the nominal interest rate offered on those securities. However, the actual return to investors who invest in a foreign money market security depends not only on the foreign interest rate (i_f) but also the percentage change in the value of the foreign currency (e_f) denominating that security. The formula for the actual or "effective" (exchange rate–adjusted) return on a foreign bank deposit, or any other money market security, is

$$r = 1(1 + i_f)(1 + e_f) - 1$$

The IFE theory states that the effective return on a foreign investment should, on average, be equal to the interest rate on a local money market investment:

$$E(r) = i_h$$

where r is the effective return on the foreign deposit and i_h is the interest rate on the home deposit. Hence we can determine the degree by which the foreign currency must change in order to make investments in both countries generate similar returns. Take the previous formula defining r and set it equal to i_h as follows:

$$r = i_h$$
$$(1 + i_f)(1 + e_f) - 1 = i_h$$

Now solve for e_f

$$(1 + i_f)(1 + e_f) = 1 + i_h$$
$$1 + e_f = \frac{1 + i_h}{1 + i_f}$$
$$e_f = \frac{1 + i_h}{1 + i_f} - 1$$

As verified here, the IFE theory contends that if $i_h > i_f$, then e_f will be positive because the relatively low foreign interest rate reflects relatively low inflationary expectations in the foreign country. That is, the foreign currency will appreciate when the foreign interest rate is lower than the home interest rate. This appreciation will improve the foreign return to investors from the home country, making returns on foreign securities similar to returns on home securities. Conversely, if $i_f > i_h$, then e_f will be negative. That is, the foreign currency will depreciate when the foreign interest rate exceeds the home interest rate. This depreciation will reduce the return on foreign securities from the perspective of investors in the home country, making returns on foreign securities no higher than returns on home securities.

Numerical Example Based on Derivation of the IFE   Given two interest rates, the value of e_f can be determined from the formula just derived and then used to forecast the exchange rate.

EXAMPLE

Assume that the interest rate on a one-year insured home country bank deposit is 11 percent, and the interest rate on a one-year insured foreign bank deposit is 12 percent. For the actual returns of these two investments to be similar from the perspective of investors in the home country, the foreign currency would have to change over the investment horizon by the following percentage:

$$e_f = \frac{1 + i_h}{1 + i_f} - 1$$
$$= \frac{1 + .11}{1 + .12} - 1$$
$$= -.0089, \text{ or } -89\%$$

In other words, the foreign currency denominating the foreign deposit would need to depreciate by .89 percent to make the actual return on the foreign deposit equal to 11 percent from the perspective of investors in the home country. That amount of depreciation would make the return on the foreign investment equal to the return on a domestic investment. ●

The theory of the international Fisher effect is summarized in Exhibit 8.5. Notice that this exhibit is similar to the summary of PPP in Exhibit 8.1. In particular, international trade is the mechanism by which the nominal interest rate differential affects the

Exhibit 8.5   Summary of International Fisher Effect

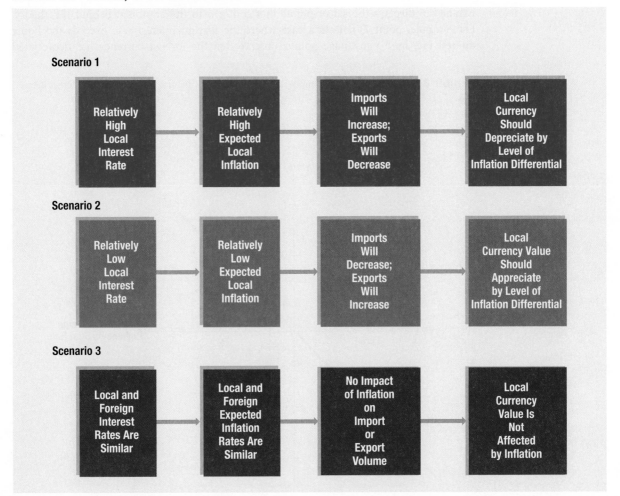

exchange rate (according to IFE theory). This means that the IFE is more applicable when the two countries of concern engage in considerable international trade with each other. If there is not much trade between the two countries, their inflation differential should not have a major impact on that trade, and there is no reason for expecting that the exchange rate will change in response to the interest rate differential. So in this case, even a large interest rate differential (which signals a large differential in expected inflation) would have a negligible effect on trade between the countries. Investors might then be more willing to invest in a foreign country with a high interest rate, although the currency of that country could still weaken for other reasons.

Simplified Relationship   A simplified (but less precise) relationship specified by the IFE is

$$e_f \approx i_h - i_f$$

That is, the percentage change in the exchange rate over the investment horizon will equal the interest rate differential between two countries. This approximation provides reasonable estimates only when the interest rate differential is small.

8-2e Graphic Analysis of the International Fisher Effect

Exhibit 8.6 displays the set of points that conform to the argument behind IFE theory. For example, point E reflects a case where the foreign interest rate exceeds the home interest rate by 3 percentage points; observe that the foreign currency has depreciated

Exhibit 8.6   Illustration of IFE Line (When Exchange Rate Changes Perfectly Offset Interest Rate Differentials)

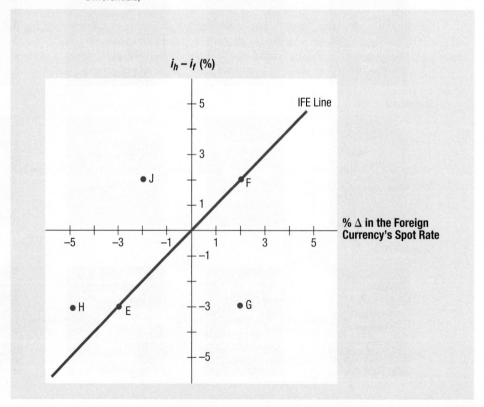

by 3 percent to offset its interest rate advantage. Thus an investor setting up a deposit in the foreign country achieves a return similar to what is possible domestically. Point F represents a home interest rate that is 2 percent above the foreign interest rate. In this case, investors from the home country who establish a foreign deposit must accept a lower interest rate; however, IFE theory suggests that the currency should appreciate by 2 percent to offset that interest rate disadvantage.

Point F in Exhibit 8.6 also illustrates the IFE from a foreign investor's perspective, for whom the home interest rate will appear attractive. However, IFE theory suggests that the foreign currency will appreciate by 2 percent; from the foreign investor's perspective, this implies that the home country's currency denominating the investment instruments will depreciate to offset the interest rate advantage.

Points on the IFE Line   All the points along the **international Fisher effect (IFE) line** in Exhibit 8.6 reflect exchange rate adjustments to offset the differential in interest rates. This means that when accounting for the exchange rate movements, investors will end up achieving the same return (yield) whether they invest at home or in a foreign country.

Points below the IFE Line   Points below the IFE line generally reflect the higher returns from investing in foreign deposits. For example, point G in Exhibit 8.6 indicates that the foreign interest rate exceeds the home interest rate by 3 percent. In addition, the foreign currency has appreciated by 2 percent. The combination of the higher foreign interest rate plus the appreciation of the foreign currency will cause the foreign return to be higher than what is possible domestically. If actual data were compiled and plotted and if the vast majority of points were below the IFE line, this would suggest that home country investors could consistently increase their investment returns by establishing foreign bank deposits. Such results would refute the IFE theory.

Points above the IFE Line   Points above the IFE line generally reflect returns from foreign deposits that are lower than the returns that are possible domestically. For example, point H reflects a foreign interest rate that is 3 percent above the home interest rate. Yet point H also indicates that the exchange rate of the foreign currency has depreciated by 5 percent, more than offsetting its interest rate advantage.

As another example, point J represents the case where a home country investor is discouraged from investing in a foreign deposit for two reasons. First, the foreign interest rate is lower than the home interest rate. Second, the foreign currency depreciates during the time the foreign deposit is held. If actual data were compiled and plotted and if the vast majority of points were above the IFE line, this would suggest that home country investors would consistently receive lower returns from foreign than from home country investments. Such results would also refute the IFE theory.

WEB

www.economagic.com
U.S. inflation and
exchange rate data.

8-2f Testing the International Fisher Effect

If the actual points (one for each period) of interest rates and exchange rate changes were plotted over time on a graph such as Exhibit 8.6, we could determine whether the points are systematically below the IFE line (suggesting higher returns from foreign investing than domestic investing), above the line (suggesting lower returns from foreign investing than domestic investing), or evenly scattered on both sides (suggesting a balance of higher returns from foreign investing than domestic investing in some periods and lower foreign returns than domestic investing in other periods). If foreign money market securities (such as bank deposits) are expected to provide about the same yield as domestic money market securities on average, then a U.S. firm would probably prefer domestic money market securities. The firm would know its return on domestic money market securities in advance, whereas the return to be attained from foreign money market securities would be uncertain because of fluctuations in the spot exchange rate.

Statistical Test of the IFE   A simple statistical test of the IFE can be developed by applying regression analysis to historical exchange rates and the nominal interest rate differential:

$$e_f = a_0 + a_1 \left(\frac{1 + i_{U.S.}}{1 + i_f} - 1 \right) + \mu$$

Here a_0 is a constant, a_1 is the coefficient's slope, and μ is an error term. Regression analysis would determine the regression coefficients. It is hypothesized that $a_0 = 0$ and $a_1 = 1$.

Just as in the case of testing the PPP, here the appropriate t-test for each regression coefficient requires a comparison to the hypothesized value and then division by the standard error (s.e.) of the coefficients.

$$\text{Test for } a_0 = 0 : \quad \text{Test for } a_1 = 1 :$$
$$t = \frac{a_0 - 0}{s.e. \text{of } a_0} \qquad t = \frac{a_1 - 1}{s.e. \text{of } a_1}$$

The t-table is then used to find the critical t-value. If either t-test finds that the coefficients differ significantly from what was hypothesized, then the IFE is refuted.

8-2g Limitations of the IFE Theory

The IFE theory is subject to some limitations that explain why it does not consistently hold. Recall that the IFE proposes (1) how each country's nominal interest rate can be used to derive its expected inflation rate, and (2) how the difference in inflation rates between two countries signals an expected change in the exchange rate. There are limitations to each of these components, as explained next.

Limitation of Deriving the Expected Inflation Rate   The derivation of a country's expected inflation rate from its nominal interest rate will not always be accurate. If you compare the expected inflation rate of a country (derived from the nominal interest rate) in any given period to the country's actual inflation rate in that same period, you will find that there is sometimes a discrepancy. If a country's nominal interest rate does not properly predict its level of inflation over a period, the difference in nominal interest rates between two countries may not serve as an accurate predictor of the exchange rate movement, even if exchange rates move exactly as suggested when applying PPP. That is, an estimate will be subject to error if the input used in the estimation procedure is itself subject to error.

Limitation of PPP   The IFE is limited because it relies on the PPP relationship between inflation and exchange rates, which is subject to error. In particular, there are other country characteristics besides inflation (such as income levels and government controls) that can affect exchange rate movements. Thus even if the expected inflation derived from the nominal interest rate (according to the Fisher effect) properly reflects the actual inflation rate over the period, relying solely on inflation to forecast the future exchange rate is subject to error.

8-2h IFE Theory versus Reality

The IFE theory contradicts the arguments in Chapter 4 about how a country with a high interest rate can attract more capital flows and therefore cause the local currency's value to strengthen. The IFE theory also contradicts the arguments in Chapter 6 about how a central bank may purposely try to raise interest rates in order to attract funds and strengthen the value of its local currency. In reality, a currency with a high interest rate strengthens in some situations, which is consistent with the points made in Chapters 4 and 6 but contrary to the IFE. Many MNCs frequently invest in money market securities in developed foreign countries where they can earn a slightly higher interest rate. They may believe that the higher interest rate advantage of the foreign money market securities is due to factors other than higher expected inflation or that any impact of inflation will not offset the interest rate advantage over the investment horizon.

Whether the IFE actually holds depends on the countries involved and also on the periods that are assessed. The IFE theory may be especially meaningful in cases when MNCs and large investors consider investing in countries where prevailing interest rates are extremely high. These countries tend to be less developed and to have higher inflation, and their currencies tend to weaken substantially over time. The depreciation in the currencies of these countries could more than offset the interest rate advantage and might even cause U.S. investors to experience a loss on their money market investments. Investors could also experience a loss on money market investments in developed countries, but the likelihood of inflation causing a substantial depreciation of their currencies is much lower.

8-2i Comparison of IRP, PPP, and IFE Theories

At this point, it may be helpful to compare three related theories of international finance: interest rate parity (IRP), discussed in Chapter 7; purchasing power parity (PPP); and the international Fisher effect (IFE). Exhibit 8.7 summarizes the main themes of each theory. Even though all three of these theories relate to the determination of exchange rates, they have different implications. The IRP theory focuses on why the forward rate differs from the spot rate and on how much the difference should be at a specific point in time. In contrast, the PPP theory and IFE theory both focus on how a currency's spot rate will change over time. Whereas PPP theory suggests that the spot rate will change in accordance with the inflation differential between two countries, IFE theory suggests that it will change in accordance with the nominal interest rate differential (and therefore in accordance with the expected inflation rate differential) between two countries. The IFE relies on the Fisher effect to determine how the differential in expected inflation rates between two countries can be measured based on the prevailing nominal interest rate differential, and then it applies PPP theory to predict how the exchange rate between the two countries will change based on the differential in expected inflation rates.

Some generalizations about countries can be made by applying these theories. High-inflation countries tend to have high nominal interest rates (due to the Fisher effect). Their currencies tend to weaken over time (because of the PPP and IFE), and the forward rates of their currencies normally have large discounts (due to IRP).

Financial managers who believe in PPP recognize that the exchange rate movement in any particular period will not always move according to the inflation differential between the two countries of concern. Even so, these managers may still rely on the inflation differential in order to derive their best guess of the expected exchange rate movement. Financial managers who believe in the IFE recognize that the exchange rate in any

Exhibit 8.7   Comparison of the IRP, PPP, and IFE Theories

THEORY	KEY VARIABLES OF THEORY		SUMMARY OF THEORY
Interest rate parity (IRP)	Forward rate premium (or discount)	Nominal interest rate differential	The forward rate of one currency with respect to another will contain a premium (or discount) that is determined by the differential in interest rates between the two countries. As a result, covered interest arbitrage will provide a return that is no higher than a domestic return.
Purchasing power parity (PPP)	Percentage change in spot exchange rate	Inflation rate differential	The spot rate of one currency with respect to another will change in reaction to the differential in inflation rates between the two countries. Consequently, the purchasing power for consumers when purchasing products in their own country will be similar to their purchasing power when importing products from the foreign country.
International Fisher effect (IFE)	Percentage change in spot exchange rate	Nominal interest rate differential	The spot rate of one currency with respect to another will change in accordance with the differential in nominal interest rates between the two countries (and thus with the expected inflation rate differential). Consequently, the return to investors from investing in foreign money market securities will, on average, be no higher than the return on domestic money market securities.

particular period will not always move according to the nominal interest rate differential between the two countries of concern; yet they may still rely on the nominal interest rate differential in order to derive their best guess of the expected exchange rate movement.

SUMMARY

- Purchasing power parity (PPP) theory specifies a precise relationship between the relative inflation rates of two countries and their exchange rate. PPP theory suggests that the equilibrium exchange rate will adjust by about the same magnitude as the difference between the two countries' inflation rates. While there is evidence of significant real-world deviations from the theory, PPP offers a logical explanation for why currencies of countries with high inflation tend to weaken over time.

■ The international Fisher effect (IFE) specifies a precise relationship between relative nominal interest rates of two countries and their exchange rates. It suggests that an investor who periodically invests in interest-bearing foreign securities will, on average, achieve a return similar to what is possible domestically. This implies that the currency of the country with high nominal interest rates will depreciate to offset the interest rate advantage achieved by foreign investments. Yet there is evidence that the IFE does not hold during all periods, which means that investment in foreign short-term securities may achieve a higher return than what is possible domestically. However, a firm that attempts to achieve this higher return also incurs the risk that the currency denominating the foreign security depreciates against the investor's home currency during the investment period by more than the nominal interest rate differential. In that case, the foreign security would generate a lower return than a domestic security even though it has a higher nominal interest rate.

POINT COUNTER-POINT

Does PPP Eliminate Concerns about Long-Term Exchange Rate Risk?

Point   Yes. Studies have shown that exchange rate movements are related to inflation differentials in the long run. Based on PPP, the currency of a high-inflation country will depreciate against the dollar. A subsidiary in that country should generate inflated revenue from the inflation, which will help offset the adverse exchange effects when its earnings are remitted to the parent. If a firm is focused on long-term performance, the deviations from PPP will offset over time. In some years, the exchange rate effects may exceed the inflation effects, and in other years the inflation effects will exceed the exchange rate effects.

Counter-Point   No. Even if the relationship between inflation and exchange rate effects is consistent, this does not guarantee that the effects on the firm will be offsetting. A subsidiary in a high-inflation country will not necessarily be able to adjust its price level to keep up with the increased costs of doing business there. The effects vary with each MNC's situation. Even if the subsidiary can raise its prices to match the rising costs, there are short-term deviations from PPP. The investors who invest in an MNC's stock may be concerned about short-term deviations from PPP because they will not necessarily hold the stock for the long term. Thus investors may prefer that firms manage in a manner that reduces the volatility in their performance in short-run and long-run periods.

Who Is Correct?   Use the Internet to learn more about this issue. Which argument do you support? Offer your own opinion on this issue.

SELF-TEST

Answers are provided in Appendix A at the back of the text.

1.   A U.S. importer of Japanese computer components pays for the components in yen. The importer is not concerned about a possible increase in Japanese prices (charged in yen) because of the likely offsetting effect caused by purchasing power parity (PPP). Explain what this means.

2.   Use what you know about tests of PPP to answer this question. Using the information in the first question, explain why the U.S. importer of Japanese computer components should be concerned about its future payments.

3.   Use PPP to explain how the values of the currencies of Eastern European countries might change if those countries experience high inflation, while the United States experiences low inflation.

4.   Assume that the Canadian dollar's spot rate is $.85 and that the Canadian and U.S. inflation rates are similar. Then assume that Canada experiences 4 percent inflation, while the United States experiences 3 percent inflation. According to PPP, what will be the new value of the Canadian dollar after it adjusts to the inflationary changes? (You may use the approximate formula to answer this question.)

5. Assume that the Australian dollar's spot rate is $.90 and that the Australian and U.S. one-year interest rates are initially 6 percent. Then assume that the Australian one-year interest rate increases by 5 percentage points, while the U.S. one-year interest rate remains unchanged. Using this information and the international Fisher effect (IFE) theory, forecast the spot rate for one year ahead.

6. In the previous question, the Australian interest rates increased from 6 to 11 percent. According to the IFE, what is the underlying factor that would cause such a change? Give an explanation based on the IFE of the forces that would cause a change in the Australian dollar. If U.S. investors believe in the IFE, will they attempt to capitalize on the higher Australian interest rates? Explain.

QUESTIONS AND APPLICATIONS

1. PPP Explain the theory of purchasing power parity (PPP). Based on this theory, what is a general forecast of the values of currencies in countries with high inflation?

2. Rationale of PPP Explain the rationale of the PPP theory.

3. Testing PPP Explain how you could determine whether PPP exists. Describe a limitation in testing whether PPP holds.

4. Testing PPP Inflation differentials between the United States and other industrialized countries have typically been a few percentage points in any given year. Yet, in many years annual exchange rates between the corresponding currencies have changed by 10 percent or more. What does this information suggest about PPP?

5. Limitations of PPP Explain why PPP does not hold.

6. Implications of IFE Explain the international Fisher effect (IFE). What is the rationale for the existence of the IFE? What are the implications of the IFE for firms with excess cash that consistently invest in foreign Treasury bills? Explain why the IFE may not hold.

7. Implications of IFE Assume U.S. interest rates are generally above foreign interest rates. What does this suggest about the future strength or weakness of the dollar based on the IFE? Should U.S. investors invest in foreign securities if they believe in the IFE? Should foreign investors invest in U.S. securities if they believe in the IFE?

8. Comparing Parity Theories Compare and contrast interest rate parity (discussed in the previous chapter), purchasing power parity (PPP), and the international Fisher effect (IFE).

9. Real Interest Rate One assumption made in developing the IFE is that all investors in all countries have the same real interest rate. What does this mean?

10. Interpreting Inflationary Expectations If investors in the United States and Canada require the same real interest rate, and the nominal rate of interest is 2 percent higher in Canada, what does this imply about expectations of U.S. inflation and Canadian inflation? What do these inflationary expectations suggest about future exchange rates?

11. PPP Applied to the Euro Assume that several European countries that use the euro as their currency experience higher inflation than the United States, while two other European countries that use the euro as their currency experience lower inflation than the United States. According to PPP, how will the euro's value against the dollar be affected?

12. Source of Weak Currencies Currencies of some Latin American countries, such as Brazil and Venezuela, frequently weaken against most other currencies. What concept in this chapter explains this occurrence? Why don't all U.S.-based MNCs use forward contracts to hedge their future remittances of funds from Latin American countries to the United States if they expect depreciation of the currencies against the dollar?

13. PPP Japan has typically had lower inflation than the United States. How would one expect this to affect the Japanese yen's value? Why does this expected relationship not always occur?

14. IFE Assume that the nominal interest rate in Mexico is 48 percent and the interest rate in the United States is 8 percent for one-year securities that are free from default risk. What does the IFE suggest about the differential in expected inflation in these two countries? Using this information and the PPP theory, describe the expected nominal return to U.S. investors who invest in Mexico.

15. IFE Shouldn't the IFE discourage investors from attempting to capitalize on higher foreign interest rates? Why do some investors continue to invest overseas, even when they have no other transactions overseas?

16. Changes in Inflation Assume that the inflation rate in Brazil is expected to increase substantially. How will this affect Brazil's nominal interest rates and the value of its currency (called the real)? If the IFE holds, how will the nominal return to U.S. investors who invest in Brazil be affected by the higher inflation in Brazil? Explain.

17. Comparing PPP and IFE How is it possible for PPP to hold if the IFE does not?

18. Estimating Depreciation Due to PPP Assume that the spot exchange rate of the British pound is $1.73. How will this spot rate adjust according to PPP if the United Kingdom experiences an inflation rate of 7 percent while the United States experiences an inflation rate of 2 percent?

19. Forecasting the Future Spot Rate Based on IFE Assume that the spot exchange rate of the Singapore dollar is $.70. The one-year interest rate is 11 percent in the United States and 7 percent in Singapore. What will the spot rate be in one year according to the IFE? What is the force that causes the spot rate to change according to the IFE?

20. Deriving Forecasts of the Future Spot Rate As of today, assume the following information is available:

	U.S.	MEXICO
Real rate of interest required by investors	2%	2%
Nominal interest rate	11%	15%
Spot rate	—	$.20
One-year forward rate	—	$.19

a. Use the forward rate to forecast the percentage change in the Mexican peso over the next year.

b. Use the differential in expected inflation to forecast the percentage change in the Mexican peso over the next year.

c. Use the spot rate to forecast the percentage change in the Mexican peso over the next year.

21. Inflation Effects in Russia Russia commonly experiences a high rate of inflation.

a. Explain why the high Russian inflation typically places severe downward pressure on the value of the Russian ruble.

b. In some periods, the Russian government intervenes in the foreign exchange market and imposes some restrictions on international trade. Why might these conditions prevent purchasing power parity (PPP)?

c. Will the effects of the high Russian inflation and the decline in the ruble offset each other for U.S. importers? That is, how will U.S. importers of Russian products be affected by the conditions?

22. IFE Application to Brazil Brazil commonly has a much higher nominal interest rate than the United States. Yet some large institutional investors do not invest in Brazilian money market securities, even when they believe the securities have no credit (default) risk. Use the international Fisher effect (IFE) to explain why the Brazilian money market securities may not be a good investment for U.S. investors.

23. IFE Applied to the Euro Given the conversion of several European currencies to the euro, explain what would cause the euro's value to change against the dollar according to the IFE.

Advanced Questions

24. IFE Beth Miller does not believe that the international Fisher effect (IFE) holds. Current one-year interest rates in Europe are 5 percent, while one-year interest rates in the United States are 3 percent. Beth converts $100,000 to euros and invests them in Germany. One year later, she converts the euros back to dollars. The current spot rate of the euro is $1.10.

a. According to the IFE, what should the spot rate of the euro in one year be?

b. If the spot rate of the euro in one year is $1.00, what is Beth's percentage return from her strategy?

c. If the spot rate of the euro in one year is $1.08, what is Beth's percentage return from her strategy?

d. What must the spot rate of the euro be in one year for Beth's strategy to be successful?

25. Integrating IRP and IFE Assume the following information is available for the United States and Europe:

	U.S.	EUROPE
Nominal interest rate	4%	6%
Expected inflation	2%	5%
Spot rate	—	$1.13
One-year forward rate	—	$1.10

a. Does IRP hold?

b. According to PPP, what is the expected spot rate of the euro in one year?

c. According to the IFE, what is the expected spot rate of the euro in one year?

d. Reconcile your answers to parts (a) and (c).

26. IRP The one-year risk-free interest rate in Mexico is 10 percent. The one-year risk-free rate in the United States is 2 percent. Assume that interest rate parity exists. The spot rate of the Mexican peso is $.14.

a. What is the forward rate premium?

b. What is the one-year forward rate of the peso?

c. Based on the international Fisher effect, what is the expected change in the spot rate over the next year?

d. If the spot rate changes as expected according to the IFE, what will be the spot rate in one year?

e. Compare your answers to (b) and (d) and explain the relationship.

27. Testing the PPP How could you use regression analysis to determine whether the relationship specified by PPP exists on average? Specify the model, and describe how you would assess the regression results to determine if there is *a significant* difference from the relationship suggested by PPP.

28. Testing the IFE Describe a statistical test for the IFE.

29. Impact of Barriers on PPP and IFE Would PPP be more likely to hold between the United States and Hungary if trade barriers were completely removed and if Hungary's currency were allowed to float without any government intervention? Would the IFE be more likely to hold between the United States and Hungary if trade barriers were completely removed and if Hungary's currency were allowed to float without any government intervention? Explain.

30. Interactive Effects of PPP Assume that the inflation rates of the countries that use the euro are very low, while other European countries that have their own currencies experience high inflation. Explain how and why the euro's value could be expected to change against these currencies according to the PPP theory.

31. Applying IRP and IFE Assume that Mexico has a one-year interest rate that is higher than the U.S. one-year interest rate. Assume that you believe in the international Fisher effect (IFE) and interest rate parity. Assume zero transaction costs.

Ed is based in the United States and attempts to speculate by purchasing Mexican pesos today, investing the pesos in a risk-free asset for a year, and then converting the pesos to dollars at the end of one year.

Ed did not cover his position in the forward market. Maria is based in Mexico and attempts covered interest arbitrage by purchasing dollars today and simultaneously selling dollars one year forward, investing the dollars in a risk-free asset for a year, and then converting the dollars back to pesos at the end of one year.

Do you think the rate of return on Ed's investment will be higher than, lower than, or the same as the rate of return on Maria's investment? Explain.

32. Arbitrage and PPP Assume that locational arbitrage ensures that spot exchange rates are properly aligned. Also assume that you believe in purchasing power parity. The spot rate of the British pound is $1.80. The spot rate of the Swiss franc is .3 pounds. You expect that the one-year inflation rate is 7 percent in the United Kingdom, 5 percent in Switzerland, and 1 percent in the United States. The one-year interest rate is 6 percent in the United Kingdom, 2 percent in Switzerland, and 4 percent in the United States. What is your expected spot rate of the Swiss franc in one year with respect to the U.S. dollar? Show your work.

33. IRP versus IFE You believe that interest rate parity and the international Fisher effect hold. Assume that the U.S. interest rate is presently much higher than the New Zealand interest rate. You have receivables of 1 million New Zealand dollars that you will receive in one year. You could hedge the receivables with the one-year forward contract. Or, you could decide to not hedge. Is your expected U.S. dollar amount of the receivables in one year from hedging higher, lower, or the same as your expected U.S. dollar amount of the receivables without hedging? Explain.

34. IRP, PPP, and Speculation The U.S. 3-month interest rate (unannualized) is 1 percent. The Canadian 3-month interest rate (unannualized) is 4 percent. Interest rate parity exists. The expected inflation over this period is 5 percent in the United States and 2 percent in Canada. A call option with a 3-month expiration date on Canadian dollars is available for a premium of $.02 and a strike price of $.64. The spot rate of the Canadian dollar is $.65. Assume that you believe in purchasing power parity.

a. Determine the dollar amount of your profit or loss from buying a call option contract specifying C$100,000.

b. Determine the dollar amount of your profit or loss from buying a futures contract specifying C$100,000.

35. Implications of PPP Today's spot rate of the Mexican peso is $.10. Assume that purchasing power parity holds. The U.S. inflation rate over this year is expected to be 7 percent, while the Mexican inflation over this year is expected to be 3 percent. Wake Forest Co. plans to import from Mexico and will need 20 million Mexican pesos in one year. Determine the expected amount of dollars to be paid by the Wake Forest Co. for the pesos in one year.

36. Investment Implications of IRP and IFE The Argentine one-year CD (deposit) rate is 13 percent, while the Mexican one-year CD rate is 11 percent and the U.S. one-year CD rate is 6 percent. All CDs have zero default risk. Interest rate parity holds, and you believe that the international Fisher effect holds.

> Jamie (based in the United States) invests in a one-year CD in Argentina.
> Ann (based in the United States) invests in a one-year CD in Mexico.
> Ken (based in the United States) invests in a one-year CD in Argentina and sells Argentine pesos one year forward to cover his position.
> Juan (who lives in Argentina) invests in a one-year CD in the United States.
> Maria (who lives in Mexico) invests in a one-year CD in the United States.
> Nina (who lives in Mexico) invests in a one-year CD in Argentina.
> Carmen (who lives in Argentina) invests in a one-year CD in Mexico and sells Mexican pesos one year forward to cover her position.
> Corio (who lives in Mexico) invests in a one-year CD in Argentina and sells Argentine pesos one year forward to cover his position.

Based on this information and assuming the international Fisher effect holds, which person will be expected to earn the highest return on the funds invested? If you believe that multiple persons will tie for the highest expected return, name each of them. Explain.

37. Investment Implications of IRP and the IFE Today, a U.S. dollar can be exchanged for 3 New Zealand dollars. The one-year CD (deposit) rate in New Zealand is 7 percent, and the one-year CD rate in the United States is 6 percent. Interest rate parity exists between the United States and New Zealand. The international Fisher effect exists between the United States and New Zealand. Today a U.S. dollar can be exchanged for 2 Swiss francs. The one-year CD rate in Switzerland is 5 percent. The spot rate of the Swiss franc is the same as the one-year forward rate.

> Karen (based in the United States) invests in a one-year CD in New Zealand and sells New Zealand dollars one year forward to cover her position.
> James (based in the United States) invests in a one-year CD in New Zealand and does not cover his position.
> Brian (based in the United States) invests in a one-year CD in Switzerland and sells Swiss francs one year forward to cover his position.
> Eric (who lives in Switzerland) invests in a one-year CD in Switzerland.
> Tonya (who lives in New Zealand) invests in a one-year CD in the United States and sells U.S. dollars one year forward to cover her position.

Based on this information, which person will be expected to earn the highest return on the funds invested? If you believe that multiple persons will tie for the highest expected return, name each of them. Explain.

38. Real Interest Rates, Expected Inflation, IRP, and the Spot Rate The United States and the country of Rueland have the same real interest rate of 3 percent. The expected inflation over the next year is 6 percent in the United States versus 21 percent in Rueland. Interest rate parity exists. The one-year currency futures contract on Rueland's currency (called the ru) is priced at $.40 per ru. What is the spot rate of the ru?

39. PPP and Real Interest Rates The nominal (quoted) U.S. one-year interest rate is 6 percent, while the nominal one-year interest rate in Canada is 5 percent. Assume you believe in purchasing power parity. You believe the real one-year interest rate is 2 percent in the United States, and that the real one-year interest rate is 3 percent in Canada. Today the Canadian dollar spot rate is $.90. What do you think the spot rate of the Canadian dollar will be in one year?

40. IFE, Cross Exchange Rates, and Cash Flows
Assume the Hong Kong dollar (HK$) value is tied to the U.S. dollar and will remain tied to the U.S. dollar. Assume that interest rate parity exists. Today an Australian dollar (A$) is worth $.50 and HK$3.9. The one-year interest rate on the Australian dollar is 11 percent, while the one-year interest rate on the U.S. dollar is 7 percent. You believe in the international Fisher effect.

You will receive A$1 million in one year from selling products to Australia, and will convert these proceeds into Hong Kong dollars in the spot market at that time to purchase imports from Hong Kong. Forecast the amount of Hong Kong dollars that you will be able to purchase in the spot market one year from now with A$1 million. Show your work.

41. PPP and Cash Flows Boston Co. will receive 1 million euros in one year from selling exports. It did not hedge this future transaction. Boston believes that the future value of the euro will be determined by purchasing power parity (PPP). It expects that inflation in countries using the euro will be 12 percent next year, while inflation in the United States will be 7 percent next year. Today the spot rate of the euro is $1.46, and the one-year forward rate is $1.50.

a. Estimate the amount of U.S. dollars that Boston will receive in one year when converting its euro receivables into U.S. dollars.

b. Today, the spot rate of the Hong Kong dollar is pegged at $.13. Boston believes that the Hong Kong dollar will remain pegged to the dollar for the next year. If Boston Co. decides to convert its 1 million euros into Hong Kong dollars instead of U.S. dollars at the end of one year, estimate the amount of Hong Kong dollars that Boston will receive in one year when converting its euro receivables into Hong Kong dollars.

42. PPP and Currency Futures Assume that you believe purchasing power parity (PPP) exists. You expect that inflation in Canada during the next year will be 3 percent and inflation in the United States will be 8 percent. Today the spot rate of the Canadian dollar is $.90 and the one-year futures contract of the Canadian dollar is priced at $.88. Estimate the expected profit or loss if an investor sold a one-year futures contract today on 1 million Canadian dollars and settled this contract on the settlement date.

43. PPP and Changes in the Real Interest Rate
Assume that you believe exchange rate movements are mostly driven by purchasing power parity. The U.S. and Canada presently have the same nominal (quoted) interest rate. The central bank of Canada just made an announcement that causes you to revise your estimate of Canada's real interest rate downward. Nominal interest rates were not affected by the announcement. Do you expect that the Canadian dollar to appreciate, depreciate, or remain the same against the dollar in response to the announcement? Briefly explain your answer.

44. IFE and Forward Rate The one-year Treasury (risk-free) interest rate in the United States is presently 6 percent, while the one-year Treasury interest rate in Switzerland is 13 percent. The spot rate of the Swiss franc is $.80. Assume that you believe in the international Fisher effect. You will receive 1 million Swiss francs in one year.

a. What is the estimated amount of dollars you will receive when converting the francs to U.S. dollars in one year at the spot rate at that time?

b. Assume that interest rate parity exists. If you hedged your future receivables with a one-year forward contract, how many dollars will you receive when converting the francs to U.S. dollars in one year?

45. PPP You believe that the future value of the Australian dollar will be determined by purchasing power parity (PPP). You expect that inflation in Australia will be 6 percent next year, while inflation in the United States will be 2 percent next year. Today the spot rate of the Australian dollar is $.81, and the one-year forward rate is $.77. What is the expected spot rate of the Australian dollar in one year?

46. Logic behind IFE Investors based in the United States can earn 11 percent interest on a one-year bank deposit in Argentina (with no default risk) or 2 percent on a one-year bank deposit in the United States (with no default risk). Assess the following statement: "According to the international Fisher effect (IFE), if U.S. investors invest 1,000 Argentine pesos in an Argentine bank deposit, they are expected to receive only 20 pesos (2% × 1,000 pesos) as interest." Is this statement a correct explanation of why the international Fisher effect would discourage U.S. investors from investing in Argentina? If not, provide a more accurate explanation for why investors who believe in IFE would not pursue the Argentine investment in this example.

47. Influence of PPP The United States has expected inflation of 2 percent, while Country A, Country B, and Country C have expected inflation of 7 percent. Country A engages in much international trade with the United States. The products that are traded between Country A and the United States can easily be produced by either country. Country B engages in much international trade with the United States. The products that are traded between Country B and the United States are important health products, and there are no substitutes for these products that are exported from the United States to Country B or from Country B to the United States. Country C engages in considerable international financial flows with the United States but very little trade. If you were to use PPP to predict the future exchange rate over the next year for the local currency of each country against the dollar, do you think PPP would provide the most accurate forecast for the currency of Country A, Country B, or Country C? Briefly explain.

Critical Thinking

Integrating IRP and PPP   Assume that interest rate parity exists. Assume that you have payables in Argentine pesos. You have noticed that historically the forward rate of the Argentine peso quoted by the banks exhibits a large discount. Write a short essay on the likely reason why the peso exhibits a discount over time. Does the discount mean that the forward rate is underpriced (that the banks should quote a higher forward rate)? Do you think that you may be more likely to hedge your payables when the Argentine peso exhibits a more pronounced discount? Explain.

Discussion in the Boardroom

This exercise can be found in Appendix E at the back of this textbook.

Running Your Own MNC

This exercise can be found on the *International Financial Management* text companion website. Go to www.cengagebrain.com (students) or www.cengage.com/login (instructors) and search using **ISBN 9781133947837**.

BLADES, INC. CASE

Assessment of Purchasing Power Parity

Blades, the U.S.-based roller blades manufacturer, is currently both exporting to and importing from Thailand. The company has chosen Thailand as an export target for its primary product, Speedos, because of Thailand's growth prospects and the lack of competition from both Thai and U.S. roller blade manufacturers in Thailand. Under an existing arrangement, Blades sells 180,000 pairs of Speedos annually to Entertainment Products, Inc., a Thai retailer. The arrangement involves a fixed, baht-denominated price and will last for three years.

Blades generates approximately 10 percent of its revenue in Thailand. Blades has also decided to import certain rubber and plastic components needed to manufacture Speedos because of cost and quality considerations. Specifically, the weak economic conditions in Thailand resulting from recent events have allowed Blades to import components from the country at a relatively low cost. However, Blades did not enter into a long-term arrangement to import these components and pays market prices (in baht) prevailing in Thailand at the time of purchase. Currently, Blades incurs about 4 percent of its cost of products sold in Thailand.

Although Blades has no immediate plans for expansion in Thailand, it may establish a subsidiary there in the future. Moreover, even if Blades does not establish a subsidiary in Thailand, it will continue exporting to and importing from the country for several years. Due to these considerations, Blades' management is very concerned about recent events in Thailand and neighboring countries, as they may affect both Blades' current performance and its future plans.

Ben Holt, Blades' CFO, is particularly concerned about the level of inflation in Thailand. Blades' export arrangement with Entertainment Products, while allowing for a minimum level of revenue to be generated in Thailand in a given year, prevents Blades from adjusting prices according to the level of inflation in Thailand. In retrospect, Holt is wondering whether Blades should have entered into the export arrangement at all. Because Thailand's economy was growing very fast when Blades agreed to the arrangement, strong consumer spending there resulted in a high level of inflation and high interest rates. Naturally, Blades would have preferred an agreement whereby the price per pair of Speedos would be adjusted for the Thai level of inflation. However, to take advantage of the growth opportunities in Thailand, Blades accepted the arrangement when Entertainment Products insisted on a fixed price level. Currently, however, the baht is freely floating, and Holt is wondering how a relatively high level of Thai inflation may affect the baht-dollar exchange rate and, consequently, Blades' revenue generated in Thailand.

Holt is also concerned about Blades' cost of products sold incurred in Thailand. Because no fixed-price arrangement exists and the components are invoiced in Thai baht, Blades has been subject to increases in the prices of rubber and plastic. Holt is wondering how a potentially high level of inflation will impact the baht-dollar exchange rate and the cost of products sold incurred in Thailand now that the baht is freely floating.

When Holt started thinking about future economic conditions in Thailand and the resulting impact on Blades, he found that he needed your help. In particular, he is vaguely familiar with the concept of purchasing power parity (PPP) and is wondering about this theory's implications, if any, for Blades. Furthermore, Holt also remembers that relatively high interest rates in Thailand will attract capital flows and put upward pressure on the baht.

Because of these concerns, and to gain some insight into the impact of inflation on Blades, Holt has asked you to provide him with answers to the following questions:

1. What is the relationship between the exchange rates and relative inflation levels of the two countries? How will this relationship affect Blades' Thai revenue and costs given that the baht is freely floating? What is the net effect of this relationship on Blades?

2. What are some of the factors that prevent PPP from occurring in the short run? Would you expect PPP to hold better if countries negotiate trade arrangements under which they commit themselves to the purchase or sale of a fixed number of products over a specified time period? Why or why not?

3. How do you reconcile the high level of interest rates in Thailand with the expected change of the baht-dollar exchange rate according to PPP?

4. Given Blades' future plans in Thailand, should the company be concerned with PPP? Why or why not?

5. PPP may hold better for some countries than for others. The Thai baht has been freely floating for more than a decade. How do you think Blades can gain insight into whether PPP holds for Thailand? Offer some logic to explain why the PPP relationship may not hold here.

Small Business Dilemma

Assessment of the IFE by the Sports Exports Company

Every month, the Sports Exports Company receives a payment denominated in British pounds for the footballs it exports to the United Kingdom. Jim Logan, owner of the Sports Exports Company, decides each month whether to hedge the payment with a forward contract for the following month. Now, however, he is questioning whether this process is worth the trouble. He suggests that if the international Fisher effect (IFE) holds, the pound's value should change (on average) by an amount that reflects the differential between the interest rates of the two countries of concern. Because the forward premium reflects that same interest rate differential, the results from hedging should equal the results from not hedging on average.

1. Is Logan's interpretation of the IFE theory correct?

2. If you were in Logan's position, would you spend time trying to decide whether to hedge the receivables each month, or do you believe that the results would be the same (on average) whether you hedged or not?

Internet/Excel Exercises

The "Market" section of the Bloomberg website (www .bloomberg.com) provides interest rate quotations for numerous currencies.

1. Review the section of the website that provides interest rates for various countries. Determine the prevailing one-year interest rate of the Australian dollar, the Japanese yen, and the British pound. Assuming a 2 percent real rate of interest for savers in any country, determine the expected rate of inflation over the next year in each of these three countries that is implied by the nominal interest rate (according to the IFE).

2. What is the approximate expected percentage change in the value of each of these currencies against the dollar over the next year when applying PPP to the inflation level of each of these currencies versus the dollar?

ONLINE ARTICLES WITH REAL-WORLD EXAMPLES

Find a recent article online that describes an actual international finance application or a real-world example about a specific MNC's actions that reinforces one or more concepts covered in this chapter.

If your class has an online component, your professor may ask you to post your summary there and provide the web link of the article so that other students can access it. If your class is live, your professor may ask you to summarize your application in class. Your professor may assign specific students to complete this assignment for this chapter, or may allow any students to do the assignment on a volunteer basis.

For recent online articles and real-world examples applied to this chapter, consider using the following search terms and include the current year as a search term to ensure that the online articles are recent:

1. purchasing power parity
2. U.S. AND purchasing power parity
3. euro AND purchasing power parity
4. inflation AND exchange rate
5. inflation AND currency effects
6. inflationary pressure AND exchange rate
7. international Fisher effect
8. interest rate differential AND currency effects
9. interest rate differential AND exchange rate
10. international interest rate AND expected inflation

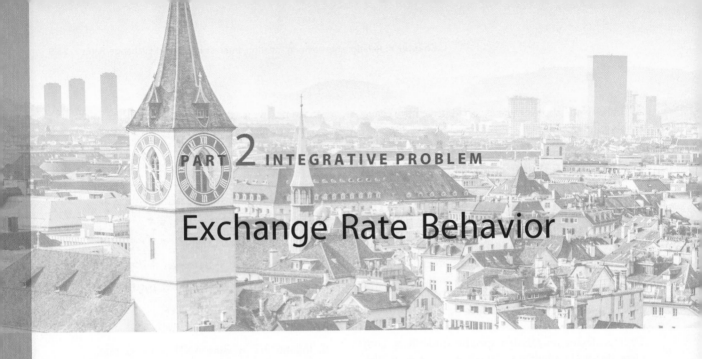

Exchange Rate Behavior

Questions

1. As an employee of the foreign exchange department for a large company, you have been given the following information:

    Beginning of Year
    Spot rate of £ = $1.596
    Spot rate of Australian dollar (A$) = $.70
    Cross exchange rate: £1 = A$2.28
    One-year forward rate of A$ = $.71
    One-year forward rate of £ = $1.58004
    One-year U.S. interest rate = 8.00%
    One-year British interest rate = 9.09%
    One-year Australian interest rate = 7.00%
    Determine whether triangular arbitrage is feasible and, if so, how it should be conducted to make a profit.

2. Using the information in question 1, determine whether covered interest arbitrage is feasible and, if so, how it should be conducted to make a profit.

3. Based on the information in question 1 for the beginning of the year, use the international Fisher effect (IFE) theory to forecast the annual percentage change in the British pound's value over the year.

4. Assume that at the beginning of the year, the pound's value is in equilibrium. Assume that over the year the British inflation rate is 6 percent, while the U.S. inflation rate is 4 percent. Assume that any change in the pound's value due to the inflation differential has occurred by the end of the year. Using this information and the information provided in question 1, determine how the pound's value changed over the year.

5. Assume that the pound's depreciation over the year was attributed directly to central bank intervention. Explain the type of direct intervention that would place downward pressure on the value of the pound.

Midterm Self-Exam

Midterm Review

You have just completed all the chapters focused on the macro- and market-related concepts. Here is a brief summary of some of the key points in those chapters. Chapter 1 explains the role of financial managers to focus on maximizing the value of the MNC and how that goal can be distorted by agency problems. MNCs use various incentives to ensure that managers serve shareholders rather than themselves. Chapter 1 explains that an MNC's value is the present value of its future cash flows and how a U.S.-based MNC's value is influenced by its foreign cash flows. Its dollar cash flows (and therefore its value) are enhanced when the foreign currencies received appreciate against the dollar, or when foreign currencies of outflows depreciate. The MNC's value is also influenced by its cost of capital, which is influenced by its capital structure and the risk of the projects that it pursues. The valuation is dependent on the environment in which MNCs operate, along with their managerial decisions.

Chapter 2 focuses on international transactions in a global context, with emphasis on international trade and capital flows. International trade flows are sensitive to relative prices of products between countries, while international capital flows are influenced by the potential return on funds invested. They can have a major impact on the economic conditions of each country and the MNCs that operate there. Net trade flows to a country may create more jobs there, while net capital flows to a country can increase the amount of funds that can be channeled to finance projects by firms or government agencies.

Chapter 3 introduces the international money, bond, and stock markets and explains how they facilitate the operations of MNCs. It also explains how the foreign exchange market facilitates international transactions. Chapter 4 explains how a currency's direct exchange rate (value measured in dollars) may rise when its country has relatively low inflation and relatively high interest rates (if expected inflation is low) compared with the United States. Chapter 5 introduces currency derivatives and explains how they can be used by MNCs or individuals to capitalize on expected movements in exchange rates.

Chapter 6 describes the role of central banks in the foreign exchange market and how they can use direct intervention to affect exchange rate movements. They can attempt to raise the value of their home currency by using dollars or another currency in their reserves to purchase their home currency in the foreign exchange market. The central banks can also attempt to reduce the value of their home currency by using their home currency reserves to purchase dollars in the foreign exchange market. Alternatively, they could use indirect intervention by affecting interest rates in a manner that will affect the appeal of their local money market securities relative to other countries. This action affects the supply of their home currency for sale and/or the demand for their home currency in the foreign exchange market and therefore affects the exchange rate.

Chapter 7 explains how the forces of arbitrage allow for parity conditions and more orderly foreign exchange market quotations. Specifically, locational arbitrage ensures that exchange rate quotations are similar among locations. Triangular arbitrage ensures that cross exchange rates are properly aligned. Covered interest arbitrage tends to ensure that the spot and forward exchange rates maintain a relationship that reflects interest rate parity, whereby the forward rate premium reflects the interest rate differential. Chapter 8 gives special attention to the impact of inflation and interest rates on exchange rate movements. Purchasing power parity suggests that a currency will depreciate to offset its country's inflation differential above the United States (or will appreciate if its country's inflation is lower than in the United States). The international Fisher effect suggests that if nominal interest rate differentials reflect the expected inflation differentials (the real interest rate is the same in each country), the exchange rate will move in accordance with purchasing power parity as applied to expected inflation. That is, a currency will depreciate to offset its country's expected inflation differential above the United States (or will appreciate if its country's expected inflation is lower than in the United States).

Midterm Self-Exam

This self-exam allows you to test your understanding of some of the key concepts covered up to this point. Chapters 1 to 8 are macro- and market-oriented, while Chapters 9 to 21 are micro-oriented. This is a good opportunity to assess your understanding of the macro and market concepts, before moving on to the micro concepts in Chapters 9 to 21.

This exam does not replace all the end-of-chapter self-tests, nor does it test all the concepts that have been covered up to this point. It is simply intended to let you test yourself on a general overview of key concepts. Try to simulate taking an exam by answering all questions without using your book and your notes. The answers to this exam are provided just after the exam so that you can grade your exam. If you have any wrong answers, you should reread the related material and then redo any exam questions that you had wrong.

This exam may not necessarily match the level of rigor in your course. Your instructor may offer you specific information about how this Midterm Self-Exam relates to the coverage and rigor of the midterm exam in your course.

1. An MNC's cash flows and therefore its valuation can be affected by expected exchange rate movements (as explained in Chapter 1). Sanoma Co. is a U.S.-based MNC that wants to assess how its valuation is affected by expected exchange rate movements. Given Sanoma's business transactions and its expectations of exchange rates, fill out the table on the next page.

2. The United States has a larger balance-of-trade deficit each year (as explained in Chapter 2). Do you think a weaker dollar would reduce the balance-of-trade deficit? Offer a convincing argument for your answer.

3. Is outsourcing by U.S. firms to foreign countries beneficial to the U.S. economy? Weigh the pros and cons, and offer your conclusions.

4. a. The dollar is presently worth .8 euros. What is the direct exchange rate of the euro?
   b. The direct exchange rate of the euro is presently valued higher than it was last month. What does this imply about the movement of the indirect exchange rate of the euro over the last month?

EACH QUARTER DURING THE YEAR, SANOMA'S MAIN BUSINESS TRANSAC-TIONS WILL BE TO:	CURRENCY USED IN TRANSACTION	EXPECTED MOVEMENT IN CURRENCY'S VALUE AGAINST THE U.S. DOLLAR DURING THIS YEAR	HOW THE EXPECTED CURRENCY MOVEMENT WILL AFFECT SANOMA'S NET CASH FLOWS (AND THEREFORE VALUE) THIS YEAR
a. Import materials from Canada	Canadian dollar	Depreciate	
b. Export products to Germany	Euro	Appreciate	
c. Receive remitted earnings from its foreign subsidiary in Argentina	Argentine peso	Appreciate	
d. Receive interest from its Australian cash account	Australian dollar	Depreciate	
e. Make loan payments on a loan provided by a Japanese bank	Japanese yen	Depreciate	

c. The quote for the Australian dollar according to the *Wall Street Journal* website is $.50, while the one-year forward rate of the Australian dollar is $.51. What is the forward rate premium? What is the expected rate of appreciation (or depreciation) if the one-year forward rate is used to predict the value of the Australian dollar in 1 year?

5. Assume that the Polish currency (called zloty) is worth $.32. The U.S. dollar is worth .7 euros. A U.S. dollar can be exchanged for 8 Mexican pesos.

Last year a dollar was valued at 2.9 Polish zloty, and the peso was valued at $.10.

a. Would U.S. exporters to Mexico that accept pesos as payment be favorably or unfavorably affected by the change in the Mexican peso's value over the last year?

b. Would U.S. importers from Poland that pay for imports in zloty be favorably or unfavorably affected by the change in the zloty's value over the last year?

c. What is the percentage change in the cross exchange rate of the peso in zloty over the last year? How would firms in Mexico that sell products to Poland denominated in zloty be affected by the change in the cross exchange rate?

6. Explain how each of the following conditions would be expected to affect the value of the Mexican peso.

SITUATION	EXPECTED IMPACT ON THE EXCHANGE RATE OF THE PESO
a. Mexico suddenly experiences a high rate of inflation.	
b. Mexico's interest rates rise, while its inflation is expected to remain low.	
c. Mexico's central bank intervenes in the foreign exchange market by purchasing dollars with pesos.	
d. Mexico imposes quotas on products imported from the United States.	

7. One year ago, you sold a put option on 100,000 euros with an expiration date of one year. You received a premium on the put option of $.05 per unit. The exercise price was $1.22. Assume that one year ago, the spot rate of the euro was $1.20. One year ago, the one-year forward rate of the euro exhibited a discount of 2 percent, and the one-year futures price of the euro was the same as the one-year forward rate of the euro. From one year ago to today, the euro depreciated against the dollar by 4 percent. Today the put option will be exercised (if it is feasible for the buyer to do so).

    a. Determine the total dollar amount of your profit or loss from your position in the put option.

    b. One year ago, Rita sold a futures contract on 100,000 euros with a settlement date of one year. Determine the total dollar amount of her profit or loss.

8. Assume that the Federal Reserve wants to reduce the value of the euro with respect to the dollar. How could it attempt to use indirect intervention to achieve its goal? What is a possible adverse effect from this type of intervention?

9. Assume that interest rate parity exists. The one-year nominal interest rate in the United States is 7 percent, while the one-year nominal interest rate in Australia is 11 percent. The spot rate of the Australian dollar is $.60. Today you purchase a one-year forward contract on 10 million Australian dollars. How many U.S. dollars will you need in one year to fulfill your forward contract?

10. You go to a bank and are given these quotes:

You can buy a euro for 14 Mexican pesos.
The bank will pay you 13 pesos for a euro.
You can buy a U.S. dollar for .9 euros.
The bank will pay you .8 euros for a U.S. dollar.
You can buy a U.S. dollar for 10 pesos.
The bank will pay you 9 pesos for a U.S. dollar.

    You have $1,000. Can you use triangular arbitrage to generate a profit? If so, explain the order of the transactions that you would execute and the profit that you would earn. If you cannot earn a profit from triangular arbitrage, explain why.

11. Today's spot rate of the Mexican peso is $.10. Assume that purchasing power parity holds. The U.S. inflation rate over this year is expected to be 7 percent, while the Mexican inflation over this year is expected to be 3 percent. Carolina Co. plans to import from Mexico and will need 20 million Mexican pesos in one year. Determine the expected amount of dollars to be paid by the Carolina Co. for the pesos in one year.

12. Tennessee Co. purchases imports that have a price of 400,000 Singapore dollars, and it has to pay for the imports in 90 days. It will use a 90-day forward contract to cover its payables. Assume that interest rate parity exists and will continue to exist. This morning, the spot rate of the Singapore dollar was $.50. At noon, the Federal Reserve reduced U.S. interest rates. There was no change in the Singapore interest rates. The Singapore dollar's spot rate remained at $.50 throughout the day. But the Fed's actions immediately increased the degree of uncertainty surrounding the future value of the Singapore dollar over the next three months.

    a. If Tennessee Co. locked in a 90-day forward contract this afternoon, would its total U.S. dollar cash outflows be *more than*, *less than*, or *the same as* the total U.S. dollar cash outflows if it had locked in a 90-day forward contract this morning? Briefly explain.

    b. Assume that Tennessee uses a currency options contract to hedge rather than a forward contract. If Tennessee Co. purchased a currency call option contract at the money on Singapore dollars this afternoon, would its total U.S. dollar cash outflows be *more than, less than,* or *the same as* the total U.S. dollar cash outflows if it had purchased a currency call option contract at the money this morning? Briefly explain.

c. Assume that the U.S. and Singapore interest rates were the same as of this morning. Also assume that the international Fisher effect holds. If Tennessee Co. purchased a currency call option contract at the money this morning to hedge its exposure, would you expect that its total U.S. dollar cash outflows would be *more than, less than, or the same* as the total U.S. dollar cash outflows if it had negotiated a forward contract this morning? Briefly explain.

13. Today, a U.S. dollar can be exchanged for 3 New Zealand dollars or for 1.6 Canadian dollars. The one-year CD (deposit) rate is 7 percent in New Zealand, 6 percent in the United States, and 5 percent in Canada. Interest rate parity exists between the United States and New Zealand and between the United States and Canada. The international Fisher effect exists between the United States and New Zealand. You expect that the Canadian dollar will be worth $.61 at the end of one year.

Karen (based in the United States) invests in a one-year CD in New Zealand and sells New Zealand dollars one year forward to cover her position.
Marcia (who lives in New Zealand) invests in a one-year CD in the United States and sells U.S. dollars one year forward to cover her position.
William (who lives in Canada) invests in a one-year CD in the United States and does not cover his position.
James (based in the United States) invests in a one-year CD in New Zealand and does not cover his position.

Based on this information, which person will be expected to earn the highest return on the funds invested? If you believe that multiple people will tie for the highest expected return, name each of them. Briefly explain.

14. Assume that the United Kingdom has an interest rate of 8 percent versus an interest rate of 5 percent in the United States.

a. Explain what the implications are for the future value of the British pound according to the theory in Chapter 4 that a country with high interest rates may attract capital flows versus the theory of the international Fisher effect (IFE) in Chapter 8.

b. Compare the implications of the IFE from Chapter 8 versus interest rate parity (IRP) as related to the information provided here.

Answers to Midterm Self-Exam

1. a. Increase
   b. Increase
   c. Increase
   d. Decrease
   e. Increase

2. One argument is that a weak dollar will make U.S. products imported by foreign countries cheaper, which will increase the demand for U.S. exports. In addition, a weaker dollar may discourage U.S. firms from importing foreign products because the cost will be higher. Both factors result in a smaller balance-of-trade deficit.

However, a weak dollar might not improve the balance-of-trade deficit because it is unlikely to weaken against all countries simultaneously. Foreign firms may compare the price they would pay for U.S. products to the price paid for similar products in other countries. Even if the dollar weakens, products produced in China or some other countries where there is cheap labor may still be cheaper for customers based in the United States or other countries.

3. Outsourcing can be beneficial to the U.S. economy because it may allow U.S. firms to produce their products at a lower cost and increase their profits (which increases income earned by the U.S. owners of those firms). It also allows U.S. customers to purchase products and services at a lower cost.

However, outsourcing eliminates some jobs in the United States, which reduces or eliminates income for people whose job was outsourced. The overall effect on the U.S. economy is based on a comparison of these two forces. It is possible to make arguments for either side. Also, the effects will vary depending on the location. For example, outsourcing may be more likely in a high-wage city in the United States where firms provide services that can be handled by phone or by electronic interaction. These jobs are easier to outsource than some other jobs.

4. a. A euro = $1.25.
b. The indirect value of the euro must have declined over the last month.
c. The forward premium is 2 percent. If the forward rate is used to forecast, the expected degree of appreciation over the next year is ($.51 − $.50)/$.50 = 2%, which is the same as the forward rate premium.

5. a. The peso is valued at $.125 today. Because the peso appreciated, the U.S. exporters are favorably affected.
b. The zloty was worth about $.345 last year. Because the zloty depreciated, the U.S. importers were favorably affected.
c. Last year, the cross rate of the peso in zloty = $.10/$.345 =.2898. Today, the cross rate of the peso in zloty = $.125/$.32 =.391. The percentage change is (.391 − .2898)/.2898 = 34.92%.

6. a. Depreciate
b. Appreciate
c. Depreciate
d. Appreciate

7. a. The spot rate depreciated from $1.20 to $1.152. You receive $.05 per unit. The buyer of the put option exercises the option, and you buy the euros for $1.22 and sell them in the spot market for $1.152. Your gain on the put option per unit is ($1.152 − $1.22) + $.05 = −$.018. Total gain = −$.018 × 100,000 = −$1,800.
b. The futures rate one year ago was equal to: $1.20 × (1 − .02) = $1.176. So the futures rate is $1.176. The gain per unit is $1.176 − $1.152 = $.024 and the total gain is $.024 × 100,000 = $2,400.

8. The Fed could use indirect intervention by raising U.S. interest rates so that the United States would attract more capital flows, which would place upward pressure on the dollar. However, the higher interest rates could make borrowing too expensive for some firms, and would possibly reduce economic growth.

9. [(1.07)/(1.11)] − 1 = −3.60%. So the one-year forward rate is $.60 × [1 + (−.036)] = $.5784. You will need 10,000,000 × $.5784 = $5,784,000.

10. Yes, you can generate a profit by converting dollars to euros, and then euros to pesos, and then pesos to dollars. First convert the information to direct quotes:

	BID	ASK
Euro in $	$1.11	$1.25
Pesos in $	$.10	$.11
Euro in pesos	13	14

Use $1,000 to purchase euros: $1,000/$1.25 = 800 euros.
Convert 800 euros to buy pesos: 800 euros × 13 = 10,400 pesos.
Convert the 10,400 pesos to U.S. dollars: 10,400 × $.10 = $1,040.
There is profit of $40 on a $1,000 investment.

The alternative strategy that you could attempt is to first buy pesos:

Use $1,000 to purchase pesos: $1,000/$.11 = 9,090.9 pesos.
Convert 9,090.9 pesos to euros: 9,090.9/14 = 649.35 euros.
Convert 649.35 euros to dollars: 649.35 euros × $1.11 = $720.78.

This strategy results in a loss.

11. [(1.07)/(1.03)] − 1 = 3.8835%. So the expected future spot rate is $.1038835. Carolina will need to pay $.1038835 × 20 million pesos = $2,077,670.

12. a. Less than because the discount would be more pronounced or the forward premium would be reduced.
  b. More than because the option premium increased due to more uncertainty.
  c. More than because there is an option premium on the option and the forward rate has no premium in this example, and the expectation is that the future spot rate will be no higher than today's forward rate. The option is at the money, so the exercise price is the same as the expected spot rate but you have to pay the option premium.

13. The expected returns of each person are as follows:

Karen earns 6 percent due to interest rate parity, and earns the same return as she could earn locally.
Marcia earns 7 percent due to interest rate parity, and earns the same return as she could earn locally.
William earns 8.6 percent. If he converts, C$ = $.625 today. After 1 year, C$ = $.61. So if William invests C $1,000, it converts to $625. At the end of 1 year, he has $662.50. He converts to C$ and has C$1,086.
James is expected to earn 6 percent, because the international Fisher effect (IFE) suggests that on average, the exchange rate movement will offset the interest rate differential.

14. a. The IFE disagrees with the theory from Chapter 4 that a currency will appreciate if it has a high interest rate (holding other factors such as inflation constant). The IFE says that capital flows will not go to where the interest rate is higher because the higher interest rate reflects a higher expectation of inflation, which means the currency will weaken over time.
  If you believe the higher interest rate reflects higher expected inflation, then the IFE makes sense. However, in many cases (such as this case), a higher interest rate may be caused by reasons other than inflation (perhaps the U.K. economy is strong

and many firms are borrowing money right now), and if so, then there is no reason to think the currency will depreciate in the future. Therefore, the IFE would not make sense.

The key is that you can see the two different arguments, so that you can understand why a high interest rate may lead to local currency depreciation in some cases and appreciation in other cases.

b. If U.S. investors attempt to capitalize on the higher rate without covering, they do not know what their return will be. However, if they believe in the IFE, then this means that the United Kingdom's higher interest rate of 3 percent above that in the United States reflects a higher expected inflation rate in the United Kingdom of about 3 percent. This implies that the best guess of the change in the pound will be −3 percent for the pound (because the IFE relies on PPP), which means that the best guess of the U.S. investor return is about 5 percent, the same as is possible domestically. It may be better, it may be worse, but on average, it is not expected to be any better than what investors can get locally.

The IFE is focused on situations in which you are trying to anticipate the movement in a currency and you know the interest rate differentials.

Interest rate parity uses interest rate differentials to derive the forward rate. The one-year forward rate would be exactly equal to the expected future spot rate if you use the IFE to derive a best guess of the future spot rate in one year. But if you invest and cover with the forward rate, you know exactly what your outcome will be. If you invest and do not cover, the IFE gives you a prediction of what the outcome will be, but it is just a guess. The result could be 20 percent above or below that guess or even farther away from the guess.

PART 3
Exchange Rate Risk Management

Part 3 (Chapters 9 through 12) explains the various functions involved in managing exposure to exchange rate risk. Chapter 9 describes various methods used to forecast exchange rates and explains how to assess forecasting performance. Chapter 10 demonstrates how a multinational corporation can measure its exposure to exchange rate movements. Given its forecasts of future exchange rates and its exposure to exchange rate movements, an MNC can decide whether and how to hedge that exposure. Chapters 11 and 12 describe this hedging by MNCs.

9

Forecasting Exchange Rates

The specific objectives of this chapter are to:

- explain why firms forecast exchange rates,
- describe the common techniques used for forecasting,
- explain how forecast performance can be evaluated, and
- explain how to account for uncertainty surrounding forecasts.

Both the cost of an MNC's operations and the revenue it receives from operations are affected by exchange rate movements. An MNC's forecasts of exchange rate movements can influence its managerial decisions.

9-1 Why Firms Forecast Exchange Rates

The following corporate functions typically require exchange rate forecasts.

- *Hedging decision.* Multinational corporations constantly face the decision of whether to hedge future payables and receivables in foreign currencies. Whether or not a firm hedges may be determined by its forecasts of foreign currency values.

EXAMPLE

Laredo Co., based in the United States, plans to pay for clothing imported from Mexico in 90 days. If the forecasted value of the peso in 90 days is sufficiently below the 90-day forward rate, then the MNC may decide not to hedge. Forecasting may enable the firm to make a decision that will increase its cash flows. ●

- *Short-term investment decision.* Corporations sometimes have a substantial amount of excess cash available for a short time period. Large deposits can be established in several currencies. The ideal currency for deposits will (1) exhibit a high interest rate and (2) strengthen in value over the investment period.

EXAMPLE

Lafayette Co. has excess cash and considers depositing the cash into a British bank account. If the British pound appreciates against the dollar by the end of the deposit period when pounds will be withdrawn and exchanged for U.S. dollars, more dollars will be received. Thus the firm can use forecasts of the pound's exchange rate when determining whether to invest the short-term cash in a British versus a U.S. account. ●

- *Capital budgeting decision.* When an MNC assesses whether to invest funds in a foreign project, the firm takes into account that the project may periodically require the exchange of currencies. The capital budgeting analysis can be completed only when all estimated cash flows are measured in the MNC's local currency.

EXAMPLE

Evansville Co. wants to determine whether to establish a subsidiary in Thailand. The earnings to be generated by the proposed subsidiary in Thailand would need to be periodically converted into dollars to be remitted to the U.S. parent. The capital budgeting process requires estimates of future dollar cash flows to be received by the U.S. parent. These dollar cash flows depend on the forecasted exchange rate of Thailand's currency (the baht) against the dollar over time. Accurate forecasts of currency values will improve the accuracy of the estimated cash flows and therefore enhance the MNC's decision making. ●

■ *Earnings assessment.* An MNC's decision about whether a foreign subsidiary should reinvest earnings in a foreign country or instead remit those earnings back to the parent may be influenced by exchange rate forecasts. If a strong foreign currency is expected to weaken substantially against the MNC's home country currency, then the parent may prefer to expedite the remittance of subsidiary earnings before the foreign currency weakens.

Exchange rate forecasts are also useful for forecasting an MNC's earnings. When earnings of an MNC are reported, subsidiary earnings are consolidated and translated into the currency representing the parent firm's home country.

■ *Long-term financing decision.* Multinational corporations that issue bonds to secure long-term funds may consider denominating those bonds in foreign currencies. They prefer that the currency borrowed depreciate over time against the currency they are receiving from sales. To estimate the cost of issuing bonds denominated in a foreign currency, forecasts of exchange rates are required.

Most forecasting is applied to currencies whose exchange rates fluctuate continuously, and that is the focus of this chapter. However, some forecasts are also derived for currencies whose exchange rates are pegged. MNCs recognize that a pegged exchange rate today does not necessarily serve as a good forecast because the government might devalue the currency in the future.

An MNC's motives for forecasting exchange rates are summarized in Exhibit 9.1. The motives are distinguished according to whether they can enhance the MNC's value by

Exhibit 9.1   Corporate Motives for Forecasting Exchange Rates

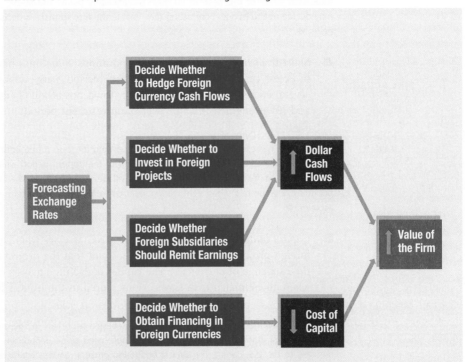

influencing its cash flows or its cost of capital. The need for accurate exchange rate projections should now be clear. The following section describes the forecasting methods available.

9-2 Forecasting Techniques

The numerous methods available for forecasting exchange rates can be categorized into four general groups: (1) technical, (2) fundamental, (3) market-based, and (4) mixed.

WEB

www.ny.frb.org/markets
/foreignex.html
Historical exchange rate
data that can be used to
create technical forecasts
of exchange rates.

9-2a Technical Forecasting

Technical forecasting involves the use of historical exchange rate data to predict future values. There may be a trend of successive daily exchange rate adjustments in the same direction, which could lead to a continuation of that trend. Alternatively, there may be some technical indication that a correction in the exchange rate is likely, which would result in a forecast that the exchange rate will reverse its direction.

EXAMPLE   Tomorrow Kansas Co. must pay 10 million Mexican pesos for supplies that it recently received from Mexico. Today, the peso has appreciated by 3 percent against the dollar. Based on an analysis of historical time series, Kansas has determined that whenever the peso appreciates against the dollar by more than 1 percent, it experiences a reversal of about 60 percent of that change on the following day. Given this forecast, Kansas Co. decides that it will make its payment tomorrow instead of today so that it can benefit from the expected depreciation of the peso. ●

Technical forecasting is sometimes cited as the main technique used by investors who speculate in the foreign exchange market, especially when their investment is for a very short time period.

Limitations of Technical Forecasting   Multinational corporations make only limited use of technical forecasting because it typically focuses on the near future, which is not that helpful for developing corporate policies. Most technical forecasts apply to very short-term periods (e.g., one day) because patterns in exchange rate movements may be more predictable over such periods. Because such patterns are likely less reliable for forecasting long-term movements (e.g., over a quarter, a year, or five years), technical forecasts are less useful for forecasting exchange rates in the distant future. Thus technical forecasting may not be suitable for firms that require a long-range forecast of exchange rates.

Furthermore, a technical forecasting model that has worked well in one particular period may not work well in another period. Unless historical trends in exchange rate movements can be identified, examination of past movements will not be useful for indicating future movements.

If the foreign exchange market is **weak-form efficient**, then historical and current exchange rate information is not useful for forecasting exchange rate movements because today's exchange rates already reflect this information. In other words, technical analysis would not be able to improve upon today exchange rates when forecasting rates in the near future.

9-2b Fundamental Forecasting

Fundamental forecasting is based on fundamental relationships between economic variables (such as inflation, income level, and interest rates) and exchange rates.

Use of purchasing power parity (PPP) for Fundamental Forecasting

Recall that the theory of purchasing power parity specifies the fundamental relationship between two countries' inflation differential and the exchange rate. In simple terms, purchasing power parity (PPP) states that the currency of the higher-inflation country will depreciate by an amount that reflects the countries' inflation differential. If PPP holds, then the percentage change in the foreign currency's value (e_f) over a given period should reflect the differential between the home inflation rate (I_h) and the foreign inflation rate (I_f) over that period.

EXAMPLE   Based on PPP, Drake Co. believes that the Australian dollar will move in accordance with the difference between the U.S. inflation rate and the Australian inflation rate. Drake relies on government reports that the U.S. inflation rate will be 1 percent over the next year and the Australian inflation rate will be 6 percent. According to PPP, the percentage change in the Australian dollar's exchange rate (denoted as e) should be:

$$e_f = \frac{1 + I_{U.S}}{1 + I_f} - 1$$
$$= \frac{1.01}{1.06} - 1$$
$$\approx -4.7\%$$

This forecast of the percentage change in the Australian dollar can be applied to its existing spot rate to forecast the future spot rate at the end of one year. The existing spot rate S_t of the Australian dollar is $.50, so the expected spot rate at the end of one year, $E(S_{t+1})$, will be about

$$E(S_{t+1}) = S_t(1 + e_f)$$
$$= \$.50[1 + (-.047)]$$
$$= \$.4765$$ ●

Fundamental Forecasting with a Lagged Impact

Fundamental forecasting sometimes has to account for a lagged (delayed) impact, in which changes in variables in an earlier period affect exchange rate movements in a future period. For example, when the inflation differential has a lagged impact on exchange rates, the inflation differential in the previous period may be used to forecast the percentage change in the exchange rate over the future period. The logic behind this lagged effect is that adjustments in international trade occur in response to the inflation differential with a one-quarter lag, and the exchange rate responds to the adjustments in trade.

EXAMPLE   Alcorn Co. wants to forecast the percentage change (rate of appreciation or depreciation) in the British pound with respect to the U.S. dollar during the next quarter. It believes that movements in the British pound are dependent only on the U.S. inflation rate minus the British inflation rate in the previous quarter; this variable is denoted INF_{t-1}.

Alcorn Co. must first determine the historical relationship between INF and the quarterly percentage change in the pound's value, a task for which regression analysis is well suited. For the previous values of the pound and INF, Alcorn obtains a set of historical data representing the last 50 quarters. Then it applies the following regression model, in which the dependent variable is the quarterly percentage change in the value of the exchange rate (e), which is dependent on (influenced by) the movements of the independent variable INF_{t-1}:

$$e = b_0 + b_1 INF_{t-1} + \mu_t$$

where b_0 is a constant, b_1 measures the sensitivity of quarterly exchange rate movements (e) to changes in INF_{t-1}, and μ_t is an error term.

The regression model used by Alcorn specifies a *lagged* relationship between the independent variable and the dependent variable, as the exchange rate movement per quarter is influenced by the inflation differential in the previous quarter. When applied to the data, the model generates the values of the regression coefficients (b_0 and b_1). The regression coefficient b_1 is expected to be positive because e_f should move in the same direction as INF_{t-1}. That is, when U.S. inflation increases relative to U.K. inflation, there is upward pressure on the pound's value.

Assume that Alcorn's application of regression analysis generates the following estimates of the coefficients: $b_0 = .00$, $b_1 = .9$. The coefficient $b_1 = .9$ suggests that for a one-unit percentage change in INF_{t-1} (the inflation differential in the previous quarter), the British pound is expected to change by .9 percent in the same direction.

Now that the historical relationship between INF_{t-1} and e has been determined by regression analysis, Alcorn Co. can forecast the British pound's exchange rate movement in the next quarter. Because the independent variable in the model has a lagged impact on e, Alcorn can apply the estimated regression coefficient b_1 to the actual value of the independent variable in the previous quarter in order to derive a forecast for the British pound for the next quarter. Assume that the most recent quarterly percentage change in INF_{t-1} (the inflation differential) is 3 percent. Using this information along with the estimated regression coefficients, Alcorn's forecast for e is

$$e_f = b_0 + b_1 INF_{t-1}$$
$$= .00 + .9(3\%)$$
$$= .00\% + 2.7\%$$
$$= 2.7\% \qquad \bullet$$

Instantaneous Influences in Fundamental Forecasting   In the previous example, the independent variable in the model was presumed to have a lagged impact on the pound's exchange rate. This allowed the use of actual values of the independent variable in the model used to forecast the pound's value. However, some independent variables may have an instantaneous influence on exchange rates. Because the values of these variables would not be known at the time the MNC wants to forecast the exchange rate, forecasts for these independent variables must be used.

EXAMPLE   Like Alcorn Co. in the previous example, Mercer Co. also wants to forecast the value of the British pound. It also believes that the quarterly percentage change in the pound (denoted as e_f) is primarily influenced by the differential between U.S. and U.K. inflation rates, but believes this relationship is instantaneous rather than lagged. Consequently, it applies the following regression model:

$$e_f = b_0 + b_1 INF_t + \mu_t$$

The only difference between this model and the previous model is that the subscript t is used for INF, reflecting the instantaneous relationship between INF and the British pound.

Assume that Mercer's application of regression analysis generates the following estimates of the coefficients: $b_0 = .00$, $b_1 = .7$. The coefficient $b_1 = .7$ suggests that for a one-unit percentage change in INF_t (the inflation differential in the same quarter), the British pound is expected to change by .7 percent in the same direction.

Now that the historical relationship between INF_t and e has been determined by regression analysis, Mercer Co. can forecast the British pound's exchange rate movement in the next quarter. However, because the independent variable in the model has an instantaneous impact on the pound's exchange rate, Mercer applies the estimated regression coefficient b_1 to a predicted value of INF for the next quarter in order to forecast the percentage change in the pound for the next quarter. Assume that it predicts that INF_t (the inflation differential) will be 2 percent. Using this information along with the estimated regression coefficients, Mercer's forecast for the percentage change in the pound is

$$e = b_0 + b_1 INF_t$$
$$= .00 + .7(2\%)$$
$$= .00\% + 1.4\%$$
$$= 1.4\% \qquad \bullet$$

Forecasting with a Comprehensive Model   The previous examples were simplified to illustrate how fundamental analysis can be implemented for forecasting. A more comprehensive model might include many more factors as described here, but the application would still be similar. A large time-series database would be necessary to warrant any confidence in the relationships detected by such a model.

Recall from Chapter 4 that a change in a currency's spot rate is influenced by the following factors:

$$e = f(\Delta INF, \Delta INT, \Delta INC, \Delta GC, \Delta EXP)$$

Where

e_f = **percentage change in the spot rate**

ΔINF = **change in the differential between U.S. inflation and the foreign country's inflation**

ΔINT = **change in the differential between the U.S. interest rate and the foreign country's interest rate**

ΔINC = **change in the differential between the U.S. income level and the foreign country's income level**

ΔGC = **change in government controls**

ΔEXP = **change in expectations of future exchange rates**

Given current values of these variables along with their historical impact on a currency's value, a corporation can develop exchange rate projections.

A forecast may also arise simply from a subjective assessment of the degree to which general movements in economic variables in one country are expected to affect exchange rates. From a statistical perspective, a forecast would be based on quantitatively measured impacts of factors on these rates.

Limitations of Fundamental Forecasting

Although fundamental forecasting accounts for the expected fundamental relationships between factors and currency values, it has four main limitations.

1. The precise timing of the impact of some factors on a currency's value is not known. It is possible that the full impact of factors on exchange rates will not occur until two, three, or four quarters later. The regression model would need to be adjusted accordingly.

2. As mentioned previously, some factors have an immediate impact on exchange rates. Yet such factors can be usefully included in a fundamental forecasting model only if forecasts can be obtained for them. Those forecasts should be developed for a period corresponding to that for which an exchange rate forecast is needed. In this case, the accuracy of the exchange rate forecasts is affected by the accuracy of these factors. Even if a firm knows exactly how their movements affect exchange rates, its exchange rate projections may be inaccurate if it cannot predict the factors' values.

3. Some factors that deserve consideration in the fundamental forecasting process cannot be easily quantified. For example, if large Australian exporting firms experience an unanticipated labor strike that causes shortages, this will reduce the availability of Australian goods for U.S. consumers and therefore reduce U.S. demand for Australian dollars. Such an event, which would put downward pressure on the Australian dollar's value, normally is not incorporated into a forecasting model.

WEB

www.cmegroup.com
Quotes on currency
futures that can be used
to create market-based
forecasts.

4. Coefficients derived from the regression analysis may not remain constant over time. If a country imposes new trade barriers (or eliminates existing barriers), the impact of the inflation differential on trade could change.

These limitations of fundamental forecasting have been discussed to emphasize that even the most sophisticated forecasting techniques (fundamental or otherwise) cannot provide consistently accurate forecasts. Consequently, exchange rate forecasts developed by MNCs must allow for some margin of error when implementing corporate policies.

9-2c Market-Based Forecasting

The process of developing forecasts from market indicators, which is known as **market-based forecasting**, is usually based on either the spot rate or the forward rate.

Using the Spot Rate   Today's spot rate may be used as a forecast of the spot rate that will exist on a future date. To see why the spot rate can be a useful market-based forecast, suppose that many participants (including speculators) in the foreign exchange market expect the British pound to appreciate against the dollar in the next 2 days. This expectation will encourage speculators to buy the pound with U.S. dollars today in anticipation of its appreciation, and these purchases can force the pound's value up immediately. Once the exchange rate has reached the point at which the prevailing spot rate is equal to the spot rate expected in 2 days, speculators would no longer purchase pounds because they would no longer view the currency as undervalued. But the speculative trading boosted the exchange rate to equal the market's expectations for two days ahead. Conversely, if the pound is expected to depreciate against the dollar, speculators will sell pounds now, hoping to purchase them back at a lower price after they decline in value. Such actions can force the pound to depreciate immediately. Thus the current value of the pound should reflect the expectation of the pound's value in the near future. When the spot rate is used as the forecast of the future spot rate, the implication is that the expected percentage change in the currency will be zero over the forecast period:

$$E(e_f) = 0$$

Of course, MNCs realize that the currency's value will not remain constant. Even so, they might use today's spot rate as their best guess of the spot rate at a future point in time.

Using the Forward Rate   A forward rate quoted for a specific date in the future is commonly used as the forecasted spot rate on that future date. Thus a 30-day forward rate forecasts the spot rate in 30 days, a 90-day forward rate forecasts the spot rate in 90 days, and so on. Recall that the forward rate is measured as

$$F = S(1 + p)$$

where p denotes the forward premium. Because p represents the percentage by which the forward rate exceeds the spot rate, it serves as the expected percentage change in the exchange rate:

$$E(e_f) = p$$
$$= (F/S) - 1 \text{ [by rearranging terms]}$$

EXAMPLE   If the one-year forward rate of the Australian dollar is $.63 while the spot rate is $.60, then the expected percentage change in the Australian dollar is

$$E(e_f) = p$$
$$= (F/S) - 1$$
$$= (.63/.60) - 1$$
$$= .05, \text{ or } 5\% \qquad \bullet$$

Rationale for Using the Forward Rate If the foreign exchange markets are **semistrong-form efficient**, then not only historical and current information but also all relevant *public* information is reflected in today's exchange rates. If today's exchange rates fully reflect any historical trends in exchange rate movements but do not reflect other public information on expected interest rate movements, then the foreign exchange markets are weak-form efficient but not semistrong-form efficient. Much research has tested the efficient market hypothesis for foreign exchange markets. Most of this research indicates that foreign exchange markets are weak-form efficient and semistrong-form efficient, which suggests that the market-based forward rate should be a reasonable indicator of the future spot rate. However, there is some evidence of inefficiencies for some currencies in certain periods.

If the forward rate consistently over- or underestimates the future spot rate, speculators should take positions in forward contracts (or futures contracts) to capitalize on the mispricing. That is, if they think the forward rate underestimates the future spot rate, they could purchase forward contracts and then sell the currency received at the end of the period at the prevailing spot rate. Alternatively, if they believe the forward rate consistently overestimates the future spot rate, they could sell forward contracts and purchase the currency in the spot market just before they would need to fulfill the forward contract.

WEB

www.fxstreet.com/rate
-charts/forward-rates/
Forward rates for the
euro, British pound,
Canadian dollar,
Japanese yen, and other
currencies for various
maturities ranging from
one week to two years.
These forward rates may
serve as forecasts of
future spot rates.

EXAMPLE Assume that most speculators expect the spot rate of the British pound in 30 days to be $1.45, and suppose the prevailing forward rate is $1.40. The speculators would buy pounds 30 days forward at $1.40 and, when received 30 days later, sell them at the prevailing spot rate. As speculators implement this strategy today, the substantial demand to purchase pounds 30 days forward will cause today's 30-day forward rate to increase. Once the forward rate reaches $1.45 (the expected future spot rate in 30 days), there is no incentive for additional speculation in the forward market. Thus the forward rate should move toward the market's general expectation of the future spot rate. In this sense, the forward rate serves as a market-based forecast because it reflects the market's expectation of the spot rate at the end of the forward horizon (in this example, 30 days from now). ●

Although the focus of this chapter is on corporate forecasting rather than speculation, it is speculation that helps to push the forward rate to the level that reflects the general expectation of the future spot rate. If corporations are convinced that the forward rate is a reliable indicator of the future spot rate, then they can simply monitor this publicly quoted rate to develop exchange rate projections. Forward rates are commonly quoted on financial websites for short-term periods (such as 30 days or 90 days) for currencies of developed countries, and these rates can be used to derive short-term forecasts for those currencies.

Long-Term Forecasting with Forward Rates Long-term exchange rate forecasts can analogously be derived from long-term forward rates.

EXAMPLE Assume that the spot rate of the euro is currently $1.00 while its five-year forward rate is $1.06. This forward rate can serve as a forecast of $1.06 for the euro in five years, which reflects a 6 percent appreciation in the euro over that period.

Forward rates are normally available for periods of two to five years or even longer, but the bid/ask spread is wide because of the limited trading volume. Although such rates are not always available on financial websites, the quoted interest rates on risk-free instruments of various countries can be used to determine what the forward rates would be under conditions of interest rate parity. ●

EXAMPLE

The U.S. five-year interest rate is currently 10 percent (annualized) while the British five-year interest rate is 13 percent. If interest rate parity holds, then the five-year compounded return on investments in each of these countries is computed as follows:

COUNTRY	FIVE-YEAR COMPOUNDED RETURN
United States	$(1.10)^5 - 1 = 61\%$
United Kingdom	$(1.13)^5 - 1 = 84\%$

Therefore, the appropriate five-year forward rate premium (or discount) of the British pound would be

$$p = \frac{1 + i_{U.S.}}{1 + i_{U.K.}} - 1$$
$$= \frac{1.61}{1.84} - 1$$
$$= -.125, \text{ or } -12.5\%$$

So if the five-year forward rate of the pound is used as a forecast, then the spot rate of the pound is expected to depreciate by 12.5 percent over the five-year period. ●

The governments of some emerging markets (such as those in Latin America) seldom issue long-term fixed rate bonds. Consequently, long-term interest rates are not available and so long-term forward rates cannot be derived in the manner shown here.

Like any method of forecasting exchange rates, the forward rate is typically more accurate when forecasting exchange rates for short-term than for long-term horizons. Exchange rates tend to wander farther from expectations over longer periods of time.

Implications of the IFE for Forecasts   Recall that if the international Fisher effect holds, a currency with a higher quoted (nominal) interest rate than the U.S. interest rate should depreciate against the dollar; the reason is that the higher interest rate implies a higher level of expected inflation in that country than in the United States. Because the forward rate captures the difference in interest rates (and thus in expected inflation rates) between two countries, it should provide more accurate forecasts for currencies in high-inflation countries than does the spot rate.

EXAMPLE

Alves, Inc., is a U.S. firm that does business in Brazil, and it needs to forecast the exchange rate of the Brazilian currency (the real) for one year ahead. It considers using either the spot rate or the forward rate to forecast the real. The spot rate of the Brazilian currency is $.40. The one-year interest rate in Brazil is 20 percent, versus 5 percent in the United States. The one-year forward rate of the Brazilian real is $.35, which reflects a discount to offset the interest rate differential (according to IRP; check this yourself). Alves believes that the real's future exchange rate will be driven by the inflation differential between Brazil and the United States. It also believes that the real rate of interest in both Brazil and the United States is 3 percent. These values imply that the expected inflation rate for next year is 17 percent in Brazil and 2 percent in the United States. The pronounced forward rate discount is based on the interest rate differential, which in turn is related to the inflation differential.

In contrast, using the spot rate of the real as a forecast would imply that the exchange rate at the end of the year will be the same as it is today. Because the forward rate forecast (indirectly) captures the differential in expected inflation rates, Alves considers it a more appropriate forecast metric than the spot rate. ●

An MNC that does not believe in the IFE may well disagree that using the forward rate is a more appropriate forecast method than using the spot rate. One could argue either that the high Brazilian interest rates do not reflect high expected inflation or that, even if the inflation occurs, it will not depress the Brazilian real. In either case, the preceding example's use of the forward rate as a forecast would be a mistake.

When a country's interest rate is similar to the U.S. interest rate, the forward rate premium or discount of that country's currency will be close to zero. That currency's forward rate is therefore similar to its spot rate, so the two will yield similar forecasts.

9-2d Mixed Forecasting

Because no single forecasting technique has been found to be consistently superior to the others, some MNCs prefer to use a combination of forecasting techniques. This method is referred to as **mixed forecasting**. Various forecasts for a particular currency value are developed using several forecasting techniques. The techniques used are assigned relative weights that total 100 percent, with the techniques considered more reliable being assigned higher weights. The actual forecast of the currency is a weighted average of the various forecasts developed.

EXAMPLE   College Station, Inc., needs to assess the value of the Mexican peso because it is considering expanding its business in that country. The conclusions that would be drawn from each forecasting technique are listed in Exhibit 9.2, which reveals that the forecasted direction of the peso's value depends on the technique used. The fundamental forecast predicts the peso will appreciate, whereas the technical and market-based forecasts predict it will depreciate. It is noteworthy that, even though the fundamental and market-based forecasts are both driven by the same factor (interest rates), the results are distinctly different. ●

An MNC might decide that only the technical and market-based forecasts are relevant when forecasting in one period but that, in some other period, only the fundamental forecast is relevant. The selection of a forecasting technique may also vary with the particular currency involved. At any given time the MNC may decide, for instance, that a market-based forecast provides the best prediction for the pound whereas fundamental forecasting generates the best prediction for the New Zealand dollar and technical forecasting the best prediction for the Mexican peso.

Consideration of Other Sources of Forecasts   Because forecasting exchange rates is subject to considerable error, MNCs may complement their forecast with forecasts from outside sources, such as a bank or securities firm that provides forecasting services. Some forecasting services specialize in technical forecasts while others specialize

Exhibit 9.2   Forecasts of the Mexican Peso Drawn from Each Forecasting Technique

FORECAST TECHNIQUE	FACTORS CONSIDERED	SITUATION	FORECAST
Technical	Recent movement in peso	The peso's value declined below a specific threshold level in the last few weeks.	The peso's value will continue to fall now that it is beyond the threshold level.
Fundamental	Economic growth, inflation, interest rates	Mexico's interest rates are high, and inflation should remain low.	The peso's value will rise as U.S. investors capitalize on the high interest rates by investing in Mexican securities.
Market-based	Spot rate, forward rate	The peso's forward rate exhibits a significant discount, which is attributed to Mexico's relatively high interest rates.	Based on the forward rate, which provides a forecast of the future spot rate, the peso's value will decline.

in fundamental forecasts. These services can accommodate a wide range of forecast horizons ranging from one month to ten years.

There is no guarantee that a forecasting service will provide more accurate forecasts than those that the MNCs can generate on their own. Some MNCs might prefer forecasts generated from outside sources because inside forecasts by some of the managers might be purposely biased to create more support for their specific expansion agendas.

Whatever forecasts are considered by an MNC should be consistently applied by all of its managers. Otherwise, one manager may be making decisions based on forecasted appreciation of a currency while another is making decisions based on forecasted depreciation of the same currency. For this reason, forecasts should normally be established by a centralized department and not by a department focused on the sales of a particular product.

9-3 Assessment of Forecast Performance

Regardless of which method is used or which service is hired to forecast exchange rates, it is important to recognize that forecasted exchange rates are rarely perfect. Multinational corporations commonly assess their past forecast errors to evaluate the accuracy of their forecasting techniques.

9-3a Measurement of Forecast Error

An MNC that forecasts exchange rates must monitor its performance over time to determine whether the forecasting procedure is satisfactory. For this purpose, a measurement of the forecast error is required. There are various ways to compute forecast errors. One popular measurement is discussed here and is defined as follows:

$$\text{Absolute forecast error as a percentage of the realized value} = \frac{|\text{Forecasted value} - \text{Realized value}|}{\text{Realized value}}$$

The error is computed using an absolute value (in the numerator) because this avoids a possible offsetting effect when determining the mean forecast error. For example, if the forecast error is .05 in the first period and −.05 in the second period (i.e., if the absolute value is not taken), the mean error is zero. Yet that would be misleading because the forecast was not perfectly accurate in either period. Taking the absolute value avoids distortions of this type.

When comparing a forecasting technique's performance among different currencies, examine the relative size of the discrepancy between the forecasted and realized value.

EXAMPLE Consider the following forecasted and realized values by New Hampshire Co. during one period:

	FORECASTED VALUE	REALIZED VALUE
British pound	$1.35	$1.50
Mexican peso	$.12	$.10

In this case, the difference between the forecasted and realized value is $.15 for the pound versus $.02 for the peso. This does not mean that the forecast for the peso is more accurate. When measured as a percentage of the realized value, the forecast error of the British pound is

$$\frac{|\$1.35 - \$1.50|}{\$1.50} = \frac{\$.15}{\$1.50} = .10, \text{ or } 10\%$$

In contrast, the forecast error of the Mexican peso is

$$\frac{|.12 - .10|}{.10} = \frac{.02}{.10} = .20, \text{ or } 20\%$$

Thus the peso's value was predicted with less accuracy. ●

9-3b Forecast Errors among Time Horizons

The potential forecast error for a particular currency depends on the forecast horizon. A forecast of the spot rate of the euro for tomorrow will have a relatively small error because tomorrow's spot rate probably will not deviate much from today's rate. However, a forecast of the euro in one month is more difficult because there is more time for economic conditions to change, which can cause the euro's value to stray farther from today's spot rate. A forecast of the euro for one year ahead is even more difficult, and a forecast of 10 years ahead will likely be subject to very large error.

9-3c Forecast Errors over Time Periods

The forecast error for a given currency changes over time. In periods when a country is experiencing economic and political problems, its currency is more volatile and more difficult to predict. The size of the errors changes over time, because the errors are larger in periods when the currency's value is more volatile.

9-3d Forecast Errors among Currencies

The ability to forecast currency values may vary with the currency of concern. From a U.S. perspective, the currencies that are more stable are susceptible to less error. As an extreme example, for a currency whose value is pegged to an exact dollar level, the spot rate would always be a perfect forecast of the future spot rate, and the forecast error would be zero. The central bank of China maintains the value of the Chinese yuan within narrow boundaries, so the yuan is quite stable and should be subject to a lower forecast error. In contrast, currencies (e.g., Australian dollar, Brazilian real, New Zealand dollar) that are volatile should be subject to larger forecast errors. Some currencies, including the Canadian dollar and Japanese yen, usually exhibit moderate volatility (even without central bank intervention) and hence should be subject to moderate forecast errors.

Exhibit 9.3 compares the mean absolute forecast error to the volatility (standard deviation of exchange rate movements) for selected currencies over time. The monthly forecasts for each currency were derived using the currency's prevailing spot rate as the forecast for one month ahead. The exhibit demonstrates how forecast errors are generally lower for less volatile currencies, including the Chinese yuan and Singapore dollar (S\$), and higher for more volatile currencies, which include the Australian dollar (A\$), the Brazilian real, and the New Zealand dollar (NZ\$). Financial managers of U.S.-based MNCs should be especially concerned if they are exposed to these more volatile currencies because they are subject to greater forecast errors. Managers may therefore wish to hedge that exposure, as discussed in detail in the next chapter.

Exhibit 9.3   How Forecast Error Is Affected by Volatility

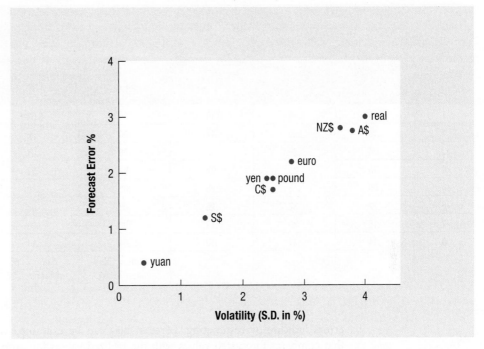

9-3e Comparing Forecast Errors among Forecast Techniques

An MNC may compare the forecast error produced by two or more techniques used to derive forecasted exchange rates for a particular currency so that it can decide which technique to use in the future.

EXAMPLE

Xavier Co. uses a fundamental forecasting method to forecast the exchange rate of the Polish currency (zloty), which it will need to purchase to buy imports from Poland. Xavier also derives a second forecast for each period based on an alternative forecasting model. Its forecasts of the zloty, using Model 1 (the fundamental method) and Model 2 (the alternative method), are shown in columns 2 and 3, respectively, of Exhibit 9.4; column 4 gives the realized value of the zloty.

The absolute forecast errors of forecasting with Model 1 and Model 2 are shown in columns 5 and 6, respectively. Notice that Model 1 outperformed Model 2 in six of the eight periods. The mean absolute forecast error when using Model 1 is $.04, so this model's forecasts are off by $.04 on average. Model 1 is not perfectly accurate but does a better job than Model 2, which had a mean absolute forecast error of $.07. Overall, predictions with Model 1 are (on average) $.03 closer to the realized value. ●

For a complete comparison of performance among forecasting methods, an MNC should evaluate as many periods as possible. Only eight periods are used in our example because that is enough to illustrate how to compare forecasting performance. If the MNC has a large number of periods to evaluate, it could statistically test for significant differences in forecasting errors.

9-3f Graphic Evaluation of Forecast Bias

MNCs may want to assess whether their forecasts are biased (consistently underestimating or overestimating), because by doing so they may be able to correct the bias to improve their forecasting accuracy. When a forecast error is measured as the forecasted value minus the realized value, negative errors indicate underestimating whereas positive

Exhibit 9.4   Comparison of Forecast Techniques

(1)	(2)	(3)	(4)	(5)	(6)	(7) = (5) − (6)
PERIOD	PREDICTED VALUE OF ZLOTY BY MODEL 1	PREDICTED VALUE OF ZLOTY BY MODEL 2	REALIZED VALUE OF ZLOTY	ABSOLUTE FORECAST ERROR USING MODEL 1	ABSOLUTE FORECAST ERROR USING MODEL 2	DIFFERENCE IN ABSOLUTE FORECAST ERRORS (MODEL 1 − MODEL 2)
1	$.20	$.24	$.16	$.04	$.08	$−.04
2	.18	.20	.14	.04	.06	−.02
3	.24	.20	.16	.08	.04	.04
4	.26	.20	.22	.04	.02	.02
5	.30	.18	.28	.02	.10	−.08
6	.22	.32	.26	.04	.06	−.02
7	.16	.20	.14	.02	.06	−.04
8	.14	.24	.10	.04	.14	−.10
				Sum = .32 Mean = .04	Sum = .56 Mean = .07	Sum = −.24 Mean = −.03

errors indicate overestimating. Forecast bias can be examined with the use of a graph that compares forecasted values with the realized values for various time periods.

EXAMPLE

Tunek Co. is a U.S.-based MNC that commonly imports products from the island of Zedan, which are denominated in Zedan's currency (called the zed). Because the zed's value in dollars is very volatile, Tunek Co. is concerned about how its expenses associated with importing could rise abruptly if the zed's value increases. For eight consecutive quarters, Tunek Co. hired a consultant to forecast the zed's spot rate in dollars three months ahead. The consultant's predictions and the realized exchange rate values are shown in Exhibit 9.5. Tunek's assessment is shown in Exhibit 9.6, where the predicted and realized values in Exhibit 9.5 are compared graphically.

The 45-degree line in Exhibit 9.6 represents perfect forecasts. If the realized value turned out to be exactly what was predicted over several periods, then all points would be located on that 45-degree line in Exhibit 9.6. For this reason, this line is known as the **perfect forecast line**. The closer the points reflecting the eight periods are to the 45-degree line, the better the forecast; the vertical distance between each point and the 45-degree line is the forecast error. A point that is $.04 above the 45-degree line indicates that the realized spot rate was $.04 higher than the exchange rate forecasted.

Exhibit 9.5   Evaluation of Forecast Performance by Tunek Co.

PERIOD	PREDICTED VALUE OF CURRENCY FOR END OF PERIOD	REALIZED VALUE OF CURRENCY AT END OF PERIOD
1	$.20	$.16
2	.18	.14
3	.24	.16
4	.26	.22
5	.30	.28
6	.22	.26
7	.16	.14
8	.14	.10

Exhibit 9.6   Graphical Evaluation of Forecast Performance

All points above the 45-degree line reflect underestimation, while all points below the 45-degree line reflect overestimation. If points appear to be scattered evenly on both sides of the 45-degree line, then the forecasts are said to be *unbiased* because they are not consistently above or below the realized values. Because most of the points are below the perfect forecast line, the forecasts have typically overestimated the actual spot rate three months later. If Tunek Co. continues to use the consultant to obtain forecasts and also believes that a similar forecast bias will persist in the future, it might consider adjusting future forecasts to correct for the possible bias. ●

9-3g Statistical Test of Forecast Bias

If a forecast is biased, there is a systematic forecast error whose correction may be able to improve forecast accuracy. One statistical test of forecast bias is to apply the following regression model to historical data:

$$S_t = a_0 + a_1 \text{FORECAST}_{t-1} + \mu_t$$

where

$$S_t = \text{spot rate at time } t$$
$$\text{FORECAST}_{t-1} = \text{forecasted exchange rate at time } t - 1$$
$$\mu_t = \textit{error term}$$
$$a_0 = \text{intercept}$$
$$a_1 = \text{regression coefficient}$$

If the forecast is unbiased, the intercept a_0 should equal 0, and the regression coefficient a_1 should equal 1. The t-test for a_1 is

$$t = \frac{a_1 - 1}{\text{Standard error of } a_1}$$

If $a_0 = 0$ and if a_1 is significantly less than 1, this implies that the forecasted spot rate is systematically overestimating the spot rate. For example, if $a_0 = 0$ and $a_1 = .90$, the future spot rate is estimated to be 90 percent of the forecasted spot rate.

If $a_0 = 0$ and a_1 is significantly greater than 1, this implies that the forward rate is systematically underestimating the spot rate. For example, if $a_0 = 0$ and $a_1 = 1.1$, the future spot rate is estimated to be 110 percent of the forecast generated by the forecasted spot rate.

When a bias is detected and anticipated to persist in the future, future forecasts may incorporate that bias. For instance, if $a_1 = 1.1$, future forecasts of the spot rate may incorporate this information, multiplying the forecasted spot rate by 1.1 to create a forecast of the future spot rate.

9-3h Shifts in Forecast Bias over Time

Detecting a forecast bias from historical data is easier than determining how long the bias will continue in the future, because the forecast bias of a currency tends to shift over time. For this reason, MNCs must use caution when attempting to correct a forecast to reflect a bias found in historical data.

EXAMPLE   Consider the use of the spot rate of the euro to forecast the euro's value one month later. During the period from August 2012 to April 2014, the euro consistently appreciated against the U.S. dollar; hence the one-month forecast typically underestimated the spot rate one month ahead over that period. However, from April 2014 to April 2015, the euro consistently depreciated against the dollar, so the one-month forecast typically overestimated the euro's value one month later over that period.

Even if the one-month forward rate of the euro (rather than its prevailing spot rate) had been used to predict the spot rate one month ahead in these periods, the forecast bias would have been similar because the one-month forward rate was usually close to the prevailing spot rate. ●

If an MNC detected the forecast bias in the first few months when the bias initially existed, it could have benefited from correcting for the bias. However, if it detected the forecast bias just as the euro's trend was reversing, its attempt to correct for the bias could have caused a more pronounced forecast error.

9-4 Accounting for Uncertainty Surrounding Forecasts

It is nearly impossible to predict future exchange rates with perfect accuracy. For this reason, MNCs do not rely just on point estimates of future exchange rates that could influence their decisions on how to expand their business. They account for the uncertainty surrounding exchange rate forecasts that could affect their decisions. An MNC can be more confident about such managerial project decisions when the project is determined to be feasible under alternative exchange rate forecasts. Furthermore, by considering a range of possible exchange rate movements in its analysis of a proposed project, an

MNC can assess the extent to which its operating performance could be affected by various possible exchange rate outcomes.

9-4a Sensitivity Analysis Applied to Fundamental Forecasting

As described earlier in the chapter, when MNCs use fundamental forecasting to predict exchange rate movements based on variables that affect exchange rates instantaneously, they must first forecast the values of those variables. Thus, even if an MNC properly estimates the relationship between that factor and the exchange rate movement, its forecast of the exchange rate movement could be subject to error if its forecast for that factor is inaccurate. An MNC can use sensitivity analysis to attempt to account for the possible error in the forecasted value of the factor and improve its forecasts. Sensitivity analysis is valuable because it allows the MNC to derive a variety of forecasts based on alternative scenarios. This allows the MNC to review the distribution or range of possible outcomes that might occur.

EXAMPLE   Mercer Co. was forced to use a forecast for INF_t when predicting the exchange rate movements of the British pound in the example earlier in the chapter. Mercer recognizes that its forecast of INF_t could be wrong and therefore applies sensitivity analysis by considering other possible outcomes for INF_t as shown in the first column of Exhibit 9.7. Assume that Mercer decides that its initial forecast for INF_t has a 50 percent chance of occurring, while the two other possible outcomes listed in the first column each have a 25 percent chance of occurring. These probabilities are listed in column 2 of the exhibit. Column 3 shows the estimate of the quarterly percentage change in the British pound for each of the three possible outcomes. Although Mercer's best guess is that the British pound will appreciate by 1.40 percent over the next quarter, it recognizes that its forecast may be wrong. Its sensitivity analysis suggests that the pound's appreciation may be as low as .70 percent under one inflation scenario, and as high as 2.80 percent in response to an alternative inflation scenario. ●

9-4b Interval Forecasts

When MNCs derive a single point estimate of an exchange rate, they may recognize that their point estimate will not be perfectly accurate. To account for this uncertainty, they can create an interval around the point estimate forecast and have much confidence that the actual value will be within that interval.

EXAMPLE   Harp, Inc., which is based in Oklahoma, imports products from Canada. It uses the spot rate of the Canadian dollar (currently $.70) to forecast the value of the Canadian dollar one month from now. In addition, Harp specifies an interval around its forecasts that is based on the Canadian dollar's historical volatility. The more volatile the currency, the more likely it is to deviate significantly from its forecasted value (i.e., the larger is the expected forecast error). Harp determines that the standard deviation of the Canadian dollar's movements over the last 12 months is 2 percent. So assuming the movements are normally distributed, there is a 68 percent chance that the actual value will be within a single standard deviation (2 percent) of its forecasted value; the resulting interval ranges from $.686 to $.714.

Exhibit 9.7   Illustration of Sensitivity Analysis Applied to Forecasting

POSSIBLE VALUE OF INFLATION DIFFERENTIAL (INF_t)	PROBABILITY OF THIS SCENARIO OCCURRING	EXPECTED EXCHANGE RATE MOVEMENT (e_t) IF THIS SCENARIO OCCURS
1.0%	25%	$.7 \times 1\% = 0.70\%$
2.0%	50%	$.7 \times 2.0\% = 1.40\%$
4.0%	25%	$.7 \times 4.0\% = 2.80\%$

Furthermore, Harp assumes there is a 95 percent chance that the Canadian dollar will be within two standard deviations (4 percent) of the predicted value; this results in an interval ranging from $.672 to $.728. By specifying an interval, Harp can anticipate more specifically how much the currency's actual value might deviate from its predicted value. For currencies that are more volatile, the standard deviation is larger and the interval surrounding the point estimate forecast is wider. ●

WEB

www.fednewyork.org
/markets/implied
volatility.html
Implied volatilities of
major currencies. The
implied volatility can be
used to measure the
market's expectations of
a specific currency's
volatility in the future.

As this example shows, knowing a currency's volatility is useful when specifying an interval around a forecast. Yet because a currency's volatility can change over time, past volatility levels may not be the best way to establish an interval around a point estimate forecast. Hence MNCs may prefer forecasting exchange rate volatility to determine this interval.

The first step in forecasting exchange rate volatility is to determine the relevant period of concern. If an MNC is forecasting the value of the Canadian dollar each day over the next quarter, then it may also attempt to forecast the standard deviation of daily exchange rate movements over this quarter. That information could be combined with the point estimate forecast of the Canadian dollar for each day to derive confidence intervals around each day's forecast.

An interval forecast requires values for the volatility of exchange rate movements. These values can be forecast using (1) recent exchange rate volatility, (2) historical time series of volatilities, and (3) the implied standard deviation derived from currency option prices.

Using Recent Levels of Volatility   The volatility of historical exchange rate movements over a recent period can be used to forecast the future. In our example, the standard deviation of monthly exchange rate movements in the Canadian dollar during the previous 12 months could be used to estimate the volatility of the Canadian dollar over the next month.

Using Historical Patterns of Volatilities   Historical volatility can change over time, so the standard deviation of monthly exchange rate movements in the last 12 months is not necessarily an accurate predictor of such volatility in the next month. To the extent that there is a pattern to changes in the exchange rate's volatility, a series of time periods may be used to forecast volatility in the subsequent period.

EXAMPLE   The standard deviation of monthly exchange rate movements in the Canadian dollar can be determined for each of the last several years. Then, a time-series trend of these standard deviation levels can be used to form an estimate for the volatility of the Canadian dollar over the next month. The forecast may be based on a time-based weighting scheme such as 60 percent times the standard deviation in the last year *plus* 30 percent times the standard deviation in the year before that *plus* 10 percent times the standard deviation in the year before that. This scheme places more weight on the most recent data to derive the forecast but allows data from previous years to influence the forecast as well. The weights that achieved the most accuracy (lowest forecast error) over previous periods are normally used when applying this method to forecast exchange rate volatility. ●

Because various economic and political factors can cause exchange rate volatility to change abruptly, not even sophisticated time-series models can necessarily forecast it accurately. A poor forecast of exchange rate volatility can lead to an improper interval surrounding a point estimate forecast.

Using the Implied Standard Deviation   A third method for forecasting exchange rate volatility is to derive the exchange rate's implied standard deviation (ISD) from the currency option pricing model. Recall that the premium on a call option for a currency depends on such factors as the relationship between the spot exchange rate and the exercise (strike) price of the option, the number of days until the option's expiration date, and the anticipated volatility of the denominating currency's exchange rate movements.

There is a currency option pricing model for estimating the call option premium based on various factors. The actual values of these factors are all known *except* for the anticipated volatility. By considering the existing option premium paid by investors for a specific currency option, MNCs can derive the anticipated volatility (also known as implied volatility or implied standard deviation) of a currency that they are forecasting. After accounting for the currency's existing spot rate (relative to the option's exercise price) and the time until expiration of the option, a larger premium must be paid for options on currencies that are expected to be volatile before the option expires. The logic is that investors who sell the option would demand a sufficiently high premium to reflect the degree of anticipated volatility before the option expires because they are subject to greater losses when the currency is more volatile. The higher the implied volatility (as determined by the currency option pricing model), the more dispersed it is in the probability distribution that surrounds a forecast of the currency's exchange rate; in other words, the interval surrounding the forecast is wider.

SUMMARY

- Multinational corporations need exchange rate forecasts to make decisions on hedging payables and receivables, short-term financing and investment, capital budgeting, and long-term financing.
- The most common forecasting techniques can be classified as (1) technical, (2) fundamental, (3) market based, or (4) mixed. Each technique has limitations, and the quality of the forecasts produced varies. Yet exchange rates are very difficult to forecast accurately, because their movements can be volatile over time.
- Forecast performance can be evaluated by comparing the actual values of currencies to the values predicted. To be meaningful, this comparison should be conducted over several periods. Two criteria used to evaluate performance of a forecast method are bias and accuracy. When comparing the accuracy of forecasts for two currencies, the absolute forecast error should be divided by the realized value of the currency in order to control for differences in the currencies' relative values.
- MNCs specify an interval around their point estimate forecast to account for uncertainty. Such an interval can be derived from the recent exchange rate volatility, the historical time series of volatilities, and the implied standard deviation from currency option prices.

POINT COUNTER-POINT

Which Exchange Rate Forecast Technique Should MNCs Use?

Point   Use the spot rate to forecast. When a U.S.-based MNC firm conducts financial budgeting, it must estimate the values of its foreign currency cash flows that will be received by the parent. Because it is well documented that firms cannot accurately forecast future values, MNCs should use the spot rate for budgeting. Changes in economic conditions are difficult to predict, and the spot rate reflects the best guess of the future spot rate if there are no changes in economic conditions.

Counter-Point   Use the forward rate to forecast. The spot rates of some currencies do not represent accurate or even unbiased estimates of the future spot rates. Many currencies of developing countries have generally declined over time. These currencies tend to be in countries that have high inflation rates. If the spot rate had been used for budgeting, the dollar cash flows resulting from cash inflows in these currencies would have been highly overestimated. The expected inflation in a country can be accounted for by using the nominal interest rate. A high nominal interest rate implies a high level of expected inflation. Based on interest rate parity, these currencies will have pronounced discounts. Thus the forward rate captures the expected inflation differential between countries because it is influenced by the nominal interest rate differential. Because it captures the inflation differential, it should provide a more accurate forecast of currencies, especially those currencies in high-inflation countries.

Who Is Correct?   Use the Internet to learn more about this issue. Which argument do you support? Offer your own opinion on this issue.

SELF-TEST

Answers are provided in Appendix A at the back of the text.

1. Assume that the annual U.S. return is expected to be 7 percent for each of the next four years, while the annual interest rate in Mexico is expected to be 20 percent. Determine the appropriate four-year forward rate premium or discount on the Mexican peso, which could be used to forecast the percentage change in the peso over the next four years.

2. Consider the following information:

CURRENCY	90-DAY FORWARD RATE	SPOT RATE THAT OCCURRED 90 DAYS LATER
Canadian dollar	$.80	$.82
Japanese yen	$.012	$.011

Assuming the forward rate was used to forecast the future spot rate, determine whether the Canadian dollar or the Japanese yen was forecasted with more accuracy, based on the absolute forecast error as a percentage of the realized value.

3. Assume that the forward rate and spot rate of the Mexican peso are normally similar at a given point in time. Assume that the peso has depreciated consistently and substantially over the last three years. Would the forward rate have been biased over this period? If so, would it typically have overestimated or underestimated the future spot rate of the peso (in dollars)? Explain.

4. An analyst has stated that the British pound seems to increase in value over the two weeks following announcements by the Bank of England (the British central bank) that it will raise interest rates. If this statement is true, what are the inferences regarding weak-form or semistrong-form efficiency?

5. Assume that Mexican interest rates are much higher than U.S. interest rates. Also assume that interest rate parity (discussed in Chapter 7) exists. If you use the forward rate of the Mexican peso to forecast the Mexican peso's future spot rate, would you expect the peso to appreciate or depreciate? Explain.

6. Warden Co. is considering a project in Venezuela that will be very profitable if the local currency (bolivar) appreciates against the dollar. If the bolivar depreciates, the project will result in losses. Warden Co. forecasts that the bolivar will appreciate. The bolivar's value historically has been very volatile. As a manager of Warden Co., would you be comfortable with this project? Explain.

QUESTIONS AND APPLICATIONS

1. Motives for Forecasting Explain corporate motives for forecasting exchange rates.

2. Technical Forecasting Explain the technical technique for forecasting exchange rates. What are some limitations of using technical forecasting to predict exchange rates?

3. Fundamental Forecasting Explain the fundamental technique for forecasting exchange rates. What are some limitations of using a fundamental technique to forecast exchange rates?

4. Market-Based Forecasting Explain the market-based technique for forecasting exchange rates. What is the rationale for using market-based forecasts? If the euro appreciates substantially against the dollar during a specific period, would market-based forecasts have overestimated or underestimated the realized values over this period? Explain.

5. Mixed Forecasting Explain the mixed technique for forecasting exchange rates.

6. Detecting a Forecast Bias Explain how to assess performance in forecasting exchange rates. Explain how to detect a bias in forecasting exchange rates.

7. Measuring Forecast Accuracy You are hired as a consultant to assess a firm's ability to forecast. The firm has developed a point forecast for two different currencies presented in the following table. The firm asks you to determine which currency was forecasted with greater accuracy.

PERIOD	YEN FORE-CAST	ACTUAL YEN VALUE	POUND FORE-CAST	ACTUAL POUND VALUE
1	$.0050	$.0051	$1.50	$1.51
2	.0048	.0052	1.53	1.50
3	.0053	.0052	1.55	1.58
4	.0055	.0056	1.49	1.52

8. Limitations of a Fundamental Forecast Syracuse Corp. believes that future real interest rate movements will affect exchange rates, and it has applied regression analysis to historical data to assess the relationship. It will use regression coefficients derived from this analysis along with forecasted real interest rate movements to predict exchange rates in the future. Explain at least three limitations of this method.

9. Consistent Forecasts Lexington Co. is a U.S.-based MNC with subsidiaries in most major countries. Each subsidiary is responsible for forecasting the future exchange rate of its local currency relative to the U.S. dollar. Comment on this policy. How might Lexington Co. ensure consistent forecasts among the different subsidiaries?

10. Forecasting with a Forward Rate Assume that the four-year annualized interest rate in the United States is 9 percent and the four-year annualized interest rate in Singapore is 6 percent. Assume interest rate parity holds for a four-year horizon. Assume that the spot rate of the Singapore dollar is $.60. If the forward rate is used to forecast exchange rates, what will be the forecast for the Singapore dollar's spot rate in four years? What percentage appreciation or depreciation does this forecast imply over the four-year period?

11. Foreign Exchange Market Efficiency Assume that foreign exchange markets were found to be weak-form efficient. What does this suggest about utilizing technical analysis to speculate in euros? If MNCs believe that foreign exchange markets are strong-form efficient, why would they develop their own forecasts of future exchange rates? That is, why wouldn't they simply use today's quoted rates as indicators about future rates? After all, today's quoted rates should reflect all relevant information.

12. Forecast Error The director of currency forecasting at Champaign-Urbana Corp. says, "The most critical task of forecasting exchange rates is not to derive a point estimate of a future exchange rate but to assess how wrong our estimate might be." What does this statement mean?

13. Forecasting Exchange Rates of Currencies That Previously Were Fixed When some countries in Eastern Europe initially allowed their currencies to fluctuate against the dollar, would the fundamental technique based on historical relationships have been useful for forecasting future exchange rates of these currencies? Explain.

14. Forecast Error Royce Co. is a U.S. firm with future receivables one year from now in Canadian dollars and British pounds. Its pound receivables are known with certainty, and its estimated Canadian dollar receivables are subject to a 2 percent error in either direction. The dollar values of both types of receivables are similar. There is no chance of default by the customers involved. Royce's treasurer says that the estimate of dollar cash flows to be generated from the British pound receivables is subject to greater uncertainty than that of the Canadian dollar receivables. Explain the rationale for the treasurer's statement.

15. Forecasting the Euro Cooper, Inc., a U.S.-based MNC, periodically obtains euros to purchase German products. It assesses U.S. and German trade patterns and inflation rates to develop a fundamental forecast for the euro. How could Cooper possibly improve its method of fundamental forecasting as applied to the euro?

16. Forward Rate Forecast Assume that you obtain a quote for a one-year forward rate on the Mexican peso. Assume that Mexico's one-year interest rate is 40 percent, while the U.S. one-year interest rate is 7 percent. Over the next year, the peso depreciates by 12 percent. Do you think the forward rate overestimated the spot rate one year ahead in this case? Explain.

17. Forecasting Based on PPP versus the Forward Rate You believe that the Singapore dollar's exchange rate movements are mostly attributed to purchasing power parity. Today the nominal annual interest rate in Singapore is 18 percent. The nominal annual interest rate in the United States is 3 percent. You expect that annual inflation will be about 4 percent in Singapore and 1 percent in the United States. Assume that interest rate parity holds. Today the spot rate of the Singapore dollar is $.63. Do you think the one-year forward rate would underestimate, overestimate, or be an unbiased estimate of the future spot rate in one year? Explain.

18. Interpreting an Unbiased Forward Rate

Assume that the forward rate is an unbiased but not necessarily accurate forecast of the future exchange rate of the yen over the next several years. Based on this information, do you think Raven Co. should hedge its remittance of expected Japanese yen profits to the U.S. parent by selling yen forward contracts? Why would this strategy be advantageous? Under what conditions would this strategy backfire?

Advanced Questions

19. Probability Distribution of Forecasts

Assume that the following regression model was applied to historical quarterly data:

$$e_f = a_0 + a_1 INT_t + a_2 INF_{t-1} + \mu_t$$

where

$e_f =$ **percentage change in the exchange rate of the Japanese yen in period t**

$INT_t =$ **average real interest rate differential (U.S. interest rate minus Japanese interest rate) over period t**

$INF_{t-1} =$ **inflation differential (U.S. inflation rate minus Japanese inflation rate) in the previous period**

$a_0, a_1, a_2 =$ **regression coefficients**

$\mu_t =$ **error term**

Assume that the regression coefficients were estimated as follows:

$$a_0 = .0$$
$$a_1 = .9$$
$$a_2 = .8$$

Also assume that the inflation differential in the most recent period was 3 percent. The real interest rate differential in the upcoming period is forecasted as follows:

INTEREST RATE DIFFERENTIAL	PROBABILITY
0%	30%
1	60
2	10

If Stillwater, Inc., uses this information to forecast the Japanese yen's exchange rate, what will be the probability distribution of the yen's percentage change over the upcoming period?

20. Testing for a Forecast Bias

You must determine whether there is a forecast bias in the forward rate. You apply regression analysis to test the relationship between the actual spot rate and the forward rate forecast (F):

$$S = a_0 + a_1(F)$$

The regression results are as follows:

COEFFICIENT	STANDARD ERROR
$a_0 = .006$	.011
$a_1 = .800$	.05

Based on these results, is there a bias in the forecast? Verify your conclusion. If there is a bias, explain whether it is an overestimate or an underestimate.

21. Effect of 9/11 on Forward Rate Forecasts

The September 11, 2001, terrorist attack on the United States was quickly followed by lower interest rates in the United States. How would this affect a fundamental forecast of foreign currencies? How would this affect the forward rate forecast of foreign currencies?

22. Interpreting Forecast Bias Information

The treasurer of Glencoe, Inc., detected a forecast bias when using the 30-day forward rate of the euro to forecast future spot rates of the euro over various periods. He believes he can use this information to determine whether imports ordered every week should be hedged (payment is made 30 days after each order). Glencoe's president says that in the long run the forward rate is unbiased and that the treasurer should not waste time trying to "beat the forward rate" but should just hedge all orders. Who is correct?

23. Forecasting Latin American Currencies

The value of each Latin American currency relative to the dollar is dictated by supply and demand conditions between that currency and the dollar. The values of Latin American currencies have generally declined substantially against the dollar over time. Most of these countries have high inflation rates and high interest rates. The data on inflation rates, economic growth, and other economic indicators are subject to error, as limited resources are used to compile the data.

a. If the forward rate is used as a market-based forecast, will this rate result in a forecast of appreciation, depreciation, or no change in any particular Latin American currency? Explain.

b. If technical forecasting is used, will this result in a forecast of appreciation, depreciation, or no change in the value of a specific Latin American currency? Explain.

c. Do you think that U.S. firms can accurately forecast the future values of Latin American currencies? Explain.

24. Selecting between Forecast Methods Bolivia currently has a nominal one-year risk-free interest rate of 40 percent, which is primarily due to the high level of expected inflation. The U.S. nominal one-year risk-free interest rate is 8 percent. The spot rate of Bolivia's currency (called the boliviano) is $.14. The one-year forward rate of the boliviano is $.108. What is the forecasted percentage change in the boliviano if the spot rate is used as a one-year forecast? What is the forecasted percentage change in the boliviano if the one-year forward rate is used as a one-year forecast? Which forecast do you think will be more accurate? Why?

25. Comparing Market-based Forecasts For all parts of this question, assume that interest rate parity exists, that the prevailing one-year U.S. nominal interest rate is low, and that you expect U.S. inflation to be low this year.

a. Assume that the country Dinland engages in much trade with the United States and the trade involves many different products. Dinland has had a zero trade balance with the United States (the value of exports and imports is about the same) in the past. Assume that you expect a high level of inflation (about 40 percent) in Dinland over the next year because of a large increase in the prices of many products that it produces. Dinland presently has a one-year risk-free interest rate of more than 40 percent. Do you think that the prevailing spot rate or the one-year forward rate would result in a more accurate forecast of Dinland's currency (the din) one year from now? Explain.

b. Assume that the country Freeland engages in much trade with the United States and the trade involves many different products. Freeland has had a zero trade balance with the United States (the value of exports and imports is about the same) in the past. You expect high inflation (about 40 percent) in Freeland over the next year because of a large increase in the cost of land (and therefore housing) in Freeland. You believe that the prices of products that Freeland produces will not be affected. Freeland presently has a one-year risk-free interest rate of more than 40 percent. Do you think that the prevailing one-year forward rate of Freeland's currency (the fre) would overestimate, underestimate, or be a reasonably accurate forecast of the spot rate one year from now? (Presume a direct quotation of the exchange rate, so that if the forward rate underestimates, it means that its value is less than the realized spot rate in one year. If the forward rate overestimates, it means that its value is more than the realized spot rate in one year.)

26. IRP and Forecasting New York Co. has agreed to pay 10 million Australian dollars (A$) in two years for equipment that it is importing from Australia. The spot rate of the Australian dollar is $.60. The annualized U.S. interest rate is 4 percent, regardless of the debt maturity. The annualized Australian dollar interest rate is 12 percent regardless of the debt maturity. New York plans to hedge its exposure with a forward contract that it will arrange today. Assume that interest rate parity exists. Determine the amount of U.S. dollars that New York Co. will need in two years to make its payment.

27. Forecasting Based on the International Fisher Effect Purdue Co. (based in the United States) exports cable wire to Australian manufacturers. It invoices its product in U.S. dollars and will not change its price over the next year. There is intense competition between Purdue and the local cable wire producers based in Australia. Purdue's competitors invoice their products in Australian dollars and will not be changing their prices over the next year. The annualized risk-free interest rate is presently 8 percent in the United States versus 3 percent in Australia. Today the spot rate of the Australian dollar is $.55. Purdue Co. uses this spot rate as a forecast of the future exchange rate of the Australian dollar. Purdue expects that revenue from its cable wire exports to Australia will be about $2 million over the next year.

If Purdue decides to use the international Fisher effect rather than the spot rate to forecast the exchange rate of the Australian dollar over the next year, will its expected revenue from its exports be higher, lower, or unaffected? Explain.

28. IRP, Expectations, and Forecast Error

Assume that interest rate parity exists and it will continue to exist in the future. Assume that interest rates of the United States and the United Kingdom vary substantially in many periods. You expect that interest rates at the beginning of each month have a major effect on the British pound's exchange rate at the end of each month because you believe that capital flows between the United States and the United Kingdom influence the pound's exchange rate. You expect that money will flow to whichever country has the higher nominal interest rate. At the beginning of each month, you will either use the spot rate or the one-month forward rate to forecast the future spot rate of the pound that will exist at the end of the month. Will the use of the spot rate as a forecast result in smaller, larger, or the same mean absolute forecast error as the forward rate when forecasting the future spot rate of the pound on a monthly basis? Explain.

29. Deriving Forecasts from Forward Rates

Assume that interest rate parity exists. Today the one-year U.S. interest rate is equal to 8 percent, while Mexico's one-year interest rate is equal to 10 percent. Today the two-year annualized U.S. interest rate is equal to 11 percent, while the two-year annualized Mexican interest rate is equal to 11 percent. West Virginia Co. uses the forward rate to predict the future spot rate. Based on forward rates for one year ahead and two years ahead, will the peso appreciate or depreciate from the end of year 1 until the end of year 2?

30. Forecast Errors from Forward Rates

Assume that interest rate parity exists. One year ago, the spot rate of the euro was $1.40, and the spot rate of the Japanese yen was $.01. At that time, the one-year interest rate of the euro and the Japanese yen was 3 percent, and the one-year U.S. interest rate was 7 percent. One year ago, you used the one-year forward rate of the euro to derive a forecast of the future spot rate of the euro and the yen one year ahead. Today the spot rate of the euro is $1.39, while the spot rate of the yen is $.009. Which currency did you forecast more accurately?

31. Forward versus Spot Rate Forecasts

Assume that interest rate parity exists and it will continue to exist in the future. Kentucky Co. wants to forecast the value of the Japanese yen in one month. The Japanese interest rate is lower than the U.S. interest rate.

Kentucky Co. will either use the spot rate or the one-month forward rate to forecast the future spot rate of the yen at the end of one month. Your opinion is that net capital flows between countries tend to move toward whichever country has the higher nominal interest rate and that these capital flows are the primary factor that affects the value of the currency. Will the forward rate as a forecast result in a smaller, larger, or the same absolute forecast error as the use of today's spot rate when forecasting the future spot rate of the yen in one month? Briefly explain.

32. Forward versus Spot Rate Forecast

Assume that interest rate parity exists. The one-year risk-free interest rate in the United States is 3 percent versus 16 percent in Singapore. You believe in purchasing power parity, and you also believe that Singapore will experience a 2 percent inflation rate and the United States will experience a 2 percent inflation rate over the next year. If you wanted to forecast the Singapore dollar's spot rate for one year ahead, do you think that the forecast error would be smaller when using today's one-year forward rate of the Singapore dollar as the forecast or using today's spot rate as the forecast? Briefly explain.

33. Forecasting Based on the IFE

The prevailing one-year risk-free interest rate in Argentina is higher than the interest rate in the United States and will continue to be higher over time. Sycamore Co. believes the international Fisher effect (IFE) can be used to derive the best forecast of the Argentine peso's exchange rate movement over time. However, you believe that the prevailing spot rate is the best forecast of the future spot rate. Based on your opinion, will Sycamore Co. typically overestimate the future spot rate, underestimate the future spot rate, or create an unbiased forecast (similar chance of overestimating or underestimating the future spot rate) of the Argentine peso? Briefly explain.

Critical Thinking

Forecasting Exchange Rates of Currencies in Developing Countries   Some U.S.-based MNCs have business in developing countries and have difficulty hedging their exposure to exchange rate risk. Their forecasts of future exchange rates are subject to much error because the currencies in these countries tend to be very volatile and could possibly depreciate by 20 percent or more in a given year.. Write a short essay on how MNCs that have receivables in such currencies might be able to use exchange rate forecasts to prepare for possible weak currency scenarios, so that they can assess whether they will have sufficient dollar cash inflows to cover their debt payments.

Discussion in the Boardroom

This exercise can be found in Appendix E at the back of this textbook.

Running Your Own MNC

This exercise can be found on the *International Financial Management* text companion website. Go to www .cengagebrain.com (students) or www.cengage.com/login (instructors) and search using **ISBN 9781133947837.**

BLADES, INC. CASE

Forecasting Exchange Rates

Recall that Blades, Inc., the U.S.-based manufacturer of roller blades, is currently both exporting to and importing from Thailand. Ben Holt, Blades' chief financial officer (CFO), and you, a financial analyst at Blades, Inc., are reasonably happy with Blades' current performance in Thailand. Entertainment Products, Inc., a Thai retailer for sporting goods, has committed itself to purchase a minimum number of Blades' Speedos annually. The agreement will terminate after three years. Blades also imports certain components needed to manufacture its products from Thailand. Both Blades' imports and exports are denominated in Thai baht. Because of these arrangements, Blades generates approximately 10 percent of its revenue and 4 percent of its cost of goods sold in Thailand.

Currently, Blades' only business in Thailand consists of this export and import trade. Holt, however, is thinking about using Thailand to augment Blades' U.S. business in other ways as well in the future. For example, Holt is contemplating establishing a subsidiary in Thailand to increase the percentage of Blades' sales to that country. Furthermore, by establishing a subsidiary in Thailand, Blades will have access to Thailand's money and capital markets. For instance, Blades could instruct its Thai subsidiary to invest excess funds or to satisfy its short-term needs for funds in the Thai money market. Furthermore, part of the subsidiary's financing could be obtained by utilizing investment banks in Thailand.

Due to Blades' current arrangements and future plans, Holt is concerned about recent developments in Thailand and their potential impact on the company's future in that country. Economic conditions in Thailand have been unfavorable recently. Movements

in the value of the baht have been highly volatile, and foreign investors in Thailand have lost confidence in the baht, causing massive capital outflows from Thailand. Consequently, the baht has been depreciating.

When Thailand was experiencing a high economic growth rate, few analysts anticipated an economic downturn. Consequently, Holt never found it necessary to forecast economic conditions in Thailand even though Blades was doing business there. Now, however, his attitude has changed. A continuation of the unfavorable economic conditions prevailing in Thailand could affect the demand for Blades' products in that country. Consequently, Entertainment Products may not renew its commitment for another three years.

Because Blades generates net cash inflows denominated in baht, a continued depreciation of the baht could adversely affect Blades, as these net inflows would be converted into fewer dollars. Thus Blades is also considering hedging its baht-denominated inflows.

Because of these concerns, Holt has decided to reassess the importance of forecasting the baht-dollar exchange rate. His primary objective is to forecast the baht-dollar exchange rate for the next quarter. A secondary objective is to determine which forecasting technique is the most accurate and should be used in future periods. To accomplish this, he has asked you, as the financial analyst at Blades, for help in forecasting the baht-dollar exchange rate for the next quarter.

Holt is aware of the forecasting techniques available. He has collected some economic data and conducted a preliminary analysis for you to use in your analysis. For example, he has conducted a time-series analysis for the exchange rates over numerous quarters. He then used this analysis to forecast the baht's value next quarter. The technical forecast indicates a depreciation of the baht by 6 percent over the next quarter from the baht's current level of $.023 to $.02162. He has also conducted a fundamental forecast of the baht-dollar exchange rate using historical inflation and interest rate data. The fundamental forecast, however, depends on what happens to Thai interest rates during the next quarter and therefore reflects a probability distribution. Based on the inflation and interest rates, there is a 30 percent chance that the baht will depreciate by 2 percent, a 15 percent chance that the baht will depreciate by 5 percent, and a 55 percent chance that the baht will depreciate by 10 percent.

Holt has asked you to answer the following questions:

1. Considering both Blades' current practices and future plans, how can it benefit from forecasting the baht-dollar exchange rate?

2. Which forecasting technique (i.e., technical, fundamental, or market-based) would be easiest to use in forecasting the future value of the baht? Why?

3. Blades is considering using either current spot rates or available forward rates to forecast the future value of the baht. Available forward rates currently exhibit a large discount. Do you think the spot or the forward rate will yield a better market-based forecast? Why?

4. The current 90-day forward rate for the baht is $.021. By what percentage is the baht expected to change over the next quarter according to a market-based forecast using the forward rate? What will be the value of the baht in 90 days according to this forecast?

5. Assume that the technical forecast has been more accurate than the market-based forecast in recent weeks. What does this indicate about market efficiency for the baht-dollar exchange rate? Do you think this means that technical analysis will always be superior to other forecasting techniques in the future? Why or why not?

6. What is the expected value of the percentage change in the value of the baht during the next quarter based on the fundamental forecast? What is the forecasted value of the baht using the expected value as the forecast? If the value of the baht 90 days from now turns out to be $.022, which forecasting technique is the most accurate? (Use the absolute forecast error as a percentage of the realized value to answer the last part of this question.)

7. Do you think the technique you have identified in question 6 will always be the most accurate? Why or why not?

SMALL BUSINESS DILEMMA

Exchange Rate Forecasting by the Sports Exports Company

The Sports Exports Company converts British pounds into dollars every month. The prevailing spot rate is about $1.65, but there is much uncertainty about the future value of the pound. Jim Logan, owner of the Sports Exports Company, expects that British inflation will rise substantially in the future. In previous years when British inflation was high, the pound depreciated. The prevailing British interest rate is slightly higher than the prevailing U.S. interest rate. The pound has risen slightly over each of the last several months. Logan wants to forecast the value of the pound for each of the next 20 months.

1. Explain how Logan can use technical forecasting to forecast the future value of the pound. Based on the information provided, do you think that a technical forecast will predict future appreciation or depreciation in the pound?

2. Explain how Logan can use fundamental forecasting to forecast the future value of the pound. Based on the information provided, do you think that a fundamental forecast will predict appreciation or depreciation in the pound?

3. Explain how Logan can use a market-based forecast to forecast the future value of the pound. Do you think the market-based forecast will predict appreciation, depreciation, or no change in the value of the pound?

4. Does it appear that all of the forecasting techniques will lead to the same forecast of the pound's future value? Which technique would you prefer to use in this situation?

INTERNET/EXCEL EXERCISES

The website of the CME Group (www.cmegroup.com), which now owns the Chicago Mercantile Exchange among others, provides information about the exchange and the futures contracts offered on the exchange.

Use this website to review the historical quotes of futures contracts and to obtain a recent quote for contracts on the Japanese yen and the British pound. Then go to www.oanda.com/currency/historical-rates/. Obtain the spot exchange rate for the Japanese yen and British pound on the same date for which you have futures contract quotations. Does the Japanese yen futures price reflect a premium or a discount relative to its spot rate? Does this futures price imply appreciation or depreciation of the Japanese yen? Answer these two questions also for the British pound.

Obtain the direct exchange rate of the Canadian dollar at the beginning of each of the last seven years. Insert this information in a column on an electronic spreadsheet. (See Appendix C for help on conducting analyses with Excel.) Repeat the process to obtain the direct exchange rate of the euro. Assume that you use the spot rate to forecast the future spot rate one year ahead. Determine the forecast error (measured as the absolute forecast error as a percentage of the realized value for each year) for the Canadian dollar in each year. Then determine the mean of the annual forecast error over all years. Repeat this process for the euro. Which currency has a lower forecast error on average? Would you have expected this result? Explain.

ONLINE ARTICLES WITH REAL-WORLD EXAMPLES

Find a recent article online that describes an actual international finance application or a real-world example about a specific MNC's actions that reinforces one or more concepts covered in this chapter.

If your class has an online component, your professor may ask you to post your summary there and provide the web link of the article so that other students can access it. If your class is live, your professor may ask you to summarize your application in class. Your professor may assign specific students to complete this assignment for this chapter, or may allow any students to do the assignment on a volunteer basis.

For recent online articles and real-world examples applied to this chapter, consider using the following search terms and include the current year as a search term to ensure that the online articles are recent:

1. forecast AND exchange rate
2. currency AND forecast
3. company AND exchange rate forecast
4. Inc. AND currency forecast
5. expected currency movements
6. forecast accuracy AND exchange rate
7. exchange rate AND forecast bias
8. currency AND forecast bias
9. forward rate AND forecast
10. currency AND forecast services

10

Measuring Exposure to Exchange Rate Fluctuations

CHAPTER OBJECTIVES

The specific objectives of this chapter are to:

■ discuss the relevance of an MNC's exposure to exchange rate risk,

■ explain how transaction exposure can be measured,

■ explain how economic exposure can be measured, and

■ explain how translation exposure can be measured.

Financial managers of MNCs must understand how to measure the exposure to exchange rate fluctuations so that they can determine whether and how to protect their operations from that exposure. In this way, they can reduce the sensitivity of their MNC's value to exchange rate movements.

10-1 Relevance of Exchange Rate Risk

Because exchange rate movements can affect an MNC's cash flow, they can affect its performance and value. When an MNC is exposed to exchange rate risk, its cash flows (and therefore its performance and value) could be adversely affected by exchange rate movements. Thus MNCs that can reduce their exchange rate exposure may be able to stabilize their earnings and cash flows. This can reduce the risk that the MNC's stock valuation may decline. It can also increase the MNC's ability to repay its debt over the long run, thereby reducing the possibility of failure and allowing the MNC to borrow funds at a lower cost.

Arguments have been made to suggest that under some assumptions, the exchange rate exposure of MNCs should not matter. Yet, for each argument as to why exchange rate risk might be irrelevant for MNCs (as briefly described in the first column of Exhibit 10.1), there is an argument for why exchange rate risk is relevant for MNCs (as described in the second column of Exhibit 10.1). In general, the assumptions used to argue for exchange rate irrelevance are not realistic. Consequently, the arguments for exchange rate relevance are clearly superior.

Furthermore, the relevance of exchange rate risk is well documented in the financial reports that MNCs distribute to investors. Many financial reports (especially annual reports) of MNCs acknowledge how their cash flows can be adversely affected by exchange rate movements. Examples are provided here:

> In general, we are a net receiver of currencies other than the U.S. dollar. Accordingly, changes in exchange rates, and in particular a strengthening of the U.S. dollar, will negatively affect our revenue and other operating results as expressed in U.S. dollars.
>
> *Facebook*

> Because we manufacture and sell products in a number of countries throughout the world, we are exposed to the impact on revenue and expenses of movements in currency exchange rates.
>
> *Procter & Gamble Co.*

Exhibit 10.1 Is Exchange Rate Risk Relevant for MNCs?

ARGUMENT FOR WHY EXCHANGE RATE RISK IS IRRELEVANT FOR MNCS	ARGUMENT FOR WHY EXCHANGE RATE RISK IS RELEVANT FOR MNCS
An MNC with cash flows in numerous currencies should not be affected by exchange rate risk if the adverse effects due to some currency movements are offset by the favorable effects of other currency movements.	Exchange rate effects on an MNC will not be offsetting, because exchange rate movements of many currencies against the dollar are in the same direction over a specific period of time. Therefore, an MNC cannot ignore exchange rate risk, even when it has cash flows in numerous currencies.
If stakeholders (such as stockholders or creditors) have stakes in a well-diversified portfolio of MNCs, then their portfolio's value might be insulated if the adverse effects of exchange rates on some MNCs are offset by favorable effects of exchange rates on other MNCs. If these stakeholders can insulate their portfolio from exchange rate effects, then MNCs should not worry about exchange rate risk.	Many MNCs are similarly affected by exchange rate movements, so it would be difficult for stakeholders to create a diversified portfolio of MNCs that will be insulated from exchange rate movements. Because stakeholders cannot diversify away the exposure of their portfolios to exchange rate risk, MNCs should be concerned about their exposure to exchange rate risk.
Investors who invest in MNCs can hedge exchange rate risk on their own. If they believe that their investments in U.S.-based MNCs would be adversely affected when foreign currencies weaken against the dollar, they could take their own positions in currency derivatives that would increase in value if foreign currencies weaken against the dollar. Thus if investors can hedge the exposure of their investments to exchange rate risk on their own, the MNCs may not need to worry about exchange rate risk.	Investors who invest in MNCs do not have complete information on each MNC's exposure to exchange rate fluctuations, so they may not have the ability to hedge the exposure of their individual investments to exchange rate risk. MNCs are more informed about their exposure to exchange rate risk and should have more expertise in managing that risk. Thus investors should benefit if MNCs manage their own exchange rate risk.

Increased volatility in foreign exchange rates ... may have an adverse impact on our business results and financial condition.

PepsiCo

10-2 Transaction Exposure

Perhaps the most obvious way in which most MNCs are exposed to exchange rate risk is through contractual transactions that are invoiced in foreign currencies. The sensitivity of the firm's contractual transactions in foreign currencies to exchange rate movements is referred to as **transaction exposure**. A U.S.-based MNC's concern about transaction exposure is that any currencies that it will need in the future to cover international transactions could appreciate by the time it obtains them, while any currencies it will receive in the future could depreciate by the time it receives them. Thus the exchange rate movements of the currencies the MNC will need or receive in the near future for international transactions could adversely affect its dollar cash flows.

Because many contractual international transactions tend to be in the near future (such as within the next quarter), MNCs naturally focus on the near future when assessing their transaction exposure. Therefore, the following discussion of transaction exposure is focused on a short-term period (the next quarter) when most contractual transactions occur. If an MNC wanted to assess transaction exposure over a shorter time horizon (such as one month) or a longer time horizon (such as one year) in the future, the process described here for assessing transaction exposure could still be applied.

EXAMPLE

Seahawk Co. is a U.S. firm that wants to assess its transaction exposure over the next quarter. It has only one international transaction pending. It just received an order from Spain for its products, and it will receive 1 million euros in one quarter (90 days). While the euro's spot rate is presently $1.35, Seahawk is more concerned about the spot rate that will exist when it exchanges 1 million euros for dollars at the end of one quarter.

Exhibit 10.2 shows the amount of dollars that Seahawk Co. will receive when exchanging 1 million euros at various possible exchange rates that could exist at that time. If the euro's value appreciates to $1.50 by the end of the quarter, Seahawk will receive $1,500,000 (computed as 1,000,000 euros × $1.50 per euro) in exchange for 1 million euros. However, if the euro's value depreciates to $1.20 by the end of the quarter, Seahawk Co. will receive only $1,200,000 when exchanging its 1 million euros. Exhibit 10.2 illustrates how Seahawk Co. is subject to transaction exposure, because the dollar cash flows it will receive is uncertain, and dependent on the future exchange rate when the international transaction is completed. The greater the uncertainty surrounding the future exchange rate of the currency, the greater is Seahawk's transaction exposure (potential adverse effects of its international transactions that could be caused by the future exchange rate movements).

Now that Seahawk has assessed its transaction exposure, it can decide whether to hedge this exposure. If Seahawk Co. believes that the euro will appreciate to $1.50 in one quarter, it will not hedge because it will benefit from the appreciation of the euro. Conversely, if it believes that the euro will depreciate to $1.20 in one quarter, it may consider hedging its transaction exposure. The techniques commonly used for hedging are described in the following chapter. ●

For most MNCs, the assessment of transaction exposure is not as simple as in the previous example. A typical MNC will have multiple orders for its products for which it will receive euros at the end of the quarter. It may also have made multiple purchases of supplies for which it will owe euros at the end of the quarter. Another factor complicating an MNC's assessment of its exposure is that a typical MNC will have international transactions in more than one currency over the next quarter. Thus an MNC should (1) estimate the expected net cash flows for each currency over the next quarter, and then (2) assess its exposure to all these currencies as a portfolio over the next quarter. The first step is illustrated in the following example, and the second step is discussed in the sections that follow.

Exhibit 10.2   Amount of Dollars to be Received from Exports (transaction value = 1 million euros) at Possible Exchange Rates Existing at the Time of Payment

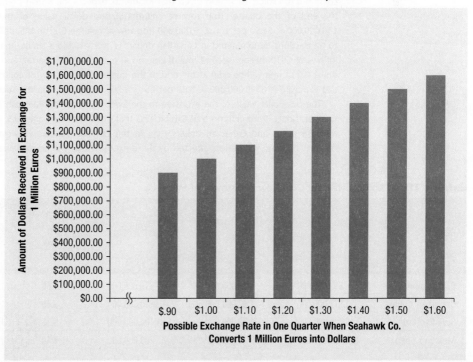

10-2a Estimating "Net" Cash Flows in Each Currency

To measure transaction exposure over the next quarter, an MNC should identify all transactions denominated in a foreign currency that will occur during the quarter and categorize the transactions by whether they are cash inflows or cash outflows. Because cash outflows that must be paid in a particular currency at the end of the quarter partially offset the cash inflows that will be received in that same currency at the end of the quarter, the MNC's transaction exposure focuses only on the "net" cash flows, measured as cash inflows minus cash outflows for a particular currency.

EXAMPLE

Miami Co. conducts its international business in four currencies. It wants to measure its exposure in each currency over the next quarter, so that it can decide whether to hedge that exposure. Miami should measure the dollar value of net cash flows for each currency over the next quarter, so that it can compare the exposure per currency using a standardized measurement.

Exhibit 10.3 shows that Miami expects British pound inflows of £17 million (shown in the top row of column 2) and outflows of £7 million over the next quarter (shown in the top row of column 3). Thus Miami expects net inflows of £10 million, as shown in the top row of column 4. Miami Co. uses the same process to determine the net cash flows of each of the other three currencies over the next quarter.

Notice in column 4 of Exhibit 10.3 that the expected net cash flows in three of the currencies are positive but that the net cash flows in the Swedish krona are negative (reflecting cash outflows). Thus Miami will be favorably affected by appreciation of the British pound, Canadian dollar, and Mexican peso against the dollar over the next quarter. Conversely, it will be adversely affected by appreciation of the Swedish krona against the dollar over the next quarter.

Miami's exposure to each foreign currency cannot be directly compared to that of the other three foreign currencies, because the values of the currencies differ. Transaction exposure of 1 million British pounds is not the same as transaction exposure of 1 million Mexican pesos, because the value of the British pound may be about 15 times the value of one Mexican peso. For this reason, Miami determines its dollar value of exposure to each foreign currency in column 6 of Exhibit 10.3, measured as the net inflow or outflow in foreign currency for the quarter (shown in column 4) times the spot exchange rate expected at the end of the quarter (shown in column 5).

Because Miami Co. has net cash flows of £10 million over the next quarter (shown in the top row of column 4 of Exhibit 10.3), and given that Miami Co. expects the British pound's spot rate will be $1.50 at the end of the quarter (top row of column 5), the dollar value of the British pound exposure is £10,000,000 × $1.50 per £ = $15,000,000 (top row of column 6). The U.S. dollar value of Miami's exposure to transactions denominated in Canadian dollars is estimated in a similar manner. Because Miami has net inflows of C$10 million (second row of column 4) over the next quarter, and it expects that the Canadian dollar's spot rate will be $.80 at the end of the quarter (second row of column 5), the U.S. dollar value of this exposure is C$10,000,000 × $.80 per C$ = $8,000,000 (shown in the second row of column 6).

The U.S. dollar value of the exposure to the Swedish krona and Mexican peso are derived in the same manner. Notice from column 6 of Exhibit 10.3 that Miami has a smaller U.S. dollar amount of exposure in Mexican pesos and Canadian dollars than in the other currencies. However, this does not necessarily mean that Miami will be less affected by these exposures, as will be explained shortly. ●

Exhibit 10.3 Consolidated Net Cash Flow Assessment of Miami Co.

(1) CURRENCY	(2) TOTAL INFLOW	(3) TOTAL OUTFLOW	(4) NET INFLOW OR OUTFLOW	(5) EXPECTED EXCHANGE RATE AT END OF QUARTER	(6) NET INFLOW OR OUTFLOW AS MEASURED IN U.S. DOLLARS
British pound	£17,000,000	£7,000,000	+£10,000,000	$1.50	+$15,000,000
Canadian dollar	C$12,000,000	C$2,000,000	+C$10,000,000	$.80	+$8,000,000
Swedish krona	SK20,000,000	SK120,000,000	−SK100,000,000	$.15	−$15,000,000
Mexican peso	MXP90,000,000	MXP10,000,000	+MXP80,000,000	$.10	+$8,000,000

10-2b Transaction Exposure of an MNC's Portfolio

After estimating net dollar cash flows per currency for an upcoming period (such as the next quarter), an MNC can assess the degree of transaction exposure of its portfolio of currencies. The transaction exposure of the currency portfolio represents the degree of uncertainty surrounding the portfolio's value, which is caused by the uncertain exchange rate movements of the currencies in the portfolio. A currency portfolio that is subject to more uncertainty is more exposed to a pronounced reduction in value over the next quarter.

The MNC is concerned about the uncertainty of its currency portfolio in the same manner that individual investors are concerned about the uncertainty of their respective investment portfolios. Just as individual investors use portfolio theory principles to assess the uncertainty of their investment portfolios, an MNC can assess its transaction exposure by using portfolio theory principles to assess the uncertainty surrounding its currency portfolio. Specifically, the MNC must consider each currency's volatility (the degree to which its value changes over time) and the correlations among currencies (degree to which movements in currencies are related).

Consider a U.S.-based MNC that will generate net cash inflows in currencies X and Y over the next quarter. It expects that currency X will convert into $100,000 and that currency Y will also convert into $100,000. Thus, at the end of the quarter, it will have a portfolio of these two currencies that it will convert into $200,000, with each currency accounting for half of the portfolio value. The MNC is subject to transaction exposure, because it is uncertain about the exchange rates at which currencies X and Y will convert to dollars at the end of the quarter. It is possible that each of the currencies may weaken against the dollar, so that by the end of the quarter, the MNC's portfolio might be worth less than the $200,000 that it is expecting.

If the dollar value of this two-currency portfolio has been very stable (low volatility) over the past several quarters, there is little risk that the portfolio value will decline substantially when converting the two currencies to dollars at the end of the next quarter. Conversely, if the dollar value of the two-currency portfolio has been very volatile over the past several quarters, there is much risk that the portfolio value will decline substantially when converting the two currencies to dollars at the end of the next quarter. In this case, the transaction exposure of the MNC's portfolio is relatively high.

The volatility of the MNC's two-currency portfolio over the past several quarters can be measured by its standard deviation (denoted σ_p), as shown here:

WEB

www.fednewyork.org
/markets/implied
volatility.html
Measure of exchange
rate volatility.

$$\sigma_p = \sqrt{w_X^2 \sigma_X^2 + w_Y^2 \sigma_Y^2 + 2w_X w_Y \sigma_X \sigma_Y \mathbf{CORR}_{XY}}$$

where

W_X = **proportion of total portfolio value that represented by currency X**

W_Y = **proportion of total portfolio value that represented by currency Y**

σ_X = **standard deviation of quarterly percentage changes in the dollar value of currency X**

σ_Y = **standard deviation of quarterly percentage changes in the dollar value of currency Y**

$\mathbf{CORR}_{XY}$ = **correlation coefficient of quarterly percentage changes in the dollar values of currencies X and Y**

The equation shows that the volatility of an MNC's currency portfolio is positively related to each individual currency's volatility and positively related to the correlation between currencies. Thus the MNC's two-currency portfolio is subject to a higher degree of transaction exposure when each currency is very volatile and when the movements of the two currencies against the dollar are highly correlated.

The transaction exposure of an MNC that has international transactions in more than two currencies over the next quarter can be assessed by the volatility of its currency portfolio over the past several quarters. The volatility of a portfolio containing more than two currencies is more difficult to estimate, but it is also positively related to the volatility of each individual currency, and to the degree of correlation between each pair of currencies in the portfolio. The means by which currency volatilities and correlations can be used to assess the transaction exposure of an MNC's currency portfolio follows.

Measurement of Currency Volatility The standard deviation statistic measures the degree of movement (or volatility) for each currency. To estimate the volatility of a currency's movements against the dollar, the first step is to access quarterly exchange rates of that currency against the dollar over the past several quarters, using a source such as a Federal Reserve website. Download the quarterly exchange rates to an electronic spreadsheet.

Second, derive the percentage change in the exchange rate of the currency from one quarter to the next (use a different period than a quarter if you are interested in a different time horizon). Then compute the standard deviation of the quarterly percentage changes. Spreadsheets such as Excel can easily compute the percentage changes in the currency's value and the standard deviation.

In any given period, exchange rates of some currencies fluctuate much more than others. The quarterly exchange rate movements of currencies in emerging countries tend to be more pronounced than the movements of currencies in developed countries. Thus if an MNC has a large net position in only one currency, it is generally more susceptible to major losses stemming from exchange rate movements if the currency is that of a developing rather than a developed country.

The volatility (as measured by the standard deviation) of any currency is dependent on the time horizon that is used to measure the exchange rate movements. In general, the longer the time horizon, the more volatile a currency's exchange rate movements. Thus a currency's exchange rate movements generally will be more volatile (have a higher standard deviation) on a quarterly basis than on a daily basis, and that currency's exchange rate movements will be more volatile on an annual basis than on a quarterly basis.

Currency Volatility over Time The volatility of a currency normally will not remain constant over time. That is, if you measure the standard deviation of quarterly movements in the euro against the dollar this year, it will not be equal to the standard deviation of quarterly movements in the euro against the dollar next year. However, an MNC can at least attempt to compare volatility levels among currencies in recent periods to anticipate which currencies will have a relatively high or low level of volatility in the future. From a U.S. perspective, the Canadian dollar's volatility has changed over time but is normally less than the volatility of other currencies. The Brazilian real's volatility has changed over time, but it tends to be consistently higher than the volatility of currencies of developed countries. During global financial crises (such as the credit crisis in 2008–2009), exchange rate movements of most currencies tend to be more volatile.

Assessing How Volatility Affects Transaction Exposure Once an MNC estimates the volatility of each individual currency, it can determine whether the currency's potential movements over the next period are cause for concern.

EXAMPLE   Recall that Miami Co. is assessing its transaction exposure. It recognizes that the Canadian dollar's exchange rate movements against the U.S. dollar tend to be less pronounced than the exchange rate movements of the other three currencies. Also, it recognizes that the Mexican peso's exchange rate movements against the dollar tend to be more pronounced than the exchange rate movements of the other three currencies. Miami's initial conclusion is that the potential exchange rate movement of each currency over the next quarter is large enough to have significant adverse effects on Miami's dollar cash flows. Before Miami can come to any final conclusions, it needs to consider the correlations between the exchange rate movements of these currencies, described in the following section. ●

Measurement of Currency Correlations   The correlations among currency movements can be measured by their *correlation coefficients*, which indicate the extent to which two currencies move in tandem with each other. The extreme case is perfect positive correlation, which is represented by a correlation coefficient equal to 1. A negative correlation coefficient suggests an inverse relationship between the exchange rate movements of two currencies.

To estimate the correlation coefficient between two currencies against the dollar, download quarterly exchange rates of those two currencies against the dollar to an electronic spreadsheet and derive the percentage change in the exchange rate of each currency from one quarter to the next, as described above (use a different period than a quarter if you are interested in a different time horizon). Spreadsheets such as Excel can easily compute the correlation coefficient. You can apply this process to many currencies and then estimate the correlation coefficients for each pair of currencies.

From a U.S. perspective, currency correlations are generally positive; this implies that currencies tend to move in the same direction against the U.S. dollar (though not always by the same degree). For example, the quarterly movements in the euro and other currencies of European countries not in the eurozone against the U.S. dollar are highly positively correlated (the correlation coefficient between any pair of these currencies is commonly .80 or higher).

The Canadian dollar's quarterly movements against the U.S. dollar are typically positively correlated with quarterly movements of European currencies against the U.S. dollar, but the correlation is not as high as that of any pair of European currencies against the dollar. The Japanese yen's quarterly movements against the U.S. dollar are also typically positively correlated with quarterly movements of European currencies against the U.S. dollar, but the correlation is not as high as that of any pair of European currencies against the dollar.

The correlation coefficient between a given pair of currencies can vary with the time horizon assessed. In general, correlation coefficients are lower when using a daily time horizon to measure the percentage changes in the currency values against the dollar over time than when using a quarterly time horizon. This suggests that while values of currencies may move more independently against the dollar on a given day, they tend to move in tandem to some degree over longer quarterly time horizons. Most MNCs give more attention to the longer time horizons, because they are more concerned about their exchange exposure over the next few months or quarters than the next few days.

Applying Currency Correlations to Net Cash Flows   The implications of currency correlations for a particular MNC depend on its cash flow characteristics. If an MNC has positive net cash flows over the next quarter in various currencies that are highly correlated, it may be subject to a higher degree of transaction exposure in that quarter. If the values of these currencies move in the same direction, and by similar degrees, they could all depreciate against the dollar in the quarter without any offsetting effects.

However, many MNCs have negative net cash flow positions (meaning that their cash outflows exceed their cash inflows) in one or more currencies. An MNC's transaction exposure is reduced if its negative net cash flow currencies are highly correlated with its positive net cash flow currencies. While depreciation of currencies has an adverse effect on the positive net cash flows (the inflows will convert to fewer dollars), it will favorably affect the negative net cash flow positions because the MNC will need fewer dollars to obtain these currencies. Conversely, whereas currency appreciation would adversely affect the MNC's negative net cash flows (more dollars would be needed to obtain those currencies), it would favorably affect the MNC's positive net cash flows (the inflows will convert to more dollars).

EXAMPLE   Recall from Exhibit 10.3 that Miami Co. anticipates net cash inflows in the British pound equivalent to $15 million and net cash outflows in the Swedish krona equivalent to $15 million at the end of the quarter. These currencies are highly positively correlated against the dollar. Thus one possible scenario is that these two currencies appreciate against the U.S. dollar over the next quarter, whereby Miami Co. would be adversely affected by its exposure to the krona but favorably affected by its pound exposure. An alternative scenario is that these two currencies depreciate against the dollar over the next quarter, whereby Miami Co. would be adversely affected by its pound exposure but favorably affected by its krona exposure. Thus, although Miami does not know which of the two scenarios will take place, it has determined that offsetting effects would occur with either scenario.

Given these offsetting effects, Miami is not concerned about its transaction exposure to the British pound or the Swedish krona over the next quarter. However, it is somewhat concerned about its exposure to the Canadian dollar and the Mexican peso. Therefore, Miami Co. decides to conduct some additional analysis to determine its transaction exposure to these two currencies, as described later in this chapter. ●

Exhibit 10.4 offers some insight about the transaction exposure of an MNC over the next period (such as the next quarter) based on some specific scenarios.

Currency Correlations over Time   Because currency correlations change over time, previous correlations are not perfect predictors of future correlations. Nevertheless, some general relationships tend to hold over time. For example, quarterly movements in values of the pound, the euro, and other European currencies against the U.S. dollar are consistently highly correlated in most one-, two-, or three-year periods regardless of the specific period that is assessed. Thus MNCs can predict with a high level of confidence that the high correlations will persist in the future. If they have inflows in one European currency and outflows of about the same value in another European currency, they may not be so concerned about their exposure because of the likely offsetting exchange rate effects.

10-2c Transaction Exposure Based on Value at Risk

A related method for assessing exposure is the value-at-risk (VaR) method, which can estimate the maximum possible loss on the value of currency positions that are exposed to exchange rate movements.

Exhibit 10.4 Impact of Cash Flow and Correlation Conditions on an MNC's Exposure over the Next Period

IF THE MNC'S EXPECTED CASH FLOW SITUATION IS	AND IF THE CURRENCIES ARE	THEN THE MNC'S EXPOSURE IS RELATIVELY
Equal amounts of net inflows in two currencies	Highly correlated	High
Equal amounts of net inflows in two currencies	Slightly positively correlated	Moderate
Equal amounts of net inflows in two currencies	Negatively correlated	Low
A net inflow in one currency and a net outflow of about the same amount in another currency	Highly correlated	Low
A net inflow in one currency and a net outflow of about the same amount in another currency	Slightly positively correlated	Moderate
A net inflow in one currency and a net outflow of about the same amount in another currency	Negatively correlated	High

EXAMPLE

Recall that Miami Co. (from the earlier examples) was attempting to assess its transaction exposure over the next quarter and has determined that its exposures to the British pound and Swedish krona are off-setting. Thus it only needs to be concerned about the exposure of its net cash flows in Canadian dollars and Mexican pesos.

Assume for the moment that Miami only needs to worry about its transaction exposure to Canadian dollar net cash flows. It can use the VaR method to estimate the maximum expected loss. Assume that Miami estimates the standard deviation of quarterly percentage changes of the Canadian dollar to be 4 percent over the last 40 quarters. If these quarterly percentage changes are normally distributed, then the maximum one-quarter loss is determined by the lower boundary (the left tail) of the probability distri-bution, which, based on a 95 percent confidence level, is about 1.65 standard deviations away from the expected percentage change in the Canadian dollar. Assume that Miami expects that the Canadian dollar will depreciate by 1 percent against the U.S. dollar over the next quarter. Based on this forecast along with the estimated standard deviation of 4 percent, the maximum expected loss due to Miami's transac-tion exposure in Canadian dollars over the next quarter is:

$$\text{Maximum one-quarter loss} = E(e_t) - (1.65 \times \sigma_{C\$})$$
$$= -1\% - (1.65 \times 4\%)$$
$$= -.01 - .066$$
$$= -.076 \text{ or } -7.6\%.$$

Recall that the U.S. dollar value of Miami's net cash flow position over the next quarter is $8 million. Therefore, a decline of 7.6 percent in the Canadian dollar's value over the next quarter would cause Miami's Canadian dollar position to experience a loss of $8,000,000 \times -.076 = -$608,000.

Now assume that Miami is only concerned about the maximum one-quarter loss due to a potential decline in the Mexican peso's value. Assume that Miami believes the expected percentage change in the Mexican peso is -1 percent during the next quarter, and that Miami estimated the standard deviation of exchange rate movements of the Mexican peso to be 6 percent over the past 40 quarters. Based on these assumptions, Miami's maximum expected one-quarter loss due to its transaction exposure in Mexican pesos over the next quarter is:

$$\text{Maximum one-quarter loss} = E(e_t) - (1.65 \times \sigma_{MXP})$$
$$= -1\% - (1.65 \times 6\%)$$
$$= -.109, \text{ or } -10.9\%$$

Recall that the dollar value of Miami's net cash flows in Mexican pesos is estimated to be $8 million. Therefore, a decline of 10.9 percent in the Mexican peso's value over the next quarter would result in a loss of $8,000,000 \times -10.9\% = -$872,000. ●

Factors That Affect the Maximum One-Day Loss   The maximum expected loss on a currency over the next quarter depends on three factors. First, it depends on the expected percentage change in the currency for the next quarter. If the expected per-centage change in the currency's value was more pronounced than the 1 percent depre-ciation assumed in the previous example, the maximum expected loss would be more pronounced. Second, a higher confidence level (such as 99 percent confidence instead of 95 percent confidence) will lead to a greater maximum expected loss (when all other factors are held constant).

Third, the maximum expected loss over the next quarter depends on the standard deviation of the currency's quarterly exchange rate movements over a previous period. Notice that the maximum expected loss in the Mexican peso is more pronounced than that of the Canadian dollar. This is due to the higher volatility (larger standard devia-tion) of the Mexican peso's quarterly exchange rate movements in the past, which makes Miami Co. believe that the Mexican peso could possibly depreciate to a greater degree than the Canadian dollar in the following quarter.

Because the VaR method provides Miami with a specific estimate of the maximum expected loss, it offers additional information to supplement Miami's previous assess-ment of its transaction exposure over the next quarter. If Miami Co. is uncomfortable with the magnitude of the possible maximum loss for either currency over the next quarter, it can hedge its position as explained in the next chapter.

However, it should also use VaR to assess the maximum loss of the portfolio (Canadian dollars and Mexican pesos) in the event that it does not hedge either currency's net cash flows, as described in the next section.

Applying VaR to the Transaction Exposure of a Portfolio

Because MNCs are commonly exposed to more than one currency, they may wish to apply the VaR method to a portfolio of currencies. When considering multiple currencies, software packages can be used to perform the computations. An example of applying VaR to a two-currency portfolio is given next.

EXAMPLE

Recall that Miami Co. is concerned about the transaction exposure of its Canadian dollar cash flows and its Mexican peso cash flows over the next quarter. Also recall that the U.S. dollar value of the net cash flows in Canadian dollars at the end of the quarter is $8 million, and the U.S. dollar value of the net cash flows in Mexican pesos is also $8 million. Thus Miami is exposed to a currency portfolio weighted 50 percent in Canadian dollars and 50 percent in Mexican pesos. Miami Co. wants to determine the maximum expected one-quarter loss in its portfolio of these two currencies (based on a 95 percent confidence level). Recall from previous examples that Miami estimates the standard deviation of quarterly percentage changes to be 4 percent for the Canadian dollar and 6 percent for the Mexican peso. Also assume that Miami estimates a correlation coefficient of .20 between these two currencies. Recall that the portfolio's standard deviation is estimated to be:

$$\sigma_p = \sqrt{w_{C\$}^2 \sigma_{C\$}^2 + w_{MXP}^2 \sigma_{MXP}^2 + 2w_{C\$} w_{MXP} \sigma_{C\$} \sigma_{MXP} \text{CORR}}$$

where

$w_{C\$}$ = proportion of total portfolio value represented by the Canadian dollar

w_{MXP} = proportion of total portfolio value represented by the Mexican peso

$\sigma_{C\$}$ = standard deviation of quarterly percentage changes in the Canadian dollar

σ_{MXP} = standard deviation of quarterly percentage changes in the value of the Mexican peso

CORR = correlation coefficient of quarterly percentage changes between the Canadian dollar and Mexican peso

Based on the assumptions,

$$\sigma_p = \sqrt{(.25)(.0016) + (.25)(.0036) + 2(.50)(.50)(.04)(.06)(.20)}$$
$$= \sqrt{.0004 + .0009 + .00024}$$
$$= .0392$$

If the quarterly percentage changes of each currency are normally distributed, then the quarterly percentage changes of the portfolio should be normally distributed. The maximum one-quarter loss of the currency portfolio is determined by the lower boundary (the left tail) of the probability distribution, which based on a 95 percent confidence level is about 1.65 standard deviations away from the expected percentage change in the currency portfolio. Assuming an expected percentage change of −1 percent for the currency portfolio, the maximum expected one-quarter loss is

$$\text{Maximum one-quarter loss of currency portfolio} = E(e_t) - (1.65 \times \sigma_p)$$
$$= -1\% - (1.65 \times 3.92\%)$$
$$= \text{about } -.0747, \text{ or about } -7.47\%$$

Notice that the maximum one-quarter loss for the portfolio is much smaller than the maximum loss for the Mexican peso by itself, which can be attributed to low correlation between the Mexican peso's movements and the Canadian dollar movements (diversification effects). In other words, because the two currencies do not move in perfect tandem, it is unlikely that both currencies would experience a maximum loss at the same time.

Given the maximum losses calculated here for individual currency positions and for the portfolio, Miami Co. may decide to hedge its transaction exposure in Canadian dollars, its transaction exposure in Mexican pesos, neither position, or both positions. An MNC's decision of whether to hedge and how to hedge is discussed in the next chapter. ●

Estimating VaR with a Spreadsheet   You can use Excel (or another spreadsheet) to facilitate estimates of VaR for a portfolio of currencies by taking these steps.

1. Obtain the series of exchange rates for all relevant dates for each currency of concern and list each currency in its own column.
2. Compute the percentage changes per period (from one date to the next) for each exchange rate in a column.
3. Estimate the standard deviation of the column of percentage changes for each exchange rate.
4. In a separate column, compute the periodic percentage change in the portfolio value by applying weights to the individual currency returns. For instance, if the portfolio is equal weighted (50 percent allocated to each currency), then the percentage change in the portfolio value per period is equal to 50 percent of the percentage change in value of one exchange rate *plus* 50 percent of the percentage change of the other exchange rate.
5. Use a "compute" statement to determine the standard deviation of the column of percentage changes in the portfolio value.

Once you have determined the standard deviation of percentage changes in the portfolio value, you can estimate the VaR of the portfolio in the manner explained earlier.

Limitations of VaR   The VaR method presumes that the distribution of exchange rate movements is normal. If the distribution of exchange rate movements is not normal, then estimating the maximum expected loss is subject to error. In addition, the VaR method typically relies on an estimate of volatility (standard deviation) of exchange rate movements from historical data. If past exchange rate movements are less volatile than future movements, then the estimated maximum expected loss derived from the VaR method will be underestimated.

10-3 Economic Exposure

The overall sensitivity of a firm's cash flows to exchange rate movements is referred to as **economic exposure** (also sometimes referred to as operating exposure), which is a broader concept than transaction exposure. Indeed, transaction exposure can be thought of as a subset of economic exposure. But whereas transaction exposure focuses on the impact of exchange rate movements on an MNC's contractual international transactions (as illustrated earlier in this chapter), economic exposure encompasses all of the ways that an MNC's cash flows can be affected by exchange rate movements.

EXAMPLE

Intel (a U.S.-based MNC) invoices many of its computer chip exports in U.S. dollars, which avoids transaction exposure. Yet if the euro weakens against the dollar, European importers will need more euros to pay for Intel's chips and therefore might decide to purchase computer chips from European manufacturers instead. While Intel's decision to price exports in dollars can avoid transaction exposure, its cash flows could still be reduced when the euro weakens. Thus it is still subject to economic exposure. ●

Even a U.S. firm that has no international business can be subject to economic exposure. If a foreign competitor's invoice currency depreciates against the dollar, some customers may shift their purchases to the foreign competitor. Thus the demand for the U.S. firm's products will decrease, and its net cash inflows will decrease as well.

Although MNCs use a short-term perspective when assessing their transaction exposure, they tend to use a long-term perspective when assessing their economic exposure. For example, U.S.-based MNCs may conduct an assessment of their economic exposure to determine how their dollar cash flows are affected in general when foreign currencies appreciate against the dollar over time. Their assessment will allow them to consider various possible strategies to reduce their economic exposure, as discussed in Chapter 12.

10-3a Exposure to Foreign Currency Depreciation

The means by which a U.S. firm's cash inflows and outflows are affected by exchange rate movements are summarized in Exhibit 10.5. The exhibit is simplified in that it focuses on a single foreign currency, whereas many firms are exposed to multiple currencies. However, the exhibit is intended simply to offer some general relationships between a foreign currency's exchange rate movements and cash flows resulting from specific business operations.

The impact of depreciation in the foreign currency on the U.S. firm's cash inflows and outflows is shown in the second column of Exhibit 10.5. The following discussion is based on this column. A U.S. firm's local sales (in the United States) are expected to decrease if the foreign currency depreciates because the firm will face increased foreign competition. That is, local customers will be able to obtain foreign substitute products cheaply if the foreign currency depreciates. Cash inflows from the firm's exports denominated in dollars will also likely be reduced as a result of depreciation in the foreign currency because foreign importers will likely demand fewer products when they need more of their own currency to pay for these products. Cash inflows from the firm's exports denominated in the foreign currency will convert to a reduced amount of dollars if the foreign currency has weakened. Any interest or dividends received from foreign investments by the U.S. firm will also convert to a reduced amount of dollars if the foreign currency has weakened.

With regard to the U.S. firm's cash outflows, the cost of imported supplies denominated in dollars will not be directly affected by changes in exchange rates. However, if

Exhibit 10.5 Economic Exposure of a U.S. Firm to Exchange Rate Fluctuations

SOURCES OF U.S. FIRM'S DOLLAR CASH FLOWS	IMPACT OF FOREIGN CURRENCY DEPRECIATION ON U.S. FIRM'S DOLLAR CASH FLOWS	IMPACT OF FOREIGN CURRENCY APPRECIATION ON U.S. FIRM'S DOLLAR CASH FLOWS
Local sales (relative to foreign competition in local markets)	Decrease	Increase
Firm's exports denominated in dollars	Decrease	Increase
Firm's exports denominated in foreign currency	Decrease	Increase
Interest received from foreign investments	Decrease	Increase
SOURCES OF DOLLAR CASH OUTFLOWS		
Firm's imported supplies denominated in dollars	No change	No change
Firm's imported supplies denominated in foreign currency	Decrease	Increase
Interest owed on foreign funds borrowed	Decrease	Increase

the imported supplies are denominated in the foreign currency, the cost will be reduced if the foreign currency depreciates. In addition, any interest to be paid by the U.S. firm on financing in a foreign currency will be reduced if the foreign currency depreciates.

Overall, depreciation in the foreign currency causes a reduction in both cash inflows and outflows for the U.S. firm. The impact on the U.S. firm's net cash flows will depend on whether the cash inflows or outflows are more sensitive to depreciation in the foreign currency. If, for example, the U.S firm is in the exporting business but obtains its supplies and borrows funds locally, its cash inflows will be reduced to a greater extent than its cash outflows, causing a reduction in its net cash flows. Conversely, if the U.S. firm concentrates on local sales (and has limited foreign competition) and obtains supplies and borrows funds overseas, its cash outflows will be reduced. Overall, this firm's net cash flows will be enhanced by depreciation of the foreign currency.

10-3b Exposure to Foreign Currency Appreciation

The impact of appreciation in the foreign currency on the U.S. firm's cash inflows and outflows is shown in the third column of Exhibit 10.5. The following discussion is based on this column. If the foreign currency appreciates, the U.S. firm's sources of cash inflows or outflows will be affected in a manner opposite to how they are influenced by foreign currency depreciation. Local sales by the U.S. firm should increase due to reduced foreign competition because prices denominated in the foreign currency will seem high to U.S. customers. The U.S. firm's exports denominated in dollars will appear cheap to foreign importers, thereby increasing foreign demand for those products. Even exports denominated in the foreign currency will increase cash flows because foreign currency inflows will convert to a larger amount of dollars. In addition, interest or dividends from foreign investments will convert to more dollars.

The amount of the U.S. firm's cash outflows due to imported supplies denominated in dollars will not be directly affected by the change in exchange rates. The cost of imported supplies denominated in the foreign currency will rise in response to the appreciation of the foreign currency. Any interest payments paid on financing in the foreign currency will also increase.

In general, appreciation of the foreign currency causes an increase in both cash inflows and outflows for the U.S. firm. If the firm concentrates on exporting and obtains supplies and borrows funds locally, it will likely benefit from the appreciation of the foreign currency. This would be the case for Caterpillar, Ford, and DuPont during periods in which foreign currencies appreciate against the dollar. Conversely, a U.S. firm that concentrates on local sales, has very little foreign competition, and obtains foreign supplies (denominated in foreign currencies) will likely suffer negative effects from appreciation of the foreign currency.

10-3c Measuring Economic Exposure

The preceding discussion suggests that MNCs should be able to determine how their cash inflows or outflows in general would be affected by exchange rate movements. However, MNCs commonly conduct a more thorough assessment of their economic exposure. They prefer to know precisely how their net cash flows would be affected as a result of specific exchange rate scenarios that could occur in the following period.

One method of doing this is to set up a spreadsheet showing the MNC's primary sources of cash inflows or outflows. The MNC then estimates its cash flows over the following period (such as the following quarter) based on the most likely exchange rate scenario. It then applies sensitivity analysis by estimating its cash flows again over the following period based on alternative exchange rate scenarios that could occur. Even though the MNC is not sure how exchange rates will move in the following period, its sensitivity analysis will indicate the sensitivity of its estimated net cash flows to the alternative scenarios. If its estimated net cash flows are very similar regardless of the exchange rate scenario, this implies that the firm's net cash flows in the following quarter are not sensitive to possible exchange rate movements. Thus the firm may conclude that its economic exposure is low and that it does not need to worry about implementing a strategy to reduce its exposure. However, if the firm's sensitivity analysis determines that its estimated net cash flows for the following period are very sensitive to an exchange rate scenario, this implies that the firm has a high degree of economic exposure. In this case, it may consider possible strategies to reduce its economic exposure, as explained in Chapter 12.

The following example illustrates how an MNC could implement its sensitivity analysis to assess its degree of economic exposure. The example is simplified in that the MNC is only exposed to one foreign currency. In addition, the example focuses only on the next quarter. In reality, an MNC would prefer to assess economic exposure for a period longer than one quarter. However, to the extent that the firm's operations and expected cash flows in this quarter are typical, the assessment of this single quarter could offer useful insight about the firm's economic exposure over a longer time frame.

EXAMPLE

Madison Co. is a U.S.-based MNC that purchases most of its materials from Canada and generates a small portion of its sales from exporting to Canada. Its U.S. sales are denominated in U.S. dollars whereas its Canadian sales are denominated in Canadian dollars (C$). The quarterly estimates of its cash flows, by country, are shown in Exhibit 10.6. Madison wants to assess its economic exposure, which is the exposure of its total cash flows to exchange rate movements.

Assume that Madison Co. expects three possible exchange rates for the Canadian dollar over the period of concern: $.75, $.80, or $.85. These scenarios are separately analyzed in (respectively) the second, third, and fourth columns of Exhibit 10.7. Row 1 is constant across scenarios because the company's sales to U.S. businesses are not affected by exchange rate movements. In row 2, the estimated U.S. dollar sales to Canadian businesses are determined by converting the estimated Canadian dollar sales into U.S. dollars. Row 3 gives the sum of the U.S. dollar sales in rows 1 and 2.

Row 4 is constant across scenarios because the cost of materials in the United States is not affected by exchange rate movements. In row 5, the estimated U.S. dollar cost of materials purchased in Canada is determined by converting the estimated Canadian cost of materials into U.S. dollars. Row 6 is the sum of the U.S. dollar cost of materials in rows 4 and 5.

Row 7 is constant across scenarios because U.S. operating expenses are not affected by exchange rate movements, and row 8 is constant across scenarios because the interest expense on U.S. debt is not affected by exchange rate movements. In row 9, the estimated U.S. dollar interest expense from Canadian debt is determined by converting the estimated Canadian interest expenses into U.S. dollars. Row 10 is the sum of the U.S. dollar interest expenses in rows 8 and 9.

The effect of exchange rates on Madison's revenues and costs can now be reviewed. Exhibit 10.7 illustrates how the dollar value of Canadian sales and Canadian cost of materials would increase as a result of

Exhibit 10.6 Estimated Sales and Expenses for Madison's U.S. and Canadian Business Segments (millions of currency units)

	U.S. BUSINESS	CANADIAN BUSINESS
Sales	$320	C$4
Cost of materials	$50	C$200
Operating expenses	$60	—
Interest expenses	$3	C$10
Cash flows	$207	−C$206

Exhibit 10.7   Impact of Possible Exchange Rates on Cash Flows of Madison Co. (millions of currency units)

		EXCHANGE RATE SCENARIO				
		C$1 = $.75		C$1 = $.80		C$1 = $.85
Sales						
(1) U.S. sales		$320.00		$320.00		$320.00
(2) Canadian sales	C$4 =	$ 3.00	C$4 =	$ 3.20	C$4 =	$ 3.40
(3) Total sales in U.S. $		$323.00		$323.20		$323.40
Cost of Materials and Operating Expenses						
(4) U.S. cost of materials		$ 50.00		$ 50.00		$ 50.00
(5) Canadian cost of materials	C$200 =	$150.00	C$200 =	$160.00	C$200 =	$170.00
(6) Total cost of materials in U.S. $		$200.00		$210.00		$220.00
(7) Operating expenses		$ 60.00		$ 60.00		$ 60.00
Interest Expenses						
(8) U.S. interest expenses		$ 3		$ 3		$ 3
(9) Canadian interest expenses	C$10 =	$ 7.5	C$10 =	$ 8	C$10 =	$ 8.50
(10) Total interest expenses in U.S. $		$ 10.50		$ 11.00		$ 11.50
Cash Flows in U.S. $ before Taxes		$ 52.50		$ 42.20		$ 31.90

a stronger Canadian dollar. Because Madison's Canadian cost of materials exposure (C$200 million) is much greater than its Canadian sales exposure (C$4 million), a strong Canadian dollar has a negative overall impact on its cash flow. The total amount in U.S. dollars needed to make interest payments is also higher when the Canadian dollar is stronger. In general, Madison Co. would be adversely affected by a stronger Canadian dollar. It would be favorably affected by a weaker Canadian dollar because the reduced value of total sales would be more than offset by the reduced cost of materials and interest expenses. ●

The example is based on a one-period time horizon. A firm that has developed forecasts of sales, expenses, and exchange rates for several periods ahead can assess its economic exposure over time.

Use of Regression Analysis   A firm may complement its spreadsheet analysis with some statistical analysis that offers more insight about its economic exposure to a currency's exchange rate movements. Specifically, it can apply regression analysis to historical cash flow and exchange rate data as follows:

$$PCF_t = a_0 + a_1 e_t + \mu_t$$

where

PCF_t = **percentage change in inflation-adjusted cash flows measured in the firm's home currency over period t**

e_t = **percentage change in the direct exchange rate of the currency over period t**

μ_t = **random error term**

a_0 = **intercept**

a_1 = **slope coefficient**

The regression coefficient a_1, which is estimated by regression analysis, indicates the sensitivity of PCF_t to e_t. If the coefficient is positive and significant, the implication is that an increase in the currency's value has a favorable effect on the firm's cash flows. A coefficient that is negative and significant implies an inverse relationship between the change in the currency's value and the firm's cash flows. If the firm anticipates no major adjustments in its operating structure, then it will expect the sensitivity detected from regression analysis to be similar in the future.

This regression model can be revised to handle more complex situations. An MNC that is affected by numerous currencies may prefer to measure the sensitivity of PCF_t to an index (or composite) of currencies.

The analysis just described for a single period can also be extended over separate subperiods, as the sensitivity of a firm's cash flows to a currency's movements may change over time. Such a change would be indicated by a corresponding shift in the regression coefficient.

Some MNCs may prefer to use their stock price as a proxy for the firm's value and then assess how their stock price changes in response to currency movements. Regression analysis could also be used in this approach by replacing PCF_t with the percentage change in stock price in the model specified here. Some MNCs may also conduct similar analyses to assess the impact of exchange rates on their earnings, exports, and/or total sales.

10-4 Translation Exposure

An MNC creates its financial statements by consolidating all of its individual subsidiaries' financial statements. A subsidiary's financial statement is normally measured in its local currency. To be consolidated, each subsidiary's financial statement must be translated into the currency of the MNC's parent. Because exchange rates vary over time, the translation of the subsidiary's financial statement into a different currency is affected by exchange rate movements. The exposure of the MNC's consolidated financial statements to exchange rate fluctuations is known as **translation exposure**. In particular, subsidiary earnings translated into the reporting currency on the consolidated income statement are subject to fluctuations in the exchange rates.

To translate earnings, MNCs use a process established by the Financial Accounting Standards Board (FASB). The guidelines for translation are set by FASB 52.

10-4a Determinants of Translation Exposure

Some MNCs have more translation exposure than others. The extent of an MNC's translation exposure depends mainly on three factors:

■ the proportion of its business conducted by foreign subsidiaries,
■ the locations of its foreign subsidiaries, and
■ the accounting methods that it uses.

Proportion of Business by Foreign Subsidiaries   The greater the percentage of an MNC's business conducted by its foreign subsidiaries, the larger the percentage of a given financial statement item that is susceptible to translation exposure.

EXAMPLE   Locus Co. and Zeuss Co. each generate about 30 percent of their sales from foreign countries. However, Locus Co. generates all of its international business by exporting whereas Zeuss Co. has a large Mexican subsidiary that generates all of its international business. Locus Co. is not subject to translation exposure (although it is subject to economic exposure), while Zeuss has substantial translation exposure. ●

Locations of Foreign Subsidiaries   The countries in which subsidiaries are located can also influence the degree of translation exposure because the financial statement items of each subsidiary are typically measured by the respective subsidiary's home currency.

EXAMPLE

Zeuss Co. and Canton Co. each have one large foreign subsidiary that generates about 30 percent of their respective sales. However, Zeuss Co. is subject to a much higher degree of translation exposure because its subsidiary is based in Mexico and the peso's value is subject to significant depreciation. In contrast, Canton's subsidiary is based in Canada, and the Canadian dollar is very stable against the U.S. dollar. ●

Accounting Methods   An MNC's degree of translation exposure is strongly affected by the accounting procedures used to translate when consolidating financial statement data. Many important consolidated accounting rules for U.S.-based MNCs are based on FASB 52, which includes the following provisions.

1. The functional currency of an entity is the currency of the economic environment in which the entity operates.
2. The current exchange rate as of the reporting date is used to translate the assets and liabilities of a foreign entity from its functional currency into the reporting currency.
3. The weighted average exchange rate over the relevant period is used to translate revenue, expenses, and gains and losses of a foreign entity from its functional currency into the reporting currency.
4. Translated income gains or losses due to changes in foreign currency values are not recognized in current net income but are reported as a second component of stockholder's equity; an exception to this rule is a foreign entity located in a country with high inflation.
5. Realized income gains or losses due to foreign currency transactions are recorded in current net income, although there are some exceptions.

Under FASB 52, consolidated earnings are sensitive to the functional currency's weighted average exchange rate.

EXAMPLE

Providence, Inc., is a U.S.-based MNC whose British subsidiary earned £10 million in year 1 and £10 million in year 2. When these earnings are consolidated along with other subsidiary earnings, they are translated into U.S. dollars at the weighted average exchange rate for the year in question. Suppose the weighted average exchange rate is $1.70 in year 1 and $1.50 in year 2. Then the translated earnings (in U.S. dollars) for each reporting period are determined as follows:

REPORTING PERIOD	LOCAL EARNINGS OF BRITISH SUBSIDIARY	WEIGHTED AVERAGE EXCHANGE RATE OF POUND OVER THE REPORTING PERIOD	TRANSLATED U.S. DOLLAR EARNINGS OF BRITISH SUBSIDIARY
Year 1	£10,000,000	$1.70	$17,000,000
Year 2	£10,000,000	$1.50	$15,000,000

Note that even though the subsidiary's earnings in pounds were the same each year, the translated consolidated dollar earnings were reduced by $2 million in year 2. This discrepancy is due to the change in the weighted average of the British pound exchange rate. The drop in earnings is not the fault of the subsidiary but rather of the weakened British pound, which makes the subsidiary's year-2 earnings look small (when measured in U.S. dollars). The effect reported in the table occurs even if all of the earnings generated by the subsidiary are reinvested in the United Kingdom. ●

Translation exposure can explain some of the variation in earnings for any particular U.S.-based MNC over time because the reported consolidated earnings are boosted in periods when the currencies of foreign subsidiaries strengthen against the dollar and are reduced in periods when these currencies weaken against the dollar. Consolidated earnings of Black & Decker, The Coca-Cola Co., and many other large MNCs are highly sensitive to exchange rates because more than a third of their assets and sales are overseas. In some quarters, more than half of the change in reported earnings by MNCs is due to the translation effect. The potential impact of this effect on consolidated earnings is especially pronounced when foreign subsidiaries generate a relatively high proportion of the MNC's total earnings and when the local currencies used by those subsidiaries have changed substantially in value over the quarter.

10-4b Exposure of an MNC's Stock Price to Translation Effects

Many investors tend to use earnings when valuing the stock of MNCs, either by deriving estimates of expected cash flows from previous earnings or by applying an industry price/earnings (P/E) ratio to expected annual earnings in order to derive a value per share of stock. Because the translation exposure of each MNC affects its consolidated earnings, that exposure can also affect the MNC's valuation.

EXAMPLE Recall the previous example, in which Providence earned consolidated earnings (translated to dollars) of $17 million in year 1 but only $15 million in year 2 (because of depreciation in the British pound during that year). Providence has 10 million shares of stock outstanding. Assume that all consolidated earnings for Providence come from its subsidiaries (the U.S. parent had no earnings). Suppose the market valuation of Providence's stock is usually near the mean P/E ratio in its industry multiplied by its prevailing earnings per share (EPS), and suppose the mean P/E ratio in its industry was 20 in year 1 and also in year 2.

Given this information, the translation effect on earnings per share and on the stock price of Providence is determined in Exhibit 10.8. In year 1, its EPS is estimated to be $1.70; hence the stock valuation is $1.70 × 20 = $34 per share in that year. In year 2, however, the company's consolidated earnings (in dollars) are only $1.50 per share, which results in a stock value of only $30 per share. Thus its stock valuation declined over the last year because its consolidated earnings declined over that period, which in turn resulted from a decline in the exchange rate used to translate the British pound earnings into dollar earnings. These results hold regardless of whether the subsidiary earnings are remitted to the U.S. parent or reinvested by the subsidiary in the United Kingdom. ●

Signals That Complement Translation Effects The exchange rate conditions that cause a translation effect can also signal changes in expected cash flows in future years. Such changes could also influence the stock price.

EXAMPLE In the previous example, the pound weakened from year 1 to year 2. Providence's British subsidiary could possibly retain all of its earnings (rather than remit them to the parent) as long as the pound is weak. However, there is no guarantee that the pound's value will revert to its higher level of the previous year; in fact, the pound might even weaken further. The prevailing weak exchange rate may serve as a reasonable guess of the pound's future spot rate when the pound cash flows are converted to dollars. Consequently, stock analysts may expect a reduction in dollar cash flows that Providence will receive from its

Exhibit 10.8 How Translation Exposure Can Affect an MNC's Stock Price

YEAR	CONSOLIDATED EARNINGS	EARNINGS PER SHARE (EPS), COMPUTED AS CONSOLIDATED EARNINGS DIVIDED BY 10 MILLION SHARES OUTSTANDING	PREVAILING PRICE-EARNINGS (P/E) RATIO IN THE INDUSTRY	VALUATION OF PROVIDENCE CO. STOCK [EPS BASED ON PREVAILING P/E RATIO × EPS]
1	$17,000,000	$1.70	20	$1.70 × 20 = $34
2	$15,000,000	$1.50	20	$1.50 × 20 = $30

British subsidiary in the future years. This expectation complements the weaker reported consolidated earnings and provides further evidence that Providence's stock price will decline. ●

Just as an unfavorable translation effect that reduces consolidated earnings may also reduce the MNC's stock price, a favorable translation effect that boosts consolidated earnings could boost the stock price. Specifically, if the British pound appreciates against the dollar in the next period, there would be a favorable effect on Providence's consolidated earnings. In addition, the prevailing strong exchange rate may serve as a reasonable estimate of the pound's future spot rate when pound cash flows are converted to dollars. Stock analysts may therefore expect an increase in dollar cash flows Providence will receive from its British subsidiary in the future years. This expectation complements the higher reported consolidated earnings and provides further evidence that Providence's stock price will increase in response to a favorable translation effect.

Exposure of Managerial Compensation to Translation Effects   Because an MNC's stock may be subject to translation effects and because managerial compensation is often tied to the MNC's stock price, it follows that managerial compensation is affected by translation effects. Managers of one U.S.-based MNC may receive more compensation in a particular quarter than managers of other MNCs in its industry simply because its foreign subsidiaries are located in countries where the local currencies appreciated against the dollar over that quarter. Analogously, managers of some U.S.-based MNCs may receive low compensation because the currencies of their foreign subsidiaries depreciated against the dollar, thereby reducing earnings and stock price performance.

SUMMARY

- Exchange rate movements can affect an MNC's cash flows and therefore can affect its performance and value. MNCs with less risk can obtain funds at lower financing costs. Because they may experience more volatile cash flows due to exchange rate movements, exchange rate risk can also affect their financing costs. Thus MNCs frequently attempt to measure their exposure to exchange rate risk (as explained in this chapter), so that they can decide whether and how to hedge that risk (as explained in the next two chapters).

- Transaction exposure is the exposure of an MNC's contractual transactions to exchange rate movements. MNCs can measure their transaction exposure by determining their future payables and receivables positions in various currencies, along with the volatility levels and correlations of these currencies. From this information, they can assess how their revenue and costs may change in response to various exchange rate scenarios.

- Economic exposure is any exposure of an MNC's cash flows (direct or indirect) to exchange rate movements. MNCs can attempt to measure their economic exposure by determining the extent to which their cash flows will be affected by their exposure to each foreign currency.

- Translation exposure is the exposure of an MNC's consolidated financial statements to exchange rate movements. To measure translation exposure, MNCs can forecast their earnings in each foreign currency and then determine how their consolidated earnings could be affected by the potential exchange rate movements of each currency.

POINT COUNTER-POINT

Should Investors Care about an MNC's Translation Exposure?

Point   No. The present value of an MNC's cash flows is based on the cash flows that the parent receives. Any

impact of the exchange rates on the financial statements is not important unless cash flows are affected.

MNCs should focus their energy on assessing the exposure of their cash flows to exchange rate movements and should not be concerned with the exposure of their financial statements to exchange rate movements. Value is about cash flows, and investors focus on value.

Counter-Point   Yes. Investors do not have sufficient financial data to derive cash flows. They commonly use earnings as a base, and if earnings are distorted, their estimates of cash flows will be also. If they underestimate cash flows because of how exchange rates affected the reported earnings, they may underestimate the value of the MNC. Even if the value is corrected in the future once the market realizes how the earnings were distorted, some investors may have sold their stock by the time the correction occurs. Investors should be concerned about an MNC's translation exposure. They should recognize that the earnings of MNCs with large translation exposure may be more distorted than the earnings of MNCs with low translation exposure.

Who Is Correct?   Use the Internet to learn more about this issue. Which argument do you support? Offer your own opinion on this issue.

SELF-TEST

Answers are provided in Appendix A at the back of the text.

1.   Given that shareholders can diversify away an individual firm's exchange rate risk by investing in a variety of firms, why are firms concerned about exchange rate risk?

2.   Bradley, Inc., considers importing its supplies from either Canada (denominated in C$) or Mexico (denominated in pesos) on a monthly basis. The quality is the same for both sources. Once the firm completes the agreement with a supplier, it will be obligated to continue using that supplier for at least three years. Based on existing exchange rates, the dollar amount to be paid (including transportation costs) will be the same. The firm has no other exposure to exchange rate movements. Given that the firm prefers to have less exchange rate risk, which alternative is preferable? Explain.

3.   Assume your U.S. firm currently exports to Mexico on a monthly basis. The goods are priced in pesos. Once material is received from a source, it is quickly used to produce the product in the United States, and then the product is exported. Currently, you have no other exposure to exchange rate risk. You have a choice of purchasing the material from Canada (denominated in C$), from Mexico (denominated in pesos), or from within the United States (denominated in U.S. dollars). The quality and your expected cost are similar across the three sources. Which source is preferable, given that you prefer minimal exchange rate risk?

4.   Using the information in the previous question, consider a proposal to price the exports to Mexico in dollars and to use the U.S. source for material. Would this proposal eliminate the exchange rate risk?

5.   Assume that the dollar is expected to strengthen against the euro over the next several years. Explain how this will affect the consolidated earnings of U.S.-based MNCs with subsidiaries in Europe.

QUESTIONS AND APPLICATIONS

1.   Transaction versus Economic Exposure Compare and contrast transaction exposure and economic exposure. Why would an MNC consider examining only its "net" cash flows in each currency when assessing its transaction exposure?

2.   Assessing Transaction Exposure Your employer, a large MNC, has asked you to assess its transaction exposure. Its projected cash flows are as follows for the next year. Danish krone inflows equal DK50,000,000 while outflows equal DK40,000,000. British pound inflows equal £2,000,000 while outflows equal £1,000,000. The spot rate of the krone is $.15, while the spot rate of the pound is $1.50. Assume that the movements in the Danish krone and the British pound are highly correlated. Provide your assessment as to your firm's degree of transaction exposure (as to whether the exposure is high or low). Substantiate your answer.

3.   Factors That Affect a Firm's Transaction Exposure What factors affect a firm's degree of transaction exposure in a particular currency? For each factor, explain the desirable characteristics that would reduce transaction exposure.

4. Currency Correlations Kopetsky Co. has net receivables in several currencies that are highly correlated with each other. What does this imply about the firm's overall degree of transaction exposure? Are currency correlations perfectly stable over time? What does your answer imply about Kopetsky Co. or any other firm using past data on correlations as an indicator for the future?

5. Currency Effects on Cash Flows How should appreciation of a firm's home currency generally affect its cash inflows? How should depreciation of a firm's home currency generally affect its cash outflows?

6. Transaction Exposure Fischer, Inc., exports products from Florida to Europe. It obtains supplies and borrows funds locally. How would appreciation of the euro likely affect its net cash flows? Why?

7. Exposure of Domestic Firms Why are the cash flows of a purely domestic firm exposed to exchange rate fluctuations?

8. Measuring Economic Exposure Memphis Co. hires you as a consultant to assess its degree of economic exposure to exchange rate fluctuations. How would you handle this task? Be specific.

9. Factors That Affect a Firm's Translation Exposure What factors affect a firm's degree of translation exposure? Explain how each factor influences translation exposure.

10. Translation Exposure Consider a period in which the U.S. dollar weakens against the euro. How will this affect the reported earnings of a U.S.-based MNC with European subsidiaries? Consider a period in which the U.S. dollar strengthens against most foreign currencies. How will this affect the reported earnings of a U.S.-based MNC with subsidiaries all over the world?

11. Transaction Exposure Aggie Co. produces chemicals. It is a major exporter to Europe, where its main competition is from other U.S. exporters. All of these companies invoice the products in U.S. dollars. Is Aggie's transaction exposure likely to be significantly affected if the euro strengthens or weakens? Explain. If the euro weakens for several years, can you think of any change that might occur in the global chemicals market?

12. Economic Exposure Longhorn Co. produces hospital equipment. Most of its revenues are in the United States. About half of its expenses require outflows in Philippine pesos (to pay for Philippine materials). Most of Longhorn's competition is from U.S. firms that have no international business at all. How will Longhorn Co. be affected if the peso strengthens?

13. Economic Exposure Lubbock, Inc., produces furniture and has no international business. Its major competitors import most of their furniture from Brazil and then sell it out of retail stores in the United States. How will Lubbock, Inc., be affected if Brazil's currency (the real) strengthens over time?

14. Economic Exposure Sooner Co. is a U.S. wholesale company that imports expensive high-quality luggage and sells it to retail stores around the United States. Its main competitors also import high-quality luggage and sell it to retail stores. None of these competitors hedge their exposure to exchange rate movements. Why might Sooner's market share be more volatile over time if it hedges its exposure?

15. PPP and Economic Exposure Boulder, Inc., exports chairs to Europe (invoiced in U.S. dollars) and competes against local European companies. If purchasing power parity exists, why would Boulder not benefit from a stronger euro?

16. Measuring Changes in Economic Exposure Toyota Motor Corp. measures the sensitivity of its exports to the yen exchange rate (relative to the U.S. dollar). Explain how regression analysis could be used for such a task. Identify the expected sign of the regression coefficient if Toyota primarily exports to the United States. If Toyota established more plants in the United States, how might the regression coefficient on the exchange rate variable change?

17. Impact of Exchange Rates on Earnings Cieplak, Inc., is a U.S.-based MNC that has expanded into Asia. Its U.S. parent exports to some Asian countries, with its exports denominated in the Asian currencies. It also has a large subsidiary in Malaysia that serves that market. Offer at least two reasons related to exposure to exchange rates that explain why Cieplak's earnings were reduced during the Asian crisis in 1997.

Advanced Questions

18. Speculating Based on Exposure Periodically, there are rumors that China will weaken its currency (the yuan) against the U.S. dollar and many European currencies. This causes investors to sell stocks in Asian countries such as Japan, Taiwan, and Singapore. Offer an intuitive explanation for such an effect. What types of Asian firms would be affected the most?

19. Comparing Transaction and Economic Exposure

Erie Co. has most of its business in the United States, except that it exports to Belgium. Its exports were invoiced in euros (Belgium's currency) last year. It has no other economic exposure to exchange rate risk. Its main competition when selling to Belgium's customers is a company in Belgium that sells similar products, denominated in euros. Starting today, Erie Co. plans to adjust its pricing strategy to invoice its exports in U.S. dollars instead of euros. Based on the new strategy, will Erie Co. be subject to economic exposure to exchange rate risk in the future? Briefly explain.

20. Using Regression Analysis to Measure Exposure

a. How can a U.S. company use regression analysis to assess its economic exposure to fluctuations in the British pound?

b. In using regression analysis to assess the sensitivity of cash flows to exchange rate movements, what is the purpose of breaking the database into subperiods?

c. Assume the regression coefficient based on assessing economic exposure was much higher in the second subperiod than in the first subperiod. What does this tell you about the firm's degree of economic exposure over time? Why might such results occur?

21. Transaction Exposure

Vegas Corp. is a U.S. firm that exports most of its products to Canada. It historically invoiced its products in Canadian dollars to accommodate the importers. However, it was adversely affected when the Canadian dollar weakened against the U.S. dollar. Because Vegas did not hedge, its Canadian dollar receivables were converted into a relatively small amount of U.S. dollars. After a few more years of continual concern about possible exchange rate movements, Vegas called its customers and requested that they pay for future orders with U.S. dollars instead of Canadian dollars. At this time, the Canadian dollar was valued at $.81. The customers decided to oblige as the number of Canadian dollars to be converted into U.S. dollars when importing the goods from Vegas was still slightly smaller than the number of Canadian dollars that would be needed to buy the product from a Canadian manufacturer. Based on this situation, has transaction exposure changed for Vegas Corp.? Has economic exposure changed? Explain.

22. Measuring Economic Exposure

Using the cost and revenue information shown for DeKalb, Inc., determine how the costs, revenue, and cash flow items would be affected by three possible exchange rate scenarios for the New Zealand dollar (NZ$): (1) NZ$ = $.50, (2) NZ$ = $.55, and (3) NZ$ = $.60. (Assume U.S. sales will be unaffected by the exchange rate.) Assume that NZ$ earnings will be remitted to the U.S. parent at the end of the period. Ignore possible tax effects.

REVENUE AND COST ESTIMATES: DEKALB, INC. (IN MILLIONS OF U.S. DOLLARS AND NEW ZEALAND DOLLARS)		
	U.S. BUSINESS	NEW ZEALAND BUSINESS
Sales	$800	NZ$800
Cost of materials	500	100
Operating Expenses	300	0
Interest expense	100	0
Cash flow	−100	NZ$700

23. Changes in Economic Exposure

The Walt Disney Company built an amusement park in France that opened in 1992. How do you think this project has affected Disney's economic exposure to exchange rate movements? Think carefully before you give your final answer. There is more than one way in which Disney's cash flows may be affected. Explain.

24. Lagged Effects of Exchange Rate Movements

Cornhusker Co. is an exporter of products to Singapore. It wants to know how its stock price is affected by changes in the Singapore dollar's exchange rate. It believes that the impact may occur with a lag of one to three quarters. How could regression analysis be used to assess the impact?

25. Potential Effects if the United Kingdom Adopted the Euro

The United Kingdom still has its own currency, the pound. The pound's interest rate has historically been higher than the euro's interest rate. The United Kingdom has considered adopting the euro as its currency. There have been many arguments about whether it should do so.

Use your knowledge and intuition to discuss the likely effects if the United Kingdom adopts the euro. For each of the 10 statements below, insert either *increase* or *decrease* in the first blank and complete the statement by adding a clear, short explanation (perhaps one to three sentences) of why the United Kingdom's adoption of the euro would have that effect.

To help you narrow your focus, follow these guidelines. Assume that the pound is more volatile than the euro. Do not base your answer on whether the pound would have been stronger than the euro in the future. Also, do not base your answer on an unusual change in economic growth in the United Kingdom or in the eurozone if the euro is adopted.

a. The economic exposure of British firms that are heavy exporters to the eurozone would ___ because ___.

b. The translation exposure of firms based in the eurozone that have British subsidiaries would ___ because ___.

c. The economic exposure of U.S. firms that conduct substantial business in the United Kingdom and have no other international business would ___ because ___.

d. The translation exposure of U.S. firms with British subsidiaries would ___ because ___.

e. The economic exposure of U.S. firms that export to the United Kingdom and whose only other international business is importing from firms based in the eurozone would ___ because ___.

f. The discount on the forward rate paid by U.S. firms that periodically use the forward market to hedge payables of British imports would ___ because ___.

g. The earnings of a foreign exchange department of a British bank that executes foreign exchange transactions desired by its European clients would ___ because ___.

h. Assume that the Swiss franc is more highly correlated with the British pound than with the euro. A U.S. firm has substantial monthly exports to the United Kingdom denominated in the British currency and also has substantial monthly imports of Swiss supplies (denominated in Swiss francs). The economic exposure of this firm would ___ because ___.

i. Assume that the Swiss franc is more highly correlated with the British pound than with the euro. A U.S. firm has substantial monthly exports to the United Kingdom denominated in the British currency and also has substantial monthly exports to Switzerland (denominated in Swiss francs). The economic exposure of this firm would ___ because ___.

j. The British government's reliance on monetary policy (as opposed to fiscal policy) as a means of fine-tuning the economy would ___ because ___.

26. Invoicing Policy to Reduce Exposure Celtic Co. is a U.S. firm that exports its products to England. It faces competition from many firms in England. Its price to customers in England has generally been lower than those of the competitors, primarily because the British pound has been strong. It has priced its exports in pounds and then converts the pound receivables into dollars. All of its expenses are in the United States and are paid with dollars. It is concerned about its economic exposure. It considers a change in its pricing policy, in which it will price its products in dollars instead of pounds. Offer your opinion on why this will or will not significantly reduce its economic exposure.

27. Exposure to Cash Flows Raton Co. is a U.S. company that has net inflows of 100 million Swiss francs and net outflows of 100 million British pounds. The present exchange rate of the Swiss franc is about $.70 while the present exchange rate of the pound is $1.90. Raton Co. has not hedged these positions. The Swiss franc and British pound are highly correlated in their movements against the dollar. Explain whether Raton will be favorably or adversely affected if the dollar weakens against foreign currencies over time.

28. Assessing Exposure Washington Co. and Vermont Co. have no domestic business. They have a similar dollar equivalent amount of international exporting business. Washington Co. exports all of its products to Canada. Vermont Co. exports its products to Poland and Mexico, with about half of its business in each of these two countries. Each firm receives the currency of the country where it sends its exports. You obtain the end-of-month spot exchange rates of the currencies mentioned above during the end of each of the last 6 months.

END OF MONTH	CANADIAN DOLLAR	MEXICAN PESO	POLISH ZLOTY
1	$.8142	$.09334	$.29914
2	.8176	.09437	.29829
3	.8395	.09241	.30187
4	.8542	.09263	.3088
5	.8501	.09251	.30274
6	.8556	.09448	.30312

You want to assess the data in a logical manner to determine which firm has a higher degree of exchange rate risk. Show your work and write your conclusion. (*Hint*: The percentage change in the portfolio of currencies is a weighted average of the percentage change in each currency in the portfolio.)

29. Exposure to Pegged Currency System

Assume that the Mexican peso and the Brazilian currency (the real) have depreciated against the U.S. dollar recently due to the high inflation rates in those countries. Assume that inflation in these two countries is expected to continue and that it will have a major effect on these currencies if they are still allowed to float. Assume that the government of Brazil decides to peg its currency to the dollar and will definitely maintain the peg for the next year. Milez Co. is based in Mexico. Its main business is to export supplies from Mexico to Brazil. It invoices its supplies in Mexican pesos. Its main competition is from firms in Brazil that produce similar supplies and sell them locally. How will the sales volume of Milez Co. be affected (if at all) by the Brazilian government's actions? Explain.

30. Assessing Currency Volatility
Zemart is a U.S. firm that plans to establish international business in which it will export to Mexico (these exports will be denominated in pesos) and to Canada (these exports will be denominated in Canadian dollars) once a month and will therefore receive payments once a month. It is concerned about exchange rate risk. It wants to compare the standard deviation of exchange rate movements of these two currencies against the U.S. dollar on a monthly basis. For this reason, it asks you to:

a. Estimate the standard deviation of the monthly movements in the Canadian dollar against the U.S. dollar over the last 12 months.

b. Estimate the standard deviation of the monthly movements in the Mexican peso against the U.S. dollar over the last 12 months.

c. Determine which currency is less volatile. You can use the website www.oanda.com (or any legitimate website that has currency data) to obtain the end-of-month direct exchange rate of the peso and the Canadian dollar in order to do your analysis. Show your work. You can use a calculator or a spreadsheet (like Excel) to do the actual computations.

31. Exposure of Net Cash Flows
Each of the following U.S. firms is expected to generate $40 million in net cash flows (after including the estimated cash flows from international sales if there are any) over the next year. Ignore any tax effects. Each firm has the same level of expected earnings. None of the firms has taken any position in exchange rate derivatives to hedge

exchange rate risk. All payments for the international trade by each firm will occur one year from today.

Sunrise Co. has ordered imports from Austria, and its imports are invoiced in euros. The dollar value of the payables (based on today's exchange rate) from its imports during this year is $10 million. It has no international sales.

Copans Co. has ordered imports from Mexico, and its imports are invoiced in U.S. dollars. The dollar value of the payables from its imports during this year is $15 million. It has no international sales.

Yamato Co. ordered imports from Italy, and its imports are invoiced in euros. The dollar value of the payables (based on today's exchange rate) from its imports during this year is $12 million. In addition, Yamato exports to Portugal, and its exports are denominated in euros. The dollar value of the receivables (based on today's exchange rate) from its exports during this year is $8 million.

Glades Co. ordered imports from Belgium, and these imports are invoiced in euros. The dollar value of the payables (based on today's exchange rate) from its imports during this year is $7 million. Glades also ordered imports from Luxembourg, and these imports are denominated in dollars. The dollar value of these payables is $30 million. Glades has no international sales.

Based on this information, which firm is exposed to the most exchange rate risk? Explain.

32. Cash Flow Sensitivity to Exchange Rate Movements
The Central Bank of Poland is about to engage in indirect intervention later today in which it will lower Poland's interest rates substantially. This will have an impact on the value of the Polish currency (zloty) against most currencies because it will immediately affect capital flows. Missouri Co. has a subsidiary in Poland that sells appliances. The demand for its appliances is not affected much by the local economy. Most of its appliances produced in Poland are typically invoiced in zloty and are purchased by consumers from Germany. The subsidiary's main competition is from appliance producers in Portugal, Spain, and Italy, which also export appliances to Germany.

a. Explain how the impact on the zloty's value will affect the sales of appliances by the Polish subsidiary.

b. The subsidiary owes a British company 1 million British pounds for some technology that the British company provided. Explain how the impact on the zloty's value will affect the cost of this technology to the subsidiary.

c. The subsidiary plans to take 2 million zloty from its recent earnings and will remit it to the U.S. parent in the near future. Explain how the impact on the zloty's value will affect the amount of dollar cash flows received by the U.S. parent due to this remittance of earnings by the subsidiary.

33. Applying the Value-at-Risk Method You use today's spot rate of the Brazilian real to forecast the spot rate of the real for one month ahead. Today's spot rate is $.4558. Use the value-at-risk method to determine the maximum percentage loss of the Brazilian real over the next month based on a 95 percent confidence level. Use the spot exchange rates at the end of each of the last six months to conduct your analysis. Forecast the exchange rate that would exist under these conditions.

34. Assessing Translation Exposure Kanab Co. and Zion Co. are U.S. companies that engage in much business within the United States and are about the same size. They both conduct some international business as well.

Kanab Co. has a subsidiary in Canada that will generate earnings of about C$20 million in each of the next five years. Kanab Co. also has a U.S. business that will receive about C$1 million (after costs) in each of the next five years as a result of exporting products to Canada that are denominated in Canadian dollars.

Zion Co. has a subsidiary in Mexico that will generate earnings of about 1 million pesos in each of the next five years. Zion Co. also has a business in the United States that will receive about 300 million pesos (after costs) in each of the next five years as a result of exporting products to Mexico that are denominated in Mexican pesos.

The salvage value of Kanab's Canadian subsidiary and Zion's Mexican subsidiary will be zero in five years. The spot rate of the Canadian dollar is $.60 while the spot rate of the Mexican peso is $.10. Assume the Canadian dollar could appreciate or depreciate against the U.S. dollar by about 8 percent in any given year, while the Mexican peso could appreciate or depreciate against the U.S. dollar by about 12 percent in any given year. Which company is subject to a higher degree of translation exposure? Explain.

35. Cross-Currency Relationships The Hong Kong dollar (HK$) is presently pegged to the U.S.

dollar and is expected to remain pegged. Some Hong Kong firms export products to Australia that are denominated in Australian dollars and have no other business in Australia. The exports are not hedged. The Australian dollar is presently worth .50 U.S. dollars, but you expect that it will be worth .45 U.S. dollars by the end of the year. Based on your expectations, will the Hong Kong exporters be affected favorably or unfavorably? Briefly explain.

36. Interpreting Economic Exposure Spratt Co. (a U.S. firm) attempts to determine its economic exposure to movements in the British pound by applying regression analysis to data over the last 36 quarters:

$$SP = b_0 + b_1e + \mu$$

where SP represents the percentage change in Spratt's stock price per quarter, e represents the percentage change in the pound value per quarter, and μ is an error term. Based on the analysis, the b_0 coefficient is zero and the b_1 coefficient is $-.4$ and is statistically significant. Assume that interest rate parity exists. Today, the spot rate of the pound is $1.80, the 90-day British interest rate is 3 percent, and the 90-day U.S. interest rate is 2 percent. Assume that the 90-day forward rate is expected to be an accurate forecast of the future spot rate. Do you expect that Spratt's value will be favorably affected, unfavorably affected, or not affected by its economic exposure over the next quarter? Explain.

37. Assessing Translation Exposure Assume the euro's spot rate is presently equal to $1.00. All of the following firms are based in New York and are the same size. While these firms concentrate on business in the United States, their entire foreign operations for this quarter are provided here.

Company A expects its exports to cause cash inflows of 9 million euros and imports to cause cash outflows equal to 3 million euros.

Company B has a subsidiary in Portugal that expects revenue of 5 million euros and has expenses of 1 million euros.

Company C expects exports to cause cash inflows of 9 million euros and imports to cause cash outflows of 3 million euros, and will repay the balance of an existing loan equal to 2 million euros.

Company D expects zero exports and imports to cause cash outflows of 11 million euros.

Company E will repay the balance of an existing loan equal to 9 million euros.

Which of the five companies described here has the highest degree of translation exposure?

38. Exchange Rates and Market Share Minnesota Co. is a U.S. firm that exports computer parts to Japan. Its main competition is from firms that are based in Japan, which invoice their products in yen. Minnesota's exports are invoiced in U.S. dollars. The prices charged by Minnesota and its competitors will not change during the next year. Will Minnesota's revenue increase, decrease, or be unaffected if the spot rate of the yen appreciates over the next year? Briefly explain.

39. Exchange Rates and Market Share Harz Co. (a U.S. firm) has an arrangement with a Chinese company in which it purchases products from them every week at the prevailing spot rate, and then sells the products in the United States invoiced in dollars. All of its competition is from U.S. firms that have no international business. The prices charged by Harz and its competitors will not change over the next year. Will the net cash flows generated by Harz increase, decrease, or be unaffected if the Chinese yuan depreciates over the next year? Briefly explain.

40. IFE and Exposure Assume that Maine Co. (a U.S. firm) measures its economic exposure to movements in the British pound by applying regression analysis to data over the last 36 quarters:

$$SP = b_0 + b_1 e + \mu$$

where SP represents the percentage change in Maine's stock price per quarter, e represents the percentage change in the British pound value per quarter, and μ is an error term. Based on the analysis, the b_0 coefficient is estimated to be zero and the b_1 coefficient is estimated to be 0.3 and is statistically significant. Maine Co. believes that the movement in the value of the pound over the next quarter will be mostly driven by the international Fisher effect. The prevailing quarterly interest rate in the United Kingdom is lower than the prevailing quarterly interest rate in the United States. Would you expect that Maine's value to be favorably affected, unfavorably affected, or not affected by the pound's movement over the next quarter? Explain.

41. PPP and Exposure Layton Co. (a U.S. firm) attempts to determine its economic exposure to movements in the Japanese yen by applying regression analysis to data over the last 36 quarters:

$$SP = b_0 + b_1 e + \mu$$

where SP represents the percentage change in Layton's stock price per quarter, e represents the percentage

change in the yen value per quarter, and μ is an error term. Based on the analysis, the b_0 coefficient is zero and the b_1 coefficient is 0.4 and is statistically significant. Layton believes that the inflation differential has a major effect on the value of the yen (based on purchasing power parity). The inflation in Japan is expected to rise substantially while the U.S. inflation will remain at a low level. Would you expect that Layton's value to be favorably affected, unfavorably affected, or not affected by its economic exposure over the next quarter? Explain.

42. Exposure to Cash Flows Lance Co. is a U.S. company that has exposure to the Swiss franc (SF) and Danish krone (DK). It has net inflows of SF100 million and net outflows of DK500 million. The present exchange rate of the SF is about $.80 while the present exchange rate of the DK is $.10. Lance Co. has not hedged these positions. The SF and DK are highly correlated in their movements against the dollar. Explain whether Lance will be favorably or adversely affected if the dollar strengthens against foreign currencies over time.

43. Assessing Transaction Exposure Zebra Co. is a U.S. firm that obtains products from a U.S. supplier and then exports them to Canadian firms. Its exports are denominated in U.S. dollars. Its main competitor is a local company in Canada that sells similar products denominated in Canadian dollars. Is Zebra subject to transaction exposure? Briefly explain.

44. Assessing Translation Exposure Quartz Co. has its entire operations in Miami, Florida, and is an exporter of products to eurozone countries. All of its earnings are derived from its exports. The exports are denominated in euros. Reed Co. (of the United States) is about the same size as Quartz Co. and generates about the same amount of earnings in a typical year. It has a subsidiary in Germany that typically generates about 40 percent of its total earnings. All earnings are reinvested in Germany and therefore not remitted. The rest of Reed's business is in the United States. Which company has a higher degree of translation exposure? Briefly explain.

45. Estimating Value at Risk Yazoo, Inc., is a U.S. firm that has substantial international business in Japan and has cash inflows in Japanese yen. The spot rate of the yen today is $.01. The yen exchange rate was $.008 three months ago, $.0085 two months ago, and $.009 one month ago. Yazoo uses today's spot rate of the yen as its forecast of the spot rate in one month. However, it wants to determine the maximum expected percentage decline in the value of the Japanese yen in one month based on the value-at-risk (VaR) method and a 95 percent probability. Use the exchange rate information provided to derive the maximum expected decline in the yen over the next month.

46. Assessing Exposure to Net Cash Flows Reese Co. will pay 1 million British pounds for materials imported from the United Kingdom in one month. Reese Co. sells some goods to Poland and will receive 3 million zloty (the Polish currency) for those goods in one month. The spot rate of the pound is $1.50, while the spot rate of the zloty is about $.30. Assume that the pound and zloty are both expected to depreciate substantially against the dollar over the next month and by the same degree (percentage). Will this have a favorable effect, unfavorable effect, or no effect on Reese Co. over the next year? Explain.

47. Impact of Translation Exposure on Stock Valuation Spencer Co. is a U.S. firm that has a large subsidiary in Singapore that generates a large amount of earnings. Spencer's stock is commonly valued at about 16 times its reported earnings per share. The earnings generated by the Singapore subsidiary in this period are the same as in the previous period. The Singapore dollar has depreciated substantially against the U.S. dollar during this period. None of the earnings generated by the Singapore subsidiary in this period will be remitted to the U.S. parent at this time. How will the stock price of Spencer Co. be affected (if at all) when the earnings are reported at the end of this period? Explain.

48. Assessing Translation Exposure Milwaukee Co. has an Australian subsidiary that earned 40 million Australian dollars (A$) this year. Little Rock Co. has an Australian subsidiary that earned A$30 million this year. The subsidiary of Milwaukee plans to reinvest its earnings in Australia while the subsidiary of Little Rock Co. plans to remit its earnings to the U.S. parent. Cincinnati Co. does not have an Australian subsidiary but it received revenue of A$50 million this year from exporting to Australia. All three companies have the same total revenue and total earnings levels (when considering their U.S. business as well), and are the same size, and do not have any other international business. Which company is subject to the highest degree of translation exposure? Briefly explain.

49. Measuring Economic Exposure Bag Company of the U.S. has a business of offering cruises along the coast of Argentina that are solely for American tourists. The company charges American tourists in U.S. dollars, but all of its expenses such as payments to its employees are in Argentine pesos. You want to measure Bag's economic exposure to movements in the peso by applying regression analysis to data over the last 60 quarters

$$SP = b_0 + b_1 e + \mu$$

where SP represents the percentage change in Bag's stock price per quarter, e represents the percentage change in the Argentine peso's value per quarter, μ is an error term, while b_0 and b_1 are regression coefficients. Do you think the expected sign of the b_1 coefficient in the model would be positive and significant, negative and significant, or zero (not significant)? Briefly explain.

Critical Thinking

Managerial Exposure to Exchange Rate Risk

The managers of many U.S.-based MNCs have heard arguments that an MNC's exposure to currency movements will have unfavorable effects on its cash flows and earnings in some periods, and favorable effects on its cash flows and earnings in other periods, and that these effects will offset in the long run. Yet the managers' compensation (including bonuses) for this quarter or year is based on the reported earnings. Because the earnings are influenced by exchange rate movements, their own compensation is influenced by exchange rate movements. Write a short essay on how MNCs could revise their bonus structure so that bonuses are not influenced by exchange rate movements. Alternatively, offer arguments to support leaving the bonus structure as it is.

Discussion in the Boardroom

This exercise can be found in Appendix E at the back of this textbook.

Running Your Own MNC

This exercise can be found on the *International Financial Management* text companion website. Go to www.cengagebrain.com (students) or www.cengage.com/login (instructors) and search using **ISBN 9781133947837**.

BLADES, INC. CASE

Assessment of Exchange Rate Exposure

Blades, Inc., is currently exporting roller blades to Thailand and importing certain components needed to manufacture roller blades from that country. Under a fixed contractual agreement, Blades' primary customer in Thailand has committed itself to purchase 180,000 pairs of roller blades annually at a fixed price of 4,594 Thai baht (THB) per pair. Blades is importing rubber and plastic components from various suppliers in Thailand at a cost of approximately THB2,871 per pair, although the exact price (in baht) depends on current market prices. Blades imports materials sufficient to manufacture 72,000 pairs of roller blades from Thailand each year. The decision to import materials from Thailand was reached because rubber and plastic components needed to manufacture Blades' products are inexpensive, yet of high quality, in Thailand.

Blades also has conducted business with a Japanese supplier in the past. Although Blades' analysis indicates that the Japanese components are of a lower quality than the Thai components, Blades has occasionally imported components from Japan when the prices were low enough. Currently, Ben Holt, Blades' chief financial officer (CFO), is considering importing components from Japan more frequently. Specifically, he would like to reduce Blades' baht exposure by taking advantage of the recently high correlation between the baht and the yen. Because Blades has net inflows denominated in baht and would have outflows denominated in yen, its net transaction exposure would be reduced if these two currencies were highly correlated. If Blades decides to import components from Japan, it would probably import materials sufficient to manufacture 1,700 pairs of roller blades annually at a price of 7,440 yen per pair.

Holt is also contemplating further expansion into foreign countries. Although he would eventually like to establish a subsidiary or acquire an existing business overseas, his immediate focus is on increasing Blades' foreign sales. Holt's primary reason for this plan is that the profit margin from Blades' imports and exports exceeds 25 percent, while the profit margin from Blades' domestic production is below 15 percent. Consequently, he believes that further foreign expansion will be beneficial to the company's future.

Though Blades' current exporting and importing practices have been profitable, Holt is contemplating extending Blades' trade relationships to countries in different regions of the world. One reason for this decision is that various Thai roller blade manufacturers have recently established subsidiaries in the United States. Furthermore, various Thai roller blade manufacturers have recently targeted the U.S. market by advertising their products over the Internet. As a result of this increased competition from Thailand, Blades is uncertain whether its primary customer in Thailand will renew the current commitment to purchase a fixed number of roller blades annually. The current agreement will terminate in three years. Another reason for engaging in transactions with other, non-Asian countries is that the Thai baht has depreciated substantially recently, which has somewhat reduced Blades' profit margins. The sale of roller blades to other countries with more stable currencies may increase Blades' profit margins.

While Blades will continue exporting to Thailand under the current agreement for the next two years, it may also export roller blades to Jogs, Ltd., a British retailer. Preliminary negotiations indicate that Jogs would be willing to commit itself to purchase 200,000 pairs of Speedos, Blades' primary product, for a fixed price of £80 per pair.

Holt is aware that further expansion would increase Blades' exposure to exchange rate fluctuations, but he believes that Blades can supplement its profit margins by expanding. He is vaguely familiar with the different types of exchange rate exposure but has asked you, a financial analyst at Blades, Inc., to help him assess how the contemplated changes would affect Blades' financial position. Among other concerns, Holt is aware that recent economic problems in the region have had an effect on Thailand and on other Asian countries. Although the correlation between Asian currencies such as the Japanese yen and the Thai baht is generally not very high and very unstable, these recent problems have increased the correlation among most Asian currencies. In contrast, the correlation between the British pound and the Asian currencies is quite low.

To aid you in your analysis, Holt has provided you with the following data:

CURRENCY	EXPECTED EXCHANGE RATE	RANGE OF POSSIBLE EXCHANGE RATES
British pound	$1.50	$1.47 to $1.53
Japanese yen	$.0083	$.0079 to $.0087
Thai baht	$.024	$.020 to $.028

Holt has asked you to answer the following questions:

1. What type(s) of exposure (transaction, economic, or translation exposure) is Blades subject to? Why?

2. Using a spreadsheet, conduct a consolidated net cash flow assessment of Blades, Inc., and estimate the range of net inflows and outflows for Blades for the coming year. Assume that Blades enters into the agreement with Jogs, Ltd.

3. If Blades does not enter into the agreement with the British firm and continues to export to Thailand and import from Thailand and Japan, do you think the increased correlations between the Japanese yen and the Thai baht will increase or reduce Blades' transaction exposure?

4. Do you think Blades should import components from Japan to reduce its net transaction exposure in the long run? Why or why not?

5. Assuming Blades enters into the agreement with Jogs, Ltd., how will its overall transaction exposure be affected?

6. Given that Thai roller blade manufacturers located in Thailand have begun targeting the U.S. roller blade market, how do you think Blades' U.S. sales were affected by the depreciation of the Thai baht? How do you think its exports to Thailand and its imports from Thailand and Japan were affected by the depreciation?

SMALL BUSINESS DILEMMA

Assessment of Exchange Rate Exposure by the Sports Exports Company

At the current time, the Sports Exports Company is willing to receive payments in British pounds for the monthly exports it sends to the United Kingdom. Although all of its receivables are denominated in pounds, it has no payables in pounds or in any other foreign currency. Jim Logan, owner of the Sports Exports Company, wants to assess his firm's exposure to exchange rate risk.

1. Would you describe the exposure of the Sports Exports Company to exchange rate risk as transaction exposure? Economic exposure? Translation exposure?

2. Logan is considering a change in the pricing policy in which the importer must pay in dollars so that

Logan will not have to worry about converting pounds to dollars every month. If implemented, would this policy eliminate the transaction exposure of the Sports Exports Company? Would it eliminate Sports Exports' economic exposure? Explain.

3. If Logan decides to implement the policy described in the previous question, how would the Sports Exports Company be affected (if at all) by appreciation of the pound? By depreciation of the pound? Would these effects on Sports Exports differ if Logan retained his original policy of pricing the exports in British pounds?

INTERNET/EXCEL EXERCISES

1. Go to www.oanda.com and obtain the direct exchange rate of the Canadian dollar and euro at the beginning of each of the last seven years.
a. Assume you received C$2 million in earnings from your Canadian subsidiary at the beginning of each year over the last seven years. Multiply this amount by the direct exchange rate of the Canadian dollar at the beginning of each year to determine how many U.S. dollars you received. Determine the percentage change

in the dollar cash flows received from one year to the next. Determine the standard deviation of these percentage changes. This measures the volatility of movements in the dollar earnings resulting from your Canadian business over time.

b. Now assume that you also received 1 million euros at the beginning of each year from your German subsidiary. Repeat the same process for the euro to measure the volatility of movements in the dollar cash flows resulting from your German business over time. Are the movements in dollar cash flows more volatile for the Canadian business or the German business?

c. Now consider the dollar cash flows you received from the Canadian subsidiary and the German subsidiary combined. That is, add the dollar cash flows received from both businesses for each year. Repeat the process to measure the volatility of movements in the dollar cash flows resulting from both businesses over time. Compare the volatility in the dollar cash flows of the portfolio to the volatility in cash flows resulting from the German business. Does it appear that diversification of businesses across two countries results in more stable cash flows than the business in Germany? Explain.

d. Compare the volatility in the dollar cash flows of the portfolio to the volatility in cash flows resulting from the Canadian business. Does it appear that diversification of businesses across two countries results in more stable cash flow movements than the business in Canada? Explain.

2. The following website contains annual reports of many MNCs: www.annualreportservice.com. Review the annual report of your choice. Look for any comments in the report that describe the MNC's transaction exposure, economic exposure, or translation exposure. Summarize the MNC's exposure based on the comments in the annual report.

Online Articles with Real-World Examples

Find a recent article online that describes an actual international finance application or a real-world example about a specific MNC's actions that reinforces one or more of the concepts covered in this chapter.

If your class has an online component, your professor may ask you to post your summary there and provide the web link of the article so that other students can access it. If your class is live, your professor may ask you to summarize your application in class. Your professor may assign specific students to complete this assignment for this chapter or may allow any students to do the assignment on a volunteer basis.

For recent online articles and real-world examples applied to this chapter, consider using the following search terms (and include the current year as a search term to ensure that the online articles are recent).

1. company AND exchange rate effects
2. Inc. AND exchange rate effects
3. company AND currency effects
4. Inc. AND currency effects
5. exposure to currency effects
6. exposure to exchange rate effects
7. exchange rate volatility
8. currency volatility
9. [name of an MNC] AND exchange rate effects
10. [name of an MNC] AND currency exposure

11
Managing Transaction Exposure

The specific objectives
of this chapter are to:

■ describe common
policies for hedging
transaction
exposure,

■ compare the
techniques
commonly used to
hedge payables,

■ compare the
techniques
commonly used to
hedge receivables,

■ describe limitations
of hedging, and

■ suggest other
methods of reducing
exchange rate risk
when hedging
techniques are not
available.

Transaction exposure exists when there are contractual transactions that cause a multinational corporation to either need or receive a specified amount of a foreign currency at a specified time in the future. The dollar value of payables could easily increase by 10 percent or more within a month. The dollar value of receivables could easily decline by 10 percent or more within a month, which might completely eliminate the profit margin on the sale of the product. For this reason, most MNCs may consider hedging contractual transactions denominated in foreign currencies. By managing transaction exposure, financial managers may increase the MNC's future cash flows, or at least reduce the uncertainty surrounding the MNC's cash flows, and thereby enhance the value of the MNC.

11-1 Policies for Hedging Transaction Exposure

An MNC's policy for hedging transaction exposure depends in part on its management's degree of risk aversion. An MNC may choose to hedge most of its transaction exposure or to hedge selectively.

11-1a Hedging Most of the Exposure

Some MNCs hedge most of their exposure so that their value is not strongly influenced by exchange rates. Multinational corporations that hedge most of their exposure do not necessarily expect that hedging will always be beneficial. In fact, they might even use some hedges that will likely result in slightly worse outcomes than no hedges at all, just to avoid the possibility of a major adverse movement in exchange rates. Hedging most of the transaction exposure allows MNCs to more accurately forecast future cash flows (in their home currency) so that they can make better decisions regarding the amount of financing they will need.

11-1b Selective Hedging

Many MNCs use selective hedging, in which they consider each type of transaction separately. Multinational corporations that are well diversified across many countries may forgo hedging their exposure except in rare circumstances. They might believe that a diversified set of exposures will limit the actual impact that exchange rates will have on their cash flows during any period.

355

Some MNCs, such as Black & Decker, Honeywell, and Merck, hedge transactions when they believe that it will improve their expected cash flows. The following quotations from annual reports illustrate the strategy of selective hedging.

> *We do not comprehensively hedge the exposure to currency rate risk, although we may choose to selectively hedge exposure to foreign currency rate risk.*
>
> —*ConocoPhillips*

> *Decisions regarding whether or not to hedge a given commitment are made on a case-by-case basis by taking into consideration the amount and duration of the exposure, market volatility, and economic trends.*
>
> —*DuPont Co.*

> *We selectively hedge the potential effect of the foreign currency fluctuations related to operating activities.*
>
> —*General Mills Co.*

When an MNC considers hedging transaction exposure, it must first assess the extent of its transaction exposure (as discussed in the previous chapter). Next, it must consider the various techniques to hedge this exposure so that it can decide which hedging technique is optimal and whether to hedge its transaction exposure. This chapter explains the process by which an MNC identifies the optimal hedging technique for a particular transaction and determines whether or not to hedge that transaction.

11-2 Hedging Exposure to Payables

An MNC may decide to hedge part or all of its known payables transactions as a way of insulating itself from possible appreciation of the currency. It may select from the following hedging techniques to hedge its payables:

- forward or futures hedge,
- money market hedge, and
- currency option hedge.

Before selecting a hedging technique, MNCs normally compare the cash flows that would be expected when using each technique. The selection of the optimal hedging technique can vary over time as the relative advantages of the various techniques change. Each technique is discussed in turn, with examples provided.

11-2a Forward or Futures Hedge on Payables

Forward contracts and futures contracts allow an MNC to lock in a specific exchange rate at which it can purchase a specific currency, thereby hedging payables denominated in that currency. A forward contract is negotiated between the firm and a financial institution such as a commercial bank, so it can be tailored to meet the firm's specific needs. The contract will specify:

- the currency that the firm will pay,
- the currency that the firm will receive,
- the amount of currency to be received by the firm,
- the rate at which the MNC will exchange currencies (the "forward" rate), and
- the future date at which the exchange of currencies will occur.

EXAMPLE

WEB

www.bankofcanada.ca
/rates/exchange/
Forward rates for the
euro, British pound,
Canadian dollar, and
Japanese yen for
1-month, 3-month,
6-month, and 12-month
maturities. These forward
rates indicate the
exchange rates at which
positions in these
currencies can be
hedged for specific
time periods.

Coleman Co. is a U.S.-based MNC that will need 100,000 euros in one year. It could obtain a forward contract to purchase the euros one year from now. The one-year forward rate is $1.20, the same rate as currency futures contracts on euros. If Coleman purchases euros one year forward, its dollar cost in one year is:

$$\text{Cost in \$} = \text{Payables} \times \text{Forward rate}$$
$$= 100{,}000 \text{ euros} \times \$1.20$$
$$= \$120{,}000 \qquad \bullet$$

The same process would apply if futures contracts were used instead of forward contracts. The futures rate is normally close to the forward rate, so the main difference is that futures contracts are standardized and can be purchased on an exchange whereas the forward contract is negotiated between the MNC and a commercial bank.

Forward contracts are frequently used by large corporations that desire to hedge. DuPont Co. and Merck & Co. often have the equivalent of $300 million to $500 million in forward contracts at any one time to cover transaction exposure.

11-2b Money Market Hedge on Payables

A money market hedge on payables involves taking a money market position to cover a future payables position. If a firm has excess cash, it can create a simplified money market hedge. However, many MNCs prefer to hedge payables without using their cash balances. A money market hedge can still be used in this situation, but it requires two money market positions: (1) borrowed funds in the home currency and (2) a short-term investment in the foreign currency.

EXAMPLE   If Coleman Co. needs 100,000 euros in one year, it could convert dollars to euros and deposit the euros in a bank today. Assuming that it could earn 5 percent on this deposit, it would need to establish a deposit of 95,238 euros in order to have 100,000 euros in one year:

$$\text{Deposit amount to hedge payables} = \frac{100{,}000 \text{ euros}}{1 + .05} = 95{,}238 \text{ euros}$$

Assuming a spot rate today of $1.18, the dollars needed to make the deposit today can be estimated as

$$\text{Deposit amount in dollars} = 95{,}238 \text{ euros} \times \$1.18 = \$112{,}381$$

Assuming that Coleman can borrow dollars at an interest rate of 8 percent, it would borrow the funds needed to make the deposit and then, at the end of the year, repay the loan:

$$\text{Dollar amount of loan repayment} = \$112{,}381 \times (1 + .08) = \$121{,}371 \qquad \bullet$$

Money Market Hedge versus Forward Hedge   Should an MNC implement a forward contract hedge or a money market hedge to cover its payables? Because the results of both hedges are known beforehand, the firm can implement the hedge that results in lower dollar cash outflows. If interest rate parity (IRP) holds and there are no transaction costs, the money market hedge will yield the same results as the forward hedge. This is because the forward premium on the forward rate reflects the interest rate differential between the two currencies. The hedging of future payables with a forward purchase is therefore similar to borrowing at the home interest rate and investing at the foreign interest rate.

11-2c Call Option Hedge on Payables

A currency call option provides the right to buy a specified amount of a particular currency at a specified price (called the *strike price* or *exercise price*) within a given period of time. Yet unlike a futures or forward contract, the currency call option does not obligate its owner to buy the currency at that price. The MNC has the flexibility to let the option expire and obtain the currency at the existing spot rate when payables are due. However, a firm must assess whether the advantages of a currency option hedge are worth the price (premium) paid for it. Details on currency options are provided in Chapter 5. The following discussion illustrates how they can be used in hedging.

Applying a Contingency Graph   The dollar cash outflows from hedging with call options are not known with certainty at the time that the options are purchased. The amount is determined once the payables are due and the spot rate at that time is known. The dollar cash outflows include the price paid for the currency as well as the premium paid for the call option. If the spot rate of the currency when the payables are due is less than the exercise price, the MNC would let the option expire because it could purchase the currency in the foreign exchange market at the spot rate. If the spot rate is either equal to or greater than the exercise price, the MNC would exercise the option and pay the exercise price for the currency.

An MNC can develop a contingency graph that determines the dollar cash outflows from hedging with call options for each of several possible spot rates when payables are due.

EXAMPLE   Recall that Coleman Co. considers hedging its payables of 100,000 euros in one year. It could purchase call options on 100,000 euros so that it can hedge its payables. Assume that the call options have an exercise price of $1.20, a premium of $.03, and an expiration date of one year from now (when the payables are due). Coleman can create a contingency graph for the call option hedge, as shown in Exhibit 11.1. The horizontal axis shows several possible spot rates of the euro that could occur at the time the payables are due, while the vertical axis shows the dollar cash flows from hedging per euro for each of those possible spot rates.

If the spot rate at the time the payables are due is less than the exercise price of $1.20, Coleman would not exercise the call option, so the dollar cash outflows from hedging would be equal to the spot rate at that time plus the premium paid for the call option. For example, if the spot rate is $1.16 when the payables are due, Coleman would pay that spot rate along with the $.03 premium per unit.

Exhibit 11.1   Contingency Graph for Hedging Payables with Call Options

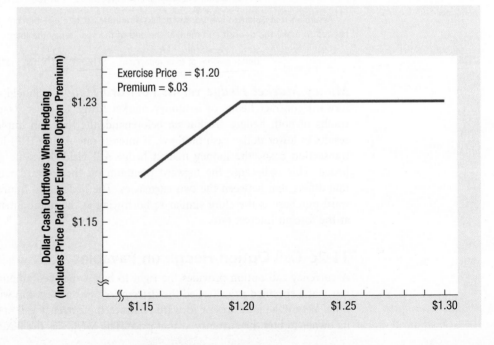

At any spot rate that is *not* less than the exercise price of $1.20, Coleman would exercise the call option; in this case, the dollar cash outflows from hedging would be equal to the price paid per euro ($1.20) plus the premium ($.03 per euro) paid for the call option. Thus the dollar cash outflows would be $1.23 if the spot rate when the payables are due equals or exceeds the exercise price of $1.20. ●

Exhibit 11.1 illustrates the advantages and disadvantages of a call option for hedging payables. The advantages are that it provides an effective hedge and allows the MNC to let the option expire if the spot rate at the time the payables are due is lower than the exercise price. Of course, the main disadvantage of the call option is that a premium must be paid for it.

To compare hedging with a call option and hedging with a forward contract, recall from a previous example that Coleman Co. could purchase a forward contract on euros for $1.20. This would result in dollar cash outflows of $1.20 per euro, regardless of the spot rate at the time the payables are due, because a forward contract (unlike a call option) creates an irrevocable obligation to execute. This could be plotted on the Exhibit 11.1 contingency graph as a horizontal line beginning at the $1.20 point on the vertical axis and extending straight across for all possible spot rates. In general, the dollar cash outflows are lower when hedging with a forward contract than when hedging with currency call options if the spot rate is relatively high when the payables are due; the reverse is true if the spot rate is relatively low at the time the payables are due.

Applying Currency Forecasts   An MNC may wish to incorporate its own forecasts of the spot rate at the time payables are due so that it can estimate more accurately the dollar cash outflows when hedging with call options.

EXAMPLE

Recall that Coleman Co. considers hedging its payables of 100,000 euros with a call option that has an exercise price of $1.20, a premium of $.03, and an expiration date of one year from now. Suppose that Coleman's forecast for the spot rate of the euro at the time payables are due is as follows:

■ $1.16 (20 percent probability),
■ $1.22 (70 percent probability),
■ $1.24 (10 percent probability).

The effect of each of these scenarios on Coleman's dollar cash outflows is shown in Exhibit 11.2. Columns 1 and 2 simply identify the scenario to be analyzed. Column 3 shows the premium per unit paid on the option, which is the same regardless of the spot rate prevailing when the payables are due. Column 4 shows the amount that Coleman would pay per euro for the payables under each scenario, assuming that it owned call options. If Scenario 1 occurs, Coleman will let the options expire and purchase euros in the spot market for $1.16 each.

Exhibit 11.2 Using Currency Call Options to Hedge Euro Payables (exercise price = $1.20, premium = $.03)

(1) SCENARIO	(2) SPOT RATE WHEN PAYABLES ARE DUE	(3) PREMIUM PER UNIT PAID ON CALL OPTIONS	(4) AMOUNT PAID PER UNIT WHEN OWNING CALL OPTIONS	(5) = (4) + (3) TOTAL AMOUNT PAID PER UNIT (INCLUDING THE PREMIUM) WHEN OWNING CALL OPTIONS	(6) $ AMOUNT PAID FOR 100,000 EUROS WHEN OWNING CALL OPTIONS
1	$1.16	$.03	$1.16	$1.19	$119,000
2	1.22	.03	1.20	1.23	123,000
3	1.24	.03	1.20	1.23	123,000

If Scenario 2 or 3 occurs, Coleman will exercise the options (purchasing euros for $1.20 per unit) and then use the euros to make its payment. Column 5, which is the sum of columns 3 and 4, shows the amount paid per unit when the $.03 premium paid on the call option is included. Column 6 converts column 5 into a total dollar cost based on the 100,000 euros hedged. ●

Consideration of Alternative Call Options Several different types of call options may be available, with different exercise prices and premiums for a given currency and expiration date. The trade-off is that an MNC must either pay a higher premium for a call option with a lower exercise price or accept a higher exercise price on an option with a lower premium. The call option perceived to be most desirable for hedging a particular payables position will be analyzed (as explained in the preceding example) so that it can be compared with the other hedging techniques.

11-2d Comparison of Techniques for Hedging Payables

The methods of hedging payables are summarized in Exhibit 11.3, which also illustrates how the dollar cash outflows for each technique were measured for Coleman Co. (based on the previous examples). Note that the dollar cash outflows when using the forward hedge or money market hedge can be determined with certainty, whereas the dollar cash outflows associated with the currency call option hedge differ depending on the future spot rate at the time the payables are due.

Exhibit 11.3 Comparison of Hedging Alternatives for Coleman Co.

Forward Hedge

Purchase euros (€) one year forward.

$$\text{Dollars needed in one year} = \text{payables in € × forward rate of euro}$$
$$= \text{100,000 euros} \times \$1.20$$
$$= \$120{,}000$$

Money Market Hedge

Borrow $, convert to €, invest €, repay $ loan in one year.

$$\text{Amount in € to be invested} = \frac{€100{,}000}{1 + .05}$$
$$= \text{95.238 euros}$$
$$\text{Amount in \$ needed to convert into € for deposit} = €95{,}238 \times \$1.18$$
$$= \$112{,}381$$
$$\text{Interest and principal owed on \$ loan after one year} = \$112{,}381 \times (1 + .08)$$
$$= \$121{,}371$$

Call Option

Purchase call option. (The following computations assume that the option is to be exercised on the day euros are needed, or not at all; exercise price = $1.20, premium = $.03.)

POSSIBLE SPOT RATE IN ONE YEAR	PREMIUM PER UNIT PAID FOR OPTION	EXERCISE OPTION?	TOTAL PRICE (INCLUDING OPTION PREMIUM) PAID PER UNIT	TOTAL PRICE PAID FOR 100,000 EUROS	PROBABILITY
$1.16	$.03	No	$1.19	$119,000	20%
1.22	.03	Yes	1.23	123,000	70
1.24	.03	Yes	1.23	123,000	10

Optimal Technique for Hedging Payables   An MNC can select the optimal technique for hedging payables by following these steps. First, because the futures and forward hedge are similar, the MNC need only consider which of these two techniques it prefers. Second, when comparing the forward (or futures) hedge to the money market hedge, the MNC can easily determine which hedge is more desirable because the dollar cash outflows associated with each hedge can be determined with certainty. Then, the MNC can determine the distribution of the estimated dollar cash outflows resulting from the currency call option hedge. It can use this distribution to estimate the expected value of dollar cash outflows from using this hedge and the likelihood that the dollar cash outflows associated with the currency call option hedge will be lower than the best alternative hedging technique.

EXAMPLE

Recall that Coleman Co. needs to hedge payables of 100,000 euros. Coleman's dollar cash outflows associated with different hedging techniques can be compared to determine which technique is optimal for hedging the payables. Exhibit 11.4 provides a graphic comparison of the dollar cash outflows associated with different hedging techniques (as determined in the previous examples in this chapter). For Coleman, the forward hedge is preferable to the money market hedge because it results in lower dollar cash outflows when hedging the payables.

The dollar cash outflows associated with the call option hedge are described by a probability distribution because they depend on the exchange rate at the time the payables are due. The expected value of the dollar cash outflows if using the currency call option hedge is

$$\text{Expected value of dollar cash outflows} = (\$119,000 \times 20\%) + (\$123,000 \times 80\%)$$
$$= \$122,200$$

The probability of the future spot rate being $1.22 (70 percent) and the probability of its being $1.24 (10 percent) are combined in the calculation because they result in the same dollar cash outflows. The expected dollar cash outflows when hedging with call options exceed the dollar cash outflows when using the forward rate hedge.

Comparing the distribution of the dollar cash outflows when hedging with call options versus the forward hedge shows that there is only a 20 percent chance that the currency call option hedge will be cheaper than the forward hedge; there is an 80 percent chance that it will be more expensive. Therefore, given the data in this specific example, the forward hedge is the optimal hedge. ●

The optimal technique to hedge payables may vary over time depending on the prevailing forward rate, interest rates, call option premium, and the forecast of the future spot rate at the time payables are due.

Optimal Hedge versus No Hedge on Payables   Even when an MNC knows what its future payables will be, it may decide not to hedge in some cases. In that event it should determine the probability distribution of its dollar cash outflows when not hedging, as explained next.

EXAMPLE

Coleman Co. has already determined that the forward rate is the optimal hedging technique if it decides to hedge its payables position. Now it wants to compare the forward hedge to using no hedge at all.

Based on its expectations of the euro's spot rate in one year (as described previously), Coleman Co. can estimate its dollar cash outflows when unhedged as follows:

POSSIBLE SPOT RATE OF EURO IN ONE YEAR	DOLLAR PAYMENTS WHEN NOT HEDGING = 100,000 EUROS × POSSIBLE SPOT RATE	PROBABILITY
$1.16	$116,000	20%
$1.22	$122,000	70%
$1.24	$124,000	10%

Exhibit 11.4 Graphic Comparison of Techniques to Hedge Payables

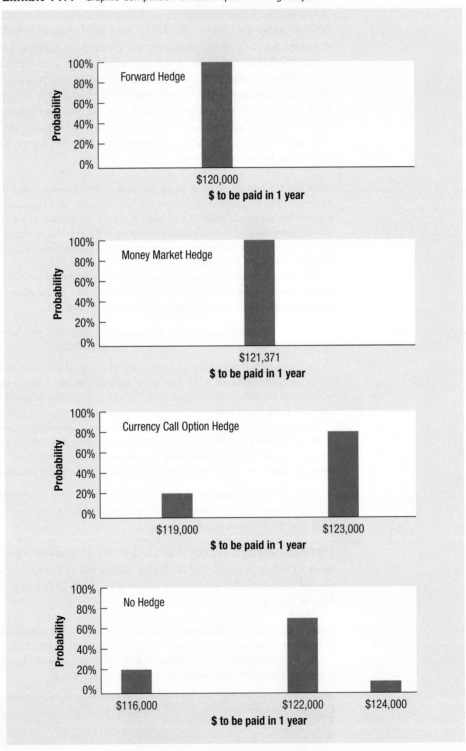

This probability distribution of the dollar cash outflows when not hedging is shown in the bottom graph of Exhibit 11.4 and can be compared to the dollar cash outflows associated with the forward hedge in that exhibit.

The expected dollar cash outflows when not hedging are now estimated as

$$\text{Expected dollar cash outflows} = (\$116{,}000 \times 20\%) + (\$122{,}000 \times 70\%) + (\$124{,}000 \times 10\%)$$
$$= \$121{,}000$$

These expected dollar cash outflows are $1,000 more than if Coleman uses a forward hedge. In addition, the probability distribution suggests an 80 percent probability that Coleman's dollar cash outflows when unhedged will exceed the dollar cash outflows when hedging with a forward contract. Therefore, Coleman decides to hedge its payables position with a forward contract. ●

For contractual transactions involving future payments, if the known cash outflows from hedging are equal to the expected cash outflows from not hedging, then an MNC will usually hedge. The cash outflows when not hedging the payables are uncertain and could be higher than expected. Most MNCs are willing to remain unhedged only if they are confident that the expected dollar cash outflows will be lower than the known cash outflows from hedging.

11-2e Evaluating Past Decisions on Hedging Payables

MNCs can evaluate past hedging decisions by estimating the real cost of hedging payables, which is measured as follows:

RCHp = Cash outflows when hedging payables – Cash outflows when unhedged

After the payables transaction has occurred, an MNC may assess the outcome of its decision to hedge.

EXAMPLE

Recall that Coleman Co. decided to hedge its payables with a forward contract, resulting in a dollar cost of $120,000. Suppose that, on the day that it makes its payment (one year after it hedged its payables), the spot rate of the euro is $1.18. Notice that this spot rate is different from all of the three possible spot rates that Coleman Co. predicted. This is not unusual, as it is difficult to predict the spot rate even when allowing for a distribution of possible outcomes. If Coleman Co. had not hedged, its dollar cash outflows associated with payables would have been $118,000 (computed as 100,000 euros × $1.18). Thus Coleman's real cost of hedging is

$$\text{RCH}p = \text{Dollar cash outflows when hedging payables} - \text{Dollar cash outflows}$$
$$= \$120{,}000 - \$118{,}000$$
$$= \$2{,}000$$

In this example, Coleman's dollar cash outflows when hedging payables turned out to be $2,000 more than if it had not hedged. However, Coleman is not necessarily disappointed in its decision to hedge. That decision allowed it to know exactly how many dollars it would need to cover its payables position and insulated the payment from adverse movements in the euro. ●

11-3 Hedging Exposure to Receivables

An MNC may decide to hedge part or all of its receivables transactions denominated in foreign currencies so that it is insulated from the possible depreciation of those currencies. It can apply the same techniques available for hedging payables to hedge receivables. The application of each hedging technique to receivables is discussed next.

11-3a Forward or Futures Hedge on Receivables

Forward contracts and futures contracts allow an MNC to lock in a specific exchange rate at which it can sell a specific currency, thereby enabling it to hedge receivables denominated in a foreign currency.

EXAMPLE

Viner Co. is a U.S.-based MNC that will receive 200,000 Swiss francs (SF) in six months. It could obtain a forward contract to sell SF200,000 in six months. The six-month forward rate is $.71, the same rate as currency futures contracts on Swiss francs. If Viner sells Swiss francs six months forward, it can estimate the amount of dollars to be received in six months as follows:

$$\textbf{Cash inflow in \$} = \textbf{Receivables} \times \textbf{Forward rate}$$
$$= \textbf{SF200,000} \times \textbf{\$.71}$$
$$= \textbf{\$142,000} \qquad \bullet$$

The same process would apply if futures contracts were used instead of forward contracts. The futures rate is normally close to the forward rate, so the main difference is that a futures contract would be standardized and sold on an exchange whereas a forward contract would be negotiated between the MNC and a commercial bank.

11-3b Money Market Hedge on Receivables

A money market hedge on receivables involves borrowing the currency that will be received and then using the receivables to pay off the loan.

EXAMPLE

Recall that Viner Co. will receive SF200,000 in six months. Assume that it can borrow funds denominated in Swiss francs at a rate of 3 percent over a six-month period. The amount that it should borrow so that it can use all of its receivables to repay the entire loan in six months is

$$\textbf{Amount to borrow} = \textbf{SF200,000}/(1 + .03)$$
$$= \textbf{SF194,175}$$

If Viner Co. obtains a six-month loan of SF194,175 from a bank, then it will owe the bank SF200,000 in six months. It can use its receivables to repay the loan. The funds that it borrowed can be converted to dollars and used to support existing operations. ●

If the MNC does not need any short-term funds to support existing operations, it can still obtain a loan as just explained, convert the funds to dollars, and invest the dollars in the money market.

EXAMPLE

If Viner Co. does not need any funds to support existing operations, it can convert the Swiss francs that it borrowed into dollars. Suppose the spot exchange rate is presently $.70. When Viner Co. converts the Swiss francs, it will receive:

$$\textbf{Amount of dollars received from loan} = \textbf{SF194,175} \times \textbf{\$.70} = \textbf{\$135,922}$$

These dollars can then be invested in the money market. Assume that Viner Co. can earn 2 percent interest over a six-month period. In six months, the investment will be worth

$$\textbf{\$135,922} \times \textbf{1.02} = \textbf{\$138,640}$$

Thus if Viner Co. uses a money market hedge, its receivables will be worth $138,640 in six months. ●

11-3c Put Option Hedge on Receivables

A put option allows an MNC to sell a specific amount of currency at a specified exercise price by a specified expiration date. An MNC can purchase a put option on the currency denominating its receivables and thus lock in the minimum amount that it would receive when converting the receivables into its home currency. However, the put option differs from a forward or futures contract in that it is an option, not an obligation. If the spot rate of the currency denominating the receivables is higher than the exercise price at the time of expiration, then the MNC can let the put option expire and can sell the currency in the foreign exchange market at the prevailing spot rate. The MNC must also consider the premium that it must pay for the put option.

Applying a Contingency Graph   The dollar cash inflows when hedging receivables with put options are not known with certainty at the time the options are purchased; the cash inflows are determined once the receivables are due and the spot rate at that time is known. An estimate of the cash to be received from a put option hedge is the estimated cash received from selling the currency minus the premium paid for the put option. If the spot rate of the currency when the receivables arrive is lower than the exercise price, then the MNC would exercise the option and receive the exercise price when selling the currency. If the spot rate at that time is equal to or higher than the exercise price, the MNC would let the option expire and would sell the currency at the spot rate in the foreign exchange market.

An MNC can develop a contingency graph that determines the cash received from hedging with put options depending on each of several possible spot rates when the receivables arrive.

EXAMPLE   Recall that Viner Co. considers hedging its receivables of SF200,000 in six months. It could do this by purchasing put options on SF200,000. Assume that the put options have an exercise price of $.70, a premium of $.02, and an expiration date of six months from now (when the receivables arrive). Viner can create a contingency graph for the put option hedge, as in Exhibit 11.5. The horizontal axis shows several possible values of the Swiss franc spot rate prevailing when Viner's receivables arrive, while the vertical axis shows the cash to be received from the put option hedge based on each of those possible spot rates.

At any spot rate less than or equal to the exercise price of $.70, Viner Co. would exercise the put option, selling the Swiss francs at the exercise price of $.70. After subtracting the $.02 premium per unit, Viner would receive $.68 per unit from selling the francs. At any spot rate higher than the exercise price, Viner would let the put option expire and simply sell the francs at the spot rate in the foreign exchange market. For example, if the spot rate was $.75 when the receivables were due, Viner would sell the Swiss francs at that rate; it would receive $.73 after subtracting the $.02 premium per unit. ●

Exhibit 11.5   Contingency Graph for Hedging Receivables with Put Options

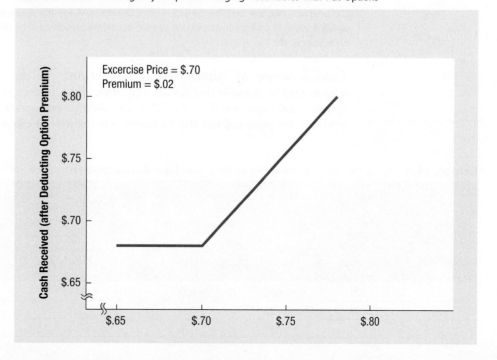

Exhibit 11.5 illustrates the advantages and disadvantages of a put option for hedging receivables. The advantage is that the put option provides an effective hedge while allowing the MNC to let the option expire if its exercise price is less than the spot rate. However, the put option's obvious disadvantage is that a premium must be paid for it.

Recall from a previous example that Viner Co. could sell a forward contract on Swiss francs for $.71; this would allow it to receive $.71 per Swiss franc regardless of the spot rate at the time the receivables arrive. This action could be plotted on the contingency graph of Exhibit 11.5 as a horizontal line that starts at the $.71 point on the vertical axis and extends straight across for all possible spot rates. In general, the forward rate hedge will provide a larger amount of cash than the put option hedge if the spot rate is relatively low when the Swiss francs are received.

Applying Currency Forecasts An MNC may wish to incorporate its own forecasts of the spot rate when estimating the dollar cash inflows to be received when hedging with put options.

EXAMPLE
Viner Co. considers purchasing a put option contract on Swiss francs; the option has an exercise price of $.72 and a premium of $.02. The company has developed the following probability distribution for the spot rate of the Swiss franc in six months:

- $.71 (30 percent probability),
- $.74 (40 percent probability),
- $.76 (30 percent probability).

The expected dollar cash flows to be received from purchasing a put option on Swiss francs are shown in Exhibit 11.6. The second column lists the possible spot rates that may (according to Viner's projections) occur in six months; the third column gives the option premium, which remains the same regardless of the future spot rate. The fourth column shows the amount to be received per unit as a result of owning the put options. If the future spot rate is $.71 (first row of the exhibit), the put option will be exercised at the exercise price of $.72. If the spot rate is higher than $.72 in six months (rows 2 and 3), Viner Co. will not exercise the option; instead it will sell the Swiss francs at the prevailing spot rate. Column 5 shows the cash received per unit, which adjusts the figures in column 4 by subtracting the premium paid per unit for the put option. Column 6 shows the amount of dollars to be received, which is equal to cash received per unit (shown in column 5) multiplied by the amount of units (200,000 Swiss francs). ●

Consideration of Alternative Put Options Several different types of put options may be available that feature different exercise prices and premiums for a given currency and expiration date. An MNC can obtain a put option with a higher exercise price, but the premium will also be higher. Alternatively, it can select a put option with

Exhibit 11.6 Use of Currency Put Options for Hedging Swiss Franc Receivables (exercise price = $.72; premium = $.02)

(1) SCENARIO	(2) SPOT RATE WHEN PAYMENT ON RECEIVABLES IS RECEIVED	(3) PREMIUM PER UNIT ON PUT OPTIONS	(4) AMOUNT RECEIVED PER UNIT WHEN OWNING PUT OPTIONS	(5) = (4) − (3) NET AMOUNT RECEIVED PER UNIT (AFTER ACCOUNTING FOR PREMIUM PAID)	(6) DOLLAR AMOUNT RECEIVED FROM HEDGING SF200,000 RECEIVABLES WITH PUT OPTIONS
1	$.71	$.02	$.72	$.70	$140,000
2	.74	.02	.74	.72	144,000
3	.76	.02	.76	.74	148,000

a lower premium but also a lower exercise price. The put option selected as most desirable for hedging a particular receivables position would be analyzed (as explained previously) and then compared to other hedging techniques.

11-3d Comparison of Techniques for Hedging Receivables

The techniques that can be used to hedge receivables are summarized in Exhibit 11.7, with an illustration of how the cash inflows from each hedging technique were measured for Viner Co. (based on previous examples).

Optimal Technique for Hedging Receivables   The optimal technique for hedging receivables may vary over time depending on the specific quotations, such as the forward rate quoted on a forward contract, the interest rates quoted on a money market loan, and the premium quoted on a put option. The optimal technique for hedging a specific future receivables position can be determined by comparing the cash to be received from the various hedging techniques. Just as when hedging payables, the MNC first considers either the futures or forward hedge according to its preferences. For our example, the forward hedge is considered. Second, it is again easy to compare the forward (or futures) hedge and the money market hedge because the cash to be received from either type can be determined with certainty.

Exhibit 11.7   Comparison of Hedging Alternatives for Viner Co.

Forward Hedge

Sell Swiss francs six months forward.

$$\text{Dollars to be received in six months} = \text{receivables in SF} \times \text{forward rate of SF}$$
$$= \text{SF200,000} \times \$.71$$
$$= \$142,000$$

Money Market Hedge

Borrow SF, convert to $, invest $, use receivables to pay off loan in six months.

$$\text{Amount in SF borrowed} = \frac{\text{SF200,000}}{1 + .03}$$
$$= \text{SF194,175}$$
$$\$ \text{ received from converting SF} = \text{SF194,175} \times \$70 \text{ per SF}$$
$$= \$135,922$$
$$\$ \text{ accumulated after six months} = \$135,922 \times (1 + .02)$$
$$= \$138,640$$

Put Option Hedge

Purchase put option. (Assume the options will be exercised on the day SF are to be received, or not at all; exercise price = $.72, premium = $.02.)

POSSIBLE SPOT RATE IN SIX MONTHS	PREMIUM PER UNIT PAID FOR OPTION	EXERCISE OPTION?	RECEIVED PER UNIT (AFTER ACCOUNTING FOR THE PREMIUM)	TOTAL DOLLARS RECEIVED FROM CONVERTING SF200,000	PROBABILITY
.71	$.02	Yes	$.70	$140,000	30%
.74	.02	No	.72	144,000	40
.76	.02	No	.74	148,000	30

Once that comparison is completed, the MNC can assess the dollar cash inflows from the currency put option hedge. Because the amount of cash to be received from the currency put option depends on the spot rate prevailing when the receivables arrive, this amount is best described by a probability distribution. That distribution of cash to be received when hedging with put options can be derived by estimating the expected value and then determining the likelihood of the currency put option hedge resulting in more cash inflows than an alternative method of hedging.

EXAMPLE

When attempting to hedge receivables of SF200,000, Viner Co. can compare the cash to be received as the result of applying different hedging techniques in order to determine which one is optimal. Exhibit 11.8 gives a graphic summary of the cash to be received from each hedging technique based on the previous examples for Viner Co. In this example, the forward hedge is better than the money market hedge because it will generate more cash.

The graph for the put option hedge confirms that the cash to be received is a function of the exchange rate at the time that receivables are due. The expected value of the cash to be received from the put option hedge is

$$\text{Expected value of cash to be received} = (\$140{,}000 \times 30\%)$$
$$+ (\$144{,}000 \times 40\%)$$
$$+ (\$148{,}000 \times 30\%)$$
$$= \$144{,}000$$

The expected value of the cash to be received when hedging with put options exceeds the cash amount that would be received from the forward rate hedge.

As Exhibit 11.8 shows, when the distribution of cash to be received from the put option is compared to the certain cash from the forward hedge, there is a 30 percent chance that the currency put option hedge will result in less cash than the forward hedge; there is also a 70 percent chance that the put option hedge will result in more cash than the forward hedge. Consequently, Viner Co. decides that the optimal hedge is the one using put options. ●

Optimal Hedge versus No Hedge on Receivables

An MNC may know what its future receivables will be yet still decide not to hedge. In that case, the MNC needs to determine the probability distribution of its revenue from receivables when not hedging. This determination is illustrated in the following example.

EXAMPLE

Viner Co. has already established that the put option hedge is the optimal technique for hedging its receivables position, so now it wants to compare using that hedge to using no hedge. Given its expectations of the Swiss franc's spot rate in one year, the company can estimate the cash to be received (if it remains unhedged) as follows:

POSSIBLE SPOT RATE OF SWISS FRANC IN ONE YEAR	DOLLAR PAYMENTS WHEN NOT HEDGING = SF200,000 × POSSIBLE SPOT RATE	PROBABILITY
$.71	$142,000	30%
$.74	$148,000	40%
$.76	$152,000	30%

The expected cash inflows that Viner will receive when not hedging are estimated as

$$\text{Expected value of cash inflows to be received} = (\$142{,}000 \times 30\%)$$
$$= (\$148{,}000 \times 40\%)$$
$$= (\$152{,}000 \times 30\%)$$
$$= \$147{,}400$$

Exhibit 11.8   Graph Comparison of Techniques to Hedge Receivables

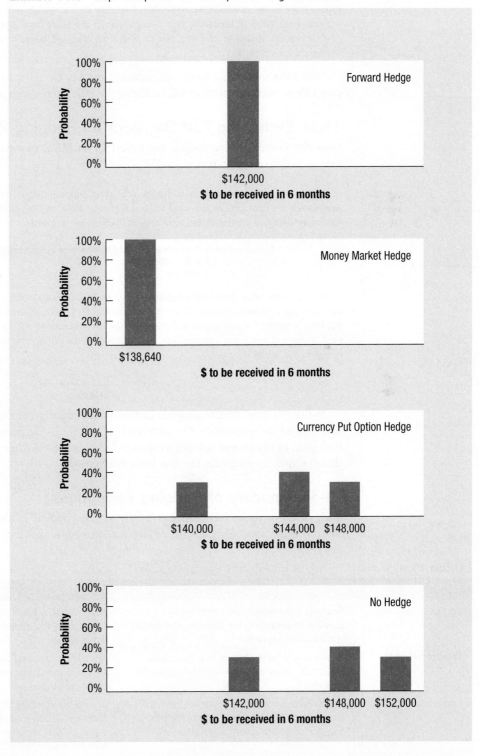

When comparing these expected cash inflows to the expected cash inflows that Viner Co. would receive from its put option hedge ($144,000), Viner decides to remain unhedged. That decision reflects the company's hope of benefiting from appreciation in the Swiss franc against the U.S. dollar over the next six months as well as its willingness to accept the trade-off: being susceptible to adverse effects if the franc depreciates. ●

Most MNCs will hedge future receivables unless they are extremely confident that expected cash inflows from not hedging will be higher than the known cash inflows from hedging.

11-3e Evaluating Past Decisions on Hedging Receivables

Once the receivables transaction has occurred, an MNC can evaluate its previous decision to hedge or not to hedge.

EXAMPLE Recall that Viner Co. decided not to hedge its receivables. Suppose that six months later, when the receivables arrive, the spot rate of the Swiss franc is $.75 (as before, this rate differs from the three possible spot rates Viner had predicted). Because Viner did not hedge, it receives

$$\text{Cash received} = \text{Spot rate of SF} \times \text{SF200,000 at time of receivables transaction}$$
$$= \$.75 \times \text{SF200,000}$$
$$= \$150,000$$

Now consider what would have happened if Viner Co. had hedged the receivables position using its preferred put options technique. Given the spot rate of $.75 when the receivables arrived, Viner would not have exercised the put option. It would therefore have exchanged the Swiss francs in the spot market for $.75 per unit minus the $.02 premium per unit paid for the put option. Its cash received from the put option hedge would have been

$$\text{Cash received} = \$.73 \times \text{SF200,000}$$
$$= \$146,000$$ ●

In this example, Viner's decision to remain unhedged generated $4,000 more than if it had hedged its receivables. The difference of $4,000 is the premium that Viner would have paid to obtain put options. Although Viner benefited from remaining unhedged in this example, it recognizes the risk from not hedging.

11-3f Summary of Hedging Techniques

Each of the hedging techniques is briefly summarized in Exhibit 11.9. When using a futures hedge, forward hedge, or money market hedge, an MNC can estimate the funds

Exhibit 11.9 Review of Techniques for Hedging Transaction Exposure

TECHNIQUE	TO HEDGE PAYABLES	TO HEDGE RECEIVABLES
Futures hedge	Purchase a currency futures contract (or contracts) representing the currency and amount related to the payables.	Sell a currency futures contract (or contracts) representing the currency and amount related to the receivables.
Forward hedge	Negotiate a forward contract to purchase the amount of foreign currency needed to cover the payables.	Negotiate a forward contract to sell the amount of foreign currency that will be received as a result of the receivables.
Money market hedge	Borrow local currency and convert to the currency denominating payables. Invest these funds until they are needed to cover the payables.	Borrow the currency denominating the receivables, convert it to the local currency, and invest it. Then pay off the loan with cash inflows from the receivables.
Currency option hedge	Purchase a currency call option (or options) representing the currency and amount related to the payables.	Purchase a currency put option (or options) representing the currency and amount related to the receivables.

(denominated in its home currency) that it will need for future payables or the funds that it will receive after converting foreign currency receivables. The outcome is certain, so the firm can compare the costs or revenue and determine which of these hedging techniques is appropriate. In contrast, the cash flow associated with the currency option hedge cannot be determined with certainty because neither the costs of purchasing payables nor the revenue generated from receivables is known ahead of time. Hence firms must forecast cash flows from the option hedge based on possible exchange rate outcomes. A fee (premium) must be paid for the option, but the option offers flexibility because it does not have to be exercised.

11-4 Limitations of Hedging

Although hedging transaction exposure can be effective, there are some limitations that deserve to be mentioned here.

11-4a Limitation of Hedging an Uncertain Payment

Some international transactions involve an uncertain amount of products to be ordered and therefore involve an uncertain transaction payment in a foreign currency. In this case an MNC may create a hedge for a larger number of units than it will actually need, which results in the opposite form of exposure.

EXAMPLE

Recall the previous example on hedging receivables, which assumed that Viner Co. will receive SF200,000 in six months. Now assume that the receivables amount could actually be much lower. If Viner uses the money market hedge on SF200,000 and the receivables amount to only SF120,000, then it will have to make up the difference by purchasing SF80,000 in the spot market to achieve the SF200,000 needed to pay off the loan. And if the Swiss franc has appreciated over the six-month period, Viner will need a large amount in dollars to obtain the SF80,000. ●

This example shows how **overhedging** (hedging a larger payment in a currency than the actual transaction payment) can adversely affect a firm. One way to avoid overhedging is to hedge only the minimum known payment in the future transaction. In our example, if the future receivables could be as low as SF120,000 then Viner could hedge only that amount. Under these conditions, however, the firm may not have completely hedged its position. If the actual transaction payment turns out to be SF200,000 as expected, then Viner will be only partially hedged and will need to sell the extra SF80,000 in the spot market.

Alternatively, Viner Co. may consider hedging the minimum level of receivables with a money market hedge and hedging the additional amount of receivables that may occur with a put option hedge. In this way, it is covered if the receivables exceed the minimum amount. If the receivables do not exceed the minimum, then Viner could either let the put option expire or exercise it (if feasible) and then exchange the additional Swiss francs received in the spot market.

Firms face this kind of dilemma because the precise payment to be received in a foreign currency at the end of a period is often uncertain, especially for firms heavily involved in exporting. It should be clear from this example that an MNC cannot completely hedge all of its transactions. Yet by hedging a portion of those transactions, the firm can reduce the sensitivity of its cash flows to exchange rate movements.

11-4b Limitation of Repeated Short-Term Hedging

The repeated hedging of near-term transactions has limited effectiveness in the long run.

EXAMPLE

Winthrop Co. is a U.S. firm that specializes in importing a single large shipment of flat-screen televisions each year and then selling the units to retail stores throughout the year. Assume that today's exchange rate of the Japanese yen (¥) is $.005 and that the televisions are worth ¥60,000, or $300 each. The forward rate of the yen generally exhibits a premium of 2 percent. Exhibit 11.10 shows the yen–dollar exchange rate to be paid by the importer over time. As the spot rate changes, the forward rate will often change by a similar amount. Thus if the spot rate increases by 10 percent over the year, then the forward rate may increase by about the same amount; in that case, the importer will pay 10 percent more for next year's shipment (assuming no change in the yen price quoted by the Japanese exporter). The use of a one-year forward contract when the yen is strong would be preferable to no hedge in this case, but it could not eliminate increases in prices paid by the importer each year. Therefore, the use of short-term hedging techniques does not completely insulate a firm from exchange rate exposure, even if the hedges are used repeatedly over time. ●

Hedging techniques that are applied over longer-term periods can more effectively insulate the firm from exchange rate risk in the long run. That is, Winthrop Co. could, at time 0, create a hedge for shipments to arrive at the end of each of the next several years. The forward rate for each hedge would be based on today's spot rate, as shown in Exhibit 11.11. If the yen is appreciating, then such a strategy would save a substantial amount of money.

This strategy is limited, however, in that the amount of yen to be hedged further into the future is more uncertain because the shipment size will depend on economic conditions or other factors at that time. If a recession occurs, Winthrop Co. may reduce the number of televisions ordered, but the amount in yen to be received by the importer is dictated by the forward contract created previously. The manufacturer may go bankrupt or simply experience stockouts, but in any case Winthrop Co. remains obligated to purchase the yen.

Long-Term Hedging as a Solution Despite the limitations of long-term hedging just described, some MNCs (including Procter & Gamble and Walt Disney Company) view it as a way to overcome the limitations of repeated short-term hedging. These firms

Exhibit 11.10 Repeated Hedging of Foreign Payables When the Foreign Currency Is Appreciating

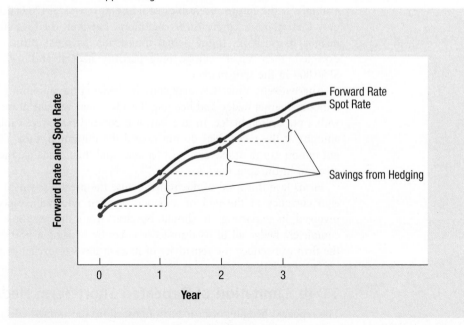

Exhibit 11.11   Long-Term Hedging of Payables When the Foreign Currency Is Appreciating

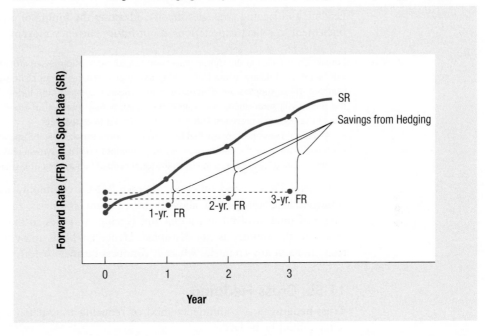

commonly use long-term forward contracts to hedge long-term transaction exposure. Some banks offer forward contracts for up to 5 or 10 years on some commonly traded currencies. Because the bank is forced to trust that the firm will fulfill its long-term obligation specified in the forward contract, only the most creditworthy bank customers are considered.

Another alternative to repeated short-term hedging is a **parallel loan** (or "back-to-back loan"), which involves an exchange of currencies between two parties with a promise to re-exchange currencies at a specified exchange rate on a future date. This long-term hedging technique involves two currency swaps: one at the inception of the loan contract and another swap at the specified future date. The arrangement is interpreted by accountants as a loan and so is recorded on financial statements; it is covered in more detail in Chapter 18.

Although the methods discussed here are usually preferable to repeated short-term hedging, they could cause an MNC to be overhedged if the long-term transaction exposure turns out to be less than expected. Therefore, these solutions are most effective when the MNC has a long-term contract with a client firm that guarantees the long-term transaction exposure.

11-5 Alternative Methods to Reduce Exchange Rate Risk

When a perfect hedge is not available (or is too expensive) to eliminate transaction exposure, the firm should consider methods that can at least reduce exposure. Such methods include

- leading and lagging,
- cross-hedging, and
- currency diversification.

Each method is discussed in turn.

11-5a Leading and Lagging

Leading and lagging strategies involve adjusting the timing of a payment request or disbursement to reflect expectations about future currency movements.

EXAMPLE
Corvalis Co. is based in the United States and has subsidiaries dispersed around the world. The focus here will be on a subsidiary in the United Kingdom that purchases some of its supplies from a subsidiary in Hungary. These supplies are denominated in Hungary's currency (the forint). If Corvalis Co. expects that the pound will soon depreciate against the forint, it may attempt to expedite its payment to Hungary before the pound depreciates. This strategy is referred to as **leading.**

As a second scenario, suppose that the British subsidiary expects that the pound will soon appreciate against the forint. In this case, the British subsidiary may attempt to stall its payment until after the pound appreciates, thereby requiring fewer pounds to obtain the forint needed for payment. This strategy is known as **lagging.** ●

General Electric and other well-known MNCs commonly use leading and lagging strategies in countries that allow them. In some countries, the government limits the length of time involved in leading and lagging strategies so that the flow of funds into or out of the country is not disrupted. Hence an MNC must be aware of government restrictions in any countries where it conducts business before using these strategies.

11-5b Cross-Hedging

Cross-hedging is a common method of reducing transaction exposure when the currency cannot be hedged.

EXAMPLE
Greeley Co., a U.S. firm, has payables in zloty (Poland's currency) 90 days from now. Because it is worried that the zloty may appreciate against the U.S. dollar, the company may want to hedge this position. If forward contracts and other hedging techniques are not available for the zloty, then Greeley may consider cross-hedging.

The first step is to identify a currency that can be hedged and that also is highly correlated with the zloty. Greeley observes that the euro has recently been moving in tandem with the zloty and decides to set up a 90-day forward contract on the euro. If the movements in the zloty and euro continue to be highly correlated (i.e., if the two currencies continue to move in the same similar direction and to a similar extent), then the exchange rate between them should be fairly stable over time. The next step is for Greeley to purchase euros 90 days forward, which enables the company to exchange euros for the zloty when zloty are required for payment. ●

This type of hedge is sometimes referred to as a *proxy hedge* because the hedged position is in a currency that serves as a proxy for the currency in which the MNC is exposed. The effectiveness of this strategy depends on the degree to which the two currencies are positively correlated: the greater the positive correlation, the more effective will be the cross-hedging strategy.

11-5c Currency Diversification

A third method for reducing transaction exposure is **currency diversification**, which can limit the potential effect of any single currency's movements on the value of an MNC. Some MNCs such as The Coca-Cola Co., PepsiCo, and Altria claim that their exposure to exchange rate movements is significantly reduced because they diversify their business among numerous countries.

The dollar value of future inflows in foreign currencies will be more stable if the foreign currencies received are *not* highly correlated. The reason is that lower (positive or negative) correlations can reduce variability in the dollar value of all foreign currency inflows. When foreign currencies are highly correlated with each other, diversifying among them is not an effective way to reduce risk. If one of the currencies substantially depreciated, then, given their strong correlation, the others would likely do so as well.

SUMMARY

- An MNC may choose to hedge most of its transaction exposure or to selectively hedge. Some MNCs hedge most of their transaction exposure so that they can more accurately predict their future cash inflows or outflows and make better decisions regarding the amount of financing they will need. Many MNCs use selective hedging, in which they consider each type of transaction separately.

- To hedge payables, a futures or forward contract on the foreign currency can be purchased. Alternatively, a money market hedge strategy can be used; in this case, the MNC borrows its home currency and converts the proceeds into the foreign currency that will be needed in the future. Finally, call options on the foreign currency can be purchased.

- To hedge receivables, a futures or forward contract on the foreign currency can be sold. Alternatively, a money market hedge strategy can be used. In this case, the MNC borrows the foreign currency to be received and converts the funds into its home currency; the loan is to be repaid by the receivables. Finally, put options on the foreign currency can be purchased. The currency option hedge has an advantage over the other hedging techniques in that the options do not have to be exercised. However, a premium must be paid to purchase the currency option, so there is a cost for the flexibility they provide.

- One limitation of hedging is that if the actual payment on a transaction is less than the expected payment, the MNC overhedged and is partially exposed to exchange rate movements. Alternatively, if an MNC hedges only the minimum possible payment in the transaction, it will be partially exposed to exchange rate movements if the transaction involves a payment that exceeds the minimum.

  Another limitation of hedging is that a short-term hedge is only effective for the period in which it was applied. One potential solution to this limitation is for an MNC to use long-term hedging rather than repeated short-term hedging. This choice is more effective if the MNC can be sure that its transaction exposure will persist into the distant future.

- When hedging techniques like forward and currency option contracts are not available, there are still some methods of reducing transaction exposure, such as leading and lagging, cross-hedging, and currency diversification.

POINT COUNTER-POINT

Should an MNC Risk Overhedging?

Point   Yes. MNCs have some "unanticipated" transactions that occur without any advance notice. They should attempt to forecast the net cash flows in each currency due to unanticipated transactions based on the previous net cash flows for that currency in a previous period. Even though it would be impossible to forecast the volume of these unanticipated transactions per day, it may be possible to forecast the volume on a monthly basis. For example, if an MNC has net cash flows between 3 million and 4 million Philippine pesos every month, it may presume that it will receive at least 3 million pesos in each of the next few months unless conditions change. Thus it can hedge a position of 3 million in pesos by either selling that amount of pesos forward or buying put options on that amount of pesos. Any amount of net cash flows in excess of 3 million pesos will not be hedged, but at least the MNC was able to hedge the minimum expected net cash flows.

Counter-Point   No. MNCs should not hedge unanticipated transactions. When they overhedge the expected net cash flows in a foreign currency, they are still exposed to exchange rate risk. If they sell more currency as a result of forward contracts than their net cash flows, they will be adversely affected by an increase in the value of the currency. Their initial reasons for hedging were to protect against the weakness of the currency, but the overhedging described here would cause a shift in their exposure. Overhedging does not insulate an MNC against exchange rate risk. It just changes the means by which the MNC is exposed.

Who Is Correct?   Use the Internet to learn more about this issue. Which argument do you support? Offer your own opinion on this issue.

SELF-TEST

Answers are provided in Appendix A at the back of the text.

1. Montclair Co., a U.S. firm, plans to use a money market hedge to hedge its payment of 3 million Australian dollars for Australian goods in one year. The U.S. interest rate is 7 percent, while the Australian interest rate is 12 percent. The spot rate of the Australian dollar is $.85, while the one-year forward rate is $.81. Determine the amount of U.S. dollars needed in one year if a money market hedge is used.

2. Using the information in the previous question, would Montclair Co. be better off hedging the payables with a money market hedge or with a forward hedge?

3. Using the information about Montclair from the first question, explain the possible advantage of a currency option hedge over a money market hedge for Montclair Co. What is a possible disadvantage of the currency option hedge?

4. Sanibel Co. purchases British goods (denominated in pounds) every month. It negotiates a one-month forward contract at the beginning of every month to hedge its payables. Assume the British pound appreciates consistently over the next five years. Will Sanibel be affected? Explain.

5. Using the information from question 4, suggest how Sanibel Co. could more effectively insulate itself from the possible long-term appreciation of the British pound.

6. Hopkins Co. transported goods to Switzerland and will receive 2 million Swiss francs in three months. It believes the three-month forward rate will be an accurate forecast of the future spot rate. The three-month forward rate of the Swiss franc is $.68. A put option is available with an exercise price of $.69 and a premium of $.03. Would Hopkins prefer a put option hedge to no hedge? Explain.

QUESTIONS AND APPLICATIONS

1. Hedging in General Explain the relationship between this chapter on hedging and the previous chapter on measuring exposure.

2. Money Market Hedge on Receivables Assume that Stevens Point Co. has net receivables of 100,000 Singapore dollars in 90 days. The spot rate of the Singapore dollar is $.50, and the Singapore interest rate is 2 percent over 90 days. Suggest how the U.S. firm could implement a money market hedge. Be precise.

3. Money Market Hedge on Payables Assume that Hampshire Co. has net payables of 200,000 Mexican pesos in 180 days. The Mexican interest rate is 7 percent over 180 days, and the spot rate of the Mexican peso is $.10. Suggest how the U.S. firm could implement a money market hedge. Be precise.

4. Net Transaction Exposure Why should an MNC identify net exposure before hedging?

5. Hedging with Futures Explain how a U.S. corporation could hedge net receivables in euros with futures contracts. Explain how a U.S. corporation could hedge net payables in Japanese yen with futures contracts.

6. Hedging with Forward Contracts Explain how a U.S. corporation could hedge net receivables in Malaysian ringgit with a forward contract. Explain how a U.S. corporation could hedge payables in Canadian dollars with a forward contract.

7. Real Cost of Hedging Payables Assume that Loras Corp. imported goods from New Zealand and needs 100,000 New Zealand dollars 180 days from now. It is trying to determine whether to hedge this position. Loras has developed the following probability distribution for the New Zealand dollar:

POSSIBLE VALUE OF NEW ZEALAND DOLLAR IN 180 DAYS	PROBABILITY
$.40	5%
.45	10
.48	30
.50	30
.53	20
.55	5

The 180-day forward rate of the New Zealand dollar is $.52. The spot rate of the New Zealand dollar is $.49. Develop a table showing a feasibility analysis for hedging. That is, determine the possible differences between the costs of hedging versus no hedging. What is the probability that hedging will be more costly to the firm than not hedging? Determine the expected value of the additional cost of hedging.

8. Benefits of Hedging If hedging is expected to be more costly than not hedging, why would a firm even consider hedging?

9. Real Cost of Hedging Payables Assume that Suffolk Co. negotiated a forward contract to purchase 200,000 British pounds in 90 days. The 90-day forward rate was $1.40 per British pound. The pounds to be purchased were to be used to purchase British supplies. On the day the pounds were delivered in accordance with the forward contract, the spot rate of the British pound was $1.44. What was the real cost of hedging the payables for this U.S. firm?

10. Forward Hedge Decision Kayla Co. imports products from Mexico, and it will make payment in pesos in 90 days. Interest rate parity holds. The prevailing interest rate in Mexico is very high, which reflects the high expected inflation there. Kayla expects that the Mexican peso will depreciate over the next 90 days. Yet it plans to hedge its payables with a 90-day forward contract. Why may Kayla believe that it will pay a smaller amount of dollars when hedging than if it remains unhedged?

11. Hedging Decision on Payables Assume the following information:

90-day U.S. interest rate	4%
90-day Malaysian interest rate	3%
90-day forward rate of Malaysian ringgit	$.400
Spot rate of Malaysian ringgit	$.404

Assume that the Santa Barbara Co. in the United States will need 300,000 ringgit in 90 days. It wishes to hedge this payables position. Would it be better off using a forward hedge or a money market hedge? Substantiate your answer with estimated costs for each type of hedge.

12. Hedging Decision on Receivables Assume the following information:

180-day U.S. interest rate	8%
180-day British interest rate	9%
180-day forward rate of British pound	$1.50
Spot rate of British pound	$1.48

Assume that Riverside Corp. from the United States will receive 400,000 pounds in 180 days. Would it be better off using a forward hedge or a money market hedge? Substantiate your answer with estimated revenue for each type of hedge.

13. Currency Options Relate the use of currency options to hedging net payables and receivables. That is, when should currency puts be purchased, and when should currency calls be purchased? Why would Cleveland, Inc., consider hedging net payables or net receivables with currency options rather than forward contracts? What are the disadvantages of hedging with currency options as opposed to forward contracts?

14. Currency Options Can Brooklyn Co. determine whether currency options will be more or less expensive than a forward hedge when considering both hedging techniques to cover net payables in euros? Why or why not?

15. Long-Term Hedging How can a firm hedge long-term currency positions? Elaborate on each method.

16. Leading and Lagging Under what conditions would Zona Co.'s subsidiary consider using a leading strategy to reduce transaction exposure? Under what conditions would Zona Co.'s subsidiary consider using a lagging strategy to reduce transaction exposure?

17. Cross-Hedging Explain how a firm can use cross-hedging to reduce transaction exposure.

18. Currency Diversification Explain how a firm can use currency diversification to reduce transaction exposure.

19. Hedging with Put Options As treasurer of Tucson Corp. (a U.S. exporter to New Zealand), you must decide how to hedge (if at all) future receivables of 250,000 New Zealand dollars 90 days from now. Put options are available for a premium of $.03 per unit and an exercise price of $.49 per New Zealand dollar. The forecasted spot rate of the NZ$ in 90 days follows:

FUTURE SPOT RATE	PROBABILITY
$.44	30%
.40	50
.38	20

Given that you hedge your position with options, create a probability distribution for U.S. dollars to be received in 90 days.

20. Forward Hedge Would Oregon Co.'s real cost of hedging Australian dollar payables every 90 days have been positive, negative, or about zero on average over a period in which the Australian dollar strengthened consistently? What does this imply about the forward rate as an unbiased predictor of the future spot rate? Explain.

21. Implications of IRP for Hedging If interest rate parity exists, would a forward hedge be more favorable, the same as, or less favorable than a money market hedge on euro payables? Explain.

22. Real Cost of Hedging Would Montana Co.'s real cost of hedging Japanese yen payables have been positive, negative, or about zero on average over a period in which the yen weakened consistently? Explain.

23. Forward versus Options Hedge on Payables If you are a U.S. importer of Mexican goods and you believe that today's forward rate of the peso is a very accurate estimate of the future spot rate, do you think Mexican peso call options would be a more appropriate hedge than the forward hedge? Explain.

24. Forward versus Options Hedge on Receivables You are an exporter of goods to the United Kingdom, and you believe that today's forward rate of the British pound substantially underestimates the future spot rate. Company policy requires you to hedge your British pound receivables in some way. Would a forward hedge or a put option hedge be more appropriate? Explain.

25. Forward Hedging Explain how a Malaysian firm can use the forward market to hedge periodic purchases of U.S. goods denominated in U.S. dollars. Explain how a French firm can use forward contracts to hedge periodic sales of goods sold to the United States that are invoiced in dollars. Explain how a British firm can use the forward market to hedge periodic purchases of Japanese goods denominated in yen.

26. Continuous Hedging Cornell Co. purchases computer chips denominated in euros on a monthly basis from a Dutch supplier. To hedge its exchange rate risk, this U.S. firm negotiates a three-month forward contract three months before the next order will arrive. In other words, Cornell is always covered for the next three monthly shipments. Because Cornell consistently hedges in this manner, it is not concerned with exchange rate movements. Is Cornell insulated from exchange rate movements? Explain.

27. Hedging Payables with Currency Options Malibu, Inc., is a U.S. company that imports British goods. It plans to use call options to hedge payables of 100,000 pounds in 90 days. Three call options are available that have an expiration date 90 days from now. Fill in the number of dollars needed to pay for the payables (including the option premium paid) for each option available under each possible scenario in the following table:

SCENARIO	SPOT RATE OF POUND 90 DAYS FROM NOW	EXERCISE PRICE = $1.74; PREMIUM = $.06	EXERCISE PRICE = $1.76; PREMIUM = $.05	EXERCISE PRICE = $1.79; PREMIUM = $.03
1	$1.65			
2	1.70			
3	1.75			
4	1.80			
5	1.85			

If each of the five scenarios had an equal probability of occurrence, which option would you choose? Explain.

28. Forward Hedging Wedco Technology of New Jersey exports plastics products to Europe. Wedco decided to price its exports in dollars. Telematics International, Inc. (of Florida), exports computer network systems to the United Kingdom (denominated in British pounds) and other countries. Telematics

decided to use hedging techniques such as forward contracts to hedge its exposure.

a. Does Wedco's strategy of pricing its materials for European customers in dollars avoid economic exposure? Explain.

b. Explain why the earnings of Telematics International, Inc., were affected by changes in the value of the pound. Why might Telematics sometimes leave its exposure unhedged?

29. The Long-Term Hedge Dilemma St. Louis, Inc., which relies on exporting, denominates its exports in pesos and receives pesos every month. It expects the peso to weaken over time. St. Louis recognizes the limitation of monthly hedging. It also recognizes that it could remove its transaction exposure by denominating its exports in dollars, but it would still be subject to economic exposure. The long-term hedging techniques are limited, and the firm does not know how many pesos it will receive in the future, so it would have difficulty even if a long-term hedging method were available. How can this business realistically reduce its exposure over the long term?

30. Long-Term Hedging Because Obisbo, Inc., conducts much business in Japan, it is likely to have cash flows in yen that will periodically be remitted by its Japanese subsidiary to the U.S. parent. What are the limitations of hedging these remittances one year in advance over each of the next 20 years? What are the limitations of creating a hedge today that will hedge these remittances over each of the next 20 years?

31. Hedging during a Crisis Describe how a crisis in Asia could reduce the cash flows of a U.S. firm that exports products (denominated in U.S. dollars) to Asian countries. How could a U.S. firm that exports products (denominated in U.S. dollars) to Asia insulate itself from any currency effects of a future crisis while continuing to export to Asia?

Advanced Questions

32. Comparison of Techniques for Hedging Receivables

a. Assume that Carbondale Co. expects to receive S$500,000 in one year. The existing spot rate of the Singapore dollar is $.60. The one-year forward rate of the Singapore dollar is $.62. Carbondale created a probability distribution for the future spot rate in one year as follows:

FUTURE SPOT RATE	PROBABILITY
$.61	20%
.63	50
.67	30

Assume that one-year put options on Singapore dollars are available, with an exercise price of $.63 and a premium of $.04 per unit. One-year call options on Singapore dollars are available with an exercise price of $.60 and a premium of $.03 per unit. Assume the following money market rates:

	U.S.	SINGAPORE
Deposit rate	8%	5%
Borrowing rate	9	6

Given this information, determine whether a forward hedge, a money market hedge, or a currency options hedge would be most appropriate. Then compare the most appropriate hedge to an unhedged strategy, and decide whether Carbondale should hedge its receivables position.

b. Assume that Baton Rouge, Inc., expects to need S$1 million in one year. Using any relevant information in part (a) of this question, determine whether a forward hedge, a money market hedge, or a currency options hedge would be most appropriate. Then compare the most appropriate hedge to an unhedged strategy, and decide whether Baton Rouge should hedge its payables position.

33. Techniques for Hedging Receivables

SMU Corp. has future receivables of 4 million New Zealand dollars (NZ$) in one year. It must decide whether to use options or a money market hedge to hedge this position. Use any of the following information to make the decision. Verify your answer by determining the estimate (or probability distribution) of dollar revenue to be received in one year for each type of hedge.

Spot rate of NZ$	$.54	
One-year call option	Exercise price = $.50; premium = $.07	
One-year put option	Exercise price = $.52; premium = $.03	
	U.S.	NEW ZEALAND
One-year deposit rate	9%	6%
One-year borrowing rate	11	8
	RATE	PROBABILITY
Forecasted spot rate of NZ$	$.50	20%
	.51	50
	.53	30

34. Exposure of U.S. Importers

If you were a U.S. importer of products from Europe, explain whether a weak U.S. economy would cause you to hedge your payables (denominated in euros) due a few months later if you expected that the weak economy would cause a major reduction in U.S. interest rates.

35. Forward versus Option Hedge As treasurer of Tempe Corp., you are confronted with the following problem. Assume the one-year forward rate of the British pound is $1.59. You plan to receive 1 million pounds in one year. A one-year put option is available. It has an exercise price of $1.61. The spot rate as of today is $1.62, and the option premium is $.04 per unit. Your forecast of the percentage change in the spot rate was determined from the following regression model:

$$e_t = a_0 + a_1 DINF_{t-1} + a_2 DINT_t + \mu$$

where

$$e_t = \text{percentage change in British pound value over period } t$$

$$DINF_{t-1} = \text{differential in inflation between the United States and the United Kingdom in period } t-1$$

$$DINT_t = \text{average differential between U.S. interest rate and British interest rate over period } t$$

$$a_0, a_1, \text{ and } a_2 = \text{regression coefficients}$$

$$\mu = \text{error term}$$

The regression model was applied to historical annual data, and the regression coefficients were estimated as follows:

$$a_0 = 0.0$$
$$a_1 = 1.1$$
$$a_2 = 0.6$$

Assume last year's inflation rates were 3 percent for the United States and 8 percent for the United Kingdom. Also assume that the interest rate differential ($DINT_t$) is forecasted as follows for this year:

FORECAST OF DINT$_t$	PROBABILITY
1%	40%
2	50
3	10

Using any of the available information, should the treasurer choose the forward hedge or the put option hedge? Show your work.

36. Hedging Decision You believe that IRP presently exists. The nominal annual interest rate in Mexico is 14 percent. The nominal annual interest rate in the United States is 3 percent. You expect that annual inflation will be about 4 percent in Mexico and

5 percent in the United States. The spot rate of the Mexican peso is $.10. Put options on pesos are available with a one-year expiration date, an exercise price of $.1008, and a premium of $.014 per unit.

You will receive 1 million pesos in one year.

a. Determine the expected amount of dollars that you will receive if you use a forward hedge.

b. Determine the expected amount of dollars that you will receive if you do not hedge and believe in purchasing power parity (PPP).

c. Determine the amount of dollars that you will expect to receive if you believe in PPP and use a currency put option hedge. Account for the premium you would pay on the put option.

37. Forecasting with IFE and Hedging Assume that Calumet Co. will receive 10 million pesos in 15 months. It does not have a relationship with a bank at this time and, therefore, cannot obtain a forward contract to hedge its receivables at this time. However, in three months, it will be able to obtain a one-year (12-month) forward contract to hedge its receivables. Today the three-month U.S. interest rate is 2 percent (not annualized), the 12-month U.S. interest rate is 8 percent, the three-month Mexican peso interest rate is 5 percent (not annualized), and the 12-month peso interest rate is 20 percent.

Assume that interest rate parity exists. Assume the international Fisher effect exists. Assume that the existing interest rates are expected to remain constant over time. The spot rate of the Mexican peso today is $.10. Based on this information, estimate the amount of dollars that Calumet Co. will receive in 15 months.

38. Forecasting from Regression Analysis and Hedging You apply a regression model to annual data in which the annual percentage change in the British pound is the dependent variable, and INF (defined as annual U.S. inflation minus U.K. inflation) is the independent variable. Results of the regression analysis show an estimate of 0.0 for the intercept and +1.4 for the slope coefficient. You believe that your model will be useful to predict exchange rate movements in the future.

You expect that inflation in the United States will be 3 percent, versus 5 percent in the United Kingdom. There is an 80 percent chance of that scenario. However, you think that oil prices could rise, and if so, the annual U.S. inflation rate will be 8 percent instead of 3 percent (and the annual U.K. inflation will still be

5 percent). There is a 20 percent chance that this scenario will occur. You think that the inflation differential is the only variable that will affect the British pound's exchange rate over the next year. The spot rate of the pound as of today is $1.80. The annual interest rate in the United States is 6 percent versus an annual interest rate in the United Kingdom of 8 percent. Call options are available with an exercise price of $1.79, an expiration date of one year from today, and a premium of $.03 per unit.

Your firm in the United States expects to need 1 million pounds in one year to pay for imports. You can use any one of the following strategies to deal with the exchange rate risk:

a. Unhedged strategy

b. Money market hedge

c. Call option hedge

Estimate the dollar cash flows you will need as a result of using each strategy. If the estimate for a particular strategy involves a probability distribution, show the distribution. Which hedge is optimal?

39. Forecasting Cash Flows and Hedging Decision Virginia Co. has a subsidiary in Hong Kong and in Thailand. Assume that the Hong Kong dollar (HK$) is pegged at $.13 per Hong Kong dollar and it will remain pegged. The Thai baht fluctuates against the U.S. dollar and is presently worth $.03. Virginia Co. expects that during this year, the U.S. inflation rate will be 2 percent, the Thailand inflation rate will be 11 percent, while the Hong Kong inflation rate will be 3 percent. Virginia Co. expects that purchasing power parity will hold for any exchange rate that is not fixed (pegged). Virginia Co. will receive 10 million Thai baht and 10 million Hong Kong dollars at the end of one year from its subsidiaries.

a. Determine the expected amount of dollars to be received from the Thai subsidiary in one year when the baht receivables are converted to U.S. dollars.

b. The Hong Kong subsidiary will send HK$1 million to make a payment for supplies to the Thai subsidiary. Determine the expected amount of baht that will be received by the Thai subsidiary when the Hong Kong dollar receivables are converted to Thai baht.

c. Assume that interest rate parity exists. Also assume that the real one-year interest rate in the United States is 10 percent, while the real interest rate in Thailand is 3 percent. Determine the expected amount of dollars to be received by Virginia Co. if it uses a one-year forward

contract today to hedge the receivables of 10 million baht that will arrive in one year.

40. Hedging Decision Indiana Co. expects to receive 5 million euros in one year from exports, and it wants to consider hedging its exchange rate risk. The spot rate of the euro as of today is $1.10. Interest rate parity exists. Indiana Co. uses the forward rate as a predictor of the future spot rate. The annual interest rate in the United States is 8 percent versus an annual interest rate of 5 percent in the eurozone. Put options on euros are available with an exercise price of $1.11, an expiration date of one year from today, and a premium of $.06 per unit. Estimate the dollar cash flows that Indiana Co. will receive as a result of using each of the following strategies:

a. unhedged strategy

b. money market hedge

c. call option hedge

Which hedge is optimal?

41. Overhedging Denver Co. is about to order supplies from Canada that are denominated in Canadian dollars (C$). It has no other transactions in Canada and will not have any other transactions in the future. The supplies will arrive in one year and payment is due at that time. There is only one supplier in Canada. Denver submits an order for three loads of supplies, which will be priced at C$3 million. Denver Co. purchases C$3 million one year forward, because it anticipates that the Canadian dollar will appreciate substantially over the year.

The existing spot rate is $.62, while the one-year forward rate is $.64. The supplier is not sure if it will be able to provide the full order, so it only guarantees Denver Co. that it will ship one load of supplies. In this case, the supplies will be priced at C$1 million. Denver Co. will not know whether it will receive one load or three loads until the end of the year.

Determine Denver's total cash outflows in U.S. dollars under the scenario that the Canadian supplier only provides one load of supplies and that the spot rate of the Canadian dollar at the end of one year is $.59. Show your work.

42. Long-Term Hedging with Forward Contracts Tampa Co. will build airplanes and export them to Mexico for delivery in three years. The total payment to be received in three years for these exports is 900 million pesos. Today the peso's spot rate is $.10. The annual U.S. interest rate is 4 percent, regardless of the debt maturity. The annual interest rate in Mexico is 9 percent regardless of the debt maturity. Tampa plans to hedge its exposure with a forward contract that it will arrange today. Assume that interest rate parity exists. Determine the dollar amount that Tampa will receive in three years.

43. Timing the Hedge Red River Co. (a U.S. firm) purchases imports that have a price of 400,000 Singapore dollars, and it has to pay for the imports in 90 days. It will use a 90-day forward contract to cover its payables. Assume that interest rate parity exists. This morning, the spot rate of the Singapore dollar was $.50. At noon, the Federal Reserve reduced U.S. interest rates, while there was no change in interest rates in Singapore. The Fed's actions immediately increased the degree of uncertainty surrounding the value of the Singapore dollar over the next three months. The Singapore dollar's spot rate remained at $.50 throughout the day. Assume that the U.S. and Singapore interest rates were the same as of this morning. Also assume that the international Fisher effect holds. If Red River Co. purchased a currency call option contract at the money this morning to hedge its exposure, would its total U.S. dollar cash outflows be more than, less than, or the same as the total U.S. dollar cash outflows if it had negotiated a forward contract this morning? Explain.

44. Hedging with Forward versus Option Contracts Assume interest rate parity exists. Today the one-year interest rate in Canada is the same as the one-year interest rate in the United States. Utah Co. uses the forward rate to forecast the future spot rate of the Canadian dollar that will exist in one year. It needs to purchase Canadian dollars in one year. Will the expected cost of its payables be lower if it hedges its payables with a one-year forward contract on Canadian dollars or a one-year at-the-money call option contract on Canadian dollars? Explain.

45. Hedging with a Bull Spread (See the chapter appendix.) Evar Imports, Inc., buys chocolate from Switzerland and resells it in the United States. It just purchased chocolate invoiced at SF62,500. Payment for the invoice is due in 30 days. Assume that the current exchange rate of the Swiss franc is $.74. Also assume that three call options for the franc are available. The first option has a strike price of $.74 and a premium of $.03; the second option has a strike price of $.77 and a premium of $.01; the third option has a strike price of $.80 and a premium of $.006. Evar Imports is concerned about a modest appreciation in the Swiss franc.

a. Describe how Evar Imports could construct a bull spread using the first two options. What is the cost of this hedge? When is this hedge most effective? When is it least effective?

b. Describe how Evar Imports could construct a bull spread using the first option and the third option. What is the cost of this hedge? When is this hedge most effective? When is it least effective?

c. Given your answers to parts (a) and (b), what is the trade-off involved in constructing a bull spread using call options with a higher exercise price?

46. Hedging with a Bear Spread (See the chapter appendix.) Marson, Inc., has some customers in Canada and frequently receives payments denominated in Canadian dollars (C$). The current spot rate for the Canadian dollar is $.75. Two call options on Canadian dollars are available. The first option has an exercise price of $.72 and a premium of $.03. The second option has an exercise price of $.74 and a premium of $.01. Marson, Inc., would like to use a bear spread to hedge a receivable position of C$50,000, which is due in a month. Marson is concerned that the Canadian dollar may depreciate to $.73 in one month.

a. Describe how Marson, Inc., could use a bear spread to hedge its position.

b. Assume the spot rate of the Canadian dollar in one month is $.73. Was the hedge effective?

47. Hedging with Straddles (See the chapter appendix.) Brooks, Inc., imports wood from Morocco. The Moroccan exporter invoices in Moroccan dirham. The current exchange rate of the dirham is $.10. Brooks just purchased wood for 2 million dirham and should pay for the wood in three months. It is also possible that Brooks will receive 4 million dirham in three months from the sale of refinished wood in Morocco. Brooks is currently in negotiations with a Moroccan importer about the refinished wood. If the negotiations are successful, Brooks will receive the 4 million dirham in three months for a net cash inflow of 2 million dirham. The following option information is available:

■ Call option premium on Moroccan dirham = $.003.
■ Put option premium on Moroccan dirham = $.002.
■ Call and put option strike price = $.098.
■ One option contract represents 500,000 dirham.

a. Describe how Brooks could use a straddle to hedge its possible positions in dirham.

b. Consider three scenarios. In the first scenario, the dirham's spot rate at option expiration is equal to the exercise price of $.098. In the second scenario, the dirham depreciates to $.08. In the third scenario, the dirham appreciates to $.11. For each scenario, consider both the case when the negotiations are successful and the case when the negotiations are not successful. Assess the effectiveness of the long straddle in each of these situations by comparing it to a strategy of using long call options to hedge.

48. Hedging with Straddles versus Strangles (See the chapter appendix.) Refer to the previous problem. Assume that Brooks believes the cost of a long straddle is too high. However, call options with an exercise price of $.105 and a premium of $.002 and put options with an exercise price of $.09 and a premium of $.001 are also available on Moroccan dirham. Describe how Brooks could use a long strangle to hedge its possible dirham positions. What is the trade-off involved in using a long strangle versus a long straddle to hedge the positions?

49. Comparison of Hedging Techniques You own a U.S. exporting firm and will receive 10 million Swiss francs in one year. Assume that interest parity exists. Assume zero transaction costs. Today the one-year interest rate in the United States is 7 percent, and the one-year interest rate in Switzerland is 9 percent. You believe that today's spot rate of the Swiss franc (which is $.85) is the best predictor of the spot rate one year from now. You consider these alternatives:

- hedge with one-year forward contract,
- hedge with a money market hedge,
- hedge with at-the-money put options on Swiss francs with a one-year expiration date, or
- remain unhedged.

Which alternative will generate the highest expected amount of dollars? If multiple alternatives are tied for generating the highest expected amount of dollars, list each of them.

50. PPP and Hedging with Call Options Visor, Inc. (a U.S. firm), has agreed to purchase supplies from Argentina and will need 1 million Argentine pesos in one year. Interest rate parity presently exists. The annual interest rate in Argentina is 19 percent. The annual interest rate in the United States is 6 percent. You expect that annual inflation will be about 11 percent in Argentina and 4 percent in the United States. The spot rate of the Argentine peso is $.30. Call options on pesos are available with a one-year expiration date, an exercise price of $.29, and a premium of $.03 per unit. Determine the expected amount of dollars that you will pay from hedging with call options (including the premium paid for the options) if you expect that the spot rate of the peso will change over the next year based on purchasing power parity (PPP).

51. Long-Term Forward Contracts Assume that interest rate parity exists. The annualized interest rate is presently 5 percent in the United States for any term to maturity and is 13 percent in Mexico for any term to maturity. Dokar Co. (a U.S. firm) has an agreement in which it will develop and export software to Mexico's government two years from now and will receive 20 million Mexican pesos in two years. The spot rate of the peso is $.10. Dokar uses a two-year forward contract to hedge its receivables in two years. How many dollars will Dokar Co. receive in two years? Show your work.

52. Money Market versus Put Option Hedge Narto Co. (a U.S. firm) exports to Switzerland and expects to receive 500,000 Swiss francs in one year. The one-year U.S. interest rate is 5 percent when investing funds and 7 percent when borrowing funds. The one-year Swiss interest rate is 9 percent when investing funds and 11 percent when borrowing funds. The spot rate of the Swiss franc is $.80. Narto expects that the spot rate of the Swiss franc will be $.75 in one year. There is a put option available on Swiss francs with an exercise price of $.79 and a premium of $.02.

a. Determine the amount of dollars that Narto Co. will receive at the end of one year if it implements a money market hedge.

b. Determine the amount of dollars that Narto Co. expects to receive at the end of one year (after accounting for the option premium) if it implements a put option hedge.

53. Forward versus Option Hedge Assume that interest rate parity exists. Today the one-year interest rate in Japan is the same as the one-year interest rate in the United States. You use the international Fisher effect when forecasting how exchange rates will change over the next year. You will receive Japanese yen in one year. You can hedge receivables with a one-year forward contract on Japanese yen or a one-year at-the-money put option contract on Japanese yen. If you use a forward hedge, will your expected dollar cash flows in 1 year be higher than, lower than, or the same as if you had used put options? Explain.

54. Long-Term Hedging Rebel Co. (a U.S. firm) has a contract with the government of Spain and will receive payments of 10,000 euros in exchange for consulting services at the end of each of the next 10 years. The annualized interest rate in the United States is 6 percent regardless of the term to maturity. The annualized interest rate for the euro is 6 percent regardless of the term to maturity. Assume that you expect that the interest rates for the U.S. dollar and for the euro will be the same at any future time, regardless of the term to maturity. Assume that interest rate parity exists. Rebel considers two alternative strategies:

Strategy 1 It can use forward hedging one year in advance of the receivables, so that at the end of each year, it creates a new one-year forward hedge for the receivables.

Strategy 2 It can establish a hedge today for all future receivables (a one-year forward hedge for receivables in one year, a two-year forward hedge for receivables in two years, and so on).

a. Assume that the euro depreciates consistently over the next 10 years. Will Strategy 1 result in higher, lower, or the same cash flows for Rebel Co. as Strategy 2?

b. Assume that the euro appreciates consistently over the next 10 years. Will Strategy 1 result in higher, lower, or the same cash flows for Rebel Co. as strategy 2?

55. Long-Term Hedging San Fran Co. imports products. It will pay 5 million Swiss francs for imports in one year. Mateo Co. will also pay 5 million Swiss francs for imports in one year. San Fran Co. and Mateo Co. will also need to pay 5 million Swiss francs for imports arriving in two years.

Today Mateo Co. uses a one-year forward contract to hedge its payables in one year. A year from today, it will use a one-year forward contract to hedge the payables that it must pay two years from today. Today, San Fran Co. uses a one-year forward contract to hedge its payables due in one year. Today, it also uses a two-year forward contract to hedge its payables in two years.

Interest rate parity exists and it will continue to exist in the future. The Swiss franc will consistently depreciate over the next two years.

Switzerland and the United States have similar interest rates, regardless of their maturity, and those rates will continue to be the same in the future.

Will the total expected dollar cash outflows that San Fran Co. will pay for its payables be higher than, lower than, or the same as the total expected dollar cash outflows that Mateo Co. will pay? Explain.

56. Comparison of Hedging Techniques Today the spot rate of the euro is $1.20. The one-year forward rate is $1.16. A one-year call option on euros exists with a premium of $.04 per unit and an exercise price of $1.17. You think the spot rate is the best forecast of future spot rates. You will need to pay 10 million euros in one year. Determine whether a money market hedge or a call option hedge would be more appropriate to hedge your payables.

57. IRP, PPP, and the Hedging Decision The one-year U.S. interest rate is presently higher than the Japanese interest rate. Assume a real rate of interest of 0 percent in each country. Assume that interest rate parity exists. You believe in purchasing power parity (PPP). You have receivables of 10 million Japanese yen that you will definitely receive in one year. Should you hedge? Briefly explain.

58. Cross-Hedging Strategy Assume that the country of Dreeland has a currency (called the dree) that tends to move in tandem with the Chilean peso and is expected to continue to move in tandem with the Chilean peso in the future. Indianapolis Co., a U.S. firm, has a large amount of receivables denominated in dree. It expects that the dree will depreciate against the dollar over time. There are no derivatives available on the dree. Indianapolis Co. considers the following strategies to reduce its exchange rate risk:

a. use a money market hedge in which it converts dollars into dree and maintains a deposit denominated in dree for one year,

b. use a forward contract to purchase Chilean pesos forward,

c. sell a put option hedge on Chilean pesos,

d. purchase a call option on Chilean pesos, and
e. use a forward contract in which it sells Chilean pesos forward.

Which strategy is most appropriate?

59. Estimating the Hedged Cost of Payables Grady Co. is a manufacturer of hockey equipment in Chicago, and it will need 3 million Swiss francs in one year to pay for imported supplies. The U.S. one-year interest rate is 2 percent. Switzerland's one-year interest rate is 7 percent. The spot rate of the Swiss franc is $.90. The one-year forward rate of the Swiss franc is $.88. A one-year call option on Swiss franc exists with an exercise price of $.90 and a premium of $.03 per unit.

As the treasurer of Grady Co., you think the spot rate of the Swiss franc is the best forecast of the future spot rate of the Swiss franc.

a. If you use a money market hedge, determine the amount of dollars that you will pay for the payables.

b. If you use a call option hedge, determine the expected amount of dollars that you will pay for the payables (account for the option premium within your estimate).

Critical Thinking

Currency Options versus Forward Contracts

Write a short essay briefly summarizing the advantages and disadvantages of currency options as compared to forward contracts when hedging payables. Explain the conditions (regarding your expectations of the future exchange rate and the uncertainty surrounding the future exchange rate) that might cause you to use currency options instead of forward contracts if you were exposed to payables. Do you think you would use currency options or forward contracts more frequently?

Discussion in the Boardroom

This exercise can be found in Appendix E at the back of this textbook.

Running Your Own MNC

This exercise can be found on the *International Financial Management* text companion website. Go to www .cengagebrain.com (students) or www.cengage.com/login (instructors) and search using **ISBN 9781133947837**.

BLADES, INC. CASE

Management of Transaction Exposure

Blades, Inc., has recently decided to expand its international trade relationship by exporting to the United Kingdom. Jogs, Ltd., a British retailer, has committed itself to the annual purchase of 200,000 pairs of Speedos, Blades' primary product, for a price of £80 per pair. The agreement is to last for two years, at which time it may be renewed by Blades and Jogs.

In addition to this new international trade relationship, Blades continues to export to Thailand. Its primary customer there, a retailer called Entertainment Products, is committed to the purchase of 180,000 pairs of Speedos annually for another three years at a fixed price of 4,594 Thai baht per pair. When the agreement terminates, it may be renewed by Blades and Entertainment Products.

Blades also incurs costs of goods sold denominated in Thai baht. It imports materials sufficient to manufacture 72,000 pairs of Speedos annually from Thailand. These imports are denominated in baht, and the price depends on current market prices for the rubber and plastic components imported.

Under the two export arrangements, Blades sells quarterly amounts of 50,000 and 45,000 pairs of Speedos to Jogs and Entertainment Products, respectively. Payment for these sales is made on the first of January, April, July, and October. The annual amounts are spread over quarters in order to avoid excessive inventories for the British and Thai retailers. Similarly, in order to avoid excessive inventories, Blades usually imports materials sufficient to manufacture 18,000 pairs of Speedos quarterly from Thailand. Although payment terms call for payment within 60 days of delivery, Blades generally pays for its Thai imports upon delivery on the first day of each quarter in order to maintain its trade relationships with the Thai suppliers. Blades feels that early payment is beneficial, as other customers of the Thai supplier pay for their purchases only when it is required.

Because Blades is relatively new to international trade, Ben Holt, Blades' chief financial officer, is concerned with the potential impact of exchange rate fluctuations on Blades' financial performance. Holt is vaguely familiar with various techniques available to hedge transaction exposure, but he is not certain whether one technique is superior to the others.

Holt would like to know more about forward, money market, and option hedges and has asked you, a financial analyst at Blades, to help him identify the hedging technique most appropriate for Blades. Unfortunately, no options are available for Thailand, but British call and put options are available for £31,250 per option. Holt has gathered and provided you with the following information for Thailand and the United Kingdom:

	THAILAND	UNITED KINGDOM
Current spot rate	$.0230	$1.50
90-day forward rate	$.0215	$1.49
Put option premium	Not available	$.020 per unit
Put option exercise price	Not available	$1.47
Call option premium	Not available	$.015 per unit
Call option exercise price	Not available	$1.48
90-day borrowing rate (nonannualized)	4%	2%
90-day lending rate (nonannualized)	3.5%	1.8%

In addition to this information, Holt has informed you that the 90-day borrowing and lending rates in the United States are 2.3 and 2.1 percent, respectively, on a nonannualized basis. He has also identified the following probability distributions for the exchange rates of the British pound and the Thai baht in 90 days:

PROBABILITY	SPOT RATE FOR THE THAI BAHT IN 90 DAYS	SPOT RATE FOR THE BRITISH POUND IN 90 DAYS
5%	$1.45	$.0200
20	1.47	.0213
30	1.48	.0217
25	1.49	.0220
15	1.50	.0230
5	1.52	.0235

Blades' next sales to and purchases from Thailand will occur one quarter from now. If Blades decides to hedge, Holt will want to hedge the entire amount subject to exchange rate fluctuations, even if it requires overhedging (i.e., hedging more than the needed amount). Currently, Holt expects the imported components from Thailand to cost approximately 3,000 baht per pair of Speedos. Holt has asked you to answer the following questions for him:

1. Using a spreadsheet, compare the hedging alternatives for the Thai baht with a scenario under which Blades remains unhedged. Do you think Blades should hedge or remain unhedged? If Blades should hedge, which hedge is most appropriate?

2. Using a spreadsheet, compare the hedging alternatives for the British pound receivables with a scenario under which Blades remains unhedged. Do you think Blades should hedge or remain unhedged? Which hedge is the most appropriate for Blades?

3. In general, do you think it is easier for Blades to hedge its inflows or its outflows denominated in foreign currencies? Why?

4. Would any of the hedges you compared in question 2 for the British pounds to be received in 90 days require Blades to overhedge? Given Blades' exporting arrangements, do you think it is subject to overhedging with a money market hedge?

5. Could Blades modify the timing of the Thai imports in order to reduce its transaction exposure? What is the trade-off of such a modification?

6. Could Blades modify its payment practices for the Thai imports in order to reduce its transaction exposure? What is the trade-off of such a modification?

7. Given Blades' exporting agreements, are there any long-term hedging techniques Blades could benefit from? For this question only, assume that Blades incurs all of its costs in the United States.

SMALL BUSINESS DILEMMA

Hedging Decisions by the Sports Exports Company

Jim Logan, owner of the Sports Exports Company, will be receiving about 10,000 British pounds about one month from now as payment for exports produced and sent by his firm. Logan is concerned about his exposure because he believes that there are two possible scenarios: (1) the pound will depreciate by 3 percent over the next month or (2) the pound will appreciate by 2 percent over the next month. There is a 70 percent chance that (1) will occur. There is a 30 percent chance that (2) will occur. Logan notices that the prevailing spot rate of the pound is $1.65, and the one-month forward rate is about $1.645.

Logan can purchase a put option over the counter from a securities firm that has an exercise (strike) price of $1.645, a premium of $.025, and an expiration date of one month from now.

1. Determine the amount of dollars received by the Sports Exports Company if the receivables to be received in one month are not hedged under each of the two exchange rate scenarios.

2. Determine the amount of dollars received by the Sports Exports Company if a put option is used to hedge receivables in one month under each of the two exchange rate scenarios.

3. Determine the amount of dollars received by the Sports Exports Company if a forward hedge is used to hedge receivables in one month under each of the two exchange rate scenarios.

4. Summarize the results of dollars received based on an unhedged strategy, a put option strategy, and a forward hedge strategy. Select the strategy that you prefer based on the information provided.

INTERNET/EXCEL EXERCISES

1. The following website contains annual reports of many MNCs: www.annualreportservice.com. Review the annual report of your choice. Look for any comments in the report that describe the MNC's hedging of transaction exposure. Summarize the MNC's hedging of transaction exposure based on the comments in the annual report.

2. The following website provides exchange rate movements against the dollar over recent months: www.federalreserve.gov/releases. Based on the exposure of the MNC you assessed in question 1, determine whether the exchange rates of whatever currency (or currencies) it is exposed to moved in a favorable or unfavorable direction over the last few months.

ONLINE ARTICLES WITH REAL-WORLD EXAMPLES

Find a recent article online that describes an actual international finance application or a real-world example about a specific MNC's actions that reinforces one or more of the concepts covered in this chapter.

If your class has an online component, your professor may ask you to post your summary there and provide the web link of the article so that other students can access it. If your class is live, your professor may ask you to summarize your application in class. Your professor may assign specific students to complete this assignment for this chapter or may allow any students to do the assignment on a volunteer basis.

For recent online articles and real-world examples applied to this chapter, consider using the following search terms (and include the current year as

a search term to ensure that the online articles are recent).

1. company AND hedge

2. Inc. AND hedge

3. hedge AND currency

4. hedge AND exchange rate

5. forward contract AND hedge

6. currency futures AND hedge

7. money market AND hedge

8. currency option AND hedge

9. [name of an MNC] AND forward contract

10. company AND hedging policy

Nontraditional Hedging Techniques

Although traditional hedging techniques were covered in the chapter, many other techniques may be appropriate for an MNC's particular situation. Some of these nontraditional techniques are described in this appendix.

Hedging with Currency Straddles

In reality, some MNCs do not know whether they will have net cash inflows or outflows as a result of their transactions in a specific currency over a particular period of time. A long straddle (purchase of a call option and put option with the same exercise price) is an effective tool to hedge under these conditions.

EXAMPLE   Houston Co. conducts business in Mexico and expects to need 4 million Mexican pesos (MXP) to cover specific expenses. If it is unable to renew a business deal with the Mexican government (its biggest customer), it will receive a total of MXP3 million in revenue in one month, which will result in net cash flows of –MXP1 million. If it is able to renew the business deal with the government, it will receive a total of MXP5 million, which will result in net cash flows of +MXP1 million. The prevailing spot rate of the Mexican peso is $.09. If Houston has excess pesos in one month, it will convert them to dollars. If Houston does not have enough pesos in one month, it will use dollars to obtain the amount that it needs. Houston would like to hedge its exchange rate risk, regardless of which scenario occurs.

Currently, call options for Mexican pesos with expiration dates in one month are available with an exercise price of $.09 and a premium of $.004 per peso. Put options for Mexican pesos with an expiration date of one month are available with an exercise price of $.09 and a premium of $.005 per peso. Options for Mexican pesos are denominated in 250,000 pesos per option contract.

Houston could hedge its possible position of having positive net cash flows of MXP1 million by purchasing put options. It would pay a premium of $5,000 (1,000,000 units × $.005). It could hedge its possible position of needing MXP1 million by purchasing call options. It would pay a premium of $4,000 (1,000,000 units × $.004). Assume that Houston constructs a straddle to hedge both possible outcomes and pays $9,000 for the call options and put options on pesos. Assume that Houston exercises the options in one month, if at all.

Consider the following scenarios that could occur one month from now.

1. If Houston has net cash flows of + MXP1 million and the peso's value is $.10, the company would let its put options expire and would convert its pesos to dollars in the spot market, receiving $100,000

(1,000,000 units × $.10) from this transaction. It would also exercise its call option by purchasing 1 million pesos at $.09 and selling them in the spot market for $.10. This transaction would generate a gain of $10,000. Overall, Houston would receive $110,000, minus the $9,000 in premiums paid for the options.

2. If Houston has net cash flows of + MXP1 million and the peso depreciates to $.08, the company would exercise its put options and let the call options expire. Overall, Houston would receive $90,000 (1,000,000 units × $.09) from exercising the options minus the $9,000 in premiums paid for the options.

3. If Houston has net cash flows of + MXP1 million and the peso is $.09, the company would let its call and put options expire. It would receive $90,000 (1,000,000 × $.09) from selling pesos in the spot market minus the $9,000 in premiums paid for the options.

4. If Houston has net cash flows of −MXP1 million and the peso's value is $.10, the company would exercise its call options and let its put options expire. Overall, Houston would pay a total of $99,000, which consists of the $90,000 (1,000,000 × $.09) from exercising the call option plus the $9,000 in premiums paid for the options.

5. If Houston has net cash flows of −MXP1 million and the peso's value is $.08, the company would let its call options expire and buy pesos in the spot market. It would also buy 1 million pesos and then sell them by exercising its put options. This transaction would generate a gain of $10,000. Overall, Houston would pay a total of $79,000, which consists of the $80,000 paid to obtain the pesos it needs plus the $9,000 in premiums paid for the options minus the $10,000 gain generated from its put options.

6. If Houston has net cash flows of −MXP1 million and the peso's value is $.09, the company would let its call and put options expire. It would pay a total of $99,000, which consists of the $90,000 paid to obtain pesos and the $9,000 in premiums paid for the options. ●

Many other scenarios could also occur. A summary of possible scenarios, and the actions taken by Houston Co., is given in Exhibit 11A.1.

Exhibit 11A.1   Possible Scenarios for Houston Co. When Hedging with a Straddle

PANEL A: HOUSTON HAS NET CASH FLOWS OF + MXP1,000,000 IN 1 MONTH	
MXP value > $.09 in one month	• Houston converts excess pesos to dollars in the spot market. • It lets the put options expire. • It exercises its call options and sells the pesos obtained from this transaction in the spot market; the proceeds recapture part of the premiums that were paid for the options.
MXP value < $.09 in one month	• Houston converts excess pesos to dollars at $.09 by exercising its put options. • It lets the call options expire.
MXP value = $.09 in one month	• Houston converts excess pesos to dollars in the spot market. • It lets its call options and put options expire.
PANEL B: HOUSTON HAS NET CASH FLOWS OF − MXP1,000,000 IN 1 MONTH	
MXP value > $.09 in one month	• Houston converts dollars to pesos by exercising its call options. • It lets the put options expire.
MXP value < $.09 in one month	• Houston lets the call options expire. • It buys pesos in the spot market and sells pesos obtained by exercising the put options; the proceeds recapture part of the premiums that were paid for the options.
MXP value = $.09 in one month	• Houston converts dollars to pesos in the spot market. • It lets its call and put options expire.

Hedging with Currency Strangles

In the hedging example just provided for Houston Co., consider that the expected value of the amount that Houston would pay or receive based on today's spot rate is $90,000 (MXP1,000,000 × $.09). The option premiums paid for the options ($9,000) represent 10 percent of that expected value. Thus the straddle is an expensive means of hedging. The exercise price at which Houston hedged was equal to the spot rate ("at the money"). If Houston is willing to accept exposure to small exchange rate movements in the peso, it could reduce the premiums paid for the options. Specifically, it would use a *long strangle* by purchasing a call option and a put option that have different exercise prices. By purchasing a call option that has an exercise price higher than $.09 and a put option that has an exercise price lower than $.09, Houston can reduce the premiums it will pay on the options.

EXAMPLE

Reconsider the example in which Houston Co. expects that it will have net cash flows of either +MXP1 million or –MXP1 million in one month. To reduce the premiums it pays for hedging with options, it can purchase options that are out of the money. Assume that it can obtain call options for Mexican pesos with an expiration date of one month, an exercise price of $.095, and a premium of $.002 per peso. It can also obtain put options for Mexican pesos with an expiration date of one month, an exercise price of $.085, and a premium of $.003 per peso.

Houston Co. could hedge its possible position of needing MXP1 million by purchasing call options. It would pay a premium of $2,000 (1,000,000 units × $.002). It could also hedge its possible position of having positive net cash flows of MXP1 million by purchasing put options. It would pay a premium of $3,000 (1,000,000 units × $.003). Overall, Houston would pay $5,000 for the call options and put options on pesos, which is substantially less than the $9,000 it would pay for the straddle in the previous example. However, the options do not offer protection until the spot rate deviates by more than $.005 from its existing level. If the spot rate remains within the range of the two exercise prices (from $.085 to $.095), Houston will not exercise either option.

This example of hedging with a strangle is a compromise between hedging with the straddle in the previous example and not hedging. For the range of possible spot rates between $.085 and $.095, there is no hedge. For scenarios in which the spot rate moves outside the range, Houston is hedged. It will have to pay no more than $.095 if it needs to obtain pesos and will be able to sell pesos for at least $.085 if it has pesos to sell. ●

Hedging with Currency Bull Spreads

In certain situations, MNCs can use currency bull spreads to hedge their cash outflows denominated in a foreign currency, as the following example illustrates.

EXAMPLE

Peak, Inc., needs to order Canadian raw materials to use in its production process. The Canadian exporter typically invoices Peak in Canadian dollars. Assume that the current exchange rate for the Canadian dollar (C$) is $.73 and that Peak needs C$100,000 in three months. Two call options for Canadian dollars with expiration dates in three months and the following additional information are available:

- Call option 1 premium on Canadian dollars = $.015.
- Call option 2 premium on Canadian dollars = $.008.
- Call option 1 strike price = $.73.
- Call option 2 strike price = $.75.
- One option contract represents C$50,000.

To lock into a future price for the C$100,000, Peak could buy two option 1 contracts, paying 2 × C$50,000 × $.015 = $1,500. This would effectively lock in a maximum price of $.73 that Peak would pay in three months for a total maximum outflow of $74,500 (C$100,000 × $.73 + $1,500). If the spot price for Canadian dollars at option expiration is below $.73, Peak has the right to let the options expire and buy the C$100,000 in the open market for the lower price. Naturally, Peak would still have paid the $1,500 total premium in this case.

Historically, the Canadian dollar has been relatively stable against the U.S. dollar. If Peak believes that the Canadian dollar will appreciate in the next three months but is very unlikely to appreciate above the higher exercise price of $.75, it should consider constructing a bull spread to hedge its Canadian dollar payables. To do so, Peak would purchase two option 1 contracts and write two option 2 contracts. The total cash outflow necessary to construct this bull spread is $2 \times$ C$50,000 $\times$ ($.015 - $.008) = $700, because Peak would receive the premiums from writing the two option 2 contracts. Constructing the bull spread has reduced the cost of hedging by $800 ($1,500 - $700).

If the spot price of the Canadian dollar at option expiration is below the $.75 strike price, the bull spread will have provided an effective hedge. For example, if the spot price at option expiration is $.74, Peak will exercise the two option 1 contracts it purchased, for a total maximum outflow of $73,700 (C$100,000 $\times$ $.73 + $700). The buyer of the two option 2 contracts Peak wrote would let those options expire. If the Canadian dollar depreciates substantially below the lower strike price of $.73, the hedge will also be effective, as both options will expire worthless. Peak would purchase the Canadian dollars at the prevailing spot rate, having paid the difference in option premiums.

Now consider what will happen if the Canadian dollar appreciates above the higher exercise price of $.75 prior to option expiration. In this case, the bull spread will still reduce the total cash outflow and therefore provide a partial hedge. However, the hedge will be less effective.

As an illustration, assume the Canadian dollar appreciates to a spot price of $.80 in three months. Peak will still exercise the two option 1 contracts it purchased. However, the two option 2 contracts it wrote will also be exercised. Recall that this is a situation in which the maximum profit from the bull spread is realized, which is equal to the difference in exercise prices less the difference in the two premiums, or $2 \times$ C$50,000 $\times$ ($.75 - $.73 - $.015 + $.008) = $1,300. Note that Peak must now purchase the C$100,000 it needs in the open market, because it needs to sell the Canadian dollars purchased by exercising the option 1 contracts to the buyer of the option 2 contracts it wrote. Therefore, Peak's total cash outflow in three months, when it needs the Canadian dollars, will be $78,700 (C$100,000 $\times$ $.80 - $1,300). Although Peak has successfully reduced its cash outflow in three months by $1,300, it would have fared much better by buying only two option 1 contracts to hedge its payables, which would have resulted in a maximum cash outflow of $74,500. Consequently, MNCs should use bull spreads to hedge only for relatively stable currencies that are not expected to appreciate drastically prior to option expiration. ●

Hedging with Currency Bear Spreads

In certain situations, MNCs can use currency bear spreads to hedge their receivables denominated in a foreign currency.

EXAMPLE Weber, Inc., has some Canadian customers. Weber typically bills these customers in Canadian dollars. Assume that the current exchange rate for the Canadian dollar (C$) is $.73 and that Weber expects to receive C$50,000 in three months. The following options for Canadian dollars are available.

■ Call option 1 premium on Canadian dollars = $.015.
■ Call option 2 premium on Canadian dollars = $.008.
■ Call option 1 strike price = $.73.
■ Call option 2 strike price = $.75.
■ One option contract represents C$50,000.

If Weber believes the Canadian dollar will not depreciate much below the lower exercise price of $.75, it can construct a bear spread to hedge the receivable. Weber will buy call option 2 and write call option 1 to establish this bear spread. The total cash inflow resulting from this bear spread is C$50,000 $\times$ ($.015 - $.008) = $350. Constructing a bear spread will always result in a net cash inflow, because the spreader writes the call option with the lower exercise price and, therefore, the higher premium.

What will happen if the Canadian dollar appreciates above the higher exercise price of $.75 prior to option expiration? For example, assume that the spot rate for the Canadian dollar is $.80 at option expiration. In this case, the bear spread would result in a maximum loss of $.013 ($.75−$.73−$.015 + $.008) per Canadian dollar, for a total maximum loss of $650. However, Weber can now sell the receivables at the prevailing spot rate of $.80, netting $39,350 (C$50,000 × $.80−$650). Furthermore, while the maximum loss remains at $650 for the bear spread, Weber can benefit if the Canadian dollar appreciates even more.

The bear spread also provides an effective hedge if the spot price of the Canadian dollar at option expiration is above the lower strike price of $.73 but below the higher strike price of $.75. In this case, however, the benefit is reduced. For instance, if the spot price at option expiration is $.74, Weber will let option 2 expire. The buyer of option 1 will exercise it, and Weber will sell the receivables at the exercise price of $.73 to fulfill its obligation. This will result in a total cash inflow of $36,850 (C$50,000 × $.73 + $350) after including the net premium received from establishing the spread.

If the Canadian dollar depreciates below the lower strike price of $.73, Weber will realize the maximum gain from the bear spread but will have to sell the receivables at the low prevailing spot rate. For example, if the spot rate at option expiration is $.70, both options will expire worthless, but Weber will have received $350 from establishing the spread. If Weber sells the receivables at the spot rate, the net cash inflow will be $35,350 (C $50,000 × $.70 + $350). ●

In summary, MNCs should hedge receivables using bear spreads only for relatively stable currencies that are expected to depreciate modestly, but not drastically, prior to option expiration.

12

Managing Economic Exposure and Translation Exposure

CHAPTER
OBJECTIVES

The specific objectives
of this chapter are to:

■ explain how an
MNC's economic
exposure can be
hedged and

■ explain how an
MNC's translation
exposure can be
hedged.

As the previous chapter described, multinational corporations can manage the exposure of their international contractual transactions to exchange rate movements (referred to as transaction exposure) in various ways. Nevertheless, cash flows of MNCs may still be sensitive to exchange rate movements (economic exposure) even if anticipated international contractual transactions are hedged. Furthermore, the consolidated financial statements of MNCs may still be exposed to exchange rate movements (translation exposure). By managing economic exposure and translation exposure, financial managers may increase the value of their MNCs.

In general, it is more difficult to hedge economic or translation exposure than to hedge transaction exposure. The reasons are explained in this chapter.

12-1 Managing Economic Exposure

From a U.S. firm's perspective, transaction exposure represents only the exchange rate risk when converting net foreign cash inflows to U.S. dollars or when purchasing foreign currencies to send payments. Economic exposure represents any impact of exchange rate fluctuations on a firm's future cash flows. Thus while an MNC's management of transaction exposure may focus on a single transaction, its management of economic exposure must consider all operations that are responsible for its cash flows. Furthermore, an MNC's management of transaction exposure is typically focused on the next period (such as the next quarter or year), while its management of economic exposure is focused on numerous periods far into the future. Thus while an MNC's management of transaction exposure may be viewed as a repetitive short-term strategy (focused on transactions occurring in the next period), its management of economic exposure is typically viewed as a long-term strategy.

The means by which an MNC's management of its exposure to exchange rate movements can increase its value are summarized in Exhibit 12.1. By properly managing its exposure over the long run, it may be able to stabilize its cash flows, which can reduce its financing costs and therefore lower its cost of capital. It may also be able to stabilize its earnings over the long run, which can reduce its risk and thereby reduce its cost of capital.

Exhibit 12.1 How Managing Exposure Can Increase an MNC's Value

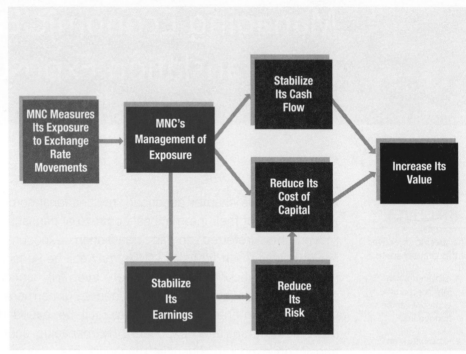

12-1a Assessing Economic Exposure

An MNC must determine how it is subject to exchange rate movements before it can manage its economic exposure. Specifically, it should first determine how its cash flows may be affected by various possible exchange rate scenarios in the future. Then it can decide whether and how to change its business operations so that its cash flows will be less sensitive to possible exchange rate scenarios in future periods.

EXAMPLE Recall from Chapter 10 that Madison Co. is subject to economic exposure. Madison can assess its economic exposure to exchange rate movements by determining the sensitivity of its expenses and revenue (and therefore its cash flows) to various possible exchange rate scenarios. Exhibit 12.2 reproduces financial information for Madison, as previously shown in Exhibit 10.10. This exhibit reflects expected revenue, expenses, and cash flows for the next quarter, based on three possible exchange rate scenarios. By reviewing how its expected cash flows change in response to the possible exchange rate scenarios, Madison can assess how its cash flows are affected by exchange rate movements. Because Madison's expected revenue and expenses next quarter are representative of a typical quarter, it can use the information in Exhibit 12.2 to assess its economic exposure (exposure of its cash flows to exchange rate movements) over the long run.

Exhibit 12.2 shows that Madison's sales in the United States (row 1) are not sensitive to exchange rate scenarios. Canadian sales (row 2) are expected to be C$4 million, but the dollar amount received from these sales will depend on the exchange rate scenario shown in each column. The cost of materials purchased in the United States (row 4) is assumed to be $50 million and insensitive to exchange rate movements. The cost of materials purchased in Canada (row 5) is assumed to be C$200 million. Operating expenses (row 7) are assumed to be $60 million and insensitive to exchange rate scenario. The interest owed to U.S. banks (row 8) is insensitive to the exchange rate scenario, but the projected amount of dollars needed to pay interest on existing Canadian loans (row 9) varies with the exchange rate scenario.

Exhibit 12.2 enables Madison to assess how its cash flows before taxes will be affected by three possible exchange rate scenarios. Notice from Exhibit 12.2 that a strong Canadian dollar (C$ = $.85) increases Madison's cash inflows received from Canadian sales. However, it also increases Madison's cash outflows

Exhibit 12.2 Original Impact of Possible Exchange Rates on Cash Flows of Madison Co. (in millions)

	EXCHANGE RATE SCENARIO					
	C$1 = $.75		C$1 = $.80		C$1 = .85	
Sales						
(1) U.S. sales		$320.00		$320.00		$320.00
(2) Canadian sales	C$4 =	3.00	C$4 =	3.20	C$4 =	3.40
(3) Total sales in U.S. $		$323.00		$323.20		$323.40
Cost of Materials and Operating Expenses						
(4) U.S. cost of materials		$ 50.00		$ 50.00		$ 50.00
(5) Canadian cost of materials	C$200 =	150.00	C$200 =	160.00	C$200 =	170.00
(6) Total cost of materials in U.S. $		$200.00		$210.00		$220.00
(7) Operating expenses		$ 60.00		$ 60.00		$ 60.00
Interest Expenses						
(8) U.S. interest expenses		$ 3		$ 3		$ 3
(9) Canadian interest expenses	C$10 =	7.5	C$10 =	8	C$10 =	8.50
(10) Total interest expenses in U.S. $		$ 10.5		$ 11		$ 11.50
Cash flows in U.S. $ before taxes		$ 52.50		$ 42.20		$ 31.90

when purchasing Canadian materials and paying interest on loans from Canadian banks. The higher cash outflows (due to higher expenses) more than offset the higher cash inflows (due to higher revenue) when the Canadian dollar is strong. Thus Madison's net cash flows are adversely affected by a stronger Canadian dollar. Because the financial information shown in Exhibit 12.2 is indicative of a typical quarter for Madison, it suggests that Madison's cash flows will likely be adversely affected if the Canadian dollar is strong (appreciates against the U.S. dollar) in any future quarter. ●

12-1b Restructuring to Reduce Economic Exposure

When MNCs notice that their cash flows will be adversely affected in a somewhat consistent manner over time by a particular exchange rate scenario, they may attempt to restructure their operations to reduce their economic exposure. Such restructuring involves shifting the sources of revenue or expenses in order to match cash inflows and outflows in foreign currencies. The restructuring is not just a temporary change for one quarter, but is maintained over several quarters in order to reduce the exposure of the MNC's cash flows to exchange rate movements over a longer time frame.

EXAMPLE   Reconsider the previous example of Madison Co., which has more cash outflows than cash inflows in Canadian dollars in a typical quarter. Madison could create more balance by increasing its Canadian sales. It believes that it can achieve Canadian sales of C$20 million if it spends $2 million more on advertising (which is part of Madison's operating expenses). The increased sales will also require an additional expenditure of $10 million on materials from U.S. suppliers. In addition, it plans to reduce its reliance on Canadian suppliers and increase its reliance on U.S. suppliers. Madison anticipates that this strategy will reduce the cost of materials from Canadian suppliers by C$100 million and increase the cost of materials from U.S. suppliers by $80 million (not including the $10 million increase resulting from increased sales to the Canadian market). Furthermore, it plans to borrow additional funds in the United States and retire some existing loans from Canadian banks. The result will be an additional interest expense of $4 million to U.S. banks and a reduction of C$5 million owed to Canadian banks. Exhibit 12.3 shows the anticipated impact of these strategies on Madison's cash flows in one quarter. For each of the three exchange rate scenarios, the initial projections are in the left column and the revised projections (as a result of the proposed strategy) are in the right column.

Exhibit 12.3 Impact of Possible Exchange Rate Movements on Earnings under Two Alternative Operational Structures (millions of currency units)

	EXCHANGE RATE SCENARIO CS = $.75		EXCHANGE RATE SCENARIO CS = $.80		EXCHANGE RATE SCENARIO CS = $.85	
	ORIGINAL OPERATIONAL STRUCTURE	PROPOSED OPERATIONAL STRUCTURE	ORIGINAL OPERATIONAL STRUCTURE	PROPOSED OPERATIONAL STRUCTURE	ORIGINAL OPERATIONAL STRUCTURE	PROPOSED OPERATIONAL STRUCTURE
Sales						
(1) U.S. sales	$320.0	$320.0	$320.0	$320.0	$320.0	$320.0
(2) Canadian sales	C$4 = 3.0	C$20 = 15.00	C$4 = 3.20	C$20 = 16	C$4 = 3.40	C$20 = 17.00
(3) Total sales in U.S. $	$323.0	$335.00	$323.20	$336.00	$323.40	$337.00
Cost of Materials and Operating Expenses						
(4) U.S. cost of materials	$ 50.0	$140.00	$ 50.00	$140	$ 50.00	$140.00
(5) Canadian cost of materials	C$200 = 150.0	C$100 = 75.00	C$200 = 160.00	C$100 = 80	C$200 = 170.00	C$100 = 85.00
(6) Total cost of materials in U.S. $	$200.0	$215.00	$210.00	$220	$220.00	$225.00
(7) Operating expenses	$ 60	$ 62	$ 60	$ 62	$ 60	$ 62
Interest Expenses						
(8) U.S. interest expenses	$ 3.0	$ 7.00	$ 3.00	$ 7.00	$ 3.00	$ 7.00
(9) Canadian interest expenses	C$10 = 7.5	C$5 = 3.75	C$10 = 8.00	C$5 = 4	C$10 = 8.50	C$5 = 4.25
(10) Total interest expenses in U.S. $	$ 10.5	$ 10.75	$ 11.00	$ 11	$ 11.50	$ 11.25
(11) Cash flows in U.S. $ before taxes	$ 52.5	$ 47.25	$ 42.20	$ 43	$ 31.90	$ 38.75

Note first the projected total sales increase in response to Madison's plan to penetrate the Canadian market (see row 3). Second, the U.S. cost of materials is now $90 million higher as a result of the $10 million increase to accommodate increased Canadian sales and the $80 million increase due to the shift from Canadian suppliers to U.S. suppliers (see row 4). The Canadian cost of materials decreases from C$200 million to C$100 million as a result of this shift (see row 5). The revised operating expenses of $62 million include the $2 million increase in advertising expenses necessary to penetrate the Canadian market (see row 7). The interest expenses are revised because of the increased loans from the U.S. banks and reduced loans from Canadian banks (see rows 8 and 9).

If Madison increases its Canadian dollar inflows and reduces its Canadian dollar outflows as proposed, then its quarterly revenue and expenses will be affected by movements of the Canadian dollar in a somewhat similar manner. A review of row 11 of Exhibit 12.3 shows that Madison's quarterly cash flows are more similar across the three exchange rate scenarios if it restructures its operations than if it retains the original operational structure. Thus its cash flows are less susceptible to movements in the Canadian dollar if it restructures than if it retains the original operational structure. Exhibit 12.4 illustrates the sensitivity of Madison's cash flows to the three exchange rate scenarios (derived from Exhibit 12.3). A perfectly horizontal line in Exhibit 12.4 would reflect the extreme case in which the expected quarterly cash flows would be exactly the same regardless of the exchange rate scenario. The line representing the proposed operational structure is not perfectly horizontal, but is more horizontal than the line representing the original operational structure. The reduced sensitivity of Madison's cash flows to exchange rate movements under the proposed operational structure is obvious.

Exhibits 12.3 and 12.4 focus on financial information for a single quarter just to illustrate how restructuring can reduce exchange rate risk. However, the restructuring would be intended to reduce economic exposure not just for one quarter but for a long-term period. If Madison decides to restructure its operations as proposed here, it would maintain the new operational structure so that its net cash flows would be less susceptible to exchange rate movements every quarter for several quarters into the future. If conditions change, Madison can make additional revisions to its operations over time. ●

Determining the sensitivity of cash flows (ignoring tax effects) to alternative exchange rate scenarios based on a proposed operational structure can be expedited by using a

Exhibit 12.4 Economic Exposure Based on the Original and Proposed Operating Structures

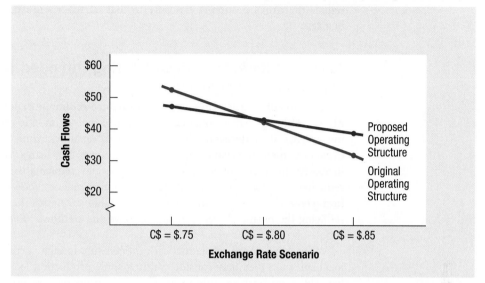

computer to create a spreadsheet similar to Exhibit 12.3. Furthermore, an MNC can revise the input for expected revenue or expenses on the spreadsheet to reflect various possible restructurings, so that it can determine the type of operational structure that will best reduce its economic exposure.

How Restructuring Is Dependent on the Form of Economic Exposure

The way a firm restructures its operations to reduce economic exposure to exchange rate risk depends on the form of exposure. For Madison Co., future expenses are more sensitive than future revenue to the possible values of the Canadian dollar. Therefore, Madison's solution for reducing its economic exposure is to increase the sensitivity of its revenue and reduce the sensitivity of its expenses to possible exchange rate scenarios for the Canadian dollar. However, MNCs that have a greater level of exchange rate–sensitive revenue than expenses would reduce their economic exposure by decreasing the level of exchange rate–sensitive revenue or by increasing the level of exchange rate–sensitive expenses.

Some of the more common solutions to balancing a foreign currency's inflows and outflows are summarized in Exhibit 12.5. Any restructuring of operations that can

Exhibit 12.5 Restructuring Operations to Balance the Impact of Currency Movements on Cash Inflows and Outflows

TYPE OF OPERATION	RECOMMENDED ACTION WHEN A FOREIGN CURRENCY HAS A GREATER IMPACT ON CASH INFLOWS	RECOMMENDED ACTION WHEN A FOREIGN CURRENCY HAS A GREATER IMPACT ON CASH OUTFLOWS
Sales in foreign currency units	Consider pricing foreign sales in the MNC's local currency.	Increase foreign sales.
Reliance on foreign supplies	Increase foreign supply orders.	Reduce foreign supply orders.
Proportion of debt structure representing foreign debt	Restructure debt to increase debt payments in foreign currency.	Restructure debt to reduce debt payments in foreign currency.

reduce the difference between a foreign currency's inflows and outflows can consistently reduce the firm's economic exposure to that currency's movements over several future quarters.

12-1c Limitations of Restructuring Intended to Reduce Economic Exposure

Some forms of restructuring intended to reduce economic exposure can adversely affect MNCs. Although MNCs may desire to reduce their economic exposure to exchange rate movements, their decisions should be focused on maximizing their value. Many MNCs expanded their international business to boost the firm's value, and this decision increased their economic exposure. They could reduce their economic exposure by reducing their foreign sales, but that would also reduce their cash flows. An ideal solution would be to use a form of restructuring that maintains their existing business, while reducing the mismatch between cash inflows and outflows in each foreign currency over time.

When MNCs have substantial cash inflows in a foreign currency and outflows in their local currency, they may consider shifting some production facilities to the foreign country. On a spreadsheet, this form of restructuring may appear to be a good solution, because it will create cash outflows in the foreign currency to offset some of the cash inflows in the foreign currency. However, moving some production facilities to foreign countries could prevent an MNC from fully capitalizing on economies of scale (if all production can be focused at one facility). In addition, moving production to a foreign country may also require layoffs in the home country, which could lead to protests by citizens and a damaged reputation for the MNC.

Some forms of restructuring such as moving production facilities may require much time and effort. Furthermore, these forms of restructuring cannot be easily reversed. Therefore, MNCs must be confident about the potential benefits before they decide to restructure their operations in this manner.

12-2 A Case Study on Hedging Economic Exposure

In reality, most MNCs are not able to reduce their economic exposure as easily as Madison Co. in the earlier example. First, an MNC's economic exposure may not be so obvious. An analysis of the income statement for an entire MNC may not necessarily detect its economic exposure. The MNC may be composed of various business units, each of which has a unique cost and revenue structure.

Although an MNC is mostly concerned with the effect of exchange rates on its performance and value overall, it can more effectively hedge its economic exposure if it can pinpoint the underlying source of the exposure. Yet even if the MNC can do so, there may not be a perfect hedge against that exposure. No textbook formula can provide the perfect solution. However, a combination of actions may reduce the economic exposure to a tolerable level, as illustrated in the following example. This example is more difficult than the previous example of Madison Co., but it may be more realistic for many MNCs.

12-2a Savor Co.'s Assessment of Economic Exposure

Savor Co., a U.S. firm, is primarily concerned with its exposure to the euro because its businesses offer services to consumers based in eurozone countries. It wants to pinpoint the source of that exposure so that it can determine how to hedge it. Savor has three business units. Because each unit has established a wide variety of business arrangements, it is not obvious whether all three units have a similar exposure. Savor may want to hedge its economic exposure, but it must first determine whether it is exposed and the source of the exposure.

Process Used to Detect Economic Exposure   Because the exact nature of its economic exposure to the euro is not obvious, Savor attempts to assess the relationship between the euro's movements and each unit's cash flows over the last nine quarters. A firm may want to use more data, but nine quarters are sufficient to illustrate the point. The cash flows and movements in the euro are shown in Exhibit 12.6. First, Savor applies regression analysis (as discussed in the previous chapter) to determine whether the quarterly percentage change in its total cash flow (PCF, shown in column 5) is related to the quarterly percentage change in the euro's value (PCE, shown in column 6) over time:

$$PCF_t = a_0 + a_1(PCE_t) + \mu_t$$

That is, the percentage change in Savor's cash flows (column 5 of Exhibit 12.6) is the dependent variable, while the percentage change in the euro (column 6) is the independent variable. Regression analysis derives the values of the constant a_0 and the slope coefficient a_1. The slope coefficient represents the sensitivity of PCF_t to movements in the euro. When applying the regression model specified above to Savor's total cash flows (apply the analysis yourself as an exercise), the slope coefficient is positive and statistically significant, which implies that the percentage changes in cash flows are positively related to the percentage changes in the euro. That is, depreciation of the euro (a negative PCE) reduces Savor's total cash flows (causes a negative PCF).

The R^2 statistic from applying the regression model specified above is .31, which suggests that 31 percent of the variation in Savor's total cash flows can be explained by movements in the euro. The evidence presented so far strongly suggests that Savor's total cash flows are exposed to exchange rate movements of the euro but does not pinpoint the source of that exposure.

Assessment of Each Unit's Exposure   Savor Co. wants to determine whether and how each of its business units is subject to movements in the euro, so that it can

Exhibit 12.6   Assessment of Savor Co.'s Cash Flows and the Euro's Movements

(1)	(2)	(3)	(4)	(5)	(6)
QUARTER	% CHANGE IN UNIT A'S CASH FLOWS	% CHANGE IN UNIT B'S CASH FLOWS	% CHANGE IN UNIT C'S CASH FLOWS	% CHANGE IN TOTAL CASH FLOWS	% CHANGE IN VALUE OF THE EURO
1	−3	2	1	0	2
2	0	1	3	4	5
3	6	−6	−1	−1	−3
4	−1	1	−1	−1	0
5	−4	0	−1	−5	−2
6	−1	−2	−2	−5	−5
7	1	−3	3	1	4
8	−3	2	1	0	2
9	4	−1	0	3	−4

then consider how it might reduce that exposure. Savor applies the regression model separately to each individual unit's cash flows. First, it assesses the exposure of Unit A by assigning Unit A's quarterly percentage change in cash flows (column 2 of Exhibit 12.6) as the dependent variable, with the quarterly percentage change in the euro (column 6) as the independent variable. Second, it assesses the exposure of Unit B by assigning column 3 as the dependent variable, while still using column 6 as the independent variable. Third, it assesses the exposure of Unit C by assigning column 4 as the dependent variable, while still using column 6 as the independent variable. The results are shown here (apply the regression analysis yourself as an exercise):

UNIT	REGRESSION COEFFICIENT
A	Not significant
B	Not significant
C	Coefficient = .45, which is statistically significant (R^2 = .80)

These results suggest that the cash flows of Units A and B are not subject to economic exposure. However, Unit C is subject to economic exposure. According to the R^2 statistic, approximately 80 percent of Unit C's cash flows can be explained by movements in the value of the euro over time, which suggests a very close relationship between the unit's cash flows and exchange rate movements. The regression coefficient for Unit C indicates that a 1 percent decrease in the value of the euro is associated with an estimated 0.45 percent decline in Unit C's cash flows.

Identifying the Source of the Unit's Exposure   Now that Savor has determined that one unit is the cause of the exposure, it attempts to understand the reasons behind the statistical results. Unit C's main business is providing travel tours in the United States for European tourists. It charges fees in U.S. dollars, so European travelers' demand for its tours declines when the euro is weak, because more euros are needed to pay for the service. Although Savor is not surprised that this type of exposure exists, it is surprised at the extent of the relationship between the value of the euro and the cash flows generated by Unit C. Because Savor's analysis also determined that its other two units are not subject to economic exposure, it can focus on reducing the exposure of Unit C, as explained next.

12-2b Possible Strategies for Hedging Economic Exposure

Now that Savor has identified Unit C as the source of its economic exposure, it wants to develop a strategy to reduce that exposure. Savor Co. considers ways to restructure its business so that it can benefit when the euro weakens in order to offset the adverse effects of a weak euro on Unit C's cash flows.

Pricing Policy   Savor considers lowering its prices to European tourists when the euro depreciates, so that Unit C could attract more European tourists when the euro is weak. However, it does not believe that this strategy will reduce exposure because Unit C's cash flows would still be low (as a result of lowering its prices) when the euro is weak.

Hedging with Forward Contracts   Savor could have Unit C sell euros forward and purchase euros in the spot market at the time the forward contract matures. If the euro depreciates, this forward contract would generate a gain that could hedge against the adverse effects of the weak euro on Savor's business operations. However, the use of a forward contract as described here would hedge only for the period of the contract. It would not serve as a continuous long-term hedge against Savor's economic exposure, which is likely to continue indefinitely.

Purchasing Foreign Supplies Some MNCs reduce their exposure to a weak foreign currency by purchasing materials in the foreign country (instead of purchasing them domestically) because the cost of the materials should decline when the foreign currency is weak. However, Savor sells services rather than products, and it does not need to obtain materials for its business.

Financing with Foreign Funds Assume that Savor's Unit C needs to finance its operations and that the interest rate on euros is not much different than the U.S. interest rate. In this case, Unit C can partially hedge its economic exposure by financing a portion of its business with loans in euros rather than in dollars. It could convert the loan proceeds to dollars and use the dollars to support its business. It would need to make periodic loan repayments in euros. If the euro weakens, the unit will need fewer dollars to cover the loan repayments. This favorable effect can partially offset the adverse effect of a weak euro on the unit's revenue. If the euro strengthens, the unit will need more dollars to cover the loan repayments, but this adverse effect will be offset by the favorable effect of the strong euro on the unit's revenue.

This hedging strategy makes sense only if Savor needs some debt financing. Also, Savor might consider this hedging strategy only if the expected cost from financing with euros is not higher than financing with dollars.

Revising Operations of Other Units Even if Unit C decides to finance its operations in euros, this strategy might only partially offset its exposure to the weak euro. Savor's top management may suggest that Units A and B also obtain their financing in euros rather than in dollars, so that the MNC's overall economic exposure is reduced to a greater degree.

However, the financial managers of Units A and B will not necessarily desire to finance their operations in euros. Recall that these units are not subject to economic exposure. By agreeing to finance in euros, Units A and B could become exposed to movements in the euro, even though Savor Co.'s overall economic exposure may be reduced. If they finance with euros and the euro strengthens, their cost of financing increases. So, by helping to offset the exposure of Unit C, Units A and B could experience poor performance, and perhaps their respective managers would receive lower compensation as a result.

A solution is still possible if Savor's top managers who are not affiliated with any unit can remove the hedging activity from the compensation formula for the units' managers. That is, top management could instruct Units A and B to borrow funds in euros, but could reward the managers of those units based on an assessment of the units' performance that *excludes* the effect of the euro on financing costs. The unit managers would then be more willing to engage in a strategy that increases their economic exposure while reducing Savor's overall exposure.

12-3 **Managing Exposure to Fixed Assets**

Up to this point, the focus has been on how economic exposure can affect periodic cash flows. The effects of exchange rate movements may extend beyond periodic cash flows, however. When an MNC has fixed assets (such as buildings or machinery) in a foreign country, the dollar cash flows to be received from the ultimate sale of these assets are subject to exchange rate risk.

EXAMPLE   Wagner Co., a U.S. firm, pursued a six-year project in Russia. It purchased a manufacturing plant from the Russian government six years ago for 500 million rubles. Because the ruble was worth $.16 at the time of the investment, Wagner needed $80 million to purchase the plant. The Russian government guaranteed that it would repurchase the plant for 500 million rubles in six years when the project was completed. At that time, however, the ruble was worth only $.034, so Wagner received only $17 million (computed as 500 million × $.034) from selling the plant. Even though the price of the plant in rubles at the time of the sale was the same as the price at the time of the purchase, the sales price of the plant in dollars at the time of the sale was about 79 percent less than the purchase price. ●

A sale of fixed assets can be hedged by selling the currency forward in a long-term forward contract. However, long-term forward contracts may not be available for currencies in emerging markets. An alternative solution is to create a liability in that currency that matches the expected value of the assets at the time in the future when they may be sold. In essence, the sale of the fixed assets generates a foreign currency cash inflow that can be used to pay off the liability that is denominated in the same currency.

EXAMPLE   In the previous example, Wagner could have financed part of its investment in the Russian manufacturing plant by borrowing rubles from a local bank, with the loan structured to have zero interest payments and a lump-sum repayment value equal to the expected sales price set for the date when Wagner expected to sell the plant. Thus the loan could have been structured to have a lump-sum repayment value of 500 million rubles in six years. ●

The limitations of hedging a sale of fixed assets are that an MNC does not necessarily know (1) the date when it will sell the assets or (2) the price in local currency at which it will sell them. Consequently, it is unable to create a liability that perfectly matches the date and amount of the sale of the fixed assets. Nevertheless, these limitations should not prevent a firm from hedging.

EXAMPLE   Even if the Russian government would not guarantee a purchase price for the plant, Wagner Co. could create a liability that reflects the earliest possible sales date and the lowest expected sales price. If the sales date turns out to be later than the earliest possible sales date, Wagner might be able to extend its loan period to match the sales date. In this way, it can still rely on the funding from the loan to support operations in Russia until the assets are sold. By structuring the lump-sum loan repayment to match the minimum sales price, Wagner will not be perfectly hedged if the fixed assets turn out to be worth more than the minimum expected amount. Even so, Wagner would at least have reduced its exposure by offsetting a portion of the fixed assets with a liability in the same currency. ●

12-4 **Managing Translation Exposure**

Recall from Chapter 10 that when a U.S.-based MNC reports its overall financial condition, it must consolidate each foreign subsidiary's financial statements with the parent's financial statements so that there is only one consolidated balance sheet and only one consolidated income statement for the entire MNC. Because exchange rates vary over time, the translation of the subsidiary's financial statements into a different currency is affected by exchange rate movements. Even if this translation exposure does not affect cash flows, it is a concern for many MNCs because it can reduce an MNC's consolidated earnings and thereby cause a decline in its stock price.

EXAMPLE   Columbus Co. is a U.S.-based MNC with a subsidiary in the United Kingdom. The subsidiary typically accounts for about half of the total revenue and earnings generated by Columbus. In the last three quarters, the value of the British pound declined, and the reported dollar level of earnings attributable to the

British subsidiary was weak simply because of the relatively low rate at which the British earnings were translated into U.S. dollars. During this period, Columbus's stock price declined because of the decline in consolidated earnings. The high-level managers and the board were criticized in the media for poor performance, even though the only reason for the decline in earnings was the translation effect. In addition, employee compensation levels are tied to consolidated earnings and therefore were low this year because of the translation effect. Consequently, Columbus decided that it would attempt to hedge translation exposure in the future. ●

12-4a Hedging Translation Exposure with Forward Contracts

Multinational corporations can use forward contracts or futures contracts to hedge translation exposure. Specifically, they can sell the currency forward that their foreign subsidiaries receive as earnings. In this way, they create a cash outflow in the currency to offset the earnings received in that currency.

EXAMPLE | Recall that Columbus Co. has one subsidiary based in the United Kingdom. While there is no foreseeable transaction exposure in the near future from the future earnings (because the pounds will remain in the United Kingdom), Columbus is vulnerable to translation exposure. The subsidiary forecasts that its earnings next year will be £20 million. To hedge its translation exposure, Columbus can implement a forward hedge on the expected earnings by selling £20 million one year forward. Assume the forward rate at that time is $1.60, the same as the spot rate. At the end of the year, Columbus can buy £20 million at the spot rate and fulfill its forward contract obligation to sell £20 million. If the pound depreciates during the fiscal year, then Columbus will be able to purchase pounds at the end of the fiscal year to fulfill the forward contract at a cheaper rate than it can sell them ($1.60 per pound). Thus it will have generated a gain from its forward hedge position that can offset the translation loss.

If the pound depreciates such that the average weighted exchange rate is $1.50 over the year, the subsidiary's earnings will be translated as follows:

$$\text{Translated earnings} = \text{Subsidiary earnings} \times \text{Weighted average exchange rate}$$
$$= 20 \text{ million pounds} \times \$1.50$$
$$= \$30 \text{ million}$$

If the exchange rate had not declined over the year, the translated amount of earnings would have been $32 million (computed as 20 million pounds × $1.60), so the exchange rate movements caused the reported earnings to be reduced by $2 million.

However, there is a gain from the forward contract because the spot rate declined over the year. If we assume that the spot rate is $1.50 at the end of the year, then the gain on the forward contract would be:

$$\text{Gain on forward contract} = (\text{Amount received from forward sale})$$
$$- (\text{Amount paid to fulfill forward contract obligation})$$
$$= (20 \text{ million pounds} \times \$1.60) - (20 \text{ million pounds} \times \$1.50)$$
$$= \$32 \text{ million} - \$30 \text{ million}$$
$$= \$2 \text{ million} \qquad \bullet$$

In reality, a perfect offsetting effect is unlikely. However, when there is a relatively large reduction in the weighted average exchange rate, there will likely be a large reduction in the spot rate over that same period. Consequently, the larger the adverse translation effect, the larger the gain on the forward contract. Thus the forward contract is normally effective in hedging a portion of the translation exposure.

12-4b Limitations of Hedging Translation Exposure

There are four limitations in hedging translation exposure.

Inaccurate Earnings Forecasts   A subsidiary's earnings in a future period are uncertain. In the previous example involving Columbus Co., British earnings were projected to be £20 million. If the actual earnings turned out to be much higher and if the pound weakened during the year, then the translation loss would likely exceed the gain generated from the forward contract strategy.

Inadequate Forward Contracts for Some Currencies

A second limitation is that forward contracts are not available for all currencies. Thus an MNC with subsidiaries in some smaller countries may not be able to obtain forward contracts for the currencies of concern.

Accounting Distortions

A third limitation is that the forward rate gain or loss reflects the difference between the forward rate and the future spot rate, whereas the translation gain or loss is caused by the change in the average exchange rate over the period in which the earnings are generated. In addition, the translation losses are not tax deductible, whereas gains on forward contracts used to hedge translation exposure are taxed.

Increased Transaction Exposure

The fourth and most critical limitation with using a forward contract to hedge translation exposure is that doing so may increase the MNC's transaction exposure. For example, consider a situation in which the subsidiary's currency appreciates during the fiscal year, resulting in a translation gain. If the MNC enacts a hedge strategy at the start of the fiscal year, this strategy will generate a transaction loss that will somewhat offset the translation gain.

Some MNCs may not be comfortable with this offsetting effect. The translation gain is simply a paper gain; that is, the reported dollar value of earnings is higher simply because of the subsidiary currency's appreciation. However, if the subsidiary reinvests the earnings, then the parent does not receive any more income due to this appreciation. The MNC's net cash flow is not affected. In contrast, the loss resulting from a hedge strategy is a true loss; that is, the net cash flow to the parent will be reduced due to this loss. Thus in this situation, the MNC reduces its translation exposure at the expense of increasing its transaction exposure.

SUMMARY

- Economic exposure can be managed by balancing the sensitivity of revenue and expenses to exchange rate fluctuations. To accomplish this, however, the firm must first recognize how its revenue and expenses are affected by exchange rate fluctuations. For some firms, revenue is more susceptible. These firms are most concerned that their home currency will appreciate against foreign currencies as the unfavorable effects on revenue will more than offset the favorable effects on expenses. Conversely, firms whose expenses are more sensitive to exchange rates than their revenue are most concerned that their home currency will depreciate against foreign currencies. When firms reduce their economic exposure, they reduce not only these unfavorable effects but also the favorable effects if the home currency value moves in the opposite direction.

- Translation exposure can be reduced by selling forward the foreign currency used to measure a subsidiary's income. If the foreign currency depreciates against the home currency, the adverse impact on the consolidated income statement can be offset by the gain on the forward sale in that currency. If the foreign currency appreciates over the time period of concern, there will be a loss on the forward sale that is offset by a favorable effect on the reported consolidated earnings. However, many MNCs would not be satisfied with a "paper gain" that offsets a "cash loss."

Point Counter-Point

Can an MNC Reduce the Impact of Translation Exposure by Communicating?

Point Yes. Investors commonly use earnings to derive an MNC's expected future cash flows. Investors do not necessarily recognize how an MNC's translation exposure could distort their estimates of the MNC's future cash flows. Therefore, the MNC could clearly communicate in its annual report and elsewhere how the earnings were affected by translation gains and losses in any period. If investors have this information, they will not overreact to earnings changes that are primarily attributed to translation exposure.

Counter-Point No. Investors focus on the bottom line and should ignore any communication regarding the translation exposure. Moreover, they may believe that translation exposure should be accounted for anyway. If foreign earnings are reduced because of a weak currency, the earnings may continue to be weak if the currency remains weak.

Who Is Correct? Use the Internet to learn more about this issue. Which argument do you support? Offer your own opinion on this issue.

Self-Test

Answers are provided in Appendix A at the back of the text.

1. Salem Exporting Co. purchases chemicals from U.S. sources and uses them to make pharmaceutical products that are exported to Canadian hospitals. Salem prices its products in Canadian dollars and is concerned about the possibility of the long-term depreciation of the Canadian dollar against the U.S. dollar. It periodically hedges its exposure with short-term forward contracts, but this does not insulate against the possible trend of continuing Canadian dollar depreciation. How could Salem offset some of its exposure resulting from its export business?

2. Using the information in question 1, give a possible disadvantage of offsetting exchange rate exposure from the export business.

3. Coastal Corp. is a U.S. firm with a subsidiary in the United Kingdom. It expects that the pound will depreciate this year. Explain Coastal's translation exposure. How could Coastal hedge its translation exposure?

4. Everhart Co. has substantial translation exposure in European subsidiaries. The treasurer of Everhart Co. suggests that the translation effects are not relevant because the earnings generated by the European subsidiaries are not being remitted to the U.S. parent but are simply being reinvested in Europe. Nevertheless, the vice president of finance of Everhart Co. is concerned about translation exposure because the stock price is highly dependent on the consolidated earnings, which are dependent on the exchange rates at which the earnings are translated. Who is correct?

5. Lincolnshire Co. exports 80 percent of its total production of goods in New Mexico to Latin American countries. Kalafa Co. sells all the products it produces in the United States, but it has a subsidiary in Spain that usually generates about 20 percent of its total earnings. Compare the translation exposure of these two U.S. firms.

Questions and Applications

1. Reducing Economic Exposure Colorado, Inc., is a U.S.-based MNC that obtains 10 percent of its supplies from European manufacturers. Sixty percent of its revenues are due to exports to Europe, where its product is invoiced in euros. Explain how Colorado can attempt to reduce its economic exposure to exchange rate fluctuations in the euro.

2. Reducing Economic Exposure UVA Co. is a U.S.-based MNC that obtains 40 percent of its foreign supplies from Thailand. It also borrows Thailand's currency (the baht) from Thai banks and converts the baht to dollars to support U.S. operations. It currently receives about 10 percent of its revenue from Thai customers. Its sales to Thai customers are denominated in baht. Explain how

UVA Co. can reduce its economic exposure to exchange rate fluctuations.

3. Reducing Economic Exposure Albany Corp. is a U.S.-based MNC that has a large government contract with Australia. The contract will continue for several years and generate more than half of Albany's total sales volume. The Australian government pays Albany in Australian dollars. About 10 percent of Albany's operating expenses are in Australian dollars; all other expenses are in U.S. dollars. Explain how Albany Corp. can reduce its economic exposure to exchange rate fluctuations.

4. Trade-offs When Reducing Economic Exposure When an MNC restructures its operations to reduce its economic exposure, it may sometimes forgo economies of scale. Explain.

5. Exchange Rate Effects on Earnings Explain how a U.S.-based MNC's consolidated earnings are affected when foreign currencies depreciate.

6. Hedging Translation Exposure Explain how a firm can hedge its translation exposure.

7. Limitations of Hedging Translation Exposure Bartunek Co. is a U.S.-based MNC that has European subsidiaries and wants to hedge its translation exposure to fluctuations in the euro's value. Explain some limitations when it hedges translation exposure.

8. Effective Hedging of Translation Exposure Would a more established MNC or a less established MNC be better able to effectively hedge its given level of translation exposure? Why?

9. Comparing Degrees of Economic Exposure Carlton Co. and Palmer, Inc., are U.S.-based MNCs with subsidiaries in Mexico that distribute medical supplies (produced in the United States) to customers throughout Latin America. Both subsidiaries purchase the products at cost and sell the products at 90 percent markup. The other operating costs of the subsidiaries are very low. Carlton Co. has a research and development center in the United States that focuses on improving its medical technology. Palmer, Inc., has a similar center based in Mexico. Each firm subsidizes its respective research and development center on an annual basis. Which firm is subject to a higher degree of economic exposure? Explain.

10. Comparing Degrees of Translation Exposure Nelson Co. is a U.S. firm with annual export sales to Singapore of about S$800 million. Its main competitor is Mez Co., also based in the United States, with a subsidiary in Singapore that generates about S$800 million in annual sales. Any earnings generated by the subsidiary are reinvested to support its operations. Based on the information provided, which firm is subject to a higher degree of translation exposure? Explain.

Advanced Questions

11. Managing Economic Exposure St. Paul Co. does business in the United States and New Zealand. In attempting to assess its economic exposure, it compiled the following information.

a. St. Paul's U.S. sales are somewhat affected by the value of the New Zealand dollar (NZ$) because it faces competition from New Zealand exporters. It forecasts the U.S. sales based on the following three exchange rate scenarios:

EXCHANGE RATE OF NEW ZEALAND DOLLARS	REVENUE FROM U.S. BUSINESS (IN MILLIONS)
NZ$ = $.48	$100
NZ$ = .50	105
NZ$ = .54	110

b. Its New Zealand dollar revenues on sales to New Zealand invoiced in New Zealand dollars are expected to be NZ$600 million.

c. Its anticipated cost of materials is estimated at $200 million from the purchase of U.S. materials and NZ$100 million from the purchase of New Zealand materials.

d. Fixed operating expenses are estimated at $30 million.

e. Variable operating expenses are estimated at 20 percent of total sales (after including New Zealand sales, translated to a dollar amount).

f. Interest expense is estimated at $20 million on existing U.S. loans, and the company has no existing New Zealand loans.

Forecast net cash flows for St. Paul Co. under each of the three exchange rate scenarios. Explain how St. Paul's net cash flows are affected by possible exchange rate movements. Explain how it can restructure its operations to reduce the sensitivity of its net cash flows to exchange rate movements without reducing its volume of business in New Zealand.

12. Assessing Economic Exposure Alaska, Inc., plans to create and finance a subsidiary in Mexico that produces computer components at a low cost and exports them to other countries. It has no other international business. The subsidiary will produce computers and export them to Caribbean islands and will invoice the products in U.S. dollars. The values of the currencies in the islands are expected to remain very stable against the dollar. The subsidiary will pay wages, rent, and other operating costs in Mexican pesos. The subsidiary will remit earnings monthly to the parent.

a. Would Alaska's cash flows be favorably or unfavorably affected if the Mexican peso depreciates over time?

b. Assume that Alaska considers partial financing of this subsidiary with peso loans from Mexican banks instead of providing all the financing with its own funds. Would this alternative form of financing increase, decrease, or have no effect on the degree to which Alaska is exposed to exchange rate movements of the peso?

13. Hedging Continual Exposure Clearlake, Inc., produces its products in its factory in Texas and exports most of the products to Mexico each month. The exports are denominated in pesos. Clearlake recognizes that hedging on a monthly basis does not really protect against long-term movements in exchange rates. It also recognizes that it could eliminate its transaction exposure by denominating the exports in dollars, but that it still would have economic exposure (because Mexican consumers would reduce demand if the peso weakened). Clearlake does not know how many pesos it will receive in the future, so it would have difficulty even if a long-term hedging method were available. How can Clearlake realistically deal with this dilemma and reduce its exposure over the long term? (There is no perfect solution, but in the real world, there rarely are perfect solutions.)

14. Sources of Supplies and Exposure to Exchange Rate Risk Laguna Co. (a U.S. firm) will be receiving 4 million British pounds in one year. It will need to make a payment of 3 million Polish zloty in one year. It has no other exchange rate risk at this time. However, it needs to buy supplies and can purchase them from Switzerland, Hong Kong, Canada, or Ecuador. Another alternative is that it could also purchase one-fourth of the supplies from each of the four countries mentioned in the previous sentence.

The supplies will be invoiced in the currency of the country from which they are imported. Laguna Co. believes that none of the sources of the imports would provide a clear cost advantage. As of today, the dollar cost of these supplies would be about $6 million regardless of the source that will provide the supplies.

The spot rates today are as follows:

British pound = $1.80
Swiss franc = $.60
Polish zloty = $.30
Hong Kong dollar = $.14
Canadian dollar = $.60

The movements of the pound and the Swiss franc and the Polish zloty against the dollar are highly correlated. The Hong Kong dollar is tied to the U.S. dollar, and you expect that it will continue to be tied to the dollar. The movements in the value of the Canadian dollar against the U.S. dollar are not correlated with the movements of the other currencies. Ecuador uses the U.S. dollar as its local currency.

Which alternative should Laguna Co. select in order to minimize its overall exchange rate risk?

15. Minimizing Exposure Lola Co. (a U.S. firm) expects to receive 10 million euros in one year. It does not plan to hedge this transaction with a forward contract or other hedging techniques. This is its only international business, and it is not exposed to any other form of exchange rate risk. Lola Co. plans to purchase materials for future operations, and it will send its payment for these materials in one year. The value of the materials to be purchased is about equal to the expected value of the receivables. Lola Co. can purchase the materials from Switzerland, Hong Kong, Canada, or the United States. Another alternative is that it could also purchase one-fourth of the materials from each of the four countries mentioned in the previous sentence. The supplies will be invoiced in the currency of the country from which they are imported.

The movements of the euro and the Swiss franc against the dollar are highly correlated and will continue to be highly correlated. The Hong Kong dollar is tied to the U.S. dollar and you expect that it will continue to be tied to the dollar. The movements in the value of Canadian dollar against the U.S. dollar are independent of (not correlated with) the movements of other currencies against the U.S. dollar.

Lola Co. believes that none of the sources of the imports would provide a clear cost advantage.

Which alternative should Lola Co. select for obtaining supplies that will minimize its overall exchange rate risk?

16. Financing to Reduce Exchange Rate Exposure Nashville Co. presently incurs costs of about 12 million Australian dollars (A$) per year for research and development expenses in Australia. It sells the products that are designed each year, and all of the products sold each year are invoiced in U.S. dollars. Nashville anticipates revenue of about $20 million per year, and about half of the revenue will be from sales to customers in Australia. The Australian dollar is presently valued at $1 (1 U.S. dollar), but it fluctuates a lot over time. Nashville Co. is planning a new project that will expand its sales to other regions within the United States, and the sales will be invoiced in dollars. Nashville can finance this project with a five-year loan by (1) borrowing only Australian dollars, (2) borrowing only U.S. dollars, or (3) borrowing one-half of the funds from each of these sources. The five-year interest rates on an Australian dollar loan and a U.S. dollar loan are the same.

a. If Nashville wants to use the form of financing that will reduce its exposure to exchange rate risk the most, what is the optimal form of financing? Briefly explain (one or two sentences should be sufficient if your explanation is clear).

b. Now assume that Nashville expects that the Australian dollar will appreciate over time. Suppose the company wants to maximize its expected net present value of its new project and is not concerned about its exposure to exchange rate risk. Under these conditions, which financing alternative is most appropriate? Briefly explain.

Critical Thinking

Creating Cash Outflows to Match Inflows in the Same Currency Consider MNCs that produce products in the United States and export the products to developing countries. The MNCs could reduce their exposure to exchange rate risk if they set up their operations in the countries to which they export. Such a restructuring would cause a shift in expenses to the developing countries, and those expenses could be paid for with revenue earned in the same currency. Write a short essay in which you explain the practical limitations of this solution, which can help to explain why some MNCs do not pursue this strategy.

Discussion in the Boardroom

This exercise can be found in Appendix E at the back of this textbook.

Running Your Own MNC

This exercise can be found on the *International Financial Management* text companion website. Go to www.cengagebrain.com (students) or www.cengage.com/login (instructors) and search using **ISBN 9781133947837**.

BLADES, INC. CASE

Assessment of Economic Exposure

Blades, Inc., has been exporting to Thailand since its decision to supplement its declining U.S. sales by exporting there. Furthermore, Blades has recently begun exporting to a retailer in the United Kingdom. The suppliers of the components needed by Blades for roller blade production (such as rubber and plastic) are located in the United States and Thailand. Blades decided to use Thai suppliers for rubber and plastic components needed to manufacture roller blades because of cost and quality considerations. All of Blades' exports and imports are denominated in the respective foreign currency; for example, Blades pays for the Thai imports in baht.

The decision to export to Thailand was supported by the fact that Thailand had been one of the world's fastest growing economies in recent years. Furthermore, Blades found an importer in Thailand that was willing to commit itself to the annual purchase of 180,000 pairs of Blades' Speedos, which are among the highest quality roller blades in the world. The commitment began last year and will last another two years, at which time it may be renewed by the two parties. Due to this commitment, Blades is selling its roller blades for 4,594 baht per pair (approximately $100 at current exchange rates) instead of the usual $120 per pair. Although this price represents a substantial discount from the regular price for a pair of Speedo blades, it still constitutes a considerable markup above cost. Because importers in other Asian countries were not willing to make this type of commitment, this was a decisive factor in the choice of Thailand for exporting purposes. Although Ben Holt, Blades' chief financial officer (CFO), believes the sports product market in Asia has very high future growth potential, Blades has recently begun exporting to Jogs, Ltd., a British retailer. Jogs has committed itself to purchase 200,000 pairs of Speedos annually for a fixed price of £80 per pair.

For the coming year, Blades expects to import rubber and plastic components from Thailand sufficient to manufacture 80,000 pairs of Speedos at a cost of approximately 3,000 baht per pair of Speedos.

You, as Blades' financial analyst, have told Holt that recent events in Asia have fundamentally affected the economic condition of Asian countries, including Thailand. For example, you have pointed out that the high level of consumer spending on leisure products such as roller blades has declined considerably. Thus the Thai retailer may not renew its commitment with Blades in two years. Furthermore, you are worried that the current economic conditions in Thailand may lead to a substantial depreciation of the Thai baht, which would affect Blades negatively.

Despite recent developments, however, Holt remains optimistic; he is convinced that Southeast Asia will exhibit high potential for growth when the impact of recent events in Asia subsides. Consequently, Holt has no doubt that the Thai customer will renew its commitment for another three years when the current agreement terminates. In your opinion, Holt is not considering all of the factors that might directly or indirectly affect Blades. Moreover, you are worried that he is ignoring Blades' future in Thailand even if the Thai importer renews its commitment for another three years. In fact, you believe that a renewal of the existing agreement with the Thai customer may affect Blades negatively due to the high level of inflation in Thailand.

Because Holt is interested in your opinion and wants to assess Blades' economic exposure in Thailand, he has asked you to conduct an analysis of the impact of the value of the baht on next year's earnings to assess Blades' economic exposure. You have gathered the following information:

■ Blades has forecasted sales in the United States of 520,000 pairs of Speedos at regular prices; exports to Thailand of 180,000 pairs of Speedos for 4,594 baht a pair; and exports to the United Kingdom of 200,000 pairs of Speedos for £80 per pair.

■ Cost of goods sold for 80,000 pairs of Speedos are incurred in Thailand; the remainder is incurred in the United States, where the cost of goods sold per pair of Speedos runs approximately $70.

■ Fixed costs are $2 million, and variable operating expenses other than costs of goods sold represent approximately 11 percent of U.S. sales. All fixed and variable operating expenses other than cost of goods sold are incurred in the United States.

■ Recent events in Asia have increased the uncertainty regarding certain Asian currencies considerably, making it extremely difficult to forecast the value of the baht at which the Thai revenues will be converted. The current spot rate of the baht is $.022, and the current spot rate of the pound is $1.50. You have created three scenarios and derived an expected value on average for the upcoming year based on each scenario (see the following table):

SCENARIO	EFFECT ON THE AVERAGE VALUE OF BAHT	AVERAGE VALUE OF BAHT	AVERAGE VALUE OF POUND
1	No change	$.0220	$1.530
2	Depreciate by 5%	.0209	1.485
3	Depreciate by 10%	.0198	1.500

■ Blades currently has no debt in its capital structure. However, it may borrow funds in Thailand if it establishes a subsidiary in the country.

Holt has asked you to answer the following questions:

1. How will Blades be negatively affected by the high level of inflation in Thailand if the Thai customer renews its commitment for another three years?

2. Holt believes that the Thai importer will renew its commitment in two years. Do you think his assessment is correct? Why or why not? Also, assume that the Thai economy returns to the high growth level that existed prior to the recent unfavorable economic events. Under this assumption, how likely is it that the Thai importer will renew its commitment in two years?

3. For each of the three possible values of the Thai baht and the British pound, use a spreadsheet to estimate cash flows for the next year. Briefly comment on the level of Blades' economic exposure. Ignore possible tax effects.

4. Now repeat your analysis in question three but assume that the British pound and the Thai baht are perfectly correlated. For example, if the baht depreciates by 5 percent, the pound will also depreciate by 5 percent. Under this assumption, is Blades subject to a greater degree of economic exposure? Why or why not?

5. Based on your answers to the previous three questions, what actions could Blades take to reduce its level of economic exposure to Thailand?

SMALL BUSINESS DILEMMA

Hedging the Sports Exports Company's Economic Exposure to Exchange Rate Risk

Jim Logan, owner of the Sports Exports Company, remains concerned about his exposure to exchange rate risk. Even if he hedges his transactions from one month to another, he recognizes that a long-term trend of depreciation in the British pound could have a severe impact on his firm. He believes that he must continue to focus on the British market for selling his footballs.

However, Logan plans to consider various ways in which he can reduce his economic exposure. At the current time, he obtains material from a local manufacturer and uses a machine to produce the footballs, which are then exported. He still uses his garage as a place of production and would like to continue using his garage to maintain low operating expenses.

1. How could Logan adjust his operations to reduce his economic exposure? What is a possible disadvantage of such an adjustment?

2. Offer another solution to hedging the economic exposure in the long run as Logan's business grows. What are the disadvantages of this solution?

INTERNET/EXCEL EXERCISES

1. Review an annual report of an MNC of your choice. Many MNCs provide their annual report on their websites. Look for any comments that relate to the MNC's economic or translation exposure. Does it appear that the MNC hedges its economic exposure or translation exposure? If so, what methods does it use to hedge its exposure?

2. Go to finance.yahoo.com and insert the ticker symbol IBM (or use a different MNC if you wish) in the stock quotations box. Then scroll down and click on Historical Prices. Set the date range so that you can access data for least the last 20 quarters. Obtain the stock price of IBM at the beginning of the last 20 quarters and insert the data on your spreadsheet. Compute the percentage change in the stock price of IBM from one quarter to the next. Then go to www.oanda.com/currency/historical-rates/ and obtain direct exchange rates of the Canadian dollar and the euro that match up with the stock price data. Run a regression analysis with the quarterly percentage change in IBM's stock price as the dependent variable and the quarterly change in the Canadian dollar's value as the independent variable. (Appendix C explains how Excel can be used to run regression analysis.) Does it appear that IBM's stock price is affected by changes in the value of the Canadian dollar? If so, what is the direction of the relationship? Is the relationship strong? (Check the R-squared statistic.) Based on this relationship, do you think IBM should attempt to hedge its economic exposure to movements in the Canadian dollar?

3. Repeat the process using the euro in place of the Canadian dollar. Does it appear that IBM's stock price is affected by changes in the value of the euro? If so, what is the direction of the relationship? Is the relationship strong? (Check the R-squared statistic.) Based on this relationship, do you think IBM should attempt to hedge its economic exposure to movements in the euro?

ONLINE ARTICLES WITH REAL-WORLD EXAMPLES

Find a recent article online that describes an actual international finance application or a real-world example about a specific MNC's actions that reinforces one or more of the concepts covered in this chapter.

If your class has an online component, your professor may ask you to post your summary there and provide the web link of the article so that other students can access it. If your class is live, your professor may ask you to summarize your application in class. Your professor may assign specific students to complete this assignment for this chapter or may allow any students to do the assignment on a volunteer basis.

For recent online articles and real-world examples applied to this chapter, consider using the following search terms (and include the current year as a search term to ensure that the online articles are recent).

1. hedge AND [name of an MNC]

2. hedge AND exchange rate effects

3. hedge AND currency effects

4. exposure AND exchange rate

5. exposure AND currency

6. hedge AND translation exposure

7. hedge AND translation effect

8. forward contract AND translation

9. managing translation exposure

10. reducing translation exposure

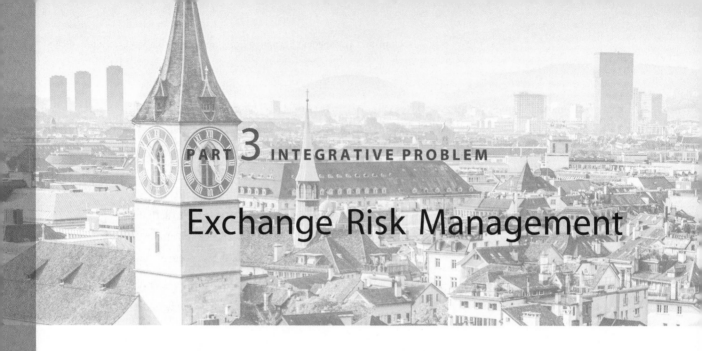

Exchange Risk Management

Vogl Co. is a U.S. firm conducting a financial plan for the next year. It has no foreign subsidiaries, but more than half of its sales are from exports. Its foreign cash inflows to be received from exporting and cash outflows to be paid for imported supplies over the next year are shown in the following table:

CURRENCY	TOTAL INFLOW	TOTAL OUTFLOW
Canadian dollar (C$)	C$32,000,000	C$32,000,000
New Zealand dollar (NZ$)	NZ$5,000,000	NZ$1,000,000
Mexican peso (MXP)	MXP11,000,000	MXP10,000
Singapore dollar (S$)	S$4,000,000	S$8,000,000

The spot rates and one-year forward rates as of today are shown below.

CURRENCY	SPOT RATE	ONE-YEAR FORWARD RATE
C$	$.90	$.93
NZ$	.60	.59
MXP	.18	.15
S$	.65	.64

Questions

1. Based on the information provided, determine Vogl's net exposure to each foreign currency in dollars.
2. Assume that today's spot rate is used as a forecast of the future spot rate one year from now. The New Zealand dollar, Mexican peso, and Singapore dollar are expected to move in tandem against the U.S. dollar over the next year. The Canadian dollar's movements are expected to be unrelated to movements of the other currencies. Because exchange rates are difficult to predict, the forecasted net dollar cash flows per currency may be inaccurate. Do you anticipate any offsetting exchange rate effects from whatever exchange movements do occur? Explain.
3. Given the forecast of the Canadian dollar along with the forward rate of the Canadian dollar, what is the expected increase or decrease in dollar cash flows

that would result from hedging the net cash flows in Canadian dollars? Would you hedge the Canadian dollar position?

4. Assume that the Canadian dollar net inflows may range from C$20 million to C$40 million over the next year. Explain the risk of hedging C$30 million in net inflows. How can Vogl Co. avoid such a risk? Is there any trade-off resulting from your strategy to avoid that risk?

5. Vogl Co. recognizes that its year-to-year hedging strategy hedges the risk only over a given year and does not insulate it from long-term trends in the Canadian dollar's value. It has considered establishing a subsidiary in Canada. The goods would be sent from the United States to the Canadian subsidiary and distributed by the subsidiary. The proceeds received would be reinvested by the Canadian subsidiary in Canada. In this way, Vogl Co. would not have to convert Canadian dollars to U.S. dollars each year. Has Vogl eliminated its exposure to exchange rate risk by using this strategy? Explain.

PART 4
Long-Term Asset and Liability Management

Part 4 (Chapters 13 through 18) focuses on how multinational corporations (MNCs) manage long-term assets and liabilities. Chapter 13 explains how MNCs can benefit from international business. Chapter 14 describes the information MNCs must have when considering multinational projects and demonstrates how capital budgeting analysis is conducted. Chapter 15 explains how MNCs engage in corporate control and restructuring on an international basis, which are special cases of capital budgeting. Chapter 16 explains how MNCs assess country risk associated with their prevailing and proposed international projects, which must be considered within the capital budgeting analysis. Chapter 17 explains the capital structure decision for MNCs, which affects the cost of financing new projects. Chapter 18 describes the long-term financing decision for MNCs. Overall, Chapters 13 through 16 identify the various factors that can affect cash flows in international investments by MNCs, whereas Chapters 17 and 18 focus on the cost of financing international investments by MNCs.

13
Direct Foreign Investment

The specific objectives of this chapter are to:

■ describe common motives for initiating direct foreign investment (DFI),

■ illustrate the benefits of international diversification,

■ describe how the host government can encourage DFI with incentives for MNCs or discourage DFI by imposing barriers, and

■ explain how MNCs can assess their potential DFI projects to determine which projects should be given serious consideration.

Multinational corporations frequently capitalize on foreign business opportunities by engaging in direct foreign investment, which is investment in real assets (such as land, buildings, or even existing plants) in foreign countries. They engage in joint ventures with foreign firms, acquire foreign firms, and form new foreign subsidiaries. Financial managers must understand the potential return and risk associated with DFI so that they can make investment decisions that maximize the MNC's value.

13-1 Motives for Direct Foreign Investment

Multinational corporations often consider direct foreign investment because it can improve their profitability and enhance shareholder wealth. They are normally focused on investing in real assets such as machinery or buildings that can support operations, rather than financial assets. When MNCs review various foreign investment opportunities, they must consider whether the opportunity is compatible with their operations. In most cases, MNCs engage in DFI because they are interested in boosting revenues, reducing costs, or both.

13-1a Revenue-Related Motives

The following are typical motives of MNCs that are attempting to boost revenues.

■ *Attract new sources of demand.* Multinational corporations commonly pursue DFI in countries experiencing economic growth so that they can benefit from the increased demand for products and services there. The increased demand is typically driven by local residents' higher income levels. Higher income allows for higher consumption, and higher consumption within the country results in higher demand.

When Twitter went public in 2013, it announced plans to expand internationally. It specifically identified Argentina, France, Japan, and South Africa as some of the countries where it had much potential to expand.

Many developing countries, such as Argentina, Chile, Mexico, Hungary, and China, have been perceived as attractive sources of new demand. Many MNCs have penetrated these countries since barriers to trade have been removed.

EXAMPLE   China has been a major target of MNCs because of its economic growth and rapidly increasing income. The Coca-Cola Co. and PepsiCo have invested hundreds of millions of dollars in bottling facilities in China. Yum! Brands, Inc. has KFC franchises and Pizza Hut franchises in China. Other MNCs such as Ford

Motor Co., United Technologies, General Electric, Hewlett-Packard, and IBM have also invested heavily in China to attract demand by consumers there. ●

■ *Enter profitable markets.* When an MNC observes that other corporations in its industry are generating high earnings in a particular country, it may decide to sell its own products in those markets. Several U.S.-based MNCs including Twitter, Facebook, LinkedIn, and Apple have pursued DFI in Ireland where taxes are lower and potential profits may be higher.

   Some MNCs may penetrate markets where prices and profits appear to be high, and undercut prices. However, one limitation with this strategy is that previously established sellers in those markets may respond to the new competition by lowering their prices.

■ *Exploit monopolistic advantages.* Firms may become internationalized if they possess resources or skills not available to competing firms. If a firm possesses advanced technology and has exploited this advantage successfully in local markets, then the firm may attempt to exploit it internationally as well. In fact, the firm may have a more distinct advantage in markets that have less advanced technology.

EXAMPLE

In recent years, Google has acquired businesses in Canada, China, Finland, Greece, Israel, South Korea, Spain, and Sweden. The company is effective at using its technology to improve the capabilities of other businesses. In this way, it expands its technology internationally. ●

■ *React to trade restrictions.* In some cases, MNCs use DFI as a defensive rather than an aggressive strategy. Specifically, MNCs may pursue DFI to circumvent trade barriers.

EXAMPLE

Japanese automobile manufacturers established plants in the United States in anticipation that their exports to the United States would be subject to more stringent trade restrictions. Japanese companies recognized that the United States might impose trade barriers that would limit or prohibit their exports. By producing automobiles in the United States, Japanese manufacturers could circumvent those barriers. ●

■ *Diversify internationally.* Because the economies of countries do not move perfectly in tandem over time, net cash flow from sales of products across countries should be more stable than comparable sales of the products in a single country. By diversifying sales (and possibly even production) internationally, an MNC can make its net cash flows less volatile. As shareholders and creditors perceive its risk to be lower because of the more stable cash flows, the MNC may enjoy a lower cost of capital. Thus diversification may reduce the likelihood that the MNC experiences financial problems.

EXAMPLE

Several MNCs that experienced weak sales because of reduced U.S. demand for their products responded by increasing their expansion in foreign markets. AT&T and Starbucks pursued new business in China. United Technologies and Wal-Mart expanded in Europe and Asia. IBM increased its presence in China, India, South Korea, and Taiwan. Cisco Systems expanded substantially in China, Japan, and South Korea. Foreign expansion diversifies an MNC's sources of revenue and thus reduces its reliance on the U.S. economy. ●

Potential benefits to MNCs that diversify internationally are examined more thoroughly later in the chapter.

13-1b Cost-Related Motives

MNCs also engage in DFI in an effort to reduce costs. The following are typical motives of MNCs that are trying to cut costs.

■ *Fully benefit from economies of scale.* An MNC that attempts to expand its primary production in new markets may be able to achieve **economies of scale** (lower average cost per unit resulting from increased production). MNCs that provide online products and services may also be able to capitalize on economies of scale because they may incur a large fixed cost when they establish their website and online platform, but their average cost per customer is reduced when they attract more customers in international markets.

EXAMPLE   Facebook benefits from economies of scale by allowing people outside the United States to access its platform. It developed a tool that enables users to translate the service into their own language, which allowed it to achieve substantial growth in many countries, including Brazil, Poland, and Turkey. Because much of its cost of operations is due to its platform, increasing international access to that platform reduces the company's cost per customer. ●

WEB

www.cia.gov
The CIA's home page, which provides a link to the *World Factbook*, is a valuable resource for information about countries that MNCs might be considering for direct foreign investment.

■ *Use foreign factors of production.* Labor and land costs can vary dramatically among countries. Multinational corporations often attempt to set up production in locations where land and labor are cheap. Because of market imperfections (as discussed in Chapter 1) such as imperfect information, relocation transaction costs, and barriers to industry entry, specific labor costs are seldom equal among markets. Thus it is worthwhile for MNCs to survey markets to determine whether they can benefit from cheaper costs by producing in those markets.

EXAMPLE   Many U.S.-based MNCs, including Black & Decker, Ford Motor Co., General Electric, Procter & Gamble, and 3M, have established subsidiaries in Mexico to achieve lower labor costs. Workers at automobile plants in Mexico earn daily wages that are less than the average hourly rate for similar workers in the United States. Ford produces trucks at subsidiaries based in Mexico. Baxter International has established manufacturing plants in Mexico to capitalize on lower costs of production (primarily wage rates).

Honeywell has joint ventures in countries such as Korea and India, where production costs are low, and has also established subsidiaries in Malaysia. Many U.S. companies including Avon, Banana Republic, Emerson Electric, Gerber Foods, and Merck have established manufacturing plants in China. ●

However, when an MNC desires to capitalize on low-cost production, it should also consider other factors such as the skills of the local people, infrastructure such as highways and airports, and the degree of government protection of human rights.

EXAMPLE   Most of Nike's shoe production is concentrated in China, Indonesia, Thailand, and Vietnam. Government regulation of labor in these countries is limited. Thus if Nike wants to ensure that employees receive fair treatment, it may have to supervise the factories itself. Thus Nike incurs additional costs of oversight to prevent unfair treatment of employees. Although its expenses from having products produced in Asia are still significantly lower than if they were produced in the United States, it needs to recognize these other expenses when determining where to manufacture its products. ●

■ *Use foreign raw materials.* Because of transportation costs, a corporation may attempt to avoid importing raw materials from a given country, especially when it plans to sell the finished product back to consumers in that country. Under such circumstances, a more feasible solution may be to develop the product in the country where the raw materials are located.

■ *Use foreign technology.* Corporations are increasingly establishing or acquiring existing overseas plants to learn about unique technologies in foreign countries. This technology is then used to improve their own production processes and increase production efficiency at all subsidiary plants around the world.

Cisco recently planned a $1 billion investment in Russia to create innovative business ideas. Cisco has previously invested heavily in India and other markets to tap into unique technologies and innovation. ●

■ *React to exchange rate movements.* When a firm perceives that a foreign currency is undervalued, the firm may consider DFI in that country because the initial outlay should be relatively low. If the foreign currency appreciates over time after an MNC has engaged in DFI, the firm will benefit because the earnings from its foreign subsidiary will convert into more U.S. dollars.

EXAMPLE Wyoming Co. (a U.S. firm) is a distributor of ski equipment that wants to acquire a Canadian business that produces snowmobiles. Wyoming Co. thinks that the Canadian dollar is undervalued and will appreciate against the U.S. dollar over the next several years. Because the Canadian dollar is presently very weak, Wyoming is able to acquire the Canadian company with fewer U.S. dollars. In addition, if the Canadian dollar appreciates against the U.S. dollar as expected, the earnings that would be periodically remitted from the Canadian company to Wyoming will convert into a larger amount of U.S. dollars. ●

13-1c Comparing Benefits of DFI among Countries

Exhibit 13.1 summarizes the possible benefits of DFI and explains how MNCs can use DFI to achieve those benefits. Most MNCs pursue DFI based on their expectations of capitalizing on one or more of the potential benefits summarized in Exhibit 13.1.

Exhibit 13.1 Summary of Motives for Direct Foreign Investment

BENEFIT	MEANS OF USING DFI TO ACHIEVE THIS BENEFIT
Revenue-Related Motives	
1. Attract new sources of demand.	Establish a subsidiary or acquire a competitor in a new market.
2. Enter markets where superior profits are possible.	Acquire a competitor that has control of its local market.
3. Exploit monopolistic advantages.	Establish a subsidiary in a market where competitors are unable to produce the identical product; sell products in that country.
4. React to trade restrictions.	Establish a subsidiary in a market where tougher trade restrictions will adversely affect the firm's export volume.
5. Diversify internationally.	Establish subsidiaries in markets whose business cycles differ from those where existing subsidiaries are based.
Cost-Related Motives	
6. Fully benefit from economies of scale.	Establish a subsidiary in a new market that can sell products produced elsewhere; this allows for increased production and possibly greater production efficiency.
7. Use foreign factors of production.	Establish a subsidiary in a market that has relatively low costs of labor or land; sell the finished product to countries where the cost of production is higher.
8. Use foreign raw materials.	Establish a subsidiary in a market where raw materials are cheap and accessible; sell the finished product to countries where the raw materials are more expensive.
9. Use foreign technology.	Participate in a joint venture in order to learn about a production process or other operations.
10. React to exchange rate movements.	Establish a subsidiary in a new market where the local currency is weak but is expected to strengthen over time.

WEB

www.weforum.org
/reports
The World Economic
Forum has analyses,
discussions, statistics,
and forecasts related to
non-U.S. economies.

WEB

finance.yahoo.com/
Information about
economic growth and
other macroeconomic
indicators used when
considering direct
foreign investment in a
foreign country.

WEB

www.worldbank.org
Valuable updated
country data that can be
considered when making
DFI decisions.

The potential benefits from DFI vary with the country. Countries in Western Europe have well-established markets where the demand for most products and services is large. Thus these countries may appeal to MNCs that want to penetrate markets because they have better products than those already being offered. Countries in Eastern Europe, Asia, and Latin America tend to have relatively low costs of land and labor.

13-2 Benefits of International Diversification

An international project can reduce a firm's overall risk as a result of international diversification benefits. The key to international diversification is selecting foreign projects whose performance levels are not highly correlated over time. In this way, the various international projects should not experience poor performance simultaneously.

EXAMPLE

Merrimack Co., a U.S. firm, plans to invest in a new project in either the United States or the United Kingdom. Once the project is completed, it will constitute 30 percent of the firm's total funds invested in its business. The remaining 70 percent of its investment in its business is exclusively in the United States. Characteristics of the proposed project are forecasted for a five-year period for both a U.S. and a British location, as shown in Exhibit 13.2.

Merrimack Co. plans to assess the feasibility of each proposed project based on expected risk and return and using a five-year time horizon. Its expected annual after-tax return on investment on its prevailing business is 20 percent, and its variability of returns (as measured by the standard deviation) is expected to be .10. The firm can assess its expected overall performance based on developing the project in the United States and in the United Kingdom. In doing so, it is essentially comparing two portfolios. In the first portfolio, 70 percent of its total funds are invested in its existing U.S. business, with the remaining 30 percent invested in a new project located in the United States. In the second portfolio, again 70 percent of the firm's total funds are invested in its existing business, but the remaining 30 percent are invested in a new project located in the United Kingdom. Therefore, 70 percent of the portfolios' investments are identical. The difference is in the remaining 30 percent of funds invested.

If the new project is located in the United States, the firm's overall expected after-tax return (r_p) is:

$r_p =$	[(70%)	$\times$	(20%)]	$+$	[(30%)	$\times$	(25%)]	$=$	21.5%
	% of funds invested in existing business		Expected return on existing business		% of funds invested in new U.S. project		Expected return on new U.S. project		Firm's overall expected return

Exhibit 13.2 Evaluation of Proposed Projects in Alternative Locations

		CHARACTERISTICS OF PROPOSED PROJECT	
	EXISTING BUSINESS	IF LOCATED IN THE UNITED STATES	IF LOCATED IN THE UNITED KINGDOM
Mean expected annual return on investment (after taxes)	20%	25%	25%
Standard deviation of expected annual after-tax returns on investment	.10	.09	.11
Correlation of expected annual after-tax returns on investment with after-tax returns of prevailing U.S. business	—	.80	.02

This computation is based on weighting the returns according to the percentage of total funds invested in each investment.

If the firm calculates its overall expected return with the new project located in the United Kingdom instead of the United States, the results are unchanged. This is because the new project's expected return is the same regardless of the country of location. Therefore, in terms of return, neither new project has an advantage.

With regard to risk, the new project is expected to exhibit slightly less variability in returns during the five-year period if it is located in the United States (see Exhibit 13.2). Because firms typically prefer more stable returns on their investments, this is an advantage. However, estimating the risk of the individual project without considering the overall firm would be a mistake. The expected correlation of the new project's returns with those of the existing business must also be considered. Recall that portfolio variance is determined by the individual variability of each component as well as their pairwise correlations. The variance of σ_p^2, a portfolio comprising just two investments (A and B), is computed as

$$\sigma_p^2 = w_A^2 \sigma_A^2 + w_B^2 \sigma_B^2 + 2w_A w_B \sigma_A \sigma_B (\text{CORR}_{AB})$$

Here w_A and w_B represent the percentage of total funds allocated to investments A and B, respectively; σ_A and σ_B are the standard deviations of returns on investments A and B; and CORR_{AB} is the correlation coefficient of returns between investments A and B. This equation for portfolio variance can be applied to the problem at hand. The portfolio reflects the overall firm. First, compute the overall firm's variance in returns while assuming it locates the new project in the United States (based on the information provided in Exhibit 13.2). This variance is

$$
\begin{aligned}
\sigma_p^2 &= (.70)^2 (.10)^2 + (.30)^2 (.09)^2 + 2(.70)(.30)(.10)(.09)(.80) \\
&= (.49)(.01) + (.09)(.0081) + .003024 \\
&= .0049 + .000729 + .003024 \\
&= .008653
\end{aligned}
$$

If Merrimack Co. decides to locate the new project in the United Kingdom instead of the United States, its overall variability in returns will be different because that project differs from the new U.S. project in terms of individual variability in returns and correlation with the existing business. The overall variability of the firm's returns based on locating the new project in the United Kingdom is estimated by the variance in portfolio returns:

$$
\begin{aligned}
\sigma_p^2 &= (.70)^2 (.10)^2 + (.30)^2 (.11)^2 + 2(.70)(.30)(.10)(.11)(.02) \\
&= (.49)(.01) + (.09)(.0121) + .0000924 \\
&= .0049 + .001089 + .0000924 \\
&= .0060814
\end{aligned}
$$

Thus Merrimack will generate more stable returns if the new project is located in the United Kingdom. The firm's overall variability in returns is almost 29.7 percent less if the new project is located in the United Kingdom rather than in the United States.

The variability is reduced when locating in a foreign country because of the correlation between the new project's expected returns and the expected returns of the existing business. If the new project is located in Merrimack's home country (the United States), its returns are expected to be more highly correlated with those of the existing business than they would be if the project were located in the United Kingdom. When economic conditions of two countries (such as the United States and the United Kingdom) are not highly correlated, a firm may reduce its risk by diversifying its business in both countries instead of concentrating in just one. ●

WEB

www.trade.gov/data.asp
Outlook of international trade conditions for various industries.

13-2a Diversification Analysis of International Projects

Like any investor, an MNC with investments positioned around the world is concerned with the risk and return characteristics of its investments. The global investments of the MNC are focused on real assets (such as production facilities), not financial assets (securities). It wants to create a portfolio of real assets that achieves high returns with limited risk. Effective diversification among projects can enable an MNC to achieve its goals.

Exhibit 13.3   Risk–Return Analysis of International Projects Diagram

Virginia, Inc., considers a global strategy of developing projects as shown in Exhibit 13.3. Each point on the graph reflects a specific project that either has been implemented or is being considered. The return (vertical axis) may be measured by potential return on assets or return on equity. The risk (horizontal axis) may be measured by potential fluctuation in the returns generated by each project.

Exhibit 13.3 shows that Project A has the highest expected return of all the projects. Although Virginia, Inc., could devote most of its resources to this project in attempting to achieve such a high return, its risk may be too high to invest in this project exclusively. In addition, such a project may not be able to absorb all the available capital if its potential market for customers is limited. Virginia, Inc., therefore develops a portfolio of projects. By combining Project A with several other projects, the company may decrease its expected return; on the other hand, it may also reduce its risk substantially.

If Virginia, Inc., appropriately combines projects, then its project portfolio may be able to achieve the risk–return trade-off exhibited by any of the points on the curve in Exhibit 13.3. This curve represents a frontier of efficient project portfolios that exhibit desirable risk–return characteristics in that no single project could outperform any of these portfolios. The term *efficient* refers to a minimum risk for a given expected return. Project portfolios outperform the individual projects considered by Virginia, Inc., because of the diversification attributes discussed earlier. The lower (or more negative) the correlation in project returns over time, the lower will be the project portfolio risk. As new projects are proposed, the frontier of efficient project portfolios available to Virginia, Inc., may shift. ●

WEB

www.treasury.gov
Links to international information that should be considered by MNCs that are contemplating direct foreign investment.

Comparing Portfolios along the Frontier

Along the frontier of efficient project portfolios, no portfolio can be singled out as "optimal" for all MNCs. This is because MNCs vary in their willingness to accept risk. If the MNC is very conservative and has the choice of any portfolios represented by the frontier in Exhibit 13.3, it will probably prefer one that exhibits low risk (near the bottom of the frontier). In contrast, a more aggressive strategy would be to implement a portfolio of projects that exhibits risk–return characteristics such as those near the top of the frontier.

Comparing Frontiers among MNCs

The actual location of the frontier of efficient project portfolios depends on the business in which the firm is involved. Some MNCs have frontiers of possible project portfolios that are more desirable than the frontiers of other MNCs.

Exhibit 13.4 Risk–Return Advantage of a Diversified MNC

EXAMPLE Eurosteel, Inc., sells steel solely to European nations and is considering other related projects. Its frontier of efficient project portfolios exhibits considerable risk (because it sells just one product to countries whose economies move in tandem). In contrast, Global Products, Inc., which sells a wide range of products to countries all over the world, has a lower degree of project portfolio risk. Its frontier of efficient project portfolios is therefore closer to the vertical axis, as illustrated in Exhibit 13.4. Of course, this comparison assumes that Global Products, Inc., is knowledgeable about all of its products and the markets where it sells. ●

Our discussion suggests that MNCs can achieve more desirable risk–return characteristics from their project portfolios if they diversify sufficiently among products and geographic markets. This capacity also relates to the MNC's advantage over a purely domestic firm serving a strictly local market. The MNC may be able to develop a more efficient portfolio of projects than its domestic counterpart.

13-2b Diversification among Countries

Economic conditions vary among countries. Therefore, when an MNC diversifies its business among countries rather than focusing on only one foreign country, it reduces its exposure to any single foreign country. However, because economic conditions are integrated among countries over time, the weakness of one country may spread to other countries. Thus diversification across economies may be less effective when there are global economic conditions that adversely affect most countries.

13-3 Host Government Impact on DFI

Each government must weigh the advantages and disadvantages of direct foreign investment in its country. The most frequently cited advantage is that DFI will create local jobs and thereby reduce the unemployment rate. In addition, DFI may attract more funds from other countries and may advance the technology in a country. DFI may be especially desirable to the host country government if it relies on local labor to produce products that are not direct substitutes for other locally produced products. In this case, the DFI might not cause a reduction in sales by local firms.

13-3a Incentives to Encourage DFI

In some cases, a government will offer incentives to MNCs that consider DFI in its country. Common incentives offered by the host government include tax breaks on the income earned there, rent-free land and buildings, low-interest loans, subsidized energy, and reduced environmental regulations. The extent to which a government will offer such incentives depends on how much it benefits from the MNC's DFI.

EXAMPLE   The decision by Allied Research Associates, Inc., a U.S.-based MNC, to build a production facility and office in Belgium was highly motivated by Belgian government subsidies. The Belgian government subsidized a large portion of the expenses incurred by Allied Research Associates and offered tax concessions and favorable interest rates on loans to Allied. ●

Many governments encourage DFI, and they use different types of incentives. France has periodically sold government land at a discount, whereas Finland, Ireland, and Mexico have attracted MNCs by imposing a low corporate tax rate on specific businesses.

13-3b Barriers to DFI

A host government is less anxious to encourage DFI that adversely affects locally owned companies unless it believes that the increased competition is needed to serve consumers. Governments tend to regulate closely any DFI that may adversely affect local firms, consumers, the local environment, and economic conditions.

Protective Barriers   When MNCs consider engaging in DFI by acquiring a foreign company, they may face various barriers imposed by host government agencies. All countries have one or more government agencies that monitor mergers and acquisitions. These agencies may prevent an MNC from acquiring companies in their country if they believe it will attempt to lay off employees. They may even restrict foreign ownership of any local firms.

"Red Tape" Barriers   An implicit barrier to DFI in some countries is the "red tape" involved, such as procedural and documentation requirements. An MNC pursuing DFI is subject to a different set of requirements in each country. Therefore, it is difficult for an MNC to become proficient at the process unless it concentrates on DFI within a single foreign country. The current efforts to make regulations uniform across Europe have simplified the process of acquiring European firms.

Industry Barriers   In certain countries, local firms in some industries have substantial influence on the government and will likely use their influence to prevent competition from MNCs that attempt DFI. A government may also impose requirements on any DFI to ensure that more local jobs are created and that effects on local competitors are limited.

EXAMPLE   MNCs that pursue DFI in Mexico to produce automobiles may be required to use a large proportion of domestically produced parts in the production of the automobiles. The required proportion may be lower for those automobiles that are to be exported.

Spain's government allowed Ford Motor Co. to set up production facilities in Spain only if Ford agreed to limit its local market share to a maximum of 10 percent and to export at least two-thirds of all automobiles that it produced in Spain. The idea behind these provisions was to create jobs for workers in Spain without seriously affecting local competitors. ●

Environmental Barriers

Each country enforces its own environmental regulations. Some countries may impose more stringent restrictions on a subsidiary whose parent is based in a different country. Building codes, disposal of production waste materials, and pollution controls are examples of restrictions that force subsidiaries to incur additional costs. Many European countries have recently imposed tougher antipollution laws.

Regulatory Barriers

Each country also enforces its own regulatory constraints pertaining to taxes, currency convertibility, earnings remittance, employee rights, and other policies that can affect cash flows of a subsidiary established there. These barriers can discourage an MNC from establishing a new subsidiary in a foreign country. Because regulations can influence a subsidiary's cash flows, financial managers must seriously consider them when deciding whether to pursue DFI in a particular country.

EXAMPLE

Facebook would like to penetrate China, which has a population of over 1.4 billion and more than 600 million Internet users. The government of China grants online operating licenses but can still restrict content and information. These restrictions have kept Facebook from penetrating China, which prevents the company from generating advertising revenue there. ●

Some MNCs are subject to changes in regulations after they engage in DFI.

EXAMPLE

Uber Technologies, Inc. (based in San Francisco), was created in 2009 to offer transportation services (as an alternative to taxis) in the United States. By 2015, it had expanded its business to more than 50 foreign countries. It was challenged in France, however, where new regulations were implemented by the French government. The government felt pressure from conflicting forces. Although Uber's business created jobs in France, it threatened the employment of French taxi drivers and the profitability of local taxi companies. Uber's performance in France and in some other countries could be adversely affected by new government regulations that restrict its business. ●

Ethical Differences

There is no standard of business conduct that applies to all countries. A business practice that is perceived to be unethical in one country may be considered totally ethical in another. Most U.S.-based MNCs are well aware that certain business practices that are accepted in some less developed countries are illegal in the United States. For example, bribes to governments in order to receive special tax breaks or other favors are common in some countries.

The Securities and Exchange Commission has recently established a specialized unit to enforce the Foreign Corrupt Practices Act (FCPA). Some U.S.-based MNCs have recently been charged with violating the FCPA. The charges typically reflect illegal payments provided in order to pursue some types of international business. These MNCs would likely argue that they could not compete for specific international government contracts in certain countries unless they offered bribes.

An MNC that does not engage in such practices may be at a competitive disadvantage when attempting DFI in some countries. Hence the firm may wish to forgo competing for some types of international business when it knows that illegal payments will be expected.

Political Instability

The governments of some countries may prevent DFI. If a country is susceptible to abrupt changes in government and political conflicts, the feasibility of DFI may depend on the outcome of those conflicts. Multinational corporations prefer to avoid direct investment in a foreign country whose government is likely to be removed after the DFI is made.

Government-imposed conditions do not necessarily prevent an MNC from pursuing DFI in a specific foreign country, but they can be costly. Therefore, MNCs should not consider DFI that requires costly conditions unless the potential benefits outweigh the costs.

13-4 Assessing Potential DFI

When an MNC considers a specific direct foreign investment, it should attempt to assess the feasibility based on diversification benefits and host government incentives, along with any country barriers that might discourage DFI. This process is intended to screen various DFI opportunities so that an MNC can focus on those opportunities that have the most potential.

13-4a A Case Study of Assessing Potential DFI

Monterey Co. created a facility 20 years ago to produce and sell health care products in the United States. For the last several years, the U.S. demand for Monterey's products has been stagnant due to increasing competition. In recent years, Monterey has promoted its health care products in the country of Zuva because there was not much competition there. Its promotion strategy in Zuva has been successful. Last year it generated $40 million from its exports to Zuva. However, this year the government of Zuva imposed a quota on imports that has the effect of limiting the volume of products that Monterey can export to Zuva. Consequently, Monterey Co. generated only $10 million (one-fourth of last year's level) from its exports to Zuva.

Monterey Co. considers establishing a production facility in Zuva to accommodate the foreign demand for its health care products, while also circumventing the quota. Monterey reviews Zuva's characteristics, as shown in Exhibit 13.5. It wants to identify the possible benefits from DFI in Zuva, along with the possible barriers or risks. Review Exhibit 13.5, and develop your own opinion about whether Monterey should further consider Zuva for possible DFI.

Financial managers recognize that DFI in Zuva should be seriously considered for the following reasons. First, by establishing a subsidiary in Zuva, Monterey could circumvent the quota imposed by Zuva's government. Monterey believes that if it established a production facility in Zuva, it might generate more than the $40 million in sales that it achieved before the quota was imposed.

Exhibit 13.5   Assessment by Monterey Co. to Determine Whether DFI in the Country of Zuva Should Be Considered

TYPE OF CHARACTERISTIC	DESCRIPTION FOR THE COUNTRY OF ZUVA
Existing demand in Zuva for Monterey's products	Demand is restricted because of a quota that restricts Monterey's exports to Zuva.
Potential demand in Zuva for Monterey's products	Demand would be at least four times higher without the quota. But the government of Zuva plans to maintain the quota for a long-term period.
Competition in Zuva for Monterey's products	There is only one local competitor that is in the same industry as Monterey Co. This competitor is partially owned by Zuva's government.
Labor characteristics in Zuva	The sole competitor in Zuva pays very high wages to its employees and offers very high retirement benefits, which partially explains why its operating costs are very high.
Government tax incentives	The government of Zuva typically offers foreign firms a tax incentive to establish a local subsidiary that employs its local citizens. The corporate income tax imposed on income earned in Zuva is reduced from 25% to 15%.

Second, the only local producer of health care products in Zuva is partially owned by Zuva's government, and Monterey Co. believes that this competitor is more concerned about satisfying its employees than its customers. The competitor is very inefficient, which may allow Monterey Co. to easily increase its market share for health care products in Zuva by offering lower prices or better quality products than the local competitor.

Third, this local competitor provides very high wages and retirement benefits to its employees. Monterey's operating expenses in the United States are much lower, so Monterey expects that it might be able to produce products in Zuva at a much lower cost than the competitor. Fourth, the government of Zuva normally allows a tax break on corporate income earned by foreign-owned subsidiaries to attract more DFI in Zuva.

However, there are counterarguments that need to be considered. First, given that the potential demand for health care products is so strong in Zuva and that the existing local firm that produces them is very inefficient, why haven't other MNCs that produce health care products outside of Zuva pursued DFI there? Furthermore, why haven't local entrepreneurs in Zuva started new businesses to produce health care products to capitalize on the opportunity? Because the one local competitor is partially owned by Zuva's government, Monterey Co. would need to carefully consider how it would be treated by the government, given that its goal would be to take away some of the local competitor's business.

Given the potential benefits and risks of pursuing DFI in Zuva, Monterey decides to have its top financial managers meet with government officials in Zuva, so that it can address the following questions:

- Will Monterey be able to obtain a business license to produce and sell its health care products in Zuva? Monterey would not even consider DFI in Zuva unless it receives a clear signal from the government that Monterey would be allowed to produce and sell its health care products there. Monterey also still needs to assess whether Zuva's government might slow the licensing process to protect the local company that it partially owns.
- Is the government of Zuva planning to privatize the sole local competitor? If so, this could be beneficial to Monterey because it may mean that the competitor will not be protected by government restrictions imposed on Monterey in the future. However, privatization might also allow the competitor to become more efficient, so that it might be much more difficult for Monterey to take business away from the competitor.
- Does the country of Zuva have specific labor laws that cause high labor costs for all companies there? Local labor laws could force Monterey to provide very favorable retirement benefits to its employees in Zuva. In fact, these laws might partially explain why the existing competitor is very inefficient. Monterey might be just as inefficient under those laws. In addition, Monterey's employees in the United States. might expect to receive similar retirement benefits.
- Would Zuva's government allow Monterey a tax break on income earned by a subsidiary in Zuva? Even if Monterey Co. is allowed an income tax break, this benefit would be meaningless if Monterey cannot obtain a business license to operate a subsidiary in Zuva, or if high labor costs prevent it from generating much income there, or even if Monterey faces extensive red tape that prevent it from operating efficiently. Furthermore, if Monterey pays a lower tax rate on its income in Zuva, it might have to pay a higher tax rate to the U.S. government on remitted earnings (this concept is explained in the appendix of Chapter 14).
- Would the government of Zuva want to buy a stake in any subsidiary established by Monterey? Monterey might be willing to allow this if it believed that doing so would ensure that the government of Zuva would treat the subsidiary fairly.

As Monterey considers DFI in Zuva, it must also recognize the possible impact on its U.S. operations. If it builds a subsidiary in Zuva, its U.S. facility will no longer need to produce the health care products that it currently exports to Zuva. Thus Monterey might need to lay off some employees in the United States if it stops exporting to Zuva.

13-4b Evaluating DFI Opportunities That Pass the First Screen

Because there are so many possible DFI opportunities, an MNC can apply a general analysis like the one described above to screen out many of the opportunities so that it can focus on a few opportunities that may offer the largest benefits. For those DFI opportunities that deserve more attention, the MNC should develop detailed plans for its proposed international project so that it can quantify the potential benefits.

Exhibit 13.6 shows a set of steps that an MNC might use when it evaluates potential DFI. It applies a multinational capital budgeting process to compare the benefits and costs of international projects (as explained in Chapter 14). It must determine the corporate governance structure that would be needed to oversee the foreign operations (Chapter 15). It must identify the potential country risk characteristics surrounding the foreign operations that could affect the expected cash flows of the international project (Chapter 16). It also needs to assess the cost of capital (Chapter 17) and debt financing possibilities (Chapter 18) in order to determine the required rate of return on an international project.

The steps in Exhibit 13.6 are listed in an orderly manner and coincide with the order of topics covered in the next five chapters of this textbook. Yet in reality, an MNC must consider all of these steps simultaneously when determining whether and how to expand internationally.

Even after MNCs engage in DFI, they apply these tasks to continuously assess their existing foreign operations. Their expected future cash flows associated with any existing foreign operations change in response the changing industry conditions (such as

Exhibit 13.6 Steps Taken by MNCs to Determine Whether to Pursue Direct Foreign Investment

Identify Motives. Review the revenue and cost-related motives for DFI, and determine which motives may apply (as explained in this chapter).
Capital Budgeting. Identify a particular international project that may be feasible, and estimate the cash flows and the initial investment associated with that project. Apply a capital budgeting analysis in order to determine whether the proposed project is feasible (as explained in Chapter 14).
International Corporate Control. Determine the appropriate corporate control structure to oversee any international subsidiaries that would be created. In addition, assess potential corporate control targets in foreign countries that could be acquired. Apply capital budgeting analysis of corporate control candidates and to any existing subsidiaries that could be sold (as explained in Chapter 15).
Country Risk Analysis. Analyze the country risk of countries where the MNC presently does business as well as in countries where the MNC plans to expand. Incorporate any conclusions from the country risk analysis into the capital budgeting analysis for those proposed projects in which the country risk may affect cash flows or the cost of financing projects (as explained in Chapter 16).
Capital Structure. Assess the existing capital structure of existing and newly proposed international subsidiaries, and determine whether it is suitable based on the MNC's existing operations and its ability to repay debt. Estimate the cost of capital that could be obtained to finance new international projects, and incorporate that estimate within the capital budgeting analysis (as explained in Chapter 17).
Long-Term Financing. Consider sources of long-term funds in foreign countries that could be used to finance existing or proposed international projects. Determine whether to revise the financing in order to hedge exchange rate risk (match loan repayment currency with cash inflow currency) or to reduce the cost of capital (as explained in Chapter 18).

competition), economic conditions, and country risk conditions. An MNC's capital structure and cost of capital can also change in response to these conditions. Consequently, MNCs periodically assess whether they should retain, divest (sell), or restructure their existing foreign operations.

SUMMARY

- MNCs may be motivated to initiate direct foreign investment in order to attract new sources of demand or to enter markets where superior profits are possible. These two motives are normally based on opportunities to generate more revenue in foreign markets. Other motives for using DFI are typically related to cost efficiency, such as using foreign factors of production, raw materials, or technology. In addition, MNCs may engage in DFI to protect their foreign market share, to react to exchange rate movements, or to avoid trade restrictions.

- International diversification is a common motive for direct foreign investment. It allows an MNC to reduce its exposure to domestic economic conditions. In this way, the MNC may be able to stabilize its cash flows and reduce its risk. Such a goal is desirable because it may reduce the firm's cost of financing. International projects may allow MNCs to achieve lower risk than is possible from only

domestic projects without reducing their expected returns. International diversification tends to be better able to reduce risk when the DFI is targeted to countries whose economies are somewhat unrelated to an MNC's home country economy.

- Some host governments boost DFI in its country by offering incentives to MNCs, such as tax breaks. However, host governments sometimes impose barriers to DFI if they are concerned that the DFI might adversely affect local competitors or the environment.

- When an MNC considers a specific form of DFI, it must measure the potential benefits, including possible diversification benefits and host government incentives. It must also consider country barriers that make the DFI more risky. If its initial assessment leads to a conclusion that DFI might be worthwhile, it can then apply a capital budgeting analysis to determine whether DFI is feasible, as described in the following chapter.

POINT COUNTER-POINT

Should MNCs Avoid DFI in Countries without Strict Child Labor Laws?

Point   Yes. An MNC should maintain its hiring standards, regardless of what country it is in. Even if a foreign country allows children to work, an MNC should not lower its standards. Although the MNC forgoes the use of low-cost labor, it maintains its global credibility.

Counter-Point   No. An MNC will not only benefit its shareholders but also create employment for

some children who need support. The MNC can provide reasonable working conditions and perhaps may even offer educational programs for its employees.

Who Is Correct?   Use the Internet to learn more about this issue. Which argument do you support? Offer your own opinion on this issue.

SELF-TEST

Answers are provided in Appendix A at the back of the text.

1. Offer some reasons why U.S. firms might prefer to engage in direct foreign investment (DFI) in Canada rather than Mexico.

2. Offer some reasons why U.S. firms might prefer to direct their DFI to Mexico rather than Canada.

3. One U.S. executive said that Europe was not considered as a location for DFI because the euro's value was presently too strong. Interpret this statement.

4. Why do you think U.S. firms commonly use joint ventures as a strategy to enter China?

5. Why would the U.S. government offer large incentives to a foreign automobile manufacturer for establishing a production subsidiary in the United States? Isn't this strategy indirectly subsidizing the foreign competitors of U.S. firms?

QUESTIONS AND APPLICATIONS

1. Motives for DFI Describe some potential benefits to an MNC as a result of direct foreign investment (DFI). Elaborate on each type of benefit. Which motives for DFI do you think encouraged Nike to expand its footwear production in Latin America?

2. Impact of a Weak Currency on Feasibility of DFI Packer, Inc., a U.S. producer of tablet computers, plans to establish a subsidiary in Mexico in order to penetrate the Mexican market. Packer's executives believe that the Mexican peso's value is relatively strong and will weaken against the dollar over time. If their expectations about the peso's value are correct, how will this affect the feasibility of the project? Explain.

3. DFI to Achieve Economies of Scale Bear Co. and Viking, Inc., are automobile manufacturers that desire to benefit from economies of scale. Bear Co. has decided to establish distributorship subsidiaries in various countries, while Viking, Inc., has decided to establish manufacturing subsidiaries in various countries. Which firm is more likely to benefit from economies of scale?

4. DFI to Reduce Cash Flow Volatility Raider Chemical Co. and Ram, Inc., had similar intentions to reduce the volatility of their cash flows. Raider implemented a long-range plan to establish 40 percent of its business in Canada. Ram, Inc., implemented a long-range plan to establish 30 percent of its business in Europe and Asia, scattered among 12 different countries. Which company will more effectively reduce cash flow volatility once the plans are achieved?

5. Impact of Import Restrictions If the United States imposed long-term restrictions on imports, would the amount of DFI by non-U.S. MNCs in the United States increase, decrease, or be unchanged? Explain.

6. Capitalizing on Low-Cost Labor Some MNCs establish a manufacturing facility where there is a relatively low cost of labor, but they sometimes close the facility later because the cost advantage dissipates. Why do you think the relative cost advantage of these countries is reduced over time? (Ignore possible exchange rate effects.)

7. Opportunities in Less Developed Countries Offer your opinion on why economies of some less developed countries with strict restrictions on international trade and DFI are somewhat independent from economies of other countries. Why would MNCs desire to enter such countries? If these countries relaxed their restrictions, would their economies continue to be independent of other economies? Explain.

8. Effects of Potential Terrorism Ohio, Inc., considers establishing a manufacturing plant in central Asia, which would be used to cover its exports to Japan and Hong Kong. If Ohio was concerned about possible terrorism, how might this affect the estimated expenses of the plant?

9. DFI Strategy Bronco Corp. has decided to establish a subsidiary in Taiwan that will produce MP3 players and sell them there. It expects that its cost of producing these MP3 players will be one-third the cost of producing them in the United States. Assuming that its production cost estimates are accurate, is Bronco's strategy sensible? Explain.

10. Risk Resulting from International Business This chapter concentrates on possible benefits to a firm that increases its international business.

a. What are some risks of international business that may not exist for local business?

b. What does this chapter reveal about the relationship between an MNC's degree of international business and its risk?

11. Motives for DFI Starter Corp. of New Haven, Connecticut, produces sportswear that is licensed by professional sports teams. It recently decided to expand in Europe. What are the potential benefits for this firm from using DFI?

12. Disney's DFI Motives What potential benefits do you think were most important in the decision of the Walt Disney Co. to build a theme park in France?

13. DFI Strategy Once an MNC establishes a subsidiary, DFI remains an ongoing decision. What does this statement mean?

14. Host Government Incentives for DFI Why would foreign governments provide MNCs with incentives to undertake DFI there?

Advanced Questions

15. DFI Strategy JCPenney has recognized numerous opportunities to expand in foreign countries and has assessed many foreign markets, including Brazil, Greece, Mexico, Portugal, Singapore, and Thailand. It has opened new stores in Europe, Asia, and Latin America. In each case, the firm was aware that it did not have sufficient understanding of the culture of each country that it had targeted. Consequently, it engaged in joint ventures with local partners who knew the preferences of the local customers.

a. What comparative advantage does JCPenney have when establishing a store in a foreign country, relative to an independent variety store?

b. Why might the overall risk of JCPenney decrease or increase as a result of its recent global expansion?

c. JCPenney has been more cautious about entering China. Explain the potential obstacles associated with entering China.

16. DFI Location Decision Decko Co. is a U.S. firm with a Chinese subsidiary that produces smartphones in China and sells them in Japan. This subsidiary pays its wages and its rent in Chinese yuan, which is stable relative to the dollar. The smartphones sold to Japan are denominated in Japanese yen. Assume that Decko Co. expects that the Chinese yuan will continue to stay stable against the dollar. The subsidiary's main goal is to generate profits for itself and reinvest the profits. It does not plan to remit any funds to Decko, the U.S. parent.

a. Assume that the Japanese yen strengthens against the U.S. dollar over time. How would this be expected to affect the profits earned by the Chinese subsidiary?

b. If Decko Co. had established its subsidiary in Tokyo, Japan, instead of in China, would the subsidiary's profits be more exposed or less exposed to exchange rate risk?

c. Why do you think that Decko Co. established the subsidiary in China instead of Japan? Assume no major country risk barriers.

d. If the Chinese subsidiary needs to borrow money to finance its expansion and wants to reduce its exchange rate risk, should it borrow U.S. dollars, Chinese yuan, or Japanese yen?

17. Foreign Investment Decision Trak Co. (of the United States) presently serves as a distributor of products by purchasing them from other U.S. firms and selling them in Japan. It wants to purchase a manufacturer in India that could produce similar products at a low cost (due to low labor costs in India) and export the products to Japan. The operating expenses would be denominated in Indian rupees. The products would be invoiced in Japanese yen. If Trak Co. can acquire a manufacturer, it will discontinue its existing distributor business. If the yen is expected to appreciate against the dollar and the rupee is expected to depreciate against the dollar, how would this affect Trak's direct foreign investment?

18. Foreign Investment Strategy Myzo Co. (based in the United States) sells basic household products that many other U.S. firms produce at the same quality level, and these other U.S. firms have about the same production cost as Myzo. Myzo is considering direct foreign investment. It believes that the market in the United States is saturated and wants to pursue business in a foreign market where it can generate more revenue. It decides to create a subsidiary in Mexico that will produce household products and sell its products only in Mexico. This subsidiary would definitely not export its products to the United States because exports to the United States could reduce the parent's market share and Myzo wants to ensure that its U.S. employees remain employed. The labor costs in Mexico are very low. Myzo will comply with some international labor laws. By complying with the laws, the total costs of Myzo's subsidiary will be 20 percent higher than other Mexican producers of household products in Mexico that are of similar quality. However, Myzo's subsidiary will be able to produce household products at a cost that is 40 percent lower than its cost of producing household products in the United States. Briefly explain whether you think Myzo's strategy for DFI is feasible.

Critical Thinking

Motives for Facebook's International Expansion Facebook has expanded its business internationally, as described by various web links (based on online search terms "Facebook" and "international expansion"). Write a short essay explaining Facebook's motivation for its international expansion. Discuss the possible risks of international expansion by Facebook.

Discussion in the Boardroom

This exercise can be found in Appendix E at the back of this textbook.

Running Your Own MNC

This exercise can be found on the *International Financial Management* text companion website. Go to www .cengagebrain.com (students) or www.cengage.com /login (instructors) and search using **ISBN 9781133947837**.

BLADES, INC. CASE

Consideration of Direct Foreign Investment

For the last year, Blades, Inc., has been exporting to Thailand in order to supplement its declining U.S. sales. Under the existing arrangement, Blades sells 180,000 pairs of roller blades annually to Entertainment Products, a Thai retailer, for a fixed price denominated in Thai baht. The agreement will last for another two years. Furthermore, to diversify internationally and to take advantage of an attractive offer by Jogs, Ltd., a British retailer, Blades has recently begun exporting to the United Kingdom. Under the resulting agreement, Jogs will purchase 200,000 pairs of Speedos, Blades' primary product, annually at a fixed price of £80 per pair.

Blades' suppliers of the needed components for its roller blade production are located primarily in the United States, where Blades incurs the majority of its cost of goods sold. Although prices for inputs needed to manufacture roller blades vary, recent costs have run approximately $70 per pair. Blades also imports components from Thailand because of the relatively low price of rubber and plastic components and because of their high quality. These imports are denominated in Thai baht, and the exact price (in baht) depends on prevailing market prices for these components in Thailand. Currently, inputs sufficient to manufacture a pair of roller blades cost approximately 3,000 Thai baht per pair of roller blades.

Although Thailand had been among the world's fastest growing economies, recent events in Thailand have increased the level of economic uncertainty. Specifically, the Thai baht, which had been pegged to the dollar, is now a freely floating currency and has depreciated substantially in recent months. Furthermore, recent levels of inflation in Thailand have been very high. Hence, future economic conditions in Thailand are highly uncertain.

Ben Holt, Blades' chief financial officer (CFO), is seriously considering DFI in Thailand. He believes

that this is a perfect time to either establish a subsidiary or acquire an existing business in Thailand because the uncertain economic conditions and the depreciation of the baht have substantially lowered the initial costs required for DFI. Holt believes the growth potential in Asia will be extremely high once the Thai economy stabilizes.

Although Holt has also considered DFI in the United Kingdom, he would prefer that Blades invest in Thailand as opposed to the United Kingdom. Forecasts indicate that the demand for roller blades in the United Kingdom is similar to that in the United States; because Blades' U.S. sales have recently declined due to the high prices it charges, Holt expects that DFI in the United Kingdom will yield similar results, especially as the components required to manufacture roller blades are more expensive in the United Kingdom than in the United States. Furthermore, both domestic and foreign roller blade manufacturers are relatively well established in the United Kingdom, so the growth potential there is limited. Holt believes the Thai roller blade market offers more growth potential.

Blades can sell its products at a lower price but generate higher profit margins in Thailand than it can in the United States. This is because the Thai customer has committed itself to purchase a fixed number of Blades' products annually only if it can purchase Speedos at a substantial discount from the U.S. price. Nevertheless, because the cost of goods sold incurred in Thailand is substantially below that incurred in the United States, Blades has managed to generate higher profit margins from its Thai exports and imports than in the United States.

As a financial analyst for Blades, Inc., you generally agree with Holt's assessment of the situation. However, you are concerned that Thai consumers have not been affected yet by the unfavorable economic conditions. You believe that they may reduce their spending on leisure products within the next year. Therefore, you think it would be beneficial to wait until next year, when the unfavorable economic conditions in Thailand may subside, to make a decision regarding DFI in Thailand. However, if economic conditions in Thailand improve over the next year, DFI may become more expensive both because target firms will be more expensive and because the baht may appreciate. You are also aware that several of Blades' U.S. competitors are considering expanding into Thailand in the next year.

If Blades acquires an existing business in Thailand or establishes a subsidiary there by the end of next year, it would fulfill its agreement with Entertainment Products for the subsequent year. The Thai retailer has expressed an interest in renewing the contractual agreement with Blades at that time if Blades establishes operations in Thailand. However, Holt believes that Blades could charge a higher price for its products if it establishes its own distribution channels.

Holt has asked you to answer the following questions:

1. Identify and discuss some of the benefits that Blades, Inc., could obtain from DFI.

2. Do you think Blades should wait until next year to undertake DFI in Thailand? What is the trade-off if Blades undertakes the DFI now?

3. Do you think Blades should renew its agreement with the Thai retailer for another three years? What is the trade-off if Blades renews the agreement?

4. Assume a high level of unemployment in Thailand and a unique production process employed by Blades, Inc. How do you think the Thai government would view the establishment of a subsidiary in Thailand by firms such as Blades? Do you think the Thai government would be more or less supportive if firms such as Blades acquired existing businesses in Thailand? Why?

SMALL BUSINESS DILEMMA

Direct Foreign Investment Decision by the Sports Exports Company

Jim Logan's business, the Sports Exports Company, continues to grow. His primary product is the footballs he produces and exports to a distributor in the United Kingdom. However, his recent joint venture with a British firm has also been successful. Under this arrangement, a British firm produces other sporting goods for Logan's firm; these goods are then delivered to that distributor. Logan intentionally started his international business by exporting because it was easier and cheaper to export than to establish a place of business in the United Kingdom. However, he is considering establishing a firm in the United Kingdom to

produce the footballs there instead of in his garage (in the United States). This firm would also produce the other sporting goods that he now sells, so he would no longer have to rely on another British firm (through the joint venture) to produce those goods.

1. Given the information provided here, what are the advantages to Logan of establishing a firm in the United Kingdom?

2. Given the information provided here, what are the disadvantages to Logan of establishing a firm in the United Kingdom?

INTERNET/EXCEL EXERCISES

IBM has substantial operations in many countries, including the United States, Canada, and Germany. Go to finance.yahoo.com/q?s=ibm.

1. Click on Historical Prices. (Or apply this exercise to a different MNC.) Set the date range so that you can obtain quarterly values of the U.S. stock index for the last 20 quarters. Insert the quarterly data on a spreadsheet. Compute the percentage change in IBM's stock price for each quarter. Next go to finance.yahoo .com/stock-center/ and click (under U.S.) on S&P

Composite 1500 Index, which represents the U.S. stock market index, so that you can derive the quarterly percentage change in the U.S. stock index over the last 20 quarters. Then run a regression analysis with IBM's quarterly return (percentage change in stock price) as the dependent variable and the quarterly percentage change in the U.S. stock market's value as the independent variable. (Appendix C explains how Excel can be used to run regression analysis.) The slope coefficient serves as an estimate of the sensitivity of IBM's value to the U.S. market returns. Also, check the fit of the relationship based on the R-squared statistic.

2. Go to finance.yahoo.com/stock-center/ and click (under "Europe") on DAX, which represents the German stock market index. Repeat the process described in exercise 1 so that you can assess IBM's sensitivity to the German stock market. Compare the slope coefficient between the two analyses. Is IBM's value more sensitive to the U.S. market or the German market? Does the U.S. market or the German market explain a higher proportion of the variation in IBM's returns (check the R-squared statistic)? Offer an explanation of your results.

ONLINE ARTICLES WITH REAL-WORLD EXAMPLES

Find a recent article online that describes an actual international finance application or a real-world example about a specific MNC's actions that reinforces one or more of the concepts covered in this chapter.

If your class has an online component, your professor may ask you to post your summary there and provide the web link of the article so that other students can access it. If your class is live, your professor may ask you to summarize your application in class. Your professor may assign specific students to complete this assignment for this chapter or may allow any students to do the assignment on a volunteer basis.

For recent online articles and real-world examples applied to this chapter, consider using the following search terms (and include the current year as a search term to ensure that the online articles are recent).

1. direct foreign investment AND motive
2. direct foreign investment AND production cost
3. direct foreign investment AND economies of scale
4. international expansion AND motive
5. international expansion AND production cost
6. international expansion AND economies of scale
7. direct foreign investment AND [name of an MNC]
8. direct foreign investment AND government incentives
9. direct foreign investment AND government barriers
10. direct foreign investment AND regulation

14
Multinational Capital Budgeting

CHAPTER OBJECTIVES

The specific objectives of this chapter are to:

- compare the capital budgeting analysis of an MNC's subsidiary versus its parent,

- demonstrate how multinational capital budgeting can be applied to determine whether an international project should be implemented,

- show how multinational capital budgeting can be adapted to account for special situations such as alternative exchange rate scenarios or when subsidiary financing is considered, and

- explain how the risk of international projects can be assessed.

Multinational corporations (MNCs) evaluate international projects by using multinational capital budgeting, which compares the benefits and costs of these projects. More specifically, MNCs determine whether an international project is feasible by comparing the present value of that project's expected future cash flows to the initial investment that would be necessary for that project. This type of evaluation of international projects is similar to the evaluation of domestic projects. However, special circumstances of international projects that affect the expected future cash flows or the discount rate used to discount cash flows make multinational capital budgeting more complex than domestic capital budgeting.

Given that many MNCs spend more than $100 million per year on international projects, multinational capital budgeting is a critical function. Many international projects are irreversible and cannot be easily sold to other corporations at a reasonable price. Financial managers must understand how to apply capital budgeting to international projects so they can maximize the value of the MNC. This chapter provides an overview of the capital budgeting process and identifies the type of information used.

14-1 Subsidiary versus Parent Perspective

Normally, multinational capital budgeting should be based on the parent's perspective. Some projects might be feasible for a subsidiary but not feasible for the parent, as net after-tax cash inflows to the subsidiary can differ substantially from those to the parent. Such differences in cash flows between the subsidiary and the parent can be due to several factors, some of which are discussed here.

14-1a Tax Differentials

If the earnings from the project will someday be remitted to the parent, then the MNC needs to consider how the parent's government taxes these earnings. If the parent's government imposes a high tax rate on the remitted funds, the project may be feasible from the subsidiary's point of view but not from the parent's point of view.

WEB

www.kpmg.com
Detailed information on
the tax regimes, rates,
and regulations of more
than 75 countries.

14-1b Restrictions on Remitted Earnings

Host governments may impose restrictions on remitted earnings by subsidiaries. Consider a potential project to be implemented in a country where host government restrictions require that a percentage of the subsidiary earnings remain in the country. Because the parent may never have access to these funds, the project is not attractive to the parent although it may be attractive to the subsidiary.

14-1c Exchange Rate Movements

When earnings are remitted to the parent, the amount received by the parent is influenced by the existing exchange rate. Therefore, a project that appears to be feasible to the subsidiary may not be feasible to the parent if the subsidiary's currency is expected to weaken substantially over time.

14-1d Summary of Factors That Distinguish the Parent Perspective

Exhibit 14.1 illustrates the process from the time earnings are generated by the subsidiary until the parent receives the remitted funds. The exhibit shows how the cash flows of the subsidiary may be reduced by the time they reach the parent. The subsidiary's earnings

Exhibit 14.1   Process of Remitting Subsidiary Earnings to the Parent

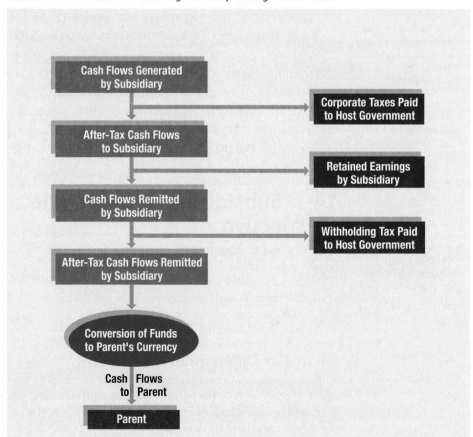

are reduced initially by corporate taxes paid to the host government. Then, some of the earnings are retained by the subsidiary (either by the subsidiary's choice or according to the host government's rules), with the residual targeted as funds to be remitted. Those funds that are remitted may be subject to a withholding tax by the host government. The remaining funds are converted to the parent's currency (at the prevailing exchange rate) and remitted to the parent.

Given the various factors shown in Exhibit 14.1 that can drain subsidiary earnings, the cash flows actually remitted by the subsidiary may represent only a small portion of the earnings it generates. The feasibility of the project from the parent's perspective depends not on the subsidiary's cash flows but on the cash flows that the parent ultimately receives.

The parent's perspective is appropriate in attempting to determine whether a project will enhance the firm's value. Given that the parent's shareholders are its owners, it should make decisions that satisfy its shareholders. Each project, whether foreign or domestic, should ultimately generate sufficient cash flows to the parent to enhance shareholder wealth. Any changes in the parent's expenses should also be included in the analysis. The parent may incur additional expenses for monitoring the new foreign subsidiary's management or consolidating the subsidiary's financial statements. Any project that can create a positive net present value for the parent should enhance shareholder wealth.

One exception to the rule of using the parent's perspective occurs when the foreign subsidiary is not wholly owned by the parent and the foreign project is partially financed with retained earnings of the parent and of the subsidiary. In this case, managers should make decisions that serve the interests of both the parent and the subsidiary shareholders.

Although this exception occasionally occurs, most foreign subsidiaries of MNCs are wholly owned by the parents. Examples in this text implicitly assume that the subsidiary is wholly owned by the parent (unless noted otherwise) and therefore focus on the parent's perspective.

WEB

http://finance.yahoo
.com/stock-center
Information on the
recent performance of
country stock indexes.
This is sometimes used
as a general indicator of
economic conditions in
various countries and
may be considered by
MNCs that assess the
feasibility of foreign
projects.

14-2 Input for Multinational Capital Budgeting

Capital budgeting for an MNC is necessary for all long-term projects that deserve consideration. The projects may range from a small expansion of a subsidiary division to the creation of a new subsidiary. Regardless of the long-term project to be considered, an MNC will normally require forecasts of the financial characteristics that influence the initial investment or cash flows of the project. Each of these characteristics is briefly described here:

1. *Initial investment.* The parent's initial investment in a project may constitute the major source of funds to support a particular project. Funds initially invested in a project may include not only those necessary to start the project but also additional funds, such as working capital, to support the project over time. Such funds are needed to finance inventory, wages, and other expenses until the project begins to generate revenue. Because cash inflows will not always be sufficient to cover upcoming cash outflows, working capital is needed throughout a project's lifetime.

2. *Price and consumer demand.* The price at which the product could be sold can be forecast using competitive products in the markets as a comparison. The future prices will most likely be responsive to the future inflation rate in the host country (where the project is to take place), but the future inflation rate is not known.

Thus future inflation rates must be forecast in order to develop projections of the product price over time.

When projecting a cash flow schedule, an accurate forecast of consumer demand for a product is quite valuable. The future demand is usually influenced by economic conditions, which are uncertain.

3. *Costs.* Variable-cost forecasts can be developed from comparative costs of the components (such as hourly labor costs and the cost of materials). Such costs should normally move in tandem with the future inflation rate of the host country. Even if the variable cost per unit can be accurately predicted, the projected total variable cost (variable cost per unit times quantity produced) may be wrong if the consumer demand is inaccurately forecast.

    Fixed costs are expenses that are not affected by consumer demand, so they can be estimated without a forecast of that demand. Rent or leasing expense is an example of a fixed cost. On a periodic basis, the fixed cost may be easier to predict than the variable cost. It is, however, sensitive to any change in the host country's inflation rate from the time the forecast is made until the time the fixed costs are incurred.

4. *Tax laws.* The tax laws affecting earnings generated by a foreign subsidiary or remitted to the MNC's parent vary among countries (see the chapter appendix for more details). Because after-tax cash flows are necessary for an adequate capital budgeting analysis, international tax effects must be considered when assessing the feasibility of any proposed foreign projects.

5. *Remitted funds.* The MNC's policy for remitting funds to the parent is relevant input because it influences the estimated cash flows generated by a foreign project that will be remitted to the parent each period. In some cases, a host government will prevent a subsidiary from remitting its earnings to the parent. If the parent is aware of these restrictions, it can incorporate them when projecting net cash flows.

6. *Exchange rates.* Any international project will be affected by exchange rate fluctuations *during* the life of the project, but these movements are usually difficult to forecast. Although it is possible to hedge foreign currency cash flows, there is normally much uncertainty surrounding the amount of those flows.

7. *Salvage (liquidation) value.* The after-tax salvage value of most projects will depend on several factors, including the success of the project and the attitude of the host government toward the project. Some projects have indefinite lifetimes that can be difficult to assess; other projects have designated specific lifetimes, following which they will be liquidated. This makes the capital budgeting analysis easier to apply. The MNC does not always have complete control over the lifetime decision. In some cases, political events may force the firm to liquidate the project earlier than planned. The probability that such events will occur varies among countries.

8. *Required rate of return.* Once the relevant cash flows of a proposed project are estimated, they can be discounted at the project's required rate of return. The MNC should first estimate its cost of capital, after which it can derive its required rate of return on a project based on the risk of that project. If a particular project has higher risk than other operations of the MNC, then the required return on that project should be higher than the MNC's cost of capital. The manner in which an MNC determines its cost of capital is discussed in Chapter 17.

WEB

www.weforum.org
Information on global
competitiveness and
other details of interest
to MNCs that implement
projects in foreign
countries.

The challenge of multinational capital budgeting is to accurately forecast the financial variables just described that are used to estimate cash flows. If garbage (inaccurate forecasts) is input into a capital budgeting analysis, then the output of that analysis will also be garbage. Consequently, an MNC may take on a project by mistake. Because such a mistake may cost millions of dollars, MNCs need to assess the degree of uncertainty for any input that is used in the project evaluation. This is discussed more thoroughly later in this chapter.

14-3 Multinational Capital Budgeting Example

This section illustrates how multinational capital budgeting can be applied. It begins with assumptions that simplify the capital budgeting analysis. Then, additional considerations are introduced to emphasize the potential complexity of such an analysis.

14-3a Background

Spartan, Inc., is considering the development of a subsidiary in Singapore that would manufacture and sell tennis rackets locally. Spartan's financial managers have asked the manufacturing, marketing, and financial departments to provide them with relevant input so they can apply a capital budgeting analysis to this project. In addition, some Spartan executives have met with government officials in Singapore to discuss the proposed subsidiary. The project would end in four years. All relevant information follows.

1. *Initial investment.* The project would require an initial investment of 20 million Singapore dollars (S$), which includes funds to support working capital. Given the existing spot rate of $.50 per Singapore dollar, the U.S. dollar amount of the parent's initial investment is S$20 million × $.50 = $10 million.

2. *Price and consumer demand.* The estimated price and demand schedules during each of the next four years are shown here:

	YEAR 1	YEAR 2	YEAR 3	YEAR 4
Price per tennis racket	S$350	S$350	S$360	S$380
Demand in Singapore	60,000 units	60,000 units	100,000 units	100,000 units

3. *Costs.* The variable costs (for materials, labor, etc.) per unit have been estimated and consolidated as shown here:

	YEAR 1	YEAR 2	YEAR 3	YEAR 4
Variable costs per tennis racket	S$200	S$200	S$250	S$260

The expense of leasing extra office space is S$1 million per year. Other annual overhead expenses are expected to be S$1 million per year.

4. *Tax laws. The* Singapore government will allow Spartan's subsidiary to depreciate the cost of the plant and equipment at a maximum rate of S$2 million per year, which is the rate the subsidiary will use.

The Singapore government will impose a 20 percent tax rate on income. In addition, it will impose a 10 percent withholding tax on any funds remitted by the subsidiary to the parent.

The U.S. government will allow a tax credit on taxes paid in Singapore; therefore, earnings remitted to the U.S. parent will not be taxed by the U.S. government.

5. *Remitted funds.* The Spartan subsidiary plans to send all net cash flows received back to the parent firm at the end of each year. The Singapore government promises no restrictions on the cash flows to be sent back to the parent firm but does impose a 10 percent withholding tax on any funds sent to the parent, as mentioned previously.

6. *Exchange rates.* The spot exchange rate of the Singapore dollar is $.50. Spartan uses the spot rate as its forecast for all future periods.

7. *Salvage value.* The Singapore government will pay the parent S$12 million to assume ownership of the subsidiary at the end of four years. Assume that there is no capital gains tax on the sale of the subsidiary.

8. *Required rate of return.* Spartan, Inc., requires a 15 percent return on this project.

14-3b Analysis

Spartan, Inc., will approve this proposed project only if the present value of estimated future cash flows (including the salvage value) to be received by the parent exceeds the initial outlay.

The capital budgeting analysis to determine whether Spartan, Inc., should establish the subsidiary is provided in Exhibit 14.2 (review this exhibit as you read on). The first step is to use demand and price estimates to forecast total revenue earned by the subsidiary (see rows 1 through 3). Then, the expenses incurred by the subsidiary are summed up to forecast total expenses (see rows 4 through 9). Next, before-tax earnings are computed (in row 10) by subtracting total expenses (row 9) from total revenue (row 3). Host government taxes (row 11) are then deducted from before-tax earnings to determine after-tax earnings for the subsidiary (row 12).

Exhibit 14.2 Capital Budgeting Analysis: Spartan, Inc.

		YEAR 0	YEAR 1	YEAR 2	YEAR 3	YEAR 4
1.	Demand		60,000	60,000	100,000	100,000
2.	Price per unit		S$350	S$350	S$360	S$380
3.	Total revenue = (1) × (2)		S$21,000,000	S$21,000,000	S$36,000,000	S$38,000,000
4.	Variable cost per unit		S$200	S$200	S$250	S$260
5.	Total variable cost = (1) × (4)		S$12,000,000	S$12,000,000	S$25,000,000	S$26,000,000
6.	Annual lease expense		S$1,000,000	S$1,000,000	S$1,000,000	S$1,000,000
7.	Other fixed annual expenses		S$1,000,000	S$1,000,000	S$1,000,000	S$1,000,000
8.	Noncash expense (depreciation)		S$2,000,000	S$2,000,000	S$2,000,000	S$2,000,000
9.	Total expenses = (5) + (6) + (7) + (8)		S$16,000,000	S$16,000,000	S$29,000,000	S$30,000,000
10.	Before-tax earnings of subsidiary = (3) − (9)		S$5,000,000	S$5,000,000	S$7,000,000	S$8,000,000
11.	Host government tax (20%)		S$1,000,000	S$1,000,000	S$1,400,000	S$1,600,000
12.	After-tax earnings of subsidiary = (10) − (11)		S$4,000,000	S$4,000,000	S$5,600,000	S$6,400,000
13.	Net cash flow to subsidiary = (12) + (8)		S$6,000,000	S$6,000,000	S$7,600,000	S$8,400,000
14.	S$ remitted by subsidiary (100% of net cash flow)		S$6,000,000	S$6,000,000	S$7,600,000	S$8,400,000
15.	Withholding tax on remitted funds (10%)		S$600,000	S$600,000	S$760,000	S$840,000
16.	S$ remitted after withholding taxes = (14) − (15)		S$5,400,000	S$5,400,000	S$6,840,000	S$7,560,000
17.	Salvage value					S$12,000,000
18.	Exchange rate of S$		$.50	$.50	$.50	$.50
19.	Cash flows to parent = [(16) + (17)] × (18)		$2,700,000	$2,700,000	$3,420,000	$9,780,000
20.	PV of parent cash flows (15% discount rate)		$2,347,826	$2,041,588	$2,248,706	$5,591,747
21.	Initial investment by parent	$10,000,000				
22.	Cumulative NPV		−$7,652,174	−$5,610,586	−$3,361,880	$2,229,867

The depreciation expense is added to the after-tax subsidiary earnings to compute the net cash flow to the subsidiary (row 13). The remitted cash flows are shown in row 14. Because all after-tax earnings are to be remitted by the subsidiary in this example, row 14 is the same as row 13. The subsidiary can afford to send all net cash flow to the parent because the initial investment provided by the parent includes working capital. The funds remitted to the parent (row 14) are subject to a 10 percent withholding tax (row 15), so the actual amount of funds to be sent after these taxes is shown in row 16. The salvage value of the project is shown in row 17. The funds to be remitted must first be converted into dollars at the exchange rate (row 18) existing at that time. The parent's cash flow (in U.S. dollars) from the subsidiary is shown in row 19. The periodic funds received from the subsidiary are not subject to U.S. corporate taxes because it was assumed that the parent would receive credit for the taxes paid in Singapore.

Calculation of Net Present Value   The net present value (NPV) of the project is estimated as the present value of the net cash flows to the parent as a result of the project less the initial outlay for the project, as shown here:

$$NPV = -IO + \sum_{t=1}^{n} \frac{CF_t}{(1+k)^t} + \frac{SV_n}{(1+k)^n}$$

where

$$IO = \text{initial outlay (investment)}$$
$$CF_t = \text{cash flow in period } t$$
$$SV_n = \text{salvage value}$$
$$k = \text{required rate of return on the project}$$
$$n = \text{lifetime of the project (number of periods)}$$

The net cash flow per period (row 19) is discounted at the required rate of return (15 percent in this example) to derive the present value (PV) of each period's net cash flow (row 20). Finally, the cumulative NPV (row 22) is determined by consolidating the discounted cash flows for each period and then subtracting the initial investment (in row 21). At the end of year 2, the cumulative NPV was −$5,610,586. This amount was determined by consolidating the $2,347,826 in year 1 and the $2,041,588 in year 2 and then subtracting the initial investment of $10,000,000. The cumulative NPV in each period measures how much of the initial outlay has been recovered up to that point by the receipt of discounted cash flows. Thus it can be used to estimate how many periods it will take to recover the initial outlay. For some projects, the cumulative NPV remains negative in all periods, which means that the initial outlay is never fully recovered.

The critical value in row 22 is in the last period because it reflects the NPV of the project. In our example, the cumulative NPV at the end of the last period is $2,229,867. Because the NPV is positive, Spartan, Inc., may accept this project if the discount rate of 15 percent has fully accounted for the project's risk. If the analysis has not yet accounted for risk, however, then Spartan may decide to reject the project. The way an MNC can account for risk in capital budgeting is discussed shortly.

14-4 Other Factors to Consider

The example of Spartan, Inc., ignored a variety of factors that may affect the capital budgeting analysis, such as:

■ exchange rate fluctuations,
■ inflation,

- financing arrangement,
- blocked funds,
- uncertain salvage value,
- impact of project on prevailing cash flows,
- host government incentives, and
- real options

Each of these factors will be discussed in turn.

14-4a Exchange Rate Fluctuations

Recall that Spartan, Inc., uses the Singapore dollar's current spot rate ($.50) as a forecast for all future periods of concern. The company realizes that the exchange rate will typically change over time, but it does not know whether the Singapore dollar will strengthen or weaken in the future. Although the difficulty of accurately forecasting exchange rates is well known, a multinational capital budgeting analysis could at least incorporate other scenarios for exchange rate movements, such as a pessimistic scenario and an optimistic scenario. From the parent's point of view, appreciation of the Singapore dollar would be favorable because the earnings received by the subsidiary and remitted to the parent would be converted to more U.S. dollars. Conversely, depreciation of the Singapore dollar would be unfavorable because the earnings received by the subsidiary and remitted to the parent would be converted to fewer U.S. dollars.

Exhibit 14.3 illustrates both a weak Singapore dollar (weak-S$) scenario and a strong Singapore dollar (strong-S$) scenario. The top row of the table shows the anticipated after-tax Singapore dollar cash flows (including salvage value) for the subsidiary from rows 16 and 17 in Exhibit 14.2. The remaining rows are numbered just as they were in the original example (Exhibit 14.2). The total amount of Singapore dollars to be sent to the parent multiplied by the forecasted exchange rate determines the estimated amount of U.S. dollars to be received by the parent.

Notice in Exhibit 14.3 how the cash flows received by the parent differ depending on the scenario. A strong Singapore dollar results in higher U.S. dollar cash flows received

Exhibit 14.3 Analysis Using Different Exchange Rate Scenarios: Spartan, Inc.

	YEAR 0	YEAR 1	YEAR 2	YEAR 3	YEAR 4
S$ remitted after withholding taxes (including salvage value)		S$5,400,000	S$5,400,000	S$6,840,000	S$19,560,000
Strong-S$ Scenario					
18. Exchange rate of S$		$.54	$.57	$.61	$.65
19. Cash flows to parent		$2,916,000	$3,078,000	$4,172,400	$12,714,000
20. PV of cash flows (15% discount rate)		$2,535,652	$2,327,410	$2,743,421	$7,269,271
21. Initial investment by parent	$10,000,000				
22. Cumulative NPV		−$7,464,348	−$5,136,938	−$2,393,517	$4,875,754
Weak-S$ Scenario					
18. Exchange rate of S$		$.47	$.45	$.40	$.37
19. Cash flows to parent		$2,538,000	$2,430,000	$2,736,000	$7,237,200
20. PV of cash flows (15% discount rate)		$2,206,957	$1,837,429	$1,798,964	$4,137,893
21. Initial investment by parent	$10,000,000				
22. Cumulative NPV		−$7,793,043	−$5,955,614	−$4,156,650	−$18,757

Exhibit 14.4   Sensitivity of the Project's NPV to Different Exchange Rate Scenarios: Spartan, Inc.

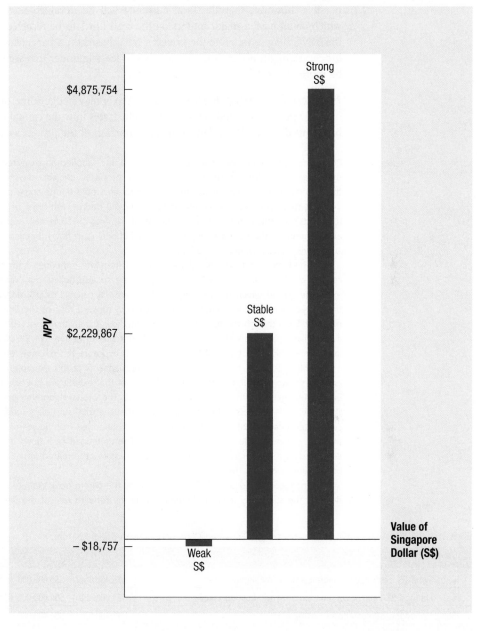

by the parent than a weak Singapore dollar scenario. The estimated NPVs based on projections for exchange rates are illustrated in Exhibit 14.4. The estimated NPV is negative for the weak-S$ scenario but positive for the stable-S$ and strong-S$ scenarios (the original example and Exhibit 14.2 illustrated the stable S$-scenario). Thus the feasibility of this project depends on the probability distribution of these three scenarios for the Singapore dollar during the project's lifetime. If there is a high probability that the weak-S$ scenario will occur, then this project should not be accepted.

Exchange Rates Tied to Parent Currency   Some U.S.-based MNCs consider projects in countries where the local currency is tied to the dollar. They may conduct a capital budgeting analysis that presumes the exchange rate will remain fixed. It is possible, however, that the local currency will be devalued at some point in the future, which could have a major impact on the cash flows to be received by the parent. Therefore, the MNC may re-estimate the project's NPV based on a particular devaluation scenario that it believes might occur. If the project is still feasible under this scenario, then the MNC may be more comfortable pursuing the project.

Hedged Exchange Rates

Some MNCs may hedge some of the expected cash flows of a new project. The following example illustrates how the capital budgeting analysis should be changed if the MNC plans to hedge a portion of the project's expected cash flows.

EXAMPLE

Reconsider the original example in which Spartan, Inc., applied an expected future spot rate of $.50 for the Singapore dollar for all four years of the proposed project. However, assume that because of the uncertainty of the Singapore dollar (S$), Spartan would hedge some of its expected cash flows if it implements the project. Specifically, assume it would hedge cash flows of S$4,000,000 per year because it expects that this is the minimum amount of earnings that the new subsidiary would receive and be able to remit to the parent in any year. Any additional cash flows (beyond S$4,000,000) received by the subsidiary per year would not be hedged.

The hedged cash flows should be separated from the unhedged cash flows because the exchange rate at which the hedged cash flows will convert to U.S. dollars may differ from the forecasted spot exchange rate at which the unhedged cash flows will convert to U.S. dollars. Assume that at the time the project would be implemented, the prevailing forward rate of the Singapore dollar is $.48 for any maturity. Even though the forward rate is slightly lower than the expected future spot rate of the Singapore dollar, Spartan is willing to use forward contracts to hedge S$4,000,000 of cash flows per year if it implements this project so that it could reduce its exposure to exchange rate risk.

Exhibit 14.5 shows how the capital budgeting analysis of this example would differ from the original analysis shown in Exhibit 14.2. The first 16 rows of that exhibit are not affected by this new example, so Exhibit 14.5 begins with row 16 from Exhibit 14.2. The capital budgeting process for this new example is the same as the process in Exhibit 14.2 except that the total subsidiary funds to be remitted (row 16) are segmented into hedged cash flows (row 16a) and unhedged cash flows (row 16b) before being converted into U.S. dollar cash flows for the U.S. parent. The unhedged cash flows of the subsidiary (row 16b) are estimated as the difference between the total funds to be remitted (row 16) and the hedged cash flows of the subsidiary (row 16a).

The hedged U.S. dollar cash flows received by the parent (row 19a) are estimated as the hedged cash flows of the subsidiary (row 16a) multiplied by the forward rate of the Singapore dollar (row 18a). The

Exhibit 14.5 Analysis When a Portion of the Expected Cash Flows Are Hedged: Spartan, Inc.

			YEAR 1	YEAR 2	YEAR 3	YEAR 4
16.	Total S$ cash flows remitted after withholding taxes		S$5,400,000	S$5,400,000	S$6,840,000	S$7,560,000
16a.	Hedged S$ cash flows remitted after withholding taxes		S$4,000,000	S$4,000,000	S$4,000,000	S$4,000,000
16b.	Unhedged S$ cash flows = (16) − (16a)		S$1,400,000	S$1,400,000	S$2,840,000	S$3,560,000
17.	Salvage value					S$12,000,000
18a.	Forward rate of S$		$.48	$.48	$.48	$.48
18b.	Expected future spot rate of S$		$.50	$.50	$.50	$.50
19a.	Hedged cash flows to parent = (16a) × (18a)		$1,920,000	$1,920,000	$1,920,000	$1,920,000
19b.	Unhedged cash flows to parent = [(16b) + (17)] × (18b)		$700,000	$700,000	$1,420,000	$7,780,000
19c.	Total cash flows to parent = (19a) + (19b)		$2,620,000	$2,620,000	$3,340,000	$9,700,000
20.	PV of parent cash flows (based on 15% discount rate)		$2,278,261	$1,981,096	$2,196,104	$5,546,006
21.	Initial investment by parent	$10,000,000				
22.	Cumulative NPV		−$7,721,739	−$5,740,643	−$3,544,539	$2,001,467

unhedged U.S. dollar cash flows (row 19b) are estimated as the unhedged cash flows of the subsidiary (row 16b) and the salvage value (row 17) multiplied by the expected future spot rate of the Singapore dollar (row 18b). The relatively large unhedged cash flows in year 4 shown in row 19b are due to the salvage value, which would not be hedged. The total U.S. dollar cash flows to the parent (row 19c) are the sum of the hedged U.S. dollar cash flows (row 19a) and the unhedged U.S. dollar cash flows (row 19b). The net present value of the proposed project in this new example is lower than it was for the original example in Exhibit 14.2 because the partial hedging strategy in this new example would cause some Singapore dollars to be converted into U.S. dollars at the forward rate, which is less than the expected future spot rate that was used in the original example. However, Spartan might still consider the partial hedging strategy if it pursues the project, because it may prefer to reduce the uncertainty surrounding the future cash flows to be generated by this project.

In this example, the payment for salvage value was not hedged. Because Spartan knows at the time that it implements the project when it is going to divest its subsidiary, it might seriously consider hedging at least a portion of the expected proceeds from the sale of the subsidiary.

The discount rate was not changed in this new example. However, it is possible that Spartan would apply a slightly lower discount rate in this example than in the original example because the hedging reduces uncertainty surrounding the U.S. dollar cash flows to be received by the parent. If so, then the net present value of the project in this example could be higher than it was in the original example. ●

The hedging assumptions used for this example are intended to illustrate how the capital budgeting analysis can be revised when an MNC plans to partially hedge future remitted earnings that are generated by an international project. However, these assumptions will not be used in any other examples in this chapter. Instead, the original example will be used and adapted to illustrate how to account for other factors in multinational capital budgeting.

14-4b Inflation

Capital budgeting analysis implicitly considers inflation because the variable cost per unit and product prices generally have been rising over time. In some countries, yearly inflation can be volatile and thus can strongly influence a project's net cash flows. In countries where the inflation rate is both high and volatile, it will be virtually impossible for an MNC to accurately forecast inflation. Inaccurate inflation forecasts can lead to inaccurate net cash flow forecasts.

Although fluctuations in inflation should affect both costs and revenue in the same direction, the magnitude of their changes may be very different. This is especially true when the project involves importing partially manufactured components and selling the finished product locally. The local economy's inflation will most likely have a stronger effect on revenue than on costs in such cases.

The effects of inflation and exchange rate fluctuations may be partially offsetting from the parent's viewpoint. The exchange rates of highly inflated currencies tend to weaken over time. Thus, even if subsidiary earnings are boosted by high inflation, the local currency may have weakened as a result (according to purchasing power parity as discussed in Chapter 8), and these earnings will be deflated when converted into the parent's home currency. However, MNCs cannot presume that exchange rate effects will perfectly offset inflation effects in a host country.

14-4c Financing Arrangement

Many foreign projects are partially financed by foreign subsidiaries. To illustrate how this foreign financing can influence a project's feasibility, consider the following revisions to the original example of Spartan, Inc.

Subsidiary Financing Assume that instead of leasing office space as in the initial example, the subsidiary borrows S$10 million to purchase the office building. Assume that the subsidiary will make interest payments on this loan (of S$1 million) annually and will pay the principal (S$10 million) at the end of year 4, when the project is terminated. Because the Singapore government permits a maximum of S$2 million per year in depreciation for this project, the subsidiary's depreciation rate will remain unchanged. Assume the office building is expected to be sold for S$10 million after taxes at the end of year 4.

Domestic capital budgeting problems would not include debt payments in the measurement of cash flows because all financing costs are captured by the discount rate. However, it is important to account for debt payments in multinational capital budgeting in order to accurately estimate the amount of cash flows that are ultimately remitted to the parent and converted into the parent's home currency. When a subsidiary uses a portion of its funds to pay interest expenses on its debt, the amount of funds to be converted into the parent's currency will be overstated if the payment of foreign interest expenses is not explicitly considered. Given the revised assumptions in this new example, the following revisions must be made to the capital budgeting analysis.

1. Because the subsidiary is borrowing funds to purchase the office building, the lease payments of S$1 million per year will not be necessary. However, the subsidiary will pay interest of S$1 million per year as a result of the loan. Thus the annual cash outflows for the subsidiary are still the same.
2. The subsidiary must pay the S$10 million in loan principal at the end of four years. However, because the subsidiary expects to receive S$10 million (in four years) from the sale of the office building that it purchases with the funds provided by the loan, it can use the proceeds of the sale to pay the loan principal.

Because the subsidiary has already taken the maximum depreciation expense allowed by the Singapore government before the office building is considered, it cannot increase its annual depreciation expenses. In this example, the cash flows ultimately received by the parent when the subsidiary obtains financing to purchase the office building are similar to the cash flows determined in the original example (when the office space was to be leased). Therefore, the NPV under the condition of subsidiary financing is the same as the NPV in the original example. If the numbers were not offsetting, then the capital budgeting analysis would be repeated to determine whether the NPV from the parent's perspective is higher than in the original example.

Parent Financing Consider one more alternative financing arrangement in which the parent uses its own funds to purchase the office building (instead of having the subsidiary lease the offices or borrow funds to purchase the building). Thus the parent's initial investment would be $15 million, which consists of the original $10 million investment as explained before plus an additional $5 million needed to obtain an extra S$10 million to purchase the offices. Assume that the parent can sell the office building for S$10 million after taxes in four years. Also assume the original exchange rate projections of $.50 per Singapore dollar for each period.

If the parent rather than the subsidiary purchases the office building, then the following revisions must be made to the capital budgeting analysis as shown in Exhibit 14.6:

■ The subsidiary will not have any loan payments (because it will not need to borrow funds) or lease payments if the parent purchases the office building.
■ The parent's initial investment is $15 million instead of $10 million.

Exhibit 14.6 Analysis if Spartan's Parent Finances the Project (Subsidiary Does Not Need to Lease Offices or Borrow Funds)

		YEAR 0	YEAR 1	YEAR 2	YEAR 3	YEAR 4
1.	Demand		60,000	60,000	100,000	100,000
2.	Price per unit		S$350	S$350	S$360	S$380
3.	Total revenue = (1) × (2)		S$21,000,000	S$21,000,000	S$36,000,000	S$38,000,000
4.	Variable cost per unit		S$200	S$200	S$250	S$260
5.	Total variable cost = (1) × (4)		S$12,000,000	S$12,000,000	S$25,000,000	S$26,000,000
6.	Annual lease expense		[S$0]	[S$0]	[S$0]	[S$0]
7.	Other fixed annual expenses		S$1,000,000	S$1,000,000	S$1,000,000	S$1,000,000
8.	Noncash expense (depreciation)		S$2,000,000	S$2,000,000	S$2,000,000	S$2,000,000
9.	Total expenses = (5) + (6) + (7) + (8)		S$15,000,000	S$15,000,000	S$28,000,000	S$29,000,000
10.	Before-tax earnings of subsidiary = (3) − (9)		S$6,000,000	S$6,000,000	S$8,000,000	S$9,000,000
11.	Host government tax (20%)		S$1,200,000	S$1,200,000	S$1,600,000	S$1,800,000
12.	After-tax earnings of subsidiary = (10) − (11)		S$4,800,000	S$4,800,000	S$6,400,000	S$7,200,000
13.	Net cash flow to subsidiary = (12) + (8)		S$6,800,000	S$6,800,000	S$8,400,000	S$9,200,000
14.	S$ remitted by subsidiary (100% of S$)		S$6,800,000	S$6,800,000	S$8,400,000	S$9,200,000
15.	Withholding tax on remitted funds (10%)		S$680,000	S$680,000	S$840,000	S$920,000
16.	S$ remitted after withholding taxes = (14) − (15)		S$6,120,000	S$6,120,000	S$7,560,000	S$8,280,000
17.	Salvage value					[S$22,000,000]
18.	Exchange rate of S$		$.50	$.50	$.50	$.50
19.	Cash flows to parent = [(16) + (17)] × (18)		$3,060,000	$3,060,000	$3,780,000	$15,140,000
20.	PV of parent cash flows (15% discount rate)		$2,660,870	$2,313,800	$2,485,411	$8,656,344
21.	Initial investment by parent	[$15,000,000]				
22.	Cumulative NPV		−$12,339,130	−$10,025,330	−$7,539,919	$1,116,425

■ The salvage value to be received by the parent is S$22 million instead of S$12 million, because the building purchased by the parent is expected to be sold for S$10 million, which can be added to the S$12 million to be received from selling the rest of the subsidiary.

The numbers in Exhibit 14.6 that are directly affected by the revised financing arrangement are bracketed. Other numbers are also affected indirectly as a result. For example, the subsidiary's after-tax earnings increase as a result of avoiding debt or lease payments. The NPV of the project under this alternative financing arrangement is positive but less than in the original arrangement. Given the lower NPV, this financing arrangement is less appealing than the arrangement in which the subsidiary either leases office space or purchases the building with borrowed funds.

Comparison of Parent and Subsidiary Financing One reason that the subsidiary financing is more desirable than the parent providing the entire financing is that the financing rate on the loan to the subsidiary is lower than the parent's required rate of return on its investment in the subsidiary. If local loans had a relatively high interest rate, however, then the use of local financing by the subsidiary would likely not be as attractive.

In general, this revised example shows that the increased investment by the parent increases its exchange rate exposure for the following reasons. First, because the parent provides the entire investment, no subsidiary financing is required. Consequently, the subsidiary makes no local interest payments in Singapore and therefore remits larger cash flows to the parent each year. Second, the salvage value to be remitted to the parent is larger if the parent owns the office building that is to be sold after four years. Given the larger payments denominated in Singapore dollars that need to be converted into U.S. dollars, the cash flows ultimately received by the parent are more susceptible to exchange rate movements.

When the subsidiary finances the office purchase, it incurs some financing expenses in Singapore. The subsidiary financing essentially shifts some of the expenses to the same currency that the subsidiary will receive as revenue, which reduces the amount of funds that will ultimately be converted into U.S. dollars for the parent, and therefore reduces the exchange rate risk.

Financing with Other Subsidiaries' Retained Earnings Some foreign projects are completely financed with retained earnings of one or more existing foreign subsidiaries of the MNC. This type of financing is unusual because the parent does not make an initial investment. The parent can evaluate the feasibility of this financing arrangement by viewing a subsidiary's investment in the new project as an opportunity cost, because those funds could have been remitted to the parent rather than invested in the foreign project. Thus the initial outlay for the new project from the parent's perspective is the amount of funds that the parent would have received from the subsidiary if the funds had been remitted rather than invested in the project. From the parent's perspective, the relevant cash flows of this new project are separate from the expected cash flows to be received from the subsidiary's other existing operations. If the net present value of this new project is positive, it implies that the subsidiary should invest the funds in the new project rather than remit the funds to the parent.

14-4d Blocked Funds

In some cases, the host country may block funds that the subsidiary attempts to send to the parent. Some countries require that earnings generated by the subsidiary be reinvested locally for at least three years before they can be remitted. Such restrictions can affect the accept/reject decision on a project.

EXAMPLE

Reconsider the example of Spartan, Inc., but now assume that all funds are blocked until the subsidiary is sold. Thus the subsidiary must reinvest those funds until that time. Blocked funds penalize a project if the return on the reinvested funds is less than the required rate of return on the project.

Suppose the subsidiary uses the funds to purchase marketable securities that are expected to yield 5 percent annually after taxes. Exhibit 14.7 shows how the blocked-funds restriction affects the original analysis of Spartan's cash flows (from Exhibit 14.2). The key difference between Exhibit 14.7 and Exhibit 14.2 is that a new row 14a has been added to show how funds are reinvested by the subsidiary until they can be remitted to the parent at the end of year 4. This affects the numbers in many other rows below row 14a. Notice that the withholding tax (row 15) is not applied until the funds are remitted to the parent, which is in year 4. The original exchange rate projections (row 18) are used here, with the key exchange rate forecast being in year 4 because that is when all the funds are remitted to the parent. Exhibit 14.7 shows that the NPV of the project (row 22) with blocked funds is positive, but it is substantially less than the NPV in the original example (Exhibit 14.2).

Furthermore, the feasibility of this project with blocked funds is highly influenced by the exchange rate forecast for year 4, because all the cash flows are to be remitted by the subsidiary at that time. Spartan would not jump to a final conclusion from the analysis in Exhibit 14.7 based on the convenient assumption that today's spot rate of the Singapore dollar (which is $.50) is an accurate forecast of the future spot rate in four years. In fact, if the spot rate of the Singapore dollar declined by just 3 percent a

Exhibit 14.7 Capital Budgeting with Blocked Funds: Spartan, Inc.

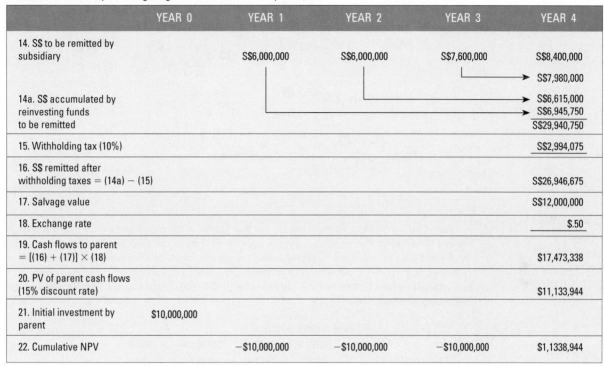

	YEAR 0	YEAR 1	YEAR 2	YEAR 3	YEAR 4
14. S$ to be remitted by subsidiary		S$6,000,000	S$6,000,000	S$7,600,000	S$8,400,000
					S$7,980,000
14a. S$ accumulated by reinvesting funds to be remitted					S$6,615,000
					S$6,945,750
					S$29,940,750
15. Withholding tax (10%)					S$2,994,075
16. S$ remitted after withholding taxes = (14a) − (15)					S$26,946,675
17. Salvage value					S$12,000,000
18. Exchange rate					$.50
19. Cash flows to parent = [(16) + (17)] × (18)					$17,473,338
20. PV of parent cash flows (15% discount rate)					$11,133,944
21. Initial investment by parent	$10,000,000				
22. Cumulative NPV		−$10,000,000	−$10,000,000	−$10,000,000	$1,1338,944

year over the next four years, the spot rate would be about $.44 in four years. Even if all the other estimates in Exhibit 14.7 were correct, if the exchange rate at the end of year 4 was $.44 instead of $.50, this project would have a negative NPV (you can verify this by replacing $.50 with $.44 for year 4 in row 18 and recalculating the NPV).

If the foreign subsidiary in this example has a loan outstanding, it may be able to better utilize the blocked funds by repaying the local loan. For example, the S$6 million at the end of year 1 could be used to reduce the outstanding loan balance instead of being invested in marketable securities, assuming that the lending bank allows early repayment. ●

An MNC may also face other situations that deserve to be considered in multinational capital budgeting, such as political conditions in the host country and restrictions that may be imposed by a country's host government. These country risk characteristics are discussed in more detail in Chapter 16.

14-4e Uncertain Salvage Value

The salvage value of an MNC's project typically has a significant impact on the project's NPV. When the salvage value is uncertain, the MNC may incorporate various possible outcomes for the salvage value and re-estimate the NPV based on each possible outcome. It may even estimate the break-even salvage value (also called break-even terminal value), which is the salvage value necessary to achieve a zero NPV for the project. If the actual salvage value is expected to equal or exceed the break-even salvage value, then the project is feasible. The break-even salvage value, SV_n, can be determined by setting NPV equal to 0 and then rearranging the capital budgeting equation:

$$NPV = -IO + \sum_{t=1}^{n} \frac{CF_t}{(1+k)^t} + \frac{SV_n}{(1+k)^n}$$

$$0 = -IO + \sum_{t=1}^{n} \frac{CF_t}{(1+k)^t} + \frac{SV_n}{(1+k)^n}$$

$$IO - \sum_{t=1}^{n} \frac{CF_t}{(1+k)^t} = \frac{SV_n}{(1+k)^n}$$

$$\left[IO - \sum_{t=1}^{n} \frac{CF_t}{(1+k)^t} \right] (1+k)^n = SV_n$$

EXAMPLE

Reconsider the Spartan, Inc., example and assume that Spartan is not guaranteed a price for the project at the end of four years. The break-even salvage value for the project can be determined by (1) estimating the present value of future cash flows (excluding the salvage value), (2) subtracting this present value of cash flows from the initial outlay, and (3) multiplying the difference by $(1 + k)^n$. Using the original cash flow information from Exhibit 14.2, the present value of cash flows (excluding the salvage value) can be determined as follows:

PV of parent cash flows

$$= \frac{\$2,700,000}{(1.15)^1} + \frac{\$2,700,000}{(1.15)^2} + \frac{\$3,420,000}{(1.15)^3} + \frac{\$3,780,000}{(1.15)^4}$$

$$= \$2,347,826 + \$2,041,588 + \$2,248,706 + \$2,161,227$$

$$= \$8,799,347$$

Given the present value of cash flows and the estimated initial outlay, the break-even salvage value is calculated as

$$SV_n = \left[IO - \sum \frac{CF_t}{(1+k)^t} \right] (1+k)^n$$

$$= (\$10,000,000 - \$8,799,347)(1.15)^4$$

$$= \$2,099,950$$

Given the original information in Exhibit 14.2, Spartan, Inc., will accept the project only if the salvage value is estimated to be at least \$2,099,950 (assuming that the project's required rate of return is 15 percent). ●

14-4f Impact of Project on Prevailing Cash Flows

Thus far, in our example, we have assumed that the new project has no impact on Spartan's existing cash flows. In reality, however, there may often be an impact.

EXAMPLE

Reconsider the Spartan, Inc., example, assuming this time that (1) Spartan currently exports tennis rackets from its U.S. plant to Singapore; (2) Spartan's export business to Singapore is expected to generate net cash flows of \$1 million over the next four years; and (3) Spartan still considers establishing a subsidiary in Singapore because it expects production costs to be lower in Singapore than in the United States. However, if it decides to establish a subsidiary in Singapore, it will no longer need to export tennis rackets to Singapore and will shut down its export business. The previously estimated cash flows to the parent from the subsidiary from the original example (Exhibit 14.2) are revised to reflect this new example in Exhibit 14.8. The first 18 rows of Exhibit 14.2 reflecting the original example are not affected. Exhibit 14.8 begins with row 19 from Exhibit 14.2. However, row 19a has been added to Exhibit 14.8 to account for

Exhibit 14.8 Capital Budgeting When Existing Cash Flows Are Affected: Spartan, Inc.

	YEAR 0	YEAR 1	YEAR 2	YEAR 3	YEAR 4
19. Cash flows to parent, ignoring impact on existing cash flows		$2,700,000	$2,700,000	$3,420,000	$9,780,000
19a. Impact of project on existing cash flows		−$1,000,000	−$1,000,000	−$1,000,000	−$1,000,000
19b. Cash flows to parent, incorporating impact on existing cash flows = (19) − (19a)		$1,700,000	$1,700,000	$2,420,000	$8,780,000
20. PV of cash flows to parent (15% discount rate)		$1,478,261	$1,285,444	$1,591,189	$5,019,994
21. Initial investment	$10,000,000				
22. Cumulative NPV		−$8,521,739	−$7,236,295	−$5,645,106	−$625,112

the cash flows generated by the export business that will be eliminated if a subsidiary is established in Singapore. Row 19b has also been added to Exhibit 14.8; it represents the estimated cash flows of the proposed project after deducting the existing cash flows that would be eliminated if the subsidiary is established. Notice in row 22 that the project has a negative NPV, which suggests that the project should be rejected. This example illustrates how a project might have a positive NPV when it has no impact on the MNC's existing businesses (as in Exhibit 14.2), but could have a negative NPV if it would reduce the cash flows generated by the MNC's existing businesses. ●

Some foreign projects may have a favorable impact on existing cash flows. For example, if a manufacturer of computer components establishes a foreign subsidiary to assemble computers, it may instruct the subsidiary to order the components from the parent. In this case, the foreign subsidiary may generate cash flows to the parent not only by remitting cash flows to the parent due to its sales of assembled computers to customers, but also by purchasing its computer components from its parent (generating more sales volume for the parent).

14-4g Host Government Incentives

Foreign projects proposed by MNCs may have a favorable impact on economic conditions in the host country and are therefore encouraged by the host government. Any incentives offered by the host government must be incorporated into the capital budgeting analysis. For example, a low-rate host government loan or a reduced tax rate offered to the subsidiary will enhance periodic cash flows. If the government subsidizes the initial establishment of the subsidiary, the MNC's initial investment will be reduced.

14-4h Real Options

A real option is an option on specified real assets such as machinery or a facility. Some capital budgeting projects contain real options in that they may provide opportunities to obtain or eliminate real assets. Because these opportunities can generate cash flows, they can enhance the value of a project.

EXAMPLE   Reconsider the Spartan example and assume that the Singapore government promised that if Spartan established the subsidiary to produce tennis rackets in Singapore, the company would be allowed to purchase some government buildings in the future at a discounted price. This offer does not directly affect the cash flows of the project that is being assessed, but it reflects an implicit call option that Spartan could exercise in the future. In some cases, real options can be so valuable that MNCs consider accepting a project that they would have rejected without the real option. ●

The value of a real option within a project is primarily influenced by two factors: (1) the probability that the real option will be exercised and (2) the NPV that would result from exercising the real option. In the example just considered, Spartan's real option is influenced by (1) the probability that Spartan will capitalize on the opportunity to purchase government buildings at a discount and (2) the NPV that would be generated from this opportunity.

14-5 Adjusting Project Assessment for Risk

If an MNC is unsure of the estimated cash flows of a proposed project, it needs to incorporate an adjustment for this risk. Three methods are commonly used to adjust the evaluation for risk:

- risk-adjusted discount rate,
- sensitivity analysis, and
- simulation

Each method will be described in a separate section.

14-5a Risk-Adjusted Discount Rate

The greater the uncertainty about a project's forecasted cash flows, the larger should be the discount rate applied to the cash flows (other things being equal). The application of a risk-adjusted discount rate is easy, but is criticized for being somewhat arbitrary. Some managers might use a higher discount rate than other managers for a particular project with a given level of expected cash flows. Hence, the project might be feasible when assessed by some managers but rejected when assessed by other managers.

In addition, an equal adjustment to the discount rate over all periods does not reflect differences in uncertainty from one period to another. If the projected cash flows among periods have different degrees of uncertainty, the risk adjustment of the cash flows should vary also. Consider a country where the political situation is slowly destabilizing. The probability of blocked funds, expropriation, and other adverse events is increasing over time. Thus cash flows sent to the parent are less certain in the distant future than they are in the near future. A different discount rate should therefore be applied to each period in accordance with its corresponding risk. Even so, the adjustment will be subjective and may not accurately reflect the actual risk.

Despite its subjectivity, the risk-adjusted discount rate is a commonly used method—perhaps because of the ease with which the discount rate can be arbitrarily adjusted. In addition, there is no alternative technique that will perfectly adjust for risk, although in certain cases some others (discussed next) may better reflect a project's risk.

14-5b Sensitivity Analysis

Once the MNC has estimated the NPV of a proposed project, it may want to consider alternative estimates for its input variables.

EXAMPLE   Recall that the demand for the Spartan subsidiary's tennis rackets was originally estimated to be 60,000 in the first two years and 100,000 in the next two years. If demand turns out to be 60,000 in all four years, how will the NPV results change? Alternatively, what if demand is 100,000 in all four years? The use of such *what-if* scenarios is referred to as sensitivity analysis. The objective is to determine how sensitive the NPV is to alternative values of the input variables. The estimates of any input variables can be revised to create new estimates for NPV. If the NPV is consistently positive during these revisions, the MNC should feel more comfortable about the project; if it is negative in many cases, the accept/reject decision for the project becomes more difficult. ●

Sensitivity analysis can be more useful than simple point estimates because it reassesses the project based on various circumstances that may occur.

Using Electronic Spreadsheets By using an electronic spreadsheet such as Excel, financial managers of MNCs can quickly derive a new estimate of NPV based on alternative assumptions about the project. Thus spreadsheets facilitate the application of sensitivity analysis to multinational capital budgeting. To illustrate, Exhibit 14.9 converts

Exhibit 14.9 Conversion of Exhibit 14.2 into Electronic Spreadsheet Format

COLUMN A	COLUMN B YEAR 0	COLUMN C YEAR 1	COLUMN D YEAR 2	COLUMN E YEAR 3	COLUMN F YEAR 4
1. Demand		INPUT	INPUT	INPUT	INPUT
2. Price per unit		INPUT	INPUT	INPUT	INPUT
3. Total revenue		C1*C2	D1*D2	E1*E2	F1*F2
4. Variable cost per unit		INPUT	INPUT	INPUT	INPUT
5. Total variable cost		C1*C4	D1*D4	E1*E4	F1*F4
6. Annual lease expense	INPUT: Annual Lease Expense	B6	B6	B6	B6
7. Other fixed annual expenses	INPUT: Other Fixed Annual Expenses	B7	B7	B7	B7
8. Noncash expense (depreciation)	INPUT: Annual Depreciation Expense	B8	B8	B8	B8
9. Total expenses		C5+C6+C7+C8	D5+D6+D7+D8	E5+E6+E7+E8	F5+F6+F7+F8
10. Before-tax earnings of subsidiary		C3−C9	D3−D9	E3−E9	F3−F9
11. Host government tax	INPUT: Host Government Tax Rate	B11*C10	B11*D10	B11*E10	B11*F10
12. After-tax earnings of subsidiary		C10−C11	D10−D11	E10−E11	F10−F11
13. Net cash flow to subsidiary		C8+C12	D8+D12	E8+E12	F8+F12
14. S$ remitted by subsidiary	INPUT: Proportion of Funds Remitted	B14*C13	B14*D13	B14*E13	B14*F13
15. Withholding tax on remitted funds	INPUT: Withholding Tax Rate	B15*C14	B15*D14	B15*E14	B15*F14
16. S$ remitted after withholding taxes		C14−C15	D14−D15	E14−E15	F14−F15
17. Salvage value					INPUT
18. Exchange rate S$		INPUT	INPUT	INPUT	INPUT
19. Cash flows to parent		C16*C18	D16*D18	E16*E18	(F16+F17)*F18
20. PV of parent cash flows	INPUT: [1 + DISCOUNT RATE]	C19/POWER (B20,1)	D19/POWER (B20,2)	E19/POWER (B20,3)	F19/POWER (B20,4)
21. Initial investment	INPUT: INITIAL INVESTMENT				
22. Cumulative NPV		C20−B21	(C20+D20)−B21	(C20+D20+ E20)−B21	(C20+D20+ E20+F20)−B21

Note: All letters followed by numbers identify specific cells in the spreadsheet. Columns are identified at the top of the spreadsheet by letter, while rows are identified on the left side of the spreadsheet by number.

Exhibit 14.2 (Spartan's assessment of whether to build a subsidiary in Singapore) into a spreadsheet and shows how each variable that was used to estimate the project's NPV (identified in a particular row) is determined.

Exhibit 14.9 labels the six columns A to F, identified at the top of the spreadsheet, and labels the 22 rows identified on the left side of the spreadsheet. The Excel spreadsheet refers to a specific cell location with the letter representing the column, followed by the number representing the row. For example, cell B7 represents the second column (Column B) and seventh row, while cell C2 represents the third column (Column C) and the second row.

Some variables in this spreadsheet (such as demand in row 1 and price per unit in row 2) require input based on the original assumptions provided in the example. For these variables, the term "INPUT" is shown in the cells on the spreadsheet in Exhibit 14.9. Other variables are determined by computations involving specific cells on the spreadsheet. Review Exhibit 14.9 while reading the following description of how the variables in the spreadsheet were determined.

Demand (row 1) and price per unit (row 2) require input. Total revenue (row 3) in any year is derived by multiplying rows 1 and 2 for that year. The variable cost per unit (row 4) requires input. Total variable cost (row 5) for any year is derived by multiplying demand (row 1) by the variable cost per unit (row 4) for that year.

The annual lease expense (row 6) is shown in cell B6, and because it is assumed that this expense does not change from year to year, the input in cell B6 represents the lease expense for every year in row 6. The other fixed expenses (row 7) are shown in cell B7, and because it is assumed that these expenses do not change from year to year, the input in cell B7 represents the other fixed expenses for every year in row 7.

The depreciation expense (row 8) is shown in cell B8, and because it is assumed that this expense does not change from year to year, the input in cell B8 represents the depreciation for every year in row 8. Total expenses (row 9) for any year are estimated by adding rows 5 through 8 for that year.

The subsidiary's before-tax earnings (row 10) in any year are computed as its total revenue (row 3) minus its total expenses (row 9) for that year. The host government tax paid by the subsidiary (row 11) for any year is estimated as the assumed host government tax rate (input for cell B11) multiplied by the before-tax earnings (row 10) for that year. The after-tax earnings of the subsidiary (row 12) in any year are computed as the before-tax earnings (row 10) minus the taxes paid to the host government (row 11) for that year. The net cash flow to the subsidiary (row 13) is derived for any year by adding the depreciation expense (row 8) to the after-tax earnings (row 12) for that year.

The amount of funds to be remitted by the subsidiary to the parent (row 14) for any year is computed as the proportion of net cash flow to be remitted (input in cell B14) multiplied by its net cash flow (row 13) for that year. The withholding tax paid by the subsidiary to the host government (row 15) for any year is computed as the withholding tax rate (input in cell B15) multiplied by the amount of funds to be remitted (row 14) for that year. The amount of funds remitted after payment of withholding tax (row 16) for any year is computed as the amount of funds to be remitted (row 14) minus the withholding tax paid (row 15) for that year. The salvage value (row 17) at the end of the four-year period requires input in cell F17.

The exchange rate of the Singapore dollar (row 18) requires input in each year. The estimated net cash flow received by the parent (row 19) for any year is computed as the amount of funds remitted after payment of withholding taxes (row 16) multiplied by the exchange rate of the Singapore dollar (row 18) for that year. The estimated net cash flows must also account for the salvage value in the last year of the project (cell F17) multiplied by the exchange rate at that time (cell F18).

The present value of the net cash flow to the parent (row 20) for any year is computed by discounting the net cash flow to the parent (row 19) in that year back to the present. The first step is to insert input for $(1 + k)$ in cell B20. Then, a compute statement can be inserted for each year in row 20 to estimate the present value of the parent's net cash flow in that year. Thus the present value of the net cash flow in year 1 (cell C20) is estimated as the net cash flow in year 1 (cell C19) divided by cell B20 (which represents $1 + k$, the discount rate) raised to the first power. The present value of the net cash flow in year 2 (cell D20) is estimated as the net cash flow in year 2 (cell D19) divided by cell B20 (which represents $1 + k$, the discount rate) raised to the second power. The power is changed in each year to reflect the number of years that the net cash flow must be discounted back to the present. The cumulative NPV (row 22) for any year is computed by accumulating the annual present values of cash flows (in row 22) up to that year, and subtracting the initial outlay (input in cell B21).

The benefit of the spreadsheet is that an MNC can see how its estimate of NPV changes when it considers alternative assumptions for specific variables. First, it may want to consider different input for variables like demand (row 1) or price per unit (row 2).

Second, the MNC may consider alternative possible tax rates such as the host government corporate tax rate (cell B11) or the withholding tax rate (cell B15). This allows the MNC to determine how the NPV would be affected if tax rates are changed.

Third, the MNC can determine how its estimate of NPV would change if it uses a higher required rate of return (cell B20). Once the spreadsheet is completed with either the original input or compute statements in all cells, financial managers can revise their original assumption for any cell requiring input in less than a minute, and the spreadsheet will immediately re-estimate the proposed project's NPV in response to changes in that assumption. Using the spreadsheet offers insight about whether the project's NPV is consistently positive even after considering a variety of possible scenarios for some of the input variables. Such insight can boost the MNC's confidence in the feasibility of the proposed project.

14-5c Simulation

Simulation can be used for a variety of tasks, including the generation of a probability distribution for NPV based on a range of possible values for one or more input variables. Simulation is typically performed with the aid of a computer package.

EXAMPLE   Reconsider Spartan, Inc., and assume that it expects the exchange rate to depreciate by 3 to 7 percent per year (with an equal probability of all values in this range occurring). Unlike a single point estimate, simulation can consider the range of possibilities for the Singapore dollar's exchange rate at the end of each year. It considers all point estimates for the other variables and randomly picks one of the possible values of the Singapore dollar's depreciation level for each of the four years. Based on this random selection process, the NPV is determined.

The procedure just described constitutes one iteration. Then the process is repeated: the Singapore dollar's depreciation for each year is again randomly selected (within the range of possibilities assumed earlier), and the NPV of the project is computed. The simulation program may be run for, say, 100 iterations. This means that 100 different possible scenarios are created for the possible exchange rates of the Singapore dollar during the four-year project period.

Each iteration reflects a different scenario. The NPV of the project based on each scenario is then computed. In this way, simulation generates a distribution of NPVs for the project. The major advantage of simulation is that the MNC can examine a range of possible NPVs that might occur. From this information, it can determine the probability that the NPV will be positive (or greater than a particular level). The greater the uncertainty of the exchange rate, the greater will be the uncertainty of the NPV. The risk of a project will be greater if it involves transactions in more volatile currencies, other things being equal. ●

In reality, many or all of the input variables necessary for multinational capital budgeting may be uncertain in the future. Probability distributions can be developed for all variables with uncertain future values. The final result is a distribution of possible NPVs that might occur for the project. The simulation technique does not put all of its emphasis on any one NPV forecast but instead provides a distribution of the possible outcomes that may occur. Some spreadsheets (such as Excel) are capable of providing a range of estimates for NPV in response to a range of possible estimates for any particular variable. The project's cost of capital can be used as a discount rate when simulation is performed. The probability that the project will be successful can be estimated by measuring the area within the probability distribution for which NPV > 0. This area represents the probability that the present value of future cash flows will exceed the initial outlay. An MNC can also use the probability distribution to estimate the probability that the project will backfire by measuring the area for which NPV < 0.

Computer programs can run 100 iterations and generate results within a matter of seconds. The user of a simulation program must provide the probability distributions for the input variables that will affect the project's NPV. As with any model, the accuracy of results generated by simulation will depend on the accuracy of the input.

SUMMARY

- Capital budgeting may generate different results and a different conclusion depending on whether it is conducted from the perspective of an MNC's subsidiary or from the perspective of the MNC's parent. When a parent is deciding whether to implement an international project, it should determine whether the project is feasible from its own perspective.

- Multinational capital budgeting requires any input that will help estimate the initial outlay, periodic cash flows, salvage value, and required rate of return on the project. Once these factors are estimated, the international project's net present value can be estimated, just as if it were a domestic project.

- It is normally more difficult to estimate cash flows for an international project. Exchange rates create an additional source of uncertainty because they affect the cash flows ultimately received by the parent as a result of the project. Other international conditions that can influence the cash flows ultimately received by the parent include the financing arrangement (parent versus subsidiary financing of the project), blocked funds by the host government, and host government incentives.

- The risk of international projects can be accounted for by estimating the net present value based on various possible scenarios for exchange rates or any other uncertain factors. This method is facilitated by the use of sensitivity analysis or simulation.

POINT COUNTER-POINT

Should MNCs Use Forward Rates to Estimate Dollar Cash Flows of Foreign Projects?

Point   Yes. An MNC's parent should use the forward rate for each year in which it will receive net cash flows in a foreign currency. The forward rate is market determined and serves as a useful forecast for future years.

Counter-Point   No. An MNC should use its own forecasts for each year in which it will receive net cash

flows in a foreign currency. If the forward rates for future time periods are higher than the MNC's expected spot rates, the MNC may accept a project that it should not accept.

Who Is Correct?   Use the Internet to learn more about this issue. Which argument do you support? Offer your own opinion on this issue.

SELF-TEST

Answers are provided in Appendix A at the back of the text.

1. Two managers of Marshall, Inc., assessed a proposed project in Jamaica. Each manager used exactly the same estimates of the earnings to be generated by the project, as these estimates were provided by other employees. The managers agree on the proportion of funds to be remitted each year, the life of the project, and the discount rate to be applied. Both managers also assessed the project from the U.S. parent's perspective. Nevertheless, one manager determined that this project had a large net present value, while the other manager determined that the project had a negative net present value. Explain the possible reasons for such a difference.

2. Pinpoint the parts of a multinational capital budgeting analysis for a proposed sales distribution center in Ireland that are sensitive when the forecast of a stable economy in Ireland is revised to predict a recession.

3. New Orleans Exporting Co. produces small computer components, which are then sold to Mexico. It plans to expand by establishing a plant in Mexico that will produce the components and sell them locally. This plant will reduce the amount of goods that are transported from New Orleans. The firm has determined that the cash flows to be earned in Mexico would yield a positive net present value after accounting for tax and exchange rate effects, converting cash flows to dollars, and discounting them at the proper discount rate. What other major factor must be considered to estimate the project's NPV?

4. Explain how the present value of the salvage value of an Indonesian subsidiary will be affected (from the U.S. parent's perspective) by (a) an increase in the risk of the foreign subsidiary and (b) an expectation that Indonesia's currency (rupiah) will depreciate against the dollar over time.

5. Wilmette Co. and Niles Co. (both from the United States) are assessing the acquisition of the same firm in Thailand and have obtained the future cash flow estimates (in Thailand's currency, baht) from the firm. Wilmette would use its retained earnings from U.S. operations to acquire the subsidiary. Niles Co. would finance the acquisition mostly with a term loan (in baht) from Thai banks. Neither firm has any other business in Thailand. Which firm's dollar cash flows would be affected more by future changes in the value of the baht (assuming that the Thai firm is acquired)?

6. Review the capital budgeting example of Spartan, Inc., discussed in this chapter. Identify the specific variables assessed in the process of estimating a foreign project's net present value (from a U.S. perspective) that would cause the most uncertainty about the NPV.

QUESTIONS AND APPLICATIONS

1. MNC Parent's Perspective Why should capital budgeting for subsidiary projects be assessed from the parent's perspective? What additional factors that normally are not relevant for a purely domestic project deserve consideration in multinational capital budgeting?

2. Accounting for Risk What is the limitation of using point estimates of exchange rates in the capital budgeting analysis?

List the various techniques for adjusting risk in multinational capital budgeting. Describe any advantages or disadvantages of each technique.

Explain how simulation can be used in multinational capital budgeting. What can it do that other risk adjustment techniques cannot?

3. Uncertainty of Cash Flows Using the capital budgeting framework discussed in this chapter, explain the sources of uncertainty surrounding a proposed project in Hungary by a U.S. firm. In what ways is the estimated net present value of this project more uncertain than that of a similar project in a more developed European country?

4. Accounting for Risk Your employees have estimated the net present value of Project X to be $1.2 million. Their report says that they have not accounted for risk but that, with such a large NPV, the project should be accepted because even a risk-adjusted NPV would likely be positive. You have the final decision as to whether to accept or reject the project. What is your decision?

5. Impact of Exchange Rates on NPV

a. Describe in general terms how future appreciation of the euro will likely affect the value (from the parent's perspective) of a project established in Germany today by a U.S.-based MNC. Will the sensitivity of the project value be affected by the percentage of earnings remitted to the parent each year?

b. Repeat this question, but assume the future depreciation of the euro.

6. Impact of Financing on NPV Explain how the financing decision can influence the sensitivity of the net present value to exchange rate forecasts.

7. Change in Required Return on Projects Woodsen, Inc., of Pittsburgh, Pennsylvania, considered the development of a large subsidiary in Greece. In response to a crisis in Greece, its expected cash flows and earnings from this acquisition were reduced only slightly. Yet the firm decided to retract its offer because of an increase in its required rate of return on the project, which caused the NPV to be negative. Explain why the required rate of return on its project may have increased.

8. Assessing a Foreign Project Huskie Industries, a U.S.-based MNC, considers purchasing a small manufacturing company in France that sells products only within France. Huskie has no other existing business in France and no cash flows in euros. Would the proposed acquisition likely be more feasible if the euro is expected to appreciate or depreciate over the long run? Explain.

9. Relevant Cash Flows in Disney's French Theme Park When Walt Disney World considered establishing a theme park in France, were the forecasted revenues and costs associated with the French park sufficient to assess the feasibility of this project? Were there any other "relevant cash flows" that deserved to be considered?

10. Capital Budgeting Logic Athens, Inc., established a subsidiary in the United Kingdom that was independent of its operations in the United States. The subsidiary's performance was well above what was expected. Consequently, when a British firm approached Athens about the possibility of acquiring the subsidiary, Athens' chief financial officer replied that the subsidiary was performing so well that it was not for sale. Comment on this strategy.

11. Capital Budgeting Logic Lehigh Co. established a subsidiary in Switzerland that was performing below the cash flow projections developed before the subsidiary was established. Lehigh anticipated that future cash flows would also be lower than the original cash flow projections. Consequently, Lehigh decided to inform several potential acquiring firms of its plan to sell the subsidiary. Lehigh then received a few bids. Even the highest bid was very low, but Lehigh accepted the offer. It justified its decision by stating that any existing project whose cash flows are not sufficient to recover the initial investment should be divested. Comment on this statement.

12. Impact of Reinvested Foreign Earnings on NPV Flagstaff Corp. is a U.S.-based firm with a subsidiary in Mexico. It plans to reinvest its earnings in Mexican government securities for the next 10 years because the interest rate earned on these securities is so high. Then, after 10 years, it will remit all accumulated earnings to the United States. What is a drawback of using this approach? (Assume the securities have no default or interest rate risk.)

13. Capital Budgeting Example Brower, Inc., just constructed a manufacturing plant in Ghana. The construction cost 9 billion Ghanaian cedi. Brower intends to leave the plant open for three years. During the three years of operation, cedi cash flows are expected to be 3 billion cedi, 3 billion cedi, and 2 billion cedi, respectively. Operating cash flows will begin one year from today and are remitted back to the parent at the end of each year. At the end of the third year, Brower expects to sell the plant for 5 billion cedi. Brower has a required rate of return of 17 percent. It currently takes 8,700 cedi to buy 1 U.S. dollar, and the cedi is expected to depreciate by 5 percent per year.

a. Determine the NPV for this project. Should Brower build the plant?

b. How would your answer change if the value of the cedi was expected to remain unchanged from its current value of 8,700 cedi per U.S. dollar over the course of the three years? Should Brower construct the plant then?

14. Impact of Financing on NPV Ventura Corp., a U.S.-based MNC, plans to establish a subsidiary in Japan. It is confident that the Japanese yen will appreciate against the dollar over time. The subsidiary will retain only enough revenue to cover expenses and will remit the rest to the parent each year. Will Ventura benefit more from exchange rate effects if its parent provides equity financing for the subsidiary or if the subsidiary is financed by local banks in Japan? Explain.

15. Accounting for Changes in Risk Santa Monica Co., a U.S.-based MNC, was considering establishing a consumer products division in Germany, which would be financed by German banks. Santa Monica completed its capital budgeting analysis in August. Then, in November, the government leadership stabilized and political conditions improved in Germany. In response, Santa Monica increased its expected cash flows by 20 percent but did not adjust the discount rate applied to the project. Should the discount rate be affected by the change in political conditions?

16. Estimating the NPV Assume that a less developed country called LDC encourages direct foreign investment (DFI) in order to reduce its unemployment rate, currently at 15 percent. Also assume that several MNCs are likely to consider DFI in this country. The inflation rate in recent years has averaged 4 percent. The hourly wage in LDC for manufacturing work is the equivalent of about $5 per hour. When Piedmont Co. develops cash flow forecasts to perform a capital budgeting analysis for a project in LDC, it assumes a wage rate of $5 in year 1 and applies a 4 percent increase for each of the next 10 years. The components produced are to be exported to Piedmont's headquarters in the United States, where they will be used in the production of computers. Do you think Piedmont will overestimate or underestimate the net present value of this project? Why? (Assume that LDC's currency is tied to the dollar and will remain that way.)

17. PepsiCo's Project in Brazil PepsiCo recently decided to invest more than $300 million for expansion in Brazil. Brazil offers considerable potential because it has 150 million people and their demand for soft drinks is increasing. However, the soft drink consumption is still only about one-fifth of the soft drink consumption in the United States. PepsiCo's initial outlay was used to purchase three production plants and a distribution network of almost 1,000 trucks to distribute its products to retail stores in Brazil. The expansion in Brazil was expected to make PepsiCo's products more accessible to Brazilian consumers.

a. Given that PepsiCo's investment in Brazil was entirely in dollars, describe its exposure to exchange rate risk resulting from the project. Explain how the size of the parent's initial investment and the exchange rate risk would have been affected if PepsiCo had financed much of the investment with loans from banks in Brazil.

b. Describe the factors that PepsiCo likely considered when estimating the future cash flows of the project in Brazil.

c. What factors did PepsiCo likely consider in deriving its required rate of return on the project in Brazil?

d. Describe the uncertainty that surrounds the estimate of future cash flows from the perspective of the U.S. parent.

e. PepsiCo's parent was responsible for assessing the expansion in Brazil. Yet PepsiCo already had some existing operations in Brazil. When capital budgeting analysis was used to determine the feasibility of this project, should the project have been assessed from a Brazilian perspective or a U.S. perspective? Explain.

18. Impact of Asian Crisis Assume that Fordham Co. was evaluating a project in Thailand (to be financed with U.S. dollars). All cash flows generated from the project were to be reinvested in Thailand for several years. Explain how the Asian crisis in 1997 would have affected the expected cash flows of this project and the required rate of return on this project. If the cash flows were to be remitted to the U.S. parent, explain how the Asian crisis would have affected the expected cash flows of this project.

19. Tax Effects on NPV When considering the implementation of a project in one of various possible countries, what types of tax characteristics should be assessed among the countries? (See the chapter appendix.)

20. Capital Budgeting Analysis A project in South Korea requires an initial investment of 2 billion South Korean won. The project is expected to generate net cash flows to the subsidiary of 3 billion and 4 billion won in the two years of operation, respectively. The project has no salvage value. The current value of the won is 1,100 won per U.S. dollar, and the value of the won is expected to remain constant over the next two years.

a. What is the NPV of this project if the required rate of return is 13 percent?

b. Repeat the question, except assume that the value of the won is expected to be 1,200 won per U.S. dollar after two years. Further assume that the funds are blocked and that the parent company will only be able to remit them back to the United States in two years. How does this affect the NPV of the project?

21. Accounting for Exchange Rate Risk Carson Co. is considering a 10-year project in Hong Kong, where the Hong Kong dollar is tied to the U.S. dollar. Carson Co. uses sensitivity analysis that allows for alternative exchange rate scenarios. Why would Carson use this approach rather than using the pegged exchange rate as its exchange rate forecast in every year?

22. Decisions Based on Capital Budgeting

Marathon, Inc., considers a one-year project with the Belgian government. Its euro revenue would be guaranteed. Its consultant states that the percentage change in the euro is represented by a normal distribution and that, based on a 95 percent confidence interval, the percentage change in the euro is expected to be between 0 and 6 percent. Marathon uses this information to create three scenarios: 0, 3, and 6 percent for the euro. It derives an estimated NPV based on each scenario and then determines the mean NPV. The NPV was positive for the 3 and 6 percent scenarios, but it was slightly negative for the 0 percent scenario. This led Marathon to reject the project. Its manager stated that it did not want to pursue a project that had a one-in-three chance of having a negative NPV. Do you agree with the manager's interpretation of the analysis? Explain.

23. Estimating Cash Flows of a Foreign Project

Assume that Nike decides to build a shoe factory in Brazil; half the initial outlay will be funded by the parent's equity and half by borrowing funds in Brazil. Assume that Nike wants to assess the project from its own perspective to determine whether the project's future cash flows will provide a sufficient return to the parent to warrant the initial investment. Why will the estimated cash flows be different from the estimated cash flows of Nike's shoe factory in New Hampshire? Why will the initial outlay be different? Explain how Nike can conduct multinational capital budgeting in a manner that will achieve its objective.

Advanced Questions

24. Break-Even Salvage Value

A project in Malaysia costs $4 million. Over the next three years, the project will generate total operating cash flows of $3.5 million, measured in today's dollars using a required rate of return of 14 percent. What is the break-even salvage value of this project?

25. Capital Budgeting Analysis

Zistine Co. considers a one-year project in New Zealand so that it can capitalize on its technology. It is risk averse but is attracted to the project because of a government guarantee. The project will generate a guaranteed NZ$8 million in revenue, paid by the New Zealand

government at the end of the year. The payment by the New Zealand government is also guaranteed by a credible U.S. bank. The cash flows earned on the project will be converted to U.S. dollars and remitted to the parent in one year. The prevailing nominal one-year interest rate in New Zealand is 5 percent, while the nominal one-year interest rate in the United States is 9 percent. Zistine's chief executive officer believes that the movement in the New Zealand dollar is highly uncertain over the next year, but his best guess is that the change in its value will be in accordance with the international Fisher effect (IFE). He also believes that interest rate parity holds. He provides this information to three recent finance graduates that he just hired as managers and asks them for their input.

a. The first manager states that due to the parity conditions, the feasibility of the project will be the same whether the cash flows are hedged with a forward contract or are not hedged. Is this manager correct? Explain.

b. The second manager states that the project should not be hedged. Based on the interest rates, the IFE suggests that Zistine Co. will benefit from the future exchange rate movements, so the project will generate a higher NPV if Zistine does not hedge. Is this manager correct? Explain.

c. The third manager states that the project should be hedged because the forward rate contains a premium and, therefore, the forward rate will generate more U.S. dollar cash flows than the expected amount of dollar cash flows if the firm remains unhedged. Is this manager correct? Explain.

26. Accounting for Uncertain Cash Flows

Blustream, Inc., considers a project in which it will sell the use of its technology to firms in Mexico. It already has received orders from Mexican firms that will generate 3 million Mexican pesos (MXP) in revenue at the end of the next year. However, it might also receive a contract to provide this technology to the Mexican government. In this case, it will generate a total of MXP5 million at the end of the next year. It will not know whether it will receive the government order until the end of the year.

Today's spot rate of the peso is $.14. The one-year forward rate is $.12. Blustream expects that the spot rate of the peso will be $.13 one year from now. The only initial outlay will be $300,000 to cover development expenses (regardless of whether the Mexican government purchases the technology). Blustream will pursue the project only if it can satisfy its required rate of return of 18 percent. Ignore possible tax effects. It decides to hedge the maximum amount of revenue that it will receive from the project.

a. Determine the NPV if Blustream receives the government contract.

b. If Blustream does not receive the contract, it will have hedged more than it needed to and will offset the excess forward sales by purchasing pesos in the spot market at the time the forward sale is executed. Determine the NPV of the project assuming that Blustream does not receive the government contract.

c. Now consider an alternative strategy in which Blustream only hedges the minimum peso revenue that it will receive. In this case, any revenue due to the government contract would not be hedged. Determine the NPV based on this alternative strategy and assume that Blustream receives the government contract.

d. If Blustream uses the alternative strategy of only hedging the minimum peso revenue that it will receive, determine the NPV assuming that it does not receive the government contract.

e. If there is a 50 percent chance that Blustream will receive the government contract, would you advise Blustream to hedge the maximum amount or the minimum amount of revenue that it may receive? Explain.

f. Blustream recognizes that it is exposed to exchange rate risk whether it hedges the minimum amount or the maximum amount of revenue it will receive. It considers a new strategy of hedging the minimum amount it will receive with a forward contract and hedging the additional revenue it might receive with a put option on Mexican pesos. The one-year put option has an exercise price of $.125 and a premium of $.01. Determine the NPV if Blustream uses this strategy and receives the government contract. Also, determine the NPV if Blustream uses this strategy and does not receive the government contract. Given that there is a 50 percent probability that Blustream will receive the government contract, would you use this new strategy or the strategy that you selected in question (e)?

27. Capital Budgeting Analysis Wolverine Corp. currently has no existing business in New Zealand but is considering establishing a subsidiary there. The following information has been gathered to assess this project:

■ The initial investment required is $50 million in New Zealand dollars (NZ$). Given the existing spot rate of $.50 per New Zealand dollar, the initial investment in U.S. dollars is $25 million. In addition to the NZ$50 million initial investment for plant and equipment, NZ$20 million is needed for working capital and will be borrowed by the subsidiary from a New Zealand bank. The New Zealand subsidiary will pay interest only on the loan each year, at an interest rate of 14 percent. The loan principal is to be paid in 10 years.

■ The project will be terminated at the end of year 3, when the subsidiary will be sold.

■ The price, demand, and variable cost of the product in New Zealand are as follows:

YEAR	PRICE	DEMAND	VARIABLE COST
1	NZ$500	40,000 units	NZ$30
2	NZ$511	50,000 units	NZ$35
3	NZ$530	60,000 units	NZ$40

■ The fixed costs, such as overhead expenses, are estimated to be NZ$6 million per year. The exchange rate of the New Zealand dollar is expected to be $.52 at the end of year 1, $.54 at the end of year 2, and $.56 at the end of year 3.

■ The New Zealand government will impose an income tax of 30 percent on income. In addition, it will impose a withholding tax of 10 percent on earnings remitted by the subsidiary. The U.S. government will allow a tax credit on the remitted earnings and will not impose any additional taxes.

■ All cash flows received by the subsidiary are to be sent to the parent at the end of each year. The subsidiary will use its working capital to support ongoing operations.

■ The plant and equipment are depreciated over 10 years using the straight-line depreciation method. Because the plant and equipment are initially valued at NZ$50 million, the annual depreciation expense is NZ$5 million.

■ In three years, the subsidiary is to be sold. Wolverine plans to let the acquiring firm assume the existing New Zealand loan. The working capital will not be liquidated but will be used by the acquiring firm that buys the subsidiary. Wolverine expects to receive NZ$52 million after subtracting capital gains taxes. Assume that this amount is not subject to a withholding tax.

■ Wolverine requires a 20 percent rate of return on this project.

a. Determine the net present value of this project. Should Wolverine accept this project?

b. Assume that Wolverine is also considering an alternative financing arrangement in which the parent would invest an additional $10 million to cover the working capital requirements so that the subsidiary would not need the New Zealand loan. If this arrangement is used, the selling price of the subsidiary (after subtracting any capital gains taxes) is expected to be NZ$18 million higher. Is this alternative financing arrangement more feasible for the parent than the original proposal? Explain.

c. From the parent's perspective, would the NPV of this project be more sensitive to exchange rate movements if the subsidiary uses New Zealand financing to cover the working capital or if the parent invests more of its own funds to cover the working capital? Explain.

d. Assume Wolverine used the original financing proposal and that funds are blocked until the subsidiary is sold. The funds to be remitted are reinvested at a rate of 6 percent (after taxes) until the end of year 3. How is the project's NPV affected?

e. What is the break-even salvage value of this project if Wolverine uses the original financing proposal and funds are not blocked?

f. Assume that Wolverine decides to implement the project using the original financing proposal. Also assume that after one year, a New Zealand firm offers Wolverine a price of $27 million after taxes for the subsidiary and that Wolverine's original forecasts for years 2 and 3 have not changed. Compare the present value of the expected cash flows if Wolverine keeps the subsidiary to the selling price. Should Wolverine divest the subsidiary? Explain.

28. Capital Budgeting with Hedging Baxter Co. considers a project with Thailand's government. If it accepts the project, it will definitely receive one lump-sum cash flow of 10 million Thai baht in five years. The spot rate of the Thai baht is presently $.03. The annualized interest rate for a five-year period is 4 percent in the United States and 17 percent in Thailand. Interest rate parity exists. Baxter plans to hedge its cash flows with a forward contract. What is the dollar amount of cash flows that Baxter will receive in five years if it accepts this project?

29. Capital Budgeting and Financing Cantoon Co. is considering the acquisition of a unit from the French government. Its initial outlay would be $4 million. It will reinvest all the earnings in the unit. It expects that at the end of eight years, it will sell the unit for 12 million euros after capital gains taxes are paid. The spot rate of the euro is $1.20 and is used as the forecast of the euro in the future years. Cantoon has no plans to hedge its exposure to exchange rate risk. The annualized U.S. risk-free interest rate is 5 percent regardless of the maturity of the debt, and the annualized risk-free interest rate on euros is 7 percent, regardless of the maturity of the debt. Assume that interest rate parity exists. Cantoon's cost of capital is 20 percent. It plans to use cash to make the acquisition.

a. Determine the NPV under these conditions.

b. Rather than use all cash, Cantoon could partially finance the acquisition. It could obtain a loan of 3 million euros today that would be used to cover a portion of the acquisition. In this case, it would have to pay a lump-sum total of 7 million euros at the end of eight years to repay the loan. There are no interest payments on this debt. This financing deal is structured such that none of the payment is tax deductible. Determine the NPV if Cantoon uses the forward rate instead of the spot rate to forecast the future spot rate of the euro and elects to partially finance the acquisition. You need to derive the eight-year forward rate for this question.

30. Sensitivity of NPV to Conditions Burton Co., based in the United States, considers a project in which it has an initial outlay of $3 million and expects to receive 10 million Swiss francs (SF) in one year. The spot rate of the franc is $.80. Burton Co. decides to purchase put options on Swiss francs with an exercise price of $.78 and a premium of $.02 per unit to hedge its receivables. It has a required rate of return of 20 percent.

a. Determine the net present value of this project for Burton Co. based on the forecast that the Swiss franc will be valued at $.70 at the end of one year.

b. Assume the same information as in part (a), but with the following adjustment. While Burton expected to receive 10 million Swiss francs, assume that there were unexpected weak economic conditions in Switzerland after Burton initiated the project. Consequently, Burton received only 6 million Swiss francs at the end of the year. Also assume that the spot rate of the franc at the end of the year was $.79. Determine the net present value of this project for Burton Co. if these conditions occur.

31. Hedge Decision on a Project Carlotto Co. (a U.S. firm) will definitely receive 1 million British pounds in one year based on a business contract it has with the British government. Like most firms, Carlotto Co. is risk averse and only takes risk when the potential benefits outweigh the risk. It has no other international business and is considering various methods to hedge its exchange rate risk. Assume that interest rate parity exists. Carlotto Co. recognizes that exchange rates are very difficult to forecast with accuracy, but it believes that the one-year forward rate of the pound yields the best forecast of the pound's spot rate in one year. Today the pound's spot rate is $2.00, while the one-year forward rate of the pound is $1.90. Carlotto Co. has determined that a forward hedge is better than alternative forms of hedging. Should Carlotto Co. hedge with a forward contract or should it remain unhedged? Briefly explain.

32. NPV of Partially Hedged Project Sazer Co. (a U.S. firm) is considering a project in which it produces special safety equipment. It will incur an initial outlay of $1 million for the research and development of this equipment. It expects to receive 600,000 euros in one year from selling the products in Portugal where it already does much business. In addition, it also expects to receive 300,000 euros in one year from sales to Spain, but these cash flows are very uncertain because it has no existing business in Spain. Today's spot rate of the euro is $1.50, and the one-year forward rate is $1.50. Sazer expects that the euro's spot rate will be $1.60 in one year. It will pursue the project only if it can satisfy its required rate of return of 24 percent. It decides to hedge all the expected receivables due to business in Portugal but none of the expected receivables due to business in Spain. Estimate the net present value of the project.

33. Project Financing Strategy Konk Co., a U.S. firm, considers a project in which it would build a subsidiary in Belgium that would generate net cash flows of about 10 million euros per year for five years and would remit that amount to the parent each year. Konk Co. has no other international business. It needs about 20 million euros as the initial outlay to establish the subsidiary. It can finance this initial outlay in the following ways and the subsidiary would repay the amount of the investment evenly over the next five years: (a) the parent can borrow dollars from a U.S. bank and convert them to euros, (b) the parent can borrow euros from a Belgian bank, (c) the parent can use its equity (retained earnings from existing business in the United States) and convert the funds into euros, (d) the parent can borrow dollars from a Belgian bank and convert them to euros, and (e) the parent can diversify its financing by obtaining one-fourth of the funds from each of the preceding sources. Assume that there is no cost advantage to any financing method. If Konk Co. wants to use a financing method to minimize its project's exposure to exchange rate risk, which method should it use? Briefly explain.

34. NPV and Financing Louisville Co. is a U.S. firm considering a project in Austria which it has an initial cash outlay of $7 million. Louisville will accept the project only if it can satisfy its required rate of return of 18 percent. The project would definitely generate 2 million euros in one year from sales to a large corporate customer in Austria. In addition, it also expects to receive 4 million euros in one year from sales to other customers in Austria. Louisville's best guess is that the euro's spot rate will be $1.26 in one year. Today, the spot rate of the euro is $1.40, while the one-year forward rate of the euro is $1.34. If Louisville accepts the project, it would hedge all the receivables resulting from sales to the large corporate customer but none of the expected receivables due to expected sales to other customers.

a. Estimate the net present value of the project.

b. Assume that Louisville considers alternative financing for the project in which it would use $5 million cash while the remaining initial outlay would come from borrowing euros. In this case, it would need 1,600,000 euros to repay the loan (principal plus interest) at the end of one year. Assume no tax effects due to this alternative financing. Estimate the NPV of the project under these conditions.

c. Do you think the Louisville's exposure to exchange rate risk due to the project if it uses the alternative financing (explained in part b) is higher, lower, or the same as if it has an initial cash outlay of $7 million (and does not borrow any funds)? Briefly explain.

35. Influence of Tax Laws on Cash Flow to MNC Parents The appendix to this chapter explains how tax laws can affect how much earnings subsidiaries remit to parents. Explain how U.S. tax laws may encourage foreign subsidiaries to reinvest their earnings in their location rather than remit the earnings to the United States.

36. Influence of Tax Laws on MNC's Choice of Home Base Explain how U.S. corporate income tax laws have encouraged some U.S.-based MNCs to consider moving their parent to another country.

Critical Thinking

Influence of Tax Laws on MNC's Choice of Home Base   As explained in the appendix, U.S. tax laws have encouraged U.S.-based MNCs to consider moving their parent to another country in order to reduce their taxes. Write a short essay that presents your opinion of this issue. Should U.S.-based MNCs be allowed to move their parent without consequences? Should the U.S. government lower the corporate income tax rate? For whatever solution you propose, explain the possible adverse effects as well.

Discussion in the Boardroom

This exercise can be found in Appendix E at the back of this textbook.

Running Your Own MNC

This exercise can be found on the *International Financial Management* text companion website. Go to www.cengagebrain.com (students) or www.cengage.com/login (instructors) and search using **ISBN 9781133947837**.

BLADES, INC. CASE

Decision by Blades, Inc., to Invest in Thailand

Because Ben Holt, Blades' chief financial officer, believes the growth potential for the roller blade market in Thailand is very high, he has decided to invest in Thailand. The investment would involve establishing a subsidiary in Bangkok consisting of a manufacturing plant to produce Speedos, Blades' high-quality roller blades. Holt believes that economic conditions in Thailand will be relatively strong in 10 years, when he expects to sell the subsidiary.

Blades will continue exporting to the United Kingdom under an existing agreement with Jogs, Ltd., a British retailer. Furthermore, it will continue its sales in the United States. Under an existing agreement with Entertainment Products, Inc., a Thai retailer, Blades is committed to selling 180,000 pairs of Speedos to the retailer at a fixed price of 4,594 Thai baht per pair. Once operations in Thailand commence, the agreement will last another year, at which time it may be renewed. Thus, during its first year of operations in Thailand, Blades will sell 180,000 pairs of roller blades to Entertainment Products under the existing agreement whether it has operations in the country or not. If it establishes the plant in Thailand, Blades will produce 108,000 of the 180,000 Entertainment Products Speedos at the plant during the last year of the agreement. Therefore, the new subsidiary would need to import 72,000 pairs of Speedos from the United States so that it can accommodate its agreement with Entertainment Products. It will save the equivalent of 300 baht per pair in variable costs on the 108,000 pairs not previously manufactured in Thailand.

Entertainment Products has already declared its willingness to renew the agreement for another three years under identical terms. Because of recent delivery delays, however, it is willing to renew the agreement only if Blades has operations in Thailand. Moreover, if Blades has a subsidiary in Thailand, Entertainment Products will keep renewing the existing agreement as long as Blades operates in Thailand. If the agreement is renewed, Blades expects to sell a total of 300,000 pairs of Speedos annually during its first two years of operation in Thailand to various retailers, including 180,000 pairs to Entertainment Products. After this time, it expects to sell 400,000 pairs annually (including 180,000 to Entertainment Products). If the agreement is not renewed, Blades will be able to sell only 5,000 pairs to Entertainment Products annually but not at a fixed price. Thus if the agreement is not renewed, Blades expects to sell a total of 125,000 pairs of Speedos annually during its first two years of operation in Thailand and 225,000 pairs annually thereafter. Pairs not sold under the contractual agreement with Entertainment Products will be sold for 5,000 Thai baht per pair, because Entertainment Products had required a lower price to compensate it for the risk of being unable to sell the pairs it purchased from Blades.

Holt wishes to analyze the financial feasibility of establishing a subsidiary in Thailand. As a Blades' financial analyst, you have been given the task of analyzing the proposed project. Because future economic conditions in Thailand are highly uncertain, Holt has also asked you to conduct some sensitivity analyses. Fortunately, he has provided most of the information you need to conduct a capital budgeting analysis. This information is detailed here:

- The building and equipment needed will cost 550 million Thai baht. This amount includes additional funds to support working capital.
- The plant and equipment, valued at 300 million baht, will be depreciated using straight-line depreciation. Thus 30 million baht will be depreciated annually for 10 years.
- The variable costs needed to manufacture Speedos are estimated to be 3,500 baht per pair next year.
- Blades' fixed operating expenses, such as administrative salaries, will be 25 million baht next year.
- The current spot exchange rate of the Thai baht is $ .023. Blades expects the baht to depreciate by an average of 2 percent per year for the next 10 years.
- The Thai government will impose a 25 percent tax rate on income and a 10 percent withholding tax on any funds remitted by the subsidiary to Blades. Any earnings remitted to the United States will not be taxed again.
- After 10 years, Blades expects to sell its Thai subsidiary. It expects to sell the subsidiary for about 650 million baht, after considering any capital gains taxes.
- The average annual inflation in Thailand is expected to be 12 percent. Unless prices are contractually fixed, revenue, variable costs, and fixed costs are subject to inflation and are expected to change by the same annual rate as the inflation rate.

Blades could continue its current operations of exporting to and importing from Thailand, which have generated a return of about 20 percent. Blades requires a return of 25 percent on this project in order to justify its investment in Thailand. All excess funds generated by the Thai subsidiary will be remitted to Blades and will be used to support U.S. operations.

Holt has asked you to answer the following questions:

1. Should the sales and the associated costs of 180,000 pairs of roller blades to be sold in Thailand under the existing agreement be included in the capital budgeting analysis to decide whether Blades should establish a subsidiary in Thailand? Should the sales resulting from a renewed agreement be included? Why or why not?

2. Using a spreadsheet, conduct a capital budgeting analysis for the proposed project, assuming that Blades renews the agreement with Entertainment Products. Should Blades establish a subsidiary in Thailand under these conditions?

3. Using a spreadsheet, conduct a capital budgeting analysis for the proposed project assuming that Blades does not renew the agreement with Entertainment Products. Should Blades establish a subsidiary in Thailand under these conditions? Should Blades renew the agreement with Entertainment Products?

4. Because future economic conditions in Thailand are uncertain, Holt would like to know how critical the salvage value is in the alternative you think is most feasible.

5. The future value of the baht is highly uncertain. Under a worst-case scenario, the baht may depreciate by as much as 5 percent annually. Revise your spreadsheet to illustrate how this would affect Blades' decision to establish a subsidiary in Thailand. (Use the capital budgeting analysis you have identified as the most favorable from questions 2 and 3 to answer this question.)

SMALL BUSINESS DILEMMA

Multinational Capital Budgeting by the Sports Exports Company

Jim Logan, owner of the Sports Exports Company, has been pleased with his success in the United Kingdom. He began his business by producing footballs and exporting them to the United Kingdom. While American-style football is still not nearly as popular in the United Kingdom as it is in the United States, his firm controls the market in the United Kingdom. Logan is considering an application of the same business in Mexico. He would produce the footballs in the United States and export them to a distributor of sporting goods in Mexico, who would sell the footballs to retail stores. The distributor likely would want to pay for the product each month in Mexican pesos. Logan would need to hire one full-time employee in the United States to produce the footballs. He would also need to lease one warehouse.

1. Describe the capital budgeting steps that would be necessary to determine whether this proposed project is feasible, as related to this specific situation.

2. Explain why there is uncertainty surrounding the cash flows of this project.

INTERNET/EXCEL EXERCISES

Assume that you invested equity to establish a project in Portugal in January about seven years ago. At the time the project began, you could have supported it with a seven-year loan either in dollars or in euros. If you borrowed U.S. dollars, your annual loan payment (including principal) would have been $2.5 million. If you borrowed euros, your annual loan payment (including principal) would have been 2 million euros. The project has generated 5 million euros per year in revenue.

1. Use an Excel spreadsheet to determine the dollar net cash flows (after making the debt payment) that you would have received at the end of each of the last seven years if you partially financed the project by borrowing dollars.

2. Determine the standard deviation of the dollar net cash flows that you would have received at the end of each of the last seven years if you partially financed the project by borrowing dollars.

3. Re-estimate the dollar net cash flows and the standard deviation of the dollar net cash flows if you partially financed the project by borrowing euros. (You can obtain the end-of-year exchange rate of the euro for the last seven years at www.oanda.com or similar websites.) Are the project's net cash flows more volatile if you borrowed dollars or euros? Explain your results.

ONLINE ARTICLES WITH REAL-WORLD EXAMPLES

Find a recent article online that describes an actual international finance application or a real-world example about a specific MNC's actions that reinforces one or more of the concepts covered in this chapter.

If your class has an online component, your professor may ask you to post your summary there and provide the web link of the article so that other students can access it. If your class is live, your professor may ask you to summarize your application in class. Your professor may assign specific students to complete this assignment for this chapter or may allow any students to do the assignment on a volunteer basis.

For recent online articles and real-world examples applied to this chapter, consider using the following search terms (and include the current year as a search term to ensure that the online articles are recent).

1. policy for repatriating earnings
2. tax on foreign earnings
3. company AND international expansion
4. Inc. AND international expansion
5. foreign subsidiary AND expansion
6. [name of an MNC] AND international project
7. Inc. AND international project
8. [name of an MNC] AND foreign project
9. company AND foreign project
10. Inc. AND foreign project

Incorporating International Tax Law in Multinational Capital Budgeting

Tax laws can vary among countries in many ways, but any type of tax causes an MNC's after-tax cash flows to differ from its before-tax cash flows. To estimate the future cash flows that are to be generated by a proposed foreign project (such as the establishment of a new subsidiary or the acquisition of a foreign firm), MNCs must first estimate the taxes that they will incur due to the foreign project. This appendix provides a general background on some of the more important international tax characteristics that an MNC must consider when assessing foreign projects. Financial managers do not necessarily have to be international tax experts because they may be able to rely on the MNC's international tax department or on independent tax consultants for guidance. Nevertheless, they should at least be aware of international tax characteristics that can affect the cash flows of a foreign project and recognize how those characteristics can vary among the countries where foreign projects are considered.

Variation in Tax Laws among Countries

Each country generates tax revenue in different ways. The United States relies on corporate and individual income taxes for federal revenue. Other countries may depend more on a *value-added tax* (VAT) or excise taxes. Because each country has its own philosophy on whom to tax and how much, it is not surprising that the tax treatment of corporations differs among countries. Because each country has a unique tax system and tax rates, MNCs need to recognize the various tax provisions of each country where they consider investing in a foreign project. The more important tax characteristics of a country to be considered in an MNC's international tax assessment are (1) corporate income taxes, (2) withholding taxes, (3) personal and excise tax rates, (4) provision for carrybacks and carryforwards, (5) tax treaties, (6) tax credits, and (7) taxes on income from intercompany transactions. A discussion of each characteristic follows.

Corporate Income Taxes

In general, countries impose taxes on corporate income generated within their borders even if the parents of those corporations are based in other countries. Each country has its unique corporate income tax laws. The United States, for example, taxes the worldwide income of U.S. "persons," a term that includes corporations. As a general rule, however, foreign income of a foreign subsidiary of a U.S. company is not taxed until it is transferred to the U.S. parent by payment of dividends or a liquidation distribution. This is the concept of *deferral*.

An MNC planning direct foreign investment in foreign countries must determine how the anticipated earnings from a foreign project will be affected. Tax rates imposed on income earned by businesses (including foreign subsidiaries of MNCs) or income remitted to a parent are shown in Exhibit 14A.1 for several countries. The tax rates may be lower than what is shown for corporations that have relatively low levels of earnings. This exhibit shows the extent to which corporate income tax rates can vary among host countries and illustrates why MNCs closely assess the tax guidelines in any foreign country where they consider conducting direct foreign investment. Given differences in tax deductions, depreciation, business subsidies, and other factors, corporate tax differentials cannot be measured simply by comparing quoted tax rates across countries.

Corporate tax rates can also differ within a country depending on whether the entity is a domestic corporation. Also, if an unregistered foreign corporation is considered to have a permanent establishment in a country, it may be subject to that country's tax laws on income earned within its borders. Generally, a permanent establishment includes an office or fixed place of business or a specified kind of agency (independent agents are normally excluded) through which active and continuous business is conducted. In some cases, the tax depends on the industry or on the form of business used (e.g., corporation, branch, partnership).

Exhibit 14A.1 Comparison of Tax Characteristics among Countries

COUNTRY	CORPORATE INCOME TAX	COUNTRY	CORPORATE INCOME TAX
Argentina	35%	Israel	27
Australia	30	Italy	31
Austria	25	Japan	38
Belgium	34	Korea	24
Brazil	34	Malaysia	25
Canada	26	Mexico	30
Chile	20	Netherlands	25
China	25	New Zealand	28
Czech Republic	19	Singapore	17
France	33	Spain	30
Germany	30	Switzerland	18
Hong Kong	17	Taiwan	17
Hungary	19	United Kingdom	23
India	34	United States	40
Indonesia	25	Venezuela	34
Ireland	12		

Source: KPMG, 2014. *The numbers provided are for illustrative purposes only, as the actual tax rate may depend on specific characteristics of the MNC.*

Withholding Taxes

The following types of payments by an MNC's subsidiary are commonly subject to a withholding tax by the host government. (1) A subsidiary may remit a portion of its earnings, referred to as *dividends*, to its parent because the parent is the shareholder of the subsidiary. (2) The subsidiary may pay interest to the parent or to other nonresident debt holders from which it received loans. (3) The subsidiary may make payments to the parent or to other nonresident firms in return for the use of patents (such as technology) or other rights. The payment of dividends reduces the amount of reinvestment by the subsidiary in the host country. The payments by the subsidiary to nonresident firms to cover interest or use of patents reflect expenses by the subsidiary, which will normally reduce its taxable income and therefore will reduce the corporate income taxes paid to the host government. Thus withholding taxes may be a way for host governments to tax MNCs that make payments for interest or use of patents to nonresident firms.

Because withholding taxes imposed on the subsidiary can reduce the funds remitted by the subsidiary to the parent, the withholding taxes must be accounted for in a capital budgeting analysis conducted by the parent. As with corporate tax rates, the withholding tax rate can vary substantially among countries.

Reducing Exposure to Withholding Taxes   Withholding taxes can be reduced by income tax treaties (discussed shortly). Because of tax treaties between some countries, the withholding taxes may be lower when the MNC is based in a county participating in the treaties.

If the host country government of a particular subsidiary imposes a high withholding tax on subsidiary earnings remitted to the parent, then the MNC may instruct the subsidiary to temporarily refrain from remitting earnings and to reinvest them in the host country instead. As an alternative approach, the MNC may instruct the subsidiary to set up a research and development division that will enhance subsidiaries elsewhere. The main purpose of this strategy is to efficiently use the funds abroad when the funds cannot be sent to the parent without excessive taxation. Because international tax laws can influence the timing of the transfer of funds to the parent, they affect the timing of cash flows on proposed foreign projects. Therefore, the international tax implications must be understood before the cash flows of a foreign project can be estimated.

Personal and Excise Tax Rates

An MNC is more likely to be concerned with corporate tax rates and withholding tax rates than individual tax rates because its cash flows are directly affected by the taxes incurred. However, a country's individual tax rates can indirectly affect an MNC's cash flows because the MNC may have to pay higher wages to employees in countries where personal income is taxed at a relatively high rate (such as many European countries). In addition, a country's value-added tax or excise tax may affect cash flows to be generated from a foreign project because it may make the products less competitive on a global basis (reducing the expected quantity of products to be sold).

Provision for Carrybacks and Carryforwards

Negative earnings from operations can often be carried back or forward to offset earnings in other years. The laws pertaining to these so-called **net operating loss carrybacks** and **carryforwards** can vary among countries. An MNC generally does not plan to generate negative earnings in foreign countries. If negative earnings do occur, however, it is desirable to be able to use them to offset positive earnings in other years. Most foreign countries do not allow negative earnings to be carried back but allow some flexibility in carrying losses forward. Because many foreign projects are expected to result in negative earnings in the early years, the tax laws for the country of concern will affect the future tax deductions resulting from these losses and will therefore affect the future cash flows of the project.

Tax Treaties

Countries often establish income tax treaties, whereby one partner will reduce its taxes by granting a credit for taxes imposed on corporations operating within the other treaty partner's tax jurisdiction. Income tax treaties help corporations avoid exposure to double taxation. Some treaties apply to taxes paid on income earned by MNCs in foreign countries. Other treaties apply to withholding taxes imposed by the host country on foreign earnings that are remitted to the parent.

Without such treaties, subsidiary earnings could be taxed by the host country and then again by the parent's country when received by the parent. To the extent that the parent uses some of these earnings to provide cash dividends for shareholders, triple taxation could result (because the dividend income is also taxed at the shareholder level). Because income tax treaties reduce taxes on earnings generated by MNCs, they help stimulate direct foreign investment. Many foreign projects that are perceived as feasible would not be feasible without income tax treaties because the expected cash flows would be reduced by excessive taxation.

Tax Credits

Even without income tax treaties, an MNC may be allowed a credit for income and withholding taxes paid in another country against taxes owed in the home country if it meets certain requirements. Like income tax treaties, tax credits help to avoid double taxation and stimulate direct foreign investment.

Tax credit policies vary somewhat among countries, but they generally work like this. Consider a U.S.-based MNC subject to a U.S. tax rate of 35 percent. Assume that a foreign subsidiary of this corporation has generated earnings taxed at less than 35 percent by the host country's government. The earnings remitted to the parent from the subsidiary will be subject to an additional amount of U.S. tax to bring the total tax up to 35 percent. From the parent's point of view, the tax on its subsidiary's remitted earnings is 35 percent overall, so it does not matter whether the host country of the subsidiary or the United States receives most of the taxes. From the perspective of the governments of these two countries, however, the allocation of taxes is very important. If a subsidiary is established in a foreign country that taxes income at nearly 35 percent, that country can generate large tax revenues from income earned by the subsidiary. The host country receives the tax revenues at the expense of the parent's country (the United States, in this example).

The corporate income tax rate in a foreign country could exceed 35 percent, although that is not common. In this case, the United States generally does not impose any additional taxes on earnings remitted to a U.S. parent by foreign subsidiaries in that country. In fact, under current law, the United States allows the excess foreign tax to be credited against other taxes owed by the parent on the same type of income generated by subsidiaries in other lower-tax countries. This suggests that some host countries could charge abnormally high corporate income tax rates to foreign subsidiaries and still attract direct foreign investment. If the MNC in our example has subsidiaries located in some countries with low corporate income taxes, then the U.S. tax on earnings remitted to the

U.S. parent will normally bring the total tax up to 35 percent. However, credits against excessive income taxes by high-tax countries on foreign subsidiaries could offset these taxes that would otherwise be paid to the U.S. government. Thus tax credits could make an MNC more willing to invest in a project in a country with high tax rates. However, U.S. tax laws require corporations to allocate expenses against foreign source income, which reduces the parent's ability to capitalize on tax credits from high-tax jurisdictions.

Basic information on a country's current taxes may not be sufficient for determining the tax effects of a particular foreign project because tax incentives may be offered in particular circumstances and tax rates can change over time. Consider an MNC that plans to establish a manufacturing plant in Country Y rather than Country X. Assume that while many economic characteristics favor Country X, the current tax rates in Country Y are lower. However, whereas tax rates in Country X have been historically stable and are expected to continue that way, they have been changing every few years in Country Y. In this case, the MNC must assess the future uncertainty of the tax rates. It cannot treat the current tax rate of Country Y as a constant when conducting a capital budgeting analysis. Instead, it must consider possible changes in the tax rates over time and, based on these possibilities, determine whether Country Y's projected tax advantages *over time* sufficiently outweigh the advantages of Country X. One approach to account for possible changes in the tax rates is to use sensitivity analysis, which measures the sensitivity of the net present value (NPV) of after-tax cash flows to various possible tax changes over time. For each tax scenario, a different NPV is projected. By accounting for each possible tax scenario, the MNC can develop a distribution of possible NPVs that may occur and can then compare these for each country.

Two critical and broadly defined functions are necessary to determine how international tax laws affect the cash flows of a foreign project. The first is to be aware of all the current (and possible future) tax laws that exist for each country where the MNC does (or plans to do) business. The second is to take the information generated from the first function and apply it to forecasted earnings and remittances to determine the taxes, so that the proposed project's cash flows can be estimated.

Taxes on Income from Intercompany Transactions

Many of an MNC's proposed foreign projects will involve intercompany transactions. For example, a U.S.-based MNC may consider acquiring a foreign firm that will produce and deliver supplies to its U.S. subsidiaries. Under these conditions, the MNC must use transfer pricing, which involves pricing the transactions between two entities (such as subsidiaries) of the same corporation. When MNCs consider new foreign projects, they must incorporate their transfer pricing to properly estimate cash flows that will be generated from these projects. This means that, before the feasibility of a foreign project can be determined, transfer pricing decisions must be made on any anticipated intercompany transactions that would result from the new project. Multinational corporations are subject to certain guidelines on transfer pricing, but they usually have some flexibility and tend to use a transfer pricing policy that will minimize taxes while satisfying the guidelines.

EXAMPLE   Oakland Corp. has established two subsidiaries to capitalize on low production costs. One of these subsidiaries (called Hitax Sub) is located in a country whose government imposes a 30 percent tax rate on before-tax earnings. Hitax Sub produces partially finished products and sends them to the other subsidiary (called Lotax Sub) where the final assembly takes place. The host government of Lotax Sub imposes a 10 percent tax on before-tax earnings. To simplify the example, assume that no earnings are to be

Exhibit 14A.2   Impact of Transfer Pricing Adjustment on Pro Forma Earnings and Taxes: Oakland Corp. (in Thousands)

	ORIGINAL ESTIMATES		
	HITAX SUB	LOTAX SUB	COMBINED*
Sales	$100,000	$150,000	$250,000
Less: Cost of goods sold	50,000	100,000	150,000
Gross profit	50,000	50,000	100,000
Less: Operating expenses	20,000	20,000	40,000
Earnings before interest and taxes	30,000	30,000	60,000
Interest expense	5,000	5,000	10,000
Earnings before taxes	25,000	25,000	50,000
Taxes (30% for Hitax and 10% for Lotax)	7,500	2,500	10,000
Earnings after taxes	$17,500	$22,500	$40,000
	REVISED ESTIMATES BASED ON ADJUSTING TRANSFER PRICING POLICY		
	HITAX SUB	LOTAX SUB	COMBINED
Sales	$80,000	$150,000	$230,000
Less: Cost of goods sold	50,000	80,000	130,000
Gross profit	30,000	70,000	100,000
Less: Operating expenses	20,000	20,000	40,000
Earnings before interest and taxes	10,000	50,000	60,000
Interest expense	5,000	5,000	10,000
Earnings before taxes	5,000	45,000	50,000
Taxes (30% for Hitax and 10% for Lotax)	1,500	4,500	6,000
Earnings after taxes	$3,500	$40,500	$44,000

*The combined numbers are shown here for illustrative purposes only and do not reflect the firm's official consolidated financial statements. When consolidating sales for financial statements, intercompany transactions (between subsidiaries) would be eliminated. This example is intended simply to illustrate how total taxes paid by subsidiaries are lower when transfer pricing is structured to shift some gross profit from a high-tax subsidiary to a low-tax subsidiary.

remitted to the parent in the near future. Given this information, pro forma income statements would be as shown in the top part of Exhibit 14A.2 for Hitax Sub (second column), Lotax Sub (third column), and the combined subsidiaries (last column). The income statement items are reported in U.S. dollars to more easily illustrate how a revised transfer pricing policy can affect earnings and cash flows.

The sales level shown for Hitax Sub matches the cost of goods sold for Lotax Sub, indicating that all Hitax Sub sales are to Lotax Sub. The additional expenses incurred by Lotax Sub to complete the product are classified as operating expenses.

Notice from Exhibit 14A.2 that both subsidiaries have the same earnings before taxes. Yet, because of the different tax rates, Hitax Sub's after-tax income is $5 million less than Lotax Sub's. If Oakland Corp. can revise its transfer pricing, its combined earnings after taxes will be increased. To illustrate, suppose that the price of products sent from Hitax Sub to Lotax Sub is reduced, causing Hitax Sub's sales to decline from $100 million to $80 million. This also reduces Lotax Sub's cost of goods sold by $20 million. The revised pro forma income statement resulting from the change in the transfer pricing policy is shown in the bottom part of Exhibit 14A.2. The two subsidiaries' forecasted earnings before taxes now differ by

$40 million, although the combined amount has not changed. Because earnings have been shifted from Hitax Sub to Lotax Sub, the total tax payments are reduced to $6 million from the original estimate of $10 million. Thus the corporate taxes imposed on earnings are now forecasted to be $4 million lower than originally expected. ●

It should be mentioned that possible adjustments in an MNC's transfer pricing policies may be limited because host governments may restrict such practices when the intent is to avoid taxes. Transactions between subsidiaries of a firm are supposed to be priced using the principle of "arm's-length" transactions. That is, the price should be set as if the buyer is unrelated to the seller and should not be adjusted simply to shift tax burdens. Nevertheless, there is some flexibility on transfer pricing policies, enabling MNCs from all countries to attempt to establish policies that are within legal limits, but also reduce tax burdens. Even if the transfer price reflects the "fair" price that would normally be charged in the market, one subsidiary can still charge another for technology transfers, research and development expenses, or other forms of overhead expenses incurred. The actual mechanics of international transfer pricing go far beyond the example provided here. The U.S. laws in this area are particularly strict, requiring that MNCs be able to justify their transfer pricing policies with reasons unrelated to the tax burden. For example, if the parent charges its high-tax subsidiary a high price for a particular service (such as research and development provided by the parent) and charges its low-tax subsidiary a lower price for a similar service, the parent must be able to justify the difference with a reason that is not related to taxes.

Despite such requirements, there is substantial evidence that MNCs based in numerous countries use transfer pricing strategies to reduce their taxes. There are various ways that MNCs can justify increasing prices at one subsidiary and reducing them at another. Moreover, transfer pricing restrictions can be circumvented in several ways. Various fees can be implemented for services, research and development, royalties, and administrative duties. Although the fees may be imposed to shift earnings and minimize taxes, they have the effect of distorting the actual performance of each subsidiary. To correct for any distortion, the MNC can use a centralized approach to account for the transfer pricing strategy when assessing the performance of each subsidiary.

Influence of Tax Laws on MNCs

Tax laws can have additional effects on MNCs and may influence not only an MNC's treatment of its subsidiaries' earnings but also its choice of a home base.

Influence of Tax Laws on Cash Flow to MNC Parents

The tax laws on remitted earnings have a major impact on the amount of earnings that subsidiaries remit to parents. The parents of many U.S.-based MNCs such as Google and Microsoft commonly allow their subsidiaries to reinvest the earnings locally rather than remit them, because the remitted earnings would often be subject to some degree of corporate taxation by the U.S. government. The simplest example is the case in which the foreign subsidiaries were subject to a very low corporate income tax in the foreign country, which causes the U.S. government to tax the remitted earnings in order to bring the total corporate income taxes of the MNC to the level required by U.S. law. The MNC can avoid this tax as long as the subsidiaries do not remit the earnings back to the United States.

Some politicians criticize the U.S. tax system because it discourages subsidiaries from remitting their earnings back to their U.S.-based parents. These critics suggest that the

U.S. tax system should implement a **territorial tax system**, in which the taxes imposed are based solely on the country where the corporate income is earned. Under this system, subsidiaries of U.S.-based MNCs would pay corporate income taxes where they are based (as they do now), but remitted earnings would not be taxed by the U.S. government. Some countries apply this type of tax law, and the parents of MNCs based in those countries do not have to pay additional taxes when receiving remitted earnings from their respective foreign subsidiaries. For this reason, remitted earnings tend to flow back to the parents of MNCs in these countries more quickly than remitted earnings flow back to parents of MNCs based in the United States. However, an obvious concern raised by a territorial tax system is that it would encourage U.S.-based MNCs to move their operations to whatever country had the lowest corporate income tax rates.

Influence of Tax Laws on MNC's Choice of Home Base (Country)

Because of the relatively high corporate tax rates in the United States, some U.S.-based MNCs have moved their parent to a home base in another country where taxes are lower. These MNCs argue that by moving to a country with lower tax rates, they can increase their after-tax cash flows and therefore increase their stock valuations for their shareholders. One method of achieving this goal is for the U.S. firm to engage in a merger with a firm based in a different country and designate the other firm as the parent of the newly merged corporation. Just as individuals search for strategies to reduce their taxes, so do MNCs. Recently, U.S. government officials have been looking for a way to prevent MNCs from engaging in this behavior. The U.S. government could lower its corporate tax rate to encourage MNCs to remain in the United States, but individuals would also demand lower income tax rates as well. Such a solution might be possible only if the U.S. government is willing to reduce its expenditures.

15

International Corporate Governance and Control

CHAPTER OBJECTIVES

The specific objectives of this chapter are to:

- describe the common forms of corporate governance by MNCs,

- explain how MNCs use corporate control as a form of governance,

- identify the factors that are considered when valuing a foreign target,

- describe the process of valuing a foreign target,

- explain why valuations of a foreign target firm vary among MNCs that consider corporate control strategies,

- identify other types of international corporate control decisions, and

- explain how some corporate control decisions can be evaluated in a real options framework.

When multinational corporations (MNCs) expand internationally, they are subject to various types of agency problems. Many of the agency problems occur because incentives for managers of the parent or its subsidiaries are not properly structured to ensure that managers focus on maximizing the value of the firm (and therefore shareholder wealth). International corporate governance and corporate control can ensure that managerial goals are aligned with those of shareholders.

15-1 International Corporate Governance

Most MNCs use a number of methods to ensure that their foreign subsidiary managers own shares of the firm in order to align their interests with those of the corporation. They may offer bonuses in the form of stock that cannot be sold for a few years, which encourages the managers of foreign subsidiaries to focus on the goal of maximizing the MNC's stock price when making decisions for the subsidiaries. However, because the stock ownership by high-level managers of an MNC is typically limited, managers' first priority in decision making may be to protect their jobs even if doing so reduces the stock price. For example, they might make decisions that will expand their subsidiary in order to justify their position, even if these decisions adversely affect the value of the MNC overall. Furthermore, expansion might increase their responsibility and potentially lead to a promotion. Thus governance may be needed to ensure that managerial decisions serve shareholder interests. Forms of governance of MNCs are described next.

15-1a Governance by Board Members

The board of directors is responsible for appointing the firm's high-level managers, including the chief executive officer (CEO). It oversees major decisions of the firm such as restructuring and expansion, and it is supposed to make sure that key management decisions are in the best interest of shareholders. However, boards of MNCs are not always effective at governance.

First, some boards of directors allow the firm's CEO to serve as the chair of the board, which may reduce the board's ability to control management because the chair may have sufficient power to control the board. For example, the chair normally sets the agenda for a board meeting and may establish the process by which decisions are made. Second, boards typically include insiders (managers working for the firm) who tend to prefer policies that favor managerial power. Boards may be more effective if they contain a larger number of outside board members that do not work for the firm. Third, board members who are employees of a foreign subsidiary may attempt to make decisions that maximize the benefits to the subsidiary and not to the MNC overall.

15-1b Governance by Institutional Investors

A large proportion of many publicly traded firms' shares of stock are held by institutional investors such as pension funds, mutual funds, hedge funds, and insurance companies. Although institutional investors together may own a large number of a firm's shares, a single institutional investor rarely owns more than 1 or 2 percent of the shares. Thus institutional investors have limited ability to influence a firm's management. If investors believe that a firm's management is weak, they will sell their shares, but that is not likely to change the firm's policies.

The ability or willingness to enforce governance varies among types of institutional investors. For example, some public pension funds and mutual funds may plan to hold the stock that they purchase for a long time. Thus they do not actively govern the companies in which they invest.

In contrast, hedge funds frequently use an investment strategy of investing in companies that have performed poorly (and therefore have a low stock price) but have the potential to improve. The hedge funds will actively govern the companies in which they invest because they benefit from their investments only if these companies improve their performance.

Private equity firms, which pool money from institutional investors such as pension funds or insurance companies, often use the money to invest in privately held companies. However, they participate in international governance because many MNCs are privately held. In addition, private equity funds commonly invest in companies based in foreign countries. They may invest in a portion of a business and offer advice to management, or they may even take over the management of a business. Private equity firms attempt to improve the operations of the companies in which they invest while they have an equity investment in those companies. They typically invest in a business for a period of four to eight years. They sell their equity interest to other investors after they have improved the management and increased the value of the companies.

Private equity firms have a natural incentive to invest in companies, particularly in countries where companies are less efficient and poorly managed. Assuming government regulations allow for entrance, the private equity firms can purchase those companies at a low price, improve their management, and sell their shares for a profit. In this way, private equity firms help to improve the level of international governance.

15-1c Governance by Shareholder Activists

Some institutional investors or individual shareholders of publicly traded MNCs are called *blockholders* because they hold a large proportion (such as at least 5 percent) of the firm's stock. Blockholders often become shareholder activists; that is, they take actions to influence management. Investors do not have to be blockholders to become activists, but there is more motivation for investors to be activists if they have a lot at stake and can possibly influence management with their voting power. If shareholder activists dislike a new policy by management, they may contact the board and voice their opinion. They may also engage in proxy contests and attempt to change the composition of the board of directors. They may even attempt to serve on the board if they have sufficient support from other shareholders. In addition, they may file lawsuits against the firm in an attempt to influence managerial decisions.

15-2 International Corporate Control

Even with these various forms of governance, managers may still be able to make decisions that serve themselves rather than shareholders. To the extent that a firm's decisions are focused on serving its managers rather than shareholders, its stock price should be relatively low as a reflection of these poor decisions. This creates an opportunity for another MNC to take over the mismanaged firm at a low price in the so-called international market for corporate control and then restructure it by removing the inefficient managers.

A firm that is subjected to a takeover attempt is referred to as a *target*. The target may be contacted by another firm that wants to engage in discussions regarding a takeover. If the target declines this request, the other firm might still acquire it by engaging in a tender offer whereby it stands willing to purchase shares from the target's shareholders. The existing shareholders of a mismanaged firm might be very willing to sell their shares if the offer price is reasonable. Even if a firm's managers are attempting to serve their shareholders, it could still become a target if it has not reached its full potential.

15-2a Motives for International Acquisitions

Many international acquisitions are motivated by the desire to increase global market share or to capitalize on economies of scale through global consolidation. Some MNCs may have a comparative advantage in terms of their technology or image in a foreign market where competition is not as intense as in their domestic market. Many U.S.-based MNCs including Oracle Corp., Google, Inc., and Dow Chemical Co. have engaged in international acquisitions. Announcements of acquisitions of foreign targets lead to neutral or slightly favorable stock price effects for acquirers, on average, whereas acquisitions of domestic targets generally lead to negative effects. The stock price of a publicly traded foreign target almost always rises considerably at the time of the acquisition, which is attributed to the large premium that the acquirer pays to obtain control of the target.

Multinational corporations may view international acquisitions as a better form of direct foreign investment (DFI) than establishing a new subsidiary. However, there are distinct differences between these two forms of DFI. Through an international acquisition, the firm can immediately expand its international business because the target is already in place. An international acquisition may also enable a firm to obtain access to new technology.

EXAMPLE

Both Google and Facebook recently acquired technology start-up companies in India. Google acquired Imperium, a cyber security firm with offices in Bangalore, India, and in California. Facebook purchased Bangalore-based Little Eye Labs, which builds mobile app analysis tools. Bangalore is the center of India's information technology industry and provides technology services for U.S. firms, mostly on an outsourcing basis. ●

An international acquisition usually generates quicker and larger cash flows than the establishment of a new subsidiary, but it also requires a larger initial outlay. International acquisitions also necessitate the integration of the parent's management style with that of the foreign target.

WEB

www.worldbank.org
Data on socioeconomic development and performance indicators as well as links to statistical and project-oriented publications and analyses.

15-2b Trends in International Acquisitions

Traditionally, MNCs in various countries tend to focus on specific geographic regions and use stocks or cash to make their purchases depending on shareholder power.

Multinational corporations based in the United States acquire more firms in the United Kingdom than in any other country. British and Canadian firms are the most common acquirers of companies in the United States. In general, Europe has been a popular target for U.S. firms, especially since many European countries adopted the euro and allowed easier entry for firms that want to do business there.

When a U.S. firm attempts to acquire a target firm in a country where shareholder rights are weak, it usually uses its own stock as payment. The target shareholders are willing to accept the stock as payment because they will now own shares in a company in which they enjoy stronger shareholder rights. However, if a firm in a country where shareholder rights are weak wants to acquire a U.S. firm, it would likely need to use cash because the shareholders of the target firm would not want to hold stock of a firm where shareholder rights are weak.

International acquisitions have generally increased over time. However, the pace is typically reduced when global economic conditions are weak, because MNCs tend to limit their expansion during such periods. The stock valuations of MNCs are low when economic conditions are weak, so they would not want to issue additional stock at that time to pay for acquisitions.

15-2c Barriers to International Corporate Control

The international market for corporate control is limited by barriers that a target firm or its host government can implement to protect against a takeover.

Anti-Takeover Amendments Implemented by Target   The target may implement an anti-takeover amendment that requires a large proportion of shareholders to approve the takeover. This type of amendment could help a firm prevent a takeover.

Poison Pills Implemented by Target   An alternative method of protecting against a takeover is a poison pill, which grants special rights to managers or shareholders under specified conditions. For example, a poison pill might grant existing shareholders of the target additional stock if a takeover is initiated. A poison pill does not require the shareholders' approval, so it can be easily implemented by the target firm. In some cases, a poison pill is used not to prevent a takeover but rather as a bargaining tool by the target firm. Because a poison pill can make it very expensive for another firm to acquire the target, it essentially forces the MNC to negotiate with the target's management.

In most cases, the target's management and board will be unwilling to give up control unless an MNC is willing to pay a premium (above the existing share price) of perhaps 30 to 50 percent. For example, if a firm wants to acquire a target that has a current market value of $100 million (based on today's stock price), it may have to pay $130 to $150 million to obtain control of the target. When an MNC must pay such a high price for the target, its board may decide that the takeover cannot be justified.

Alternatively, an MNC might pursue the takeover anyway, which normally causes some of its shareholders to sell their shares because they believe the MNC is paying too much for the target. Consequently, the share price of the MNC could decline in response to its announced intentions to take over a target, especially when the premium that it plans to pay is very high.

Host Government Barriers   Governments of some countries restrict foreign firms from taking control of local firms, or they may allow foreign ownership of local firms only if specific guidelines are satisfied. For example, foreign firms might be allowed to acquire a local firm only if they retain all its employees. If the local firm was an appealing takeover target because it was inefficient and could be acquired at a low price, then the inability to reduce its employment level means the foreign acquirer may be prevented from improving the target. Thus this type of restriction could serve as a major barrier to international corporate control.

15-2d Model for Valuing a Foreign Target

WEB

www.cia.gov
Provides a link to the
World Factbook, which
has valuable information
about countries that
would be considered by
MNCs seeking to acquire
foreign targets.

Recall from Chapter 1 that the value of an MNC is based on the present value of expected cash flows to be received. An MNC that engages in restructuring alters the structure of its assets, which will ultimately affect the present value of its cash flows. For example, if it acquires a company it will incur a large initial outlay this year, but its expected annual cash flows will now be larger. An MNC's decision to acquire a foreign company is similar to the decision to invest in other projects in that it is based on a comparison of benefits and costs as measured by net present value (as explained in Chapter 14). From the MNC's perspective, the foreign target's value can be estimated as the present value of cash flows that the MNC would receive from the target.

The MNC would consider investing in the target only if the estimated present value of the cash flows it would receive from the target over time exceeds the initial outlay necessary to purchase the target. Thus capital budgeting analysis can be used to determine whether a firm should be acquired. The net present value of a company from the acquiring firm's perspective (NPV_a) is

$$\text{NPV}_a = -\text{IO}_a + \sum_{t=1}^{n} \frac{\text{CF}_{a,t}}{(1+k)^t} + \frac{\text{SV}_a}{(1+k)^n}$$

where

IO_a = initial outlay needed by the acquiring firm to acquire the target

$\text{CF}_{a,t}$ = cash flow to be generated by the target for the acquiring firm

k = required rate of return on the acquisition of the target

SV_a = salvage value of the target (expected selling price of the target at a point in the future)

n = time when the target will be sold by the acquiring firm

Estimating the Initial Outlay The initial outlay reflects the price to be paid for the target. When firms acquire publicly traded foreign targets, they commonly pay premiums of at least 30 percent above the prevailing stock price of the target in order to gain ownership. This premium must be accounted for when deriving an accurate estimate of the estimated initial outlay.

For an acquisition to be successful, the acquirer must substantially improve the target's cash flows so that it can overcome the large premium it pays for the target. The capital budgeting analysis of a foreign target must also account for the exchange rate of concern. The dollar initial outlay (IO_a) needed by the U.S. firm is determined by the acquisition price in foreign currency units (IO_f) and the spot rate of the foreign currency (S):

$$\text{IO}_a = \text{IO}_f(S)$$

Estimating the Cash Flows The dollar amount of cash flows to the U.S. firm is calculated as the foreign currency cash flows ($\text{CF}_{f,t}$) per period remitted to the United States multiplied by the spot rate at that time (S_t):

$$\text{CF}_{a,t} = (\text{CF}_{f,t})S_t$$

The estimated foreign currency cash flows that are to be converted must account for any taxes or blocked-funds restrictions imposed by the host government. Some international acquisitions backfire because the MNC overestimates the net cash flows of the target. That is, the MNC's managers are excessively optimistic when estimating the target's future cash flows, which leads them to make acquisitions that are not feasible.

The dollar amount of salvage value to the U.S. firm is determined by the salvage value in foreign currency units (SV_f) and the spot rate at the time (period n) when it is converted to dollars (S_n) as follows:

$$SV_a = (SV_f) S_n$$

Estimating the NPV The net present value of a foreign target can be derived by substituting the equalities just described into the capital budgeting equation:

$$NPV_a = -IO_a + \sum_{t=1}^{n} \frac{CF_{a,t}}{(1+k)^t} + \frac{SV_a}{(1+k)^n}$$

$$= -(IO_f) S + \sum_{t=1}^{n} \frac{(CF_{f,t}) S_t}{(1+k)^t} + \frac{(SV_f) S_n}{(1+k)^n}$$

Impact of the SOX Act on the Valuation of Targets When estimating the target's net present value and pursuing an acquisition, the MNC must ensure that the target's financial information is accurate. Under the Sarbanes-Oxley (SOX) Act of 2002, executives and board members can be held accountable for the reporting process and major decisions of the firm. Executives of the MNC must conduct a thorough review of the foreign target's operations and risk (called due diligence). In addition, the MNC's board of directors must conduct a thorough review of any proposed acquisitions before agreeing to them. MNCs commonly hire outside legal and financial advisers to offer their assessment of proposed acquisitions.

15-3 Factors Affecting Target Valuation

When an MNC estimates the future cash flows that it will ultimately receive after acquiring a foreign target, it considers several factors about the target or its respective country.

15-3a Target-Specific Factors

The following characteristics of the foreign target are typically considered when estimating the cash flows that the target will provide to the parent.

Target's Previous Cash Flows Because the foreign target has been conducting business, it has a history of cash flows that it has generated. The recent cash flows per period may serve as an initial base from which future cash flows per period can be estimated after accounting for other factors. Such recent data may also make it easier to estimate the cash flows the target will generate than to estimate the cash flows that would be generated by a new foreign subsidiary.

However, a company's previous cash flows are not necessarily an accurate indicator of future cash flows to the acquirer because the target's future cash flows must be converted into the acquirer's home currency when they are remitted to the parent. The acquirer needs to carefully consider all the factors that could influence the amount of funds that the target will need to continue its operations so that the cash flows remitted to the parent can be more accurately estimated.

Managerial Talent of the Target   An acquiring firm must assess the target's existing management so that it can determine how the target firm will be managed after the acquisition. If the MNC acquires the target, it may allow the target firm to be managed as it was before the acquisition. Under these conditions, however, the acquiring firm may have less potential for enhancing the target's cash flows.

A second alternative for the MNC is to downsize the target firm after acquiring it. For example, if the acquiring firm introduces new technology that reduces the need for some of the target's employees, it can attempt to downsize the target. Downsizing reduces expenses but may also reduce productivity and revenue, so the effect on cash flows can vary with the situation.

A third alternative for the MNC is to maintain the existing employees of the target but restructure the operations so that labor is used more efficiently. For example, the MNC may infuse its own technology into the target firm and then restructure operations so that many of the employees receive new job assignments. This strategy may cause the acquirer to incur some additional expenses, but there is potential for improved cash flows over time.

15-3b Country-Specific Factors

An MNC typically considers the following country-specific factors when estimating the cash flows that will be provided by the foreign target to the parent.

Target's Local Economic Conditions   Potential targets in countries where economic conditions are strong are more likely to experience strong demand for their products in the future and may generate higher cash flows. However, some firms are more sensitive to economic conditions than others. Also, some acquisitions of firms are intended to focus on exporting from the target's home country, so the economic conditions in the target's country may not be as important. Economic conditions are difficult to predict over a long-term period, especially for emerging countries.

Target's Local Political Conditions   Potential targets in countries where political conditions are favorable are less likely to experience adverse shocks to their cash flows. The sensitivity of cash flows to political conditions depends on the firm's type of business. Political conditions are also difficult to predict over a long-term period, especially for emerging countries.

If an MNC plans to improve the efficiency of a target by laying off employees who are not needed, it must make sure that the government would allow layoffs before it makes the acquisition. Some countries protect employees from layoffs, which may cause many local firms to be inefficient. An MNC might not be capable of improving efficiency if it is not allowed to lay off employees.

Target's Industry Conditions   Industry conditions within a country can cause some targets to be more desirable than others. Some industries in a particular country may be extremely competitive while others are not. In addition, some industries exhibit strong potential for growth in a particular country, whereas others exhibit very little potential. When an MNC assesses targets among countries, it would prefer a country where the growth potential for its industry is high and the competition within the industry is low.

Target's Currency Conditions   If a U.S.-based MNC plans to acquire a foreign target, it must consider how future exchange rate movements may affect the target's local currency cash flows. It must also consider how exchange rates will affect the conversion of the target's remitted earnings to the U.S. parent. Holding other factors constant, MNCs that acquire a foreign target may prefer that the foreign currency is weak at the time of the acquisition (so that the MNC's initial outlay is low) but strengthens over time as funds are periodically remitted to the U.S. parent. The MNC forecasts future exchange rates and then applies the forecasts to estimate the effect of those rates on cash flows.

Target's Local Stock Market Conditions   Potential target firms that are publicly held are continuously valued in the market, so their stock prices can change rapidly. As the target firm's stock price changes, the bid price required to buy that firm will likely change as well. Thus there can be substantial swings in the purchase price that would be acceptable to a target. This is especially true for publicly traded firms in emerging markets in Asia, Eastern Europe, and Latin America, where stock prices often change by 5 percent or more in a week. Therefore, an MNC that plans to acquire a target would prefer to make its bid at a time when the local stock market prices are generally low.

Taxes Applicable to the Target   When an MNC assesses a foreign target, it must estimate the expected after-tax cash flows that it will ultimately receive in the form of funds remitted to the parent. Thus the tax laws applicable to the foreign target are used to derive the after-tax cash flows. First, the applicable corporate tax rates are applied to the estimated future earnings of the target to determine the after-tax earnings. Second, the after-tax proceeds are determined by applying any withholding tax rates to the funds that are expected to be remitted to the parent in each period. Third, if the acquiring firm's government imposes an additional tax on remitted earnings or allows a tax credit, that tax or credit must be applied.

15-4 A Case Study of Valuing a Foreign Target

Lincoln Co. desires to expand in Latin America or Canada. The methods Lincoln uses to screen targets in various countries and then to estimate a target's value are discussed next.

15-4a International Screening Process

Lincoln Co. considers the factors just described when it conducts an initial screening of prospective targets. It has identified prospective targets in Mexico, Brazil, Colombia, and Canada, as shown in Exhibit 15.1. The target in Mexico has no plans to sell its business

Exhibit 15.1 Example of Process Used to Screen Foreign Targets

TARGET BASED IN:	IS THE TARGET RECEPTIVE TO AN ACQUISITION?	LOCAL ECONOMIC AND INDUSTRY CONDITIONS	LOCAL POLITICAL CONDITIONS	LOCAL CURRENCY CONDITIONS	PREVAILING STOCK MARKET PRICES	TAX LAWS
Mexico	No	Favorable	OK	OK	OK	May change
Brazil	Maybe	OK	OK	OK	Too high	May change
Colombia	Yes	Favorable	Volatile	Favorable	OK	Reasonable
Canada	Yes	OK	Favorable	Slightly unfavorable	OK	Reasonable

and is unwilling to even consider an offer from Lincoln Co. Therefore, this firm is no longer considered. Lincoln anticipates potential political problems that could create barriers to an acquisition in Colombia, even though the Colombian target is willing to be acquired. Stock market conditions are not favorable in Brazil, as the stock prices of most Brazilian companies have recently risen substantially, causing the Brazilian target to be overvalued. Lincoln does not want to pay as much as the Brazilian target is now worth based on its prevailing market value.

Based on this screening process, the only foreign target that deserves a closer assessment is the target in Canada. According to Lincoln's assessment, Canadian currency conditions are slightly unfavorable, but this is not a reason to eliminate the target from further consideration. Thus the next step would be for Lincoln to obtain as much information as possible about the target and conditions in Canada. Then Lincoln can use this information to derive the target's expected cash flows and to determine whether the target's value exceeds the initial outlay that would be required to purchase it, as explained next.

15-4b Estimating the Target's Value

Continuing with our simplified example, Lincoln's screening process resulted in only one eligible target, a Canadian firm. Assume that Lincoln believes that it can make the target more efficient, which will result in higher revenue and lower expenses for the target. The target's expected cash flows can be measured by first determining the revenue and expense levels in recent years and then adjusting those levels to reflect the changes that would occur after the acquisition, as shown in Exhibit 15.2.

Estimated Revenue of Target The target's annual revenue has ranged between C$80 million and C$90 million in Canadian dollars (C$) over the last four years. Lincoln Co. expects that it can improve sales, and it forecasts revenue to be C$100 million next

Exhibit 15.2 Valuation of Canadian Target Based on the Assumptions Provided (millions of dollars)

		LAST YEAR	YEAR 1	YEAR 2	YEAR 3
1.	Revenue	C$90	C$100	C$93.3	C$121
2.	Cost of goods sold	C$45	C$40	C$37.3	C$48.4
3.	Gross profit = (1) − (2)	C$45	C$60	C$56	C$72.6
4.	Selling & administrative expenses	C$20	C$15	C$15	C$15
5.	Depreciation	C$10	C$10	C$10	C$10
6.	Earnings before taxes = (3) − (4) − (5)	C$15	C$35	C$31	C$47.6
7.	Tax (30%)	C$4.5	C$10.5	C$9.3	C$14.28
8.	Earnings after taxes = (6) − (7)	C$10.5	C$24.5	C$21.7	C$33.32
9.	+ Depreciation		C$10	C$10	C$10
10.	− Funds to reinvest		C$5	C$5	C$5
11.	Sale of firm after capital gains taxes				C$230
12.	Cash flows in C$ = (8) + (9) − (10) + (11)		C$29.5	C$26.7	C$268.32
13.	Exchange rate of C$		$.80	$.80	$.80
14.	Cash flows in $ = (12) × (13)		$23.6	$21.36	$214.66
15.	PV (20% discount rate)		$19.67	$14.83	$124.22
16.	Cumulative PV		$19.67	$34.50	$158.72

year, C$93.3 million in the following year, and C$121 million in the year after (see row 1 of Exhibit 15.2).

Estimated Expenses of Target   The cost of goods sold has been about 50 percent of revenue in the past, but Lincoln expects it will fall to 40 percent of revenue because of improvements in efficiency. Thus the cost of goods sold in row 2 is 40 percent of the estimated revenue in row 1. Gross profit (row 3) is equal to revenue (row 1) minus cost of goods sold (row 2). Selling and administrative expenses have been about C$20 million annually, but Lincoln believes that through restructuring it can reduce these expenses to C$15 million in each of the next three years (see row 4). Depreciation expenses have been about C$10 million in the past and are expected to remain at that level for the next three years (see row 5).

Estimated Earnings of Target   Earnings before taxes are estimated in row 6 as gross profit (row 3) minus selling and administrative expenses (row 4) and depreciation (row 5). The taxes to be paid by the target (row 7) are expected to be 30 percent of forecasted earnings before taxes, and they are subtracted from before-tax earnings in order to estimate earnings after taxes (row 8).

Cash Flows to Parent   Because Lincoln's parent wishes to assess the target from its own perspective, it focuses on the dollar cash flows that it expects to receive. Assume that the target will need C$5 million in cash each year to support existing operations (including the repair of existing machinery) and that the remaining cash flow can be remitted to the U.S. parent. The cash flows generated by the target (row 12) are determined by adding the depreciation expenses (row 9) back to the after-tax earnings, accounting for the amount of funds to be reinvested to maintain existing operations (row 10) and accounting for the salvage value (row 11) when the target business is sold. Assume that Lincoln expects to receive C$230 million (after capital gains taxes) from the sale of the target in three years.

Assuming no additional taxes, the expected cash flows generated in Canada that are to be remitted to Lincoln are converted into U.S. dollars at the expected exchange rate at the end of each year. Lincoln uses the prevailing exchange rate of the Canadian dollar (which is $.80) as the expected exchange rate for the Canadian dollar in future years (row 13) when estimating the U.S. dollar cash flows to be received by the parent (row 14).

Present Value of Estimated Cash Flows   Assuming a required rate of return of 20 percent (row 15), the present value of the target is estimated to be $158.72 million after three years (last column of row 16). Given that the target presently has 10 million shares outstanding, and that its shares are currently valued at C$17 per share, the 10 million shares are worth C$170 million. At the prevailing exchange rate of $.80 per Canadian dollar, the target is currently valued at $136 million by the market (computed as C$170 million × $.80). However, Lincoln would likely have to pay a premium of at least 30 percent on the shares to persuade the target's board of directors to approve the acquisition, which means that the acquisition price would be about $177 million (computed as $136 million × 1.3). Because Lincoln's valuation of the target ($159 million) is less than the amount it would likely need to pay to acquire the target, it decides not to submit a bid for the target. It may still consider acquiring the target in the future, but would need to redo its analysis of the target at that time. As the country conditions (economic growth, industry competition, exchange rates, etc.) that affect the target's expected cash flows change over time, so will the valuation of the target.

15-4c Uncertainty Surrounding the Target's Valuation

When MNCs pursue a target company that they wish to acquire, they attempt to determine the present value of that target's future cash flows. Although they can utilize public financial statements disclosed by the target, the future cash flows of the target are still subject to uncertainty.

To identify the sources of uncertainty that could cause Lincoln to overestimate the target's valuation, review the factors in Exhibit 15.2 that influence estimated cash flows, starting with the top row and moving down. The target's revenue is subject to uncertainty because economic growth is difficult to forecast. Second, the cost of goods sold could exceed the assumed level of 40 percent of revenue, which would reduce cash flows remitted to the parent. Third, the selling and administrative expenses could exceed the assumed amount of C$15 million, especially when considering that the annual expenses were C$20 million prior to the acquisition. Fourth, Canada's corporate tax rate could increase, which would reduce the cash flows remitted to the parent. Fifth, the exchange rate of the Canadian dollar may be weaker than assumed, which would reduce the cash flows received by the parent. Sixth, the estimated selling price of the target three years from now could be incorrect for any of these five reasons, and this estimate has a strong effect on the current valuation of the target.

To account for uncertainty, the capital budgeting analysis could be reapplied by allowing for possible alternative scenarios. For example, the future cash flows to be received by Lincoln could be re-estimated based on alternative assumptions about revenue, cost, future exchange rates, or salvage value.

15-4d Changes in Market Valuation of Target over Time

Just as changes in the target's country conditions affect an MNC's valuation of the target, they also affect the market valuation of the target. This is very important because the price that an MNC must pay to acquire a publicly traded target is heavily influenced by the target's market valuation. Specific country conditions that can have a major impact on the market valuation of a target over time are identified here.

Impact of Stock Market Conditions   A change in stock market conditions affects the price per share of stock for each firm in that market. This affects the values of publicly traded firms whose shares are traded in that market, and the price to acquire any of those firms will change as well.

EXAMPLE

Recall from the previous example that Lincoln Co. valued the Canadian target at about $159 million, but that valuation was not high enough to justify an acquisition of the target. Assume that three months after that initial valuation, Canada's economy improves, which causes Lincoln to reassess whether to acquire the Canadian target. Lincoln's new analysis determines that the target's valuation is now $200 million. Lincoln's new valuation of the target would justify the acquisition if it could pay the price that it would have paid for the target three months ago (recall that this price was $177 million).

However, the target's market valuation has changed in the last three months. As the economy has improved, prices in the Canadian stock market have surged, and the target's stock price has increased by 20 percent. Assuming that the exchange rate from the original example has not changed, the market valuation of the target is now about $163 million. Furthermore, because Lincoln still expects that it would need to pay at least a 30 percent premium above the market valuation to entice the target shareholders to sell their shares, it would now have to pay about $212 million (computed as $163 million × 1.3) to acquire the target. While Lincoln has substantially increased its valuation of the target, the new acquisition price exceeds its new valuation. Therefore, Lincoln decides not to submit a bid for the target at this time. ●

Even if a target is privately held, general stock market conditions will affect the price that an acquirer has to pay for the target because the valuation of a privately held company is influenced by the market price multiples of related firms in the same country. A simple method of valuing a private company is to apply the price/earnings (P/E) ratios of publicly traded firms in the same industry to the private company's annual earnings. If stock prices rise in a particular country, then the P/E ratios of publicly traded firms in that country usually rise and so a higher P/E ratio would be applied to value a private firm.

Impact of Credit Availability   The availability of credit in a country has a strong effect on the ability of MNCs to make acquisitions, and therefore has an effect on the demand for target firms. When economic conditions are weak, financial institutions commonly impose higher standards for providing loans, because they are more concerned that loans will not be repaid. Some potential acquirers might not be able to obtain sufficient funds to execute an acquisition when financial institutions restrict the amount of credit available. Conversely, when economic conditions are more favorable, more credit is available, and MNCs can more easily obtain funds to pursue acquisitions. Under these conditions, the frequency of acquisitions is higher, and the price offered for a target may be higher as well.

Impact of Market Anticipation Regarding the Target   In some countries, information about planned acquisitions tends to leak because laws against insider trading are not strictly enforced. If such inside information becomes public, the stock price of the target will likely increase because investors are aware that stock prices of targets rise abruptly after a bid by an acquiring firm. As investors purchase shares in anticipation of a takeover bid, the target's stock price rises, and this could make the acquisition more expensive for the acquiring firm. Thus the price that an acquiring firm has to pay for a target may be relatively higher in countries where inside information is commonly leaked. Any MNC considering an acquisition should attempt to keep its plans confidential, but it may be difficult to keep inside information from spreading.

15-5 Disparity in Foreign Target Valuations

Most MNCs that consider acquiring a specific target will attempt to estimate the present value of the cash flows that the target would generate for them. Nevertheless, if multiple MNCs were considering the acquisition of a specific target, their valuations of that target will vary because of differences in (1) estimated cash flows to be generated by the target, (2) exchange rate effects on funds remitted to the MNC's parent, and (3) the MNC's required rate of return in order to acquire the target.

15-5a Expected Cash Flows of the Foreign Target

The target's expected future cash flows will vary among any MNCs that would consider acquiring it because the cash flows to the acquirer will depend on its management or oversight of the target's operations. Each MNC may have a different plan as to how the target will fit within its structure and how the target will conduct future operations. The target's expected cash flows will be influenced by the way it is utilized. An MNC with production plants in Asia that purchases another Asian production plant may simply be attempting to increase its market share and production capacity. This MNC's cash flows change because of a higher production and sales level. In contrast, an MNC with all of its production plants in the United States may purchase an Asian production plant to shift its production where costs are lower. This MNC's cash flows change because of lower expenses.

Tax laws can create competitive advantages for acquirers that are based in some countries. Acquirers based in low-tax countries may be able to generate higher cash flows from acquiring a foreign target than acquirers in high-tax countries simply because they are subject to lower taxes on the future earnings remitted by the target (after it is acquired).

15-5b Exchange Rate Effects on Remitted Earnings

The valuation of a target can vary among MNCs simply because of differences in the exchange rate effects on earnings remitted by the foreign target to the MNC's parent. On the one hand, if the MNC would require the target to remit most of its earnings shortly after being acquired, then the target's value will depend in part on the expected exchange rate of the target's local currency when the earnings are remitted to the MNC. On the other hand, if the MNC would prefer that the target reinvest its earnings to expand operations in the host country, then the target's valuation depends more on its local growth strategy and on exchange rates in the distant future.

The exchange rate effects are also dependent on the local country (and currency) of the acquirer. For acquirers based in countries with a weak currency, the target's currency may be expected to appreciate against the acquirer's local currency in the future, which could boost the future cash flows received by the acquirer when earnings are remitted from the target (after being acquired). For acquirers based in countries with a strong currency, the target's currency may be expected to depreciate against the acquirer's local currency in the future, which could reduce the future cash flows received by the acquirer when earnings are remitted from the target (after being acquired).

15-5c Required Return of Acquirer

The valuation of the target could also vary among MNCs because of differences in their required rate of return from investing funds to acquire the target. If an MNC pursues a successful foreign company and plans to continue the target's local business in a more efficient manner, then the risk of the business will be relatively low. In that case, the MNC's required return from acquiring the target will be relatively low. But if an MNC seeks to convert the target into a major exporter, the risk is much higher because the cash flows from the new exporting business are very uncertain. Under these conditions, the MNC's required return from acquiring the target will be relatively high.

If potential acquirers are based in different countries, their required rates of return from a specific target will vary even if they plan to use the target in similar ways. Recall that an MNC's required rate of return on any project depends on the local risk-free interest rate (because that rate influences the cost of funds for the MNC). Therefore, the required rate of return for MNCs based in countries with relatively high interest rates (such as Brazil and Venezuela) may differ from MNCs based in countries with low interest rates (such as the United States and Japan). The higher required rate of return for MNCs based in Latin American countries will not necessarily lead to a lower valuation. The target's currency might be expected to appreciate substantially against Latin American currencies (given that some Latin American currencies have consistently weakened over time), which would enhance the amount of cash flows received as a result of remitted funds and could possibly offset the effects of the higher required rate of return.

15-6 Other Corporate Control Decisions

Besides acquiring foreign firms, MNCs may also pursue international partial acquisitions, acquisitions of privatized businesses, and international divestitures. Each type is described in turn.

15-6a International Partial Acquisitions

An MNC may consider a partial international acquisition in which it purchases part of the existing stock of a foreign firm. A partial international acquisition requires fewer funds because only a portion of the foreign target's shares are purchased. With this type of investment, the foreign target normally continues operating and may not experience the employee turnover that usually occurs after a target's ownership changes. Nevertheless, by acquiring a substantial fraction of the shares, the MNC may have some influence on the target's management and is in a position to complete the acquisition in the future. Some MNCs buy substantial stakes in foreign companies to maintain control over their operations. For example, Coca-Cola has purchased stakes in many foreign bottling companies that bottle its beverages. In this way, it can ensure that the bottling operations meet its standards.

Valuation Process   When an MNC considers a partial acquisition in which it will purchase enough shares to control the firm, the MNC can conduct its valuation of the target in much the same way as when it purchases the entire firm. If the MNC buys only a small proportion of the firm's shares, however, the MNC cannot restructure the firm's operations to make it more efficient. Therefore, its estimates of the target's cash flows must be made from the perspective of a passive investor rather than as a decision maker for the firm.

15-6b International Acquisitions of Privatized Businesses

In recent years, government-owned businesses in many developing countries in Eastern Europe and South America have been sold to individuals or corporations. Many MNCs have capitalized on this wave of so-called privatization by taking control of businesses that are sold by governments. These businesses may be attractive because of the potential for MNCs to increase their efficiency.

Valuation Process   An MNC can conduct a valuation of a foreign business that was owned by the government in a developing country by using capital budgeting analysis, as illustrated earlier. However, the valuation of such businesses is difficult for the following reasons.

- The future cash flows are uncertain because the businesses were previously operating in environments of little or no competition. Thus previous sales volume figures may not be useful indicators of future sales.
- Data concerning what businesses are worth are limited in some countries because there are not many publicly traded firms in their markets and there is limited disclosure of prices paid for targets in other acquisitions. Consequently, there may not be any benchmarks to use when valuing a privatized business.
- Economic conditions in these countries are uncertain during the transition to a market-oriented economy.
- Political conditions tend to be volatile during the transition because government policies for businesses are sometimes unclear or subject to abrupt changes.

■ If the government retains a portion of the firm's equity, it may attempt to exert some control over the firm. Its objectives may be very different from those of the acquirer, which could lead to conflict.

Despite these difficulties, MNCs such as IBM and PepsiCo have acquired privatized businesses as a means of entering new markets. Hungary serves as a model country for privatizations. Hungary's government was quick and efficient at selling off its assets to MNCs. More than 25,000 MNCs have a foreign stake in Hungary's businesses.

15-6c International Divestitures

Multinational corporations periodically reassess foreign projects that they previously implemented to determine whether they should be continued or sold (divested). Some foreign projects that were previously implemented may no longer be feasible if today's present value of the project's future cash flows is lower than the price for which the project could now be sold. External forces that could reduce the present value of a foreign subsidiary's future cash flows include the following.

■ A weakening economy in the host country could reduce expected cash flows to be generated by the subsidiary.
■ A reduction in the value of the local currency of the host country could reduce the exchange rate at which the cash flows generated by the subsidiary would be converted to the parent's home currency.
■ Higher taxes imposed by the host government would reduce the expected cash flows of the subsidiary.
■ An increase in the parent's cost of capital would increase the discount rate at which expected future cash flows are discounted when determining the present value of the subsidiary.

Valuation Process   The valuation of a proposed international divestiture requires comparing the present value of the cash flows if the project is continued to the proceeds that would be received (after taxes) if the project is divested.

EXAMPLE

Recall the example from the previous chapter in which Spartan, Inc., considered establishing a Singapore subsidiary, with plans to sell the subsidiary after four years. Assume that the Singapore subsidiary was created and, after two years, the spot rate of the Singapore dollar (S$) has declined to $.46. In addition, forecasts have been revised for the remaining two years of the project, and these forecasts project that the Singapore dollar will be worth $.44 next year (which is year 3 of the project) and $.40 in the following year (the project's final year). Because these forecasted exchange rates have an adverse effect on the project, Spartan, Inc., considers divesting the subsidiary now rather than waiting for two more years to sell the subsidiary. Assume that the original forecasts of the other variables as described in the previous chapter remain unchanged and that a potential acquirer has offered S$13 million (after adjusting for any capital gains taxes) for the subsidiary if the acquirer can retain the existing working capital.

Spartan can conduct a divestiture analysis by comparing the after-tax proceeds from divesting the subsidiary (in U.S. dollars) today to the present value of the expected U.S. dollar inflows that the subsidiary will generate if it is not sold. This comparison will determine the net present value of the divestiture (NPV$_d$), as illustrated in Exhibit 15.3. This exhibit shows that if Spartan divests the subsidiary, it would receive $5,980,000 now (after converting the S$13 million into U.S. dollars at the prevailing exchange rate of S$ = $.46). The exhibit also shows that if Spartan retains the subsidiary for the next two years, the present value of the remaining cash flows of the project is estimated to be $8,533,112. Because the present value of the subsidiary's remaining cash flows exceeds the price at which Spartan can sell the subsidiary, the divestiture is not feasible. Thus Spartan should not divest the subsidiary at the price offered. Spartan may still search for another firm that is willing to acquire the subsidiary for a price that exceeds its present value. ●

Exhibit 15.3 Divestiture Analysis: Spartan, Inc.

	END OF YEAR 2 (TODAY)	END OF YEAR 3 (I YEAR FROM TODAY)	END OF YEAR 4 (2 YEARS FROM TODAY)
1. S$ remitted after withholding taxes		S$6,840,000	S$19,560,000
2. Selling price in S$	S$13,000,000		
3. Exchange rate	$.46	$.44	$.40
4. U.S. dollars received from divestiture = (2) × (3)	$5,980,000		
5. U.S. dollar cash flows forgone because of divestiture = (1) × (3)		$3,009,600	$7,824,000
6. PV of forgone cash flows (15% discount rate)		$2,617,044	$5,916,068

$$NPV_d = \$5,980,000 - (\$2,617,044 + \$5,916,068)$$
$$= \$5,980,000 - \$8,533,112$$
$$= -\$2,553,112$$

Market Value of Assets to Be Divested   Even though subsidiaries are expected to perform poorly, MNCs may not divest them if potential buyers of the subsidiaries have the same expectation and offer only a low price. In this case, the price that potential buyers would pay for the subsidiaries reflects the expected weak performance.

EXAMPLE

During the crisis in Greece, TCU Co. (based in the United States) assessed whether to keep or divest its subsidiary in Greece. TCU revised the expected cash flows of this subsidiary downward because of the weak Greek economy. TCU was also concerned that the subsidiary might be subjected to higher corporate tax rates as the Greek government searched for ways to correct its budget deficit. The future exchange rate (used to estimate future dollar cash flows to TCU's parent) was subject to more uncertainty because of TCU's concern that Greece might abandon the euro as its currency.

For all of these reasons, TCU believed that the subsidiary would not be profitable, and it decided to search for a potential buyer. However, other MNCs that considered purchasing the subsidiary had the same outlook for the subsidiary's business. Thus these potential buyers were not willing to buy the subsidiary unless TCU would sell it at a heavily discounted price. TCU was faced with the choice of essentially giving the subsidiary away or keeping the subsidiary even though it was expected to perform poorly. Because the present value of the subsidiary's future cash flows was higher than the price at which the subsidiary could be sold, TCU decided to keep the subsidiary and hope that its business might improve in the future if the Greece crisis is resolved. ●

15-7 Corporate Control Decisions as Real Options

Some international corporate control decisions by MNCs involve real options, or implicit options on real assets (such as buildings, machinery, and other assets used by MNCs to facilitate their production). A real option can be classified as a call option on real assets or a put option on real assets, as explained next.

15-7a Call Option on Real Assets

A **call option on real assets** represents a proposed project that contains an option of pursuing an additional venture. Some possible forms of restructuring by MNCs contain a call option on real assets. Multinational capital budgeting can be conducted in a way that accounts for the option.

EXAMPLE

Coral, Inc., an Internet firm in the United States, is considering the acquisition of an Internet business in Mexico. Coral estimates and discounts the expected dollar cash flows that would result from acquiring this business and compares them to the initial outlay. At this time, the present value of the future cash flows that are directly attributable to the Mexican business is slightly lower than the initial outlay that would be required to purchase that business, so the business appears to be an infeasible investment.

A Brazilian Internet firm is also for sale. However, its owners will sell the business only to a firm that they know and trust, and Coral, Inc., has no relationship with this business. A possible advantage of the Mexican firm that is not measured by the traditional multinational capital budgeting analysis is that it frequently does business with the Brazilian Internet firm and could use its relationship to help Coral acquire the Brazilian firm. Thus if Coral purchases the Mexican business, it will have an option to also acquire the Internet firm in Brazil. In essence, Coral will have a call option on real assets (of the Brazilian firm) because it will have the option (not the obligation) to purchase the Brazilian firm. The expected purchase price of the Brazilian firm over the next few months serves as the exercise price in the call option on real assets. If Coral acquires the Brazilian firm, it now has a second initial outlay and will generate a second stream of cash flows.

When the call option on real assets is considered, the acquisition of the Mexican Internet firm may now be feasible even though it was not feasible when considering only the cash flows directly attributable to that firm. The project can be analyzed by segmenting it into two scenarios. In the first scenario, Coral, Inc., acquires the Mexican firm but, after taking a closer look at the Brazilian firm, decides not to exercise its call option (decides not to purchase the Brazilian firm). The net present value in this scenario is simply a measure of the present value of expected dollar cash flows directly attributable to the Mexican firm minus the initial outlay necessary to purchase that firm. In the second scenario, Coral, Inc., acquires the Mexican firm and then exercises its option by also purchasing the Brazilian firm. In this case, the present value of combined (Mexican firm plus Brazilian firm) cash flow streams (in dollars) would be compared to the combined initial outlays.

If the outlay necessary to acquire the Brazilian firm was made after the initial outlay of the Mexican firm, then the outlay for the Brazilian firm should be discounted to determine its present value. If Coral, Inc., knows the probability of the two scenarios, it can determine the probability of each one and then determine the expected value of the proposed project's NPV by summing the products of the probability of each scenario by the respective net present value for that scenario. ●

15-7b Put Option on Real Assets

A **put option on real assets** represents a proposed project that contains an option of divesting part or all of the project. Like a call option on real assets, a put option on real assets can be accounted for by multinational capital budgeting.

EXAMPLE

Jade, Inc., an office supply firm in the United States, is considering the acquisition of a similar business in Italy. Jade believes that if future economic conditions in Italy are favorable, then the net present value of this project is positive. However, given that weak economic conditions in Italy are more likely, the proposed project appears to be infeasible.

Assume now that Jade, Inc., knows that it can sell the Italian firm at a specified price to another firm at any time during the next four years. Thus Jade has an implied put option attached to the project.

The feasibility of this project can be assessed by determining the net present value under both the scenario of strong economic conditions and the scenario of weak economic conditions. The expected value of the net present value of this project can be estimated as the sum of the products of the probability of each scenario by its respective net present value. If economic conditions are favorable, the net present value is positive. If economic conditions are weak, Jade, Inc., may sell the Italian firm at the locked-in sales price (which resembles the exercise price of a put option) and therefore may still achieve a positive net present value over the short time that it owned the Italian firm. Thus the put option on real assets may turn an infeasible project into a feasible one. ●

SUMMARY

- An MNC's board of directors is responsible for ensuring that its managers focus on maximizing the wealth of the shareholders. A board should be more effective if the chair is an outside board member and if the board is dominated by outside members. Institutional investors monitor an MNC, but some institutional investors (such as hedge funds) tend to be more effective monitors than others. Blockholders who have a large stake in the firm may also serve as effective monitors and can influence the management because of their voting power.

- The international market for corporate control serves as another form of governance because public firms that do not serve their shareholders may become subject to takeovers. However, managers of public firms can implement some tactics such as anti-takeover provisions and poison pills to protect against takeovers.

- The valuation of a firm's target is influenced by target-specific factors (such as the target's previous cash flows and its managerial talent) and country-specific factors (such as economic conditions, political conditions, currency conditions, and stock market conditions).

- In the typical valuation process, an MNC initially screens prospective targets based on willingness to be acquired and country barriers. Each prospective target is valued by estimating its cash flows, based on target-specific characteristics and the target's country characteristics, and by discounting the expected cash flows. Then the perceived value is compared to the target's market value to determine whether the target can be purchased at a price that is below the perceived value from the MNC's perspective.

- Valuations of a foreign target may vary among potential acquirers because of differences in estimates of the target's cash flows or exchange rate movements or differences in the required rate of return among acquirers. These differences may be especially pronounced when the potential acquirers are from different countries.

- Besides international acquisitions of firms, international corporate control transactions include international partial acquisitions, international acquisitions of privatized businesses, and international divestitures. The feasibility of these types of transactions can be assessed by applying multinational capital budgeting.

- Some international corporate control decisions by MNCs involve implicit options on real assets. An MNC's capital budgeting analysis of these decisions should account for these options.

POINT COUNTER-POINT

Can a Foreign Target Be Assessed Like Any Other Asset?

Point   Yes. The value of a foreign target to an MNC is the present value of the future cash flows to the MNC. The process of estimating a foreign target's value is the same as the process of estimating a machine's value. A target has expected cash flows, which can be derived from information about previous cash flows.

Counter-Point   No. A target's behavior will change after it is acquired by an MNC. Its efficiency may improve depending on the ability of the MNC to integrate the target with its own operations. The morale of the target employees could either improve or worsen after the acquisition, depending on their treatment by the acquirer. Thus a proper estimate of cash flows generated by the target must consider the changes in the target due to the acquisition.

Who Is Correct?   Use the Internet to learn more about this issue. Which argument do you support? Offer your own opinion on this issue.

SELF-TEST

Answers are provided in Appendix A at the back of the text.

1.   If the government of an emerging market suddenly allows foreign ownership of its local companies, why might its local companies become attractive targets to MNCs outside of this country?

2. What are some of the barriers to international acquisitions?

3. Why might a U.S.-based MNC prefer to establish a foreign subsidiary rather than acquire an existing firm in a foreign country?

4. Provo, Inc. (based in Utah), has been considering the divestiture of a Swedish subsidiary that produces ski equipment and sells it locally. A Swedish firm has already offered to acquire this Swedish subsidiary. Assume that the U.S. parent has just revised its projections of the Swedish krona's value downward. Will the proposed divestiture now seem more or less feasible than it did before? Explain.

QUESTIONS AND APPLICATIONS

1. **Motives for Restructuring** Why do you think MNCs continuously assess possible forms of multinational restructuring, such as foreign acquisitions or downsizing of a foreign subsidiary?

2. **Exposure to Country Regulations** Maude, Inc., a U.S.-based MNC, has recently acquired a firm in Singapore. To eliminate inefficiencies, Maude downsized the target substantially, eliminating two-thirds of the workforce. Why might this action affect the regulations imposed on the subsidiary's business by the Singapore government?

3. **Global Expansion Strategy** Poki, Inc., a U.S.-based MNC, is considering expanding into Thailand because of decreasing profit margins in the United States. The demand for Poki's product in Thailand is very strong. However, forecasts indicate that the baht is expected to depreciate substantially over the next three years. Should Poki expand into Thailand? What factors may affect its decision?

4. **Valuation of a Private Target** Rastell, Inc., a U.S.-based MNC, is considering the acquisition of a Russian target to produce tablet computers and market them throughout Russia, where demand for tablets has increased substantially in recent years. Assume that the stock prices of most Russian companies rose substantially just prior to Rastell's assessment of the target. If Rastell, Inc., acquires a private target in Russia, will it be able to avoid the impact of the high stock prices on business valuations in Russia?

5. **Comparing International Projects** Savannah, Inc., a manufacturer of clothing, wants to increase its market share by acquiring a target producing a popular clothing line in Europe. This clothing line is well established. Forecasts indicate a relatively stable euro over the life of the project. Marquette, Inc., wants to increase its market share in the tablet computer market by acquiring a target in Thailand that currently produces radios and converting the operations to produce tablets. Forecasts indicate a depreciation of the baht over the life of the project. Funds resulting from both projects will be remitted to the respective U.S. parent on a regular basis. Which target do you think will result in a higher net present value? Why?

6. **Privatized Business Valuations** Why are valuations of privatized businesses previously owned by the governments of developing countries more difficult than valuations of existing firms in developed countries?

7. **Valuing a Foreign Target** Blore, Inc., a U.S.-based MNC, has screened several targets. Based on economic and political considerations, only one eligible target remains in Malaysia. Blore would like you to value this target and has provided you with the following information:

■ Blore expects to keep the target for three years, at which time it expects to sell the firm for 300 million Malaysian ringgit (MYR) after any taxes.

■ Blore expects a strong Malaysian economy. The estimates for revenue for the next year are MYR200 million. Revenues are expected to increase by 8 percent in each of the following two years.

■ Cost of goods sold is expected to be 50 percent of revenue.

■ Selling and administrative expenses are expected to be MYR30 million in each of the next three years.

■ The Malaysian tax rate on the target's earnings is expected to be 35 percent.

■ Depreciation expenses are expected to be MYR20 million per year for each of the next three years.

■ The target will need MYR7 million in cash each year to support existing operations.

■ The target's stock price is currently MYR30 per share. The target has 9 million shares outstanding.

■ Any remaining cash flows will be remitted by the target to Blore, Inc. Blore uses the prevailing exchange rate of the Malaysian ringgit as the expected exchange rate for the next three years. This exchange rate is currently $.25.

■ Blore's required rate of return on similar projects is 20 percent.

a. Prepare a worksheet to estimate the value of the Malaysian target based on the information provided.

b. Will Blore, Inc., be able to acquire the Malaysian target for a price lower than its valuation of the target?

8.   Uncertainty Surrounding a Foreign Target Refer to question 7. What are some of the key sources of uncertainty in Blore's valuation of the target? Identify two reasons why the expected cash flows from an Asian subsidiary of a U.S.-based MNC would be lower if Asia experienced a new crisis.

9.   Divestiture Strategy A crisis in a foreign country will commonly cause a substantial reduction in cash flows (and valuations) of an MNC's subsidiaries based in that country. Explain why the MNC will not necessarily sell its subsidiaries even if these subsidiaries are not profitable.

10.   Why a Foreign Acquisition May Backfire Provide two reasons why an MNC's strategy of acquiring a foreign target could backfire. That is, explain why the acquisition might result in a negative NPV.

Advanced Questions

11.   Pricing a Foreign Target Alaska, Inc., would like to acquire Estoya Corp., which is located in Peru. In initial negotiations, Estoya has asked for a purchase price of 1 billion Peruvian new sol. If Alaska completes the purchase, it would keep Estoya's operations for two years and then sell the company. In the recent past, Estoya has generated annual cash flows of 500 million new sol per year, but Alaska believes that it can increase these cash flows 5 percent each year by improving the operations of the plant. Given these improvements, Alaska believes it will be able to resell Estoya in two years for 1.2 billion new sol. The current exchange rate of the new sol is $.29, and exchange rate forecasts for the next two years indicate values of $.29 and $.27, respectively. Given these facts, should Alaska, Inc., pay 1 billion new sol for Estoya Corp. if the required rate of return is 18 percent? What is the maximum price Alaska should be willing to pay?

12.   Global Strategy Senser Co. established a subsidiary in Russia two years ago. Under its original plans, Senser intended to operate the subsidiary for a total of four years. However, it would like to reassess the situation because exchange rate forecasts for the Russian ruble indicate that it may depreciate from its current level of $.033 to $.028 next year and to $.025 in the following year. Senser could sell the subsidiary today for 5 million rubles to a potential acquirer. If Senser continues to operate the subsidiary, it will generate cash flows of 3 million rubles next year and 4 million rubles in the following year. These cash flows would be remitted back to the parent in the United States. The required rate of return of the project is 16 percent. Should Senser continue operating the Russian subsidiary?

13.   Divestiture Decision Colorado Springs Co. plans to divest either its Singapore or its Canadian subsidiary. Assume that if exchange rates remain constant, the dollar cash flows each of these subsidiaries would provide to the parent over time would be somewhat similar. However, the company expects the Singapore dollar to depreciate against the U.S. dollar and the Canadian dollar to appreciate against the U.S. dollar. The firm can sell either subsidiary for about the same price today. Which one should it sell?

14.   Divestiture Decision San Gabriel Corp. recently considered divesting its Italian subsidiary and determined that the divestiture was not feasible. The required rate of return on this subsidiary was 17 percent. In the last week, San Gabriel's required return on that subsidiary increased to 21 percent. If the sales price of the subsidiary has not changed, explain why the divestiture may now be feasible.

15.   Divestiture Decision Ethridge Co. of Atlanta, Georgia, has a subsidiary in India that produces products and sells them throughout Asia. In response to the September 11, 2001, terrorist attack on the United States, Ethridge Co. decided to conduct a capital budgeting analysis to determine whether it should divest the subsidiary. Why might this decision be different after the attack as opposed to before the attack? Describe the general method for determining whether the divestiture is financially feasible.

16.   Feasibility of a Divestiture Merton, Inc., has a subsidiary in Bulgaria that it fully finances with its own equity. Last week, a firm offered to buy the subsidiary from Merton for $60 million in cash, and the offer is still available this week as well. The annualized long-term risk-free rate in the United States increased from 7 to 8 percent this week. The expected monthly cash flows to be generated by the subsidiary have not changed since last week. The risk premium that Merton applies to its projects in Bulgaria was reduced from 11.3 to 10.9 percent this week. The annualized long-term risk-free rate in Bulgaria declined from 23 to 21 percent this week. Would the NPV to Merton, Inc., from divesting this unit be more or less than the NPV determined last week? Why? (No analysis is necessary, but make sure that your explanation is very clear.)

17. Accounting for Government Restrictions
Sunbelt, Inc., plans to purchase a firm in Indonesia. It believes that it can install its operating procedure in this firm, which would significantly reduce the firm's operating expenses. However, the Indonesian government will approve the acquisition only if Sunbelt agrees not to lay off any workers. How can Sunbelt possibly increase efficiency without laying off workers? How can Sunbelt account for the Indonesian government's position as it assesses the NPV of this possible acquisition?

18. Foreign Acquisition Decision Florida Co. produces software. Its primary business in Boca Raton is expected to generate cash flows of $4 million at the end of each of the next three years, and Florida expects that it could sell this business for $10 million (after accounting for capital gains taxes) at the end of three years. Florida Co. also has a side business in Pompano Beach that takes the software created in Boca Raton and exports it to Europe. As long as the side business distributes this software to Europe, it is expected to generate $2 million in cash flows at the end of each of the next three years. This side business in Pompano Beach is separate from Florida's main business.

Recently, Florida was contacted by Ryne Co., located in Europe, which specializes in distributing software throughout Europe. If Florida acquires Ryne Co., it would rely on Ryne instead of its side business to sell its software in Europe because Ryne could easily reach all of Florida Co.'s existing European customers and additional potential European customers. By acquiring Ryne, Florida would be able to sell much more software in Europe than it can sell with its side business, but it has to determine whether the acquisition would be feasible. The initial investment to acquire Ryne Co. would be $7 million. Ryne would generate 6 million euros per year in profits and would be subject to a European tax rate of 40 percent. All after-tax profits would be remitted to Florida Co. at the end of each year, and the profits would not be subject to any U.S. taxes because they were already taxed in Europe. The spot rate of the euro is $1.10, and Florida Co. believes

the spot rate is a reasonable forecast of future exchange rates. Florida Co. expects that it could sell Ryne Co. at the end of three years for 3 million euros (after accounting for any capital gains taxes). Florida Co.'s required rate of return on the acquisition is 20 percent. Determine the net present value of this acquisition. Should Florida Co. acquire Ryne Co.?

19. Foreign Acquisition Decision Idaho Co. consists of two businesses. Its local business is expected to generate cash flows of $1 million at the end of each of the next three years. It also owns a foreign subsidiary based in Mexico, whose business is selling technology in Mexico. This business is expected to generate $2 million in cash flows at the end of each of the next three years. The main competitor of the Mexican subsidiary is Perez Co., a privately held firm that is based in Mexico. Idaho Co. just contacted Perez Co. and wants to acquire it. If it acquires Perez, Idaho would merge the operations of Perez Co. with its Mexican subsidiary's business. It expects that these merged operations in Mexico would generate a total of $3 million in cash flows at the end of each of the next three years. Perez Co. is willing to be acquired for a price of 40 million pesos. The spot rate of the Mexican peso is $.10. The required rate of return on this project is 24 percent. Determine the net present value of this acquisition by Idaho Co. Should Idaho Co. pursue this acquisition?

20. Decision to Sell a Business Kentucky Co. has an existing business in Italy that it is trying to sell. It receives one offer today from Rome Co. for $20 million (after capital gains taxes are paid). Alternatively, Venice Co. wants to buy the business but will not have the funds to make the acquisition until two years from now. It is meeting with Kentucky Co. today to negotiate the acquisition price that it will pay for Kentucky in two years. If Kentucky Co. retains the business for the next two years, it expects that the business will generate 6 million euros per year in cash flows (after taxes are paid) at the end of each of the next two years, which would be remitted to the United States. The euro is presently $1.20, and that rate can be used as a forecast of future spot rates. Kentucky would only retain the business if it can earn a rate of return of at least 18 percent by keeping the firm for the next two years rather than selling it to Rome Co. now. Determine the minimum price in dollars at which Kentucky should be willing to sell its business (after accounting for capital gain taxes paid) to Venice Co. in order to satisfy its required rate of return.

21. **Foreign Divestiture Decision** Baltimore Co. considers divesting its six foreign projects as of today. Each project will last one year. Its required rate of return on each project is the same. The cost of operations for each project is denominated in dollars and is the same. Baltimore believes that each project will generate the equivalent of $10 million in one year based on today's exchange rate. However, each project generates its cash flow in a different currency. Baltimore believes that interest rate parity (IRP) exists. Baltimore forecasts exchange rates as explained in the table below.

PROJECT	COMPARISON OF 1-YEAR U.S. AND FOREIGN INTEREST RATES	METHOD USED TO FORECAST THE SPOT RATE 1 YEAR FROM NOW
Country A	U.S. interest rate is higher than currency A's interest rate	Spot rate
Country B	U.S interest rate is higher than currency B's interest rate	Forward rate
Country C	U.S. interest rate is the same as currency C's interest rate	Forward rate
Country D	U.S. interest rate is the same as currency D's interest rate	Spot rate
Country E	U.S. interest rate is lower than currency E's interest rate	Forward rate
Country F	U.S. interest rate is lower than currency F's interest rate	Spot rate

a. Based on this information, which project will Baltimore be most likely to divest? Why?

b. Based on this information, which project will Baltimore be least likely to divest? Why?

22. **Factors That Affect the NPV of a Divestiture** Clemson Co. (a U.S. firm) has a subsidiary in Germany that generates substantial earnings in euros each year. One week ago, it received an offer from a company to purchase the subsidiary, and it has not yet responded to this offer.

a. Since last week, the expected stream of euro cash flows has not changed, but the forecasts of the euro's value in future periods have been revised downward. Will the NPV of the divestiture be larger or smaller or the same as it was last week? Briefly explain.

b. Since last week, the expected stream of euro cash flows has not changed, but the long-term interest rate in the United States has declined. Will the NPV of the divestiture be larger or smaller or the same as it was last week? Briefly explain.

23. **Impact of Country Perspective on Target Valuation** Targ Co. of the United States has been targeted by three firms that consider acquiring it: (1) Americo (from the United States), Japino (of Japan), and Canzo (of Canada). These three firms do not have any other international business, have similar risk levels, and have a similar capital structure. Each of the three potential acquirers has derived similar expected dollar cash flow estimates for Targ Co. The long-term risk-free interest rate is 6 percent in the United States, 9 percent in Canada, and 3 percent in Japan. The stock market conditions are similar in each of the countries. There are no potential country risk problems that would result from acquiring Targ Co. All potential acquirers expect that the Canadian dollar will appreciate by 1 percent a year against the U.S. dollar and will be stable against the Japanese yen. Which firm will likely have the highest valuation of Targ Co.? Explain.

24. **Valuation of a Foreign Target** Gaston Co. (a U.S. firm) is considering the purchase of a target company based in Mexico. The net cash flows to be generated by this target firm are expected to be 300 million pesos at the end of one year. The existing spot rate of the peso is $.14, while the expected spot rate in one year is $.12. All cash flows will be remitted to the parent at the end of one year. In addition, Gaston hopes to sell the company for 800 million pesos (after taxes) at the end of one year. The target has 10 million shares outstanding. If Gaston purchases this target, it would require a 25 percent return. The maximum value that Gaston should pay for this target company today is ___ pesos per share. Show your work.

25. **Divestiture of a Foreign Subsidiary** Rudecki Co. (a U.S. firm) has a Polish subsidiary that it is considering divesting. The subsidiary is completely focused on research and development for Rudecki's other business. Rudecki has cash outflows (paid in zloty, the Polish currency) for the laboratories and scientists in Poland. Although the subsidiary does not generate any sales, its research and development lead to new products and higher sales of products that are sold solely in the United States and denominated in dollars.

There is no foreign competition. Last week, a firm offered to purchase the subsidiary for $10 million, and the offer is still available. Today Rudecki has revised its forecasts of the zloty upward for all future periods. Will today's adjustment in exchange rate forecasts increase, decrease, or have no effect on the net present value of a divestiture of this subsidiary from Rudecki's perspective? Briefly explain. (Keep in mind that the NPV of the divestiture is not the same as the NPV that results from acquiring a project.)

26. Poison Pills and Takeovers Explain how a foreign target could use poison pills to prevent a takeover or change the terms of a takeover.

27. Governance of MNCs by Shareholders Explain the various ways in which large shareholders can attempt to govern an MNC and improve its management.

28. Divestiture of a Foreign Subsidiary Ved Co. (a U.S. firm) has a subsidiary in Germany that generates substantial earnings in euros each year. It will soon decide whether to divest the subsidiary. One week ago, a company offered to purchase the subsidiary from Ved Co., and Ved has not yet responded to this offer.

a. Since last week, the expected stream of euro cash flows has not changed, but the forecasts of the euro's value in future periods have been revised downward. When deciding whether a divestiture is feasible, Ved Co. estimates the NPV of the divestiture. Will Ved's estimated NPV of the divestiture be larger or smaller or the same as it was last week? Briefly explain.

b. If the long-term interest rate in the United States suddenly declines and all other factors are unchanged, will the NPV of the divestiture be larger, smaller, or the same as it was last week? Briefly explain.

29. Valuation of a Planned Divestiture Dallen Co. has a subsidiary in Mexico that does research and development and produces prescription pills that are transported to and sold in the United States. The parent used its own funds to build the subsidiary. Dallen Co. pays for the operations in Mexico in Mexican pesos, but all of its revenue from selling the pills in the United States is denominated in dollars. It has no other international business. Dallen's competitors are local firms in the United States that have no international operations. Two days ago, - Dallen received an offer from a firm to buy Dallen's subsidiary, and the offer is in effect for a few days.

a. Yesterday, an event occurred that makes the parent of Dallen Co. believe that the Mexican peso will weaken substantially in the future. Do you think the event that occurred yesterday will increase, decrease, or have no impact on the likelihood that Dallen will accept the offer and sell its subsidiary at the existing offer price? Briefly explain.

b. Today, an event occurred that caused the risk-free interest rate in the United States to increase. Do you think the event that just occurred today will increase, decrease, or have no impact on the likelihood that Dallen will accept the offer and sell its subsidiary at the existing offer price? Briefly explain.

30. Divestiture Decision Kylee Co. (a U.S. firm) has a British subsidiary that will generate cash flows of 3 million pounds at the end of each of the next two years. It uses the prevailing spot rate of the British pound of $1.80 as a forecast of the future value of the pound. Its required rate of return on this business is 16 percent. Kylee just received an offer from a British company who wants to buy the subsidiary for $8,000,000. Assume that Kylee would not be subject to any tax on the sale.

a. Should Kylee Co. sell the business? Show your work.

b. Assume that there is news today that causes Kylee to think that the British pound will strengthen substantially the next two years. Assume the offer price remains unchanged. If Kylee reassesses whether to divest based on this information, do you think the potential news will increase the net present value of the divestiture (make the divestiture more beneficial for Kylee), reduce the net present value of the divestiture, or have no impact on the estimated net present value of the divestiture? Briefly explain.

c. Assume that today the prevailing long-term U.S. risk-free interest rate decreased and that this has no effect on Kylee's cash flows from operations. Assume the offer price remains unchanged. Do you think this information about the decline in the U.S. risk-free interest rate will increase the net present value of the divestiture, reduce the net present value of the divestiture, or have no impact on the estimated net present value of the divestiture? Briefly explain.

Critical Thinking

Valuation of Foreign Target Companies In 2011, Microsoft acquired Skype (based in Luxembourg) for about $8.5 billion. Write a short essay that describes the general process that Microsoft would have used to determine how much it was willing to pay for Skype. Some analysts claim that Skype as an independent company was not worth $8.5 billion, but that it is worth more than $8.5 billion to Microsoft. Explain this point in your essay.

Discussion in the Boardroom

This exercise can be found in Appendix E at the back of this textbook.

Running Your Own MNC

This exercise can be found on the *International Financial Management* text companion website. Go to www .cengagebrain.com (students) or www.cengage.com/login (instructors) and search using **ISBN 9781133947837**.

BLADES, INC. CASE

Assessment of an Acquisition in Thailand

Recall that Ben Holt, Blades' chief financial officer (CFO), has suggested to the board of directors that Blades proceed with the establishment of a subsidiary in Thailand. Due to the high growth potential of the roller blade market in Thailand, his analysis suggests that the venture will be profitable. Specifically, his view is that Blades should establish a subsidiary in Thailand to manufacture roller blades, whether an existing agreement with Entertainment Products (a Thai retailer) is renewed or not. Under this agreement, Entertainment Products is committed to the purchase of 180,000 pairs of Speedos, Blades' primary product, annually. The agreement was initially for three years and will expire two years from now. At this time, the agreement may be renewed. Due to delivery delays, Entertainment Products has indicated that it will renew the agreement only if Blades establishes a subsidiary in Thailand. In this case, the price per pair of roller blades would be fixed at 4,594 Thai baht per pair. If Blades decides not to renew the agreement, Entertainment Products has indicated that it would purchase only 5,000 pairs of Speedos annually at prevailing market prices.

According to Holt's analysis, renewing the agreement with Entertainment Products and establishing a subsidiary in Thailand will result in a net present value (NPV) of $2,638,735. However, if the agreement is not renewed and a subsidiary is established, the resulting NPV will be $8,746,688. Consequently, Holt has suggested to the board of directors that Blades establish a subsidiary without renewing the existing agreement with Entertainment Products.

Recently, a Thai roller blade manufacturer called Skates'n'Stuff contacted Holt regarding the potential sale of the company to Blades. Skates'n'Stuff entered the Thai roller blade market a decade ago and has generated a profit in every year of operation. Furthermore, Skates'n'Stuff has established distribution channels in

Thailand. Consequently, if Blades acquires the company, it could begin sales immediately and would not require an additional year to build the plant in Thailand. Initial forecasts indicate that Blades would be able to sell 280,000 pairs of roller blades annually. These sales are incremental to the acquisition of Skates'n'Stuff. Furthermore, all sales resulting from the acquisition would be made to retailers in Thailand. Blades' fixed expenses would be 20 million baht annually. Although Holt has not previously considered the acquisition of an existing business, he is now wondering whether acquiring Skates'n'Stuff may be a better course of action than building a subsidiary in Thailand.

Holt is also aware of some disadvantages associated with such an acquisition. Skates'n'Stuff's CFO has indicated that he would be willing to accept a price of 1 billion baht in payment for the company, which is clearly more expensive than the 550 million baht outlay that would be required to establish a subsidiary in Thailand. However, Skates'n'Stuff's CFO has indicated that it is willing to negotiate. Furthermore, Blades employs a high-quality production process, which enables it to charge relatively high prices for roller blades produced in its plants. If Blades acquires Skates'n'Stuff, which uses an inferior production process (resulting in lower quality roller blades), it would have to charge a lower price for the roller blades it produces there. Initial forecasts indicate that Blades will be able to charge a price of 4,500 Thai baht per pair of roller blades without affecting demand. However, because Skates'n'Stuff uses a production process that results in lower quality roller blades than Blades' Speedos, operating costs incurred would be similar to the amount incurred if Blades establishes a subsidiary in Thailand. Thus Blades estimates that it would incur operating costs of about 3,500 baht per pair of roller blades.

Holt has asked you, a financial analyst for Blades, Inc., to determine whether the acquisition of Skates'n'-Stuff is a better course of action for Blades than the establishment of a subsidiary in Thailand. Acquiring Skates'n'Stuff will be more favorable than establishing a subsidiary if the present value of the cash flows generated by the company exceeds the purchase price by more than $8,746,688, the NPV of establishing a new subsidiary. Thus Holt has asked you to construct a spreadsheet that determines the NPV of the acquisition. To aid you in your analysis, Holt has provided the following additional information, which he gathered from various sources, including unaudited financial statements of Skates'n'Stuff for the last three years:

- Blades, Inc., requires a return on the Thai acquisition of 25 percent, the same rate of return it would require if it established a subsidiary in Thailand.
- If Skates'n'Stuff is acquired, Blades, Inc., will operate the company for 10 years, at which time Skates'n'-Stuff will be sold for an estimated 1.1 million baht.
- Of the 1 billion baht purchase price, 600 million baht constitutes the cost of the plant and equipment. These items are depreciated using straight-line depreciation. Thus 60 million baht will be depreciated annually for 10 years.
- Sales of 280,000 pairs of roller blades annually will begin immediately at a price of 4,500 baht per pair.
- Variable costs per pair of roller blades will be 3,500 per pair.
- Fixed operating costs, including salaries and administrative expenses, will be 20 million baht annually.
- The current spot rate of the Thai baht is $.023. Blades expects the baht to depreciate by an average of 2 percent per year for the next 10 years.
- The Thai government will impose a 25 percent tax on income and a 10 percent withholding tax on any funds remitted by Skates'n'Stuff to Blades, Inc. Any earnings remitted to the United States will not be taxed again in the United States. All

earnings generated by Skates'n'Stuff will be remitted to Blades, Inc.
- The average inflation rate in Thailand is expected to be 12 percent annually. Revenues, variable costs, and fixed costs are subject to inflation and are expected to change by the same annual rate as the inflation rate.

In addition to the information outlined above, Holt has informed you that Blades, Inc., will need to manufacture all of the 180,000 pairs to be delivered to Entertainment Products this year and next year in Thailand. Because Blades previously only used components from Thailand (which are of a lower quality but cheaper than U.S. components) sufficient to manufacture 72,000 pairs annually, it will incur cost savings of 32.4 million baht this year and next year. However, because Blades will sell 180,000 pairs of Speedos annually to Entertainment Products this year and next year whether it acquires Skates'n'Stuff or not, Holt has urged you not to include these sales in your analysis. The agreement with Entertainment Products will not be renewed at the end of next year.

Holt would like you to answer the following questions:

1. Using a spreadsheet, determine the NPV of the acquisition of Skates'n'Stuff. Based on your numerical analysis, should Blades establish a subsidiary in Thailand or acquire Skates'n'Stuff?

2. If Blades negotiates with Skates'n'Stuff, what is the maximum amount (in Thai baht) Blades should be willing to pay?

3. Are there any other factors Blades should consider in making its decision? In your answer, you should consider the price Skates'n'Stuff is asking relative to your analysis in question 1, other potential businesses for sale in Thailand, the source of the information your analysis is based on, the production process that will be employed by the target in the future, and the future management of Skates'n'Stuff.

SMALL BUSINESS DILEMMA

Multinational Restructuring by the Sports Exports Company

The Sports Exports Company has been successful in producing footballs in the United States and exporting them to the United Kingdom. Recently, Jim Logan (owner of the Sports Exports Company) has considered restructuring his company by expanding throughout Europe. He plans to export footballs and other sporting goods that were not already popular in Europe to one large sporting goods distributor in Germany; the goods will then be distributed to any retail sporting goods stores throughout Europe that are willing to purchase these goods. This distributor will make payments in euros to the Sports Exports Company.

1. Are there any reasons why the business that has been so successful in the United Kingdom might not be successful in other European countries?

2. If the business is diversified throughout Europe, will this substantially reduce the exposure of the Sports Exports Company to exchange rate risk?

3. Now that several countries in Europe participate in a single currency system, will this affect the performance of new expansion throughout Europe?

INTERNET/EXCEL EXERCISES

1. Use an online news source to review an international acquisition in the last month. Describe the motive for this acquisition. Explain how the acquirer could benefit from this acquisition.

2. You consider acquiring a target in Argentina, Brazil, or Canada. You realize that the value of a target is partially influenced by stock market conditions in a country. Go to finance.yahoo.com/stock-center/ and, under "Americas" click on Merval Index (the Argentina stock market index). Click on 1y just below the chart provided. Then, at the left, click on "Historical Prices." Set the date range so that you can obtain the

stock index value as of three years ago, two years ago, one year ago, and as of today. Insert the data on a spreadsheet. Compute the annual percentage change in the stock value. Also compute the annual percentage change in the stock value from three years ago until today. Repeat the process for the Brazilian stock index Ibovespa and the Canadian stock index S&P/TSX Composite. Based on this information, in which country have values of corporations increased the most? In which country have the values of corporations increased the least? Why might this information influence your decision on where to pursue a target?

ONLINE ARTICLES WITH REAL-WORLD EXAMPLES

Find a recent article online that describes an actual international finance application or a real-world example about a specific MNC's actions that reinforces one or more of the concepts covered in this chapter.

If your class has an online component, your professor may ask you to post your summary there and provide the web link of the article so that other students can access it. If your class is live, your professor may ask you to summarize your application in class. Your professor may assign specific students to complete this assignment for this chapter or may allow any students to do the assignment on a volunteer basis.

For recent online articles and real-world examples applied to this chapter, consider using the following

search terms (and include the current year as a search term to ensure that the online articles are recent).

1. international corporate governance

2. multinational AND board member

3. multinational AND shareholder activist

4. multinational AND corporate control

5. international acquisition

6. foreign target

7. acquire AND foreign company

8. partial acquisition AND international

9. divestiture AND foreign

10. takeover AND foreign

16
Country Risk Analysis

CHAPTER OBJECTIVES

The specific objectives of this chapter are to:

■ identify the common factors used by MNCs to measure country risk,

■ explain how to measure country risk,

■ explain how MNCs use the assessment of country risk when making financial decisions, and

■ explain how MNCs can prevent host government takeovers.

Country risk involves the potentially adverse impact of a country's environment on an MNC's cash flows. Annual reports of MNCs document their exposure to country risk, illustrated as follows:

> *We have significant international operations and plan to continue expanding our operations abroad where we have limited operating experience, and this may subject us to increased business and economic risks that could affect our financial results.*
>
> *Facebook*

> *We could be subject to economic, political, regulatory and other risks arising from our international operations.*
>
> *Netflix*

   MNCs periodically conduct a country risk analysis to determine the exposure of their existing foreign business operations to country risk. They also conduct a country risk analysis when considering new direct foreign investment. Financial managers must understand how to measure country risk and incorporate country risk within their capital budgeting analysis so that they can make investment decisions that maximize their MNC's value.

16-1 Country Risk Characteristics

Country risk characteristics can be partitioned into political risks and financial risks.

16-1a Political Risk Characteristics

Political risk can impede the performance of a local subsidiary. An extreme form of political risk is the possibility that the host country will take over a subsidiary. In some cases of expropriation, compensation (in an amount determined by the host country government) is awarded. In other cases, the assets are confiscated and no compensation is provided. Expropriation can take place peacefully or by force. The following are some of the more common characteristics of political risk:

■ attitude of consumers in the host country,
■ actions of host government,
■ blockage of fund transfers,

- currency inconvertibility,
- war,
- inefficient bureaucracy, and
- corruption.

Each of these characteristics will be discussed in turn.

Attitude of Consumers in the Host Country

A mild form of political risk (to an exporter) is the tendency of residents to purchase only locally produced products. Even if the exporter decides to set up a subsidiary in the foreign country, that tendency could prevent its success. Country governments commonly encourage local consumers to purchase from locally owned manufacturers. An MNC that considers entering a foreign market (or has already entered that market) must monitor the general attitude of consumers toward locally produced products. If consumers are very loyal to local products, then a joint venture with a local company may be more feasible than an exporting strategy.

Actions of Host Government

Various actions of the host government can affect an MNC's cash flow. A host government might impose pollution control standards (which affect costs) and additional corporate taxes (which affect after-tax earnings) as well as withholding taxes and fund transfer restrictions (which affect after-tax cash flows sent to the parent). A government's attempt at censorship may also affect an MNC's business.

EXAMPLE

WEB

www.cia.gov
Valuable information about political risk that should be considered by MNCs engaging in direct foreign investment.

Google's search engine has been generally unavailable in mainland China since 2010 when Google withdrew most of its operations due to the Chinese government's censorship of its search results and cyberattacks on its Gmail system. As a result, Google's share of the Internet search market in China has fallen from about one-third to less than 2 percent, and its revenues in China also declined substantially.

When Facebook went public in 2012, its registration statement disclosed its exposure to political risk as follows: "It is possible that governments of one of more countries may seek to censor content available on Facebook in their country, restrict access to Facebook from their country entirely, or impose other restrictions that may affect the accessibility in their country…. In the event that access to Facebook is restricted, …we may not be able to maintain or grow our revenue as anticipated and our financial results could be adversely affected." ●

Some MNCs use turnover in government members or change in government philosophy as a proxy for a country's political risk. Although such change can significantly influence the MNC's future cash flows, it alone does not serve as a suitable representation of political risk. A subsidiary is not necessarily affected by changing governments. Furthermore, a subsidiary can be affected by new policies of the host government or by a changed attitude toward the subsidiary's home country (and therefore the subsidiary) even when the host government has no risk of being overthrown.

A host government can use various means to make an MNC's operations coincide with its own goals. It may, for example, require the use of local employees for managerial positions at a subsidiary. Furthermore, a host government may impose extra taxes or restrictions on a subsidiary or take actions that protect or subsidize competitors. It may also impose restrictions on an MNC in response to actions taken by the MNC's government.

EXAMPLE

In 2014, Russia announced that it had temporarily closed four McDonald's restaurants due to health and safety violations. The closures may have been prompted by the U.S. sanctions that were imposed on Russia as a result of Russia's conflict with Ukraine. Surveys of executives of U.S.-based MNCs doing business in Russia at the time found that they were concerned that their Russian subsidiaries might be subjected to restrictions by the Russian government as a form of retaliation against the U.S. government. ●

In some cases, MNCs are adversely affected by a *lack* of restrictions in a host country, which allows illegitimate businesses to capture market share. One of the most troubling issues for MNCs is the failure by host governments to enforce copyright laws against local firms that illegally copy the MNC's product. For example, local firms in Asia commonly copy software produced by MNCs and sell it to customers at lower prices. Software producers lose an estimated $3 billion in sales annually in Asia for this reason. MNCs with subsidiaries in any country (including the United States) could argue that they lose some sales due to a lack of enforcement of copyright laws. This risk is especially pronounced in countries where the laws do not adequately cover copyright violations or where the legal system is not adequate to enforce the laws.

Blockage of Fund Transfers   Subsidiaries of MNCs often send funds back to headquarters to repay loans, purchase supplies, pay administrative fees, remit earnings, or other purposes. In some cases, a host government may block fund transfers, which could force subsidiaries to undertake projects in the host country that are not optimal (just to make use of the funds). Alternatively, the MNC may invest the funds in local securities that provide some return while the funds are blocked. But this return may be inferior to what could have been earned on funds remitted to the parent.

Currency Inconvertibility   Some governments do not allow the home currency to be exchanged into other currencies. Thus the earnings generated by a subsidiary in these countries cannot be remitted to the parent through currency conversion. When the currency is inconvertible, an MNC's parent may need to spend it in the host country.

War   Some countries tend to engage in conflicts with neighboring countries or to experience internal turmoil. This can affect the safety of employees hired by an MNC's subsidiary or by salespeople who attempt to establish export markets for the MNC. In addition, countries plagued by the threat of war typically have volatile business cycles, which make cash flows generated from such countries more uncertain. Multinational corporations in all countries have some exposure to terrorist attacks, but this exposure is much higher in certain countries than in others. Even if an MNC is not directly damaged due to a war, it may incur costs from ensuring the safety of its employees. If a country's risk of war is high, MNCs do not need to analyze the feasibility of the proposed project any further.

WEB

finance.yahoo.com
Assessments of various
political risks by outside
evaluators.

Inefficient Government Bureaucracy   An inefficient government bureaucracy can delay an MNC's efforts to establish a new subsidiary or expand business in a country. In general, bureaucracy is a bigger problem in some emerging countries. The problem is commonly caused by a lack of government organization, so the development of a new business is delayed until various applications are approved by different sections of the bureaucracy. Delays can also be caused by government employees who expect "gifts" before they will approve an MNC's applications.

WEB

www.heritage.org
Interesting insight into
international political risk
issues that should be
considered by MNCs
conducting international
business.

Corruption   Corruption can adversely affect an MNC's international business because it can increase the cost of conducting business or reduce revenue. Various forms of corruption can occur at the firm level or as a result of relationships between firms and government agencies. For example, an MNC may lose revenue because a government contract is awarded to a local firm that paid off a government official. Laws defining corruption and their enforcement vary among countries. In the United States, for instance, it is illegal to pay a high-ranking government official in return for political favors, but it is legal for U.S. firms to contribute to a politician's election campaign.

Transparency International is a global nongovernmental organization that has developed a Corruption Perceptions Index for most countries (see www.transparency.org). The index,

Exhibit 16.1 Corruption Perceptions Index Ratings for Selected Countries (maximum rating = 100; high ratings indicate low corruption)

COUNTRY	CORRUPTION INDEX	COUNTRY	CORRUPTION INDEX
Denmark	92	Portugal	63
New Zealand	91	Taiwan	61
Finland	89	Spain	60
Sweden	87	South Korea	55
Norway	86	Malaysia	52
Switzerland	86	Czech Republic	51
Singapore	84	Saudi Arabia	49
Netherlands	83	Brazil	43
Luxembourg	82	Greece	43
Canada	81	Italy	43
Australia	80	India	38
Germany	79	Thailand	38
United Kingdom	78	Colombia	37
Belgium	76	Mexico	35
Japan	76	Indonesia	34
Hong Kong	74	Ecuador	33
Ireland	74	Pakistan	29
United States	74	Iran	27
Chile	73	Russia	27
Uruguay	73	Venezuela	19
Austria	72	Iraq	16
France	69	Afghanistan	12

Source: Transparency International, 2015.

which ranks countries according to their perceived level of public-sector corruption, is based on surveys of businesses and institutions. The index for selected countries is shown in Exhibit 16.1. Emerging countries tend to have lower ratings. Corruption ratings change over time in response to the factors that influence a country's rating. Therefore, MNCs need to periodically update their assessments of each country where they do business.

16-1b Financial Risk Characteristics

Along with political characteristics, financial characteristics should be considered when assessing country risk. Financial characteristics can have a strong impact on international projects that MNCs have proposed or implemented.

Economic Growth The most obvious financial characteristic is the current and potential state of the country's economy. An MNC that exports to a country or develops a subsidiary there is naturally concerned about that country's demand for its products, which is influenced by the country's economy. A recession could severely reduce demand for the MNC's exports or for products sold by the MNC's local subsidiary.

Recent levels of a country's gross domestic product (GDP) may be used to measure recent economic growth; in some cases, these levels may be used to forecast future economic growth. A country's economic growth is influenced by interest rates, exchange rates, and inflation.

- *Interest rates.* Higher interest rates tend to slow the growth of an economy and reduce demand for the MNC's products. Governments commonly attempt to maintain low interest rates when they want to stimulate the economy. Low interest rates can encourage more borrowing by firms and consumers and thus can result in more spending.
- *Exchange rates.* Exchange rates can influence the demand for the country's exports, which affects the country's production and income level. A strong currency may reduce demand for the country's exports, increase the volume of products imported by the country, and therefore reduce the country's production and national income.
- *Inflation.* Inflation can affect consumers' purchasing power and their demand for an MNC's products. In addition, it affects the expenses associated with operations in the country. Inflation may also influence a country's financial condition by affecting the country's interest rates and currency value.

A country's financial risk characteristics are strongly influenced by the government's fiscal policy. Some countries use expansionary fiscal policies that involve massive spending and low taxes in order to stimulate their economy. However, this type of policy results in a large national budget deficit and therefore increases the amount of funds borrowed by the government. An expansionary fiscal policy can have long-term adverse effects if the level of government borrowing is so high that it causes concerns about the government's ability to repay its loans.

EXAMPLE

During the 2008–2015 period, the government of Greece continued to pay generous salaries and pensions to government employees, and it spent much more money than it received in taxes. The government finally had to take actions to correct its debt problems so that it could obtain new loans from creditors. To reduce its budget deficit, the government was forced to reduce its spending and to raise taxes, which adversely affected the economy. Many MNCs did not pursue new business in Greece because they recognized that economic conditions might be weak and that corporate tax rates might be increased to pay for the huge budget deficit. ●

16-2 Measuring Country Risk

WEB

www.loc.gov/collections
/country-studies/
Detailed studies of more
than 80 countries
provided by the Library
of Congress.

A **macro-assessment of country risk** is an overall risk assessment of a country and involves consideration of all variables that affect country risk *except* those that are unique to a particular firm or industry. This type of assessment is convenient because it remains the same for a given country regardless of the firm or industry of concern; however, it excludes relevant information that could improve the assessment's accuracy. A macro-assessment of country risk serves as a foundation that can be modified to reflect the particular business of the MNC, as explained next.

A **micro-assessment of country risk** involves the assessment of a country as it relates to the MNC's type of business. It is used to determine how the country risk relates to the specific MNC. The specific impact of a particular form of country risk can affect MNCs in different ways, which is why a micro-assessment of country risk is needed.

EXAMPLE

Country Z has been assigned a relatively low macro-assessment by most experts because of its poor financial condition. Two MNCs are deciding whether to set up subsidiaries in Country Z. Carco, Inc., is considering developing a subsidiary that would produce automobiles and sell them locally, while Milco, Inc., plans to build a subsidiary that would produce military supplies. Carco's plan to build an automobile subsidiary does not appear to be feasible unless Country Z does not already have enough automobile producers.

Country Z's government may be committed to purchasing a given amount of military supplies, regardless of how weak the economy is. Thus Milco's plan to build a military supply subsidiary may still be feasible even though Country Z's financial condition is poor.

It is possible, however, that Country Z's government will order its military supplies from a locally owned firm because it wants information about its military supplies to remain confidential for security purposes. This possibility is an element of country risk because it is a country characteristic (or attitude) that can affect the feasibility of a project. Yet that particular characteristic is relevant only to Milco, Inc., and not to Carco, Inc. ●

This example illustrates how an appropriate country risk assessment varies with the firm, industry, and project of concern, so it also illustrates the limitations of using only a macro-assessment of country risk. Thus a micro-assessment is also necessary when evaluating the country risk related to a specific project proposed by a particular firm.

16-2a Techniques for Assessing Country Risk

Once a firm identifies all the macro- and micro-factors that deserve consideration in the country risk assessment, it may wish to implement a system for evaluating these factors and determining a country risk rating. Various techniques are available to achieve this objective. Among the most popular techniques are the following:

- checklist approach,
- Delphi technique,
- quantitative analysis,
- inspection visits, and
- a combination of techniques.

Each technique is briefly discussed in turn.

Checklist Approach   A checklist approach involves making a judgment on all the political and financial factors (both macro and micro) that contribute to a firm's assessment of country risk. Ratings are assigned to a list of various financial and political factors, and these ratings are then consolidated to derive an overall assessment of country risk. Some factors (such as real GDP growth) can be measured from available data, whereas others (such as probability of entering a war) must be subjectively measured.

A substantial amount of information about countries is available on the Internet. This information can be used to develop ratings of various factors used to assess country risk. The factors are then converted to a numerical rating in order to assess a particular country. Those factors thought to have a greater influence on country risk should be assigned greater weights. Both the measurement of some factors and the weighting scheme implemented are subjective.

Delphi Technique   The **Delphi technique** involves the collection of independent opinions without group discussion. As applied to country risk analysis, the MNC could survey specific employees or outside consultants who have some expertise in assessing a given country's risk characteristics. After the MNC receives responses from its survey, it attempts to determine some consensus opinions (without attaching names to any of the opinions) about the country's perceived risk. The firm then sends this summary of the survey back to the survey respondents and asks for additional feedback regarding its summary of the country's risk.

Quantitative Analysis   Once the financial and political variables have been measured for a period of time, quantitative models can attempt to identify the country risk characteristics that have influenced an MNC's sales or earnings in a specific country.

Results from such an analysis will indicate the susceptibility of a particular business to a country's economy. This is valuable information to incorporate into the overall evaluation of country risk.

However, quantitative models cannot always indicate a country's problems *before* they actually occur (preferably before the firm's decision to pursue a project in that country). Nor can such models evaluate subjective data that cannot be quantified within models. In addition, historical trends of various country characteristics are not always useful for anticipating an upcoming crisis.

Inspection Visits   Inspection visits involve traveling to a country and meeting with government officials, business executives, and/or consumers. Such meetings can help clarify any uncertain opinions the firm has about a country. Indeed, some variables (such as intercountry relationships) may be difficult to assess without a trip to the host country.

Combination of Techniques   Many MNCs do not have a formal method to assess country risk, because there is no proven method that is always most appropriate. Consequently, many MNCs use a combination of techniques to assess country risk.

16-2b Deriving a Country Risk Rating

An overall country risk rating using a checklist approach can be developed from separate ratings for political and financial risk. First, the political factors are assigned values within some arbitrarily chosen range (such as values from 1 to 5, where 5 is the lowest risk and thus the best value). Next, these political factors are assigned weights (representing relative degree of importance), which should add up to 100 percent. The assigned values of the factors multiplied by their respective weights can then be summed to derive a political risk rating.

The process is then repeated to derive the financial risk rating. All financial factors are assigned values from 1 to 5 and, just as for political risk, the assigned values of the factors multiplied by their respective weights are summed to derive a financial risk rating.

Once the political and financial ratings have been derived, a country's overall country risk rating as it relates to a specific project can be determined by assigning weights to the overall political and financial ratings according to their perceived importance. The importance of political risk versus financial risk varies with the intent of the MNC. An MNC considering direct foreign investment to attract demand in that country must be highly concerned about financial risk. An MNC establishing a foreign manufacturing plant and planning to export the products from there should be more concerned with political risk.

If a project's political risk is considered to be much more relevant than its financial risk, then the political risk rating will receive a higher weight than the financial risk rating (as before, both weights must sum to 100 percent). The political and financial ratings multiplied by their respective weights will determine the overall country risk rating for a country as it relates to a particular project.

EXAMPLE   Assume that Cougar Co. plans to build a steel plant in Mexico. It has used the Delphi technique and quantitative analysis to derive ratings for various political and financial factors. The discussion here focuses on how to consolidate the ratings to derive an overall country risk rating.

Exhibit 16.2 illustrates Cougar's country risk assessment of Mexico. The exhibit shows that two political factors and five financial factors contribute to the overall country risk rating in this example. Cougar Co. will consider projects only in countries for which its country risk rating is 3.5 or higher.

Cougar Co. has assigned the values and weights to the factors as shown in Exhibit 16.3. In this example, the company generally assigns the financial factors higher ratings than the political factors. The

Exhibit 16.2   Determining the Overall Country Risk Rating Diagram

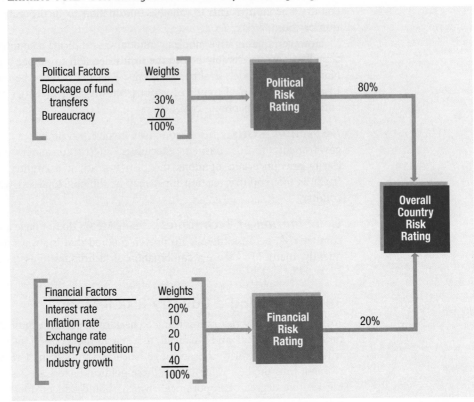

financial condition of Mexico has therefore been assessed more favorably than the political condition. Industry growth is the most important financial factor in Mexico, based on its 40 percent weighting. The bureaucracy is thought to be the most important political factor, based on a weighting of 70 percent; regulation of international fund transfers receives the remaining 30 percent weighting. The political risk rating is estimated at 3.3 by adding the products of the assigned ratings (column 2) and weights (column 3) of the political risk factors.

The financial risk is computed to be 3.9, based on adding the products of the assigned ratings and the weights of the financial risk factors. Once the political and financial ratings are determined, the overall country risk rating can be derived (as shown at the bottom of Exhibit 16.3), given the weights assigned to political and financial risk. Column 3 at the bottom of Exhibit 16.3 indicates that Cougar perceives political risk (receiving an 80 percent weight) to be much more important than financial risk (receiving a 20 percent weight) in Mexico for the proposed project. The overall country risk rating of 3.42 may appear low given the individual category ratings. This is because of the heavy weighting given to political risk, which in this example is crucial from the firm's perspective. In particular, Cougar views Mexico's bureaucracy as a critical factor and assigns it a low rating. Given that Cougar considers projects only in countries that have a rating of at least 3.5, it decides not to pursue the project in Mexico. ●

The weighting procedure described here is just one of many that could be used to derive an overall measure of country risk. Most procedures are similar, though, in that they somehow assign ratings and weights to all individual characteristics relevant to country risk assessment.

Governance of the Country Risk Assessment   Many international projects by MNCs last for 20 years or more. When managers want to pursue a project because of its potential success during the next few years, they may overlook the potential for increased

Exhibit 16.3 Derivation of the Overall Country Risk Rating Based on Assumed Information

(1)	(2)	(3)	(4) = (2) × (3)
POLITICAL RISK FACTORS	RATING ASSIGNED BY COMPANY TO FACTOR (WITHIN A RANGE OF 1–5)	WEIGHT ASSIGNED BY COMPANY TO FACTOR ACCORDING TO IMPORTANCE	WEIGHTED VALUE OF FACTOR
Blockage of fund transfers	4	30%	1.2
Bureaucracy	3	70	2.1
		100%	3.3 = Political risk rating
FINANCIAL RISK FACTORS			
Interest rate	5	20%	1.0
Inflation rate	4	10	.4
Exchange rate	4	20	.8
Industry competition	5	10	.5
Industry growth	3	40	1.2
		100%	3.9 = Financial risk rating

(1)	(2)	(3)	(4) = (2) × (3)
CATEGORY	RATING AS DETERMINED ABOVE	WEIGHT ASSIGNED BY COMPANY TO EACH RISK CATEGORY	WEIGHTED RATING
Political risk	3.3	80%	2.64
Financial risk	3.9	20	.78
		100%	3.42 = Overall country risk rating

country risk surrounding the project over time. They may believe that they will no longer be held accountable if the project fails several years from now. Consequently, MNCs need a proper governance system to ensure that managers fully consider country risk when assessing potential projects. One solution is to require that major long-term projects use input from an external source (such as a consulting firm) regarding the country risk assessment of a specific project and that this assessment be directly incorporated into the project analysis. This procedure might allow for a better assessment of country risk over the long term.

16-2c Comparing Risk Ratings among Countries

WEB

www.eulerhermes.com /economic-research /country-risks/

This site provides risk ratings for 241 countries and territories.

An MNC may evaluate country risk for several countries, perhaps to determine where to establish a subsidiary. One approach to comparing political and financial ratings among countries, advocated by some foreign risk managers, is a **foreign investment risk matrix** (**FIRM**) that displays the financial (or economic) and political risk by intervals ranging across the matrix from "poor" to "good." Each country can be positioned in its appropriate location on the matrix based on its political rating and financial rating.

16-3 Incorporating Risk in Capital Budgeting

When MNCs assess the feasibility of a proposed project, country risk can be incorporated in the capital budgeting analysis by adjusting the discount rate or by adjusting the estimated cash flows. Each method is discussed here.

16-3a Adjustment of the Discount Rate

The discount rate of a proposed project is supposed to reflect the required rate of return on that project. Thus the discount rate can be adjusted to account for the country risk. The lower the country risk rating, the higher the perceived risk and the higher the discount rate applied to the project's cash flows. This approach is convenient in that one adjustment to the capital budgeting analysis can capture country risk. However, there is no precise formula for adjusting the discount rate to incorporate country risk. The adjustment is somewhat arbitrary and may therefore cause feasible projects to be rejected or infeasible projects to be accepted.

16-3b Adjustment of the Estimated Cash Flows

Perhaps the most appropriate method for incorporating forms of country risk in a capital budgeting analysis is to estimate how the cash flows would be affected by each form of country risk. For example, if there is a 20 percent probability that the host government will temporarily block funds from the subsidiary to the parent, the MNC should estimate the project's net present value (NPV) under these circumstances, realizing that there is a 20 percent chance that this NPV will occur.

If there is a chance that a host government will impose higher taxes on the subsidiary, then the foreign project's NPV to the MNC should be estimated under these conditions. Each possible form of risk has an estimated effect on the foreign project's cash flows and therefore on the project's NPV. By analyzing each possible effect, the MNC can determine the probability distribution of NPVs for the project. Its accept/reject decision on the project will be based on its assessment of the probability that the project will generate a positive NPV and of the size of possible NPV outcomes.

EXAMPLE   Reconsider the example of Spartan, Inc., introduced in Chapter 14, in which Spartan plans to establish a subsidiary in Singapore. Assume for the moment that all the initial assumptions regarding Spartan's initial investment, project life, pricing policy, exchange rate projections, and so on still apply. Now, however, assume two forms of country risk situation that Spartan must consider.

1. *Higher withholding tax.* The original example (shown in Exhibit 14.2 in Chapter 14) assumed that Singapore would impose a 10 percent withholding tax on any funds remitted by the subsidiary to the parent (with 100 percent certainty). Now assume that there is a 30 percent chance that Singapore will impose a 20 percent withholding tax rate instead of the 10 percent rate. This means that the probability of the originally assumed 10 percent withholding tax is reduced from 100 percent to 70 percent, because the sum of probabilities of possible outcomes for the withholding tax must add to 100 percent:

POSSIBLE TAX RATE OUTCOME	PROBABILITY OF OUTCOME OCCURRING
10%	70%
20%	30%
	100%

2. *Lower salvage value.* The original example assumed that the Singapore government will buy the subsidiary from Spartan (salvage value) for S$12 million after four years. Now assume that there is a 40 percent chance that the Singapore government might be experiencing budget problems in four years, and will only be willing to pay Spartan S$7 million instead of S$12 million for the subsidiary. Thus the probability distribution of possible outcomes for the salvage value is now as follows:

POSSIBLE SALVAGE VALUE OUTCOME	PROBABILITY OF OUTCOME OCCURRING
S$12 million	60%
S$7 million	40%
	100%

Given two possible outcomes for withholding tax (tax = 10% or 20%), and given two possible outcomes for salvage value (salvage value =S$12 million or S$7 million), there are four possible scenarios that Spartan, Inc., must consider:

SCENARIO	WITHHOLDING TAX	SALVAGE VALUE
1 (the original example in Exhibit 14.2)	10%	S$12 million
2	20%	S$12 million
3	10%	S$7 million
4	20%	S$7 million

Spartan should conduct a capital budgeting analysis for each of the four scenarios. It already estimated the NPV for the first scenario in Exhibit 14.2. It can revise Exhibit 14.2 to re-estimate NPV for each of the other three scenarios. If the analysis for Exhibit 14.2 is already on a spreadsheet, then the NPV can easily be re-estimated for each of the other scenarios by adjusting row 15 (withholding tax on remitted funds) and/or row 17 (salvage value).

Exhibit 16.4 shows how Exhibit 14.2 is revised based on scenario 2, in which the withholding tax rate increases to 20 percent while the salvage value remains at S$12 million. Because the rows above row 14 in Exhibit 14.2 are not affected by the new analysis, these rows are not shown in Exhibit 16.4. Notice in Exhibit 16.4 that if the 20 percent withholding tax rate is imposed, the NPV of the project is estimated to be $1,252,160, which is lower than the NPV estimated for scenario 1 because the higher withholding tax reduces the cash flows received by the parent.

Exhibit 16.4   Analysis of Project Based on a 20 Percent Withholding Tax: Spartan, Inc.

	YEAR 0	YEAR 1	YEAR 2	YEAR 3	YEAR 4
14. S$ remitted by subsidiary		S$6,000,000	S$6,000,000	S$7,600,000	S$8,400,000
15. Withholding tax imposed on remitted funds (20%)		S$1,200,000	S$1,200,000	S$1,520,000	S$1,680,000
16. S$ remitted after withholding taxes = (14)−(15)		S$4,800,000	S$4,800,000	S$6,080,000	S$6,720,000
17. Salvage value					S$12,000,000
18. Exchange rate of S$		$.50	$.50	$.50	$.50
19. Cash flows to parent= [(16) + (17)] × (18)		$2,400,000	$2,400,000	$3,040,000	$9,360,000
20. PV of parent cash flows (15% discount rate)		$2,086,956	$1,814,745	$1,998,849	$5,351,610
21. Initial investment by parent	$10,000,000				
22. Cumulative NPV		−$7,913,044	−$6,098,299	−$4,099,450	$1,252,160

Exhibit 16.5 Analysis of Project Based on a Reduced Salvage Value: Spartan, Inc.

	YEAR 0	YEAR 1	YEAR 2	YEAR 3	YEAR 4
14. S$ remitted by subsidiary		S$6,000,000	S$6,000,000	S$7,600,000	S$8,400,000
15. Withholding tax imposed on remitted funds (10%)		S$600,000	S$600,000	S$760,000	S$840,000
16. S$ remitted after withholding taxes = (14) − (15)		S$5,400,000	S$5,400,000	S$6,840,000	S$7,560,000
17. Salvage value					S$7,000,000
18. Exchange rate of S$		$.50	$.50	$.50	$.50
19. Cash flows to parent = [(16) + (17)] × (18)		$2,700,000	$2,700,000	$3,420,000	$7,280,000
20. PV of parent cash flows (15% discount rate)		$2,347,826	$2,041,588	$2,248,706	$4,162,364
21. Initial investment by parent	$10,000,000				
22. Cumulative NPV		−$7,652,174	−$5,610,586	−$3,361,880	$800,484

Now consider scenario 3, which retains the original 10 percent withholding tax, but assumes that the salvage value is only S$7 million. Exhibit 16.5 shows that if this scenario occurs, the estimated NPV is $800,484, which is lower than the NPV estimated for scenario 1 because the lower salvage value reduces the cash flows received by the parent in year 4.

Finally, consider scenario 4, which assumes a 20 percent withholding tax and a S$7 million salvage value. Exhibit 16.6 shows that if this scenario occurs, the NPV is estimated to be −177,223. The NPV for this scenario is worse than that of any of the other three scenarios, because it reflects a relatively bad outcome for the withholding tax and for the salvage value.

Now that Spartan, Inc., has estimated its NPV for all four scenarios, it can attempt to determine whether the project is feasible. Exhibit 16.7 summarizes the analysis of the four scenarios. Notice that each scenario is based on one outcome for the withholding tax (withholding tax = 10% or 20%) and one outcome for the salvage value (salvage value = S$12 million or S$7 million). When the probability for a scenario is based on two outcomes (such as one outcome for the withholding tax and one outcome for the salvage value), it is sometimes referred to as a "joint probability." Assuming that the withholding tax outcome is independent of the salvage value outcome, the joint probability of any specific scenario occurring can be determined by multiplying the probability of the tax outcome by the probability of the salvage value outcome. The probability of each scenario is computed in the fifth column of Exhibit 16.7. Scenario 1 (the original example in Chapter 14, assuming a 10 percent withholding tax and S$12 million salvage value) has a

Exhibit 16.6 Analysis of Project Based on a 20 Percent Withholding Tax and a Reduced Salvage Value: Spartan, Inc.

	YEAR 0	YEAR 1	YEAR 2	YEAR 3	YEAR 4
14. 5$ remitted by subsidiary		S$6,000,000	S$6,000,000	S$7,600,000	S$8,400,000
15. Withholding tax imposed on remitted funds (20%)		S$1,200,000	S$1,200,000	S$1,520,000	S$1,680,000
16. S$ remitted after withholding taxes = (14) − (15)		S$4,800,000	S$4,800,000	S$6,080,000	S$6,720,000
17. Salvage value					S$7,000,000
18. Exchange rate of S$		$50	$0.50	$0.50	$0.50
19. Cash flows to parent = [(16) + (17)] ×(18)		$2,400,000	$2,400,000	$3,040,000	$6,860,000
20. PV of parent cash flows (15% discount rate)		$2,086,956	$1,814,745	$1,998,849	$3,922,227
21. Initial investment by parent	$10,000,000				
22. Cumulative NPV		−$7,913,044	−$6,098,299	−$4,099,450	−$177,223

Exhibit 16.7   Summary of Estimated NPVs across the Possible Scenarios: Spartan, Inc.

SCENARIO	WITHHOLDING TAX IMPOSED BY SINGAPORE GOVERNMENT	SALVAGE VALUE OF PROJECT	NPV	PROBABILITY
1	10%	S$12,000,000	$2,229,867	(70%)(60%) = 42%
2	20%	S$12,000,000	$1,252,160	(30%)(60%) = 18%
3	10%	S$7,000,000	$800,484	(70%)(40%) = 28%
4	20%	S$7,000,000	−$177,223	(30%)(40%) = 12%
E(NPV) = $2,229,867(42%) + $1,252,160(18%) + $800,484(28%) − $177,223(12%) = $1,364,801				

probability of 70% × 60% = 42%; this is the probability that *both* outcomes will occur. The probabilities for the other three scenarios shown in Exhibit 16.7 are determined in the same manner.

In Exhibit 16.7, scenario 4 is the only scenario in which there is a negative NPV. Because this scenario has a 12 percent chance of occurring, there is a 12 percent chance that the project will adversely affect the value of Spartan, Inc. Put another way, there is an 88 percent chance that the project will enhance Spartan's value.

The expected value of the project's NPV can be measured as the sum of each scenario's estimated NPV multiplied by its respective probability across all four scenarios, as shown at the bottom of Exhibit 16.7. Most MNCs would accept the proposed project, given the likelihood that the project will have a positive NPV and the limited loss that would occur under even the worst-case scenario. ●

Accounting for Uncertainty   Although MNCs cannot anticipate all changes in country risk conditions that may happen, they should at least consider various scenarios that might occur, especially when considering a long-term project in a foreign country. In the previous example, the initial assumptions for most input variables were used as if they were known with certainty. However, Spartan, Inc., could account for the uncertainty of country risk characteristics while also allowing for uncertainty in the other variables as well. This process is facilitated by performing the analysis with the aid of a computer spreadsheet.

EXAMPLE   If Spartan, Inc., wishes to allow for three possible exchange rate trends, it can adjust the exchange rate projections for each of the four scenarios assessed. Each scenario will reflect a specific withholding tax outcome, a specific salvage value outcome, and a specific exchange rate trend. There will now be a total of 12 scenarios, each with its associated NPV estimate and probability of occurrence. Based on the estimated NPV and the probability of each scenario, Spartan, Inc., can then measure the expected NPV and the probability that it will be positive, which leads to a decision regarding whether the project is feasible. ●

16-3c Analysis of Existing Projects

An MNC should not only consider country risk when assessing a new project but should also review the country risk periodically after a project has been implemented. If an MNC has a subsidiary in a country that experiences adverse political conditions, it may need to reassess the feasibility of maintaining this subsidiary.

EXAMPLE   Three years ago, California Co. established a subsidiary in Zinland. As a result of a new higher tax imposed by the government of Zinland, the cash flows generated by the subsidiary are reduced. Based on a new capital budgeting analysis, California Co. determines that the present value of the subsidiary is 30 percent less than before the higher tax rate was imposed. Because it believes that the high tax rate will continue in Zinland, California Co. decides to seek a buyer for its subsidiary. If it can find a buyer that is willing to pay more than the subsidiary's present value, it will sell its subsidiary and do its future business in Zinland by exporting products there. ●

16-4 Preventing Host Government Takeovers

The most severe country risk is that the host government will take over the MNC's subsidiary. This type of takeover may result in major losses, especially when the MNC does not have any power to negotiate with the host government.

The following are the most common strategies used to reduce exposure to a host government takeover:

- Use a short-term horizon.
- Rely on unique supplies or technology.
- Hire local labor.
- Borrow local funds.
- Purchase insurance.
- Use project finance.

16-4a Use a Short-Term Horizon

An MNC may concentrate on recovering cash flow quickly so that losses are minimized in the event of expropriation. An MNC might make only a minimum effort to replace worn-out equipment and machinery at the subsidiary. It may even phase out its overseas investment by selling off its assets to local investors or the government in stages over time. As a result, there would be little incentive for a host government to take over the MNC's subsidiary.

16-4b Rely on Unique Supplies or Technology

If the subsidiary can bring in supplies from its headquarters (or a sister subsidiary) that cannot be duplicated locally, the host government will not be able to take over and operate the subsidiary without those supplies. The MNC can also cut off supplies if the subsidiary is treated unfairly.

If the subsidiary can hide the technology in its production process, a government takeover will be less likely. A takeover would be successful in this case only if the MNC would provide the necessary technology, and the MNC would do so only under conditions of a friendly takeover that would ensure it received adequate compensation.

16-4c Hire Local Labor

If local employees of the subsidiary would be affected by the host government's takeover, they can pressure the government to avoid such action. This strategy has only limited effectiveness in preventing a takeover, however, because the government could keep those employees after taking over the subsidiary.

16-4d Borrow Local Funds

If the subsidiary borrows funds locally, local banks will be concerned about its future performance. If for any reason a government takeover would reduce the probability that the banks would receive their loan repayments promptly, they might attempt to prevent a takeover by the host government. However, the host government may guarantee repayment to the banks, so this strategy has only limited effectiveness. Nevertheless, it could still be preferable to a situation in which the MNC not only loses the subsidiary but also still owes home country creditors.

16-4e Purchase Insurance

Insurance can be purchased to cover the risk of expropriation. For example, the U.S. government provides insurance through the Overseas Private Investment Corporation (OPIC). The insurance premiums paid by a firm depend on the extent of insurance coverage and the risk associated with the firm. Typically, however, any insurance policy will cover only a portion of the company's total exposure to country risk.

Many home countries of MNCs have investment guarantee programs that provide some insurance against the risks of expropriation, wars, or currency blockage. Some guarantee programs have a one-year waiting period (or longer) before compensation is paid on losses due to expropriation. Also, some insurance policies do not cover all forms of expropriation. Furthermore, to be eligible for such insurance, the subsidiary might be required to concentrate on exporting rather than on local sales. Even if a subsidiary qualifies for insurance, there is a cost. Any insurance will typically cover only a portion of the assets and may specify a maximum duration of coverage, such as 15 or 20 years. A subsidiary must weigh the benefits of this insurance against the cost of the policy's premiums and potential losses in excess of coverage. The insurance can be helpful, but it does not by itself prevent losses due to expropriation.

The World Bank has established an affiliate, called the Multilateral Investment Guarantee Agency (MIGA), to provide political insurance for MNCs with direct foreign investment in less developed countries. This agency offers insurance against expropriation, breach of contract, currency inconvertibility, war, and civil disturbances.

16-4f Use Project Finance

Many of the world's largest infrastructure projects are structured as "project finance" deals, which limit the exposure of the MNCs. First, project finance deals are heavily financed with credit. Thus the MNC's exposure is limited because it invests only a limited amount of equity in the project. Second, a bank may guarantee the payments to the MNC. Third, project finance deals are unique in that they are secured by the project's future revenues from production. That is, the project is separate from the MNC that manages the project. The loans are "nonrecourse" so that the creditor is entitled only to the assets and cash flows of the project itself. Given the transparency of the process, which arises from the single purpose and finite plan for termination, project finance enables funding for projects that might not obtain financing under conventional terms. A host government is unlikely to take over this type of project because it would have to assume the existing liabilities due to the credit arrangement.

SUMMARY

- The characteristics used by MNCs to measure a country's political risk include the attitude of consumers toward purchasing locally produced products, the host government's actions toward the

MNC, the blockage of fund transfers, currency inconvertibility, war, bureaucratic problems, and corruption. These characteristics can increase the costs of international business.

The characteristics used by MNCs to measure a country's financial risk are the country's gross domestic product, interest rate, exchange rate, and inflation rate.

- The techniques typically used by MNCs to measure the country risk are the checklist approach, the Delphi technique, quantitative analysis, and inspection visits. Because no one technique covers all aspects of country risk, a combination of these techniques may be used. An overall measure of country risk is essentially a weighted average of the political or financial factors that are perceived to constitute country risk. Each MNC has its own view as to the weights that should be assigned to each factor and its own view about each factor's importance as related to its business. Thus the overall rating for a country varies among MNCs.

- Once country risk is measured, it can be incorporated into a capital budgeting analysis by adjustment of the discount rate. The adjustment is somewhat arbitrary, however, and may lead to improper decision making. An alternative method of incorporating country risk analysis into capital budgeting is to explicitly account for each factor that affects country risk. For each possible form of risk, the MNC can recalculate the foreign project's net present value under the condition that the event (such as blocked funds or increased taxes) occurs.

- MNCs can reduce the likelihood of a host government takeover of their subsidiary by using a short-term horizon for their operations whereby the investment in the subsidiary is limited. In addition, reliance on unique technology (that cannot be copied), local citizens for labor, and local financial institutions for financing may create some protection from the host government.

POINT COUNTER-POINT

Does Country Risk Matter for U.S. Projects?

Point   No. U.S.-based MNCs should consider country risk for foreign projects only. A U.S.-based MNC can account for U.S. economic conditions when estimating cash flows of a U.S. project or deriving the required rate of return on a project, but it does not need to consider country risk.

Counter-Point   Yes. Country risk should be considered for U.S. projects. Country risk can indirectly affect the cash flows of a U.S. project. Consider a U.S. project in which supplies are produced and sent to a U.S. exporter. The demand for the supplies will be dependent on the demand for the exports over time, and the demand for exports over time may be dependent on country risk.

Who Is Correct?   Use the Internet to learn more about this issue. Which argument do you support? Offer your own opinion on this issue.

SELF-TEST

Answers are provided in Appendix A at the back of the text.

1. Key West Co. exports highly advanced home entertainment system components to its subsidiary shops on islands in the Caribbean. The components are purchased by consumers to improve their home entertainment systems. These components are not produced in other countries. Explain how political risk factors could adversely affect the profitability of Key West Co.

2. Using the information in question 1, explain how financial risk factors could adversely affect the profitability of Key West Co.

3. Given the information in question 1, do you expect that Key West Co. is more concerned about the adverse effects of political risk or financial risk?

4. Explain what types of firms would be most concerned about an increase in country risk as a result of the terrorist attack on the United States on September 11, 2001.

5. Rockford Co. plans to expand its successful business by establishing a subsidiary in Canada. However, it is concerned that after two years the Canadian government will either impose a special tax on any income sent back to the U.S. parent or order the subsidiary to be sold at that time. The executives have estimated that each of these scenarios has a 15 percent chance of occurring. They have decided to add four percentage points to the project's required rate of return to incorporate the country risk that they are concerned

about in the capital budgeting analysis. Is there a better way to more precisely incorporate the country risk of concern here?

QUESTIONS AND APPLICATIONS

1. Forms of Country Risk List some forms of political risk other than a takeover of a subsidiary by the host government, and briefly elaborate on how each factor can affect the risk to the MNC. Identify common financial factors for an MNC to consider when assessing country risk. Briefly elaborate on how each factor can affect the risk to the MNC.

2. Country Risk Assessment Describe the steps involved in assessing country risk once all relevant information has been gathered.

3. Uncertainty Surrounding the Country Risk Assessment Describe the possible errors involved in assessing country risk. In other words, explain why country risk analysis is not always accurate.

4. Diversifying Away Country Risk Why do you think that an MNC's strategy of diversifying projects internationally could achieve low exposure to country risk?

5. Monitoring Country Risk Once a project is accepted, country risk analysis for the foreign country involved is no longer necessary, assuming that no other proposed projects are being evaluated for that country. Do you agree with this statement? Why or why not?

6. Country Risk Analysis If the potential return is high enough, any degree of country risk can be tolerated. Do you agree with this statement? Why or why not? Do you think that a proper country risk analysis can replace a capital budgeting analysis of a project considered for a foreign country? Explain.

7. Country Risk Analysis Niagara, Inc., has decided to call a well-known country risk consultant to conduct a country risk analysis in a small country where it plans to develop a large subsidiary. Niagara prefers to hire the consultant because it plans to use its employees for other important corporate functions. The consultant uses a computer program that has assigned weights of importance linked to the various factors. The consultant will evaluate the factors for this small country and insert a rating for each factor into the computer. The weights assigned to the factors are not adjusted by the computer, but the factor ratings are adjusted for each

country that the consultant assesses. Do you think Niagara, Inc., should use this consultant? Why or why not?

8. Micro-Assessment Explain the micro-assessment of country risk.

9. Incorporating Country Risk in Capital Budgeting How could a country risk assessment be used to adjust a project's required rate of return? How could such an assessment be used instead to adjust a project's estimated cash flows?

10. Reducing Country Risk Explain some methods of reducing exposure to existing country risk while maintaining the same amount of business within a particular country.

11. Managing Country Risk Why do some subsidiaries maintain a low profile as to where their parents are located?

12. Country Risk Analysis When NYU Corp. considered establishing a subsidiary in Zenland, it performed a country risk analysis to help make the decision. It first retrieved a country risk analysis performed about one year earlier, when it had planned to begin a major exporting business to Zenland firms. Then it updated the analysis by incorporating all current information on the key variables that were used in that analysis, such as Zenland's willingness to accept exports, its existing quotas, and existing tariff laws. Is this country risk analysis adequate? Explain.

13. Reducing Country Risk MNCs such as Alcoa, DuPont, Heinz, and IBM donated products and technology to foreign countries where they had subsidiaries. How could these actions have reduced some forms of country risk?

14. Country Risk Ratings Assauer, Inc., would like to assess the country risk of Glovanskia. Assauer has identified various political and financial risk factors, as shown below. Assauer has assigned an overall rating of 80 percent to political risk factors and of 20 percent to financial risk factors. Assauer is not willing to consider Glovanskia for investment if the country risk rating is below 4.0. Should Assauer consider Glovanskia for investment?

POLITICAL RISK FACTOR	ASSIGNED RATING	ASSIGNED WEIGHT
Blockage of fund transfers	5	40%
Bureaucracy	3	60%

FINANCIAL RISK FACTOR	ASSIGNED RATING	ASSIGNED WEIGHT
Interest rate	1	10%
Inflation	4	20%
Exchange rate	5	30%
Competition	4	20%
Growth	5	20%

15. Exposure to Terrorism Arkansas, Inc., exports to various less developed countries, and its receivables are denominated in the foreign currencies of the importers. It considers reducing its exchange rate risk by establishing small subsidiaries to produce products. By incurring some expenses in the countries where it generates revenue, it reduces its exposure to exchange rate risk. In recent months, several countries to which it exports have experienced terrorist attacks. Now Arkansas is questioning whether it should restructure its operations. Its CEO believes that its cash flows may be less exposed to exchange rate risk but more exposed to other types of risk as a result of restructuring. What is your opinion?

Advanced Questions

16. How Country Risk Affects NPV Hoosier, Inc., is planning a project in the United Kingdom. It would lease space for one year in a shopping mall to sell expensive clothes manufactured in the United States. The project would end in one year, when all earnings would be remitted to Hoosier, Inc. Assume that no additional corporate taxes are incurred beyond those imposed by the British government. Because Hoosier, Inc., would rent space, it would not have any long-term assets in the United Kingdom and expects the salvage (terminal) value of the project to be about zero.

Assume that the project's required rate of return is 18 percent. Also assume that the initial outlay required by the parent to fill the store with clothes is $200,000. The pretax earnings are expected to be £300,000 at the end of one year. The British pound is expected to be worth $1.60 at the end of one year, when the after-tax earnings are converted to dollars and remitted to the United States. The following forms of country risk must be considered:

- The British economy may weaken (probability = 30 percent), which would cause the expected pretax earnings to be £200,000.
- The British corporate tax rate on income earned by U.S. firms may increase from 40 to 50 percent (probability = 20 percent).

These two forms of country risk are independent. Calculate the expected value of the project's net present value (NPV) and determine the probability that the project will have a negative NPV.

17. How Country Risk Affects NPV Explain how the capital budgeting analysis in the previous question would need to be adjusted if there were three possible outcomes for the British pound along with the possible outcomes for the British economy and corporate tax rate.

18. JCPenney's Country Risk Analysis Recently, JCPenney decided to consider expanding into various foreign countries; it applied a comprehensive country risk analysis before making its expansion decisions. Initial screenings of 30 foreign countries were based on political and economic factors that contribute to country risk. For the remaining 20 countries where country risk was considered to be tolerable, specific country risk characteristics of each country were considered. One of JCPenney's biggest targets is Mexico, where it planned to build and operate seven large stores.

a. Identify the political factors that you think may possibly affect the performance of the JCPenney stores in Mexico.

b. Explain why the JCPenney stores in Mexico and in other foreign markets are subject to financial risk (a subset of country risk).

c. Assume that JCPenney anticipated that there was a 10 percent chance that the Mexican government would temporarily prevent conversion of peso profits into dollars because of political conditions. This event would prevent JCPenney from remitting earnings generated in Mexico and could adversely affect the performance of these stores (from the U.S. perspective).

d. Offer a way in which this type of political risk could be explicitly incorporated into a capital budgeting analysis when assessing the feasibility of these projects.

e. Assume that JCPenney decides to use dollars to finance the expansion of stores in Mexico. Second, assume that JCPenney decides to use one set of dollar cash flow estimates for any project that it assesses. Third, assume that the stores in Mexico are not subject to political risk. Do you think that the required rate of return on these projects would differ from the required rate of return on stores built in the United States at that same time? Explain.

f. Based on your answer to the previous question, does this mean that proposals for any new stores in the United States have a higher probability of being accepted than proposals for any new stores in Mexico?

19. How Country Risk Affects NPV Monk, Inc., is considering a capital budgeting project in Tunisia. The project requires an initial outlay of 1 million Tunisian dinars; the dinar is currently valued at $.70. In the first and second years of operation, the project will generate 700,000 dinars in each year. After two years, Monk will terminate the project, and the expected salvage value is 300,000 dinars. Monk has assigned a discount rate of 12 percent to this project. The following additional information is available:

- There is currently no withholding tax on remittances to the United States, but there is a 20 percent chance that the Tunisian government will impose a withholding tax of 10 percent beginning next year.
- There is a 50 percent chance that the Tunisian government will pay Monk 100,000 dinar after two years instead of the 300,000 dinars it expects.
- The value of the dinar is expected to remain unchanged over the next two years.

a. Determine the net present value of the project in each of the four possible scenarios.

b. Determine the joint probability of each scenario.

c. Compute the expected NPV of the project and make a recommendation to Monk regarding its feasibility.

20. How Country Risk Affects NPV In the previous question, assume that instead of adjusting the estimated cash flows of the project, Monk had decided to adjust the discount rate from 12 to 17 percent. Reevaluate the NPV of the project's expected scenario using this adjusted discount rate.

21. Risk and Cost of Potential Kidnapping During a conflict in the Middle East, some MNCs capitalized on opportunities to rebuild the damaged areas. However, some of their employees were kidnapped by local militant groups. How should an MNC account for this potential risk when it considers direct foreign investment (DFI) in any particular country? Should it avoid DFI in any country in which such an event could occur? If so, how would it screen the countries to determine which are acceptable? For whatever countries the MNC is willing to consider, should it adjust its feasibility analysis to account for the possibility of kidnapping? Should it attach a cost to reflect this possibility or increase the discount rate when estimating the net present value? Explain.

22. Integrating Country Risk and Capital Budgeting Tovar Co. is a U.S. firm that has been asked to provide consulting services to help Grecia Co. (in Greece) improve its performance. Tovar would need to spend $300,000 today on expenses related to this project. In one year, Tovar will receive payment from Grecia, which will be tied to Grecia's performance during the year. There is uncertainty about Grecia's performance and about Grecia's tendency for corruption.

Tovar expects that it will receive 400,000 euros if Grecia achieves strong performance following the consulting job. However, there are two forms of country risk that are a concern to Tovar Co. There is an 80 percent chance that Grecia will achieve strong performance. There is a 20 percent chance that Grecia will perform poorly, and in this case, Tovar will receive a payment of only 200,000 euros.

While there is a 90 percent chance that Grecia will make its payment to Tovar, there is a 10 percent chance that Grecia will become corrupt, and in this case, Grecia will not submit any payment to Tovar.

Assume that the outcome of Grecia's performance is independent of whether Grecia becomes corrupt. The prevailing spot rate of the euro is $1.30, but Tovar expects that the euro will depreciate by 10 percent in one year, regardless of Grecia's performance or whether it is corrupt.

Tovar's cost of capital is 26 percent. Determine the expected value of the project's net present value. Determine the probability that the project's NPV will be negative.

23. Capital Budgeting and Country Risk Wyoming Co. is a nonprofit educational institution that wants to import educational software products from Hong Kong and sell them in the United States. It wants to assess the net present value of this project because any profits it earns will be used for its foundation. It expects to pay HK$5 million for the imports. Assume the existing exchange rate is HK$1 = $.12. It would also incur selling expenses of $1 million to sell the products in the United States. It would be able to sell the products in the United States for $1.7 million. However, it is concerned about two forms of country risk. First, there is a 60 percent chance that the Hong Kong dollar will be revalued to be worth HK$1 = $.16 by the Hong Kong government. Second, there is a 70 percent chance that the Hong Kong government will impose a special tax of 10 percent on the amount that U.S. importers must pay for Hong Kong exports. These two forms of country risk are independent, meaning that the probability that the Hong Kong dollar will be revalued is independent of the probability that the Hong Kong government will impose a special tax. Wyoming's required rate of return on this project is 22 percent. What is the expected value of the project's net present value? What is the probability that the project's NPV will be negative?

24. Accounting for Country Risk of a Project
Kansas Co. wants to invest in a project in China. It would require an initial investment of 5 million yuan. It is expected to generate cash flows of 7 million yuan at the end of one year. The spot rate of the yuan is $.12, and Kansas thinks this exchange rate is the best forecast of the future. However, there are two forms of country risk.

First, there is a 30 percent chance that the Chinese government will require that the yuan cash flows earned by Kansas at the end of one year be reinvested in China for one year before they can be remitted (so that cash would not be remitted until two years from today). In this case, Kansas would earn 4 percent after taxes on a bank deposit in China during that second year.

Second, there is a 40 percent chance that the Chinese government will impose a special remittance tax of 400,000 yuan at the time that Kansas Co. remits cash flows earned in China back to the United States.

The two forms of country risk are independent. The required rate of return on this project is 26 percent. There is no salvage value. What is the expected value of the project's net present value?

25. Accounting for Country Risk of a Project
Slidell Co. (a U.S. firm) considers a foreign project in which it expects to receive 10 million euros at the end of this year. It plans to hedge receivables of 10 million euros with a forward contract. Today, the spot rate of the euro is $1.20, the one-year forward rate of the euro is presently $1.24, and the expected spot rate of the euro in one year is $1.19. The initial outlay is $7 million. Slidell has a required return of

18 percent.

There is a 20 percent chance that political problems will cause a reduction in foreign business, such that Slidell would only receive 4 million euros at the end of one year. Determine the expected value of the net present value of this project.

26. Political Risk and Currency Derivative Values
Assume that interest rate parity exists. At 10:30 a.m., the media reported that the Mexican government's political problems had been solved, which reduced the expected volatility of the Mexican peso against the dollar over the next month. However, this news had no effect on the prevailing one-month interest rates of the U.S. dollar or Mexican peso, or on the expected exchange rate of the Mexican peso in one month. The spot rate of the Mexican peso was $.13 as of 10 a.m. and remained at that level all morning.

a. At 10 a.m., Piazza Co. purchased a call option at the money on 1 million Mexican pesos with a December expiration date. At 11:00 a.m., Corradetti Co. purchased a call option at the money on 1 million pesos with a December expiration date. Did Corradetti Co. pay more, less, or the same as Piazza Co. for the options? Briefly explain.

b. Teke Co. purchased futures contracts on 1 million Mexican pesos with a December settlement date at 10 a.m. Malone Co. purchased futures contracts on 1 million Mexican pesos with a December settlement date at 11 a.m. Did Teke Co. pay more, less, or the same as Malone Co. for the futures contracts? Briefly explain.

27. Political Risk and Project NPV
Drysdale Co. (a U.S. firm) is considering a new project that would result in cash flows of 5 million Argentine pesos in one year under the most likely economic and political conditions. The spot rate of the Argentina peso in one year is expected to be $.40 based on these conditions. However, it wants to also account for the 10 percent probability of a political crisis in Argentina, which would change the expected cash flows to 4 million Argentine pesos in one year. In addition, it wants to account for the 20 percent probability that the exchange rate may only be $.36 at the end of one year. These two forms of country risk are independent. Drysdale's required rate of return is 25 percent, and its initial outlay for this project is $1.4 million. Show the distribution of possible outcomes for the project's net present value.

28. Country Risk and Project NPV
Atro Co. (a U.S. firm) considers a foreign project in which it expects to receive 10 million euros at the end of one

year. Although it realizes that its receivables are uncertain, it decides to hedge receivables of 10 million euros with a forward contract today. As of today, the spot rate of the euro is $1.20, while the one-year forward rate of the euro is presently $1.24, and the expected spot rate of the euro in one year is $1.19. The initial outlay of this project is $7 million. Atro has a required return of 18 percent.

a. Estimate the NPV of this project based on the expectation of 10 million euros in receivables.

b. Now estimate the NPV based on the possibility that country risk could cause a reduction in foreign business such that Atro Co. only receives 4 million euros instead of 10 million euros at the end of one year. Estimate the net present value of the project if this form of country risk occurs.

29. Accounting for Political Risk and the Hedging Decision

a. Duv Co. (a U.S. firm) is planning to invest $2.5 million in a project in Portugal that will exist for one year. Its required rate of return on this project is 18 percent. It expects to receive cash flows of 2 million euros in one year from this project. The spot rate of the euro in one year is expected to be $1.50. The one-year forward rate of the euro is presently $1.40. Duv Co. wants to account also for the 20 percent probability of a crisis in Portugal. If this crisis occurs, Duv would reduce its expected cash flows to 1 million euros in one year. Duv Co. does not plan to hedge its expected cash flows. Show the distribution of possible outcomes for the project's estimated net present

value, including the probability of each possible outcome.

b. Now assume that Duv plans to hedge the cash flows that it believes it will receive if a crisis in Portugal occurs. However, it decides not to hedge additional cash flows that it would receive if the crisis does not occur. Estimate what the net present value of the project will be based on the hedging strategy described here and assuming that a crisis in Portugal does not occur.

Critical Thinking

Recognizing Exposure to Country Risk   Select a U.S.-based MNC (such as ExxonMobil or General Electric) that does considerable business in Russia. Write a short essay describing the MNC's business in Russia and how its cash flows are exposed to country risk due to the Russia-Ukraine conflict. Many MNCs engaged in direct foreign investment in Russia several years before this conflict began. Explain the difficulty in predicting possible country risk issues such as this conflict several years into the future.

Discussion in the Boardroom

This exercise can be found in Appendix E at the back of this textbook.

Running Your Own MNC

This exercise can be found on the *International Financial Management* text companion website. Go to www.cengagebrain.com (students) or www.cengage.com/login (instructors) and search using **ISBN 9781133947837**.

BLADES, INC. CASE

Country Risk Assessment

Recently, Ben Holt, Blades' chief financial officer, has assessed whether it would be more beneficial for Blades to establish a subsidiary in Thailand to manufacture roller blades or to acquire an existing manufacturer, Skates'n'Stuff, which has offered to sell the business to Blades for 1 billion Thai baht. In Holt's view, establishing a subsidiary in Thailand yields a higher net present value than acquiring the existing business. Furthermore, the Thai manufacturer has rejected an offer by Blades, Inc., of 900 million baht. A purchase price of 900 million baht for Skates'n'Stuff would make the acquisition as attractive as the establishment of a subsidiary in Thailand in terms of NPV Skates'n'Stuff has

indicated that it is not willing to accept less than 950 million baht.

Although Holt is confident that the NPV analysis was conducted correctly, he is troubled by the fact that the same discount rate, 25 percent, was used in each analysis. In his view, establishing a subsidiary in Thailand may be associated with a higher level of country risk than acquiring Skates'n'Stuff. Although either approach would result in approximately the same level of financial risk, the political risk associated with establishing a subsidiary in Thailand may be higher than the political risk of operating Skates'n'Stuff. If the establishment of a subsidiary in Thailand is associated with a higher level of country risk overall, then a higher discount rate should have been used in the analysis. Based on these considerations, Holt wants to measure the country risk associated with Thailand on both a macro and a micro level and then to reexamine the feasibility of both approaches.

First, Holt has gathered some more detailed political information for Thailand. For example, he believes that consumers in Asian countries prefer to purchase goods produced by Asians, which might prevent a subsidiary in Thailand from being successful. This cultural characteristic might not prevent an acquisition of Skates'n'Stuff from succeeding, however, especially if Blades retains the company's management and employees. Furthermore, the subsidiary would have to apply for various licenses and permits to be allowed to operate in Thailand, whereas Skates'n'Stuff obtained these licenses and permits long ago. However, the number of licenses required for Blades' industry is relatively low compared to other industries. Moreover, there is a high possibility that the Thai government will implement capital controls in the near future, which would prevent funds from leaving Thailand. Because Blades, Inc., has planned to remit all earnings generated by its subsidiary or by Skates'n'Stuff back to the United States, regardless of which approach to direct foreign investment it takes, capital controls may force Blades to reinvest funds in Thailand.

Holt has also gathered some information regarding the financial risk of operating in Thailand. Thailand's economy has been weak lately, and recent forecasts indicate that a recovery may be slow. A weak economy may affect the demand for Blades' products, roller blades. The state of the economy is of particular concern to Blades because it produces a leisure product. In the case of an economic turndown, consumers will first eliminate these types of purchases. Holt is also worried about the high interest rates in Thailand, which may further slow economic growth if Thai citizens begin saving more. Furthermore, Holt is also aware that inflation levels in Thailand are expected to remain high. These high inflation levels can affect the purchasing power of Thai consumers, who may adjust their spending habits to purchase more essential products than roller blades. However, high levels of inflation also indicate that consumers in Thailand are still spending a relatively high proportion of their earnings.

Another financial factor that may affect Blades' operations in Thailand is the baht-dollar exchange rate. Current forecasts indicate that the Thai baht may depreciate in the future. However, recall that Blades will sell all roller blades produced in Thailand to Thai consumers. Therefore, Blades is not subject to a lower level of U.S. demand resulting from a weak baht. Blades will remit the earnings generated in Thailand back to the United States, however, and a weak baht would reduce the dollar amount of these translated earnings. Based on these initial considerations, Holt feels that the level of political risk of operating may be higher if Blades decides to establish a subsidiary to manufacture roller blades (as opposed to acquiring Skates'n'Stuff). The financial risk of operating in Thailand will be roughly the same whether Blades establishes a subsidiary or acquires Skates'n'Stuff. Holt is not satisfied with this initial assessment, however, and would like to have numbers at hand when he meets with the board of directors next week. Thus he would like to conduct a quantitative analysis of the country risk associated with operating in Thailand. He has asked you, a financial analyst at Blades, to develop a country risk analysis for Thailand and to adjust the discount rate for the riskier venture (i.e., establishing a subsidiary or acquiring Skates'n'Stuff). Holt has provided the following information for your analysis:

- Because Blades produces leisure products, it is more susceptible to financial risk factors than political risk factors. You should use weights of 60 percent for financial risk factors and 40 percent for political risk factors in your analysis.
- You should use the attitude of Thai consumers, capital controls, and bureaucracy as political risk factors in your analysis. Holt perceives capital controls as the most important political risk factor. In his view, the consumer attitude and bureaucracy factors are of equal importance.
- You should use interest rates, inflation levels, and exchange rates as the financial risk factors in your analysis. In Holt's view, exchange rates and interest rates in Thailand are of equal importance, while inflation levels are slightly less important.
- Each factor used in your analysis should be assigned a rating in a range of 1 to 5, where 5 indicates the most unfavorable rating.

Holt has asked you to provide answers to the following questions for him, which he will use in his meeting with the board of directors:

1. Based on the information provided in the case, do you think the political risk associated with Thailand is higher or lower for a manufacturer of leisure products such as Blades as opposed to, say, a food producer? That is, conduct a micro-assessment of political risk for Blades, Inc.

2. Do you think the financial risk associated with Thailand is higher or lower for a manufacturer of leisure products such as Blades as opposed to, say, a food producer? That is, conduct a micro-assessment of financial risk for Blades, Inc. Do you think a leisure product manufacturer such as Blades will be more affected by political or financial risk factors?

3. Without using a numerical analysis, do you think establishing a subsidiary in Thailand or acquiring Skates'n'Stuff will result in a higher assessment of political risk? Of financial risk? Substantiate your answer.

4. Using a spreadsheet, conduct a quantitative country risk analysis for Blades, Inc., based on the information Holt has provided for you. Use your judgment to assign weights and ratings to each political and financial risk factor and determine an overall country risk rating for Thailand. Conduct two separate analyses for the establishment of a subsidiary in Thailand and the acquisition of Skates'n'Stuff.

5. Which method of direct foreign investment should utilize a higher discount rate in the capital budgeting analysis? Would this strengthen or weaken the tentative decision of establishing a subsidiary in Thailand?

SMALL BUSINESS DILEMMA

Country Risk Analysis at the Sports Exports Company

The Sports Exports Company produces footballs in the United States and exports them to the United Kingdom. It also has an ongoing joint venture with a British firm that produces some sporting goods for a fee. The Sports Exports Company is considering the establishment of a small subsidiary in the United Kingdom.

1. Under the current conditions, is the Sports Exports Company subject to country risk?

2. If the firm does decide to develop a small subsidiary in the United Kingdom, will its exposure to country risk change? If so, how?

INTERNET/EXCEL EXERCISE

Go to the website (www.cia.gov/library/publications/resources/the-world-factbook/index.html) of the CIA *World Factbook*. Select a country and review the information about the country's political conditions.

Explain whether these conditions would likely discourage an MNC from engaging in direct foreign investment. Explain how the political conditions could adversely affect the cash flows of the MNC.

ONLINE ARTICLES WITH REAL-WORLD EXAMPLES

Find a recent article online that describes an actual international finance application or a real-world example about a specific MNC's actions that reinforces one or more of the concepts covered in this chapter.

If your class has an online component, your professor may ask you to post your summary there and provide the web link of the article so that other students can access it. If your class is live, your professor may ask you to summarize your application in class. Your professor may assign specific students to complete this assignment for this chapter or may allow any students to do the assignment on a volunteer basis.

For recent online articles and real-world examples applied to this chapter, consider using the following search terms (and include the current year as a

search term to ensure that the online articles are recent).

1. company AND political risk

2. Inc. AND political risk

3. [name of an MNC] AND political risk

4. [name of an MNC] AND country risk

5. exposure to political risk

6. exposure to country risk

7. country risk rating

8. risk AND foreign project

9. risk AND foreign subsidiary

10. multinational AND government takeover

17

Multinational Capital Structure and Cost of Capital

CHAPTER OBJECTIVES

The specific objectives of this chapter are to:

- describe the key components of an MNC's capital,

- identify the factors that affect an MNC's capital structure,

- explain the interaction between a subsidiary and parent in capital structure decisions,

- explain how the cost of capital is estimated, and

- explain why the cost of capital varies among countries.

Multinational corporations rely on capital to finance their expansion of existing subsidiaries, the creation of new subsidiaries, and other projects. Because the MNC's decisions regarding its capital structure determine its cost of capital and the cost of capital affects the profitability of its projects, the MNC's capital structure decisions affect its value.

17-1 Components of Capital

An MNC needs capital to expand its operations. In general, an MNC can increase its capital internally by retaining earnings or externally with debt or equity. These sources of capital are described in turn.

17-1a Retained Earnings

An MNC's parent and its subsidiaries commonly generate earnings, which can be retained and reinvested to support existing operations or expansion. There are many different ways in which an MNC might use retained earnings. First, the MNC might allow each subsidiary to retain sufficient earnings to cover its expected operating expenses denominated in the same currency in the near future. This strategy allows each subsidiary to use its recent cash inflows to cover its future cash outflows. Because this strategy minimizes the earnings remitted to the parent and parent financing of subsidiary operations, it minimizes the amount of cash flows between subsidiary and parent that must be converted into a different currency. However, this strategy will not always be a perfect solution because some subsidiaries may need more funding than can be covered by recent earnings. Alternatively, the parent might require that the subsidiaries remit their earnings to cover the parent's operating expenses in the near future. If the parent invested its own cash to create each subsidiary, it may view the remitted earnings as a return on its initial investment in the subsidiary.

The MNC might also use retained earnings to further expand its operations internationally by establishing a new subsidiary in another country, in which it again invests some cash to create an equity investment. This subsidiary uses the cash infusion to develop its business operations, and it will ultimately add to its capital by retaining some earnings and by obtaining loans from local banks. This subsidiary has its own capital structure, which may vary substantially from that of the other subsidiaries and the parent. When an MNC has foreign subsidiaries, its overall (or "global") capital structure is the combination of the capital structures of the parent and all subsidiaries.

17-1b Sources of Debt

When MNCs wish to finance their operations with debt, they consider the following sources.

Domestic Bond Offering Multinational corporations often engage in a domestic bond offering in their home country in which the funds are denominated in their local currency. They hire an investment bank to help determine the amount of the offering and the price at which the bonds can be sold. The investment bank also provides distribution by selling the bonds to many institutional investors. Maturities on the debt typically range from 10 to 20 years. Investors who purchase the bonds do not have to hold them until maturity because the bonds can be sold to other investors in the secondary market.

The proceeds of a domestic bond offering are initially denominated in the parent's local currency. Thus if the parent plans to use a portion of the proceeds to provide financing to any of its foreign subsidiaries, it would convert the funds into the subsidiary's local currency at the prevailing exchange rate.

Global Bond Offering An MNC can engage in a global bond offering (with the help of an investment bank) in which it simultaneously sells bonds denominated in the currencies of multiple countries. The focus is on obtaining funds from a few countries where large subsidiaries are in need of financing.

For example, an offering by a U.S.-based MNC may consist of $20 million in bonds sold to U.S. investors to finance its home operations, British pound–denominated bonds valued at 15 million British pounds sold to British investors to finance its subsidiaries that conduct business in the United Kingdom, and Swiss franc–denominated bonds valued at 10 million Swiss francs sold to Swiss investors to finance its subsidiaries that conduct business in Switzerland. Investors who purchase any of these bonds can sell them before maturity to other investors in the secondary market. The U.S. parent would rely on revenue from its own operations to make coupon payments on the dollar-denominated bonds, while the British subsidiaries would use some of their pound-denominated revenue to make coupon payments on the pound-denominated bonds and the Swiss subsidiaries would use some of their Swiss franc–denominated revenue to make coupon payments on the Swiss franc–denominated bonds.

Private Placement of Bonds Another source of debt for MNCs is to offer a private placement of bonds to financial institutions in their home country or in the foreign country where they are expanding. Private placements of debt may reduce transaction costs because the debt is placed with a small number of large investors. However, MNCs may not be able to obtain all the funds that they need with a private placement of debt. Privately placed bonds may carry some restrictions on their resale in the secondary market. Thus they may offer limited liquidity to investors.

Loans from Financial Institutions An MNC commonly borrows funds from financial institutions. It not only benefits from access to funds but also establishes a business relationship with the financial institutions, giving it access to other services such as foreign exchange and cash management. Subsidiaries of an MNC borrow funds from local financial institutions in their respective host country and may also rely on other services from these financial institutions.

Loans from financial institutions to MNCs typically specify an adjustable interest rate that changes every six months or every year in accordance with the annualized interbank loan rate (called the London Interbank Offer Rate, or LIBOR) in the same currency. For example, the interest rate on a loan denominated in British pounds may be reset every year for loans denominated in pounds, plus an annualized premium of 3 percent. The interest rate on a loan denominated in Swiss francs may be reset every year at the prevailing LIBOR for interbank loans denominated in Swiss francs, plus an annualized premium of 3 percent. Although the formula is the same for both loans, their interest rates may vary substantially because the prevailing interbank loan rate on one currency might be much higher than the interbank loan rate on the other currency. For example, if the prevailing LIBOR for British pound–denominated loans is higher than the prevailing LIBOR for Swiss franc–denominated loans, then the interest rate on a loan to an MNC denominated in pounds would be higher than the interest rate on a loan denominated in Swiss francs.

The size of the premium paid by the MNC above the interbank interest rate depends on the MNC's credit risk. A profitable MNC seeking a loan that is backed by collateral would be charged a relatively low loan premium (such as 2 percent), whereas a financially weaker MNC seeking a loan that is not backed by collateral would be charged a much higher premium (such as 5 percent).

If the MNC wants to borrow a large amount of funds, it may rely on a syndicate of lenders rather than a single lender. The structure of a syndicated loan can be tailored to meet the MNC's needs. For example, the loan can be segmented into portions so that each portion is denominated in a currency that is needed by a particular foreign subsidiary. The interest rate on the loan per currency will be periodically reset every six months or every year based on that currency's prevailing LIBOR.

The term of a loan can be set to fit the preferences of the MNC. Although MNCs normally rely on long-term loans to finance their operations, they may also obtain short-term loans and lines of credit (as described in Chapter 20) to ensure access to cash and their ability to cover short-term funding needs. Some MNCs continually roll over their short-term loans upon maturity so that they essentially rely on some short-term debt as a permanent form of financing to complement their other sources of capital.

17-1c External Sources of Equity

When MNCs need to obtain external equity, they consider the following sources.

Domestic Equity Offering Multinational corporations can engage in a domestic equity offering in their home country in which the funds are denominated in their local currency. They may distribute a portion of the proceeds to their subsidiaries. Any funds transferred to subsidiaries must be converted into the subsidiary's local currency at the prevailing exchange rate.

Global Equity Offering Most MNCs obtain equity funding in their home country, but some pursue a global equity offering in which they can simultaneously access equity from multiple countries. Their efforts in placing the stock are focused on a few countries where they have large subsidiaries that need financing. The stock will be listed on an exchange in the foreign country and denominated in the local currency so that investors there can sell their holdings of the stock in the local stock market. Investors in a foreign country will be more willing to purchase shares in a global equity offering if the MNC places a large number of shares in that country because this ensures a more active and liquid secondary market for the stock in that country. Hence those investors can more easily sell their shares in the secondary market in the future.

EXAMPLE   Georgia Co. engages in a global offering in which a portion of the stock is denominated in dollars. The proceeds received from selling the dollar-denominated stock are used to support the operations of subsidiaries in the United States. This stock is placed with investors in the United States, who can easily sell the stock in the future because it is listed on U.S. stock exchanges.

Another portion of the global stock offering is denominated in Japanese yen, and the proceeds of this portion are used to support operations by Georgia's Japanese subsidiary. This stock is placed with Japanese investors who can easily sell the stock in the future because it is listed on a Japanese stock exchange.

Another portion of Georgia's global stock offering is denominated in euros, and the proceeds of this portion are to be used to support operations by Georgia's European subsidiary. This stock is placed with European investors who can easily sell the stock in the future because it is listed on a European stock exchange. ●

Multinational corporations that issue stock on a global basis are typically more capable of issuing new stock at the stock's prevailing market price than are MNCs that issue stock only in their home country. MNCs are better able to issue stock globally if they are large and have global name recognition. A global equity offering may be ineffective in countries where there are weak disclosure laws, weak shareholder protection laws, and weak enforcement of the securities laws because there may be limited demand for stock by investors in such countries.

In addition, an MNC would consider raising funds from a stock offering in a foreign country only if the country's prevailing stock market valuations are relatively high. If the valuations are low, a stock offering would not attract much interest and would not generate a sufficient amount of funds for the MNC.

Private Placement of Equity   Another source of equity for MNCs is to offer a private placement of equity to financial institutions in their home country or in the foreign country where they are expanding. Like private placements of debt, private placements of equity may reduce transaction costs. However, MNCs may not be able to obtain all the funds that they need with a private placement. The funding must come from a limited number of large investors who are willing to maintain the investment for a long period of time because the equity may be subject to conditions regarding its resale.

Subsidiary's Offering of Its Own Stock   A foreign subsidiary of the MNC could engage in a public offering of its own stock, assuming that it receives approval from the parent. If shares of the subsidiary stock are sold to investors in the host country, the subsidiary would no longer be wholly owned by the parent, although the parent would likely remain as the majority owner.

If an MNC allows a subsidiary to issue its own stock, the parent may offer the managers of the subsidiary shares of this stock as partial compensation to encourage them to make decisions that maximize the stock's value. However, there is a potential conflict of interest when a foreign subsidiary is partially financed with its own stock and its managers are minority shareholders. These managers may make decisions that benefit the subsidiary at the expense of the MNC overall. For example, they may use funds for projects that are feasible from their perspective but not from the parent's perspective. Although some subsidiaries have issued their own stock, most MNC parents prefer to own all the equity of their subsidiaries. Thus the subsidiary is more likely to increase its equity over time by retaining earnings than by issuing its own stock.

17-2 The MNC's Capital Structure Decision

An MNC's capital structure decision involves the choice of debt versus equity financing within all of its subsidiaries. The advantages of using debt as opposed to equity vary with corporate characteristics specific to each MNC and specific to the countries where the MNC has established subsidiaries.

17-2a Influence of Corporate Characteristics

Characteristics unique to each MNC can influence its capital structure, as described next.

MNC's Cash Flow Stability   Multinational corporations with more stable cash flows can handle more debt because there is a constant stream of cash inflows to cover periodic interest payments on debt. Conversely, MNCs with erratic cash flows may prefer less debt because they are not assured of generating enough cash in each period to make larger interest payments on debt. An MNC that is diversified across several countries may have more stable cash flows because the conditions in any single country should not have a major impact on cash flows. Consequently, such MNCs may be able to handle a more debt-intensive capital structure.

MNC's Credit Risk   Multinational corporations that have lower credit risk (risk of default on loans provided by creditors) have more access to credit. An MNC with assets that serve as acceptable collateral (such as buildings and adaptable machinery) can more easily secure loans and so may prefer to emphasize debt financing. In contrast, MNCs with assets that do not serve as adequate collateral may need to use a higher proportion of equity financing.

MNC's Access to Retained Earnings   Highly profitable MNCs may be able to finance most of their investment with retained earnings and therefore use an equity-intensive capital structure; MNCs that generate small levels of earnings may rely mainly on debt financing. Growth-oriented MNCs may commonly need more funds than can be accessed from retained earnings, so they tend to rely on debt financing. In contrast, MNCs with less growth may be able to rely on retained earnings (equity) rather than debt.

MNC's Guarantees on Debt   If the parent backs the debt of its subsidiary, the subsidiary's borrowing capacity should be increased. In that case, the subsidiary would need less equity financing. At the same time, however, the parent's borrowing capacity might be reduced because creditors will be less willing to provide funds to the parent if those funds might be needed to rescue the subsidiary.

MNC's Agency Problems   If a subsidiary in a foreign country cannot easily be monitored by investors from the parent's country, agency costs are higher. The parent may require the subsidiary to rely more on debt financing, because this will force the subsidiary to be disciplined in order to cover its periodic loan payments.

17-2b Influence of Host Country Characteristics

In addition to characteristics unique to each MNC, the following characteristics unique to each host country can influence the MNC's choice of debt versus equity financing and thereby influence the MNC's capital structure.

Interest Rates in Host Countries   The price of loanable funds (the interest rate) can vary across countries. Consequently, an MNC's preference for debt may depend on the cost of debt in the countries where it operates. If the interest rate in a subsidiary's country appears excessive, the parent may prefer to provide its own financing for projects implemented by the subsidiary.

Strength of Host Country Currencies   If an MNC is concerned about the potential weakness of the currencies in its subsidiaries' host countries, it may instruct these subsidiaries to finance a large proportion of their operations by borrowing in

WEB

www.worldbank.org
Country profiles, analyses, and sectoral surveys.

those currencies instead of relying on parent financing. In this way, the subsidiaries will remit a smaller amount in earnings because they will be making interest payments on local debt. This strategy reduces the MNC's exposure to exchange rate risk.

If the parent believes that a subsidiary's local currency will appreciate against the parent's currency, then it may have the subsidiary retain and reinvest more of its earnings. As a result, the subsidiary will reduce its reliance on local debt financing.

Country Risk in Host Countries   A relatively mild form of country risk is the possibility that the host government will temporarily block funds to be remitted by the subsidiary to the parent. Subsidiaries that are prevented from remitting earnings over a period may prefer to use local debt financing. This strategy reduces the amount of funds that are blocked because the subsidiary can use some of the funds to pay interest on local debt.

If an MNC's subsidiary is exposed to the risk that the host government might confiscate its assets, then the subsidiary may rely mostly on debt financing in that host country. Then local creditors that have loaned funds will have a genuine interest in ensuring that the subsidiary is treated fairly by the host government. In addition, if the MNC's operations in a foreign country are terminated by the host government, it will not lose as much if its operations are financed by local creditors. Under these circumstances, the local creditors will have to negotiate with the host government to obtain all or part of the funds they have loaned after the host government liquidates the assets it confiscates from the MNC.

Alternatively, the subsidiary could issue stock in the host country. Local investors who are minority shareholders benefit directly from a profitable subsidiary. Therefore, they could pressure their local government to refrain from imposing excessive taxes, environmental constraints, or any other provisions that would reduce the subsidiary's profits. Having local investors own a minority interest in a subsidiary may also offer some protection against threats of adverse actions by the host government. Another advantage of a partially owned subsidiary is that it may open up additional opportunities in the host country. The subsidiary's name will become better known when its shares are acquired by minority shareholders in that country. As noted earlier, however, if the subsidiary's managers are minority shareholders, a conflict of interest between parent and subsidiary could arise if the managers make decisions that benefit the subsidiary at the expense of the parent.

Tax Laws in Host Countries   Foreign subsidiaries of an MNC may be subject to a withholding tax when they remit earnings. By using local debt financing instead of relying on parent financing, they will make interest payments on the local debt that should reduce the amount to be remitted periodically. Thus the subsidiary reduces the withholding taxes by using more local debt financing.

17-2c Response to Changing Country Characteristics

The country characteristics just described vary among countries and also can change over time in any particular country. Thus these characteristics explain not only *why* the ideal capital structure may vary among countries but also *how* the ideal capital structure could change within any particular country over time.

EXAMPLE

Plymouth Co. has subsidiaries in several countries that have just revised their capital structure levels as follows:

■   Plymouth Co. is concerned that the Japanese yen will depreciate substantially over the next two years. The company instructs its subsidiary in Japan to remit all earnings to the parent over the next year, before the yen depreciates. Consequently, the Japanese subsidiary cannot rely on retained earnings (equity) to support its operations and must rely more heavily on local debt.

■ Plymouth Co. has a subsidiary in India, where the government has announced it will eliminate its withholding tax on remitted funds. This subsidiary will now remit more of its earnings to the parent. Thus the subsidiary will rely less on retained earnings and more on local debt to support its operations.

■ Plymouth Co. has a subsidiary in Chile, where the government has announced it will block the remission of funds for the next year. This subsidiary will use the blocked funds that it would otherwise have remitted to pay off its local debt in Chile. This subsidiary's capital structure will become more equity intensive.

■ Plymouth Co. has a subsidiary in Argentina that will rely more on retained earnings because local interest rates have increased, thereby boosting the cost of local debt. The subsidiary's capital structure will become more equity intensive.

Overall, country conditions caused two of the subsidiaries to use a more debt-intensive capital structure, while causing two other subsidiaries to use a more equity-intensive capital structure. ●

WEB

http://finance.yahoo.com
Capital repatriation
regulations imposed by
each country.

17-3 Subsidiary versus Parent Capital Structure Decisions

The capital structure of an MNC's subsidiaries may vary because some subsidiaries are subject to conditions that favor debt financing whereas others are subject to conditions that favor equity financing. Because the subsidiary's capital structure decision affects the amount of retained earnings that are remitted to the parent, that decision affects the amount of equity contributed to the parent and so affects the parent's capital structure. Thus the capital structure decisions of subsidiaries affect the capital structure of the parent and should be made in consultation with the parent. The potential impact of subsidiary financing on the parent's capital structure is illustrated next.

17-3a Impact of Increased Subsidiary Debt Financing

When a subsidiary relies heavily on debt financing, its need for internal equity financing (retained earnings) is reduced. Because these "extra" internal funds are remitted to the parent, the parent will itself have a larger amount of internal funds to use before resorting to external financing. Assuming that the parent's operations absorb all internal funds and require some debt financing, there are offsetting effects on the capital structures of the subsidiary and the parent. The increased use of debt financing by the subsidiary is offset by the reduced debt financing of the parent. Because the subsidiary may have more financial leverage than is desired for the MNC overall, the parent may use less financial leverage to finance its own operations in order to achieve its overall ("global") target capital structure.

17-3b Impact of Reduced Subsidiary Debt Financing

When global conditions encourage the subsidiary to use less debt financing, it will need to use more internal financing. The subsidiary will therefore remit fewer funds, reducing the amount of internal funds available to the parent. If the parent's operations absorb all internal funds and require some debt financing, then there are offsetting effects on the capital structures of the subsidiary and parent. The subsidiary's reduced use of debt financing is offset by the parent's increased use. Thus even though a local (specific subsidiary) capital structure has changed, it is seldom necessary for the MNC's global capital structure to change. An MNC can still achieve its target capital structure by offsetting one subsidiary's change in financial leverage with an opposite change in the financial leverage of another subsidiary or of the parent.

17-3c Limitations in Offsetting a Subsidiary's Leverage

The strategy of offsetting a subsidiary's shift in financial leverage to achieve a global target capital structure is rational as long as it is acceptable to foreign creditors and investors. However, foreign creditors may charge higher loan rates to a subsidiary that uses a highly leveraged local capital structure (even if the MNC's global capital structure is more balanced) because they believe that the subsidiary may be unable to meet its high debt repayments. If the parent plans to back the subsidiaries, however, it could guarantee debt repayment to the creditors in the foreign countries; doing so might reduce their risk perception and lower the cost of the debt. Many MNC parents stand ready to financially back their subsidiaries because, if they did not, their subsidiaries would be unable to obtain adequate financing.

17-4 Multinational Cost of Capital

Because an MNC's capital represents its debt and its equity, its cost of capital is based on its cost of debt and its cost of equity.

17-4a MNC's Cost of Debt

An MNC's cost of debt depends on the interest rate that it pays when borrowing funds. The interest rate that it pays is equal to the risk-free rate at the time it borrows funds along with a credit risk premium that compensates creditors for accepting credit (default) risk when extending credit to the MNC. Because interest expenses incurred by corporations are deductible when determining a corporation's taxable income, there is a tax advantage associated with debt.

17-4b MNC's Cost of Equity

An MNC creates equity by retaining earnings or by issuing new stock. The firm's cost of retained earnings reflects an opportunity cost, which represents what the existing shareholders could have earned if they had received the earnings as dividends and invested the funds themselves. The MNC's cost of new equity (from issuing new common stock) also reflects an opportunity cost of what the new shareholders could have earned if they had invested their funds elsewhere instead of in the stock. This cost exceeds that of retained earnings because it also includes the expenses (known as "flotation costs") associated with selling the new stock.

An MNC's cost of equity contains a risk premium (above the risk-free interest rate) that compensates the equity investors for their willingness to invest in the equity. If investors thought the MNC would offer a future return on equity that was no higher than the prevailing risk-free rate, then they would not invest in its equity because they would rather earn that same return without any exposure to risk by investing in a risk-free Treasury security. When investing in an MNC's equity, there is uncertainty surrounding the return on that investment. Thus the price of equity must be low enough that investors can expect it to increase and thus offer them a return that reflects a premium above the risk-free rate.

The equity risk premium that investors would expect in order to invest in an MNC's equity (instead of investing in a risk-free security or in other securities) depends on the risk of the MNC. Those MNCs with higher levels of uncertainty surrounding their cash flows exhibit a higher level of risk. Thus, to entice investors, the stock price of an MNC with high risk must be low enough so that the investment can potentially offer a large enough return to compensate for the risk involved.

17-4c **Estimating an MNC's Cost of Capital**

The cost of an MNC's capital (denoted k_c) can be measured as the cost of its debt plus the cost of its equity, with appropriate weights applied in order to reflect the percentage of the MNC's capital represented by debt and equity, respectively:

$$ k_c = \left(\frac{D}{D+E} \right) k_d (1-t) + \left(\frac{E}{D+E} \right) k_e $$

where

$D =$ amount of the firm's debt
$k_d =$ before-tax cost of the firm's debt
$t =$ corporate tax rate
$E =$ amount of the firm's equity
$k_e =$ cost of financing with equity

The weights assigned to debt and equity appear within large parentheses in the preceding equation.

17-4d **Comparing Costs of Debt and Equity**

There is an advantage to using debt rather than equity as capital because the interest payments on debt are tax deductible. The greater the use of debt, however, the greater the interest expense and the higher the probability that the firm will be unable to meet its expenses. Consequently, as an MNC increases its proportion of debt, the rate of return required by potential new shareholders or creditors will increase to reflect the greater likelihood of bankruptcy.

The trade-off between debt's advantage (tax deductibility of interest payments) and its disadvantage (increased likelihood of bankruptcy) is illustrated in Exhibit 17.1. The graph shows the relationship between the firm's degree of financial leverage (as measured by the ratio of debt to total capital on the horizontal axis) and the cost of capital (on the vertical axis). When the ratio of debt to total capital is low, there is not much concern that the firm will go bankrupt because the firm should be able to cover its debt payments easily. Under these conditions, the tax advantage of debt overwhelms the disadvantage of debt (potential concerns about bankruptcy).

Yet at some point (labeled X in Exhibit 17.1), the debt ratio is high enough to trigger concern by creditors and shareholders about the firm's potential bankruptcy. The larger amount of debt would require the firm to make higher debt payments, which would increase the probability of the firm going bankrupt. At such a higher level of debt, the firm would incur a higher cost of additional debt to reflect the higher level of credit risk. In addition, investors might require higher returns (which means a higher cost of equity from the firm's perspective) in order to invest because of the firm's higher risk of bankruptcy. Consequently, when the ratio of debt to total capital is beyond point X on the horizontal axis, the cost of capital rises as the ratio of debt to total capital

Exhibit 17.1   Searching for the Appropriate Capital Structure

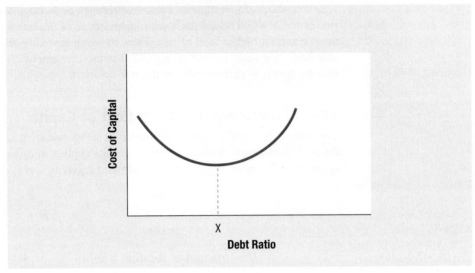

increases. The firm's cost of capital is minimized at point X, where it benefits from the tax advantage of debt but does not use so much debt that its tax advantage is overwhelmed by concerns about the firm's bankruptcy.

17-4e Cost of Capital for MNCs versus Domestic Firms

The cost of capital for MNCs may differ from that for domestic firms because of the following characteristics that distinguish MNCs from domestic firms.

Size of Firm   An MNC that often borrows substantial amounts may receive preferential treatment from creditors, thereby reducing its cost of capital. Furthermore, its relatively large issues of stocks or bonds allow for reduced flotation costs (as a percentage of the amount of financing). Note, however, that these advantages are due to the MNC's size and not to its internationalized business. A domestic corporation may receive the same treatment if it is large enough. Nevertheless, a firm's growth is more restricted if it is not willing to operate internationally. Because MNCs may more easily achieve growth, they may be more able than purely domestic firms to become large enough to receive preferential treatment from creditors.

Access to International Capital Markets   Multinational corporations are normally able to obtain funds through the international capital markets. Because the cost of funds can vary among markets, the MNC's access to the international capital markets may allow it to obtain funds at a lower cost than that paid by domestic firms. In addition, subsidiaries may be able to obtain funds locally at a lower cost than that available to the parent if the prevailing interest rates in the host country are relatively low.

EXAMPLE   The Coca-Cola Co.'s recent annual report stated: "Our global presence and strong capital position afford us easy access to key financial markets around the world, enabling us to raise funds with a low effective cost. This posture, coupled with the aggressive management of our mix of short-term and long-term debt, results in a lower overall cost of borrowing." ●

International Diversification   As explained earlier, a firm's cost of capital is affected by the probability that it will go bankrupt. If a firm's cash inflows come from sources all over the world, those cash inflows may be more stable because the firm's total sales will not be strongly influenced by a single economy. To the extent that individual economies are independent of each other, net cash flows from a portfolio of subsidiaries should exhibit less variability, which may reduce the probability of bankruptcy and therefore reduce the cost of capital.

Exposure to Exchange Rate Risk An MNC's cash flows could be more volatile than those of a domestic firm in the same industry if it is highly exposed to exchange rate risk. If foreign earnings are remitted to the U.S. parent, they will not be worth as much when the U.S. dollar is strong against major currencies. This reduces the firm's ability to make interest payments on its outstanding debt, which increases the likelihood of bankruptcy. In addition, an MNC that is more exposed to exchange rate fluctuations will usually have a wider (more dispersed) distribution of possible cash flows in future periods. This could lead creditors and shareholders to require a higher return, which would increase the MNC's cost of capital.

Exposure to Country Risk An MNC that establishes foreign subsidiaries is subject to the possibility that a host country government may seize a subsidiary's assets. The probability of such an occurrence is influenced by many factors, including the industry in which the MNC operates and the attitude of the host country government. If assets are seized and fair compensation is not provided, the probability of the MNC's going bankrupt increases. The higher the percentage of an MNC's assets invested in foreign countries and the higher the overall country risk of operating in these countries, the higher will be the MNC's probability of bankruptcy (and therefore its cost of capital), other things being equal.

Other more moderate forms of country risk, such as changes in a host government's tax laws, could also affect an MNC's subsidiary's cash flows. Because it is possible that these events will occur, the capital budgeting process should incorporate such risk.

EXAMPLE   ExxonMobil has much experience in assessing the feasibility of potential projects in foreign countries. If it detects a radical change in government or tax policy, it adds a premium to the required return of related projects. The adjustment also reflects a possible increase in its cost of capital. ●

The five factors that distinguish the cost of capital for an MNC and the cost for a domestic firm in a particular industry are summarized in Exhibit 17.2. In general, the first three factors listed (size, access to international capital markets, and international diversification) have a favorable effect on an MNC's cost of capital; the next two factors (exposure to exchange rate risk and country risk) have an unfavorable effect. It is impossible to generalize about whether MNCs have an overall cost-of-capital advantage over domestic firms. Each MNC should be assessed separately to determine whether the net effects of its international operations on the cost of capital are favorable.

17-4f Cost-of-Equity Comparison Using the CAPM

To assess how the cost of equity for an MNC differs from that cost for a purely domestic firm, the capital asset pricing model (CAPM) can be applied. This model defines the required return (k_e) on a stock as

$$k_e = R_f + B(R_m - R_f)$$

where

$$R_f = \text{risk-free rate of return}$$
$$R_m = \text{market return}$$
$$B = \text{beta of stock}$$

Exhibit 17.2   Summary of Factors That Cause the Cost of Capital to Differ for MNCs versus Domestic Firms

The CAPM suggests that the required return on a firm's stock is a positive function of (1) the risk-free rate of interest, (2) the market rate of return, and (3) the stock's beta. The *beta* refers to the sensitivity of a stock's returns to market returns (a U.S. stock index is normally used as a proxy for the market when assessing the stock of a U.S. company).

Implications of the CAPM for an MNC's Risk   A U.S.-based MNC that increases the amount of its international business may be able to reduce the sensitivity of its stock returns to a stock index, thereby reducing its stock's beta. According to the previous equation, an MNC that can reduce its beta (for example, by increasing its international business) will be able to reduce the return required by investors. In this way, the MNC can reduce its cost of equity and therefore its cost of capital.

Implications of the CAPM for an MNC's Projects   Advocates of the CAPM may suggest that a project's beta can be used to determine the required rate of return for that project. The beta of a U.S.-based firm's project represents the sensitivity of the project's cash flow to U.S. market conditions. For a well-diversified firm with cash flows generated by several projects, each project contains two types of risk: (1) systematic risk, which is the project risk due to general market conditions; and (2) unsystematic risk, which is the risk unique to the specific project. Capital asset pricing theory suggests that the unsystematic risk of projects can be ignored because it will be diversified away if a firm engages in many projects. However, the systematic risk of the firm's projects cannot be diversified away because all the firm's projects are exposed to this risk.

Because many projects of U.S.-based MNCs are in foreign countries, their cash flows are less sensitive to general U.S. market conditions. Thus the betas of their projects should be relatively low, which means that the rate of return required by investors should be low. This translates into a lower cost of equity and thus a lower overall cost of capital.

However, some investors may consider unsystematic project risk to be relevant. For example, when a U.S.-based MNC has projects in Asia and South America, the cash flows of these projects may not be very sensitive to U.S. market conditions, which means that the systematic risk of the projects is low. Yet the project cash flows may be very uncertain because of unsystematic risk, such as high country risk associated with a particular project. Investors will not necessarily ignore the unsystematic risk, even if the MNC is well diversified, because they recognize that it could affect the overall cash flows and profitability of the MNC. Under these conditions, the required rate of return by investors will not necessarily be lower for an MNC's projects than for projects of domestic firms.

Applying the CAPM with a World Market Index   The CAPM as presented here is based on the sensitivity of project cash flows to a U.S. stock index. If U.S. investors invest mostly in the United States, then their investments are systematically affected by the U.S. market. Thus MNCs may be more capable of pursuing international projects with cash flows that are *not* sensitive to the U.S. market.

However, a world market may be more appropriate than a U.S. market for determining the betas of U.S.-based MNCs. That is, if investors purchase stocks across many countries, their stocks will be substantially affected by world market conditions and not only by U.S. market conditions. Consequently, to achieve more diversification benefits, they will prefer to invest in firms with low sensitivity to world market conditions, not just to U.S. market conditions. When MNCs adopt projects that are isolated from general world market conditions, they may be able to reduce their overall sensitivity to such conditions and so might be viewed as more desirable investments by investors. However, it may be more difficult for MNCs (than for domestic firms) to achieve lower betas on projects if the beta is based on sensitivity to general world market conditions.

In summary, we cannot say with certainty whether an MNC will have a lower cost of capital than a purely domestic firm in the same industry. However, this discussion illustrates how the conclusion from comparing the cost of equity for MNCs versus domestic firms depends on the measurement of risk chosen.

WEB

www.pwc.com
Access to country-specific information such as general business rules and regulations, tax environments, and other useful statistics and surveys.

17-5 Cost of Capital across Countries

An understanding of why the cost of capital can vary among countries is relevant for three reasons. First, it can explain why MNCs based in some countries may have a competitive advantage over others. Multinational corporations based in some countries with a low cost of capital will have a larger set of feasible (positive-NPV) projects; thus these MNCs can more easily increase their world market share.

Second, MNCs may be able to adjust their international operations and sources of funds to capitalize on differences in the cost of capital among countries. Third, differences in the costs of each capital component (debt and equity) can help explain why MNCs based in some countries tend to use a more debt-intensive capital structure than MNCs based elsewhere. Country differences in the cost of debt are discussed next, followed by country differences in the cost of equity.

17-5a Country Differences in the Cost of Debt

The cost of debt to a firm is primarily determined by the prevailing risk-free interest rate in the currency borrowed and the debt risk premium required by creditors. The cost of debt for firms is higher in some countries than in others because the corresponding risk-free rate is higher at a certain time or because the credit risk premium is higher. Explanations for country differences in the risk-free rate and in the credit risk premium follow.

Differences in the Risk-Free Rate   The risk-free rate is the interest rate charged on loans to a country's government that is perceived to have no risk of defaulting on the loans. Many country governments are presumed to have no credit risk because they can increase taxes or reduce expenditures if necessary in order to have sufficient funds to repay debt.

Any factors that influence the supply of or the demand for loanable funds within a country will affect the risk-free rate. These factors include tax laws, demographics, monetary policies, and economic conditions, all of which differ among countries. Tax laws in some countries offer more incentives to save than those in others; this can influence the supply of savings and, by extension, interest rates. A country's corporate tax laws may affect the corporate demand for loanable funds and thus may affect interest rates.

A country's demographics influence the supply of savings available and the amount of loanable funds demanded. Because demographics differ among countries, so will supply and demand conditions and, as a result, nominal interest rates. Countries with younger populations are likely to experience higher interest rates because younger households tend to save less and borrow more.

Because economic conditions influence interest rates, they can cause interest rates to vary across countries. The cost of debt is much higher in many less developed countries than in industrialized countries, primarily because of economic conditions. Countries such as Brazil and Russia have a high risk-free interest rate, which is due in part to higher levels of expected inflation. Investors in these countries will invest in a firm's debt securities only if they are compensated beyond the degree to which prices of products are expected to increase.

The monetary policy implemented by a country's central bank influences the supply of loanable funds and therefore influences interest rates. Each central bank implements its own monetary policy, and this can cause interest rates to differ among countries. One exception is the set of European countries that rely on the European Central Bank to control the supply of euros. Most of these countries have a similar risk-free rate because they use the same currency.

Differences in the Credit Risk Premium   Most MNCs must pay a credit premium above the prevailing risk-free rate in the country where they obtain loans. The credit risk premium paid by an MNC must be large enough to compensate creditors for taking the risk that the MNC may not meet its payment obligations.

The credit risk premium on an MNC's loans is strongly affected by characteristics of the creditors' country, such as its economic conditions, the relationship between its creditors and borrowers, and its government's willingness to rescue troubled companies. When a country's economic conditions tend to be stable, the risk of a recession in that country is relatively low. Hence the probability that a firm might not meet its debt obligations is lower, which allows for a lower credit risk premium.

Corporations and creditors have closer relationships in some countries than in others. Creditors in Japan stand ready to extend credit in the event of a corporation's financial distress, which reduces the risk of illiquidity. The cost of a Japanese firm's financial problems may be shared in various ways by the firm's management, business customers, and consumers. Because the financial problems are not borne entirely by creditors, all parties involved have more incentive to see that the problems are resolved. Thus there is less likelihood (for a given level of debt) that Japanese firms will go bankrupt, allowing for a lower risk premium on the debt of Japanese firms.

Some countries' governments are more willing than others to intervene and rescue local failing firms. For example, in the United Kingdom many firms are partially owned by the government. It may be in the government's best interest to rescue firms that it partially owns. Even if the government is not a partial owner, it may provide direct subsidies or extend loans to failing firms based in that country. In the United States, government rescues are less likely because taxpayers prefer not to bear the cost of corporate mismanagement. Although the U.S. government has intervened occasionally (such as during the credit crisis of 2008) to protect particular industries, the probability that a failing firm will be rescued by the government is lower in the United States than in other countries.

Firms in some countries have greater borrowing capacity because their creditors are willing to tolerate a higher degree of financial leverage. For example, firms in Japan and Germany have a higher degree of financial leverage than firms in the United States. If all other factors were equal, these high-leverage firms would have to pay a higher risk premium. However, all other factors are not equal. In fact, these firms are allowed to use a higher degree of financial leverage because of their unique relationships with the creditors and governments.

WEB

www.bloomberg.com
Latest information from
financial markets around
the world.

Comparative Costs of Debt across Countries   The before-tax cost of debt (as measured by high-rated corporate bond yields) for various countries is displayed in Exhibit 17.3. There is some positive correlation between country cost-of-debt levels over time. Notice how interest rates in various countries tend to move in the same direction. However, some rates change to a greater degree than others. The disparity in the cost of debt among the countries is due primarily to the disparity in their risk-free interest rates.

17-5b Country Differences in the Cost of Equity

A firm's cost of equity represents an opportunity cost: what shareholders could earn on investments with similar risk if the equity funds were distributed to them. The cost of equity among firms per country can vary because of differences in country characteristics.

Differences in the Risk-Free Rate   Because risk-free interest rates vary among countries, so does the cost of equity. When the country's risk-free interest rate is high, local investors would invest in equity only if the potential return is sufficiently higher than what they can earn at the risk-free rate. Thus firms that wish to attract equity funding must compensate the local investors by offering a high return. In contrast, if the country's interest rate is low, local investors may be more willing to consider equity investments because they do not give up much by switching away from risk-free government securities.

Differences in the Equity Risk Premium   The equity risk premium is partially based on investment opportunities in the country of concern. In a country where firms have many investment opportunities, potential returns may be relatively high. Firms are able to sell stock at relatively high prices, which means that they can obtain equity funding at a low cost (they pay a relatively small equity premium). Conversely, in a country where investment opportunities are limited, investors will be less willing to invest in

Exhibit 17.3 Costs of Debt across Countries

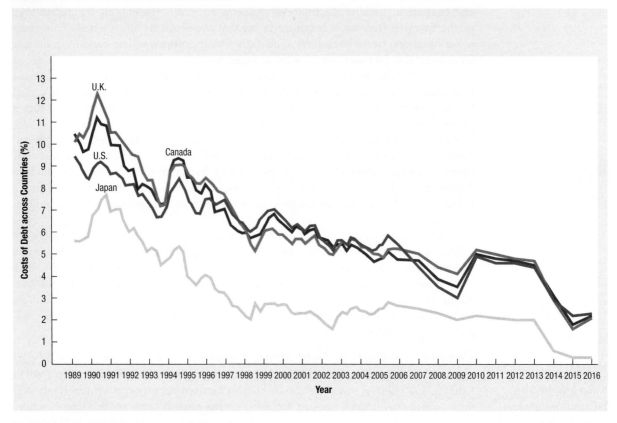

Source: U.S. Federal Reserve.

equity. Firms would have to sell stock at relatively low prices, which means that they can obtain equity funding only at a high cost (they pay a large equity premium). In other words, they must offer a relatively large amount of stock in order to obtain adequate funding to pursue a particular project.

A second factor that can influence the equity risk premium is the country risk. In a country where the government is stable and is not viewed as a threat to business expansion, local firms are more capable of selling stock easily. They can issue stock at relatively high prices because of the large number of investors who are willing to buy stock, which allows the firms to access equity funding at a relatively low cost. Conversely, in a country where country risk problems (such as government corruption, political instability, and government bureaucracy) are severe, local firms may be able to sell stock only at a relatively low price. That is, they would have to pay a high equity premium to attract investors because of concerns that the local environment could disrupt business opportunities.

In addition, the country's laws on corporate disclosure, legal protection of local shareholders, and enforcement of securities laws can affect the cost of equity. Laws on corporate disclosure can ensure that local firms are transparent and can be more easily monitored by shareholders. Strong legal protection of shareholders and enforcement of securities laws may encourage more investors to invest in equity without concern about fraud. This enables firms to issue stock at relatively high prices, so that they incur a relatively low cost of equity. Conversely, a lack of disclosure, legal protection, and enforcement in a country will discourage investors from investing in local stocks, so local firms will have to sell stock at relatively low prices (incur a high cost of equity).

One method of comparing the cost of equity among countries is to review the stock price/earnings ratio of firms in various countries. This ratio measures the market value of a firm's equity in proportion to the firm's recent performance (as measured by earnings). A high price/earnings ratio implies that the firm could receive a relatively high price for its stock, based on a given level of earnings. Thus its cost of equity financing is low. The price/earnings ratio varies among firms, but the *mean* price/earnings ratio should be higher in countries that exhibit the favorable country characteristics of promoting business expansion and shareholder rights.

SUMMARY

- An MNC's capital consists of debt and equity. MNCs can access debt through domestic debt offerings, global debt offerings, private placements of debt, and loans from financial institutions. They can access equity by retaining earnings and by issuing stock through domestic offerings, global offerings, and private placements of equity.

- An MNC's capital structure decision is influenced by corporate characteristics such as the stability of the MNC's cash flows, its credit risk, and its access to earnings. The capital structure is also influenced by characteristics of the countries where the MNC conducts business, such as interest rates, strength of local currencies, country risk, and tax laws. Some characteristics favor an equity-intensive capital structure because they discourage the use of debt. Other characteristics favor a debt-intensive structure because of the desire to protect against risks by creating foreign debt.

- If a foreign subsidiary's financial leverage deviates from the parent MNC's global target capital structure, the MNC can still achieve the target if either another subsidiary or the parent takes an offsetting position in financial leverage. However, even with these offsetting effects, the cost of capital might be affected.

- The cost of capital may be lower for an MNC than for a domestic firm because of characteristics peculiar to the MNC, including its size, its access to international capital markets, and its degree of international diversification. Yet some characteristics peculiar to an MNC can increase the MNC's cost of capital, such as exposure to exchange rate risk and to country risk.

- Costs of capital vary across countries because of country differences in the components that constitute the cost of capital. Specifically, there are differences in the risk-free rate, the risk premium on debt, and the cost of equity among countries. Countries with a higher risk-free rate tend to exhibit a higher cost of capital.

POINT COUNTER-POINT

Should a Reduced Tax Rate on Dividends Affect an MNC's Capital Structure?

Point No. A change in the tax law reduces the taxes that investors pay on dividends. It does not change the taxes paid by the MNC. Thus it should not affect the capital structure of the MNC.

Counter-Point Yes. A dividend income tax reduction may encourage a U.S.-based MNC to offer dividends to its shareholders or to increase the dividend payment. This strategy reflects an increase in the cash outflows of the MNC. To offset these

outflows, the MNC may have to adjust its capital structure. For example, the next time that it raises funds, it may prefer to use equity rather than debt so that it can free up some cash outflows (the outflows to cover dividends would be less than outflows associated with debt).

Who Is Correct? Use the Internet to learn more about this issue. Which argument do you support? Offer your own opinion on this issue.

SELF-TEST

Answers are provided in Appendix A at the back of the text.

1. When Goshen, Inc., focused only on domestic business in the United States, it had a low debt level. As it expanded into other countries, it increased its degree of financial leverage (on a consolidated basis). What factors would have caused Goshen to increase its financial leverage (assuming that country risk was not a concern)?

2. Lynde Co. is a U.S.-based MNC with a large subsidiary in the Philippines financed with equity from the parent. In response to news about a possible change in the Philippine government, the subsidiary revised its capital structure by borrowing from local banks and transferring the equity investment back to the U.S. parent. Explain the likely motive behind these actions.

3. Duever Co. (a U.S. firm) noticed that its financial leverage was substantially lower than that of most successful firms in Germany and Japan in the same industry. Is Duever's capital structure less than optimal?

4. Atlanta, Inc., has a large subsidiary in Venezuela, where interest rates are very high and the currency is expected to weaken. Assume that Atlanta perceives the country risk to be high. Explain the trade-off involved in financing the subsidiary with local debt versus an equity investment from the parent.

5. Reno, Inc., is considering a project to establish a plant for producing and selling consumer goods in an undeveloped country. Assume that the host country's economy is very dependent on oil prices, the local currency of the country is very volatile, and the country risk is very high. Also assume that the country's economic conditions are unrelated to U.S. conditions. Should the required rate of return (and therefore the risk premium) on the project be higher or lower than that of alternative projects in the United States?

QUESTIONS AND APPLICATIONS

1. Capital Structure of MNCs Present an argument in support of an MNC favoring a debt-intensive capital structure. Present an argument in support of an MNC favoring an equity-intensive capital structure.

2. Optimal Financing Wizard, Inc., has a subsidiary in a country where the government allows only a small amount of earnings to be remitted to the United States each year. Should Wizard finance the subsidiary with debt financing by the parent, equity financing by the parent, or financing by local banks in the foreign country?

3. Country Differences Describe general differences between the capital structures of firms based in the United States and those of firms based in Japan. Offer an explanation for these differences.

4. Local versus Global Capital Structure Why might a firm use a "local" capital structure at a particular subsidiary that differs substantially from its "global" capital structure?

5. Cost of Capital Explain how characteristics of MNCs can affect the cost of capital.

6. Capital Structure and Agency Issues Explain why managers of a wholly owned subsidiary may be more likely to satisfy the shareholders of the MNC.

7. Target Capital Structure LaSalle Corp. is a U.S.-based MNC with subsidiaries in various less developed countries where stock markets are not well established. How can LaSalle still achieve its "global" target capital structure of 50 percent debt and 50 percent equity if it plans to use only debt financing for the subsidiaries in these countries?

8. Financing Decision Drexel Co. is a U.S.-based company that is establishing a project in a politically unstable country. It is considering two possible sources of financing. Either the parent could provide most of the financing, or the subsidiary could be supported by local loans from banks in that country. Which financing alternative is more appropriate to protect the subsidiary?

9. Financing Decision Veer Co. is a U.S.-based MNC that has most of its operations in Japan. Because the Japanese companies with which it competes use more financial leverage, it has decided to adjust its financial leverage to be in line with theirs. With this heavy emphasis on debt, Veer should reap more tax advantages. It believes that the market's perception of its risk will remain unchanged, because its financial leverage will still be no higher than that of its Japanese competitors. Comment on this strategy.

10. Financing Trade-Offs Pullman, Inc., a U.S. firm, has been highly profitable but prefers not to pay out higher dividends because its shareholders want the funds to be reinvested. It plans for large growth in several less developed countries. Pullman would like to finance the growth with local debt in the host countries of concern to reduce its exposure to country risk. Explain the dilemma faced by Pullman, and offer possible solutions.

11. Costs of Capital across Countries Explain why the cost of capital for a U.S.-based MNC with a large subsidiary in Brazil is higher than for a U.S.-based MNC in the same industry with a large subsidiary in Japan. Assume that the subsidiary operations for each MNC are financed with local debt in the host country.

12. Cost of Capital An MNC has total assets of $100 million and debt of $20 million. The firm's before-tax cost of debt is 12 percent, and its cost of financing with equity is 15 percent. The MNC has a corporate tax rate of 40 percent. What is this firm's cost of capital?

13. Cost of Equity Wiley, Inc., an MNC, has a beta of 1.3. The U.S. stock market is expected to generate an annual return of 11 percent. Currently, Treasury bonds yield 2 percent. Based on this information, what is Wiley's estimated cost of equity?

14. Cost of Capital Blues, Inc., is an MNC located in the United States. Blues would like to estimate its weighted average cost of capital (WACC). On average, bonds issued by Blues yield 9 percent. Currently, Treasury security rates are 3 percent. Furthermore, Blues' stock has a beta of 1.5, and the return on the Wilshire 5000 stock index is expected to be 10 percent. Blues' target capital structure is 30 percent debt and 70 percent equity. If Blues is in the 35 percent tax bracket, what is its weighted average cost of capital?

15. Effects of September 11 Rose, Inc., of Dallas, Texas, needed to infuse capital into its foreign subsidiaries to support their expansion. As of August 2001, it planned to issue stock in the United States. However, after the September 11, 2001, terrorist attack, it decided that long-term debt was a cheaper source of capital. Explain how the terrorist attack could have altered the two forms of capital.

16. Nike's Cost of Capital If Nike decides to expand further in South America, why might its capital structure be affected? Why will its overall cost of capital be affected?

Advanced Questions

17. Interaction between Financing and Investment Charleston Corp. is considering establishing a subsidiary in either Germany or the United Kingdom. The subsidiary will be mostly financed with loans from the local banks in the host country chosen. Charleston has determined that the revenue generated from the British subsidiary will be slightly more favorable than the revenue generated by the German subsidiary, even after considering tax and exchange rate effects. The initial outlay will be the same, and both countries appear to be politically stable. Charleston decides to establish the subsidiary in the United Kingdom because of the revenue advantage. Do you agree with its decision? Explain.

18. Financing Decision In recent years, several U.S. firms have penetrated Mexico's market. One of the biggest challenges is the cost of capital to finance businesses in Mexico. Mexican interest rates tend to be much higher than U.S. interest rates. In some periods, the Mexican government does not attempt to lower the interest rates because higher rates may attract foreign investment in Mexican securities.

a. How might U.S.-based MNCs expand in Mexico without incurring the high Mexican interest expenses when financing their expansion? Are any disadvantages associated with this strategy?

b. Are there any additional alternatives for the Mexican subsidiary to finance its business itself after it has been well established? How might this strategy affect the subsidiary's capital structure?

19. Financing Decision The subsidiaries of Forest Co. produce goods in the United States, Germany, and Australia and sell those goods in the areas where they are produced. Foreign earnings are periodically remitted to the U.S. parent. As the euro's interest rates have declined to a very low level, Forest has decided to finance its German operations with borrowed funds in place of the parent's equity investment. Forest will transfer its equity investment in the German subsidiary over to its Australian subsidiary. These funds will be used to pay off a floating rate loan, as Australian interest rates have been high and are rising. Explain the expected effects of these actions on the consolidated capital structure and cost of capital of Forest Co.

Given the strategy to be used by Forest, explain how its exposure to exchange rate risk may have changed.

20. Financing in a High-Interest Rate Country Fairfield Corp., a U.S. firm, recently established a subsidiary in a less developed country that consistently experiences an annual inflation rate of 80 percent or more. The country does not have an established stock market, but loans by local banks are available with a 90 percent interest rate. Fairfield has decided to use a strategy in which the subsidiary is financed entirely with funds from the parent. It believes that in this way it can avoid the excessive interest rate in the host country. What is a key disadvantage of using this strategy that may cause Fairfield to be no better off than if it paid the 90 percent interest rate?

21. Cost of Foreign Debt versus Equity Carazona, Inc., is a U.S. firm that has a large subsidiary in Indonesia. It wants to finance the subsidiary's operations in Indonesia. However, the cost of debt is currently about 30 percent there for firms like Carazona or government agencies that have a very strong credit rating. A consultant suggests to Carazona that it should use equity financing there to avoid the high interest expense. He suggests that because Carazona's cost of equity in the United States is about 14 percent, the Indonesian investors should be satisfied with a return of about 14 percent as well. Clearly explain why the consultant's advice is not logical. That is, explain why Carazona's cost of equity in Indonesia would not be less than Carazona's cost of debt in Indonesia.

22. Integrating Cost of Capital and Capital Budgeting Zylon Co. is a U.S. firm that provides technology software for the government of Singapore. It will be paid S$7 million at the end of each of the next five years. The entire amount of the payment represents earnings because Zylon created the technology software years ago. Zylon is subject to a 30 percent corporate income tax rate in the United States. Its other cash inflows (such as revenue) are expected to be offset by its other cash outflows (due to operating expenses) each year, so its profits on the Singapore contract represent its expected annual net cash flows. Its financing costs are not considered within its estimate of cash flows. The Singapore dollar (S$) is presently worth $.60, and Zylon uses that spot exchange rate as a forecast of future exchange rates.

The risk-free interest rate in the United States is 6 percent while the risk-free interest rate in Singapore is 14 percent. Zylon's capital structure is 60 percent debt and 40 percent equity. Zylon is charged an interest rate of 12 percent on its debt. Zylon's cost of equity is based on the CAPM. It expects that the U.S. annual market return will be 12 percent per year. Its beta is 1.5.

Quiso Co., a U.S. firm, wants to acquire Zylon and offers Zylon a price of $10 million.

Zylon's owner must decide whether to sell the business at this price and hires you to make a recommendation. Estimate the NPV to Zylon as a result of selling the business, and make a recommendation about whether Zylon's owner should sell the business at the price offered.

23. Financing with Foreign Equity Orlando Co. has its U.S. business funded in dollars with a capital structure of 60 percent debt and 40 percent equity. It has its Thailand business funded in Thai baht with a capital structure of 50 percent debt and 50 percent equity. The corporate tax rate on U.S. earnings and on Thailand earnings is 30 percent. The annualized 10-year risk-free interest rate is 6 percent in the United States and 21 percent in Thailand. The annual real rate of interest is about 2 percent in the United States and 2 percent in Thailand. Interest rate parity exists. Orlando pays 3 percentage points above the risk-free rates when it borrows, so its before-tax cost of debt is 9 percent in the United States and 24 percent in Thailand. Orlando expects that the U.S. stock market return will be 10 percent per year, and expects that the Thailand stock market return will be 28 percent per year. Its business in the United States has a beta of.8 relative to the U.S. market, while its business in Thailand has a beta of 1.1 relative to the Thai market. The equity used to support Orlando's Thai business was created from retained earnings by the Thailand subsidiary in previous years. However, Orlando Co. is considering a stock offering in Thailand that is denominated in Thai baht and targeted at Thai investors. Estimate Orlando's cost of equity in Thailand that would result from issuing stock in Thailand.

24. Assessing Foreign Project Funded with Debt and Equity Nebraska Co. plans to pursue a project in Argentina that will generate revenue of 10 million Argentine pesos (AP) at the end of each of the next four years. It will have to pay operating expenses of AP3 million per year. The Argentine government will charge a 30 percent tax rate on profits. All after-tax profits each year will be remitted to the U.S. parent and no additional taxes are owed. The spot rate of the AP is presently $.20. The AP is expected to depreciate by 10 percent each year for the next four years. The salvage value of the assets will be worth AP40 million in four years after capital gains taxes are paid. The initial investment will require $12 million, half of which will be in the form of equity from the U.S. parent and half of which will come from borrowed funds. Nebraska will borrow the funds in Argentine pesos. The annual interest rate on the funds borrowed is 14 percent. Annual interest (and zero principal) is paid on the debt at the end of each year, and the interest payments can be deducted before determining the tax owed to the Argentine government. The entire principal of the loan will be paid at the end of year 4. Nebraska requires a rate of return of at least 20 percent on its invested equity for this project to be worthwhile. Determine the NPV of this project. Should Nebraska pursue the project?

25. Sensitivity of Foreign Project Risk to Capital Structure Texas Co. produces drugs and plans to acquire a subsidiary in Poland. This subsidiary is a lab that would perform biotech research. Texas Co. is attracted to the lab because of the cheap wages of scientists in Poland. The parent of Texas Co. would review the lab research findings of the subsidiary in Poland when deciding which drugs to produce and would then produce the drugs in the United States. The expenses incurred in Poland will represent about half of the total expenses incurred by Texas Co. All drugs produced by Texas Co. are sold in the United States, and this situation would not change in the future. Texas Co. has considered three ways to finance the acquisition of the Polish subsidiary if it buys it. First, it could use 50 percent equity funding (in dollars) from the parent and 50 percent borrowed funds in dollars. Second, it could use 50 percent equity funding (in dollars) from the parent and 50 percent borrowed funds in Polish zloty. Third, it could use 50 percent equity funding by selling new stock to Polish investors denominated in Polish zloty and 50 percent borrowed funds denominated in Polish zloty. Assuming that Texas Co. decides to acquire the Polish subsidiary, which financing method for the Polish subsidiary would minimize the exposure of Texas to exchange rate risk? Explain.

26. Cost of Capital and Risk of Foreign Financing Nevada Co. is a U.S. firm that conducts major importing and exporting business in Japan, and all transactions are invoiced in dollars. It obtained debt in the United States at an interest rate of 10 percent per year. The long-term risk-free rate in the United States is 8 percent. The stock market return in the United States is expected to be 14 percent annually. Nevada's beta is 1.2. Its target capital structure is 30 percent debt and 70 percent equity. Nevada Co. is subject to a 25 percent corporate tax rate.

a. Estimate the cost of capital to Nevada Co.

b. Nevada has no subsidiaries in foreign countries but plans to replace some of its dollar-denominated debt with Japanese yen–denominated debt because Japanese interest rates are low. It will obtain yen-denominated debt at an interest rate of 5 percent. It cannot effectively hedge the exchange rate risk resulting from this debt because of parity conditions that make the price of derivatives contracts reflect the interest rate differential. How could Nevada Co. reduce its exposure to the exchange rate risk resulting from the yen-denominated debt without moving its operations?

27. Measuring the Cost of Capital Messan Co. (a U.S. firm) borrows U.S. funds at an interest rate of 10 percent per year. Its beta is 1.0. The long-term annualized risk-free rate in the United States is 6 percent. The stock market return in the United States is expected to be 16 percent annually. Messan's target capital structure is 40 percent debt and 60 percent equity. Messan Co. is subject to a 30 percent corporate tax rate. Estimate the cost of capital to Messan Co.

28. MNC's Cost of Capital Newark Co. is based in the United States. About 30 percent of its sales are from exports to Portugal. Newark Co. has no other international business. It finances its operations with 40 percent equity and 60 percent dollar-denominated debt. It borrows its funds from a U.S. bank at an interest rate of 9 percent per year. The long-term risk-free rate in the United States is 6 percent. The long-term risk-free rate in Portugal is 11 percent. The stock market return in the United States is expected to be 13 percent annually. Newark's stock price typically moves in the same direction and by the same degree as the U.S. stock market. Its earnings are subject to a 20 percent corporate tax rate. Estimate the cost of capital to Newark Co.

29. MNC's Cost of Capital Slater Co. is a U.S.-based MNC that finances all operations with debt and equity. It borrows U.S. funds at an interest rate of 11 percent per year. The long-term risk-free rate in the United States is 7 percent. The stock market return in the United States is expected to be 15 percent annually. Slater's beta is 1.4. Its target capital structure is 20 percent debt and 80 percent equity. Slater Co. is subject to a 30 percent corporate tax rate. Estimate the cost of capital to Slater Co.

30. Change in Cost of Capital Assume that Naperville Co. will use equity to finance a project in Switzerland, that Lombard Co. will rely on a dollar-denominated loan to finance a project in Switzerland, and that Addison Co. will rely on a Swiss franc–denominated loan to finance a project in Switzerland. The firms will arrange their financing in one month.

This week, the U.S. risk-free long-term interest rate declined, but interest rates in Switzerland did not change. Do you think the estimated cost of capital for the projects by each of these three U.S. firms increased, decreased, or remained unchanged? Explain.

31. **Cost of Equity** Illinois Co. is a U.S. firm that plans to expand its business overseas. It plans to use all the equity to be obtained in the United States to finance a new project. The project's cash flows are not affected by U.S. interest rates. Just before Illinois Co. obtains new equity, the U.S. risk-free interest rate rises. Will the change in interest rates increase, decrease, or have no effect on the required rate of return on the project? Briefly explain.

32. **Debt Financing Decision** Marks Co. (a U.S. firm) considers a project in which it will establish a subsidiary in Zinland, and it expects that the subsidiary will generate large earnings in zin (the currency). However, it is the Zinland government's policy to block all funds so that earnings cannot be remitted to the U.S. parent for at least 10 years; furthermore, the blocked funds cannot earn interest. The zin is expected to weaken by 20 percent per year against the dollar over time. Marks Co. will borrow some funds to finance the subsidiary. Should the company (a) obtain a dollar-denominated loan and convert the loan into zin, (b) obtain a zin-denominated loan, or (c) obtain half of the funds needed from each possible source? (Assume that the interest rate from borrowing zin is

the same as the interest rate from borrowing dollars.) Briefly explain.

Critical Thinking

Trade-offs Involved in an MNC's Capital Structure Decisions   In recent years, some U.S.-based MNCs (such as Apple) have taken advantage of the very low interest rates in the United States by borrowing large amounts of dollars to finance their operations. Write a short essay that explains the advantages and possible disadvantages (if any) of this type of financing. Consider how it affects the cost of capital. Consider how it affects the capital structure, but keep in mind that the interest payments on debt borrowed at an interest rate of 3 percent are different from interest payments on debt borrowed at 10 percent. Also consider how this type of financing affects the MNC's exposure to exchange rate risk if the funds borrowed are used to finance foreign operations.

Discussion in the Boardroom

This exercise can be found in Appendix E at the back of this textbook.

Running Your Own MNC

This exercise can be found on the *International Financial Management* text companion website. Go to www .cengagebrain.com (students) or www.cengage.com/login (instructors) and search using **ISBN 9781133947837**.

BLADES, INC. CASE

Assessment of Cost of Capital

Recall that Blades has tentatively decided to establish a subsidiary in Thailand to manufacture roller blades. The new plant will be utilized to produce Speedos, Blades' primary product. Once the subsidiary has been established in Thailand, it will be operated for 10 years, at which time it is expected to be sold. Ben Holt, Blades' chief financial officer, believes the growth potential in Thailand will be extremely high over the next few years. However, his optimism is not shared by most economic forecasters, who predict a slow recovery of the Thai economy, which has been very negatively affected by recent events in that country. Furthermore, forecasts for the future value of the baht indicate that the currency may continue to depreciate over the next few years.

Despite the pessimistic forecasts, Holt believes Thailand is a good international target for Blades' products

because of the high growth potential and lack of competitors in Thailand. At a recent meeting of the board of directors, Holt presented his capital budgeting analysis and pointed out that the establishment of a subsidiary in Thailand had a net present value (NPV) of over $8 million even when a 25 percent required rate of return is used to discount the cash flows resulting from the project. Blades' board of directors, although favorable to the idea of international expansion, remained skeptical. Specifically, the directors wondered where Holt obtained the 25 percent discount rate to conduct his capital budgeting analysis and whether this discount rate was high enough. Consequently, the decision to establish a subsidiary in Thailand has been delayed until the directors' meeting next month.

The directors also asked Holt to determine how operating a subsidiary in Thailand would affect Blades' required rate of return and its cost of capital. The directors would like to know how Blades' characteristics would affect its cost of capital relative to roller blade manufacturers operating solely in the United States. Furthermore, the capital asset pricing model (CAPM) was mentioned by two directors, who would like to know how Blades' systematic risk would be affected by expanding into Thailand. Another issue that was raised is how the cost of debt and equity in Thailand differ from the corresponding costs in the United States and whether these differences would affect Blades' cost of capital. The last issue that was raised during the meeting was whether Blades' capital structure would be affected by expanding into Thailand. The directors have asked Holt to conduct a thorough analysis of these issues and report back to them at their next meeting.

Holt's knowledge of cost of capital and capital structure decisions is somewhat limited, and he requires your help. You are a financial analyst for Blades, Inc. Holt has gathered some information regarding Blades' characteristics that distinguish it from roller blade manufacturers operating solely in the United States, its systematic risk, and the costs of debt and equity in Thailand, and he wants to know whether and how this information will affect Blades' cost of capital and its capital structure decision.

Regarding Blades' characteristics, Holt has gathered information regarding Blades' size, its access to the Thai capital markets, its diversification benefits from a Thai expansion, its exposure to exchange rate risk, and its exposure to country risk. Although Blades' expansion into Thailand classifies the company as an MNC, Blades is still relatively small compared to other U.S. roller blade manufacturers. Also, Blades' expansion into Thailand will give it access to the capital and money markets there. However, negotiations with various commercial banks in Thailand indicate that Blades will have to borrow at interest rates of approximately 15 percent, versus 8 percent in the United States.

Expanding into Thailand will diversify Blades' operations. As a result of this expansion, Blades would be subject to economic conditions in Thailand as well as in the United States. Holt sees this as a major advantage because Blades' cash flows would no longer be solely dependent on the U.S. economy. Consequently, he believes that Blades' probability of bankruptcy would be reduced. Nevertheless, if Blades establishes a subsidiary in Thailand, all of the subsidiary's earnings will be remitted back to the U.S. parent, which would create a high level of exchange rate risk.

This is of particular concern because current economic forecasts for Thailand indicate that the baht will depreciate over the next few years. Furthermore, Holt has already conducted a country risk analysis for Thailand that resulted in an unfavorable country risk rating.

Regarding Blades' level of systematic risk, Holt has determined how Blades' beta, which measures systematic risk, would be affected by the establishment of a subsidiary in Thailand. He believes that Blades' beta would drop from its current level of 2.0 to 1.8 because the firm's exposure to U.S. market conditions would be reduced by its expansion into Thailand. Moreover, Holt estimates that the risk-free interest rate is 5 percent and the required return on the market is 12 percent.

Holt has also determined that the costs of both debt and equity are higher in Thailand than in the United States. Lenders such as commercial banks in Thailand require interest rates higher than U.S. rates. This is partially attributed to a higher risk premium, which reflects the larger degree of economic uncertainty in Thailand. The cost of equity is also higher in Thailand than in the United States. Thailand is not as developed as the United States in many ways, and various investment opportunities are available to Thai investors, which increases the opportunity cost. However, Holt is not sure that this higher cost of equity in Thailand would affect Blades, as all of Blades' shareholders are located in the United States.

Holt has asked you to analyze this information and to determine how it may affect Blades' cost of capital and its capital structure. To help you in your analysis, he would like you to provide answers to the following questions:

1. If Blades expands into Thailand, do you think its cost of capital will be higher or lower than the cost of capital of roller blade manufacturers operating solely in the United States? Substantiate your answer by outlining how Blades' characteristics distinguish it from domestic roller blade manufacturers.

2. According to the CAPM, how would Blades' required rate of return be affected by an expansion into Thailand? How do you reconcile this result with your answer to question 1? Do you think Blades should use the required rate of return resulting from the CAPM to discount the cash flows of the Thai subsidiary to determine its NPV?

3. If Blades borrows funds in Thailand to support its Thai subsidiary, how would this affect its cost of capital? Why?

4. Given the high level of interest rates in Thailand, the high level of exchange rate risk, and the high (perceived) level of country risk, do you think Blades will be more or less likely to use debt in its capital structure as a result of its expansion into Thailand? Why?

SMALL BUSINESS DILEMMA

Multinational Capital Structure Decision at the Sports Exports Company

The Sports Exports Company has considered a variety of projects, but all of its business is still in the United Kingdom. Because most of its business comes from exporting footballs (denominated in pounds), it remains exposed to exchange rate risk. On the favorable side, the British demand for its footballs has risen consistently every month. Jim Logan, the owner of the Sports Exports Company, has retained more than $100,000 (after the pounds were converted into dollars) in earnings since he began his business. At this point in time, his capital structure is mostly his own equity with very little debt. Logan has periodically considered establishing a very small subsidiary in the United Kingdom to produce the footballs there (so that he would not have to export them from the United States). If he does establish this subsidiary, he has several options for the capital structure that would be used to support it: (1) use all of his equity to invest in the firm, (2) use pound-denominated long-term debt, or (3) use dollar-denominated long-term debt. The interest rate on British long-term debt is slightly higher than the interest rate on U.S. long-term debt.

1. What is an advantage of using equity to support the subsidiary? What is a disadvantage?

2. If Logan decides to use long-term debt as the primary form of capital to support this subsidiary, should he use dollar-denominated debt or pound-denominated debt?

3. How can the equity proportion of this firm's capital structure increase over time after it is established?

INTERNET/EXCEL EXERCISE

The Bloomberg website (www.bloomberg.com) provides interest rate data for many countries and various maturities. Go to the "Markets" section and then click on "Rates and Bonds." Assume that an MNC would pay 1 percent more on borrowed funds than the risk-free (government) rates shown on the Bloomberg website. Determine the cost of debt (use a 10-year maturity) for the U.S. parent that borrows dollars. Click on Japan and determine the cost of funds for a foreign subsidiary in Japan that borrows funds locally. Then click on Germany and determine the cost of debt for a subsidiary in Germany that borrows funds locally. Offer some explanations as to why the cost of debt may vary among the three countries.

ONLINE ARTICLES WITH REAL-WORLD EXAMPLES

Find a recent article online that describes an actual international finance application or a real-world example about a specific MNC's actions that reinforces one or more of the concepts covered in this chapter.

If your class has an online component, your professor may ask you to post your summary there and provide the web link of the article so that other students can access it. If your class is live, your professor may ask you to summarize your application in class. Your professor may assign specific students to complete this assignment for this chapter or may allow any students to do the assignment on a volunteer basis.

For recent online articles and real-world examples applied to this chapter, consider using the following search terms (and include the current year as a search term to ensure that the online articles are recent).

1. [name of an MNC] AND debt

2. multinational AND equity

3. multinational AND capital

4. international AND capital structure

5. international AND cost of capital

6. company AND foreign financing

7. Inc. AND foreign financing

8. subsidiary AND repatriates

9. subsidiary AND financing

10. international AND financing

18

Long-Term Debt Financing

CHAPTER
OBJECTIVES

The specific objectives
of this chapter are to:

■ explain the debt
denomination
dilemma for MNCs
that need long-term
debt financing,

■ illustrate how MNCs
conduct analysis to
make the debt
denomination
decision,

■ explain how currency
swaps and parallel
loans facilitate long-
term debt financing,

■ explain how an MNC
determines the
optimal maturity
when obtaining
debt, and

■ explain how an MNC
decides between
using fixed rate
versus floating
rate debt.

Multinational corporations (MNCs) typically use long-term sources of funds to finance long-term projects. They have access to both domestic and foreign sources of funds. It is worthwhile for MNCs to consider all possible forms of financing before making their final decisions. Financial managers must be aware of their sources of long-term funds so that they can finance international projects in a manner that maximizes the wealth of the MNC.

The MNC's cost of debt affects its required rate of return when it assesses proposed projects. Features of debt such as currency of denomination, maturity, and whether the rate is fixed or floating can affect the cost of debt and thereby affect the feasibility of projects that are supported with the debt. Thus MNCs can enhance their value by determining specific debt features that can reduce their cost of debt.

18-1 Debt Denomination Decision of Foreign Subsidiaries

When a U.S.-based MNC's foreign subsidiary needs to borrow funds to support existing operations or expand, it typically considers the following choices:

1. Borrow funds denominated in the local currency where it is located, and use funds generated from its local sales in the same currency to repay the debt.
2. Borrow funds denominated in dollars, and convert the dollars into the local currency in order to support existing operations or expansion there. As cash inflows are generated in the local currency due to local sales, a portion of those funds can be converted into dollars to make periodic debt repayments.

Each of these financing methods may have advantages and disadvantages that should be considered, as explained next.

18-1a Foreign Subsidiary Borrows Its Local Currency

Many subsidiaries of MNCs finance their operations or expansion by borrowing in their respective local currency that they use to invoice their products. This strategy allows a foreign subsidiary to match the currency received from its sales with the currency that is needed to repay its debt. Because the subsidiary does not need to convert its currency received from sales into another currency in order to repay its debt, it avoids any exchange rate risk on its debt repayments.

EXAMPLE   Many MNCs, including Honeywell, The Coca-Cola Co., and General Electric, issue bonds in some of the foreign currencies they receive from operations. PepsiCo issues bonds in several foreign currencies and uses some of its revenue (in those same currencies) resulting from foreign operations to make interest and principal payments. IBM and Nike have issued bonds denominated in Japanese yen at low-interest rates and use yen-denominated revenue from sales in Japan to make the interest payments. Spectra Energy Corp. (based in Houston) issues bonds in Canadian dollars and uses some of its revenue denominated in Canadian dollars (from its Canadian operations) to make payments on the bonds. ●

The matching strategy just described is especially desirable when the foreign subsidiaries are based in countries where interest rates are relatively low. The MNC achieves a low financing rate and also reduces its exchange rate risk by matching its debt outflow payments with the currency denominating its cash inflows. China's government has only recently allowed MNCs to issue debt denominated in the Chinese yuan. The MNCs can now match yuan inflows that they receive from their Chinese subsidiaries with yuan outflows that are used to make coupon payments on the bonds they issued. Another attractive feature of the yuan-denominated loans is that interest rates are low, and there is a large pool of Chinese investors interested in purchasing yuan-denominated bonds issued by credible MNCs.

Comparison of Long-term Interest Rates among Countries

If subsidiaries of MNCs match the currency they borrow with the currency they use to invoice products, then their cost of debt will depend on the prevailing local interest rate of their host country. Exhibit 18.1 illustrates how long-term risk-free bond yields can vary among countries. The cost of debt to a subsidiary in any of these countries would be slightly higher than the risk-free rates shown here because it would contain a credit risk premium.

A subsidiary's cost of debt financing in Germany and Japan is typically very low because interest rates in these countries are typically very low. At the other extreme, the cost of debt financing in developing countries such as Brazil and India can be high. While a subsidiary's matching strategy of borrowing the same currency as its local invoice currency avoids exchange rate risk on the repayment of debt, it results in a high cost of debt for subsidiaries of a U.S.-based MNC that are located in developing countries.

Exhibit 18.1   Annualized Bond Yields among Countries (as of October 2015)

COUNTRY	ANNUALIZED BOND YIELD
Australia	1.5%
Brazil	6.5
Canada	1.5
Germany	0.6
India	7.6
Japan	0.4
New Zealand	3.3
Singapore	2.5
South Korea	2.1
United Kingdom	1.8
United States	2.1

18-1b Foreign Subsidiary Borrows Dollars

If a foreign subsidiary of a U.S.-based MNC is located in a developing country that has a high local interest rate, it can borrow dollars instead of the local currency. The advantage of this strategy is that because the U.S. interest rate is typically much lower than the interest rate in the developing country, the foreign subsidiary can borrow funds at a lower rate of interest.

However, the disadvantage is that the subsidiary will have to convert its local currency into dollars to repay the loan. If its local currency depreciates against the U.S. dollar over time, it will need more of its currency to obtain the dollars needed to make its periodic debt repayments. Consequently, even though the interest rate on the dollar loan is lower than on a local loan in the host country, the actual cost of the dollar-denominated debt could be higher than the cost of debt denominated in the subsidiary's local currency.

Recall from Chapter 8 that countries with high nominal interest rates tend to have high expected inflation (the Fisher effect). In addition, currencies of countries with relatively high inflation tend to over time (as suggested by purchasing power parity, in Chapter 8). Thus by attempting to avoid the high cost of debt in a developing country, the subsidiary of a U.S.-based MNC becomes more exposed to exchange rate risk.

Foreign Subsidiary Borrows Dollars and Hedges Exchange Rate Risk A foreign subsidiary in a developing country could attempt to hedge its future loan payments in dollars. It would need to sell its local currency forward in exchange for dollars at future points in time to make the periodic loan repayments. However, recall from Chapter 7 that according to interest rate parity, the forward rate on a currency of a country with a high nominal interest rate will contain a discount (relative to the prevailing spot rate) that reflects the differential between that country's interest rate and the U.S. interest rate. Thus the subsidiary's cost of debt financing with dollars will be no cheaper than its cost of debt financing in its local currency. Even if a subsidiary cannot effectively hedge its financing position, it might still consider financing with a currency that differs from its host country currency. Its final debt denomination decision will likely be based on its forecasts of exchange rates, as illustrated next.

18-2 Debt Denomination Analysis: A Case Study

When an MNC's subsidiaries are based in developing countries such as Brazil, Indonesia, Malaysia, Mexico, and Thailand, they may be subject to relatively high interest rates. So even though the matching strategy described earlier reduces exchange rate risk, it would force these subsidiaries to incur a high cost of debt. A U.S.-based MNC may consider providing a loan in dollars so that the subsidiary can avoid the high cost of local debt. However, doing so will force the subsidiary to convert some of its funds to dollars to repay the loan.

18-2a Identifying Debt Denomination Alternatives

Consider the case of Boise Co. (a U.S. company), which has a Mexican subsidiary that will need about 200 million Mexican pesos (MXP) for three years to finance its Mexican operations. Although the Mexican subsidiary will continue to exist after the three years are up, focusing on a three-year period is sufficient to illustrate a common subsidiary financing dilemma when the host country interest rate is high. The peso's spot rate is

$.10, so the financing represents $20 million (computed as MXP200 million × $.10). To finance its operations, Boise considers two possible financing alternatives:

1. *Peso Loan.* Boise's Mexican subsidiary can borrow MXP200 million to finance the Mexican operations. The interest rate on a three-year fixed rate peso-denominated loan is 12 percent. If the Mexican subsidiary borrows Mexican pesos, it can match its cash inflow currency (from sales generated in Mexico) with the currency needed to repay the loan.
2. *Dollar Loan.* The Mexican subsidiary can borrow $20 million and convert the funds into MXP200 to finance the Mexican operations. The interest rate on a three-year fixed rate dollar-denominated loan is 7 percent.

Thus Boise's Mexican subsidiary can lock in a cost of debt of 12 percent by borrowing pesos. It recognizes that it could reduce its cost of debt by borrowing dollars at a 7 percent interest rate. However, if the peso depreciates substantially against the dollar over the financing period, the subsidiary's cost of borrowing dollars may exceed the 12 percent cost of debt from borrowing pesos. The proper debt denomination decision can only be made by conducting an analysis that estimates the cost of debt financing in dollars.

18-2b Analyzing Debt Denomination Alternatives

Assume that all loan principal is repaid at the end of three years. An analysis of the cash outflows associated with each debt financing method is shown in Exhibit 18.2. If Boise Co.'s Mexican subsidiary obtains a MXP200 million loan at an annualized interest rate of 12 percent, it would have cash outflows of MXP24 million per year (computed as .12 × MXP200 million) over the next three years, along with the principal payment in year 3. The subsidiary's payments on the peso-denominated loan are simply based on the interest rate (12 percent) applied to the loan amount, because there is no exchange rate risk to the subsidiary when borrowing its local currency.

Alternatively, if the subsidiary borrows $20 million at an annualized interest rate of 7 percent, it would need to obtain $1,400,000 per year to make interest payments, along with the principal of $20 million in year 3. Because its revenue is denominated in Mexican pesos, it would need to convert pesos into dollars to make payments on the loan. Because the payments are in the future, it needs to forecast the exchange rate of the peso on the future dates when payments must be made. Assume that it forecasts that the Mexican peso's spot rate will be $.10 at the end of year 1, $.09 at the end of year 2, and $.09 at the end of year 3.

Given the required loan repayments in dollars and the forecasted exchange rate of the peso, the amount of pesos needed to repay the loan per year can be estimated as shown in Exhibit 18.2. Next, the Mexican subsidiary's estimated cost of financing with a dollar loan can be determined: it is the discount rate that equates the payments to the loan proceeds ($20 million) at the time the loan is created. Applying a calculator, the discount rate is 10.82 percent.

Exhibit 18.2 Comparison of Two Alternative Loans with Different Debt Denominations for the Foreign Subsidiary

	YEAR 1	YEAR 2	YEAR 3
PESO LOAN OF MXP200,000,000 at 12%:	MXP24,000,000	MXP24,000,000	MXP24,000,000 + loan principal repayment of MXP200,000,000
U.S. DOLLAR LOAN OF $20,000,000 at 7%: Loan repayment in U.S. dollars	$1,400,000	$1,400,000	$1,400,000 + loan principal repayment of $20,000,000
Forecasted exchange rate of peso	$.10	$.09	$.09
Pesos needed to repay dollar loan	MXP14,000,000	MXP15,555,556	MXP237,777,778

Although the annualized cost of financing is slightly lower when dollars are used, this cost is only an estimate based on forecasted exchange rates. If the Mexican peso weakens more than expected and the realized spot rates in the future turn out to be lower than the forecasted exchange rates, the cost of financing with dollars could be higher than the cost of financing with pesos. In contrast, the Mexican subsidiary's cost of the peso-denominated loan is certain. Because the subsidiary is not confident about its forecasts of the peso's future exchange rate, it decides that the potential cost savings from debt financing in dollars are not worth the risk that the cost might actually be higher than the cost of the peso-denominated loan.

Accounting for Uncertainty of Financing Costs   The estimated cost of debt financing by the subsidiary when it borrows a different currency than that of its host country is highly sensitive to the forecasted exchange rates. An MNC can at least account for the uncertainty surrounding the point estimates of exchange rates by using sensitivity analysis, in which alternative exchange rate scenarios are considered. This would allow the MNC to estimate how high the subsidiary's annual cost of financing could be if its local currency weakens substantially against the currency that it borrowed.

Alternatively, an MNC can apply simulation in which it develops a probability distribution for the exchange rate for each period in which a loan payment must be made. A simulation program uses this input to generate a probability distribution of annual financing costs that can then be compared with the known cost of financing if the subsidiary borrows its local currency. Through this comparison, the MNC can determine the probability that borrowing a currency other than its local currency (of its host country) will achieve a lower annualized cost of financing than if it borrows its local currency.

18-3 Loans Facilitate Financing

In some cases, an MNC may not be able to borrow a currency that matches its invoice currency. Under these conditions, the MNC may want to engage in a currency swap or a parallel loan to execute the matching strategy, as described next.

18-3a Using Currency Swaps

A currency swap specifies the exchange of currencies at periodic intervals. A currency swap may allow the MNC's cash outflows to be denominated in the same currency as the one in which it receives most or all of its revenue, which reduces the MNC's exposure to exchange rate movements.

EXAMPLE   Miller Co., a U.S. firm, has a European subsidiary that desires to issue a bond denominated in euros because it could make payments with euro inflows to be generated from existing operations. However, Miller Co. is not well known to the investors who would consider purchasing euro-denominated bonds. Meanwhile, Beck Co. of Germany desires to issue dollar-denominated bonds because its cash inflows are mostly in dollars. However, it is not well known to the investors who would purchase these bonds.

At If Miller is known in the dollar-denominated market and if Beck is known in the euro-denominated market, then the following transactions are appropriate. Miller issues dollar-denominated bonds while Beck issues euro-denominated bonds. Miller will provide euro payments to Beck in exchange for dollar payments. This swap of currencies allows the companies to make payments to their respective bondholders without concern about exchange rate risk. This type of currency swap is illustrated in Exhibit 18.3. ●

The swap just described eliminates exchange rate risk for both Miller Co. and Beck Co. because both firms are able to match their cash outflow currency with their cash inflow currency. Miller essentially passes the euros it receives from ongoing operations through to Beck and passes the dollars it receives from Beck through to investors in the

Exhibit 18.3   Illustration of a Currency Swap

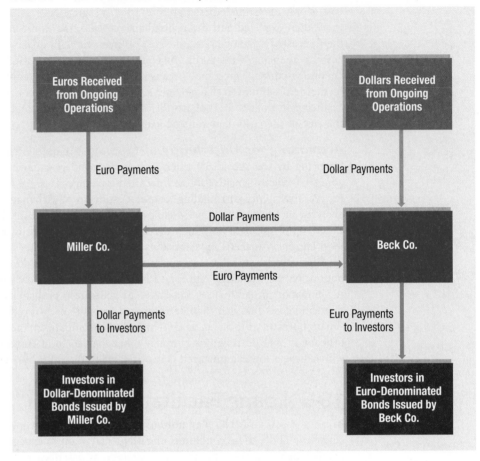

dollar-denominated bonds. So even though Miller receives euros from its ongoing operations, the currency swap allows it to make dollar payments to the investors without having to be concerned about exchange rate risk.

Caterpillar, Ford Motor Co., Johnson & Johnson, PepsiCo, and many other MNCs use currency swaps. The large commercial banks that serve as financial intermediaries for currency swaps sometimes take positions. That is, they may agree to swap currencies with firms rather than searching for suitable swap candidates.

18-3b Using Parallel Loans

If an MNC is not able to borrow a currency that matches its invoice currency, it might consider financing with a parallel (or back-to-back) loan so that it can match its invoice currency. In a parallel loan, two companies provide simultaneous loans with an agreement to repay at some specified future time.

EXAMPLE

Ann Arbor Co. (a U.S.-based MNC) desires to expand its British subsidiary, while Brit Ltd. (a British-based MNC) desires to expand its American subsidiary. Ann Arbor Co. can more easily obtain a loan in U.S. dollars, while Brit Ltd. has easier access to loans in British pounds. The two companies can engage in a parallel loan as follows. Brit Ltd. provides a loan in pounds to the British subsidiary of Ann Arbor Co., while Ann Arbor Co. provides a loan in dollars to the American subsidiary of Brit Ltd. (see Exhibit 18.4). At the time

Exhibit 18.4 Illustration of a Parallel Loan

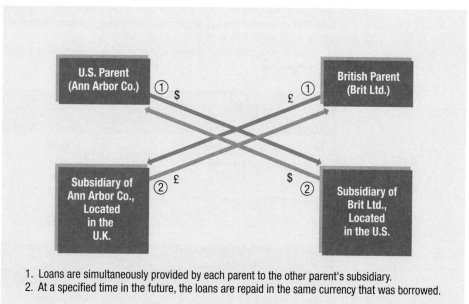

1. Loans are simultaneously provided by each parent to the other parent's subsidiary.
2. At a specified time in the future, the loans are repaid in the same currency that was borrowed.

specified by the loan contract, the loans are repaid. The British subsidiary of Ann Arbor Co. uses its pound-denominated revenues to repay Brit Ltd. for the loan; at the same time, the American subsidiary of Brit Ltd. uses its dollar-denominated revenues to repay the loan from Ann Arbor Co. ●

The use of parallel loans is particularly attractive if the MNC is conducting a project in a foreign country, will receive the cash flows in the foreign currency, and is worried that the foreign currency will depreciate substantially.

EXAMPLE

Schnell, Inc., has been approached by the government of Malaysia to engage in a project there over the next year. Schnell would need to invest 1 million Malaysian ringgit (MR) in the project now, and the project is expected to generate cash flows of MR1.4 million next year. The project will terminate at that time.

The current value of the ringgit is $.25, but Schnell believes that the ringgit will depreciate and have a value of $.20 next year. Furthermore, Schnell will have to borrow for one year in order to pursue the project and will incur financing costs of 13 percent over the next year.

If Schnell pursues the project, it will incur a net outflow now of MR1,000,000 × $.25 = $250,000. Next year, it will also have to pay the financing costs of $250,000 × 13% = $32,500. If the ringgit depreciates to $.20, then Schnell will receive MR1,400,000 × $.20 = $280,000 next year. Schnell's cash flows are summarized below.

	YEAR 0	YEAR 1
Investment	−$250,000	
Financing cost to Schnell		−$32,500
Project cash flow	0	$280,000
Net	−$250,000	$247,500

The cash inflows to Schnell in one year (shown in the bottom row for year 1) would be less than Schnell's initial investment, even if the time value of money is ignored.

However, a parallel loan may improve the outcome for Schnell. Assume that Schnell and the Malaysian government engage in a parallel loan in which the Malaysian government gives Schnell MR1 million in exchange for a loan of $250,000 (the exchange of loans is based on the current exchange rate). Both parties will repay the loans at the end of one year when the project is completed. Assume that next year Schnell will repay the loan (MR1,000,000) plus 15 percent interest to the Malaysian government, while the Malaysian government repays its loan ($250,000) plus 7 percent interest to Schnell. Graphically, the parallel loan is shown in Exhibit 18.5.

By using the parallel loan, Schnell is able to more closely match its cash inflows and outflows in ringgit, as shown here:

	SCHNELL DOLLAR CASH FLOWS	
	YEAR 0	YEAR 1
Loan from Schnell to Malaysia	−$250,000	
Financing cost to Schnell		−$32,500
Interest received on loan ($250,000 × 7%)		$17,500
Repayment of loan principal to Schnell		$250,000
Net cash flow	−$250,000	$235,000

	SCHNELL RINGGIT CASH FLOWS	
	YEAR 0	YEAR 1
Loan from Malaysia to Schnell	MR1,000,000	
Investment in project	−MR1,000,000	
Interest paid on loan (MR1,000,000 × 15%)		−MR150,000
Repayment of loan principal by Schnell		−MR1,000,000
Project cash flow		MR1,400,000
Net cash flow		MR250,000

Exhibit 18.5   Illustration of a Parallel Loan

Based on the forecasted spot rate of $.20 in one year, the net cash flow in year 1 of MR250,000 is expected to be MR250,000 × $.20 = $50,000. Thus the total dollar cash flows when using the parallel loan are $235,000 + $50,000 = $285,000. Overall, Schnell's net cash flows in year 1 more than offset its initial cash outflow of $250,000. In addition, the parallel loan reduces the ringgit amount that Schnell must convert to dollars at project termination from MR1.4 million to MR250,000. Thus the parallel loan reduces Schnell's exposure to the potential depreciation of the ringgit. ●

18-4 Debt Maturity Decision

Regardless of the currency that an MNC uses to finance its international operations, it must also decide on the maturity that it should use for its debt. An MNC normally uses a long-term maturity when financing subsidiary operations that will continue for a long-term period. But the firm might consider a maturity that is shorter than the time period in which it will need funds, especially when the annualized interest rates on debt are relatively low for particular maturities.

18-4a Assessment of the Yield Curve

Before making the debt maturity decision, MNCs assess the yield curve of the country in which they need funds.

The shape of the yield curve, which illustrates the relationship between annualized yield and debt maturity, can vary among countries. Some countries tend to have an upward-sloping yield curve, which means that the annualized yields are lower for short-term debt maturities than for long-term debt maturities. One explanation given for the upward slope is that investors may require a higher rate of return on long-term debt as compensation for lower liquidity (tying up their funds for a longer period of time).

18-4b Financing Costs of Loans with Different Maturities

When there is an upward-sloping yield curve, the MNC may be tempted to finance the project with debt over a shorter maturity in order to achieve a lower cost of debt financing, even if doing so means that funds will still be required beyond the life of the loan. However, the MNC may incur higher financing costs when it attempts to obtain additional funding after the existing loan matures if market interest rates are higher at that time. It must therefore decide whether to obtain a loan with a maturity that perfectly fits its needs or one with a shorter maturity and a more favorable interest rate and then seek additional financing when this loan matures.

When selecting a shorter loan maturity than what is needed, an MNC is subject to the risk that the future loan rate at the time it pursues a loan extension is higher than expected. Consequently, it might incur a cost of financing that is higher than with a loan with a longer maturity.

EXAMPLE — Scottsdale Co. (a U.S.-based MNC) has a Swiss subsidiary that needs to borrow 40 million Swiss francs (SF) for five years. A Swiss bank offers a loan that would require annual interest payments of 8 percent for a five-year period, which results in interest expenses of SF3,200,000 per year (computed as SF40,000,000 × .08). Assume that the subsidiary could achieve an annualized cost of debt of only 6 percent if it borrows for a period of three years instead of five years. In this case, its interest expenses would be SF2,400,000 per year (computed as SF40,000,000 × .06) over the first three years. Thus the subsidiary can reduce its interest expenses by SF80,000 per year over the first three years by securing a three-year loan. If it accepts a three-year loan, it would be able to extend the loan in three years for two additional years, but the loan rate for those remaining years would be based on the prevailing market interest rate on Swiss francs at the time. The

Exhibit 18.6   Loans of Different Maturities Made to Foreign Subsidiary

	YEAR 1	YEAR 2	YEAR 3	YEAR 4	YEAR 5
5-year loan: Repayments based on fixed rate loan of 8% for 5 years	SF3,200,000	SF3,200,000	SF3,200,000	SF3,200,000	SF3,200,000 + Repayment of SF40,000,000 in loan principal
3-year loan plus extension: Repayments based on fixed rate loan of 6% for 3 years + forecasted interest rate of 9% in years 4 and 5	SF2,400,000	SF2,400,000	SF2,400,000	SF3,600,000	SF3,600,000 + Repayment of SF40,000,000 in loan principal

subsidiary believes that the interest rate on Swiss francs in years 4 and 5 will be 9 percent. In that case, it would pay SF3,600,000 in annual interest expenses during years 4 and 5.

The payments involved with the two financing alternatives are shown in Exhibit 18.6. Row 1 shows the payments that would be required for the five-year loan, and row 2 shows the payments for the three-year loan plus the estimated payments for the loan extension (in years 4 and 5). The annualized cost of financing for the two alternatives can be measured as the discount rate that equates the payments to the loan proceeds of SF40 million. This discount rate is 8.00 percent for the five-year loan versus 7.08 percent for the three-year loan plus the loan extension. Because the annualized cost of financing is expected to be lower for the three-year loan plus loan extension, Scottsdale prefers that loan. ●

When Scottsdale Co. assesses the annualized cost of financing for the three-year loan plus the loan extension, there is uncertainty surrounding the interest rate to be paid during the loan extension (in years 4 and 5). It could consider alternative possible interest rates that may exist over that period and then estimate the annualized cost of financing based on those scenarios. In this way, it could develop a probability distribution for the annualized cost of financing and compare that to the known annualized cost of financing if it pursues the fixed rate five-year loan.

18-5 Fixed versus Floating Rate Debt Decision

Multinational corporations that wish to use a long-term maturity but wish to avoid paying the prevailing fixed rate on long-term bonds may consider floating rate bonds or loans. In this case, the coupon rate on bonds (or interest rate on loans) will fluctuate over time in accordance with market interest rates. For example, the coupon rate on a floating rate bond is frequently tied to the London Interbank Offer Rate (LIBOR), which is the rate at which banks lend funds to each other. As LIBOR increases, so does the coupon rate of a floating rate bond. A floating coupon rate can be an advantage to the bond issuer during periods of decreasing interest rates, when the firm would otherwise be locked in at a higher coupon rate over the life of the bond. However, a floating rate is a disadvantage during periods of rising interest rates. In some countries, such as those in South America, most long-term debt has a floating interest rate.

18-5a Financing Costs of Fixed versus Floating Rate Loans

If an MNC considers financing with floating rate loans whose rate is tied to LIBOR, then it can forecast the LIBOR for each year to estimate its annual interest rate. This allows the firm to forecast interest payments for all years of the loan. It can then estimate the annualized cost of financing based on the anticipated loan interest payments and repayment of loan principal.

EXAMPLE   Reconsider the case of Scottsdale Co., which plans to borrow SF40 million at a fixed rate for three years and to obtain a loan extension for two additional years. It is now considering an alternative financing

Exhibit 18.7 Alternative Financing Arrangement with a Floating Rate Loan

	YEAR 1	YEAR 2	YEAR 3	YEAR 4	YEAR 5
Forecast of LIBOR	3%	4%	4%	6%	6%
Forecast of interest rate applied to the floating rate loan	6%	7%	7%	9%	9%
5-year floating rate loan: Repayments based on floating rate loan of LIBOR + 3%	SF2,400,000	SF2,800,000	SF2,800,000	SF3,600,000	SF3,600,000 + Repayment of SF40,000,000 in loan principal

arrangement in which it obtains a floating rate loan from a bank at an interest rate equal to LIBOR + 3 percent. The company's analysis of this loan is provided in Exhibit 18.7.

To forecast the interest payments paid on the floating rate loan, Scottsdale must first forecast the LIBOR for each year. Assume the forecasts are as given in the first row. The interest rate applied to its loan each year is LIBOR + 3 percent, as shown in row 2. Row 3 discloses the results when the loan amount of SF40,000,000 is multiplied by this interest rate in order to estimate the interest expenses each year, and the repayment of principal is also included in year 5.

The annualized cost of financing is determined as the discount rate that equates the payments to the loan proceeds of SF40,000,000. For the floating rate loan, the annualized cost of financing is 7.48 percent. This value is lower than the 8 percent annualized cost of the five-year fixed rate loan in the previous example, but it is higher than the 7.08 percent annualized cost of that example's three-year fixed rate loan plus loan extension. Based on this comparison, Scottsdale decides to obtain the three-year fixed rate loan with the loan extension. ●

18-5b Hedging Interest Payments with Interest Rate Swaps

In some cases, MNCs may finance with floating rather than fixed rate debt because the prevailing floating rate terms at the time of the debt offering were more favorable. However, if the MNCs are concerned that interest rates will rise over time, they may complement their floating rate debt with interest rate *swaps* in order to hedge the risk of rising interest rates. The interest rate swaps allow them to reconfigure their future cash flows in a manner that offsets their outflow payments to creditors (lenders or bondholders). In this way, MNCs can reduce their exposure to interest rate movements. Many MNCs use interest rate swaps, including Ashland, Inc., Campbell Soup Co., Intel Corp., and Johnson Controls.

Financial institutions such as commercial and investment banks and insurance companies often act as dealers in interest rate swaps. Financial institutions can also act as brokers in the interest rate swap market. As a broker, the financial institution simply arranges an interest rate swap between two parties while charging a fee for this service, but it does not actually take a position in the swap.

In a "plain vanilla" interest rate swap, one participating firm makes fixed rate payments periodically (every 6 or 12 months) in exchange for floating rate payments. The fixed rate payments remain fixed over the life of the contract. The floating interest rate payment per period is based on a prevailing interest rate, such as LIBOR at that time. The payments in an interest rate swap are typically determined using some **notional value** agreed upon by the parties to the swap in order to determine the swap payments.

The fixed rate payer is typically concerned that interest rates may rise in the future. Perhaps it recently issued a floating rate bond and is worried that its coupon payments will rise if interest rates increase. If these expectations are correct, then the fixed rate payer can benefit from swapping fixed interest payments in exchange for floating rate payments, and the gains from this interest rate swap can offset its higher expenses from

WEB

www.bloomberg.com
Information about international financing, including the issuance of debt in international markets.

having to make higher coupon payments on the bonds it issued. Conversely, a floating rate payer that expects interest rates to decline over time can benefit (if these expectations are correct) from swapping floating interest payments in exchange for fixed interest payments.

EXAMPLE

Two firms, Quality Co. and Risky Co., plan to issue bonds.

■   Quality Co. is a highly rated firm that prefers to borrow at a variable (floating) interest rate because it expects that interest rates will decline over time.

■   Risky Co. is a low-rated firm that prefers to borrow at a fixed interest rate.

Assume that the rates these companies would pay for issuing either floating rate or fixed rate bonds are as follows:

	FIXED RATE BOND	FLOATING RATE BOND
Quality Co.	9%	LIBOR + 0.5%
Risky Co.	10.5%	LIBOR + 1.0%

Based on the information given, Quality Co. has an advantage when issuing either fixed rate or floating rate bonds but more of an advantage when issuing fixed rate bonds. Even so, Quality Co. prefers to issue floating rate bonds because it anticipates declining interest rates. If Quality Co. issues fixed rate bonds and Risky Co. issues floating rate bonds, then Quality can make floating rate payments to Risky in exchange for fixed rate payments.

Assume that Quality Co. negotiates with Risky Co. to provide variable rate payments at LIBOR + 0.5 percent in exchange for fixed rate payments of 9.5 percent. This interest rate swap arrangement is shown in Exhibit 18.8. Quality Co. benefits because the fixed rate payments of 9.5 percent it receives on the swap exceed the payments it owes (9.0 percent) to bondholders by 0.5 percent. At the same time, its floating rate payments (LIBOR + 0.5 percent) to Risky Co. are the same as what it would have paid if it had issued floating rate bonds.

Exhibit 18.8   Illustration of an Interest Rate Swap

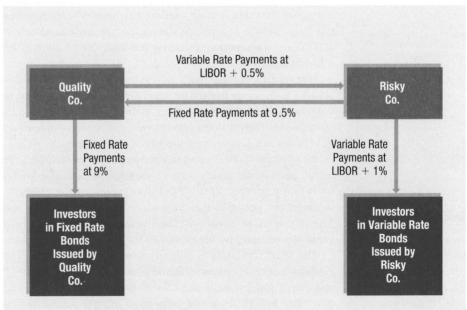

Exhibit 18.9 Expected Payments Resulting from Interest Rate Swap

YEAR	LIBOR	QUALITY CO.'S PAYMENT	RISKY CO.'S PAYMENT	NET PAYMENT
1	8.0%	8.5% × $50 million = $4.25 million	9.5% × $50 million = $4.75 million	Risky pays Quality $0.5 million
2	7.0%	7.5% × $50 million = $3.75 million	9.5% × $50 million = $4.75 million	Risky pays Quality $1 million
3	5.5%	6.0% × $50 million = $3 million	9.5% × $50 million = $4.75 million	Risky pays Quality $1.75 million
4	9.0%	9.5% × $50 million = $4.75 million	9.5% × $50 million = $4.75 million	No payment is made
5	10.0%	10.5% × $50 million = $5.25 million	9.5% × $50 million = $4.75 million	Quality pays Risky $0.5 million

Risky Co. is receiving LIBOR + 0.5 percent on the swap, which is 0.5 percent less than what it must pay (LIBOR + 1 percent) on its floating rate bonds. Yet it is making fixed rate payments of 9.5 percent, which is 1 percent less than what it would have paid if it had issued fixed rate bonds. Overall, Risky Co. saves 0.5 percent per year in financing costs.

Assume that the notional value agreed upon by the parties is $50 million and that the two firms exchange net payments annually. From Quality Co.'s viewpoint, the complete swap arrangement now involves payment of LIBOR + 0.5 percent annually based on a notional value of $50 million; from Risky Co.'s viewpoint, the swap arrangement involves a fixed payment of 9.5 percent annually based on the same notional value of $50 million. Exhibit 18.9 illustrates the payments based on forecasted values for LIBOR. ●

Limitations of Interest Rate Swaps Two limitations of the swap just described are worth mentioning. First, there is a cost of time and resources associated with searching for a suitable swap candidate and negotiating the swap terms. Second, each swap participant faces the risk that its counterpart could default on its payments.

Other Types of Interest Rate Swaps Continuing financial innovation has resulted in various additional types of interest rate swaps in recent years. Listed below are some examples.

- *Accreting swap.* An accreting swap is a swap in which the notional value is increased over time.
- *Amortizing swap.* An amortizing swap is essentially the opposite of an accreting swap. In an amortizing swap, the notional value is reduced over time.
- *Basis (floating-for-floating) swap.* A basis swap involves the exchange of two floating rate payments. For example, a swap between one-year LIBOR and six-month LIBOR is a basis swap.
- *Callable swap.* As the name suggests, a callable swap gives the fixed rate payer the right to terminate the swap. The fixed rate payer would exercise this right if interest rates fall substantially.
- *Forward swap.* A forward swap is an interest rate swap that is entered into today. However, the swap payments do not start until a specified future time.
- *Putable swap.* A putable swap gives the floating rate payer the right to terminate the swap. The floating rate payer would exercise this right if interest rates rise substantially.
- *Zero-coupon swap.* In a zero-coupon swap, all fixed interest payments are postponed until maturity and are paid in one lump sum when the swap matures. However, the floating rate payments are due periodically.

■ *Swaption.* A swaption gives its owner the right to enter into a swap. The exercise price of a swaption is a specified fixed interest rate at which the swaption owner can enter the swap at a specified future date. A payer swaption gives its owner the right to switch from paying floating to paying fixed interest rates at the exercise price; a receiver swaption gives its owner the right to switch from receiving floating rate to receiving fixed rate payments at the exercise price.

Standardization of the Swap Market   As the swap market has grown in recent years, one association in particular is frequently credited with its standardization. The **International Swaps and Derivatives Association (ISDA)** is a global trade association that represents leading participants in privately negotiated derivatives, such as interest rate, currency, commodity, credit, and equity swaps as well as related products.

The ISDA's two primary objectives are (1) developing and maintaining documentation on derivatives to promote efficient business conduct practices and (2) encouraging the development of sound risk management practices. One of the ISDA's most notable accomplishments is the development of the ISDA **Master Agreement**. This agreement provides participants in the private derivatives markets with the opportunity to establish the legal and credit terms between them for an ongoing business relationship. The key advantage of such an agreement is that the general legal and credit terms do not have to be renegotiated each time the parties enter into a transaction. Consequently, the ISDA Master Agreement has contributed greatly to the standardization of the derivatives market.[1]

SUMMARY

■ An MNC's subsidiary may prefer to use debt financing in a currency that matches the currency it receives from cash inflows. The cash inflows can be used to cover its interest payments on its existing loans. When a subsidiary issues debt in a currency that differs from the local currency it receives from sales, it is exposed to the risk that the local currency may depreciate over time.

■ An MNC's subsidiary may consider long-term financing in a foreign currency different from its local (host country) currency in order to reduce financing costs. It can forecast the exchange rates for the periods in which it will make loan payments and then can estimate the annualized cost of financing in that currency. However, the actual cost of debt financing is uncertain because the subsidiary's forecasts of future exchange rate movements may not be accurate.

■ MNCs can use currency swaps or parallel loans to hedge the exchange rate risk resulting from long-term debt financing.

■ An MNC's subsidiary can select among various available debt maturities when financing its operations. It can estimate the annualized cost of financing for alternative maturities and then determine which maturity will result in the lowest expected annualized cost of financing.

■ For debt that has floating interest rates, the interest (or coupon) payment to be paid to investors is frequently dependent on the future LIBOR and is therefore uncertain. An MNC can forecast LIBOR so it can derive the expected interest rates that it would be charged on the loan in future periods. It can apply these expected interest rates to estimate expected loan payments and can then derive the expected annualized cost of financing for the floating rate loan. Finally, it can compare the expected cost of financing on a floating rate loan to the known cost of financing on a fixed rate loan. In some cases, an MNC may engage in a floating rate loan, and use interest rate swaps to hedge the interest rate risk.

---

[1]For more information about interest rate swaps, see Robert A. Strong, *Derivatives: An Introduction*, 2e (Mason, Ohio: South-Western, 2005), and the ISDA (www.isda.org).

POINT COUNTER-POINT

Will Currency Swaps Result in Low Financing Costs?

Point   Yes. Currency swaps have created greater participation by firms that need to exchange their currencies in the future. Thus firms that finance in a low interest rate currency can more easily establish an agreement to obtain the currency that has the low interest rate.

Counter-Point   No. Currency swaps will establish an exchange rate that is based on market forces. If a forward rate exists for a future period, the swap rate should be somewhat similar to the forward rate. If it were not as attractive as the forward rate, the participants would use the forward market instead. If a

forward market does not exist for the currency, the swap rate should still reflect market forces. The exchange rate at which a low-interest currency could be purchased will exceed the prevailing spot rate because otherwise MNCs would borrow the low-interest currency and simultaneously purchase the currency forward so that they could hedge their future interest payments.

Who Is Correct?   Use the Internet to learn more about this issue. Which argument do you support? Offer your own opinion on this issue.

SELF-TEST

Answers are provided in Appendix A at the back of the text.

1. Explain why a firm may issue a bond denominated in a currency different from its home currency to finance local operations. Explain the risk involved.

2. Tulane, Inc. (based in Louisiana), considers issuing a 20-year Swiss franc–denominated bond. The proceeds are to be converted to British pounds to support the firm's British operations. Tulane, Inc., has no Swiss operations but prefers to issue the bond in francs rather than pounds because the coupon rate is 2 percentage points lower. Explain the risk involved in this strategy. Do you think the risk here is greater or less than it would be if the bond proceeds were used to finance U.S. operations? Why?

3. Some large companies based in Latin American countries could borrow funds (through issuing bonds or borrowing from U.S. banks) at an interest rate that would be substantially less than the interest rates in their own countries. Assuming that they are perceived

to be creditworthy in the United States, why might they still prefer to borrow in their local countries when financing local projects (even if they incur interest rates of 80 percent or more)?

4. A respected economist recently predicted that, even though Japanese inflation would not rise, Japanese interest rates would rise consistently over the next five years. Paxson Co., a U.S. firm with no foreign operations, has recently issued a Japanese yen–denominated bond to finance U.S. operations. It chose the yen denomination because the coupon rate was low. Its vice president stated, "I'm not concerned about the prediction because we issued fixed rate bonds and are therefore insulated from risk." Do you agree? Explain.

5. Long-term interest rates in some Latin American countries tend to be much higher than those of industrialized countries. Why do you think some projects in these countries are feasible for local firms even though the cost of funding the projects is so high?

QUESTIONS AND APPLICATIONS

1. Floating Rate Bonds

a. What factors should be considered by a U.S. firm that plans to issue a floating rate bond denominated in a foreign currency?

b. Is the risk of issuing a floating rate bond higher or lower than the risk of issuing a fixed rate bond? Explain.

c. How would an investing firm differ from a borrowing firm in the features (i.e., interest rate and currency's future exchange rates) it would prefer a floating rate foreign currency–denominated bond to exhibit?

2. Risk from Issuing Foreign Currency-Denominated Bonds What is the advantage of using simulation to assess the bond financing position?

3. Exchange Rate Effects

a. Explain the difference in the cost of financing with foreign currencies during a strong-dollar period versus a weak-dollar period for a U.S. firm.

b. Explain how a U.S.-based MNC issuing bonds denominated in euros may be able to offset a portion of its exchange rate risk.

4. Bond Offering Decision
Columbia Corp. is a U.S. company with no foreign currency cash flows. It plans to issue either a bond denominated in euros with a fixed interest rate or a bond denominated in U.S. dollars with a floating interest rate. It estimates its periodic dollar cash flows for each bond. Which bond do you think would have greater uncertainty surrounding these future dollar cash flows? Explain.

5. Borrowing Combined with Forward Hedging
Cedar Falls Co. has a subsidiary in Brazil, where local interest rates are high. It considers borrowing dollars and hedging the exchange rate risk by selling the Brazilian real forward in exchange for dollars for the periods in which it would need to make loan payments in dollars. Assume that forward contracts on the real are available. What is the limitation of this strategy?

6. Financing That Reduces Exchange Rate Risk
Kerr, Inc., a major U.S. exporter of products to Japan, denominates its exports in dollars and has no other international business. It can borrow dollars at 9 percent to finance its operations or borrow yen at 3 percent. If it borrows yen, it will be exposed to exchange rate risk. How can Kerr borrow yen and possibly reduce its economic exposure to exchange rate risk?

7. Exchange Rate Effects
Katina, Inc., is a U.S. firm that plans to finance with bonds denominated in euros to obtain a lower interest rate than is available on dollar-denominated bonds. What is the most critical point in time when the exchange rate will have the greatest impact?

8. Financing Decision
Cuanto Corp. is a U.S. drug company that has attempted to capitalize on new opportunities to expand in Eastern Europe. The production costs in most Eastern European countries are very low, often less than one-fourth of the cost in Germany or Switzerland. Furthermore, there is a strong demand for drugs in Eastern Europe. Cuanto penetrated Eastern Europe by purchasing a 60 percent stake in Galena, a Czech firm that produces drugs.

a. Should Cuanto finance its investment in the Czech firm by borrowing dollars from a U.S. bank that would then be converted into koruna (the Czech currency) or by borrowing koruna from a local Czech bank? What information do you need to know to answer this question?

b. How can borrowing koruna locally from a Czech bank reduce the exposure of Cuanto to exchange rate risk?

c. How can borrowing koruna locally from a Czech bank reduce the exposure of Cuanto to political risk caused by government regulations?

Advanced Questions

9. Bond Financing Analysis
Sambuka, Inc., can issue bonds either in U.S. dollars or in Swiss francs. Dollar-denominated bonds would have a coupon rate of 15 percent; Swiss franc–denominated bonds would have a coupon rate of 12 percent. Assuming that Sambuka can issue bonds worth $10 million in either currency, that the current exchange rate of the Swiss franc is $.70, and that the forecasted exchange rate of the franc in each of the next three years is $.75, what is the annual cost of financing for the franc-denominated bonds? Which type of bond should Sambuka issue?

10. Bond Financing Analysis
Hawaii Co. just agreed to a long-term deal in which it will export products to Japan. It needs funds to finance the production of the products that it will export. The products will be denominated in dollars. The prevailing U.S. long-term interest rate is 9 percent versus 3 percent in Japan. Assume that interest rate parity exists and that Hawaii Co. believes that the international Fisher effect holds.

a. Should Hawaii Co. finance its production with yen and leave itself open to exchange rate risk? Explain.

b. Should Hawaii Co. finance its production with yen and simultaneously engage in forward contracts to hedge its exposure to exchange rate risk?

c. How could Hawaii Co. achieve low-cost financing while eliminating its exposure to exchange rate risk?

11. Cost of Financing
Assume that Seminole, Inc., considers issuing a Singapore dollar–denominated bond at its present coupon rate of 7 percent, even though it has no incoming cash flows to cover the bond payments. It is attracted to the low financing rate because U.S. dollar–denominated bonds issued in the

United States would have a coupon rate of 12 percent. Assume that either type of bond would have a four-year maturity and could be issued at par value. Seminole needs to borrow $10 million. Therefore, it will issue either U.S. dollar–denominated bonds with a par value of $10 million or bonds denominated in Singapore dollars with a par value of S$20 million. The spot rate of the Singapore dollar is $.50. Seminole has forecasted the Singapore dollar's value at the end of each of the next four years, when coupon payments are to be paid. Determine the expected annual cost of financing with Singapore dollars. Should Seminole, Inc., issue bonds denominated in U.S. dollars or Singapore dollars? Explain.

END OF YEAR	EXCHANGE RATE OF SINGAPORE DOLLAR
1	$.52
2	.56
3	.58
4	.53

12. Interaction between Financing and Invoicing Policies Assume that Hurricane, Inc., is a U.S. company that exports products to the United Kingdom, invoiced in dollars. It also exports products to Denmark, invoiced in dollars. It currently has no cash outflows in foreign currencies, and it plans to issue bonds in the near future. Hurricane could likely issue bonds at par value in (1) dollars with a coupon rate of 12 percent, (2) Danish krone with a coupon rate of 9 percent, or (3) pounds with a coupon rate of 15 percent. It expects the krone and pound to strengthen over time. How could Hurricane revise its invoicing policy and make its bond denomination decision to achieve low financing costs without excessive exposure to exchange rate fluctuations?

13. Swap Agreement Grant, Inc., is a well-known U.S. firm that needs to borrow 10 million British pounds to support a new business in the United Kingdom. However, it cannot obtain financing from British banks because it is not yet established within the United Kingdom. It decides to issue dollar-denominated debt (at par value) in the United States, for which it will pay an annual coupon rate of 10 percent. It then will convert the dollar proceeds from the debt issue into British pounds at the prevailing spot rate (the prevailing spot rate is one pound = $1.70). Over each of the next three years, it plans to use the revenue in pounds from the new business in the United

Kingdom to make its annual debt payment. Grant, Inc., engages in a currency swap in which it will convert pounds to dollars at an exchange rate of $1.70 per pound at the end of each of the next three years. How many dollars must be borrowed initially to support the new business in the United Kingdom? How many pounds should Grant, Inc., specify in the swap agreement that it will swap over each of the next three years in exchange for dollars so that it can make its annual coupon payments to the U.S. creditors?

14. Interest Rate Swap Janutis Co. has just issued fixed rate debt at 10 percent. Yet it prefers to convert its financing to incur a floating rate on its debt. It engages in an interest rate swap in which it swaps variable rate payments of LIBOR plus 1 percent in exchange for payments of 10 percent. The interest rates are applied to an amount that represents the principal from its recent debt issue in order to determine the interest payments due at the end of each year for the next three years. Janutis Co. expects that the LIBOR will be 9 percent at the end of the first year, 8.5 percent at the end of the second year, and 7 percent at the end of the third year. Determine the financing rate that Janutis Co. expects to pay on its debt after considering the effect of the interest rate swap.

15. Financing and the Currency Swap Decision Bradenton Co. is considering a project in which it will export special contact lenses to Mexico. It expects that it will receive 1 million pesos after taxes at the end of each year for the next four years and after that time its business in Mexico will end as its special patent will be terminated. The peso's spot rate is presently $.20. The U.S. annual risk-free interest rate is 6 percent, while Mexico's annual risk-free interest rate is 11 percent. Interest rate parity exists. Bradenton Co. uses the one-year forward rate as a predictor of the exchange rate in one year. Bradenton Co. also presumes the exchange rates in each of years 2 through 4 will also change by the same percentage as it predicts for year 1. Bradenton searches for a firm with which it can swap pesos for dollars over each of the next four years. Briggs Co. is an importer of Mexican products. It is willing to take the 1 million pesos per year from Bradenton Co. and will provide Bradenton Co. with dollars at an exchange rate of $.17 per peso. Ignore tax effects. Bradenton Co. has a capital structure of 60 percent debt and 40 percent equity. Its corporate tax rate is 30 percent. It borrows funds from a bank and pays 10 percent interest on its debt. It expects that the U.S. annual stock market return will be 18 percent per year. Its beta is .9.

Bradenton would use its cost of capital as the required return for this project.

a. Determine the NPV of this project if Bradenton engages in the currency swap.

b. Determine the NPV of this project if Bradenton does not hedge the future cash flows.

16. Financing and Exchange Rate Risk The parent of Nester Co. (a U.S. firm) has no international business but plans to invest $20 million in a business in Switzerland. Because the operating costs of this business are very low, Nester Co. expects this business to generate large cash flows in Swiss francs that will be remitted to the parent each year. Nester will finance half of this project with debt. It has these choices for financing the project:

- obtain half of the funds needed from parent equity and the other half by borrowing dollars,
- obtain half of the funds needed from parent equity and the other half by borrowing Swiss francs, or
- obtain half of the funds that are needed from parent equity and obtain the remainder by borrowing an equal amount of dollars and Swiss francs.

    The interest rate on dollars is the same as the interest rate on Swiss francs.

a. Which choice will result in the most exchange rate exposure?

b. Which choice will result in the least exchange rate exposure?

c. If the Swiss franc were expected to appreciate over time, which financing choice would result in the highest expected net present value?

17. Financing and Exchange Rate Risk Vix Co. (a U.S firm) presently serves as a distributor of products by purchasing them from other U.S. firms and selling them in Europe. It wants to purchase a manufacturer in Thailand that could produce similar products at a low cost (due to low labor costs in Thailand) and export the products to Europe. The operating expenses would be denominated in Thai currency (the baht). The products would be invoiced in euros. If Vix Co. can acquire a manufacturer, it will discontinue its existing distributor business. If Vix Co. purchases a company in Thailand, it expects that its revenue might not be sufficient to cover its operating expenses during the first eight years. It will need to borrow funds for an eight-year term to ensure that it has enough funds to pay all of its operating expenses in Thailand. It can borrow funds denominated in U.S. dollars, in Thai baht, or in euros. Assuming that its financing decision will be primarily intended to minimize its exposure to exchange rate risk, which currency should it borrow? Briefly explain.

18. Financing and Exchange Rate Risk Compton Co. has a subsidiary in Thailand that produces computer components. The subsidiary sells the components to manufacturers in the United States. The components are invoiced in U.S. dollars. Compton pays employees of the subsidiary in Thai baht and makes a large monthly lease payment in Thai baht. Compton financed the investment in the Thai subsidiary by borrowing dollars from a U.S. bank. Compton has no other international business.

a. Given the conditions, is Compton affected favorably, unfavorably, or not at all by depreciation of the Thai baht? Briefly explain.

b. Assume that interest rates in Thailand declined recently, so the Compton subsidiary considers obtaining a new loan in Thai baht. Compton would use the proceeds to pay off its existing loan from a U.S. bank. Will this form of financing increase, reduce, or have no impact on its economic exposure to exchange rate movements? Briefly explain.

19. Selecting a Loan Maturity Omaha Co. has a subsidiary in Chile that wants to borrow from a local bank at a fixed rate over the next 10 years.

a. Explain why Chile's term structure of interest rates (as reflected in its yield curve) might cause the subsidiary to borrow for a different term to maturity.

b. If Omaha is offered a more favorable interest rate for a term of 6 years, explain the potential disadvantage compared to a 10-year loan.

c. Explain how the subsidiary can determine whether to select the 6-year loan or the 10-year loan.

20. Project Financing Dryden Co. is a U.S. firm that plans a foreign project in which it needs $8 million as an initial investment. The project is expected to generate cash flows of 10 million euros in one year after the complete repayment of the loan (including the loan interest and principal). The project has zero salvage value and is terminated at the end of one year. Dryden considers financing this project with:

- all U.S. equity,
- all U.S. debt (loans) denominated in dollars provided by U.S. banks,
- all debt (loans) denominated in euros provided by European banks, or

■ half of funds obtained from loans denominated in euros and half obtained from loans denominated in dollars.

Which form of financing will cause the project's NPV to be the least sensitive to exchange rate risk?

Critical Thinking

Financing Foreign Business with Foreign Debt Spectra Energy Corp. (based in Houston) has substantial operations in Canada and generates much revenue in Canadian dollars. It borrows funds denominated in Canadian dollars (rather than U.S. dollars) to finance its Canadian operations. Write a short essay that explains the potential benefits from such a strategy. Explain the possible disadvantages that might occur when some U.S.-based MNCs attempt this strategy in a country where interest rates are high. Also consider the alternative solutions such as not hedging, or selling forward contracts.

Discussion in the Boardroom

This exercise can be found in Appendix E at the back of this textbook.

Running Your Own MNC

This exercise can be found on the *International Financial Management* text companion website. Go to www.cengagebrain.com (students) or www.cengage.com/login (instructors) and search using **ISBN 9781133947837**.

BLADES, INC. CASE

Use of Long-Term Financing

Recall that Blades, Inc., is considering the establishment of a subsidiary in Thailand to manufacture Speedos, Blades' primary roller blade product. Alternatively, Blades could acquire an existing manufacturer of roller blades in Thailand, Skates'n'Stuff. At the most recent meeting of the board of directors of Blades, Inc., the directors voted to establish a subsidiary in Thailand because of the relatively high level of control it would afford Blades.

The Thai subsidiary is expected to begin production by early next year, and the construction of the plant in Thailand and the purchase of necessary equipment to manufacture Speedos are to commence immediately. Initial estimates of the plant and equipment required to establish the subsidiary in Bangkok indicate costs of approximately 550 million Thai baht. Because the current exchange rate of the baht is $0.023, this translates to a dollar cost of $12.65 million. Blades currently has $2.65 million available in cash to cover a portion of the costs. The remaining $10 million (434,782,609 baht), however, will have to be obtained from other sources.

The board of directors has asked Ben Holt, Blades' chief financial officer, to line up the necessary financing to cover the remaining construction costs and purchase of equipment. Holt realizes that Blades is a relatively small company whose stock is not widely held. Furthermore, he believes that Blades' stock is currently undervalued because the company's expansion into Thailand has not been widely publicized at this point.

Because of these considerations, Holt would prefer debt to equity financing to raise the funds necessary to complete construction of the Thai plant.

Holt has identified two alternatives for debt financing: issue the equivalent of $10 million yen-denominated notes or issue the equivalent of approximately $10 million baht-denominated notes. Both types of notes would have a maturity of 5 years. In the fifth year, the face value of the notes will be repaid together with the last annual interest payment. Notes denominated in yen (¥) are available in increments of ¥125,000, while baht-denominated notes are issued in increments of 50,000 baht. Because the baht-denominated notes are issued in increments of 50,000 baht (THB), Blades needs to issue THB434,782,609/50,000 = 8,696 baht-denominated notes. Furthermore, because the current exchange rate of the yen in baht is THB0.347826/¥, Blades needs to obtain THB434,782,609/THB0.347826 = ¥1,250,000,313. Because yen-denominated notes would be issued in increments of 125,000 yen, Blades would have to issue ¥1,250,000,313/¥125,000 = 10,000 yen-denominated notes.

Due to recent unfavorable economic events in Thailand, expansion into Thailand is viewed as relatively risky; Holt's research indicates that Blades would have to offer a coupon rate of approximately 10 percent on the yen-denominated notes to induce investors to purchase these notes. Blades could issue baht-denominated notes at a coupon rate of 15 percent. Whether Blades decides to issue baht- or yen-denominated notes, it would use the cash flows generated by the Thai subsidiary to pay the interest on the notes and to repay the principal in five years. For example, if Blades decides to issue yen-denominated notes, it would convert baht into yen to pay the interest on these notes and to repay the principal in five years.

Although Blades can finance with a lower coupon rate by issuing yen-denominated notes, Holt suspects that the effective financing rate for the yen-denominated notes may actually be higher than for the baht-denominated notes. This is because forecasts for the future value of the yen indicate an appreciation of the yen (versus the baht) in the future. Although the precise future value of the yen is uncertain, Holt has compiled the following probability distribution for the annual percentage change of the yen versus the baht:

ANNUAL % CHANGE IN YEN (AGAINST THE BAHT)	PROBABILITY
0%	20%
2	50
3	30

Holt suspects that the effective financing cost of the yen-denominated notes may actually be higher than for the baht-denominated notes once the expected appreciation of the yen (against the baht) is taken into consideration.

Holt has asked you, a financial analyst at Blades, Inc., to answer the following questions for him:

1. Given that Blades expects to use the cash flows generated by the Thai subsidiary to pay the interest and principal of the notes, would the effective financing cost of the baht-denominated notes be affected by exchange rate movements? Would the effective financing cost of the yen-denominated notes be affected by exchange rate movements? How? Construct a spreadsheet to determine the annual effective financing percentage cost of the yen-denominated notes issued in each of the three scenarios for the future value of the yen. What is the probability that the financing cost of issuing yen-denominated notes is higher than the cost of issuing baht-denominated notes?

2. Using a spreadsheet, determine the expected annual effective financing percentage cost of issuing yen-denominated notes. How does this expected financing cost compare with the expected financing cost of the baht-denominated notes?

3. Based on your answers to the previous questions, do you think Blades should issue yen- or baht-denominated notes?

4. What is the trade-off involved?

Small Business Dilemma

Long-Term Financing Decision by the Sports Exports Company

The Sports Exports Company continues to focus on producing footballs in the United States and exporting them to the United Kingdom. The exports are denominated in pounds, which has continually exposed the firm to exchange rate risk. It is now considering a new form of expansion where it would sell specialty sporting goods in the United States. If it pursues this U.S. project, it will need to borrow long-term funds. The dollar-denominated debt has an interest rate that is slightly lower than the pound-denominated debt.

1. Jim Logan, owner of the Sports Exports Company, needs to determine whether dollar-denominated debt

or pound-denominated debt would be most appropriate for financing this expansion, if he does expand. He is leaning toward financing the U.S. project with dollar-denominated debt because his goal is to avoid exchange rate risk. Is there any reason why he should consider using pound-denominated debt to reduce exchange rate risk?

2. Assume that Logan decides to finance his proposed U.S. business with dollar-denominated debt, if he does implement the U.S. business idea. How could he use a currency swap along with the debt to reduce the firm's exposure to exchange rate risk?

Internet/Excel Exercises

1. The Bloomberg website (www.bloomberg.com) provides interest rate data for many countries and

various maturities. Go to the Markets section of the website and then to Rates & Bonds and then click on

"Australia." Consider a subsidiary of a U.S.-based MNC that is located in Australia. Assume that when it borrows in Australian dollars, it would pay 1 percent more than the risk-free (government) rates shown on the website. What rate would the subsidiary pay for 1-year debt? For 5-year debt? For 10-year debt? Assuming that it needs funds for 10 years, do you think it should use 1-year debt, 5-year debt, or 10-year debt? Explain your answer.

2. Assume that you conduct business in Argentina, Brazil, and Canada. You consider expanding your business overseas. You want to estimate the annual cost of equity in these countries in case you decide to obtain equity funding there. Go to finance.yahoo.com /stock-center and select "Americas" and then "Central & South America." Click on Merval Index (which represents the Argentina stock market index). Click on "1y" just below the chart provided. Then click on "Historical Prices." Obtain the stock market index value eight years ago, seven years ago, . . . one year ago, and as of today. Insert the data on a spreadsheet. Use the mean annual return (percentage change in value) over the last eight years as a rough estimate of your cost of equity in each of these countries.

Then start over and repeat the process for Brazil (click on Ibovespa Index). Then start over and repeat the process for Canada (click on S&PTSX). Which country has the lowest estimated cost of equity? Which country has the highest estimated cost of equity?

ONLINE ARTICLES WITH REAL-WORLD EXAMPLES

Find a recent article available that describes an actual international finance application or a real-world example about a specific MNC's actions that reinforces one or more of the concepts covered in this chapter.

If your class has an online component, your professor may ask you to post your summary there and provide the web link of the article so that other students can access it. If your class is live, your professor may ask you to summarize your application in class. Your professor may assign specific students to complete this assignment for this chapter or may allow any students to do the assignment on a volunteer basis.

For recent online articles and real-world examples applied to this chapter, consider using the following search terms (and include the current year as a search term to ensure that the online articles are recent).

1. company AND foreign debt
2. Inc. AND foreign debt
3. [name of an MNC] AND debt
4. international AND debt
5. international AND financing
6. Company AND foreign financing
7. Inc. AND foreign financing
8. subsidiary AND debt
9. subsidiary AND financing
10. subsidiary AND leverage

Long-Term Asset and Liability Management

Gandor Co. is a U.S. firm that is considering a joint venture with a Chinese firm to produce and sell DVDs. Gandor will invest $12 million in this project, which will help to finance the Chinese firm's production. For each of the first three years, 50 percent of the total profits will be distributed to the Chinese firm, while the remaining 50 percent will be converted to dollars to be sent to the United States. The Chinese government intends to impose a 20 percent income tax on the profits distributed to Gandor. The Chinese government has guaranteed that the after-tax profits (denominated in yuan, the Chinese currency) can be converted to U.S. dollars at an exchange rate of $.20 per yuan and sent to Gandor Co. each year. At the current time, no withholding tax is imposed on profits sent to the United States as a result of joint ventures in China. Assume that after considering the taxes paid in China, an additional 10 percent tax is imposed by the U.S. government on profits received by Gandor Co. After the first three years, all profits earned are allocated to the Chinese firm.

The expected total profits resulting from the joint venture per year are as follows:

YEAR	TOTAL PROFITS FROM JOINT VENTURE (YUAN)
1	60 million
2	80 million
3	100 million

Gandor's average cost of debt is 13.8 percent before taxes. Its average cost of equity is 18 percent. Assume that the corporate income tax rate imposed on Gandor is normally 30 percent. Gandor uses a capital structure composed of 60 percent debt and 40 percent equity. Gandor automatically adds 4 percentage points to its cost of capital when deriving its required rate of return on international joint ventures. Though this project has particular forms of country risk that are unique, Gandor plans to account for these forms of risk within its estimation of cash flows.

Gandor is concerned about two forms of country risk. First, there is the risk that the Chinese government will increase the corporate income tax rate from 20 to 40 percent (20 percent probability). If this occurs, additional tax credits will be allowed, resulting in no U.S. taxes on the profits from this joint venture. Second, there is the risk that the Chinese government will impose a withholding tax of 10 percent on the profits that are sent to the United States (20 percent probability). In this case, additional tax credits will not be allowed, and Gandor will still be subject to a 10 percent U.S. tax on profits received from China. Assume that the two types of country risk are mutually exclusive. That is, the Chinese government will adjust only one of its taxes (the income tax or the withholding tax), if any.

Questions

1. Determine Gandor's cost of capital. Also, determine Gandor's required rate of return for the joint venture in China.

2. Determine the probability distribution of Gandor's net present values for the joint venture. Capital budgeting analyses should be conducted for these three scenarios:

   ■ *Scenario 1.* Based on original assumptions
   ■ *Scenario 2.* Based on an increase in the corporate income tax by the Chinese government
   ■ *Scenario 3.* Based on the imposition of a withholding tax by the Chinese government

3. Would you recommend that Gandor participate in the joint venture? Explain.

4. What do you think would be the key underlying factor that would have the most influence on the profits earned in China as a result of the joint venture?

5. Is there any reason for Gandor to revise the composition of its capital (debt and equity) obtained from the United States when financing joint ventures like this?

6. When Gandor was assessing this proposed joint venture, some of its managers recommended that Gandor borrow the Chinese currency rather than dollars to obtain some of the necessary capital for its initial investment. They suggested that such a strategy could reduce Gandor's exchange rate risk. Do you agree? Explain.

Short-Term Asset and Liability Management

Part 5 (Chapters 19 through 21) focuses on the multinational corporation's management of short-term assets and liabilities. Chapter 19 describes methods by which MNCs can finance their international trade. Chapter 20 identifies sources of short-term funds and explains the criteria used by MNCs to make their short-term financing decisions. Chapter 21 describes how MNCs optimize their cash flows and explains the criteria used to make their short-term investment decisions.

19

Financing International Trade

The specific objectives of this chapter are to:

■ describe methods of payment for international trade,

■ explain common trade finance methods, and

■ describe the major agencies that facilitate international trade with export insurance and/or loan programs.

The international trade activities of MNCs have grown in importance over time. This trend is attributable to the increased globalization of the world economies and the availability of trade finance from the international banking community.

19-1 Payment Methods for International Trade

The payment for a transaction between an exporter (seller) and importer (buyer) is complicated because of concerns that one party might not fulfill its obligation to the other party. First, the exporter may be concerned that it will not receive the payment from the importer. Second, even if the importer is willing to make payment, its government might impose exchange controls that prevent it from paying the exporter. Third, the importer may not trust the exporter to ship the products ordered. Financial managers must be aware of methods that they can use to ensure delivery of the products or the payment in international trade.

In general, five basic methods of payment are used to settle international transactions, each with a different degree of risk to the exporter and importer (see Exhibit 19.1):

■ prepayment,
■ letters of credit,
■ drafts,
■ consignment, and
■ open account.

19-1a Prepayment

Under the **prepayment** method, the exporter will not ship the products until it has received payment from the importer. Payment is usually made in the form of an international wire transfer to the exporter's bank account or a foreign bank draft. International electronic payment systems also allow firms engaged in international trade to make electronic credits and debits through an intermediary bank. This method provides the exporter with the most protection. Thus exporters normally require prepayment when dealing for the first time with importers whose creditworthiness is unknown or whose countries are in financial difficulty. Most importers, however, may not be willing to prepay because of concerns that the exporter might not ship the products ordered.

Exhibit 19.1 Comparison of Payment Methods for International Trade

METHOD	USUAL TIME OF PAYMENT	PRODUCTS AVAILABLE TO IMPORTERS	RISK TO EXPORTER	RISK TO IMPORTER
Prepayment	Before shipment	After payment	None	Relies completely on exporter to ship products as ordered
Letter of credit	When shipment is made	After payment	Very little or none, depending on credit terms	Is assured that shipment has been made, but relies on exporter to ship products described in documents
Sight draft; documents against payment	On presentation of draft to importer	After payment	If draft unpaid, must dispose of products	Same as above unless importer can inspect products before payment
Time draft; documents against acceptance	On maturity of drafts	Before payment	Relies on importer to pay drafts	Same as above
Consignment	At time of sale by importer	Before payment	Allows importer to sell inventory before paying exporter	None; improves cash flow of importer
Open account	As agreed	Before payment	Relies completely on importer to pay account as agreed	None

19-1b Letters of Credit

The **letter of credit (L/C)** is a written obligation to ensure that the importer makes payment to the exporter once it receives proof that the products have been shipped. Specifically, the importer's bank (also referred to as the "issuing bank") issues an L/C by making a written commitment on behalf of the importer to pay the exporter when the importer's bank receives shipping documents confirming that the exporter has shipped the products to the importer. The exporter benefits from the L/C because it may trust the importer's bank more than the importer itself to make payment.

Normally, the exporter's bank (also referred to as the "advising bank") will send the shipping documents to the importer's bank to verify that the products have been shipped. The importer benefits from the L/C because it does not have to make payment until the exporter has shipped the products, and because it may trust the exporter's bank more than the exporter itself to verify shipment of the products.

Even if the importer's bank is well known worldwide, the exporter may be concerned that the foreign government will impose foreign exchange controls or other restrictions that would prevent payment by the importer's bank. For this reason, the exporter may request that its bank assure that all the responsibilities of the importer's bank will be met. In this case, the exporter only needs to worry about the credibility of its bank rather than the importer's bank.

EXAMPLE   Nike can attribute part of its international business growth in the 1970s to the use of L/Cs. In 1971, Nike (which was then called BSR) was not well known to businesses in Japan or anywhere else. It wanted to subcontract the production of athletic shoes in Japan that could be shipped to and sold within the United States. By using L/Cs, Nike could be assured that it would receive the shoes that it ordered. Furthermore, the L/Cs assured the Japanese shoe producer that it would receive payment for the shoes sent to the United States. ●

Exhibit 19.2   Example of an Irrevocable Letter of Credit

Name of importer's bank
Address of importer's bank

Name of exporter
Address of exporter

We establish our irrevocable letter of credit:

for the account of *(importer name)*,

in the amount of (value of exports),

expiring *(date)*,

available by your draft at *(time period)* days sight and accompanied by:

(any invoices, packing lists, bills of lading, etc., that
need to be presented with the letter of credit)

Insurance provided by *(exporter or importer)*

covering shipment of (merchandise description)

From: (port of shipment)

To: (port of arrival)

(Authorized Signature)

Key Documents in Shipments Facilitated by a Letter of Credit   The key document in an international shipment under an L/C is the **bill of lading** (**B/L**). It serves as a receipt for shipment and a summary of freight charges; most importantly, it conveys title to the merchandise. If the merchandise is to be shipped by boat, the carrier will create an **ocean bill of lading**. When the merchandise is shipped by air, the carrier will create an **airway bill**. The carrier presents the bill to the exporter (shipper), who in turn presents the bill to its bank along with the other required documents.

The L/Cs used in international trade are **irrevocable letters of credit**, meaning that they cannot be canceled or amended without the exporter's consent (see Exhibit 19.2). Letters of credit are normally issued in accordance with the provisions contained in "Uniform Customs and Practice for Documentary Credits," which is published by the International Chamber of Commerce.

The bill of lading usually includes the following documents:

- a description of the merchandise,
- identification marks on the merchandise,
- evidence of loading (receiving) ports,
- name of the exporter (shipper),
- name of the importer,
- status of freight charges (prepaid or collect), and
- date of shipment.

The exporter's description of the merchandise being sold to the importer is the **commercial invoice**, which normally contains the following information:

- name and address of exporter;
- name and address of importer;
- date;
- terms of payment;
- price (including freight, handling, and insurance if applicable);

Exhibit 19.3 Documentary Credit Procedure

quantity, weight, packaging, etc.; and

shipping information.

Under an L/C shipment, the description of the merchandise outlined in the invoice must correspond exactly to that contained in the L/C. The documentary credit procedure involved with an L/C is depicted in Exhibit 19.3.

19-1c Drafts

A **draft** (or **bill of exchange**) represents a written order from the exporter instructing the importer to pay the face amount of the draft either when it is presented or at a specified future date. The documents for an L/C generally include a draft, but a draft may also be used without an L/C. However, a draft without an L/C affords the exporter less protection than an L/C because no bank is obligated to make the payment on the importer's behalf.

Most trade transactions handled on a draft basis are processed through banking channels. In these transactions, which are known as **documentary collections**, banks on both ends act as intermediaries in processing the shipping documents and collecting payment. If the products are shipped under a *sight draft*, the exporter is paid once the shipment has been made and the draft is presented to the importer for payment. This method of payment is known as **documents against payment**. It provides the exporter with some protection because the exporter's bank will release the shipping documents only according to the exporter's instructions. The importer needs the shipping documents to pick up the merchandise. The importer does not have to pay for the merchandise until the draft has been presented.

If a shipment is made under a *time draft*, the exporter instructs the importer's bank to release the shipping documents when the importer accepts (signs) the draft. This method of payment is sometimes referred to as **documents against acceptance**. By accepting the draft, the importer is promising to pay the exporter at the specified future date. The time period, or **tenor**, of most time drafts usually ranges from 30 to 180 days. The accepted draft is also known as a **trade acceptance**.

With a time draft, the importer is able to obtain the merchandise prior to paying for it. The exporter provides the financing and relies on the importer's financial integrity to pay the draft at maturity. If the importer fails to pay, its bank is not obligated to do so. Thus the exporter is assuming all the risk and must analyze the importer accordingly. A draft is a binding financial obligation, so the exporter could file a lawsuit to try to collect the amount owed if the importer does not pay.

19-1d Consignment

Under a **consignment** arrangement, the exporter ships the products to the importer while still retaining actual title to the merchandise. The importer has access to the products but does not have to pay for them until they have been sold to a third party. The exporter trusts the importer to remit payment for the products sold at that time. If the importer fails to pay, the exporter has limited recourse because no draft is involved and the products have already been sold. As a result of the high risk, consignments are seldom used except by affiliated and subsidiary companies trading with the parent company. Some equipment suppliers allow importers to hold some equipment on the sales floor as demonstrator models. Once the models are sold or after a specified period, payment is sent to the supplier.

19-1e Open Account

In an **open account transaction**, the exporter ships the merchandise and expects the importer to send payment according to the agreed-upon terms. The exporter is relying fully upon the financial creditworthiness and integrity of the importer. This method is used only when the exporter and importer have mutual trust and a great deal of experience with each other. Despite the risks, open account transactions are widely utilized, particularly among the industrialized countries in North America and Europe.

19-1f Impact of the Credit Crisis on Payment Methods

When the credit crisis intensified in the fall of 2008, international trade transactions stalled. Commercial banks facilitate trade transactions because they are normally trusted to guarantee payment on behalf of an importer. However, during the credit crisis, many financial institutions experienced financial problems. Consequently, exporters lost trust in commercial banks, and did not want to export products even if an importer's bank would guarantee payment. The crisis illustrated how international trade is so reliant on the soundness and integrity of commercial banks.

19-2 Trade Finance Methods

In any international trade transaction, credit is provided by the exporter, the importer, one or more financial institutions, or any combination of these. The exporter may have sufficient cash flow to finance the entire trade cycle, beginning with the production of the product until payment is eventually made by the importer. This form of credit is known as **supplier credit** because the exporter that supplies the products is also providing credit.

If the exporter does not have sufficient cash to fund the entire cycle, it may require bank financing, or the importer will have to finance the transaction. Thus commercial banks commonly play an integral role in trade financing on both sides of a transaction.

The following are some of the more popular methods of financing international trade:

- accounts receivable financing,
- factoring,
- letters of credit (L/Cs),
- banker's acceptances,
- medium-term capital goods financing (forfaiting), and
- countertrade.

Each of these methods is described in turn.

19-2a Accounts Receivable Financing

An exporter may be willing to ship products to an importer without an assurance of payment from a bank. This could take the form of an open account shipment or a time draft. Prior to shipment, the exporter should conduct a credit check of the importer to determine its creditworthiness. If the exporter is willing to wait for payment, it will extend credit to the importer.

If the exporter needs funds immediately, it may obtain financing from a bank. In what is referred to as **accounts receivable financing**, the bank will provide a loan to the exporter secured by the account receivable. The bank's loan is made to the exporter based on its creditworthiness. If the importer fails to pay the exporter for any reason, the exporter is still responsible for repaying the bank.

International accounts receivable financing involves additional risks, such as government restrictions and exchange controls that may prevent the importer from paying the exporter. As a result, the loan rate is often higher than for domestic accounts receivable financing. The length of a financing term is usually one to six months. To reduce the additional risk of a foreign receivable, exporters and banks often require export credit insurance before financing foreign receivables.

19-2b Factoring

When an exporter ships products before receiving payment, its accounts receivable balance increases. Unless the exporter has received a loan from a bank, it is initially financing the transaction and must monitor the collections of receivables. Because there is a danger that the importer will never pay at all, the exporter may decide to sell the accounts receivable to a third party, known as a **factor**. The factor then assumes all responsibility for collecting from the importer and the associated credit risk. The factor usually purchases the receivable at a discount and also receives a flat processing fee.

Before purchasing the receivable, the factor conducts a credit check on the importer. In international transactions, **cross-border factoring** is often used. This involves a network of factors in various countries that assess credit risk. The exporter's factor contacts a correspondent factor in the importer's country to assess the importer's creditworthiness and handle the collection of the receivable.

Factoring provides several benefits to the exporter. First, by selling the accounts receivable, the exporter does not have to worry about the costs of maintaining and monitoring an accounts receivable accounting ledger. Second, the factor assumes the credit risk, so the exporter does not have to assess the creditworthiness of the importer. Finally, by selling the receivable to the factor, the exporter receives immediate payment and improves its cash flow.

Factoring services are usually provided by the factoring subsidiaries of commercial banks, commercial finance companies, and other specialized finance houses. Factors often utilize export credit insurance to mitigate the additional risk of a foreign receivable.

19-2c Letters of Credit (L/Cs)

Letters of credit are not only an important payment method in international trade (as described earlier), but are also a source of financing. Many L/Cs are payable at a specified future date, so the exporter is providing financing to the importer until the importer (or the importer's bank) makes its payment to the exporter.

The importer's bank may also provide financing. When an importer obtains an L/C, it must pay its bank the amount of the L/C plus fees. The importer usually has an account at its bank to be drawn upon for payment. However, if the importer does not have sufficient funds in its account, the importer's bank is still obligated to make the payments due under the L/C. In doing so, the bank is extending credit to the importer. Consequently, the bank's willingness to create an L/C on behalf of an importer only occurs if the bank trusts the importer.

Another form of financing involves a **standby letter of credit,** in which the importer's bank promises to pay the exporter if the importer fails to pay as agreed. Internationally, standby L/Cs often are used with government-related contracts and serve as bid bonds, performance bonds, or advance payment guarantees.

19-2d Banker's Acceptances

A **banker's acceptance** (shown in Exhibit 19.4) is a bill of exchange, or time draft, that is issued by a firm and guaranteed by a bank. As the first step in creating a banker's acceptance in international trade, the importer orders products from the exporter. The importer then requests its local bank to create an L/C on its behalf that will ensure payment to the exporter. The exporter presents a time draft along with the shipping

WEB

www.huntington.com/
Click on "Commercial,"
then on "Industries," and
then on "International
Trade Services," to see
the various types of trade
financing that a bank can
provide for MNCs.

WEB

www.economagic.com
/fedbog.htm
Provides yield quotations
on banker's acceptances.

Exhibit 19.4 Banker's Acceptance

documents to its local bank, and the exporter's bank sends the time draft along with the shipping documents to the importer's bank. The importer's bank accepts (agrees to) the conditions of the draft, thereby creating a banker's acceptance.

If the exporter holds the acceptance until maturity, it provides the financing for the importer just as it does with accounts receivable financing. The key difference between a banker's acceptance and accounts receivable financing is that a banker's acceptance guarantees payment to the exporter by the importer's bank.

An exporter can sell the banker's acceptance in the money market if it does not want to hold the banker's acceptance until maturity. In this case, the exporter will receive less from the sale of the banker's acceptance than if it had waited to receive payment; this discount reflects the time value of money. An investor may be willing to buy the banker's acceptance at a discount and hold it until the specified payment date. The bank will make full payment at the date specified to the investor because it expects to receive this amount plus an additional fee from the importer.

A banker's acceptance can be beneficial to the exporter, importer, and the importer's bank. The exporter does not need to worry about the credit risk of the importer and can therefore penetrate new foreign markets without concern about the credit risk of potential customers. In addition, the exporter faces little exposure to political risk or to foreign exchange controls imposed by a government because banks normally are allowed to meet their payment commitments even if controls are imposed. In contrast, foreign exchange controls could prevent an importer from paying, so, without a banker's acceptance, an exporter might not receive payment even though the importer is willing to pay. Finally, the exporter can sell the banker's acceptance at a discount before payment is due and thus obtain funds up front.

The importer benefits from a banker's acceptance by obtaining greater access to foreign markets when purchasing supplies and other products. Without banker's acceptances, exporters may be unwilling to accept the credit risk of importers. In addition, the documents presented along with the acceptance assure the importer that the products have been shipped. Finally, because the banker's acceptance allows the importer to pay at a later date, the importer's payment is financed until the maturity date of the banker's acceptance. Without an acceptance, the importer would likely be forced to pay in advance, thereby tying up funds.

The importer's bank that accepts the draft benefits from the commission it earns from creating an acceptance. The commission that the bank charges the importer reflects the importer's perceived creditworthiness. The fee charged to the importer, referred to as the **all-in rate**, consists of the interest rate plus the acceptance commission. In general, the all-in rate for acceptance financing is lower than prime-based borrowings, as shown in the following comparison:

	LOAN	ACCEPTANCE
Amount	$1,000,000	$1,000,000
Term	180 days	180 days
Rate	Prime + 1.5%	B/A rate + 1.5%
	10.0% + 1.5% = 11.5%	7.60% + 1.5% = 9.10%
Interest cost	$57,500	$45,500

In this case, the interest savings for a six-month period are $12,000. Because the banker's acceptance is a marketable instrument with an active secondary market, the rates on acceptances usually fall between the rates on short-term Treasury bills and the rates on commercial paper. Investors are usually willing to purchase acceptances

Exhibit 19.5   Life Cycle of a Typical Banker's Acceptance (B/A)

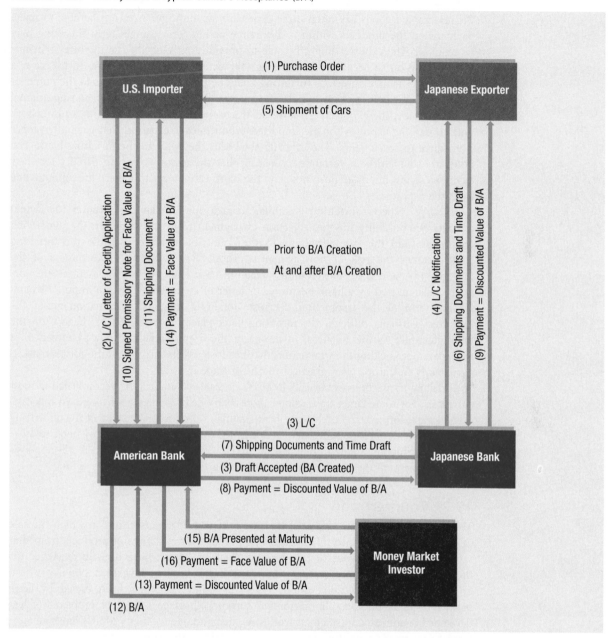

as an investment because of their yield, safety, and liquidity. When the importer's bank creates, accepts, and sells the acceptance, it is actually using the investor's money to finance the importer. Banker's acceptance financing can also be arranged through the refinancing of a sight letter of credit. In this case, the exporter may insist on payment at sight (immediately upon presenting the shipping documents). The importer's bank arranges to finance the payment of the sight L/C under a separate acceptance financing agreement. The life cycle of a banker's acceptance is illustrated in Exhibit 19.5.

19-2e Medium-Term Capital Goods Financing (Forfaiting)

Because capital goods are often quite expensive, an importer may not be able to make payment on the products within a short time period. Thus longer-term financing may be required. The exporter might be able to provide financing for the importer but may not desire to do so because the financing may extend over several years. In this case, a type of trade finance known as **forfaiting** could be used. Forfaiting refers to the purchase of financial obligations, such as bills of exchange or promissory notes, from the original holder (usually, the exporter). In a forfait transaction, the importer issues a promissory note to pay the exporter for the imported products over a period that generally ranges from three to seven years. The exporter then sells the notes to the forfaiting bank. The notes are sold "without recourse," meaning that the exporter has no liability for their payment; if the importer does not pay, the bank cannot try to collect the amount due from the exporter.

In some respects, forfaiting is similar to factoring in that the forfaiter (or factor) assumes responsibility for the collection of payment from the importer, the underlying credit risk, and the risk pertaining to the countries involved. Because the forfaiting bank assumes the risk of nonpayment, it should assess the creditworthiness of the importer just as if it were extending a medium-term loan. Forfait transactions are normally collateralized by a bank guarantee or letter of credit issued by the importer's bank for the term of the transaction. Because obtaining financial information about the importer is usually difficult, the forfaiting bank places a great deal of reliance on the bank guarantee as the collateral in the event the importer fails to pay as agreed. It is this guarantee backing the transaction that has fostered the growth of the forfait market, particularly in Europe, as a practical means of trade finance.

Forfaiting transactions are usually in excess of $500,000 and can be denominated in most currencies. For some larger transactions, more than one bank may be involved. In this case, a syndicate is formed, and each participant assumes a proportionate share of the underlying risk and profit. A forfaiting firm may decide to sell the importer's promissory notes to other financial institutions willing to purchase them. However, the forfaiting firm is still responsible for payment on the notes in the event the importer is unable to pay.

19-2f Countertrade

The term **countertrade** denotes all types of foreign trade transactions in which the sale of products to one country is linked to the purchase or exchange of products from that same country. Some types of countertrade, such as barter, have been in existence for thousands of years. Only recently, however, has countertrade gained popularity and importance. The growth in various types of countertrade has been fueled by large balance-of-payment disequilibria, foreign currency shortages, the debt problems of less developed countries, and stagnant worldwide demand. Hence many MNCs have encountered countertrade opportunities, especially in Asia, Latin America, and Eastern Europe. The most frequently used types of countertrade include barter, compensation, and counterpurchase.

Barter is the exchange of products between two parties without the use of any currency as a medium of exchange. Most barter arrangements are one-time transactions governed by a single contract. An example would be the exchange of 100 tons of wheat from Canada for 20 tons of shrimp from Ecuador.

In a **compensation** or clearing-account arrangement, the delivery of products to one party is compensated for by the exporter buying back a certain amount of the product from that same party. The transaction is governed by one contract, and the value of the products is expressed in monetary terms. The buyback arrangement could be for a fraction of the original sale (**partial compensation**) or for 100 percent of the original sale (**full compensation**). An example of compensation would be the sale of phosphate from Morocco to France in exchange for Morocco purchasing a specific amount of fertilizer from France. In some countries, this is also referred to as an industrial cooperation arrangement. Such arrangements often involve the construction of large projects, such as power plants, in exchange for the purchase of the project's output over an extended period of time. For example, Brazil sold a hydroelectric plant to Argentina and, in exchange, gained the right to purchase a percentage of the plant's output under a long-term contract.

The term **counterpurchase** denotes the exchange of products between two parties under two distinct contracts expressed in monetary terms. Delivery and payment of both products are technically separate transactions.

Despite the economic inefficiencies of countertrade, it has become much more important in recent years. The primary participants are governments and MNCs, with assistance provided by specialists in the field (such as attorneys, financial institutions, and trading companies). The transactions are usually large and complex. Many variations of countertrade exist, and the terminology used by the various market participants is still forming as the countertrade market continues to develop.

19-3 Agencies That Facilitate International Trade

Given the inherent risks of international trade, government institutions and the private sector offer various forms of export credit, export finance, and guarantee programs to reduce risk and stimulate foreign trade.

Three prominent agencies provide these services in the United States:

- the Export-Import Bank of the United States (Ex-Im Bank),
- the Private Export Funding Corporation (PEFCO), and
- the Overseas Private Investment Corporation (OPIC).

Each of these agencies will be described in this section.

WEB

www.exim.gov
Information about the Export-Import Bank of the United States.

19-3a Export-Import Bank of the United States

The **Export-Import Bank** (Ex-Im Bank) was established in 1934 with the original goal of facilitating Soviet–American trade. Its missions today are to finance and facilitate the export of American products and services and to maintain the competitiveness of American companies in overseas markets. It operates as an independent agency of the U.S. government and, as such, carries the full faith and credit of the United States.

Most of the Ex-Im Bank's programs are designed to encourage the private sector to finance export trade by assuming some of the underlying credit risk and providing direct financing to foreign importers when private lenders are unwilling to do so. To satisfy these objectives, the Ex-Im Bank offers programs that are classified as (1) guarantees, (2) loans, (3) bank insurance, and (4) export credit insurance.

Guarantee Programs   The two most widely used guarantee programs are the **Working Capital Guarantee Program** and the **Medium-Term Guarantee Program**. The Working Capital Guarantee Program encourages commercial banks to extend short-term export financing to eligible exporters by providing a comprehensive guarantee that covers 90 to 100 percent of the loan's principal and interest. This guarantee protects the lender against the risk of default by the exporter, but it does not protect the exporter against the risk of nonpayment by the importer. The loans are fully collateralized by export receivables and export inventory, and they require the payment of guarantee fees to the Ex-Im Bank. The export receivables are usually supported with export credit insurance or a letter of credit.

The Medium-Term Guarantee Program encourages commercial lenders to finance the sale of U.S. capital equipment and services to approved importers. The Ex-Im Bank guarantees 100 percent of the loan's principal and interest. The financed amount cannot exceed 85 percent of the contract price. This program is designed to finance products sold on a medium-term basis, with repayment terms of generally between one and five years. The guarantee fees paid to the Ex-Im Bank are determined by the repayment terms and the importer's risk. The Ex-Im Bank now offers a leasing program to finance capital equipment and related services.

WEB

www.bloomberg.com
Quotations of short-term foreign interest rates; this information is useful to an MNC that needs to finance its short-term liquidity needs.

Loan Programs   Two of the most popular loan programs are the **Direct Loan Program** and the **Project Finance Loan Program**. Under the Direct Loan Program, the Ex-Im Bank offers fixed rate loans directly to the importer to purchase U.S. capital equipment and services on a medium-term or long-term basis. The total financed amount cannot exceed 85 percent of the contract price. Repayment terms depend on the amount but are typically one to five years for medium-term transactions and seven to ten years for long-term transactions. The Ex-Im Bank's lending rates are generally below market rates.

The Project Finance Loan Program allows banks, the Ex-Im Bank, or a combination of both to extend long-term financing for capital equipment and related services for major projects. These are typically large infrastructure projects, such as power generation projects, whose repayment depends on project cash flow. Major U.S. corporations are often involved in these types of projects. The program typically requires a 15 percent cash payment by the importer and allows for guarantees of up to 85 percent of the contract amount. The fees and interest rates vary depending on the project risk.

Bank Insurance Programs   The Ex-Im Bank offers several insurance policies to banks. The most widely used is the **Bank Letter of Credit Policy**. This policy enables banks to confirm letters of credit issued by foreign banks supporting a purchase of U.S. exports. Without this insurance, some banks would not be willing to assume the underlying commercial and political risk associated with confirming an L/C. The banks are insured up to 100 percent for sovereign (government) banks and 95 percent for all other banks. The insurance premium is based on the type of importer, repayment term, and country.

The **Financial Institution Buyer Credit Policy** is issued in the name of the bank. This policy provides insurance coverage for loans by banks to foreign buyers (importers) on a short-term basis. A variety of short-term and medium-term insurance policies are available to exporters, banks, and other eligible applicants. Basically, all the policies provide insurance protection against the risk of nonpayment by importers. If the importer fails to pay the exporter because of commercial reasons such as cash flow problems or insolvency, the Ex-Im Bank will reimburse the exporter between 90 and 100 percent of the insured amount, depending on the type of policy and importer.

If the loss is due to political factors, such as foreign exchange controls or war, the Ex-Im Bank will reimburse the exporter for 100 percent of the insured amount. Exporters can use the insurance policies as a marketing tool because the insurance enables them to offer more competitive terms while protecting them against the risk of nonpayment. An exporter can also use the insurance policy as a financing tool by assigning the proceeds of the policy to a bank as collateral. Certain restrictions may apply to particular countries, depending on the Ex-Im Bank's experience and also on existing economic and political conditions.

Export Credit Insurance   The **Small Business Policy** provides enhanced coverage to new exporters and small businesses. The policy insures short-term credit sales (under 180 days) to approved importers. In addition to providing 95 percent coverage against commercial risk defaults and 100 percent coverage against political risk, the policy offers lower premiums. The exporter can assign the policy to a bank as collateral.

The **Umbrella Policy** operates in a slightly different manner. The policy itself is issued to an "administrator," such as a bank, trading company, insurance broker, or government agency. The policyholder administers the policy for multiple exporters and relieves the exporters of the administrative responsibilities associated with the policy. The short-term insurance protection is similar to that provided by the Small Business Policy and does not have a commercial risk deductible. The proceeds of the policy may be assigned to a bank for financing purposes.

The **Multibuyer Policy** is used primarily by experienced exporters. It provides insurance coverage on short-term export sales to many different buyers. Premiums are based on an exporter's sales profile, credit history, terms of repayment, country, and other factors. Based on the exporter's experience and the importer's creditworthiness, the Ex-Im Bank may grant the exporter authority to preapprove specific buyers up to a certain limit.

The **Single-Buyer Policy** allows an exporter to selectively insure certain short-term transactions to preapproved importers. Premiums are based on repayment terms and transaction risk. There is also a Medium-Term Policy to cover sales to a single importer for terms of between one and five years.

The Ex-Im Bank has also entered into partnership arrangements with more than 30 U.S. states to disseminate government trade promotion services to a broader audience. For example, the Florida Export Finance Corp. provides export credit insurance consulting, trade finance, and guarantees to exporters based in Florida.

Several private insurance carriers, such as AIG, also provide various types of insurance policies that may be used to mitigate risk. They are frequently employed when Ex-Im Bank insurance is not available or desirable.

19-3b Private Export Funding Corporation

The Private Export Funding Corporation (PEFCO) is a private corporation owned by a consortium of commercial banks and industrial companies. In cooperation with the Ex-Im Bank, PEFCO provides medium- and long-term fixed rate financing to importers. The Ex-Im Bank guarantees all export loans made by PEFCO. Most PEFCO loans are to finance large projects, such as aircraft and power generation equipment, and therefore have relatively long terms (sometimes as long as 25 years). Because commercial banks usually do not extend such long terms, PEFCO fills a void in the market while also serving as a secondary market importer of export loans originated by U.S. banks. PEFCO raises its funds in the capital markets through the issuance of long-term bonds. These bonds are readily marketable because they are, in effect, secured by Ex-Im Bank–guaranteed loans.

19-3c Overseas Private Investment Corporation

The Overseas Private Investment Corporation (OPIC) was formed in 1971 as a self-sustaining federal agency responsible for insuring direct U.S. investments in foreign countries against the risks of currency inconvertibility, expropriation, and other political risks. Through the direct loan or guaranty program, OPIC will provide medium- to long-term financing to U.S. investors undertaking an overseas venture. In addition to general insurance and finance programs, OPIC offers specific types of coverage for exporters bidding on or performing foreign contracts. American contractors can insure themselves against contractual disputes and even against the wrongful calling of standby letters of credit.

SUMMARY

- The common methods of payment for international trade are (1) prepayment (before products are sent), (2) letters of credit, (3) drafts, (4) consignment, and (5) open account.
- The most popular methods of financing international trade are (1) accounts receivable financing, (2) factoring, (3) letters of credit, (4) banker's

acceptances, (5) medium-term capital goods financing (forfaiting), and (6) countertrade.

- The major agencies that facilitate international trade with export insurance and/or loan programs are (1) the Export-Import Bank, (2) the Private Export Funding Corporation, and (3) the Overseas Private Investment Corporation.

POINT COUNTER-POINT

Do Agencies That Facilitate International Trade Prevent Free Trade?

Point Yes. The Export-Import Bank of the United States provides many programs to help U.S. exporters conduct international trade. The government is essentially subsidizing the exports. Governments in other countries have various programs as well. Thus some countries may have a trade advantage because their exporters are subsidized in various ways. These subsidies distort the notion of free trade.

Counter-Point No. It is natural for any government to facilitate exporting for relatively inexperienced exporting firms. All governments provide a

variety of services for their firms, including public services and tax breaks for producing products that are ultimately exported. There is a difference between facilitating the exporting process and protecting an industry from foreign competition. The protection of an industry violates the notion of free trade, but facilitating the exporting process does not.

Who Is Correct? Use the Internet to learn more about this issue. Which argument do you support? Offer your own opinion on this issue.

SELF-TEST

Answers are provided in Appendix A at the back of the text.

1. Explain why so many international transactions require international trade credit facilitated by commercial banks.

2. Explain the difference in the risk to the exporter between accounts receivable financing and factoring.

3. Explain how the Export-Import Bank can encourage U.S. firms to export to less developed countries where there is political risk.

QUESTIONS AND APPLICATIONS

1. Banker's Acceptances

a. Describe how foreign trade would be affected if banks did not provide trade-related services.

b. How can a banker's acceptance be beneficial to an exporter, an importer, and a bank?

2. Export Financing

a. Why would an exporter provide financing for an importer?

b. Is there much risk in this activity? Explain.

3. Role of Factors What is the role of a factor in international trade transactions?

4. Export-Import Bank

a. What is the role today of the Export-Import Bank of the United States?

b. Describe the Direct Loan Program administered by the Export-Import Bank.

5. Bills of Lading What are bills of lading, and how do they facilitate international trade transactions?

6. Forfaiting What is forfaiting? Specify the type of traded products for which forfaiting is applied.

7. PEFCO Briefly describe the role of the Private Export Funding Corporation (PEFCO).

8. Government Programs This chapter described many forms of government insurance and guarantee programs. What motivates a government to establish such programs?

9. Countertrade What is countertrade?

10. Impact of Foreign Exchange Controls Every quarter, Bronx Co. ships computer chips to a firm in central Asia. It has not used any trade financing because the importing firm always pays its bill in a timely manner upon receipt of the computer chips. However, Bronx Co. was concerned that the foreign government may impose foreign exchange controls. Bronx Co. reconsidered whether it should use some form of trade financing that would ensure that it would be paid for its exports upon delivery. How could Bronx Co. have achieved its goal?

11. Working Capital Guarantee Program Briefly describe the Working Capital Guarantee Program administered by the Export-Import Bank.

12. Small Business Policy Describe the Small Business Policy.

13. OPIC Describe the role of the Overseas Private Investment Corporation (OPIC).

Advanced Questions

14. Letters of Credit Ocean Traders of North America is a firm based in Mobile, Alabama, that specializes in seafood exports and commonly uses letters of credit (L/Cs) to ensure payment. It recently experienced a problem, however. Ocean Traders had an irrevocable L/C issued by a Russian bank to ensure that it would receive payment upon shipment of 16,000 tons of fish to a Russian firm. This bank backed out of its obligation, however, stating that it was not authorized to guarantee commercial transactions.

a. Explain how an irrevocable L/C would normally facilitate the business transaction between the Russian importer and Ocean Traders of North America (the U.S. exporter).

b. Explain how the cancellation of the L/C could create a trade crisis between the U.S. and Russian firms.

c. Why do you think situations like this (the cancellation of the L/C) are rare in industrialized countries?

d. Can you think of any alternative strategy that the U.S. exporter could have used to protect itself better when dealing with a Russian importer?

Critical Thinking

Limitations of Payment Methods for International Trade Write a short essay expressing your opinion about whether the traditional payment methods for international trade insulate an MNC's business when there are strained relations between two countries.

Discussion in the Boardroom

This exercise can be found in Appendix E at the back of this textbook.

Running Your Own MNC

This exercise can be found on the *International Financial Management* text companion website. Go to www.cengagebrain.com (students) or www.cengage.com/login (instructors) and search using **ISBN 9781133947837**.

BLADES, INC. CASE

Assessment of International Trade Financing in Thailand

Blades, Inc., has recently decided to establish a subsidiary in Thailand to produce Speedos, Blades' primary roller blade product. In establishing the subsidiary in Thailand, Blades was motivated by the high growth potential of the Thai roller blade market. Furthermore,

Blades has decided to establish a subsidiary, as opposed to acquiring an existing Thai roller blade manufacturer for sale, in order to maintain its flexibility and control over the operations in Thailand. Moreover, Blades has decided to issue yen-denominated notes to partially finance the cost of establishing the subsidiary. Blades has decided to issue notes denominated in yen instead of baht to avoid the high effective interest rates associated with the baht-denominated notes.

Currently, Blades plans to sell all roller blades manufactured in Thailand to retailers in Thailand. Furthermore, Blades plans to purchase all components for roller blades manufactured in Thailand from Thai suppliers. Similarly, all of Blades' roller blades manufactured in the United States will be sold to retailers in the United States and all components needed for Blades' U.S. production will be purchased from suppliers in the United States. Consequently, Blades will have no exports and imports once the plant in Thailand is operational, which is expected to occur early next year.

Construction of the plant in Thailand has already begun, and Blades is currently in the process of purchasing the machinery necessary to produce Speedos. Besides these activities, Ben Holt, Blades' chief financial officer, has been actively lining up suppliers of the needed rubber and plastic components in Thailand and identifying Thai customers, which will consist of various sports product retailers in Thailand.

Although Holt has been successful in locating both interested suppliers and interested customers, he is discovering that he has neglected certain precautions for operating a subsidiary in Thailand. First, although Blades is relatively well known in the United States, it is not recognized internationally. Consequently, the suppliers Blades would like to use in Thailand are not familiar with the firm and have no information about its reputation. Moreover, Blades' previous activities in Thailand were restricted to the export of a fixed number of Speedos annually to one customer, a Thai retailer called Entertainment Products. Holt has little information about the potential Thai customers that would buy the roller blades produced by the new plant. He is aware, however, that although letters of credit (L/Cs) and drafts are usually employed for exporting purposes, these instruments are also used for trade within a country between relatively unknown parties.

Of the various potential customers Blades has identified in Thailand, four retailers of sports products appear particularly interested. Because Blades is not familiar with these firms and their reputations, it would like to receive payment from them as soon as possible. Ideally, Blades would like its customers to prepay for their purchases, as this would involve the least risk for Blades. Unfortunately, none of the four potential customers has agreed to a prepayment arrangement. In fact, one potential customer, Cool Runnings,

Inc., insists on an open account transaction. Payment terms in Thailand for purchases of this type are typically "net 60," indicating that payment for the roller blades would be due approximately two months after a purchase was made. Two of the remaining three retailers, Sports Equipment, Inc., and Major Leagues, Inc., have indicated that they would also prefer an open account transaction; however, both of these retailers would have their banks act as intermediaries for a time draft. The fourth retailer, Sports Gear, Inc., is indifferent as to the specific payment method but finds a prepayment arrangement unacceptable.

Blades also needs a suitable arrangement with its various potential suppliers of rubber and plastic components in Thailand. Because Blades' financing of the Thai subsidiary involved a U.S. bank, it has virtually no contacts in the Thai banking system. Because Blades is relatively unknown in Thailand, Thai suppliers have indicated that they would prefer prepayment or at least a guarantee from a Thai bank that Blades will be able to make payment within 30 days of purchase. Blades does not currently have accounts receivable in Thailand. It does, however, have accounts receivable in the United States resulting from its U.S. sales.

Holt would like to please Blades' Thai customers and suppliers in order to establish strong business relationships in Thailand. However, he is worried that Blades may be at a disadvantage if it accepts all of the Thai firms' demands. Consequently, he has asked you, a financial analyst for Blades, Inc., to provide him with some guidance regarding international trade financing. Specifically, Holt has asked you to answer the following questions for him:

1. Assuming that banks in Thailand issue a time draft on behalf of Sports Equipment, Inc., and Major Leagues, Inc., would Blades receive payment for its roller blades before it delivers them? Do the banks issuing the time drafts guarantee payment on behalf of the Thai retailers if they default on the payment?

2. What payment method should Blades suggest to Sports Gear, Inc.? Substantiate your answer.

3. What organization could Blades contact in order to insure its sales to the Thai retailers? What type of insurance does this organization provide?

4. How could Blades use accounts receivable financing or factoring, considering that it does not currently have accounts receivable in Thailand? If Blades uses a Thai bank to obtain this financing, how do you think the fact that Blades does not have receivables in Thailand would affect the terms of the financing?

5. Assuming that Blades is unable to locate a Thai bank that is willing to issue an L/C on Blades' behalf, can you think of a way Blades could utilize its bank in the United States to effectively obtain an L/C from a Thai bank?

6. What organizations could Blades contact to obtain working capital financing? If Blades is unable to obtain working capital financing from these organizations, what are its other options to finance its working capital needs in Thailand?

SMALL BUSINESS DILEMMA

Ensuring Payment for Products Exported by the Sports Exports Company

The Sports Exports Company produces footballs and exports them to a distributor in the United Kingdom. It typically sends footballs in bulk and then receives payment after the distributor receives the shipment. The business relationship with the distributor is based on trust. Although the relationship has worked thus far, Jim Logan (owner of the Sports Exports Company) is concerned about the possibility that the distributor will not make its payment.

1. How could Logan use a letter of credit to ensure that he will be paid for the products he exports?

2. Logan has discussed the possibility of expanding his export business through a second sporting goods distributor in the United Kingdom; this second distributor would cover a different territory than the first distributor. The second distributor is only willing to engage in a consignment arrangement when selling footballs to retail stores. Explain the risk to Logan beyond the typical types of risk he incurs when dealing with the first distributor. Should he pursue this type of business?

INTERNET/EXCEL EXERCISE

The website of the Export-Import Bank of the United States (www.exim.gov) offers information about trade financing. Summarize what the Ex-Im Bank does to facilitate trade by businesses.

ONLINE ARTICLES WITH REAL-WORLD EXAMPLES

Find a recent article online that describes an actual international finance application or a real-world example about a specific MNC's actions that reinforces one or more of the concepts covered in this chapter.

If your class has an online component, your professor may ask you to post your summary there and provide the web link of the article so that other students can access it. If your class is live, your professor may ask you to summarize your application in class. Your professor may assign specific students to complete this assignment for this chapter or may allow any students to do the assignment on a volunteer basis.

For recent online articles and real-world examples applied to this chapter, consider using the following search terms (and include the current year as a search term to ensure that the online articles are recent).

1. international trade AND payment
2. international trade AND financing
3. company AND trade financing
4. Inc. AND trade financing
5. international AND trade financing
6. multinational AND trade financing
7. international AND letter of credit
8. multinational AND letter of credit
9. Export-Import Bank
10. export credit insurance

20
Short-Term Financing

CHAPTER OBJECTIVES

The specific objectives of this chapter are to:

■ identify sources of short-term financing for MNCs,

■ explain how MNCs determine whether to use foreign financing, and

■ illustrate the possible benefits of financing with a portfolio of currencies.

All firms make short-term financing decisions periodically. Beyond the international trade financing discussed in the previous chapter, MNCs obtain short-term financing to support other operations. Because MNCs have access to additional sources of funds, their short-term financing decisions are more complex than those of other companies. Financial managers must understand the possible advantages and disadvantages of short-term financing with foreign currencies so that they can make short-term financing decisions that maximize the value of the MNC.

20-1 Sources of Foreign Financing

Multinational corporations may sometimes experience a temporary shortage of funds, so they rely on short-term financing until they receive sufficient cash inflows to cover the shortage. They may first attempt internal short-term financing, but if internal funds are not available, they access funds externally. Both financing types are discussed next.

20-1a Internal Short-Term Financing

Before an MNC or subsidiary in need of funds searches for outside funding, it should check other subsidiaries' cash flow positions to determine whether any internal funds are available.

EXAMPLE   The Canadian subsidiary of Shreveport, Inc., has experienced strong earnings and invested a portion of the earnings locally in money market securities. It does not expect that it will need these funds for the next six months. Meanwhile, Shreveport's Mexican subsidiary normally relies on earnings to support its expansion, but its earnings were relatively low this quarter. Consequently, it does not have adequate funds to support its expansion at this time. Shreveport instructs the Canadian subsidiary to loan some of its excess funds to the Mexican subsidiary for the next six months. Because the Mexican subsidiary is expected to generate positive cash flows over the next two quarters, it will be able to repay the loan within six months. ●

Multinational corporations can also attempt to obtain financing from their subsidiaries by increasing the markups on supplies that they send to them. In this case, the funds the subsidiary gives to the parent will never be returned. This method of supporting the parent can sometimes be more feasible than obtaining loans from the subsidiary because it may circumvent restrictions or taxes imposed by national governments. In some cases, though, this method itself may be restricted or limited by the host governments where the subsidiaries are located.

Internal Control over Funds   An MNC should have an internal system that constantly monitors the amount of short-term financing by all of its subsidiaries. This may allow it to recognize which subsidiaries have cash available in the same currency that another subsidiary needs to borrow. Furthermore, the monitoring system can govern the extent of short-term financing by each subsidiary. Without such controls, one subsidiary may borrow excessively, which may ultimately affect the amount that other subsidiaries can borrow if all subsidiary borrowing from banks is backed by the parent's guarantee. Thus the MNC can use internal controls both to monitor the short-term financing at its subsidiaries and to impose a maximum short-term debt level at each subsidiary.

20-1b External Short-Term Financing

If MNCs and their subsidiaries cannot access short-term funds internally, they can consider the following external sources of short-term funds to satisfy their liquidity needs.

Short-Term Notes   One method increasingly used in recent years is the issuing of short-term notes, or unsecured debt securities. In Europe, the securities are referred to as **Euronotes**. The interest rates on these notes are based on LIBOR, the interest rate charged on interbank loans among European and other countries. Short-term notes typically have maturities of one, three, or six months. Some MNCs continually roll them over as a form of intermediate-term financing. Commercial banks underwrite the notes for MNCs, and some commercial banks purchase them for their own investment portfolios.

Commercial Paper   In addition to short-term notes, MNCs also issue commercial paper. In Europe, this is sometimes referred to as **Euro–commercial paper**. Dealers issue commercial paper for MNCs without the backing of an underwriting syndicate, so the issuer is not guaranteed a selling price. Maturities can be tailored to the issuer's preferences. Dealers may make a secondary market by offering to repurchase commercial paper before maturity.

Bank Loans   Direct loans from banks, which are often used to maintain bank relationships, are another popular source of short-term funds for MNCs. If alternative sources of short-term funds become unavailable, MNCs rely more heavily on direct loans from banks. Most MNCs maintain credit arrangements with various banks around the world; some have credit arrangements with more than 100 foreign and domestic banks.

20-1c Access to Funding during a Credit Crisis

During a credit crisis, financial institutions tend to reduce the amount of credit they are willing to extend to MNCs because of concerns that the borrowers will not repay the loans. For example, during the credit crisis of 2008–2009, the markets for short-term notes, commercial paper, and bank loans were less active. Many financial institutions that had provided funds in these markets shifted funds to risk-free (government) debt securities because they were concerned about the credit risk of MNCs. Some MNCs had to pay a higher risk premium to obtain short-term debt. Other MNCs were unable to obtain short-term debt and had to rely more on cash or retained earnings (internal financing) during the credit crisis.

20-2 Financing with a Foreign Currency

When MNCs obtain short-term financing, they usually borrow the currency that matches their future cash inflows. If an MNC has a net receivables position in a foreign

Exhibit 20.1 Comparison of Short-term Interest Rates among Countries (as of January 2016)

COUNTRY	ANNUALIZED INTEREST RATE
Australia	2.5%
Brazil	14.7
Canada	1.1
Chile	3.5
China	5.0
Eurozone countries	1.1
India	6.3
Indonesia	8.2
Japan	0.5
Mexico	3.5
New Zealand	3.3
Russia	11.5
Taiwan	2.4
Turkey	8.0
United Kingdom	1.0
United States	1.2

currency, it may obtain a short-term loan in that currency so that it can access short-term funds and also hedge its receivables against exchange rate risk. This strategy is especially appealing if the interest rate of the foreign currency is low.

20-2a Motive for Financing with a Foreign Currency

Even when an MNC or its subsidiary is not attempting to cover foreign net receivables, it may still consider borrowing a foreign currency if the interest rate on the currency is relatively low. By shaving 1 percentage point off its financing rate, an MNC can save $1 million in annual interest expense on debt of $100 million. Such savings motivate MNCs to consider various currencies when financing their operations.

Exhibit 20.1 compares short-term interest rates among countries. The interest rates in many developing countries are usually higher than the interest rates in developed countries. For example, Exhibit 20.1 shows that interest rates in Brazil and India are much higher than the interest rates of the developed countries. The developing countries tend to have higher inflation and a low level of saving, and these factors cause interest rates to be relatively high. The interest rate in Japan is almost always low compared to other countries because the very high rate of saving by households allows a large supply of funds to be channeled to borrowers.

Given the disparity in interest rates among countries, MNCs may naturally consider financing with a foreign currency that has a low interest rate. They must weigh the potential cost savings against the risk, as explained in the next sections.

WEB

www.bloomberg.com
Short-term interest rates
for major currencies such
as the Canadian dollar,
Japanese yen, and British
pound for various
maturities.

20-2b Potential Cost Savings from Financing with a Foreign Currency

When an MNC borrows a currency that differs from its local currency, the actual or "effective" financing rate will depend on (1) the interest rate charged by the bank providing the loan and (2) the movement in the borrowed currency's value over the life of the loan. Specifically, the MNC's effective financing rate (denoted r_f) can be derived as follows:

$$r_f = (1 + i_f)(1 + e_f) - 1$$

where i_f represents the interest rate of the foreign currency over the loan period, and e_f represents the percentage change in the value of the foreign currency over the loan period. Although the interest rate is known before the loan period begins, the movement in the borrowed currency's value over the life of the loan is uncertain. Thus the effective financing rate from financing with a foreign currency is not known until the loan period is over. However, an MNC can forecast the exchange rate movement in the foreign currency that it may borrow, as illustrated in the following example.

EXAMPLE

Cobra Co. (based in the United States) needs a one-year loan to support its U.S. operations. Its bank currently offers an annual interest rate of 8 percent on a loan in U.S. dollars. The bank also offers an interest rate of 3 percent on a loan denominated in Canadian dollars, because the Canadian market interest rates are currently very low. Cobra could obtain a one-year loan in Canadian dollars and convert the funds into U.S. dollars to support its U.S. operations. In one year, Cobra Co. would need to convert U.S. dollars into Canadian dollars to repay the loan principal plus 3 percent interest.

Assume that Cobra Co. expects that the Canadian dollar will depreciate by 1 percent against the U.S. dollar over the life of the loan. Given the 3 percent interest rate on the loan, and 1 percent depreciation in the Canadian dollar over the loan life, the effective financing rate on the loan denominated in Canadian dollars can be computed as

$$r_f = (1 + i_f)(1 + e_f) - 1$$
$$= (1 + .03)[1 + (-.01)] - 1$$
$$= .0197 \text{ or } 1.97\%$$

Cobra Co. would benefit not only from the low interest rate on the loan, but also from the slight depreciation in the Canadian dollar. ●

The example shows how the effective financing rate is reduced if the currency depreciates over the loan period. Cobra Co.'s effective financing rate could even be negative if the degree of depreciation in the Canadian dollar over the loan period was greater than the loan's interest rate of 3 percent. A negative effective financing rate means that the amount of funds needed to repay the loan is less than the amount borrowed.

20-2c Risk of Financing with a Foreign Currency

Although an MNC can benefit from financing in a currency with a low interest rate that differs from the currency that it needs, the strategy could backfire if the currency that is borrowed substantially appreciates over the loan period.

EXAMPLE

Cobra Co. wants to consider an alternative scenario in which the Canadian dollar appreciates by 10 percent over the one-year loan period. Given the quoted interest rate (i_f) of 3 percent and the percentage change in the Canadian dollar (e_f) of 10 percent over the loan period, the effective financing rate on the loan to Cobra Co. would be

$$r_f = (1 + .03)[1 + (.10)] - 1$$
$$= .133 \text{ or } 13.3\%$$

In this example, Cobra would incur a higher cost of financing with Canadian dollars than if it borrows U.S. dollars. ●

This scenario illustrates the potential exchange rate risk from financing with a foreign currency, even when that currency has a low interest rate. The exchange rate risk is especially high when the foreign currency tends to have volatile exchange rate movements and is therefore subject to much uncertainty in the future.

20-2d Hedging the Foreign Currency Borrowed

To avoid exposure to exchange rate risk when borrowing a foreign currency, an MNC could hedge its position by purchasing the borrowed currency forward (for the time at which the loan is to be repaid). In this case, the MNC's cost of financing will be affected by the percentage difference between the spot rate at which the foreign currency was converted to the local currency at the time it received the loan and the forward rate that it pays to purchase the foreign currency when paying off the loan. This percentage difference reflects the forward premium (p), which can be substituted for the percentage change in the exchange rate (e_f) in the equation representing the effective financing rate:

$$r_f = (1 + i_f)(1 + p) - 1$$

Recall from Chapter 7 that under conditions of interest rate parity, a foreign currency's forward premium is determined by the differential between its interest rate and the home interest rate:

$$p = \frac{1 + i_h}{1 + i_f} - 1$$

where i_h denotes the home currency's interest rate. Substitute this formula for p to determine the effective financing rate of a foreign currency under conditions of interest rate parity:

$$
\begin{aligned}
r_f &= (1 + i_f)(1 + p) - 1 \\
&= (1 + i_f)\left(1 + \frac{1 + i_h}{1 + i_f} - 1\right) - 1 \\
&= i_h
\end{aligned}
$$

So, if interest rate parity exists, the attempt to finance with a low–interest rate currency and simultaneously hedge that position will result in an effective financing rate that is similar to the local interest rate.

EXAMPLE

Recall that Cobra Co. needs to finance its U.S. operations over the next year and would prefer to borrow Canadian dollars at the prevailing interest rate of 3 percent rather than borrow U.S. dollars at the prevailing interest rate of 8 percent. Because Cobra does not want to be exposed to exchange rate risk, it considers borrowing Canadian dollars for one year at the interest rate of 3 percent and simultaneously purchasing a one-year forward contract on Canadian dollars in order to repay the loan in one year. However, if interest rate parity exists, the one-year forward rate of the Canadian dollar presently has a premium that is determined by the differential between the U.S. interest rate and the Canadian interest rate:

$$
\begin{aligned}
p &= \frac{1 + i_h}{1 + i_f} - 1 \\
&= \frac{1.08}{1.03} - 1 \\
&= \text{about } 4.85\%
\end{aligned}
$$

Therefore, Cobra's effective financing rate from implementing this strategy would be:

$$
\begin{aligned}
r_f &= (1 + i_f)(1 + p) - 1 \\
r_f &= (1 + .03)(1 + 1.0485) - 1 \\
&= .08 \text{ or } 8\%
\end{aligned}
$$

Thus if interest rate parity exists, the strategy of financing with a loan denominated in Canadian dollars and hedging that position would not allow Cobra Co. to achieve a lower cost of financing than a loan in U.S. dollars. Cobra Co. can still attempt to reduce its cost of financing by borrowing a foreign currency, but it will have to leave its position unhedged. ●

20-2e Reliance on the Forward Rate for Forecasting

Although an MNC might not benefit from using the forward rate to hedge when financing with a foreign currency (as illustrated in the previous example), it might still use the forward rate to forecast the future value of the foreign currency that it plans to borrow. Recall from Chapter 9 that the forward rate is frequently used as a means of forecasting the currency's future spot rate. If the prevailing one-year forward rate is used to forecast the spot rate one year from now, this means that the prevailing forward rate premium represents the forecast of the percentage change in the spot rate over the next year.

Recall from the previous example that if interest rate parity exists, the forward rate premium is determined by the differential in interest rates between the two currencies. Thus, if interest rate parity exists, the forward premium used to forecast the percentage change in the exchange rate is determined by the differential in interest rates between the two currencies. If the forward rate is an accurate estimator of the future spot rate, then the foreign financing rate will be similar to the cost of borrowing funds locally.

In reality, the forward rate does not forecast the future spot rate with perfect accuracy. But if it represents an unbiased forecast of the future spot rate, this would suggest that the forward rate premium represents an unbiased forecast of the percentage change in the foreign currency over the life of a loan. If interest rate parity exists, the effective financing rate from foreign financing would be lower than the cost of borrowing locally in some periods, and higher in other periods, but would be similar to the cost of borrowing locally on average over several periods. Consequently, MNCs that believe the forward rate is an unbiased predictor of the future spot rate will prefer borrowing their home currency, because the cost of financing is known with certainty and is not expected to be any higher on average than foreign financing.

Exhibit 20.2 summarizes the implications of a variety of scenarios relating to interest rate parity. Even if interest rate parity holds, financing with a foreign currency may still be feasible; however, it would have to be conducted on an uncovered basis (i.e., without using a forward hedge). In other words, an MNC such as Cobra Co. in the previous

Exhibit 20.2 Implications of Interest Rate Parity for Foreign Financing

SCENARIO	IMPLICATIONS
1. Interest rate parity holds.	Foreign financing and a simultaneous hedge of that position in the forward market will result in financing costs similar to those incurred in domestic financing.
2. Interest rate parity holds, and the forward rate is an accurate forecast of the future spot rate.	Uncovered foreign financing will result in financing costs similar to those incurred in domestic financing.
3. Interest rate parity holds, and the forward rate is expected to overestimate the future spot rate.	Uncovered foreign financing is expected to result in lower financing costs than those incurred in domestic financing.
4. Interest rate parity holds, and the forward rate is expected to underestimate the future spot rate.	Uncovered foreign financing is expected to result in higher financing costs than those incurred in domestic financing.

example may be able to obtain foreign financing at a lower cost than domestic financing, but that result cannot be guaranteed unless the firm has receivables in that same currency.

Many MNCs would still consider financing with a foreign currency because they do not necessarily expect that the forward rate is an unbiased predictor of the future spot rate. Given the influence of the exchange rate movement on the cost of foreign financing, an MNC such as Cobra Co. may attach probabilities to possible exchange rate scenarios in order to make its financing decision, as explained next.

20-2f Use of Probability Distributions to Enhance the Financing Decision

Using the probability distribution of possible percentage changes in the currency's value along with the currency's interest rate, an MNC can determine the probability distribution of the possible effective financing rates for the currency. It can then compare this distribution to the known financing rate of the home currency in order to make its financing decision.

EXAMPLE   Recall that Cobra Co. is considering short-term financing with a loan denominated in Canadian dollars. Assume that Cobra develops a probability distribution of the Canadian dollar's exchange rate over the next year, as shown in Exhibit 20.3. The first row in that exhibit shows that Cobra believes there is a 60 percent probability that the Canadian dollar will depreciate by 1 percent over the loan's life. If the Canadian dollar depreciates by 1 percent, then the effective financing rate would be 1.97 percent. Thus there is a 60 percent probability that Cobra will incur a 1.97 percent effective financing rate on its loan.

The second row shows that there is a 40 percent probability of a 10 percent appreciation in the Canadian dollar over the life of the loan. In this case, the effective financing rate would be 13.3 percent. Thus there is a 40 percent probability that Cobra will incur a 13.3 percent effective financing rate on its loan.

By multiplying each possible effective financing rate by its probability, Cobra Co. can estimate the expected value for the effective financing rate of the Canadian dollar loan. Based on the information in Exhibit 20.3, the expected value of the effective financing rate, or $E[r_f]$, is computed as

$$E[r_f] = [60\%(1.97\%)] + [40\%(13.3\%)]$$
$$= 1.182\% + 5.32\%$$
$$= 6.502\%$$

Thus the expected value of the effective financing rate of the Canadian dollar loan is lower than the 8 percent cost of funds if Cobra Co. borrows U.S. dollars.

The information in Exhibit 20.3 can also be used to determine the risk that the effective financing rate of the foreign loan will exceed the 8 percent domestic cost of financing. For Cobra Co., the risk reflects the 40 percent probability that the effective financing rate on the Canadian dollar loan will be substantially higher than if it borrows U.S. dollars. ●

Put yourself in the position of Cobra Co. Would you pursue the loan denominated in Canadian dollars, or would you prefer to borrow U.S. dollars at 8 percent with certainty? Some financial managers of MNCs might be attracted to the Canadian dollar loan

Exhibit 20.3 Analysis of Financing with a Foreign Currency

POSSIBLE RATE OF CHANGE IN THE CANADIAN DOLLAR OVER THE LIFE OF THE LOAN (e_f)	PROBABILITY OF OCCURRENCE	EFFECTIVE FINANCING RATE IF THIS RATE OF CHANGE IN THE CANADIAN DOLLAR DOES OCCUR (r_f)
−1%	60%	(1.03)[1 + (−.01)] − 1 = 1.97%
+10%	40%	(1.03)[1 + (.10)] − 1 = 13.3%

because of the 60 percent probability that their MNC's cost of financing could be more than 6 percentage points lower than if they borrowed U.S. dollars. However, they should also be very concerned that their strategy could backfire if the alternative scenario occurs (with 40 percent probability); in that case, their MNC's cost of financing would be more than 5 percentage points higher than with a loan in U.S. dollars. Many financial managers would prefer the loan in U.S. dollars at a cost of 8 percent (with certainty), rather than expose their MNC to the 40 percent probability that their Canadian loan backfires.

Assume that Cobra Co. wants to consider an additional loan offer (discussed in the following section) before it finalizes its short-term financing decision.

20-3 Financing with a Portfolio of Currencies

Multinational corporations may be able to achieve lower financing costs without excessive risk by financing with a portfolio of foreign currencies instead of a single foreign currency, as demonstrated here.

EXAMPLE Recall that Cobra Co. needs to finance its U.S. operations, and its bank offered a loan in U.S. dollars at an interest rate of 8 percent, or a loan denominated in Canadian dollars at 3 percent. Now assume that the bank also offers a loan denominated in Japanese yen at an interest rate of 4 percent. Cobra Co. wants to consider borrowing a portfolio of Canadian dollars and Japanese yen. Recall that Cobra Co. forecasted possible percentage changes in the spot rate of the Canadian dollar (as described in the previous example). Assume that Cobra also forecasts possible percentage changes in the spot rate of the Japanese yen over the loan life. Specifically, it forecasts that the Japanese yen will depreciate by 2 percent, with a 70 percent probability, or that the yen will appreciate by 8 percent, with a 30 percent probability. Exhibit 20.4 shows the effective financing rate for each currency based on the forecasts. The third column shows the probability of each possible outcome for each currency.

Assume that Cobra considers borrowing half of its needed funds in Canadian dollars and half in Japanese yen. Because there are two possible outcomes for the Canadian dollar (as shown in the top two rows of Exhibit 20.4), and two possible outcomes for the Japanese yen (as shown in the bottom two rows of Exhibit 20.4), this means that there are four possible outcomes for the portfolio's effective financing rate, shown in Exhibit 20.5.

Columns 1 and 2 of Exhibit 20.5 list all possible joint effective financing rates. Column 3 computes the joint probability of that occurrence assuming that exchange rate movements of the Canadian dollar and Japanese yen are independent. Finally, column 4 shows the computation of the portfolio's effective financing rate based on each currency having a 50 percent weight in the portfolio.

Exhibit 20.4 Possible Effective Financing Rates for Each Currency

CURRENCY	POSSIBLE PERCENTAGE CHANGE IN THE SPOT RATE OVER THE LOAN LIFE	PROBABILITY OF THAT PERCENTAGE CHANGE IN THE SPOT RATE OCCURRING	COMPUTATION OF EFFECTIVE FINANCING RATE BASED ON THAT PERCENTAGE CHANGE IN THE SPOT RATE
Outcome 1 for Canadian dollar	−1%	60%	(1.03) [1 + (−.01)] − 1 = .0197, or 1.97%
Outcome 2 for Canadian dollar	10%	40%	(1.03) [1 + (.10)] − 1 = .133, or 13.3%
		100%	
Outcome 1 for Japanese yen	−2%	70%	(1.04) [1 + (−.02)] − 1 = .0192 or 1.92%
Outcome 2 for Japanese yen	8%	30%	(1.04) [1 + (.08)] − 1 = .1232 or 12.32%,
		100%	

Exhibit 20.5 Analysis of Financing with Two Foreign Currencies

(1) POSSIBLE JOINT EFFECTIVE FINANCING RATES		(3) COMPUTATION OF JOINT PROBABILITY	(4) COMPUTATION OF EFFECTIVE FINANCING RATE OF PORTFOLIO (50% OF TOTAL FUNDS BORROWED IN EACH CURRENCY)
CANADIAN DOLLAR	JAPANESE YEN		
1.97%	1.92%	(60%)(70%) = 42%	.5(1.97%) + .5(1.92%) = 1.945%
1.97	12.32	(60%)(30%) = 18%	.5(1.97%) + .5(12.32%) = 7.145%
13.3	1.92	(40%)(70%) = 28%	.5(13.3%) + .5(1.92%) = 7.61%
13.3	12.32	(40%)(30%) = 12%	.5(13.3%) + .5(12.32%) = 12.81%
		100%	

An examination of the top row will help to clarify the table. This row indicates that one possible outcome of borrowing both Canadian dollars and Japanese yen is that the Canadian dollar will have an effective financing rate of 1.97 percent (with a probability of 60 percent), while the Japanese yen will have an effective financing rate of 1.92 percent (with a probability of 70 percent). The joint probability that both of these outcomes will occur simultaneously is (60 percent) × (70 percent) = 42 percent. Assuming that half (50 percent) of the funds needed are to be borrowed from each currency, the portfolio's effective financing rate if both of these outcomes occur is estimated in the fourth column to be 1.945 percent.

A similar procedure was used to develop the remaining three rows in Exhibit 20.5. Notice that there is a 42 percent chance that the portfolio's effective financing rate will be 1.945 percent (as shown in the first row), an 18 percent chance that it will be 7.145 percent (as shown in the second row), and so on.

When both foreign currencies are borrowed, the only way the portfolio will have a higher effective financing rate than a loan in U.S. dollars is if *both* currencies appreciate simultaneously against the U.S. dollar. If only one currency appreciates, the adverse impact of its appreciation will be somewhat offset by the other currency's movement. As shown in the bottom row of Exhibit 20.5, the probability that the currencies appreciate is 40 percent for the Canadian dollar and 30 percent for the Japanese yen, so the joint probability of these events occurring simultaneously is only 12 percent. This diversification effect is an advantage of financing in a portfolio of foreign currencies. Cobra Co. decides that because it has an 88 percent chance of attaining lower costs of financing with the foreign portfolio than with domestic financing, it will finance with the foreign portfolio. ●

MNCs have different ways of forecasting exchange rates, which would lead to different anticipated effective financing rates per currency, and perhaps to different short-term financing decisions. Yet, even if all MNCs derived the same probability distribution of effective financing rates as in Exhibit 20.5, their final short-term financing decision may vary because of differences in their degree of risk aversion. Some MNCs (like Cobra Co.) would likely decide to borrow in the currency portfolio, given that the odds of financing a lower cost than the U.S. dollar loan are heavily in their favor. However, other MNCs may be unwilling to take the chance (probability of 12 percent) that both currencies will appreciate against the dollar and cause a substantially higher cost of funds than the U.S. dollar loan.

In the example, the computation of joint probabilities assumes that the two currencies move independently. If instead the movements of the two currencies are highly positively correlated, then financing with a portfolio of currencies will not be as beneficial because it is much more likely that both currencies would experience a high level of appreciation at the same time. If the two currencies are not highly correlated, they are less likely to

WEB

www.commerzbank.com Information about how Commerzbank provides financing services to firms and about its current views about conditions in the foreign exchange market.

appreciate simultaneously to that extent. Thus the chances that the portfolio's effective financing rate will exceed the U.S. rate are reduced when the currencies included in the portfolio are *not* correlated.

The example included only two currencies in the portfolio. Financing with a more diversified portfolio of additional currencies that have low interest rates might increase the probability that foreign financing will be less costly than domestic financing; several currencies are unlikely to move in tandem and therefore unlikely to simultaneously appreciate enough to offset the advantage of their low interest rates.

SUMMARY

- MNCs may first consider internal sources of funds for short-term financing, including foreign subsidiaries that might have excess funds. They also commonly rely on external sources such as short-term notes, commercial paper, or bank loans.

- MNCs may use foreign financing in an attempt to reduce their financing costs. They can determine whether to use foreign financing by estimating the effective financing rate for any foreign currency over the period in which financing will be needed. The expected effective financing rate is dependent on the quoted interest rate of the foreign currency and the forecasted percentage change in the currency's value over the financing period.

- When MNCs borrow a portfolio of currencies that have low interest rates, they can increase the probability of achieving relatively low financing costs if the currencies' values are not highly correlated.

POINT COUNTER-POINT

Do MNCs Increase Their Risk When Borrowing Foreign Currencies?

Point   Yes. MNCs should borrow the currency that matches their cash inflows. If they borrow a foreign currency to finance business in a different currency, they are essentially speculating on the future exchange rate movements. The results of this strategy are uncertain, which represents risk to the MNC and its shareholders.

Counter-Point   No. If MNCs expect that they can reduce the effective financing rate by borrowing a foreign currency, they should consider borrowing that currency. This enables them to achieve lower costs and improves their ability to compete. If they take the most conservative approach by borrowing whatever currency matches their inflows, they may incur higher costs and have a greater chance of failure.

Who Is Correct?   Use the Internet to learn more about this issue. Which argument do you support? Offer your own opinion on this issue.

SELF-TEST

Answers are provided in Appendix A at the back of the text.

1. Assume that the interest rate in New Zealand is 9 percent. A U.S. firm plans to borrow New Zealand dollars, convert them to U.S. dollars, and repay the loan in one year. What will be the effective financing rate if the New Zealand dollar depreciates by 6 percent? If the New Zealand dollar appreciates by 3 percent?

2. Using the information in question 1 and assuming a 50 percent chance of either scenario occurring, determine the expected value of the effective financing rate.

3. Assume that the Japanese one-year interest rate is 5 percent while the U.S. one-year interest rate is 8 percent. What percentage change in the Japanese yen would cause a U.S. firm borrowing yen to incur the same effective financing rate as it would if it borrowed dollars?

4. The spot rate of the Australian dollar is $.62. The one-year forward rate of the Australian dollar is $.60. The Australian one-year interest rate is 9 percent. Assume that the forward rate is used to forecast the future spot rate. Determine the expected effective financing rate for a U.S. firm that borrows Australian dollars to finance its U.S. business.

5. Cleveland, Inc., plans to finance its U.S. operations by borrowing two currencies with low interest rates whose exchange rate movements are highly correlated. The movements in the two currencies against the dollar are highly correlated. While it recognizes that each currency could possibly appreciate substantially against the dollar over the period in which it borrows funds, it is hoping that by diversifying between two currencies, it will not be adversely affected by possible exchange rate movements. Offer your opinion of Cleveland's strategy and logic.

QUESTIONS AND APPLICATIONS

1. Financing from Subsidiaries Explain why an MNC parent would consider financing from its subsidiaries.

2. Foreign Financing

a. Explain how a firm's degree of risk aversion enters into its decision of whether to finance in a foreign currency or a local currency.

b. Assume that interest rate parity exists. If the forward rate is an unbiased forecast of the future spot rate, explain the implications from borrowing a foreign currency (versus local financing) over time.

3. Probability Distribution

a. Discuss the development of a probability distribution of effective financing rates when financing in a foreign currency. How is this distribution developed?

b. Once the probability distribution of effective financing rates from financing in a foreign currency is developed, how can this distribution be used in deciding whether to finance in the foreign currency or the home currency?

4. Financing and Exchange Rate Risk How can a U.S. firm finance in euros and not necessarily be exposed to exchange rate risk?

5. Short-Term Financing Analysis Assume that Davenport, Inc., needs $3 million for a one-year period. Within one year, it will generate enough U.S. dollars to pay off the loan. It is considering three options: (1) borrowing U.S. dollars at an interest rate of 6 percent, (2) borrowing Japanese yen at an interest rate of 3 percent, or (3) borrowing Canadian dollars at an interest rate of 4 percent. Davenport expects that the Japanese yen will appreciate by 1 percent over the next year and that the Canadian dollar will appreciate by 3 percent. What is the expected "effective" financing rate for each of the three options? Which option appears to be most feasible? Why might Davenport, Inc., not necessarily choose the option reflecting the lowest effective financing rate?

6. Effective Financing Rate How is it possible for a firm to incur a negative effective financing rate?

7. IRP Application to Short-Term Financing Connecticut Co. plans to finance its U.S. operations. It can borrow euros on a short-term basis at a lower interest rate than if it borrowed dollars.

a. If interest rate parity does not hold, what strategy should Connecticut Co. consider when it needs short-term financing?

b. Assume that Connecticut Co. needs dollars. It borrows euros at a lower interest rate than that for dollars. If interest rate parity exists and if the forward rate of the euro is a reliable predictor of the future spot rate, what does this suggest about the feasibility of such a strategy?

c. If Connecticut Co. expects the current spot rate to be a more reliable predictor of the future spot rate, what does this suggest about the feasibility of such a strategy?

8. IRP Application to Short-term Financing Seabreeze Co. needs to finance some dollar-denominated expenses for one year. It can borrow euros cheaper than dollars. Interest rate parity exists. The one-year forward rate of the euro contains a premium of 4 percent. If it believes the euro will appreciate by 6 percent over the next year, would its expected financing expense be lower if it borrowed dollars or euros?

9. IRP Application to Short-Term Financing

Assume that interest rate parity exists. If a firm believes that the forward rate is an unbiased predictor of the future spot rate, will it expect to achieve lower financing costs by consistently borrowing a foreign currency with a low interest rate?

10. Effective Financing Rate

Greensboro, Inc., needs $4 million for one year. It currently has no business in Japan but plans to borrow Japanese yen from a Japanese bank because the Japanese interest rate is 3 percentage points lower than the U.S. rate. Assume that interest rate parity exists; also assume that Greensboro believes that the one-year forward rate of the Japanese yen will exceed the future spot rate one year from now. Will the expected effective financing rate be higher, lower, or the same as financing with dollars? Explain.

11. IRP Application to Short-Term Financing

Assume that the U.S. interest rate is 7 percent and the euro's interest rate is 4 percent. Assume that the euro's forward rate has a premium of 4 percent. Determine whether the following statement is true: "Interest rate parity does not hold; therefore, U.S. firms could lock in a lower financing cost by borrowing euros and purchasing euros forward for one year." Explain your answer.

12. Implications of the Forward Rate for Foreign Financing.

Mizner, Inc., is a U.S.-based MNC with a subsidiary in Mexico. Its Mexican subsidiary needs a one-year loan of 10 million pesos for operating expenses. It can borrow pesos at 11 percent and can use peso revenues to be received over the year to repay the loan. Alternatively, it can borrow dollars at 6 percent. Interest rate parity exists. The forward rate of the peso is expected to overestimate the spot rate of the peso in one year. Should the subsidiary borrow pesos or dollars?

13. Financing During a Crisis

Bradenton, Inc., has a foreign subsidiary in Asia that commonly obtains short-term financing from local banks. If Asia suddenly experiences a crisis, explain why Bradenton may not be able to easily obtain funds from the local banks.

14. Impact of Credit Crisis on Risk of Financing.

Homewood Co. commonly finances some of its U.S. expansion by repeatedly borrowing on a short-term basis. Explain how a global credit crisis might limit the firm's ability to repeatedly borrow short-term funds and increase the cost of borrowing.

Advanced Questions

15. Probability Distribution of Financing Costs

Missoula, Inc., decides to borrow Japanese yen for one year. The interest rate on the borrowed yen is 8 percent. Missoula has developed the following probability distribution for the yen's degree of fluctuation against the dollar:

POSSIBLE DEGREE OF FLUCTUATION OF YEN PERCENTAGE AGAINST THE DOLLAR	PROBABILITY
−4%	20%
−1	30
0	10
3	40

Given this information, what is the expected value of the effective financing rate of the Japanese yen from Missoula's perspective?

16. Analysis of Short-Term Financing

Jacksonville Corp. is a U.S.-based firm that needs $600,000. It has no business in Japan but is considering one-year financing with Japanese yen because the annual interest rate would be 5 percent versus 9 percent in the United States. Assume that interest rate parity exists.

a. Can Jacksonville benefit from borrowing Japanese yen and simultaneously purchasing yen one year forward to avoid exchange rate risk? Explain.

b. Assume that Jacksonville does not cover its exposure and uses the forward rate to forecast the future spot rate. Determine the expected effective financing rate. Should Jacksonville finance with Japanese yen? Explain.

c. Assume that Jacksonville does not cover its exposure and expects that the Japanese yen will appreciate by 5, 3, or 2 percent, and with equal probability of each occurrence. Use this information to determine the probability distribution of the effective financing rate. Should Jacksonville finance with Japanese yen? Explain.

17. Financing with a Portfolio

Pepperdine, Inc., considers obtaining 40 percent of its one-year financing in Canadian dollars and 60 percent in Japanese yen. The forecasts of appreciation in the

Canadian dollar and Japanese yen for the next year are as follows:

CURRENCY	POSSIBLE PERCENTAGE CHANGE IN THE SPOT RATE OVER THE LOAN LIFE	PROBABILITY OF THAT PERCENTAGE CHANGE IN THE SPOT RATE OCCURRING
Canadian dollar	4%	70%
Canadian dollar	7	30
Japanese yen	6	50
Japanese yen	9	50

The interest rate on the Canadian dollar is 9 percent, and the interest rate on the Japanese yen is 7 percent. Develop the possible effective financing rates of the overall portfolio and the probability of each possibility based on the use of joint probabilities.

18. Financing with a Portfolio
a. Does borrowing a portfolio of currencies offer any possible advantages over the borrowing of a single foreign currency?
b. If a firm borrows a portfolio of currencies, what characteristics of the currencies will affect the potential uncertainty of the portfolio's effective financing rate? What characteristics would be desirable from a borrowing firm's perspective?

19. Financing with a Portfolio Raleigh Corp. needs to borrow funds for one year to support its operations in the United States. The following interest rates are available:

COUNTRY	BORROWING RATE
United States	10%
Canada	6
Japan	5

The percentage changes in the spot rates of the Canadian dollar and Japanese yen over the next year are as follows:

CANADIAN DOLLAR		JAPANESE YEN	
PROB-ABILITY	PER-CENTAGE CHANGE IN SPOT RATE	PROB-ABILITY	PER-CENTAGE CHANGE IN SPOT RATE
10%	5%	20%	6%
90%	2%	80%	1%

If Raleigh Corp. borrows a portfolio that has 50 percent of funds from Canadian dollars and 50 percent of funds from yen, determine the probability distribution of the effective financing rate of the portfolio.

What is the probability that Raleigh will incur a higher effective financing rate from borrowing this portfolio than from borrowing U.S. dollars?

Critical Thinking

MNC's Use of Dollar-Denominated Short-term Debt In recent years, U.S. short-term interest rates have been close to zero. Write a short essay to provide your opinion on whether you (as a manager of an MNC) might be more willing to use dollar-denominated short-term debt to cover short-term funding needs for subsidiaries in foreign countries that generate positive earnings. Explain the possible trade-offs involved.

Discussion in the Boardroom

This exercise can be found in Appendix E at the back of this textbook.

Running Your Own MNC

This exercise can be found on the *International Financial Management* text companion website. Go to www.cengagebrain.com (students) or www.cengage.com/login (instructors) and search using **ISBN 9781133947837**.

BLADES, INC. CASE

Use of Foreign Short-Term Financing

Blades, Inc., just received a special order for 120,000 pairs of Speedos, its primary roller blade product. Ben Holt, Blades' chief financial officer (CFO), needs short-term financing to finance this large order from the time Blades orders its supplies until the time it will receive payment. Blades will charge a price of 5,000 baht per pair of Speedos. The materials needed to manufacture these 120,000 pairs will be purchased from Thai suppliers. Blades expects the cost of the components for one pair of Speedos to be approximately 3,500 baht in its first year of operating the Thai subsidiary.

Because Blades is relatively unknown in Thailand, its suppliers have indicated that they would like to receive payment as early as possible. The customer that placed this order insists on open account transactions, which means that Blades will receive payment for the roller blades approximately three months subsequent to the sale. Furthermore, the production cycle necessary to produce Speedos, from purchase of the materials to the eventual sale of the product, is approximately three months. Because of these considerations, Blades expects to collect its revenues approximately six months after it has paid for the materials, such as rubber and plastic components, needed to manufacture Speedos.

Holt has identified at least two alternatives for satisfying Blades' financing needs. First, Blades could borrow Japanese yen for six months, convert the yen to Thai baht, and use the baht to pay the Thai suppliers. When the accounts receivable in Thailand are collected, Blades would convert the baht received to yen and repay the Japanese yen loan. Second, Blades could borrow Thai baht for six months in order to pay its Thai suppliers. When Blades collects its accounts receivable, it would use these receipts to repay the baht loan. Thus Blades will use revenue generated in Thailand to repay the loan, whether it borrows the money in yen or in baht.

Holt's initial research indicates that the 180-day interest rates available to Blades in Japan and in Thailand are 4 and 6 percent, respectively. Consequently, Holt favors borrowing the Japanese yen, as he believes this loan will be cheaper than the baht-denominated loan. He is aware that he should somehow incorporate the future movements of the yen-baht exchange rate in his analysis, but he is unsure how to accomplish this. However, he has identified the following probability distribution of the change in the value of the Japanese yen with respect to the Thai baht and of the change in the value of the Thai baht with respect to the dollar over the six-month period of the loan:

POSSIBLE RATE OF CHANGE IN THE JAPANESE YEN RELATIVE TO THE THAI BAHT OVER THE LIFE OF THE LOAN	POSSIBLE RATE OF CHANGE IN THE THAI BAHT RELATIVE TO THE DOLLAR OVER THE LIFE OF THE LOAN	PROBABILITY OF OCCURRENCE
2%	−3%	30%
1	−2	30
0	−1	20
1	0	15
2	1	5

Holt has also informed you that the current spot rate of the yen (in Thai baht) is THB.347826, while the current spot rate of the baht (in dollars) is $.023.

As a financial analyst for Blades, you have been asked to answer the following questions for Holt:

1. What is the amount, in baht, that Blades needs to borrow to cover the payments due to the Thai suppliers? What is the amount, in yen, that Blades needs to borrow to cover the payments due to the Thai suppliers?

2. Given that Blades will use the receipts from the receivables in Thailand to repay the loan and that the subsidiary plans to remit all baht-denominated cash flows to the U.S. parent whether it borrows in baht or yen, does the future value of the yen with respect to the baht affect the cost of the loan if Blades borrows in yen?

3. Using a spreadsheet, compute the expected amount (in U.S. dollars) that will be remitted to the United States in six months if Blades finances its working capital requirements by borrowing baht versus borrowing yen. Based on your analysis, should Blades obtain a yen- or baht-denominated loan?

SMALL BUSINESS DILEMMA

Short-Term Financing by the Sports Exports Company

At the current time, the Sports Exports Company focuses on producing footballs and exporting them to a distributor in the United Kingdom. The exports are denominated in British pounds. Jim Logan, the owner, plans to develop other sporting goods products besides the footballs that he produces. His entire expansion will be focused on the United Kingdom, where he is trying to make a name for his firm. He remains concerned about his firm's exposure to exchange rate risk but does not plan to let that get in the way of his expansion plans because he believes that his firm can continue to penetrate the British sporting goods market. He has just negotiated a joint venture with a British firm that will produce other sporting goods products that are more popular in the United States (such as basketballs) but will be sold in the United Kingdom. Logan will pay the British manufacturer in British pounds. These products will be delivered directly to the British distributor rather than to Jim, and the distributor will pay Logan with British pounds.

Logan's expansion plans will result in the need for additional funding. Logan would prefer to borrow on a short-term basis now. He has an excellent credit rating and collateral and therefore should be able to obtain short-term financing. The British interest rate is one-fourth of a percentage point above the U.S. interest rate.

1. Should Logan borrow dollars or pounds to finance his joint venture business? Why?

2. Logan could also borrow euros at an interest rate that is lower than the U.S. or British rate. The values of the euro and pound tend to move in the same direction against the dollar but not always by the same degree. Would borrowing euros to support the British joint venture result in more exposure to exchange rate risk than borrowing pounds? Would it result in more exposure to exchange rate risk than borrowing dollars?

INTERNET/EXCEL EXERCISES

The Bloomberg website (www.bloomberg.com) provides interest rate data for many different foreign currencies over various maturities.

1. Go to the Markets section and then to Rates & Bonds and look at the listing of countries for which yields of different foreign currencies are shown. Review the three-month yields of currencies. Assume that you could borrow at a rate 1 percentage point above the quoted yield for each currency. Which currency would offer you the lowest quoted yield?

2. As a cash manager of a U.S.-based MNC that needs dollars to support U.S. operations, where would you borrow funds for the next three months? Explain.

3. Assume that at the beginning of each of the last seven years, you had the choice of a one-year loan in U.S. dollars or Japanese yen. Your business is in the United States, but you considered borrowing yen because the yen annual interest rate was 2 percent versus a dollar annual interest rate of 7 percent. Go to www.oanda.com /currency/historical-rates and obtain the annual percentage change in the yen's exchange rate for each of the last seven years. Determine the effective financing rate of the yen in each of the last seven years. Based on your results, was the annual effective financing rate lower for the yen or dollar on average over the seven years? In how many of the years would you have been better off financing in yen rather than in dollars? Explain.

ONLINE ARTICLES WITH REAL-WORLD EXAMPLES

Find a recent article online that describes an actual international finance application or a real-world example about a specific MNC's actions that reinforces one or more of the concepts covered in this chapter.

If your class has an online component, your professor may ask you to post your summary there and provide the web link of the article so that other students can access it. If your class is live, your professor may ask you to summarize your application in class. Your professor may assign specific students to complete this assignment for this chapter or may allow any students to do the assignment on a volunteer basis.

For recent online articles and real-world examples applied to this chapter, consider using the following search terms (and include the current year as a search term to ensure that the online articles are recent).

1. [name of an MNC] AND short-term financing
2. multinational AND short-term financing
3. parent AND short-term financing
4. subsidiary AND short-term financing
5. short-term financing AND exchange rate risk
6. foreign financing
7. multinational financing
8. multinational AND funding
9. subsidiary AND funding
10. international AND short-term financing

21
International Cash Management

CHAPTER OBJECTIVES

The specific objectives of this chapter are to:

- explain working capital management from a subsidiary perspective versus a parent perspective,

- explain how cash management can be centralized in order to ensure that cash is used more efficiently,

- explain the various techniques used to optimize cash flows, and

- explain the decision to invest cash internationally.

Cash management can be broadly defined to mean optimization of cash flows and investment of excess cash. Financial managers need to understand the advantages and disadvantages of investing cash in foreign markets so that they can make international cash management decisions that maximize the value of the MNC.

21-1 Multinational Working Capital Management

Multinational corporations tie up funds when investing in their working capital, which includes short-term assets such as inventory, accounts receivable, and cash. They attempt working capital management by maintaining sufficient short-term assets to support their operations. However, they do not want to invest excessively in short-term assets because these funds might be put to better use.

The management of working capital is more complex for MNCs that have foreign subsidiaries because each subsidiary must have adequate working capital to support its operations. If a subsidiary experiences a deficiency in inventory, its production may be delayed. If it is short of cash, it may be unable to purchase supplies or materials. If the MNC is aware of the working capital situation at every subsidiary, then it may be able to transfer working capital from one subsidiary to another in order to solve temporary deficiencies at any subsidiary.

21-1a Subsidiary Expenses

Begin by considering the typical cash flow situation of a single foreign subsidiary. The subsidiary will normally have a more difficult time forecasting future outflow payments if its purchases are international rather than domestic because of exchange rate fluctuations. In addition, there is a possibility that payments will be substantially higher due to appreciation of the invoice currency. Hence it may wish to maintain a large inventory of supplies and raw materials so that it can draw from its inventory and cut down on purchases if the invoice currency appreciates. Still another possibility is that imported products from another country could be restricted by the host government (through quotas, etc.). In this event, a larger inventory would give a firm more time to search for alternative sources of supplies or raw materials. A subsidiary with domestic supply sources would not experience such a problem, so it would not need such a large inventory.

Outflow payments for supplies will be influenced by future sales. If sales volume is substantially influenced by exchange rate fluctuations, its future level becomes more uncertain, which makes the need for supplies more uncertain. Such uncertainty may force the subsidiary to maintain larger cash balances to cover any unexpected increase in supply requirements.

21-1b Subsidiary Revenue

If subsidiaries export their products, their sales volume may be more volatile than if the products were only sold domestically, especially if their invoice currency is volatile. Importers' demand for finished products will most likely decrease if the invoice currency appreciates. If the products are sold domestically, exchange rate fluctuations will not have a direct impact on sales, although there will still be an indirect impact because the fluctuations will influence prices paid by local customers for imports from foreign competitors.

Sales can often be increased by relaxing credit standards. However, it is important to focus on cash inflows due to sales rather than on sales themselves. Looser credit standards may cause a slowdown in cash inflows from sales, which could offset the benefits of increased sales volume. Accounts receivable management is an important part of the subsidiary's working capital management because of its potential impact on cash inflows.

21-1c Subsidiary Dividend Payments

The subsidiary may be expected to periodically send dividend payments and other fees to the parent. These fees could represent royalties or charges for overhead costs incurred by the parent that benefit the subsidiary. An example is research and development costs incurred by the parent, which improve the quality of products produced by the subsidiary. Whatever the reason, payments by the subsidiary to the parent are often necessary. When dividend payments and fees are known in advance and denominated in the subsidiary's currency, forecasting cash flows is easier for the subsidiary. The level of dividends paid by subsidiaries to the parent depends on the liquidity needs of each subsidiary, potential uses of funds at various subsidiary locations, expected movements in the currencies of the subsidiaries, and regulations of the host country government.

21-1d Subsidiary Liquidity Management

After accounting for all outflow and inflow payments, the subsidiary may have either excess or deficient cash. It uses liquidity management to either invest its excess cash or borrow to cover its cash deficiencies. If it anticipates a cash deficiency, short-term financing is necessary, as described in the previous chapter. If it anticipates excess cash, it must determine how the excess cash should be used. Investing in foreign currencies can sometimes be attractive, but exchange rate risk makes the effective yield uncertain. This issue is discussed later in the chapter.

Liquidity management is a crucial component of a subsidiary's working capital management. Most subsidiaries have access to numerous lines of credit and overdraft facilities in various currencies. Therefore, they may maintain adequate liquidity without substantial cash balances. Although liquidity is important for the MNC, it cannot be properly measured by liquidity ratios. Potential access to funds is more relevant than cash on hand.

21-2 Centralized Cash Management

A key component of working capital management is cash management. Multinational corporations have large cash inflows and outflows in various currencies, and the cash inflows and outflows will not balance in any currency in any given month. Each subsidiary's management may naturally focus on managing its own cash positions. However, such decentralized management is not optimal because it will force the MNC overall to maintain a larger investment in cash than is necessary. Thus MNCs normally use **centralized cash management** to monitor and manage the parent–subsidiary and intersubsidiary cash flows.

Exhibit 21.1 illustrates how funds might flow between the parent and its subsidiaries. The subsidiaries may periodically send loan repayments and dividends to the parent or send excess cash to the parent (where the centralized cash management process is assumed to take place). The parent's cash outflows to the subsidiaries can include loans and the return of cash previously invested by the subsidiaries. The subsidiaries may also have cash flows between themselves because they purchase supplies from each other.

Exhibit 21.1   Cash Flow of the MNC

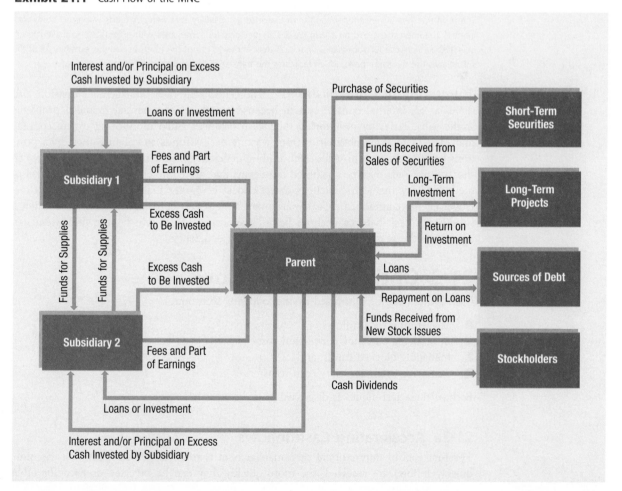

21-2a Accommodating Cash Shortages

The centralized cash management division of an MNC cannot always accurately forecast cash flows of the parent or each subsidiary. It should, however, be ready to react whenever the parent or a subsidiary has a shortage of funds by considering whether any subsidiary has excess funds that can be transferred to cover the shortage. A key role of the centralized cash management division is to facilitate the transfer of funds from subsidiaries with excess funds to those that need funds. This requires updated information on the cash situation at each subsidiary as well as the power to instruct one subsidiary to provide loans to another. Because a subsidiary that experiences a cash shortage may not be able to rely on other subsidiaries for funding, it needs to have other sources of funds (credit lines) available.

Technology Used to Facilitate Fund Transfers A centralized cash management system needs a continual flow of information about currency positions so that it can determine whether one subsidiary's shortage of cash can be covered by another subsidiary's excess of cash in that currency.

Utah Co. created a cash balances website that specifies the cash balance of every currency for each subsidiary. Near the end of each day, each subsidiary updates the website to provide its latest cash balance for each currency. Each subsidiary also specifies the period of time in which the excess or deficiency will persist. The parent's treasury department monitors the updated data and determines whether any cash needs identified by a subsidiary in a particular currency can be accommodated by another subsidiary that has excess cash in that same currency. The treasury department then e-mails instructions to the subsidiaries about fund transfers. The fund transfers are essentially short-term loans, so a subsidiary that borrows funds will repay them with interest. The interest charged on a loan creates an incentive for subsidiaries with excess cash to make it available and an incentive for subsidiaries with cash deficiencies to return the funds as soon as possible. All of the subsidiaries use the same bank, which facilitates the transfer of funds among subsidiaries. ●

Monitoring of Cash Positions The centralized cash management division also serves as an internal control system because it can detect potential financial problems at the subsidiaries by monitoring their cash balances. Such monitoring can discourage managers of foreign subsidiaries from wasting excess funds to enhance their own positions because the system will detect funding deficiencies. In some cases, the deficiency in short-term funds may be attributed to reasons that are completely beyond the control of the subsidiary managers, such as a weak local economy that caused sales to decline. However, the centralized cash management system can be designed to identify when a subsidiary's cash balance declines below a specific level, at which time the parent can investigate the reasons for the subsidiary's cash deficiency.

21-3 Optimizing Cash Flows

Cash inflows can be optimized by the following techniques:

- accelerating cash inflows,
- minimizing currency conversion costs,
- managing blocked funds, and
- managing intersubsidiary cash transfers.

Each of these techniques is discussed in turn.

21-3a Accelerating Cash Inflows

The first goal in international cash management is to accelerate cash inflows: the more quickly inflows are received, the more quickly they can be invested or used for other purposes. Several managerial practices may be implemented by the individual subsidiaries to achieve this. First, a corporation may establish **lockboxes** around the world, which are post office boxes to which customers are instructed to send payment. When set up in appropriate locations, lockboxes can help reduce mailing time (**mail float**). A bank usually processes incoming checks at a lockbox on a daily basis and deposits the funds in the firm's account. Lockbox services today also often include processing electronic payments as well as checks. Second, cash inflows can be accelerated by using **preauthorized payments**, which allow a corporation to charge a customer's bank account up to some limit. Both preauthorized payments and lockboxes are also used in a domestic setting. Because international transactions may have a relatively long mailing time, these methods of accelerating cash inflows can be quite valuable for an MNC.

21-3b Minimizing Currency Conversion Costs

Netting is a technique that optimizes cash flows by reducing the administrative and transaction costs that result from currency conversion. It can be implemented through the joint effort of subsidiaries or by the centralized cash management group.

EXAMPLE   Montana, Inc., has subsidiaries located in France and in the United Kingdom. Whenever the French subsidiary purchases supplies from the British subsidiary, it needs to convert euros into British pounds to make payment. Similarly, the British subsidiary must convert pounds into euros whenever it purchases supplies from the French subsidiary. Montana, Inc., has instructed both subsidiaries to net their transactions on a monthly basis so that only one net payment is made at the end of each month. By using this approach, both subsidiaries avoid (or at least reduce) the transaction costs of currency conversion. ●

Netting has become increasingly popular because it offers several key benefits. First, it reduces the number of cross-border transactions between subsidiaries, thereby reducing the overall administrative cost of such cash transfers. Second, because transactions occur less frequently, there is less need for foreign exchange conversion, so the transaction costs associated with such conversions are reduced. Third, the netting process imposes tight control over information on transactions between subsidiaries. Thus all subsidiaries engage in a more coordinated effort to accurately report and settle their various accounts. Finally, cash flow forecasting is easier because only net cash transfers are made at the end of each period, rather than individual cash transfers throughout the period. Improved cash flow forecasting can enhance financing and investment decisions.

A **bilateral netting system** involves transactions between two units either between the parent and a subsidiary or between two subsidiaries. A **multilateral netting system** usually involves a more complex interchange among the parent and several subsidiaries. For most large MNCs, a multilateral netting system would be necessary to effectively reduce administrative and currency conversion costs. Such a system is typically centralized so that all necessary information is consolidated. From the consolidated cash flow information, net cash flow positions for each pair of units (subsidiaries, or whatever) are determined, and the actual reconciliation at the end of each period can be dictated. The centralized group may even maintain inventories of various currencies so that currency conversions for the end-of-period net payments can be completed without significant transaction costs.

Most MNCs monitor the cash flows between their subsidiaries with the use of an intersubsidiary payments matrix. A U.S.-based MNC will normally translate the payments into dollars (based on the prevailing spot rate) so that the net payments can be easily determined. If the Canadian subsidiary of the MNC normally makes payments to the French subsidiary in euros but the French subsidiary normally makes payments to the Canadian subsidiary in Canadian dollars, then the payments need to be translated into a common currency so that the net payment owed can be determined. Translating the amounts into dollars allows a U.S.-based MNC to assess the relative size of each net payment owed between subsidiaries, as illustrated below.

EXAMPLE

Exhibit 21.2 is an example of an intersubsidiary payments matrix that totals each subsidiary's individual payments to each of the other subsidiaries. The first row indicates that the Canadian subsidiary owes the equivalent of $40,000 to the French subsidiary, the equivalent of $90,000 to the Japanese subsidiary, and so on. During this same period, these subsidiaries have also received products from the Canadian subsidiary, for which payment is due. The second column (under Canada) shows that the Canadian subsidiary is owed the equivalent of $60,000 by the French subsidiary, the equivalent of $100,000 by the Japanese subsidiary, and so on.

Because subsidiaries owe each other, currency conversion costs can be reduced by requiring that only the net payment be extended. Using the intersubsidiary table, the schedule of net payments is determined as shown in Exhibit 21.3. Because the Canadian subsidiary owes the French subsidiary the equivalent of $40,000 but is owed the equivalent of $60,000 by the French subsidiary, the net payment required is the equivalent of $20,000 from the French subsidiary to the Canadian subsidiary. Exhibits 21.2 and 21.3 convert all figures to U.S. dollar equivalents to allow for consolidating payments in both directions so that the net payment can be determined.

The net amount owed by each subsidiary to all other subsidiaries is shown in the last column in Exhibit 21.3, while the net amount to be received by each subsidiary from all other subsidiaries is shown in the bottom row. The Canadian subsidiary owes net payments totaling $40,000, while it will receive net payments totaling $30,000. Therefore, its overall balance of net cash flows based on payments to and from subsidiaries is a net outflow of $10,000 for this period. The Canadian subsidiary may use this information along with its expectations of other cash flows not related to other subsidiaries to determine whether it will have sufficient cash during this period. ●

There can be some limitations to multilateral netting due to foreign exchange controls. Although the major industrialized countries typically do not impose such controls, some other countries do, and some countries prohibit netting altogether. Thus an MNC

Exhibit 21.2   Intersubsidiary Payments Matrix

PAYMENTS OWED BY SUBSIDIARY LOCATED IN	U.S. DOLLAR VALUE (IN THOUSANDS) OWED TO SUBSIDIARY LOCATED IN				
	CANADA	FRANCE	JAPAN	SWITZERLAND	U.S.
Canada	—	40	90	20	40
France	60	—	30	60	50
Japan	100	30	—	20	30
Switzerland	10	50	10	—	50
U.S.	10	60	20	20	—

Exhibit 12.3   Netting Schedule

NET PAYMENTS TO BE MADE BY SUBSIDIARY LOCATED IN	NET U.S. DOLLAR VALUE (IN THOUSANDS) OWED TO SUBSIDIARY LOCATED IN					
	CANADA	FRANCE	JAPAN	SWITZERLAND	U.S.	TOTAL
Canada	—	0	0	10	30	40
France	20	—	0	10	0	30
Japan	10	0	—	10	10	30
Switzerland	0	0	0	—	30	30
U.S.	0	10	0	0	—	10
Total	30	10	0	30	70	

with subsidiaries around the world may not be able to include all of its subsidiaries in its multilateral netting system. Obviously, this will limit the degree to which the netting system can reduce administration and transaction costs.

21-3c Managing Blocked Funds

Cash flows can also be affected by a host government's blockage of funds, which might occur if the government requires all funds to remain within the country in order to create jobs and reduce unemployment. To deal with funds blockage, the MNC may implement the same strategies used when a host country government imposes high taxes. To make efficient use of these funds, the MNC may instruct the subsidiary to set up a research and development division, which incurs costs and possibly generates revenues for other subsidiaries.

Another strategy is to use transfer pricing in a manner that will increase the expenses incurred by the subsidiary. A host country government is likely to be more lenient on funds sent to cover expenses than on earnings remitted to the parent.

When subsidiaries are restricted from transferring funds to the parent, the parent may instruct the subsidiary to obtain financing from a local bank rather than from the parent. By borrowing through a local intermediary, the subsidiary is assured that its earnings can be distributed to pay off previous financing. Overall, most methods of managing blocked funds are intended to make efficient use of the funds by using them to cover expenses that are transferred to that country.

EXAMPLE   Wittenberg, Inc., a U.S.-based MNC, has a subsidiary in the Philippines. During a turbulent period, the subsidiary was prevented from exchanging its Philippine pesos into U.S. dollars to be sent home. Wittenberg held its corporate meeting in Manila so that it could use the pesos to pay the expenses of the meeting (hotel, food, etc.) in pesos. In this way, it was able to use local funds to cover an expense that it would have incurred anyway. Ordinarily, the corporate meeting would have been held in the parent's country, and the parent would have paid the expenses. ●

21-3d Managing Intersubsidiary Cash Transfers

Proper management of cash flows can also be beneficial to a subsidiary in need of funds.

EXAMPLE   Texas, Inc., has two foreign subsidiaries called Short Sub and Long Sub. Short Sub needs funds while Long Sub has excess funds. If Long Sub purchases supplies from Short Sub, it can provide financing by paying for its supplies earlier than necessary. This technique is often called **leading**. Alternatively, if Long Sub sells supplies to Short Sub, it can provide financing by allowing Short Sub to delay its payments. This technique is called **lagging**. ●

The leading or lagging strategy can make efficient use of cash and thereby reduce debt. Some host governments prohibit the practice by requiring that subsidiaries pay for supplies from another subsidiary at the time they are transferred. Thus an MNC needs to be aware of any laws that restrict the use of this strategy.

21-3e Complications in Optimizing Cash Flow

Most complications encountered when optimizing cash flow can be classified into three categories:

- company-related characteristics,
- government restrictions, or
- limitations of banking systems.

Each complication will be discussed in this section.

Company-Related Characteristics In some cases, optimizing cash flow can become complicated because of the MNC's characteristics. If one of the subsidiaries delays payments to other subsidiaries for supplies received, the other subsidiaries may be forced to borrow until the payments arrive. A centralized approach that monitors all intersubsidiary payments should be able to minimize such problems.

Government Restrictions The existence of government restrictions can disrupt a cash flow optimization policy. Some governments prohibit the use of a netting system, as noted earlier. In addition, some countries periodically prevent cash from leaving the country, thereby preventing net payments from being made. These problems can arise even for MNCs that do not experience any company-related problems. Countries in Latin America often impose restrictions that affect an MNC's cash flows.

Limitations of Banking Systems The abilities of banks to facilitate cash transfers for MNCs vary among countries. Banks in the United States are advanced in this field, but banks in some other countries do not offer these services. Multinational corporations prefer some form of a zero-balance account, where excess funds can be used to make payments but earn interest until they are used. Most MNCs can benefit from the use of lockboxes, but such services are not available in some countries.

In addition, a bank may not update the MNC's bank account information sufficiently or provide a detailed breakdown of fees for banking services. Without full use of banking resources and information, the effectiveness of international cash management is limited. Moreover, an MNC with subsidiaries in, say, eight different countries will typically be dealing with eight different banking systems. Much progress has been made in foreign banking systems in recent years. As time passes and a more uniform global banking system emerges, such problems may be alleviated.

21-4 Investing Excess Cash

Many MNCs have at least $100 million in cash balances across banks in various countries. If they can find a way to earn an extra 1 percent on those funds, they will generate an extra $1 million each year. Thus their short-term investment decisions affect the amount of their cash inflows. Multinational corporations typically invest in large deposits at commercial banks. They also purchase foreign Treasury securities and commercial paper.

An MNC can usually earn a higher interest rate on short-term investments that are in larger amounts. If two subsidiaries have excess cash of $50,000 each for one month, the rates on their individual bank deposits may be lower than the rate they could obtain if they pooled their cash into a single $100,000 bank deposit. For this reason, MNCs commonly pool excess cash among subsidiaries to generate a higher rate of return on their short-term investments.

21-4a Benefits of Investing in a Foreign Currency

An MNC's excess funds can be invested in domestic or foreign short-term securities. In some periods, the foreign short-term securities will have higher interest rates than domestic interest rates, and may therefore deserve consideration by MNCs that have excess short-term funds available. A U.S.-based MNC may invest in a deposit that is denominated in a foreign currency with a high interest rate and then convert the funds back to dollars when the deposit matures. In this case, its return on its investment (called its *effective yield*) must account for the exchange rate movement of the foreign currency from the time the MNC converts dollars into the foreign currency until the end of the deposit period when the MNC converts the foreign currency back into dollars. The effective yield of a bank deposit (denoted as r) is dependent on both the interest rate of the foreign currency (i_f) and the rate of appreciation (e_f) of the currency over the deposit period. (The term i_f was used in Chapter 20 to represent the interest rate when borrowing a foreign currency. In this chapter, the term i_f is still used to represent the interest rate of a foreign currency, but it represents the interest rate earned on a deposit in the foreign currency.) The effective yield can be computed as:

$$r = (1 + i_f)(1 + e_f) - 1$$

The effective yield can be very different from the quoted interest rate on a deposit denominated in a foreign currency.

EXAMPLE Utah Co. (a U.S.-based MNC) has excess funds in U.S. dollars that it wants to invest for one year. It can invest in a one-year deposit in U.S. dollars at 4 percent but is attracted to a deposit denominated in Australian dollars that offers an interest rate of 7 percent. Utah Co. forecasts that the Australian dollar will appreciate by 4 percent over the one-year deposit period. Based on this forecast, the effective yield on the deposit denominated in Australian dollars is:

$$r = (1 + i_f)(1 + e_f) - 1$$
$$r = (1 + .07)(1 + .04) - 1$$
$$= .1128 \text{ or } 11.28\%$$

Thus the effective yield on the deposit is expected to be significantly higher than the interest rate on the deposit (i_f) because of the expected positive percentage change in the value of the foreign currency (e_f). In this example, Utah Co. expects to benefit from the relatively high interest rate and from the appreciation of the Australian dollar during the deposit period. ●

21-4b Risk of Investing in a Foreign Currency

While an MNC might earn a higher effective yield from investing in a deposit denominated in a foreign currency, its investment is subject to risk, or uncertainty surrounding the effective yield. Among other things, the investment could be subject to credit (default) risk. However, MNCs typically attempt to invest their cash in short-term securities that are free from credit risk. Therefore, all examples of short-term investments in this chapter are assumed to be in bank deposits that are free from credit risk. Our discussion will focus on bank deposits for short-term foreign investment, but the implications of the discussion can be applied to other risk-free short-term securities (such as government securities) as well.

Even if the short-term investments in foreign deposits cannot default, they are subject to exchange rate risk. If the currency denominating the deposit depreciates over the life of the deposit, the effective yield would be less than the interest rate on that deposit. The advantage of a higher interest rate may be more than offset by the depreciation in the currency denominating the deposit. Consequently, the effective yield on the foreign deposit could be less than what the MNC could have earned from investing in its local currency.

WEB

www.bloomberg.com
Latest information from financial markets around the world.

EXAMPLE Recall that Utah Co. considers investing in an Australian deposit that offers an interest rate of 7 percent, which is more attractive than the U.S. deposit interest rate of 4 percent. While Utah Co. forecasted that the Australian dollar would appreciate by 4 percent over the deposit period, it also recognizes that this forecast could be wrong. It considers one alternative scenario in which the Australian dollar depreciates by 5 percent. Based on this scenario, the effective yield on the deposit denominated in Australian dollars would be:

$$r = (1 + i_f)(1 + e_f) - 1$$
$$= (1 + .07)[1 + (-.05)] - 1$$
$$= .0165, \text{ or } 1.65\%$$

Thus, if this scenario occurs, Utah Co. will earn a lower return on its Australian deposit than it could have earned by investing domestically in a U.S. dollar deposit. ●

The effective yield on a foreign deposit can even be negative if the currency denominating the deposit depreciates to an extent that more than offsets the interest accrued from the deposit. This means that the MNC would have a smaller amount of funds at the end of the investment period than it had at the beginning of the period.

21-4c Hedging the Investment in a Foreign Currency

MNCs that want to invest their cash in deposits with a high foreign interest rate may consider hedging their investment in an attempt to avoid exposure to exchange rate risk. On the day that they make their investment in the foreign deposit, they could sell a forward contract that will allow them to sell the foreign currency at the end of the deposit period.

In this case, the MNC's effective yield will be affected by the percentage difference between the spot rate at which the MNC could obtain the foreign currency at the time it initiated its investment, and the forward rate (negotiated at the time it initiated the investment) at which it sells the foreign currency when the deposit period is over. This percentage difference reflects the forward premium (p), which can be substituted for the percentage change in the exchange rate (e_f) in the equation representing the effective yield:

$$r = (1 + i_f)(1 + p) - 1$$

Recall from Chapter 7 that under conditions of interest rate parity, a foreign currency's forward premium is determined by the differential between its interest rate and the home interest rate:

$$p = \frac{1 + i_h}{1 + i_f} - 1$$

where i_h denotes the home currency's interest rate. Substitute the formula for p to determine the effective yield of a foreign currency under conditions of interest rate parity:

$$r = (1 + i_f)(1 + p) - 1$$
$$= (1 + i_f)\left(1 + \frac{1 + i_h}{1 + i_f} - 1\right) - 1$$
$$= i_h$$

So, if interest rate parity exists, the attempt to invest in a high–interest rate currency and simultaneously hedge that position will result in an effective yield that is similar to the local interest rate.

EXAMPLE

Recall that Utah Co. wants to invest excess cash over the next year and would prefer to invest in a deposit denominated in Australian dollars at the prevailing interest rate of 7 percent rather than invest in U.S. dollars at the prevailing interest rate of 4 percent. Because Utah does not want to be exposed to exchange rate risk, it considers a strategy of investing in the deposit denominated in Australian dollars and simultaneously selling a forward contract on Australian dollars in order to lock in the rate at which it can convert the Australian dollars to U.S. dollars in one year. However, if interest rate parity exists, the one-year forward rate of the Australian dollar presently has a premium (a negative value for a premium represents a discount) that is determined by the differential between the Australian interest rate and the U.S. interest rate:

$$p = \frac{1 + i_h}{1 + i_f} - 1$$
$$= \frac{1.04}{1.07} - 1$$
$$= \text{about } - .028, \text{ or } - 2.8\%$$

The negative value of the premium (p) suggests that the forward rate of the Australian dollar contains a discount. Thus Utah's effective yield from implementing its strategy would be:

$$r = (1 + i_f)(1 + p) - 1$$
$$r = (1 + .07)[(1 + (-.028)] - 1$$
$$= .04 \text{ or } 4\%$$

Thus if interest rate parity exists, the strategy of investing in a deposit denominated in Australian dollars and hedging that position would not allow Utah Co. to achieve a higher effective yield than an investment in a domestic deposit. ●

Even if interest rate parity does hold, short-term investing in a foreign deposit may still be feasible if the position is not hedged, but the MNC is subject to exchange rate risk.

21-4d Break-Even Point from Investing in a Foreign Currency

The discussion of interest rate parity and hedging in the previous section can be used to provide insight about the forward rate as a forecast when an MNC attempts to invest in a foreign deposit without hedging its position. If interest rate parity holds, and if the forward rate was an accurate forecast of the future spot rate at the end of the deposit period, the effective yield on the deposit would be equal to the yield on a domestic deposit. The reason is that if interest rate parity exists, the forward rate discount (which represents the forecasted percentage change in the spot rate over the deposit period) reflects the differential between the foreign interest rate and the domestic interest rate. If the currency depreciates as predicted by the forward discount, this means that the degree of depreciation will offset the interest rate advantage. Thus the forward rate can be viewed as a break-even point because if it serves as an accurate forecast, the effective yield on the foreign deposit will be equal to the yield from investing domestically.

Given that the forward rate can be viewed as a break-even point, forecasts that are higher or lower than the forecast derived from the forward rate offer relevant implications for short-term investing. If an MNC's forecast of the future spot rate (that will exist at the end of the deposit period) is higher than the forward rate when it invests in a deposit, the MNC would expect the effective yield of the foreign deposit to exceed the domestic yield. Conversely, if an MNC's forecast of the future spot rate (that will exist at the end of the deposit period) is lower than the forward rate when it invests in a deposit, the MNC would expect the effective yield of the foreign deposit to be lower than the domestic yield.

WEB

http://global.broad.msu
.edu/ibc/
Links to numerous sites
related to international
business.

Relationship with the International Fisher Effect When interest rate parity exists, MNCs that use the forward rate to forecast the future spot rate would expect the yield on foreign deposits to equal that on their local deposits. Although the forward rate is not necessarily an accurate predictor, it may provide unbiased forecasts of the future spot rate. A forward rate that is *unbiased* will underestimate and overestimate the future spot rate with nearly equal frequency, in which case the effective yield on foreign deposits is (on average) equal to the domestic yield. Therefore, MNCs that consistently invest in foreign short-term securities would earn a yield similar to what they could earn on domestic deposits.

The discussion here is closely related to the international Fisher effect (IFE). Recall that the IFE suggests that the exchange rate of a foreign currency is expected to change by an amount reflecting the difference between its interest rate and the U.S. interest rate. The rationale behind this theory is that a high nominal interest rate reflects an expectation of high inflation, which could weaken the currency (according to purchasing power parity).

If interest rate parity holds, then the forward premium or discount reflects that interest rate difference and so represents the expected percentage change in the currency's value when the forward rate is used as a predictor of the future spot rate. The IFE suggests that firms cannot consistently earn short-term yields on foreign deposits that are higher than those on domestic deposits because the exchange rate is expected to adjust, on average, to the interest rate difference. If interest rate parity holds and if the forward rate is an unbiased predictor of the future spot rate, then we can expect the IFE to hold.

A look back in time reveals that the IFE is supported for some currencies in some periods. However, it may be difficult for an MNC to anticipate when the IFE will hold and when it will not. For virtually any currency, it is possible to identify previous periods an MNC would have earned very high returns from investing short-term funds in a foreign deposit. Yet it is also possible to identify other periods when an MNC would have earned low (or even negative) returns from investing in that same foreign deposit.

Conclusions about the Forward Rate   The key implications of interest rate parity and the forward rate as a predictor of future spot rates for foreign investing are summarized in Exhibit 21.4. This exhibit explains the conditions under which investment in foreign short-term deposits is feasible. Because some MNCs do not believe that the forward rate is an accurate or even an unbiased forecast of the future spot rate, they seriously consider investing excess cash in foreign deposits that have high interest rates.

21-4e Using a Probability Distribution to Enhance the Investment Decision

MNCs that consider investing in foreign deposits may benefit from developing a probability distribution of exchange rate movements of the currency denominating the deposit. The development of a probability distribution acknowledges the difficulty of forecasting exchange rates and allows an MNC to consider the impact of alternative possible outcomes of the exchange rate movement over the deposit period. An example of how a probability distribution can be applied follows.

Exhibit 21.4   Considerations When Investing Excess Cash

SCENARIO	IMPLICATIONS FOR INVESTING IN FOREIGN DEPOSITS
1. Interest rate parity exists.	Covered interest arbitrage is not worthwhile.
2. Interest rate parity exists, and the forward rate is an accurate forecast of the future spot rate.	An uncovered investment in a foreign deposit is not worthwhile.
3. Interest rate parity exists, and the forward rate is an unbiased forecast of the future spot rate.	An uncovered investment in a foreign deposit will on average earn an effective yield similar to an investment in a domestic deposit.
4. Interest rate parity exists, and the forward rate is expected to overestimate the future spot rate.	An uncovered investment in a foreign deposit is expected to earn a lower effective yield than an investment in a domestic deposit.
5. Interest rate parity exists, and the forward rate is expected to underestimate the future spot rate.	An uncovered investment in a foreign deposit is expected to earn a higher effective yield than an investment in a domestic deposit.
6. Interest rate parity does not exist, and the forward premium (discount) exceeds (is less than) the interest rate differential.	Covered interest arbitrage is feasible for investors residing in the home country.
7. Interest rate parity does not exist, and the forward premium (discount) is less than (exceeds) the interest rate differential.	Covered interest arbitrage is feasible for foreign investors but not for investors residing in the home country.

EXAMPLE

Recall that Utah Co. is deciding whether to invest in a deposit denominated in Australian dollars with a 7 percent interest rate for one year versus a U.S. dollar deposit with a 4 percent interest rate. Recall from earlier examples that Utah considered two possible outcomes for the exchange rate movement in the Australian dollar. Now it decides to assign a probability to each of those outcomes. It believes there is a 70 percent probability that the Australian dollar will appreciate by 4 percent and a 30 percent probability that the Australian dollar will depreciate by 5 percent.

Utah can use these probabilities of exchange rate movements to create a probability distribution for the effective yield on the Australian dollar deposit, as displayed in Exhibit 21.5. From the first row in the exhibit, there is a 70 percent probability of a 4 percent appreciation in the Australian dollar over the deposit's life. If the Australian dollar does appreciate by 4 percent, then the effective yield will be 11.28 percent. This indicates that there is a 70 percent probability that Utah Co. will earn an effective yield of 11.28 percent on its funds. From the second row in the exhibit, there is a 30 percent probability of a 5 percent depreciation in the Australian dollar over the deposit period. If the Australian dollar does depreciate by 5 percent, then the effective yield will be 1.65 percent, which means there is a 30 percent probability that Utah will generate an effective yield of 1.65 percent on this deposit.

Utah can derive an *expected value* of the effective yield of the Australian dollar deposit by multiplying the probability of each possible outcome for the exchange rate movement by the effective yield if that outcome occurs. Based on the information in Exhibit 21.5, the expected value of the effective yield, $E[r]$, is computed as follows:

$$E[r] = 70\%(11.28\%) + 30\%(1.65\%)$$
$$= 7.896\% + .495\%$$
$$= 8.391\%$$

To further assess the question of which currency to invest in, the information in the second and third columns from Exhibit 21.5 is used to develop a probability distribution for the effective yield. If Utah Co. invests in Australian dollars, it is exposed to the risk (with 30 percent probability) that the investment only earns 1.65 percent. It could earn 4 percent with certainty by investing in U.S. dollars. Before it finalizes its decision for investing excess cash, Utah Co. plans to consider one other possible strategy of investing in a portfolio of foreign currencies, as explained in the following section. ●

21-4f Investing in a Portfolio of Currencies

Because an MNC is not sure how exchange rates will change over time, it may prefer to diversify its cash among deposits denominated in different currencies. Limiting the percentage of excess cash invested in each foreign currency will reduce the MNC's exposure to exchange rate risk.

EXAMPLE

Recall that Utah Co. can invest funds for one year in U.S. dollars to earn a 4 percent interest rate or in Australian dollars to earn an interest rate of 7 percent. Assume that it could also invest in a one-year deposit denominated in Mexican pesos and earn an interest rate of 6 percent. It wants to consider the possible outcomes if it invests in a currency portfolio, with half of its funds invested in an Australian dollar deposit and the other half in a Mexican peso deposit. Utah Co. determines possible outcomes for the

Exhibit 21.5 Analysis of Investing in a Foreign Currency

POSSIBLE RATE OF CHANGE IN THE AUSTRALIAN DOLLAR OVER THE LIFE OF THE INVESTMENT (e_f)	PROBABILITY OF OCCURRENCE	EFFECTIVE YIELD IF THIS RATE OF CHANGE IN THE AUSTRALIAN DOLLAR OCCURS
+4%	70%	$(1.07)[1 + (.04)] - 1 = .1128$, or 11.28%
−5%	30%	$(1.07)[1 + (- .05)] - 1 = .1.65$, or 1.65%
	100%	

Exhibit 21.6 Development of Possible Effective Yields

CURRENCY	POSSIBLE PERCENTAGE CHANGE IN THE SPOT RATE OVER THE DEPOSIT LIFE	PROBABILITY OF THAT PERCENTAGE CHANGE IN THE SPOT RATE OCCURRING	COMPUTATION OF EFFECTIVE YIELD BASED ON THAT PERCENTAGE CHANGE IN THE SPOT RATE
Australian dollar	+4%	70%	$(1.07)[1 + (.04)] - 1 = 11.28\%$
Australian dollar	−5%	30	$(1.07)[1 + (-.05)] - 1 = 1.65\%$
		100%	
Mexican peso	+2%	60%	$(1.06)[1 + (.02)] - 1 = .0812$ or 8.12%
Mexican peso	−4%	40%	$(1.06)[1 + (-.04)] - 1 = .0176$ or 1.76%
		100%	

Australian dollar in the first two rows of Exhibit 21.6, which are based on its expectations described in the previous example.

Assume that Utah Co. also forecasts that the Mexican peso will appreciate by 2 percent with a 60 percent probability, or depreciate by 4 percent with a 40 percent probability. The bottom two rows of Exhibit 21.6 determine the effective yield from investing in the Mexican peso deposit for each possible exchange rate outcome. Notice from these two rows that Utah Co. expects that the effective yield from investing in a Mexican peso deposit will be 8.12 percent with a 60 percent probability, or 1.76 percent with a 40 percent probability.

Because there are two possible outcomes for the Australian dollar and two possible outcomes for the Mexican peso, there are four possible outcomes for a portfolio containing the Australian dollar and the Mexican peso. Utah Co. estimates the effective yield of the portfolio for each possible outcome if it invests half of its available funds in each of the foreign currencies. In making the estimates, it assumes that the outcome for the Australian dollar is independent of the outcome for the Mexican peso. Utah's estimates are shown in Exhibit 21.7. The first two columns list all possible joint effective yields. The third column computes the joint probability of each possible occurrence. The fourth column shows the computation of the portfolio's effective yield based on the possible rates for the individual currencies shown in the first two columns. The top row of the table indicates that one possible outcome is that the Australian dollar deposit will earn an effective yield of 11.28 percent (with 70 percent probability) while the Mexican peso deposit will earn an effective yield of 8.12 percent (with 60 percent probability). The joint probability that these effective yields will occur simultaneously is $(.70)(.60) = 42$ percent. Assuming that half of the funds available are invested in each currency, the portfolio's effective yield will be $.5(11.28$ percent$) + .5(8.12$ percent$) = 9.70$ percent (if those individual effective yields do occur).

A similar procedure was used to develop the remaining three rows in Exhibit 21.7. There is a 42 percent chance the portfolio's effective yield will be 9.70 percent, a 28 percent chance that it will be 6.52 percent, and so on.

Exhibit 21.7 Analysis of Investing in Two Foreign Currencies

POSSIBLE JOINT EFFECTIVE YIELD			
AUSTRALIAN DOLLAR	MEXICAN PESO	COMPUTATION OF JOINT PROBABILITY	COMPUTATION OF EFFECTIVE YIELD OF PORTFOLIO (50% OF TOTAL FUNDS INVESTED IN EACH CURRENCY)
11.28%	8.12%	$(70\%)(60\%) = 42\%$	$.5(11.28\%) + .5(8.12\%) = 9.70\%$
11.28%	1.76%	$(70\%)(40\%) = 28\%$	$.5(11.28\%) + .5(1.76\%) = 6.52\%$
1.65%	8.12%	$(30\%)(60\%) = 18\%$	$.5(1.65\%) + .5(8.12\%) = 4.885\%$
1.65%	1.76%	$(30\%)(40\%) = 12\%$	$.5(1.65\%) + .5(1.76\%) = 1.705\%$
		100%	

Exhibit 21.7 shows that in three of the four possible outcomes, Utah Co. would earn a higher effective yield on the currency portfolio than if it invests in a deposit denominated in U.S. dollars. The only scenario in which the currency portfolio earns a lower effective yield is shown in the bottom row, which represents the outcome if both the Australian dollar and the Mexican peso depreciate.

To recognize the benefits of investing in a currency portfolio versus investing in only one foreign currency, compare the results among the possible investing strategies. If Utah Co. invests only in an Australian dollar deposit, there is a 30 percent probability that its effective yield will be lower than that of the U.S. dollar deposit. If Utah Co. invests only in Mexican pesos, there is a 40 percent probability that its effective yield will be lower than that of the U.S. dollar deposit. Yet if Utah Co. invests in the currency portfolio of Australian dollars and Mexican pesos, there is only a 12 percent probability that its effective yield on the currency portfolio will be lower than investing in a U.S. dollar deposit. These results for the currency portfolio illustrate the potential benefits of diversification.

If the outcomes for the exchange rate movements in the Australian dollar and Mexican peso are independent, there is a good chance that the most unfavorable outcomes will not occur simultaneously for both currencies. If the unfavorable outcome occurs for one of the currencies, this may be partially offset by a more favorable outcome for the other currency. ●

In our example, the computation of joint probabilities required the assumption that the movements in the two currencies were independent. If the movements of the two currencies were actually highly correlated, then investing in a portfolio of currencies would not be as beneficial as demonstrated here because there would be a strong likelihood that both currencies would experience a high level of depreciation simultaneously. If the two currencies are not highly correlated, they will not be expected to simultaneously depreciate to such a degree.

Our example included only two currencies in the portfolio. Investing in a more diversified portfolio of additional currencies that exhibit high interest rates can increase the probability that foreign investing will be more rewarding than the U.S. deposit. This is because of the low probability that all currencies will move in tandem and therefore simultaneously depreciate to offset their high interest rate advantages. Again, the degree to which these currencies are correlated with each other is important. If all currencies are highly positively correlated with each other, then investing in such a portfolio will not be very different from investing in a single foreign currency.

21-4g Dynamic Hedging

Some MNCs continually adjust their short-term positions in currencies in response to revised expectations of each currency's future movement. This is the strategy of **dynamic hedging**, which involves applying a hedge when the currencies held are expected to depreciate and removing any hedge when the currencies held are expected to appreciate. In essence, the objective is to protect against downside risk while still benefiting from the favorable movement of exchange rates.

For example, consider a treasurer of a U.S. firm who plans to invest in British deposits. If the British pound begins to decline and is expected to depreciate further, then the treasurer may sell pounds forward in the foreign exchange market for a future date at which the pound's value is expected to turn upward. If the treasurer can be confident that the pound will depreciate in the short run, then most or all of the position will be hedged.

Now assume that the pound begins to appreciate before the forward contract date. Because the contract will preclude the potential benefits from the pound's appreciation, the treasurer may buy pounds forward to offset the existing forward sale contracts. In this way, the treasurer has removed the existing hedge. Of course, if the forward rate at the time of the forward purchase exceeds the forward rate that existed at the time of the forward sale, a cost is incurred to offset the hedge.

The treasurer may decide to remove only part of the hedge, offsetting only some of the existing forward sales with forward purchases. With this approach, the position is still partially protected if the pound depreciates further. Overall, the performance from using dynamic hedging depends on the treasurer's ability to forecast the direction of exchange rate movements.

SUMMARY

- MNCs manage their working capital, which includes short-term assets such as inventory, accounts receivable, and cash. Multinational management of working capital is complex for MNCs that have foreign subsidiaries because each subsidiary must have adequate working capital to support its operations. The MNC may use a centralized perspective to monitor cash positions and to ensure that funds can be transferred among subsidiaries to accommodate cash deficiencies.

- An MNC's centralized cash management can monitor cash flows between subsidiaries and between each subsidiary and the parent. It can facilitate the transfer of funds from subsidiaries with excess funds to those that need funds so that the MNC uses its funds efficiently.

- The common techniques to optimize cash flows are (1) accelerating cash inflows, (2) minimizing currency conversion costs, (3) managing blocked funds, and (4) implementing intersubsidiary cash transfers. The efforts by MNCs to optimize cash flows are complicated by company-related characteristics, government restrictions, and characteristics of banking systems.

- MNCs can possibly achieve higher returns when investing excess cash in foreign currencies that either have relatively high interest rates or may appreciate over the investment period. If the foreign currency depreciates over the investment period, however, this may offset any interest rate advantage of that currency.

POINT COUNTER-POINT

Should Interest Rate Parity Prevent MNCs from Investing in Foreign Currencies?

Point   Yes. Currencies with high interest rates have large forward discounts according to interest rate parity. To the extent that the forward rate is a reasonable forecast of the future spot rate, investing in a foreign country is not feasible.

Counter-Point   No. Even if interest rate parity holds, MNCs should still consider investing in a

foreign currency. The key is their expectations of the future spot rate. If their expectations of the future spot rate are higher than the forward rate, the MNCs would benefit from investing in a foreign currency.

Who Is Correct?   Use the Internet to learn more about this issue. Which argument do you support? Offer your own opinion on this issue.

SELF-TEST

Answers are provided in Appendix A at the back of the text.

1.   Country X typically has a high interest rate, and its currency is expected to strengthen against the dollar over time. Country Y typically has a low interest rate, and its currency is expected to weaken against the dollar over time. Both countries have imposed a "blocked funds" restriction over the next

four years on the two subsidiaries owned by a U.S. firm. Which subsidiary will be more adversely affected by the blocked funds, assuming that there are limited opportunities for corporate expansion in both countries?

2.   Assume that the Australian one-year interest rate is 14 percent. Also assume that the Australian dollar is expected to appreciate by 8 percent over the next year against the U.S. dollar. What is the expected effective yield on a one-year deposit in Australia by a U.S. firm?

3. Assume that the one-year forward rate is used as the forecast of the future spot rate. The Malaysian ringgit's spot rate is $.20 while its one-year forward rate is $.19. The Malaysian one-year interest rate is 11 percent. What is the expected effective yield on a one-year deposit in Malaysia by a U.S. firm?

4. Assume that the Venezuelan one-year interest rate is 90 percent while the U.S. one-year interest rate is 6 percent. Determine the break-even value for the percentage change in Venezuela's currency (the bolivar) that would cause the effective yield to be the same for a one-year deposit in Venezuela as for a one-year deposit in the United States.

5. Assume interest rate parity exists. Would U.S. firms possibly consider investing in deposits in countries with high interest rates? Explain.

QUESTIONS AND APPLICATIONS

1. **International Cash Management** Discuss the general functions involved in international cash management. Explain how the MNC's optimization of cash flow can distort the profits of each subsidiary.

2. **Netting** Explain the benefits of netting. How can a centralized cash management system be beneficial to the MNC?

3. **Leading and Lagging** How can an MNC implement leading and lagging techniques to help subsidiaries in need of funds?

4. **International Fisher Effect** If a U.S. firm believes that the international Fisher effect holds, what are the implications regarding a strategy of continually attempting to generate high returns from investing in currencies with high interest rates?

5. **Investing Strategy** Tallahassee Co. has $2 million in excess cash that it has invested in Mexico at an annual interest rate of 60 percent. The U.S. interest rate is 9 percent. By how much would the Mexican peso have to depreciate to cause such a strategy to backfire?

6. **Investing Strategy** Why would a U.S. firm consider investing short-term funds in euros even when it does not have any future cash outflows in euros?

7. **Covered Interest Arbitrage** Evansville, Inc., has $2 million in cash available for 90 days. It is considering the use of covered interest arbitrage because the euro's 90-day interest rate is higher than the U.S. interest rate. What will determine whether this strategy is feasible?

8. **Effective Yield** Fort Collins, Inc., has $1 million in cash available for 30 days. It can earn 1 percent on a 30-day investment in the United States. Alternatively, if it converts the dollars to Mexican pesos, it can earn 1.5 percent on a Mexican deposit. The spot rate of the Mexican peso is $.12. The spot rate 30 days from now is expected to be $.10. Should Fort Collins invest its cash in the United States or in Mexico? Substantiate your answer.

9. **Effective Yield** Rollins, Inc., has $3 million in cash available for 180 days. It can earn 7 percent on a U.S. Treasury bill or 9 percent on a British Treasury bill. The British investment requires conversion of dollars to British pounds. Assume that interest rate parity holds and that Rollins believes the 180-day forward rate is a reliable predictor of the spot rate to be realized 180 days from now. Would the British investment provide an effective yield that is below, above, or equal to the yield on the U.S. investment? Explain your answer.

10. **Effective Yield** Repeat question 9, but this time assume that Rollins, Inc., expects the 180-day forward rate of the pound to substantially overestimate the spot rate to be realized in 180 days.

11. **Effective Yield** Repeat question 9, but this time assume that Rollins, Inc., expects the 180-day forward rate of the pound to substantially underestimate the spot rate to be realized in 180 days.

12. **Effective Yield** Assume that the one-year U.S. interest rate is 10 percent and the one-year Canadian interest rate is 3 percent. If a U.S. firm invests its funds in Canada, by what percentage will the Canadian dollar have to depreciate to make its effective yield the same as the U. S. interest rate from the U.S. firm's perspective?

13. **Investing in a Currency Portfolio** Why would a firm consider investing in a portfolio of foreign currencies instead of just a single foreign currency?

14. **Interest Rate Parity** Dallas Co. has determined that the interest rate on euros is 16 percent while the U.S. interest rate is 11 percent for one-year Treasury bills. The one-year forward rate of the euro has a discount of 7 percent. Does interest rate parity exist? Can Dallas achieve a higher effective yield by using covered

interest arbitrage than by investing in U.S. Treasury bills? Explain.

15. Diversified Investments Hofstra, Inc., has no European business and has cash invested in six European countries, each of which uses the euro as its local currency. Are Hofstra's short-term investments well diversified and subject to a low degree of exchange rate risk? Explain.

16. Investing Strategy Should McNeese Co. consider investing funds in Latin American countries where it may expand facilities? The interest rates are high, and the proceeds from the investments could be used to help support the expansion. When would this strategy backfire?

17. Impact of September 11 Palos Co. commonly invests some of its excess dollars in foreign government short-term securities in order to earn a higher short-term interest rate on its cash. Describe how the potential return and risk of this strategy may have changed after the September 11, 2001, terrorist attack on the United States.

Advanced Questions

18. Investing in a Portfolio Pittsburgh Co. plans to invest its excess cash in Mexican pesos for one year. The one-year Mexican interest rate is 19 percent. The probability of the peso's percentage change in value during the next year is shown next:

POSSIBLE RATE OF CHANGE IN THE MEXICAN PESO OVER THE LIFE OF THE INVESTMENT	PROBABILITY OF OCCURRENCE
−15%	20%
−4	50
0	30

What is the expected value of the effective yield based on this information? Given that the U.S. interest rate for one year is 7 percent, what is the probability that a one-year investment in pesos will generate a lower effective yield than could be generated if Pittsburgh Co. simply invested domestically?

19. Effective Yield of Portfolio Ithaca Co. considers placing 30 percent of its excess funds in a one-year Singapore dollar deposit and the remaining 70 percent of its funds in a one-year Canadian dollar deposit. The Singapore one-year interest rate is 15 percent, while the Canadian one-year interest rate is

13 percent. The possible percentage changes in the two currencies for the next year are forecasted as follows:

CURRENCY	HORIZON	PROBABILITY OF THAT CHANGE IN THE SPOT RATE OCCURRING
Singapore dollar	−2%	20%
Singapore dollar	1	60
Singapore dollar	3	20
Canadian dollar	1	50
Canadian dollar	4	40
Canadian dollar	6	10

Given this information, determine the possible effective yields of the portfolio and the probability associated with each possible portfolio yield. Given a one-year U.S. interest rate of 8 percent, what is the probability that the portfolio's effective yield will be lower than the yield achieved from investing in the United States?

Critical Thinking

Optimal Use of Cash in Foreign Countries
Some U.S.-based MNCs have been maintaining a very large amount of cash in foreign countries, because they would be subject to a corporate income tax on these funds if they were remitted to the parent. The tax is implemented to cover the difference between the corporate tax rate imposed by the U.S. government and the tax rate imposed by the foreign country. In recent years, short-term interest rates in many countries have been very low, although not as low as in the United States. Write a short essay to explain whether the low interest rates may cause MNCs to make better use of their funds. What is an obvious alternative use of funds in a foreign country that an MNC would likely consider? Why might the MNC continue to just maintain funds in cash accounts (earning very low interest) rather than using the funds in a manner that could earn a higher expected return?

Discussion in the Boardroom

This exercise can be found in Appendix E at the back of this textbook.

Running Your Own MNC

This exercise can be found on the *International Financial Management* text companion website. Go to www.cengagebrain.com (students) or www.cengage.com/login (instructors) and search using **ISBN 9781133947837**.

BLADES, INC. CASE

International Cash Management

Recall from Chapter 20 that the new Thailand subsidiary of Blades, Inc., received a one-time order from a customer for 120,000 pairs of Speedos, Blades' primary product. There is a six-month lag between the time when Blades needs funds to purchase material for the production of the Speedos and the time when it will be paid by the customer. Ben Holt, Blades' chief financial officer (CFO), has decided to finance the cost by borrowing Thai baht at an interest rate of 6 percent over a six-month period. Because the average cost per pair of Speedos is approximately 3,500 baht, Blades will borrow 420 million baht. The payment for the order will be used to repay the loan's principal and interest.

Holt is currently planning to instruct the Thai subsidiary to remit any remaining baht-denominated cash flows back to the United States. Just before Blades receives payment for the large order, however, Holt notices that interest rates in Thailand have increased substantially. Blades would be able to invest funds in Thailand at a relatively high interest rate compared to the U.S. rate. Specifically, Blades could invest the remaining baht-denominated funds for one year in Thailand at an interest rate of 15 percent.

If the funds are remitted back to the U.S. parent, the excess dollar volume resulting from the conversion of baht will either be used to support the U.S. production of Speedos, if needed, or be invested in the United States. Specifically, the funds will be used to cover cost of products sold in the U.S. manufacturing plant, located in Omaha, Nebraska. Because Blades used a significant amount of cash to finance the initial investment to build the plant in Thailand and purchase the necessary equipment, its U.S. operations are strapped for cash. Consequently, if the subsidiary's earnings are not remitted back to the United States, Blades will have to borrow funds at an interest rate of 10 percent to support its U.S. operations. Any funds remitted by the subsidiary that are not used to support U.S. operations will be invested in the United States at an interest

rate of 8 percent. Holt estimates that approximately 60 percent of the remitted funds will be needed to support U.S. operations and that the remaining 40 percent will be invested in the United States.

Consequently, Holt must choose between two alternative plans. First, he could instruct the Thai subsidiary to repay the baht loan (with interest) and invest any remaining funds in Thailand at an interest rate of 15 percent. Second, he could instruct the Thai subsidiary to repay the baht loan and remit any remaining funds back to the United States, where 60 percent of the funds would be used to support U.S. operations and 40 percent would be invested at an interest rate of 8 percent. Assume no income or withholding taxes on the earnings generated in Thailand.

Holt has contacted you, a financial analyst at Blades, Inc., to help him analyze these two options. He has informed you that the current spot rate of the Thai baht is .0225 and that the baht is expected to depreciate by 5 percent over the coming year. He has provided you with the following list of questions he would like you to answer.

1. There is a trade-off between the higher interest rates in Thailand and the delayed conversion of baht into dollars. What does this mean?

2. If the net baht received from the Thailand subsidiary are invested in Thailand, how will U.S. operations be affected?

3. Construct a spreadsheet that compares the cash flows resulting from the two plans. Under the first plan, net baht-denominated cash flows (received today) will be invested in Thailand at 15 percent for a one-year period, after which the baht will be converted to dollars. Under the second plan, net baht-denominated cash flows are converted to dollars immediately and 60 percent of the funds will be used to support U.S. operations, while 40 percent are invested in the United States for one year at 8 percent. Which plan is superior given the expectation of the baht's value in one year?

SMALL BUSINESS DILEMMA

Cash Management at the Sports Exports Company

Ever since Jim Logan began his Sports Exports Company, he has been concerned about his exposure to exchange rate risk. The firm produces footballs and

exports them to a distributor in the United Kingdom, with the exports being denominated in British pounds. Logan has just entered into a joint venture in the

United Kingdom in which a British firm produces sporting goods for Logan's firm and sells the goods to the British distributor. The distributor pays pounds to Logan's firm for these products. Logan recently borrowed pounds to finance this venture, which created some cash outflows (interest payments) that partially offset his cash inflows in pounds. The interest paid on this loan is equal to the British Treasury bill rate plus 3 percentage points. His original business of exporting has been very successful recently, which has caused him to have revenue (in pounds) that will be retained as excess cash. Logan must decide whether to pay off part of the existing British loan, invest the cash

in the U.S. Treasury bills, or invest the cash in British Treasury bills.

1. If Logan invests the excess cash in U.S. Treasury bills, would this reduce the firm's exposure to exchange rate risk?

2. Logan decided to use the excess cash to pay off the British loan. However, a friend advised him to invest the cash in British Treasury bills, stating that "the loan provides an offset to the pound receivables, so you would be better off investing in British Treasury bills than paying off the loan." Is the friend correct? What should Logan do?

INTERNET/EXCEL EXERCISES

The Bloomberg website (www.bloomberg.com) provides interest rate data for many different foreign currencies over various maturities.

1. Go to the Markets section and then to Rates & Bonds, and click on a country to review its interest rates. Review the one-year yields of currencies. Assume that you could invest at the quoted yield for each currency. Which currency would offer you the highest quoted yield?

2. As a cash manager of an MNC based in the United States that has extra dollars that can be invested for one year, where would you invest funds for the next year? Explain.

3. If you were working for a foreign subsidiary based in Japan and could invest Japanese yen for one year until the yen are needed to support local operations, where would you invest the yen? Explain.

4. Assume that at the beginning of each of the last seven years, you had the choice of a one-year investment in U.S. dollars or Australian dollars. Your business is in the United States, but you considered investing in Australian dollars because the Australian dollar's annual interest rate was 9 percent versus the U.S. dollar's annual interest rate of 6 percent. Go to www.oanda.com/currency/historical-rates and obtain the annual percentage change in the Australian dollar's exchange rate for each of the last seven years. Determine the effective yield from investing in Australian dollars in each of the last seven years. Based on your results, was the annual effective yield higher for the Australian dollar or the U.S. dollar on average over the seven years? In how many of the years would you have been better off investing in Australian dollars rather than U.S dollars? Explain.

ONLINE ARTICLES WITH REAL-WORLD EXAMPLES

Find a recent article online that describes an actual international finance application or a real-world example about a specific MNC's actions that reinforces one or more of the concepts covered in this chapter.

If your class has an online component, your professor may ask you to post your summary there and provide the web link of the article so that other students can access it. If your class is live, your professor may ask you to summarize your application in class. Your professor may assign specific students to complete this assignment for this chapter or may allow any students to do the assignment on a volunteer basis.

For recent online articles and real-world examples applied to this chapter, consider using the following

search terms (and include the current year as a search term to ensure that the online articles are recent).

1. [name of an MNC] AND cash management

2. multinational AND cash

3. parent AND liquidity

4. subsidiary AND liquidity

5. cash AND exchange rate risk

6. cash AND foreign

7. parent AND cash

8. subsidiary AND cash

9. intersubsidiary AND cash

10. subsidiary AND liquidity

Short-Term Asset and Liability Management

Kent Co. is a large U.S. firm with no international business. It has two branches within the United States, an eastern branch and a western branch. Each branch currently makes investing or financing decisions independently, as if it were a separate entity. The eastern branch has excess cash of $15 million to invest for the next year. It can invest its funds in Treasury bills denominated in dollars or in any of four foreign currencies. The only restriction enforced by the parent is that a maximum of $5 million can be invested or financed in any foreign currency.

The western branch needs to borrow $15 million over one year to support its U.S. operations. It can borrow funds in any of these same currencies (although any foreign funds borrowed would need to be converted to dollars to finance the U.S. operations). The only restriction enforced by the parent is that a maximum equivalent of $5 million can be borrowed in any single currency. A large bank serving the international money market has offered Kent Co. the following terms:

CURRENCY	ANNUAL INTEREST RATE ON DEPOSITS	ANNUAL INTEREST RATE CHARGED ON LOANS
U.S. dollar	6%	9%
Australian dollar	11	14
Canadian dollar	7	10
New Zealand dollar	9	12
Japanese yen	8	11

Kent Co. has created one-year forecasts of each currency for the branches to use in making their investing or financing decisions:

CURRENCY	TODAY'S SPOT EXCHANGE RATE	FORECASTED ANNUAL PERCENTAGE CHANGE IN EXCHANGE RATE
Australian dollar	$.70	−4%
Canadian dollar	.80	−2
New Zealand dollar	.60	+3
Japanese yen	.008	0

Questions

1. Determine the investment portfolio composition for Kent's eastern branch that would maximize the expected effective yield while satisfying the restriction imposed by the parent.

2. What is the expected effective yield of the investment portfolio?

3. Based on the expected effective yield for the portfolio and the initial investment amount of $15 million, determine the annual interest to be earned on the portfolio.

4. Determine the financing portfolio composition for Kent's western branch that would minimize the expected effective financing rate while satisfying the restriction imposed by the parent.

5. What is the expected effective financing rate of the total amount borrowed?

6. Based on the expected effective financing rate for the portfolio and the total amount of $15 million borrowed, determine the expected loan repayment amount beyond the principal borrowed.

7. When the expected interest received by the eastern branch and paid by the western branch of Kent Co. are consolidated, what is the net amount of interest received?

8. If the eastern branch and the western branch worked together, the eastern branch could loan its $15 million to the western branch. Nevertheless, one could argue that the branches could not take advantage of interest rate differentials or expected exchange rate effects among currencies. Given the data provided in this example, would you recommend that the two branches make their short-term investment and financing decisions independently, or should the eastern branch lend its excess cash to the western branch? Explain.

Final Self-Exam

Final Review

This self-exam focuses on the managerial chapters (Chapters 9 through 21). Here is a brief summary of some of the key points in those chapters. Chapter 9 describes various methods that are used to forecast exchange rates. Chapter 10 explains how transaction exposure is based on transactions involving different currencies, while economic exposure is any form of exposure that can affect the value of the MNC, and translation exposure is due to the existence of foreign subsidiaries whose earnings are translated to consolidated income statements. Chapter 11 explains how transaction exposure in payables can be managed by purchasing forward or futures contracts, purchasing call options, or using a money market hedge that involves investing in the foreign currency. Transaction exposure in receivables can be managed by selling forward or futures contracts, purchasing put options, or using a money market hedge that involves borrowing the foreign currency. Chapter 12 explains how economic exposure can be hedged by restructuring operations to match foreign currency inflows and outflows. The translation exposure can be hedged by selling a forward contract on the foreign currency of the foreign subsidiary. However, though this hedge may reduce translation exposure, it also may result in a cash loss.

Chapter 13 explains how direct foreign investment can be motivated by foreign market conditions that may increase demand and revenue or conditions that reflect lower costs of production. Chapter 14 explains how the net present value of a multinational project is enhanced when the foreign currency to be received in the future is expected to appreciate but is reduced when that currency is expected to depreciate. It explains how financing with a foreign currency can offset inflows and reduce exchange rate risk. Chapter 15 explains how the net present value framework can be applied to acquisitions, divestitures, or other forms of restructuring. Chapter 16 explains how the net present value framework can be used to incorporate country risk conditions when assessing a project's feasibility. Chapter 17 explains how an MNC's cost of capital is influenced by its home country's risk-free interest rate and its risk premium. The MNC's capital structure decision will likely result in a heavier emphasis toward debt if it has stable cash flows, has less retained earnings available, and has more assets that it can use as collateral.

Chapter 18 explains how the cost of long-term financing with foreign currency–denominated debt is subject to exchange rate movements. When the debt payments are not offset by cash inflows in the same currency, the cost of financing increases if the value of the foreign currency denominating the debt increases over time.

Chapter 19 explains how international trade can be facilitated by various forms of payment and financing. Chapter 20 explains how an MNC's short-term financing in foreign currencies can reduce exchange rate risk if it is offset by foreign currency inflows at the end of the financing period. When there are not offsetting currency inflows, the effective financing rate of a foreign currency is more favorable (lower) when its interest rate is low and when the currency depreciates over the financing period.

Chapter 21 explains how an MNC's short-term investment in foreign currencies can reduce exchange rate risk if the proceeds can be used at the end of the period to cover foreign currency outflows. When there are not offsetting currency outflows, the effective yield from investing in a foreign currency is more favorable (higher) when its interest rate is high and when the currency appreciates over the investment period.

This self-exam allows you to test your understanding of some of the key concepts covered in the managerial chapters. This is a good opportunity to assess your understanding of the managerial concepts. This final self-exam does not replace all the end-of-chapter self-tests, nor does it cover all the concepts. It is simply intended to let you test yourself on a general overview of key concepts. Try to simulate taking an exam by answering all questions without using your book and your notes. The answers to this exam are provided just after the exam questions. If you have any wrong answers, you should reread the related material and then redo any exam questions that you answered incorrectly.

This exam may not necessarily match the level of rigor in your course. Your instructor may offer you specific information about how this final self-exam relates to the coverage and rigor of the final exam in your course.

Final Self-Exam

1. New Hampshire Co. expects that monthly capital flows between the United States and Japan will be the major factor that affects the monthly exchange rate movements of the Japanese yen in the future, as money will flow to whichever country has the higher nominal interest rate. At the beginning of each month, New Hampshire Co. will use either the spot rate or the forward rate to forecast the future spot rate that will exist at the end of the month. Will the spot rate result in smaller, larger, or the same mean absolute forecast error as the forward rate when forecasting the future spot rate of the yen on a monthly basis? Explain.

2. California Co. will need 1 million Polish zloty in two years to purchase imports. Assume interest rate parity holds. Assume that the spot rate of the Polish zloty is $.30. The two-year annualized interest rate in the United States is 5 percent, and the two-year annualized interest rate in Poland is 11 percent. If California Co. uses a forward contract to hedge its payables, how many dollars will it need in two years?

3. Minnesota Co. uses regression analysis to assess its economic exposure to fluctuations in the Canadian dollar. The dependent variable in the regressions is the monthly percentage change in the company's stock price, and the independent variable is the monthly percentage change in the Canadian dollar. The analysis estimated the intercept to be zero and the coefficient of the monthly percentage change in the Canadian dollar to be −0.6. Assume the interest rate in Canada is consistently higher than the interest rate in the United States. Assume that interest rate parity exists. You use the forward rate to forecast future exchange rates of the Canadian dollar. Do you think Minnesota's stock price will be (a) favorably affected, (b) adversely affected, or (c) not affected by the expected movement in the Canadian dollar? Explain the logic behind your answer.

4. Iowa Co. has most of its business in the United States, except that it exports to Portugal. Its exports were invoiced in euros (Portugal's currency) last year. It has no other economic exposure to exchange rate risk. Its main competition when selling to Portugal's customers is a company in Portugal that sells similar products, denominated in euros. Starting today, Iowa Co. plans to adjust its pricing strategy to invoice its exports in U.S. dollars instead of euros. Based on the new strategy, will the company be exposed to exchange rate risk in the future? Briefly explain.

5. Maine Co. has a facility that produces basic clothing in Indonesia (where labor costs are very low), and the clothes produced there are sold in the United States. Its facility is subject to a tax in Indonesia because it is not owned by local citizens. This tax increases its cost of production by 20 percent, but its cost is still 40 percent less than what it would be if it produced the clothing in the United States (because of Indonesia's low cost of labor). Maine wants to achieve geographical diversification and decides to sell its clothing in Indonesia. Its competition would be from several existing local firms in Indonesia. Briefly explain whether you think Maine's strategy for direct foreign investment is feasible.

6. Assume that interest rate parity exists and will continue to exist in the future. The U.S. and Mexican interest rates are the same regardless of the maturity of the interest rate, and they will continue to be the same in the future. Tucson Co. and Phoenix Co. will each receive 1 million Mexican pesos in one year and will receive 1 million Mexican pesos in two years. Today, Tucson uses a one-year forward contract to hedge its receivables that will arrive in one year. Today it also uses a two-year forward contract to hedge its receivables that will arrive in two years.

Phoenix uses a one-year forward contract to hedge the receivables that will arrive in one year. A year from today, Phoenix will use a one-year forward contract to hedge the receivables that will arrive two years from today. The Mexican peso is expected to consistently depreciate substantially over the next two years.

Will Tucson receive more, less, or the same amount of dollars as Phoenix? Explain.

7. Assume that Jarret Co. (a U.S. firm) expects to receive 1 million euros in one year. The existing spot rate of the euro is $1.20. The one-year forward rate of the euro is $1.21. Jarret expects the spot rate of the euro to be $1.22 in one year.

Assume that one-year put options on euros are available, with an exercise price of $1.23 and a premium of $.04 per unit. Assume the following money market rates:

	UNITED STATES	EUROZONE
Deposit rate	8%	5%
Borrowing rate	9%	6%

a. Determine the dollar cash flows to be received if Jarret uses a money market hedge. (Assume Jarret does not have any cash on hand.)

b. Determine the dollar cash flows to be received if Jarret uses a put option hedge.

8. a. Portland Co. is a U.S. firm with no foreign subsidiaries. In addition to much business in the United States, its exporting business results in annual cash inflows of 20 million euros. Briefly explain how Portland Co. is subject to translation exposure (if at all).

b. Topeka Co. is a U.S. firm with no exports or imports. It has a subsidiary in Germany that typically generates earnings of 10 million euros each year, and none of the earnings are remitted to the United States. Briefly explain how Topeka Co. is subject to translation exposure (if at all).

9. Lexington Co. is a U.S. firm. It has a subsidiary in India that produces computer chips and sells them to European countries. The chips are invoiced in dollars. The subsidiary pays wages, rent, and other operating costs in India's currency (rupee). Every month, the subsidiary remits a large amount of earnings to the U.S. parent. This is the only international business that Lexington Co. has. The subsidiary wants to borrow funds to expand its facilities, and it can borrow dollars at 9 percent annually or borrow rupee at 9 percent annually. Which currency should the parent tell the subsidiary to borrow if the parent's main goal is to minimize exchange rate risk? Explain.

10. Illinois Co. (of the United States) and Franco Co. (based in France) are separately considering the acquisition of Podansk Co. (of Poland). Illinois Co. and Franco Co. have similar estimates of cash flows (in the Polish currency, the zloty) to be generated by Podansk in the future. The U.S. long-term risk-free interest rate is presently 8 percent, while the long-term risk-free rate of the euro is presently 3 percent. Illinois Co. and Franco Co. expect that the return of the U.S. stock market will be much better than the return of the French market. Illinois Co. has about the same amount of risk as a typical firm in the United States. Franco Co. has about the same amount of risk as a typical firm in France. The zloty is expected to depreciate against the euro by 1.2 percent per year and against the dollar by 1.4 percent per year. Which firm will likely have a higher valuation of the target Podansk? Explain.

11. A year ago, the spot exchange rate of the euro was $1.20. At that time, Talen Co. (a U.S. firm) invested $4 million to establish a project in the Netherlands. It expected that this project would generate cash flows of 3 million euros at the end of the first and second years.

Talen Co. always uses the spot rate as its forecast of future exchange rates. It uses a required rate of return of 20 percent on international projects.

Because conditions in the Netherlands are weaker than expected, the cash flows in the first year of the project were 2 million euros, and Talen now believes the expected cash flows for next year will be 1 million euros. A company offers to buy the project from Talen today for $1.25 million. Assume no tax effects. Today, the spot rate of the euro is $1.30. Should Talen accept the offer? Show your work.

12. Everhart, Inc., is a U.S. firm with no international business. It issues debt in the United States at an interest rate of 10 percent per year. The risk-free rate in the United States is 8 percent. The stock market return in the United States is expected to be 14 percent annually. Everhart's beta is 1.2. Its target capital structure is 30 percent debt and 70 percent equity. It is subject to a 25 percent corporate tax rate. Everhart plans a project in the Philippines in which it would receive net cash flows in Philippine pesos on an annual basis. The risk of the project would be similar to the risk of its other businesses. The existing risk-free rate in the Philippines is 21 percent, and the stock market return there is expected to be 28 percent annually. Everhart plans to finance this project with either its existing equity or by borrowing Philippine pesos.

    a. Estimate the cost to Everhart if it uses dollar-denominated equity. Show your work.

    b. Assume that Everhart believes that the Philippine peso will appreciate substantially each year against the dollar. Do you think it should finance this project with its dollar-denominated debt or by borrowing Philippine pesos? Explain.

    c. Assume that Everhart receives an offer from a Philippine investor who is willing to provide equity financing in Philippine pesos. Do you think this form of financing would be preferable to Everhart than financing with debt denominated in Philippine pesos? Explain.

13. Assume that a euro is equal to $1.00 today. A U.S. firm could engage in a parallel loan today in which it borrows 1 million euros from a firm in Belgium and provides a $1 million loan to the Belgian firm. The loans will be repaid in one year with interest.

Which of the following U.S. firms could most effectively use this parallel loan in order to reduce its exposure to exchange rate risk? (Assume that these U.S. firms have no other international business than what is described here.) Explain.

Sacramento Co. will receive a payment of 1 million euros from a French company in one year.

Stanislaus Co. needs to make a payment of 1 million euros to a German supplier in one year.

Los Angele Co. will receive 1 million euros from the Netherlands government in one year. It just engaged in a forward contract in which it sold 1 million euros one year forward.

San Mateo Co. will receive a payment of 1 million euros today and will owe a supplier 1 million euros in one year.

San Francisco Co. will make a payment of 1 million euros to a firm in Spain today and will receive $1 million from a firm in Spain for some consulting work in one year.

14. Assume the following direct exchange rate of the Swiss franc and Argentine peso at the beginning of each of the last 7 years.

BEGINNING OF YEAR	SWISS FRANC (SF)	ARGENTINE PESO (AP)
1	$.60	$.35
2	$.64	$.36
3	$.60	$.38
4	$.66	$.40
5	$.68	$.39
6	$.72	$.37
7	$.76	$.36

a. Suppose you forecast that the Swiss franc will appreciate by 3 percent over the next year, but you realize that there is much uncertainty surrounding your forecast. Use the value-at-risk method to estimate (based on a 95 percent confidence level) the maximum level of depreciation in the Swiss franc over the next year, based on the data you were provided.

b. Assume that you forecast that the Argentine peso will depreciate by 2 percent over the next year but realize there is much uncertainty surrounding your forecast. Use the value-at-risk method to estimate (based on a 95 percent confidence level) the maximum level of depreciation in the Argentine peso over the next year, based on the data you were provided.

15. Brooks Co. (a U.S. firm) considers a project in which it will have computer software developed. It would sell the software to Razon Co., an Australian company, and would receive payment of 10 million Australian dollars (A$) at the end of one year. To obtain the software, Brooks would have to pay a local software producer $4 million today.

Brooks Co. might also receive an order for the same software from Zug Co. in Australia. It would receive A$4 million at the end of this year if it receives this order, and it would not incur any additional costs because it is the same software that would be created for Razon Co.

The spot rate of the Australian dollar is $.50, and the spot rate is expected to depreciate by 8 percent over the next year. The one-year forward rate of the Australian dollar is $.47.

If Brooks decides to pursue this project (have the software developed), it would hedge the expected receivables due to the order from Razon Co. with a one-year forward contract, but it would not hedge the order from Zug Co. Brooks would require a 24 percent rate of return in order to accept the project.

   a. Determine the net present value of this project under the conditions that Brooks receives the order from Zug and from Razon and that Brooks receives payments from these orders in one year.

   b. Brooks recognizes there are some country risk conditions that could cause Razon Co. to go bankrupt. Determine the net present value of this project under the conditions that Brooks receives both orders but that Razon goes bankrupt and defaults on its payment to Brooks.

16. Austin Co. needs to borrow $10 million for the next year to support its U.S. operations. It can borrow U.S. dollars at 7 percent or Japanese yen at 1 percent. It has no other cash flows in Japanese yen. Assume that interest rate parity holds, so the one-year forward rate of the yen exhibits a premium in this case. Austin expects that the spot rate of the yen will appreciate but not as much as suggested by the one-year forward rate of the yen.

   a. Should Austin consider financing with yen and simultaneously purchasing yen one year forward to cover its position? Explain.

   b. If Austin finances with yen without covering this position, is the effective financing rate expected to be above, below, or equal to the Japanese interest rate of 1 percent? Is the effective financing rate expected to be above, below, or equal to the U.S. interest rate of 7 percent?

   c. Explain the implications if Austin finances with yen without covering its position and the future spot rate of the yen in one year turns out to be higher than today's one-year forward rate on the yen.

17. Provo Co. has $15 million that it will not need until one year from now. It can invest the funds in U.S. dollar–denominated securities and earn 6 percent or in New Zealand dollars (NZ$) at 11 percent. It has no other cash flows in New Zealand dollars. Assume that interest rate parity holds, so the one-year forward rate of the NZ$ exhibits a discount in this case. Provo expects that the spot rate of the NZ$ will depreciate but not as much as suggested by the one-year forward rate of the NZ$.

   a. Should Provo consider investing in NZ$ and simultaneously selling NZ$ 1 year forward to cover its position? Explain.

   b. If Provo invests in NZ$ without covering this position, is the effective yield expected to be above, below, or equal to the U.S. interest rate of 6 percent? Is the effective yield expected to be above, below, or equal to the New Zealand interest rate of 11 percent?

   c. Explain the implications if Provo invests in NZ$ without covering its position and the future spot rate of the NZ$ in one year turns out to be lower than today's one-year forward rate on the NZ$.

Answers to Final Self-Exam

1. The accuracy from forecasting with the spot rate will be better. The forward rate is higher than the spot rate (it has a premium) when the interest rate is lower. So, if the forward rate is used as a forecast, it would suggest that a currency with the lower interest rate will appreciate (in accordance with the international Fisher effect). However, because money is assumed to flow where interest rates are higher, this implies that the spot rate will rise when a currency has a relatively high interest rate. This relationship is in contrast to the IFE. Thus a forward rate will suggest depreciation of the currencies that should appreciate (and vice versa) based on the information in the question. The spot rate as a forecast reflects a forecast of no change in the exchange rate. The forecast of no change in a currency value (when the spot rate is used as the forecast) is better than a forecast of depreciation for a currency that appreciates. The spot rate forecast results in a smaller mean absolute forecast error.

2. The two-year forward premium is $1.1025/1.2321 - 1 = -.10518$. The two-year forward rate is $\$.30 \times (1 - .10518) = \$.26844$. The amount of dollars needed is $\$.26844 \times 1,000,000$ zloty $= \$268,440$.

3. Minnesota's stock price will be favorably affected. When the Canadian interest rate is higher, the forward rate of the Canadian dollar will exhibit a discount, which implies expected depreciation of the C$ if the forward rate is used to predict the future spot rate. The negative coefficient in the regression model suggests that the firm's stock price will be inversely related to the forecast. Thus the expected depreciation of the C$ will result in a higher stock price.

4. Iowa will still be subject to economic exposure because Portugal's demand for its products would decline if the euro weakens against the dollar. Thus Iowa's cash flows are still affected by exchange rate movements.

5. Maine Co. does not have an advantage over the other producers in Indonesia because the competitors also capitalize on cheap land and labor.

6. Tucson will receive more cash flows. The one-year and two-year forward rates today are equal to today's spot rate. Thus it hedges receivables at the same exchange rate as today's spot rate. Phoenix also hedges the receivables one year from now at that same exchange rate. But one year from now, it will hedge the receivables in the following year. In one year, the spot rate will be lower, so the one-year forward rate at that time will be lower than today's forward rate. Thus the receivables in two years will convert to a smaller amount of dollars for Phoenix than for Tucson.

7. **a.** Money market hedge:
Borrow euros:

$$\frac{1,000,000}{1.06} = 943,396 \text{ euros to be borrowed}$$

Convert the euros to dollars:

$$943,396 \text{ euros} \times \$1.20 = \$1,132,075$$

Invest the dollars:

$$\$1,132,075 \times 1.08 = \$1,222,641$$

b. Put option: Pay premium of

$$\$.04 \times 1,000,000 = \$40,000$$

If the spot rate in one year is $1.22 as expected, then the put option would be exercised at the strike price of $1.23. The cash flows would then be

$$1,000,000 \times (1.23 - \$.04 \text{ premium}) = \$1,190,000$$

Thus the money market hedge would be most appropriate.

8. **a.** Portland Co. is not subject to translation exposure because it has no foreign subsidiaries.

b. Topeka's consolidated earnings will increase if the euro appreciates against the dollar over the reporting period.

9. The subsidiary should borrow dollars because it already has a new cash outflow position in rupee so borrowing rupee would increase its exposure.

10. Franco Co. will offer a higher bid because its existing valuation of Podansk should be higher (because its risk-free rate is much lower).

11. As of today, the NPV from selling the project is
Proceeds received from selling the project − Present value of the forgone cash flows.
Proceeds = $1.25 million.
PV of forgone cash flows = (1,000,000 × $1.30)/1.2 = $1,083,333.
The NPV from selling the project is $1,250,000 − $1,083,333 = $166,667. Therefore, selling the project is feasible.

12. a. Based on the CAPM, Everhart's cost of equity = 8% + 1.2(14% − 8%) = 15.2%.
    b. Philippine debt has a high interest rate. Also, the peso will appreciate so the debt is even more expensive. Everhart should finance with dollar-denominated debt.
    c. Philippine debt is cheaper than Philippine equity. The Philippine investor would require a higher return than if Everhart uses debt. Also, there is no tax advantage if Everhart accepted an equity investment.

13. Sacramento could benefit from the parallel loan because its receivables in one year could be used to pay off the loan principal in euros.

14. a. The standard deviation of the annual movements in the Swiss franc is .0557, or 5.57 percent. It is necessary to focus on the volatility of the movements, not the actual values.
    The maximum level of annual depreciation of the Swiss franc is:

$$3\% - (1.65 \times .0557) = -.0619 \text{ or } -6.19\%$$

    b. The standard deviation of the annual movements in the Argentine peso is .0458, or 4.58 percent.
    The maximum level of annual depreciation of the Argentine peso is:

$$-2\% - (1.65 \times .0458) = -.09557 \text{ or } -9.557\%$$

15. a. Order from Razon:

$$\$.47 \times A\$10 \text{ million} = \$4,700,000$$

Order from Zug:

$$\$.46 \times A\$4 \text{ million} = \$1,840,000$$
$$\text{Present value} = \frac{\$6,540,000}{1.24} = \$5,274,193$$
$$\text{NPV} = \$5,274,193 - \$4,000,000 = \$1,274,193$$

    b. Order from Zug is $1,840,000 as just calculated.
    The expected cost of offsetting the hedged cash flows is $100,000 as explained next.
    Brooks sold A$1 million forward. It will purchase them in the spot market and then will fulfill its forward contract. The expected future spot rate in one year is $.46, so it would be expected to pay $.46 and sell A$ at the forward rate of $.47 for a $.01 profit per unit. For A$10 million, the profit is $.01 × 10 million = $100,000.

$$\text{Cash flows in 1 year} = \$1,840,000 + \$100,000 = \$1,940,000$$

$$\text{Present value} = \frac{\$1,940,000}{1.24} = \$1,564,516$$

$$\text{NPV} = \$1,564,516 - \$4,000,000 = -\$2,435,484$$

(An alternative method would be to apply the $.47 to Zug for A$4 million, which would leave a net of A$6 million to fulfill on the forward contract. The answer will be the same for either method.)

16. **a.** Austin should not consider financing with yen and simultaneously purchasing yen one year forward because the effective financing rate would be 7 percent, the same as the financing rate in the United States.

   b. If Austin finances with yen without covering this position, then its effective financing rate is expected to exceed the interest rate on the yen because of the expected appreciation of the yen over the financing period. However, the effective financing rate is not expected to be as high as the interest rate on the dollar.

   c. If the yen's spot rate in one year is higher than today's forward rate, then the effective financing rate will be higher than the U.S. interest rate of 7 percent.

17. **a.** Provo should not consider investing in NZ$ and simultaneously selling NZ$ one year forward because the effective yield would be 6 percent, the same as the yield in the United States.

   b. If Provo invests in NZ$, then its yield is expected to exceed the U.S. interest rate but be less than the NZ$ interest rate.

   c. If the NZ$ spot rate in one year is lower than today's forward rate, the effective yield will be lower than the U.S. interest rate of 6 percent.

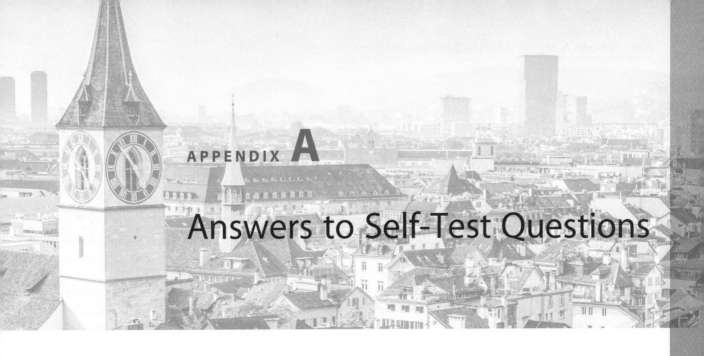

APPENDIX A

Answers to Self-Test Questions

Chapter 1

1. Multinational corporations can capitalize on comparative advantages (such as a technology or cost of labor) that they have relative to firms in other countries, which allows them to penetrate those other countries' markets. Given a world of imperfect markets, comparative advantages across countries are not freely transferable. Therefore, MNCs may be able to capitalize on comparative advantages. Many MNCs initially penetrate markets by exporting but ultimately establish a subsidiary in foreign markets and attempt to differentiate their products as other firms enter those markets (product cycle theory).

2. Weak economic conditions or unstable political conditions in a foreign country can reduce cash flows received by the MNC, or they can result in a higher required rate of return for the MNC. Either of these effects results in a lower valuation of the MNC.

3. First, there is the risk of poor economic conditions in the foreign country. Second, there is country risk, which reflects the risk of changing government or public attitudes toward the MNC. Third, there is exchange rate risk, which can affect the performance of the MNC in the foreign country.

Chapter 2

1. Each of the economic factors is described, holding other factors constant.

   a. *Inflation.* A relatively high U.S. inflation rate relative to other countries can make U.S. goods less attractive to U.S. and non-U.S. consumers, which results in fewer U.S. exports, more U.S. imports, and a lower (or more negative) current account balance. A relatively low U.S. inflation rate would have the opposite effect.

   b. *National income.* A relatively high increase in the U.S. national income (compared with other countries) tends to cause a large increase in demand for imports and can cause a lower (or more negative) current account balance. A relatively low increase in the U.S. national income would have the opposite effect.

   c. *Exchange rates.* A weaker dollar tends to make U.S. products cheaper to non-U.S. firms and makes non-U.S. products expensive to U.S. firms. Thus U.S. exports are expected to increase while U.S. imports are expected to decrease. However, some conditions can prevent these effects from occurring, as explained in the chapter. Normally, a stronger dollar causes U.S. exports to decrease and U.S. imports to increase because it makes U.S. goods more expensive to non-U.S. firms and makes non-U.S. goods less expensive to U.S. firms.

d. *Government restrictions.* When the U.S. government imposes new barriers on imports, U.S. imports decline, causing the U.S. balance of trade to increase (or be less negative). When non-U.S. governments impose new barriers on imports from the United States, the U.S. balance of trade may decrease (or be more negative). When governments remove trade barriers, the opposite effects are expected.

2. When the United States imposes tariffs on imported goods, foreign countries may retaliate by imposing tariffs on goods exported by the United States. Thus there is a decline in U.S. exports that may offset any decline in U.S. imports.

3. A global recession might cause governments to impose trade restrictions so that they can protect local firms from intense competition and prevent additional layoffs within the country. However, if other countries impose more barriers in retaliation, this strategy could backfire.

Chapter 3

1. ($.80 − $.784)/$.80 = .02, or 2 percent.

2. ($.19 − $.188)/$.19 = .0105, or 1.05 percent.

3. Multinational corporations use the spot foreign exchange market to exchange currencies for immediate delivery. They use the forward foreign exchange market and the currency futures market to lock in the exchange rate at which currencies will be exchanged at a future time. They use the currency options market when they wish to lock in the maximum (minimum) amount to be paid (received) in a future currency transaction but maintain flexibility in the event of favorable exchange rate movements.

Multinational corporations use the international money markets to engage in short-term investing or financing and use the Eurocredit market to engage in medium-term financing. They can obtain long-term financing by issuing bonds in the Eurobond market or by issuing stock in the international markets.

Chapter 4

1. Economic factors affect the yen's value as follows.

a. If U.S. inflation is higher than Japanese inflation, then the U.S. demand for Japanese goods may increase (to avoid the higher U.S. prices) and the Japanese demand for U.S. goods may decrease (to avoid the higher U.S. prices). Consequently, there is upward pressure on the value of the yen.

b. If U.S. interest rates increase and exceed Japanese interest rates, then the U.S. demand for Japanese interest-bearing securities may decline (because U.S. interest-bearing securities are more attractive) while the Japanese demand for U.S. interest-bearing securities may rise. Both forces place downward pressure on the yen's value.

c. If U.S. national income increases more than Japanese national income, then the U.S. demand for Japanese goods may increase more than the Japanese demand for U.S. goods. Assuming that the change in national income levels does not affect exchange rates indirectly through effects on relative interest rates, the forces should place upward pressure on the yen's value.

d. If government controls reduce the U.S. demand for Japanese goods, they place downward pressure on the yen's value. If the controls reduce the Japanese demand for U.S. goods, they place upward pressure on the yen's value.

The opposite scenarios of those described here would cause the expected pressure to be in the opposite direction.

2. The U.S. capital flows with Country A may be larger than U.S. capital flows with Country B. Therefore, the change in the interest rate differential has a larger effect on the capital flows with Country A, causing the exchange rate to change. If the capital flows with Country B are nonexistent, then interest rate changes do not change the capital flows and so do not change the demand and supply conditions in the foreign exchange market.

3. Smart Banking Corp. should not pursue the strategy because a loss would result, as shown here.

    a. Borrow $5 million.

    b. Convert $5 million to C$5,263,158 (based on the spot exchange rate of $.95 per C$).

    c. Invest the C$ at 9 percent annualized, which represents a return of .15 percent over 6 days, so the C$ received after six days is C$5,271,053 (computed as C$5,263,158 × [1 + .0015]).

    d. Convert the C$ received back to U.S. dollars after six days: C$5,271,053 = $4,954,789 (based on anticipated exchange rate of $.94 per C$ after six days).

    e. The interest rate owed on the U.S. dollar loan is .10 percent over the six-day period. Thus the amount owed as a result of the loan is $5,005,000 [computed as $5,000,000 × (1 + .001)].

    f. The strategy is expected to cause a gain of $4,954,789 − $5,005,000 = −$50,211.

Chapter 5

1. The net profit to the speculator is −$.01 per unit.

The net profit to the speculator for one contract is −$500 (computed as −$.01 × 50,000 units).

The spot rate would need to be $.66 for the speculator to break even.

The net profit to the seller of the call option is $.01 per unit.

2. The speculator should exercise the option.

The net profit to the speculator is $.04 per unit.

The net profit to the seller of the put option is −$.04 per unit.

3. The premium paid is higher for options with longer expiration dates (other things being equal). Firms may prefer not to pay such high premiums.

4. a. The expected profit for Jarrod is $.02 per unit.

    b. The expected profit for Laurie is $.03 per unit, which represents the premium she received when selling the put options.

5. a. Your loss is −$.04 per unit.

    b. Your profit is the premium of $.02 per unit that you received from selling the call options.

Chapter 6

1. Market forces cause the demand and supply of yen in the foreign exchange market to change, which causes a change in the equilibrium exchange rate. The central banks could intervene to affect the demand or supply conditions in the foreign exchange market, but they would not always be able to offset the changing market forces. For example, if there were a large increase in the U.S. demand for yen and no increase in the supply of yen for sale, then the central banks would have to increase the supply of yen in the foreign exchange market to offset the increased demand.

2. The Fed could use direct intervention by selling some of its dollar reserves in exchange for pesos in the foreign exchange market. It could also use indirect intervention by attempting to reduce U.S. interest rates through monetary policy. Specifically, it could increase the U.S. money supply, which places downward pressure on U.S. interest rates (assuming that inflationary expectations do not change). The lower U.S. interest rates should discourage foreign investment in the United States and encourage increased investment by U.S. investors in foreign securities. Both forces tend to weaken the dollar's value.

3. A weaker dollar tends to increase the demand for U.S. goods because the price paid for a specified amount in dollars by non-U.S. firms is reduced. In addition, the U.S. demand for foreign goods is reduced because it takes more dollars to obtain a specified amount in foreign currency once the dollar weakens. Both forces tend to stimulate the U.S. economy and therefore improve productivity and reduce unemployment in the United States.

4. a. If the euro depreciates against the dollar, it must also depreciate against the slu (because the value of the slu is tied to the dollar). Therefore, Sluban's exports will become more expensive to importers in the eurozone, and the volume of Sluban's exports to the eurozone should decline.

b. If the euro depreciates against the dollar, U.S. importers may prefer to purchase products from the eurozone rather than Sluban, so Sluban's exports to the U.S. should decrease.

Chapter 7

1. No. The cross exchange rate between the pound and the C$ is appropriate, based on the other exchange rates. There is no discrepancy to capitalize on.

2. No. Covered interest arbitrage involves the exchange of dollars for pounds. Assuming that the investors begin with $1 million (the starting amount will not affect the final conclusion), the dollars would be converted to pounds as shown here:

$$\$1 \text{ million}/\$1.60 \text{ per } £ = £625,000$$

The British investment would accumulate interest over the 180-day period, resulting in

$$£625,000 \times 1.04 = £650,000$$

After 180 days, the pounds would be converted to dollars:

$$£650,000 \times \$1.56 \text{ per pound} = \$1,014,000$$

This amount reflects a return of 1.4 percent above the amount with which U.S. investors initially started. The investors could simply invest the funds in the United States at 3 percent. Thus U.S. investors would earn less using the covered interest arbitrage strategy than investing in the United States.

3. No. The forward rate discount on the pound does not perfectly offset the interest rate differential. In fact, the discount is 2.5 percent, which is larger than the interest rate differential. Hence U.S. investors do worse when attempting covered interest arbitrage than when investing their funds in the United States because the interest rate advantage on the British investment is more than offset by the forward discount.

Further clarification may be helpful here. Whereas U.S. investors could not benefit from covered interest arbitrage, British investors could capitalize on covered interest arbitrage. Although British investors would earn 1 percent less interest on the U.S. investment, they would be purchasing pounds forward at a discount of 2.5 percent at the end of the investment period. If interest rate parity does not hold, then investors from only one of the two countries of concern could benefit from using covered interest arbitrage.

4. If there is a discrepancy in the pricing of a currency, one may capitalize on it by using the various forms of arbitrage described in the chapter. As arbitrage occurs, the exchange rates will be pushed toward their appropriate levels because arbitrageurs will buy an underpriced currency in the foreign exchange market (an increase in demand for currency places upward pressure on its value) and will sell an overpriced currency in the foreign exchange market (an increase in the supply of currency for sale places downward pressure on its value).

5. The one-year forward discount on pounds would become more pronounced (by about 1 percentage point more than before) because the spread between the British interest rates and U.S. interest rates would increase.

Chapter 8

1. If Japanese prices rise because of inflation in that country, then the value of the yen should decline. Thus even though the importer might need to pay more yen, it would benefit from a weaker yen value (it would pay fewer dollars for a given amount in yen). Thus there could be an offsetting effect if PPP holds.

2. Purchasing power parity does not necessarily hold. In our example, Japanese inflation could rise (causing the importer to pay more yen), and yet the Japanese yen would not necessarily depreciate by an offsetting amount, or at all. Therefore, the dollar amount to be paid for Japanese supplies could increase over time.

3. High inflation will cause a balance-of-trade adjustment, whereby the United States will reduce its purchases of goods in these countries, while the demand for U.S. goods by these countries should increase (according to PPP). Consequently, there will be downward pressure on the values of these currencies.

4.
$$e_f = I_h - I_f$$
$$= 3\% - 4\%$$
$$= -.01, \text{ or } -1\%$$
$$S_{t+1} = S(1 + e_f)$$
$$= \$.85[1 + (-.01)]$$
$$= \$.8415$$

5.
$$e_f = \frac{1 + i_h}{1 + i_f} - 1$$
$$= \frac{1 + .06}{1 + .11} - 1$$
$$\cong -.045, \text{ or } -4.5\%$$
$$S_{t+1} = S(1 + e_f)$$
$$= \$.90[1 + (-.045)]$$
$$= \$.8595$$

6. According to the IFE, the increase in interest rates by 5 percentage points reflects an increase in expected inflation by 5 percentage points.

If the inflation adjustment occurs, then the balance of trade should be affected because Australian demand for U.S. goods rises while the U.S. demand for Australian goods declines. Thus the Australian dollar should weaken.

If U.S. investors believed in the IFE, they would not attempt to capitalize on higher Australian interest rates because they would expect the Australian dollar to depreciate over time.

Chapter 9

1. U.S. four-year interest rate $= (1 + .07)^4 = 131.08$ percent, or 1.3108. Mexican four-year interest rate $= (1 + .20)^4 = 207.36$ percent, or 2.0736.

$$p = \frac{1 + i_b}{1 + i_f} - 1 = \frac{1.3108}{2.0736} - 1$$
$$= -.3679, \text{ or } -36.79\%$$

2. Canadian dollar

$$\frac{|\$.80 - \$.82|}{\$.82} = 2.44\%$$

Japanese yen

$$\frac{|\$0.12 - \$.011|}{\$.011} = 9.09\%$$

The forecast error was larger for the Japanese yen.

3. The forward rate of the peso would have overestimated the future spot rate because the spot rate would have declined by the end of each month.

4. Semistrong-form efficiency would be refuted because the currency values do not adjust immediately to useful public information.

5. The peso would be expected to depreciate because its forward rate would exhibit a discount (be less than the spot rate). Thus the forecast derived from the forward rate is less than the spot rate, which implies anticipated depreciation of the peso.

6. As the chapter suggests, forecasts of currencies are subject to a high degree of error. Thus if a project's success is very sensitive to the future value of the bolivar, there is much uncertainty. This project could easily backfire because the future value of the bolivar is very uncertain.

Chapter 10

1. Managers have more information about the firm's exposure to exchange rate risk than do shareholders and may be able to hedge it more easily than shareholders could. Shareholders may prefer that the managers hedge for them. Also, cash flows may be stabilized as a result of hedging, which can reduce the firm's cost of financing.

2. The Canadian supplies would have less exposure to exchange rate risk because the Canadian dollar is less volatile than the Mexican peso.

3. The Mexican source would be preferable because the firm could use peso inflows to make payments for material that is imported.

4. No. If exports are priced in dollars, then the dollar cash flows received from exporting will depend on Mexico's demand, which will be affected by the peso's value. If the peso depreciates, Mexican demand for the exports would likely decrease.

5. The earnings generated by the European subsidiaries will be translated to a smaller amount in dollar earnings if the dollar strengthens. Thus the consolidated earnings of the U.S.-based MNCs will be reduced.

Chapter 11

1.

$$\text{Amount of A\$ to be invested today} = \text{A\$3,000,000}/(1 + .12)$$
$$= \text{A\$2,678,571}$$
$$\text{Amount of U.S.\$ to be borrowed to convert to A\$} = \text{A\$2,678,571} \times \text{\$.85}$$
$$= \text{\$2,276,785}$$
$$\text{Amount of U.S.\$ needed in one year to pay off loan} = \text{\$2,276,785} \times (1 + .07)$$
$$= \text{\$2,436,160}$$

2. The forward hedge would be more appropriate. Given a forward rate of $.81, Montclair would need $2,430,000 in one year (computed as A$3,000,000 × $.81) when using a forward hedge.

3. Montclair could purchase a currency call option in Australian dollars. The option could hedge against the possible appreciation of the Australian dollar. If the Australian dollar depreciates, Montclair could let the option expire and purchase the Australian dollars at the spot rate at the time it needs to send payment. A disadvantage of the currency call option is that a premium must be paid for it. Thus if Montclair expects the Australian dollar to appreciate over the year, the money market hedge would probably be a better choice because the flexibility provided by the option would not be useful in this case.

4. Even though Sanibel Co. is insulated from the beginning of a month to the end of the month, the forward rate will become higher each month because the forward rate moves with the spot rate. Thus the firm will pay more dollars each month even though it is hedged during the month. Sanibel will be adversely affected by the consistent appreciation of the pound.

5. Sanibel Co. could engage in a series of forward contracts today to cover the payments in each successive month. In this way, it locks in the future payments today and does not have to agree to the higher forward rates that may exist in future months.

6. A put option on SF2 million would cost $60,000. If the spot rate of the SF reaches $.68 as expected, the put option would be exercised, which would yield $1,380,000 (computed as SF2,000,000 × $.69). Accounting for the premium costs of $60,000, the receivables amount would convert to $1,320,000. If Hopkins remains unhedged, it expects to receive $1,360,000 (computed as SF2,000,000 × $.68). Thus the unhedged strategy is preferable.

Chapter 12

1. Salem could attempt to purchase its chemicals from Canadian sources. Then, if the Canadian dollar depreciates, the reduction in dollar inflows resulting from its exports to Canada will be partially offset by a reduction in dollar outflows needed to pay for the Canadian imports. An alternative possibility for Salem is to finance its business with Canadian dollars, but this would probably be a less efficient solution.

2. A possible disadvantage is that Salem would forgo some of the benefits if the Canadian dollar appreciated over time.

3. The consolidated earnings of Coastal Corp. will be adversely affected if the pound depreciates because the British earnings will be translated into dollar earnings for the consolidated income statement at a lower exchange rate. Coastal could attempt to hedge its translation exposure by selling pounds forward. If the pound depreciates, the company will benefit from its forward position, which could help offset the translation effect.

4. This argument has no perfect solution. It appears that shareholders penalize the firm for poor earnings even when the reason for poor earnings is a weak euro that has adverse translation effects. It is possible that translation effects could be hedged to stabilize earnings, but Everhart may consider informing the shareholders that the major earnings changes have been due to translation effects and not to changes in consumer demand or other factors. Perhaps shareholders would not respond so strongly to earnings changes if they were well aware that the changes were primarily caused by translation effects.

5. Lincolnshire has no translation exposure because it has no foreign subsidiaries. Kalafa has translation exposure resulting from its subsidiary in Spain.

Chapter 13

1. Possible reasons include

- more demand for the product (depending on the product),
- better technology in Canada, and
- fewer restrictions (less political interference).

2. Possible reasons include

- more demand for the product (depending on the product),
- greater probability of earning superior profits (because many goods have not been marketed in Mexico in the past),
- cheaper factors of production (such as land and labor), and
- possible exploitation of monopolistic advantages.

3. U.S. firms prefer to enter a country when the foreign country's currency is weak, so that they need fewer dollars to engage in DFI. U.S. firms normally would prefer that the foreign currency appreciate after they invest their dollars to develop the subsidiary. The executive's comment suggests that the euro is too strong, so DFI in in Europe would be too expensive.

4. It may be easier to engage in a joint venture with a Chinese firm, which is already well established in China, to circumvent barriers.

5. The government may attempt to stimulate the economy in this way.

Chapter 14

1. In addition to earnings generated in Jamaica, the NPV is based on some factors not controlled by the firm; these factors include the expected host government tax on profits, the withholding tax imposed by the host government, and the salvage value to be received when the project is terminated. Furthermore, exchange rate projections will affect the estimates of dollar cash flows received by the parent as earnings are remitted.

2. The most obvious effect is on the cash flows that will be generated by the sales distribution center in Ireland. These cash flow estimates will likely be revised downward (due to lower sales estimates). It is also possible that the estimated salvage value could be reduced. Exchange rate estimates could be revised as a result of revised economic conditions. Estimated tax rates imposed on the center by the Irish government could also be affected by the revised economic conditions.

3. New Orleans Exporting Co. must account for the cash flows that will be forgone as a result of the plant because some of the cash flows that used to be received by the parent through its exporting operation will be eliminated. The NPV estimate will be reduced after this factor is accounted for.

4. a. An increase in the risk will cause an increase in the required rate of return on the subsidiary, which results in a lower discounted value of the subsidiary's salvage value.

b. If the rupiah depreciates over time, the subsidiary's salvage value will be reduced because the proceeds will convert to fewer dollars.

5. The dollar cash flows of Wilmette Co. would be affected more because the periodic remitted earnings from Thailand to be converted to dollars would be larger. The dollar cash flows of Niles would not be affected so much because interest payments would be made on the Thai loans before earnings could be remitted to the United States. Thus a smaller amount in earnings would be remitted.

6. The demand for the product in the foreign country may be very uncertain, causing the total revenue to be uncertain. The exchange rates can be very uncertain, creating uncertainty about the dollar cash flows received by the U.S. parent. The salvage value may be very uncertain; this will have a larger effect if the lifetime of the project is short (for projects with a very long life, the discounted value of the salvage value is small anyway).

Chapter 15

1. If the government restricted foreign ownership of companies in the past, this may have protected all the local companies from the market for corporate control. Some of the local companies might be mismanaged (and therefore have the potential for improvement) but were protected by the government in the past. These companies might be attractive targets now.

2. Common restrictions include government regulations such as antitrust restrictions, environmental restrictions, and red tape.

3. The establishment of a new subsidiary allows an MNC to create the subsidiary it desires without assuming existing facilities or employees. However, the process of building a new subsidiary and hiring employees will normally take longer than the process of acquiring an existing foreign firm.

4. The divestiture is now more feasible because the dollar cash flows to be received by the U.S. parent are reduced as a result of the revised projections of the krona's value.

Chapter 16

1. First, consumers on the islands could develop a philosophy of purchasing homemade goods. Second, they could discontinue their purchases of exports by Key West Co. as a form of protest against specific U.S. government actions. Third, the host governments could impose severe restrictions on the subsidiary shops owned by Key West Co. (including the blockage of funds to be remitted to the U.S. parent).

2. First, the islands could experience poor economic conditions, which would cause lower income for some residents. Second, residents could be subject to higher inflation or higher interest rates, which would reduce the income that they could allocate to exports. Depreciation of the local currencies could also raise the local prices to be paid for goods exported from the United States. All these factors could reduce the demand for goods exported by Key West Co.

3. Financial risk is probably a bigger concern. The political risk factors are unlikely, given that the product is produced by Key West Co. and because there are no substitute products available in other countries. The financial risk factors deserve serious consideration.

4. This event has heightened the perceived country risk for any firms that have offices in populated areas (especially next to government or military offices). It has also heightened the risk for firms whose employees commonly travel to other countries and for firms that provide office services or travel services.

5. Rockford Co. could estimate the net present value (NPV) of the project under three scenarios: (1) include a special tax when estimating cash flows back to the parent (probability of scenario = 15%), (2) assume the project ends in two years and include a salvage value when estimating the NPV (probability of scenario = 15%), and (3) assume no Canadian government intervention (probability = 70%). This results in three estimates of NPV, one for each scenario. This method is less arbitrary than the one considered by Rockford's executives.

Chapter 17

1. Growth may have caused Goshen to require a large amount for financing that could not be completely provided by retained earnings. In addition, the interest rates may have been low in these foreign countries to make debt financing an attractive alternative. Finally, the use of foreign debt can reduce the exchange rate risk because the amount in periodic remitted earnings is reduced when interest payments are required on foreign debt.

2. If country risk has increased, Lynde can attempt to reduce its exposure to that risk by removing its equity investment from the subsidiary. When the subsidiary is financed with local funds, the local creditors have more to lose than the parent if the host government imposes any severe restrictions on the subsidiary.

3. Not necessarily. German and Japanese firms tend to have more support from other firms or from the government if they experience cash flow problems and can therefore afford to use a higher degree of financial leverage than firms from the same industry in the United States.

4. Local debt financing is favorable because it can reduce the MNC's exposure to country risk and exchange rate risk. However, the high interest rates will make the local debt very expensive. If the parent makes an equity investment in the subsidiary to avoid the high cost of local debt, it will be more exposed to country risk and exchange rate risk.

5. The answer to this question depends on whether or not you believe that unsystematic risk is relevant. If the CAPM is used as a framework for measuring risk, then the foreign project's risk is determined to be low because the systematic risk is low. That is, the risk is specific to the host country and is not related to U.S. market conditions. However, if the project's unsystematic risk is relevant, then the project is considered to have a high degree of risk. The project's cash flows are very uncertain even though the systematic risk is low.

Chapter 18

1. A firm may be able to obtain a lower coupon rate by issuing bonds denominated in a different currency. The firm converts the proceeds from issuing the bond to its local currency in order to finance local operations. However, there is exchange rate risk because the firm will need to make coupon payments (and the principal payment) in the currency denominating the bond. If that currency appreciates against the firm's local currency, then the financing costs could become larger than expected.

2. The risk is that the Swiss franc would appreciate against the pound over time because the British subsidiary will periodically convert some of its pound cash flows to francs to make the coupon payments.

The risk here is less than it would be if the proceeds were used to finance U.S. operations. The Swiss franc's movement against the dollar is much more volatile than the Swiss franc's movement against the pound. The Swiss franc and the pound have historically moved in tandem to some degree against the dollar, which means that there is a fairly stable exchange rate between the two currencies.

3. If these firms borrow U.S. dollars and convert them to finance local projects, then they will need to use their own currencies to obtain dollars and make coupon payments. These firms would be highly exposed to exchange rate risk.

4. Paxson Co. is exposed to exchange rate risk. If the yen appreciates, the number of dollars needed for conversion into yen will increase. To the extent that the yen strengthens, Paxson's cost of financing when financing with yen could be higher than when financing with dollars.

5. The nominal interest rate incorporates expected inflation (according to the international Fisher effect). Therefore, the high interest rates reflect high expected inflation. Cash flows can be enhanced by inflation because a given profit margin converts into larger profits as a result of inflation, even if costs increase at the same rate as revenues.

Chapter 19

1. The exporter may not trust the importer or may be concerned about the government imposing exchange controls that prevent payment to the exporter. Meanwhile, the importer may not trust that the exporter will ship the goods ordered and therefore may not pay until the goods are received. Commercial banks can help by providing guarantees to the exporter in case the importer does not pay.

2. In accounts receivable financing, the bank provides a loan to the exporter secured by the accounts receivable. If the importer fails to pay the exporter, the exporter is still responsible for repaying the bank. Factoring involves the sale of accounts receivable by the exporter to a so-called factor, in which the exporter is no longer responsible for the importer's payment.

3. The guarantee programs of the Export-Import Bank provide medium-term protection against the risk of nonpayment by the foreign buyer due to political risk.

Chapter 20

1. $r_f = (1 + i_f)(1 + e_f) - 1$

    If $e_f = -6\%$, $r_f = (1 + .09)[1 + (-.06)] - 1$
    $= .0246$, or 2.46%

    If $e_f = 3\%$, $r_f = (1 + .09)(1 + .03) - 1$
    $= .1227$, or 12.27%

2. $E[r_f] = 50\%(2.46\%) + 50\%(12.27\%)$
    $= 1.23\% + 6.135\%$
    $= 7.365\%$

3. $e_f = \dfrac{1 + r_f}{1 + i} - 1$
    $= \dfrac{1 + .08}{1 + .05} - 1$
    $= .0286$, or 2.86%

4. $E[e_f] = (\text{Forward rate} - \text{Spot rate})/\text{Spot rate}$
    $= (\$.60 - \$.62)/\$.62$
    $= -.0322$, or -3.22%

    $E[e_f] = (1 + i_f)[1 + E[e_f]] - 1$
    $= (1 + .09)[1 + (-.0322)] - 1$
    $= .0548$, or 5.48%

5. Because the movements in the two currencies against the dollar are highly correlated, both currencies could appreciate substantially against the dollar at the same time. Thus Cleveland's logic is flawed. The potential diversification effect is very limited.

Chapter 21

1. The subsidiary in Country Y should be more adversely affected because the blocked funds will not earn as much interest over time. In addition, the funds will likely be converted to dollars at an unfavorable exchange rate because the currency is expected to weaken over time.

2. $E[r] = (1 + i_f)[1 + E[e_f]] - 1$
    $= (1 + .14)(1 + .08) - 1$
    $= .2312$, or 23.12%

3. $E[e_f] = (\text{Forward rate} - \text{Spot rate})/\text{Spot rate}$
    $= (\$.19 - \$.20)/\$.20$
    $= -.05$, or -5%

    $E[r] = (1 + i_f)[1 + E[e_f]] - 1$
    $= (1 + .11)[1 + (-.05)] - 1$
    $= .0545$, or 5.45%

4. $e_f = \dfrac{1+r}{1+i_f} - 1$

$= \dfrac{1+.06}{1+.90} - 1$

$= -.4421,$ or -44.21%

If the bolivar depreciates by less than 44.21 percent against the dollar over the one-year period, then a one-year deposit in Venezuela will generate a higher effective yield than a one-year U.S. deposit.

5. Yes. Interest rate parity would discourage U.S. firms only from covering their investments in foreign deposits by using forward contracts. As long as the firms believe that the currency will not depreciate to offset the interest rate advantage, they may consider investing in countries with high interest rates.

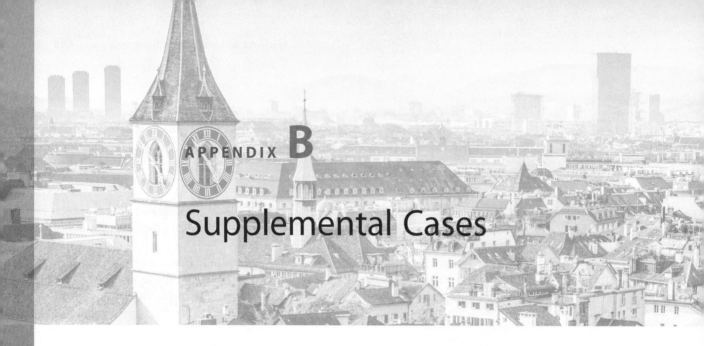

Supplemental Cases

Chapter 1 Ranger Supply Company

Motivation for International Business

Ranger Supply Company is a large manufacturer and distributor of office supplies. It is based in New York but sends supplies to firms throughout the United States. It markets its supplies on its website and through periodic mass mailings of catalogs to those firms. Its clients can make orders at the website or over the phone, and Ranger ships the supplies upon demand. Ranger has had very high production efficiency in the past. This is attributed partly to low employee turnover and high morale, as employees are guaranteed job security until retirement.

Ranger already holds a large proportion of the market share in distributing office supplies in the United States. Its main competition in the United States comes from one U.S. firm and one Canadian firm. A British firm has a small share of the U.S. market but is at a disadvantage because of its distance. The British firm's marketing and transportation costs in the U.S. market are relatively high.

Although Ranger's office supplies are similar to those of its competitors, it has been able to capture most of the U.S. market because its high efficiency enables it to charge low prices to retail stores. It expects a decline in the aggregate demand for office supplies in the United States in future years. However, it anticipates strong demand for office supplies in Canada and in Eastern Europe over the next several years. Ranger's executives have begun to consider exporting as a way to offset the possible decline in domestic demand for its products.

a. Ranger plans to attempt penetrating either the Canadian market or the Eastern European market through exporting. What factors deserve to be considered in deciding which market is more feasible?

b. One financial manager has been responsible for developing a contingency plan in case whichever market is chosen imposes trade barriers over time. This manager proposes that Ranger establish a subsidiary in the country of concern under such conditions. Is this a reasonable strategy? Are there any obvious reasons why this strategy could fail?

Chapter 2 Savanta Company

Assessing the Effects of Possible Trade Barriers

Savanta Company is based in the United States. Its sales of jewelry have consistently increased, primarily because the stones used in the production process are imported from the country of Ketraz at a very low cost. Savanta's major competitors are U.S. companies that do not import their stones.

The country of Ketraz has a free trade agreement with the United States. In addition, Savanta Company has an excellent business relationship with Ketraz, and even considered setting up a subsidiary in Ketraz that would produce the jewelry in Ketraz before shipping the jewelry to the United States.

Recently, the government of Ketraz has received some negative publicity for not enforcing its child labor laws.

a. Why might the negative news about the government of Ketraz adversely affect Savanta Company's business?

b. Assume that Savanta wishes to continue to rely on stones from Ketraz. Savanta Company cannot influence the government's enforcement of child labor laws. Offer a possible solution for Ketraz that could possibly allow it to rely on stones from Ketraz while ensuring that its business with Ketraz causes no violation of child labor laws in Ketraz.

c. Explain a possible disadvantage of your solution in answer b, in which it might stop one form of criticism but then be subject to another form of criticism.

Chapter 3 Gretz Tool Company

Using International Financial Markets

Gretz Tool Company is a large U.S.-based multinational corporation with subsidiaries in eight different countries. The company provided an initial cash infusion to establish each subsidiary. However, each subsidiary has had to finance its own growth since then. The parent and subsidiaries of Gretz typically use Citigroup (with branches in numerous countries) when possible to facilitate any flow of funds necessary.

a. Explain the various ways in which Citigroup could facilitate Gretz's flow of funds, and identify the type of financial market where that flow of funds occurs. For each type of financing transaction, specify whether Citigroup would serve as the creditor or would simply be facilitating the flow of funds to Gretz.

b. Recently, the British subsidiary called on Citigroup for a medium-term loan and was offered the following alternatives:

LOAN DENOMINATED IN	ANNUALIZED RATE
British pounds	13%
U.S. dollars	11%
Canadian dollars	10%
Japanese yen	8%

What characteristics do you think would help the British subsidiary determine which currency to borrow?

Chapter 4 Bruin Aircraft, Inc.

Factors Affecting Exchange Rates

Bruin Aircraft, Inc., is a designer and manufacturer of airplane parts. Its production plant is based in California. About one-third of its sales are exports to the United Kingdom. Though Bruin invoices its exports in dollars, the demand for its exports is highly sensitive to the value of the British pound. In order to maintain its parts inventory at a proper level, it must forecast the total demand for its parts, which is somewhat dependent on the forecasted value of the pound. Bruin's treasurer has been assigned the task of forecasting the value of the pound (against the dollar) for each of the next five years. He plans to ask the firm's chief economist for forecasts on all the relevant factors that could affect the pound's future exchange rate. The treasurer has organized his worksheet by separating demand-related factors from supply-related factors, as illustrated by the headings below:

Factors that can affect the value of the pound	Check (✓) here if the factor influences the U.S. demand for pounds	Check (✓) here if the factor influences the supply of pounds for sale

Help the treasurer by identifying the factors in the first column and then checking the second or third (or both) columns. Include any possible government-related factors and be specific (tie your description to the specific case background provided here).

Chapter 5 Capital Crystal, Inc.

Using Currency Futures and Options

Capital Crystal, Inc., is a major importer of crystal glassware from the United Kingdom. The crystal is sold to prestigious retail stores throughout the United States. The imports are denominated in British pounds (£). Every quarter, Capital needs £500 million. It is currently attempting to determine whether it should use currency futures or currency options to hedge imports three months from now, if it will hedge at all. The spot rate of the pound is $1.60. A three-month futures contract on the pound is available for $1.59 per unit. A call option on the pound is available with a three-month expiration date and an exercise price of $1.60. The premium to be paid on the call option is $.01 per unit.

Capital is confident that the value of the pound will rise to at least $1.62 in three months. Its previous forecasts of the pound's value have been very accurate. Capital's management is extremely risk averse. Managers receive a bonus at the end of the year if they satisfy minimal performance standards. The bonus is the same, regardless of how high above the minimum level a manager's performance is. If performance is below the minimum, then there is no bonus and future advancement within the company is unlikely.

a. As a financial manager of Capital, you have been assigned the task of choosing among three possible strategies: (1) hedge the pound's position by purchasing futures, (2) hedge the pound's position by purchasing call options, or (3) do not hedge. Offer your recommendation and justify it.

b. Assume the previous information provided, except for this difference: Capital has revised its forecast of the pound to be worth $1.57 three months from now. Given this revision, recommend whether Capital should (1) hedge the pound's position by purchasing futures, (2) hedge the pound's position by purchasing call options, or (3) not hedge. Justify your recommendation. Is your recommendation consistent with maximizing shareholder wealth?

Chapter 6 Hull Importing Company

Effects of Intervention on Import Expenses

Hull Importing Company is a U.S.-based firm that imports small gift items and sells them to retail gift shops across the United States. About half of the value of Hull's purchases comes from the United Kingdom, while the remaining purchases are from Mexico. The imported products are denominated in the currency of the country where they are produced. Hull normally does not hedge its purchases.

In previous years, the Mexican peso and the pound fluctuated substantially against the dollar (although not by the same degree). Hull's expenses are directly tied to these currency values because all of its products are imported. It has been successful because the imported gift items are unique and are attractive to U.S. consumers. However, Hull has been unable to pass on higher costs (due to a weaker dollar) to its gift shop clients, because the shops fear that if they raise prices, their customers will switch to different gift items sold at other stores.

a. Hull expects that Mexico's central bank will increase interest rates and that Mexico's inflation will not be affected. Offer any insight on how the peso's value may change and how Hull's profits would be affected as a result.

b. Hull closely monitors government intervention by the Bank of England (the British central bank). Assume that the Bank of England intervenes to strengthen the pound's value with respect to the dollar by 5 percent. Would this have a favorable or unfavorable effect on Hull's business?

Chapter 7 Crayson Co.

Using Covered Interest Arbitrage

Crayson Co. is a U.S.-based MNC that has $5 million in cash available. It will not need the funds for one quarter. Crayson notices that the quarterly bank deposit interest rate in the country of Zynland is 2% (not annualized) versus only 1% in the United States. Also, there is no credit risk because the bank deposit is fully backed by the Zynland government. The currency in Minland (called the zyn) has been tied to the value of the euro (2 zyn = 1 euro) for the last eight years. The quarterly interest rate in the eurozone is 1 percent. The spot rate of euro is presently $1, while the quarterly forward rate of the euro is $1. The zyn is presently valued at $.50, so that 2 zyn are presently equal to $1. Because the zyn is tied to the euro, it fluctuates against the dollar over time in the same manner that the euro fluctuates against the dollar over time.

a. Explain how Crayson Co. could possibly earn a higher return on its funds by a form of covered interest arbitrage in which it invests in the zyn and covers its position with a forward sale in euros. What would be its expected return over the quarter if the zyn remains tied to the euro?

b. Explain the risk to Crayson Co. of engaging in the form of covered interest arbitrage described in the previous question.

Chapter 8 Flame Fixtures, Inc.

Business Application of Purchasing Power Parity

Flame Fixtures, Inc., is a small U.S. business in Arizona that produces and sells lamp fixtures. Its costs and revenues have been very stable over time. Its profits have been adequate, but Flame has been searching for a way to increase profits in the future. It has recently been negotiating with a Mexican firm called Corón Company, from which it will purchase some necessary parts. Every three months, Corón Company will send a specified number of parts with the bill invoiced in Mexican pesos. By having the parts produced by Corón, Flame expects to save about 20 percent on production costs. Corón is willing to work out a deal only if it is assured that it will receive a minimum specified amount of orders every three months over the next 10 years, for a minimum specified amount. Flame will be required to use its assets to serve as collateral in case it does not fulfill its obligation.

The price of the parts will change over time in response to the costs of production. Flame recognizes that the cost to Corón will increase substantially over time as a result of the very high inflation rate in Mexico. Therefore, the price charged in pesos likely will rise substantially every three months. However, Flame feels that, because of the concept of purchasing power parity (PPP), its dollar payments to Corón will be stable. According to PPP, if Mexican inflation is much higher than U.S. inflation, the peso will weaken against the dollar by that difference. Because Flame does not have much liquidity, it could experience a severe cash shortage if its expenses are much higher than anticipated.

The demand for Flame's product has been stable and is expected to continue that way. Because the U.S. inflation rate is expected to be very low, Flame likely will continue pricing its lamps at today's prices (in dollars). It believes that by saving 20 percent on production costs, it will substantially increase its profits. It is about ready to sign a contract with Corón Company.

a. Describe a scenario that could cause Flame to save even more than 20 percent on production costs.

b. Describe a scenario that could cause Flame to actually incur higher production costs than if it simply had the parts produced in the United States.

c. Do you think that Flame will experience stable dollar outflow payments to Corón over time? Explain. (Assume that the number of parts ordered is constant over time.)

d. Do you think that Flame's risk changes at all as a result of its new relationship with Corón Company? Explain.

Chapter 9 Whaler Publishing Company

Forecasting Exchange Rates

Whaler Publishing Company specializes in producing textbooks in the United States and marketing these books in foreign universities where the English language is used. Its sales are invoiced in the currency of the country where the textbooks are sold. The expected revenues from textbooks sold to university bookstores are shown in Exhibit B.1.

Whaler is comfortable with the estimated foreign currency revenues in each country. However, it is uncertain about the U.S. dollar revenues to be received from each country. At this time (which is the beginning of year 16), Whaler is using today's spot rate as its best guess of the exchange rate at which the revenues from each country will be converted into U.S. dollars at the end of this year (which implies a zero percentage change in the value of each currency). Yet it recognizes the potential error associated with this

Exhibit B.1   Expected Revenues from Textbooks Sold to University Bookstores

UNIVERSITY BOOKSTORES IN	LOCAL CURRENCY	TODAY'S SPOT EXCHANGE RATE	EXPECTED REVENUES FROM BOOKSTORES THIS YEAR
Australia	Australian dollars (A$)	$.7671	A$38,000,000
Canada	Canadian dollars (C$)	.8625	C$35,000,000
New Zealand	New Zealand dollars (NZ$)	.5985	NZ$33,000,000
United Kingdom	Pounds (£)	1.9382	£34,000,000

type of forecast. Therefore, it desires to incorporate the risk surrounding each currency forecast by creating confidence intervals for each currency. First, it must derive the annual percentage change in the exchange rate over each of the last 15 years for each currency to derive a standard deviation in the percentage change of each foreign currency. By assuming that the percentage changes in exchange rates are normally distributed, it plans to develop two ranges of forecasts for the annual percentage change in each currency: (1) one standard deviation in each direction from its best guess to develop a 68 percent confidence interval, and (2) two standard deviations in each direction from its best guess to develop a 95 percent confidence interval. These confidence intervals can then be applied to today's spot rates to develop confidence intervals for the future spot rate one year from today.

The exchange rates at the beginning of each year over a 16-year period for each currency (with respect to the U.S. dollar) are shown here:

BEGINNING OF YEAR	AUSTRALIAN DOLLAR	CANADIAN DOLLAR	NEW ZEALAND DOLLAR	BRITISH POUND
1	$1.2571	$.9839	$1.0437	£2.0235
2	1.0864	.9908	.9500	1.7024
3	1.1414	.9137	1.0197	1.9060
4	1.1505	.8432	1.0666	2.0345
5	1.1055	.8561	.9862	2.2240
6	1.1807	.8370	.9623	2.3850
7	1.1279	.8432	.8244	1.9080
8	.9806	.8137	.7325	1.6145
9	.9020	.8038	.6546	1.4506
10	.8278	.7570	.4776	1.1565
11	.6809	.7153	.4985	1.4445
12	.6648	.7241	.5235	1.4745
13	.7225	.8130	.6575	1.8715
14	.8555	.8382	.6283	1.8095
15	.7831	.8518	.5876	1.5772
16	.7671	.8625	.5985	1.9382

The confidence intervals for each currency can be applied to the expected book revenues to derive confidence intervals in U.S. dollars to be received from each country. Complete this assignment for Whaler Publishing Company, and also rank the currencies in terms of uncertainty (degree of volatility). The analysis will indicate (1) how volatile currencies can be, (2) how much more volatile some currencies are than others, and (3) how estimated revenues can be subject to a high degree of uncertainty as a result of uncertain exchange rates. (If you use a spreadsheet to do this case, you may want to retain it because the next chapter's case is an extension of this one.)

Chapter 10 Whaler Publishing Company
Measuring Exposure to Exchange Rate Risk

Recall the situation of Whaler Publishing Company from the previous chapter. Whaler needed to develop confidence intervals of four exchange rates in order to derive confidence intervals for U.S. dollar cash flows to be received from four different countries. Each confidence interval was isolated on a particular country.

Assume that Whaler would like to estimate the range of its aggregate dollar cash flows to be generated from other countries. A spreadsheet should be developed to facilitate this exercise. Whaler plans to simulate the conversion of the expected currency cash flows to dollars, using each of the previous years as a possible scenario (recall that exchange rate data are provided in the original case in Chapter 9). Specifically, Whaler will determine the annual percentage change in the spot rate of each currency for a given year. Then it will apply that percentage to the respective existing spot rates to determine a possible spot rate in one year for each currency. Recall that today's spot rates are assumed to be as follows:

- Australian dollar = $.7671
- Canadian dollar = $.8625
- New Zealand dollar = $.5985
- British pound = £1.9382

Once the spot rate is forecast for one year ahead for each currency, the U.S. dollar revenues received from each country can be forecast. For example, from year 1 to year 2, the Australian dollar declined by about 13.6 percent. If this percentage change occurs this year, the spot rate of the Australian dollar will decline from today's rate of $.7671 to about $.6629. In this case, the A$38 million to be received would convert to $25,190,200. The same tasks must be done for the other three currencies as well in order to estimate the aggregate dollar cash flows under this scenario.

This process can be repeated, using each of the previous years as a possible future scenario. There will be 15 possible scenarios, or 15 forecasts of the aggregate U.S. dollar cash flows. Each of these scenarios is expected to have an equal probability of occurring. By assuming that these cash flows are normally distributed, Whaler uses the standard deviation of the possible aggregate cash flows for all 15 scenarios to develop 68 percent and 95 percent confidence intervals surrounding the "expected value" of the aggregate level of U.S. dollar cash flows to be received in one year.

a. Perform these tasks for Whaler in order to determine these confidence intervals on the aggregate level of U.S. dollar cash flows to be received. Whaler uses the methodology described here, rather than simply combining the results for individual countries (from the previous chapter) because exchange rate movements may be correlated.

b. Review the annual percentage changes in the four exchange rates. Do they appear to be positively correlated? Estimate the correlation coefficient between exchange rate movements with either a calculator or a spreadsheet package. Based on this analysis, you can fill out the following correlation coefficient matrix:

	A$	C$	NZ$	£
A$	1.00	—	—	—
C$		1.00	—	—
NZ$			1.00	—
£				1.00

Would aggregate dollar cash flows to be received by Whaler be more risky than they would if the exchange rate movements were completely independent? Explain.

c. One Whaler executive has suggested that a more efficient way of deriving the confidence intervals would be to use the exchange rates instead of the percentage changes as the scenarios and derive U.S. dollar cash flow estimates directly from them. Do you think this method would be as accurate as the method now used by Whaler? Explain.

Chapter 11 Blackhawk Company

Forecasting Exchange Rates and the Hedging Decision

This case is intended to illustrate how forecasting exchange rates and hedging decisions are related. Blackhawk Company imports products from New Zealand and plans to purchase NZ$800,000 one quarter from now to pay for imports. As the treasurer of Blackhawk, you are responsible for determining whether and how to hedge this payables position. Several tasks will need to be completed before you can make these decisions. The entire analysis can be performed using Excel spreadsheets. Your first goal is to assess three different models for forecasting the value of NZ$ at the end of the quarter (also called the future spot rate, or FSR).

■ Using the forward rate (FR) at the beginning of the quarter.
■ Using the spot rate (SR) at the beginning of the quarter.
■ Estimating the historical influence of the inflation differential during each quarter on the percentage change in the NZ$ (which leads to a forecast of the FSR of the NZ$).

   The historical data to be used for this analysis are provided in Exhibit B.2.

a. Use regression analysis to determine whether the forward rate is an unbiased estimator of the spot rate at the end of the quarter.

b. Use the simplified approach of assessing the signs of forecast errors over time. Do you detect any bias when using the FR to forecast? Explain.

c. Determine the average absolute forecast error when using the forward rate to forecast.

d. Determine whether the spot rate of the NZ$ at the beginning of the quarter is an unbiased estimator of the SR at the end of the quarter using regression analysis.

e. Use the simplified approach of assessing the signs of forecast errors over time. Do you detect any bias when using the spot rate to forecast? Explain.

f. Determine the average absolute forecast error when using the spot rate to forecast. Is the spot rate or the forward rate a more accurate forecast of the future spot rate? Explain.

g. Use the following regression model to determine the relationship between the inflation differential (DIFF, defined as U.S. inflation minus New Zealand inflation) and the percentage change in the NZ$ (denoted PNZ$):

$$PNZ\$ = b_0 + b_1(DIFF)$$

Exhibit B.2   Historical Data for Hedging Analysis

QUARTER	SPOT RATE OF NZ$ AT BEGINNING OF QUARTER	90-DAY FORWARD RATE OF NZ$ AT BEGINNING OF QUARTER	SPOT RATE OF NZ$ AT END OF QUARTER	LAST QUARTER'S INFLATION DIFFERENTIAL	PERCENTAGE CHANGE IN NZ$ OVER QUARTER
1	$.3177	$.3250	$.3233	−.05%	1.76%
2	.3233	.3272	.3267	−.46	1.05
3	.3267	.3285	.3746	.66	14.66
4	.3746	.3778	.4063	.94	8.46
5	.4063	.4093	.4315	.58	6.20
6	.4315	.4344	.4548	.23	5.40
7	.4548	.4572	.4949	.02	8.82
8	.4949	.4966	.5153	1.26	4.12
9	.5153	.5169	.5540	.86	7.51
10	.5540	.5574	.5465	.54	−1.35
11	.5465	.5510	.5440	1.00	−.46
12	.5440	.5488	.6309	1.09	15.97
13	.6309	.6365	.6027	.78	−4.47
14	.6027	.6081	.5409	.23	−10.25
15	.5491	.5538	.5320	.71	−3.11
16	.5320	.5365	.5617	1.18	5.58
17	.5617	.5667	.5283	.70	−5.95
18	.5283	.5334	.5122	−.31	−3.05
19	.5122	.5149	.5352	.62	4.49
20	.5352	.5372	.5890	.87	10.05
21 (Now)	.5890	.5878	(to be forecasted)	.28	(to be forecasted)

Once you have determined the coefficients b_0 and b_1, use them to forecast PNZ$ based on a forecast of 2 percent for DIFF in the upcoming quarter. Then, apply your forecast for PNZ$ to the prevailing spot rate (which is $.589) to derive the expected FSR of the NZ$.

h. Blackhawk plans to develop a probability distribution for the FSR. First, it will assign a 40 percent probability to the forecast of FSR derived from the regression analysis in the previous question. Second, it will assign a 40 percent probability to the forecast of FSR based on either the forward rate or the spot rate (whichever was more accurate according to your earlier analysis). Third, it will assign a 20 percent probability to the forecast of FSR based on either the forward rate or the spot rate (whichever was less accurate according to your earlier analysis).

Fill in the table that follows:

PROBABILITY	FSR
40% based on regression analysis	
40% based on FR or SR	
20% based on FR or SR	

i. Assuming that Blackhawk does not hedge, fill in the following table:

PROBABILITY	FORECASTED DOLLAR AMOUNT NEEDED TO PAY FOR IMPORTS IN 90 DAYS
40%	
40	
20	

j. Based on the probability distribution for the FSR, use the table that follows to determine the probability distribution for the real cost of hedging if a forward contract is used for hedging (recall that the prevailing 90-day forward rate is $.5878).

PROBABILITY	FORECASTED DOLLAR AMOUNT NEEDED IF HEDGED WITH A FORWARD CONTRACT	FORECASTED AMOUNT NEEDED IF UNHEDGED	FORECASTED REAL COST OF HEDGING PAYABLES
40%			
40			
20			

k. If Blackhawk hedges its position, it will use either a 90-day forward rate, a money market hedge, or a call option. The following data are available at the time of its decision.

- Spot rate = $.589.
- 90-day forward rate = $.5878.
- 90-day U.S. borrowing rate = 2.5 percent.
- 90-day U.S. investing rate = 2.3 percent.
- 90-day New Zealand borrowing rate = 2.4 percent.
- 90-day New Zealand investing rate = 2.1 percent.
- Call option on NZ$ has a premium of $.01 per unit.
- Call option on NZ$ has an exercise price of $.60.

Determine the probability distribution of dollars needed for a call option if used (include the premium paid) by filling out the following table:

PROBABILITY	FSR	DOLLARS NEEDED TO PAY FOR PAYABLES
40%		
40		
20		

l. Compare the forward hedge with the money market hedge. Which is superior? Why?

m. Compare either the forward hedge or the money market hedge (whichever is better) with the call option hedge. If you hedge, which technique should you use? Why?

n. Compare the hedge you believe is the best with an unhedged strategy. Should you hedge or remain unhedged? Explain.

Chapter 12 Madison, Inc.
Assessing Economic Exposure

The situation for Madison, Inc., was described in this chapter to illustrate how alternative operational structures could affect economic exposure to exchange rate movements. Ken Moore, the vice president of finance at Madison, Inc., was seriously considering a shift to the proposed operational structure described in the text. He was determined to stabilize the earnings before taxes and believed that the proposed approach would achieve this objective. The firm expected that the Canadian dollar would consistently depreciate over the next several years. Over time, its forecasts have been very accurate. Moore paid little attention to the forecasts, stating that regardless of how the Canadian dollar changed, future earnings would be more stable under the proposed operational structure. He also was constantly reminded of how the strengthened Canadian dollar in some years had adversely affected the firm's earnings. In fact, he was somewhat concerned that he might even lose his job if the adverse effects from economic exposure continued.

a. Would a revised operational structure at this time be in the best interests of the shareholders? Would it be in the best interests of the vice president?

b. How could a revised operational structure be feasible from the vice president's perspective but not from the shareholders' perspective? Explain how the firm might be able to ensure that the vice president will make decisions related to economic exposure that are in the best interests of the shareholders.

Chapter 13 Blues Corporation
Capitalizing on New Markets in Eastern Europe

Having done business in the United States for over 50 years, Blues Corporation has an established reputation. Most of Blues' business is in the United States. It has a subsidiary in the western section of Germany, which produces products and exports them to other European countries. Blues Corporation produces many consumer products that could possibly be produced or marketed in Eastern European countries. The following issues were raised at a recent executive meeting. Offer your comments about each issue.

a. Blues Corporation is considering shifting its European production facility from western Germany to eastern Germany. There are two key factors motivating this shift. First, labor costs are lower in eastern Germany. Second, there is an existing facility in eastern Germany that is for sale at a low price because it has not been modernized. Blues would like to renovate the facility and install new technology to increase its production efficiency. Blues estimates that it would need only one-fourth of the workers in that facility. What other factors deserve to be considered before the decision is made?

b. Blues Corporation believes that it could penetrate the Eastern European markets. It would need to invest considerable funds in promoting its consumer products in Eastern Europe, because its products are not well known there. Yet it believes that this strategy could pay off in the long run because Blues could underprice the competition. At the current time, the main competition consists of businesses that are perceived to be inefficiently run. The lack of competitive pricing in this market is the primary reason for Blues Corporation to consider marketing its products in Eastern Europe. What other factors deserve to be considered before a decision is made?

c. Blues Corporation is currently experiencing a cash squeeze because of a reduced demand for its products in the United States (although management expects the demand in the United States to increase soon). It is currently near its debt capacity and prefers not to issue stock at this time. Blues Corporation will purchase a facility in Eastern Europe or implement a heavy promotion program in Eastern Europe only if it can raise funds by divesting a significant amount of its U.S. assets. The market values of its assets are temporarily depressed, but some executives think an immediate move is necessary in order to fully capitalize on the Eastern European market. Would you recommend that Blues Corporation divest some of its U.S. assets? Explain.

Chapter 14 North Star Company

Capital Budgeting

This case is intended to illustrate that the value of an international project is sensitive to various types of input. It also is intended to show how a computer spreadsheet format can facilitate capital budgeting decisions that involve uncertainty.

This case can be performed using a spreadsheet such as Excel. The following present value factors may be helpful input for discounting cash flows:

YEARS FROM NOW	PRESENT VALUE INTEREST FACTOR AT 18%
1	.8475
2	.7182
3	.6086
4	.5158
5	.4371
6	.3704

For consistency in discussion of this case, you should develop your spreadsheet in a format that resembles the one used in Chapter 14, with each year representing a column across the top. The use of a spreadsheet will significantly reduce the time needed to complete this case.

North Star Company is considering establishing a subsidiary to manufacture clothing in Singapore. Its sales would be invoiced in Singapore dollars (S$). It has forecast net cash flows to the subsidiary as follows:

YEAR	NET CASH FLOWS TO SUBSIDIARY
1	S$8,000,000
2	10,000,000
3	14,000,000
4	16,000,000
5	16,000,000
6	16,000,000

These cash flows do not include financing costs (interest expenses) on any funds borrowed in Singapore. North Star Company also expects to receive S$30 million after taxes as a result of selling the subsidiary at the end of year 6. Assume that there will not be any withholding taxes imposed on this amount.

Exhibit B.3 Three Scenarios of Economic Conditions

END OF YEAR	SCENARIO I: FAIRLY STABLE S$	SCENARIO II: WEAK S$	SCENARIO III: STRONG S$
1	.50	.49	.52
2	.51	.46	.55
3	.48	.45	.59
4	.50	.43	.64
5	.52	.43	.67
6	.48	.41	.71

The exchange rate of the Singapore dollar is forecasted in Exhibit B.3 based on three possible scenarios of economic conditions. The probability of each scenario is shown below:

	FAIRLY STABLE S$	WEAK S$	STRONG S$
Probability	60%	30%	10%

Fifty percent of the net cash flows to the subsidiary would be remitted to the parent, while the remaining 50 percent would be reinvested to support ongoing operations at the subsidiary. North Star Company anticipates a 10 percent withholding tax on funds remitted to the United States.

The initial investment (including investment in working capital) by North Star in the subsidiary would be S$40 million. Any investment in working capital (such as accounts receivable, inventory, etc.) is to be assumed by the buyer in year 6. The expected salvage value has already accounted for this transfer of working capital to the buyer in year 6. The initial investment could be financed completely by the parent ($20 million, converted at the present exchange rate of $.50 per Singapore dollar to achieve S$40 million). North Star Company will go forward with its intentions to build the subsidiary only if it expects to achieve a return on its capital of 18 percent or higher.

North Star is considering an alternative financing arrangement. With this arrangement, the parent would provide $10 million (S$20 million), which means that the subsidiary would need to borrow S$20 million. Under this scenario, the subsidiary would obtain a 20-year loan and pay interest on the loan each year. The interest payments are S$1.6 million per year. In addition, the forecasted proceeds to be received from selling the subsidiary (after taxes) at the end of six years would be S$20 million (the forecast of proceeds is revised downward here because the equity investment of the subsidiary is less; the buyer would be assuming more debt if part of the initial investment in the subsidiary were supported by local bank loans). Assume that the parent's required rate of return would still be 18 percent.

a. Which of the two financing arrangements would you recommend for the parent? Assess the forecasted NPV for each exchange rate scenario to compare the two financing arrangements and substantiate your recommendation.

b. In the first question, an alternative arrangement of partial financing by the subsidiary was considered while assuming that the required rate of return by the parent would not be affected. Is there any reason why the parent's required rate of return might increase when using this financing arrangement? Explain. How would you revise the analysis in the previous question under this situation? (This question requires discussion, not analysis.)

c. Would you recommend that North Star Company establish the subsidiary even if the withholding tax is 20 percent?

d. Assume that there is some concern about the economic conditions in Singapore that could reduce net cash flows to the subsidiary. Explain how Excel could be used to reevaluate the project based on alternative cash flow scenarios. That is, how can this form of country risk be incorporated into the capital budgeting decision? (This question requires discussion, not analysis.)

e. Assume that North Star Company does implement the project, investing $10 million of its own funds with the remainder borrowed by the subsidiary. Two years later, a U.S.-based corporation notifies North Star that it would like to purchase the subsidiary. Assume that the exchange rate forecasts for the fairly stable scenario are appropriate for years 3 through 6. Also assume that the other information already provided on net cash flows, financing costs, the 10 percent withholding tax, the salvage value, and the parent's required rate of return is still appropriate. What would be the minimum dollar price (after taxes) that North Star should receive to divest the subsidiary? Substantiate your opinion.

Chapter 15   Redwing Technology Company

Assessing Subsidiary Performance

Redwing Technology Company is a U.S.-based firm that makes a variety of high-tech components. Five years ago, it established subsidiaries in Canada, South Africa, and Japan. The earnings generated by each subsidiary as translated (at the average annual exchange rate) into U.S. dollars per year are shown in Exhibit B.4.

Each subsidiary had an equivalent amount in resources with which to conduct operations. The wage rates for the labor needed were similar across countries. The inflation rates, economic growth, and degree of competition were also similar across countries.

The average exchange rates of the respective currencies over the last five years are given below:

YEARS AGO	CANADIAN DOLLAR	SOUTH AFRICAN RAND	JAPANESE YEN
5	$.84	$.10	$.0040
4	.83	.12	.0043
3	.81	.16	.0046
2	.81	.20	.0055
1	.79	.24	.0064

The earnings generated by each country were reinvested rather than remitted. There were no plans to remit any future earnings, either.

A committee of vice presidents met to evaluate the performance of each subsidiary in the last five years. The purpose of the assessment was to determine whether Redwing

Exhibit B.4   Translated Dollar Value of Annual Earnings in Each Subsidiary (millions)

YEARS AGO	CANADA	SOUTH AFRICA	JAPAN
5	$20	$21	$30
4	24	24	32
3	28	24	35
2	32	36	41
1	36	42	46

should be restructured to focus future growth on any particular subsidiary or to divest any subsidiaries that might experience poor performance. Because exchange rates of the related currencies were affected by so many different factors, the treasurer acknowledged that there was much uncertainty about their future direction. The treasurer did suggest, however, that last year's average exchange rate would probably serve as at least a reasonable guess of exchange rates in future years. He did not anticipate that any of the currencies would experience consistent appreciation or depreciation.

a. Use whatever means you think are appropriate to rank the performance of each subsidiary. That is, which subsidiary do you think did the best job over the five-year period? Justify your opinion.

b. Use whatever means you think are appropriate to determine which subsidiary deserves additional funds from the parent to push for additional growth. (Assume no constraint on potential growth in any country.) Where would you recommend the parent's excess funds be invested, based on the information available? Justify your opinion.

c. Repeat question b but now assume that all earnings generated from the parent's investment will be remitted to the parent every year. Would your recommendation change? Explain.

d. A final task of the committee was to recommend whether any of the subsidiaries should be divested. One vice president suggested that a review of the earnings translated into dollars shows that the performances of the Canadian and South African subsidiaries are highly correlated. She concluded that having both of these subsidiaries did not achieve much in diversification benefits and suggested that either one could be sold without forgoing any diversification benefits. Do you agree? Explain.

Chapter 16 King, Inc.

Country Risk Analysis

King, Inc., a U.S. firm, is considering the establishment of a small subsidiary in Bulgaria that would produce food products. All ingredients can be obtained or produced in Bulgaria. The final products to be produced by the subsidiary would be sold in Bulgaria and other Eastern European countries. King, Inc., is very interested in this project, as there is little competition in that area. Three of King's high-level managers have been assigned the task of assessing the country risk of Bulgaria. Specifically, the managers were asked to list all characteristics of Bulgaria that could adversely affect the performance of this project. The decision on whether or not to undertake this project will be made only after this country risk analysis is completed and accounted for in the capital budgeting analysis. Because King, Inc., has focused exclusively on domestic business in the past, it is not accustomed to country risk analysis.

a. What factors related to Bulgaria's government deserve to be considered?

b. What country-related factors can affect the demand for the food products to be produced by King, Inc.?

c. What country-related factors can affect the cost of production?

Chapter 17 Sabre Computer Corporation

Cost of Capital

Sabre Computer Corporation is a U.S.-based company that plans to participate in joint ventures in Mexico and in Hungary. Each joint venture involves the development of a small subsidiary that helps produce computers. Sabre's main contributions are the technology and a few key computer components used in the production process. The joint venture in Mexico specifies joint production of computers with a Mexican company owned by the government. The computers have already been ordered by educational institutions and government agencies throughout Mexico. Sabre has a contract to sell all the computers it produces in Mexico to these institutions and agencies at a price that is tied to inflation. Given the very high and volatile inflation levels in Mexico, Sabre wanted to ensure that the contracted price would adjust to cover rising costs over time.

The venture will require a temporary transfer of several managers to Mexico plus the manufacturing of key computer components in a leased Mexican plant. Most of these costs will be incurred in Mexico and will therefore require payment in pesos. Sabre will receive 30 percent of the revenue generated (in pesos) from computer sales. The Mexican partner will receive the remainder.

The joint venture in Hungary specifies joint production of personal computers with a Hungarian computer manufacturer. The computers will then be marketed to consumers throughout Eastern Europe. Similar computers are produced by some competitors, but Sabre believes it can penetrate these markets because its products will be competitively priced. Although the economies of the Eastern European countries are expected to be somewhat stagnant, demand for personal computers is reasonably strong. The computers will be priced in Hungary's currency, the forint, and Sabre will receive 30 percent of the revenue generated from sales.

a. Assume that Sabre plans to finance most of its investment in the Mexican subsidiary by borrowing Mexican pesos and to finance most of its investment in the Hungarian subsidiary by borrowing forint. The cost of financing is influenced by the risk-free rates in the respective countries and the risk premiums on funds borrowed. Explain how these factors will affect the relative costs of financing both ventures. Address this question from the perspective of the subsidiary, not from the perspective of Sabre.

b. Will the joint venture experiencing the higher cost of financing (as determined in the previous question) necessarily experience lower returns to the subsidiary? Explain.

c. The Hungarian subsidiary has a high degree of financial leverage, but the parent's capital structure is mostly equity. What will determine whether the creditors of the Hungarian subsidiary charge a high risk premium on borrowed funds because of the high degree of financial leverage?

d. One Sabre executive has suggested that, because the cost of debt financing by highly leveraged Hungarian-owned companies is about 14 percent, its Hungarian subsidiary should be able to borrow at about the same interest rate. Do you agree? Explain. (Assume that the chances of the subsidiary's experiencing financial problems are the same as those for these other Hungarian-owned firms.)

e. There is some concern that the economy in Hungary could become inflated. Assess the relative magnitude of an increase in inflation on (1) the cost of funds, (2) the cost of production, and (3) revenue from selling the computers.

Chapter 18 Devil Corporation

Long-Term Debt Financing

Devil Corporation is a U.S.-based company that produces high-definition DVD players. Three years ago, Devil established a production facility in the United Kingdom, because it sells DVD players there. Devil has excess capacity there and will use that facility to produce the DVD players that are to be marketed in Singapore. The DVD players will be sold to distributors in Singapore and invoiced in Singapore dollars (S$). If the exporting program is successful, Devil Corporation will probably build a facility in Singapore, but it plans to wait at least 10 years.

Prior to this exporting program, Devil Corporation decided to develop a hedging strategy to hedge any cash flows from its subsidiaries. Its plan is to issue bonds to finance the entire investment in the exporting program. Virtually all expenses associated with this program are denominated in pounds, yet the revenue generated by the program is denominated in Singapore dollars. Any revenue above and beyond expenses is to be remitted to the United States on an annual basis. Aside from the exporting program, the British subsidiary will generate just enough in cash flows to cover expenses and therefore will not be remitting any earnings to the parent. Devil Corporation is considering three different ways to finance the program for 10 years.

- Issue 10-year, Singapore dollar–denominated bonds at par value; coupon rate = 11 percent.
- Issue 10-year, pound-denominated bonds at par value; coupon rate = 14 percent.
- Issue 10-year, U.S. dollar–denominated bonds at par value; coupon rate = 11 percent.

a. Describe the exchange rate risk if Devil finances with Singapore dollars.

b. Describe the exchange rate risk if Devil finances with British pounds.

c. Describe the exchange rate risk if Devil finances with U.S. dollars.

Chapter 19 Ryco Chemical Company

Using Countertrade

Ryco Chemical Company produces a wide variety of chemical products that are sold to manufacturing firms. Some of the chemicals used in its production process are imported from Concellos Chemical Company in Brazil. Concellos uses some chemicals in its production process that are produced by Ryco (although Concellos has historically purchased these chemicals from another U.S. chemical company rather than from Ryco). The Brazilian currency, the real, has been depreciating continuously against the dollar, so Concellos's cost of obtaining chemicals is always rising. Concellos will probably pay twice as much for these chemicals this year because of the weak real. It probably will attempt to pass on most of its higher costs to its customers in the form of higher prices. However, it may not always be able to pass on higher costs from a weak real: its competitors make all their chemicals locally, and their costs are directly tied to Brazil's inflation. Its competitors sell all their goods locally. This year, Concellos planned to charge Ryco a price in real that was substantially above last year's price.

Representatives from Ryco are flying to Brazil to discuss its trade problems with Concellos. Specifically, Ryco wants to avoid its exposure to the high inflation rate in Brazil. This adverse effect is somewhat offset by the consistent decline in the value of the real, which allows Ryco to obtain more real with a given amount of dollars every year. However, the offset is not perfect, and Ryco wants to create a better hedge against Brazilian inflation.

a. Describe a countertrade strategy that could reduce Ryco's exposure to Brazilian inflation.

b. Would Concellos be willing to consider this strategy? Is there any favorable effect on Concellos that may motivate it to accept the strategy?

c. Assume that both parties agree on countertrade. Why would the cost of obtaining imports still rise over time for Concellos? Would Concellos earn lower profits as a result?

Chapter 20 Flyer Company

Composing the Optimal Currency Portfolio for Financing

As the treasurer for Flyer Company, you must develop a strategy for short-term financing. The firm, based in the United States, currently has no transaction exposure to currency movements. Assume the following data as of today:

CURRENCY	SPOT EXCHANGE RATE	ANNUALIZED INTEREST RATE
Australian dollar	$.75	13.0%
British pound	1.70	12.5
Canadian dollar	.86	11.0
Japanese yen	.006	8.0
Mexican peso	.17	11.5
New Zealand dollar	.60	7.0
Singapore dollar	.50	6.0
South African rand	.16	9.0
U.S. dollar	1.00	9.0
Venezuelan bolivar	.0008	12.0

Your forecasting department has provided you with the following forecasts of the spot rates one year from now:

CURRENCY	STRONG $ SCENARIO	STABLE $ SCENARIO	WEAK $ SCENARIO
Australian dollar	$.66	$.76	$.85
British pound	1.58	1.73	1.83
Canadian dollar	.85	.85	.91
Japanese yen	.0055	.0062	.0072
Mexican peso	.14	.173	.18
New Zealand dollar	.53	.59	.63
Singapore dollar	.45	.48	.52
South African rand	.15	.155	.17
U.S. dollar	1.00	1.00	1.00
Venezuelan bolivar	.00073	.00079	.00086

The probability of the strong-dollar scenario is 30 percent, the probability of the stable-dollar scenario is 40 percent, and the probability of the weak-dollar scenario is 30 percent. Based on the information provided, prescribe the composition of the portfolio that would achieve the minimum expected effective financing rate based on each of the following risk preferences.

- *Risk neutral.* Focus on minimizing the expected value of your effective financing rate without any constraints.
- *Balanced.* Borrow no more than 25 percent of the funds in any foreign currency.
- *Conservative.* Borrow at least 60 percent U.S. dollars and no more than 10 percent of the funds from any individual foreign currency.
- *Ultraconservative.* Do not create any exposure to exchange rate risk.

Fill out the following table:

RISK PREFERENCE	PORTFOLIO'S EFFECTIVE FINANCING RATE BASED ON			EXPECTED VALUE OF EFFECTIVE FINANCING RATE
	STRONG $ SCENARIO	STABLE $ SCENARIO	WEAK $ SCENARIO	
Risk-neutral portfolio				
Balanced portfolio				
Conservative portfolio				
Ultraconservative portfolio				

Which portfolio would you prescribe for your firm? Why?

Chapter 21 Islander Corporation

Composing the Optimal Currency Portfolio for Investing

As the treasurer for the Islander Corporation, you must develop a strategy for investing the excess cash that will be available for the next year. The firm, based in the United States, currently has no transaction exposure to foreign currency movements. Assume the following data as of today:

CURRENCY	SPOT EXCHANGE RATE	ANNUALIZED INTEREST RATE
Australian dollar	.75	13.00
British pound	1.70	12.5
Canadian dollar	.86	11.0
Japanese yen	.006	8.0
U.S. dollar	1.00	9.0

Your forecasting department has provided you with the following forecasts of the spot rates one year from now:

CURRENCY	STRONG $ SCENARIO	FAIRLY STABLE $ SCENARIO	WEAK $ SCENARIO
Australian dollar	$.66	$.76	$.85
British pound	1.58	1.73	1.83
Canadian dollar	.85	.85	.91
Japanese yen	.0055	.0062	.0072
U.S. dollar	1.00	1.00	1.00

The probability of the strong-dollar scenario is 30 percent, the probability of the fairly stable-dollar scenario is 40 percent, and the probability of the weak-dollar scenario is 30 percent. Based on the information provided, prescribe the composition of the investment portfolio that would maximize the expected value of the effective yield for each of four possible risk preferences.

- *Risk neutral.* Focus on maximizing the expected value of your effective yield without any constraints.
- *Balanced.* Invest no more than 25 percent in any foreign currency.
- *Conservative.* Invest at least 50 percent of the funds in the U.S. dollar and no more than 10 percent of the funds in any individual foreign currency.
- *Ultraconservative.* Do not create any exposure to exchange rate risk.

Fill out the following table:

RISK PREFERENCE	FORECASTED EFFECTIVE YIELD FOR			
	STRONG $ SCENARIO	FAIRLY STABLE $ SCENARIO	WEAK $ SCENARIO	EXPECTED VALUE OF EFFECTIVE YIELD
Risk-neutral portfolio				
Balanced portfolio				
Conservative portfolio				
Ultraconservative portfolio				

Which portfolio would you prescribe for your firm? Why? (You may find it helpful to draw bar charts that show the probability distribution of effective yields for each of the portfolios, placing one bar chart above another.)

RISK PREFERENCE	FORECASTED EFFECTIVE YIELD FOR			
	STRONG $ SCENARIO	FAIRLY STABLE $ SCENARIO	WEAK $ SCENARIO	EXPECTED VALUE OF EFFECTIVE YIELD
First row here …				

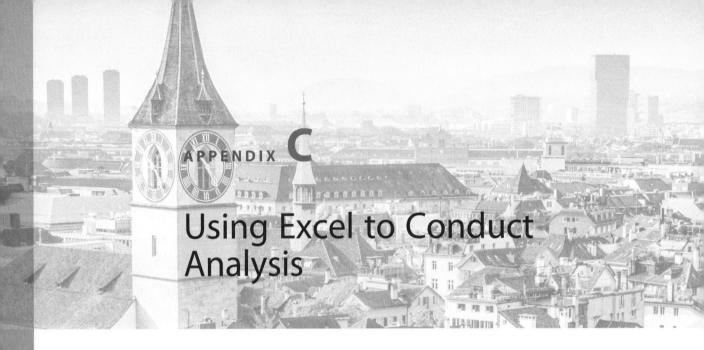

Using Excel to Conduct Analysis

Computing with Excel

Excel spreadsheets are useful for organizing numerical data. In addition, they can execute computations for you. Excel not only allows you to compute general statistics such as average and standard deviation of cells but also can be used to conduct regression analysis. This appendix starts by describing how Excel can be used to compute general statistics. This is followed by a background on regression analysis and then an example of the application of Excel to run a regression analysis.

General Statistics

Some of the more popular computations are discussed here.

Creating a COMPUTE Statement If you want to determine the percentage change in a value from one period to the next, type the COMPUTE statement in a cell where you want to see the result. For example, assume that you have months listed in column A and the corresponding exchange rate of the euro (with respect to the dollar) at the beginning of each month in column B. Assume you want to insert the monthly percentage change in the exchange rate for each month in column C. In cell C2 (the second row of column C), you want to determine the percentage change in the exchange rate as of the month in cell B2 from the previous month in cell B1. Thus you would type the COMPUTE statement in cell C2 that reflects the computation you want. A COMPUTE statement begins with an $=$ sign. The proper COMPUTE statement to compute a percentage change for cell C2 is $=(B2-B1)/B1$ in this case. If you want cell C3 to report the percentage change in the exchange rate as of the month in cell B3 from the previous month in cell B2, then type the COMPUTE statement $=(B3-B2)/B2$ in cell C3.

Using the COPY Command If you need to repeat a particular COMPUTE statement for several different cells, you can use the COPY command as follows.

- Place the cursor in the cell with the COMPUTE statement that you want to copy to other cells.
- Click the Home Tab on the menu.
- Click Copy.

■ Highlight the cells where you want that COMPUTE statement copied.
■ Press the Enter key.

For example, suppose that you have 30 monthly exchange rates of the euro in column B and you already calculated the percentage change in the exchange rate in cell C2 as explained previously. (You did not have a percentage change in cell C1 because you needed two dates, cells B1 and B2, to derive your first percentage change.) You could then place the cursor on cell C2, click the Home Tab on the menu, click Copy, highlight cells C3 to C30, and then press the Enter key.

Computing an Average   You can compute the average of a set of cells in the following way. Suppose you want to determine the average exchange rate of the 30 monthly exchange rates of the euro that you have listed from cell B1 to cell B30. In cell B31 (or in any blank cell where you want to see the result), type the COMPUTE statement =AVERAGE(B1:B30). Likewise, if you want to determine the average of the monthly percentage changes in the euro then go to column C (where you have monthly percentage changes in the euro from cells C2 through C30). In cell C31, say, type the COMPUTE statement =AVERAGE(C2:C30).

Computing a Standard Deviation   You can compute the standard deviation of a set of cells as follows. Assume that you wanted to determine the standard deviation of the 30 monthly exchange rates of the euro that you have listed from cell B1 to cell B30. In cell B31 (or in any blank cell where you want to see the result), type the COMPUTE statement =STDEV(B1:B30). Similarly, to determine the standard deviation of the monthly percentage changes in the euro, go to column C (where you have monthly percentage changes in the euro from cells C2 through C30). In cell C31 (or in any other blank cell), type the COMPUTE statement =STDEV(C2:C30).

Fundamentals of Regression Analysis

Businesses often use **regression analysis** to measure relationships between variables when establishing policies. For example, a firm may measure the historical relationship between its sales and its accounts receivable. Using the relationship detected, it can then forecast the future level of accounts receivable based on a forecast of sales. Alternatively, it may measure the sensitivity of its sales to economic growth and interest rates so that it can assess how susceptible its sales are to future changes in these economic variables. In international financial management, regression analysis can be used to measure the sensitivity of a firm's performance (as proxied by sales, earnings, or stock price) to currency movements or the economic growth of various countries.

Regression analysis can be applied to measure the sensitivity of exports to various economic variables. This example will be used to explain the fundamentals of regression analysis. The main steps involved in regression analysis are

1. specifying the regression model,
2. compiling the data,
3. estimating the regression coefficients, and
4. interpreting the regression results.

Specifying the Regression Model

Assume that your main goal is to determine the relationship between percentage changes in U.S. exports to Australia (denoted CEXP) and percentage changes in the value of the

Australian dollar (CAUS). The percentage change in the exports to Australia is the **dependent variable** because it is hypothesized to be influenced by another variable. Although you are most concerned with how CAUS affects CEXP, the regression model should include any other factors (the so-called **independent variables**) that could also affect CEXP. Assume that the percentage change in the Australian GDP (denoted CGDP) is also hypothesized to influence CEXP. This factor should also be included in the regression model. To simplify the example, assume that CAUS and CGDP are the only factors expected to influence CEXP. Also assume that there is a lagged impact of one quarter. In this case, the regression model can be specified as

$$CEXP_t = b_0 + b_1(CAUS_{t-1}) + b_2(CGDP_{t-1}) + \mu_t$$

where

$b_0 =$ **a constant**

$b_1 =$ **regression coefficient that measures the sensitivity of CEXP$_t$ to CAUS$_{t-1}$**

$b_2 =$ **regression coefficient that measures the sensitivity of CEXP$_t$ to CGDP$_{t-1}$**

$\mu_t =$ **an error term**

The t subscript represents the time period. Some models, such as this one, specify a lagged impact of an independent variable on the dependent variable and therefore use a $t - 1$ subscript.

Compiling the Data

Now that the model has been specified, data on the variables must be compiled. The data are normally input onto a spreadsheet as follows:

PERIOD (t)	CEXP	CAUS	CGDP
1	.03	.01	.04
2	.01	.02	.01
3	.04	.03	.02
4	.00	.02	.01
5	.01	.02	.02
...	...	...	...
...	...	...	...
...	...	...	...

The column specifying the period is not necessary to run the regression model, but it is normally included in the data set for convenience.

The difference between the number of observations (periods) and the regression coefficients (including the constant) represents the degrees of freedom (often denoted df). For our example, assume that the data covered 40 quarterly periods. The degrees of freedom for this example are $40 - 3 = 37$. As a general rule, analysts usually try to have at least 30 degrees of freedom when using regression analysis.

Some regression models involve only a single period. For example, if you desired to determine whether there was a relationship between a firm's degree of international sales (as a percentage of total sales) and earnings per share of MNCs, then last year's data on these two variables could be gathered for many MNCs, after which regression analysis could be applied. This would be an example of **cross-sectional analysis**, whereas our original treatment is an example of **time-series analysis**.

Estimating the Regression Coefficients

Once the data have been input into a data file, a regression program can be applied to the data to estimate the **regression coefficients**. There are various packages such as Excel that contain a regression analysis application.

The actual steps conducted to estimate regression coefficients are rather complex. For more details on how regression coefficients are estimated, see any econometrics textbook.

Interpreting the Regression Results

Most regression programs provide estimates of the regression coefficients along with additional statistics. For our example, suppose that the following information was provided by the regression program:

	ESTIMATED REGRESSION COEFFICIENT	STANDARD ERROR OF REGRESSION COEFFICIENT	t-STATISTIC
Constant	.002		
$CAUS_{t-1}$	.80	.32	2.50
$CGDP_{t-1}$	.36	.50	.72
Coefficient of determination (R^2) =	.33		

The independent variable $CAUS_{t-1}$ has an estimated regression coefficient of .80, which indicates that a 1 percent increase in CAUS is associated with an .8 percent increase in the dependent variable CEXP in the following period. This implies a positive relationship between $CAUS_{t-1}$ and $CEXP_t$. The independent variable $CGDP_{t-1}$ has an estimated coefficient of .36, which suggests that a 1 percent increase in the Australian GDP is associated with a .36 percent increase in CEXP one period later.

Many analysts attempt to determine whether a coefficient is statistically different from zero. Regression coefficients may be different from zero simply because of a coincidental relationship between the independent variable of concern and the dependent variable. One can have more confidence that a negative or positive relationship actually exists by testing the coefficient for significance. A t-test is commonly used for this purpose, as described next.

Test to determine whether $CAUS_{t-1}$ affects $CEXP_t$

$$\text{Calculated } t\text{-statistic} = \frac{\text{Estimated regression coefficient for } CAUS_{t-1}}{\text{Standard error of the regression coefficient}} = \frac{.80}{.32} = 2.50$$

Test to determine whether $CGDP_{t-1}$ affects $CEXP_t$

$$\text{Calculated } t\text{-statistic} = \frac{\text{Estimated regression coefficient for } CGDP_{t-1}}{\text{Standard error of the regression coefficient}} = \frac{.36}{.50} = .72$$

The calculated t-statistic is sometimes provided along with the regression results. It can be compared to the critical t-statistic to determine whether the coefficient is significant. The value of the *critical t-statistic* depends on the degrees of freedom and confidence level chosen. For our example, assume that there are 37 degrees of freedom and that a 95 confidence level is desired. The critical t-statistic would then be 2.02, which can be verified by using a t-table from any statistics book. Based on the regression results, the coefficient for $CAUS_{t-1}$ is significantly different from zero whereas the coefficient for $CGDP_{t-1}$ is not. This implies that one can be confident of a positive relationship between $CAUS_{t-1}$ and $CEXP_t$, but the positive relationship between $CGDP_{t-1}$ and $CEXP_t$ may have arisen simply by chance.

In some particular cases, one may be interested in determining whether the regression coefficient differs significantly from some value other than zero. In these cases, the t-statistic reported in the regression results would not be appropriate. See an econometrics text for more information on this subject.

The regression results indicate the **coefficient of determination** (denoted R^2 and often called "R-squared") of a regression model, which measures the percentage of variation in the dependent variable that can be explained by the regression model. The R^2 value can range from 0 to 100 percent. It is unusual for regression models to generate an R^2 of close to 100 percent, because the movement in any dependent variable is partially random and not associated with movements in independent variables. In our example the R^2 is 33 percent, which suggests that one-third of the variation in CEXP can be explained by movements in $CAUS_{t-1}$ and $CGDP_{t-1}$.

Some analysts use regression analysis as a forecasting tool. In this case, the regression results could be used (along with data for CAUS and CGDP) to forecast CEXP. Assume that, in the most recent period, CAUS was 5 percent and CGDP was -1 percent. The forecast of CEXP in the following period is derived by inserting this information into the regression model as follows:

$$
\begin{aligned}
CEXP_t &= b_0 + b_1(CAUS_{t-1}) + b_2(CGDP_{t-1}) \\
&= .002 + (.80)(.05) + (.36)(-.01) \\
&= .002 + .0400 - .0036 \\
&= .0420 - .0036 \\
&= .0384
\end{aligned}
$$

Thus the CEXP is forecast to be 3.84 percent in the following period. Some analysts might prefer to omit $CGDP_{t-1}$ from the model because its regression coefficient was not significantly different from zero. This would alter the forecasted value of CEXP.

When there is not a lagged relationship between independent variables and the dependent variable, the independent variables must be forecast in order to derive a forecast of the dependent variable. In this case, if the forecasts of the independent variables are inaccurate, an analyst might derive a poor forecast of the dependent variable, even when the regression model is properly specified.

As with most statistical techniques, there are some limitations that should be recognized when using regression analysis. These limitations are described in most statistics and econometrics textbooks.

Using Excel to Conduct Regression Analysis

Various software packages are available to run regression analysis. The following example is run on Excel to illustrate the ease with which regression analysis can be run.

Suppose that a firm wants to assess the influence of changes in the value of the Australian dollar on changes in its exports to Australia based on the following data:

PERIOD	VALUE (IN THOUSANDS OF DOLLARS) OF EXPORTS TO AUSTRALIA	AVERAGE EXCHANGE RATE OF AUSTRALIAN DOLLAR OVER THAT PERIOD
1	110	$0.50
2	125	.54
3	130	.57
4	142	.60
5	129	.55
6	113	.49
7	108	.46
8	103	.42
9	109	.43
10	118	.48
11	125	.49
12	130	.50
13	134	.52
14	138	.50
15	144	.53
16	149	.55
17	156	.58
18	160	.62
19	165	.66
20	170	.67
21	160	.62
22	158	.62
23	155	.61
24	167	.66

Assume that the firm applies the following regression model to the data:

$$CEXP = b_0 + b_1 CAUS + \mu$$

where

CEXP = percentage change in the firm's export value from one period to the next

CAUS = percentage change in the average exchange rate from one period to the next

μ = error term

The first step is to input the data for the two variables in two columns on a file using Excel. Then the data can be converted into percentage changes. This can be easily performed with a COMPUTE statement in the third column (column C) to derive CEXP and another COMPUTE statement in the fourth column (column D) to derive CAUS. These two columns will have a blank first row because the percentage change cannot be computed without the previous period's data.

Once you have derived CEXP and CAUS from the raw data, you can perform regression analysis as follows. First, click the Data Tab and see if you have the Data Analysis option. If not, you must install the free Analysis ToolPak add-in within Excel. Next, click Data Analysis; this leads to a new menu, in which you should click on Regression. Next to the Input Y Range, identify the range C2 to C24 for the dependent variable as C2:C24. Next to the Input X Range, identify the range D2 to D24 for the independent variable as D2:D24. The Output Range specifies the location on the screen where the output of the regression analysis should be displayed. In our example, F1 would be an appropriate location as it represents the upper left section of the output. Then click on OK and, within a few seconds, the regression analysis will be complete. For our example, the output is listed below:

SUMMARY OUTPUT

REGRESSION STATISTICS	
Multiple R	0.8852
R-square	0.7836
Adjusted R-square	0.7733
Standard error	2.9115
Observations	23.0000

ANOVA

	df	SS	MS	F	SIGNIFICANCE F
Regression	1.0000	644.6262	644.6262	76.0461	0.0000
Residual	21.0000	178.0125	8.4768		
Total	22.0000	822.6387			

	COEFFICIENTS	STANDARD ERROR	t-STAT	p-VALUE
Intercept	0.7951	0.6229	1.2763	0.2158
X variable 1	0.8678	0.0995	8.7204	0.0000

	LOWER 95%	UPPER 95%	LOWER 95%	UPPER 95%
Intercept	−0.5004	2.0905	−0.5004	2.0905
X variable 1	0.6608	1.0747	0.6608	1.0747

The estimate of the so-called slope coefficient is about .8678, which indicates that every 1 percent change in the Australian dollar's exchange rate is associated with a .8678 percent change (in the same direction) in the firm's exports to Australia. The t-statistic is also estimated to determine whether the slope coefficient is significantly different than zero. Because the standard error of the slope coefficient is about .0995, the t-statistic is .8678/.0995 = 8.72. This value suggests a significant relationship between CAUS and CEXP. The R-square statistic suggests that about 78 percent of the variation in CEXP is explained by CAUS. The correlation between CEXP and CAUS can also be measured by the correlation coefficient, which is the square root of the R-square statistic.

If you have more than one independent variable (multiple regression), place the independent variables next to each other in the file. Then, for the X-RANGE, identify this block of data. The output for the regression model will display the coefficient, standard error, and t-statistic for each of the independent variables. For multiple regression, the R-square statistic is interpreted as the percentage of variation in the dependent variable explained by the model as a whole.

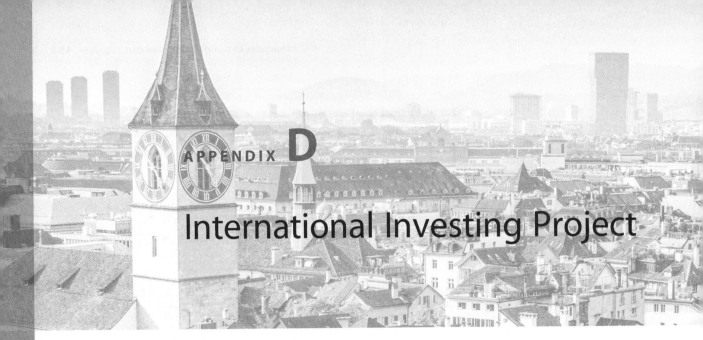

International Investing Project

Note to the Professor: *You may want to assign this as a project to be completed by the end of the semester. This project helps students to understand the factors that influence the performance of MNCs and foreign stocks. This project can also be done with teams of students and may be used for class presentations near the end of the semester. If you allow students to share their results in class, the students will learn that relationships cannot necessarily be generalized, as some MNCs are more exposed than others to economic conditions and exchange rate movements. The focus in grading this project will be on the explanations provided by the students, not on the movements in the stock prices or exchange rates.*

This project allows you to learn more about international investing and about firms that compete in the global arena. You will be asked to create a stock portfolio of at least two U.S.-based multinational corporations (MNCs) and two foreign stocks. You will monitor the performance of your portfolio over the school term and ultimately will attempt to explain why your portfolio performed well or poorly relative to the portfolios created by other students in your class. The explanations will offer insight into what is driving the valuations of the U.S.-based MNCs and the foreign stocks over time.

Select two stocks of U.S.-based MNCs that you want to include in your portfolio. If you do not know the ticker symbol of the stocks you want to invest in, go to the website finance.yahoo.com and type the company's name in the search box and click on "Search Finance." If you want to review a list of possible stocks, go to biz.yahoo.com/p (which lists stocks by sectors or industries). Make sure that your firms conduct a substantial amount of international business.

Next, select two foreign stocks that are traded on U.S. stock exchanges and are not from the same foreign country. Many foreign stocks are traded on U.S. stock exchanges as American depository receipts (ADRs), which are securities that represent ownership of foreign stock. The ADRs are denominated in dollars but reflect the value of a foreign stock, so an increase in the value of the foreign currency can have a favorable effect on the ADR's value. To review a list of ADRs in which you may invest, go to www.adr.com; under Investors, click on "Search DRs." You can choose a company from the alphabetical list of ADRs, or you can click on Industry, Sector, Country, and the like in the menu to obtain a list of companies with particular characteristics. Click on any company listed to review background information, including a description of its business and its stock price trend over the last year. It is assumed that you will invest $10,000 in each stock that you purchase.

List your portfolio in the following format:

U.S.-BASED MNCS			
NAME OF FIRM	TICKER SYMBOL	AMOUNT OF YOUR INVESTMENT	PRICE PER SHARE AT WHICH YOU PURCHASED THE STOCK
		$10,000	
		$10,000	

FOREIGN STOCKS (ADRS)				
NAME OF FIRM	TICKER SYMBOL	COUNTRY WHERE FIRM IS BASED	AMOUNT OF YOUR INVESTMENT	PRICE PER SHARE OF ADR AT WHICH YOU PURCHASED THE STOCK
			$10,000	
			$10,000	

You can easily monitor your portfolio using various Internet tools. If you do not already use a specific website for this purpose, go to finance.yahoo.com/?u and register for free. Follow the instructions, and in a few minutes you can create your own portfolio tracking system. This system not only updates the values of your stocks but also provides charts, recent news, and other information on the stocks in your portfolio.

Evaluation

At the end of each month during the school term (or a date specified by your professor), you should evaluate the performance and behavior of your stocks.

1. **a.** Determine the percentage increase or decrease in each of your stocks over the period of your investment and report that percentage in a table like the one below. In addition, offer the primary reason for this change in the stock price based on news about that stock or your own intuition. To review the recent news about each of your stocks, go to the site finance.yahoo.com/?u and insert the ticker symbol for each firm. Recent news is provided at the bottom of the screen.

NAME OF FIRM	PERCENTAGE CHANGE IN STOCK PRICE	PRIMARY REASON
1.		
2.		
3.		
4.		
Portfolio (average)		

b. How does your portfolio's performance compare to the portfolios of some other students? (Your professor may survey class members on their performances so that you can see how your performance differs from those of others.) Why do you think your performance was relatively high or low compared to other students' performances? Was it because of the markets where your firms do their business or because of firm-specific conditions?

2. Determine whether the performance of each of your U.S.-based MNCs is driven by the U.S. market. Go to the site finance.yahoo.com/?u and insert the symbol for your stock. Once the quote is provided, click on "Interactive" under Chart. Click on "Comparison" above the chart and then select S&P (which represents the S&P 500 Index). Then, assess the relationship between the U.S. market index movements and the stock's price movements. Explain whether the stock's price movements appear to be driven by U.S. market conditions. Repeat this task for each U.S.-based MNC in which you invested.

3. **a.** Determine whether the performance of each of your foreign stocks is driven by the corresponding market where the firm is based. First, go to the site finance.yahoo.com/stock-center and find the name of the country index of concern. For example, Brazil's index is the Ibovespa Index. Next, go to finance.yahoo.com/?u and insert the symbol for your stock. Click on "Interactive" under Chart; next, click on "Comparison" above the chart and then type the name of the index in the "compare symbol" box. (The box will automatically list the index's symbol; thus if you type "Ibovespa Index," the box will list ^BVSP, which is the index symbol.) Then, assess the relationship between the market index movements and the stock's price movements. Explain whether the stock's price movements appear to be driven by local market conditions. Repeat this exercise for each foreign stock in which you invested.

   b. Determine whether your foreign stock prices are highly correlated. Repeat the process just described, except insert the symbol representing one of the foreign stocks you own in the "compare symbol" box.

   c. Determine whether your foreign stock's performance is driven by the U.S. market (using the S&P 500 as a market proxy). Erase the symbol you typed in the "compare symbol" box, and click on S&P.

4. **a.** Review annual reports and news about each of your U.S.-based MNCs to determine where it does most of its business and the foreign currency to which it is most exposed. Determine whether your U.S.-based MNC's stock performance is influenced by the exchange rate movements of the foreign currency (against the U.S. dollar) to which it is most exposed. Go to www.oanda.com; under Currency Converter, click on "Historical Rates." You can convert the foreign currency to which the MNC is most exposed into U.S. dollars and determine the exchange rate movements over the period in which you invested in the stock. Provide your assessment of the relationship between the currency's exchange rate movements and the performance of the stock over the investment period. Attempt to explain the relationship that you just found.

   b. Repeat the steps in 4a for each U.S.-based MNC in which you invested.

5. **a.** Determine whether the stock performance of each of your foreign firms is influenced by the exchange rate movements of the firm's local currency against the U.S. dollar (you can obtain this information from www.oanda.com). You can convert the foreign currency of concern to U.S. dollars and determine the exchange rate movements over the period in which you invested in the stock. Provide your assessment of the relationship between the currency's exchange rate movements and the performance of the stock over the investment period. Attempt to explain the relationship that you just found.

   b. Repeat the steps in 5a for each of the foreign stocks in which you invested.

APPENDIX E

Discussion in the Boardroom

This exercise is intended to apply many of the key concepts presented in the text to broad issues that are discussed by managers who make financial decisions. It does not replace the more detailed questions and problems at the end of the chapters. Instead, it focuses on broad financial issues to facilitate class discussion and simulate a boardroom discussion. It serves as a running case in which concepts from every chapter are applied to the same business throughout the school term. The exercise not only enables students to apply concepts to the real world but also develops their intuitive and communication skills.

This exercise can be used in a course in several ways.

1. Apply it on a chapter-by-chapter basis to ensure that the broad chapter concepts are understood before moving on to the next chapter.
2. Use it to encourage online discussion for courses taught online.
3. Use it as a review before each exam, covering all chapters assigned for that exam.
4. Use it as a comprehensive case discussion, near the end of the semester, as a means of reviewing the key concepts that were described throughout the course.
5. Use it for presentations in which individuals or teams present their views on the questions assigned to them.

This exercise has been placed on the course website so that students can download it and insert their answers after the questions. By the end of the course, students will have applied all the major concepts of the text to a single firm. The focus on a single firm will allow students to recognize how some of their decisions in the earlier chapters interact with decisions to be made in later chapters.

Background

One of the best ways to learn the broad concepts presented in this text is to put yourself in the position of an MNC manager or board member and apply the concepts to financial decisions. Although board members normally do not make the decisions discussed here, they must have the conceptual skills to monitor the policies that are implemented by the MNC's managers. Thus they must frequently consider what they would do if they were making the managerial decisions or setting corporate policies.

This exercise is based on a business that you could easily create: a business that teaches individuals in a non-U.S. country to speak English. Although this business is very basic, it still requires the same types of decisions faced by large MNCs.

Assume that you live in the United States and invest $60,000 to establish a language school called Escuela de Inglés in Mexico City, Mexico. You set up a small subsidiary in Mexico with an office and an attached classroom that you lease. You hire local individuals in Mexico who can speak English and teach it to others. Your school offers two types of courses: a one-month structured course in English and a one-week intensive course for individuals who already know English but want to improve their skills before visiting the United States. You advertise both types of teaching services in local newspapers.

All revenue and expenses associated with your business are denominated in Mexican pesos. Your subsidiary sends most of the profits from the business in Mexico to you at the end of each month. Although your expenses are fairly stable, your revenue varies with the number of clients who sign up for the courses in Mexico.

This background is sufficient to enable you to answer the questions that are asked about your business throughout the term. Answer each question as if you were serving on the board or as a manager of the business. The questions in the early chapters force you to assess the firm's opportunities and exposure, and those in later chapters force you to consider potential strategies that your business might pursue.

Chapter 1

a. Discuss the corporate control of your business. Explain why your business in Mexico is exposed to agency problems.

b. How would you attempt to monitor the ongoing operations of the business?

c. Explain how you might be able to use a compensation plan that limits the potential agency problems.

d. Assume that you have been approached by a competitor in Mexico to engage in a joint venture. The competitor would offer the classroom facilities (so that you would not need to rent classroom facilities), while your employees would provide the teaching. You would split the profits with this business. Discuss how your potential return and your risk would change if you pursue the joint venture.

e. Explain the conditions that would cause your business to be adversely affected by exchange rate movements.

f. Explain how your business could be adversely affected by political risk.

Chapter 2

Your business provides DVDs for free to customers who pay for the English courses that you offer in Mexico. You consider the idea of mass production of the DVDs in the United States so that you can sell (export) them to distributors or to retail stores throughout Mexico. You would price the DVDs in dollars when exporting them. The DVDs are not as effective without the teaching, but can be useful to individuals who want to learn the basics of the English language.

a. If you pursue this idea, explain how the factors that affect international trade flows (identified in Chapter 2) could affect the Mexican demand for your DVDs. Which of these factors would likely have the largest impact on the Mexican demand for your DVDs? What other factors would affect the Mexican demand for the DVDs?

b. If you believe the Mexican government would impose a tariff on the DVDs exported to Mexico, how could you still execute this business idea at a relatively low cost while avoiding the tariff? Describe any disadvantages of this idea that would avoid the tariff.

Chapter 3

Assuming that the business in Mexico grows, explain how financial markets could help to finance the growth of the business.

Chapter 4

Given the factors that affect the value of a foreign currency, describe the type of economic or other conditions in Mexico that could cause the Mexican peso to weaken, and therefore to adversely affect your business.

Chapter 5

Explain how currency futures could be used to hedge your business in Mexico. Explain how currency options could be used to hedge your business in Mexico.

Chapter 6

a. Explain how your business would likely be affected (at least in the short run) if the central bank of Mexico intervened in the foreign exchange market by exchanging Mexican pesos for dollars in the foreign exchange market.

b. Explain how your business would likely be affected if the central bank of Mexico used indirect intervention by lowering Mexican interest rates (assume inflationary expectations have not changed).

Chapter 7

Mexican interest rates are normally substantially higher than U.S. interest rates.

a. What does this imply about the forward premium or discount of the Mexican peso?

b. What does this imply about your business using the forward or futures contracts to hedge your periodic profits in pesos that must be converted into dollars?

c. Do you think you would frequently hedge your exposure to Mexican pesos? Explain your answer.

Chapter 8

Mexican interest rates are normally substantially higher than U.S. interest rates.

a. What does this imply about the inflation differential (Mexico inflation minus U.S. inflation), assuming that the peso interest rate is the same in both countries? Does this imply that the Mexican peso will appreciate or depreciate? Explain.

b. It may be argued that the high Mexican interest rate should entice U.S. investors to invest in Mexican money market securities, which could cause the peso to appreciate. Reconcile this theory with your answer in part a. If you believe that the high Mexican interest rate does not entice U.S. investors, explain why.

c. Assume that the difference between Mexican and U.S. interest rates is typically attributed to a difference in expected inflation in the two countries. Also assume that purchasing power parity holds. Do you think that your business cash flows would be adversely affected? In reality, purchasing power parity does not hold consistently. Assume that the inflation differential (Mexico inflation minus U.S. inflation) is not fully offset by the exchange rate movement of the peso. Would this benefit or hurt your business? Now assume that the inflation differential is more than offset by the exchange rate movement of the peso. Would this benefit or hurt your business?

d. Assume that the nominal interest rate in Mexico is presently much higher than the interest rate in the United States, which is due to a high rate of expected inflation in Mexico. You consider implementing a marketing campaign in which you would hire a local firm to promote your business, but you would have to borrow funds to finance this campaign. A consultant advises you to delay the marketing campaign for a year, so that you can capitalize on the high nominal interest rate in Mexico. He suggests that you retain the profits that you would normally have remitted to the United States and deposit them in a Mexican bank. The Mexican peso cash flows that your business deposits will grow at a high rate of interest over the year. Should you follow the consultant's advice?

Chapter 9

a. Mexican interest rates are normally substantially higher than U.S. interest rates. What does this imply about the forward rate as a forecast of the future spot rate?

b. Does the forward rate reflect a forecast of appreciation or depreciation of the Mexican peso? Explain how the degree of the expected change implied by the forward rate forecast is tied to the interest rate differential.

c. Do you think that today's forward rate or today's spot rate of the peso would be a better forecast of the future spot rate of the peso?

Chapter 10

Recall that your Mexican business invoices in Mexican pesos.

a. You are already aware that a decline in the value of the peso could reduce your dollar cash flows. Yet, according to purchasing power parity, a weak peso should only occur in response to a high level of Mexican inflation, and such high inflation should increase your profits. If this theory holds precisely, your cash flows would not really be exposed. Should you be concerned about your exposure, or not? Explain.

b. If you shift your invoicing policy to be only in dollars, how will your transaction exposure be affected?

c. Why might the demand for your business change if you shift your invoice policy? What are the implications for economic exposure?

Chapter 11

Mexican interest rates are normally substantially higher than U.S. interest rates.

a. Assuming that interest rate parity exists, do you think hedging with a forward rate would be beneficial if the spot rate of the Mexican peso was expected to decline slightly over time?

b. Would hedging with a money market hedge be beneficial if the spot rate of the Mexican peso was expected to decline slightly over time (assume zero transaction costs)? Explain.

c. What are some limitations on using currency futures or options that may make it difficult for you to perfectly hedge against exchange rate risk over the next year or so?

d. In general, there is a lack of long-term currency futures and options on the Mexican pesos. A consultant suggests that this is no problem because you can hedge your position a quarter at a time. In other words, the profits that you remit at any point in the future can be hedged by taking a currency futures or options position three months or so before that time. Thus, although the consultant recognizes that the peso could weaken substantially in the long term, he sees no reason why you should worry about it as long as you continually create a short-term hedge. Do you agree?

Chapter 12

a. Explain how your business is subject to translation exposure.

b. How could you hedge against this translation exposure?

c. Is it worthwhile for your business to hedge the translation exposure?

Chapter 13

Assume that you wanted to expand your learning English business to other non-U.S. countries where some individuals may want to speak English.

a. Explain why you might be able to stabilize the profits of your total business in this manner. Review the motives for direct foreign investment that are identified in this chapter. Which of these motives are most important?

b. Why would a city such as Montreal be a less desirable site for your business than a city such as Mexico City?

c. Describe the conditions in which your total business would experience weak effects even if the business was spread across three or four countries.

d. What factors affect the probability of these conditions occurring? (In other words, explain why the conditions could occur in one set of countries, but not another set of countries.)

e. What data would you review to assess the probability of these conditions occurring?

f. Consider that the prevailing service you offer is teaching individuals in Mexico to speak English, and your business has already created some supplemental pamphlets and DVDs that translate common Spanish terms into English. How could you expand your business in a manner that may allow you to benefit from economies of scale (and perhaps even benefit from your existing business reputation)? When you attempt to benefit from economies of scale, do you forgo diversification benefits? Explain.

g. How would you come to a decision on whether to pursue business expansion that capitalizes on economies of scale even if it would forgo diversification benefits? Do you think economies of scale would be more important or less important than diversification for your business?

h. Is there any way to achieve economies of scale and yet still achieve diversification benefits?

Chapter 14

a. Review the different items that are used in the multinational capital budgeting example (Spartan Inc.). Describe the items that would be included on a spreadsheet if you were to conduct a multinational capital budgeting analysis of investing dollars to expand your existing language business in a different location.

b. Assume that you recognize your limitations in predicting the future exchange rate of the invoice currency for your expanded business. You think that there are several possible exchange rate scenarios, each with equal probability of occurrence. Explain how you could use this information to estimate the future NPV and make a decision about whether to accept or reject the project.

c. Now assume that there is also much uncertainty about the demand for your service by individuals. Explain how you can attempt to incorporate this uncertainty along with the uncertainty of exchange rate movements so that you can make a decision about whether to accept or reject the project.

d. Explain how you would derive a required rate of return for your capital budgeting analysis. What type of information would you use to derive the required rate of return?

Chapter 15

You have an opportunity to purchase a private competitor called Fernand in Mexico. You will use only your funds if you decide to purchase the company.

a. When you attempt to determine the value of this company, how will you derive your required rate of return? Specifically, should you use the U.S. or Mexico risk-free rate as a base when deriving your required rate of return? Why?

b. Another Mexican firm called Vascon also considers the purchase of this firm. Explain why Vascon's required rate of return may be higher than your required rate of return. Is there any reason why Vascon's required rate of return may be lower than your required rate of return?

c. Assume that you and Vascon have the same expectations regarding the Mexican cash flows that will be generated by Fernand. Fernand's owner is willing to sell the company for 2 million Mexican pesos. You and Vascon use a similar process to determine the feasibility of acquiring a target. You both compare the present value of the target's cash flows to the purchase price of the target. Based on your analysis, Fernand would generate a positive net present value for your firm. Based on Vascon's analysis, Fernand would generate a negative net present value for Vascon. How could you determine that the acquisition of Fernand is feasible, while Vascon determines that the acquisition of Fernand is not feasible?

d. Repeat part c, except reverse the assumptions. Based on your analysis, Fernand would generate a negative net present value for your firm. Based on Vascon's analysis, Fernand would generate a positive net present value for Vascon. How could you determine that the acquisition of Fernand is not feasible, while Vascon determines that the acquisition of Fernand is feasible?

Chapter 16

a. Review the political risk factors, and identify those that could possibly affect your business. Explain how your cash flows could be affected.

b. Explain why any threats of terrorism due to friction between two countries could possibly affect your business, even if the terrorism has no effect on the relations between the United States and Mexico.

c. Assume there is an upcoming election in Mexico that may result in a complete change in government. Explain why such an election can have significant effects on your cash flows.

Chapter 17

a. Assume that your business is considering expansion within Mexico. You plan to invest a small amount of U.S. dollar equity into this project, and finance the remainder with debt. You can obtain debt financing for the expansion in Mexico, but the interest rates in Mexico are higher than in the United States. Yet if you used mostly U.S. debt financing, you are more exposed to exchange rate risk. Explain why.

b. If you pursue a new project in Mexico, you want to assess the feasibility of the project if you use mostly U.S. debt financing versus mostly Mexican debt financing. Yet you also want to capture possible exchange rate effects on your cash flows over time. How can you use capital budgeting to conduct your comparison?

c. You would prefer to avoid using Mexican debt to finance your expansion in Mexico because the interest rates are high. A consultant suggests that you seek one or more investors in Mexico who would be willing to take an equity position in your business. You would provide them with periodic dividends and they would be partial owners of your company. The consultant suggests that this strategy circumvents the high cost of capital in Mexico because it uses equity financing instead of debt financing. Is the consultant correct?

Chapter 18

Recall from the previous chapter that your business is considering expansion within Mexico. Recall that you plan to invest a small amount of U.S. dollar equity into this project, and finance the remainder with debt. You can obtain debt financing for the expansion in Mexico, but the interest rates in Mexico are higher than in the United States. Today you receive credit offers from different banks. You can either obtain a fixed-rate loan in the United States at 8 percent for the life of this project or a floating-rate loan (rate changes each year in response to market interest rates) in Mexico at 10 percent. Explain how you could estimate the net present value of the project for each alternative financing method. Include in your explanation how you would account for the uncertainty of future interest rate movements of the Mexican debt.

Chapter 19

Your business provides DVDs on learning English that complement the teaching that is provided by your employees based in Mexico. Assume that you decide to capitalize on these DVDs by selling them to a large retail store based in Mexico. The DVDs are not as effective without the teaching, but can be useful to individuals who want to learn the basics of the English language. You do not want to take the risk of sending a case of DVDs to the retail store unless you can be sure of receiving payment. Explain how you can ensure payment for the DVDs.

Chapter 20

If you decide to implement a major marketing campaign in Mexico, you will incur high expenses in Mexican pesos. You would need to finance the cost of your marketing. You could either borrow dollars at a low interest rate and convert them to Mexican pesos to cover the cost, or borrow Mexican pesos to cover the cost. You would expect to pay off the loan on a monthly basis over the next year with the use of a portion of the revenue you generate from your business in Mexico.

a. Would your business be more exposed to exchange rate risk if you borrow dollars or Mexican pesos?

b. Explain how you would make the decision to borrow dollars versus Mexican pesos. What is the key factor (other than the interest rate of each currency) that will determine whether you should borrow dollars or Mexican pesos?

Chapter 21

Assume that you decide not to implement the marketing campaign that you considered in the previous chapter. You may pursue it next year instead and will attempt to invest some of your profits this year in money market investments, and then use this money to cover the campaign next year. You can retain your profits earned this year by investing them in a Mexican bank where interest rates are high. Alternatively, you could invest the profits in a dollar-denominated bank account. That is, you could convert your Mexican peso profits to dollars periodically and accumulate the dollars over the year. At the end of the year, you could convert the dollars back to Mexican pesos, so that you can pay for the marketing campaign. Explain how you could decide between these two alternatives.

Use of Bitcoin to Conduct International Transactions

International transactions are increasingly conducted in cryptocurrencies, which are digital or virtual currencies that use encryption techniques to verify fund transfers. Cryptocurrencies are created and operate independently of national governments, so until recently they have been outside the jurisdiction of central banks and the financial regulations issued by governments. As a result of this independence and the relative anonymity of cryptocurrency transactions, cryptocurrencies have sometimes been used for illegal activities such as money laundering and tax evasion. Recently, however, governments have attempted to introduce regulations to prevent the less desirable uses of cryptocurrencies while allowing their use for legitimate payments.

Although several cryptocurrencies exist, bitcoins are the most widely used. Bitcoin was established in 2009 as a peer-to-peer payment network that is owned and controlled by its users. No corporation or other entity runs Bitcoin. The speed of transactions and the minimal fees charged have made bitcoins a viable means of exchange, especially for international transactions. Bitcoins are now accepted as a means of payment by many MNCs around the world.

Using Bitcoins

Bitcoins can be purchased on online exchanges or received as a form of payment for goods or services. The bitcoin owner receives a password that is a key to a particular bitcoin address; the owner then stores the bitcoins in a digital wallet. The owner can then spend the bitcoins at all businesses that accept them. Consumers can use their digital wallet to send payments around the world by entering the payee's bitcoin address and the amount. Most digital wallets allow the sender to enter the amount in dollars, euros, or other major currencies. The wallet software will then convert that amount into bitcoins before transmitting the payment to the payee.

Even if a particular online business does not accept bitcoins directly, consumers can still use bitcoins for purchases by opening an account at Snapcard.com. They can use this account rather than a credit card for online purchases. When shopping in person, consumers can use a mobile app on a smartphone that enables them to make a purchase by simply scanning the merchant's Quick Response code (a QR code is a matrix barcode consisting of black dots arranged in a square).

When businesses receive bitcoins, they can either store the bitcoins in their digital wallets or convert them into dollars or another currency at a bitcoin exchange. There is a quoted exchange rate between bitcoins and dollars and most other world currencies at any point in time. The exchange rate changes over time.

Advantages and Disadvantages of Bitcoins

One major advantage of bitcoins is the speed of transactions, especially international transactions. Bitcoins can be transferred from person to person or business to business anywhere in the world in 10 minutes. In addition, the fees for fund transfers are generally much lower than the fees charged by financial institutions for international payments.

A disadvantage of bitcoins is the volatility of their value. In 2013, for example, the value of a bitcoin ranged from about $100 to more than $1,200, the all-time peak value. Although the value has been more stable in recent years, this volatility demonstrates the degree to which the value of the bitcoin could decline while being held in the owner's digital wallet. Consequently, some firms that are willing to accept bitcoins quickly convert them into another currency upon receipt.

Another problem with retaining a large amount of bitcoins in an account is that there is no protection against loss. There is no deposit insurance for bitcoins. If hackers access a digital wallet and steal the bitcoins, the owner has no recourse against them. In 2014, Mt. Gox, a large Tokyo-based bitcoin exchange, went bankrupt and said that $400 million worth of customer bitcoin funds had been lost or stolen. In 2015, hackers obtained about $5 million worth of bitcoins from a bitcoin exchange in Slovenia. In 2016, Bitfinex (a digital currency exchange based in Hong Kong) lost $65 million to hackers.

Regulating Bitcoin

As the number of users of bitcoins has grown, the lack of protection for bitcoin owners and the potential for illegal activity has led to some regulations. In 2015, the state of New York granted a banking trust charter to itBit Trust Co., making it the first fully regulated bitcoin exchange. Bitcoin accounts at itBit are backed by mandatory capital reserves, and dollar accounts are insured by the Federal Deposit Insurance Corporation. Previously, some MNCs were reluctant to accept bitcoins because many banks were unwilling to set up bitcoin accounts, so an MNC had to convert the bitcoins to another currency at an exchange and then transfer the converted amount to a bank; now bitcoins can be converted to dollars at itBit and immediately moved into a dollar account. To prevent hacking, itBit keeps bitcoin owners' wallets offline and moves the bitcoins online only as needed. To obtain the charter, itBit had to meet higher consumer protection and security standards than other bitcoin exchanges meet. In addition, New York now requires bitcoin dealers to obtain a "bitlicense" to operate in the state. The U.S. Treasury is also developing rules for cryptocurrencies.

Glossary

A

absolute form of PPP: theory that explains how inflation differentials affect exchange rates. It suggests that prices of two products of different countries should be equal when measured by a common currency.

accounts receivable financing: indirect financing provided by an exporter for an importer by exporting goods and allowing for payment to be made at a later date.

advising bank: corresponding bank in the beneficiary's country to which the issuing bank sends the letter of credit.

agency problem: conflict of goals between a firm's shareholders and its managers.

airway bill: receipt for a shipment by air, which includes freight charges and title to the merchandise.

all-in rate: rate used in charging customers for accepting banker's acceptances, consisting of the discount interest rate plus the commission.

American depository receipts (ADRs): certificates representing ownership of foreign stocks, which are traded on stock exchanges in the United States.

appreciation: increase in the value of a currency.

arbitrage: action to capitalize on a discrepancy in quoted prices; in many cases, there is no investment of funds tied up for any length of time.

Asian money market: market in Asia in which banks collect deposits and make loans denominated in U.S. dollars.

ask price: price at which a trader of foreign exchange (typically a bank) is willing to sell a particular currency.

assignment of proceeds: arrangement that allows the original beneficiary of a letter of credit to pledge or assign proceeds to an end supplier.

B

balance of payments: is a summary of transactions between domestic and foreign residents for a specific country over a specified period of time.

balance of trade: difference between the value of merchandise exports and merchandise imports.

Bank for International Settlements (BIS): institution that facilitates cooperation among countries involved in international transactions and provides assistance to countries experiencing international payment problems.

Bank Letter of Credit Policy: policy that enables banks to confirm letters of credit by foreign banks supporting the purchase of U.S. exports.

banker's acceptance: bill of exchange drawn on and accepted by a banking institution; it is commonly used to guarantee exporters that they will receive payment on goods delivered to importers.

barter: exchange of goods between two parties without the use of any currency as a medium of exchange.

Basel Accord: agreement among country representatives in 1988 to establish standardized risk-based capital requirements for banks across countries.

bid price: price that a trader of foreign exchange (typically a bank) is willing to pay for a particular currency.

bid/ask spread: difference between the price at which a bank is willing to buy a currency and the price at which it will sell that currency.

bilateral netting system: netting method used for transactions between two units.

bill of exchange (draft): promise drawn by one party (usually an exporter) to pay a specified amount to another party at a specified future date, or upon presentation of the draft.

bill of lading (B/L): document serving as a receipt for shipment and a summary of freight charges and conveying title to the merchandise.

Bretton Woods Agreement: conference held in Bretton Woods, New Hampshire, in 1944, resulting in an agreement to maintain exchange rates of currencies within very narrow boundaries; this agreement lasted until 1971.

C

call option on real assets: a proposed project that contains an option of pursuing an additional venture.

capital account: represents a summary of the flow of funds between one specified country and all other countries due to purchases of goods and services or to the cash flows generated by income-producing financial assets.

cash management: optimization of cash flows and investment of excess cash.

centralized cash flow management: policy that consolidates cash management decisions for all MNC units, usually at the parent's location.

coefficient of determination: measure of the percentage variation in the dependent variable that can be explained by the independent variables when using regression analysis.

cofinancing agreements: arrangement in which the World Bank participates along with other agencies or lenders in providing funds to developing countries.

commercial invoice: exporter's description of merchandise being sold to the buyer.

commercial letters of credit: Trade-related letters of credit.

comparative advantage: theory suggesting that specialization by countries can increase worldwide production.

compensation: arrangement in which the delivery of goods to a party is compensated for by buying back a certain amount of the product from that same party.

compensatory financing facility (CFF): facility that attempts to reduce the impact of export instability on country economies.

consignment: arrangement in which the exporter ships goods to the importer while still retaining title to the merchandise.

counterpurchase: exchange of goods between two parties under two distinct contracts expressed in monetary terms.

countertrade: sale of goods to one country that is linked to the purchase or exchange of goods from that same country.

country risk: characteristics of the host country, including political and financial conditions, that can affect an MNC's cash flows.

covered interest arbitrage: investment in a foreign money market security with a simultaneous forward sale of the currency denominating that security.

cross exchange rate: exchange rate between currency A and currency B, given the values of currencies A and B with respect to a third currency.

cross-hedging: hedging an open position in one currency with a hedge on another currency that is highly correlated with the first currency. This occurs when for some reason the common hedging techniques cannot be applied to the first currency. A cross-hedge is not a perfect hedge, but can substantially reduce the exposure.

cross-sectional analysis: analysis of relationships among a cross section of firms, countries, or some other variable at a given point in time.

currency board: system for maintaining the value of the local currency with respect to some other specified currency.

currency call option: contract that grants the right to purchase a specific currency at a specific price (exchange rate) within a specific period of time.

currency diversification: process of using more than one currency as an investing or financing strategy. Exposure to a diversified currency portfolio typically results in less exchange rate risk than if all of the exposure was in a single foreign currency.

currency futures contract: contract specifying a standard volume of a particular currency to be exchanged on a specific settlement date.

currency option combination: the use of simultaneous call and put option positions to construct a unique position to suit the hedger's or speculator's needs. Two of the most popular currency option combinations are straddles and strangles.

currency put option: contract granting the right to sell a particular currency at a specified price (exchange rate) within a specified period of time.

currency swap: agreement to exchange one currency for another at a specified exchange rate and date. Banks commonly serve as intermediaries between two parties who wish to engage in a currency swap.

current account: broad measure of a country's international trade in goods and services.

D

Delphi technique: collection of independent opinions without group discussion by the assessors who provide the opinions; used for various types of assessments (such as country risk assessment).

depreciation: decrease in the value of a currency.

devaluation: a downward adjustment of the exchange rate by a central bank.

devalue: to reduce the value of a currency against the value of other currencies.

direct foreign investment (DFI): any method of increasing international business that requires a direct investment in foreign operations.

Direct Loan Program: program in which the Ex-Im Bank offers fixed rate loans directly to the foreign buyer to purchase U.S. capital equipment and services.

direct quotations: quotations that report the value of a foreign currency in dollars (number of dollars per unit of other currency).

discount: as related to forward rates, represents the percentage amount by which the forward rate is less than the spot rate.

documentary collections: trade transactions handled on a draft basis.

documents against acceptance: situation in which the buyer's bank does not release shipping documents to the buyer until the buyer has accepted (signed) the draft.

documents against payment: shipping documents that are released to the buyer once the buyer has paid for the draft.

dollarization: replacement of a foreign currency with U.S. dollars.

draft (bill of exchange): unconditional promise drawn by one party (usually the exporter) instructing the buyer to pay the face amount of the draft upon presentation.

dumping: the exporting of products that were produced with the help of government subsidies.

dynamic hedging: applying a hedge when the currencies held are expected to depreciate and removing any hedge when the currencies held are expected to appreciate.

E

economic exposure: the sensitivity of the firm's cash flows to exchange rate movements; sometimes referred to as operational exposure.

economies of scale: lower average cost per unit resulting from increased production.

equilibrium exchange rate: exchange rate at which demand for a currency is equal to the supply of the currency for sale.

Eurobonds: bonds that are sold in countries other than the country whose currency is used to denominate the bonds.

Euro-commercial paper: debt securities issued by MNCs for short-term financing.

Eurocredit loans: loans of one year or longer that are extended by banks to MNCs or government agencies in Europe.

Eurocredit market: collection of banks that accepts deposits and provides loans in large denominations and in a variety of currencies. The banks that comprise this market are the same banks that comprise the Eurocurrency market; the difference is that the Eurocredit loans are longer term than so-called Eurocurrency loans.

Eurodollars: dollar deposits in banks in Europe (and on other continents).

Euronotes: unsecured debt securities issued by MNCs for short-term financing.

European Central Bank (ECB): central bank responsible for setting monetary policy for European countries participating in the single European currency, the euro.

exchange rate mechanism (ERM): method of linking European currency values with the European Currency Unit (ECU).

exercise price (strike price): price (exchange rate) at which the owner of a currency call option is allowed to buy a specified currency; or the price (exchange rate) at which the owner of a currency put option is allowed to sell a specified currency.

Export-Import Bank (Ex-Im Bank): a bank that finances and facilitates the export of American goods and services and maintains the competitiveness of American companies in overseas markets.

F

factor: firm specializing in collection on accounts receivable; exporters sometimes sell their accounts receivable to a factor at a discount.

factor income: income (interest and dividend payments) received by investors on foreign investments in financial assets (securities).

factoring: purchase of receivables of an exporter by a factor without recourse to the exporter.

Financial account: measures the flow of funds between countries due to direct foreign investment, portfolio investment, and other capital investment.

Financial Institution Buyer Credit Policy: policy that provides insurance coverage for loans by banks to foreign buyers of exports on a short-term basis.

fixed exchange rate system: an exchange rate system in which exchange rates are either held constant or allowed to fluctuate only within very narrow boundaries.

floating rate notes (FRNs): a variable rate provision in some Eurobonds that adjusts the coupon rate over time according to prevailing market rates.

foreign bond: bond issued by a borrower foreign to the country where the bond is placed.

foreign exchange dealers: dealers who serve as intermediaries in the foreign exchange market by exchanging currencies desired by MNCs or individuals.

foreign exchange market: market composed primarily of banks, serving firms and consumers who wish to buy or sell various currencies.

foreign investment risk matrix (FIRM): matrix that displays the financial (or economic) and political risk by intervals (ranging across the matrix from "poor" to "good") so that each country can be positioned in its appropriate location on the matrix based on its political rating and financial rating.

forfaiting: refers to the purchase of financial obligations, such as bills of exchange or promissory notes, without recourse to the original holder (usually, the exporter).

forward contract: agreement to buy or sell a specified currency at a specified exchange rate on a specified future date.

forward market: market in which forward contracts are created.

forward rate: specified exchange rate within the forward contract.

I

imperfect market: the condition where, due to the costs to transfer labor and other resources used for production, firms may attempt to use foreign factors of production when they are less costly than local factors.

import/export letters of credit: trade-related letters of credit.

independent variable: term used in regression analysis to represent the variable that is expected to influence another (the "dependent") variable.

indirect quotations: exchange rate quotations representing the value measured by number of units per dollar.

International Bank for Reconstruction and Development (IBRD): also referred to as the World Bank, was established in 1944 to make loans that can reduce poverty and increase economic development.

International Development Association: was established in 1960 to make loans intended to boost economic development in less developed countries.

International Finance Corporation: was established in 1956 to promote private enterprise within countries.

International Monetary Fund (IMF): was established in 1944 to promote cooperation among countries on international monetary issues, stabilize exchange rates, and to increase international business.

intracompany trade: the process that companies adopt to purchase products that are produced by their subsidiaries.

J

J-curve effect: effect of a weaker dollar on the U.S. trade balance in which the trade balance initially deteriorates; it only improves once U.S. and non-U.S. importers respond to the change in purchasing power that is caused by the weaker dollar.

joint venture: a venture that is jointly owned and operated by two or more firms.

L

lagging: strategy used by a firm to stall payments, normally in response to exchange rate projections.

leading: strategy used by a firm to accelerate payments, normally in response to exchange rate expectations.

letter of credit (L/C): an instrument issued by a bank on behalf of the importer (buyer) promising to pay the exporter (beneficiary) upon presentation of shipping documents in compliance with the terms stipulated therein.

licensing: an arrangement whereby one firm provides its technology (copyrights, patents, trademarks, or trade names) in exchange for fees or other considerations.

locational arbitrage: the process of buying a currency at a location where it is priced cheap and then immediately selling it at some other location where it is priced higher.

lockboxes: post office boxes to which customers are instructed to send payment.

London Interbank Offer Rate (LIBOR): the rate most often charged for very short-term loans (such as for one day) between banks.

M

macro-assessment of country risk: a country's overall risk assessment involving consideration of all variables that affect country risk except those that are unique to a particular firm or industry.

mail float: mailing time involved in sending payments by mail.

managed float: exchange rate system in which governments may intervene to prevent their currencies from moving too far in a certain direction.

market-based forecasting: use of a market-determined exchange rate (such as the spot rate or forward rate) to forecast the spot rate in the future.

Master Agreement: an agreement that provides participants in the private derivatives markets with the opportunity to establish the legal and credit terms between them for an ongoing business relationship.

micro-assessment of country risk: the risk assessment of a country as related to the MNC's type of business.

mixed forecasting: development of forecasts based on a mixture of forecasting techniques.

Multibuyer Policy: policy administered by the Ex-Im Bank that provides credit risk insurance on export sales to many different buyers.

Multilateral Investment Guarantee Agency (MIGA): agency established by the World Bank that offers various forms of political risk insurance to corporations.

multilateral netting system: complex interchange for netting between a parent and several subsidiaries.

multinational corporations (MNCs): firms that engage in some form of international business.

N

net operating loss carrybacks: practice of applying losses to offset earnings in previous years.

net operating loss carryforwards: practice of applying losses to offset earnings in future years.

netting: optimizing cash flows by reducing the administrative and transaction costs that result from currency conversion.

non-deliverable forward contract (NDF): like a forward contract, represents an agreement regarding a position in a specified currency, a specified exchange rate, and a specified future settlement date, but does not result in delivery of currencies. Instead, a payment is made by one party in the agreement to the other party based on the exchange rate at the future date.

nonsterilized intervention: intervention in the foreign exchange market without adjusting for the change in money supply.

notional value: a valuation to which interest rates can be applied on a periodic basis to determine the net interest that will be paid by one party to another party.

O

ocean bill of lading: the carrier issues this if the merchandise is to be shipped by boat.

open account transaction: sale in which the exporter ships the merchandise and expects the buyer to remit payment according to agreed-upon terms.

outsourcing: represents the process of subcontracting to a third party.

overhedging: hedging an amount in a currency larger than the actual transaction amount.

P

parallel bonds: bonds placed in different countries and denominated in the respective currencies of the countries where they are placed.

parallel loan: loan involving an exchange of currencies between two parties, with a promise to re-exchange the currencies at a specified exchange rate and future date.

partial compensation: an arrangement in which the delivery of goods to one party is partially compensated for by buying back a certain amount of product from the same party.

pegged exchange rate: exchange rate whose value is pegged to another currency's value or to a unit of account.

perfect forecast line: a 45-degree line on a graph that matches the forecast of an exchange rate with the actual exchange rate.

petrodollars: deposits of dollars by countries that receive dollar revenues due to the sale of petroleum to other countries; the term commonly refers to OPEC deposits of dollars in the Eurocurrency market.

political risk: political actions taken by the host government or the public that affect the MNC's cash flows.

preauthorized payment: method of accelerating cash inflows by receiving authorization to charge a customer's bank account.

prepayment: method that exporter uses to receive payment before shipping goods.

price-elastic: sensitive to price changes.

Primary income: component of current account, mostly composed of income earned by MNCs on their direct foreign investment, and income earned by investors who invest in foreign securities.

privatization: conversion of government-owned businesses to ownership by shareholders or individuals.

product cycle theory: theory suggesting that a firm initially establishes itself locally and expands into foreign markets in response to foreign demand for its product; over time, the MNC will grow in foreign markets; after some point, its foreign business may decline unless it can differentiate its product from competitors.

Project Finance Loan Program: program that allows banks, the Ex-Im Bank, or a combination of both to extend long-term financing for capital equipment and related services for major projects.

purchasing power parity (PPP) line: diagonal line on a graph that reflects points at which the inflation differential between two countries is equal to the percentage change in the exchange rate between the two respective currencies.

purchasing power parity (PPP) theory: theory suggesting that exchange rates will adjust over time to reflect the differential in inflation rates in the two countries; in this way, the purchasing power of consumers when purchasing domestic goods will be the same as that when they purchase foreign goods.

put option on real assets: project that contains an option of divesting part or all of the project.

Q

quota: maximum limit imposed by the government on goods allowed to be imported into a country.

R

real cost of hedging: the additional cost of hedging when compared to not hedging (a negative real cost would imply that hedging was more favorable than not hedging).

real interest rate: nominal (or quoted) interest rate minus the inflation rate.

real options: implicit options on real assets.

regression analysis: statistical technique used to measure the relationship between variables and the sensitivity of a variable to one or more other variables.

regression coefficient: term measured by regression analysis to estimate the sensitivity of the dependent variable to a particular independent variable.

revaluation: an upward adjustment of the exchange rate by a central bank.

revalue: to increase the value of a currency against the value of other currencies.

revocable letter of credit: letter of credit issued by a bank that can be canceled at any time without prior notification to the beneficiary.

S

Secondary income: component of current account, mostly composed of aid, grants, and gifts from one country to another.

semistrong-form efficient: description of foreign exchange markets, implying that all relevant public information is already reflected in prevailing spot exchange rates.

sensitivity analysis: technique for assessing uncertainty whereby various possibilities are input to determine possible outcomes.

simulation: technique for assessing the degree of uncertainty. Probability distributions are developed for the input variables; simulation uses this information to generate possible outcomes.

Single European Act: act intended to remove numerous barriers imposed on trade and capital flows between European countries.

Single-Buyer Policy: policy administered by the Ex-Im Bank that allows the exporter to selectively insure certain transactions.

Small Business Policy: policy providing enhanced coverage to new exporters and small businesses.

Smithsonian Agreement: conference between nations in 1971 that resulted in a devaluation of the dollar against major currencies and a widening of boundaries (2 percent in either direction) around the newly established exchange rates.

snake: arrangement established in 1972, whereby European currencies were tied to each other within specified limits.

special drawing rights (SDRs): represent a unit of account that are allocated to member countries to supplement currency reserves in IMF financing.

spot market: market in which exchange transactions occur for immediate exchange.

spot rate: current exchange rate of currency.

standby letter of credit: document used to guarantee invoice payments to a supplier; it promises to pay the beneficiary if the buyer fails to pay.

sterilized intervention: intervention by the Federal Reserve in the foreign exchange market, with simultaneous intervention in the Treasury securities markets to offset any effects on the dollar money supply; thus, the intervention in the foreign exchange market is achieved without affecting the existing dollar money supply.

straddle: a combination of a call option and a put option with the same exercise price.

strangle: a combination of a put option and a call option, whereby the exercise prices are not the same.

strike price (exercise price): price (exchange rate) at which the owner of a currency call option is allowed to buy a specified currency; or the price (exchange rate) at which the owner of a currency put option is allowed to sell a specified currency.

strong-form efficient: description of foreign exchange markets, implying that all relevant public and private information is already reflected in prevailing spot exchange rates.

Structural Adjustment Loan (SAL): established in 1980 by the World Bank to enhance a country's long-term economic growth through financing projects.

supplier credit: credit provided by the supplier to itself to fund its operations.

syndicate: group of banks that participate in loans.

tariff: tax imposed by a government on imported goods.

technical forecasting: development of forecasts using historical prices or trends.

tenor: time period of drafts.

time-series analysis: analysis of relationships between two or more variables over periods of time.

trade acceptance: draft that allows the buyer to obtain merchandise prior to paying for it.

transaction exposure: the sensitivity of the firm's contractual transactions in foreign currencies to exchange rate movements.

Transfer payments: sometimes referred to as secondary income in balance of payments accounting; component of current account, mostly composed of aid, grants, and gifts from one country to another.

transfer pricing: policy for pricing goods sent by either the parent or a subsidiary to a subsidiary of an MNC.

transferable letter of credit: document that allows the first beneficiary on a standby letter of credit to transfer all or part of the original letter of credit to a third party.

translation exposure: degree to which a firm's consolidated financial statements are exposed to fluctuations in exchange rates.

triangular arbitrage: action to capitalize on a discrepancy where the quoted cross exchange rate is not equal to the rate that should exist at equilibrium.

U

Umbrella Policy: policy issued to a bank or trading company to insure exports of an exporter and handle all administrative requirements.

W

weak-form efficient: description of foreign exchange markets, implying that all historical and current exchange rate information is already reflected in prevailing spot exchange rates.

Working Capital Guarantee Program: program conducted by the Ex-Im Bank that encourages commercial banks to extend short-term export financing to eligible exporters; the Ex-Im Bank provides a guarantee of the loan's principal and interest.

World Bank: bank established in 1944 to enhance economic development by providing loans to countries.

World Trade Organization (WTO): organization established to provide a forum for multilateral trade negotiations and to settle trade disputes related to the GATT accord.

writer: seller of an option.

Yankee stock offerings: offerings of stock by non-U.S. firms in the U.S. markets.

Index

A

Absolute form of PPP, 257
Accounting, 4
Accounting laws, 86–87
Accounts receivable financing, 582
Accretion swap, 563
Acquisitions,
   of existing operations, 11–12
   international, 479–480
   international partial, 490
   privatized businesses, 490–491
Advising bank, 578
African Development Bank, 58
Agency costs, 5
Agency problem, 4–6
   corporate control of, 5–6
   MNC's, 531
   parent control of, 5
Airway bill, 579
All-in-rate, 584
Altria, 374
American depository receipts (ADR), 84–85, 101
   equation, 84–85
Amortizing swap, 563
Anti-takeover amendments, by target, 480
Appreciation, 103
Arbitrage, 85, 165, 166, 167, 168, 227
   comparisons, 236
   covered interest, 232–236
   international, 227–247
   locational, 227–229
   triangular, 229–232
Argentina, 41, 52, 86, 113, 151, 417, 470
Ashland, Inc., 561
Asia, 52, 76, 81, 193, 222, 484, 488, 505, 586
Asian crisis, 55, 194
   exchange rate during, 223–224
   interest rate during, 224
Asian Development Bank, 58, 221
Asian financial crisis, 218–224
Asian money market, 76
Ask, 67
Ask price, 67
Ask rate, 132
Assignment of proceeds, 588–589
AT&T, 81

Australia,
   interest rates, 77, 191, 597
Austria, 198

B

Back-to-back loan, 373, 556
Bahrain, 39
Balance of payments, 33–37
Balance of trade, 34
   trends, 42–43
Balance of trade deficit, exchange rate correcting,
   49–50
Bank for International Settlements (BIS), 57
Bank Letter of Credit Policy, 588
Banker's acceptance, 582, 583–585
   life cycle, 585
Banks, economic development agencies, 55–58
Barter, 586
Basel Accord, 79
Basel Committee, 79
Basel II Accord, 79
Basel III Accord, 79
Basis (floating-for-floating) swap, 563
Bausch & Lomb, 52
Belgium, 198
Berlin wall, 37
Best Foods, 38
Bid, 67, 132–133
Bid/ask spread, 67–69, 132–133
   accounting for, 231–232
   of banks, 67
   among currencies, 67–69
   equation, 68
   factors that affect, 69–70
Biger and Hull currency option pricing model
   equation, 166–167
Bilateral netting system, 615
Bill of exchange, 580, 583
Bill of lading (B/L), 579
Black & Decker, 342, 356
Black-Scholes stock OPM, 167
Blockage of funds transfers, 505
Blocked funds, 450–451, 617
Blockholders, 478
Bloody Thursday, 221

Board of directors, 477–478
Bodurtha and Courtadon, predictive ability,
   currency option pricing model, 167
Boeing, 10
Bolivar, 194–195
Bolivia, 66
Bond markets, 80
   international, 80–81
   other, 81–83
Bond offering,
   domestic, 528
   global, 528
Bond yields, 82, 552
Bonds, 56, 80–83
   Eurobonds, 80–81
   in eurozone, 199
   foreign, 80
   impact of Greek crisis, 82–83
   parallel, 80
   private placement, 528
Brazil, 11, 52, 222, 484–485
   interest rates, 597
Break-even salvage value, 451–452
Break-even terminal value, 451
Bretton Woods Agreement, 64, 188
Bribery, 46
Bulgaria, 4, 38, 670
Business laws, 46

C

CAFTA, 39
Call option,
   at the money, 148
   contingency graph, for buyer and seller, 147
   European style, 143
   to hedge payables, 144
   hedge on payables, 356–363
   to hedge project bidding, 144
   to hedge target bidding, 145
   hedging with, 357–360
   in the money, 148
   out of the money, 149
   premium, 143
   premium equation, 149
   on real assets, 492–493

Callable swap, 563
Campbell Soup Co., 561
Canada, 11, 39, 40–42, 52, 86, 191, 485–487
  interest rates, 55
Canon, 52
Capital,
  components of, 527–530
  cost of, 14, 21, 535
    across countries, 539–543
    vs. domestic firms, 536–537
    multinational, 534–539
Capital account, 33, 36–37
  errors and omissions in, 37
Capital asset pricing model (CAPM), 537
  cost-of-equity comparison, 537–539
Capital budgeting,
  and exchange rate forecasting, 297–298
  incorporating risk in, 512–516
  multinational, 437–458
  input, 439–441
  subsidiary *vs.* parent, 437–439
  tax law for multinational, 469–476
Capital flows, international, 52–55
Capital goods financing, medium-term, 586
Capital management, working capital, 611–612
Capital structure decision,
  corporate characteristics, 531
  host country characteristics, 531–532
  of MNC, 530–533
  subsidiary vs. parent, 533–534
Caribbean, 52
Carry trade, 120–123
  risk, 122–123
Carrybacks, net operating loss, 471–472
Carryforwards, net operating loss, 471–472
Cash, 507
  investing excess, 618–626
Cash flow,
  adjustment of the estimated, 512–515
  and correlation conditions, 331–332
  calculation, 475
  estimating, 481–482
  government restrictions, 618
  impact of project on prevailing, 452–453
  optimizing, 614–618
Cash inflows, 531, 614–615
Cash management, 611
  centralized, 613–614
  international, 611–626
Cash positions, monitoring, 614
Cash shortages, 614
Cash transfers, intersubsidiary, 617
Caterpillar, 337, 556
CBOT, 142
Cemex, 84
Central America, 39
Central American Trade Agreement (CAFTA), 39
Central bank, 209
Centralized multinational financial management, 7
Chicago Mercantile Exchange (CME), 136, 137,
    139, 142
Child labor laws, 46, 47
Chile, 39, 52, 133, 222
China, 8, 11, 42, 43, 51, 52, 54, 417, 572–573
  impact of the Asian crisis on, 222
  pegged exchange rate system, 194
China Telecom Corp., 84
Citgo Petroleum, 52

Citigroup, 65
CME Group, 136, 142–143
Coca-Cola Co., 75, 81, 342, 374, 490
Cofinancing agreement, 56
Colgate-Palmolive, 3, 52
Commercial invoice, 579
Commercial paper, 584, 596, 618
Commission, 142
Comparative advantage, 8
Compensating balance, 131
Compensation, 586–587
Compensatory financing facility (CFF), 56
Computers, 95
Conditional currency options, 152–154
Consignment, 581
Consumer demand, multinational capital
    budgeting, 439
Contract, forward, 74
Control decisions, 490–492
Conversion costs, minimizing, 615–617
Corporate control,
  barriers to international, 480–481
  international, 429, 479–482
  motives for international acquisitions, 479
  trends in international acquisitions, 479–480
Corporate governance,
  by board members, 477–478
  by institutional investors, 478
  international, 477–478
  by shareholder activities, 478
Corporate income tax comparison among
    countries, 470
Correlation coefficients, 331
Correlation conditions, and cash flow, 332
Corruption, 505–506
Cost of capital. *See* Capital, cost of
Cost of debt. *See* Debt, cost of
Cost of equity. *See* Equity, cost of
Cost of labor, 43
Costs, multinational capital budgeting, 440
Counterpurchase, 587
Countertrade, 586–587
Country, comparing risk rates, 511
Country risk,
  assessing, 508–509
  checklist approach, 508
  Delphi technique, 508
  inspection visits, 509
  quantitative analysis, 508–509
  characteristics, 503–507
  financial risk characteristics, 506–507
  measuring, 507–511
  political risk characteristics, 503–506
  rating, 509–511
Country security laws, 46–47
Covered arbitrage, bid/ask spreads, 231–232
Covered interest arbitrage, 232–236
  by non-U.S. investors, 236
Credit, 36, 37
Credit crisis,
  credit market, 79–80
  and IMF, 54
  impact on stock markets, 91
Credit crisis of 2008, 80, 148, 505, 534, 575
  access to funding, 596
  impact on payment methods, 581
Credit market,
  international, 78–80

  regulations, 79
  syndicate loans, 78–80
Credit risk, of international bonds, 82
Credit spread, 180
Credit Suisse Group, 84
Crisis, market movements in, 113–114
Croatia, 38, 81
Cross border factoring, 582
Cross exchange rate quotations, 73–74
Cross exchange rates, 73–74, 116–117, 137, 229
Cross-border factoring, 582
Cross-hedging, 374
Currency, 48–49, 96–97
  comparison of bid/ask spread among, 67–69
  demand for, 105–106
  diversifying cash, 623–624
  European, 198–203
  financing with, 596–602
  inconvertibility, 505
  inflow, 545
  investing in, example, 619–621
  minimizing conversion costs, 615–617
  money market interest rates among, 76–77
  repeated investing, 638
  supply of, 106
Currency bear spreads, 180–181
Currency boards, 195–196
Currency bull spreads,
  with call options, 177–180
  with put options, 180
  speculating with, 180
Currency call options, 75, 142
  firms use, 144–145
  hedge, 357
  premiums, 143–144
  speculating in, 145–148
Currency correlations, 331
  to net cash flows, 331–332
Currency derivatives, 74, 131–154
Currency diversification, 374
Currency diversification argument, for exchange
    rates, 374
Currency futures,
  market, 91, 136–141
  MNCs using, 139–140
  pricing, 139
  speculation, 141
  trading, 137–138
  trading platforms, 138
Currency futures contract, 75, 136
  credit risk of, 138
Currency markets, 115–116
Currency option combinations, 169–182
Currency option hedge, 356, 370
Currency option pricing, 165–168
  boundary conditions, 165–166
Currency option pricing model,
  Biger and Hull model, equation, 166
  European model, 167
  predictive ability, Bodurtha and Courtadon, 167
Currency options, 75
  basic and conditional, 152–154
  conditional, 152–154
  European, 154
Currency options exchanges, 142
Currency options market, 88, 142
  efficiency of, 152
  over-the-counter, 142

Currency put option, 75, 148
  hedging, 147
  MNCs using, 149–150
  at the money, 148
  in the money, 148
  out of the money, 149
  premiums, 149
  pricing, 167–168
  speculating, 150–152
Currency put option premiums, equation, 149
Currency risk, 69
Currency speculation, 120
Currency spot rate, equation, 108–109
Currency spreads, 177–182
Currency straddles, 169–173
  long, 169–171
  short, 171–172
  speculating with, 172–173
Currency strangles, 173–177
  long, 173–175
  short, 175–177
Currency swaps, 555–556
Currency volatility, 330
Current account, 33–35
Cyprus, 38, 198
Czech Republic, 38, 198

D

Dairy Queen, 11
Debt,
  external sources, 528–529
  cost of, 534
  country differences, 540–541
  vs. equity, 535–536
Debt decision, fixed *vs.* floating rate, 560–564
Debt denomination,
  analyzing alternatives, 554–555
  identifying alternatives, 553–554
Debt denomination analysis, 553–555
Debt denomination decision of foreign
      subsidiaries, 551–553
Debt financing,
  long-term, 551–564
  subsidiary, 533–534
  using currency swaps, 555–556
  using parallel loans, 556–559
Debt maturity decision, 559–560
Debt spread, 180
Debits, 34
Decentralized multinational financial
      management, 7
Denmark, 38, 198
Denominations, 81
Depreciation, 103, 187
Deutsche Bank, 65
Devaluation, 187
Devalue, 187
Direct foreign investment (DFI), 11, 35, 52–53, 88,
      417–430
  assessing potential, 427–430
  barriers to, 425–427
  benefits, 421–424
  cost-related motives, 418–420
  economic growth, 53
  exchange rates, 53
  factors affecting, 52–53
  government-imposed conditions, 426–427
  host government views, 424–427

incentives to encourage, 425
motives for, 417–421
privatization, 52–53
restrictions, 52
revenue-related motives, 417–418
tax rates, 53
whether to pursue, 426
Direct Loan Program, 588
Direct quotations, 70
Diversification, 104–105
  among countries, 424
  currency, 374
  international stock, 97–98
  limitations of international, 98
Diversification analysis, of international projects,
      422–424
Divestitures, international, 491–492
Dividend discount model, for valuing stocks, 98–101
Dividend payments, subsidiary, 612
Documentary collections, 580
Documents against acceptance, 580
Documents against payment, 580
Dollar cash flows, 14
Dollar initial outlay calculation, 481
Dollarization, 197
Domestic equity offering, 529
Domestic model, of valuation, 14
Dominican Republic, 39
Dow Chemical Co., 3, 83, 479
Draft, 580–581, 583–584
Due diligence, 482
Dumping, 45
DuPont Co., 10, 337, 357
Dynamic hedging, 625–626

E

Earnings,
  forecasts, 403–404
  remitted, 438, 489, 527
Earnings assessment, and exchange rate
      forecasting, 298
East Germany, 37
Eastern Europe, 37, 38, 43, 52, 198, 484
Economic exposure, 335–340
  assessing, 394–395
  to foreign currency appreciation, 337
  to foreign currency depreciation, 336–337
  managing, 393–404
  measuring, 337–340
  restructuring to reduce, 395–398
Economies of scale, 419
Effective financing rate, 597–598
  borrowing foreign currency calculation, 597–598
  calculation, 597
Effective return on foreign deposits, equation, 270
Effective yield, 618, 619–622
  on foreign deposits, calculation, 619
Electronic communication networks (ECNs), 95
E-mini futures contacts, 136
Enron, 6
Environmental barriers, to DFI, 426
Environmental restrictions, 45–46
Equilibrium exchange rate, 104, 106–107
  change in, 107–108
  determination, 107
Equity,
  cost of, 535–536

country differences, 541–543
external sources of, 529–530
private placement, 530
Equity offering, 529–530
  domestic, 529
  global, 529–530
  MNC's cost of, 534–535
Equity risk premium, 541–542
Estonia, 38, 198
Euro, 39, 63, 66, 69, 71, 72, 76, 82, 105, 120–121,
      142, 193, 198
  floating exchange rate, 191
  impact of a country abandoning, 202–203
Eurobond market, 80–81
Eurobonds, 80, 82
  denominations, 81
  features of, 81
  secondary market, 81
  underwriting, 80
Euro-commercial paper, 596
Eurocredit loans, 78
Eurocredit market, 78
Eurodollar, 76
Euronext market, 85
Euronotes, 596
Europe, 18, 37, 43, 76, 78, 79, 82, 84, 85, 222
  snake arrangement, pegged exchange rate, 192
European Bank for Reconstruction and
      Development, 58
European Central Bank (ECB), 198, 203, 540
European currency, 198–203
European currency options, 154
European Currency Unit (ECU), 192
European monetary system (EMS), 192–193
European money market, 76
European style call options, 143
European Union (EU), 38–39, 79, 198
Eurozone, 39, 69, 198, 199–202
  crisis within, 199–202
  financial flows, 199
  firms and, 199
  monetary policy, 198
Exam, final self exam, 633–641
Exchange clearinghouse, 138
Exchange rate, 48–50, 53, 63, 124–126, 255–275
  affecting earnings, 438
  changes in, 70
  correcting balance of trade deficit, 49–50
  cross, 73, 116–117, 118
  during Asian crisis, 223–224
  equilibrium, 104–108
  factors that influence, 108–116
  floating, 64
  forecasting, 297–315
  forecasting errors, 307–309
  friction, 50–52
  fundamental forecasting, 299–303
  government controls, 112
  government influence on, 187–210
  and international portfolio investment, 53
  and intervention, 203–207
  limitations of fundamental forecasting, 302–303
  market-based forecasting for, 303–306
  measuring impact, 96–97
  measuring movements, 103–104
  mixed forecasting for, 306–307
  multinational capital budgeting, 438
  pegged, 191
  reducing risk of foreign stocks, 97

Exchange rate (*continued*)
  technical forecasting, 299
  transaction exposure. *See* Transaction exposure
  volatility, forecasting, 314–315
  why, 297–299
Exchange rate boundaries, 203–204
Exchange rate determination, 103–123
Exchange rate equilibrium, 104–108
Exchange rate fluctuations, measuring exposure, 325–345
Exchange rate forecast, 297–299, 600–601
Exchange rate mechanism (ERM), 192
Exchange rate movement, 438
  expected, 117–123, 267
  measuring, 103–104
  smoothing, 203
  standard deviation of, 329
Exchange rate quotations, 70–74
  cross, 73–74
  direct, 70–72
  indirect, 70–72
  online sources, 72–73
  source of, 72–73
Exchange rate risk, 17, 77, 78, 81, 96–97, 99–100, 323–326
  alternative methods to reduce, 373–374
  exposure to, 19–20, 537
  of international bonds, 82
  of a pegged currency, 196
  relevance of, 325–326
Exchange rate system, 187–198
  fixed, 187–189
  freely floating, 189–190
  floating, 64
  managed float, 190–191
  pegged, 191–196
Exchange-traded funds (ETFs), 101
Excise tax rates, 469, 471
Exercise price, 75, 143
Expenses, subsidiary, 611–612
Expiration date, 142, 143
Export credit insurance, 589
Exporters, 577, 579–581, 583–585
  subsidies for, 45
Export-Import Bank (Ex-Im Bank), 587–589
Exporting, 10
Exports, 12, 18, 33–34, 39, 40
Exposure,
  economic, 335–340
  measuring, 337–340
  exchange rate risk, 19
  foreign currency appreciation, 337
  foreign currency depreciation, 336–337
  international economic conditions, 17–19
  international political risk, 19
  hedging translation, 403–404
  managing translation, 402–404
  operating, 335
  transaction, 326–335
  translation, 340–343
Expropriation, 503, 517, 589
External short-term financing, 596
ExxonMobil, 3

F

Facebook, 3, 17, 418
Factor, 582

Factor income, 34
Factoring, 582–583
Federal Reserve System (the Fed), 55, 64, 203, 204, 205–209
Ferro, 3
Fidelity, 100, 101
Finance, 4
Financial Accounting Standards Board (FASB), 340
Financial accounts, 35–36
Financial Institution Buyer Credit Policy, 588
Financial markets,
  international, 63–89
  serving MNCs, 88
Financial statements, 340
Financing,
  arrangement, 447–450
  with currencies, 596–604
  with currency portfolio, 602–604
  external short-term, 596
  foreign, 595–596
  foreign, sources of, 595–596
  with foreign currency, 596–602
  with foreign funds, 401
  internal short-term, 595–596
  loans facilitating, 555–559
  long-term, 429
  parent, 448–450
  short-term, 595–604
  subsidiary, 448, 449–450
Financing costs, uncertainty, 555
Finland, 38, 198, 425
Fireman's Fund, 52
Fisher effect, 111, 274–276
Fisher, Irving, 266
Fixed exchange rate, agreements, 64
Fixed exchange rate system, 187–189
Floating exchange rate, countries, 190–191
Floating exchange rate system, 64
Floating rate notes (FRNs), 81
Ford Motor Co., 556
Forecast bias, 307–310
  graphic evaluation of, 309–311
  shifts in, 312
  statistical test of, 311–312
Forecast error, for exchange rates, 307–308
  among currencies, 308–309
  bias, 309–312
  graphic evaluation, 309–311
  measurement, 307–308
  time horizons, 308
  time periods, 308
Forecasting,
  exchange rates, 297–315
  for exchange rates, interval, 313–315
  for foreign exchange market, 297–299
  fundamental, for exchange rates, 299–303
  technical, for exchange rates, 299
  why, 297–299
Forecasting techniques, for exchange rates, 299–307
Foreign bond, 80
Foreign capital, 53–55
Foreign currency speculation, 118–120
Foreign exchange,
  attributes of banks providing, 67
  dealers, 65
  history, 63–64
  quotations, 70–74
  transactions, 64–70

Foreign exchange controls, government use of, 210
Foreign exchange market, 63–75, 88
  derivative contracts in, 74–75
  direct intervention, 203–209
  forecasting, 297–299
  indirect intervention, 209–210
Foreign financing
  sources of, 595–596
Foreign government, 19
Foreign investment, 53, 97, 202–203
Foreign investment risk matrix (FIRM), 511
Foreign stock,
  reducing the exchange rate risk of, 97
  in United States, 84–85
  valuation, 98–101
Foreign stock listings, and SOX, 84
Foreign stock markets, 85
Foreign subsidiaries, 13, 340, 530, 551–553
  establishing new, 12
Foreign target valuation, disparity, 488–489
Forfaiting, 586
Fortune Brands, 3
Forward contracts, 74, 131, 135, 356, 363, 373, 400–401, 404
  comparison to currency futures, 138–139
  hedging, 400–401
  long-term, 373
  MNCs use, 131–132
  non-deliverable, 135
  offsetting, 134–135
Forward hedge, 357, 360
  on payables, 357
  on receivables, 367–370
Forward market, 74, 131–136
Forward premiums, 244–247
  changes in, 245–247
  across maturities, 244–245
  variation in, 244–247
Forward rate, 74, 131, 232, 234–235
  as a forecast, 303, 304–305, 600, 622
  changes in, 246–247
  movements, 134
  premium or discount on, 133–134
Forward swap, 563
France, 38, 40, 52, 86, 198, 236, 417, 425, 587
Franchising, 11, 12
Freely floating exchange rate system, 189–190
Fuji Co., 11
Full compensation, 587
Fund transfers
  blockage of, 505
  technology used, 614
Fundamental forecasting, 299–303
  with a comprehensive model, 302
  for exchange rates, 299–303
  instantaneous influences in, 301
  with a lagged impact, 300–301
  limitations, 302–303
  sensitivity analysis, 313
  use of PPP, 300
Funds, internal control over, 596
Funds transfers, blockage, 505
Future spot rate, 75
Futures contracts, 356, 363
  hedging, 403
Futures hedge, 356
  on payables, 356–357
  on receivables, 363–364

Futures market, currency, 136–141
Futures position, closing out, 140
Futures rate, 75
FX Connect, 65

G

Gap, 8
GATT, 38, 57
GDP, 40
General Agreement on Tariffs and Trade (GATT) accord. *See* GATT
General Electric, 10, 52, 374
General Mills, Inc., 11
General Motors, 11, 46
Germany, 37, 38, 40, 52, 65, 198, 470
    degree of financial leverage, 541
Global equity offering, 529–530
Globex system, 142
Gold standard, 64
Google, Inc., 74, 475, 479
Greece, 38, 55, 56, 82–83, 198, 200, 202
Greek crisis, 82–83
Guinness, 80

H

Hedge, 139, 140, 144, 145
    currency call option, 357–360
    forward, 356–357
    money market, 357
    proxy, 374
Hedge funds, 478
Hedging, 97, 145, 325
    cross-hedging, 374
    with currency bear spreads, 391–392
    with currency bull spreads, 390–391
    with currency straddles, 388–389
    with currency strangles, 390
    dynamic, 625–626
    and exchange rate forecasting, 297
    exposure to fixed assets, 401–402
    exposure to payables transactions, 356–363
    exposure to receivables, 363–371
    forward, 357
    forward contracts, 400–401
    futures contracts, 363–364
    interest payments with interest rate, 561–564
    leading and lagging, 374
    limitations, 371–373
    long-term, 372–373
    overhedging, 371
    selective, 355–356
    swaps, 561–564
    techniques, 370–371
    transaction exposure, 355–356, 403–404
    translation exposure, limitations, 403–404
    an uncertain payment, 371
Hedging payables
    comparison of techniques for, 360-363
    evaluating past decisions on, 363
    optimal technique for, 361
    real cost of, 363
    techniques, 360–363 Hedging receivables, techniques, 367–370
Heineken, 35, 36, 84
Hewlett-Packard, 223
Home currency, 53, 66, 76, 136, 191–192, 198, 202

weak, 50, 207
Hong Kong, 76, 221, 696
Host government barriers, 480–481
Host government incentives, 453
Host government takeovers, preventing, 516–517
Host governments, and DFI, 424–427
Hungary, 38, 52, 81, 198, 417, 491

I

IBM, 3, 8, 10, 12, 491
IMF, 55–56, 101, 194, 220, 221
    funding dilemma, 56
Imperfect market, 8
Import/export letters of credit, 578
Importers, 10, 50, 577–578, 581–584, 586–587, 588–589
Importing, 10
Imports, 12, 33–34, 39, 42
    restrictions on, 45
Income level, 44
    relative, 111–112
India, 39, 52, 113
    interest rates, 592, 597
Indirect quotations, 70–71
Indonesia, 66, 221, 224, 553
    financial crisis rescue package, 220
    floating exchange rate, 191
Industry barriers, to DFI, 425
Inefficient bureaucracy, 505
Inflation, 113, 189, 195, 198, 202, 203, 267–268
    and capital budget analysis, 447
    impact on trade, 44
Inflation rates, relative, 109–110
Information costs, 96
Information systems, 4
Initial investment, multinational capital budgeting, 439
Institutional speculation, 118–120
    based on expected appreciation, 118–119
    based on expected depreciation, 119–120
Insurance
    export credit, 589
    for expropriation, 517
    purchase, 517
Intel Corp., 8, 144, 561
Inter-American Development Bank, 58
Interbank market, 66
Interest payments, hedging with interest rate swaps, 561–564
Interest rate parity (IRP), 236–244, 600
    considerations when assessing, 243–244
    derivation of, 237–238
    and forward premium, equation, 238–240
    comparison to PPP and IFE, 275–276
    derivation of, 237–238
    graphic analysis, 240–242
    illustration of, 240
    implications of, 600
    interpretation, 242
    line, 241
    political risk, 243
    tax laws, 244
    testing, 242
    transaction costs, 243
Interest rate risk, of international bonds, 81–82
Interest rate swaps,
    hedging with interest payments, 561–564

illustration of, 562
    limitations, 563
Interest rates, 507, 531
    during Asian crisis, 223–224
    among currencies, 597
    government control of, 209–210
    and international portfolio investment, 53
    international Fisher effect, 266–275
    real, 111
    relative, 110–111
Internal short-term financing, 595–596
International arbitrage, 227–247 *See also* Arbitrage, international
International Bank for Reconstruction and Development (IBRD) (World Bank), 56–57
International bond market, 80–83
International bonds, risk, 81–82
International business,
    methods to conduct, 10–13
    pursuing, 8–9
International capital flows, 52–55
International cash management, 611–626
International Chamber of Commerce, 579
International credit market, 78–80
International Development Association (IDA), 57
International diversification, 536–537
    benefits, 421–424
    limitations of, 98
International divestitures, 491–492
International economic conditions, 17–19
International Financial Corporation (IFC), 57
International financial markets, 63–89
    investing in, 95–101
International Fisher effect (IFE), 266–276, 621–622
    derivation of, 270–272
    graphic analysis of, 272–273
    implications of, 267
    implications of the IFE for forecasts, 305–306
    implications of the IFE for two non-U.S. currencies, 268
    testing, 273–274
    theory, 266, 275–276
International Fisher effect (IFE) line, 273
International flow of funds, 33–58
International Monetary Fund (IMF), 55–56, 101, 194, 220, 221
International money market, 75–78 *See also* Money market, international
International money market securities, 77–78
International mutual funds (IMFs), 101
International political risk, 19
International product life cycle, 9
International stock diversification, 97–98
International stock exchanges, 95–98
International stock markets, 83–88
International Swaps and Derivatives Association (ISDA), 564
    Master Agreement, 564
International trade, 10, 13
    agencies that motivate, 587–590
    financing, 577–590
    flows, factors affecting, 43–52
    growth in, 37–43
    Internet facilitating, 10
    payment methods, 577–581
International trade and financial transactions, agencies that facilitate, 55–58

Internet,
  and international trade, 10
  facilitates management control, 8
Intersubsidiary cash transfers, 617
Intersubsidiary payments matrix, 615, 616
Interval forecasts, for exchange rates, 313–315
Intervention,
  in currency valuation, 209–210
  and exchange rate, 203–209
Intervention warnings, 210
Intracompany trade, 50
Investing,
  in MNC stock, 104–105
  internationally, 104–105
Investment, direct foreign, 11
Investment currency, appreciation in, 121, 122
Investor hedge argument, for exchange rates, 325–326
Investors, institutional, 478
Ireland, 198, 200, 418, 425
Irrevocable letter of credit, 579
iShares, 101
Issuing bank, 578
Italy, 38, 63, 86, 198, 200

J

J.C. Penney, 35
JPMorgan Chase & Co.,, 5, 65
Jamaica, 8
Japan, 8, 39, 40, 42, 43, 52, 63, 80, 220, 222, 241, 417
  degree of financial leverage, 540
  impact of the Asian crisis on, 222
  interest rates, 597
J-curve effect, 50
Johnson & Johnson, 556
Johnson Control, 561
Joint venture, 11, 12, 13

K

KFC, 417
Korea, 419

L

Labor laws, 46
Lagging, 374
Latin America, 52, 57, 74, 84, 210, 222, 421
Latvia, 38, 198
Leading, 374
Letters of credit (L/C), 578–580, 583
  irrevocable, 579–580
  standby, 583
  types of, 578–580
LIBOR, 77, 528–529, 560–564
Licensing, 10, 13
Licensing agreements, 12
Liquidity, 116
Liquidity management, subsidiary, 612
Liquidity risk, of international bonds, 82
Lithuania, 38, 198
Loans, 78–79, 82, 528–529
  back-to-back, 556
  bank, 596
  eurocredit, 78
  financing costs of fixed vs. floating rates, 560–561
  financing costs with different maturities, 559–560
  parallel, 373, 556–559
  programs, 588

syndicated, 78–79, 529
Locational arbitrage, 227–229
Lockboxes, 615
London Interbank Offer Rate (LIBOR), 77, 528–529, 560–564
Long straddle, 169–172
Long-term financing
  DFI, 429
  and exchange rate forecasting, 298
Long-term forward contracts, 373, 402
Luxembourg, 38, 198

M

Maastricht Treaty, 198
Macro-assessment of country risk, 507
Mail float, 615
Malta, 38, 198
Managed float, 190–191
Managed float exchange rate system, 190–191
Management, 4
Market,
  Asian money, 76
  black, 197
  currency options, 142
  eurobond, 80–81
  eurocredit, 78
  forward, 74, 131–136
  interbank, 66
  secondary, 81
  spot, 65
Market-based forecasting, for exchange rates, 303–306
Marketing, 4
McDonald's, 11, 80
Medium-Term Guarantee Program, 587–588
Medtronic, 3
Merck & Co., 356, 357
Mexican peso crisis, 193
Mexico, 8, 38, 39, 42, 51, 52, 63, 84, 133, 222, 425
  pegged exchange rate system, 193
Micro-assessment of country risk, 507
Mixed forecasting,
  for exchange rates, 306–307
Money market, 76–77, 357, 364
  Asian, 76
  currency options, 154
  European, 76
  interest rates among currencies, 76
  international, 75–77
  Money market hedge, 364
  on payables, 357
  on receivables, 364
  vs. forward hedge, 357
Morocco, 39, 587
Motorola, 223
Multibuyer Policy, 589
Multilateral Investment Guarantee Agency (MIGA), 57, 517
Multilateral netting system, 615
Multinational capital budgeting, 437–458
  example, 441
  incorporating international tax law in, 469–476
  input for, 439–441
  parent financing, 448–450
  subsidiary financing, 448, 449–450. See also
    Capital budgeting, multinational
Multinational corporations (MNCs), 3

cash flows, uncertainty, 17–20
cash flow diagram, 13
management structure, 6–8
management styles, 6, 7
managing, 4–8
size, 536
uncertainty affects cost of capital, 21
valuation model, 13–21
Multinational financial management, 3–22
Multinational model, of valuation, 14–16
Mutual funds, international, 101

N

NAFTA, 38
National income, impact on trade, 44
Nestle SA, 11, 80
Net cash flows, estimating in currencies, 328
Net operating loss carrybacks, 471
Net operating loss carryforwards, 471
Net present value (NPV), calculation, 443
  from acquiring firm's perspective, 481
  estimating, 482
Netherlands, 38, 52, 198
Netting, 615–617
New York Stock Exchange (NYSE), 85
Nike, 3, 8, 12, 223
Nokia, 84
Non-deliverable forward contracts (NDF), 135–136
Nonsterilized intervention, 206–207
North American Free Trade Agreement (NAFTA). See NAFTA
Norway, 198
Notes, short-term, 596
Notional value, 561
NYSE, 85
NYSE Euronext, 85

O

OANDA, 65
Ocean bill of lading, 579
Oman, 39
Open account transactions, 581
Operating exposure, 335
Oracle Corp., 8, 479
Organization for Economic Cooperation and Development (OECD), 58
Organization of Petroleum Exporting Countries (OPEC), 76
Outsourcing, 39–40
  impact on trade, 39–40
  managerial decisions, 40
Overhedging, 371
Overseas Private Investment Corporation (OPIC), 517, 589–590
Over-the-counter currency futures market, 137
Over-the-counter currency options market, 142
Over-the-counter (OTC) stock market, 101

P

Parallel bonds, 80
Parallel loan, 373
  using, 556–559
Parent (company), 504
Partial compensation, 587
Payables, techniques to hedge, 360–363

Payment entries, 34
Payments,
    for merchandise and services, 34
    transfer, 34
Pegged currency, interest rates, 196
Pegged exchange rate, 191
    Asian, 193–194
    China, 194
    classification of, 196
    limitations, 191–192
    Venezuela, 194–195
Pegged exchange rate system, 191–196
PepsiCo, 12, 326, 374
Peru, 39
Petrodollars, 76
Piracy, restrictions on, 45
Pizza Hut, 11
Poison pills, by target, 480
Poland, 38, 52, 198
Political risk,
    international, 19
    of interest rate parity, 243–244
Political risk characteristics for countries, 503–506
Portfolio,
    diversification, 623–625
    exposure, 329–335
    investment, 35–36
    risk of two-currency, equation, 329
Portugal, 38, 55, 83, 198, 200
Pound, trends in, 121–122
PPP. *See* Purchasing power parity
Preauthorized payments, 615
Premium, 133–134, 143, 148
    equation, 133–134
Prepayment, 577–578
Price,
    exercise, 75
    multinational capital budgeting, 439–440
    strike, 75
Price elastic, 49
Price index, 258–259
Pricing models, 166–168
Private equity firms, 478
Private Export Funding Corporation (PEFCO), 589
Private placement of equity, 530
Privatization, and direct foreign investment, 52–53
Privatized, 84
Privatized businesses, international acquisitions of,
    490–491
Probability distribution, 601–602, 622–623
Procter & Gamble Co., 325, 372
Product cycle theory, 9
Project assessment, for risk, 454–457
Project Finance Loan Program, 588
Protective barriers, to DFI, 425
Proxy hedge, 374
Purchasing power disparity, 261–262
Purchasing power parity (PPP), 257–266
    absolute form, 257–258
    comparison to IRP and IFE, 275–276
    derivation, 258–259
    estimate exchange rate movement, 265–266
    estimating exchange rate effects, 259–260
    for fundamental forecasting for exchange rates,
        300
    graphic analysis, 260–262
    interpretations of, 257–258
    limitations of, 274

    relative form, 258
    simplified, 260
Purchasing power parity line, 260–261
Purchasing power parity theory,
    testing, 263–265
Put option, 364, 366–367
    contingency graph, for buyer and seller, 151–152
    on real assets, 493
Put option hedge, 364
    on receivables, 364–367
Put option premium, 149, 165, 166
Putable swap, 563
Put-call parity, pricing currency put options,
    167–168

Q

Quota, 45
Quotations, direct and indirect, 70–72

R

Rate,
    forward, 74
    spot, 65
Raw materials, 419
Real assets, call and put options, 492–493
Real cost of hedging payables, 363
Real interest rates, equation, 111
Real options, 453–454
Receivables,
    forward hedge on, 363–364
    futures hedge on, 363–364
    hedging exposure to, 363–371
    money market hedge on, 364
    put option hedge on, 364–367
    selling futures to hedge, 139–140
Red tape barriers, to DFI, 425
Refinancing of a sight letter of credit, 585
Regional development agencies, 58
Regression analysis, 339–340
Regulatory barriers, to DFI, 426
Relative form of PPP, 258
Relative income levels, 111–112
Relative inflation rates, 109–110
Relative interest rates, 110–111
Relative PPP theory, rationale, 258
Remitted funds, multinational capital budgeting, 440
Required rate of return, 99
    multinational capital budgeting, 440
Revaluation, 187
Revalue, 187
Revenue, subsidiary, 612
Risk rates, comparing country, 511
Risk,
    adjusting project assessment for, 454–458
    of two-currency portfolio, equation, 334
Risk, country risk. *See* Country risk
Risk-adjusted discount rate, 454
Risk-free interest rates, 541
Romania, 38, 81
Royal Dutch Shell, 100
Rule 144a, 84
Russia, 66, 96, 142, 190, 210, 221

S

Salvage (liquidation) value, multinational capital
    budgeting, 440

Salvage value,
    break-even, 451
    calculation, 482
    uncertain, 451–452
Sarbanes-Oxley (SOX) Act of 2002, 6, 84, 482
Secondary market, 81
Securities and Exchange Commission, 84, 142, 426
Selective hedging, 355–356
Semi-strong-form efficient, foreign exchange
    market, 304
Sensitivity analysis, 454–457
    of fundamental forecasting for exchange rates, 313
Settlement date, 141
Shareholders, 86, 87
Shell Oil, 52
Short-term investment, and exchange rate
    forecasting, 297
Short-term notes, 596
Simulation, 457–458
Singapore, 39, 76, 441
Single European Act of 1987, 37–38, 79
Single-Buyer Policy, 589
Slovakia, 38, 198
Slovenia, 38, 198
Small Business Policy, 589
Smithsonian Agreement, 64, 188
Snake arrangement, pegged exchange rate, 192
Sony, 100
South America, 81, 490, 539
South Korea, 39, 133, 221–222, 418
Spain, 38, 83, 198, 200
Special drawing rights (SDRs), 56
Speculation,
    break-even point, 146–147
    with currency futures, 141
    foreign currency, 120
    by individuals, 120
    institutional, 118–120
    by MNCs, 147–148
Speculators, 150
Spot market, 65
    liquidity, 66–67
    structure, 65–66
    time zone, 66
    use of dollar in, 66
Spot price, 174
Spot rate, 65, 108, 166
Stakeholder diversification argument, for exchange
    rates, 326
Stakeholder, 326
Standard deviation, 97–98
Standby letter of credit, 583
Starbucks, 418
State Street Corporation, 65
Sterilized intervention, 206–207
Stock,
    diversification, 97–98
    in eurozone, 199–201
    valuations among countries, 99–100
Stock exchange, 95–98
    alliances, 96
    international, 95–98
    U.S., 84–85
Stock market, 85, 86, 487
    characteristics, 87
    comparing, 85–86
    credit markets and, 87–88
    governance among, 86–87

Stock market (*continued*)
  impact of credit crisis, 221
  international, 83–88
Stock option pricing model (OPM), 167
Stock price, exposure to translation effects,
    342–343
Stockholders, 326
Straddle, 153, 172–175
  long, 172–173 See also Currency straddles
Strangles, 169 See also Currency strangles
Strike price, 75, 180, 357
Structural Adjustment Loan (SAL), 56
Subsidiary, 530
  dividend payments, 612
  expenses, 611–612
  liquidity management, 612
  revenue, 612
Subway, 11
Supplier credit, 581
Swap market, standardization of, 564
Swap transactions, using forward contracts, 135
Swaps, types, 563–564
Swaption, 564
Sweden, 11, 38, 198
Switzerland, 198
Syndicate loans, 78–79
Syndicate, 78

T

Taiwan, 133, 220
Takeovers
  by host governments, preventing, 516–517
  target, 479
Target, 479
  of takeovers, 479
  valuation, 482–484
  valuing a foreign, 481–482
Target valuation disparity, foreign target, 488–489
Tariff, 45
Tax breaks, 46
Tax credits, 472–473
Tax differentials, 437
Tax laws,
  among countries, 469–475
  differential, 244
  MNCs, impact on, 475–476
  multinational capital budgeting, 440, 441
  regarding interest rate parity, 244
Tax rates, 53
  among countries, 471
  and international portfolio investment, 53
  personal and excise, 471
Tax treaties, 472
Taxes, 99–100
  corporate income tax among countries,
      469–470
  intercompany transactions, 473–475
  withholding, 471
Technical forecasting, for exchange rates, 299
Tenor, 581
Terminal value, break-even, 451
Text, organization of, 21–22
Thailand, 133
  financial crisis, 218–224

floating exchange rate, 191
  rescue package, 220
  and Southeast Asia, 220
3M Co., 9, 223
Trade,
  acceptance, 581
  agreements, 39
  and cost of labor, 43
  and credit conditions, 44
  and government policies, 44–45
  and inflation, 44
  and national income, 44
  barriers, 37, 38
  countertrade, 586–587
  deficit, 34
  finance methods, 581–587
  international, 10, 37–43, 587–590
  intracompany, 50
  outsourcing, 39–40
  restrictions, 45–46. See also International trade
Trade flows, international, 43–52
Trade volume, 37–39
  among countries, 40–42
  events that increased, 37–39
  between United States and other countries,
      40–42
Transaction costs,
  arbitrage reducing, 236
  of interest rate parity, 243
  reduction in, 95–96
Transaction exposure, 326–335, 393
  based on value at risk, 332–335
  hedging, 355–356
  to exchange rate risk, 326–335
  of an MNC's portfolio, 329–332
Transfer payments, 34
Translation effects, and stock price, 342–343
Translation exposure, 340–343, 393
  determinants of, 340–342
  increased, 404
  managing, 402–404
Triangular arbitrage, 229–232
  bid/ask spread, 231–232
  gains from, 230–232
  realignment due to, 232

U

Ukraine, 81
Umbrella Policy, 589
Underwriting, Eurobonds, 80
"Uniform Customs and Practice for Documentary
    Credits," 579
Unilever, 38
United Kingdom, 38, 39, 41, 42, 52, 65, 80, 84, 86,
      105 183, 190, 198, 241, 242
  interest rates, 597
  rescuing failing firms, 541
United Nations Monetary and Financial
    Conference, 55
United States, 4, 8, 14, 18, 33, 34, 36, 38, 39, 40,
      42–43, 52, 136, 190, 194, 426
  Asian crisis and, 223
  cost of debt, 541
  degree of financial leverage, 541

foreign stocks, 84–85
  interest rates, 597
  rescuing failing firms, 541
  stock exchange, 86
Uruguay Round, 38, 57
  of GATT, 38

V

Valuation,
  MNC, uncertainty, 17
  of MNC cash flows over multiple periods,
      15–16
  of MNC that uses multiple currencies, 15
Valuation equation, 14–15
  for multiple periods, 15–16
  multinational, 14–15
Valuation model, of MNC, 13–21
Value-added tax (VAT), 469
Value-at-risk (VaR) method of assessing exposure,
    332–335
  estimating, 335
  limitations, 335
  longer time horizon, 331
  transaction exposure of portfolio, 334–335
Vanguard, 101
Venezuela,
  pegged exchange rate, 194–195
Vietnam, 4, 66
Virgin Islands, 8, 52
Volatile, 104
Volkswagen, 80

W

Wal-Mart, 418
Walt Disney, 80, 372
War, 505
Weak-form efficient, foreign exchange market,
    299, 304
Websites, 10
West Germany, 37
Western Europe, 37, 38, 43, 421
Working Capital Guarantee Program, 587–588
World Bank, 56–57, 221, 517. See also
      International Bank for Reconstruction
      and Development (IBRD)
World equity benchmark shares (WEBS), 101
World Trade Organization (WTO), 57
WorldCom, 6
Writer, 145

X

Xerox, Corp., 11

Y

Yankee stock offerings, 84
Yield curve, assessment, 559
Yields, foreign and domestic, 621–622
Yuan, 51, 210
Yum Brands, 417

Z

Zero-coupon swap, 563

Direct Exchange Rates over Time *continued*